DEVELOPMENT ECONOMICS

A Critical Study of Economic Growth, Development and Environment

ABOUT THE AUTHOR

Dr H L Ahuja, a distinguished academician, is a distinction holder in MA Economics. He was the recipient of McConnel Levin prize from Punjab University for his paper "Investment Criteria in Development Planning". He continued his academic pursuit and received his doctorate from Delhi University in 1982.

An eminent professor, Dr Ahuja has taught Advanced Economic Theory (Micro and Macro), Development Economics and Problems of Indian Economy to postgraduate students at the Kurukshetra University. He subsequently taught at Zakir Husain Delhi College, Delhi University, where he taught Micro and Macro Economic Theories, Development Policy and Indian Economy. He was a member of the Academic Council of Delhi University for a period of five years (1987-92). A prolific writer, Dr Ahuja has more than a dozen books to his credit.

DEVELOPMENT ECONOMICS

A Critical Study of Economic Growth, Development and Environment

H L AHUJA
MA, PhD (DSE)
Formerly, Associate Professor
Department of Economics
Zakir Husain Delhi College
University of Delhi
Delhi

AMIT AHUJA

S. CHAND
PUBLISHING

S Chand And Company Limited
(ISO 9001 Certified Company)

S Chand And Company Limited

(ISO 9001 Certified Company)

Head Office: D-92, Sector–2, Noida – 201301, U.P. (India), Ph. 91-120-4682700

Registered Office: A-27, 2nd Floor, Mohan Co-operative Industrial Estate, New Delhi – 110 044, Phone: 011-49731800

www.**schandpublishing.com;** e-mail: **info@schandpublishing.com**

Marketing Offices:

Chennai	:	Ph: 23632120; chennai@schandpublishing.com
Guwahati	:	Ph: 2738811, 2735640; guwahati@schandpublishing.com
Hyderabad	:	Ph: 40186018; hyderabad@schandpublishing.com
Jalandhar	:	Ph: 4645630; jalandhar@schandpublishing.com
Kolkata	:	Ph: 23357458, 23353914; kolkata@schandpublishing.com
Lucknow	:	Ph: 4003633; lucknow@schandpublishing.com
Mumbai	:	Ph: 25000297; mumbai@schandpublishing.com
Patna	:	Ph: 4011400; patna@schandpublishing.com

First Edition 2016
Reprints 2018, 2020 (Twice), 2021, 2022 (Twice), 2023 (Twice), 2024, 2025

Reprint 2026

ISBN: 978-93-856-7647-5 **Product Code:** H5DEC41ECON10ENAA16O

PRINTED IN INDIA

By Shri Shyamlal Printing Press Private Limited, Plot 20/4, Site-IV, Industrial Area Sahibabad, Ghaziabad – 201 010 and Published by S Chand And Company Limited, A-27, 2nd Floor, Mohan Co-operative Industrial Estate, New Delhi – 110 044.

To Prem and Shaifali
with Love and Affection

PREFACE

It is a matter of great satisfaction for me to bring out a book on *Development Economics*. From the very beginning of my academic career, I had great interest in the subject of economics relating to the growth and development of the poor developing countries. In 1961, soon after passing MA, I wrote a paper on "Investment Criteria in Development Planning", then a popular topic, for which I was awarded McConnel-Levin Prize by the Punjab University. This further increased my interest in the subject of economics of development. Later, I worked on my PhD research topic "*Development Strategy in a Labour Surplus Economy*" at the Delhi School of Economics and was awarded PhD degree in 1982. Besides, I taught this subject to postgraduate and BA (Hons) classes at Kurukshetra University and Zakir Husain Delhi College, University of Delhi for about 4 decades. Since I remained preoccupied in teaching, writing and revising my books on Advanced Microeconomics and Macroeconomics, I could not get sufficient time to write a book on Development Economics which has been my specialised field.

On the persistent demand of fellow teachers and pressure from my publisher, I have written this book entitled *Development Economics,* which deals with the problems of economic growth, development and eradication of poverty and unemployment. Recently, the issue of environment and sustainable development has gained worldwide prominence. It has been my mission to write a comprehensive and a critical study on the subject. It has taken me more than seven years to complete the writing of this book and, during this long period, I had to take the help of my son Amit Ahuja in various ways, especially in writing and expressing the various economic concepts and propositions in mathematical forms, and estimating the regression equations through computer programming. I have made a lot of effort to produce a good textbook which not only describes and explains the models and theories of economic growth and development but also critically evaluates them and shows to what extent they are relevant to the poor developing countries. It is for the readers to judge how far I have succeeded in my mission.

It is important to note that this book is mainly based on UGC's model curriculum on the subject for postgraduate and BA (Hons) classes of Indian universities. In UGC's model curriculum, the study of three important topics, namely, *economic inequality and poverty*; their relation with economic growth and *problems of unemployment and employment generation* in developing countries is explicitly not included. I have however dealt with these subjects in detail in the end - part XII of this book.

The book is divided into the following twelve parts:

1. **Development and Underdevelopment**–In this part, I have explained not only the concepts of economic growth and development, and their measurement but also discussed Amartya Sen's Capabilities Approach to development. Besides, the various theories of perpetuation of underdevelopment and poverty in the presently developing countries and the existing development gap between the developed and developing countries have been discussed.
2. **Factors in Economic Development**–This part is concerned with the critical study of the factors that affect economic growth such as capital formation, technological progress, human capital (education, health and nutrition), population growth and economic development.
3. **Modern Theories and Models of Economic Growth**–This part provides an analytical study of the important growth models such as Harrod–Domar model, Solow's neoclassical model, Meade's neoclassical model, Joan Robinson's model and Romer's endogenous growth model (new theory of economic growth). I have also explained how these models are relevant to the problems of growth and development of the developing countries.
4. **Theories of Economic Development: Classical, Marx, Schumpeter**–This part provides a critical study of classical theories of growth and development of Adam Smith, Ricardo and Malthus, Marx's theory of capitalist development and Schumpeter's theory of development which assigns key role to the entrepreneur and his innovations in the growth process. Besides, I have explained and evaluated Lewis's model of development with unlimited labour supply.

5. **Various Approaches and Strategies of Development**–This part deals with the prominent strategies of economic development namely, Big Push, Nurkse's balanced growth and Hirschman's unbalanced growth, dualism (both sociological and technological), 'Critical Minimum Effort' thesis, Mahalanobis's basic heavy industries-based strategy and Vakil and Brahmananda's wage-goods strategy of development.
6. **Sectoral Aspects of Economic Development**–This part examines the role of agriculture in economic development, agricultural productivity and efficiency, new technology and importance of land reforms. In addition to this, the rationale and pattern of industrialisation in developing countries with special reference to *import-substituting and export-led industrial growth* are also discussed. Besides, the issue of efficiency of small-scale vs large-scale industries has also been discussed.
7. **International Aspects of Economic Development**–In this part, a critical evaluation of the following subjects relating to international trade and economic growth has been made: Trade as an engine of economic growth, Myrdal's backwash effect and Prebisch-Singer's doctrine of deteriorating terms of trade of underdeveloped countries, dual gap analysis, *export-led growth model*, theory of effective rate of protection and tariff, post-GATT international economic order and the role of WTO.
8. **Resource Allocation: Choice and Pattern of Investment**–This part presents a critical analysis of various investment criteria such as minimum capital-output criterion, social marginal productivity criterion and maximum reinvestment quotient criterion. Moreover, it also discusses *cost-benefit analysis and project evaluation.*
9. **Macroeconomic Policies and Development**–In this part, the role of monetary policy, fiscal policy (taxation, government borrowing, creation of new money), foreign capital and multinational corporations (MNCs) in resources mobilisation for development have been discussed. Besides, IMF and World Bank-directed policy of *structural adjustment reforms comprising liberalisation, privatisation and globalisation* have been critically evaluated.
10. **Environment and Development**–This important part is concerned with the study of environment use and degradation, external diseconomies and common property resources, measures for pollution control, environment accounting and *issues of sustainable development and climate change*.
11. **Planning and Development**–In this part, I have explained the role of planning in developing countries for faster and inclusive economic growth, and reviewed the objectives and development strategies of India's Five-Year Plans, both in the pre-reforms and post-reforms period. Besides, I have discussed the Indian Growth Miracle in terms of GDP growth and by overtaking China India has emerged as the *fastest growing economy of the world*. However, I have explained in detail how faster GDP growth alone is not enough for raising living standards of the people. In this connection, I have critically evaluated the views of Prof. Jagdish Bhagwati and Amartya Sen on growth, income distribution and poverty.
12. **Inequality, Poverty and Unemployment**–This crucial part explains the problems of inequality, poverty and unemployment, how their magnitudes are measured and their relationship with economic growth. Special mention has been made of Kuznets' Inverted-U Hypothesis of changes in income distribution during the process of economic growth and the discussion of various development strategies of labour-absorption in gainful employment.

I hope this comprehensive book with the analytical treatment of various subjects of development economics will fulfil the needs of both undergraduate and postgraduate students of Indian universities. Besides, it will also meet fully the requirements of those preparing for competitive examinations of IAS and allied services.

Comments and suggestions from the fellow teachers will be heartily welcomed. These should be communicated either through E-mail address (drhlahuja@gmail.com) or the residential address given below.

69, Vaishali
Pitampura
Delhi-110034

H L AHUJA

SYLLABUS

UGC MODEL CURRICULUM
M.A.
Compulsory Paper : Paper–VI

ECONOMICS OF GROWTH AND DEVELOPMENT

Module 1: Economic Growth—I

Economic growth and development—Factors affecting economic growth: capital, labour and technology; Growth models—Harrod and Domar, instability of equilibrium; Neoclassical growth models—Solow and Meade, Mrs. Joan Robinson's growth model; Cambridge criticism of neoclassical analysis of growth; The capital controversy.

Module 2: Economic Growth—II

Technological progress—Embodied and disembodied technical progress; Hicks, Harrod; learning by doing, production function approach to the economic growth; Total factor productivity and growth accounting; Growth Models of Kaldor and Pasinetti, optimal savings and Ramsay's rule, golden rule of accumulation, two-sector model of Ujawa, Stability of equilibrium, money in economic growth, Tobin, Levhari, Patinkin and Johnson; Endogenous growth; Intellectual capital; Role of learning, education and research; AK model—Explanations of cross country differentials in economic growth.

Module 3: Social and Institutional Aspects of Development

Development and underdevelopment—Perpetuation of underdevelopment; Poverty—Absolute and relative; Measuring development and development gap—Per capita income, inequality of income, Human development index and other indices of development and quality of life—Food security, education, health and nutrition; Human resource development; Population problem and growth pattern of population—Theory of demographic transition; Population as limits to growth and as ultimate source—Population, poverty and environment; Economic development and institutions —market and market failures, State and State failure; Issues of good governance.

Module 4: Theories of Development

Classical theory of development—Contributions of Adam Smith, Ricardo, Malthus and James Mill, Karl Marx and development of capitalist economy—Theory of social change, surplus value and profits; Immutable laws of capitalist development; Crisis in capitalism—Schumpeter and capitalistic development; Innovations—Role of credit, profit and degeneration of capitalism; Structural analysis of development; Imperfect market paradigm.

Module 5: Approaches to Development

Partial theories of growth and development—Vicious circle of poverty, circular causation, unlimited supply of labour, big-push, balanced growth, unbalanced growth, critical minimum effort thesis, low-income equilibrium trap; Dualism—Technical, behavioural and social; Ranis and Fei model, Dixit and Marglin model, Kelly et. al. Model; Dependency theory of development; Structural view of development.

Module 6: Sectoral Aspects of Development

Role of agriculture in economic development; Efficiency and productivity in agriculture, New technology and sustainable agriculture; Globalization and agricultural growth; Rationale and pattern of industrialization in developing countries; The choice of techniques and appropriate technology and employment; Efficiency of small-scale vs large-scale production; Terms of trade between agriculture and industry; Infrastructure and its importance; Labour markets and their functioning in developing countries.

Module 7: Trade and Economic Development

International trade as engine of growth; Static and dynamic gains from trade; Prebisch, Singer and Myrdal thesis vs free trade; Export-led growth; Dual gap analysis; Balance of payments; Tariffs and effective protection; Post-GATT international economic order; WTO and developing countries.

Module 8: Macroeconomic Policies and Development

Role of monetary and fiscal policies in developing countries—Prior savings, inflation and growth—Empirical evidence; External resources—FDI, Aid vs Trade, technology inflow; MNCs activity in developing countries; Borrowings—domestic and external; Burden of borrowing—IMF and World Bank policies in developing countries.

Module 9: Allocation of Resources

Need for investment criteria in developing countries —Present vs. future, alternative investment criteria; Cost-benefit analysis, shadow prices, project evaluation and UNIDO guidelines.

UGC MODEL CURRICULUM
B.A. & B.A (Honours)
Compulsory Paper
Paper–V

DEVELOPMENT AND ENVIRONMENTAL ECONOMICS

Module 1: Development and Economic Growth

Economic growth and development—Factors affecting economic growth: Capital, labour and technology; Growth models—Harrod and Domar, instability of equilibrium; Neoclassical growth models—Solow and Meade, Mrs. Joan Robinson's growth model; Technological progress —Embodied and disembodied technical progress—Technical progress of Hicks, Harrod; Learning by doing; Production function approach to the sources of growth.

Module 2: Economic Development, Population and Institutions

Development and underdevelopment—Perpetuation of underdevelopment; Poverty: absolute and relative; Measuring development and development gap—per capita income, inequality of income and wealth, human development index and other indices of development and quality of life; Concept of intellectual capital; Food security, education, health and nutrition—Human resource development — Population problem and growth pattern of population; Theory of demographic transition; Population, poverty and environment; Economic development and institutions; Market and market failures; State and State failure; Issues of good governance.

Module 3: Theories of Economic Development

Theories of development—Classical theory of development; Karl Marx theory of development; Theory of social change; Immutable laws of capitalist development—Crisis in capitalism; Schumpeter and capitalist development.

Module 4: Approaches to Economic Development

Partial theories of growth and development—Vicious circle of poverty, circular causation, unlimited supply of labour, big-push, balanced growth, unbalanced growth, critical minimum effort thesis—Low income equilibrium trap—Dualism: Technical, behavioural and social.

Module 5: Sectoral View of Development

Role of agriculture in economic development; Importance of land reforms; Efficiency and productivity in agriculture; New Technology and sustainable agriculture; Globalization and agriculture growth; Rationale and pattern of industrialization in developing countries; The choice of techniques and appropriate technology and employment; Efficiency of small-scale vs. large-scale production; Terms of trade between agriculture and industry; Infrastructure and its importance; Labour markets and their functioning in developing countries.

Module 6: Choice and Pattern of Investment

Need for investment criteria in LDCs; Present vs. future growth; Alternative investment criteria; Cost-benefit analysis.

Module 7: International Aspects of Economic Development

International trade as an engine of growth; Static and dynamic gains from trade; Prebisch, Singer and Myrdal thesis vs free trade; Export-led growth; Dual gap analysis; Balance of payments; tariffs and effective protection; Post-GATT International economic order; WTO and developing countries.

Module 8: Macroeconomic Policy and Economic Development

Role of monetary and fiscal policies in developing countries; External resources; FDI; Aid vs Trade; technology inflow; MNCs activity in developing countries; IMF and World Bank policies in developing countries.

Module 9: Planning and Development

Need for planning—Democratic, decentralized and indicative planning, micro level planning; Review of Indian plan models.

Module 10: Environment and Ecology

Environment-economy linkage; Environment as a necessity and luxury; Population-environment linkage; Environmental use and environmental disruption as an allocation problem; Market failure for environmental goods; Environment as a public good; The common problem; Property right approach to environmental problem; valuation of environmental damages; Land, water, air and forests.

Module 11: Pollution Control

Prevention, control and abatement of pollution; Choice of policy instruments in developing countries; Environmental legislation; Indicators of sustainable development; Environmental accounting.

CONTENTS

PART—I
DEVELOPMENT AND UNDERDEVELOPMENT

PART—II
FACTORS IN ECONOMIC DEVELOPMENT

PART—III
MODERN THEORIES AND MODELS OF ECONOMIC GROWTH

PART—IV
THEORIES OF ECONOMIC DEVELOPMENT: CLASSICAL, MARX, SCHUMPETER

PART—VI
SECTORAL ASPECTS OF ECONOMIC DEVELOPMENT

PART—VII
INTERNATIONAL ASPECTS OF ECONOMIC DEVELOPMENT

PART—IX
MACROECONOMIC POLICIES AND DEVELOPMENT

PART—XI
PLANNING AND DEVELOPMENT

PART—XII
INEQUALITY, POVERTY AND UNEMPLOYMENT

PART I

Development and Underdevelopment

- Economic Growth and Development
- Alternative Measures of Development and Human Development Index (HDI)
- Underdevelopment and Development Gap
- Common Characteristics of Developing Countries
- Perpetuation of Underdevelopment and Obstacles to Economic Development

Economic Growth and Development

Before explaining the factors which determine economic growth and development and the common characteristics of the developing countries, it is useful to describe how the terms economic growth and development are interpreted by the economists. In the fifties and sixties when the economics of growth and development were evolved, economic growth and development were considered to have the same meaning and therefore these two terms were used interchangeably. Today, however, an important distinction is drawn between economic growth and economic development. In what follows we first explain the meaning of these terms and the distinction between them.

Meaning of Economic Growth

Economic growth has been defined in two ways. In the first place, *economic growth is defined as a sustained annual increase in an economy's real national income over a long period of time.* In other words, economic growth means *rising trend of net national product at constant prices*. This definition has been criticised by some economists as inadequate and unsatisfactory. They argue that total national income may be increasing and yet the standard of living of the people may be falling. This can happen when the population is increasing at a faster rate than total national income. For instance, if national income is rising by 1% per year and population is increasing at 2% per year, the standard of living of the people will tend to fall. This is so because when population is increasing more rapidly than national income, per capita income will go on falling. Per capita income will rise when the national income increases faster than population. Therefore, the second and better way of defining economic growth is to do so in terms of per capita income. According to the second view, *"economic growth means the annual increase in real per capita income of a country over a long period.* Thus, Professor Arthur Lewis says that *"economic growth means the growth of output per head of population"*. Since the main aim of economic growth is to raise the standards of living of the people, therefore the second way of defining economic growth which runs in terms of per capita income or output is better.

Another point which is worth mentioning in regard to the definition of economic growth is that the increase in national income or more correctly increase in per capita income or output, must be a 'sustained increase' if it is to be called economic growth. By sustained increase in per capita income we mean the upward or rising trend in per capita income over a long period of time. A mere short-period rise in per capita income, such as that occurs over a business cycle, cannot be validly called economic growth.

Now, almost universally, rates of economic growth are measured both in terms of increase in overall Gross National Product (GNP) or Net National Product (NNP) and increase in per capita income. While Gross National Product (GNP) measures the total output of goods and services which an economy is capable of producing, per capita income measures how much of real goods and services which an average person of the community will have for consumption and investment, that is, average level of living of a citizen of a country.

Thus, world organisations such as World Bank and IMF have been employing both these measures of economic growth in their annual World Development Reports for comparing growth and levels of living of the developed and the developing countries. In India also our Planning Commission, Central Statistical Organisation (CSO), and Reserve Bank of India have been measuring economic growth on the basis of both overall GNP or NNP and per capita income. The recent estimates of annual growth in per capita income and GNP are given in Table 1.1. This table reveals an interesting feature *that economic growth achieved in recent years is higher in the developing countries than in the developed countries*. However, it should be noted that in the past several decades the present-day developed countries recorded much higher growth rates than the developing countries which remained static for a long period. As a result, per capita income and levels of living of the people of the developed countries are now much higher as compared to those of the developing countries. The problem of the developing countries is to catch up with the developed countries through attaining rapid economic growth so as to enjoy higher levels of living.

For the sake of comparison we have given in Table 1.1 the data of population, Gross National Product (GNP) per capita and growth rate of Gross Domestic Product (GDP) for three periods 1980-90, 1990-2000 and 2000-2012 of some developed and developing countries. It will be seen from this Table 1.1 that in the last two decades India has become the second fastest growing economy of the world.

Table 1.1. GNP Per Capita, Growth Rate and Population in Some Developed and Developing Countries

Country	Population (million) 2012	GNP per capita in 2012 (PPP US Dollars)	Average Annual Growth Rate of GDP (%)		
Developed Countries					
			1980-90	1990-2000	2000-2012
USA	314	50,610	3.0	3.6	1.7
Australia	23	43,300	3.5	3.9	3.1
UK	63	36,880	3.2	2.6	1.6
Canada	35	42,530	3.4	3.1	1.9
Japan	128	36,290	4.1	1.0	0.7
Developing Countries					
India	1,237	3,840	5.8	6.0	7.8
Brazil	199	11,720	–	2.7	3.6
China	1,351	9,210	10.2	10.6	10.6
Pakistan	179	3,030	6.3	3.8	4.4
Bangladesh	155	2,070	4.3	4.8	6.0
Sri Lanka	20	6,120	4.2	5.3	5.5

Source: World Bank, *World Development Report*, 2014 and World Development Indicators, 2014.

Meaning of Economic Development: Traditional View

As mentioned above, no distinction was drawn between economic growth and development in the beginning of the evolution of economics of development. However, since the seventies it has been thought necessary to distinguish between economic growth and economic development. There are two views even about the concept of economic development. The traditional view has been to interpret it in terms of planned changes in the structure of national product and the occupational pattern of labour force and also the institutional and technological changes that bring about such changes or accompany such changes. It may be noted that Kuznets in his study of *Modern Economic Growth* interpreted the process of modern economic growth which involves these structural changes[1]. In this view during the process of economic growth share of agriculture in both national product and employment of labour force declines and that of industries and services increases. Various strategies of development which were suggested until 'seventies' generally focussed on rapid industrialisation so that structural transformation could be achieved. For this purpose appropriate institutional and technological changes were recommended to bring about such structural changes. Thus C.P. Kindleberger writes, *Economic growth means more output and economic development implies both more output and changes in the technical and institutional arrangements by which it is produced.*[2]

Thus, according to traditional view, economic development implies growth plus structural change. Structural change refers to changes in technological and institutional factors which cause shift of labour from agriculture to modern manufacturing and services sectors and also generate self-sustaining growth of output. An aspect of structural change which is of special mention is that during the process of economic development there occurs a shift of working population from low productivity employment in agriculture to the modern industrial and services sectors having higher levels of productivity of labour. That is, during the process of economic development percentage share of working population in agriculture sharply falls whereas percentage shares of working population employed in modern industrial and services sectors substantially increase. Along with this change in sectoral distribution of labour force there occurs a change in sectoral composition of national income in which percentage contribution of agriculture to national income and declines and percentage contributions to national income of industrial and services sectors increase. This occurs due to the change in pattern of consumption of the people as economy grows and people's income increases as well as due to the changes in levels of productivity in the different sectors of the economy.

It is worth mentioning that in this view causal references were made to the role of some social factors such as growth of literacy, education and good health in economic development but they were considered to be of secondary importance. On the whole, in this view of economic development which generally prevailed till seventies, development was considered to be an economic phenomenon in which benefits from growth in overall GNP or per capita GNP and the structural changes accompanying it would trickle down to the poor and unemployed. No separate or special attention was paid to eliminate mass poverty and unemployment and to reduce inequalities in income distribution.[3]

The Concept of Economic Development: Modern View

The experience of the developing countries during the sixties and seventies showed that whereas target rates of economic growth were in fact achieved, trickle-down effect in the form of creation of more employment opportunities, rise in wages and improvement in income distribution did not operate. The problems of poverty, unemployment and income inequality further worsened instead of getting reduced during the process of growth in the nineteen fifties and sixties in the developing countries. For instance, in India, Dandekar and Rath found that 40 per cent of rural population in India lived below the poverty line in 1968-69. Using somewhat different approach, B.S. Minhas estimated that 37 per cent of rural population in India lived below the poverty line in 1967-68. Similarly, the magnitude of poverty and unemployment and the extent of income inequalities also increased in many other developing countries.[4]

Thus, due to the failure of traditional strategies of development in solving the problems of poverty, unemployment and inequality, it was realised in the seventies that the concept of development

---

1 Simon Kuznets, *Modern Economic Growth*.

2 C.P. Kindleberger, *Economic Development*, McGraw-Hill, Second Edition, 1965, p. 3.

3 Dandekar and Rath, *Poverty in India*, 1971.

4 B.S. Minhas, "Poverty, Land Redistribution and Development Strategy", *Indian Economic Review*, 1971.

should be broadened so that it should signify that well-being of the people has increased. This led to the view that economic development should not be judged on the basis of growth in GNP alone. Therefore, when we regard the well-being of the masses as the ultimate objective of development, we have to see whether poverty and unemployment are decreasing and how the increases in gross national product or national income are being distributed among the population. Economic development will take place in true terms only if the poor people are raised above the poverty line. Late Prof. Sukhamoy Chakravarty rightly writes, "*The rate of growth strategy is by itself an inadequate device to deal with the problems of generating employment opportunities and for reducing economic disparities. Much depends on the composition of the growth process and how growth is financed and how benefits from growth process are distributed.*"[5]

It is worth mentioning that there is no guarantee that when there is increase in GNP, employment will also increase. It can happen that with the use of more capital-intensive technique while production may be increasing at a rapid rate, employment may be falling instead of rising. According to the modern perception of economic development, rapid increase in GNP secured through displacing labour by machines and thus causing rise in unemployment and underemployment cannot be called true economic development. Professor Dudley Seers makes the meaning of economic development according to the new perception in the following words:

"*The questions to ask about a country's development are therefore: What has been happening to poverty? What has been happening to unemployment? What has been happening to inequality? If all three of these have declined from high levels, then beyond doubt this has been a period of development for the country concerned. If one or two of these central problems have been growing worse, especially if all three have, it would be strange to call the result development even if per capita income doubled.*"[6]

Recently, the concept of economic development has been further widened so that it now involves not only reduction in poverty, inequality and unemployment but also requires improvement in *quality of life which includes cleaner environment, better education, good health and nutrition.* Thus World Development Report 1991, published by the World Bank, asserts: "*The challenge of development is to improve the quality of life, especially in the world's poor countries, a better quality of life generally calls for higher incomes but it involves much more. It encompasses as ends in themselves better education, higher standards of health and nutrition, less poverty, a cleaner environment, more equality of opportunity*"[7] Thus the concept of economic development has been greatly broadened. Today economic development is interpreted as not only in more growth in Gross Domestic Product (GDP) but also in terms of good quality of life which, according to Prof. Amartya Sen, '*consists in enlargement of opportunities for people and freedom of human choices*'. This new concept of development includes achievement of freedom from servitude to ignorance and illiteracy. It also includes enjoyment of human rights. Thus United Nations '*Human Development Report*' of 1994 in the writing of which Prof. Amartya Sen made a significant contribution, asserts, "Human beings are born with certain potential capabilities. *The purpose of development* is *to create an environment in which all people can expand their capabilities, and opportunities can be enlarged for both present and future generations*..... .Wealth is important for human life. but to concentrate on it exclusively is wrong for two reasons. First, accumulating wealth is not necessary for the fulfilment of some important human choices .... Second, human choices extend far beyond economic well-being." In his recent book, Amartya Sen writes, "Economic growth cannot be sensibly treated as an end in itself. Development has to be more concerned with enhancing the *lives we lead and the freedoms we enjoy*."[8]

5 Sukhamoy Chakravarty, "Some Observations on Growth Process," *Seminar*, 1971.

6 Dudley Seers, "The Meaning of Development", a paper presented at the Eleventh World Conference of the Society for International Development (New Delhi), 1969.

7 World Bank, *World Development Report*, 1991.

8 Amartya Sen, *Development as Freedom,* Oxford University Press, 2001, 175.

On the basis of various ingredients of good quality of life and other criteria such as enlargement of human choices and freedom a human development index is prepared by United Nations Development Programme (UNDP). This human development index is considered as a better indicator of economic development index.

SEN'S 'CAPABILITIES' APPROACH TO DEVELOPMENT

Meaning of Development

Prof. Amartya Sen has put forward a new view of development based on his concepts of freedom and capabilities. According to Prof. Sen, "*Development can be seen as a process of expanding the real freedom that people enjoy*".[9] Development consists of the *removal of various types of unfreedoms* that leave people with little choice and little opportunity of exercising their reasoned faculty. He further elaborates "*Development requires the removal of major sources of unfreedoms*: *poverty as well as tyranny, poor economic opportunities as well as systematic social deprivation, neglect of public facilities as well as intolerance or overactivity of repressive states*". This Sen's view of development is in sharp contrast to traditional view of development in terms of growth of GNP or rise in personal incomes or industrialisation or technological advancement are important *as means* to expanding freedoms enjoyed by the people but they are not sufficient to remove unfreedoms suffered by a vast number of people in a society. In Sen's conception freedom has a very wide connotation. Thus, according to Sen, development means freedom from hunger and unourishment, freedom from illiteracy, freedom from illness, freedom from unemployment, freedom from social deprivation, freedom from political intolerance and so forth. In his view, freedom also depends on factors such as social and economic arrangements (for example, facilities for education and health) as well as civil and political rights.[10]

It is worth noting that in Sen's approach expansion of freedom is viewed as both a primary as well as the principal objective of development. To quote him again, "Viewing development in terms of expanding substantive freedom *directs attention to the ends* that make development important rather than merely some of the means that, interalia, play a prominent part in the process."[11]

Despite substantial achievement in terms of GDP and industrialisation, according to Sen, the contemporary society denies elementary freedoms to a vast number of people. Thus, despite social growth in GDP in several countries of the world (including India) there still prevails *abysmal poverty which deprives people of freedom to satisfy hunger, to get sufficient nutrition or get treatment for as various diseases they suffer from and the opportunity to get adequate clothing, clean water and sanitation facilities*. He also mentions the lack of freedom or what he calls unfreedoms of the people relating to lack of public facilities for healthcare and educational facilities and above all lack of effective public institutions for maintenance of local law and order. Though certain political and social freedoms such as freedom of political participation and dissent or opportunities to get basic education and healthcare are 'conducive to development' but their significance lies in the fact that they are 'constituents of development'.

Some critics especially Prof. Jagdish Bhagwati, have alleged that Sen is against market mechanism. This is however not correct. Like Adam Smith, Sen views market mechanism as *'freedom of exchange and transactions'*. He acknowledges that market mechanism is significant as a means of contributing to high economic growth and overall economic progress but emphasises the role of market *as a part of the process of development* in the sense of "freedom of exchange and transactions" of the people, not an end itself.

9 *Ibid.*

10 *Ibid.*

11 Amartya Sen, *op.cit*., p. 3.

Freedoms and Capabilities

Sen's view of development as freedom forms the basis of his capabilities approach to development. *Capabilities refer to what a person can or cannot do, can or cannot be*. The relevant capabilities which people can have are of various types. Being free from starvation, from hunger, from undernourishment, freedom to participate in communal life, being adequately clothed and sheltered, being free to travels etc. In this context, it is worthwhile to explain *Sen's concept of functionings* which refers to what a person does or can do with the commodities of given characteristics that he comes to possess or control. Explaining the meaning of "functionalities" Sen writes, "The concept of "functionings" reflects the various things a person may value doing or being. The value functions may vary from elementary ones, such as being adequately nourished and being free from avoidable diseases to very complex activities or personal states, such as being able to take part in the life of the community and having self-respect"[12]

Sen draws an important distinction between *realised functionings* and *capability* set. While the *realised* functionings refer to what a person is actually able to do, the capabilities is a set of alternatives open to him, that is, has freedom to choose from the opportunities available. Thus while realised functionings inform us about the things a person possesses, the "capabilities" tell us about the things a person is substantially free to do. Capability is thus a kind of freedom to achieve alternative combinations of functionings. These capabilities can be enhanced by public policy.

It follows from above that free from shackles of unfreedoms and the expansion of capabilities of persons are the central aspects of approach to development. It is because of Sen's emphasis on freedom and capabilities that in development economics today economists are laying stress on education and health, food security, nutrition, inclusive growth and empowerment of women. According to Sen, poverty must be seen as deprivation of basic capabilities rather than merely as *lowness of incomes* which is the standard criterion of identification of poverty[13]. He recognizes that major causes of poverty, but there are other factors that influence deprivation of capability that leads to poverty. Therefore, his view of development as freedom, and poverty as capability deprivation that he emphasizes that the objective of development must not be just maximisation of income or wealth as they are only one factor in the development process. Thus, according to him, "for a fuller understanding of the development process, it is simply not adequate to take as our basic objective just the maximisation of income or wealth . . . . economic growth cannot be treated as an end in itself. Development has to be more concerned with enhancing the lives we lead and the freedoms we enjoy. Expanding the freedoms that we reason to value not only make our lives richer and more unfettered but also allows us to be fuller social persons, exercising our own volitions and interacting with and influencing–the world in which we live".[14]

Prof. Amartya Sen on Growth, Poverty and Distribution in India

It will be noted from the above that Prof. Amartya Sen has been an advocate of the approach that considers building of capabilities of the people through more education and healthcare of the poor. Besides, he advocates for enlargement of job opportunities for the poor and freedom of human choice as a means of eliminating poverty and promoting well-being of the people. Unlike Jagdish Bhagwati, his chief critic, he does not consider growth first and then redistribution to share the problems of poverty and unemployment. In his latest book coauthered with Jean Dieze 'An uncertain Glory' India and its contradictions he points out that rapid growth in India has co-existed with grossly inadequate social services (education and health) and physical services (safe water electricity, roads drainage and sanitation).

12 Amartya Sen, *op.cit.*, p. 75.
13 Amartya Sen, *op.cit.*, p. 87.
14 Amartya sen, *op.cit.*, pp. 14-15.

Despite significant economic growth achieved in the last two decades (1991-2012), according to him, there still prevails widespread poverty in India. The poor and underprivileged people suffer from undernourishment, poor health, illiteracy, lack of education and skills to get gainful employment. Freedom from hunger and undernourishment freedom from illness and freedom from illiteracy are essential requirements of economic development. In his new book he argues for integrating growth and development. He thus writes, "While growth is an important tool for enhancing living conditions, its *reach and impact depend greatly on what is being done with the fruits of growth.* The relation between economic growth and advancement of living standards depends on money factors, including economic and social inequality in general, and *no less importantly on what* the government does with the public revenue that is generated by economic growth. The importance of economic growth can be adequately understood only in this broader contact"[15]. He thus writes, "It is necessary to recognise the role of growth in facilitating development in the form of enhancing human lives and freedoms, but it is also necessary in this context to appreciate how the possibilities of a country depends in turn on the advancement of human capabilities (through education healthcare and other facilities) in which the State can play a useful role.

Thus, it is the building of capabilities of the poor and gain freedom from illness and illiteracy that Sen views as development. To quote him again "*Economic growth cannot be sensibly treated as an end in itself. Development has to be more concerned with enhancing the lives we lead and freedoms*, we enjoy. Furthermore, the challenge of development is to improve the quality of life, especially in developing countries such as ours. A better quality of life generally calls for high standards of health and nutrition, less poverty, more equality of opportunity.[16] In his latest book, *An Uncertain Glory: India and its Contradictions*, he cites successful countries[17] like Korea and China to argue that fast economic growth is not sustainable without strong development of human capital and essential infrastructure. India lags behind many countries at a similar level of development and even behind poor Bangladesh. In an interview with *Times of India* at the time of publication of its above mentioned book in July 2013 he says, "Despite great success in many ways over the last two decades the fact is that India is in a dreadful state in many ways. *Inequality is the primary aspect of it*. About economic growth I think there are two things about it. First, the way the Indian dialogue has developed there seems to be basic involvement about how growth happens. *No country in the world with such a fast sustained rate of economic growth has done so little towards having an educated and healthy labour force*." The way the debate has come it is now just '*we now have growth so we have to make it inclusive*'. Now, according to him, these are not two distinct things. If growth happens it depends on how it is happening. *If it happens because you have an educated and healthy labour force then a lot of people are better placed to earn more income*".

It is evident from the above that, according to Sen, the State should begin with investment in education and healthcare of the people right away without waiting for first to become rich and then think of redistribution for achieving inclusive growth. He gives the example of Singapore, Taiwan, Korea, China which began with investment in education and healthcare of the people without waiting for first becoming rich. In their case, according to him, growth happened along with the poor benefiting from it by making earnings from the education and health acquired by them in the

---

15 Jean Dreze and Amartya Sen, *An Uncertain Glory, India and Its Contradictions*, Penguin Books, 1914, p. 38

16 Amartya Sen, *Development as Freedom*, Oxford University Press, 2001, p. 14.

17 *Ibid*, p. 39.

process of growth and in this way become a productive part of the society. He further emphasises, as mentioned above, that growth will generate more resources and if they are ploughed back for further investment in building human capabilities, it will still generate rapid economic growth. He bemoans the fact that even after 60 years of development India has not achieved universal education. In response to Bhagwati's criticism he says that he has not been against liberalisation and globalisation and did not support the license permit system. But he emphasises that while economic reforms initiated by Dr. Manmohan Singh in 1991 *attempted to correct the overactivity of government in some fields* (*i.e.*, removing licence-permit system by undertaking liberalisation and privatization), *the need to correct government underactivity in other areas has not really been addressed.* As back as in 1998, he wrote, "the success of liberalisation and closer integration with the world economy may be severely impaired by India's backwardness in basic education, elementary healthcare, gender inequality and other limitations".[18]

It is because of absence of the constructive activities of the State, namely, expansion in government spending on healthcare and nutrition of the people that he has criticised "Gujarat Model of Development".

Sen and his co-author Jean Dreze have supported the starting of *MGNREGA Scheme* because it helps the poor to obtain gainful employment giving them income which they can use to end their undernourishment which contribute to the improvement of their health. Similarly, they have supported the passage of Food Security Bill which would ensure the poor people adequate food to remove their hunger and undernourishment and therefore contribute to their capability to participate in the process of development.

Thus, Sen believes that the *State must directly deliver food, employment, education and health-care rather than relying on trickle-down effect of economic growth achieved through the dominant role of private sector in a predominantly free-market economy*. Besides, Sen is of the view that rapid economic growth achieved through liberalisation, privatisation and globalisation of the Indian economy has resulted in glaring income inequalities which besides being non-functional lead to conspicuous consumption of the few rich people. This has adversely affected resources available for growth and social spending by the government on food security, education, employment and healthcare of the poor people. Furthermore, according to him, rapid growth would have been brought about by involving in India's most abundant resource, namely, investing in education and health of its people and thereby building up their capabilities for productive work, the present glaring income inequalities would not have been there and inclusive growth in real terms would have been achieved.

Three Core Values of Development

We have explained above that, in the new view, development is used to describe the process of economic and social change in a society whereby there is not only growth in GDP but also there is wider distribution of benefits or gains of growth of GDP and expansion in employment opportunities for the people. As a result both poverty and unemployment fall. Prof. Amartya Sen, as seen above further widened the meaning of development by viewing it as enhancing of freedoms, entitlements and capabilities of the people which are not necessarily generally accompanied with growth in GDP. Related to Sen's view of development is Goulet's[19] view of *core values* or *basic components* of development which reflect the wider meaning of real development and depends on the achievement

18 Amartya Sen, "Theory and Practice of Development" in Isher Judge Ahluwalia and J.M.D. Little (eds) *India's Economic Reforms and Development*, Essays in Honour of Dr. Manmohan Singh, Oxford University Press, 1998, p. 82.

19 D. Goulet. *The Cruel Choice : A New Concept in the Theory of Development* (New York; Atheneum), 1971 and *Development Ethics at Work* (London: Routledge), 2006.

of major economic and social objectives. These three core values are : (1) Life-sustenance; (2) Self-esteem; and (3) Freedom. We explain below these core values which constitute the three components of development.

1. **Life-sustenance:** All human beings have certain *basic needs* which must be met if they have to live. These basic needs include food, clothing, shelter, and healthcare. If any of these essential things is not available or in critically short supply, it will not be possible for people to sustain their lives. A basic function of an economy is to provide people with food, clothing, shelter and healthcare to save them from miserable life. No doubt, the fulfilment of these basic needs of human beings require economic growth with right type of product composition and equitable distribution of basic goods being produced. This essential objective of development will be realised if absolute poverty is eliminated, enough employment opportunities are created and present income inequalities are reduced.
2. **Self-esteem:** A second component of good life for the people is *to live with respect, honour or dignity*. All people and societies want to live with self-respect and dignity because only then they would have a sense of their own worth. The nature and form of self-esteem may vary from society to society and from culture to culture. A country will have true development if it gains self-esteem, being free from dominance by others. This is not only true of individuals but also of the society as a whole. As Goulet put it, "*Development is legitimized as a goal because it is an important, perhaps an indispensable, way of gaining esteem*"[20] It may be noted for a nation as a whole to gain self-esteem and having a profound sense of its worth in the comity of nations it requires to grow economically and become prosperous. This is because, as Todaro and Smith write, "national prosperity has become an almost universal measure of wealths due to the significance attached to material values in developed nations, worthiness and esteem are nowadays increasingly conferred only on countries that possess economic wealth and technological power – those that have "developed".[21]
3. **Freedom:** The third core value is the freedom from servitude. Freedom involves expanded range of choice for the individuals and society at large. As noted above, Amartya Sen views development as freedom. The term freedom is here used not only in the sense of political or social freedoms such as the freedom of political participation and dissent, the rule of law, freedom of expression and equality of opportunity but also the freedom from poverty, ignorance and squalor so that people can determine their own destiny.

For example, women in the Indian society do not enjoy freedom of choice as they are dominated by men. No person can be free if he has no freedom of choice, if he is imprisoned by living in abysmal poverty with no education and healthcare. There must be expansion in the range of human choice open to individuals and societies at large, if true development has to take place. Long back W. Arthur Lewis, a development economist, stressed the importance of freedom saying that "*the advantage of economic growth is not that wealth increases happiness but that it increases the range of human choice*."[22] The increase in wealth of individuals enhances freedom as it enables people to gain greater control over nature and physical environment through, for example, production of food, clothing, shelter, etc. and to provide education and healthcare. Such freedom cannot be enjoyed by the people if they remain poor. Using some of the above criteria UNDP in its annual Human Development Reports prepares human freedom index for the various countries covered by it. However, some countries which have achieved high rate of economic growth or high incomes, such as China, Singapore, Malaysia, Saudi

20 Denis Goulet, *The Cruel Choice*, A New Concept in the Theory of Development (New York : Atheneum, 1971), p. 90.

21. Tadaro and Smith, *Economic Development*, 9th edition, p. 31.

22. W. Arthur Lewis, "Is Economic Growth Desirable" in *The Theory of Economic Growth* (London: Allen and Unwin, 1963, p. 420.

Arabia, have lower human freedom indexes as they do not meet some human freedom criteria adopted by UNDP.

THE OBJECTIVES OF DEVELOPMENT

From our study of Sen's capability approach to development and Goulet's core values of development we are in a position to explain the objectives of development. We may mention here the basic objective of development is broadbased improvement in the economic and social conditions of our people so as to achieve better quality of life for them. We explain important objectives of development.

1. To achieve a higher rate of GDP growth. The first and foremost objective of development is to achieve a higher rate of GDP growth so as to raise the living standards of our people. Rapid growth of total GDP or per capita income is considered necessary because it ensures an expansion in the productive capacity of the economy without which broad based improvement in living standards of the people is not possible. However, it should be recognised that faster economic growth, though necessary, is not a sufficient condition for raising the living standards of our teeming millions. This is because one can easily imagine a growth process which may not be sufficiently inclusive to ensure a spread of benefits to the mass of our population.

There are three reasons why GDP growth is necessary for raising the living standards of the population. First, rapid growth of GDP ensures a higher expansion in total income and production which, if growth process is sufficiently inclusive, will make available a larger output of goods and services to be consumed by the people and thus raise their living standards. Secondly, rapid economic growth generates more employment opportunities and income enhancing activities of the people, provided labour-saving technologies are not used for production of goods both in the industrial and agricultural sectors. Third, higher GDP growth is important because it generates higher revenues for government which help to finance anti-poverty programmes started by the government.

2. To eradicate poverty and unemployment. The second important objective of development is to eradicate poverty. As explained above in Amartya Sen's approach to development, poverty should be viewed as deprivation of basic capabilities rather than merely as low income. The existence of poverty or deprivation of basic capabilities is reflected in hunger, significant undernourishment/ especially of children premature mortality, permanent morbidity, widespread illness, and lack of basic education and other failures. Though economic growth is necessary for elimination of poverty but is not a sufficient condition for it because it is related to income distribution in a society as well.

Related to issue of poverty is the question of unemployment which exists on a large scale in developing countries, especially in labour-surplus countries such as ours. Chronic and long-term unemployment exists in the developing economies because due to higher population growth relative to capital formation it has not been possible to absorb the increasing number of workers in productive employment resulting in large-scale unemployment in developing countries. Gainful employment is the means of livelihood for the masses of the population. The growth of employment opportunities needs to be accelerated both in manufacturing and services sectors to provide employment to increasingly educated population which has high expectations and aspirations. Unemployment leads to the feelings of worthlessness and frustration among the youth leading to the increase in incidence of crime in the society.

3. To expand the freedoms enjoyed by the people. The other important objective of development, as has been discussed in Amartya Sen's approach to development and Goulet's core values, is to expand the freedoms that people of a society enjoy. Growth of GDP or of individual incomes or industrialisation or technological progress are merely *means* to expanding human freedoms but freedoms depend on other factors as well. As Sen stresses viewing development as expansion of substantive freedoms directs attention to end or objective of development rather than means such as GDP growth or industrialisation which play an important role in the process of development.

If the objective of expansion of freedoms is to be achieved, the various sources of unfreedoms such as lack of public facilities of education and healthcare, denial of political liberty and basic civil rights (such as liberty to participate in public discussion) and denial of equal rights to women in the society have to be removed. It is worth mentioning here that some have supported the denial of political liberty and basic civil rights to the people on the ground that they promote economic growth. However, Amartya Sen[23] has rightly pointed out that there is little evidence that authoritarian politics actually helps economic growth. Indeed, empirical evidence very strongly suggests that economic growth is more a matter of friendly economic climate than of a harsher political system.

EVOLUTION OF DEVELOPMENT ECONOMICS AS A SEPARATE DISCIPLINE

The study of development economics as a separate discipline is relatively new as about 65 years ago in 1950s the study of the problem of economic development of poor developing countries did not constitute an important distinct branch of economics. This is despite the fact that classical economists such as Adam Smith, Ricardo, Malthus, and Marx extensively dealt with the study of development of the economies. The theories of development of these classical economists will be explained and critically examined in a later chapter. However, with the appearance of neoclassical economics propounded among others by Alfred Marshall and A.C. Pigou who were mainly concerned with explaining efficient allocation of resources in a free market economy, development economics dealing with the developing economies found no place in their works. Believing in Say's law of markets they assumed that full employment of resources would prevail in the economy and further that the working of price mechanism would ensure sufficient incentives to save and invest to bring about appropriate growth of GNP. It was generally believed that neoclassical economics applied to developed and developing countries alike. Therefore the need for a special theory to explain economic growth and development for developing countries was not felt. In the 1930s and 1940s, the economists led by J.M. Keynes remained occupied with the problem of involuntary unemployment and depression as severe depression causing huge unemployment took place in 1929-33 in the industrialised countries.

The renewed interest and public concern with the development of poor countries began only after the Second World War when the poverty of the underdeveloped countries of Asia, Africa and Latin America posed a great challenge to the peace and progress of the world as a whole and also many underdeveloped countries got freedom from the colonial rule. It was felt that Keynesian economics which was concerned with the short-run problem of depression caused by fall in aggregate effective demand did not apply to the underdeveloped economies which faced a long-run and chronic problem of unemployment and mass poverty due to deficiency of cooperating factors (such as capital) and low productivity of resources. It was therefore felt that there was need for a distinct and separate branch of special economic theory which explains perpetuation of underdevelopment and general poverty and also the adoption of appropriate development strategies to initiate and accelerate economic growth in the developing countries.

It was pointed out that the problems of poverty, underemployment of underdeveloped economies were quite different and required special analysis. Therefore, development economics which is concerned with the economic growth, capital accumulation and underemployment in the developing countries became a special and distinct discipline. During 1950s and 1960s development policies in underdeveloped countries required acceleration of economic growth and eradication of poverty and chronic underemployment. For this, economists laid stress on capital accumulation, mobilisation of surplus labour for growth and industrialisation based on import-substitution through economic

23 Amartya Sen, *Development as Freedom*, pp. 15-16.

planning and with active role of the government. It was thought that due to market failures, development through free market, as emphasized by neoclassical economics, would neither achieve efficient allocation of scarce resources nor bring about desired GDP growth rate to remove poverty and employment. Since rate of domestic saving in these underdeveloped countries was inadequate to bring about a desired rate of growth, the need for foreign aid to supplement domestic saving was emphasised in early approaches to development based on application of Harrod-Domar growth model.

Furthermore, it was suggested in the early approaches to development in the 1950s and 1960s that since demand for primary products was inelastic by advanced industrialised countries, as explained by Prebisch, Singer and Myrdal, to accelerate growth through expansion of primary exports by developing countries would cause deterioration of terms of trade. This led to ***export pessimism,*** that is, little prospects of acceleration of growth through promotion of exports. Therefore, those economists who laid stress on limitations of development based on expansion of primary exports, advocated for import-substituting industrialisation to promote economic growth and solve the problems of poverty and unemployment in developing countries.[24]

Much of the thinking about development in this early period was how to break out of *poverty trap* or *vicious circle of poverty* or '*low level equilibrium trap'*. For this purpose Ragnar Nurkse[25] put forward a balanced '*growth strategy*' in which he suggested undertaking of simultaneous investment in a wide range of industries so that the workers employed in different industries could generate demand for each other's products so as to ensure balanced growth by overcoming the problem of demand deficiency. Hirschmanm,[26] on the other hand, laid stress on the scarcity of decision-making enterprise and also emphasised forward and backward linkages of different industries and to take advantage of them he proposed '*unbalanced growth strategy*' by concentrating investment in a few industries of strategic importance from the viewpoint of economic growth. Leibenstein[27] and Nelson[28] considered rapid population growth as a retarding factor of economic growth and recommended a certain '*critical minimum effort'* in terms of investment so as to break out the low level equilibrium trap.

Besides, Arthur Lewis[29] proposed a model of growth of a dual economy with surplus labour in which he emphasised industrialisation of underdeveloped countries by mobilising disguisedly unemployed labour in agriculture or subsistence sector and ploughing back of profits so earned for further capital accumulation and industrial growth. In India Mahalanobis growth model[30] on which Second Five Year and Third Five Year Plans were based gave a high priority to basic heavy industries producing fixed capital goods (*i.e*., machines) and basic intermediate goods such as steel, fertilizers and emphasised impor-substituting industrialisation to accelerate rate of growth of the Indian economy. Harrod-Domar model[31] of growth based on Keynesian framework which dealt with the problem of steady growth was applied to the growth problem of developing countries. Harrod-Domar model suggested that growth depends on the rate of saving and capital-output ratio $\left(g=\frac{s}{v}\right)$, where *s* represents ratio of saving to national income and *v* is rate of growth of GDP).

24 See Jagdish Bhagwati, "Development Economics: What Have We Learned?" *Asian Development Review*, 2 No.1 (1989), pp. 24-29.

25 Ragnar Nurkse, *Problems of Capital Formation in Underdeveloped Countries* (Oxford: Oxford University Press), 1953.

26 A Hirschman, *Strategy of Economic Development* (New Haven, CT: Yale University Press, 1958.

27 H. Leibenstein, *Economic Backwardness and EconomicGrowth (*New York : Wiley*)*, 1957.

28 R.R. Nelson, A Theory of Low-level Equilibrium, *American Economic Review*, December 1956.

29 Arthur Lewis, *Economic Development with Unlimited Supplies of Labour*, Manchester School, May 1954.

30 P.C. Mahalanobis, The Approach of Operational Research to Planning in India, *Sankhya*, Vol.16, December 1953.

31 R.F. Harrod, *Towards a Dynamic Economics*, Macmillan & Co; London, 1948, and E. Domar, Capital Accumulation, Rate of Growth, and Employment, *Economica*, Vol. 14, 1946.

Unlike the neoclassical economics which assumes smoothly working market mechanism, the early development economists adopted a more structural approach to development. They emphasise rigidities, lags, shortages and surpluses and low elasticities of demand and supply in developing countries. Prebisch[32] and Singer[33] have been prominent economists who laid stress on the limitations of development based on expansion of primary exports because of the adverse effects on terms of trade.

In the early 1970s there was realisation by economists that growth in terms of GDP, though a necessary condition, is not a sufficient condition for the reduction of poverty, inequality and unemployment. Therefore, in the second phase of the evolution of development economics when the emphasis on growth of GNP was downgraded, the focus of analysis shifted directly to the removal of poverty, unemployment and inequality in the developing countries. Mahboob ul Haq, an eminent economist of World Bank who along with Amartya Sen was pioneer in the development of the concept of *Human Development Economics Index* (HDI) wrote, "The problem of development must be defined as a selective attack on the worst forms of poverty. Development goals must be defined in terms of progressive reduction and eventual elimination of malnutrition, disease, illiteracy, squalor, unemployment and inequalities. We were taught to take care of our GNP because it would take care of poverty. Let us reverse this and take care of poverty because it will take care of the GNP. In other words, let us worry about the *content* of GNP even more than its rate of increase[34] ".

Thus in the seventies, the reliance on GDP growth alone to solve the problems of poverty and unemployment was challenged. It was pointed out by several economists that benefits of growth were not trickling down to the poor and the number of people living below the poverty line had increased in developing countries. Even the meaning of economic development was questioned. It was suggested that economic development was not the same thing as economic growth. According to the new view, *economic development means not only the increase in GNP (or GNP per capita) but also the reduction in poverty, unemployment and inequalities of incomes*. A World Bank study [35] titled '*Redistribution with Growth* laid stress on redistribution of incomes with reduction of poverty along with GDP growth for development to be meaningful. Besides, in the 1970s and 1980s ILO emphasised that for true development to take place *basic human needs* must be fulfilled. These basic human needs are food, clothing, shelter, healthcare and availability of drinking water. According to this, without these basic needs being met, development cannot be said to have taken place.

Another important change in the approach to development during 1970s and 1980s was a shift in the emphasis from industrialisation to agriculture. It was proposed that *agriculture-led growth strategy*[36] would ensure higher growth rate, larger amount of employment generation without causing inflation. Further, during 1970s and 1980s *role of human capital* (*i.e*., education and health) instead of physical capital began to be emphasised for boosting economic development. Besides, in view of the low labour intensity of technologies imported from abroad, the need for development of appropriate technologies suited to the factor endowments of developing countries was highlighted.[37] In this connection, it was pointed out that a developing country should not blindly import foreign capital-intensive technologies but should use discretion as to what technology could or should be imported.

The most significant change in the thinking of development economists came during the decade of 1980s, especially in the mid-eighties. This change was *resurgence of neoclassical economics* which gives important role to private sector and market mechanism in the process of development.

---

32 Prebisch, *The Economic Development of Latin America and Some of its Problems*, UN, New York, 1949.

33 Hans Singer, The Distribution of Gains Between Investing and Borrowing Countries, *American Economic Review*, May, 1950.

34 Mahboob ul Haq, Employment and Income Distribution in 1970s: A New Perspective," *Pakistan Economic and Social Review*, June 1971, p.6.

35 ILO, *The Basic Needs Approach to Development*, 1971.

36 See John Mellor, *The New Economics of Growth*.

37 France Stewart, *Technology and Development*, 1971.

It was felt that centralised planning and excess regulation and control over the private sector by the State and higher importance given to the public sector was obstructing growth due to its inefficiency in the use of resources. Besides, under the controlled regime, the twin crises of high fiscal deficit and external balance of payments crisis made the growth unsustainable. The policy framework of neoclassical economics such as *liberalisation, privatisation and globalisation* was suggested by prominent economists, I.M.D. Little, Jagdish Bhagwati, Bela Balarsa who were the advisors to the World Bank and IMF argued that free markets and greater role of private sector (including foreign investors) would ensure efficiency by encouraging competition. Thus the advocates of the adoption of policy framework of neoclassical economics emphasised government failures to obstruct rapid development. Similar to the neoclassical economists' approach to development Dr. Manmohan Singh who initiated economic reforms in India in 1991 in his first budget speach as Finance Minister on July 24, 1991, said, "Over-centralisation and excessive bureaucratisation of economic process have proved to be counter productive. We need to expand the scope and the area of operations of market forces. A *reformed price system* can be a superior instrument of resource allocation and qualitative control". Further, advocating for the adoption of export orientation of development strategy instead of import-substituting industrialisation be redefined "*the vision of self-reliant economy as one which can meet all its requirements through exports without undue dependence on artificial external sops such as foreign aid.*"

As a step towards economic reforms the neoclassical economics recommended the removal of price distortion introduced by government controls and getting all prices right to achieve efficient resource allocation. As Gerald Meier writes, "Markets, prices and incentives became central. Inward-looking strategies of development were to give way to liberalisation of foreign trade regime and export promotion. Inflation was to submit to stabilisation programmes.[38] State-owned enterprises were to be privatised. A poor country was now considered poor because of inappropriate policies, and good economics, that is, neoclassical economics – was good for the developing country".

Development Economics as a Separate Discipline. In the 1950s and 1960s the pioneers in development economics had asked why underdeveloped countries were poor and backward and put forward the grand theories and development strategies for starting and accelerating economic growth so as to lift them out of poverty trap. In propounding the various theories and stratagies to accelerate economic growth in developing countries, the pioneers in development economics abandoned the use of neoclassical economies which involves free working of market mechanism and role of material incentives and profit motive guiding allocation of resources and economic growth in an economy. The pioneers in development economics considered the neoclassical economics as a *special case* applicable to developed countries having not much relevance for the underdeveloped countries as the latter are *structurally different* from the developed economics. These pioneers investigated the factors that perpetulate underdevelopment and poverty in underdeveloped countries and for initiating and boosting economic growth not only rejected the principles of neoclassical economics but also found theories of development of classical economists such as Adam Smith, Ricardo, Malthus and Marx not fully applicable to the present-day developing economies. Prominent contributors to development economics are Arthur Lewis, Ragnar Nurkse, Albert Hirshman, Hans Singer, Rostow, Michael Todaro, Amartya Sen among many others.[39]

However, as explained above, from the early eighties there has been greater reliance on neoclassical economics which gives greater role to market mechanism and profit motive for efficient resource allocation and economic growth in developing countries. Further, as this neoclassical economics applies equally to rich developed countries and poor developing countries. Therefore,

38 Gerald M. Meier, *Leading Issues in Economic Development*, 8th edition.

39 For outstanding contributions made to traditional development economics see Gerald M. Meier and Dudley Seers, *Pioneers in Development Economics*, 1984.

it has been asserted by some economists prominent among whom is Albert Hirshman[40], that the development economics which was thought to be a separate and distinct subject, different from the principles of neoclassical economics has collapsed and that there is no any distinct or special subject of development economics applicable to developing countries alone. To quote Hirshman, "The sub-discipline of development economics has achieved its considerable lustre and excitement through the implicit idea that it could slay the dragon of backwardness virtually by itself or at least that its contribution to this task was central. We know that this is not so."[41]

Hirschman's view has been challenged by Prof. Amartya Sen. According to him, the original themes with which development economics has been concerned "while severely incomplete in coverage did not point entirely in the wrong direction and *the discipline of development economics does have a central role to play in the field of economic growth in developing countries*"[42]

Hirschman pointed to the main themes or ideas which formed the basis of development economics. They are (1) rural underemployment including disguised unemployment that prevailed in underdeveloped countries which became the focus utilisation of surplus labour for industrial growth or capital accumulation; (2) the subject of late industrialisation of underdeveloped countries which, according to the standard development economics required active role and guided efforts by the State and also economic planning and protection measures by the state to overcome the disadvantages of late industrialisation."[43]

While there have been differences about certain issues in development strategies to be adopted to break out of the low-level equilibrium trap but, as has been mentioned by Amartya Sen, the following three are the strategic themes in terms of economic policy with which standard development economics has been concerned to achieve rapid economic growth.[44]

1. Industrialisation
2. Capital accumulation
3. Mobilisation of underemployed or disguisedly unemployed labour for bringing about economic growth
4. Planning in an economically active State

As mentioned by Amartya Sen, the above themes used for planning and active role of the State in promoting industrialisation (or capital accumulation) and the use of surplus labour for it are parts of the standard development economics on account of which neoclassical economics has been said to be inapplicable for acceleration of economic growth in developing countries. Hirschman who explained the rise and decline of development economics hold the view that the neoclassical economics as applicable to both developed and developing countries alike. In other words, he talked of the relevance of '*mono-economics*' for both developed and developing countries and argued against the development economics as a separate and distinct subject.

The resurgence of neoclassical economics has drawn its support from the high growth performance of East Asian countries such as South Korea, Taiwan, Hong-Kong and Singapore in which higher economic growth rates have been achieved based on market mechanism, private enterprise, profit

40 See Albert Hirschman, "The Rise and Fall of Development Economics" *in Essays on Trespassing Economics*, 1981.

41 Amartya Sen, *op.cit.*, p. 48, 1983.

42 Hirschman, *op. cit.* 1981, p. 23.

43 Amartya Sen, *op.cit.* 1983.

44 These themes are the subject matter of the works of (1) Rosensteim-Rodan, "The Problem of Industrialization in Eastern and Soth Eastern Europe" *Economic Journal* (1943), 53. (2) Arthur Lewis, *Economic Development with Unlimited Supplies of Labour*, Manchester School (1964); (3) Ragnar Nurkse, *Capital Formation in Underdeveloped Countries* (4) Hans Singer, *op.cit.* (5) Albert Hirschman, *The Strategy of Development*, 1958 and (6) Amartya Sen, *Choice of Techniques.*

motive and material incentives, and liberal foreign trade. On the other hand, the lower growth in developing countries of South East Asia, Africa and Latin America has been cited as a result of the intervention in market by the government and role of planning in resource allocation in the growth process. Similarly, failure of development experience in Soviet Russia and China under activist state and centralised planning played a significant role has been cited as a proof of collapse of standard development economics with its emphasis on role of State and economic planning.

The sum and substance of the critique of development economics has been that neoclassical economics with its role of free market mechanism, private enterprise, material incentives ensure higher economic growth as against State-guided industrialisation through centralised planning.

However, the above mentioned defence of neoclassical economics and critique of development economics has been challenged, among others, by Amartya Sen. To quote Sen, "*I believe that contentuous and simplistic though development economics might have been in some respects, the main themes that were associated with the origin of development economics and have given its distinctive character are not rejectable for that reason.*"[45]

It is worth mentioning that traditional development economics has concentrated on economic growth as against economic development which is a broader concept than economic growth. However, so far as economic growth is concerned, the strategic themes such as role of capital accumulation, industrialisation and role of State and planning for acceleration of economic growth is concerned Amartya Sen using World Bank data of GNP per capita, gross domestic investment, (*i.e.*, capital formation) as per cent of GDP and percentage share of industry in GDP and growth rate during 1960-80 pertaining to 14 low-income countries and 18 middle income countries has shown that capital accumulation and industrialisation have played an important role in achieving higher GDP growth rate. As regards role of mobilisation of surplus labour he points out that high growth performance has distinguished record of labour-using growth particularly in case of China and South Korea mobilisation of labour for bringing about rapid growth is quite outstanding. Lastly, he points out that in China, Romania, Yugoslavia and South Korea State intervention and planning have played a significant role in fostering economic growth. Thus, in conclusion, Sen writes: "Despite these *average* achievements the performance of various countries is highly different. There is still much relevance in the broad policy themes which traditional development economics has emphasized." Further, in defence of traditional development economics, he writes: "The general policy prescription and strategies in this tradition have to be judged in terms of the climate of opinion and overall factual situation prevailing at the same time these theories were formulated"[46]. Development economics was born at a time when government involvement in deliberately fostering economic growth in general, and in industrialisation in particular, was very rare, and when the typical rates of capital accumulation were very low.

It may be further noted that despite the revival of importance of neoclassical economics which emphasises liberalisation and privatisation for accelerating economic growth, role of State or Government is still in two important respects, First, the Government has to play a significant role in making arrangements for the expansion of education, healthcare for the advance of human capabilities on which growth depends. Secondly, the government has an important role in building up physical infrastructure such as power, roads, railways, ports and telecommunication as lack of these facilities is holding back economic development. Thirdly, the Government has a special role in starting schemes for alleviation of poverty and unemployment in the developing countries as the free working of market mechanism will not ensure this.

45 Amartya Sen (1983), *op. cit.*

46 Amartya Sen, 1981 *op.cit.*

CHAPTER 2

ALTERNATIVE MEASURES OF DEVELOPMENT AND HUMAN DEVELOPMENT INDEX (HDI)

GNP AS A MEASURE OF DEVELOPMENT

It is now important to explain how economists measure development. Prior to 1970, economic development was generally meant to be *sustained increase* in the productive capacity of a country over a period and was interpreted in the same sense as *economic growth*. Accordingly, development was measured by the growth in gross national product (GNP) or what is also called gross national income (GNI). If population was increasing faster than gross national product (GNP), the per capita income on which average standard of living depends will be declining. This means that per cent increase in gross national product (GNP) is not a true and adequate index of change in standard of living.

Besides, GDP growth rate does not consider the distribution of income. A high GDP growth rate may be achieved but this may have benefited only the rich while the share of bottom 30 per cent of population may not have received the benefits, that is, poverty of a large section of the population may not have declined. Further, if GDP growth has been brought about by the labour-saving technologies in the production of commodities, employment will not rise and therefore unemployment may rise instead of falling. Thus there is possibility that while GDP has grown, poverty and unemployment may not fall. In other words, there may be *growth without development*.

Another important limitation of GDP growth as a true measure of development is that it pays no regard to the *composition of growing output* as between essential consumer goods (which are generally called *wage goods*) and luxuries. While there may be shortage of food output resulting in higher food inflation, there is plenty of growth of luxuries due to gross inequalities in income distribution. This would adversely affect the well-being of the people. Late Prof. Sukhamoy Chakravarty rightly writes, "*The rate of growth strategy is by itself an adequate device to deal with the problems of generating employment opportunities and for reducing economic disparities. Much depends on the composition of growth process and how growth is financed and how benefits from growth process are distributed.*"[1]

Mention may also be made of the harmful effects on environment and depletion of natural resources which result from rapid growth of GDP. As is well known, production of modern industries pollutes the environment such as pollution of air, water and calmness which significantly reduce the welfare of the people. Though modern industrialisation has greatly increased the national output of the countries but by causing environment pollution and degradation has adversely affected the well-being and quality of life of the people. This makes GDP growth as an imperfect measure and indicator of development.

Another important drawback of GDP growth as a measure and index of development is that it focuses on the *quantity* of goods and services and totally ignores the *quality of life* that development

1 Sukhamoy Chakravarty, "Some Observations on the Growth Process", in *Seminar*, 1971.

is expected to enhance. The quality f life is related to such things as increase in the expectancy of life at birth, better nutrition and healthcare, clothing, shelter and literacy which increase the well-being of the people. Commenting on the limitations of GDP growth rate as an indicator of development Jean Dreze[2] and Amartya Sen write, "While economic growth is an important tool for enhancing living conditions, its reach and impact depend greatly on what is being done with the fruits of growth. *The relation between economic growth and advancement of living standards depends on many factors, including economic and social inequality in general and no less important on what the government does with the public revenue that is generated by economic growth.* The importance of economic growth can be adequately understood only in this broader context. It is necessary to recognise the role of growth in facilitating development in the form of enhancing human lives and freedoms."

PER CAPITA INCOME AS A MEASURE OF DEVELOPMENT

Per capita income is more generally used as a measure of development and is considered as better indicator of development as increase in per capita income shows the ability of a country to increase its gross domestic product (GDP) faster than population. Increase in per capita income indicates the overall improvement in economic well-being of a population, that is, it shows how much extra goods and services are available per head in a country for consumption and investment. It is however worthwhile to note that it is *real* per capita income that is used to measure level of development and therefore growth or development was measured by the increase in real per capita income in a period. The increase in real per capita income is found by adjusting *nominal* per capita income for rate of inflation. That is, increase in GDP per capita is equal to increase in nominal GDP per capita minus the rate of inflation.

As size of population of various countries differs sharply, the overall GDP will not correctly indicate the average standard of living because the per capita income of a country may be low because of higher size of its population, though its overall GDP is much greater than others. Therefore, for making international comparisons of development across countries it is per capita income that is more often used. Further, in developed countries where per capita income is already very high but population growth is small, the use of GNP per capita as indicator of development may be correct but in developing countries with rapid increase in population as in case of India, the rise in per capita income will be a better indicator of development as it will depict increase in *average* levels of living in a country. Besides, the per capita income or changes in it enable us to keep focus on removal of poverty in the economy. Thus, income-poverty, that is, lower level of per capita income is an important component of Human Development Index (HDI) prepared by the United Nations Development Programme (UNDP).

Further, as emphasised above, increase in overall GNP or per capita GNP does not adequately reflect the problem of generating employment opportunities and for reducing economic disparities which forms the core of economic development. *For increase in the living standards of the masses, much depends* on the composition of growing overall GNP or per capita GNP and how benefits of growth are distributed among the population. Thus, the main limitation of per capita income as a measure of development is that it ignores income distribution which has an important bearing on the welfare of the people. It is implicitly assumed in per capita income as an indicator of development that each extra rupee of income is of equal importance whether earned by the rich or the poor. This, however, is not correct. In fact it matters a lot in welfare terms as to who benefits from growth in GNP per capita. An extra rupee to the poor, for example, means a much higher happiness or satisfaction than the same increase to the rich. That is why in latest reports of human development by the United Nations Development Programme (UNDP), Human Development Index (HDI) is adjusted for

2 Jean Dreze and Amartya Sen, "*An Uncertain Glory: India and its Contradictions*' Penguin Books, 2014, pp. 38-39.

inequality. It has been found that in the rankings of different countries with regard to unadjusted HDI and inequality adjusted HDI there is a lot of difference.

Besides, per capita income as an indicator of development also does not take into account the various ingredients of *physical quality of life* such as life expectancy, literacy and education, health conditions such as undernourishment and mortality rate. These basic elements of quality of life are essential for well-being of the people and are parts of new view of economic development explained earlier.

Prior to 1970s the development was viewed in terms of economic growth (*i.e.*, rise in GDP or per capita income). It was thought that benefits of economic growth would trickle down to the majority of population in the form of more employment opportunities and rise in wages. Therefore, the problems of poverty, unemployment, undernourishment and nutrition would be automatically solved if rapid economic growth was achieved. Income redistribution was given only secondary importance though in the five year plans lip service was paid to reducing income inequalities and providing equality of opportunity. Further, prior to 1970s economic development was generally considered in terms of structural change in the pattern of production and employment so that agricultural share both in GDP and workforce was planned to fall and that of industrial and services sectors to rise. This shift in labour force was expected to lead to increase in overall productivity and economic growth as productivity levels in both organised manufacturing and services sectors was found to be higher than that in agriculture. We give in Table 2.1, the average annual growth rate of GDP per capita in India and some selected developing countries in the past five decades.

It will be seen from this table that even with regard to GDP per capita, in the last decade (2000-2011) China with its annual per capita GDP growth of 9.6 %, China has emerged as the fastest growing country of the World. Next to China, India with its per capita is the second fastest growing country of the world.

Table 2.1. Average Annual Growth Rate (%) of GDP Per Capita in India and Some Selected Developing Countries Since 1960

Country	1961-70	1970-80	1980-90	1990-2000	2000-2011
India	1.8	0.9	3.3	3.6	5.5
Bangladesh	1.1	–0.5	0.7	2.7	4.4
Nepal	0.5	–0.2	1.7	2.4	2.0
Pakistan	4.5	2.2	3.2	1.3	2.5
Sri Lanka	2.2	2.6	2.8	4.1	4.7
China	2.4	5.4	7.6	8.6	9.6
South Korea	5.7	5.5	6.5	5.5	3.9
Indonesia	1.6	5.3	4.5	3.3	4.1
Thailand	5.0	4.6	5.7	4.1	3.1

Source: World Bank, Reports of World Development Indicators for the years 2006, 2011 and 2013.

However, the development experience of 1950s and 1960s in developing countries showed that the problems of poverty and unemployment remained unresolved despite the achievement in general of economic growth targets. It was therefore realised that economic growth was necessary but not sufficient for raising the living standards of the masses. As a result, as explained earlier, there was drastic change in the meaning and measurement of economic development. According to the new view of economic development, eradication of poverty and unemployment, reduction in inequality in income distribution, elimination of discrimination on the basis of gender (*i.e.*, achievement of gender equality) were considered essential for development to take place. As Amartya Sen puts it "*development is more concerned with enhancing the lives we live and the freedoms we enjoy*".[3] It is in this context that Eleventh and Twelfth Five Year Plans of India set the objective not only in terms of accelerating rate of economic growth but also to achieve *inclusive growth.* Inclusive growth implies

3 Amartya Sen, *Economic Development as Freedom,* Oxford University Press, 2001, p. 14.

that in addition to increase in GDP or per capita income the elimination of poverty and unemployment reduction in income inequalities must occur so that fruits of economic growth are equitably distributed.

It is worth noting that for measuring development the United Nations Development Programme (UNDP) has been constructing Human Development Index (HDI) for 187 countries of the world which takes into account not only income per capita but also other elements of human development such as life expectancy at birth, literacy. Life expectancy at birth represents conditions of health and literacy represents the level of education in a country. Thus human development index (HDI) is a composite measure of income per capita (*i.e.*, average standard of living), health and educational levels. In what follows we explain the concept of human development index (HDI), how it is constructed and give rankings of different countries of the world in respect of this human development index.

HUMAN DEVELOPMENT INDEX (HDI)

Growth in national income (GNP) or per capita income considered above as indicator of economic growth does not represent a true and adequate measure of welfare and economic development of the people of a country. Therefore, a need was felt to put forward an index which should truly and correctly reflect the level of economic welfare and economic development of a nation. Thus, Human Development Report (1997) states, "*Income is clearly only one option that people would like to have, though an important one. But it is not the sum total of their lives. Income is also a means, with human development, the end*". Human development index is a composite measure of three aspects of good life and well-being. Three questions were raised regarding what people want in order to have a good and cherished life. Answers provided were :

1. people want to lead a long and healthy life;
2. they want to be educated and to acquire knowledge; and
3. they want to have access to resources so that they enjoy a decent standard of living. In other words, they want to have a per capita income which is high enough to ensure them a decent standard of living.

The concept of human development has been developed by a number of economists, prominent among whom are Dr. Mehbub-ul-Haq and Nobel Laureate Dr. Amartya Sen. Explaining the concept of human development, Prof. Amartya Sen writes, "The process of *widening people's choices and the level of well-being they achieve are* the core of the notion of human development. But regardless of the level of development, the three essential choices for people are to lead a long and healthy life, to acquire knowledge and to have access to the resources needed for a decent standard of living. Human development does not end there, however, other choices highly valued by many people range from *political, economic and social freedoms to opportunities for being creative and productive and enjoying self-respect and guaranteed human rights.*"

It is clear from this that in the concept of human development Prof. Amartya Sen would like to include the social, economic and political freedoms as well as human rights they enjoy in a country. Therefore, the latest Human Development Reports consider and assess the performance of the countries in respect of these questions of freedoms and human rights along with the three indicators or criteria mentioned below.

Three Indicators of Good Life

The three criteria or indicators which represent different aspects of good life or the three goals of human development are:

1. **Longevity,** which is measured by life expectancy at birth. Life expectancy at birth means how many years a newly born infant can hope to live in this world. This represents element of health in the Human Development Index (HDI).

2. **Education or Knowledge,** which is measured by the weighted average of adult literacy and mean years of schooling. For this 2/3rd weight is given to adult literacy and 1/3rd weight is given to the mean years of schooling.
3. **Standard of living** which is measured by real per capita income of a country at purchasing power parity (PPP) prices, that is, adjusted for purchasing power of currencies of different countries.

Let us explain how Human Development Index (HDI)[4] is estimated for different countries. As mentioned above, there are three goals of development, namely, better health as measured by life expectancy at birth, better education or knowledge as measured by literacy rate and standard of living as measured by per capita income measured in terms of purchasing power parity prices (PPP) in US dollars. To construct human development index, fixed minimum and maximum values are taken for each variable or component included in the index. For example, for life expectancy at birth the range is 25 to 82 years, for literacy rate the range is 0 to 100 per cent and for per capita income the range is $ 100 to 40,000 in terms of PPP (US $). The value of each component of human development index is calculated by using the following formula :

$$\text{HDI for individual component} = \frac{\text{Actual Value} - \text{Minimum Value}}{\text{Maximum Value} - \text{Minimum Value}}$$

If the actual value of an individual variable in HDI of a country is equal to the minimum, the index of that variable for a country is zero. On the other hand, if the value of an individual component is equal to the maximum value, the index of that component will be equal to one.

For example, India's life expectancy at birth in 2011 was 65.5, the life expectancy index for India according to the above formula (with the given range of 25–85) will be :

$$\text{Life expectancy Index of India} = \frac{65.5-25}{85-25} = 0.673$$

Similarly, with 3460 PPP (US $) of India's per capita income, its individual index (with range 100 – 40,000) = $(Y_j - \overline{Y})^2$ = 0.084

With 74 per cent literacy rate of India, literacy index $\sigma = \sqrt{\sum_{j=1}^{m} \frac{n_j}{n}(Y_j - \overline{Y})^2}$

In constructing overall HDI we take average of three individual indexes with each having $\frac{1}{3}$ weight. Thus,

HDI = 1/3 (per capita income index) + 1/3 (life expectancy index) + 1/3 (literacy index)

After finding the values of Human Development Index (HDI) for various countries they are ranked from the highest to the lowest. In Table 2.2 we have given the values of HDI for 187 countries for the year 2012 as per Human Development Report 2013. The 7th column in Table 2.2 shows GNI (Gross National Income) per capita rank *minus* HDI rank.

A positive differential in this column means that a country's ranking rises when HDI is used instead of GNI per capita index. This implies that the country's non-income indicators (such as health and education indicators) in HDI are relatively better which therefore raise its overall HDI ranking. On the other hand, if differential between GNI per capita income index and HDI is *negative*, it means its non-income development indicators are relatively not so good which lowers its overall HDI ranking. Thus in case of *negative* differential between GNI per capita and HDI rankings in case

4 In the construction of HDI in recent years literacy rate or education index is prepared from the two sub-variables: (1) mean years of schooling received by the people aged 25 years and above; (2) expected years of schooling which means the number of years of schooling a child joins a school at an entrance age is expected to receive.

of a country, its ranking in respect of GNI per capita ranking will be higher. In this context it will be interesting to note that the differential between GNI per capita income ranking and HDI ranking is negative (–3). This means India's performance in respect of non-income indicators is lower which reduces its overall HDI ranking as compared to its GNI per capita ranking.

It follows from above that human development levels are different from levels of GNI per capita income. This clearly indicates the ratinale for constructing HDI for if the country's ranking in terms of HDI does not differ much from GNI per capita ranking, then the latter could be used as a proxy for human development. Human development index (HDI) shows broad-based development and not merely rise in per capita income. In this connection, it is important to note that some oil-rich Arab countries per capita income has greatly gone up without much improvements in health and education. This is because their main source of income is exports of oil-a natural resource product, but poor levels of health and education. Therefore, their case has been described as one of "growth without development". This is because development means much more than rise in per capita income. Better health and education are important factors in raising production levels and therefore GNI per capita but Arab countries have become rich because of exporting oil and not through much improvements in their levels of education and health. Commenting on the importance of constructing human development index, Todaro and Smith write :

"Health and education are inputs into the national production function in their role as components of *human capital*, meaning *productive investments embodied in persons* Improvements in health and education are also important development goals in their own rights. We cannot easily argue that a nation of high-income individuals who are not well educated and suffer from significant health problems that lead to their living much shorter lives than others around the globe has achieved a higher development than a low income country with high life expectancy and widespread literacy. A better indicator of development disparities and ranking might be found by including health and education variables in a weighted welfare measure rather than by simply looking at income levels, and the HDI offers one very useful way to get at this"[5].

Table 2.2. Human Development Index and its Components

	Human Development Index (HDI)	Life expectancy at birth	Mean years of schooling	Expected years of schooling	Gross national Income (GNI) per capita	GNI per capita rank minus HDI rank	Non-income HDI
	Value	(years)	(years)	(years)	(2005 PPP $)		value
HDI rank	2012	2012	2010*	2011*	2012	2012	2012
VERY HIGH HUMAN DEVELOPMENT							
1 Norway	0.955	81.3	12.6	17.5	48,688	4	0.977
2 Australia	0.938	82.0	12.0	19.6	34,340	15	0.978
3 United States	0.937	78.7	13.3	16.8	43,480	6	0.958
4. Netherlands	0.921	80.8	11.6	16.9	37,282	8	0.945
5 Germany	0.920	80.6	12.2	16.4	35,431	10	0.948
6 New Zealand	0.919	80.8	12.5	19.7	24,358	26	0.978
7 Ireland	0.916	80.7	11.6	18.3	28.671	19	0.960
8 Sweden	0.916	81.6	11.7	16.0	36.143	6	0.940
9 Switzerland	0.913	82.5	11.0	15.7	40,527	2	0.926
10 Japan	0.912	83.6	11.6	15.3	32,545	11	0.942

5 Todaro and Smith, *Economic Development,* pp. 51-52.

	Human Development Index (HDI)	Life expectancy at birth	Mean years of schooling	Expected years of schooling	Gross national Income (GNI) per capita	GNI per capita rank minus HDI rank	Non-income HDI
	Value	(years)	(years)	(years)	(2005 PPP $)		value
HDI rank	2012	2012	2010*	2011*	2012	2012	2012
11 Canada	0.911	81.1	12.3	15.1	35,369	5	0.934
12 Korea, Republic of	0.909	80.7	11.6	17.2	28,231	15	0.949
13 Hong Kong China (SAR)	0.906	83.0	10.0	15.5	45,598	–6	0.907
14 Iceland	0.906	81.9	10.4	18.3	29,176	12	0.943
15 Denmark	0.901	79.0	11.4	16.8	33,518	4	0.924
16 Israel	0.900	81.9	11.9	15.7	26,224	13	0.942
17 Belgium	0.897	80.0	10.9	16.4	33,429	3	0.917
18 Austria	0.895	81.0	10.8	15.3	36,438	5	0.908
19 Singapore	0.895	81.2	10.1	14.4	52,613	–15	0.880
20 France	0.893	81.7	10.6	16.1	30,277	4	0.919
21 Finland	0.892	80.1	10.3	16.9	32,510	2	0.912
22 Slovenia	0.892	79.5	11.7	16.9	23,999	12	0.936
23 Spain	0.885	81.6	10.4	16.4	25,947	8	0.919
24 Liechtenstein	0.883	79.8	10.3	11.9	84,880	–22	0.832
25 Italy	0.881	82.0	10.1	16.2	26,158	5	0.911
26 Luxembourg	0.875	80.1	10.1	13.5	48,285	–20	0.858
27 United Kingdom	0.875	80.3	9.4	16.4	32,538	–5	0.886
28 Crech Republic	0.873	77.8	12.3	15.3	22,067	10	0.913
29 Greece	0.860	80.0	10.1	16.3	20,511	13	0.899
30 Brunei Darussalam	0.855	78.1	8.6	15.0	45,690	–23	0.832
31 Cyprus	0.848	79.8	9.8	14.9	23,825	4	0.869
32 Malta	0.847	79.8	9.9	15.1	21,184	9	0.876
33 Andorra	0.846	81.1	10.4	11.7	33,918	–15	0.839
34 Estonia	0.846	75.0	12.0	15.8	17,402	13	0.892
35 Slovakia	0.840	75.6	11.6	14.7	19,696	9	0.872
36 Qatar	0.834	78.5	7.3	12.2	87,478	–35	0.761
37 Hungary	0.831	74.6	11.7	15.3	16,088	13	0.874
38 Barbados	0.825	77.0	9.3	16.3	17,308	10	0.859
39 Poland	0.821	76.3	10.0	15.2	17,776	7	0.851
40 Chile	0.819	79.3	9.7	14.7	14,987	13	0.863
41 Lithuania	0.818	72.5	10.9	15.7	16,858	7	0.850
42 United Arab Emirates	0.818	76.7	8.9	12.0	42,716	–31	0.783
43 Portugal	0.816	79.7	7.7	16.0	19,907	0	0.835
44 Latvia	0.814	73.6	11.5	14.8	14,724	10	0.856

	Human Development Index (HDI)	Life expectancy at birth	Mean years of schooling	Expected years of schooling	Gross national Income (GNI) per capita	GNI per capita rank minus HDI rank	Non-income HDI
	Value	(years)	(years)	(years)	(2005 PPP $)		value
HDI rank	2012	2012	2010*	2011*	2012	2012	2012
45 Argentina	0.811	76.1	9.3	16.1	15,347	7	0.848
46 Seychelles	0.806	73.8	9.4	14.3	22,615	–9	0.808
47 Croatia	0.805	76.8	9.8	14.1	15,419	4	0.837
48 Bahrain	0.796	75.2	9.4	13.4	19,154	–3	0.806
49 Bahamas	0.794	75.9	8.5	12.6	27,401	–21	0.777
50 Belarus	0.793	70.6	11.5	14.7	13,385	11	0.830
51 Uruguay	0.792	77.2	8.5	15.5	13,333	11	0.829
52 Montenegro	0.791	74.8	10.5	15.0	10.471	24	0.850
53 Palau	0.791	72.1	12.2	13.7	11,463	18	0.840
54 Kuwait	0.790	74.7	6.1	14.2	52,793	–51	0.730
55 Russian Federation	0.788	69.1	11.7	14.3	14,461	0	0.816
56 Romania	0.786	74.2	10.4	14.5	11,011	16	0.836
57 Bulgaria	0.782	73.6	10.6	14.0	11,474	12	0.826
58 Saudi Arabia	0.782	74.1	7.8	14.3	22,616	–21	0.774
59 Cuba	0.780	79.3	10.2	16.2	5,539	44	0.894
60 Panama	0.780	76.3	9.4	13.2	13,519	1	0.810
61 Mexico	0.775	77.1	8.5	13.7	12,947	4	0.805
62 Costa Rica	0.773	79.4	8.4	13.7	10,863	12	0.816
63 Grenada	0.770	76.1	8.6	15.8	9,257	21	0.827
64 Libya	0.769	75.0	7.3	16.2	13,765	8	0.791
65 Malaysia	0.769	74.5	9.5	12.6	13,676	7	0.791
66 Serbia	0.769	74.7	10.2	13.6	9,533	16	0.823
67 Antigua and Barbuda	0.760	72.8	8.9	13.3	13,883	–12	0.776
68 Trinidad and Tobago	0.760	70.3	9.2	11.9	21.941	–28	0.743
69 Kazakhstan	0.754	67.4	10.4	15.3	10,451	8	0.791
70 Albania	0.749	77.1	10.4	11.4	7,822	21	0.807
71 Venezuela, Bolivarian Republic of	0.748	74.6	7.6	14.4	11,475	–2	0.774
72 Dominica	0.745	77.6	7.7	12.7	10,977	–1	0.771
73 Georgia	0.745	73.9	12,1	13.2	5,005	37	0.845
74 Lebanon	0.745	72.8	7.9	13.9	12,364	–5	0.762
75 Saint Kitts and Nevis	0.745	73.3	8.4	12.9	12,460	–5	0.763
76 Iran, Islamic Republic	0.742	73.2	7.8	14.4	10,695	–1	0.769
77 Peru	0.741	74.2	8.7	13.2	9,306	6	0.780

	Human Development Index (HDI)	Life expectancy at birth	Mean years of schooling	Expected years of schooling	Gross national Income (GNI) per capita	GNI per capita rank minus HDI rank	Non-income HDI
	Value	(years)	(years)	(years)	(2005 PPP $)		value
HDI rank	2012	2012	2010*	2011*	2012	2012	2012
78 Yugoslav Republic of Macedonia	0.740	75.0	8.2	13.4	9,377	2	0.777
79 Ukraine	0.740	68.8	11.3	14.8	6,428	22	0.813
80 Mauritius	0.737	73.5	7.2	13.6	13,300	–17	0.745
81 Bosnia and Herzegovina	0.735	75.8	8.3	13.4	7,713	13	0.787
82 Azerbaijan	0.734	70.9	11.2	11.7	8,153	5	0.780
83 Saint Vincent and the Grenadines	0.733	72.5	8.6	13.3	9,367	–1	0.767
84 Oman	0.731	73.2	5.5	13.5	24,092	–51	0.694
85 Brazil	0.730	73.8	7.2	14.2	10,152	–8	0.755
86 Jamaica	0.730	73.3	9.6	13.1	6,701	14	0.792
87 Armenia	0.729	74.4	10.8	12.2	5,540	16	0.808
88 Saint Lucia	0.725	74.8	8.3	12.7	7,971	1	0.768
89 Ecuador	0.724	75.8	7.6	13.7	7,471	7	0.772
90 Turkey	0.722	74.2	6.5	12.9	13,710	–32	0.720
91 Colombia	0.719	73.9	7.3	13.6	8,711	–6	0.751
92 Sri Lanka	0.715	75.1	9.3	12.7	5,170	18	0.792
93 Algeria	0.713	73.4	7.6	13.6	7,418	4	0.755
94 Tunisia	0.712	74.7	6.5	14.5	8,103	–6	0.746
MEDIUM HUMAN DEVELOPMENT							
95 Tonga	0.710	72.5	10.3	13.7	4,153	26	0.807
96 Belize	0.702	76.3	8.0	12.5	5.327	8	0.767
97 Dominican Republic	0.702	73.6	7.2	12.3	8,506	-11	0.726
98 Fiji	0.702	69.4	10.7	13.9	4,087	24	0.794
99 Samoa	0.702	72.7	10.3	13.0	3,928	28	0.800
100 Jordan	0.700	73.5	8.6	12.7	5,272	8	0.766
101 China	0.699	73.7	7.5	11.7	7,945	-11	0.728
102 Turkmenistan	0.698	65.2	9.9	12.6	7,782	–10	0.727
103 Thailand	0.690	74.3	6.6	12.3	7,722	-10	0.715
104 Maldives	0.688	77.1	5.8	12.5	7,478	–9	0.715
105 Surinam	0.684	70.8	7.2	12.4	7,327	–7	0.710
106 Gabon	0.683	63.1	7.5	13.0	12,521	–40	0.668
107 El Salvador	0.680	72.4	7.5	12.0	5,915	–5	0.723
108 Bolivia, Plurinational State of	0.675	66.9	9.2	13.5	4,444	7	0.740

	Human Development Index (HDI)	Life expectancy at birth	Mean years of schooling	Expected years of schooling	Gross national Income (GNI) per capita	GNI per capita rank minus HDI rank	Non-income HDI
	Value	(years)	(years)	(years)	(2005 PPP $)		value
HDI rank	2012	2012	2010*	2011*	2012	2012	2012
109 Mongolia	0.675	68.8	8.3	14.3	4,245	10	0.746
110 Palestine, State of	0.670	73.0	8.0	13.5	3,359	20	0.761
111 Paraguay	0.669	72.7	7.7	12.1	4,497	4	0.730
112 Egypt	0.662	73.5	6.4	12.1	5,401	–6	0.702
113 Moldova, Republic of	0.660	69.6	9.7	11.8	3,319	19	0.747
114 Philippines	0.654	69.0	8.9	11.7	3,752	11	0.724
115 Uzbekistan	0.654	68.6	10.0	11.6	3,201	19	0.740
116 Syrian Arab Republic	0.648	76.0	5.7	11.7	4,674	–2	0.692
117 Micronesia, Federated States of	0.645	69.2	8.8	11.4	3,352	14	0.719
118 Guyana	0.636	70.2	8.5	10.3	3,387	11	0.703
119 Botswana	0.634	53.0	8.9	11.8	13,102	–55	0.596
120 Honduras	0.632	73.4	6.5	11.4	3,426	8	0.695
121 Indonesia	0.629	69.8	5.8	12.9	4,154	–3	0.672
122 Kiribati	0.629	68.4	7.8	12.0	3,079	13	0.701
123 South Africa	0.629	53.4	8.5	13.1	9,594	–42	0.608
124 Vanuatu	0.626	71.3	6.7	10.6	3,960		0.672
125 Kyrgystan	0.622	68.0	9.3	12.6	2,009	2	0.738
126 Tajikistan	0.622	67.8	9.8	11.5	2,119	1	0.731
127 Viet Nam	0.617	75.4	5.5	11.9	2,970		0.686
128 Nambia	0.608	62.6	6.2	11.3	5,973	–2	0.611
129 Nicaragua	0.599	74.3	5.8	10.8	2,551	1	0.671
130 Morocco	0.591	72.4	4.4	10.4	4,384	–1	0.608
131 Iraq	0.590	69.6	5.6	10.0	3,557	–	0.623
132 Cape Verde	0.586	74.3	3.5	12.7	3,609	–1	0.617
133 Guatemala	0.581	71.4	4.1	10.7	4,235	–1	0.596
134 Timor-Leste	0.576	62.9	4.4	11.7	5,446	–21	0.569
135 Ghana	0.558	64.6	7.0	11.4	1,684	22	0.646
136 Equatorial Guinea	0.554	51.4	5.4	7.9	21,715	–97	0.463
137 India	0.554	65.8	4.4	10.7	3,285	–3	0.575
138 Cambodia	0.543	63.6	5.8	10.5	2,095	9	0.597
139 Lao People's Democratic Republic	0.543	67.8	4.6	10.1	2,435	2	0.584
140 Bhutan	0.538	67.6	2.3	12.4	5,246	–31	0.516
141 Swaziland	0.536	48.9	7.1	10.7	5,104	–30	0.515

	Human Develop-ment Index (HDI)	Life ex-pectancy at birth	Mean years of school-ing	Expected years of school-ing	Gross national Income (GNI) per capita	GNI per capita rank mi-nus HDI rank	Non-income HDI
	Value	(years)	(years)	(years)	(2005 PPP $)		value
HDI rank	2012	2012	2010*	2011*	2012	2012	2012
LOW HUMAN DEVELOPMENT INDEX							
142 Congo	0.534	57.8	5.9	10.1	2,934	–5	0.553
143 Solomon Islands	0.530	68.2	4.5	9.3	2,172	1	0.572
144 Sao Tome and Principle	0.525	64.9	4.7	10.8	1,864	7	0.579
145 Kenya	0.519	57.7	7.0	11.1	1,541	15	0.588
146 Bangladesh	0.515	69.2	4.8	8.1	1,785	9	0.567
147 Pakistan	0.515	65.7	4.9	7.3	2,566	–9	0.534
148 Angola	0.508	51.5	4.7	10.2	4,812	–35	0.479
149 Myanmar	0.498	65.7	3.9	9.4	1,817	5	0.537
150 Cameroon	0.495	52.1	5.9	10.9	2,114	–4	0.520
151 Madagascar	0.483	66.9	5.2	10.4	828	28	0.601
152 Tanzania, United Rep. of	0.476	58.9	5.1	9.1	1,383	10	0.527
153 Nigeria	0.471	52.3	5.2	9.0	2,102	–6	0.482
154 Senegal	0.470	59.6	4.5	8.2	1,653	4	0.501
155 Mauritania	0.467	58.9	3.7	8.1	2,174	–12	0.473
156 Papua New Guinea	0.466	63.1	3.9	5.8	2,386	–15	0.464
157 Nepal	0.463	69.1	3.2	8.9	1,137	11	0.526
158 Lesotho	0.461	48.7	5.9	9.6	1,879	–8	0.476
159 Togo	0.459	57.5	5.3	10.6	928	16	0.542
160 Yemen	0.458	65.9	2.5	8.7	1,820	–7	0.474
161 Haiti	0.456	62.4	4.9	7.6	1,070	7	0.521
162 Uganda	0.456	54.5	4.7	11.1	1,168	5	0.511
163 Zambia	0.448	49.4	6.7	8.5	1,358	0	0.483
164 Djibouti	0.445	58.3	3.8°	5.7	2,350	–22	0.435
165 Gambia	0.439	58.8	2.8	8.7	1,731	–9	0.448
166 Benin	0.436	56.5	3.2	9.4	1,439	–5	0.459
167 Rwanda	0.434	55.7	3.3	10.9	1,147	0	0.476
168 Cote d'Ivoir	0.432	56.0	4.2	6.5	1,593	–9	0.444
169 Comoros	0.429	61.5	2.8	10.2	986	4	0.484
170 Malawi	0.418	54.8	4.2	10.4	774	10	0.492
171 Sudan	0.414	61.8	3.1	10.5	1,848	19	0.405
172 Zimbabwe	0.397	52.7	7.2	10.1	424	14	0.452
173 Ethiopia	0.396	59.7	2.2	8.7	1,017	–2	0.425

	Human Development Index (HDI)	Life expectancy at birth	Mean years of schooling	Expected years of schooling	Gross national Income (GNI) per capita	GNI per capita rank minus HDI rank	Non-income HDI
	Value	(years)	(years)	(years)	(2005 PPP $)		value
HDI rank	2012	2012	2010*	2011*	2012	2012	2012
174 Liberia	0.388	57.3	3.9	10.5	480	11	0.502
175 Afghanistan	0.374	49.1	3.1	8.1	1,000	3	0.393
176 Guinea-Bissau	0.364	48.6	2.3	9.5	1,042	–6	0.373
177 Sierra Leone	0.359	48.1	3.3	7.3	881	0	0.380
178 Burundi	0.355	50.9	2.7	11.3	544	4	0.423
179 Guinea	0.355	54.5	1.6	8.8	941	–4	0.368
180 Central African Republic	0.352	49.1	3.5	6.8	722	1	0.386
181 Eritrea	0.351	62.0	3.4	4.6	531	3	0.418
182 Mali	0.344	51.9	2.0	7.5	853	–4	0.359
183 Burkina Faso	0.343	55.9	1.3	6.9	1,202	–18	0.332
184 Chad	0.340	49.9	1.5	7.4	1,258	–20	0.324
185 Mozambique	0.327	50.7	1.2	9.2	906	–9	0.327
186. Cong. Dem. Republic	0.304	48.7	3.5	8.5	319	0	0.404
187. Niger	0.304	55.1	1.4	4.9	701	–4	0.313
Human Development Index Groups							
Very high human development	0.905	80.1	11.5	16.3	33,391	-	0.927
High human development	0.758	73.4	8.8	13.9	11,501	-	0.781
Medium human development	0.640	69.9	6.3	11.4	5,428	-	0.661
Low human development	0.466	59.1	4.2	8.5	1,633	–	0.487
Regions							
Arab States	0.652	71.0	6.0	10.6	8,317	–	0.658
East Asia and the Pacific	0.683	72.7	7.2	11.8	6,874	-	0.712
Europe and Central Asia	0.771	71.5	10.4	13.7	12,243	-	0.801
Latin America and the Caribbean	0.741	74.7	7.8	13.7	10,300	–	0.770
South Asia	0.558	66.2	4.7	10.2	3,343	–	0.577
Sub-Saharan Africa	0.475	54.9	4.7	9.3	2,010	–	0.479
Least developed countries	0.449	59.5	3.7	8.5	1,385	-	0.475
Small island developing states	0.648	69.8	7.3	10.7	5,397	–	0.673
World	0.694	70.1	7.5	11.6	10,184	–	0.690

Note. Life expectancy at birth: Number of years a newborn infant could expect to live if prevailing patterns of age-specific mortality rates at the time of birth stay the same throughout the infant's life. **Mean years of schooling :** Average number of years of education received by people age 25 and older, converted from educational attainment levels using official durations of each level. **Expected years of schooling:** Number of years of schooling that a child of school entrance age can expect to receive if prevailing patterns of age-specific enrolment rates persist throughout the child's life. **Gross national income (GNI) per capita:** Aggregate income of an economy generated by its production and its ownership of factors of production, less the incomes paid for the use of factors of production owned by the rest of the world converted to international dollars using PPP rates, divided by midyear population. **GNI per capita rank minus HDI rank:** Difference in rankings by GNI per capita and by the HDI. A negative value means that the country is better ranked by GNI than by the HDI.

Source: *Human Development Report*, 2013

Human development index calculated and presented in *Human Development Report*, 2013 are given in Table 2.2. It will be seen from this table that in 178 countries for which Human Development Index (HDI) 2013 has been prepared, India's ranking was 136th in 2011 which is indeed a very low position. It is important to note that human development index attempts to make ranking of different countries on a scale of 0 (lowest human development) to 1 (the highest human development). It may be noted that positions of different countries have been changing in different years depending on their index of human development calculated for the years. For example, Norway which had a 2nd ranking in 1997 and 1998 moved up to position No. 1 in the year 1999 and still occupies No. 1 position. Australia which had a 2nd position in year 1999 moved up to the 4th position in 2001. USA which had 3rd ranking in both 1997 and 1998 slided down to the 6th rank in 1999 and to 7th rank in 2001 and to 8th rank in 2004. It is noteworthy that ranking of both Pakistan and Bangladesh is lower than that of India.

Two things must be noted in regard to human development index (HDI). First, it measures relative and not absolute level of human development. Second, the focus of human development is on the goals or ends of development which are (1) long and healthy life, (2) the level of knowledge and (3) a decent standard of living and not on real per capita income alone. In fact, *human development index is a composite measure of well-being based on life expectancy, literacy level, and real per capita income*.

As China and India are the two fastest growing economies of the world, their ranking with regard to human development index is worth noting. As will be seen from Table 2.2, as compared to India's 136th ranking in overall human development index, China's ranking was 101 among 187 countries in the year 2011. Besides, while life expectancy in India in 2014 was 65.4 years, it was 73.5 years in China; adult-literacy rate was 61 per cent in India while it was 90.9 per cent in China and school enrolment ratio was 62 per cent in India as against 70 per cent in China.

HDI data reveal that India is still in the medium human development category with countries like China, Sri Lanka, Thailand, Philippines, Egypt, Indonesia, South Africa and even Vietnam having higher overall HDI ranking within the same category.[6] The existing gap in health and education compared to developed countries and also to many developing countries indicates that India needs a much faster and widespread basic health and education. Life expectancy at birth in India in 2012 was 65.8 years as against 81.3 years in Norway, 82 years in Australia, 75.1 years in Sri Lanka, 73.7 years in China and the global average of 70.1 years.

Another important fact revealed by human development Index of various countries is that HDI rises with the rise in GNI per capita index. This can be explained by relatively higher levels of investment in human resource development (*i.e.*, in education and health) by richer countries with a higher GNI per capita. Better health and education leads to higher productivity and therefore higher GNI per capita. However, there are significant differences in HDI index showing broadbased

6 Note that the data for the year 2012 indicates that India's ranking has gone down to the 136th position while it was 126th in the year 2004.

measures of well-being and index of GNI per capita. Therefore, as explained above, there is a need for constructing a separate HDI index. As mentioned above, as in case of oil-rich Arab countries, the countries may have higher per capita income but poor levels of health and education.

Shortcomings and Critique of HDI

Some shortcomings of HDI as a true indicator of well-being for purposes of estimating development disparities among nations may be noted. First, for estimating literacy rate, expected years of schooling by children at the entrance age is used which overstates the literacy rate as in many countries (including India) many children who join primary school later drop out at some stage. Secondly, in preparing HDI equal weight of 1/3 is given to each of the three variables, namely, life expectancy, literacy rate and GNI per capita. This involves some value judgement and seems to be quite arbitrary. Besides, since these three components of HDI are measured in different units, to give equal weight to each component of HDI does not make much sense.

Thirdly, in constructing human development index, role of quality has been ignored. For example, there is a big difference between extra year of life for a healthy well-educated person and extra one year life for a person who is bed-ridden and has limited capability to do work. Similarly, in constructing HDI only the *number of years of schooling* is taken into account while the quality of education also matters a lot for good living. Due to lack of adequate data about quality of health and education, it is not incorporated in the construction of HDI. But without the quality of health and education being considered, HDI does not represent the true index of human development.

But the important drawback of human development index (HDI), is that it is of composite character which makes it an imperfect indicator of development or well-being of the people. If these three components are highly correlated to each other, then a single one will serve the purpose of comparing the levels of development and well-being of the people of different countries. However, in our view it, is not proper to put the three variables reflecting development into a single composite index. It is better and much more revealing if performance of different countries is compared in respect of *various indicators separately* because putting them together obscures the performance of development of various countries in respect of some crucial areas. Thus, in our view, *human development index hides more than it reveals*. Besides, in constructing human development index (HDI) there is a problem of what to be included and what to be excluded and what weights be assigned to the various variables included for construction of the index. In fact until recently human development index was prepared taking into account three variables, namely, life expectancy, literacy and per capita income and inequality in income distribution which also determines well-being of the people was ignored. Realising the importance of inequalities in income distribution, recent *Human Development Report*, 2013 has also given '*inequality-adjusted HDI*' in addition to the HDI without such adjustment.

Besides, human development index still does not take into account social, economic and political freedoms as well as human rights on which Amartya Sen laid a great stress in his book "*Development as Freedom*". Further, human development index as it is being presently constructed is not comprehensive as it does not include the two important indicators such as poverty and unemployment as reduction in them are important indicators of development. However, UNDP which constructs human development index separately calculates '*human poverty index*' (HPI) which has now been replaced by '*multi-dimensioned poverty index*'. But the existence of unemployment which is an important aspect of human development still remains excluded. Thus in our view, the chief drawback of human development index (HDI) is that it obscures many dimensions of the concept of development. The concept of development is so much wider, deeper and richer that single composite measure like HDI cannot adequately measure it. Therefore, it is better to judge and assess the development performance of different countries by a number of indicators that reflect different aspects of development rather to judge it by a single composite index of HDI.

Chapter 3

Underdevelopment and Development Gap

Underdevelopment: Its Meaning

All economies of the world are not equally developed. Some are more developed and advanced than others. Therefore, the economies of the world have been classified into developed economies and underdeveloped economies. Previously, the undeveloped economies were called backward or poor economies and the developed economies were known as advanced or rich economies. But the terms backward and advanced are now considered unsatisfactory and misleading. Therefore, the terms developed and underdeveloped began to be used in place of advanced and backward. But it is not easy to give a precise definition of an underdeveloped economy. According to the United Nations experts, "*an underdeveloped country is one in which per capita real income is low when compared with the per capita real income of the United States of America, Canada, Australia and Western Europe. In this sense, an adequate synonym would be poor countries*."[1] This definition brings out an important feature of underdevelopment, namely, poverty. But poverty is not always an adequate criterion to judge whether a country is developed or underdeveloped. For a country to be called underdeveloped, there must be unutilised or underutilised natural resources which may be used for production to raise per capita income and standards of living of the people. If the resources of a country are meagre and scanty, then even after having fully developed them, it will remain poor.

Professor Ragnar Nurkse also gave a definition of an underdeveloped country. According to him, "underdeveloped countries are those which compared with the advanced countries are under-equipped with capital in relation to their population and natural resources."[2] But this is also not a wholly correct and adequate definition of under-developed countries. This is because lack of capital is not the only cause of under-development and poverty. There are other important factors such as lack of technological progress, deficiency of human resources such as improved health, better education of the people which are responsible for low income and poverty of the people. Growth and development do not merely depend upon physical capital accumulation. Nurkse himself has pointed out that, "*Economic development has much to do with human endowments, social attitudes, political conditions and historical accidents. Capital is necessary but not a sufficient condition of progress.*"[3]

Professor Jacob Viner has provided a more satisfactory and adequate definition of an underdeveloped economy. According to Professor Viner, an underdeveloped country is one, "which has good potential prospect for using more capital or more labour or more available natural resources, or all of these to support its present population on a higher level of living."[4] Thus, Professor Viner has emphasised that for a country to be called underdeveloped *there must be possibilities and potentialities*

1 U.N., *Measures for the Economic Development of Underdeveloped Countries*, New York, 1951.
2 Ragnar Nurkse, *Problems of Capital Formation in Underdeveloped Countries*, 1953, p. 1.
3 *Ibid.*
4 Jacob Viner, "The Economics of Development", printed in A.N. Agarwala, and S.P. Singh (ed.), The *Economics of Underdevelopment*, Oxford University Press, 1958, p. 12.

for its development. In other words, in an underdeveloped country resources must be lying unutilised which can be used for increasing the rate of production and thereby raising the level of living of the people. Thus, according to him, the basic criterion of underdevelopment is whether there exists *potential prospects for development and raising standards of living* of the people through the use of its resources. Similar to Professor Viner, Eugene Stanley has also provided a definition. According to him, an underdeveloped country is one which is "characterised (i) by mass poverty which is chronic and not the result of some temporary misfortune and (ii) by obsolete methods of production and social organisation which means that poverty is not entirely due to poor natural resources and hence could presumably be lessened by methods already proved in other countries."[5] Thus Eugene Stanley lays emphasis on the existence of poverty as well as the potentialities for development and raising standards of living. We conclude that underdeveloped country is one which is poor but which has the future possibility and prospect of removing poverty and raising the levels of living of its people by utilising the idle and underutilised resources for production.

Economic development has been associated with industrialisation. Today's developed countries such as Britain, Germany, France, the United States experienced *industrial revolution* and growth was transmitted from industrial sector to agriculture and services. The present-day developing countries could not experience industrial revolution and remained underdeveloped and poor. It is worth mentioning that many of the present-day poor and developing countries were colonies of the developed countries and were used as suppliers of raw materials and primary products and as markets for the industrial products of the developed countries. In this many of the present-day poor and developing countries were exploited by the rich or industrialised countries for promoting their own economic growth.

Now, a pertinent question is why today's developing countries have remained underdeveloped and poor for so long. In other words why there has been *perpetuation of underdevelopment* in the presently developing countries. We will explain in a later chapter the perpetuation of their underdevelopment.

Developing Countries: Recent Changes in Terminology

There have been changes in terminology of describing the poor economies that have not undergone the process of development. They were called by various names such as poor, backward, undeveloped, underdeveloped. For quite some time these countries were called underdeveloped countries and, as explained above, some prominent economists gave their own definition of underdevelopment or underdeveloped countries. However, in recent years the term '*underdeveloped*' countries has gone out of vogue as the term 'underdeveloped' gave a wrong impression that the so called underdeveloped countries are not only socially and culturally backward but also not showing any signs of further development. It is now believed that different countries are merely more developed or less developed. Assuming that all countries have development potential and differ only in the degree of development; some are more and some are less developed. Therefore, at present the terms '*developing countries*' or *less developed countries* (LDC), are most widely used for the poor countries that are currently undergoing a process of development.

Developed countries are also called '*industrial countries*' in recognition of the close association between development and industrialisation. It is important to note that several formerly poor or developing countries of Asia such as Taiwan, Hong Kong, Korea and Singapore have recorded a remarkable industrial growth in the post-World War II period are called '*Newly Industrialised Economies*' (NIE). They represent success growth stories and because of the sharp rise in their per capita income they have joined the ranks of high-income countries.

It may be further noted that some years ago, the developing countries were collectively called the '*third world*'. The developed or industrialised countries of Western Europe, North America and Pacific were the '*first word*'; which are market economies formerly centrally planned socialist

5 Eugene Stanley, *The Future of Underdeveloped Countries*, New York, 1956, p. 18.

countries such as Soviet Russia, Poland, Yugoslavia, Hungary constituted the '*second world*' and the remaining developing countries were called the '*third world*'. Now this terminology is no longer used as there has been collapse of the second world representing centrally planned socialist economies and adopting by them market-friendly approach to development. Further, as the developed countries are geographically situated in the north of the globe and the developing countries are situated in the south of the globe, the developing countries are often called countries of the South. Therefore, in various world conferences where negotiations are held between the developed and the developing countries are often described as dialogue between the North and the South.

The Developed and Developing Countries: World Bank Classification

Despite shortcomings of per capita income as a measure of development, the World Bank, International Monetary Fund (IMF) and other international agencies consider developed and developing countries in terms of Gross National Income (GNI) per capita. The World Bank classifies

Table 3.1. Classification of Economies by Region and Income, FY2014

Low Income Countries	Georgia	Ecuador	Lithuania
Afghanistan	Ghana	Hungary	Netherlands
Bangladesh	Guatemala	Iran, Islamic Rep.	New Zealand
Benin	Honduras	Iraq	Norway
Burkina Faso	**India**	Jordan	Poland
Burundi	Indonesia	Kazakhstan	Portugal
Cambodia	Lao PDR	Lebanon	Russian Federation
Central African Republic	Mauritania	Libya	Saudi Arabia
Chad	Moldova	Malaysia	Singapore
Congo, Dem. Rep.	Morocco	Mexico	Slovak Republic
Eritrea	Nicaragua	Panama	Spain
Ethiopia	Nigeria	Peru	Sweden
Guinea	Pakistan	Romania	Switzerland
Haiti	Papua New Guinea	Serbia	United Arab Emirates
Kenya	Paraguay	South Africa	United Kingdom
Kyrgyz Republic	Philippines	Thailand	United States
Liberia	Senegal	Tunisia	Uruguay
Madagascar	Sri Lanka	Turkey	**Selected Island States**
Malawi	Sudan	Turkmenistan	Antigua and Barbuda
Mali	Syrian Arab Republic	Venezuela, RB	Bahamas
Mozambique	Ukraine	**High Income**	Barbados
Myanmar	Uzbekistan	Australia	Bermuda
Nepal	Vietnam	Austria	Comoros
Niger	West Bank and Gaza	Belgium	Dominica
Rwanda	Yemen, Rep.	Canada	Dominican Rep
Sierra Leone	Zambia	Chile	Fiji
Somalia	**Upper Middle Income**	Hong Kong SAR, China	Grenada
South Sudan	Albania	Croatia	Haiti
Tajikistan	Algeria	Czech Republic	Jamaica
Tanzania	Angola	Denmark	Maldives
Togo	Argentina	Finland	Marshall Is
Uganda	Azerbaijan	France	Micronesia Fed States
Zimbabwe	Belarus	Germany	Philippines
Lower Middle Income	Bosnia and Herzegovina	Greece	Samoa
Armenia	Brazil	Ireland	Seychelles
Bolivia	Bulgaria	Israel	Solomon Is.
Cameroon	**China**	Italy	St. Kitts and Nevis
Congo, Rep.	Colombia	Japan	St. Lucia
Cote d'Ivoire	Costa Rica	Korea, Rep.	St. Vincent and The Gren-
Egypt, Arab Rep.	Dominican		adines
El Salvador	Republic		Trinidad and Tobago

Source: *World Development Report*, 2014, p. 295.

different countries of the world on the basis GNI per capita representing their development status. The figures of GNI per capita of different countries used belong to the World Bank fiscal year ending on June 30 of the year. According to this World Bank classification (i) *low income countries* are those with GNI per capita of $ 1035 or less in 2012 (the latest year which is presently available). Middle income countries are those with GNI per capita more than $ 1035 but less than $ 12,616. Middle income countries are further divided into (a) *lower middle income economies* and (b) *upper middle* income economies. (3) High income economies which have GNI per capita of $ 12, 616 or more. In Table 3.1 we give classifications of economies by region and per capita income (*i.e.*, GNI per capita in Table 3.2 we give GNI per capita and other key indicators of development such as population and its growth rate, life expectancy at birth and adult literacy rate.

It is important to note that developing countries are those *whose GNI per capita falla in low income and middle income range*. As mentioned above, low-income countries have less than $ 1035 GNI per capita and middle income countries have per capital income more than $ 1035 but less than $ 1266 *based on their official or current exchange rates* of the national currencies into US dollars. It will be seen from Table 3.2 that in 2012 India with per capita income of $ 1530 at current exchange rate falls in lower middle income category while China with $ 574 per capita income at the current exchange rate falls in the upper middle income countries. However, as defined above, both India and China are described as developing countries.

On the other hand, U.S. with per capita income of $ 5012, U.K. with per capita income of $ 38250, Germany with a per capita income of $ 44010. France with per capita income of $ 41750 in 2012 are high-income countries and are described as developed economies.

It may be noted that the terms 'developing' and 'developed' are used for convenience. It is not intended to imply that all economies in the group of developing countries are experiencing similar developments. Likewise, for describing some countries as 'developed' is not meant that they have reached a preferred or final stage of development. In fact, they too are growing and developing further. Further, classifying different countries according to the size of their per capita income does not reflect their *permanent development status*. A country's per capita may rise with time as development proceeds further and therefore its development status may shift from low income to middle income or middle income to high income category.

THE DEVELOPMENT GAP AND INCOME DISTRIBUTION IN THE WORLD ECONOMY

An important feature of world economy is that world's income is distribution extremely unequally between different countries and people. We have referred above to North-South divide which means there are wide differences of per capita income — an indicator of development — between rich industrialised countries mainly located in the northern hemisphere on the one hand on semi-industrialised development countries mainly situated in the southern hemisphere. The division in the global economy is also often made between the developed continents of Europe and North America on the one hand and poor and developing continents of Asia, Africa and Latin America on the other. It is however important to note that, developing countries of Asia, Africa and Latin America are not completely homogeneous though they have many common characteristics and impediments to development. It is often said that there is a good deal of *commonality among diversity* among the developing nations. One significant aspect of the differences among the poor and developing countries is with to regard to economic growth and development achieved by them since 1960s. While in the race of economic development South East Africa, China, India have forged ahead, the countries of Africa have left behind, and Latin America occupies a middle position with respect to its development performance.

Table 3.2. Key Indicators of Development

	Population		Population age Compo-sition	Gross national income		Gross national income, PPP		Life expectancy at birth		Adult literacy rate % ages 15 and older
	Millions	Average annual growth %	% ages 0-14	$ billions	$ per capita	$ billions	$ per capita	Years, male	Years, female	
	2012	2000-12	2012	2012	2012	2012	2012	2011	2011	2005-11
Afghanistan	30	3.1	47	16.6	570	40.7	1400	49	49	--
Albania	3	-0.4	21	12.9	4090	29.7	9390	74	80	96
Algeria	38	1.6	27	155.1	4110	285.0	7550	72	75	73
Angola	21	3.4	48	95.4	4580	114.3	5490	50	53	70
Argentina	41	0.9	24	-	-	-	-	72	80	98
Armenia	3	-0.3	20	11.1	3720	20.8	6990	71	77	100
Australia	23	14	19	1351.2	59570	982.2	43300	80	84	-
Austria	8	0.5	15	407.6	48160	373.2	44100	78	84	-
Azerbaijan	9	1.2	22	56.3	6050	87.5	9410	68	74	100
Bangladesh	155	1.3	31	129.2	840	319.9	2070	68	70	57
Belarus	9	-0.5	15	61.8	6503	143.9	15210	65	77	100
Belgium	11	0.7	17	501.3	44990	447.6	40170	78	83	-
Benin	10	3.1	43	7.5	750	15.8	1570	54	58	42
Bolivia	10	1.8	35	23.3	220	52.1	4960	64	69	91
Bosnia and Herze-	4	0.0	16	17.8	4650	36.0	9380	73	78	98
govina	199	1.1	25	2031.1	11630	2328.8	11720	70	77	90
Brazil	7	-0.9	14	50.2	6870	112.4	15390	71	78	98
Bulgaria	16	2.9	46	10.9	670	24.9	1510	54	56	29
Burkina Faso	10	3.2	44	2.4	240	5.5	560	49	52	67
Burundi	15	1.6	31	13.0	880	35.1	2360	62	64	74
Cambodia	22	2.6	43	25.4	1170	50.3	2320	51	53	71
Cameroon	35	1.0	16	1777.19	50970	1483.6	42530	79	83	--
Canada										
Central African Rep.	5	1.8	40	2.2	490	3.9	860	47	50	56
Chad	12	3.4	49	9.3	740	16.4	1320	48	51	34
Chile	17	1.0	21	2495	14280	372.1	21310	76	82	99
China	1351	0.6	18	7748.9	5740	12435.4	9210	72	75	94
Hong Kong SAR,	7	0.6	12	261.6	36500	379.6	53050	80	87	-
China	48	1.5	28	333.6	6990	482.2	10110	70	77	93
Colombia	66	2.8	45	14.8	220	24.5	370	47	50	67
Congo, Dem Rep.	4	2.7	42	11.1	2550	15.2	3510	56	59	-
Congo. Rep.	5	1.7	24	42.0	8740	60.5	12590	77	82	96
Costa Rica	20	1.7	41	24.2	1220	38.8	1960	54	57	56
Cote d'lvoire	4	-0.3	15	56.7	13290	84.3	19760	74	80	99
Croatia	11	0.2	15	190.6	18130	259.8	24710	75	81	-
Czech Republic	6	0.4	18	934.1	59770	242.3	43340	78	82	-
Denmark	10	1.4	31	56.2	5470	101.0	9820	71	76	90
Dominican Republic	15	1.8	30	80.5	5190	148.5	9590	73	79	92
Ecuador	81	1.7	31	241.8	3000	536.3	6640	71	75	72
Egypt, Arab Rep	6	0.5	31	22.5	3580	42.8	6790	67	77	84
El Salvador	6	3.7	43	2.8	450	3.4	560	59	64	68
Eritrea	92	2.7	43	37.4	410	104.2	1140	58	61	39
Ethiopia	5	0.4	16	254.1	46940	209.2	38630	77	84	--
Finalnd	66	0.6	18	2742.9	41750	2412.6	36720	78	85	--
France	5	0.2	18	14.8	3280	26.4	5860	70	77	100
Georgia										

	Population		Population age Composition	Gross national income		Gross national income, PPP		Life expectancy at birth		Adult liiteracy rate % ages 15 and older
	Millions	Average annual growth %	% ages 0-14	$ billions	$ per capita	$ billions	$ per capita	Years, male	Years, female	
	2012	2000-12	2012	2012	2012	2012	2012	2011	2011	2005-11
Germany	82	0.0	13	3603.9	44010	3430.1	41890	78	83	--
Ghana	25	2.5	39	39.3	1550	49.2	1940	63	65	67
Greece	11	0.3	15	262.4	23260	287.2	25460	79	83	97
Guatemala	15	2.5	41	47.0	3120	74.8	4960	68	75	75
Guinea	11	2.2	42	5.3	460	11.3	980	53	56	41
Haiti	10	1.4	35	7.7	760	12.6	1240	61	63	49
Honduras	8	2.0	36	16.4	2070	30.9	3890	71	75	85
Hungary	10	-0.2	15	123.4	12390	205.9	20710	71	79	99
India	1,237	1.4	29	1890.4	1530	4749.2	3840	64	67	63
Indonesia	247	1.4	29	844.0	3420	1188.0	4810	68	71	93
Iran, Islamic Rep.	76	1.2	24	--	--	--	--	71	75	85
Iraq	33	2.6	41	191.2	5870	140.2	4300	66	72	78
Ireland	5	1.6	22	178.8	38970	164.6	35870	78	83	--
Israel	8	1.9	28	224.7	28930	218.0	28070	80	84	--
Italy	61	0.6	14	2061.3	33840	2002.3	32870	80	85	99
Japan	128	0.0	13	6105.8	47870	4629.7	36290	79	86	--
Jordan	6	2.3	34	29.9	4720	38.8	6130	72	75	93
Kazakhstan	17	1.0	25	163.5	9730	200.7	11950	64	74	100
Kenya	43	2.7	42	36.2	840	76.1	1760	56	58	87
Korea, Rep.	50	0.5	15	1133.8	22670	1548.7	30970	78	84	--
Kyrgyz Republic	6	1.1	30	5.5	990	12.6	2260	66	74	90
Lao PDR	7	1.7	36	8.4	1260	18.1	2730	66	69	73
Lebanon	4	2.6	22	40.7	9190	63.7	14400	70	75	90
Liberia	4	3.1	43	1.6	370	2.5	600	56	58	61
Libya	6	1.4	29	--	--	--	--	72	78	89
Lithuania	3	-1.3	15	41.3	13850	67.9	22760	68	79	100
Madagascar	22	2.9	43	9.7	430	21.2	950	65	68	64
Malawi	16	2.8	45	5.0	320	13.9	880	54	54	75
Malaysia	29	1.8	27	286.4	9800	483.2	16530	72	77	93
Mali	15	3.1	47	9.8	660	17.2	1160	50	52	31
Mauritania	4	2.8	40	4.2	1110	9.6	2520	57	60	58
Mexico	121	1.3	29	1176.9	9740	2015.8	16680	75	79	93
Moldova	4	-0.2	17	7.4	2070	13.1	3690	66	73	99
Morocco	33	1.0	28	97.1	2940	166.6	5040	70	74	56
Mozambique	25	2.7	45	12.8	510	25.7	1,020	49	51	56
Myanmar	53	0.7	25	--	--	--	--	63	67	92
Nepal	27	1.4	36	19.2	700	41.1	1500	68	70	60
Netherlands	17	0.4	17	809.1	48250	731.5	43620	79	83	--
New Zealand	4	1.2	20	134.9	30620	132.0	29960	79	83	--
Nicaragua	6	1.3	33	9.9	1650	23.7	3960	71	77	78
Niger	17	3.7	50	6.4	370	11.2	650	54	55	29
Nigeria	169	2.6	44	241.1	1430	409.1	2420	51	53	61
Norway	5	0.9	19	496.2	98860	336.1	66960	79	84	--
Pakistan	179	1.8	34	225.4	1260	543.6	3030	65	66	55
Panama	4	1.8	29	37.7	9910	67.8	17830	74	79	94
Papua New Guinea	7	2.4	38	12.8	1790	19.9	2780	61	65	61

	Population		Population age Compo- sition	Gross national income, PPP		Gross national income, PPP		Life expectancy at birth		Adult liit- eracy rate % ages 15 and older
	Millions	Average annual growth %	% ages 0-14	$ billions	$ per capita	$ billions	$ per capita	Years, male	Years, female	
	2012	2000-12	2012	2012	2012	2012	2012	2011	2011	2005-11
Paraguay	7	1.9	33	22.0	3290	37.5	5610	70	75	94
Peru	30	1.2	29	176.5	5880	306.9	10240	71	77	90
Philippines	97	1.8	35	238.7	2470	425.2	4400	66	72	95
Poland	39	0.0	15	488.3	12670	816.0	21170	73	81	100
Portugal	11	0.2	15	216.6	20580	260.7	24770	78	84	95
Romania	21	-0.4	15	179.6	8420	347.8	16310	71	78	98
Russian Federation	144	-0.2	15	1822.7	12700	3260.6	22720	63	75	100
Rwanda	11	2.6	44	6.2	560	13.9	1250	54	57	71
Saudi Arabia	28	2.8	30	500.5	18030	694.4	25010	73	75	87
Senegal	14	2.8	44	14.2	1040	26.3	1920	58	60	50
Serbia	7	-0.3	16	38.1	5280	80.8	11180	72	77	98
Sierra Leone	6	3.1	42	3.5	580	8.1	1360	47	48	42
Singapore	5	2.3	16	250.8	47210	324.6	61100	80	84	96
Slovak Republic	5	0.0	15	92.9	17170	134.0	24770	72	80	--
Somalia	10	2.7	47	--	--	--	--	50	53	--
South Africa	51	1.3	30	389.8	7610	572.6	11190	52	53	89
South Sudan	11	4.1	42	7.0	650	--	--	--	--	--
Spain	46	1.1	15	1391.4	30110	1493.8	32320	79	85	98
Sri Lanka	20	0.5	25	59.3	2920	124.5	6120	72	78	91
Sudan	37	2.4	41	53.8	1450	75.3	2030	60	63	71
Sweeden	10	0.6	17	535.0	56210	420.1	44150	80	84	--
Switzerland	8	0.9	15	661.6	82730	449.8	56240	81	85	--
Syrian Arab Rep.	22	2.6	35	56.3	2610	116.5	5200	74	77	83
Tajikistan	8	2.2	36	6.9	860	17.8	2220	64	71	100
Tanzania	48	2.8	45	26.7	570	73.6	1590	75	59	73
Thailand	67	0.6	18	347.9	5210	630.0	9430	71	78	94
Togo	7	2.6	42	3.3	500	6.1	920	56	59	57
Tunisia	11	1.0	23	44.8	4150	100.9	9360	73	77	78
Turkey	74	1.3	26	801.1	10830	1345.7	18190	72	76	91
Turkmenistan	5	1.2	29	28.7	5550	49.9	9640	61	69	100
Uganda	36	3.4	49	16.0	440	41.4	1140	53	55	73
Ukraine	46	-0.6	14	159.6	3500	332.5	7290	66	76	100
United Arab. Emirates	9	9.3	14	321.7	36040	378.3	42380	76	78	90
United Kingdom	63	0.6	18	2418.5	38250	2331.9	36880	79	83	--
United States	314	0.9	20	15734.6	50120	15887.6	50610	76	81	--
Uruguay	3	0.2	22	45.9	13510	52.9	15570	73	80	98
Uzbekistan	30	1.6	29	51.3	1720	111.6	3750	65	71	99
Venezuela, Rep.	30	1.7	29	373.5	12470	393.0	13120	71	77	96
Vietnam	89	1.1	23	124.1	1400	305.6	3440	73	77	93
West Bank and Gaza	4	2.7	41	--	--	--	--	71	75	95
Yemen, Rep.	24	2.6	41	26.0	1110	53.7	2310	64	67	64
Zambia	14	2.8	47	19.1	1350	22.8	1620	49	49	71
Zimbabwe	14	0.8	40	9.3	680	---	--	52	50	92
World	**7046s**	**1.2w**	**26w**	**70571.6t**	**10015w**	**85463.2t**	**12129w**	68w	**72w**	**84w**

	Population		Population age Composition	Gross national income		Gross national income, PPP		Life expectancy at birth		Adult Lliteracy rate % ages 15 and older
	Millions	Average annual growth %	% ages 0-14	$ billions	$ per capita	$ billions	$ per capita	Years, male	Years, female	
	2012	2000-12	2012	2012	2012	2012	2012	2011	2011	2005-11
Middle income	4898	1.2	27	21396.9	4369	35469.4	7242	67	71	83
Lower middle income	2507	1.6	31	4706.2	1877	9808.1	3912	64	68	71
Upper middle income	2391	0.8	22	16704.9	6987	25679.4	10741	71	75	94
Low & middle income	5774	1.3	29	21902.7	3813	36624.4	6376	66	70	80
High income	1302	0.6	17	48952.3	37595	49167.5	37760	76	82	--

a. Calculated using the World Bank Atlas method
b. PPP = purchasing power parity.
c. Data are for the most recent year available.
d. The estimate is based on repression, others are extrapolated from the 2005 international Comparison Program Backmark estimates.
e. Estimated to be upper middle income ($ 4,086– S 12,615).
f. Excludes Abkhazia and South Ossetia.
g. Excludes Tranistria
h. Includes Former Spanish Sahara.
i. Estimated to be low income ($ 1,035 or less),
j. Excludes South Sudan.
k. Covers mainland Tanzania only.
l. Estimated to be lower middle income ($ 1,036–$ 4,085).

Source: World Development Report, 2014, pp. 296-297

As explained above, the World Bank in its annual *World Development Report* classifies different 188 countries of the world into (1) low income countries (LIC), (2) middle income countries (MIC) and (3) high income countries (HIC). The middle income countries are further divided into (a) Lower middle income countries and (b) Upper Middle Income Countries. Table 3.3 among other things, gives the level of per capita national income measured in PPP 2012 (column 7) in different countries of the world. It will be seen from this table that in terms of per capita income ($ PPP 2012) with $ 370 $ PPP 2012, Democratic Republic of Congo is the poorest country and with GNI per capita Norway $ 66960 is the richest country of the world. In Table 3.3 average levels of per capita national income are given separately for low, middle and high income countries of the world.

Table 3.3. Population and GNI Per Capita $ PPP in the Year 2012

	Countries	Population (millions)	Gross National Income Per Capita, PPP $ (average)
1.	Low Income	846	1,387
2.	Middle Income (a) Lower Middle Income (b) Upper Middle Income	4,898 2,507 2,391	7,242 3,912 10,741
3.	Low and Middle Income Countries	5,744	6,376
4.	High Income Countries	1302	37,760
	World	7,046	12,129

Source: *World Development Report,* 2014.

Table 3.3 reveals that a large development gap exists between low income countries (with $ 1,035 PPP or less) and high income developed countries (with $ 12,615 PPP or above) in 2012.

In low income countries containing 846 million population average per capita income of $ 1,387 PPP as against average per capita income of $ 37,760 PPP of high income countries having population of 1,302 million in 2012. This is indeed a very large development gap between the low income countries and high income countries. Developing countries as generally defined contain both low-income and middle-income countries. It will be interesting to compare the gap between the developing countries as a whole on the one side and high income developed countries. It will be seen from Table 3.3 that developing countries (*i.e.* low and middle-income countries) containing 5.74 billion population have average per capita income equal to $ 6,376 PPP in 2012 as against average per capita income of $ 37,760 PPP of high-income developed countries having total population of 1.30 billion in 2012. This too is a very large income gap which has to be bridged by developing countries by achieving a much higher rate of GDP growth than that of developed countries, if they desire to catch up with them. We will explain this in detail later and see how East Asian countries joined the rank of high-income developed countries by registering a very high rate of GDP growth after 1965 till 1990. China and India, the *two fastest growing countries* of the world, are expected to catch up with the developed countries by 2050.

Measuring International Income Inequality

We have explained above that gross national income per capita of different countries of the world varies a good deal and further that there exists a large income or development gap between the developing and the developed countries. It is important to explain how income inequalities between various countries in the world economy is exactly measured. We will explain the various methods of measuring income inequalities within an economy in a later chapter. However, methods of measuring income inequalities *between* countries are the same as the methods used for measuring inequalities *within* countries. We explain below these methods in brief only while their detailed analysis will be made in the later chapter.

Absolute Income Method. This is the simplest method of measuring international income inequality. In this we measure *absolute income gap* or *range* between the richest and poorest countries. From Table 3.2 we find that gross *national income per capita* based on purchasing power parity (PPP) prices for the year 2012, the poorest country is Democratic Republic of Congo with $ 370, whereas the GNI per capita of the richest country Norway is $ 66960 in 2012. Thus, absolute income gap is $ 66960 – $, 370 = $ 66590. In this case if the two countries *grow at the same rate*, the absolute income will grow. For example, 1 per cent growth rate will roughly add to Norway's per capita income by $ 670 whereas one per cent growth will cause only $ 3.7 increase in per capita income of Democratic Republic of Congo. In this case Congos would have to grow more than 600 per cent so as to narrow the absolute income gap between itself and Norway. However, this absolute income method of measuring international income inequality underestimates the degree of income inequality between them because it compares only the *average* incomes of the poor and rich countries. If actual income per capita of the *poorest* people of the poor countries is compared with income per capita of the *richest* people in rich countries, the income gap will be much greater.

Relative Income Method. In this method of measuring income inequality in the world economy instead of measuring the absolute income gap, the ratio of income per capita of the low income countries to the per capita income of the high income countries is found. In the data given in Table 3.3 average income per capita of low income countries in terms of purchasing power party (PPP) prices is $ 1,387 whereas the average income per capita of high income countries is $ 37,760. Therefore, the relative income ratio in the present case is $ 37,760/1,387 = 28.1. From the relative income ratio it follows that to narrow the gap, poor countries have to grow faster than the richest countries. East Asian countries, Taiwan, South Korea, Hong Kong, Singapore, recorded much higher growth rates of around 6 to 7% in per capita income between 1965 and 1990 as compared to the rich countries and therefore succeeded in reaching the level of rich countries. In the last over two decades, China and

India have registered a very high growth rate in per capita income and have narrowed the relative income gap with the rich developed countries. It is now estimated that if India maintains its 8% growth in total GDP it will reach the rank of high income developed countries by the year 2050 and will thus catch up with them.

Lorenz Curve and Gini Index. The most popular method of measuring international income inequality is to draw a Lorenz curve which in the present context relates to the distribution of income corresponding to the distribution of population across countries or groups of countries. It is worth mentioning that in this method international income inequality is measured in two ways. In the first method, international income inequality is measured treating each country as a single unit and giving equal weight in the measure. In the second method of measuring international income inequality though each country is treated as a single unit in the measure but is *weighted by its size of population.*

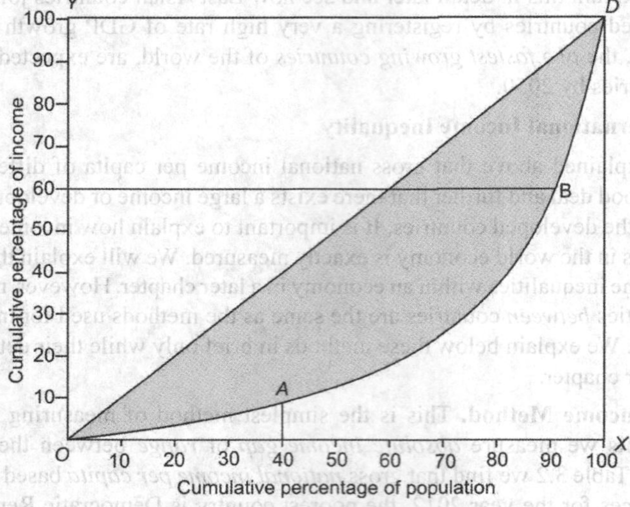

Fig. 3.1. *Lorenz curve depicting world inequality in incomes*

To draw Lorenz curve depicting distribution of income we first rank each country or groups of countries in ascending order of the percentage of gross national income of the world income they have and percentage of world population possessed by them. Then, to draw Lorenz curve in a figure we measure cumulative percentage of income of countries on the *Y*-axis and cumulative percentage of their population on the *X*-axis. By drawing so we get a box as shown in Fig. 3.1. The diagonal line *OD* represents the line of perfect equality. Now, with given data of Gross national income (based on PPP $) of various countries and their populations, such as given in Table 3.2, we can draw a Lorenz Curve by plotting the cumulative percentage of income of the countries in ascending order and the cumulative percentage of their populations. Such a Lorenz curve *OABD* has been drawn in Fig. 3.1. According to this cumulative 10 per cent of world income of the countries have 40 per cent of world population and cumulative 60 per cent of incomes of the countries contain 90 per cent of populations is represented by point A. Needless to say, 100 to per cent cumulative income of all countries would correspond to 100 per cent of world population. The Lorenz Curve *OABD roughly* represents the data of gross national income (GNI) based on PPP $ of various countries and their populations in the year 2012 given in Table 3.2. As will be seen, Lorenz curve *OABD* is much far away from line *OD* of perfect equality. This, shows there is a very high degree of international income inequality.

Gini Index or Gini Ratio. Gini Index which is widely used both for measuring international income inequality and income inequality *within* individuals countries is based on Lorenz curve measure as represented by curve *OABD*. Gini index is the ratio the shaded area within the Lorenz curve *OABD* to the total area *OXD*. The greater this area, the higher will be the value of Gini Index.

Standard Deviation and Coefficient of Variation. These are also important measures of inequality. Standard deviation measures the square root of average of the sun of squared deviations of each country's per capita income from the *mean income* of all countries. Symbolically it is written as

$$\sigma = \sqrt{\sum_{i=1}^{n} \frac{(y_i - y)^2}{n}}$$

where σ stands for standard deviation, y_1 is income of a country, $\bar{y}$ is mean income of all countries and *n* is the number of countries included in the sample.

Having calculated standard deviation (σ), *coefficient of variation* can be obtained by dividing the standard deviation by the mean of the sample ($\bar{y}$). Coefficient of variation normalises the standard deviation as there is positive correlation between the mean and standard deviation.

Catching up with Developed Countries

In fact, the *developing countries have been growing much faster than the developed countries* in the past three decades as will be seen from. Table 3.4 where we have given the growth rates of GDP for some selected developed and developing countries for 1980-90, 1990-2000 and 2000-09. For example, whereas China's GDP has been growing at more than 10 per cent in all these decades and India's annual GDP growth was 5.8% in 1980-90, 6.0 per cent in 1990-2000 and 7.9 per cent in 2000-09. China has been the fastest growing economy of the world and India is the second fastest growing country of the world. If they maintain this growth momentum, they will catch up with the present-day high per capita income countries. Newly industrialised countries (NIC) such as Taiwan, South Korea, Singapore through higher economic growth after the fifties have joined the rank of high per capita income countries.

Table 3.4. Growth Rate of GDP

Country	Annual Growth rate of GDP (%)		
	1980-90	1990-2000	2000-09
Developed Countries			
U.S.	3.0	3.5	2.0
U.K.	3.2	2.7	2.0
Germany	–	1.8	1.0
France	–	1.9	1.5
Canada	3.4	3.1	2.1
Japan	4.1	1.3	1.1
Australia	3.5	3.9	3.3
Developing Countries			
India	5.8	6.0	7.9
Brazil	–	2.7	3.6
China	10.2	10.6	10.9
Pakistan	6.3	3.8	5.2
Bangladesh	4.3	4.8	5.9
Sri Lanka	4.2	5.3	5.5

Source: *World Development Indicators*, 2006 and 2011.

Further, according to **International Comparison Progress (ICP)** report of World Bank released in April 2014, the global economy balance seems to be tilting towards the developing countries.

It will be interesting to note that India has overtaken Japan to emerge as the third largest economy of the world in terms of total GDP based on purchasing power parity (PPP $) terms after the U.S. and China according to the latest (2011) data of World Bank (ICP). Share of twelve largest economies of the world's GDP as per World Bank's ICP 2011 report is given in Table 3.5. It will be seen from Table 3.5. that with 17.1 per cent of share world's GDP the United States remains world's largest economy followed by China with 14.9 per cent share in world's GDP and India with 6.4 per cent share of world's GDP.

The previous version of the World Bank's International Comparison Progress (ICP) report had said that India was ranked 10th in 2005 in terms of PPP. PPP $ is used to compare economies and incomes of people by adjusting for differences in prices in various countries. The economies of Japan and the U.K. became relative to the U.S. while Germany increased slightly and France and Italy remained the same.

Further, the World Bank ICP report 2011 said that six of the world's largest economies were in the middle income per capita category. The dozen largest economies accounted for two-third of the world economy and 59% of the population. The six largest middle income economies, China, India, Russia, Brazil, Indonesia and Mexico, accounted for 32.3 per cent of world GDP, while the six largest high income economies – U.S., Japan, Germany, France, UK, Italy – accounted for 32.9% showing that emerging economies had reduced the gap through rapid growth in recent years.

Table 3.5. Twelve Largest Economies of World GDP, ICP 2011

Ranking by GDP (PPP-Based)	Economy	Share of World GDP (PPP-based world = 100)	Ranking by GDP per capita (PPP-based)
1	United States	17.1	**12**
2	**China**	14.9	**99**
3	**India**	6.4	**127**
4	Japan	4.8	**33**
5	Germany	3.7	**24**
6	Russian Federation	3.5	**55**
7	**Brazil**	3.1	**80**
8	France	2.6	**30**
9	United Kingdom	2.4	**32**
10	**Indonesia**	2.3	**107**
11	Italy	2.3	**34**
12	Mexico	2.1	**72**

Source: *World Bank* ICP, 2011

It is important to note that a number of largest economies in terms of GDP are not the richest in terms of GDP per capita as can be seen in Table 3.5 from their ranking of their GDP per capita (see 4th col. of the Table). For example, India is 3rd largest economy but its ranking in terms of GNP per capita is 127th. This is due to its large population which reduces its per capita GDP. The same is the case of China. Despite its second largest economy in respect of the size of its total GDP, its ranking in GDP per capita is 99th only. Both India and China have per capita GDP in the middle income category and are designated as developing countries.

It is worth mentioning that most developing countries have done well in respect of rate of economic growth (see Table 3.5), a good number of countries have done particularly well and therefore *2013 Human Development Report* calls it as "***the rise of the south***" (note that as mentioned earlier the South means developing countries). According to this *2013 Human Development Report*, the combined output of the developing world's there economic powers, China, India and Brazil together represented only 10% of the world economy (*i.e*, world's GDP) *in 1950*, while six traditional economic leaders of the North[6] (*i.e.*, developed countries) accounted for more than half. According to projections

6 World Bank, 2013 *Human Development Report*, April 2014.

made in this report by 2050 (the combined outfit of the three leading developing countries alone – China, India and Brazil – will account for 40 per cent of global output surpassing the aggregate production of present-day's group of six developed countries – Canada, France, Germany, Italy, the United Kingdom and the United States[7] (see Fig. 3.2). What is significant to note is that according to this report "*much of the expansion in output in these countries is being driven by new trade and technology partnership within the south itself*"[8]

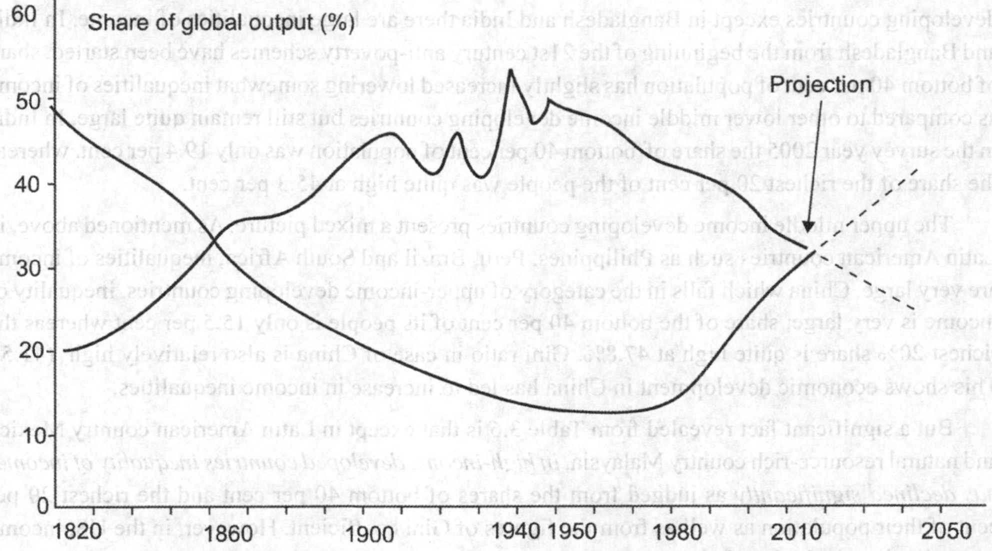

Fig. 3.2. *Brazil, China and India combined are projected to account for 40% of global output by 2050, up from 10% in 1950*

Note*: Output is measured in 1990 purchasing power parity dollars.*
Source: *Human Development Report*. 2013)

Higher Levels of Inequality and Poverty

In our analysis of international income inequality above we find that there is a very large gap *between* the per capita income of the rich and poor countries. However, to fully know the causes of poverty in developing countries, it is necessary to know the extent of inequality in income distribution *within* the developing countries. In general we find that in poor developing countries there are large inequalities of income *within* them. Thus, it is important to mention that the problem of poverty of the people in poor developing countries is not only due to their lower average per capita income as compared to the rich countries but also there exists larger inequality in the distribution of income *within* them. Prof. Debraj Ray[9] rightly writes, "*The poor are twice cursed : once for living in countries that are poor on average and then again for being on the receiving end of the high levels of inequality in those countries*". Income inequalities also exist in rich developed countries, but in developing countries where along with *average* low level of per capita income large inequality in income distribution leads to the acute problem of absolute poverty and destitution. In several African countries such as South Africa, Lesotho, Sierra Leone, there prevail very high levels of income inequality. In Latin American countries which belong to the group of middle-income countries, large income inequalities are found. Income inequality varies greatly among developing countries. In resources-rich developing countries of Middle East and Sub-Saharan Africa, income inequalities are substantially high.

---

7 See, *op. cit. Summary of 2013 Report,* p. 2.
8 *Op. cit*; p. 2.
9 Debraj Ray, *Development Economics;* New Delhi: Oxford University Press, 1998, p. 22.

Table 3.6 gives per capita income and inequality of incomes (as measured by share of poorest 40% and share of richest 20% and Gini Ratio) of low-income, lower-middle income and upper-middle income developing countries and high income developed countries. It will be seen from Table 3.6 that in low-income countries share of bottom 40 per cent of population is around only 15 to 17 per cent and the share of the richest 20 per cent of people is quite high at 47 to 54 per cent. Thus, in low-income developing countries, inequalities of income are quite large. In lower middle-income developing countries except in Bangladesh and India there are large inequalities of income. In India and Bangladesh from the beginning of the 21st century anti-poverty schemes have been started, share of bottom 40 per cent of population has slightly increased lowering somewhat inequalities of income as compared to other lower middle income developing countries but still remain quite large. In India in the survey year 2005 the share of bottom 40 per cent of population was only 19.4 per cent, whereas the share of the richest 20 per cent of the people was quite high at 45.3 per cent.

The upper middle income developing countries present a mixed picture. As mentioned above, in Latin American countries such as Philippines, Peru, Brazil and South Africa, inequalities of income are very large. China which falls in the category of upper-income developing countries, inequality of income is very large; share of the bottom 40 per cent of its people is only 15.5 per cent whereas the richest 20% share is quite high at 47.8%. Gini ratio in case of China is also relatively high (41.5). This shows economic development in China has led to increase in income inequalities.

But a significant fact revealed from Table 3.6 is that except in Latin American country Mexico and natural resource-rich country Malaysia, *in high-income developed countries inequality of incomes has declined significantly* as judged from the shares of bottom 40 per cent and the richest 20 per cent of their population as well as from the figures of Gini coefficient. However, in the US, income inequality is quite high as in it bottom 40 per cent of its people get only 16 per cent share in national income while the richest 20 per cent get around 46 per cent of national income. This shows that development in the U.S. is quite inequitable and unfair.

Table 3.6. Income Inequality within Countries

Country	Per Capita Income in US $ PPP (2005-2012)	Share of Poorest 40% (in %)	Share of Richest 20% (in %)	Gini Ratio
Less than $ 1,035				
Congo Demo. Rep.	370	14.7	50.6	44.4
Liberia	600	17.8	45.0	52.6
Niger	650	20.3	42.8	34.0
Central African Rep.	860	14.6	49.4	43.6
Malawi	880	17.8	46.4	39.0
Tongo	920	15.7	47.1	34.4
Madagascar	950	15.8	53.5	47.2
Guinea	980	16.9	46.2	39.4
Mozambique	1020	14.7	51.5	45.6
More than $ 1035 and Less than $ 4,085				

Country	Per capita Income PPP 2012 $	Share of Poorest 40% (in %)	Share of Richest 20% (in %)	Gini Ratio
Nepal	1500	15.0	54.2	47.3
Tanzania	1590	17.9	44.8	37.6
Zambia	1620	11.4	55.2	47.7
Kenya	1760	13.5	40.8	31.0
Bangladesh	2070	22.0	45.3	37.7
Yemen	2310	18.3	51.7	44.4
Cambodia	2360	16.0	48.6	42.9
Nigeria	2420	14.8	42.1	32.7
Pakistan	3030	21.4	–	37.6
Vietnam	3440	18.2	45.3	36.8
India	3840	19.4	45.3	–

Income Inequality within Countries

Country	Per capita Income PPP 2012 $	Share of Poorest 40% (in %)	Share of Richest 20% (in %)	Gini Ratio
Between $ 4,085 and $ 12,615				
Philippines	4400	14.7	50.4	44.0
Sri Lanka	6120	17.3	47.8	40.5
Jordan	6130	16.3	45.4	37.7
Egypt Arab Rep.	6640	21.6	41.5	32.1
Algeria	7750	18.4	42.4	35.3
Tunisia	9360	16.1	47.2	40.8
Thailand	9410	10.9	58.6	53.6
China	10110	15.5	47.8	41.5
Peru	10240	12.3	52.6	48.9
South Africa	11190	8.7	62.7	52.8
Brazil	11770	10.5	58.1	53.9
> $ 12,615 (High Income Countries)				
Malaysia	16680	11.8	56.2	48.0
Mexico	16680	11.8	56.2	51.7
Korea Republic	30970	21.5	37.5	31.6
Spain	32320	19.2	42.0	34.7
Italy	32870	18.5	42.0	36.0
Ireland	35870	28.6	42.0	36.0
Japan	36290	24.8	35.7	24.9
France	36720	19.8	40.2	32.7
U.K.	36880	17.5	44.0	36.0
Germany	41890	22.2	36.9	28.3
Canada	42530	19.9	39.9	32.0
Australia	43300	17.9	41.3	35.2
U.S.	50610	16.1	45.8	40.8
Switzerland	56240	19.8	41.3	33.7
Norway	66960	23.6	37.2	25.8

Source: For Per Capita Income, *World Development Report*, 2014 and for shares of Bottom 40% and Richest 20% and Gini ratio, *Human Development Report*, 2013. Note that while per capita income is of the year 2012, shares of bottom 40% and richest 20% and Gini ratios are of different years of the countries depending on the years when last income distribution surveys were conducted.

Thus, with the exception of few countries, *inequality in income distribution tends to be lower in high-income developed countries.* A World Bank study whose results are presented in **'World Development Indicators, 2013,** confirms the conclusion that in high-income developed countries, inequality in income distribution is lower as seen from Fig. 3.3. That is, ultimately with economic development as a country becomes richer inequality of income falls. Thus, in general with economic development beyond middle income status income inequality falls.

It may however be noted that from about $ 5000 till about $ 12000 (in 2005 $ PPP) per capita income World Bank study shows declining income inequality as measured by Gini coefficient but the points representing several countries in the scatter diagram underlying the income-inequality trend curve are quite far away below and above the trend curve implying that up till around $ 12000 per capita income trend curve does not truly represent the situation regarding income distribution. However, with high-income countries whose per capita income exceeds $ 12000 (in $ 2005 PPP), declining trend is quite visible.

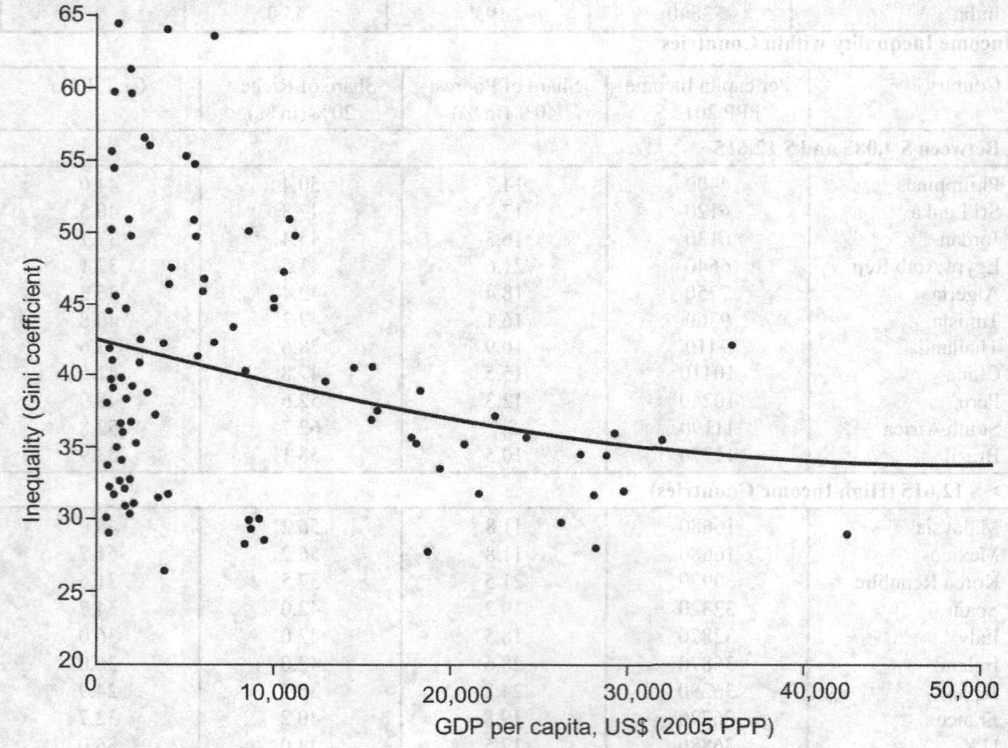

Fig. 3.3. *Inequality tends to be lower in high-income countries*

The goals of reducing income inequalities and eradicating poverty highlight the need for social, economic and institutional arrangements that foster welfare and income growth of less well-off. However, it needs to be emphasized that the *inclusive growth that helps to raise the incomes of the poor (i.e., bottom 40 per cent of population) and accelerates progress towards a just society does not come automatically* but requires mechanisms to ensure that the poor constituting bottom 40 per cent of the people not only enjoy the benefits of the growth process but are also integral to the process. Growth can be inclusive if it generates jobs and economic opportunities for the poor and unemployed. This requires adequate investment in physical and human capital accumulation and incentives for the adoption of labour-intensive technologies *Evidence also suggests that poverty reduction is higher when growth is biased towards labour-intensive sectors.*[10] The government has a key role in creating sustained growth with employment generation and accelerating investment in human capital–education and health of the people–so that the poor are integral part of the growth process.

10 See N. Loayza and C. Raddatz, *Journal of Development Studies*, 93(1), 2010.

Poverty. As explained above, low per capita income along with inequalities in income distribution has given rise to the problem of absolute poverty in low-income and middle-income developing countries. Although poverty has declined rapidly in developing countries since 1980, they still suffer from the large absolute poverty. More than 1 billion people worldwide still live in destitution, a state of affairs that is morally unacceptable, given the resources and technology available today. The World Bank has fixed $1.25 a day (2005 $ PPP) and one of its Millennium Development Goals is to reduce this poverty as measured by the people of a country having income or consumption below $1.25 a day to 16 % by the year 2015. Eradicating absolute poverty is one of the most compelling challenges facing the developing countries. Table 3.7 gives the extent of poverty prevailing in developing countries. Eradication of poverty requires not only sustained rate of economic growth but also to ensure there is adequate growth of employment opportunities in industry and services sectors. To ensure that the poor are productively absorbed, the investment by the government in human capital (*i.e.*, education and health) must be stepped up. Besides, poor must get subsidised food, cooking gas, electricity so that the poor can attain proper level of living and also preventing inequality from increasing. Further, it is imperative that inflation as measured by consumer price index (CPI) number should be checked as inflation makes even essential goods costlier and thereby makes them beyond the reach of the poor.

In Table 3.7 along with total population and GDP per capita we give the estimates of population living below the poverty line in India and some other selected developing countries both on the basis of *international poverty line of 1.25 $ PPP* and *national poverty line* (which varies between different countries depending on their own poverty-line norm). It will be noticed from Table 3.7 (column 5) that on the basis of international poverty line (*i.e.*, 1.25 $ PPP). Bangladesh has the largest ratio of 43.3% of population living below this poverty line. Next to it, India where 32.7 per cent of population live below this international poverty line. In respect of 'national poverty line also, Bangladesh tops the list with 31.5 per cent of its population living below the poverty line. Even with regard to national poverty line, India's place comes next to Bangladesh as in India 29.8 per cent of population lived below the poverty line. This about 30 per cent of India's population below the poverty line in 2009-10 was based on the poverty line fixed by the expert committee headed by Late Prof. Suresh Tendulkar.

Table 3.7. Population, per Capita Income Poverty in some Selected Developing Countries

Country	Population (Millions) 2012	Per Capita GDP in 2005 $ PPP 2012	Survey Year	Population below income Poverty line	
				1.25 $ PPP	Nation Poverty
India	1,237	3,840	2009	32.7	29.8
Bangladesh	155	2,070	2010	43.3	31.5
Nepal	27	1,500	2013	23.7	25.2 (2010)
Pakistan	170	3,030	2008	17.2	22.3
Sri Lanka	20	6,120	2007	7.0	8.9 (2010)
China	1,350	9,210	2010	9.2	12.7
Indonesia	247	4,810	2010	18.0	12.5
Thailand	67	9,430	2010	0.4	8.1
Columbia	48	10,410	2011	5.0	13.2
Peru	30	10,240	2011	3.0	25.8
Phillipines	97	4,400	2009	18.1	26.3
Brazil	199	11,728	2011	4.5	11.5
Mexico	121	16,680	2010	1.2	5.5

Source: For population and per capita GDP, World Development Report, 2014 and for poverty Estimates, World Development Indicators 2014.

Note: Data regarding population below National Poverty Line is based on the different countries own data based on their own norms of poverty line and their estimates based on the Surveys conducted between 2005-2011.

It will be further seen that as compared to India, China has succeeded in reducing its poverty problem as in around 2007-11, its only 13.1 per cent of Chinese population was living below the International Poverty Line of 1.25 $ PPP. Besides, on the basis of 'national poverty line' China's population living below the poverty line has fallen to a more 2.8 per cent. The dramatic fall in poverty in China has been attributed to labour intensive higher rate industrial growth.

Furthermore it will be observed in other developing countries such as Nepal, Pakistan, Sri Lanka, Indonesia, Thailand, percentage of population living below the International Poverty Line is very less as compared to that of India. In case of developing countries (Peru, Philippines, Brazil, Mexico) of Latin America, the incidence of poverty is also low. In Brazil, which is also one of BRICS country 6 per cent of population lived below the line on the basis of international poverty line of 1.25 $ PPP in the period 2007-11.

The issue of poverty estimates has been a subject of heated debate many people have questioned the '*low poverty line*' used by the Tendulkar Committee to find that in 2009-10 around 30 per cent of India's population lived below the poverty line (which is absolute number amounts to 350 million people). However, even these poverty numbers based on relatively low poverty line are of quite enormous size and indicate the appalling living conditions of the poor in India Jean Dreze and Amartya Sen slightly suggest that "It is all the more important to explore possible ways of *extending direct income support to the poor families* without waiting patiently for economic growth to raise their wages and incomes. There is, in fact, growing evidence that various forms of income support, economic redistribution and social security can make a substantial difference to people's living standards without delay."[11] In conformity with these views Jean Dreze and Amartya Sen have supported Mahatma Gandhi National Rural Employment Guarantee Scheme (MGNREGS) and *Food Security Bill* enacted in India to help the poor directly by offering them guaranteed employment and subsidised food.

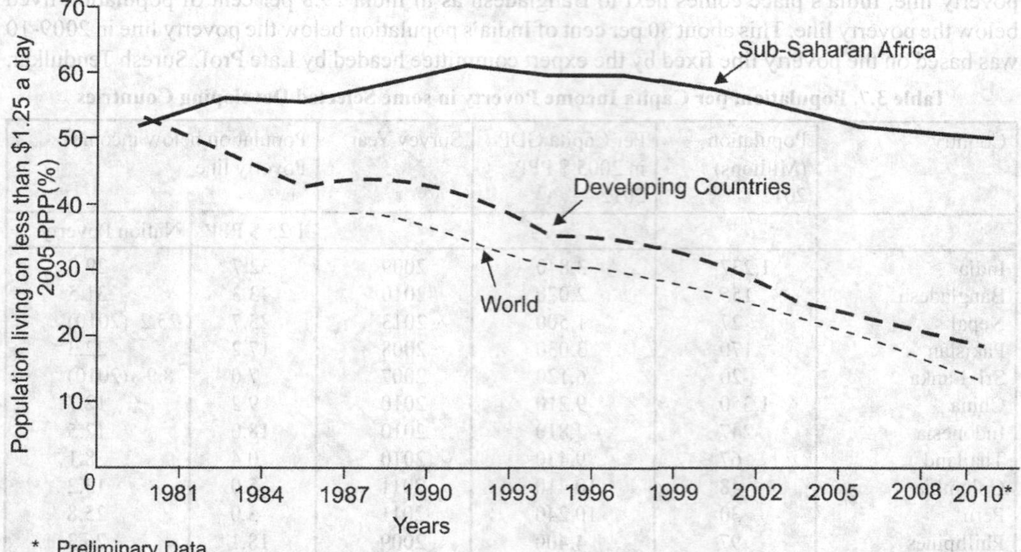

Fig. 3.4. *Poverty has fallen steadily since the 1980s except in Africa where the decline began later*

11 Jean Dreze and Amartya Sen, "*An Uncertain Glory: India and Its Contradictions*" Penguin Books, 2014, pp. 190-91.

As mentioned above, in the last three decades there has been substantial decline in poverty in the developing countries (including India). China alone accounted for more than half of the total reduction in global poverty between 1980 and 2000. Between 1981 and 2010 when the number of extreme poor in the world declined, the proportion of the poor in East Asia and Pacific (including China) fell from 57 per cent to 20 per cent.[12] However, in sub-Saharan Africa and South Asia reduction in poverty in two decades (1981-1999) has been quite disappointing. In sub Saharan Africa in the first decade of 21st century (2000-2010) reduction in poverty has been quite substantial (See Fig. 3.4). Thus extreme poverty in developing countries has declined steadily since 1980 except in Africa where the decline began after 2000. According to World Bank Report referred to above, "More than one-third of countries in sub-Sabaran Africa, many of them fragile and conflict-affected States had an extreme poverty rate of more than 50 per cent in 2010. In 12 countries in Sub-Saharan Africa, the extreme poverty rate is above 60 per cent; in four cases (Burundi, the Democratic Republic of Congo, Siberia and Madagascar) it is above 80 per cent.[13]

12 The World Bank, '*End Extreme Poverty and Promote Shared Prosperity*', Report by the World Bank Group on Shared Prosperity, 2014.

13 *Ibid,* p. 14.

Chapter 4

Common Characteristics of Developing Countries

COMMONALITY AMONG DIVERSITY

An idea of the characteristics of a developing economy must have been gathered from the above analysis of the definitions of an underdeveloped economy. Various developing countries differ a good deal from each other. Some countries such as countries of Africa do not face problem of rapid population growth, others have to cope with the consequences of rapid population growth. Some developing countries are *largely dependent on exports* of primary products, others do not show such dependence, others do not show such dependence. Some developing countries have weak institutional structure such as lack of property rights, absence of the rule of law and political instability which affect incentives to invest. Besides, there are lot of differences with regard to levels of education, health, food production and availability of natural resources. However, despite this great diversity there are many common features of the developing economies. It is because of common characteristics that their developmental problems are studied within a common analytical framework of development economics. We explain below some of the basic and important characteristics which are common to all developing economies.

Low Per Capita Income

The first important feature of the developing countries is their low per capita income. According to the World Bank estimates for the year 1995, average per capita income of the low income countries is $ 430 as compared to $ 24,930 of the high-income countries including U.S.A., U.K., France and Japan. According to these estimates for the year 1995, per capita income was $340 in India, $ 620 in China, $240 in Bangladesh, $ 700 in Sri Lanka. As against these, for the year 1995 per capita income was $ 26,980 in USA, $ 23,750 in Sweden, $ 39,640 in Japan and 40,630 in Switzerland.

It may however be noted that the extent of poverty prevailing in the developing countries is not fully reflected in the per capita income which is only an average income and also includes the incomes of the rich also. Large inequalities in income distribution prevailing in these economies have made the lives of the people more miserable. A large bulk of population of these countries live below the poverty line. For example, the recent estimates reveal that about 28 per cent of India's population (*i.e.* about 260 million people) live below the poverty line, that is, they are unable to get even sufficient calories of food needed for minimum subsistence, not to speak of minimum clothing and housing facilities. The situation in other developing countries is no better.

The low levels of per capita income and poverty in developing countries is due to low levels of productivity in various fields of production. The low levels of productivity in the developing economies has been caused by dominance of low-productivity agriculture and informal sectors in their economies, low levels of capital formation – both physical and human (education, health), lack of technological progress, rapid population growth which are in fact the very characteristics of the underdeveloped nature of the developing economies. By utilising their natural resources accelerating rate of capital formation and making progress in technology they can increase their levels of productivity and income and break the vicious circle of poverty operating in them.

It may however be noted that after the Second World War and with getting political freedom from colonial rule, in a good number of the underdeveloped countries the process of growth has been started and their gross domestic product (GDP) and per capita income are increasing.

Excessive Dependence on Agriculture

A developing country is generally predominantly agricultural. About 60 to 75 per cent of its population depends on agriculture and its allied activities for its livelihood. Further, about 30 to 50 per cent of national income of these countries is obtained from agriculture alone. This excessive dependence on agriculture is the result of low productivity and backwardness of their agriculture and lack of modern industrial growth. In the present-day developed countries, the modern industrial growth brought about structural transformation with the proportion of working population engaged in agriculture falling drastically and that employed in the modern industrial and services sectors rising enormously. This occurred due to the rapid growth of the modern sector on the one hand and tremendous rise in productivity in agriculture on the other.

The dominance of agriculture in developing countries can be known from the distribution of their workforce by sectors. According to estimates made by ILO given in Table 4.1 on an average 61 per cent of workforce of low-income developing countries was employed in agriculture whereas only 19 per cent in industry and 20 per cent in services. On the contrary, in high income, that is, developed countries only 4 per cent of their workforce is employed in agriculture, while 26 per cent of their workforce is employed in industry and 70 per cent in services.

Table 4.1. Distribution of Workforce by Sectors (percentage)

Countries	Agriculture	Industry	Services
Low-income countries	61	19	20
Middle-income countries	22	34	44
High-Income countries	4	26	70

Source: ILO 2010

In India at the time of independence about 60 per cent of population was employed in agriculture and with six decades of development the percentage of population engaged in agriculture has fallen to around 50 per cent in 2011-12. However, it is significance to note that the increase in population in non-agriculture sector has found employment not in organised industry and services sector but in *informal sector* where labour productivity is as low as in agriculture.

Besides, it is important to note though at present (20011-12) agriculture employes 50 per cent of workforce, it contributes only 13 per cent to its GDP. This shows labour productivity in agriculture and informal sector in the Indian economy, as in other developing economies, is due to the fact that the employment in organised industrial and services sector has not grown at a rate commensurate with the increase in population despite recording a higher growth rate in output. This is due to use of capital-intensive technologies in the organised industrial and services sectors. With the growth of population in the last few decades the demographic preserve on land has increased resulting in fall in land-labour ratio. With this agricultural holdings have become sub-divided into small plots which do not permit the use of efficient methods of cultivation.

In developing countries today, despite their modern industrial growth in the last four decades not much progress has been achieved towards structural transformation in the occupational structure of their economies. Due to the use of highly capital-intensive techniques very few employment opportunities have been created in their organised industrial and services sectors. When increasing population cannot obtain employment in the modern non-agricultural occupations, such as industry, transport and other services, then the people remain on land and agriculture and do some work which they are able to get. This has resulted in disguised unemployment in agriculture. During the last some decades because of population explosion the pressure of manpower on land in the developing countries has largely increased.

Low Level of Capital Formation

The insufficient amount of physical and human capital is so characteristic a feature in all undeveloped economies that they are often called simply `capital-poor' economies. One indication of the capital deficiency is the low amount of capital per head of population. Not only is the capital stock extremely small, but the current rate of capital formation is also very low. In the early 1950s in most of developing countries investment was only 5 per cent to 8 per cent of the national income, whereas in the United States, Canada, and Western Europe, it was generally from 15 per cent to 30 per cent. Since then there has been substantial increase in the rate of saving and investment in the developing countries. However, the quantity of capital per head is still very low in them and therefore productivity remains low. For example, in India rate of investment has now (2012-13) risen to about 35 per cent but it still remains a poor country with low level of productivity. This is because as a result of rapid population growth, capital per head is still very low.

The low level of capital formation in a developing country is due both to the weakness of the inducement to invest and to the low propensity and capacity to save. The rate of saving in developing countries is low primarily because of the low level of national income. In such an economy, the low level of per capita income limits the size of the market demand for manufacturing output which weakens the inducement to invest. The low level of investment also arises as a result of the lack of dynamic entrepreneurship which was regarded by Schumpeter as the focal point in the process of economic development.

At the root of capital deficiency is the shortage of savings. The level of per capita income being quite low, most of it is spent on satisfying the bare necessities of life, leaving a very little margin of income for capital accumulation. Even with an increase in the level of individual incomes in a developing economy, there does not usually follow a higher rate of accumulation because of the tendency to copy the higher levels of consumption prevailing in the advanced countries. Nurkse has called this as "*demonstration effect*". It is usually caused through media like films, television or through foreign visits.

Generally, there exist large inequalities in the distribution of incomes in developing countries. This should have resulted in a greater volume of savings available for capital formation. But most often the sector in which the greatest concentration of incomes lies is the one which derives its income primarily from non-entrepreneurial sources such as unearned incomes of rents, interests and monopoly profits. The attitudes and social values of this sector are often such that it is prone to use its income for `conspicuous consumption', investment in land and real estate, speculative transactions, inventory accumulation and hoarding of gold and jewellery. If these surpluses are channelled into productive investment, they would tend to increase substantially the level of capital formation.

Rapid Population Growth and Disguised Unemployment

The diversity among developing economies is perhaps nowhere to be seen so much in evidence as in respect of the facts of their population in respect of its size, density and growth. While we have examples of India, Pakistan and Bangladesh with their teeming millions and galloping rates of population growth, there are the Latin American countries which are very sparsely populated and whose total population in some cases numbers less than a single metropolitan city in India and China. In several newly emerging countries of Africa too and in some of the Middle Eastern countries the size of their population cannot be regarded as excessive, considering their large expanse. The South-East and Eastern Asia, on the other hand, have large populations.

However, there appears to be a common feature, namely, a rapid rate of population growth. This rate has been rising still more in recent years, thanks to the advances in medical sciences which have greatly reduced the death rate due to epidemics and diseases. While the death rate has fallen sharply, but there has been no commensurate decline in birth rate so that the natural survival rate has become much larger. The great threat of this rapid population growth rate is that it sets at nought all attempts at development in as much as much of the increased output is swallowed up by the increased population.

One important consequence of this rapid rate of population growth is that it throws more and more people on land and into informal sector to eke out their living from agriculture, since alternative occupations do not simultaneously develop and thus are not there to absorb the increasing numbers seeking gainful employment. The resultant pressure of population on land and in informal sector thus gives rise to what has been called "*disguised unemployment*". Disguised unemployment means that there are more persons engaged in agriculture than are actually needed so that the addition of such persons does not add to agricultural output, or putting it alternatively, given the technology and organisation even if some of the persons are withdrawn from land, no fall in production will follow from such withdrawal. As a result, marginal productivity of a wide range of labourers employed in agriculture is zero.

Table 4.2. Population Growth and other Features of Population

Countries	Population in 2009 Millions	Average annual population growth rate 1990-2009 (per cent)	Dependency ratio (% of working age population)		Crude death rate per 1,000 people (2009)	Crude birth rate per 1000 people (2009)
			Young 2009	Old 2009		
World	6,775	1.3	42	12	8	20
Low Income	4,846	2.3	69	6	11	34
Middle Income	4,813	1.3	41	10	8	19
Low & Middle Income	5,659	1.4	45	9	8	21
High Income	1,117	0.7	26	23	8	12

Source: *World Development Indicators*, 2011, p. 38

It will be seen from Table 4.2 that in 2009, population of the world was estimated at 6,775 million in 2009 and its annual population growth in 1990-2009 was 1.3 per cent. The population growths in *low-income developing countries* has been 2.3 per cent per annum during 1990-2009 and of *middle income developing countries* as a whole has been 1.3 per cent per annum. As against this, population growth rate in *high income countries* (*i.e.*, developed countries) was 0.7% per annum. That is, population in developing countries has been growing at a much faster rate as compared to the developed countries.

In Table 4.2, we have given the *dependency ratio* on the working population. Both children and boys below the age of 15 years (*i.e.*, young ones) and the old people above the age of 65 years and above represent *dependency burden* as they are unproductive members and are financially dependent on the working population. The bad effect of this dependency burden for developing countries is that it reduces saving rate of the community and therefore adversely affects economic growth.[1] It will be seen from Table 4.2 that the dependency burden of young persons (*i.e.*, below the age of 15 years) in case of low-income countries is very high at 69%, whereas the dependency burden of old people on the working population is much lower, only 6 per cent. As against this, for high income countries dependency burden of old persons is relatively very high being 23 per cent.

1 See A. Coale and E. Hoover, *Population Growth and Economic Development in Low Income Countries*, Princeton University Press, 1958.

Underutilisation of Natural Resources. The natural resources in an underdeveloped economy are either unutilised or underutilised. Generally speaking, under-developed countries are not deficient in land, water, mineral, forest or power resources, though they may be untapped. In other words, they constitute only potential resources. The main problem in their case is that such resources have not been fully and properly utilised due to various difficulties such as shortage of capital, primitive technology and the small size of the market.

Lower Levels of Human Capital

Human capital – education, health and skills – are of crucial importance for economic development. In our analysis of human development index (HDI) we noted that there is great disparity in human capital among the developing and developed countries. The developing countries lack in human capital that are responsible for low productivity of labour and capital in them. Lack of education manifests itself in lower enrolment rate in primary, secondary and tertiary educational institutions which impact knowledge and skills of the people. Lower levels of education and skills are not conducive for the development of new industries and for absorbing new technologies to achieve higher levels of production. Besides, lack of education and skills makes people less adaptable to change and lowers the ability to organise and manage industrial enterprises. Further, in countries like India, advantage of demographic dividend can be taken only if the younger persons can be educated, healthy and equipped with appropriate skills so that they can be employed in productive activities.

Table 4.3. Indicators Education Level

Country or Group	Gross Enrolment Rate % (relevant age group) 2005-09			Adult Literacy Rate % of age 15 years and older (2005-09)
	Primary	Secondary	Tertiary	
Low Income	104	38	6	62
Lower Middle	107	63	19	80
Upper Middle	111	88	42	92
High Income	101	100	67	98
Country				
Congo Dem. Rep.(LIC)	90	37	6	67
Egypt (LMC)	100	–	28	66
India (LMC)	117	60	13	63
China (UMC)	113	78	25	94
Brazil (LMC)	120	90	38	90
Malaysia (UMC)	95	69	36	92
United States (HI)	99	94	83	–
United Kingdom (HI)	106	99	57	–
Region				
East Asia & Pacific	111	74	–	94
Europe & Central Asia	99	89	55	98
Latin America & Caribbean	116	89	35	91
Middle East & N. Africa	105	73	27	74
South Asia	108	52	11	61
Sub-Saharan Africa	100	34	6	62

Source: World Bank, *World Development Indicators* 2011

LIC = Low Income Country, LMC = Lower Middle Income Country, UMC = Upper Middle Income Country

HI = High Income Country

The data of various education indicators is given in Table 4.3. It will be seen from this table that as compared to high income countries enrolment in secondary and tertiary educational institutions was 38% and 63% of person of relevant age group in 2009 as compared to 100 per cent in high-income developed countries. Similarly, enrolment rate in tertiary educational institutions which impart higher liberal, managerial and technical education in developing countries of low income and lower middle income is 6 per cent and 19 per cent respectively of the relevant age group as compared to 67 per cent in high-income developed countries. It will be seen from Table 4.3 that in India enrolment for secondary education is 60 per cent and in China 78 per cent of relevant age group.

Similarly, Table 4.3 reveals that adult literacy rate (percentage of population of ages 15 and older that can read and write a short simple statement in their everyday life) is much lower (62% in low income and 80% in lower middle income developing countries) in 2009 as compared to 98% in high income developed countries. In India adult literacy rate is only 63 per cent in 2009 whereas it is much higher in China (94 %) and Brazil (90 %) as compared to 98% in high-income developed countries.

It is evident from above that educational and skill levels in developing countries are much lower as compared to developed countries. This lowers the quality of the people of developing countries as productive agents and wealth creators.

Health. Likewise, health, the other important human resource, is a key factor that determines efficiency or productivity of the people. The people who are undernourished and malnourished often suffer from sickness cannot be efficient and therefore cannot contribute much to the increase in productivity. Besides, health enjoyed by the people is good in itself as it directly increases the happiness and welfare of the people, Lower health of the people of developing countries is manifested lower

Table 4.4. Health Indicators

Country or Group	Life Expectancy at birth (years)		Under 5 years Mortality rate per 1000 live births		Undernourished persons (% of population)		Children under 5 Malnourished (under-weight)	Access to Improved Sanitation Facilities (% of population)	
	1990	2009	1990	2009	1990-92	2005-09	2004-09	1990	2008
Lower Income	52	57	171	118	38	31	27.7	23	35
Lower Middle	63	68	93	57	19	15	24.0	37	50
Upper Middle	68	72	51	22	8	6	–	78	84
High Income	75	80	12	7	5	5	–	100	99
Country									
Congo Dep. Rep.(LIC)	48	48	199	199	26	69	28.2	9	23
Egypt (LMC)	63	60	90	21	<5	<5	6.8	72	94
India (LMC)	58	64	118	66	20	21	43.5	18	31
Brazil (LMC)	66	73	56	21	11	6	2.2	69	80
Malaysia (UMC)	70	75	18	6	<5	<5	–	84	96
United States (HI)	75	79	11	8	<5	<5	1.3	100	100
United Kingdom (HI)	76	80	10	8	<5	<5	–	100	100
Region									
EAst Africa & Pacific	67	72	55	26	20	11	8.8	42	59
Europe & Central Asia	68	70	52	21	7	6	–	87	89
Latin America & Caribbean	68	74	52	23	13	9	3.8	69	79
Middle E. & N. Africa	64	71	76	33	7	7	6.8	73	84
South Asia	58	64	125	71	22	22	42.5	22	36
Sub-Saharan Africa	50	53	181	130	31	26	24.7	27	31

LIC = Lower Income country; LMC = Lower Middle Income Country; UMC = Upper Middle Income Country and HI = High Income Country

Source: World Bank, *World Development Indicators*, 2011

life expectancy at birth, higher mortality rate of children under 5 years age, undernourishment and malnourishment (*i.e.*, underweight children) of the people and access to improved sanitation facilities. Though health conditions in developing countries have greatly improved in the last some decades of development, there are still important differences between them and developed countries. The data of various health indicators is given in Table 4.4.

It will be seen from Table 4.4 that life expectancy at birth in low income (LIC) and lower middle income countries (LMC) is 57% and 68% respectively in 2009 as against 80% in high income developed countries. Health conditions in South Asia and Sub-Saharan Africa are highly deplorable and they continue to suffer from problems of acute undernourishment, malnourishment and children's mortality rate. Mortality rate of under 5 years age children per 1000 live births in 2009 was 118 in low income countries (LIC) and 57 in lower middle income countries (LMC). In India which is a lower middle income country, under 5-years mortality rate in 2009 was relatively high at 66 as against only 8 per 1000 live births in the United States and United Kingdom.

Two types of statistical data regarding ***nutrition*** is given in Table 4.4. First, undernourished persons in a country as per cent of population. Undernourishment refers to dietary energy consumption that is continuously below minimum requirement for maintaining healthy life so as to carry out light physical activity with an acceptable minimum weight. Second, Child nutrition which is here measured by malnourishment of children under 5 years age who are underweight. This unnourishment impairs the working capacity of the individuals and also makes them unable to acquire education and skills needed for high productivity job. It will be seen from Table 4.4 that percentage of under weight persons to total population is very high in developing countries: 31 per cent in low income countries (LIC) and 15 per cent in lower middle income countries whereas it is very low at 5% in high income developed countries in the year 2009. In India the percentage of undernorished persons to total population was high at 21 per cent but Brazil has succeeded in lowering it to 6 per cent of the population.

As regards the prevalence of malnourishment, the condition in India is shocking as it has the highest, 43.5%, of children under 5 years age whereas it is only 1.3% in 2009. The same is the case with regard to access to improved sanitation facilities. It will be seen from Table 4.4 that in India 31 per cent of population has access to improved sanitation facilities as against 100 per cent in the United States and United Kingdom.

Dualistic Structure of the Underdeveloped Economies

An important feature of developing economies, especially those which are marked by surplus labour is that they have a dualistic structure. This dualistic character of these economies has been held to be the cause of unemployment and underemployment existing in them. Keeping in view this dualistic structure of less developed economies, important models of income and employment have been propounded. Famous Lewis model of economic development with unlimited supplies of labour and Fei-Ranis model of "*Development in a Labour Surplus Economy*" explain how in dualistic economies, the unemployed and underemployed labour in the traditional sector is drawn into a modern high productivity sector. The concept of dualism was first of all introduced into the development analysis by Dr. J.H. Boeke[2] but he emphasised the social dualism, according to which there is sharp contrast between the social systems characterising the two broad sectors of the economy, one in which the original social system with its subsistence or pre-capitalist nature, limited wants, non-economic behaviour and low level of economic and social welfare prevails, and the other where imported capitalist system with its modern system of industrial organisation, wage employment, unlimited wants and positive behaviour to economic incentives exists.

2 J.H. Boeke, *Economies and Economic Policy of Dual Societies*, New York, 1953.

However, it is technological dualism rather than Boeke's social dualism which has an important bearing on the problem of economic growth and surplus labour in the developing countries. According to the concept of technological dualism, the important difference between the traditional and the modern sectors lies in the difference between the production techniques or technologies used. In the small modern sector consisting of large-scale manufacturing and mining which provides wage employment, highly capital-intensive techniques imported from the developed countries are used. On the other hand, in the large traditional sector covering agriculture, handicrafts and allied activities, in which there exist extended family system and self-employment, labour-intensive technology is generally used. As a result of the difference in technologies used, the labour productivity and levels of earnings in the modern sector are much higher than those in the traditional sector. Moreover, since the technology used in the modern sector is highly capital-intensive, the growth of this sector has not absorbed adequate amount of labour in high productivity and high wage employment. With the explosive rate of growth of population and labour force and the limited creation of employment opportunities in the modern sectors because of the highly capital-intensive technology, surplus labour has emerged in the agriculture and services. It has been possible for agriculture to contain the surplus labour because of the prevalence of extended family system in which both work and income are shared by the family members.

We thus see that the problem of unemployment and underemployment in less developed economies has been intensified by the technological dualism caused by the use, in the modern manufacturing and mining, of capital-intensive technology imported from abroad which is wholly unsuitable to the factor endowments of these less developed economies with abundant labour and small capital. The unemployment and underemployment in these less developed economies are not only due to the slow growth of capital or low rate of investment, it is also due to the highly capital-intensive techniques used in the modern sector. This technological dualism with the fact that modern sector has limited labour-absorptive capacity contains important implications for development strategy to be framed for less developed countries like India with surplus labour.

Need for Development

There is a very urgent need for economic development in the underdeveloped or poor countries. Economic development is needed so that living standards of their people may be raised. What is more important is that economic development of the poor countries is necessary from the point of view of the richer countries. What do we find today? The world is divided into two parts: one of the poor and the other of the rich which is continuously becoming richer. Such a situation threatens the economic and political stability of the world. Unless the poor countries are enabled to share the general prosperity, their condition will become more and more difficult. It is the relative difference between the rich and poor countries which will make the poor countries discontented. Ever-increasing discontent in the poor countries is bound, sooner or later, to aggravate the already explosive situation in the world.

As the gulf between the rich and poor countries widens, the tension in the world will grow. The poor countries will agitate more and more for a share in prosperity and, consequently, their demand on the richer countries will grow louder and louder in volume and intensity. There is ample evidence in the world of the fact that when nations cannot solve their domestic problems, their governments plunge them into war with their neighbours who may be prosperous. It is thus in the interest of world peace and harmony that the poor countries are enabled to remove or reduce their poverty. There is a growing and legitimate desire of the poor nations to eradicate poverty. The desire to develop is keenly felt by different sections of their population. Their desire to develop is natural and understandable because they experience acute physical sufferings as a result of appallingly miserable economic conditions in which they live. The masses in the poor countries constantly face hunger, illiteracy, sickness and are forced to eke out a life of extreme poverty.

Note, that, according to the new view as made popular by Amartya Sen economic development is needed mainly for two reasons: (1) the removal of poverty, (2) enlargement of human capabilities and freedoms. For the removal of poverty capabilities of the poor should be enhanced so that they should be able to meet their minimum basic needs which include getting adequate food, health, clothing and shelter. To achieve these economic growth is necessary but not sufficient. Therefore, for removal of poverty, direct anti-poverty measures such as generation of enough employment opportunities be taken. Secondly, as emphasized by Amartya Sen, development is needed so that people should enjoy freedom and life of valued functioning. To quote Amartya Sen, "*The valued functioning may vary from elementary ones, such as being adequately nourished and being free from avoidable diseases to very complex activities or personal states such as being able to take part in the life of community and having self-respect*".[3] Thus, according to Amartya Sen, freedom of choice, and control of one's own life are central aspects of well-being for which true development is needed.

Times are gone when people believed in their destiny or *kismet*. They are no longer prepared to reconcile to their poverty as resulting from fate. They have now realised that the solution of the problem of poverty lies in economic development. This realisation has been further strengthened by the ever-increasing contacts and communications between such countries and the developed countries. The awareness of the possibilities of development is growing every day. Already, the upper sections of society in developing countries are imitating the living standards prevalent in the rich countries.

The desire for development has followed the political freedom of the many poor countries from foreign rule. It has now been realised that political freedom without economic freedom and prosperity has no meaning. Political independence has naturally raised expectations of the people in the economic sphere. No wonder that people of these countries which have won freedom from the colonial rule aspire to develop economically and that in the shortest possible time.

FROM UNDERDEVELOPMENT TO DEVELOPMENT: ROSTOW'S STAGES OF GROWTH

Prof. W.W. Rostow[4], an eminent economic historian, has described the historical process of transition from underdevelopment to development in terms of a series of five stages of growth through which all countries must pass to reach the ultimate destination of a developed country'. These five stages of growth are : (1) the traditional society, (2) preconditions for take-off, (3) the take-off period, (4) the drive to maturity, and (5) stage of mass consumption.

It is important to note that these stages are not merely a way of generalising certain actual historical experiences about the sequence of development of today's developed countries but they have an inner logic and continuity. In fact, they constitute both a general theory of economic development and of social modern history as a whole. Rostow emphasises that gradual economic changes result in drastic changes in economic, social and political structure and institutions. Rostow argued that today's developed nations had all passed the stage of take-off into self-sustaining growth, while the underdeveloped countries were still in either the traditional society or the "preconditions for take-off stage" and they had to follow the path defined by the next stages of growth to reach the destination of a developed nation.

We explain below briefly Rostow's five stages of growth.

1. Traditional Society. This initial stage of traditional society signifies a primitive society having no access to modern science and technology. In other words, it is a society based on primitive technology and primitive attitude towards the physical world. Thus, Rostow defines a traditional

3 Amartya Sen, *Development as Freedom*, Oxford University Press, 2001, p. 75.

4 W.W. Rostow, *The Stages of Economic Growth* : A *Non-Communist Manifesto;* Cambridge University Press, 1960.

society "as one whose structure is developed within the limited production function based on pre-Newtonian science and technology and as pre-Newtonian attitudes towards the physical world"[5]

However, Rostow does not view this traditional society as being completely static. In this stage of a society output could be increasing through the expansion of land area under cultivation or through the discovery and spread of a new crop. But the critical fact about this type of society is that there is limit to attainable output per head. This limit arises due to the absence of access to modern science and technology. This type of a society allocates a large proportion of its resources to agriculture and is characterised by a hierarchical social structure in which there is little possibility for vertical mobility. The value system that prevails in such a society is what Rostow calls a long-run fatalism. People of these societies think that not much economic progress is possible for them and for their future generations.

2. Preconditions or The Preparatory Stage. This covers a long period of a century or more during which the preconditions for take-off are established. These conditions mainly comprise fundamental changes in the social, political and economic fields; for example (a) a change in society's attitudes towards science, risk-taking and profit-earning; (b) the adaptability of the labour force; (c) political sovereignty ; (d) development of a centralised tax system and financial institutions; and (e) the construction of certain economic and social infrastructure like railways, ports, power generation and educational institutions. India did some of these things in the First Five Year plan Period (1951-56).

It is evident from above that in this second stage of growth foundations for economic transformation are laid. The people start using modern science and technology for increasing productivity in both agriculture and industry. Further, there is a change in the attitude of the people who start viewing the world where there are possibilities of future growth. A new class of entrepreneurs emerges in the society who mobilise savings and undertake investment in new enterprises and bear risks and uncertainty. In the sphere of political organisation, it is during this stage that an effective centralised nation state starts emerging.

Thus in the stage of precondition for take-off Rostow views agriculture as performing three roles; first, agriculture must produce sufficient foodgrains to meet the demand of growing population and of the workers who get employment in agriculture. Secondly, increase in agricultural incomes would lead to the demand for industrial products and stimulate industrial investment. Thirdly, expanding agriculture must provide much of the savings needed for the expansion of the industrial sector.

3. The "Take-off" Stage. This is the crucial stage which covers a relatively brief period of two to three decades in which the economy transforms itself in such a way that economic growth subsequently takes place more or less automatically. "The take-off stage" is defined as "*the interval during which the rate of investment increases in such a way that real output per capita rises and this initial increase carries with it radical changes in the techniques of production and the disposition of income flows which perpetuate the new scale of investment and prepetuate thereby the rising trend in per capita output.*"

Thus, the term "take-off " implies three things : first, the proportion of investment to national income must rise from 5% to 12% and more so as to outstrip the likely population growth; secondly, the period must be relatively short so that it should show the characteristics of an economic revolution; and thirdly, it must culminate in self-sustaining and self-generating economic growth. Thus, during the take-off stage, the desire to achieve economic growth to raise the living standards dominates the society. Revolutionary changes occur in both agriculture and industry and productivity levels sharply increase. There is greater urbanisation and urban labour force increases. In a relatively short period of a decade or two, both the basic structure of the economy and social and political structure is changed so that a self-sustaining growth rate can be maintained.

5 Rostow, *op.cit.*

It is worth noting that, in the opinion of Rostow, the rise of a new elite (*i.e.*, new entrepreneurial class) and establishment of a nation state are crucial for economic development.

4. Drive to Maturity: Period of Self-Sustained Growth. This stage of economic growth occurs when the economy becomes mature and is capable of generating self-sustained growth. The rates of saving and investment are of such a magnitude that economic development becomes automatic. Overall capital per head increases as the economy matures. The structure of the economy changes increasingly. The initial key industries which sparked the take-off decelerate as diminishing returns set in. But the average rate of growth is maintained by a succession of new rapidly-growing sectors with a new set of leading sectors. The proportion of the population engaged in agriculture and other rural pursuits declines, and the structure of the country's foreign trade undergoes a radical change.

It is with both the problems and the cyclical movements of national income in such mature growing economies in this fourth stage that the bulk of modern theoretical economics is concerned. The students of contemporary developing countries and also of economic history are more likely to be concerned with the economics of the previous two stages, that is, the economics of the preparatory and the `take-off' stages. If we are to have a useful and adequate theory of economic growth, it must obviously be comprehensive enough to embrace these two stages as well, especially the economics of the "take-off into self-sustaining growth".

5. Stage of Mass Consumption. In this stage of development per capita income of a country rises to such a high level that consumption basket of the people increases beyond food, clothing and shelters to articles of comforts and luxuries on a mass scale. Further, with progressive industrialisation and urbanization of the economy values of people change in favour of more consumption of luxuries and high styles of living. New types of industries producing durable consumer goods come into existence which satisfy the wants for more consumption. These new industries producing durable consumer goods become the new leading sectors of economic growth.

A Critique of Rostow's Stages of Growth

Rostow's stages of growth theory has come in for severe criticism. Gunar Mydral has argued that there cannot be an inevitable sequence of events described as successive stages of growth. According to him, economic growth is the result of certain economic policies adopted and not the other way round. Likewise, Meier argues that stages in the history of economic growth cannot be generalised from the development experience of some European countries as Rostow has done. To quote Meier, "Stage-making approaches are misleading when they consider a linear conception of history and imply that all economies tend to pass through the same series of stages. Although a particular sequence may correspond broadly to the historical experience of some economies, no single sequence fits the history of all countries. To maintain that every economy always follows the same course of development with a common past and the same future is to overschematize the complex forces of development, and to give the sequence of stages a generality that is unwarranted".[6]

6 G.M. Meier, *Leading Issues in Economic Development*, Oxford University Press, Sixth Edition.

Perpetuation of Underdevelopment and Obstacles to Economic Development

In the previous chapters we have explained the main common characteristics of developing countries and determinants of economic growth. Now the important question is why these countries have remained underdeveloped or, in other words, what are the causes of the perpetuation of underdevelopment and backwardness in these poor countries. Besides, the important issue is what have been the obstacles to their development and *constraints on their economic growth.* There is not one but several explanations, both economic and non-economic, for their underdevelopment. In the present chapter we are concerned with the study of some important explanations of perpetuation of their underdevelopment. A suitable strategy of development to accelerate the rate of economic growth can be framed if the correct explanation of their underdevelopment and what are the factors that hinder their development can be known. Backwardness and underdevelopment are said to be due to general shortage of some crucial factors that determine economic growth and their inefficient use. It is lack of capital accumulation or industrialisation and the use of inefficient technology that are said to be responsible for poverty and backwardness of the presently developing countries. The current development gap between the rich and poor countries has arisen mainly because in countries of Western Europe and North America rapid industrial growth and capital accumulation took place while the presently poor developing countries did not register such rapid industrial growth. Why rapid industrial development occurred in some countries and not in others or, in other words, *why poverty and underdevelopment has perpetuated* in the current poor and developing countries while some countries through rapid industrial growth became rich and affluent.

In what follows we first explain some important explanations of perpetuation of underdevelopment and backwardness in the present-day poor and underdeveloped countries. After this we will explain some additional factors which obstruct their growth and development.

IMBALANCE BETWEEN RESOURCES (CAPITAL) AND POPULATION

The first and foremost economic explanation of underdevelopment or the existence of mass unemployment and poverty of today's developing countries is that in them there has come about a serious imbalance between population and productive resources, especially the stock of capital. This imbalance between resources and population has manifested itself not only in low per capita income and poverty but also in the existence of huge open unemployment, disguised unemployment in the developing countries, especially those which have labour abundance. The present stock of capital (including land) is quite insufficient to employ all at a reasonable level of real per capita income.

In the present-day world man by himself can hardly produce anything. Even the primitive man needed some elementary tools like bow and arrow to engage in hunting for the earning of his livelihood. With the growth of technology and specialisation, he needs much more capital with which to be engaged in productive activity. If he is an agriculturist, he needs a piece of land and also a plough, a pair of oxen, seeds and some foodgrains and other necessities of life to sustain himself during the period of the sowing to the reaping of the harvest. In the industrial sector, he needs factories to work in and machines to work with. All these instruments of production belong to the nation's stock of capital. A nation's stock of capital can be enlarged by increased investment which in the absence of any unutilised resources requires additional savings on the part of the community. The rate of capital formation should be kept sufficiently high so that employment opportunities are successively enlarged to absorb the increase in the labour force. Now, if the population grows faster than the stock of capital of a country, the entire addition to labour force cannot be absorbed in productive employment because not enough instruments of production will be there to employ them.

It is important to note that the existing imbalance between capital and land resources on the one hand and population on the other is a legacy of the past. Thus, the present state of underdevelopment must be viewed in the long-run setting of these countries. For several decades in the past, especially prior to gaining political independence, the rate of investment and therefore the growth of the capital stock has not been keeping pace with the growth of population in the underdeveloped countries. This implies that opportunities for productive employment have not been increasing commensurate with the growth of population and labour force. This has resulted in mass poverty and unemployment.

It may be noted that population growth is an exogenous factor. There is nothing in the system that should keep the rate of population growth equal to the rate of investment. Nor is there any mechanism that should automatically raise the rate of investment commensurate with any given rate of population growth. Thus imbalance between resources, especially capital stock and population, emerges when population grows faster than investment.

Now, the question is when addition to labour force is unable to get employment in productive activities due to lack of capital, how is it absorbed in the economy? Unable to get employment in the organised sector on a wage basis additional workers remain in their families and share work with other members of the family on the farm and other traditional occupations *i.e.*, whatever work their families do. Since the same amount of work is done by more workers, the additional workers only share the given amount of work with the members of their families, they do not add to total output. Land, technology and capital resources remaining the same, sharing of work by more workers lowers the hours and intensity of work put in by each worker engaged in agriculture and traditional occupations, resulting in mass disguised unemployment and lowering the standards of living of the people. Agricultural family farms and traditional occupations such as cottage industries, where disguised unemployment emerges, are run on family basis, do not represent modern form of economic organisation; they do not follow the principle of employing labour productively by equating marginal product of labour with wage rate. They are, in fact, traditional forms of economic organisation. It follows therefore that "*it is through inferior forms of organisation and a reduction in the ratio of surplus to employed worker and/or through a general reduction in the levels of standards of living that the surplus population is absorbed.*"[1]

The lack of real capital per head of population is so characteristic a feature of the developing economies that they are often called "*capital-poor economies*". Low productivity of population and therefore their low income in the developing countries is mainly due to the small amount of capital per head of population. Thus an *important economic explanation for underdevelopment and poverty is the imbalance between resources (e.g. capital) and population; capital is too small in relation to the huge amount of population.*

Not only was the existing stock of capital very small, but the rate of capital formation in the 1950s when most of the developing countries started the process of development was also very low. In most underdeveloped countries rate of investment at that time was only 5% to 8% of the national income, whereas in the United States, Canada and Western European countries, it generally varied

1 Vakil and Brahmananda, *Planning for an Expanding Economy*, Vora & Co., Bombay, 1965.

from 15% to 30% of the national income. The low rate of capital formation in underdeveloped countries has been due to the following reasons: (1) The supply of domestic savings has been very small. (2) There has been a lack of daring, honest and dynamic enterpreneurs who should perform the task of making investments and bearing risks. (3) Inducement to invest for various reasons has been very weak, that is, demand for making investment has been very small.

The basic solution to the problem of the above sort is the faster rate of capital formation so as to increase employment opportunities. For this purpose, every possible encouragement should be given to the increase in savings and their productive utilisation for increasing the rate of investment. In the developing countries investment incentives are generally very low and the State can assist in the process of capital formation directly as well as indirectly. Through a fiscal policy which encourages saving and investment and a sound monetary policy it can do much to encourage investors. The State itself can participate in the process of capital formation by investing in infrastructure and basic heavy industries in which the private entrepreneurs do not find it profitable to undertake investment. Therefore, in the developing countries the State has got to assume a special role in speeding up the rate of investment. The other line of attack has got to be on the rate of population growth. If population grows at a rapid rate, then to maintain the people even at their existing per capita income (*i.e.*, levels of living) large amounts of capital are needed. Besides, more capital is required to raise the amount of capital available per man and hence raise the living standards at a faster rate.

The important point to be borne in mind is that even if at present the rate of investment is raised to keep pace with the rate of population growth, the already existing huge disguised unemployment and mass poverty which came to exist as a result of the disproportion between investment and population will remain untouched. It follows, therefore, that for the solution of existing disguised unemployment and poverty, mere raising the rate of investment equal to the current rate of population growth is not enough. "*The central problem of economic growth in the context of India and other underdveloped countries is that of the creation of those conditions under which the rate of investment can be stepped up above that of population growth.*"[2] It is heartening to note that as under the development policies pursued in the Five Year Plans in India, rate of domestic saving rose to 25.1 per cent in 1995-96 and further to 36 per cent in 2007-08. Apparently this seems to be high rate of saving for a developing country like India with a very low per capita income. Remember also that during the last 60 years of planned development, our population increased from 36 crore in 1951 to about 101 crore in 2001 and further to 121 crore in 2011. Our population is currently increasing at the rate of around 1.6 per cent per annum. For achieving adequate growth rate in per capita income, in the Twelfth Five Year Plan (2012-17), target of GDP growth rate of 8% per annum has to be achieved, for which it has been estimated that rate of saving has to be increased to 38% of GDP and rate of investment to 40% of GDP by 2016-17.

VICIOUS CIRCLE OF POVERTY

Most widely propagated explanation why poor underdeveloped countnes have failed to grow economically is that they are trapped in vicious circles of poverty. These vicious circles of poverty operate both on the supply and demand sides of capital formation. Supply side of capital formation refers to saving required to accelerate capital formation in order to raise productivity and per capita income. On the other hand, demand side of capital formation refers to inducement to invest (that is, investment demand) which depends on the size of market (*i.e.*; level of demand) which is small in the underdeveloped countries. Ragnar Nurkse in his now well known work[3] on underdeveloped countries attributed the persistence of poverty in them to these vicious circles of poverty and suggested policies to break these vicious circles. Both these vicious circles take poverty as their starting point.

2 Vakil and Brahmananda, *op. cit.*, p. 240.

3 Ragnar Nurkse, *Problems of Capital Formation in Underdeveloped Countries.*

We explain below both these types of vicious circles of poverty.

Vicious Circle of Poverty (Supply-side)

In the underdeveloped countries the rate of savings has been very low. In other words, these countries save a very small proportion of their current national income. In India the level of gross domestic savings has increased to about 30% of the national income in recent years only because of the stimulus provided by the planned development under the Five Year Plans. The level of savings in underdeveloped countries is very small mainly because their level of national income and per capita income is very low. As a result, much of the income is consumed and little is left for investment purposes. Thus underdeveloped countries are caught in the vicious circle of poverty. Because of the low level of income the capacity to save is very small. Since the capacity to save is small, rate of saving and investment must be low. Investment being low leads to a lack of capital per head. Because there is small amount of capital per head, the productivity of the people or real income per head will be low. Thus, the vicious circle is complete. Vicious circle of poverty on the supply-side of capital formation is illustrated in Fig. 5.1.

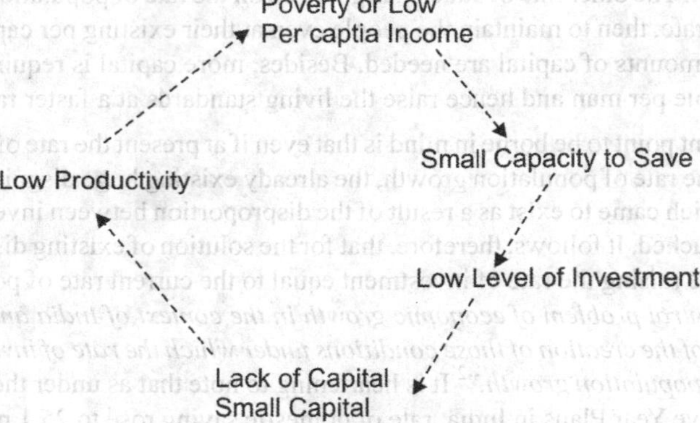

Fig. 5.1. *Vicious crcle of poverty on the supply-sde of capital formation*

In a slightly different way Professor Hicks describes the working of vicious circle in an under developed country as thus, "Productive power can be used either for the production of consumption goods or of investment goods. Now when the average productivity of a community is low, it will have the greatest difficulty in producing enough consumption goods to satisfy the basic necessities of life; so it will have little productive power to spare for the production of investment goods. Countries which are in this position are involved in a vicious circle. A large supply of capital equipment would enable them to escape from the toils of overpopulation but they are too deeply caught in those toils to be able to produce that equipment for themselves. Thus, they cannot escape without assistance from outside."[4]

Apart from the low level of per capita income, the low *relative* level of real income in underdeveloped countries as compared with the advanced and rich countries also makes their capacity to save very small. The great and growing inequalities between the income levels and, therefore, living standards of different countries, combined with increasing awareness of these inequalities have pushed up the general propensity to consume of people in the underdeveloped countries and, have, therefore, reduced their capacity to save. The tendency of the people of underdeveloped countries to copy the higher levels of consumption standards prevailing in the advanced countries has been called "***International demonstration effect***" by Nurkse.[5] This also explains why the rate of saving and capital formation in developing countries has been low which is the main cause of their underdevelopment.

4 J.R. Hicks, *Social Framework*, p. 35.
5 Ragnar Nurkse, *op. cit.*

It may be noted that Nurkse used the idea of vicious circle of poverty to advocate that *with adequate foreign aid or foreign direct investment the underdeveloped countries could succeed in breaking the vicious circle of poverty*. He argued that with injection of foreign capital, productivity of labour would rise which would lead to higher incomes and eventually will generate higher savings. With higher savings made possible by injection of foreign capital, rate of capital formation will be raised which will help to break the vicious circle of poverty. Furthermore, higher incomes generated by greater investment with foreign capital would also increase aggregate demand in the economy which will stimulate capital formation by creating profitable investment opportunities.

A Critique

However, the above thesis of Nurkse is questionable. If this thesis were valid, then it would be difficult to explain the development and capital formation in the present-day developing countries like China (until 1980s) and India which also started with low per capita income and many of them grew economically without much foreign aid. Of course, foreign aid and foreign investment can make an important contribution to economic development of the underdeveloped countries. What is being stressed here is that higher rate of capital formation and economic growth can be achieved without much inflow of foreign capital.

Though the majority of the people in poor developing countries are poor and are not in a position to save much but due to glaring inequalities in the distribution of income, there is minority of the people which is quite rich and wealthy and are in a position to save. *Savings, it is said, do not depend on per capita income but how income and wealth are distributed in a society*. For example, a poor Indian peasant may be unable to save because he has to spend all of whatever small income he earns to survive but there are many rich people in India who can save a lot. It is worth mentioning that some poor countries have managed to achieve a high rate of saving and investment. Even Japan when it began developing at the end of 19th century had an average per capita income only slightly more than India in the 1950s and still it was able raise its rate of saving and investment. Despite its poverty and low rate of economic growth (on average 3.5% per annum till the end of 1970s), even India was able to raise its rate of saving to 17 per cent in 1978-79 which far exceeded Arthur Lewis prescription of raising rate of saving to 12 to 15% of national income to achieve self-sustained high growth rate.

But it is worth mentioning that in a country like India the people who get large incomes generally use much of their incomes for conspicuous consumption, investment in land and real estate, speculative transactions, inventory accumulation and hoarding of gold and jewellery rather than using them for productive investment. Low use of savings for productive investment is one of the important factors responsible for low rate of economic growth in the developing countries. For raising the of productive investment, tendency for spending a good part of their income on conspicuous consumption and making unproductive investment be discouraged.

Vicious Circle of Poverty (Demand Side)

An important reason why investment or capital formation is low has been advanced by Nurkse. He argues that just as division of labour is limited by the size of the market, inducement to invest is also limited by the size of the market. The size of the market in underdeveloped countries is very small due to the low per capita income of the people, and the income per capita is low because there is a use of meagre amount of capital in the production processes in underdeveloped countries. The use of capital equipment in the production of goods and services for the domestic market is discouraged by the small size of the market. Thus, a vicious circle operates on the demand-side of capital formation. To quote Nurkse, "*The inducement to invest may be low because of the small buying power of the people, which is due to their small real income, which again is due to low productivity. The low level of productivity, however, is a result of the small amount of capital used in production, which its turn may be caused at least partly by the small inducement to invest.*"[6] The vicious circle of poverty operating on the demand side is illustrated in Fig. 5.2.

6 Ragnar Nurkse, *Problems of Capital Formation in Underdeveloped Countries*, p. 5.

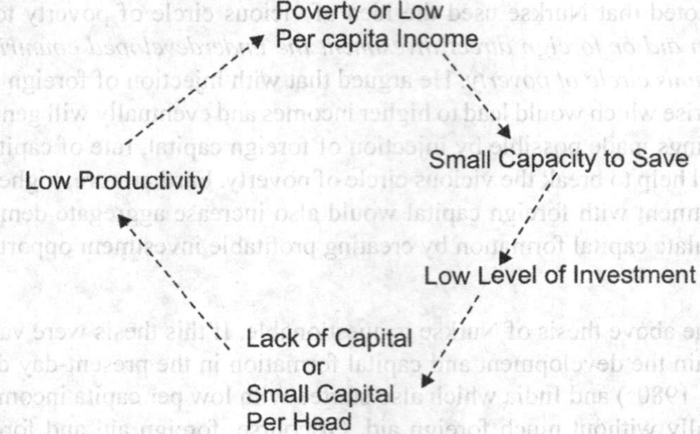

Fig. 5.2. *Vicious circle of poverty on the demand-side of capital formation*

From above it is concluded that underdeveloped countries have remained poor and economically backward because of low rate of capital accumulation as compared with the growth of population. As a result, capital per worker is very small and therefore his productivity is low. This, as seen above, gives rise to the vicious circle of poverty which is an important cause of persistent underdevelopment. If the underdeveloped countries want to accelerate the rate of capital accumulation so as to achieve rapid economic growth, then the vicious circles of poverty operating on the supply and demand sides of capital formation have to be broken. Once the vicious circles are broken and a country starts developing, economic growth becomes cumulative and these circles become beneficient.

A Critique

However, there are also flaws in the argument for the operation of vicious circle of poverty on the demand-side of capital formation. In this regard, the argument of Nurkse that limited size of the market is responsible for low rate of investment in poor underdeveloped countries is not entirely correct. The relationship between the limited size of the market and lower investment is based on the argument that *economies of scale* in industries are a key feature of their growth and for big industrial enterprises to produce on a large scale and to be economically profitable, the size of market, that is level of demand for a product must be large.

However, Nurkse and others ignore the fact that economies of scale are important only for a few industries such as basic heavy industries of machine making steel, chemicals, fertilizers etc. but it is often feasible to produce quite efficiently in small enterprises in sectors such as textiles, shoes and leather products, food processing industries, jute manufactures' etc.

Besides, while per capita income in developing countries is small but due to inequalities in income distribution prevailing in the poor developing countries, there are quite a large number of people whose incomes are high enough to demand or buy the products of large-scale industrial enterprises which make them quite profitable to be set up in developing countries.

In view of the above it is possible to argue that limited size of the market is a problem for some industries but only in rare cases, it is a major cause of persistence of underdevelopment of the poor backward countries.

Suggestions for Breaking the Vicious Circle of Poverty

In order to break the vicious circle of poverty and bring about economic growth, an important thing to be noted is that in underdeveloped countries rate of saving and investment can be increased without the reduction in consumption. As is well known, rate of saving in underdeveloped countries is low. With a given rate of saving and investment, some rate of economic growth and as a result some increment in income must be occurring in these underdeveloped countries. If out of this increment in income a proportionately greater part is saved, the rate of saving of the economy will rise. For instance, suppose as a result of 15% rate of saving and investment, an increment in income equal to ₹ 100 crore takes place. If out of these ₹ 100 crore, a greater part is saved, say 25%, and 75% is consumed, then the rate of saving will rise above 15%. It should be noted that in this process consumption will not decline, in fact it will increase by ₹ 75 crore, and along with this the rate of saving will also increase. If the increment in income of ₹ 100 crore is wholly consumed away, the rate of saving will decline.

The saving of ₹ 25 crore out of the increment of ₹ 100 crore, means that the marginal rate of saving is 25%, which is higher than the previous average rate of saving *i.e.*, 15% which means average rate of saving will go up. The sum and substance of the argument is that in *underdeveloped countries, the rate of investment and capital formation can be stepped up even without reduction in the consumption of the people, provided the marginal rate of saving is kept higher than the average rate of saving even though the current average rate of saving is low.* In this way, the rate of investment can be stepped up and standards of living of the people can be raised in future without the reduction in present consumption. This is how the vicious circle of poverty operating on the supply side of the capital formation can be broken.

As explained before, according to Nurkse, vicious circle of poverty also operates on the demand side of capital formation. To break the vicious circle on the demand side, Nurkse suggested *'the strategy of balanced growth'*. According to this, if investment is made in an individual industry, it is likely to fail owing to low income and limited size of the market. This is because investment in an individual industry does not raise the incomes of the people outside that industry. If the incomes of the people outside that industry do not rise, the demand for the product of that industry will not increase adequately to buy the larger production of the industry made possible by larger investment in it. Thus more investment in one individual industry makes possible large increase in production. But since the incomes of the people are low, the demand for the product of the firms in which more investment has been made, will not rise and therefore productive capacity of the firms will not be fully utilised. As a result of this, larger investment in them may not be profitable. This would have an adverse effect on the inducement to invest in the industry.

But, according to Nurkse, *if investment is made in several industries simultaneously*, then the workers employed in various industries will become consumers of each other's products, and will thus create demand for one another. The simultaneous investment in a large number of industries has been called *balanced growth*. The balanced growth, *i.e.*, simultaneous investment in a large number of industries creates its own demand. Thus, according to Nurkse, through the strategy of balanced growth vicious circle of poverty operating on the demand side of capital formation can be broken.

Comments. In our view, as mentioned above, Nurkse has exaggerated the vicious circle on the demand side of capital formation. Actually, there is enough demand for several products in underdeveloped countries like India and investment in the industries producing them is quite profitable. The reason for this is that in underdeveloped countries, owing to the large inequalities of income there are several people who have enough purchasing power to buy certain goods, despite the low per capita income. For instance, who can deny that in India investment in agriculture, sugar industry, refined oil, vanaspati ghee, etc., cannot be increased because of lack of demand for them. It is thus clear that production and capital formation in these countries are low not due to the lack of demand. There are other factors which are responsible for low production and capital formation in these countries.

Another important thing to note in this connection is that several commodities are imported in large quantities by developing countries, which shows that demand for them exists in these countries. Substitution of these imports by producing them at home will not face any problem of lack of demand. Therefore, for the imported products, there is generally no problem of lack of demand or inadequate size of the market. Therefore, in many Latin American countries, strategy of import substitution of consumer goods was followed under which industrial goods which were previously imported started being produced in their own countries. Thus no problem of small size of the market was faced. We thus see that vicious circle of poverty can be broken in underdeveloped countries by making larger investment in a large number of import-substituting industries. Besides, investment and industrial production can be substantially increased by producing for exports. East Asian Countries of South Korea, Taiwan, Singapore, Hong Kong accelerated their rate of capital formation and economic growth during the seventies and eighties through this route. In this way economic growth can be accelerated to raise the standards of living of the people.

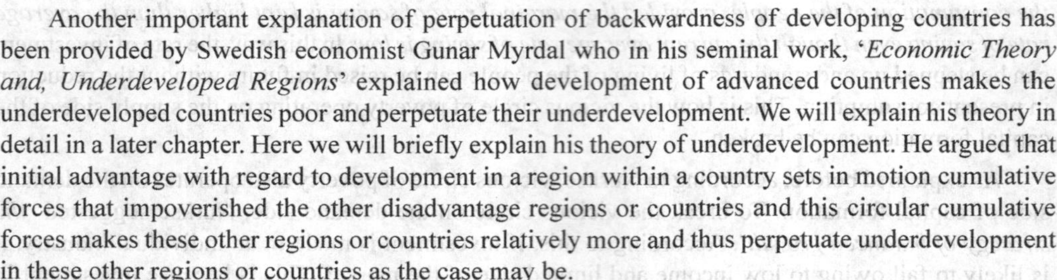

MYRDAL'S HYPOTHESIS OF CUMULATIVE CAUSATION

Another important explanation of perpetuation of backwardness of developing countries has been provided by Swedish economist Gunar Myrdal who in his seminal work, '*Economic Theory and, Underdeveloped Regions*' explained how development of advanced countries makes the underdeveloped countries poor and perpetuate their underdevelopment. We will explain his theory in detail in a later chapter. Here we will briefly explain his theory of underdevelopment. He argued that initial advantage with regard to development in a region within a country sets in motion cumulative forces that impoverished the other disadvantage regions or countries and this circular cumulative forces makes these other regions or countries relatively more and thus perpetuate underdevelopment in these other regions or countries as the case may be.

It is worth noting that Myrdal's thesis is actually about ***geographic dualism*** that equally explains persistence of underdevelopment in case of regions within a country or in nations or countries in the world. In his analysis he considers a wide variety of development indicators such as wage rate, per capita income, rates or levels of employment and unemployment regarding which sharp differences between them emerge. He points out that these inter-regional international economic differences or what has been called *spatial differences* increase when one country or one region within a country, starts developing taking initial advantage over others. Thus "*the process of cumulative causation is a direct challenge to static equilibrium theory which predicts the working of economic and social forces will cause spacial differences to narrow*"[7]

Thus, Myrdal's thesis is in sharp contrast to the neoclassical equilibrium theory according to which through the process of factor mobility (*i.e.*, movements of labour, capital etc.) wage rates and rate of profits tend to become equal across nations or regions. Thus, according to neoclassical theory, in countries or regions where labour is scarce, labour will migrate to them. Similarly, according to neoclassical theory, where capital is in plenty and therefore rate of return is low, capital will flow out resulting in rise in profits or return on it. On the other hand, according to neoclassical doctrine, in regions or countries where labour is in abundance and capital is scarce, labour will move out and capital will come in and thereby raise wages of labour and lower the rate of profit or return on capital. In this way, according to neoclassical theory, rate of profit in both types of countries or regions rewards to labour and capital are equalised.

On the contrary, according to Myrdal's theory, factor price tend to be unequal rather than becoming equal between countries or regions. According to Myrdal, in the development process started in countries or regions with some initial advantage, differences in wages or return on capital will further increase between them. Explaining Myrdal's approach to regional development, A.P. Thirlwall writes, "In a free market capital, like labour, will tend to move where the *prospective return* is the highest and this will be to the advantage of the region where demand is buoyant (not necessarily the region where the wage is lowest as in the neoclassical theory). Capital, labour and entrepreneurship will tend to migrate together.[8]

7 A.P. Thirlwall, *Economic Development*, 9th edition, 2000, p. 264.
8 *Ibid*, p. 266.

Trade also plays an important role in the process of cumulative causation. If production is subject to increasing returns, the country which is experiencing rapid growth of factor supplies will acquire comparative advantage over the relatively lagging countries where production is being done in small-scale industries. The trade between the rapidly growing countries and the lagging less developed countries will lead to the products of the underdeveloped countries being competed out in the world markets. This will lead to the destruction of small-scale industries in the underdeveloped countries making them more poor. Trade will also produce another adverse effect on the poor underdeveloped countries which produce primary products. The expansion of primary products demand for which is inelastic and trade them with the industrial products of rapidly growing countries, having income elastic demand will lead to *deterioration of terms of trade* for the poor underdeveloped countries producing and exporting primary products which have inelastic demand. Thus, trade gives the rich and rapidly growing countries unequal advantage.

Backwash Effect

An important view expressed by Myrdal causing persistent underdevelopment and poverty in the poor underdeveloped countries relates to the development gaps that emerge between countries set in motion a chain of cumulative causation through which expansion in developed countries produces unfavourable effect on the poor countries which Myrdal calls *backwash effect* causing development differences in general to persist or even wider and therefore account for the perpetuation of the poor underdeveloped countries. Advocates of free market economic system point to the *trickle-down effects* or what are called *spread effects* emanating from growth in the rich industrialised countries which benefit the underdeveloped countries in their growth process. These spread effects are in the form of increase in demand for their products as a result of rapid economic growth in the rich developed countries and the diffusion of technology and knowledge. These favourable spread effects, according to this view, will ultimately narrow down the spacial differences across various countries. However, according to Myrdal, *these favourable spread effects are weaker than backwash effect and for the special differences to be reduced the State in poor underdeveloped countries must intervene to protect their industries and agriculture by adopting suitable policy measures*.

A Critical Evaluation

In our view Myrdal's theory provides a valid explanation why there are large economic disparities between the developed and underdeveloped countries and also inter-regional differences within countries. Explaining the backwash effects on underdeveloped countries. Benjamin Higgins and Jean Downing Higgins write, "The fifteenth century had been one of the relative stagnation in Europe and Asia alike; the sixteenth century brought the first stirring of the subsequent Industrial Revolution to Europe; the transition from feudalism to commercial capitalism was well advanced and the agricultural revolution was on its way. Had Asians carried trade to Europe rather the other way round some of the "*preconditions for take off*" might have rubbed off on Asians as well. And if the Asians had suitable education system when the Westerners launched the first large-scale modern enterprises, local staff might have been engaged. Instead, Asia continued to stagnate technologically. A basically similar situation developed in Africa and to a lesser extent in Latin America"[9] However, whereas Myridal's theory convincingly explains the role of economic forces in causing interns regional differences in development, in causing the development gaps between the advanced developed countries and the poor underdeveloped countries, colonialism played a major role. We will explain the role of colonialism for perpetuation of underdevelopment and poverty in the present-day developing countries in a later section of this chapter. That is why after getting freedom from the colonical rule, these countries have started growing. In fact, China and India, the two Asian giants have emerged as the two fastest growing economies of the world.

9 Benjamin Higgins and Jean Downing Higgins, *Economic Development in a Small Planet* (New York 1979, Norton and Company, p. 98.

POPULATION GROWTH AND LOW LEVEL EQUILIBRIUM TRAP

Another important explanation of the persistence of poverty and underdevelopment in the presently developing countries has been explained with the help of rapid population growth relative to the growth of per capita income. Rapid population growth does not allow an adequate increase in per capita income to provide for sufficiently large savings to achieve necessary capital accumulation for bringing about rapid growth in per capita income. Secondly, it may happen that if population growth exceeds the labour-absorptive capacity of the economy in both the industrial and agricultural sectors of the economy, this will result in the increase in urban and rural unemployment and disguised unemployment in agriculture, Besides, the increase in demographic pressure on land will lead to lowering of agricultural productivity. As a result, it is possible that at the early stages of economic development population growth outstrips the growth in per capita income at the minimum subsitence level. This is called *low-level equilibrium trap*, also known as *Malthusian population trap* as it is based on Malthus' theory of population. The low-level equilibrium trap is illustrated in Fig. 5.3.

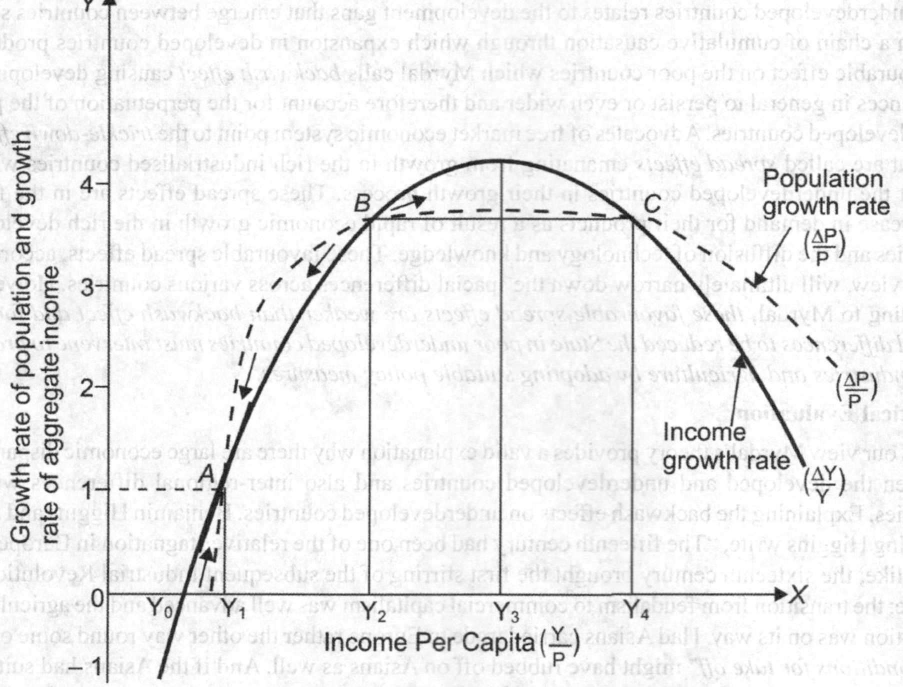

Fig. 5.3. *Low level equilibrium trap*

In Fig. 5.3 on the horizontal axis we measure per capita income $\left(\frac{Y}{P}\right)$, and on the vertical axis we measure both percentage rate of growth of per capita income $\left(\frac{\Delta Y}{P}\right)$ and percentage rate of population growth $\left(\frac{\Delta P}{P}\right)$. Y_0 represents subsistence level and at this low subsistence level of per capita income Y_0, the rate of population growth rate is zero as conceived by Mathus' theory of population.[10] Zero growth rate of per capita income is due to both the birth and death rates being

10 This theory of low level equilibrium trap has been put forward by R.R. Nelson, A Theory of the Low Level Equilibrium Trap, *American Economic Review*, Dec. 1956 and Harvey Leibenstein, *Economic Backwardness and Economic Growth.*

high and, therefore, this corresponds to the first stage of the theory of demographic transition. As a result of equal birth and death rates at per capita income Y_0, the population will remain stable at this subsistence level of per capita income Y_0.

Now, at a per capita income level greater than Y_0 (*i.e*, to the right of Y_0 on the horizontal axis), it is assumed that due to the pressure of falling death rate, population will increase at a rate higher than the growth rate of per capita income. Higher levels of per capita income beyond Y_0 will cause a fall in death rate due to the decrease in deaths on account of starvation, diseases, etc. bringing about higher growth rate of population $\left(\frac{\Delta P}{P}\right)$ to occur. With birth rate assumed at the biological maximum, the fall in death rate will bring about rapid growth in population. (This corresponds to the second stage of the demographic transition). Thus, *to the right of Y_0, the higher rate of population growth will depress per capita income to the level* Y_0 as shown by arrow. It is therefore concluded that the economy is stuck at low level equilibrium trap at the subsistence per capita income equal to Y_0.

It will be seen from Fig. 5.3 that population growth rate $\left(\frac{\Delta P}{P}\right)$ reaches its maximum rate which is assumed to be equal to around 3.3% at per capita income level Y_2 and remains at this level for long until much higher per capita income exceeds level is achieved. In Fig. 5.3 this per capita income level is Y_4. Beyond per capita income level Y_4, due to fall in birth rate in accordance with the stage 3 of demographic transition the population growth rate $\left(\frac{\Delta P}{P}\right)$ starts falling and causes population growth rate curve to slope downward.

The next step in our analysis is to plot a curve showing the relationship between the growth rate of aggregate income, that is, $\left(\frac{\Delta Y}{Y}\right)$ (*independent of population growth rate*) and per capita income levels. Having done so we can compare the population growth rate $\left(\frac{\Delta P}{P}\right)$ with growth rate of aggregate income $\left(\frac{\Delta Y}{Y}\right)$. Thus, if population grows faster than aggregate income (*i.e.*, if $\frac{\Delta P}{P} > \frac{\Delta Y}{Y}$), income per capita (measured on the horizontal axis) will fall back to per capita income level Y_1. It will be seen from Fig. 5.3 that in the beginning from income level Y_1 until per capita income level Y_2 *population growth rate exceeds growth rate of aggregate income*. As a result, per capita income will fall to Y_1. On the other hand, *if aggregate income grows faster than population* as it is happening to the *left* of per capita income level Y_1, per capita income will rise to level Y_1. Beyond income level Y_1 (corresponding to point *A*) and upto per capita income level Y_2 (corresponding to point *B*) population growth $\left(\frac{\Delta P}{P}\right)$ exceeds growth rate of aggregate income $\left(\frac{\Delta Y}{Y}\right)$ which will pull down the per capita income to the level Y_1 (that is, to point *A*). It therefore follows that ***point A (corresponding to per capita income level Y_1) represents the low level equilibrium trap.***

It is important to understand why aggregate income growth curve $\left(\frac{\Delta Y}{Y}\right)$ has the slope and shape as shown in Fig. 5.3. In the beginning and up to the per capita income level Y_3, slope of the curve of *aggregate income growth rate* (which is measured on the vertical axis) is positively related to the per capita income $\left(\frac{Y}{P}\right)$ measured on the horizontal axis. The reason for this is that the higher the level of per capita income $\left(\frac{Y}{P}\right)$, the higher the saving rate which would cause higher investment to take place which will bring about higher growth rate of aggregate income $\left(\frac{\Delta Y}{Y}\right)$. However, as will be seen from Fig. 5.3, beyond per capita income level Y_3, the growth rate of aggregate income declines due to the operation of law of diminishing marginal returns which occurs because more workers or people have now to work with the given fixed amounts of land and other natural resources. (Note that Malthus and his followers do not consider the favourable impact of technological progress on productivity that works to counter the deminishing marginal returns to take place.)

It will be seen from Fig. 5.3 that the two curves, namely growth rate of population curve $\left(\frac{\Delta P}{P}\right)$ and growth rate of aggregate income curve $\left(\frac{\Delta Y}{Y}\right)$ intersect at three points *A*, *B* and *C*. As explained above, point *A* represents low level equilibrium trap. Note that point *A* is a stable equilibrium point because any small deviation from this point will cause per capita income level to come back to this point. For example, if per capita income increases from per capita income level Y_1 towards Y_2, the rate of growth of population $\left(\frac{\Delta P}{P}\right)$ being greater than the rate of growth of aggregate income, the per capita income will fall back to the level Y_1. Similarly, if income per capita moves to the left of the level Y_1 the growth rate of aggregate income exceeds the growth rate of population. As a result, per capita income will rise to the level Y_1 (*i.e.* towards point *A*). *Thus we see that equilibrium at low level of per capita income Y_1 is stable.*

It is however important to mention that equilibrium at point *B* (*i.e.*, at per capita income Y_2) is unstable. This is because any smaller deviation from *B* towards left will cause per capita income to fall to Y_1. On the other hand, ***if through a big push in investment, per capita income is raised beyond level Y_2 (i.e. beyond equilibrium point B), per capita income will continue to grow until stable equilibrium at point C (i.e. per capita income Y_4) is reached.*** We thus see that point *B* represents an unstable equilibrium as any movement in per capita income either to the light or left will cause changes in per capita income until either *A* or *C* is reached. We will explain in a later chapter that if rate of saving and investment is increased by a big push so that the economy starts moving to the right of point *B*, the economy will start growing in a sustained manner so that the stable equilibrium is reached at point *C* at per capita income level Y_4. In other words, a minimum critical effort in terms of saving and investment is needed so that the economy starts moving to the right of point *B* or, in other words, per capita income starts increasing beyond Y_2 level. Thus, a *critical minimum effort in terms of saving and investment is needed to break out of the low-level equilibrium trap.*

Critique of Low-level Equilibrium Trap Theory

Low-level equilibrium trap which is also ***Malthusian Population Trap*** describes the relationship between population growth and economic development. However, it is based on simplistic assumptions which have been found to be untrue by empirical evidence. This low-level equilibrium trap theory has been mainly criticized on the following two grounds: First, the low-level equilibrium trap theory is based on Malthus' theory of population and ignores the beneficial effect of technological progress in neutralising the effect of inhibiting forces of rapid population growth. The history of modern economic growth of present-day developed countries reveals that rapid technological progress that occurred as a result of a series of inventions and innovations suspended the operation of diminishing marginal returns on which Malthus' theory of population and low-level equilibrium trap theory is based. As a result of technological advancement, productivity of land increased substantially. Thus Todaro and Smith aptly writes, "Increasing rather than decreasing returns to scale have been a distinguishing feature of the modern growth epoch. While Malthus was basically correct in assuming a limited supply of land, he did not anticipate the manner in which technological progress could augment the availability of land by raising its quality (its productivity) even though its quantity might roughly remain the same".[11]

The technological progress shows low level equilibrium trap theory to be invalid as it causes an upward shift in the growth of aggregate income $\left(\frac{\Delta Y}{Y}\right)$ curve at *all* levels of per capita income $\left(\frac{Y}{P}\right)$ at a vertically higher than the curve of population growth rate $\left(\frac{\Delta P}{P}\right)$ as shown in Fig. 5.4

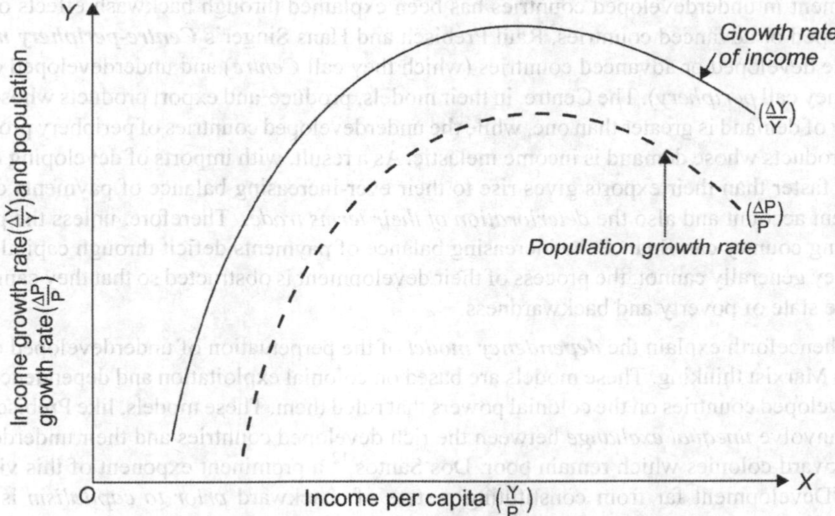

Fig. 5.4. *Technological progress ensuring growth rate of income above that of population growth rate at all levels of per capita income*

As a result of technological progress aggregate income has increased steadily over time. This has made possible for the present-day developed countries to escape the low-level equilibrium trap. This has also actually happened in developing countries of China and India – the two most populated countries of the world. Both these countries have achieved higher growth rates of GDP (*i.e.*, aggregate income) than population growth rate and has escaped from Malthusian trap despite rapid growth of population. For example, India due to high rate of saving and investment and advance in technology (*e.e.*, green revolution in agricultures) has succeeded in achieving GDP growth rate higher than population growth rate, Besides, even growth rate of food production in India has exceeded the growth rate of population.

The second weekness of low-level equilibrium trap is its wrong assumption regarding positive relationship between population growth rate and level of per capita income. According to this, starting from the subsistence level of per capita income, population increases with the increase in per capita income. This has not been borne out to be true by empirical evidence which shows that there is no any exact positive relationship between population growth rate and increase in per capita income. In fact, the Indian experience shows that population growth rate instead of rising has declined with the increase in per capita income. It has, therefore, been said that development (*i.e., increase in per capita income*) *is the best contraceptive*.

11 Todaro and Smith, *op. cit*., p. 289.

Besides, progress in modern medicine and public health programmes has brought down the death rate, especially the reduction in mortality rate of children. This has increased the *survival rate* which has worked towards reduction in fertility rate (*i.e.*, birth rate). This has therefore tended to reduce population growth rate.

COLONIALISM AND THEORIES OF DEPENDENCE

We have explained above Myrdal's theory of cumulative causation in which the perpetuation of development in underdeveloped countries has been explained through backwash effects of growth in developed or advanced countries. Raul Prebisch and Hans Singer's ***Centre-periphery models*** in which the developed or advanced countries (which they call *Centre*) and underdeveloped countries (which they call *periphery*). The Centre, in their models, produce and export products whose income elasticity of demand is greater than one, while the underdeveloped countries of periphery produce and export products whose demand is income inelastic. As a result, with imports of developing countries growing faster than their exports gives rise to their ever-increasing balance of payments deficit on the current account and also the *deterioration of their terms trade*. Therefore, unless the periphery developing country can finance the increasing balance of payments deficit through capital-inflows, which they generally cannot, the process of their development is obstructed so that they cannot break out of the state of poverty and backwardness.

We henceforth explain the ***dependency model*** of the perpetuation of underdeveloped countries based on Marxist thinking. These models are based on colonial exploitation and dependence of poor underdeveloped countries on the colonial powers that ruled them. These models, like Prebisch-Singer models, involve *unequal exchange* between the rich developed countries and their underdeveloped and backward colonies which remain poor. Dos Santos,[12] a prominent exponent of this viewpoint, writes, "Development far from constituting a state of backward *prior to capitalism* is rather a *consequence and a particular form of capitalist development known as dependency capitalism*". Furthermore, explaining this dependence of underdeveloped countries on their colonial capitalist power countries be writes 'Dependence is a *conditioning situation in which the economies of one group of countries are conditioned by the development and expansion of others*. A relationship of interdependence between one or more economies or between such economies and the world trading system becomes a dependent relationship when some countries expand through self-impulsion while others being in a dependent position can only expand as a reflection of the dominant countries which may have positive or negative effects on their immediate development. In either case basic situation of dependence causes these countries to be both backward and exploited"[13].

It is evident from above that in this viewpoint the development gap between the developed and underdeveloped countries widened as a result colonialism. The colonial powers which were endowed with technological and commercial abilities along with possession of large amount of capital exploited the poor and underdeveloped countries under their dominance and extracted a part of their produce. Development, then, was based on international division of labour which allowed industrial development to take place in some countries white preventing it in others. It thus follows that the emergence of colonialism led to a pattern of development different from that which would have occurred if their growth had occurred based mainly on their internal socioeconomic forces. According to this school of thought perpetuation of underdevelopment in the poor developed countries cannot be fully understood without analysing how they came to be conditioned and dominated by colonialism which emerged on world scene as a product of world capitalism. According to Marxist thinking, colonialism is essentially an economic phenomenon under which capitalist development

12 Dos Santos, The Crisis of Development Theory and the Problem of Dependence in Latin America, in Berstein H. (ed.) (1973), *Underdevelopment and Development*, Penguin.

13 *Ibid.*

in the Western Europe changed the entire world resulting in the existence of two groups of countries; the colonial power countries and their dependent colonies which they exploited to promote further industrial development in their own countries. With this a particular international division of labour came to prevail under which the poor underdeveloped countries became the suppliers of minerals and agricultural raw materials to their colonial powers that ruled them.

The poor and backward countries were also used as markets for industrial products of the colonial powers. Besides, the industrialists of these colonial powers started investment in mines and plantations of the poor underdeveloped countries and repatriated profits to their home countries. These industrialists of colonial powers got cheap minerals and agricultural raw materials from their dependent colonies and sold them the industrial products at higher prices. This represents what has come to be called ***unequal exchange*** through which the industrial powers exploited the people of poor countries. They invested in those lines of production *i.e.*, minerals and plantations which they exported. They made little investment in the industrial development of the poor underdeveloped countries. In fact, as has been exphasised by Gunaer Myrdal, the industrial growth of the rich countries had a '*backwash effect*' on the growth of the underdeveloped countries. The emergence of colonialism and their exploitation of the poor underdeveloped countries led to their '*de-industrialisation*'. Thus India's famous handloom industries declined due to their being unable to compete with the products of industrial powers which rendered millions of people unemployed.

The Neocolonial Dependence Model

It is worth mentioning that even after many years of independence, there has been a revival of colonial dependence in the new form called '*neocolonial dependency model*'[14] According to this, there has been emergence of small elite class consisting of big industrialists enjoying vast political power and social status, the ruling political class consisting of political leaders, landlords whose principal interest, according to Todaro and Smith, "knowingly or not, is in the perpetuation of inequality and inconformity in which they are rewarded"[15] Elaborating this. Todaro and Smith write, "These special interest groups including multinational corporations, national bilateral agencies and multinational assistance organisations like the World Bank or the International Monetary Fund (IMF) which are tied by allegiance or funding to the wealthy capitalist countries. The elite activities and viewpoints often serve to inhibit any genuine reform efforts that benefit the wider population and in some cases actually lead to even lower levels of living and to the perpetuation of underdevelopment".

In the case of India at present, the reference may be made to some economists and spokesmen of the Indian capitalist class[16] who advocate acceleration of economic growth through increasing the role of private sector, both Indian and foreign investment class and oppose even *merit or necessary subsidies* to the poor (some of them even oppose food security system meant to ensure minimum amount of food to the poor and special employment guarantee schemes to provide some employment to the poor). They advocate tax concessions by the government and lower interest rates by banks to accelerate investment to generate higher rate of economic growth. Furthermore, they advocate for *flexible labour laws* so that the industrialists can retrench workers when it is desired by them. These economists believe that the acceleration of economic growth would automatically remove poverty and unemployment through what has been called *trickle-down* effect.

Importantly, these elite groups also advocate for wooing foreign investment, both direct and portfolio, (which happen to be investment by multinational corporations (MNCs) to promote growth forgetting that the main interest of these foreign investors are to make profits and repatriate them to their

14 See Todaro and Smith, *Economic Development*, 10th edition, 2012.

15 Todaro and Smith, *op.cit.* p. 23.

16 Authors of this book do not consider it proper to name these Indian economists and spokesmen of the capitalist class. Besides, their views may be well-intentioned for acceleration of economic growth and removal of poverty in India. But in our view their approach is based on faulty reasoning.

home countries rather than promoting *inclusive economic growth*. Thus, according to Dos Santos,[17] it has become difficult for breaking out of the dependence on the advanced industrialised countries if one wishes so as they will be opposed by vested interests *within* the poor underdeveloped countries themselves. It may be noted, in the neoclassical dependence model, the multinational corporations (MNCs) are seen as the modern form or instrument for expropriation of the surplus generated by the cheap labour of underdeveloped countries. So in one form or another, the poor countries despite having achieved formal political independence remain locked in a system of economic dependence that perpetuates underdevelopment.

A Critical Evaluation of Dependency Theory

The concept of dependency has provided us a very important insight into the problem of developing countries and their relationship with the developed countries. The relationship in these two types of countries represents *dualism of the world*. While the developed countries such as US and EU which dominate the world bodies such as UN, IMF, World Bank, WTO still meant that for them trade should be faciliated by reduction of Tariffs on their industrial and agricultural products by the developing countries and reduce subsidies and other support to their farmers. However subsidies to farmers and provision of food security to the poor are necessary for elimination of poverty. Thus, the tragedy is that poor countries are still dependent on the developed countries for financial capital and technology of various kinds. Thus while the advocates of dependency theory explain the shortcomings of dependence on the advanced industrialised countries, they offer little explanation why poverty and underdevelopment still persist even after several years of gaining independence from colonial rule. They offer no explanation how to initiate and sustain rapid growth without assistance in one form or the other from the developed countries.

Second, actual experience of developing countries which started development process without the help of much foreign capital and in which public sector played an important role and pursued strategy of import substitution also did not achieve a higher rate of economic growth due to the flaws in their economic policies. Both India and China are examples of such countries. China having failed in their earlier experience of Marxist and Mao's approach to development had to give up this approach and since 1979 not only switched to the free market economy but also invited foreign investment by multinational corporations to set up industries there and mainly export the industrial products. What is important to note is that this free-market approach and with the help of foreign capital it has been able to become the fastest growing economy of the world. With the achievement of high rate of economic growth, China has been able to reduce significantly its poverty problem. This is due to the fact that its growth has been due to the expansion of labour-intensive manufacturing industries.

Furthermore, when in the early 1990s India faced problems serious balance of payments crisis and high inflation, it also switched over not only to the predominantly free-market economy by adopting IMF directed structural adjustment economic reforms but also opened up the Indian economy to foreign trade and foreign investment, both direct foreign investment and portfolio investment, by foreign institutional investors (FIIs). These policies were adopted to achieve economic stabilisation and higher rate of economic growth. Though since 1991, India, like China, has also achieved a higher rate of economic growth and has become the second fastest growing economy of the world next only to China. The growth of China and India with the help of foreign investment goes against the main thrust of neocolonial theory of dependence.

However, while in the present circumstances foreign direct investment is welcome, the dependence on foreign portfolio investment is not desirable. The porfolio investment by FIIs may help to meet current account deficit in the short run but from long-run viewpoint of healthy growth it is not good. This is because there is always uncertainty about capital flows by FIIs and create a lot of volatility in Indian stock market and foreign exchange rate of rupee.

17 Dos Santos, *op.cit.*

DEFICIENCY OF DYNAMIC ENTREPRENEURSHIP AND WEAK PROPENSITY TO SAVE

According to the classical economists, an entrepreneur or an organiser acts as an agent for bringing together the various agents of production and undertake to remunerate them for the work done. But the modern economists recognise the dynamic role that an entrepreneur plays in promoting economic development of the country. This was *specially underlined by Joseph Schumpeter who thought that entrepreneur played a key role in economic development*. According to him, the entrepreneur tries to maximise his profits by making innovations, that is, introducing new production techniques, bringing out new products, tapping new markets, tapping new sources of raw materials and by adopting a optimum or most economical combination of the factors of production. In all these ways, while he succeeds in making higher profits for himself, he is making a significant contribution to the increase in the national income.

But there is a lack of dynamic entrepreneurs in underdeveloped countries who can invest the savings in productive capital and carry out innovations. This explains why rate of economic development has been low in them and underdevelopment persists. Whatever entrepreneurs are there in underdeveloped countries, they are interested in *quick returns as monopoly rent* and are not daring enough to bear risks involved in making productive investment and in developing basic and heavy industries from whom profits accrue after a long time. The entrepreneurs in underdeveloped countries try to avoid risk and are *attracted by commerce and trade* which provide them quick returns on the capital invested.

Thus, prior to 1947 private enterprise in India did not take India any far on the road of economic development. It left untouched and undeveloped some vital sectors such as basic heavy industries like steel, fertilizers, machine making and chemical industries. They were attracted more by commerce, trade and speculative activities than by industry. That is why after independence in the Five Year Plans, it became necessary for the Government to intervene and provide right type of entrepreneurship to bring about economic development.

Weak Propensity to Save and Invest. Another characteristics of the entrepreneurs in developing countries is that they exhibit weak propensity to save and invest which is a great obstacle in the way of economic development. The entrepreneurs undertake investment and production of goods if there is a strong motivation to accumulate wealth. If instead of using wealth of income for a further investment a good part of it is consumed by the entrepreneurs, the motivation or propensity to invest will not be present in sufficient degree. The function of the capitalist (entrepreneur), according to Marx, is 'to accumulate' and this propensity to accumulate played a crucial role in the development of Western economies through promoting investment for more and more production. Marx has described capitalist (entrepreneur) as personified capital and accumulation as his passion. To quote him, "*Frantically bent upon the expansion of value, he (the capitalist) relentlessly drives human beings to production for production's sake, thus bringing about a development of social productivity and the creation of those material conditions of production which can alone form the real basis of a higher type of society . . . only as the personification of capital is the capitalist respectable.*"[18] Thus the entrepreneurs (the capitalists) played an important role in the growth of Western economies as they did not spend their acquired wealth on their personal enjoyment and consumption. Instead, they used a major part of their income for further investment and production in order to gain power. For this they relatively saved more and consumed less. This greater propensity to invest for further production as compared to the propensity to consume helped to enlarge stock of capital and productive capacity in today's Western developed countries.

18 Karl Marx, *Capital*, Vol. 1, (Everyman's edition).

But the entrepreneurs in the developing countries such as India have weak propensity to accumulate, and instead, indulge conspicuously in luxury consumption. That is why rate of capital accumulation and therefore of economic growth has been low in them and till today they remain underdeveloped. Commenting on this late Prof. A.K. Dass Gupta writes, "*It is a tragedy that the underdeveloped countries have missed the early phase of capitalism when luxury goods were yet to arrive in the market and when the urge for power spent itself solely in accumulation. The conditions which stimulated accumulation in the early phase of capitalism in the West do not exist now. We have tasted the forbidden fruit and have fallen from paradise. The capitalist's urge for accumulation is now restrained everywhere by his love for display, and commodities making for display are multiplying.*"[19]

SOME OTHER OBSTACLES TO ECONOMIC DEVELOPMENT

Lack of Infrastructure

Economic growth in the developing countries has been impeded by **inadequate availability of infrastructure.** Infrastructure includes power, irrigation, transport and communication. It may also include credit facilities available from banks and other financial institutions and also the facilities for the education and training of labour. The availability of these infrastructures facilitates production in industry, agriculture and other productive sectors of the economy. *These infrastructures give rise to external economies and thereby cause reduction in costs, facilitate production and increase efficiency in all productive sectors of the economy.* Thus power (electricity) is used in the production process these days both in industry and agriculture. It is now too well known in India that non-availability of adequate amount of power lowers industrial and agricultural development. Likewise, the existence of the means of transport is essential for transportation of raw materials to the place of production and to sell the goods produced to far off places. In fact, the availability of transport widens the market for goods and thereby encourages their production. Likewise, the availability of adequate irrigation facilities is necessary to raise agricultural output.

One of the most important hurdles in the growth of investment in developing countries is *the acute lack of external economies* which, as has been stated above, are provided by basic infrastructures such as transport, communication and power. In a developed country the economic system being highly diversified there are tremendous amounts of external economies which a new enterprise can draw upon. The various types of infrastructure in *developed countries* were generally built up by private enterprise although with the liberal help of the Government in the form of grants and loans. In contrast, the contemporary developing countries lack an adequate system of transport, communication and power. For instance, the inadequacy of railway network in most of the newly independent countries of Africa and Latin America is a bottleneck in the expansion of national market and growth of industries. Since development of power, transport, communication involves lumpy investment, has long gestation period and the returns accrue mainly in the form of external economies, the private enterprise is not attracted to build this infrastructure. The Government should therefore play an important role in undertaking the task of building up adequate infrastructure to speed up economic growth.

Likewise, there is a lack of adequate credit facilities or funds. For an entrepreneur who wishes to undertake business or set up some factory he should have sufficient funds to finance it. Credit facilities are also badly needed by farmers for agriculture. The growth of agriculture suffers if adequate credit facilities are not available. Therefore, the Government in the developing countries should give high priority to develop the facilities of providing adequate credit and finance for the development of industry and agriculture.

---

19 A.K. Dass Gupta, *The Economics of Austerity*, Oxford University Press, 1975.

Demonstration Effect and Economic Growth

In raising rate of capital formation, the developing countries have to contend against one problem which arises from demonstration effect on consumption. Demonstration effect leads to initiation and imitation of superior consumption standards stimulates consumption among the middle and upper middle class which increases their propensity to consume and consequently reduce their capacity to save.

Nurkse[20] laid great stress on this new theory of consumption and saving. We ordinarily think that a man's consumption depends on his income. But that is not quite correct. A person's consumption does not merely depend on his own income but also on the incomes and therefore the consumption behaviour of his friends and relations with whom he maintains social contacts. A man finds some of his friends using colour televisions, luxury cars, costly mobiles, refrigerators, air-conditioners, electric hot plates, electric washing machines and so on and experiences a sort of restlessness and a craving is generated in his mind to enjoy these amenities some immediately and others some later days. These desires for conspicuous consumption generally outrun the consumer's means. Thus *consumption behaviour of individuals depends not on absolute real income but on relative levels of real incomes*. It does not depend on what we can afford but what the others afford and enjoy. This is what Duesenberry calls '*demonstration effect*'. The intensity of this demonstration effect on saving seriously impairs a person's capacity to save. He may save less even if his income has gone up; the ability to save may have increased but the willingness to save has decreased. It has been estimated that 75 per cent of the Americans do not save. The reason is not that they are too poor to save but that they are adopting better ways of living seen among the upper classes. *It is thus the interdependence of consumer's preferences which determines the choice between consumption and saving*. This is Duesenberry's relative theory of consumption and saving.

What is true of individual applies also to nations. The disparities in the real incomes of nations have a profound effect on the economic development of nations. Whereas the rich nations can help the poor nations develop economically and break the vicious circle of poverty, they also pass on to them their consumption patterns. The poor countries may not find it easy to increase productivity and raise income but it is easy to imitate costly consumption standards. Thus, there is *international demonstration effect* which lowers the propensity to save of the less well-off developing countries. The demonstration effect aggravates propensity to consume and reduces capacity to save which is a serious impediment to economic development. The relative aspect of the problem need again to be emphasised. It is not the absolute level of income which determines consumption pattern but the relative levels of national income of connected countries which affect consumption of a less prosperous country. It follows therefore that even if the national income of a developing country goes up, it may not be able to save more than before simply because the income gap between this country and the other countries with which it has commercial or political intercourse has increased. The ability to save may have gone up but the willingness to save would have gone down on account of a keen desire to consume luxury goods which are consumed in the richer countries.

Thus, the interpersonal and international consumption functions are interrelated and not independent. The consumption and saving habits of the economically backward countries are greatly influenced by those of the prosperous countries. As Nurkse puts it, "*When people come into contact with superior goods or superior patterns of consumption, with new articles or new ways of meeting old wants, they are apt to feel after a while a certain restlessness and dissatisfaction. Their knowledge is extended, their imagination stimulated, new desires are aroused, the propensity to consume is shifted upward.*"[21]

---

20 Ragnar Nurkse, *Problems of Capital Formation in Underdeveloped Countries*.

21 *Op. cit*., pp. 58-59.

It is not merely the superior consumption prevalent in rich countries which exercises influence on the consumption in the poor countries but also the knowledge of it. First, we know and then we imitate. Knowledge opens eyes to the future possibilities. "It widens the horizons of imagination and desires." New products or new patterns or designs of old products are constantly being advertised and brought irresistibly to the notice of the consumer at home and abroad. These new goods enter into the standard of living of the poorer communities. "The presence or the mere knowledge of new goods and new methods of consumption tends to raise the general propensity to consume."[22]

The movies, the radio and television, spread of education and modern travel facilities are the powerful media through which new goods or new and better ways of living are communicated far and wide. In the present state of the world attraction of advanced living standards have a fairly wide influence on the consumption of the people of low-income countries.

Propensity to save is directly influenced by propensity to consume. When the poor countries copy living standards from the rich, they must pay the price. The price is that their capacity to save must diminish. This no doubt adds to the difficulties of bringing about economic development. We have already said that this saving potential can be mobilised only if consumption is kept at the same level as before. But we have seen that when such a country comes in contact with a rich country, its propensity to consume is likely to go up. The potential domestic sources of capital are seriously impaired by the impatience and dissatisfaction, which the demonstration effect tends to generate. This impatience to raise living standards curtails the capacity to save. The conflict between the need to save and the desire to consume is intensified by the demonstration effect. Thus the small rate of saving in poor developing countries may not be altogether due to low level of real income. It may also be due to allurement of superior levels of living. This throws new light on international economic relations. Prosperity in one country may breed prosperity in another but it may also create difficulties by provoking consumption that it cannot afford and which it should avoid for some time at any rate. The high consumption of a rich country in this manner hinders capital formation in developing economies.

We may conclude in Nurkse's 'words: '*The great and growing gaps between the income levels and therefore living standards of different countries, combined with increasing awareness of these gaps, may tend to push up the general propensity to save*". The entrepreneurial class in India is, in fact, aping western modes of living and squandering away profits which they should plough back into investment. The country is poorer for this senseless consumption behaviour.

How to Overcome Demonstration Effect

Curtailing the Consumption of Luxury Goods. The working of demonstration effect in developing economIes implies that wants should be regulated or curtailed. If wants of the people go on multiplying under the influence of demonstration effect, the demand for luxuries or non-basic consumption goods will increase. This will raise the propensity to consume of the economy resulting in a low ratio of saving to income. Further, the increased wants for luxuries and their consumption will divert the basic resources such as steel, cement, machines etc., towards their production. As a result, the production of basic consumption 'goods will be starved of essential resources. The use of scarce national resources to satisfy the non-basic wants of the people when millions who live below poverty line are unable to meet their basic wants for subsistence is purely a wastage of resources.

Thus, according to Prof. A. K. Dass Gupta, "*The implication of luxury consumption for an underdeveloped country is more obvious and direct. The underdeveloped countries will need a high rate of growth for quite some time to come. Their level of per capita income is too low. In India, for example, the per capita income is hardly adequate to afford a man his minimum subsistence. Even with a stationary population, the country will thus require years of capital accumulation for*

22 Ragnar Nurkse, *op. cit.*

it to attain a civilized standard. Luxury consumption slows down the rate of accumulation and thus hampers growth."[23]

Limitation of Wants. Mahatma Gandhi had warned long ago against multiplication of wants. He thus stated, "I do not believe that multiplication of wants ... is taking the world a single step nearer its goal. I whole-heartedly detest this and desire to increase animal appetites and go to the ends of the earth to satisfy them. If modern civilization stands for all this and I have understood it does, I call it satanic."[24]

It may be noted that Mahatma Gandhi was not against the satisfaction of wants for consumption goods which are absolutely needed for maintenance of health and promotion of productivity. It is the *multiplication of wants for non-basic consumption goods*, that is, luxuries against which Mahatma Gandhi wrote. According to him, there is no end to the multiplication of wants and efforts ought to be made to reduce them. To quote him again, "*The mind is a restless bird, the more it gets, the more it wants and still remains unsatisfied. Therefore, the ideal of creating an unlimited number of wants and satisfying them seems to be delusion and snare. Civilization in the real sense of the term consists not in multiplication but in the deliberate and voluntary reduction of wants.*[25]

One may not entirely agree with Mahatma Gandhi regarding the limitation of wants, but in the context of poor underdeveloped economies in which glaring inequalities of income prevail, the restraint on the multiplication of wants of the richer sections of the society is essential if economic surplus is to be generated and used for productive investment. Consumption of luxury and semi-luxury goods should therefore be controlled if rate of capital accumulation is to be stepped up. Japan and South Asian countries were able to raise the level of their saving and investment to 30 per cent and above of their national income and achieve a high rate of economic growth by cutting consumption to the minimum. Now, the question is how to regulate wants and curtail consumption of luxury goods. One way is the adoption of fiscal measures under which heavy taxes should be imposed on luxurious consumption expenditure by individuals and business companies. Heavy excise duties and sales taxes should also be imposed on luxury goods so as to curtail their consumption by the rich people. Physical controls can be imposed on the production and distribution of luxury goods such as cars, air conditioners . These goods should be distributed to the individuals on functional basis rather than on the basis of money power.

Restricting the Production of Luxury Goods. But the most effective method to curtail consumption of the affluent is to suitably restrict the production of luxury goods and a much high priority should be accorded to the production of basic consumption goods needed by the masses. This will raise the rate of capital accumulation on the one hand by releasing resources from the production of luxury goods and reduce inequalities between the rich and the poor on the other by raising the living standards of the latter. But the restriction on the production of luxury goods is easier said than done. This is because luxury consumer goods are produced by the private sector in mixed economies of underdeveloped countries. Guided as they are by the market or effective demand, the private capitalists prefer to produce luxury goods since there is ample market for them by the richer sections. Prof A.K. Dass Gupta rightly states: "The Industrial Policy Resolution of 1956 gives private capitalists complete sway over the production of consumer goods. Restrictions on imports protect them from international competition. A sheltered market is created in the country for luxury goods. These industries thus receive high priority from India's capitalists".[26]

---

23 A.K. Dass Gupta, *The Economics of Austerity*, Oxford University Press, 1975, p. 12.

24 M.K. Gandhi, *Young India*, March 19, 1927.

25 M.K. Gandhi, *Hind Swaraj*, pp. 44-45.

26 A.K. Dass Gupta, *op. cit.*

23. A.K. Dass Gupta, *The Economics of Austerity*, Oxford University Press, 1975, p. 12.
24. M.K. Gandhi, *Young India*, March 19, 1927.
25. M.K. Gandhi, *Hind Swaraj*, pp. 44-45.
26. A.K. Dass Gupta, *op.cit.*

PART II

FACTORS IN ECONOMIC DEVELOPMENT

- Factors Determining Economic Growth: An Overview
- Capital Formation: Determinants and Acceleration
- Technological Progress and Economic Development
- Human Resource Development: Education and Economic Growth
- Human Resource Development: Health and Nutrition
- Population and Economic Development: Theory of Demographic Transition and Fertility
- Population Growth: How it Affects Economic Development, Poverty and Environment

Factors Determining Economic Growth: An Overview

Economic Growth as an Objective of a Developing Economy

An important goal of an economy, especially a developing economy, is to achieve economic growth so as to raise the living standards of the people. There is a need for economic growth even in today's developed economies but in developing economies the need for economic growth is very urgent since it is through the increase in productive capacity that the problems of poverty and unemployment can be solved.

In India's Five Year Plans the most important objective has been to achieve economic growth at the rate of 5 to 9 per cent per annum in various Five Year Plans. In the first three decades (1951-80) of planned development in India on an average growth in GNP of 3.5 per cent per annum was achieved which was too low considering the annual growth rate of population which was about 2.1 per cent during 1961-81. However, during the decade (1980-1990) of the last century, growth rate of the Indian economy rose to 5.6 per cent in GDP and 4.1 per cent in per capita GDP. Keeping in view the rate of population growth which is currently equal to about 1.6 per cent per annum to raise significantly the living standards of our people, rate of growth must be accelerated. In the 10th Plan period (2002-07), actual average growth rate achieved was 7.8 per cent which during the 11th Plan period (2007-12) rose to average annual 8 per cent growth rate which is the highest growth rate ever recorded in the Indian economy. The objective of development is broad-based improvement in economic and social conditions of our people. Rapid growth is essential requirement for achieving this objective. There are two reasons why rapid GDP growth rate is important. First, rapid growth of GDP produces a large expansion in total income and production opportunities which, if growth is not brought about by labour-saving technologies, will directly raise the living standards of a vast section of our people by providing them with employment and other income-enhancing activities.

The second reason why growth is important is that it generates larger revenues for the government which can help to finance anti-poverty and employment generating programmes such as Mahatma Gandhi National Rural Employment Guarantee Scheme (MGNREGS), Mid-Day Meal programme, Sarv Shiksha Abhiyan which either provide direct benefits to the poor or *increase their ability to access employment and income generating opportunities* generated by the growth process.

FACTORS AFFECTING ECONOMIC GROWTH

The process of economic growth is a highly complex phenomenon and is influenced by numerous and varied factors such as economic, political, social and cultural factors. It is believed by some economists that the capital is the main requirement for growth and therefore the greatest emphasis be laid on capital formation to bring about economic development. But this is wrong. As Professor Nurkse rightly remarks, "*Economic development has much to do with human endowments, social attitudes, political conditions and historical accidents. Capital is a necessary but not a sufficient condition of progress.*"[1]

Growth in gross domestic product (GDP) depends on the supply of various factors such as labour, capital, natural resources and technology. Many economists use production function approach to explain the contributions to the increase in gross domestic product. This aggregate production function is written as:

$$Y = AF(K, L, R)$$

where A represents technology change in which causes a shift in the production function, K stands for capital, L for labour and R for natural resources including land. In the study of factors that determine growth natural resources are taken as given and constant, and capital is further differentiated as *physical capital* such as machines and equipment and *human capital* which represents improvement in health and education. Note that natural resources (including land) denoted by R in the aggregate production function are given and fixed. However, through better utilisation of land and other natural resources, total output can be increased. The following are various factors which affect economic growth:

(*i*) Supply of land and other natural resources;

(*ii*) Capital formation which depends upon the rate of domestic saving and investment and inflow of foreign capital;

(*iii*) Human Capital : Education and Health, and

(*iv*) Technological progress

We explain below each of these factors in turn.

Supply of Land and Other Natural Resources

The quantity and quality of natural resources play a vital role in the economic development of a country. Important natural resources are land, minerals and oil resources, water, forests, climate, etc. The quality of natural resources available in a country puts a limit on the level of output of goods which can be attained. Without a minimum of natural resources there is a not much hope for economic growth. It should, however, be noted that *resource availability is a necessary but not a sufficient condition for economic growth.* For instance, India, though rich in natural resources, has remained poor and underdeveloped. This is because resources have not been fully utilised for productive purposes. Thus it is not only the availability of natural resources but also the ability to bring them into use, which determine the growth of an economy. On the other hand, Japan has a relatively few natural resources but has shown a very high rate of economic growth and as a result has become one of the richest countries in the world. How has Japan done this miracle ? It is international trade that has made possible for Japan to achieve higher growth rate. Japan imports many of natural resources such as mineral oil it requires for production of manufactured goods. It then exports manufactured goods to the countries that are rich in natural resources. Thus experience of Japan shows that paucity of natural resources can be overcome through foreign trade for bringing about economic growth.

Supplies of natural resources can be increased as a result of new discoveries of resources within a country or technological changes which facilitate discoveries or transform certain previously useless materials into highly useful ones. It should also be noted that the scarcity of certain natural resources can be overcome by *synthetic substitutes*. For example, the synthetic rubber is being increasingly used in the place of natural rubber in advanced countries. Further, nylon which is a synthetic substance is being largely used in place of silk which is a natural substance.

It was Malthus who first pointed out the possibility of growing relative scarcity of natural resources as a binding constraint on the growth process. He argued that with a given and fixed land and due to the operation of diminishing returns to labour the growth of output of food will not keep

1 Ragnar Nurkse, *Problems of Capital Formation in Under-developed Countries*, Basil Blackwell, 1957.

pace with the exponential growth in population which will result in food shortages and famines and bring growth process to a halt. Though the present-day industrialized countries escaped from the gloomy forecast of Malthus by making technological progress, but the developing countries which made little progress in technology have often faced food-supply shortages and rising food prices. However despite the fixity of land and other natural resources, agricultural and food production can be substantially increased through *science-based agriculture*, that is, through raising productivity of land by the use of improved technology. It is through the use of green revolution technology that India has succeeded in raising food production from 100 million tonnes 1969-70 to 257 million tonnes in 2012-13. We will discuss in detail this issue of raising agricultural productivity in a separate chapter.

Like gloomy prediction made by the Malthus theory in 1972, a report by Meadows and others titled '*The Limits to Growth*' submitted to the *Club of Rome*, pointed out that there is not only the problem of food crisis but also the crisis of natural resource exhaustion and environmental degradation due to over-exploitation of natural resources by the exponential population growth. The report pointed out that if this exponential industrial growth is not curbed, economic growth would start declining by the first two decades of 21st century and death rate will increase due to food shortage and environmental pollution. Though the gloomy forecast of this report by the Club of Rome has not come true but the report correctly predicted that environmental pollution will substantially increase causing increase in death rate.

If follows from above that a pertinent question has been raised: whether economic growth and living standards will continue rising in future or the depletion of non-renewable natural resources will limit it. The economists associated with Club of *Rome* argued that non-renewable natural resources such as oil and minerals put a limit to how much economies of the world could grow. This is because exponential economic growth will eventually use up the fixed stock of these natural resources. When this stage occurs economic growth will come to a halt and living standards may fall if population goes on increasing.

Though the above argument apparently seems to be plausible but it is not fully correct to assert that natural resources will limit economic growth. Two factors save us from this disaster of depletion of natural resources that results in halting the process of economic growth. First, technological progress helps us to produce more using fewer resources. Progress in technology enables us to improve the ways in which natural resources are used. Thus, modern cars have better petrol mileage than the old cars of fifty years ago. Energy efficiency of room lighting and heating has greatly increased. Besides, recycling permits some non-renewable resources to be used again.

Second, as shortage of some specific natural resources was felt, their prices rose which led to the discovery and use of their substitutes. For example, some fifty years ago, it was feared that due to excessive use of tin and copper, their natural stocks would soon be depleted posing great problems. These were then essential commodities Tin was used to make various types of food containers and copper was used to make telephone wires. Today, plastic has replaced tin for making food containers and telephones now use fibre-optic cables which are made from sand. Ethanol is being used as substitute for gasoline. It follows from above that technological progress and growing ability to find synthetic substitutes for natural products show that there is no reason to believe that natural resources are a limit to economic growth.

The use of natural resources and the role they play in the economic growth depend, among other things, on the type of technology. The relationship of resources to the kind and level of technology is very intimate. One does not have to go back very far in history to find when an item currently as valuable as petroleum was of little or no significance. It is only recently that the various radioactive elements have come to be regarded as valuable. In many developing economies there are, no doubt, deposits of many minerals that are not being used because of technological deficiencies.

Capital Formation

Labour is combined with capital to produce goods and services. Workers need machines, tools and factories to work. In fact the use of capital makes workers more productive. Setting up of more factories equipped with machines and tools raises the productive capacity of the economy. Therefore, in the opinion of many economists, capital formation is the very core of economic development. Whatever the type of economic system, without capital accumulation the process of economic growth cannot be accelerated. Levels of productivity in the United States of America are very high mainly because American people work with more and better type of capital goods built up over the last several years. Low productivity and poverty of developing countries is largely due to the scarcity or shortage of real physical capital in these countries. Economic growth cannot be speeded up without accumulating various types of capital goods. Physical capital can be classified into two main categories. First type of physical capital is in the form of machines, equipment and plant which directly help to produce further goods. The second type of physical capital is *overhead capital* which is also called *infrastructure* which facilitates the production of goods. The examples of infrastructure are power (*i.e.*, electricity), transport (*i.e.*, roads, railways, ports, communication network). Lack of infrastructure impedes economic growth. Economic growth cannot be accelerated without accumulating these types of capital, namely, fixed capital goods such as machines, equipment, plants and infrastructure facilities such as power, roads etc. There is a third type of capital input commonly known as *circulating capital* such as irrigation, fertilizers, HYV seeds, pesticides which raise the productivity of land and are therefore called land-augmenting.

Accumulation of capital is necessary for economic growth as *it raises the productive capacity* of the economy to produce goods and services. Besides, capital accumulation is important because it generates more employment opportunities. The workers need to be equipped with capital goods to be employed for production of goods and services. Therefore, to absorb growing labour force in productive activities capital accumulation needs to be stepped up. It may be noted that in production function of the type of Cobb-Douglas production ($Y = AK^{a}L^{1-a}$), *both capital* (K) *and labour* (L) are required to increase output (Y). That is, according to this production function, labour without capital will produce nothing and similarly capital without labour will also produce nothing.

But capital formation requires saving, that is, the sacrifice of some current consumption. An increase in supplies of capital goods can only result from investment, and investment in turn is only possible if a portion of current income is saved. Thus saving is essential to economic growth. According to Professor Arthur Lewis, "*The central problem in the theory of economic growth is to understand the process by which a community is converted from being a 5 per cent saver to a 12 per cent saver with all the changes in attitudes, in institutions and in techniques which accompany this conversion.*[2]" Underdeveloped economies generally save very little; not more than 5 per cent of their national income. For instance, saving in India on the eve of independence was about 6 per cent of the national income. On the other hand, rich countries save from 15 to 30 per cent of their national income. In order to bring about economic growth, rate of savings must be stepped up to over 15 per cent of national income. But in developing countries, the rate of saving is low because income of the people is low and that they are living at the level of subsistence. Thus, the lower the per capita income, the more difficult it is to forgo current consumption. It is difficult for people living at or near subsistence level to curtail current consumption. This in large part explains the low level of saving in the poor, underdeveloped countries.

It must be emphasized, however, that savings in itself do not contribute to economic growth. It is only when savings are invested in accumulation of capital that they contribute to economic growth. If savings are hoarded in the form of gold or precious jewels, or if they are used for buying land, they do not result in an increase in supplies of capital goods and thus make no contribution to economic growth. Studies conducted to examine the relationship between investment and growth in terms of

2 Arthur Lewis, "Economic Development with Unlimited Supplies of Labour", *Machester School*, 1954.

increase in GDP have found that there exists a *strong correlation between the two*. Countries that allocate a larger fraction of their GDP to investment such as Japan and Singapore achieved high growth rates, and countries that allocate a small share of GDP to investment such as Bangladesh and Nepal have low growth rates.

That the rate of growth depends on rate of saving or investment on which capital accumulation depends has been clearly brought out by Harrod-Domar model of growth. According to this model, growth rate depends on rate of saving or investment (*i.e.*, ratio of saving or investment to national income) and capital-output ratio which means how much extra capital is required to produce an extra unit of output. This Harrod–Domar growth formula can be written as

$$g = \frac{s}{v}$$

where g is growth rate of output (that is, $\frac{\Delta Y}{Y}$), s is the saving rate (i.e., ratio of saving to national income or S/Y) and v is incremental capital-output ratio, that is, ratio of capital investment to the increase in output by one unit.

Since rate of saving is assumed to be equal to rate of investment, it follows from above formula that the higher the rate of saving or investment, the higher the rate of economic growth, capital-output ratio (v) remaining the same.

Foreign Capital: Foreign Aid and Foreign Investment

As domestic savings are not sufficient to make possible the necessary or desired accumulation of capital goods, borrowing from abroad may play an important role. Professor A.J. Brown rightly says that "*Development demands that people somewhere should refrain from spending a part of their incomes, thus allowing part of the world's productive resources to be used for accumulation of capital goods. The people who can best afford to do this are generally those who live in countries of high average income. On the other hand, the countries where development is likely to alleviate suffering and promote welfare to the greatest extent are those where average incomes are low. There is a strong general case for the rich countries lending to the poor ones*."[3] Nearly every developed state obtained the foreign assistance to supplement its own small saving during the early stages of its development. England borrowed from Holland in the seventeenth and eighteenth centuries, and in turn came to lend to almost every other country in the world in the nineteenth and twentieth centuries. The United States of America, now the richest country in the world, borrowed heavily in the nineteenth century, and has now emerged as the major lender country of the twentieth· century which is assisting the poor countries in their attempts to bring about economic growth .

It should be noted that foreign capital does not flow into the developing countries in the form of aid alone (that is, loans at concessional rates of interest) but also through direct investment by foreign companies. Foreign direct investment (FDI) is an important way for a country to accelerate its economic growth. Though the foreign companies send back profits earned, their investments in factories *increase the rate of capital accumulation* in the developing countries leading to a higher rate of economic growth and higher productivity of labour. Besides, foreign direct investment enables the developing countries *to learn the new advanced technologies* developed and used in the rich developed countries.

The importance of foreign capital is reinforced by *the need of a developing country for foreign exchange to buy imports*. A developing country has to import huge quantities of capital goods, technical know-how and essential raw materials which are required for industrial growth and building up of infrastructure such as power projects, roads, irrigation facilities, ports and telecommunication. For all these, foreign exchange is needed which can be obtained if foreign rich countries lend it to

3 A.J. Brown, *Introduction to the World Economy.*

developing economies or if foreign companies make direct investment in the developing countries. If foreign assistance is not forthcoming in adequate quantity, then the developing countries will experience serious difficulties of balance of payments. In the absence of sufficient borrowing from abroad, or direct foreign investment, rapid economic development of the developing countries will turn their balance of payments seriously adverse.

Furthermore, developing countries suffer not only from a shortage of savings but also from *a lack of technical know-how, managerial ability*, etc. Foreign capital when it comes in the form of private investment in developing countries by foreign companies, especially the multinational corporations (MNCs), bring with it these complementary factors which are very essential for development.

Due to bad experience of the colonial rule in the past, the developing countries were generally against the foreign capital, especially against private foreign investment. However, the fears of foreign investment and aid are now no longer there. Further, now *multilateral foreign aid* is available through World Bank and International Monetary Fund (IMF) which provide loans at concessional rates to the developing countries for accelerating growth. As far as private foreign investment is concerned, the developing countries (including China and India) are now competing with each other to attract private foreign investors. It has now been realised that foreign investment will not only supplement domestic saving and thereby raise the rate of investment, bring better technology and managerial know-how but will also ease the problem of foreign exchange. Through raising the rate of investment and providing foreign exchange resources, it will not only increase output but will also generate employment opportunities. Besides, like the domestic investment, *foreign investment also produces a multiplier effect on output, income and employment* in the developing countries.

In the last fifteen years, China's very high rate of economic growth which is generally described as "*Chinese growth miracle*" is due to higher inflow of foreign direct investment (FDI) as compared to India. Foreign direct investment flows to China grew from \$3.5 billion in 1990 to \$53 billion in 2002. On the other hand, FDI flow to India was a low \$0.4 billion in 1990 and rose to \$5.5 billion in 2002. Further, FDI has contributed significantly to the rapid growth of China's manufacturing exports. In India by contrast FDI has been much less important in driving India's export growth, except in information technology. For higher foreign direct investment flows China has more business-oriented and FDI-friendly attitudes, its FDI procedures are easier and decisions are taken rapidly. Besides, China has more flexible labour laws, a better labour climate and better entry and exit procedures for business. It is therefore not unexpected that China has emerged at the top in attracting FDI flows. Against this, at present (*i.e.*, in 2002) India is 15th in the world's FDI destination.

Human Capital: Education and Health

Till recently economists have been considering physical capital as the most important factor determining economic growth and have been recommending that rate of physical capital formation in developing countries must be increased to accelerate the process of economic growth and raise the living standards of the people. But the last three decades of economic research has revealed the importance of education as a crucial factor in economic development. Education refers to the development of human skills and knowledge of the labour force. It is not only the quantitative expansion of educational opportunities but also the qualitative improvement of the education which is imparted to the labour force that holds the key to economic development. Because of its significant contribution to economic development, education has been called as human capital and expenditure on education of the people as *investment in man or human capital*. Speaking of the importance of education or human capital, Prof. Harbison writes: "*Human resources ..... constitute the ultimate basis of production, human beings are the active agents who accumulate capital, exploit natural resources, build social, economic and political organisations; and carry forward national development. Clearly, a country which is unable to develop the skills and knowledge of its people and to utilise them effectively in the national economy will be unable to develop anything else.*"[4]

4 Frederick Harbison, *Human Resources as the Wealth of Nations*, Oxford University Press, 1973, p.3.

Table 6.1. Sources of US Economic Growth, 1929-1982 (per cent)

Annual growth of output (per cent)	2.9
Percentage of growth due to :	
Growth in labour input	32
Growth in labour productivity :	
(1) Education per worker	14
(2) Capital formation	19
(3) Technological change	28
(4) Economies of scale	9
(5) Other factors	–2

Source: Edward E. Denison, *Trends in American Economic Growth* (1929-82), The Brookings Instiitution, 1983, p. 30.

Several empirical studies made in developed countries, especially the U.S.A., regarding the sources of growth or, in other words, contributions made by various factors such as physical capital, manhours (*i.e.*, physical labour), education etc. have shown that education or the development of human capital is a significant source of economic growth. Professor Solow[5] who was one of the first economists to measure the contribution of human capital to economic growth estimated that for United States between 1909 and 1949, 57.5 per cent of growth in output per manhour could be attributed to the *residual factor* which represents the effect of technological change and of the improvement in the quality of labour mainly as a consequence of education.

Denison, another American economist made, further refinement in estimating the contribution to economic growth of various factors. Denison tried to separate and measure the contributions of various elements of 'residual factor'. Denison's estimates for various sources of US growth during 1929-82 are given in Table 6.l. As will be seen from the Table 6.l Gross Domestic Product in USA grew at the rate of 2.9 per cent per annum over this period. The factors determining growth in this period have been divided into two groups. It will be seen from the table that the growth in *the quantity of labour* accounted for 32 per cent of growth in GDP of the USA over this period. The other group consists of *various variables determining growth in labour productivity* has been divided into five factors. It is noteworthy that education per worker contributed 14 per cent to growth in output during this period, technoJogical change contributed 28 per cent to the growth in output. Thus, growth in education per worker and technological change together accounted for 42 per cent of growth in the output in the USA over this period whereas capital formation contributed 19 per cent to the growth rate. This shows the great importance of education and technological change as determinants of economic growth.[6]

In our above analysis we have explained that education is regarded as investment and like investment in physical capital, it raises productivity of labour and thus contributes to growth of national income. Some economists have argued that education is of crucial importance not only because education raises 'he productivity and therefore earnings of individual workers, **but it creates positive externalities**, that is, beneficial external effects. A positive *externality* occurs when the activity of a person provides benefits to *others*. For example, an educated person might generate new ideas which may lead to the improvement in methods of producing goods. When these ideas become a part of society's pool of knowledge (*i.e.*, stock of human capital), everyone can use them and derive benefits from them. These ideas are therefore external benefits of education. One problem facing the developing countries, especially India, is of *brain drain*, that is; migration of a large number of highly educated persons (such as those trained by IIT, 11M and medical colleges) to the developed countries such as USA to make higher earnings there. If education has positive external effects, then

5 Robert M. Solow, "Technical Change and Aggregate Production Function," *Review* of *Economics and Statistics*, Aug. 1957.

6 E.F. Denison, *Trends in American Growth* (1929-82), The Brookings Institution, 1983, p. 30.

this brain drain will deprive the Indian economy of the beneficial effects which these educated people would have created in India.

Health. Like education, improvement in health and nutrition is a sort of investment in human capital. Both better education and health are good in themselves and *directly* raise the well-being of the people but, according to human-capital approach, better health increases ability and productivity of the workers and therefore contributes to the growth of output. Better health and nutrition increases the life span of the people and thereby lengthens their working life and enables them to go on earning incomes for an expanded period. Besides, they complement educational investment since *returns to education* will be higher if they are able to work and earn for a longer period. Further, healthy persons especially healthy children, are in a better position to acquire more education and skills to become more productive.

Improvement in health is very difficult to measure and, therefore, its contribution to growth of output cannot be easily ascertained. However, *life expectancy at birth has been usually used as a proxy for health*; the higher life expectancy reflects better health of the people and, as mentioned above, they are able to earn a stream of income for a long time in future and along with their higher individual returns on health, they make greater contribution to growth of national output for a longer period. Development economists Haymi and Godo in their empirical study of relationship between life expectancy at birth and growth rate of GDP for the years 1965-2000 for a number of countries have found correlation coefficient to be equal to 0.43 which is quite significant.[7]

Technological Progress and Economic Growth

Another important factor in economic growth is progress in technology. Use of advanced techniques in production or *progress in technology brings about a significant increase in per capita output*. Technological advance refers to the discovery of new and better techniques of doing things. Sometimes technological advances result in an increase in available supplies of natural resources. *But more generally technological advance results in increasing the productivity or effectiveness with* which natural resources, capital and labour are used and worked to produce goods. As a result of technological advance it becomes possible to produce more output with same resources or the same amount of product with less resources.

But the question arises as to how does the technological progress take place. The technological progress takes place through *inventions and innovations*. The word invention is used for the new scientific discoveries, whereas the innovations are said to take place only when the new scientific discoveries are used for actual production processes or commercial purposes. Some inventions may not be economically profitable to be used for actual production.

It is quite well known that improvements in technology greatly increases the productivity of factors. In United States, for instance, increased use of mechanized power-driven farm equipment on land greatly raised the agricultural productivity of land per hectare. It may also be noted that some technological improvements have resulted in the increased effectiveness with which capital goods are used. Technological change raises the productivity of workers through the provision of better machines, better methods and superior skills. By bringing about increase in productivity of factors the progress in technology makes it possible to produce more output with the same amount of factors or the same amount of output with less amount of factors.

Technological progress manifests itself in the change in production function. So a simple measure of the technical progress would be the comparison of the position of production function at two points of time. The technological change may operate upon the production function through improvements of various sorts such as a superior equipment, an improved material, and superior organisational efficiency.

7 Yujiro Haymi and Yoshihiva Godo, *Development Economics*, (New Delhi : Oxford University Press, 3rd edition, 2005), p. 53.

Technological progress increases the productivity of factors, labour and capital, so that with the same amount of a factor, more output can be produced. In other words, technological change causes an upward shift in the production function. This is shown in Fig. 6.1 in which along the *X*-axis number of workers are measured and on the vertical axis total output is measured. To begin with, with production function PF_0, the number of workers *OL* produces OQ_1 amount of output. Now suppose technological progress takes place causing shift in the production function upward from PF_0 to PF_1 and as will be seen from Fig. 6.1 that now the same number of workers *OL* can produce more output OQ_2. This means technological change has raised the productivity of labour. Similarly, technological change will raise the productivity of capital.

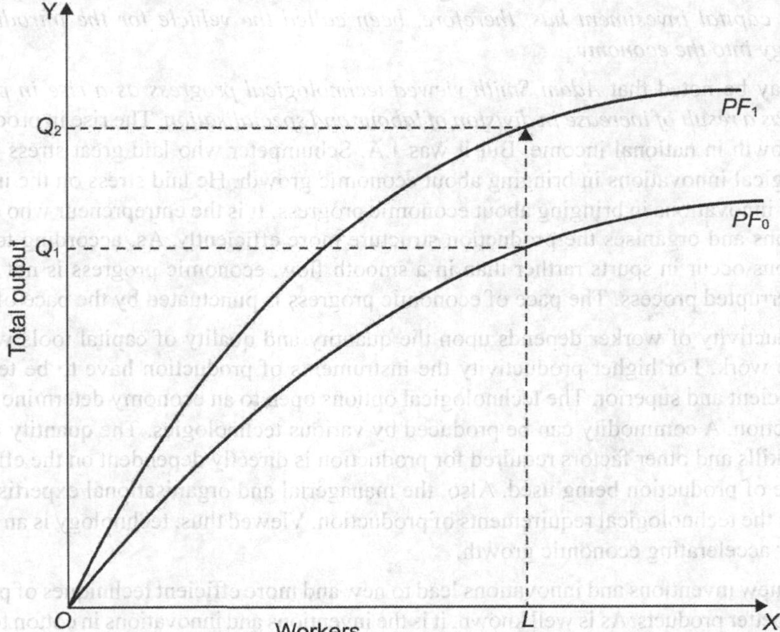

Fig. 6.1. *Upward shift in the production function due to technological progress showing increase in productivity of labour*

It will be seen from Table 6.1 that Denison in his empirical study of sources of US economic growth that between 1929-1982, technological progress contributed 28 per cent of increase in labour productivity as against 19 per cent by capital formation and 14 per cent by education per worker.

It is now widely accepted that technological change raises productivity and that a *continuous technological change will enable the economy to escape from being driven to the stationary state or economic stagnation.* Classical economists like Ricardo and J.S. Mill expressed fear that the increase in the stock of capital will sooner or later, because of the operation of diminishing returns, land the economy into stationary state beyond which economic growth will come to an end. *Classical economists remained occupied with the idea of a stationary state because they underplayed the importance of technological progress that could postpone the occurrence of a stationary state and ensure sustained economic growth.* Indeed, if technological progress continuously takes place, demon of stationary state can be put off indefinitely.

Embodied and Disembodied Technological Change. The two types of technological changes should be distinguished: (1) Embodied technological change (2) disembodied technological change. Disembodied technological change is one which permits more output to be produced from *unchanged inputs without investment in new capital goods such as machines.* Disembodied technological change is organisational in nature and not dependent on capital accumulation and assumes that productivity of *all vintages of capital goods rises equally*. On the other hand, embodied technological change refers to technological improvements that can be introduced into the production system by *investment in new capital goods* (*i.e.*, machines or equipment).

The process of technological progress is inseparably linked with the process of capital formation. In fact, both go hand in hand. Technological progress is virtually impossible without capital formation. It is because the introduction of superior or more efficient techniques requires building up of new capital equipment which incorporates new technology. In other words, new and superior technology can contribute to national product and its growth if it is first embodied in the new capital equipment. *The new capital investment has, therefore, been called the vehicle for the introduction of new technology into the economy*.

It may be noted that *Adam Smith viewed technological progress as a rise in productivity of workers as a result of increase in division of labour and specialisation*. The rise in productivity leads to the growth in national income. But it was J.A. Schumpeter who laid great stress on the role of technological innovations in bringing about economic growth. He laid stress on the introduction of technical innovations in bringing about economic progress. It is the entrepreneur who carries out the innovations and organises the production structure more efficiently. As, according to Schumpeter, innovations occur in spurts rarther than in a smooth flow, economic progress is not a smooth and an uninterrupted process. The pace of economic progress is punctuated by the pace of innovations.

Productivity of worker depends upon the quantity and quality of capital tools with which the labourers work. For higher productivity the instruments of production have to be technologically more efficient and superior. The technological options open to an economy determine the input-mix of production. A commodity can be produced by various technologies. The quantity and quality of capital, skills and other factors required for production is directly dependent on the efficiency of the technique of production being used. Also, the managerial and organisational expertise has to be in tune with the technological requirements of production. Viewed thus, technology is an indispensable factor for accelerating economic growth.

The new inventions and innovations lead to new and more efficient techniques of production and new and better products. As is well known, it is the inventions and innovations in cotton textile industry that led to the industrial revolution in England. In the olden times inventions were the work of some individuals and innovations were introduced into the production process by the private entrepreneurs. Keeping in view the importance of technological progress in the economic growth of a country, the governments of various countries are spending a lot of money on "*research and development*" (R & D) which is carried on in various laboratories and institutes to promote technological progress.

Developing countries are using the technology imported from the developed countries because they have not yet made sufficient progress in technology, nor have they developed to an adequate extent capital goods industries which produce capital goods, embodying advanced technology. But imitation and use of the technology of the advanced countries by these underdeveloped countries has produced one unfavourable result. It is that the technology of the advanced countries is not in accordance with the factor endowments of these developing countries, since they have abundance of capital while the developing countries have surplus labour. As a result of the use of the capital-intensive technology, enough employment opportunities have not been created by the large-scale industries using imported technology. As a result, unemployment in developing countries like India has been increasing despite the progress in industrialisation of the economy. In view of this not so happy experience in' regard to the creation of employment opportunities by industrial growth, an eminent English economist, Prof. Schumacher, has recommended the use of intermediate technology or what is also known as *appropriate technology* by the developing countries like India. *By Intermediate or appropriate technology is meant the technology which is labour-intensive and yet highly productive so that with its use enough employment opportunities are created along with more production.* But in order to find out this appropriate technology for several industries, a good deal of research and development (R & D) activity is required to be carried out.

The Growth of Population and Labour Force

The growth of population is another factor which determines the rate of economic growth. The growing population increases the level of output by *increasing the number of working population or labour force* provided all are absorbed in productive employment. This is because labour is a factor of production and is an essential input in the production function of various commodities. We saw above that according to estimates of Denison, increase in the quantity of labour contributed to the extent of 32 per cent to economic growth of output in the USA during 1929-1982. Moreover, the increase in population leads to the *increase in demand for goods*. Thus, growing population means growing market for goods which facilitates the process of growth. When market for goods is enlarged, they can be produced on a large scale and thus *economies of large-scale production* can be reaped. The economic history of U.S.A. and European countries shows that population growth contributed greatly to the increase in their national output.

But what has been true of U.S.A. and European countries may not be true in case of the present-day developing countries. Whether or not the growth of population contributes to economic growth depends on the existing size of population; the available supplies of natural and capital resources, and the prevailing technology. In the United States, where supplies of natural and capital resources are comparatively abundant, the growth in population raises national output by increasing the quantity of labour. In India where supplies of other economic resources, especially capital equipment, are relatively scarce, increase in population leads to the increase in unemployment of workers.

Labour is combined with capital to produce goods and services. Therefore, increase in the quantity of labour force will contribute to economic growth when the cooperating-factor capital is also increasing and technology used is not labour saving. In the modem times workers need machines, tools and factories to work. Since a developing country such as India has a lot of surplus labour but relatively a small stock of capital workers cannot be absorbed in productive activities. We thus see that a rapidly growing labour force by itself is no guarantee of economic growth. Increase in national output, that is, economic growth is possible only when the supplies of capital and other resources are increasing adequately along with the growth of labour force. If, on the other hand, when the supplies of capital and the other resources are meagre, the increase in the labour force (or population) will merely add to unemployment and will not bring about increase in national output.

As stated above, economic growth requires increasing supplies of capital goods. Increasing supplies of capital goods become possible only with higher rate of investment. And a higher rate of investment, in turn, is possible if rate of saving is high. Now, *increase in population by adding to the number of mouths to be fed tends to raise consumption and, therefore, lowers both saving and investment*. In other words, increase in population raises the ***dependency ratio*** of the households which tends to lower their savings. Thus rapid growth of population by causing lower rate of saving and investment tends to hold down the rate of economic growth in developing countries. Thus, under conditions like those in India population growth actually impedes economic development rather than facilitates it.

It is worth noting here that *changes in total GDP* which are used to measure rate of economic growth are not a good measure of economic well-being. For the purpose of evaluating changes in economic well-being or living standards of the people of a country GDP *per capita* is more important for it tells us the amount of goods and services that is available for consumption for an individual in the economy. But growth in population or labour force adversely affects growth in GDP per capita. The reason is that rapidly increasing labour force forces the economy to spread more thinly the other cooperating factors, especially capital and land over many more workers. As a result, capital or land per worker declines causing decline in productivity of workers.

Further, rapid population growth nullifies our efforts to raise the living standards of our people. In other words, *a high rate of increase in population swallows up a large part of the increase in national income so that per capita income or living standard of the people does not rise much.* This is precisely what has happened during the planning era in India. This while the gross national income of India went up by 7.6 per cent in the Tenth Plan period and 8 per cent in the Eleventh Plan period per annum, per capita income rose by only 5.9 per cent and 6.3 per cent per annum respectively. The relatively slower rate of rise in per capita income has been due to rapid population growth.

CAPITAL-OUTPUT RATIO

Capital-output ratio is the amount of capital required to produce output worth ₹ 1. If Y stands for output or income and K for the stock of capital used to produce that output, then $\frac{K}{Y}$ represents capital-output ratio. It is useful to distinguish between incremental or marginal capital-output ratio and average capital-output ratio. Whereas average capital-output ratio describes the ratio of total capital to total output or income of the economy, incremental capital-output ratIo is ratio of *increment* in the stock of capital to the *increment* in output. Therefore, marginal capital-output ratio (*ICOR*) can be written as $\frac{\Delta K}{\Delta Y}$ where ΔK is the increment in capital and ΔY is the resultant increase in income or output.

The rate of economic growth of a country depends upon the rate of capital formation and capital-output ratio. Capital-output ratio determines the rate at which output grows as a result of a given volume of capital investment. For example, a capital-output ratio of 4 would mean, in Indian rupees, that a capital investment of ₹ 4 results in the addition of output worth ₹ 1. Hence, in order to produce a given level of output, 'smaller capital investment would be needed if the capital-output ratio is lower than when it is higher.

Factors Determining Capital-Output Ratio

It is difficult to estimate the capital-output ratio of an economy. The productivity of capital depends upon many factors such as the degree of technological improvement associated with capital investment, the efficiency of handling new types of equipment, the quality of managerial and organisational skill, the existence and the extent of the utilisation of economic overheads and the pattern and rate of investment. For instance, the higher the proportion of investment devoted to the production of light consumer goods, the lower the capital-output ratio; and higher the proportion of investment devoted to public utilities, *i.e.*, economic and social overheads, the higher will be the capital-output ratio, and *vice versa*. Likewise, the greater the investment devoted to basic heavy industries, the higher will be the capital-output ratio, and *vice versa*. The superior organising ability and the use of better technology will lower the capital-output ratio. The capital-output ratio also varies with the prices of inputs. .

It is agreed that capital-output ratio in developing countries is generally higher, *i.e.*, the capital is less productive in them than in developed countries. This is so because there is a relative inefficiency of the industries in developing countries which produce capital goods. There is the greater wastage of capital in the process of production due to low level of technical knowledge. Besides, owing to indivisibilities, certain kinds of investment are bound to be initially underutilised. Further, as development proceeds in the developing countries the pattern of demand shifts towards the more capital-intensive industries which tends to raise capital-output ratio.

In order to gain the most from capital formation, a country must also undergo technological and organizational progress, so that the capital-output ratio be reduced. Thus, the growth of the rate of output depends not only on the amount of capital accumulated but also on how much capital is required per unit increase in output (*i.e*., incremental capital-output ratio). The lower the incremental capital-output ratio, the more accelerated is economic growth. A low capital-output ratio is, . thus, as significant as large capital accumulation. But it must also be pointed out that a lower incremental capital-output ratio (ICOR) requires technological and organisational progress so that capital becomes more productive.

Limitations of Capital-Output Ratio

It may, however, be pointed out that the concept of capital-output ratio suffers from certain limitations. Its precise calculation presents some formidable difficulties. Hence, the quantitative relationship between capital investment and output, which the capital-output ratio suggests, may prove to be misleading. It would, therefore, be hazardous to base the estimates of capital requirements of an industry or economy on such ratios. Neither can the capital stock be assumed with any exactitude; nor is the other side of the ratio, *i.e*., output capable of any precise measurement. Besides the index number problems, a clear distinction cannot be often made between capital goods and non-capital goods. Returns to social overheads, in particular, cannot be calculated accurately. Further, capital-output ratio is influenced by several variables, *e.g*., technological improvements, better utilisation of equipment, organisational improvements, labour efficiency, and these factors elude quantitative measurement.

Hence, the concept of capital-output ratio has only a limited practical significance, because it cannot indicate the actual contribution of capital alone in a given scheme of investment. Great caution is, therefore, necessary in making use of a particular capital-output ratio in the adoption of actual investment policy.

PRODUCTION FUNCTION APPROACH TO ECONOMIC GROWTH

In our above analysis we have explained how growth in Gross Domestic Product (GDP) depends on supply of resources such as labour, capital, natural resources. Many economists use production function approach to explain the importance of various factors for determining growth rate. The following type of production function has been used to measure the contributions of different factors to economic growth.

$$Y = AF(L, K, N)$$

where Y = Gross domestic product (GDP)

A = Total factor productivity

L = The quantity of labour input

K = The size of capital stock

N = The quantity of natural resources.

In the studies of sources of growth, the natural resources are given as constant and human capital is added as a separate factor for determining growth in Gross Domestic Product. With these changes then the production function becomes

$$Y = AF(L, K, H)$$

where H represents the quantity of human capital.

An important way to. assess the contribution of a resource to the production of goods and services is its productivity. *By productivity we mean the ratio of output produced to the quantity of input used to produce it*. We can measure productivity of a single factor such as labour or capital. To measure the productivity of all inputs together the concept of *total factor productivity* (*TFP*) is employed. The total factor productivity means the ratio of output produced to the *amount of all inputs used.* Total factor productivity is index of overall productivity of the economy. In fact, *technical progress in the economy is measured by the annual increase in total factor productivity* (TFP).

Now, the economic growth depends on the increase in factor inputs and technological progress that is taking place in the economy. Improvement in technology makes factor inputs or resources more productive. If the quantity of resources is increasing and total factor productivity is rising, then output would grow faster than the increase in the quantity of resources. Therefore, rate of economic growth achieved will depend on the growth in resources (*i.e.*, factor inputs such as labour, capital and the rate of increase in total factor productivity. Thus

Economic growth = growth rate of supply of resources + technological progress (i.e., rate of increase in total factor productivity)

Now, the amount by which output increases due to the increase in labour input depends on the contribution of labour to it. Similarly, the amount by which output increases due to accumulation of capital depends on the contribution of capital to it. Assuming no change in natural resources and taking two factor production function, then the growth in real output resulting from the increases in labour and capital inputs can be obtained from multiplying the increases in labour and capital by their respective contributions to the production of output. Following the neoclassical economists such as Solow[8] and Meade[9], the economists generally use the *shares in national income (GDP) of labour and capital to measure their contributions to output*. From the recent production function studies conducted for the US economy it has been found that labour's share is about 70 per cent and capital's share is about 30 per cent of national income. We can obtain the growth in output, (*i.e.* GDP) by using the following growth equation :

$$\% \Delta \text{ GDP} = \% \Delta\text{TFP} + 0.70 (\% \Delta L) + 0.30 (\% \Delta K)$$

where

GDP = Gross Domestic Product

ΔTFP = Change in total factor productivity

ΔL = Increase in the quantity of labour

ΔK = Increase in the capital stock

The above growth equation shows how growth in GDP depends on changes in total factor productivity (TFP) and changes in factors such as labour and capital. Recall that *change in total factor productivity measures technological progress* that is taking place in the economy. As explained earlier, technical progress, that is, changes in total factor productivity is a crucial factor in determining gross output. For example, if total factor productivity is increasing at the rate of 2 per cent per annum, then even with capital stock and labour force being held constant, gross domestic product (GDP) will increase at the rate of 2 per cent per annum. If labour input increases by 2 per cent and capital stock increases by 3 per cent per annum each, then applying the above growth equation

$$\begin{aligned} \% \Delta\text{GDP} &= 2 + 0.70 (2) + 0.30 (3) \\ &= 2 + 1.40 + 0.90 \\ &= 4.3 \end{aligned}$$

Thus, GDP will grow at the rate of 4.3 per cent per annum.

It is worth noting here that higher growth rate achieved by Japan in the past was not only due

8 Robert Solow, "A Contribution to the Theory of Economic Growth", *Quarterly Journal of Economics*, Vol. 70, Feb. 1956.

9 J.E. Meade, *A Neoclassical Theory of Economic Growth*. 1961

to rapid growth rate of capital stock but also because of relatively higher growth rate in total factor productivity (TFP), that is, technological progress: Further, from 1973 to mid-nineties, lower growth rate in the United States was due to slowdown in growth in total factor productivity. It may be further noted that differences in growth rates across countries can be explained in terms of differences in growth rates of capital stock and of total factor productivity.

EAST ASIAN COUNTRIES GROWTH MIRACLE

In recent years (between mid-sixties and the end of eighties, that is, during 1966-1990), the rate of economic growth in the four East Asian countries, namely, Hong Kong, Singapore, South Korea and Taiwan has been so remarkable that they are popularly known as Asian Tigers. It will be seen from Table 6.2 that *growth rate in GDP per capita* in these countries has been within the range of 5.7 to 6.8 per cent per annum.[10] It has been mentioned with pride by some leaders of these four East Asian countries that they have learned a 'special trick' to grow more rapidly that is worthy of emulation by the other poor developing countries.

Table 6.2. Economic Growth in Asian Tigers (Per cent per annum)

	Hong Kong (1966-1990)	Singapore (1966-1990)	South Korea (1966-1990)	Taiwan (1966-1990)
Growth in GDP per capita (per annum)	5.7	6.8	6.8	6.7
Change in labour force participation (%)	38 → 49	27 → 51	27 →36	28 →37
Change in Secondary Education or higher (%)	27.2 →71.4	15.8 → 66.3	26.5 → 75.0	25.8 → 67.6
TFP growth (%)	2.3	0.2	1.7	2.6

Source : Alwyn Young, "The *Tyranny of Numbers*: Confronting the Statistical Realities of the East Asian Growth Experience" *Quarterly Journal of Economics*, August 1995.

However, some economists, especially Alwyn Young have found that there are no '*special tricks*' used by these countries to achieve remarkably high rates of growth in per capita income. Instead, *they have relied on well-known factors determining growth, namely, using more labour input, saving and investing more, and expanding education of workforce and thereby building more human capital. An important fact about determinants of growth in four East Asian countries which is noteworthy is that growth in total factor productivity* (TFP) (by which technical progress is generally measured) has been high but not remarkably high. From the data about these variables of growth of these so called *Asian Tigers* in Table 6.2. it will be seen that all these four countries have remarkably high growth rates in GDP per capita but their growth is explained by increased inputs (that is, by use of more labour input, more human capital, (*i.e.*, increase in education) and correspondingly more physical capital) and not by much higher increase in total factor productivity (TFP). It may be noted that change in total factor productivity measures the change in output per unit increase in inputs and represents technological progress. Although the change in total factor productivity in these countries (except Singapore) is high but not remarkably high and therefore cannot explain remarkably high growth rate in per capita GDP. Total factor productivity growth rate in Singapore has been very small but still its growth in per capita GDP has been very high (6.8 per cent per annum).

It will be seen from Table 6.2 that in all these four countries there has been a very large increase in labour force participation rate indicating use of more labour input in the production of goods and services. *It is noteworthy that much of this increase in labour force participation rate has been due*

10 In contrast, it may be noted that annual growth rate of per capita income in India during this period (1965-90) was only about 2 to 2.5 per cent.

to more women joining the labour force. Each of these countries increased greatly its human capital. In fact education level of these countries reached close to those of rich industrialized countries.

Another important feature of these East Asian countries is that *they have pursued outward-looking development strategy* (*i.e.*, promoting exports to generate growth) and followed *laissez-faire* free market policies with emphasis on competition as driving force of growth with the exception of Singapore where Government played a significant role in regulating and controlling private enterprise and direction of investment. Moreover, Singapore relied more on foreign direct investment to bring in new technologies.

To sum up, in the history of economic development of *these four Asian Tigers have achieved extraordinary growth rates, and that too with the well-known way through using more labour input, more investment in capital, both physical and human and fostering competition*. It is reassuring to note that once these poor countries will soon catch up with the developed industrialized countries in per capita income level. Singapore has already achieved per capita income level of the rich industrialized nations of the world. The· other poor developing countries like India can get lessons from the growth experience of these countries to catch up with the developed countries.

Chapter 7

Capital Formation: Determinants and Acceleration

There are two important determinants of economic growth: (1) the rate of investment and (2) capital-output ratio. These factors were brought out by the growth models of Harrod and Domar. Therefore, if it is desired to step up the rate of economic growth, the rate of investment or capital formation should be raised and capital-output ratio should be lowered. An important factor which determines capital-output ratio in the economy is the technology that is being used for production in agriculture, industry and other activities. If the economy makes progress in technology, capital-output ratio will be lowered. It follows that rate of economic growth depends upon rate of investment or capital accumulation and technological progress. In the present chapter we shall discuss determinants of capital formation and measures to accelerate it. In Chapter 6 we have already discussed technological change and its effect on productivity and growth.

Meaning of Capital Formation

Capital formation means the increase in the stock of real capital in a country. In other words, capital formation involves making of more capital goods as machines, tools, factories, transport equipment, materials, electricity, etc., which are all used for further production of goods. Thus, Prof. Gill defines capital accumulation in the following words: "*Capital accumulation is the process of adding to our stock of machinery, tools, buildings, and so on, over time. If our stock of capital at the end of the year is larger than it was at the beginning, the difference represents the amount of capital we have accumulated during the year. Another name for this is investment. Annual real investment is the addition to our capital stock over the course of a year*".[1] Emphasising that for making additions to the stock of capital, saving and investment are essential, Ragnar Nurkse has defined capital formation as follows:

"The meaning of 'Capital Formation' is that society does not apply the whole of its current productive activity to the needs and desires of immediate consumption, but directs a part of it to the making of capital goods; tools and instruments, machines, and transport facilities, plant and equipment—all the various forms of real capital that can so greatly increase the efficacy of productive effort.... The essence of the process, then, is the diversion of a part of society's currently available resources to the purpose of increasing the stock of capital goods so as to make possible an expansion of consumable output in the future."[2]

Likewise, Professor J.R. Hicks remarks, "The way by which capital equipment is increased is the use of some part of the community's productive power during a period for the construction of new equipment (investment)."[3] It is thus evident that in order to accumulate capital goods some current consumption has to be sacrificed. The greater the extent that people are willing to abstain from present consumption, the greater the extent that society will devote resources to new capital

1 Richard T. Gill, *Economic Development : Past and Present*, 3rd edition, p. 14.

2 Ragnar Nurkse, *Problems of Capital Formation in Underdeveloped Countries*, p. 2.

3 J.R. Hicks, *The Social Framework*, p. 55.

formation. If society consumes all what it produces and saves nothing, future productive capacity of the economy will fall as the present capital equipment wears out. In other words, if whole of the current productive capacity is used to produce consumer goods and no new capital goods are made, production of consumer goods in the future will greatly decline. To cut down some of the consumption and to wait for more consumption in the future requires foresightedness on the part of the people. There is an old Chinese proverb: "He who cannot see beyond the dawn will have much good wine to drink at noon, much green wine to cure his headache at dusk, and only rain water to drink for the rest of days."

Widening of Capital and Deepening of Capital

A community could just go on building more transport facilities, more sources of power, more factories of the *existing type*. This process of duplicating capital of the existing technique is called "*widening of capital*", in contrast with "*deepening of capital*" which implies use of more capital-intensive techniques. In fact, capital accumulation and technological progress go hand in hand. Technological improvement is virtually impossible without capital accumulation. This is because new capital has to be built up according to the new superior techniques of production and since superior techniques are of higher capital intensity, larger investment has to be made. Thus, no nation which is not willing either to save or to get foreign aid for greater investment will enjoy the fruits of the advanced techniques and capital accumulation.

Accumulation of Human Capital

We have explained above the concept of *accumulation of physical capital*. For a long time in economics, it was thought that it was the physical capital which played a crucial role in expanding production. In recent years, a new concept of '*human capital*' has been evolved and emphasized. *By human capital is meant the stock of people equipped with education, skills, good health*, etc. It has now been found that the rate of growth achieved in the developed countries cannot be wholly explained by the increases in physical capital and advances in technology. A good part of economic growth has occurred due to the accumulation of human capital. It has now been realised that human capital formation is as important in increasing production and productivity as the physical capital formation. An educated, trained and skilled man is much more productive than an uneducated, untrained and unskilled man. Likewise, a person with good health contributes to production to a greater degree than the person with frail and poor health. Since the investment in education, skill and health adds greatly to the productivity of men, investment in human capital has also been called *investment in men*, or *investment in human beings*.

ROLE OF CAPITAL FORMATION IN ECONOMIC GROWTH

Capital plays a vital role in the modern productive system. Production without capital is hard for us even to imagine. Nature cannot furnish goods and materials to man unless he has the tools and machinery for mining, farming, forestry, fishing, etc. If man had to work with his hands on barren soil, productivity would be very low indeed. Even in the primitive stage, man used some tools and implements to assist him in the work of production. Primitive man made use of elementary tools like bow and arrow for hunting and fishing net for catching fishes. With the growth of technology and specialisation, capital has become more complex and is of superior and advanced type. More goods can be produced with the aid of capital. In fact, greater productivity of the developed economies like that of USA is mainly due to the extensive use of capital, *i.e.* machinery, tools or implements in the productive process. Capital adds greatly to the productivity of worker and hence of the economy as a whole.

Much economic development is not possible without making and using of industrial machinery, making of agricultural tools and implements, building of dams, bridges, factories, roads, railways, airports, ships, ports, harbours, etc., which are all capital. All these capital goods are man-made instruments of production and *increase the productive capacity* of the economy. Therefore, accumulation of capital goods every year greatly increases the national product or income. Capital accumulation is necessary to provide people with tools and implements of production. If the population goes on increasing and no net capital accumulation takes place, then the growing population would not be able to get necessary tools, instruments, machines and other means of production with the result that their capacity to produce would be seriously affected.

Besides this, *capital, accumulation makes possible the use of indirect or roundabout methods of production* which greatly increase the productivity of the workers. Under these indirect or roundabout methods of production, workers instead of working with bare hands, work with the aid of more productive tools, instruments and machinery. Under these indirect or roundabout methods some workers and other productive resources are first employed in producing capital goods and then with the help of these capital goods workers produce consumer goods. The greater the extent to which the methods of production would be indirect or roundabout, the greater their productivity and efficiency. But, as we have seen above, for the use of indirect or roundabout methods of production capital has to be accumulated. Therefore, we see that capital accumulation makes the use of indirect or roundabout methods of production possible and thereby greatly increases the national product and is helpful in bringing about rapid economic growth.

Moreover, *productivity of the workers depends upon the amount of capital per worker.* The greater the quantity of capital per worker, the greater the productivity of the worker. It is not capital accumulation alone that increases the amount of capital per worker. Capital per worker rises when the rate of capital accumulation is greater than the rate of population growth. With the increase in capital per worker, productivity per worker will increase with the result that national product and income will increase. Therefore, capital accumulation, by increasing the productivity of the workers, plays an important role in the growth of the economy.

From the viewpoint of economic growth capital formation is important also because *it makes large-scale production and greater degree of specialisation possible.* Thus, with capital accumulation the *advantages of large-scale production and specialisation* are obtained. The advantage of large-scale production and specialisation is that they greatly increase output and productivity and thereby bring down the *cost of production per unit.* Without adequate capital accumulation neither the scale of production can be increased nor greater specialisation and division of labour in the production process is possible. Hence, capital accumulation by enlarging the scale of production and specialisation increases the production and productivity in the economy and thereby promotes economic growth.

Another way in which capital accumulation contributes to growth is that *it makes the technological progress of the economy* possible. Different technologies need different types of capital goods. Therefore, when new, superior and better technology is discovered, its use can be made for production only if that technology is embodied in capital goods, that is, if capital goods according to that technology are made. Therefore, without capital accumulation, no technical progress can be made. If there is no capital accumulation, then the various new inventions or discoveries will remain unused for production. If is, therefore, clear that capital accumulation promotes technical progress in the country and through this accelerates the economic growth of the country.

Another important economic role of capital formation is the *creation of employment opportunities* in the country. Capital formation creates employment at two stages. First, when the capital is produced, some workers have to be employed to make capital like machinery, factories, dams, irrigation works, etc. Secondly, more men have to be employed when capital has to be used for producing further goods. In other words, many workers have to be engaged to produce goods with the help of machines, factories, etc. Thus, one sees that employment will increase as capital formation is stepped up in the economy. Now, if the population grows faster than the increase in the stock of capital, the entire addition to the labour force cannot be absorbed in productive employment because not enough instruments of production will be there to employ them. This results in unemployment. The rate of capital formation must be kept sufficiently high so that employment opportunities are enlarged to absorb the additions to the working force of the country as a result of population growth. In India the stock of capital has not been growing at a fast enough rate so as to keep pace with the growth of population. That is why there is huge unemployment and underemployment in both the urban and rural areas. The fundamental solution to this problem of unemployment and underemployment is to speed up the rate of capital formation so as to enlarge employment opportunities.

Role of Capital: Diagrammatic Illustration

A diagrammatic illustration will make it clear as to how a greater rate of capital accumulation steps up the growth rate and also what it costs to the society. A given amount of resources has to be distributed between the production of consumer goods and capital goods. But, the greater the amount of resources that are invested in production of capital goods, the smaller quantity of resources will be left for the production of consumer goods. Thus, greater accumulation and therefore greater rate of economic growth comes at the cost of present consumption. Of course, with greater rate of growth, the productive capacity and consumption in the future years will increase, but greater capital accumulation means less consumption in the present. This is what is generally described as "more jam tomorrow means less jam today". But, as said above, if a poor country wants to raise the standards of living of its people, it must step up its rate of economic growth through greater investment of resources in the production of capital goods. Consider Fig. 7.1 in which the *X*-axis measures consumers' goods and the *Y*-axis measure capital goods. With a given amount of resources we have drawn a production possibility curve *PP*′. Suppose the allocation of resources between the consumers' goods and capital goods is such that the economy is operating at point *D* on the production possibility curve so that it is producing *OC* amount of consumers' goods and *OK* amount of capital goods. With the capital accumulation the productive capacity of the economy will increase and as a result the production possibility curve will shift outwards. If the same *proportion* of resources continues to be allocated to the production of capital goods, the economy will be growing at a certain rate, say 2% as is indicated by the ray *OA*.

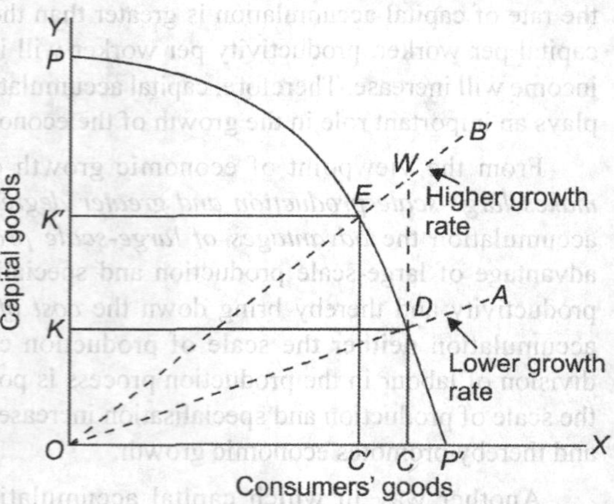

Fig. 7.1. *Capital formation and economic growth*

Now, if the economy wants to step up the rate of economic growth, say to 3%, it will have to allocate a greater proportion of its resources towards the production of capital goods than before. Thus when the economy is operating at point *D* on production possibility curve *PP*′, and wants to build up more capital, it will have to allocate more resources to the production of capital goods and less to the production of consumer goods. Suppose the economy reallocates its resources so that it produces *OK*′ capital goods and *OC*′ consumer goods on the production possibility curve *PP*′. It is clear from the figure that with greater capital accumulation, the production of consumer goods has fallen from *OC* to *OC*′. Therefore, consumption will have to be cut down for the sake of more capital.

But greater capital accumulation will mean greater growth of productive capacity with the result that production possibility curve will shift outwards more rapidly and if the same higher proportion of resources continues to be allocated, the economy will be having a higher rate of economic growth, say 3%, and will move along the ray *OB*.

Cost of Capital Formation. It is thus clear from above that the process of capital accumulation and economic growth is not a painless job. The price for it has to be paid and this price is paid in terms of the reduction in present consumption. But it should be remembered that greater capital formation will more than compensate this loss of present consumption. Thus, in our figure, when the economy has chosen the growth path of ray *OB* by having greater capital accumulation, then after some years it will reach point *W at which the consumption is OC*. Thus, at point *W*, the previous level of consumption has been restored. As the economy keeps up its higher rate of capital accumulation and moves along the growth path *OB* beyond *W*, it will be having higher consumption than along the growth path *OA*.

Role of Capital: A Dissenting View

It is generally agreed among economists that capital accumulation rate and economic growth are closely correlated. In Harrod-Domar models of economic growth as well as Lewis' model of "*economic development with unlimited supplies of labour*"[4], capital accumulation plays a crucial role in raising both output and employment. However, some economists have objected to such a great emphasis and importance being given to the physical capital. Thus, Professor Cairncross remarks, "There is a great danger that the importance of capital in relation to economic progress will be exaggerated than that it will be underrated."[5] According to Prof. Cairncross, the rate of economic growth achieved in developed countries cannot be wholly explained by increases in labour and physical capital. He points out that *technological progress has played a more important role than accumulation of physical capital in the process of economic growth*. According to him, only one quarter of the rate of economic growth can be explained with the accumulation of physical capital. To quote him, *"There seems no reason to suppose that capital accumulation does by itself exercise so predominant an influence on economic development. In most industrialized communities the rate of capital accumulation out of savings is equal to about 10 per cent of income.* If one were to assume that innovation came to a standstill and that additional investment could nevertheless yield an average return of 5 per cent, the consequential rate of increase in the national income would normally be not more than ½ per cent per annum. We are told that the national income has in fact been rising in such communities at a rate of 2.3 per cent per annum. On this showing, capital accumulation could account for, at most, one-quarter of the recorded rate of economic progress. Nor were things very different in the nineteenth century."[6]

A.K. Cairncross thinks that capital accumulation need not necessarily take place along with technological progress. Technological progress can occur independently of any net capital accumulation. What is needed is that the funds kept for depreciation may be used for building up new assets and capital equipment, embodying new technology. He points out that new capital equipment embodying new advanced technology may even cost less and therefore technological progress is possible even with decline in physical capital. Moreover, Prof. Cairncross thinks that besides technological progress, improvements in social and economic organisation, trained management, new attitudes, play an important role in raising production and promoting economic growth as the accumulation of physical capital. The process of economic development, according to him, "is a complex situation and it may exist in some underdeveloped countries. But it is by no means

4 Arthur Lewis, "Economic Development with Unimited Supplies of Labour", *The Manchester School*, 1954

5 A.K. Cairncross, "The Place of Capital in Economic Progress", printed in G. Meier, *Leading Issues in Economic Development*, 2nd edition, 1971.

6 *Ibid.*

obvious that additional capital, whether borrowed from abroad or accumulated through the exertions of surplus labour in the countryside, would by itself suffice to start off a cycle of industrialization. The problem is often one of organisation quite as much as of capital creation: of training management and men, of creating new attitudes towards industrial employment, of taking advantage of innovations that need little capital and using the resulting gains to finance investment elsewhere."

We agree with Prof. Cairncross that technological progress, human capital, *improvements in economic organisation, trained management.* etc. are also important factors in economic growth. However, the crucial importance of physical capital also cannot be denied. In our view, both physical and various forms of human capital are important in promoting economic growth.[7]

DETERMINANTS OF CAPITAL FORMATION

From above it is clear that saving is essential for capital formation. But, in a monetary economy, savings do not directly and automatically result in the production of capital goods. Savings must be invested in order to have capital goods. In a modern economy where savings and investment are done mainly by two different classes of people, there must be certain means or mechanism whereby savings of the people are obtained and mobilised in order to give them to businessmen or entrepreneurs to invest in capital goods. Therefore, in the modern free-market economy, the process of capital formation consists of the following three stages:

(*i*) An increase in the rate of real savings so that resources that would have been devoted to the production of consumption goods should be released for the purpose of capital formation.

(*ii*) Existence of a good financial system so that the available resources are obtained by private investors for capital formation.

(*iii*) The act of investment itself so that resources are actually used for the production of capital goods.

Rate of Saving

Savings in India are classified into three groups:

1. Household Savings;
2. Corporate Savings; and
3. Government Savings.

We discuss below these categories of savings and the factors determining them.

Household Savings. Household savings comprise savings of all households and individuals, both rural and urban, and non-corporate business undertakings, partnerships and non-profitable institutions like charitable trusts. Households save when they do not spend all their incomes on consumer goods. When individuals or households save, they release resources from the production of consumer goods. Resources (workers, capital, natural resources, materials, etc.) thus released are made available for the production of capital goods. The level of savings in a country depends upon *the power to save and the will to save*. The savings of the households are either in the form of *financial assets* like bank deposits, shares, bonds, provident fund, life insurance policies, national saving certificates etc, or in the form of *physical assets* such as various capital goods, houses, etc.

Level of Per Capita Income and Distribution of Income. The power to save or saving capacity of an economy mainly depends upon the level of per capita income and *the distribution of national*

7 In fact in new growth theory human capital is clubbed with physical capital to make up a single factor called '*Capital*'.

income. The greater the level of per capita income, the greater will be the amount of savings. The countries having higher levels of per capita income can save more than those with low levels of income. That is why the rate of savings in U.S.A. and Western European countries is much higher than that in developing and poor countries like India. Further, the greater the inequalities of income, the greater will be the amount of savings in the economy. If the national income is equally distributed, much of the income will be consumed and a little would be saved. On the contrary, if national income is unequally distributed, a larger amount of savings will be done by richer people.

Apart from the power to save, the total amount of savings depends upon the will to save. Various personal, family, or national considerations induce the people to save. People save in order to provide against old age and unforeseen contingencies. Some people desire to save a large sum to start their own business or to expand the existing business. Moreover, people want to make provision for education, marriages and a good start in business for their children.

Rate of Inflation. Another important factor which determines the household saving in the country is the price situation. In the economy when there is high inflation rate or prices are continuously rising, value of money declines. The rise in prices or the fall in the value of money has an adverse effect on the savings in the economy. When the value of money is declining every year due to the rise in prices, it is not profitable to save money and, therefore, propensity to save diminishes. Besides, inflation or rise in prices reduces the capacity to save of the people because a greater part of income has to be spent on essential consumption due to the rise in prices.

Growth Rate of per Capita Income. In addition to the current level of per capita income, *growth rate of per capita income* as emphasised by life cycle theory of consumption and saving is also an important determinant of household saving. If income per capita is not growing, the task of raising the marginal rate of saving is likely to be difficult because more saving in this case has to be achieved by curtailing present consumption. If per capita income is rising due to increase in productivity, it becomes possible to save relatively more out of increment in income and thereby rate of saving can be increased while increasing absolute consumption at the same time. It is noteworthy that the growth in per capita income can occur if investment in physical capital and human capital or its productivity increases. A higher rate of saving ensures higher rate of investment and thereby generates higher growth in per capita income. But the reverse is also true; a higher growth rate in per capita makes it possible to raise the rate of saving by keeping marginal rate of saving higher than average rate of saving.

Policies to Restrain Growth in Consumption. To increase the rate of saving deliberate policies to restrain the growth of consumption have also been adopted. For example, in India prior to mid –1980s industrial licensing was actively used to ensure that there was no more investment in luxury durable consumer goods like automobiles, colour TVs, air conditioners, refrigerators except in small scale sectors and existing factories. Heavy excise duties were levied on consumer goods, especially durable ones, to discourage their production. Besides, to restrain the consumption of durable consumers goods heavy tariffs were levied on imports of such goods or imports of such goods were prohibited. It may however be noted that policies of using physical controls and detailed industrial licensing obstructed the rate of industrial growth. Therefore, in India in the beginning of the Sixth Plan (1980–85) output projections for the plan periods were based on consumption requirements of the people and physical controls on the production and consumption of goods were liberalised to step up economic growth.

Interest Rate Policy. To promote savings, policy of following positive real interest rate has been suggested by several economists. Positive real rate of interest has been suggested for raising household savings. Real rate of interest rate is nominal rate of interest rate minus rate of inflation. Advocates of the policy of real rate of interest argue that negative real interest rate will divert savings to informal financial markets, unproductive investment (such as gold, jewellery, luxurious houses) and will cause flight of capital from the country. Therefore, for promoting savings nominal rate of interest should be kept above rate of inflation. Positive real rate of interest also ensures efficient utilisation of resources, particularly scarce capital. Though rise in positive real rate of interest causes the *financial savings* to increase, there is no firm evidence about its positive effect on the increase in *overall savings* of the economy.

Table 7.1. Savings and Investment in India

(As per cent of GDP at current market prices)

	GDCF	GDS	Public Savings	Private Savings	Household Savings	Private Corporate Savings
Average 1985-90	22.7	20.4	2.4	18.0	16.0	2.0
1990-91	26.3	23.1	1.1	22.0	19.3	2.7
1991-92	22.6	22.0	2.0	20.1	17.0	3.1
1992-93	23.6	21.8	1.6	20.2	17.5	2.7
1993-94	23.1	22.5	0.6	21.9	18.4	3.5
1994-95	26.0	24.8	1.7	23.2	19.7	3.5
1995-96	26.9	25.1	2.0	23.1	18.2	4.9
1996-97	24.5	23.2	1.7	21.5	17.0	4.5
1997-98	24.6	23.1	1.3	21.8	17.6	4.2
1998-99	22.7	21.5	–1.0	22.5	18.8	3.7
1999-2000	25.4	24.9	–0.9	25.7	21.3	4.5
2000-2001	23.9	23.5	–1.8	25.3	21.2	4.1
2001-2002	22.2	23.5	–2.0	25.5	22.1	3.4
2002-2003	25.0	26.4	–0.6	27.0	23.2	3.9
2003-2004	27.7	29.8	1.1	28.7	24.4	4.4
2004-2005	32.8	32.4	2.3	30.1	23.6	6.6
2005-06	33.7	33.5	2.4	31.0	23.5	7.5
2006-07	35.7	34.6	3.6	31.0	23.2	7.9
2007-08	38.1	36.8	5.0	31.9	22.5	9.4
2008-09	34.3	32.0	1.0	31.0	23.6	7.4
2009-10	36.5	33.7	0.2	33.6	25.2	8.4
2010-11	36.5	33.7	2.6	31.1	23.1	8.0
2011-12	35.5	31.3	1.2	30.1	22.8	7.3
1012-13	34.8	30.1	1.2	29.0	21.9	7.1

Public Savings. Public Savings are another source of savings. In Government savings are included the surplus of revenue obtained through taxes and surpluses from public undertakings over and above the current expenditure of the Government. Given the current consumption expenditure of the Government, the greater the revenue collected from taxes and the profits earned from public enterprises, the greater the Government or public savings. It is worth noting that all revenue earned from taxes, etc. does not constitute the public savings because a good part of the tax revenue is spent on current consumption expenditure of the Government such as civil administration, defence and other unproductive services. That part of income or revenue of the Government which is over and above the expenditure on civil administration, defence and other current consumption is called the public savings. The Government savings are used for public investment spending on building of factories, roads, irrigation facilities, and other various types of industries started by the Government.

In India public savings of both Centre and State governments was around 2.9 per cent of GDP at market price in 1970-71, it reached its peak of 4.9 per cent of GDP in 1976-77 and started declining thereafter and in 1989-90, it fell to 1.6 per cent of G.D.P. The decline in *budgetary savings* of government as distinguished from those of public enterprises was relatively much higher. It is noteworthy that trends in fiscal deficit determine the performance in public savings.

Table 7.1 shows that public savings increased to 2.0 per cent of GDP in 1995-96, the year in which revenue deficit was at the lowest mark in the nineties. Subsequently, with the increase in revenue deficit, public savings declined and even became negative. Had the household savings not increased during this period, this would have led to the decline in gross domestic saving (GDS) and would have adversely affected investment and economic growth in the economy.

However, after 2003-04 there was appreciable increase in public saving as will be seen from Table 7.1. Rate of public saving as per cent of GDP which was –0.6% in 2002-03 became positive after it. In 2003-04 it was 1.1 per cent which went on increasing and in 2007-08 it was at peak of 5 per cent of GDP. This accounts for large increase in overall gross domestic saving (GDS) and Gross Domestic Capital Formation (GDCF). On account of this large increase in gross domestic saving and capital formation rate of growth of GDP rose above 9 per cent in three successive years, 2005-08, and the Indian economy became the second highest growing economy of the world. It is worth noting that to prevent global financial crisis (2008-09) from causing drastic decline in economic growth, the Indian Government reduced its several taxes and increased its expenditure to provide fiscal stimulus to the Indian economy. As a result, revenue deficit increased and public saving drastically declined to 1.0 per cent of GDP in 2008-09, 0.2 per cent in 2009-10 but rose to 2.6% in 2010-11.

The huge combined fiscal deficit of the Centre and the States which presently constitutes about 10 per cent of Gross Domestic Product is adversely affecting saving and investment in the economy and therefore the rate of economic growth of the Indian economy. To quote Shankar Acharya, a former economic advisor to the Ministry of Finance, "It is quite interesting how the deterioration of about 3 per cent points of GDP in the consolidated revenue deficit between 1995-96 and 1998-99 is reflected strongly in the worsening of aggregate saving and investment ratios over the period. It would be hard to find more telling evidence of the adverse impact of fiscal deficit on savings and investment. Another way to look at this is that if the fiscal deficit deterioration since1995-96 had not occurred, saving and investment might well have been higher by around 3 per cent points of GDP in recent years."[8]

The above analysis underlines the importance of measures to reduce fiscal deficit, particularly revenue deficit, if rate of saving and investment in the Indian economy is to be raised to accelerate the rate of economic growth. For this purpose base of taxation must be widened by withdrawing the several exemptions in income and wealth taxes as suggested by various committees.[9] Besides, the subsidies must be well targeted so that only the poor should take advantage of them and the remaining subsidies must be phased out. Further, to reduce revenue deficit, non-plan non-essential government expenditure must be reduced along with the reforms in the taxation system. However, care should be taken to avoid any cut in Government expenditure on education and health which promote accumulation of human capital and have beneficial effect on economic growth.

It may be pointed out that savings may be either voluntary or forced. Voluntary savings are those which people make of their own free will. As explained above, voluntary savings depend upon the power to save and will to save of the people. On the other hand, taxes by the Government represent forced savings.

Private Corporate Sector Savings. Furthermore, savings may be done not only by households and Government but also by corporate business enterprises corporate business enterprises save when they do not distribute whole of their profits but retain a part of them in the form of undistributed profits. They then use these undistributed profits for investment in real capital. In advanced countries like U.S.A. and England, these corporate savings form the

8 Shankar Acharya, "Macroeconomic Management in the Nineties", *Economic and Political Weekly*, April, 20, 2000, p. 1525.

9 Recently Kelkar Committee has recommended reforms in taxation system on these lines.

largest part of the total savings. In U.S.A. and England, corporate savings, *i.e.*, undistributed profits constitute about 50% to 60% of the total annual domestic savings. Note that *savings of unincorporated business enterprises are included in household savings*. Business savings of private corporate sector in India are shown separately in Table 7.1. It will be seen from this table that the private corporate sector, which operates in the organised sector, though contribute significantly to Gross National Product, their saving makes only a small contribution to gross domestic savings. The corporate sector savings which contributed on an annual average of 2.0 per cent of GDP to gross domestic saving in 1990-91 reached its peak in 1995-96 when their savings constituted 4.9 per cent of GDP. Thereafter it declined to 3.4 per cent of GDP in 2001-02 and to 3.9 per cent in 2002-03. The lower corporate saving was attributed to high rental cost of capital (including high real rate of interest), high corporate tax rate, high rates of excise duties, tax on dividend distribution, inefficiency in use of investment funds and underutilisation of production capacity. Liberalisation regime initiated in India since 1991 providing for reduction in tariff rates on imported raw materials, reduction in corporate tax, and excise duties resulted in higher corporate saving in 1995-96 and 1997-98. Recently, lowering of lending interest rates as a result of soft interest rate policy also boosted the profits of corporate sector and therefore since 2002-2003 corporate saving has tended to rise (See Table 7.1). Corporate sector saving rose from 4.4% of GDP in 2003-04 to 6.6% in 2004-05, to 7.5% in 2005-06 and 7.9% in 2006-07 and further rose to 9.4% in 2007-08. The global financial crisis in 2008-09 affected the saving of the corporate sector which declined to 7.4 per cent in 2008-09, 8.4% per cent in 2009-10 and 8% in 2010-11.

Financial System

Next step in the process of capital formation is that the savings of households must be mobilised and transferred to businessmen or entrepreneurs who require them for investment. In the capital market, funds are supplied by the individual investors (who may buy securities or shares issued by the companies). Banks, investment trusts, life insurance companies, finance corporations, are other financial institutions which mobilise savings for investment purposes. In India there is also unorganised capital market constituting indigenous bankers and money-lenders. One reason responsible for the low rate of capital formation in India has been the absence of well-developed capital market. Indian capital is said to be very shy. If the rate of capital formation in the private sector is to be stepped up, the development of financial system is very necessary. Well-developed financial market will ensure that the savings of the society will be mobilised and transferred to the entrepreneurs or businessmen who require them for investment.

Investment

For savings to result in capital formation and economic growth they must be invested. In order that investment of savings should take place, there must be a good number of honest and dynamic entrepreneurs in a country who are willing to take risks and bear uncertainty of production. Given that a country has got enough good and venturesome entrepreneurs, investment will be made by them only if there is sufficient *inducement to invest*. Inducement to invest depends on *marginal efficiency of capital*, *i.e.*, rate of return or profit on the one hand, and real rate of interest on the other. If prospects about profit are quite bright, that is, when entrepreneurs expect large profits from investment, investment will be made on a large scale. If profits are expected to be low, investment made will also be small. It is generally believed that at a lower real rate of interest, investment is more and at a higher real rate of interest, investment is less. In other words, it means that when credit is cheaper, businessmen will borrow more funds for investment purposes.

Of the two determinants of inducement to investment, namely, marginal efficiency of capital and the rate of interest, it is the former which is of greater importance. Marginal efficiency of capital depends upon the *cost or supply price of capital* as well as the *expectations of profits*. Fluctuations in investment are mainly due to the changes in expectations regarding profits. But it is *the size of market* (*i.e.*, demand for goods) which determines the scope for profitable investment. Thus primary factor which determines the level of investment or capital formation in an economy is the *size of market* for goods. Demand for capital equipment like machinery depends upon the demand for goods it helps to produce. The inducement to invest is limited by the size of the market *i.e.* the demand for the goods. The greater the size of the market, the greater will be the inducement to invest. The small size of the market will discourage the entrepreneurs to make investment. All poor countries have a small market in everything and this is a great hurdle in the way of capital formation in underdeveloped countries.

Animal Spirits and Investment. J.M. Keynes who emphasised that marginal efficiency of capital played a crucial role in determining investment also laid stress on animal spirits of entrepreneurs for causing fluctuations in investment. By animal spirits Keynes means the waves of optimism and pessimism which quite often grip business class and greatly affect their investment behaviour. Keynes attributed the drastic fall in private investment in 1929-33 to the collapse of marginal efficiency of capital which was caused by wave of pessimism among the business class which resulted in stock market crash in England. Even in India today lack of confidence among business class resulting from their animal spirits is responsible for slowdown in private investment since 1997.

Public Investment in Infrastructure. Private investment is also affected by the availability of infrastructure such as power, good roads and means of transport, good means of communication, good ports, etc. Slowdown in the Indian economy since 1996-97 is also partly due to lack of good infrastructure. It has therefore been suggested that *public investment in infrastructure not only generates demand for the industrial products but also leads* to the expansion of infrastructural facilities such as power, ports, roads etc. Thus, in the Indian context public investment helps to solve both the supply-side and demand-side problems of private sector investment. Therefore, in India the greater public investment *crowds in* private investment rather than *crowding it out*.

Taxation Policies. Taxation policies of the Government also affect investment behaviour of the corporate sector. High corporate taxes discourage private investment. For example, high corporation income tax, tax on dividend distribution, high excise duties and tariffs adversely affect corporate sector investment by lowering the profitability of investment. Therefore, to increase corporate investment, investment-friendly taxation policies need to be adopted.

Availability of Credit. Apart from internal savings, the corporate sector gets investment funds from the capital market and banks. To meet their needs for working capital they rely on bank credit. Therefore, to ensure greater private investment adequate credit facilities must be made available.

Improvement of Stock Market. Besides, corporate sector raises its equity capital from the stock market. Therefore, the working of stock markets must be improved and made fair and transparent, so that public should have confidence in fair dealings at the stock market. For instance, stock market crash in 1992 engineered by Harshad Mehta and later by Ketan Parikh and scams involving UTI have badly shaken the confidence of small investors who have withdrawn from the market. This has created difficulties for private corporate sector for riasing investment funds from the stock market through issue of equity capital.

Size of Market or Level of Demand

Ragnar Nurkse in his now well-known work, '*Problems of Capital Formation in Underdeveloped Countries*' emphasized *size of market* (that is, *level of demand*) for a commodity is an important determinants of capital formation in developing countries. Furthermore, according to him, size of market for a commodity is determined by levels of incomes of the people. Since the production of industrial commodities in the modern times requires installation of machinery and other capital equipment which have large productive capacity. Therefore, making investment in them to be profitable there should be sufficient size of market or demand for that industrial commodity. According to Nurkse, since because of poverty in underdeveloped countries per capital income of the people is low, there will not be enough demand for an industrial product and as a result productive capacity created will remain underutilised. Therefore, it will not be profitable to make investment in the machinery and other capital equipment for the production of the commodity. Thus limited size of the market in underdeveloped countries lowers inducement to invest in them to overcome this problem of limited size of the market for commodities. Nurkse suggested '*balanced growth strategy*' under which *simultaneous investment* in a large number of industries be made so that the workers employed in various industries create demand for each other's product. We will discuss the issue of linked size of market adversely affecting inducement to invest and Nurkse's balanced growth strategy in detail in a later chapter.

Saving, Capital Formation and Economic Growth in India

In India also capital formation or rate of investment has played a significant role in generating higher economic growth rate. The higher annual growth rate of 5.8 per cent per annum during the eighties was due to higher rate of investment or capital formation as compared to the earlier decades of planned development which witnessed only 3.5 per cent average growth rate per annum.

The 1900s represent a very important period in economic growth in India because far reaching economic reforms of liberalisation and privatisation were carried out during this period. As will be seen from Table 7.2, leaving the first two years as they represent the transition period of crisis and adjustment, in the post-reform period, the growth rate in 1992-93 to 1996-97 has been quite higher (6.6 per cent average annual growth rate) as campared to 5.8 per cent in the pre-reform period. This was due to pick-up in corporate saving and investment following the abolition of industrial licensing and reduction in rental cost of capital due to reduction in tariffs on imports of raw materials, and reduction in corporate taxes which increased the profitability of private investment.

However, after 1996, higher growth rate could not be maintained and in fact Indian economy went into recession despite the continuation of economic reforms. Two factors were responsible for it. First, following the structural adjustment reforms and the need to contain fiscal deficit public investment declined between 1997-98 and 2002-03. This adversely affected the overall growth in GDP as well as the industrial growth through both adverse supply-side and demand-side factors. It will be seen from Table 7.2 that between 1992-93 and 1996-97 higher average GDP growth rate of around 6.5 per cent per annum was achieved mainly due to higher rate of gross domestic capital formation (GDCF). In the late nineties and and up till 2002-03 when investment or GDCF was less especially due to decline in public investment, growth rate of GDP also fell.

After 2003 when both public investment and private investment had picked up, growth rate of GDP rose to over 9 per cent per annum during the three years (2005-08). Now in the Eleventh Five Year (2007-12) period the average 8 per cent growth in GDP per annum was achieved. This was considered feasible as gross doemstic saving rate (GDS) had gone up to 36.4 per cent and gross domestic capital formation (GDCF) per annum in 2007-08. However, the impact of global financial crisis (2008-09) brought down the growth rate of GDP to 6.7% in 2008-09 and to 8.6% in 2009-10 and to 8.9% in 2010-11. However, for the reasons explained below, for 2011-12, estimate for GDP growth rate is lower at 6.7 per cent.

Table 7.2. GDS, Capital Formation and GDP Growth, 1990–2011

Year	Growth of GDP	(As per cent of GDP at current market prices) GDCF	GDS
1990–91	5.6	26.3	23.1
1991–92	1.3	22.6	22.0
1992–93	5.1	23.1	21.8
1993–94	5.9	26.0	22.5
1994–95	7.3	26.9	25.1
1995–96	7.3	24.5	23.2
1996–97	7.8	24.5	23.1
1997–98	4.8	24.6	21.5
1998–99	6.5	22.7	24.1
1999–2000	6.1	25.4	24.9
2000–2001	4.4	23.9	23.5
2001–2002	5.6	22.1	23.5
2002-2003	3.8	25.0	26.4
2003-2004	8.5	27.7	29.8
2004-2005	7.5	32.7	32.2
2005-2006	9.5	34.7	33.3
2006-2007	9.6	35.7	34.5
2007-2008	9.3	38.1	36.9
2008-2009	6.7	34.5	32.2
2009-2010	8.6	36.5	33.7
2010-2011	8.9	36.5	33.7
2011-2012	6.7	35.5	31.3
2012-2013	4.5	34.8	30.1

MEASURES TO ACCELERATE CAPITAL FORMATION

As explained above, rate of capital formation is an important determinant of economic growth. Therefore, all efforts should be made to raise the rate of capital formation in the country, if the twin problems of mass poverty and unemployment are to be solved. We have also discussed the various problems, namely, the operation of vicious circles of poverty, the working of demonstration effect and the growth of wants, which come in the way of our efforts to accelerate capital formation in developing economies. These problems have to be overcome if the rate of capital formation is to be raised.

In order to raise capital formation in the economy we have first to raise *ratio of surplus to capital* or rate of surplus to national income and then measures have to be adopted to mobilize this surplus for purposes of productive investment.

Raising the Ratio of Surplus to Capital

In this connection the distinction between potential economic surplus and actual economic surplus should be borne in mind. Potential economic surplus is the difference between the national income of a country and the *essential or basic* consumption (which includes also capital replacement), while the actual economic surplus is the surplus actually achieved after spending on essential and non-essential consumption and also unproductive investment.

Now, if the ratio of actual surplus to capital is to be raised, non-productive uses of potential surplus, namely, non-essential consumption and unproductive investment have to be prevented. As has been mentioned before, in developing countries wasteful use of potential economic surplus in the form of non-essential consumption and unproductive investment is quite enormous both among private individuals and the Government. The unproductive consumption is indulged in by property owners such as big landlords and rich farmers, rich businessmen and industrialists when they spend a part of their income on luxuries such as purchase of expensive motor cars, air conditioners, construction of palatial houses, gold and jewellery, etc. The high wage earners and self-employed also indulge in luxurious consumption when they spend a good part of their income on relatively luxurious items such as costly sofa sets and other furniture, expensive clothes, wine, unnecessary entertainments and lavish expenditure on births, marriages and death ceremonies, etc. Even the Government spends a lot on unnecessary or unproductive consumption expenditure when it spends excessively on police and other administrative services, defence, large size of the ministries, liberal travelling allowances and other facilities to the officers and ministers, etc.

Productive surplus is also reduced by the various forms of unproductive investment made both by the private sector and the Government. The unproductive investment by the private sector takes place when the rich businessmen and landlords invest their incomes in real estate (*i.e.,* land), palatial houses, gold and jewellery. Likewise, even Government makes unproductive type of investment when it spends money on the construction and maintenance of luxurious hotels, office buildings, houses, parks, etc. It, therefore, follows that if the actual and productive surplus is to be raised the magnitudes of non-essential and unproductive investments are to be considerably reduced.

It may be noted that the propensity of the people of underdeveloped countries to use the economic surplus for conspicuous consumption has become stronger in recent years because of the *international demonstration effect.* The concept of international demonstration effect is that people of poor developing countries try to copy the high consumption standards of the people of affluent developed countries. As a result, unproductive or non-essential consumption of these countries increases and as a result surplus available for productive investment falls. This international demonstration effect has become quite strong these days because of the greater awareness on the part of the people in underdeveloped countries regarding the living standards of the people in rich nations. This greater awareness has emerged because of wide travel by the people of the poor countries in Western countries, propaganda and advertisement in radio, television and newspapers. Therefore, if the ratio of surplus to capital is to be raised significantly, the operation of the demonstration effect should be overcome by educating the people and also by providing various incentives for saving.

Incentives for Saving

An important measure to encourage savings and raise ratio of surplus to capital is that savings be exempted wholly or substantially from income taxes. When people know that they will not have to pay income taxes on the saved portion of their income, they will be greatly tempted not to consume a good part of their income and thereby save it. Secondly, in order to encourage savings, rates of interest on savings and time deposits with the banks be raised. In order to be able to earn more income because of higher interest rates, people will be induced to save more and make deposits in the banks. Thirdly, a great incentive for saving can be provided if the prices are prevented from rising. When the prices are continuously rising and as a result value of money is rapidly falling, it will not be worthwhile to save, for the money saved will greatly depreciate with the rise in the prices of goods.

We thus see that if proper fiscal, monetary and price policies are adopted incentives to save can be greatly increased and in this way ratio of surplus to capital can be raised. But contrary to what is required to raise the rate of saving, in India in recent years liberal loans for non-essential commodities such as purchase of cars, air conditioners, refrigerators and construction of luxury houses are being given by banks at cheap rates of interest. This tends to reduce the ratio of saving to national income.

---

10 In fact, Lewis in his famous model of "*Economic Development with Unlimited Supply of Labour*" has assumed that all profits are saved and automatically invested and all wages are consumed.

Some development economists, especially Professor Arthur Lewis, that the saving rate depends on the share of profit and wages have suggested that if the national income is distributed more in favour of profits, that is, if the share of profits in national income is greater, the saving ratio will be high and *vice versa*. This is because, according to them, recipients of profits, *i.e.*, capitalists or entrepreneurs save a major part of their income, their propensity to consume being very little.[10] On the other hand, if share of wages in national income is relatively high, the saving ratio will be low as the propensity to consume of the workers is very high. Thus, according to growth models of Kaldor, Robinson and Arthur Lewis, the saving or surplus ratio of a community depends on the relative shares of profits and wages. In order to raise the savings or surplus ratio they have proposed that wages in the modern industrial sector should be kept at a certain minimum level so that with the development of the sector, profits share goes on rising and as a result growth of investment or capital accumulation becomes cumulative. In this way they have contended to achieve the growth and employment objectives in the shortest possible time.

Though the above mentioned relation between profit share and savings ratio is generally true, it may, however, be pointed out that a good part of the profits made by the capitalists in underdeveloped countries like India are spent on luxurious consumption and unproductive investment. Therefore, if rate of capital formation is to be raised through raising share of profits in national income, the tendency on the part of the capitalists to spend profits on luxurious consumption and unproductive investment has to be effectively curbed through taking suitable monetary and fiscal measures.

Mobilisation of resources for capital formation by the Government is of crucial importance in those underdeveloped countries where public sector plays an important role in the economic development. The Government can raise the resources for capital formation in the following ways: (*a*) by imposing taxes on the people, (*b*) borrowing from the people, (*c*) by ploughing back the profits by the Government of public undertakings and (*d*) by creation of new money or borrowing from the central bank of the country which is also known as deficit financing. We explain below these various ways of mobilizing surplus or resources by the Government to finance its investment expenditure.

Taxation

Taxation is an important method of raising resources by the Government formation. Taxation increases the amount of collective savings by restricting private consumption. Thus, as a result of taxation, the people is general or private sector is forced to save for accelerating capital formation. It should, however, be noted that the total tax revenue collected by the Government does not represent savings because a good deal of tax money is spent by the Government to meet its current expenditure such as defence, police and civil administration which is similar to the private consumption expenditure of the people. Therefore, it is only the surplus of tax revenue over and above such current expenditure of the Government that represents the net savings of the Government sector. Further, even the extra government savings achieved through taxation may not constitute net addition to the aggregate savings of the country. Net addition to aggregate savings will occur only to the extent the tax payments are made by sacrificing consumption. On the contrary, if taxes are paid by the individuals and firms by reducing private savings, then the increase in public savings may not result in any net increase in overall savings.

On the other hand, it has been asserted by some economists that the marginal propensity to save of the Government out of tax revenue is lower than marginal propensity to save of the private individuals and firms. This is because the government uses a greater part of income from taxation to meet its ever increasing current expenditure. If this is so, then the taxation instead of raising overall saving will actually reduce it. If the Government is to mobilise resources for development, it has to check the growth of its non-productive expenditure.

Both direct and indirect taxes play an important part in augmenting the resources of the Government for developmental purposes. It is best to levy taxes on non-entrepreneurial incomes and goods of luxury consumption. Such taxes will curtail unnecessary consumption and will have no disincentive effect on business enterprise. Hence, in order to raise adequate amount of resources, it becomes necessary to bring increasing number of '*services*' in the tax net. In addition, taxation of agricultural incomes has to play an important part in the mobilisation of resources for the public sector in a developing economy.

Taxation plays a double role in a developing economy. On the one hand, it mobilises resources for the public sector schemes and projects. On the other hand, if the taxation structure is well designed, it can direct the flow of the resources of the economy to productive channels of investment in the private sector. By discouraging speculative activity and other types of unproductive investment and also useless and luxury consumption, taxation promotes investment to accelerate economic growth.

The level of voluntary savings in underdeveloped countries is very low and the upper classes which are in a position to save prefer to invest these savings in real estate or jewellery or they simply hoard them. The result is that such savings are not available for productive investment. In these circumstances, compulsory saving enforced by taxation performs an essential function. By releasing resources from non-functional consumption and non-essential or unproductive investment, taxation makes these resources available for the public sector. In order to raise adequate resources for development, it may have to infringe on essential consumption too.

The role of taxation is not to be merely static. It has also to play a dynamic role in raising resources for capital formation. As economic development proceeds national output increases and new incomes are generated. The tax policy must make sure that these new incomes are not permitted to flow into unproductive channels. They must be directed towards productive investments. The tax structure should have *built-in flexibility* to perform this function automatically. As incomes grow, the tax base must also be deepened and broadened. For this purpose, the marginal rate of taxation will have to be kept high and Prof. Lewis suggests that the marginal rate of taxation should be considerably greater than the average rate[11]. Such a tax structure presupposes a progressive income tax and also high rates of indirect taxes on commodities having a large income elasticity of demand. In this way an increasingly larger proportion of increment in output would be converted into public savings. Considering that there is considerable non-monetised sector in backward economies and there are several institutional barriers, the tax structure will have to be considerably broadened, deepened and diversified. Otherwise there is no guarantee that adequate resources will be mobilised for developmental purposes.

Drawbacks. But taxation as a method of mobilisation of surplus presents some difficulties. In developing countries, only a narrow range of population is affected by taxation to any appreciable extent. The reason is that only a small number of people have their income reaching the level of direct taxes; and the indirect taxes on luxuries, which are the main source of income in advanced countries, fall on a small number of people. Hence the yield from taxes is small owing to their limited coverage. And the per capita revenue collected in the country is very low.

While taxation increases involuntary savings, it decreases voluntary savings to enable the people to maintain the former standard of consumption. The result is that the resources available for the private sector are thereby diminished. Another major drawback of taxation is that it has disincentive effect on business enterprises and discourages savings. The taxes on wage-earners diminish their incentive to work harder; taxes on profits of higher income groups reduce their incentive to save and to make investment in new enterprise; taxes on output or incomes of farmers diminish their incentives to improve agricultural techniques. Hence taxation militates against the efforts of those who can make an important contribution to economic growth.

Thus saving extracted from taxation is not an unmixed advantage. It is, therefore, very

11 W.A. Lewis. *The Theory of Economic Growth.*

necessary to devise a system of taxation which will not weaken the incentives to work, save and invest; nor should it violate the accepted notion of equity. Taxation should not impair the productivity of the economic system. A high marginal rate of taxation may have a considerable disincentive effect on private enterprise.

Role of Indirect Taxes. It has been found that indirect taxes are better suited to the conditions obtaining in developing countries for reducing current consumption and mobilising resources for development because in such countries quite a large proportion of national income tends to be diverted to current consumption instead of being productively invested. The average propensity to consume in such countries is much higher than is the case in advanced countries. Therefore, in developing countries, indirect taxes must thus play a more important part. They will raise the rate of savings which are so essential for economic growth. It may be noted that with the adoption of new economic policy of liberalisation since 1991 rates of customs duties and excise duties in India have been reduced in order to reduce the costs of industries and thereby to increase their competitiveness However, this has reduced the tax-revenue of the Government and has also lowered the tax-GDP ratio.

But, "High rates of taxes on commodities with a high income elasticity of demand are quite effective in siphoning a substantial proportion of increase in output into the resources of the public sector needed for development financing and a higher rate of commodity taxes on luxury articles tends to introduce an element of progressiveness in an otherwise predominantly regressive tax structure in developing countries".[12] But in order to make sure that the resources raised through commodity taxes are adequate, it will be necessary to widen their base by withdrawing various exemptions from tariff duties and excise duties[13]. In the poor countries, it is not possible to exempt entirely goods of general consumption, because they are the only goods that provide a base broad enough to assure an adequate amount of resources.

Role of Taxation in Promoting Private Investment. It is generally considered that taxation is meant to mobilise resources for the public sector. But a little thought will show that even in promoting investment in the private sector taxation plays an important role. It plays an allocative role by directing the resources to desirable and useful channels. A developing economy can adopt taxation measures which will check conspicuous and non-functional consumption, especially the consumption of luxuries. Funds so saved will then be available for investment in the private sector. This role is played by import duties and excise duties on luxury or semi-luxury articles. A steady progressive tax on the upper income brackets also promotes saving. Diversion of savings into a real estate, jewellery or other prestigious but unremunerative investment can be checked by taxes and so also investment for speculative purposes. Taxes for these purposes can be imposed on land and buildings, capital gains or increments in land values.

Thus taxation can provide incentives for desirable investments and can check undesirable and unproductive investment. For instance, there is a tax holiday for new industrial undertakings. Liberal depreciation allowances can be given on new buildings, plant and machinery. Development rebates may be given for reinvesting profits in business, income tax may be imposed on profits declared as dividends. Substantial carry-overs of business losses may be allowed.

Government Borrowing

Borrowing by the government is another method by which the savings of the community may be mobilised for economic development. In developing economies, the Governments resort to public borrowing in order to finance schemes of economic development. Public borrowing becomes necessary because taxation alone does not provide sufficient funds for economic development. Besides, too heavy taxation of income and wealth be avoided as it has an adverse effect on saving and investment.

---

12 Tripathy, R.N. *Public Finance in Underdeveloped Countries*, 1966, p. 200.

13 See Kelkar Committee Report, 2002.

Public borrowing takes two forms: (*a*) *market loans* and (*b*) *small savings*. In the case of market borrowing, the Government sells to the public negotiable Government securities of varying terms and duration and treasury bills. For financing capital projects long-term Government bonds are floated in the capital market. This form of public borrowing is more important for mobilising resources for development. The treasury bills which represent short-term borrowing are intended to meet only the current Government expenditure. New bonds may be issued for meeting old maturing bonds. The small savings represent public borrowing which is not negotiable and are not bought and sold in the capital market. For mobilising small savings, various types of savings certificates are issued, *e.g.*, National Savings Certificates, National Development Certificates, Rural Development Bonds, Postal Certificates and Postal Accounts, Compulsory Deposits, etc. A widespread campaign is necessary to attract small savings.

Borrowing is the quickest mode of raising funds. On the other hand, tax finance is not so expeditious because passing of tax laws, assessment of taxes based on those laws and their collection involves considerable delay. Besides, public debt does not involve any burden if it is devoted to productive works. The subscribers to Government loans are able to find remunerative investment whereas the Government can pay the principal and interest out of the income yielded by investment financed from loans. Thus public borrowing is not only necessary but also desirable.

There is another advantage in public borrowing. *Public borrowing in anti-inflationary*. The underdeveloped countries are victims of inflation since they have to resort to deficit financing for finding funds for economic development. Since deficit financing is inflationary, public borrowing is preferable to deficit financing. Public borrowing mops up the surplus purchasing power with the people. It thus checks consumption and so a rise in prices. At the same time idle balances are absorbed in productive activity.

Public borrowing generates additional productive capacity. The funds raised by public borrowing can be *utilised for building up the infrastructure* for the economy through schemes for the development of roads, ports, highways, irrigation, transport and power. They help in building up of the agricultural and industrial base of the economy. All such investments facilitate further economic growth. There is no doubt, therefore, that the public borrowing plays a very useful and important role in accelerating economic development of developing economies. Public debt promotes saving and investment, the two most crucial determinants of economic growth.

But there exist a number of obstacles which hinder the success of borrowing policy in an underdeveloped economy. In many such countries, there are no organized money and capital markets and in those where such markets exist, they constitute a very small proportion of total money market of the country. There may not, besides, exist any organic relationship between the organized and unorganized part of the money market. Moreover, the resources of the organized capital market may be too inadequate to fulfil the needs both of the private and of the public sector. Further, in the capital market the competition for funds between the government and the private sector will raise rate of interest and this will have a highly disincentive effect on the expansion of investment in the private sectors. Besides, for the mobilisation of savings it is necessary to check and regulate the diversion of savings into unproductive investment such as real estate, gold and jewellery and inventory accumulation.

It may be noted here that there is now ample evidence in India that the resources raised through borrowing by the Government are spent for public investment in infrastructure such as power, communication, railways, roads, highways, it *crowds in* private investment rather than *crowding out* private investment. This is because private sector investment is impeded by the non-availability of good infrastructure. Further, public sector investment creates demand for products of private sector such as cement, steel and others in addition to the expansion of aggregate demand in general.

Suitable techniques of borrowing must also be devised. For example, bonds issued by the Government should be adjusted to the preferences of the general public; bonds of large denomination and long maturity may be offered to the institutional investors, whereas those of small denomination and short maturity may be reserved for the non-institutional public. If properly devised and conducted small savings campaign can mobilise a sizable amount of resources. Further, the mobilisation of the hoardings of gold and jewellery through government programmes constitutes a highly desirable source of resource mobilisation. Of course, suitable techniques of public borrowing for the mobilisation of these resources have to be evolved.

Profits of Public Undertakings

In developing countries with a mixed economy, the public sector has been expanded in the past especially when the objective was the establishment of a socialistic pattern of society in India. The result is that a large number of projects of irrigation, power and industrial projects in heavy and basic industries are being executed by the Government. Commercial enterprises like steel plants, oil and petroleum enterprises fertilizer plants, machine tool factories and State trading organisation were set up by the Government. It was expected that these public undertakings would in course of time start yielding profits which would be available for reinvestment in the schemes of economic development. This is how public undertakings can make their contribution to self-generating growth.

The public undertakings are not to be run on no-profit no-loss basis known as the 'break-even' principle. But in the interest of a continuing process of economic growth they must be made to yield a reasonable return on investment. The price policy of State Trading Corporation must also be adjusted to mobilise resources in the form of trading profits. Like the private enterprises, they must pursue the principle of profitability implying efficiency and cost reduction to enlarge the profits accruing from such enterprises. Their working, therefore, has constantly to be reviewed and ordinary principles of accounting and auditing must be applied thereto. Thus, contrary to the usual conception, the public sector enterprises should not only pay their way but also make legitimate profits.

But it cannot be denied that the surpluses from public enterprises should constitute a reasonable proportion of the resources for development. In developing countries, where there is a paucity of investible resources, the process of accelerated economic developemnt requires that these enterprises should make reasonable return on their investment and make their maximum contribution to capital formation. It is a very convenient and desirable method of resource mobilisation. The profit is concealed in the price charged. Thus it is administratively convenient and politically feasible.

The public enterprise is not now confined to providing environmental facilities or social and economic overheads but also extended to purely industrial and commercial business. They have, therefore, to pursue price-output policies which should generate enough resources for capital formation. Dr. V.K.R.V. Rao has rightly advocated that "price policies in the public sector should be such as to yield a planned profit which will include not only depreciation expenditure but also an element of surplus for capital formation".[14]

Raising Resources through Public Sector Disinvestment. It may be noted that with the adoption of new economic policy of liberalisation and privatisation since 1991 role of public sector in Indian economy has been greatly diluted and Government has been making disinvestment in public sector enterprises in which it holds a large share of equity capital and thereby raising resources for its various future investment projects. Accordingly, Government has sold some of its share captial in many public enterprises such as BALCO, VSNL, CMC, Modern Foods, some oil companies, Maruti to private sector firms. Recently, Government sold a good part of its share capital in Maruti Car Company through open public offer in the market and raised ₹ 900 crore. In the Tenth Plan period (2002-07), it was planned to raise resources of the order of ₹ 10,000 crore annually through public sector investment. Thus, disinvestment of public sector enterprises is yielding good revenue to the Government. Resources raised through public sector disinvestment if invested in infrastructure and social services such as education and health will accelerate economic growth in India.

14 Ooty Seminar Papers, 1959, p. 33

Technological Progress and Economic Development

We have explained earlier that capital formation and technological change are two important factors that determine rate of economic growth. Having discussed capital formation in the preceding chapter, we now turn to the explanation of technological change and its role in expanding output and employment. In the beginning it may be noted that technological progress plays a more important role than capital formation. In the absence of technological progress capital formation can lead to increase in output per head only so long as all the workers in the given labour force have not been fully equipped with the capital equipment embodying the latest available techniques. Once all the workers in the labour force have been so equipped with capital, further economic growth, that is, increase in output or income per head comes to an end. *It is technological progress which can bring about continued increase in output per head of the population.* Technological progress is thus the prime-mover of economic growth.

Meaning of Technological Change

Technological change or progress refers to the discovery of the new and improved methods of producing goods. Sometimes technological advances result in the increase in available supplies of natural resources. But more generally technological changes result in increasing the productivity of labour, capital and other resources. The productivity of combined inputs of all factors is called *total factor productivity*. Thus technological progress means increase in total factor productivity. As a result of technological advance, it becomes possible to produce more output with same resources or the same amount of product with less resources.

But the question arises as to how does the technological progress take place. The technological progress takes place through *inventions and innovations*. The word invention is used for the new scientific discoveries, whereas the innovations are said to take place only when the new scientific discoveries are commercially used for actual production of goods. Some inventions may not be economically profitable to be used for actual production.

It follows from above that technological change brings about an increase in output per head. Thus technological change, or more precisely technological progress, is *the change in the production process which results in an increased output per unit of labour*. Technological change causes a shift in the production function embodying all known techniques. Technological change must be distinguished from a *change in technique*. While by technological change we mean advance in knowledge resulting in improved methods of production, change in technique refers to the use of a different but already known method of production.

TECHNOLOGICAL CHANGE AND ECONOMIC GROWTH

The process of economic growth involves the increase in the production of goods and services. Increase in production can be achieved either through the use of more resources and/or through the realisation of higher productivity by means of using the resources of labour, capital and land more efficiently. Technological change helps to promote growth in both these ways. It can help in the discovery of new natural resources in the country and thereby enhances the productive potential of the country. Technological change also increases the productivity of available resources. For instance, it can find out the productive uses of land that hitherto has been regarded as infertile or it can discover new economic use of a raw material that had previously been considered as useless. But, as stated above, *technological change more generally results in higher productivity of resources*. Technological change raises the productivity of worker through the provision of better machines, better methods and superior skills. In Table 8.1 we give the percentage increase in labour productivity in a number countries during the period 1970-1989. By bringing about increase in productivity of resources the progress in technology makes it possible to produce more output with the same resources or the same amount of output with less resources. Progress in technology causes improvement in technology through the provision of better machines, better methods and enhanced skills.

It is technology which underlies the process of producing new things with the existing resources or using the existing resources in new ways. This is what Schumpeter means when he says that, "the slow and continuous increase in the national supply of productive means and savings is obviously an important factor in explaining the course of economic history through the centuries, *but it is completely overshadowed by the fact that development consists primarily in employing existing resources in a different way, in doing new things with them, irrespective of whether those resources increase or not*."[1] It is important to emphasise that newly discovered techniques lead to the increase in output per worker.

Productivity of workers depends upon the quantity and quality of capital tools with which they work. For higher productivity the instruments of production have to be technologically efficient and superior. The technological options open to an economy determine the *input mix of production*. A commodity can be produced by various technologies. The quantity and quality of capital, skills and other factors required for production is directly dependent on the efficiency of the technique of production being used. Also, the managerial and organisational expertise has to be in line with the technological requirements of production. Viewed thus, technology in the present stage of economic development is an indispensable factor of production.

This is the age of technology. The developing countries are obssessed by the desire to make rapid progress in technology so as to catch up with the present-day developed countries. Frantic efforts are being made to install improved technology in agriculture, industries, health, sanitation and education; in fact in all walks of human life. Indeed, the newly emerging nations, have come to regard technology as a bastion of national autonomy and as a status symbol in the international community.

Table 8.1. Percentage Increase in Labour Productivity, 1970-1989

Country	Increase %
United States	2.9
Canada	2.5
Denmark	3.3
France	4.1
Italy	4.9
Japan	6.0
Netherlands	4.9
Sweden	2.9
United Kingdom	3.8
Germany	3.2

Source: H. Craig Petersen and W. Cris Lewis, *Managerial Economics*, 3rd edition, 1995, p. 538.

1 J.A. Schumpeter, *The Theory of Economic Development*, Cambridge, Harvard University Press, 1949, p. 68.

It will be noticed that during 1970-89 rate of increase in labour productivity for the United States is less than other countries except Canada and Sweden. Slow growth in productivity in the Unites States during the period (1970-89) had been a major concern and was the subject of debate among the economists. It will be further observed that during this period Japan had the highest growth rate in labour productivity of 6% followed by Italy and Netherlands.

Denison in his empirical study has estimated the sources of increase in real GNP between 1929 and 1982 of the United States. He found that technological change contributed 28% to the average annual growth in real GNP which was 2.9 per cent over this period. The estimates of contribution of various factors such as labour, education and capital are presented in Table 8.2.

Table 8.2. Sources of Growth in Real GNP in the United STates (1929-82)

Source of Growth	Percentage Contribution to growth due to
Growth in labour input	32
Growth in labour productivity	
Education per worker	14
Capital formation	19
Technological Change	28
Economics of scale	9
Other factors*	–2

* These include worker safety, pollution abatement and fewer labour disputes.

Source: E. Denison, *Trends in American Economic Growth*, Washington, Brookings Institutions, 1985, p. 30.

From the table it will be seen that increase in the *quantity* of labour contributed to 32 per cent to 2.9 per cent annual growth in the United States. The other factors contribute to the annual growth by raising productivity of labour.

Technical progress manifests itself in the change in production function, So a simple measure of the technical progress would be the comparison of the position of production function at two points of time. The technological change my operate upon the production function through improvements of various sorts such as a superior- equipment, an improved material, and superior organisational efficiency. Also, the technological progress may express itself in making available new products. The availability of a new product in many cases could be construed as a change in the production function as it can be regarded equivalent to a more efficient way of meeting an old want.

Technological Change and Capital Formation

The process of technological progress is inseparably linked with the process of capital formation. In fact, both go hand in hand. Technological progress is virtually impossible without prior capital formation. It is because the introduction of superior or more efficient techniques requires the building up of new capital equipment which incorporates new technology. In other words, new and superior technology can contribute to national product and its growth if it is first embodied in the new capital equipment. The capital accumulation has, therefore, been called the vehicle for the steady introduction of new technology into the economy:

It may be noted that Adam Smith viewed technological progress as a rise in productivity of workers as a result of increase in division of labour and specialization. This leads to the growth in national income. But it was J.A. Schumpeter who laid great stress on the role of technological innovations in bringing about economic growth. He visualised technical innovations in bringing about economic progress. It is the entrepreneur who carries out the innovations and organises the production structure more efficiently. As, according to Schumpter, the innovations occur in spurts rather than in a smooth flow, economic progress is not an uninterupted process. The pace of economic progress is punctuated by the pace of innovations. Since innovations are governed by a host of factors, therefore, it is difficult to perdict about the economic progress resulting from technological changes.

Prof. Rostow has proposed four stages in the development of an economy. These stages are : (*i*) traditional society; (*ii*) preconditions for take off; (*iii*) drive to maturity and (*iv*) stages of high mass consumption. It may be noted that the economic transformation of the society from one stage to another involves, along with other things, a change in the level and character of technology. In the present age of greater specialisation it is the technology factor that underlines all major aspects of the modern productive apparatus such as decision making, production programming, skill requirements market strategy.

The role of technological progress in economic development has not only been large but also increasing over time. It is beyond any doubt that the inventions and changes in production techniques played more important role in the late eighteenth and later centuries than in the earlier ones. The technical innovations provided the motive force for the industrial revolution in Western Europe. While the innovations mainly arose because of input shortages, they tended to overcome the impediments to mass production and the transport bottlenecks in the movement of industrial raw materials and labour. There were also improvements in managerial organisation with a view to reduce costs of production. The adjustments in the product designs also took place to meet the variations in the wants of the people.

Technical progress is the *prime mover of economic growth.* A continuing technical progress ensures a continuing growth. Where there is no technical progress, capital accumulation alone may fail to bring growth beyond a point. For capital accumulation without technical progress can bring about growth in income per head only so long as the available labour force has not been fully equipped with the latest techniques available, and only so long as all the wants of the consumers have not been supplied to the full extent. Once that point is reached where all labour has been equipped with the latest techniques and all wants of consumers have been met to the full extent, growth would come to an end unless technical progress occurs.

Technological Progress to Overcome Stationary State

It is now widely accepted that technological change raises productivity and that a continuous occurrence of technological change will enable the economy to escape from being driven to the stationary state or economic stagnation. Classical economists like David Ricardo and J.S. Mill expressed fear that the increase in the stock of capital will sooner or later land the economy into stationary state beyond which economic growth will come to an end. *Classical economists remained occupied with the idea of a stationary state because they did not take into account technological progress that could postpone the occurrence of a stationary state and ensure continued economic growth.* Indeed, if technological progress continuously takes place, demon of stationary state can be put off indefinitely.[2]

We can diagrammatically show how the technological change will raise productivity and thereby suspend the occurrence of stationary state with the help of Hicks's representation of classical model. Let us first represent the classical model of stationary state. Consider Fig. 8.1 where along the X-axis stock of capital is measured and up the Y-axis rate of return on capital is measured. This rate of return on capital is in effect the marginal productivity of capital. It may be noted that *rate of return* is here taken to be quite akin to the '*rate of interest*' which was regarded by the classical economists as the mechanism which determines investment to be made in any period of time.

Now, let us suppose that the economy has, at a particular moment, a stock of capital equal to K_1 in Fig. 8.1. Given this stock of capital, the rate of return which the businessmen would be able to earn from a *new investment* would be somewhat less than r_3. However, if the economy is to be kept growing through capital accumulation while maintaining full employment, the rate of interest must be less than r_3; let us say it is at the level r_2. In this situation, it would be profitable for the businessmen, in the given period, say, one year, to undertake investment (through borrowing or with their own funds) to an extent that results in a net addition of $K_1 K_2$ to the capital stock. Therefore, at the end of

2 J.R. Hicks, 'Thoughts on the Theory of Capital,' *Oxford Economic Papers* (New Series), 1960, p. 123.

the year, the economy would come to have K_2 amount of capital stock. It is possible now to draw a curve *CC* in Fig. 8.1 which indicates the different rates of return obtainable from the different levels of capital stock.

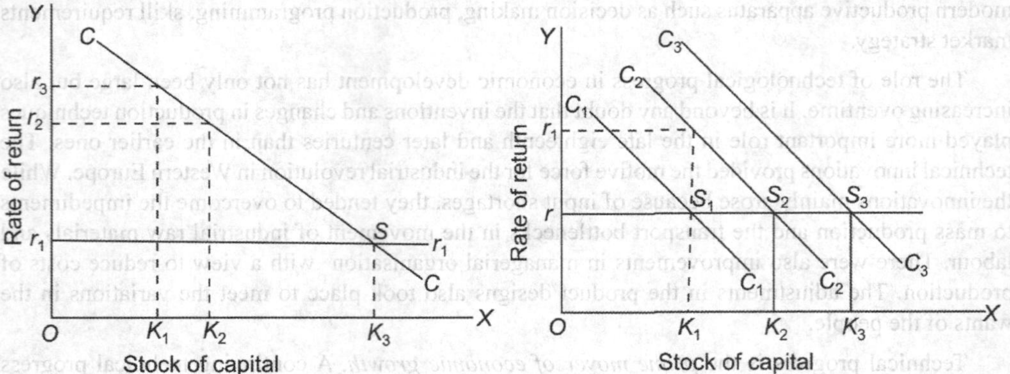

Fig. 8.1. *Classical model of stationary state* **Fig. 8.2.** *Stationary state and technological progress*

Assuming that the supply of labour is constant, in the absence of technological progress and consequently rate of return curve *CC* remaining the same, the expansion in the stock of capital from K_1 to K_2 will bring down the rate of return on capital from r_3 to r_2. As a result, the rate of return on new investment will now be slightly below r_2 after K_1K_2 investment has been undertaken in the year. Now, if there are still net *positive savings* in the community which is likely the case when capital stock has not yet sufficiently increased, then the rate of interest will fall below the level of r_2. With the fall in the rate of interest below r_2 and the rate of return on new investment being nearly equal to r_2 (*i.e.*, only slightly less than r_2), it will be worthwhile to undertake new investment in the next year and in this way to maintain full employment in the next year.

According to the classical economists, rate of interest will continue falling gradually over time till it reaches a level at which both net saving and net investment have fallen to zero. In Fig. 8.1 this will take place when the capital stock has increased to K_3 and rate of interest has fallen to r_1. Since there are no more net savings and investment, the further expansion in the stock of capital and therefore the process of economic growth will cease to occur and the economy will reach what classical economists called *stationary state*. However, according to the classical economists, the stationary state is a distant end which may not be reached at all. This view of 'classicals', according to Hicks, is based on the idea that the curve *CC* is highly elastic, so that the distances such as K_1 K_2 are, indeed, very small. Thus, capital accumulation takes place by very small steps and can go on for a very long time before the rate of return finally falls to r_1.

Stationary State can be Postponed through Technological Progress

It may be noted that the businessmen would continue undertaking investments so long as the capital stock is less than K_3. For, until K_3 level of capital stock is reached, the rate of return is high enough to induce businessmen to use the net savings for undertaking new investments. However, once the K_3 level of capital stock is reached, net savings would have fallen to the zero level and consequently both net investment and capital accumulation will cease to occur. While in this situation, net investment would necessarily have come to an end, gross investment may continue. But the gross investment does not add to capital stock; it is made just for the purposes of replacements of worn-out capital. When the stationary state has been reached, net investment would be zero because net savings are zero. Also, the population, income and standards of living would stabilise at a constant level.

Now, the importance of technological progress is that it can suspend the occurrence of stationary state equilibrium. Classical economists underestimated the role of technological progress in preventing the occurrence of stationary state equilibrium. When technical progress occurs it will raise the productivity of capital and labour. As a result of the rise in productivity, the rate of return curve *CC* (*i.e.*, marginal productivity curve of capital) will shift upward. This implies that it will be profitable to accumulate more capital and thereby suspending the occurrence of the stationary state. This is illustrated in Fig. 8.2 where to begin with economy is in stationary state equilibrium at point S_1 with rate of return on capital equal to *r*. Suppose that now a new technological advance takes place which is embodied in a new machinery with which output per unit of labour is greater than before. As a result of this technological advance, the marginal productivity curve (*i.e.*, curve of rate of return on capital) will shift upward.

As will be seen from Fig. 8.2, with the shift in the rate of return curve from C_1C_1 to C_2C_2 the rate of return on capital has risen to r_1. With the rate of return on new investment being nearly equal to r_1 and the rate of interest being equal to *r*, it will be profitable to undertake new investment. As a result, stock of capital will increase to the level K_2 and the whole of the given labour force has been equipped with new machines corresponding to the new technology. With the increase in stock of capital to K_2, the rate of return will fall to *r* . Thus when the rate of return again falls to *r* level, the net saving and the net investment will be reduced to zero and a new stationary state equilibrium will be reached at S_2. With the stock of capital equal to K_2 suppose there occurs a new burst of technical progress which causes the *CC* curve to shift further upward to C_3C_3. This will cause the capital accumulation to take place further to K_3. Thus a result of technological progress and more capital accumulation, output, income and the standards of living of the people will rise.

It follows from above that *technological progress holds the key to economic growth. As technological progress takes place, capital accumulation will proceed further and economic growth will take place*. Without technical progress, capital accumulation can raise the output and income to a limited extent. With constant labour force and the given technology, capital accumulation can lead to the increase in output so long as all the workers of the labour force are not equipped with the latest capital equipment embodying the latest technology. After this only technological progress can lead to the growth of output and income. Thus, Professors Stonier and Hague rightly state. "*Technical progress, therefore, turns out to be even more essential to economic growth than capital accumulation. Where there is no technical progress, capital accumulation can lead to growth in income per head only so long as labour force has not been fully equipped in accordance with the latest techniques. Once that happens, growth comes to an end. It is technical progress alone which ensures that the stationary state is not merely very far off but will never arrive so long as technical progress continues*."[3]

Technological Change: Disembodied and Embodied

What factors cause sustained growth of national income and per capita income is an important issue that has been the concern of economists. Capital accumulation, growth in labour force and technological progress contribute to the growth of an economy. American economist R.M. Solow[4] used the aggregate production function that relates the level of output to the levels of various inputs such as growth of capital, labour and technological progress over time. Solow used the following production function:

$$Y = A(t)F(K, L) \qquad \ldots(1)$$

where *Y* stands for output, *K* for capital and *L* for labour. The term *A*(*t*) represents technological change which is taken to depend merely on time, that is, as time passes, *A*(*t*) increases showing that over time technological progress enables more to be produced with the given quantities of capital and labour. With such specification of production function, technological progress does not cause

3 Alfred W. Stonier and Douglas C. Hague, *A Textbook of Economic Theory,* 4th edition, 1972, p. 626.

4 R.M. Solow, "Technical Change and Aggregate Production Function, *Review of Economics and Statistics*, Aug. 1957.

any change in the relative marginal productivities of capital and labour, that is, such technological progress brings about equal increases in the productivities of the two factors and is said to be *Hicks' neutral* in the sense that it favours neither capital nor labour.

But the important thing to note in the production function given above is that it represents *technological progress which is exogenous and disembodied.* By exogenous technological progress we mean it comes from outside the model and, therefore, the term $A(t)$ is shown outside the production function. Disembodied technological change raises the productivity of *both* old and new machines (*i.e.*, capital goods) and does not depend on the rate of new investment. *The disembedied technological change in purely organisational in nature which permits* more output to be produced from the given inputs without any new investment. That is, disembodied technological change causes a shift in the production function without disturbing capital-labour ratio. It is through organisational changes that disembedied technological change enables more output to be produced with existing inputs being used more effectively.

Disembodied technological change is represented in Fig. 8.3 where on the horizontal axis capital-labour ratio (K/L), that is, capital per worker is measured and along the vertical axis output per worker (Y/L) is measured. In the beginning, production function curve $Y = f_1(K/L)$ is given and,

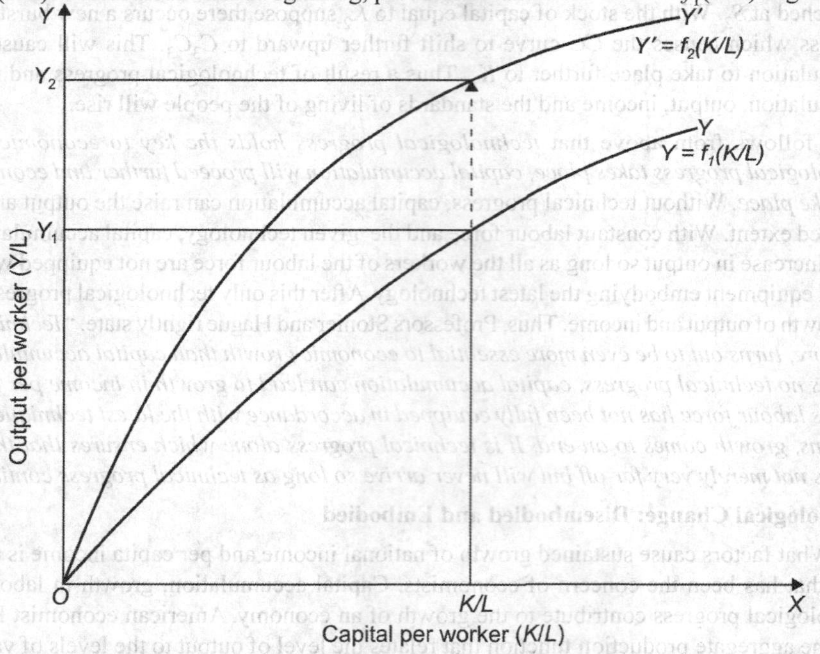

Fig. 8.3. *Shift in the production function due to disembodied technological change*

according to this, with a capital per worker equal to K/L, level of output Y_1 is being produced. Suppose now that technological progress takes place and production function curve shifts upward to OY' that is, to $Y' = f_2(K/L)$. According to the new production function curve $Y' = f_2(K/L)$, with the given capital-labour ratio, K/L more output Y_2 is produced. Similarly, with any other capital-labour ratio on the new production function curve OY', *i.e.*, $Y' = f_2(K/L)$, more output will be produced as compared to that on the production function curve OY.

Embodied Technological Change. In the embodied technological change, the increase in investment or capital accumulation, is regarded as the vehicle of technological progress. Technological progress increases the productivity of new machines built in any period compared with old machines built in the previous periods. This implies that embodied technological change does not cause increase in the productivity of machine already in existence. About embodied technological change. Hahn and Matthews in their review of the theory of economic growth write, "*Technological change is embodied in new machines. Machines unalterably embody the technology of their date of construction. Machines built in different dates ---- are therefore qualitatively dissimilar and cannot in the general case be aggregated into a single measure of capital. A separate production function is needed for each vintage. Total output is the sum of output of all vintages in use.*"[5]

Production function of embodied technology can be written as

$$Y_t = F(K_t, L_t, A_t) \qquad \ldots (2)$$

where output Y_t depends on the amount of capital (K_t), labour (L_t) and the level of technology (A_t). Note that in the production function (2), the term A_t for technology appears *inside* the production function as one of the endogenous inputs.

It is important to note that in the production function (2), the relationship between output and technology differs from the relationship between output and other inputs, capital and labour. This can be better understood by considering this production function in case of an individual firm which can be stated as under:

$$Y_{it} = F(K_{it}, L_{it}, At) \qquad \ldots (3)$$

The production function (3) of the individual firm shows that output of an individual firm depends not only on *its own level* of capital (K_{it}) and labour (L_{it}) but also on the economy-wide level of technology. Expressing production function in this way, the technological progress in the economy will increase the productivity of *all* firms including the firm whose production function (3) is given above. In this formulation of production function, the technology is assumed to progress endogenously instead of being an exogenous change. Thus, in the concept of *embodied technology, production function depends on the investment in new capital.* Technological progress fosters inventions and improvements in machines. Thus new improved technology is embodied in investment in the new machines.

NEUTRAL, CAPITAL-SAVING AND LABOUR-SAVING TECHNOLOGICAL CHANGE

It is important to know the difference between labour-saving and capital-saving technological change. But before explaining labour-saving and capital-saving technological change, it will be useful to make clear the meaning of neutral technological changes, since it is neutral technology which is the dividing line between labour-saving and capital-saving technological change. In economics neutral technological change (or innovation) has been defined in two ways, the first by J.R. Hicks and the second by R.F. Harrod. We shall explain below these two concepts of neutral technological change.

Hicks' Neutral Technological Change

Hicks defined neutral technological change in the context of static price theory, especially in connection with the theory of wages. According to Hicks, *neutral technological change* (or neutral innovation) is one where if certain ratio of two factors, say, labour and capital, is being used to produce a given output, *the effect of neutral technological change is to bring about increase in the marginal productivity of each factor in the same proportion.* Hicksian concept of neutral technological change (neutral innovation) has been shown in Fig. 8.4. where along the *X*-axis, capital per man is measured and up the *Y*-axis output per man is measured. To the left of the origin *O* along the *X*-axis we represent

5 F.H. Hahn, and R.C. Matthews, "Theory of Economic Growth" *A Survey of Economic Growth*, Vol. 74, 1964.

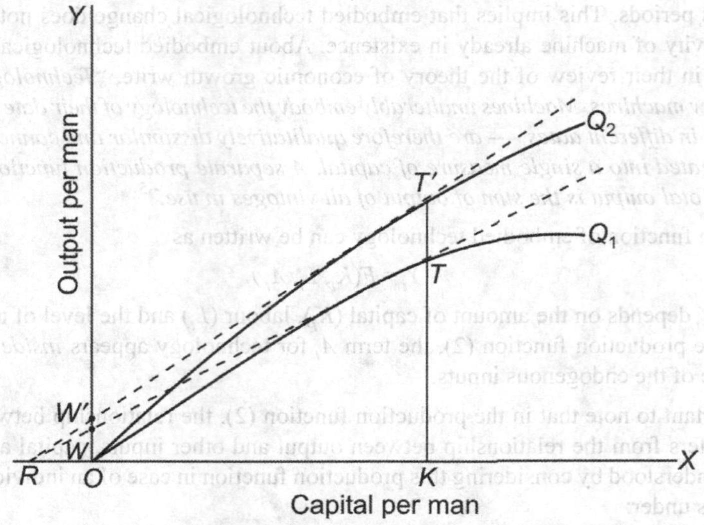

Fig. 8.4. *Hicks' Neutral Technological Change*

the ratio of marginal products of labour and capital such as *OR* The curve OQ_1 depicts the production function (total product curve) according to some existing technology. Suppose a technological change takes place and as a result production function shifts upward to OQ_2.

With production function OQ_1 and, before technological change in Fig. 8.4 the equilibrium is at point *T* on the production function OQ_1 where wage rate is equal to *OW* which is equal to the marginal product of labour. It should be noted that in Fig. 8.4 the slope of the curve *TR* represents the *marginal product of capital* as along the *X*-axis, capital per man is measured.

Now, the slope of the tangent, $TR = \frac{TK}{RK} = \frac{OW}{OR}$

It follows therefore that marginal product of capital $= \frac{OW}{OR}$

It *v* stands for marginal product of capital, then

$$v = \frac{OW}{OR}$$

Manipulating the above equation we have:

$$OR = \frac{OW}{v}$$

As stated above, *OW* represents marginal product of labour and *v* the marginal product of capital.

Therefore, $$OR = \frac{\text{Marginal Product of Labour}}{\text{Marginal Product of Capital}}$$

It is, therefore, evident that the distance *OR* measures the ratio between the marginal product of labour and the marginal product of capital in the position of equilibrium.

Now, *if technological progress is to be Hicks-neutral, then technological change causing shift in production function from OQ_1 to OQ_2 should leave the ratio between the marginal product of labour and marginal product of capital unchanged at any given value of the capital-labour ratio.* Since at the equilibrium position *T* in Fig. 8.4 the capital-labour ratio (*i.e.*, capital per man) is *OK*, Hicks' neutral technology requires that at the capital-labour ratio *OK*, the ratio of marginal product of capital to marginal product of labour remains the same (*i.e.*, equal to *OR*) when technological change has taken place and production function has sifted to OQ_2. This implies that when the new production function OQ_2 and at point

T' corresponding to capital-labour ratio *OK*, if a tangent is drawn, it should pass through the same point *R*. It will be seen that such is the case in Fig. 8.4. With the slopes of the tangents RT' and RT to production functions Q_2 and Q_1 being equal to *OR* implies that technological change brings about change in the marginal products of labour in the same proportion. It will also be observed from Fig. 8.4 that as a result of the technological progress and shift in production function, the output per man has increased and also the equilibrium wage rate has increased from *OW* to OW'. Thus both labour productivity and capital productivity has increased as a result of technological progress.

Capital-Saving and Labour-Saving Technological Change

From Hicks' definition of neutral technological change, the concepts of capital-saving and labour-saving technical change can easily be understood. We explain them below. *A capital-saving technological change (capital-saving innovation) is that which, at a given capital-labour ratio, raises the marginal productivity of labour relative to the marginal productivity of capital*. This means that it would now be possible to produce a given level of output with less capital relative to labour as a result of technological progress. Thus technological change is capital-saving in the Hicksian sense when the ratio, $\frac{\text{Marginal Product of Labour}}{\text{Marginal Product of Capital}}$ or $\frac{\Delta Q}{\Delta L} / \frac{\Delta Q}{\Delta K}$ increases, where ΔQ stands for a small change in output in response to a small change in labour input (ΔL) and a small change in capital input (ΔK). Thus $\frac{\Delta Q}{\Delta L}$ and $\frac{\Delta Q}{\Delta K}$ will measure marginal product of labour and marginal product of capital respectively. Note that *capital-saving* technological change, generally implies *labour-using* technological change as labour is substituted for capital.

In terms of Fig. 8.4 if capital-saving technological change occurs, the production function will shift in such a way that the tangent drawn at point T' (corresponding to the given capital-labour ratio *OK*) then that tangent will pass through the *left of point R* indicating that the ratio of marginal product of labour to marginal product of capital will increase. As a result, the given output can be produced with less capital relatively to labour. Therefore, it shows capital-saving innovation (*i.e.*, technological change).

Labour-Saving Technological Change. According to Hicks, labour-saving technological change is one which reduces the marginal product of labour relative to that of capital. In other words, labour-saving technological change (*i.e.*, labour-saving innovation) occurs when at a given capital-labour ratio, the ratio, $\frac{\text{Marginal Product of Labour}}{\text{Marginal Product of Capital}}$ (MP_L/MP_K) declines.

This implies that in case of labour-using technological change it would now be possible to produce a given level of output with less labour relative to capital following a change in technology. Note that *labour-saving* technological change generally implies *capital-using* technological change. In other words, in this case *capital-intensity of production* will increase. In terms of Fig. 8.4 the production function curve will shift in such a way that the tangent drawn at the new production function corresponding to the given capital-labour ratio *OK* will pass through the *right* of point *R*.

HARROD'S NEUTRAL, LABOUR-SAVING AND CAPITAL-SAVING TECHNOLOGICAL CHANGE

It has been shown by R.F. Harrod, a prominent British economist, that Hicks' concept of neutral change is heavily dependent on factors such as elasticity of demand for factors and products which are quite unrelated to the real character of technological change. Besides, Hicks' concept of neutral technology has been developed in the framework of static economic theory. Therefore, an alternative concept of neutral technological change which is extensively used in the theory of economic growth has been put forward by R.F. Harrod in his now well known work "*Towards a Dynamic Economics*".

While Hicks' concept of neutral technological change considers the ratio between the marginal products of the two factors when capital-labour ratio remains constant, Harrod states his concept of neutral technological change in terms of the relationship between rate of profit and capital-output ratio. According to Harrod, *neutral technological change is that which leaves the capital-output ratio unchanged* when rate of profit (assumed to be equal to marginal product of capital) remains constant. Thus when there is technological progress and rate of profit remains constant, technological change will be Harrod-neutral only if *capital-output ratio* also remains unchanged.

It follows from the definition of Harrod's neutral technical change that *when rate of profit remains constant after the technological change, technological progress would be labour-saving in the Harrodian sense if capital-output ratio rises.* This means that now same output can be obtained by using more capital. Given the level of output, the use of more capital implies the substitution of capital for labour.

On the other hand, *when there is technological progress and rate of profit remain the same, the technological progress would be capital-saving in the Harrodian sense if capital-output ratio falls. This implies that now the same output can be produced with less capital*. Obviously, there is saving in capital as a result of substitution of labour for it. It is worthwhile to note that since in Harrod's concept of neutral technological change, rate of profit and capital-output ratio remain constant, it means that distribution of income between profits and wages will remain unchanged following such a type of technological change. In terms of Harrod's growth model, the implication of capital-output ratio remaining constant when a neutral technological change occurs is that *relative shares of wages and profits in national income* remains constant as balanced growth of national income takes place.

Harrod's concept of neutral technological change is graphically illustrated in Fig. 8.5. In this figure, as in the previous one, capital per man is measured along the *X*-axis and output per man is measured up the *Y*-axis. Initially, the production function curve is OP_1 showing the change in total output as capital per man increases. Suppose the economy is in equilibrium at point T_1 on the production function curve OP_1. At point T_1 on the production function curve OP_1, capital-output ratio is $\frac{OK_1}{OY_1}$. The straight line *OR* passes through the origin. Therefore, all points on the straight line *OR* such as T_1 and T_2 *represent the same capital-output ratio. Thus capital-output ratio at* T_2 is equal to $\frac{OK_2}{OY_2}$.

Hence

$$\frac{OK_2}{OY_2} = \frac{OK_1}{OY_1}$$

Suppose there is technical progress and as a result production function shifts from OP_1 to OP_2. The economy will now be in equilibrium at some point, say T_2, on the new production function OP_2. As the points T_1 and T_2 lie on the same straight line *OR* passing through the origin, capital-output ratio at the equilibrium position before and after the assumed technical change has remained unchanged.

But for technological change to be neutral in the Harrodian sense, not only capital-output ratio should remain the same but also rate of profit should remain unchanged as production function changes and we move along the ray *OR* representing a given level of capital-output ratio. Now, the rate of profit which is assumed to be equal to the marginal product of capital will be given by the slopes of the production function at the relevant points. If the technological change which has raised the production function from OP_1 to OP_2 is to be Harrod-neutral, then slope at point T_1 on production function OP_1 and slope at point T_2 on production function OP_2 must be the the same. The slope of functions at T_1 and T_2 would be the same if the tangents drawn at these points are parallel to each other. This is exactly the case in Fig. 8.5 where tangent drawn at point. T_1 on the production function OP_1 before technical change and tangent drawn at point T_2 on production function OP_2 after the technical change are parallel.

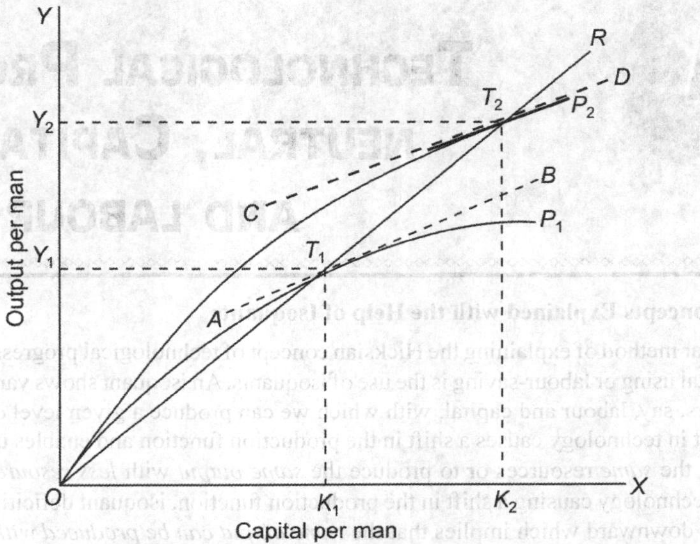

Fig. 8.5. *Harrod's neutral technological change*

Nature of Technological Change and Income Distribution

As mentioned above, in Harrod's growth model, neutrality of technological progress implies that income distribution between wages and profits will remain constant as equilibrium growth of the economy occurs. In Harrod's growth model, there are two factors of production–labour and capital – and growth with neutral technological progress causes increase in incomes of both workers and capitalists. Income of workers increase as rate of wages per man hour rises due to increase in their productivity as a result of technological change. Profits of capitalists increase because they accumulate more capital assets as growth proceeds, though rate of profit per rupee worth of capital remains the same. Thus, commenting on Harrod's growth model with neutral technological progress Stonier and Hague write, "The workers' standard of living will rise because his wage rate has risen. The capitalist's standard of living will rise too but it will do so because he gets much the same rate of return on each pound's worth of a bigger stock of capital."[6]

However, if in Harrod's growth theory *capital-saving technological progress* occurs, the share of profits in national income will fall and that of wages will rise. On the other hand, if *labour-saving technological progress* occurs the share of profits in national income will rise and share of wages will decline during the process of growth.

6 Stonier and Hague, *A Textbook of Economic Theory*, 5th edition, 1980, p. 654.

APPENDIX 8A

TECHNOLOGICAL PROGRESS: NEUTRAL, CAPITAL-USING AND LABOUR-SAVING

Hicksian Concepts Explained with the Help of Isoquants

A popular method of explaining the Hicksian concept of technological progress as to whether it is neutral, capital using or labour-saving is the use of isoquants. An isoquant shows various combinations of two factors, say, labour and capital, with which we can produce a given level of output. Now, an advancement in technology causes a shift in the production function and enables us to produce *more output* using the *same* resources or to produce the *same output* with *less resources*. When there is progress in technology causing a shift in the production function, isoquant deficiting a given level of output shifts downward which implies that the *same output can be produced with smaller amounts of factors*. A shift in the production function brings about a change in marginal products of factors and, therefore, in marginal rate of technical substitution between labour and capital. Due to its effect on $MRTS_{LK}$ or ratio of MP_L/MP_K, the technological change affects income distribution or relative shares of factors. We explain below the neutral, capital-using and labour-saving technological change with the help of isoquants.

Various Types of Technological Progress. Technological ch@anges have been classified by J. R. Hicks into three categories (*i*) neutral, (*ii*) capital-using and (*iii*) labour-using technological change. It may be noted that technological advancement implies that a given level of output can be produced with smaller quantities of factors and, therefore, isoquant shifts downward as a result of this. *Technological change is said to be neutral, if at a given and constant capital-labour ratio, marginal rate of technical substitution* $\left(=\dfrac{MP_L}{MP_K}\right)$ *remains the same when due to the progress in technology isoquants representing production function shift downward.* This is illustrated in panel (a) of Fig. 8A.1. It will be seen from panel (a) that initially a firm is at isoquant Q producing the level of output Q and OR is a linear ray drawn from the origin representing constant capital-labour ratio equal to its slope. Now, as a result of neutral technological progress isoquant representing level of output Q shifts downward to the new position Q' (dotted) and along the ray OR of constant capital-labour ratio (K/L), the firm reaches at point B. It will be found that the slope of the tangent drawn at point B on the new isoquant, Q' indicating $MRTS_{LK}$ is the same as at point A of the ray OR on the initial isoquant Q.This occurs when the nature of technological change is such that it equally increases the marginal products of both labour and capital so that marginal rate of technical substitution ($MRTS_{LK}$) which is equal to the ratio of MP_L/MP_K remains the same.

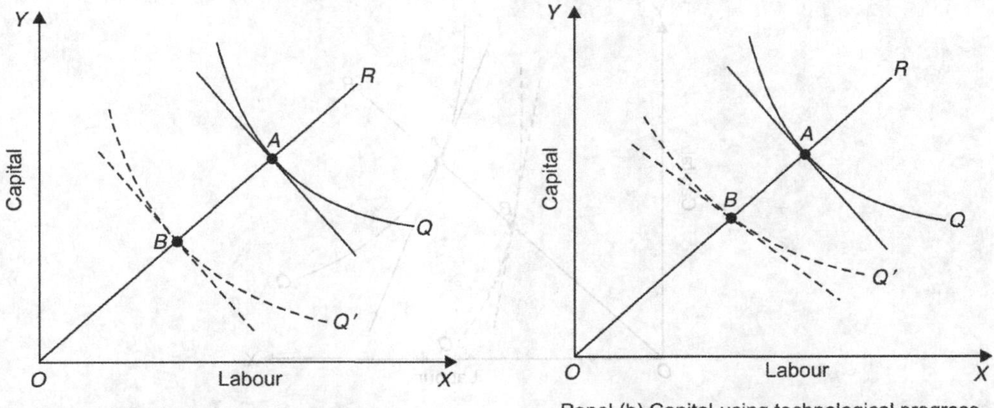

Fig. 8A.1. *Different types of technological progress*

Capital-Using Technological Progress. According to Hicks, *technological progress is capital-using (or capital deepening) if it raises the marginal product of capital relative to labour*. This means that with the shift in the isoquants representing production function, capital biased technological change will cause the marginal rate of technical substitution ($MRTS_{LK}$), which is the ratio of marginal product of labour to marginal product of capital $\left(\frac{MP_L}{MP_K}\right)$, to decrease. Panel (b) of Fig. 8A.1 illustrates the capital-using technological change. It will be seen from panel (b) that the linear ray *OR* from the origin depicting a given constant capital-labour (*K*/*L*) ratio intersects the initial isoquant *Q* at point *A* and the new isoquant *Q*′ at point *B* after its downward shift due to the technological advancement. *A* glance at panel (*b*) will reveal that the slope of the tangent depicting $MRTS_{LK}$ drawn at point *B* on the isoquant *Q*′ is less than at point *A* on the initial isoquant *Q*. This implies that marginal rate of technological substitution ($MRTS_{LK}$) has declined as a result of technological change showing that this is the case of capital-using or capital-deepening technological progress. (Note that when due to technological progress MP_K *rises* relatively to MP_L, the ratio $\frac{MP_L}{MP_K}$ will fall).

Labour-Using Technological Change. Lastly, labour-saving technological change occurs when it leads to the increase in marginal product of labour relative to marginal product of capital so that marginal rate of technical substitution of labour for capital ($MRTS_{LK}$) at the constant capital labour (*K*/*L*) ratio increases. Panel (c) of Fig. 8A.2 illustrates the case of labour-using technological change. With the improvement of technology.and consequent downward shift in the isoquant representing a given level of output shifts from *Q* to *Q*′. It will be seen at point *B* on the ray *OR* that the slope of the new isoquent *Q*′ is greater than at point *A* on the initial isoquant *Q* which means that marginal rate of technical substitution of labour for capital ($MRTS_{LK}$) has increased with the change in technology, capital-labour ratio remaining constant. Thus, panel (c) represents the case of labour-using technological progress.

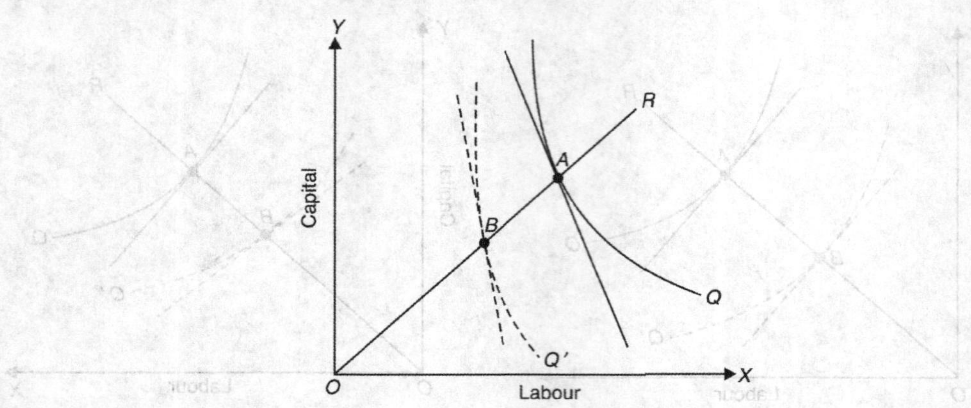

Fig. 8A.2. *Panel (c) Labour-using technological progress*

CHAPTER

9

HUMAN RESOURCE DEVELOPMENT: EDUCATION AND ECONOMIC GROWTH

The Concept of Human Capital

Capital embodied in human beings in the form of education and health which make them more productive is called human capital. As explained in an earlier chapter, like physical capital human resources or human capital plays a significant role in determining economic development. More education makes the human beings more productive through enhancing their skills, abilities, knowledge and better health enables them not only to participate in the production process but increase their capabilities to produce more. Thus education and health can add to the value of production in the economy and also to the incomes of the persons who have been educated and made healthy.

The human capital is embodied in human beings. Human capital comprises the education, knowledge, the skills, better health and the capacities of all people in the society to undertake production. On the other hand, the physical capital consists of produced means of production such as machines that are used in producing other goods. Economic development calls for both forms of capital accumulation. And both forms of capital call for investment. Investment in human capital has therefore been called '*investment in man*'. Education plays a crucial role in the ability of a country to absorb modern technology and to generate the capacity for self-sustained growth and development. Health is also essential for increase in productivity of labour and, therefore, not only raises the private incomes but also contributes to the growth of GDP. Thus, Todaro and Smith write, "Both health and education can also be seen as vital *components of growth and development* as inputs to the aggregate production function. Their role as both inputs and output gives health and education their central importance in economic development."[1] In this chapter we explain the role of education in economic development and in the next chapter we will examine the role of health in economic development of the country.

Till recently economists have been considering physical capital as the most important factor determining economic growth and have been recommending that rate of physical capital formation in developing countries must be increased to accelerate the process of economic growth and raise the living standards of the people. But in the last three decades economic research has revealed the importance of education as a crucial factor in economic development. Education refers to the development of human skills and knowledge of the people or labour force. It is not only the quantitative expansion of educational opportunities but also the qualitative improvement of the type of education which is imparted to the labour force that holds the key to economic development. Because of its significant contribution to economic development, education has been called as human capital and expenditure on education of the people as investment in man or human capital. Speaking of the importance of education or human capital. Prof. Harbison writes: *"Human resources constitute the ultimate basis of production, human beings are the active agents who accumulate capital, exploit natural resources, build social, economic and political organisations, and carry forward national*

1 Michael P. Todaro and Stephen C. Smith, *Economic Development*, Tenth edition, 2012, Pearson Education, pp. 369-70.

development. Clearly, a country which is unable to develop the skills and knowledge of its people and to utilise them effectively in the national economy will be unable to develop anything else."[2]

Important Role of Education or Human Capital in Economic Development

Gross domestic product of a country depends on not only the amount of labour (*i.e.* work-hours) used for producing goods and services but also on its productivity. *One of the important factors that determines productivity of worker is human capital, that is, education.* As seen above, in the modern economics the concept of capital is not confined to physical capital such as machines, tractors, capital equipment, etc. that raises productivity of labour but also includes what is called human capital. By human capital we mean the skills and knowledge that workers acquire through education and training. This human capital, that is, knowledge and skills, are accumulated by human beings through education during the time they spend in primary and secondary schools and up to graduation and post-graduation in colleges or universities. Besides, specialised professional education such as engineering, computer training, management education and others raises greatly the productivity of workers. Therefore, *accumulation of human capital is generally called investment in people*.

Just as a firm considers whether to invest in physical capital, individuals decide whether to invest in their own human capital. When a firm purchases a machinery and other capital equipment to produce more output and increases its future profits, individuals invest in education or acquiring skills to raise their productivity and their future earnings. *Investment in education or acquiring new skills is called investment in human capital*. While usual models of labour supply assume that wage rate of individuals is fixed, however through investment in human capital the individuals can raise their wages or earnings as investment in human capital raises their productivity and it has been found that in the United States rate of return on investment in secondary education is 10 to 13 per cent higher.

According to Prof. Amartya Sen, the improvement in the availability and quality of education result in higher level of *functionings and capability* of labour. He has shown in his works[3] that for a country a low level of education lowers the growth of GDP due to shortages of labour with appropriate skills. Besides, the empirical evidence available suggests that countries which have invested more in education as measured by average years of schooling tend to experience, other things remaining constant, higher rate of growth. Furthermore, higher technical education help to discover new inventions and innovations and thereby promote technological progress.

Human capital, though less tangible than physical capital, is similar to it in many ways. First, like physical capital, accumulation of human capital increases the ability of a country to produce more goods and services. Secondly, like physical capital, human capital is a produced factor of production. Producing human capital requires investment in inputs such as student time, teachers, books and libraries, college buildings. Thirdly, like the physical capital, the accumulation of human capital increases the productivity of workers and therefore causes their wages to rise. Fourthly, *like the accumulation of physical capital, the accumulation of human capital requires the sacrifice of some present consumption so as to have more consumption in future*.

Cost of Human Capital or of Acquiring Skills

Human capital is built through acquiring more education or skills by spending more time in school, college or university. Thus, in spending more time in acquiring more education, one not only delays one's entry into labour force but also sacrifices income or wages which he could have earned by working during the time he spends for acquiring education. *This is the opportunity cost of acquiring more education, skills and grades (i.e., accumulating more human capital*). But they spend time in acquiring more human capital with the expectation that they would be able to earn higher income or wages in the future as more education and higher skills raise the productivity of

2 Frederick Harbison, *Human Resources as the Wealth of Nations*, Oxford University Press, 1973, p. 3.

3 See his works, (1) *Development as Freedom* and (2) *An Uncertain Glory: India and its contradictions.*

the workers and therefore their wages. Thus, *the students, like the people who save, face a trade-off between less consumption today for more consumption in the future*.

Thus, "*spending more on education today (reducing consumption) raises future income but each additional investment in education provides a smaller and smaller return*"[4]. It follows from above that, like physical capital, expenditure on education also represents investment in capital which raises productivity in the future. Besides, investment in education is tied to specific human being and therefore it is called human capital. Thus, according to Mankiw, "*Like all forms of capital, education represents an expenditure of resources at one point in time to raise productivity in the future. But unlike an investment in other forms of capital, investment in education is tied to a specific person and this linkage is what makes it human capital.*"[5] It is important to note that workers endowed with higher education (*i.e.*, more human capital) earn more income or wages than those having less education. The differences in wages between those with more education and those with less education are quite large and have been increasing. For example "*College graduates in the United States earn about twice as much as those workers who end their education with a high school diploma*"[6] *It may be noted that this difference in earnings between workers with more human capital and those with less human capital on an average tends to be even larger in developing countries where educated workers are in scarce supply*."[7]

That investment in education or human capital has a cost can be easily illustrated. Economists are generally concerned with the *opportunity cost of time* spent in acquiring education or human capital. If you are attending a class acquiring education you cannot be working simultaneously at a job yielding you some income. Therefore, by attending computer classes you forgo some wages or earnings and hence some consumption which represents the cost of acquiring human capital.

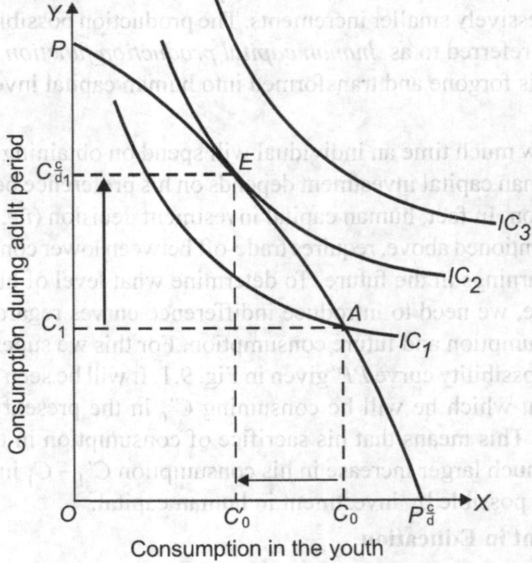

Fig. 9.1. *Trade-off between consumption in youth period and consumption in the period of adulthood*

How decision regarding more investment in education (human capital) involves trade-off between consumption in the period of youth and consumption in later working years is depicted

4 Joseph E. Stiglitz, *Principles of Economics*, W.W. Noton & Co., New York, 1997, p. 170.
5 N. Gregory Mankiw, *Principles of Economics*, Thomson, 2nd edition, 2001, p. 419.
6 Mankiw, *op. cit*., p. 419.
7 Stiglitz. *op. cit*., p. 171.

in Fig. 9.1 through production possibility curve PP'. On the horizontal axis consumption in youth is measured, while consumption in later working years (*i.e.*, the period of adulthood) is measured along the vertical axis.

Illustration of importance of investment in education and acquiring of human capital will bring out the importance of investment in human capital for raising earnings or living standards of the people. To keep things simple assume that only option before our individual is to invest in human capital, that is, acquiring education and that he has no access at all to financial capital market. Let us assume that *in the absence of any investment* in human capital the individual is at point A of the production possibility curve PP'. In this situation A individual's consumption is C_0 in the youth and C_1 in the adulthood period. Thus the situation at point A represents what is called the *endowment point*. Now suppose individual has the opportunities to attend classes of computer programming which is in fact a decision to make investment in human capital. By attending the computer programming classes the individual would have to forgo some present consumption as he would not be working to earn income during that period.

However, by acquiring the knowledge of computer programming he would be enhancing his productivity and earning capacity in the adulthood period. In fact, more time he spends in attending acquisition of computer education, the higher will be his earnings in the adulthood period. However, this process of spending more time in getting education of computer programming is subject to diminishing marginal returns. Each extra hour of computer class raises his earning ability by successively smaller marginal amount. With these assumptions, the opportunities of the individual are reflected in production possibility curve PP' in Fig. 9.1. It will be seen that this production possibility curve PP' is *concave* to the origin and its curvature implies that each rupee reduction in consumption in the present period (that is, in youth) increases the future earnings in terms of consumption by successively smaller increments. The production possibility curve PP' drawn in Fig. 9.1 is therefore often referred to as *human capital production function*. It shows how consumption in the present period is forgone and transformed into human capital investment and higher earnings in the adult period.

To determine how much time an individual will spend on obtaining computer education or skill formation, that is, human capital investment depends on his preference between present consumption and future consumption. In fact, human capital investment decision (*i.e.*, investment in education or skill formation), as mentioned above, requires trade-off between lower consumption level in the present in return for higher earnings in the future. To determine what level of human capital investment the individual will choose, we need to introduce indifference curves regarding individual's preference between present consumption and future consumption. For this we superimpose indifference curves upon his production possibility curve PP' given in Fig. 9.1. It will be seen from Fig. 9.1 that individual will choose point E at which he will be consuming C'_0 in the present period of youth and C'_1 in the adulthood period. This means that his sacrifice of consumption in the period of youth equal to $C'_0 - C_0$ has led to a much larger increase in his consumption $C'_1 - C_1$ in the adulthood as a result of higher earnings made possible by investment in human capital.

Return on Investment in Education

The studies conducted by the World Bank show that economic returns on investment in education appears to be higher than in alternative kinds of investment, especially in physical capital. Further it has been found that rate of return to education of all the three levels in developing countries is higher than in developed countries. An important study based on available statistical data of both developing and developed countries was made by George Psacharopoulos found that in the early 1990s private returns on primary, secondary and higher education were higher in developing countries of Sub-Saharan Africa, Asia and Latin America than the developed countries (see Table 9.1). For instance, private return to primary education was 41% in Sub-Saharan Africa, 39% in Asia, 26% in Latin America as compared to 22% in developed OECD countries.

Table 9.1. Private Rate of Return (%) of Different Levels of Education

Country Type and Region	Primary Education	Secondary Education	Higher Education
Developing			
Sub-Saharan Africa	41	27	28
Asia	39	19	20
Latin America	26	17	20
Developed	22	12	12

Source: George Psacharopoulos, Returns to Education: A Global update, *World Development* 22 (1994), pp. 1325-1343

Another fact worthwhile to note is that private return to education tends to fall as level of development (measured by the level of per capita income) increases.

Besides, there are *social returns* to investment in education which take into account the *externalities* which do not enter into the calculations of private individuals in their assessment of private return on education. We will explain these social returns on education later in this chapter.

Education and Sources of Economic Growth

The supply of human capital plays a crucial role in promoting economic growth. In an important study, Edward F. Denison[8] has measured the relative importance of various sources of economic growth in the United States for the 50 years period, 1929-69.

Table 9.2. Sources of US Economic Growth

Source	Per cent Contribution to Growth Rate	
	1929-1969	1948-1969
Advances in knowledge	31.1	34.1
More work done	28.7	23.9
Capital accumulation	15.8	21.6
Increased education	14.1	11.9
Others	10.3	8.5
Total	100	100

Rate of economic growth in the US economy was on an average 3.3 percent during the period 1929-69 of the study. It will be seen from Table 9.2 that the most important source of economic growth (31.1 to 34 per cent) was advances in knowledge (which includes improvement in technological knowledge) that takes place as a result of increase in education and in research and development activity. The next important source of economic growth was increase in the quantity of labour force (*i.e.*, more work done) as measured by increase in hours worked by labour which contributed about 28.7 per cent during the period of study. Contrary to expectations of economists, accumulation of physical capital contributed only 15.8 per cent during the entire period (1929-69) and 21.6 per cent during 1948-69 to the growth in GDP in the United States. For the entire period of study (1929-69) increase in education (*i.e.*, number of years spent in schools, colleges and universities) contributed almost the same as accumulation of physical capital (14.1 per cent as against 15.8 per cent of physical capital. However, if we club the contribution of increased education and advances in knowledge, their contribution is as high as about 45 per cent to growth.

Other sources include the efficient use of available resources, economies of scale, a shift of labour force from low-productivity agricultural sector to higher productivity industrial sector which contributed about 10 per cent to growth in GDP. It may however be noted that Denison could not measure directly the contribution of advances in knowledge. He measured the contributions of other four sources of growth, namely, more labour work, accumulation of physical capital, increased education, and others (as mentioned above) and assumed that all economic growth that could not be explained by other sources was the contribution of advances in knowledge.

8 Edward, E. Denison, *Accounting for US Economic Growth, 1929-1969* (Washington D.C., Brookings Institution, 1974.

As it pays to the individual to invest in human capital (education or skill formation), similarly, the community as a whole can raise its consumption or living standards by investing in human capital.

MEASURING CONTRIBUTION OF EDUCATION TO ECONOMIC GROWTH

Several empirical studies made in developed countries, especially the U.S.A., regarding the *sources of growth or*, in other words, contributions made by various factors such as physical capital, manhours, (*i.e.*, physical labour), education etc. have shown that education or the development of human capital is a significant source of economic growth.

It may be pointed out that economists generally hold that while some investments in education are '*economic*' in the sense that they promote growth directly, other expenditures on education and development of the human resources are basically of the form of '*social investment*' which, therefore, should be determined residually. It is not possible to separate out the consumption and investment parts of the expenditure on education so that it is very difficult to estimate the rate of financial return on education in the same manner as in the case of a factory or a dam. At best, one can only recognise the probable importance of the expenditure on education in the process of economic growth.

The estimation of return on investments in education or human capital is beset with many difficulties. The fact is that human resource development encompasses a wide field. It cannot be solely examined in economic terms. For instance, it is not very realistic to estimate the return on education purely in terms of the increases in individual incomes or the income of the economy taken as a whole. Also, the increases in productivity do not by themselves constitute the effectiveness of human capital. Notwithstanding these considerations, economists have attempted to measure the contribution of education to economic growth solely on the basis of economic criteria.

We may mention here, in broad outline, the basis on which return and, therefore, role of investment in human resources, particularly education, has been sought to be incorporated in the mainstream of economic analysis. The following are the main approaches that have been developed to gauge the productivity of investment in education.

The Residual Approach or Production Function Approach

There have been some attempts to estimate the proportion of the measured increase in gross national product attributable to education. This is sought to be done by first determining the increase in gross national product on account of the measurable inputs of labour and capital. Then this figure is subtracted from the figure of GNP, to get a 'residue' which represents the increase in GDP due to the improvements in the quality of labour as a consequence of education.

Professor Solow[9], who was one of the first economists to measure the contribution of human capital to economic growth, estimated that for United States between 1909 and 1949, *57.5 per cent of the growth in output per manhour could be attributed to the residual factor which represents the effect of the technological change and of the improvement in the quality of labour mainly as a consequence of education.* He estimated this residual factor determining the increase in the total output on account of the measurable inputs of capital and labour (man hours). He then subtracted this figure from the total output to get the contribution of residual factor which represented the effect of education and technological change, the physically immeasurable factors.

As explained above, Denison[10] another American economist, made further refinement in estimating the contribution to economic growth of various factors. Denison tried to separate and measure the contributions

9 Robert M. Solow, Technical Change and Aggregate Production Function. *Review of Economics and Statistics*, Aug. 1957.

10 Edward E. Denison, *Trends in American Economics Growth (1929-82)*. The Brooking Institution 1983, p. 30.

of various elements of 'residual factor'. According to the estimates of Denison, over the period 1929-82 in the USA during which total national output grew at the rate of 2.9 per cent per annum. increase in labour input accounted for 32 per cent, the remaining 68 per cent was due to the *increase in productivity per worker*. He then measured the contributions of education of per worker, capital formation, technological change and economies of scale. Denison found that 28 per cent of contribution to growth in output due to growth in labour productivity was due to technological change, 19 per cent to capital formation and 14 per cent due to education per worker and 9 per cent points due due to economies of scale. It is thus clear that education and technological progress together made 42 per cent (14 + 28) contribution to growth in national product.

Limitations. However, the above estimates are not fully reliable. The basic reason for this is that the methods used in calculating the contribution of education, are not free from flaws. Moreover, the data which have been used in the calculations applies only to formal education. *It completely ignores on-the-job training. Also, only private return on education is measured*. But education makes a considerable social contribution also in the form of increased mobility, adaptability and the growth of applied technology. In this sense, these calculations make underestimation of the contribution of education.

There being interrelation between capital formation, technology and growth of knowledge, the component in the residual ascribed to increased knowledge may, in fact, include some capital assets. But, in these methods no distinction has been made between formal and informal education. Again, the differences in the quality or content of education have been ignored.

Notwithstanding these limitations, these estimates highlight the significance of the improvements in the quality of human resources through education, in the process of economic growth.

Rate of Return Approach: Further Elaboration

The contribution of education to economic growth has also been *measured through the rate of return approach.* In this approach rate of return is calculated from expenditure made by individuals on education and the measurement of the flow of an individual's future earnings expected to result from education. The present value of these is then calculated by using appropriate discount rate. For calculating the present value of future earnings with education the appropriate present value formula is used. This method has been used by Gary S. Backer who measured income differential arising from the cost or expenditure incurred on acquiring a college education in the United States. His estimates show that the rates of return on education in the U.S.A. for urban white population were 12.5 per cent in 1940 and 10 per cent in 1950.[11]

Another study on similar lines was made by E.F. Reneshaw. He used Schultz's earlier estimates, for USA of total earnings forgone and the cost of education in high schools, colleges and university. Doing this, he found that the average return on education ranged between 5 and 10 per cent for the period 1900 to 1950.[12]

It is worth noting that *estimates of rate of return on investment in education are based upon private rates of returns to individuals receiving education.* However, by assuming that differences in earnings in a market economy reflect differences in productivity, the rate of return on investment in education is taken to be the effect of education on the output of the country.

Limitations. However, these estimates of the return on education are valid only to the extent to which the underlying assumptions are valid. The expenditure on education has two components: the future earnings and the future consumption. While the educational investment results in increase in the future earnings, it also entails the consumption element in the sense of the direct satisfaction

11 Gray S. Backer, "Underinvestment in College Education". *American Economic Review* (Papers and Proceedings). May 1960, p. 347.

12 E.F. Renshaw, "Estimating the Returns to Education", *Review of Economics and Statistics*, Aug. 1970.

derived from education so obtained. The latter, *i.e.*, the consumption component of investment in education wherein resides the source of future utilities, nowhere enters into the measured national income. To the extent these estimates ignore the future utilities and other external economies of acquiring knowledge, they underestimate the returns on education.

Moreover, the earning capacity of individuals with varying educational levels is not entirely the function of formal education. Other factors such as on-the-job training, experience, family income, social status and natural abilities also influence the earning capacity. But the estimates of return on education take no account of these other factors.

Furthermore, these estimates concentrate only on the measurement of the private rates of return on educational investment. At best, they take into account merely the indirect effects of education on the output of the country on the assumption that the earnings differentials in a market economy reflect the differentials in productivity. But the various groups such as engineers, doctors, teachers and manual workers through collective efforts or trade unionism may distort the relative earnings in the economy. What is more, it is difficult to even estimate the private returns on education where the costs of running an educational institution are negligible. For instance, in India there are a large number of single teacher schools where no fee is charged from the pupils.

Again, as has been argued by Eckaus, the cost (or price) of educated labour which is used in evaluating the rate of return ought to reflect the relative scarcities of the factors involved. However, when the primary burden of educational investment is borne by the government, the prices of educated labour fail to reflect the scarcities of factor inputs that are so used. Also, these estimates of rate of return on education undervalue the importance of education as a stepping stone to further education. The fact is that one level of education leads to another. As such, a comparison of individuals with primary education with those who lack it would simply underestimate the significance of primary education as the basic prerequisite to acquire further education. Further, these estimates of return on education provide no information as to the quantity and quality of education most conducive to economic development.

Schultz Approach: Comparing Expenditure on Education with Income Earned

Another approach to measure the contribution of education is based upon the analysis of the relationship between expenditure on education and income. Using this approach Schultz studied the relationship between expenditure on education and consumer's income and also the relationship between expenditure on education and physical capital formation for the United States during the period 1900 to 1956. He found that when measured in constant dollars, "the resources allocated to education rose about three and a half times (*a*) relative to consumer income in dollars, (*b*) relative to the gross formation of physical capital in dollars"[13].This implies that the "income elasticity" of the demand .for education was about 3.5 times over the period or in other words, *education considered as an investment could be regarded as 3.5 times* more attractive than *investment in physical capital*. It may however be noted that these estimates of Schultz only indirectly reflect the contribution of education to economic growth.[14]

In our above analysis we have explained that education is regarded as investment and like investment in physical 'capital, it raises productivity of the labour and thus contributes to growth of national income. The increased earnings or higher wages made by more educated workers have been considered as benefits not only to the private individuals, but also to the society as a whole. This is because higher earnings presumably reflect higher productivity, increased output in real as well as monetary terms.

13 Schultz, Education and Economic Growth, in Nelson B. Henry (ed.) *The Sixtieth Year book of the National Society for the Study of Education*. University of Chicago Press. 1961.

14 R.S. Eckaus, "Economic Criterion for Education" and Training Review of Economies and Statistics, May, 1964.

Consumption Benefits of Education

We have explained above the investment benefits of education and therefore its effects on productivity and national output. But investment benefits are the only benefits flowing from education. Education also yields consumption benefits for the individual as he may "enjoy" more education, derive increased satisfaction from his present and future personal life. If the welfare of society depends on the welfare of its individual members, then the society as a whole also gains in welfare as a result of the increased consumption benefits of individuals from more education. Economic theory also helps us in quantifying the consumption benefits derived from education. In economic theory, to measure the marginal value of a product or service to a consumer we consider how much he has paid for it. An individual would not have purchased a product or service if it were not worth its price to him. Besides, an individual would have bought more units of a product if he thought that the marginal utility he was getting was more than the price he was paying. Thus *relative prices of various products reflect the marginal values of different products and the amount consumed of various products multiplied by their prices would, therefore, indicate the consumption benefits derived by the individuals.*

It may, however, be pointed out that the prices in a free economy are influenced by a given income distribution and the presence of monopolies and imperfections in the market structure and therefore they do not reflect the true marginal social values of different goods. However, an objective measure of consumption benefits of education is difficult and has yet to be found out. It may also be noted that, *according to the new view, economic development is not merely concerned with the growth of output but also with the increase in consumption and well-being of the society.* Thus Prof. Amartya Sen writes, "Education can add to the value of production in economy and also to the income of the person who has been educated. But even with the same level of income, *a person may benefit from education in reading, communicating, arguing, in being able to choose in a more informed way, in being taken more seriously by others and so on.*[15] Therefore, consumption benefits of education may also be regarded as developmental benefits.

External Benefits of Education

We have explained above the investment benefits and consumption benefits flowing from more education both for the individual and the society. The analysis of benefits has been based on the assumption that private interests of individuals are consistent with the social good. However, private and social benefits do not always coincide, for instance, social benefits may exceed private benefits. This is the case with the education of an individual which not only benefits individual privately but also others. First, education makes people better neighbours and citizens and makes social and political life more healthy and meaningful. Secondly, the ,most important external benefit of more education is its effect on technological change in the economy. More education, especially higher education, stimulates research and thereby raises productivity which undoubtedly benefits the society.

The individual inventor may not receive earnings equal to his contribution to the research. Denison's study of contribution of education to growth whose main findings have been mentioned above clearly shows the external benefits of education. After estimating the contribution of labour (including educated labour) and physical capital to economic growth he obtained an average residual of about 32 percentage to annual growth of 2.9 per cent in the U.S. during the period 1929-60. Denison attributed this to the *increase in knowledge* which is the direct result of research and indirectly of higher education. This is in addition to 14 per cent contribution to the annual growth made directly by increase in education. Therefore, Harris and James concludes, "*If the entire residual indeed stemmed ultimately from education, as some human capital enthusiasts have implied, this would mean that education, directly or indirectly, contributed over 40 per cent of total output growth and 80 per cent*

15 Amartya Sen, *Development as Freedom,* Oxford University Press, 2000.

of increased productivity from 1929 to 1957."[16] If Denison's residual is regarded as mainly due to research stimulated by additional education, then this is indeed a major external benefit of education.

Education, Inequality and Poverty

An evaluation of the role of education in economic development must not be confined to judging its impact on growth in output but should also include its impact on *structure and pattern of economic development as well as on the distribution of income and removal of past poverty*. In the 1950, the most important objective of development has been the maximization of rate of economic growth, *i.e.*, growth of material output and in conformity with this the economics of education also focussed on estimating the contribution of education to the growth of national output. But nowadays policy of economic development has been increasingly concerned with the distribution of income, *i.e.*, how gains of economic growth are distributed and whether poverty is being reduced.

But recent studies have revealed that education, *given the present education system, has tended to increase the inequalities in income distribution rather than reducing them.*[17] The adverse effect of formal education on income distribution has been explained through establishing a positive correlation between level of education received by an individual and the level of his life-term earnings. It has been shown that those who are able to complete their secondary and university education earn *as high* as 300 to 800 percentage more income in their lifetime than those who complete a part or whole of their primary education. "*Since levels of earned income are so clearly dependent on years of completed schooling, it follows that large income inequalities will be reinforced and the magnitude of poverty perpetuated if students from middle and upper income brackets are represented disproportionately in secondary and university enrolments. If for financial and/or other reasons the poor are effectively denied access to secondary and higher education opportunities, then the educational system can actually perpetuate and even increase inequality in Third World nations*."[18]

There are two important economic reasons why in the present education system, children and boys belonging to the poor families cannot complete their education up to the secondary level and in many cases even up to the primary level. First, the private costs, especially 'the opportunity costs' of primary education for the children belonging to the poor families are higher than for students belonging to the rich families. Children of the poor families are needed to do work on their family farms or in other family occupations, that is, the opportunity cost of studying in school is family work sacrificed. On the other hand, benefits of education to the poor students are also lower as compared to those to the rich students. This is because it is difficult for the poor students to be selected for the jobs because of poor contacts and influences as compared to rich students, even though they may possess the same level of education. Even in agriculture where it can be said that more education can benefit all equally because it raises the labour productivity, the *more benefits of education and consequently of higher productivity in agriculture are likely to be obtained by those who own land and have adequate resources to modernise their agriculture*. The benefits of more education and consequently higher productivity of landless labour may go to the landlords for whom they work.

It follows from above that as ***a result of higher private costs and lower expected benefits from education of the poor students, the poor family's rate of return from investment in education of a child is much lower.*** As a result of this, the children of poor families are likely to 'drop out' during the course of primary education. The fact that children and boys of poor family are unable to complete their secondary education couple with the fact that there are large income or wage differentials between different persons of different levels of education explain that education in developing economies

16 S.E. Harris, and F. James, "Economics of Health and Education" in Brown, Neubergar and Palmatier (ed.), *Perspectives* in *Economics*, McGraw Hill, 1971, pp.165-166.

17 Jagdish Bhagwati, Education, Class Structure and Income Inequalities. *World Development*, Vol. 1, No.5. 1973.

18 Michael P. Todaro, *Economic Development*,. Pearson Education (Singapore), 8th edition, 2003 p. 388.

tends to increase income inequalities and perpetuates poverty rather than helps to reduce them.

Education and Rural Development

If the objective of raising the standards of living of the people in general and removal of mass poverty is to be attained in less developed countries like India, then rural development must get the highest priority. In the 1950's and 1960's in most of developing countries, the modernisation and development of the urban sector was given the highest priority in the development plans and more resources were allocated to this sector. But in recent years the thinking among economists all over the world has undergone a significant change, since the development of the large-scale industries and the urban sector has failed to solve the twin problems of poverty and unemployment. It has now been increasingly realised that it is through the emphasis on agricultural and rural development in the strategy of development that the problems of poverty and unemployment can be solved. Since over 65 per cent of the population of less developed countries directly or indirectly depends upon agriculture, rural area needs to be given the highest priority.

Now, education can play an important role in agricultural and rural development provided it is suitably modified and given a rural bias. The present system of education has a strong urban bias so that it is ill-suited to the requirements of agricultural and rural development. Moreover, the emphasis in the present education system is on *general* education rather than on *vocational* education.

A relevant and meaningful education can raise the productivity of the rural labour in agricultural work. It can create new employment opportunities if during the schooling students are educated and trained in some useful skills or vocations. Moreover, education to the poor people will induce in them desire to have fewer children with the result that not only their private level of living will rise, but it will also help the general economic development by checking the growth of population. Above all, education will bring about improvement in their health and nutrition. Phillip H. Coomb, an eminent educationist and economist, has classified different types of education that should be provided to the rural people so as to promote rapid rural and agricultural development. They are:

1. *General or Basic Education*. This should cover teaching the students about reading, writing, elementary mathematics and about understanding of basic science and one's environment. This type of education is being currently provided.

2. *Family Improvement Education*. Under this students should be provided knowledge, skills, attitudes which are useful in improving the quality of human life. Accordingly, this should cover subjects such as health and nutrition, family planning, child care, home repairs and environment improvements etc.

3. *Community Development Education*. This type of education should be so designed as to improve the working of rural institutions and processes so that rural community should be developed. This should cover subjects such as local self-government, co-operative enterprise, running rural development projects etc.

4. *Occupational Education*: Under this students should be educated and trained for performing various agricultural activities properly and efficiently and for imparting education regarding particular agricultural skills and occupations. This would enable the students to make their living through self-employed occupations in agriculture, agro-industries and other non-agricultural works after completing their education.

CHAPTER

10

HUMAN RESOURCE DEVELOPMENT: HEALTH AND NUTRITION

Introduction

Until recently improvement in health conditions like education was not given a priority by most of the developing countries though it was considered desirable for increasing welfare of the people. The improvement in conditions of health and nutrition was also not given much importance as a factor affecting economic growth in the studies of economic growth and development. Recently, more attention is being given to the health and nutrition of the people both at the national and international levels not only as important factors determining well-being of the people but also as factors determining economic growth and development. Health like education is now regarded as human capital which is as important as physical capital as determining productivity of workers. It is worth noting that it is poverty in the developing countries that is responsible for their poor health and nutrition. Mushkin rightly writes, "Improved health and education in developing countries help families escape vicious circle of poverty in which they are trapped".[1]

Basic Needs Approach

It may be noted that in the beginning, during the 1970s attention was given to the importance of health in *basic needs approach to development*. The rationale of basic needs approach has been that direct provision of such goods as health services along with elementary education, housing, access to sanitation facilities, access to safe drinking water supply was likely to alleviate absolute poverty more immediately than the alternative strategy that relies exclusively on accelerating economic growth. According to basic needs approach, benefits of rapid economic growth may trickle down to the poor. Besides, it was pointed out by the basic needs approach that it may take a very long time for economic growth to raise the incomes of the poor to enable them to spend adequately for fulfilment of their basic needs. Besides, it was pointed out that certain basic health facilities such as access to sanitation facilities, safe drinking water, can only be provided by the State.

Amartya Sen's Approach to Health and Nutrition

Amartya Sen in his now well-known work '*Development as Freedom*' and his new book '*An Uncertain Glory: India and its Contradictions*' coauthored with Jean Dreze has presented a new approach to improvement of health and nutrition. Sen's approach is based on his '*human capability approach*' to development. Improvement in health and nutrition, according to Sen, is needed to build up human capabilities for accelerating economic development. Further, according to him, the State can play a constructive role for improvement of healthcare services, as in case of promoting elementary school education. To quote Amartya Sen, "It is necessary to recognise the role of growth and development in the form of enhancing human lives and *freedoms but it is also necessary in this context to appreciate how the growth possibilities of a country depend on the advancement of*

1 Mushkin, Selma, "Health as Investment", *Journal of Political Economy*, 70, 1962, pp. 129-157.

human capabilities (through education, healthcare and other Services in which State can play a constructive role.[2]

The main thrust of Amartya Sen's approach is that improvement in healthcare and nutrition is required not only as a welfare measure but is an important factor in determining economic growth by enhancing human capabilities. With their expanded human capabilities, the people will work more efficiently and productively. Amartya Sen laments that India has not gained much achievement in respect of various health indicators such as life expectancy, infant mortality rate, maternal mortality rate, access to sanitation facilities and safe drinking water facilities as is seen from Table 10.1. It will seen from this table that various health indicators such as life expectancy at birth, infant mortality rate, maternal mortality rate improved as level of national income increases. For example, life expectancy at birth in 2009 was 57 years in low income countries, 68 years in lower middle income countries, 72 years in upper middle income countries and 80 years in high income countries. Similarly, infant mortality rate and maternal mortality rate falls as we go from low income countries to high income countries Indeed, infant mortality rate is more than 10 times higher in low-income countries as compared to the high-income developed countries.

Another important fact revealed by Table 10.1 is that as economic development takes place, there is improvement in health conditions of the countries. Of course, this improvement in health conditions varies in different countries with economic development. This improvement in health conditions can be judged by comparing the numbers of health indicators for the year 2009 with the year 1990. For example, the infant mortality rate per 1000 live births in low income countries fell from 108 in 1990 to 76 in 2009. Similarly, in case of lower middle income countries maternal mortality rate (per 100,000 live births) fell from 400 in 1990 to 230 in 2009. This improvement in health conditions occurs mainly due to increase in access to improved water sources and improved sanitation facilities whose data are given in the last two columns of Table 10.1.

Table 10.1. Levels of Income and Health Measures

Level of Income	Life Expectancy at birth		Infant Mortality rate (per 1000 live births)		Under Five Mortality rate (per 1000)		Maternal Mortality rate (per 100,000 live births)		Access to Improved water sources (% of population)		Access to Improved Sanitation Facilities (% of population)	
	1990	2009	1990	2009	1990	2009	1990	2008	1990	2008	1990	2008
Low Income	52	57	108	76	171	118	850	580	55	64	23	35
Lower Middle Income	63	68	66	43	93	57	400	230	70	86	37	50
Upper Middle Income	68	72	41	19	51	22	120	82	89	95	78	84
High Income	75	80	10	6	12	7	15	15	99	100	100	99
Euro Area	76	81	8	3	9	4	11	7	100	100	100	100
East Asia & Pacific	67	72	41	21	55	26	200	89	69	88	42	59
Europe & Central Asia	68	70	43	19	52	21	69	32	91	95	87	89
Latin America & Caribbean	68	74	42	19	52	23	140	86	85	93	69	79
Middle East & N. Africa	64	71	57	27	76	33	210	88	87	87	73	84
South Asia	58	64	89	55	125	71	610	290	74	87	22	36
Sub-Saharan Africa	50	53	109	81	181	130	870	650	49	60	27	31
World	52	57	108	76	171	118	400	260	77	87	52	61

Source: World Bank: *World Development Indicators*, 2011.

2 Amartya Sen and Jean Dreze, *An Uncertain Glory: India and its Contradictions*, Penguin Books, 2014, pp. 38-39.

Importance of Healthcare as a Factor in Economic Development

It is evident from above that in economics today expenditure on health, like on education, is regarded as a form of investment in human capital. This is because better health increases the productivity of man and therefore expenditure on health and nutrition increases the productivity of man and therefore contributes to economic development of the country. It is however important to note that better health is a basic human need and increases welfare of the people. Therefore, to promote health and nutrition of the people is an important goal in its own right apart from its productivity enhancing effect. Since better health improves the quality of life, everyone gains from the fulfilment of his basic needs. With better health the young can contribute to national output for a longer period for they live longer and work and earn for a longer duration. Further, increases in health raises the return on education by extending the working life of the young.

As health, like education, is regarded as investment in human capital, it is an important factor in economic development. The higher expenditure on health improves the quality of human resources both in the present and future. Better health increases the strength, stamina and ability to concentrate on whatever work a person is doing. This raises the productivity of workers which will lead not only to higher wages of workers but will also increase their contribution to economic growth.

Return on Investment in Health

The return on investment in health is difficult to measure. Though investment in health increases the working life of the people but the problem faced in this regard is what value is assigned to it. In private-cost analysis discounted value of additional earnings made from extended life span as a result of improved health is measured as a return from it. However, from the viewpoint of social cost and benefits, it is harder to measure the return to society of investment in health improvement of the people. In a developing economy with surplus labour where marginal productivity of labour is small or even zero, increased benefits in the form of contribution to growth of output of extended working life resulting from investment in health will be obviously small. Besides, even when workers with better health are employed, increase in their productivity that is exclusively attributable to improvement in health is hard to measure.

However, in our view the quantitative effect on output or productivity of investment in health may be difficult to measure, but it cannot be denied that improvement in health and nutrition represents investment in human capital and makes significant contribution to economic growth. Before Amartya Sen, expenditure on health was considered as a mere welfare measure or fulfilment of a basic human need. It goes to the credit of Amartya Sen that expenditure on improvement of health is regard as a means of enhancing human capability and as such is a factor in economic growth.

Two-way Relationship. It is worth noting that there is a two-way relationship between better health and economic growth. On the one hand, better health contributes to increase in rate of economic growth and, on the other hand, economic *growth not only generates* more individual incomes but also generates more resources to the government which can be used to spend more on further investment in improvement of health and nutrition of the people.

An important benefit of improved health is that *it raises the return on education in several ways*. First, the healthy children tend to have higher school attendance which helps them to learn more efficiently. Secondly, healthy children being more successful in school education are likely to get higher education which raises the chances of their getting higher paid jobs. Thirdly, by causing higher life span better health permits workers to work for a longer period resulting in higher return on education received by them. Finally, healthier persons are able to make more productive use of education at any point in life. Thus, Todaro and Smith rightly write, "Health status, once attained, also affects school performance . . . . . better health and nutrition leads to earlier and longer school enrolment, better school attendance and more effective learning."[3]

3 Todaro and Smith, *Economic Development*, Tenth Edition, 2012, p. 374.

Our analysis of the importance of health and education for economic development and their poor conditions in developing countries shows that while economic growth is an important investment for improving the living conditions of the people of a country, economic growth alone is not enough for *much depends on how the fruits of economic growth are distributed.* If economic growth helps to improve health of the poor people and meet their nutritional requirements, it will not only *directly increase their well-being* but will also give a boost to further economic growth by raising their productivity and capability. If economic growth only makes the already well-off richer, it will not promote real development.

SELECTED HEALTH INDICATORS: A COMPARATIVE STUDY

As has been explained earlier, India's economic growth, especially since 1991, has been quite impressive. In the last two decades (1991-92-2013-14) India has achieved an average GDP growth rate of 7.2 per cent. As a result, it has become the second fastest growing economy of the world, next only to China, another developing country. However, even today India does not appear to fare well in respect of health condition as compared to the other poor developing countries of the world. We have given in Table 10.2 a comparative picture of selected health standards of some poor developing countries and rich developed countries along with their per capita GDP for the years 1990 and 2011.

As regards life expectancy at birth in the year 2011, it was 65 years in India as compared to 69 in Bangladesh and Nepal, 75 in Sri Lanka, 73 in China and 70 in Brazil. It will also be noticed from. Table 10.2 that with economic growth in the last two decades (1991-2011) India succeeded in raising life expectancy by 7 years from 58 in 1990 to 65 years in 2011. This has been possible by lowering maternal mortality rate, infant mortality rate, under 5 children mortality and preventing the spread of diseases such as malaria, tuberculosis, cholera which were some of the main causes of deaths in the country. Some other developing countries have done better than us, but as a highly populated country, India's achievement in this regard in our view is quite good.

Table 10.2. Health Indicators and Per Capita GDP of Some Developing and Developed Countries

Country	Per Capita GDP in 2005 PPP$		Life Expectancy at birth		Infant Mortality rate		Under –5 Mortality rate		Maternal Mortality rate		Exp. on Health as % of GDP 2010
	1990	2011	1990	2011	1990	2011	1990	2011	1990	2011	2010
India	1,193	3,203	58	65	81	48	114	61	600	200	1.2
Bangladesh	741	1,569	59	69	97	37	139	46	800	240	1.2
Bhutan	678	5,088	53	67	96	42	138	54	1000	180	4.5
Nepal	716	1,102	54	69	94	39	135	48	770	170	1.8
Pakistan	1,624	2,424	61	65	98	59	122	72	490	260	0.8
Sri Lanka	2,017	4,529	70	75	24	11	29	12	85	35	1.3
China	1,121	7,418	69	73	37	13	49	15	120	39	2.7
Brazil	–	10,274	66	73*	46	14	56	16	120	55*	4.2
Russia	–	14,808	69	63*	23	10	27	12	74	39*	3.2
United States	–	42,488	75	79*	9	7	11	8	12	24*	9.5
Japan	–	30,680	79	83*	5	2	6	3	12	6	7.8
Korea, Rep. of	–	27,541	71	80*	8	5	9	5	18	18*	4.1
Singapore	–	53,581	74	81*	6	2	8	3	6	9*	1.4
France	–	28,809	77	81*	7	3	9	4	13	8*	9.3
U.K.	–	32,474	76	80*	8	5	10	5	10	12	8.1

Note: 1. Data marked star (*) belong to the year, 2009. 2. Infant and under –5 mortality rates are expressed as per 1000 live births 3. Maternal mortality rates are expressed as per 100,000 live births.

Source: *World Development Indicators, 2011 and* 2013, and *Human Development Report*, 2013.

The same is the situation with regard to infant mortality rate and maternal mortality rate. In 2011 infant mortality rate (per 1000 live births) was 48 in India, which was higher than even Bangladesh (37), Bhutan (42), Nepal (39), Brazil (14). Infant mortality rate was much higher than that in the rich developed countries such as 7 of the United States and 2 of Japan. The same is true of under-five mortality rae and maternal mortality rate (see Table 10.2). However, in the two decade period(1990-2011) India succeeded in lowering under –5 mortality rate (per 1,000 live births) from 114 in 1990 to 61 in 2011 and maternal mortality rate (per 100,000 live births) from 600 in 1990 to 200 in 2011. Although this achievement by India appears to be lower as compared to those of some other developing countries, its achievement according to our view, is commendable considering that India is a highly populated country with 125,000,000 population.

Making a comparative study of the above health indicators, Prof. Amartya Sen[4] and Jean Dreze in their jointly written book, *An Uncertain Glory: India and its Contradictions* (2014), have presented a highly dismal picture of India's achievement in respect of its improvement in health conditions. They thus write, "What is disturbing . . . . is how badly India does in terms of *non-income* features of living standards even with this group of poorest non-African countries." Further, they write, "Aside from GDP per capita India's rank among these 16 poor countries is 10th or worse in most cases. Not only are India's figures worse than the average for the other 15 countries for all social indicators presented here (except for the total fertility rate and male literacy rate), its rank in this group is inglorious 10th for child mortality, 11th for female literacy, 13th for access to improved sanitation and DPT immunisation and absolutely worse (along with Yemen) in terms of the proportion of underweight children." From their comparative study they conclude, "The basic concern remains that, for whatever reasons, India is not doing well at all in many respects even in comparisons with some of the poorest countries of the world. This is not to disparage India's achievements, but to put them in perspective and to focus on the deficiencies that plague India most and which have to be overcome."[5]

Evaluation of Amartya Sen and Jean Dreze

Although India's position with regard to living conditions as measured by health indicators does not appear good in a comparative study, it is not correct to draw a dismal picture of conditions in India, as has been done by Amartya Sen and Jean Dreze. This is because it is not correct to make comparisons on the average rates or ratios such as GDP per capita, infant and under – 5 mortality rate, maternal mortality rate and such other indicators because these average rates or ratios are calculated with a *large population as the base.* As India is a highly populated country with a population of 125,000,000 people, even if it makes a significant progress in absolute terms in certain fields, in terms of rate or ratio of this huge population as the base, this progress becomes too small. This is what has happened in India not only in case of per capita GDP which is a *ratio of total GDP to population* but in case of health and education indicators which are expressed as average rates. Although these ratios or rates are quite low as compared to other developing countries, it is not correct to draw dismal conclusions about India's progress in terms of these rates or ratios. As regards the other two highly populated countries, namely, China and Bangladesh, Jagdish Bhagwati and Arvind Panagariya have challenged the conclusions of Amartya Sen and Jean Dreze.[6]

However, we agree with the policy measures suggested by Sen and Jean Drez about making further progress in respect of health conditions in India. They rightly warn against "*to rely on income growth alone to bring about a transformation of living conditions*" of the people. They recommend that the State has to play a constructive role. Thus they point out "the overwhelming objective of ensuring access to health services and other requirements of good health to all members of the community irrespective of their ability to pay is intrinsically a public responsibility. Further, given the limitations

4 Amartya Sen and Jean Drez, *op.cit.*, p. 48.

5 *Ibid.* p. 50.

6 See Jagdish Bhagwati and Arvind Panagariya, *India's Tryst with Destiny,* Harper Collins, 2014, pp. 73-77.

of market arrangements and of private insurance in the field of health care, *public provision of health services* has an important foundational role to play in the realisation of universal health coverage".[7]

The need for government intervention is more strong for preventing rather than curing diseases. For this the government should take appropriate measures of immunization, improvement of sanitation, access to safe drinking water, management of waste disposal and adopt special measures to check the spread of malaria, tuberculosis etc. In India's new health policy 2014, the decision to raise health expenditure from present 1.2 per cent of GDP to 2.5 per cent of GDP is a welcome measure. With this spurt in health expenditure it is hoped that our health conditions will improve significantly. As has been stressed earlier, it is, level of poverty prevailing in India that is responsible for bad health conditions. If, in addition to increase in national expenditure on health, effective steps are taken to reduce poverty in the country, our health, parameters will definitely improve.

UNDERNUTRITION AND DISEASE PREVENTION

An important gap between the rich and poor relates to the nutrition. It is the level of nutrition that determines health, energy intake and productivity of the people. Besides, the malnourishment and undernourishment make people, especially children, more prone to diseases and determine life expectancy at birth, maternal mortality rate and infant mortality rate. It has been estimated in World Bank studies that around 2 billion people of poor countries suffer from lack of one or more micro-nutrients.

Energy Intake and Level of Productivity

Let us first explain the relationship between energy intake and level of productivity. Energy intake depends upon the calories consumed by the human beings. It is intake of calories that determines the energy level which affects the health, work effort and productivity. Prof. Partha Dasgupta[8] in his important study" on well-being of the poor in developing countries defines *undernourishment as "a state in which the physical functioning of a person is impaired to the point where he cannot maintain as adequate level of performance at physical work or at resisting or recovering from the effects of a variety of diseases*". As mentioned above, it is the daily calorie intake that determines the energy level. There is a certain minimum requirement (γ) of energy intake (*i.e.*, calorie consumption) which a person requires to perform his minimum activities of eating and maintaining essential personal hygiene. Beyond this minimum level (γ), calorie or energy intake affects his work efficiency and

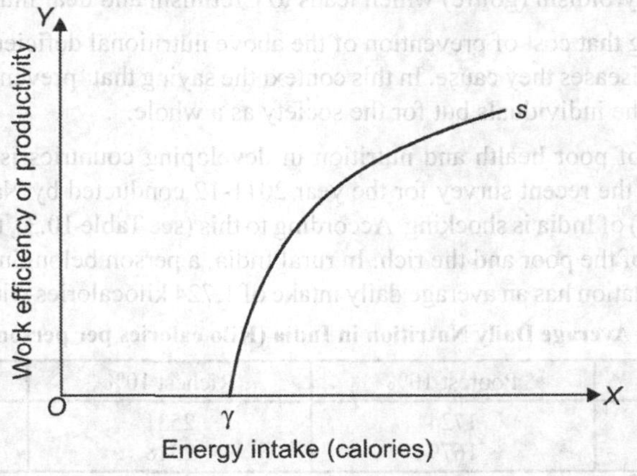

Fig. 10.1. *Relation between energy intake and productivity*

7 Amartya Sen and Jean Dreze, *op.cit.*, p. 179.
8 Partha Dasgupta, *An Enquiry into Well-Being and Destitution*, 1993.

productivity. This relation between energy intake and productivity is depicted in Fig. 10.1 where the curve γ_S traces the effect of increase in calorie intake on productivity beyond the minimum essential requirement (γ).

It will be seen from Fig. 10.1 that as energy intake increases beyond the minimum level γ, productivity or work efficiency increases but at a diminishing rate. However, the recent studies show that in the initial stages this productivity curve is linear rather than having a diminishing slope. Whatever be the case, the important fact revealed by γ curve is that *calorie intake determines the productivity level of human beings*. On the number of calories consumed depends the strength, fatigue and stamina of the people which affect their work efficiency and incomes earned by them. Prof. Partha Dasgupta points out the two-way relationship between food intake and income of the people. *The low income or poverty of the people is responsible for the undernourishment of the people which in turn is the cause of their poverty or low income as undernourishment or low food intake adversely affects their productivity and income earned.*

The root cause of many deaths in developing countries is the diseases which are attributed to malnutrition and micronutrient deficiencies. Diarrhoea, malaria, tuberculosis, acute respiratory infections, Hepatitis B, Dengu are some important diseases from which the people of a country suffer. AIDS is the latest addition to the cause of deaths in poor underdeveloped countries, especially sub-Saharan Africa. Diseases are caused by lack of food energy in terms of nutritional requirements of calorie intake and, consumption of protein and deficiency of specific nutrients in diets of the people. The deficiency of calorie intake causes the loss of body weight, fatigue and mental faculties. Therefore, the persons with deficiency of calorie intake are less productive. Lack of protein in diet causes lower physical and mental development. The recent studies show that deficiency of protein can be made up by the extra calorie intake in diet. Thus calories are now regarded as a crucial factor in nutrition of the people and therefore its deficiency should be given higher priority for maintaining health of the people.

Besides, deficiencies of certain vitamins and minerals also causes several diseases and therefore to ensure adequate nutrition of the people steps should be taken to remove these deficiencies. Deficiency of vitamin A causes blindness and thus makes the children and adults suffering from it quite crippled and unable to do any productive work. Deficiency of iron causes anemia which badly impairs the health of the people. Therefore, in order to ensure adequate nutrition proper measures should be taken and government expenditure on health must be increased. Similarly, deficiency of iodine causes hypothyroidism (goitre) which leads to Cretinism and deaf mutism.

It is worth noting that cost of prevention of the above nutritional deficiencies is much less than the treatment of the diseases they cause. In this context the saying that 'prevention is better than cure' not only applies for the individuals but for the society as a whole.

The root cause of poor health and nutrition in developing countries is poverty itself. In this regard the finding of the recent survey for the year 2011-12 conducted by National Sample Survey Organisation (NSSO) of India is shocking. According to this (see Table 10.3), there is huge difference in nutritional intake of the poor and the rich. In rural India, a person belonging to the poorest 10 per cent of the rural population has an average daily intake of 1,724 kilocalories with protein consumption

Table 10.3. Average Daily Nutrition in India (Kilo calories per person) in 2011-12

	Poorest 10%	Richest 10%	Gap (%)
Rural	1724	2531	46%
Urban	1679	2518	50%

Source: NSSO, 2011-12

at about 45g and fat about 24g. At the other end, the average daily consumption per person of the richest 10 per cent of the rural population is 2,531 K.Cal. the difference of 46 per cent over the poorest 10 per cent. The similar difference is found in case of consumption of protein and fats.

As will be seen from Table 10.3, the nutritional gap between the rich and the poor in the urban areas is worse. In the urban areas in India, the average daily kilo calories intake per person of the poorest urban 10 per cent is 1679, whereas it is 2,518 of the richest 10 per cent which is 50 per cent more than that of the poorest urban 10 per cent. Another shocking result of 2011-12 National Sample Survey is that whereas average Calorific intake per person and average daily protein consumption (gram per person) in both the rural and urban areas have declined marginally, the average fat consumption (gram per person) has increased in 2011-12 as compared to 1993-94 (see Table 10.4).

Table 10.4. Average Daily Nutrition in India, in 1993-94 and 2011-12

	1993-94	2011-12
A. Average Calorific Intake (Kcal per person)		
Rural	2153	2099
Urban	2071	2058
B. Average Protein Consumption (grams per person)		
Rural	60.2	56.5
Urban	57.2	55.7
C. Fat Consumption (grams per person)		
Rural	31.4	41.6
Urban	42	52.5

Source : NSSO Reports

Two things are worth noting in this regard, first, as against the recommendation of National Institute of Nutrition requirement of 2320 Kcal a day for a man aged 18-29 years weighing 60 kg in a sedentary job both in the rural and urban areas, average calorific intake per person is much less than this (see Table 10.4) and for the poorest 10% in both the rural and urban areas situation in this regard is worse (see Table 10.3).

The second fact revealed by the National Sample Survey 2011-12 is that in the past two decades (1993-94-2011-12), eating habits of the Indian people have significantly changed. Whereas the average calorific intake and consumption of protein per person in both the rural and urban areas have declined (see Table 10.4), the consumption of oil and fat per person has increased from 31.4 grams in 1993-94 to 41.6 grams in 2011-12 in rural areas and from 42 to 52.5 grams in urban areas during the same period.

At the national level, daily protein consumption dipped from 60.2 gm for a person in 1993-94 to 56.5 gm in 2011-12 and from 57.2 gm in 1993-94 to 55.7 gm in 2011-12 in the urban areas (see Table 10.4). On the other hand, in the total food intake, the share of items like fruits and vegetables, dairy products and eggs, meat and fish was about 9 per cent in 1993-94 which has marginally increased to 9.6 per cent in 2011-12.

As emphasised above, the root cause of deficiency of food intake of calories, proteins, vitamins and minerals in the diet of children and adults is the poverty that prevails in India and other developing countries. Therefore, the State has to play a constructive role in improving the nutrition of the people, especially children, to raise their work efficiency. In this regard, it is worthwhile to note that recently in India (in 2013) the *Food-Security Act* has been passed to ensure minimum food requirements of the people living below the poverty line. This would help to increase their calorie intake. The pulses should also be added in this food security scheme so as to meet the protein requirements of the people.

The most severe nutritional problem in the developing countries is of infants and children which are the cause of their high mortality rate. If malnutrition of infants and children is not corrected, it will reduce their energy level, physical and mental growth. This nutritional deficiency of children makes them vulnerable to various diseases and lowers their ability to learn in school. Therefore, mid-day meals scheme in school started in India is a welcome step in this direction. Suitably designed, this programme can meet the deficiency of calories, proteins, vitamins and iron and ensure their physical and mental growth. It will also help to reduce their school dropout.

Nutrition of pregnant and nursing women also needs to be increased because carrying and nursing women require extra nutrition as during this period they feed their babies as well. If their extra requirements of nutrition are not met, it would affect the health of their infants and children.

Improvement of nutrition and health of the working adults also requires attention as it will have direct and immediate effect on economic development by increasing their productivity and capability. It may be noted that at the household level the working male adults get priority in meeting their food requirements as there exists *gender inequality* in this regard, especially in India. The female members even if they are working do not get adequate share of the supply of food and other nutrients to the families. This adversely affects their health and makes them more prone to diseases which accounts for higher maternal mortality rate. Starting of Mahatma Gandhi National Rural Employment Guarantee Scheme (MGNREGS) where women also get employment at the same wages as men and *Food Security Act* which is intended to ensure minimum foodgrains to the households below the poverty line (BPL) would go a long way to improve the nutrition and health of women and increase their productivity.

The Millennium Development Goals and Improvement in Health Conditions

UNO had certain targets under its Millennium Development Goals relating to improvement of health and prevention of certain diseases which were to be achieved by 2015. It is now appropriate to know to what extent these objectives are likely to be achieved.

Improvement of Maternal Health

It has been estimated that 287,000 deaths took place worldwide in 2010 (47% decline since 1990) and out of them 2400 maternal deaths were in developing countries. In 2010 more than half of the maternal deaths occurred in Sub-Saharan Africa and a quarter in South Asia. While the number of maternal deaths worldwide has declined but remains high in South Asia. However, fall in it in South Asia has made the largest contribution to the achievement of Millennium Development Goals of reaching a maternal mortality ratio of 220 per 100,000 live births in 2011, down from 620 in 1990, a reduction of 65 per cent. The Middle East and North Africa and East Asia and Pacific have also succeeded in reducing their maternal mortality ratios more than 60 per cent (Fig. 10.2).

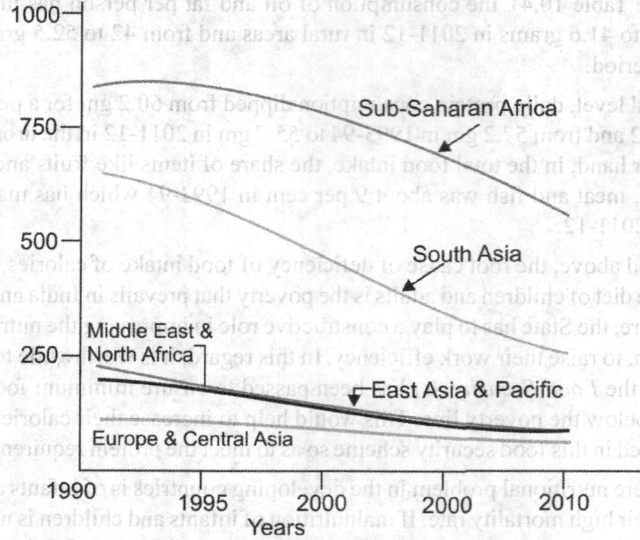

Fig. 10.2. *Decline in maternal mortality ratio since 1990 (most progress has been in regions of sub-saharan Africa and South Asia.*

Source : *World Development Indicators* 2014.

These achievements are impressive but they are less than the target of 75 per cent reduction set by the Millennium Development Goal between 1990 and 2015. Few countries will achieve this target and no developing countries is likely to achieve this

Improved maternal healthcare and lower fertility can reduce maternal deaths. Family planning and access to contraceptive devices can help avoid the large number of deaths that are unwanted and premature.

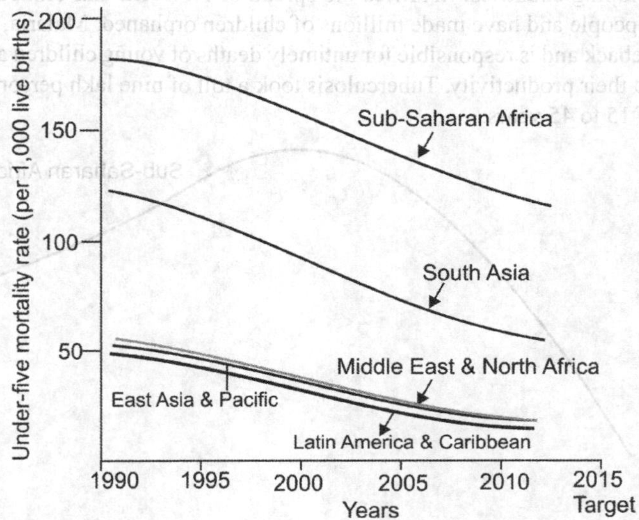

Fig. 10.3. *Under-five mortality rates continue to fall*

Source : *World Development Indicators* 2014.

Reducing Child Mortality

Worldwide in 1990, 13 million children under –5 years age died while in the year 1979 fewer than 10 million of the age under –5 years died in the world as a whole. The deaths of under –5 years age children declined to 7 million in 2012 in the whole world. During 1990-2012, under-five mortality rate in developing countries declined by 46 per cent, from an average of 99 per 1,000 live births in 1990 to 53 in 2012. However, the child mortality rates remain higher in Sub-Saharan Africa and South Asia than in the other developing country regions.

Overall progress with regard to reduction in under –5 mortality rate has been quite substantial but worldwide the rate of decline is inadequate to achieve the Millennium Development Goal to reduce the under-five mortality rate by two-thirds between 1990-2015. However, the average annual rate of decline of under –5 mortality rate accelerated from 1.2 per cent in 1990-95 to 3.9 per cent in 2005-12.

Most children die from causes readily preventable or curable with the existing means, such as pneumonia (17 per cent), diarrhoea (9 per cent) and malaria (7 per cent). Approximately 70 per cent of deaths of children under –5 years age occur in the first year of life, and 60 per cent of those in the first month. Premature birth complications account for 15 per cent of deaths and complications during birth another 10 per cent (UNICEF 2013). Reducing child mortality thus requires addressing the causes of neonatal and infant deaths such as malnutrition, poor sanitation, inadequate care at and after birth and exposure to acute and chronic diseases.

Improvement of infant and child mortality makes the biggest contribution to increase the life expectancy in most countries. Childhood vaccinations are a proven, cost-effective way of reducing childhood illness and death. But despite years of vaccination campaigns, many children in low-and lower middle-income countries remain unprotected as in case of measles. To achieve success, vaccination campaigns must reach all children and be sustained over time.

Preventing Diseases such as HIV/AIDS, Malaria, Tuberculosis and others

Epidemic diseases take a huge toll of human life and as a result of it a good number of opportunities of development are lost. Poverty, undernourishment and malnutrition are the chief causes of diseases that occur in developing countries. In Africa the spread of HIV/AID has tended to reduce the life expectancy of the people and have made millions of children orphaned. Malaria, once checked, has again made a comeback and is responsible for untimely deaths of young children and weakens adults at immense cost to their productivity. Tuberculosis took a toll of nine lakh persons in 2012, most of them of the age of 15 to 45 years.

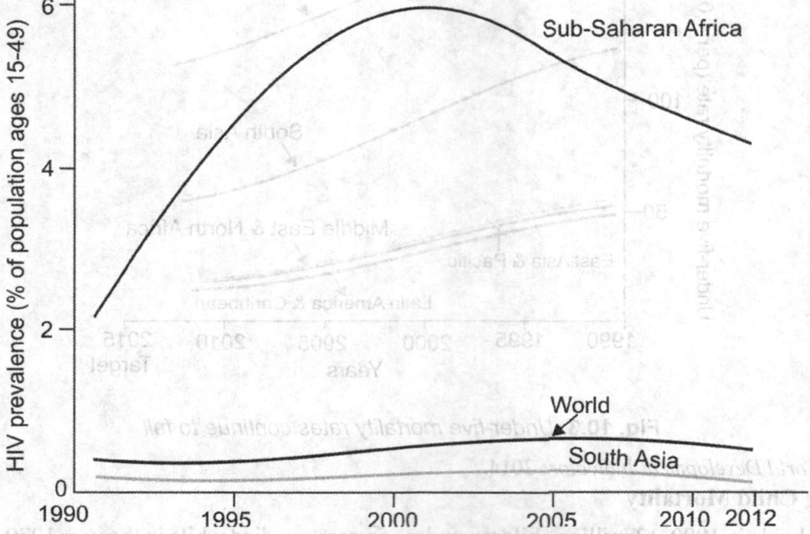

Fig. 10.4. *HIV prevalence in Sub-Saharan Africa continues to fall*

Source: *World Development Indicators* 2014

In the year 2012, worldwide 35 million people already suffered from HIV/AIDS and around 2.3 million more people acquired the disease. People suffering from HIV/AIDS are mostly found in Sub-Saharan Africa but the proportion for the adults suffering from AIDS has started falling as the survival rate of those with access to its new drugs of its treatment has increased. This has helped to halt and reverse the HIV epidemic. This is shown in Fig. 10.4. As regards tuberculosis, globally 8.6 millions people were newly diagnosed with tuberculosis but people contacting, living with and dying from tuberculosis are falling (see Fig. 10.5). If this progress continues and is sustained it has been estimated by the World Bank that the target of halting and reversing the spread of tuberculosis will be achieved by 2015.

People suffering from HIV/AIDS which reduces resistance to tuberculosis, refuges, displaced persons and prisoners living in close quarters and the insanitary conditions are particularly prone to tuberculosis. To prevent the incidence of tuberculosis well-managed policy using appropriate drug therapy to prevent the spread of tuberculosis. As regards malaria, according to WHO (2013) there were an estimated 20 million cases of malaria causing deaths of 6 lakh persons. Malaria is mainly a disease of poverty. There has been a progress in checking the spread of malaria. Although it occurs in all regions, in Sub-Saharan Africa, a most lethal type of malaria is found in plenty. To prevent malaria the insecticide-treated nets have proved to be very effective. Therefore, their use should be promoted.

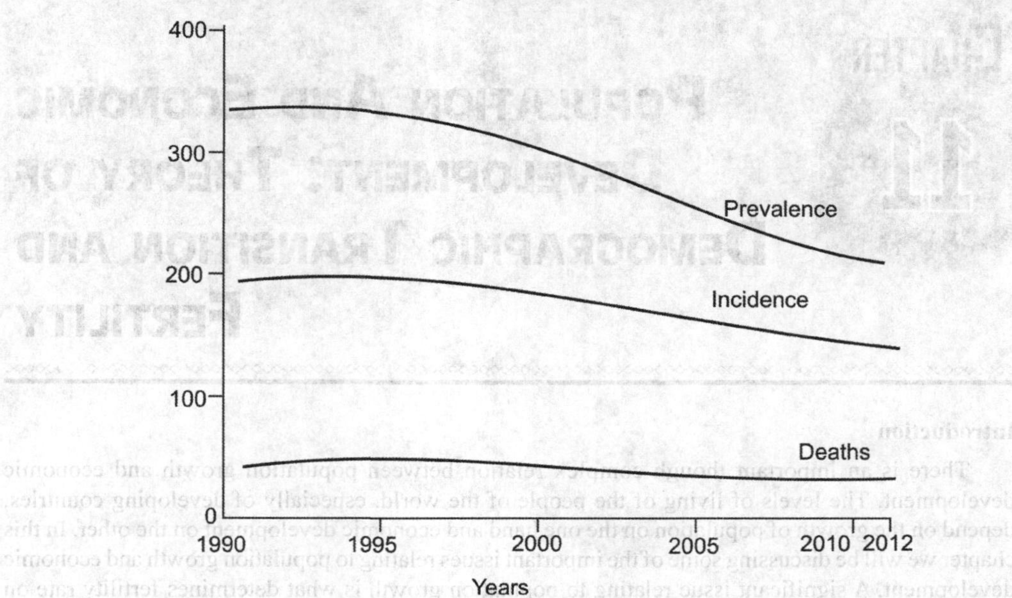

Fig. 10.5. *Tuberculosis prevalence, incidence and death in low and middle-income countries (per 100,000 people)*

Source: *World Development Indicators*, 2014

CHAPTER 11

Population And Economic Development: Theory of Demographic Transition and Fertility

Introduction

There is an important though complex relation between population growth and economic development. The levels of living of the people of the world, especially of developing countries, depend on the growth of population on the one hand and economic development on the other. In this chapter we will be discussing some of the important issues relating to population growth and economic development. A significant issue relating to population growth is what determines fertility rate on which birth rate of a country depends. The second important issue is *how economic development affects birth rate and death rate and thereby determines population growth*. This issue is dealt with in the *theory of demographic transition*. The third important issue is *how population growth affects economic development*, especially in developing countries. As shall be discussed in the next chapter, while population growth by causing increase in workforce helped economic growth in the presently developed countries, in case of labour-surplus developing countries such as India far from helping economic development retards it.

The other important issue is how population growth is responsible for the increase in the magnitude of poverty in developing countries and also cause environmental degradation. The last issue is what measures should be adopted in developing countries to check population growth rate so that economic development be speeded up. An important aspect of population, especially in case of India, is the beneficial effect of change in composition of population toward the higher ratio of young population to the total population which is described as *population dividend*. To what extent and how India can take advantage of population dividend will be explained in the appendix to this chapter.

Population of World, Low-Income, Middle-Income and High-Income Countries

We first start with the analysis of facts about population of world as a whole, low-income, middle-income and high-income countries. As will be seen from Table 11.1, population of the world as a whole was 7 billion in 2012 and according to the estimates of World Bank, world population will be more than 9.2 billion by the year 2050 and will reach a maximum of 11 billion by the end of the 21st century in the year 2200. It will be seen from Table 11.1 the world population is currently (years 2000-2012) growing at the average rate of 1.2 per cent per annum. In recent years due to advancement in medical science and expansion of healthcare facilities life expectancy at birth for the world as a whole has gone up to 68 years for males and 72 years for females. Besides, for the world as a whole adult literacy rate has also gone up to 84 per cent of population which has tended to reduce birth rate and lower the population growth.

In low-income countries population has been growing at the rate of 2.2 per cent per annum during 2000-12 which is quite a high growth rate. In low-income countries adult literacy rate is lower (61 per cent) and life expectancy at birth is also low; 58 for males and 61 for females. On the other hand, in high-income developed countries average population growth during 2000-12 has slowed down to 0.6 per cent per annum as a result of rapid fall in birth rate. This is due to the large increase in literacy rate to almost 100 per cent and large increase in incomes of the people due to economic growth achieved by them. Life expectancy at birth in high-income countries has also gone up to 76 years for men and 82 years for women.

Of special mention are the two most populous countries of the world, namely, China and India whose population data are given in the last two rows of the table. China with 1351 million people has the largest population of the world. However, it has succeeded in lowering its population growth rate to 0.6 per cent per annum in 2000-2012 as a result of the policy of *"one child per couple"* which has been implemented by it through coercive method. Because of this policy *'young dependency ratio'* (*i.e.*, age composition of population, 0-14 years) being equal to 18 per cent is also low in China.

Table 11.1. Population and Key Indicators of Development

Country	Population (in million) 2012	Average annual population growth rate (%) 2000-12	Density per sq. km.	Age composition of population % ages 0-14	GNI in $ per capita, PPP 2012	Life expectancy at birth (years) M	F	Adult literacy rate % age 15 and older
World	7046	1.2	54	26	12129	68	72	84
Low-Income Countries	846	2.2	56	39	1387	58	61	61
Middle-Income Countries	4898	1.2	77	27	7242	67	71	83
Low Middle Income	2507	1.6	122	31	3912	64	68	71
Upper Middle Income	2391	0.8	56	22	10741	71	75	94
High-Income Countries	1302	0.6	25	17	37760	76	82	–
China	1351	0.6	145	18	9210	72	75	94
India	1237	1.4	416	29	3840	64	67	73

Source: World Bank, *World Development Report, 2014.*

Next to China, India with a population of 1237 million in 2012 is the second largest populous country of the world. Its current population growth has come down to 1.4 per cent per annum after 4 decades of explosive growth rate. As shall be explained later, this has been possible because of its more rapid growth of national income and per capita income in the last over two decades and also its literacy rate (especially of women) has gone up to 73 per cent of population in 2011. Both of these factors along with the reduction in poverty have brought about decline in average birth rate to 15 per cent of population and are responsible for reducing the current growth rate of population to 1.4 per cent.

THEORY OF DEMOGRAPHIC TRANSITION

The effect of economic development on the population growth of the countries has been explained with the theory of demographic transition. The theory of demographic transition has been formulated on the basis of experience gained in the historical development of the present-day developed countries. According to this theory of demographic transition as put forward by Karl Sax economic growth has to pass through four stages. These four stages in the demographic transition are as follows :

Stage I: In stage I, birth rate is accompanied by high but varying death rate. As a result, the population of a country in this stage either remains constant or grows slowly.

Stage II: In stage II, death rate steeply declines while birth rate remains more or less at a high level which leads to rapid growth in population. This rapid growth in population above 1.5% per year has been called *population explosion.*

Stage III. In the third stage the birth rates start falling but the death rates level down at low level or show further slowing down. With this the growth of population slows down.

Stage IV. In stage IV birth rates and death rates balance at low levels with the result that population remains more or less constant.

Let us explain these stages of demographic transition in some detail.[1]

It is worth noting that various stages of demographic transition are associated with the various stages of economic growth. The first stage is regarded as a feature of agrarian underdeveloped economies, the second of the take-off period of economic growth and third of the developed countries in their mature stage of economic growth. We shall explain below these three stages in some detail.

Stage I: High Birth and Death Rates. The stage I is regarded as characteristic of pre-industrial agrarian economies which are primitive in nature. As said above, both birth rate and death rate are at high levels in the primitive pre-industrial economies. Birth rate is high because of the practice of universal early marriage, ignorance about knowledge of family planning techniques and lack of motivation to adopt them, deep-rooted social beliefs, customs and religious attitudes which are conducive to enlargement of the size of the families and involve preference for more children. Besides, in these primitive agrarian economies, children are considered as an economic asset because they start working at an early age and supplement to family income. Moreover, more children are regarded as a sort of insurance against old age. To quote Coale and Hoover, the prominent exponents of the theory of demographic transition, "Children contribute at an early age . . . and are traditional sources of security in the old age of parents. The prevalent high death rates, especially in infancy, imply that such security can be attained only when many children are born."[2]

In this stage, the death rates are high but fluctuating. The high death rate is caused by poor diet, bad sanitary conditions, absence of medical facilities. In other words, due to low per capita income, standard of living is very low and this causes a high death rate. In this stage rate of growth of population is nil or low because high birth rate is matched by high death rate. No doubt, this is a stage of high growth potential because of low population growth rate. But due to other several economic and non-economic factors, actual growth rate is very low.

Stage II: Low Death Rates, High Birth Rates: This second stage of demographic transition is regarded as characteristic of the take-off period of economic growth, during which population grows at a very rapid rate. As the economy develops and its per capita income rises, there takes place an improvement in the standards of living of the people. This rise in standard of living enables the

1 There is a lack of unanimity among demographers about the postulated number of stages. For instance, Blacker (*The Eugenics Review*. U.K., Vol. 39, No. 3, Oct. 1947, pp. 88-102) identifies five stages, viz., (i) *The High Stationary*, exhibiting high rates of both natality and mortality; (ii) *The Early Expanding*, marked by high natality but declining mortality, (iii) *The Late Expanding*, with both natality and mortality declining but the latter at a speedier rate; (iv) *The Low Stationary*, exhibiting a balance between low natality and low mortality; (v) *The Declining*, marked by low mortality and natality, the latter lower than the former. Karl Sax divides the demographic transition into four stages. See his, '*The Population, Explosion*' Foreign Policy Association Headline Series, No. 120 (Nov-Dec. 1956, pp. 17-18.

2 Coale, A.J. and Hoover, E.M., *Population Growth and Economic Development in Low-Income Countries*, Oxford University Press (1959), p.10.

people to improve their diets which increase their resistance to diseases. Moreover, as a result of the improvement in the transport system, food supply becomes more abundant and regular. With the rising incomes, there is greater availability of medical facilities and sanitary conditions also improve. All these cause death rate to decline, whereas birth rate remains at almost the previous high level. As a result of this sharp decline in death rate, with birth rate remaining at a high level, population grows rapidly. Therefore, this stage has been called the stage of *population explosion*. The currently developed countries have already crossed this stage but many presently developing countries like India are said to be passing through this stage.

Stage III: Low Birth and Death Rates. Stage III is considered as characteristic of currently developed countries in their present mature stage of economic growth in which most of the Western European countries as well as U.S.A. and Japan find themselves. In this stage, birth rate also starts declining and reaches a low level while the death rate has already reached a low level. Consequently, the two once again balance each other but now at a low level rather than at a high level. As a result, population grows at a slow rate. As the economy develops and makes progress in industrialisation, there takes place a shift of population from the rural to the urban areas. This is generally called *structural transformation* of which industrialisation and urbanisation are important features.

With the rise in incomes, as a result of the growth of urbanisation and industrialisation, standard of living of the people rises which has a favourable effect on the birth rate. In order to maintain their high standards of living and also to raise them further, people deliberately try to limit the size of their families by using contraceptive devices. In the urban setting children are regarded as more of a burden than an economic asset. Commenting on the fall in birth rate as a result of industrialisation and urbanisation, Coale and Hoover write, "*The development of economic roles for women outside the home tends to decrease the possibility of economic advantages of a large family. One of the features of economic development is typically increasing urbanisation, and children are usually more of a burden and less of an asset in an urban setting than in a rural one.*" Thus, with birth rate and death rate at almost low level, the population grows at a low rate but the economy has already reached a level of high per capita income.

Thus, the third stage is characterised by narrowing down the difference between the birth and the death rates at low levels. The birth rates decline low enough and establish a parallel with the already lowly settled death rates. Small families and low mortality becomes the typical pattern.

Countries which appear to have attained a steady rate of growth of population resemble. Western and Southern Europe, U.S.A. and Japan.

A glance at Fig. 11.1 showing the different stages of demographic transition, would reveal that the differences between fertility and mortality rates is small in the first and third stages. The main difference between the '*old balance*' (*viz*., that in the first stage) and the '*new balance*' (*viz*, that in the third stage) is that in the latter case the balancing between the death and the birth rates occurs at a much lower level than it does in the former case.

Population Explosion. As is clear from Fig. 11.1, the second and the early part the third stage constitute the period of population explosion. This is reflective of a big differential between the birth and the death rates. The duration of the '*population explosion*' depends upon the time required to clear the time-lag between the decline in birth rate and the fall in death rate. The death rate falls first and the decline in death rate occurs later.

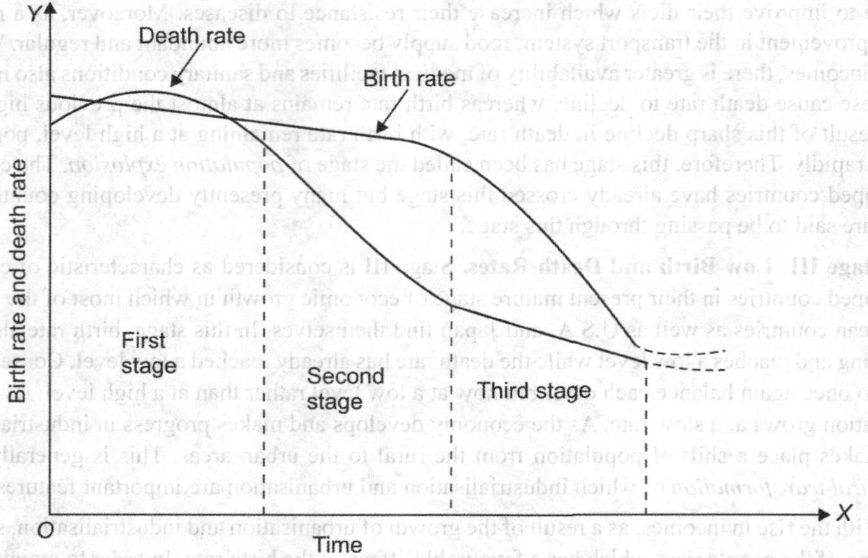

Fig. 11.1. *Three stages of demographic transition*

It may however be noted that the historical pattern of demographic transition differs country by country. In countries such as France and the USA, the birth rate began to decline with little time lag behind the fall in the death rate. "In general, the later a country started industrialisation, the faster the process of demographic transition was completed often with a shift from phase 1 to phase 3, skipping over phase 2, as observed for Japan, Russia and South and East European nations. It appears that the population explosion in developing economies today follows this trend."[3] Similarly, Thirwal writes, "The experience of the developing countries today has no historical parallel, at least in Western Europe. In nineteenth century Europe the birth rate and death rates tended to fall together and population growth never exceeded 1 per cent per annum. It could also be argued that the 'balance of nature' has been upset in today's developing countries. The introduction of public health measures and medical advances reduced death rates suddenly and dramatically but the means and knowhow to effect equally dramatically fall in death rate where not provided. "[4]

Critical Evaluation of the Theory of Demographic Transition

Theory of demographic transition and its application to developing countries has also been criticised. The following shortcomings of this theory have been pointed out.

European experience and not a theory. Firstly, the critics have pointed out the that particular demographic transition is a fact obtained from European experience and not a theory. In other words, the theory of demographic transition only describes the historical experience of population growth and economic growth in currently developed European countries. The experience and the fact of the European development cannot be generalised to formulate a theory which is applicable to developing countries. Therefore, it has been argued that demographic transition witnessed in European development cannot necessarily occur in the developing countries of today. Various reasons have been given in defence of this view. Firstly, it has been argued by Kuznets[5] that the demographic characteristics of the currently developing countries are quite different from those of Europe or other currently developed countries in their period of industrial revolution. According to him, as compared

3 Y. Hayami and Y. Godo, *Development Economics,* Oxford University Press, Delhi, 5th ed. 2005, p. 7.

4 A.P. Thirlwall, *Economic Development*, Palgrave, Macmillan, 9th Edition, 2011, p. 291.

5 Simon Kuznets, 'Underdeveloped Countries and the Pre-Industrial Phase in the Advanced Countries in United Nations, *Proceedings of the World Population Conference*, Vol. V. 1954.

to today's underdeveloped countries, pre-industrial European countries have had smaller size of the population (generally less than 15 million), lower birth and death rates and smaller rates of growth of population. For instance, in England in its period of industrial revolution, largest increase in population per decade was nearly 18% during 1811-21 which amounts to 1.7% per annum. This is substantially below the rate of population growth ranging between 2 and $3\frac{1}{2}$% per year in the currently developing countries.

Causes of decline in death rates are different. Another criticism against the theory of demographic transition as applied to developing countries is that the causes of the decline in death rate in the European countries were different from those operating in the developing countries of today. The decline in death rate in the European countries was mainly due to the rise in the standard of living, improvements in the diet of the people which increased their resistance to the diseases. Medical improvements, except in case of smallpox, was not a significant cause of decline in death rate in the growth of European countries. On the other hand, the sharp decline in the death rate in the developing countries like India is mainly due to the improvements in medicine, public health techniques, use of insecticides, mass vaccination and the discovery and use of antibiotics and sulpha drugs. *These medical improvements have caused a sharp decline in death rate even when the per capita income or standard of living of the people has not shown any significant increase*. In other words, the population explosion in Europe was caused by the rise in per capita income and consumption standards as a result of economic growth, whereas the population explosion experienced by the presently developing countries is due to the factors which are *external* to the process of economic growth. Medical improvements which have brought down the death rate have not been caused by the increase in per capita income but have led to the decline in death rate and have caused rapid increase in the rate of population growth. They are making increases in per capita income even more difficult to achieve.

THEORY OF FERTILITY

To explain the changes in birth rate witnessed during demographic transition, especially fall in the birth rate in stage 3 of the demographic transition with the development of the economy, economists have used the microeconomic theory of family fertility. According to the neoclassical theory of consumer's behaviour, to maximise his satisfaction from consumption of goods, children are treated as normal goods in this analysis of family fertility. As in case of demand for other goods economists use indifference curves between demand for children and all other goods and budget constraint to explain the family fertility. For explaining demand for surviving children and therefore fertility, like the demand for other goods, the following function is employed :

$$C_d = f(Y, P_c, P_x, t_x), \qquad x = 1, \ldots n$$

where C_d represents demand for serving children; Y represents level of family income; P_c is *net price of children* which is the difference between the anticipated cost of children (which includes the direct cost of upbringing of a child and opportunity cost of a working mother's time) on the one hand and benefits (which may consist of potential child income and age old support)[6] on the other P_x stands for price of all other goods, t_x stands for tastes or preferences for other goods relative to having children.

In Fig. 11.2 and 11.3 we graphically represent the theory of fertility. In these figures along the horizontal axis we measure the number of children desired (C_d) and along the vertical axis we measure the demand for other goods by the parents which we write G_p. Families desires and preferences

6 Note that in poor underdeveloped countries where infant *mortality rate* is high, demand for children is net of rate of children born minus infant mortality rate. That is, families take into account the infant mortality rate and therefore actual demand for children is demand for surviving children.

between demand for children (C_d) and other goods (G_p) are shown by a set of indifference curves, IC_1, IC_2, IC_3. Each indifference curve is a locus of various combinations of children and other goods which give the same amount of satisfaction to the parents and the higher the indifference curve, the greater the satisfaction of the parents.

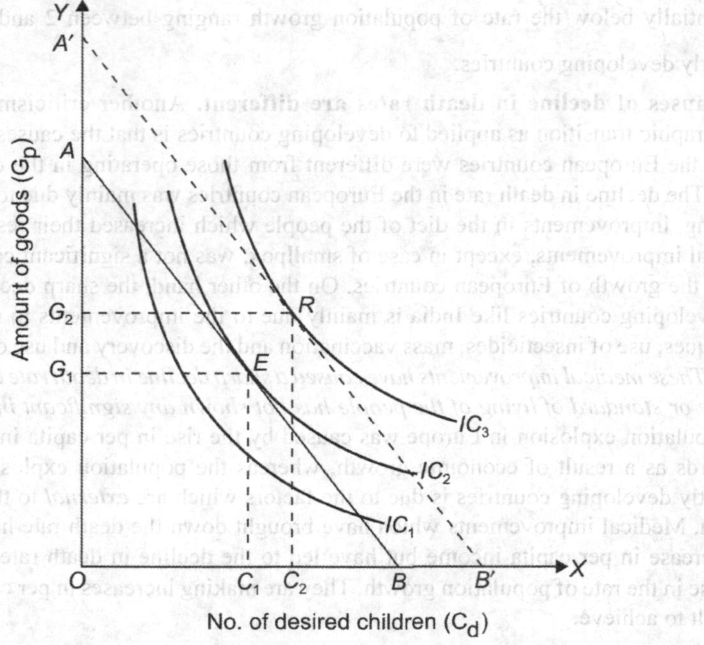

Fig. 11.2. *Family's choice of desired children and the effect of increase in its income*

The family's capacity to buy the alternative combinations of goods and children is represented by the budget constraint line *AB*. Note that the budget constraint line *AB* is determined by the perceived income by the family and prices of goods and children. The price of children is determined by the costs of upbringing of children. These costs are of two types : (1) direct cost of rearing children and as they need to be fed, clothed, kept in good health, given some education, and (2) indirect costs which are the *opportunity cost* of women who look after their children and these opportunity costs are income forgone by the working women during the time they spend for bringing up their children.

It is worth mentioning that steeper the budget constraint line (*i.e.*, the greater its slope), the higher the price of children relative to goods . Now, according to the fertility theory based on neoclassical indifference curve demand theory, from the available combination of goods and children lying on the budget constraint line the family will choose a combination that maximizes its subjective satisfaction. In Fig. 11.2 it will be seen that such a satisfaction-maximizing combination is represented by the tangency point *E* on the budget constraint line *AB*. At point *E*, the family demands C_1 children and G_1 other goods.

Now, if family's income increases, budget constraint line shifts outward, say to dotted *A′B′*. Now, new budget constraint line *A′B′* is tangent to higher indifference curve IC_3 at point *R* and is demanding C_2 children and G_2 goods. This is not surprising as children in the fertility theory are treated as a normal good whose demand increases as income increases. This is particularly relevant for poor countries where children are often demanded as a source of financial security or support.

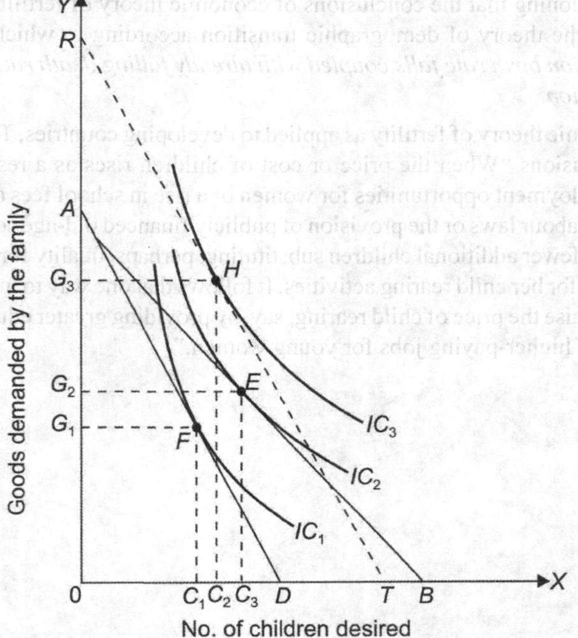

Fig. 11.3. *Impact of rise in opportunity cost of children and of simultaneous rise in cost of children and increase in family's income*

Rise in Cost of Children

Now suppose there is a rise in opportunity cost of children as female member is a working woman who will have to take the responsibility of bringing up the children and therefore she has to forgo her income in the process of upbringing of children. With the rise in opportunity cost of children, budget constraint line will rotate from *AB* to *AD* in Fig. 11.3 and the family moves from equilibrium point *E* on indifference curve IC_2 to the equilibrium at point *F* on lower indifference IC_1 and is now demanding C_1 number of children and G_1 amount of goods; $C_1 < C_3$. That is, with the rise in opportunity cost of children, the family is demanding fewer children. This is an important conclusion from the theory of fertility which has been found to be true by empirical evidence. For example, in the State of Kerala where women are quite literate and are employed, the birth rate is lower as compared to other States of India.

Now, suppose there is *simultaneous* increase in family's income (say, rise in wages) and rise in opportunity cost of children as a result of expansion in employment for women. This will cause both an *outward shift* and *downward rotation* of the budget constraint line. In Fig 11.3 to obtain such a budget line we draw a new budget line *RT* parallel to the rotated budget line *AD* at *a distance* equal to the increase in income. It will be seen from Fig. 11.3 that the new budget constraint line *RT* depicting both the increase in income and rise in opportunity cost of children is tangent to indifference curve IC_3 at point *H* at which family demands or desires OC_2 number of children which are fewer than OC_3 prior to increase in income and rise in opportunity cost of children. Further, at new equilibrium at point *H* on higher indifference curve IC_3, the family is consuming more amount G_3 of goods which makes it better off than before.

Besides, it may be noted that as income of the family increases the parents may like to spend more on each child for providing them better education and keeping then well-nourished and healthy and this would also cause the parents to prefer to have a fewer children.

It is worth mentioning that the conclusions of economic theory of fertility explained above are in conformity with the theory of demographic transition according to which in the *third stage of demographic transition birth rate falls coupled with already falling death rate brings down the rate of growth of population.*

From the economic theory of fertility as applied to developing countries, Todaro and Smith reach the following conclusions "When the price or cost of children rises as a result of, say" increased educational and employment opportunities for women or a rise in school fees or the establishment of minimum-age child labour laws or the provision of publicly financed old-age social security schemes, parents will demand fewer additional children substituting, perhaps, quality for quantity or a mother's employment income for her child rearing activities. It follows that one way to induce families *to desire fewer children* is to raise the price of child rearing, say, by providing greater educational opportunities and a wider range of higher-paying jobs for young women."[7]

7 M.P. Todaro and S.C. Smith; *Economic Development,* Pearson Education, Tenth Edition, 2012, p. 294.

CHAPTER

12

POPULATION GROWTH: HOW IT AFFECTS ECONOMIC DEVELOPMENT, POVERTY AND ENVIRONMENT

POPULATION GROWTH AS AN OBSTACLE TO ECONOMIC DEVELOPMENT

Having discussed the rapid growth of population in India we now turn to explain how population growth in India is hindering economic development. But, to begin with, it is necessary to mention that by economic development we mean not only increase in national income (GNP) or per capita income, but also reduction in unemployment as a result of the growth of employment opportunities and reduction in poverty and inequalities of income. Since economic growth depends on rate of saving and investment and productivity of labour, we will discuss the impact of population growth on these factors.

It is important to note here that in the present day's industrialised development countries, in spite of Mathus' view to the contrary, *population growth was beneficial for economic growth rather than retarding it*. It has been argued by some that population growth leads to the increase in labour force *which is an essential productive resource*. By increasing the amount of labour force population growth will help in producing more output. As someone has remarked, population growth brings in more hands to work for production and therefore contributes to economic growth. Secondly, it has been pointed out that the *increase in population leads to the increase in demand for goods*. Thus growing population means the growing market for goods is enlarged, *they can be produced on a large scale and thus economies of large-scale production can be reaped.* The economic history of the USA and European countries shows that growth of population and labour force contributed a good deal to the increase in their national output.

But wheat has been true of USA and European countries may not be true in case of other countries. Whether or not the growth of population contributes to economic growth depends on the existing size of population, the available supplies of natural and capital resources, and the prevailing technology. In the United States, where supplies of natural and capital resources are comparatively abundant, growth in labour force caused by increasing population raises national output. In India where supplies of other economic resources, especially capital equipment, are relatively scarce, increase in population or labour force does not lead to the employment of all due to scarcity of capital resources. Unemployed people do not add to national output. As for the argument that population growth leads to increase in demand or market for goods, it may be noted that the demand or market for goods increases if the real purchasing power in the hands of the people increases. The mere growth of unemployed or paupers cannot lead to greater demand for goods or expansion in their markets.

Having ruled out the beneficial effects of population growth in the context of the Indian economy we discuss below how population growth in India retards economic development.

1. Population Growth and Rate of Saving and Investment. Economic growth requires increasing supplies of capital goods. A higher rate of economic growth can be achieved by accelerating the rate of capital formation. Increasing supplies in capital goods becomes possible only with higher rate of investment. And a higher rate of investment, in turn, is possible if the rate of savings is high. Now, increase in population by adding to the number of people whose requirements of "feeding and clothing" have to be met tends to raise consumption and, therefore, lowers both saving and investment.

Coale and Hoover, in their famous work explained that saving rate was reduced by population growth because of *increase in burden of dependency.* They argued that with high fertility rate among the younger persons and declining mortality (death) rate among the old-age people in the growing population, the *proportion of non-working age groups* which depend on the working or earning members of their families increases. Since all must consume, in the absence of increase to productivity, saving per person must fall. Thus rapid growth of population by causing lower rate of savings and investment *tends to hold down* the rate of capital formation and therefore the rate of economic growth in developing countries like India. Under conditions like those in India population growth therefore actually impedes economic development rather than facilitates it.

Thus Enke writes, "The economic danger of rapid population growth lies in the consequent inability of a country both to increase its stock of capital and to improve its state of art rapidly enough for its per capita income not to be less than it otherwise would be. If the rate of technological innovation cannot be forced and is not advanced by faster population growth, a rapid proportionate growth in population can cause an actual reduction in income per capita. Rapid population growth inhibits an increase in capital per worker, especially if associated with high crude birth rate that makes for young age distribution.[1]

2. Investible Resources and Raising Per Capita Income. While, on the one hand, rapid growth in population reduces investible resources for accelerating capital formation, *it raises the requirements for investment to achieve a given target increase in per capita income.* Suppose population of country *A* is increasing at 1.5 per cent per annum and that of country *B* at 2.5 per cent per annum. Given that capital-output ratio is 4 : 1, then country *A* would have to invest 6 per cent of its current income to maintain its per capita income, while country *B* would have to invest 10 per cent of its current income even to maintain its per capita output. This can be shown by using Harrod-Domar growth formula, namely, $g = I/v$ where g is growth rate in national income, I is rate of investment as a ratio of national income and v is capital-output ratio. The formula can be restated as under:

$$I = v.g$$

For country *A* with 1.5 per cent annual growth rate of population, its national income must grow (g) at the rate of 1.5 per cent to keep per capita constant. For this investment as per cent of national income required to keep per capita constant is given by

$$I = 4 \times 1.5 = 6 \text{ per cent}$$

And for country *B* whose population is growing at the rate of 2.5 per cent per annum, its national income must also grow at the rate of 2.5% to maintain its per capita income. For this, investment required will be

$$I = 4 \times 2.5 = 10 \text{ per cent}$$

Thus, when the population is increasing at a rapid rate, comparatively larger investment is needed to maintain the current level of income. Thus, given the scarcity of investible resources, adequate resources are not left to *raise per capita income* significantly.

3. Lower Growth of Per Capita Income. Like a thief in the night, population growth robs us of most of the gains in national income made from higher investment. Rapid *population growth*

1 Enke, "Economic Consequences of Rapid Population Growth", *Economic Journal*, Dec. 1971.

nullifies our investment efforts to raise the living standards of our people. In other words, a high rate of increase in population swallows up a large part of the increase in national income so that per capita income or living standards of the people does not rise much. This is precisely what has happened during the planning era in India. Thus, while the aggregate national income of India went up by 3.6% per annum in the First Plan period and 4.1% per annum in the Second Plan period, per capita income rose by only 1.8 per cent and 2 per cent per annum respectively. Average annual growth in national income and per capita income in various Five Year Plan periods in given in Table 12.1. It will be seen from the table that the annual growth in per capita income has been much less than the annual growth rate in the national income. It is the population growing at 2 per cent per annum or more during the planning period that has caused per capita income to rise much less than the increase achieved in national income.

Table 12.1. Annual Average Growth Rate (at 2004-05 prices)

Plan Period	National Income (per cent)	Per Capita Income (per cent)
First Plan (1951-56)	4.2	2.4
Second Plan (1956-61)	4.2	2.2
Third Plan (1961-66)	2.6	0.3
Fourth Plan (1969-74)	3.2	0.9
Fifth Plan (1974-79)	4.9	2.6
Sixth Plan (1980-85)	5.4	3.1
Seventh Plan (1985-90)	5.5	3.3
Eighth Plan (1992-97)	6.7	4.6
Ninth Plan (1997-2002)	5.5	3.5
Tenth Plan (2002-07)	7.5	5.9
Eleventh Plan (2007-12)	7.7	6.3

Source: Economic Survey, 2002-03, 2007-08.

However, since 1991 population growth rate has been less than 2 per cent, it was 1.93 per cent between 1991 and 2001 and 1.6 per cent between 2001-2011 on the one hand and growth rate of national income was much higher on the other (see Table 12.1). Therefore, the growth rate of per capita income has been relatively higher. Per capita income (at 2004-05 prices) grew at the rate of 4.6 per cent in the 8th Plan period (1992-97), 3.5 per cent in the 9th Plan period (1997-2002), 5.9 per cent in the 10th Plan period and 6.3 per cent in the 11th Plan period. This higher per capita income growth rate since 1991 has tended to raise the standard of living of the people higher than before.

That the population growth prevents the rapid rise in per capita income and therefore rise in living standards of the people can be expressed by the following growth formula :

$$g = I\alpha - r$$

where g stands for the rate of growth of per capita income, I represents rate of investment, α stands for output-capital ratio (or productivity of capital) and r represents rate of population growth.

Since rate of growth in national income is given by the rate of investment multiplied by the cutput-capital ratio, $I\alpha$ will signify the rate of growth of national income. Now, it will be seen that rate of population growth r appears as a negative factor and will therefore lower the rate of growth of per capita income g. It therefore follows that if rate of growth of per capita income g and the rate of rise in living standards with a given rate of investment is to be raised, the rate of growth of population should be lowered.

4. Population Growth and Marketed Surplus of Foodgrains. Another way in which growth in population is impeding economic development is its effect on *marketed surplus of foodgrains.* The marketed surplus of foodgrains is a prerequisite for expansion in non-agricultural employment and output. When a country grows and accelerates its pace of industrialization, it requires foodgrains to feed the workers who are employed in industries. If enough surpluses of foodgrains are not forthcoming this acts as an important constraint on the industrial development. This prevents the living standards of the people to rise rapidly. Now, marketed surplus of foodgrains is the difference between the output of foodgrains by the agricultural population and their consumption of them. Thus,

$$\text{Marketed surplus of foodgrains} = (0 - C_f).$$

where *0* stands for output of foodgrains, and C_f for consumption of foodgrains by the farmers themselves. As about 50% of the population is engaged in agriculture, the most of the increase in population also takes place there. This increase in population in the agriculture raises the consumption of foodgrains, *i.e.,* C_f in the above equation and therefore reduces the marketable surplus, if output remains the same. Even if output is rising, the extra consumption by the increase in population tends to lower the growth in marketed surplus for foodgrains. We thus see that the growth in population has an adverse effect on the marketed surplus of foodgrains and this acts as a drag on the growth of output and employment in industries and to ensure food security to the people. In India, in several years, increase in agricultural output has not been enough and further that the rapid growth in population tends to reduce the growth of marketable surplus and leads to rise in food prices. Rise in food prices relative to prices of industrial goods causes *unfavourable terms of trade* for industrial sector. This has an adverse effect on industrial development in the country. Besides, over time food inflation gets generalised and causes the problem of general inflation in the country which forces Reserve Bank of India to adopt *tight* monetary policy (that is, raises its lending rates of interest. The high interest rate discourages private investment and lowers rate of economic growth).

Rapid growth in population in an already over-populated country also raises the problem of food security in the country. The cause of food problem in India is the rapid growth in population since 1951. In order to overcome the shortage of foodgrains and to prevent the occurrence of famines in the country, India was forced to import foodgrains and spend a good amount of valuable foreign exchange on them. This worsened the balance of payments problem of the country. As a result, sufficient amount of foreign exchange to import materials. machines and equipment for our industries could not be made and this obstructed the growth of industrial output. This also shows how rapid growth in population by causing food shortage inhibits the rate of industrial development.

5. Population Growth and Unproductive Investment. In his study of population growth and economic development in India, Coale and Hoover[2] focussed on the adverse effect of population growth on the resources available for productive investment. According to them. rapid population growth forces the country to make non-productive investment, that is, to invest in duplicating certain social welfare facilities such as the construction of parks. houses, social buildings, sanitation works. To the extent the Government has to increase its expenses on duplicating these social welfare facilities, investment resources for productive type of capital such as machines for industries, irrigation and fertilisers for agriculture, crucial basic goods such as steal, coal, electricity generation etc would be reduced. Thus, rapid population growth obstructs economic development by reducing the growth of productive capital.

6. Population Growth and Unemployment. Economic development requires that employment should increase adequately so that unemployment should decrease. Explosive growth in population causes serious unemployment and underemployment problem in a country. Due to explosive growth in population in India labour force has been increasing rapidly since 1951. In recent years labour force, which was estimated at 309 million in 1983, went up to 333 million in 1988, to 382 million in 1994 and to 406 million in 1999-2000. As a result of this explosive increase in labour force demographic pressure on the economy has increased resulting in increase in backlog of unemployment and under-unemployment at the beginning of each successive Five Year Plan. In view of this much of our

2 Coale and Hoover, *op. cit.*

investment efforts are directed at absorbing the growing labour force in productive employment, our ability to *raise productivity of labour* is severely constrained.

Since production processes in modem organised industrial sector is highly-capital intensive, much of the growing labour force cannot be employed there. As a result, demographic pressure on land and agriculture increases resulting in the severe drop in the net sown area per capita. In agriculture, self-employment is predominant and the joint family system prevails under which both household's income and work are shared among the family members. Therefore, in the absence of employment opportunities outside agriculture, much of the additional labour force is forced to remain in agriculture and allied activities. Agriculture performs the role of residual absorber. They share work in agriculture with other family members no matter how low the productivity per person becomes. Thus, with the fall in net sown area per person and increased population pressure, disguised unemployment emerges in agriculture. Disguised unemployment means more workers seem to be employed in it but quite a large number of additional workers do not add to agricultural output, that is, marginal productivity of workers in agriculture is zero or nearly zero. Since population growth reduces savings and investable resources, it is very difficult to withdraw any significant number of workers from agriculture so as to equip them with the required capital to provide them productive employment outside agriculture. To a certain extent lack of capital may be made up by harder work by workers in a country like India. But such a method of adjustment is not easy to achieve in India. This is because in the modern times man can produce little with bare hands. To provide them productive employment workers need to be equipped with enough capital goods. Even employment generation in agriculture apart from high yielding inputs such as fertilisers, HYV seeds. pesticides requires irrigation works, an important capital needed for extension of double cropping which is a highly employment-generating way in agriculture. Due to lack of invisible resources caused partly by population growth, it has not been possible to extend irrigation facilities to the currently known irrigation potential.

It follows from above that labour force consequences of population growth is to a good extent responsible for huge unemployment and underemployment prevailing in India.

7. **Population Growth and Poverty.** Last but not the least, as shall be explained in detail below, the important consequence of rapid population growth is that it has made very difficult to make a significant dent into the problem of mass poverty prevailing in the country. This is clear from the fact that as large as about 18 million people over and above 125 crore population estimated on March 1, 2011, are being added to our population every year as per 2011 population census. This gives rise to a huge problem of properly feeding and clothing them. Further, as has been explained in detail in the above sections such large increase in population and consequently huge increment in labour force lowers our capacity to make productive investment and thereby to increase productivity of labour to ensure eradication of poverty. Prof. K. Sundaram rightly writes, "The size of increments to population is itself of some consequence. Thus is because the resource requirements of feeding and clothing even at the current low levels are such that the incremental population itself constraints the ability of the economy to raise the living standards of the existing population."[3] A vicious circle of poverty operates in this regard. Rapid population growth leads to lower productivity which causes poverty, poverty causes high infant mortality rate which in turn causes high population growth. There is no wonder then, even after over 60 years of planned economic development, 400 million people live below the poverty line in 2011-12. as per the poverty criteria used by the Expert Committee headed by C. Rangarajan.

Demographic Changes in India and Population Dividend

India is passing through a phase of unprecedented demographic changes. These demographic changes are likely to contribute to a substantially increased labour force in the country. The census

3. K. Sundaram, *Demography and Development, 1951-2001*, A Paper presented at the Institute of Economic Growth, April 27, 1984.

projection report shows that the proportion of working age population between 15 and 59 years is likely to increase from approximately 58 per cent in 2001 to more than 64 per cent by 2021. *In absolute numbers there will be approximately 63.5 million new entrants to the working age group between 2011 and 2016*. Further, it is important to note that the *bulk of this increase is likely to take place in the relatively younger age group of 20-35 years*. Such a trend would make India one of the youngest nations in the world. In 2020 average Indian will be only 29 years old. The comparable figures for China and US are 37 and for West Europe 45 and for Japan 48 years. *This higher proportion of young labour force in India has a great production potential* and has therefore been called '*demographic dividend*'. This demographic dividend provides India large productive opportunities for rapid economic growth.

Thus it has been pointed out that demographics are in India's favour because working age population is growing faster than overall population. According to the advocates of demographic dividend, the working age population will earn by contributing to production and save more, thereby contributing to higher savings and higher investment which will lead to higher growth. However, in our view demographic dividend poses a great challenge; *its benefit will be realised only if our young population is healthy, educated and appropriately skilled and get productive employment*. There is nothing inevitable about demographic dividend. Demographic dividend will flow if we are able to find jobs for the growing labour force. According to National Sample Survey conducted between June 2011 and June 2012, the unemployment rate among youth (15-29 years) which made up a fourth (285 million) of the 1210 million total population rose by a percentage point in those two years while national rate of unemployment remained constant. According to this survey data, as presented in Table 12.2 the rate of unemployment among young Indians (15-29 years) was 8% for urban males and 13% for urban females and for both of them rate of unemployment in this survey period went up. The rate of unemployment in both rural males and females was found to be equal to 5 per cent in the two years of the survey period (2009-10 – 2011-12). Unemployment rate in this period for young women, however, fell.

Table 12.2. Unemployment Rate in India for the Period 2009-10–2011-12
(on the Usual Status Basis)

National Average Rate of Unemployment		
Urban		
	Male	2 %
	Female	2%
Rural		
	Male	3%
	Female	5%
	Unemployment Rate among the Youth (15-29) years	
Urban		
	Male	8%
	Female	13%
Rural		
	Male	5%
	Female	5%

Source: NSSO *Survey*

It follows from above that till 2011-12 no population dividend was accruing in case of India. Thus unless adequate employment opportunities are generated in the process of economic growth, benefits of population dividend will not be reaped. If the advantage of population dividend is to be availed of, high priority should be given to the generation of employment opportunities. For this the youth should be properly educated and imparted right types of skills.

POPULATION CONTROL POLICY

Over-populated developing countries are currently facing the problem of population explosion. We have explained above in this chapter how population growth is hampering economic growth in these countries. The population growth is swallowing up a large part of the gains in national income brought about by planned economic development. If we want that future generations should have at least as much good prospects of living as the present generation we must control population growth.

India's population which is presently about 1250 million is increasing at a rate of about 1.6 per cent per annum. If current trends continue, India may overtake China in 2045 to become the most populous country in the world. At present about 50 per cent of India's population is below 20 years of age. Hence, a large number of our present population will live to see by the middle of the 21st century the disastrous consequences such as acute poverty conditions, widespread unemployment a high degree of socio-economic tensions if current growth in population is not checked.

The check on the growth of population is therefore absolutely essential if we want to solve problems of mass poverty and widespread unemployment. Further, if the economy is to be prevented from reaching the stationary state, controlling population growth is essential to achieve this aim. Stressing the importance of controlling population growth in India characterised by economic growth, the existence of mass poverty and unemployment. Prof. P.R. Brahmananda writes, "a stationary economy with an open ended population expansion angle will be the greatest permanent disaster for the country. All hopes of improvement in living standard even at the meagre levels of vast masses will have been forever dashed to pieces".[4] He further adds, "Such an atmosphere cannot be conducive for economic progress. The prospect of more bread being ruled out, the flow of freedom may not flutter for long."

Now, an important question is as to what policies can be adopted to control population. Population growth depends on the fertility rate (birth rate) and death rate. Thus, policies that have to be adopted to check population growth should aim to reduce the birth rate. The increase in birth rate is ruled out for obvious reasons. Population growth can be reduced by reducing the birth rate. That is, each family should have smaller number of children. It may be noted that reducing fertility rate in under-developed countries is quite a formidable task. This is because, as has been pointed out by Kuznets, *"in underdeveloped countries people have an intense tendency to have more children because under the economic and social conditions large proportions of the population see their economic and social interests in more children as a supply of 'family labour, as a pool for a genetic lottery, and as a matter of economic and social security in a non-protecting society."*[5]

The various policies that may be adopted to control the growth of population are: *(a)* Family Planning Programme, *(b)* Sterilisation, *(c)* Promotion of education, (*d*) Social and economic development, especially of the poor sections of the society. We shall now discuss each of them briefly.

Family Planning Programme

This is an important policy measure that has been adopted by several developing countries. India is the first country in the world to adopt family planning as a State policy. Under family planning programme various contraceptive devices and health services are provided to encourage the couples to adopt *small family norm,* that is, to have fewer children. Through various communication media a wide publicity is given that couples should go in for only two or three children and no more. An appeal is made to them that their life would be happy and prosperous if they have small family.

---

4 P.R. Brahmananda, *Planning in a Futureless Economy*, Vira & Company

5 Simon Kuznets, *Underdeveloped Countries and the Pre-Industrial Phaze in the Advanced Countries, The United Nations*, 1954.

Recently, policy of providing *economic incentives and discentives* has been adopted in some countries to discourage the people from having more children beyond a certain number which is generally fixed at two or three. Some of the incentives and disincentives adopted to promote family planning are : (1) Elimination or reduction of maternity leave and benefits beyond a certain number. This will discourage the employed women to bear more children. (2) The establishment of old-age social security provisions, such as old-age pension. This greatly helps in motivating the people to have smaller number of children. As is well known, in poor countries like India, people have a tendency to bear more children so that in their old age security be ensured. (3) Money payments to those who opt for small families and voluntarily go in for sterilisation operation, (4) Allotment of scarce public houses, housing plots, flats etc. on the basis of preference to those who have a small family. Besides these several other incentives and disincentives have been devised to encourage the small family norm.

For the success of the family planning programme a variety of *medically tested and safe contraceptives* such as IUD pills, condoms, foam tablets, jellies and others should be made freely available. It may be noted that a great boost was given to the family planning programme by the discovery of IUD (intrauterine device). popularly called as loop. But after some time 'impression was created among the female population that it was not very safe. The need of the hour is to strengthen the research in contraceptive technology and such devices should be discovered which should be effective but minimise the health risk. In India, after the experience of several years, there has been some reconsideration of the various aspects of the family planning programme. Family planning programme would now be an integral part of comprehensive family welfare policy covering education, health and childcare, family planning and women's rights and nutrition. The accent in new policy is on integrating contraception with public health, medical care, maternal and child health and nutrition. In fact, the name of the ministry has been changed from Ministry for Family Planning to Ministry of Family Welfare. In so far as it goes, the new orientation may prove to be good but it needs to be stressed, as shall be brought out later, that the success of family planning programme depends heavily on the process of social and economic development.

Compulsory and Forced Sterilisation

As effective policy measure to check the growth of population, compulsory sterilisation has been suggested by many. According to this, it should be made compulsory for the couples to undergo sterilisation beyond a certain number of children, say two or three. Those who violate this, either penalties may be imposed or they are forced to undergo the operation. Admittedly, this is a drastic measure, but is considered very effective in the context of the failure of voluntary family planning programme.

Of all the measures involving several incentives and disincentives proposed ,the most controversial is the proposal of *compulsory sterilisation*. According to this proposal, compulsory sterilisation of every couple who has more than two children should be introduced. This suggestion of introducing an element of compulsion in the sterilisation programme implies that one is not hopeful of various incentives and discentives succeeding in achieving the objective of stabilising the population size. It may be noted that people of India have already rejected the policy of compulsory sterilisation adopted during the emergency period 1975-77.

In India during the dark period of emergency the policy of forced sterilisation was in fact adopted, though officially it was described as voluntary. In the name of motivation campaign, family planning camps were set up where people were forcibly driven to undergo operation. Ambitious targets were laid down which were successively revised upwards. In fact *coercion* came to be used on a large scale, especially in the States in the North, so that the programme was voluntary only in name. The State Chief Ministers vied with each other to surpass their targets and excesses were committed in the process. In 1976 while the target of sterilisation originally fixed was 43 lakhs, actually 75 Iakhs sterilisations were effected. Little wonder, the official over-enthusiasm and excesses made the whole programme highly unpopular and this was one of the main causes of Congress Party's utter rout in the Northern States in Lok Sabha elections of March 1977.

In the opinion of the present author, the policy of forced sterilisation is quite inhuman; it is treating human beings as animals. Public opinion is strongly opposed to it. Moreover, when there are several contraceptives available. recourse to compulsory sterilisation is not needed.

Promotion of Education

Empirical studies conducted in several countries reveal that there is *inverse relation between the fertility rate and education, especially of women and girls.* Therefore, an important measure to reduce the birth rate is the promotion of education, especially among female population of the country. The educated men and women accept small family norm and more readily take family planning measures such as use of contraceptives. Moreover, when educated women are employed, their tendency to bear and rear more children falls. Dr. Ashish Bose, an eminent demographer, in 1978 pointed out that India's family planning campaign has been severely handicapped because of the slow rise in the *literacy level.* To quote him, *"The sad fact remains that in large parts of India, especially in U.P., Bihar, Madhya Pradesh and Rajasthan, women literacy rate in the rural areas* is *less than 10 per cent. And these are States where the progress of family planning is slow. These four States account for 39 per cent of India's population. So their impact (or lack of it) on the national birth rate is bound to be significant."*[6] However, efforts to educate the people especially women, both formally and informally, be strengthened to achieve the target of reduction in birth rate.

Social and Economic Development

It has been said that *"development is the best contraceptive." This implies that with social and economic development, the birth rate will go down, as people with higher levels of living prefer to have fewer children.* First, people with a higher level of living do not need children to supplement the family's meagre income. Secondly, they come to prefer "quality" of children rather than "quantity". Thirdly, their desire to further improve their level of living increases and this induces them to practise family planning measures. In the opinion of the present author, if the population growth in India has remained virtually unchecked in spite of a nationwide family planning programme, the fault does not lie solely with the programme but to a much greater extent with the character of social and economic development in India which has failed to remove mass poverty and improve the levels of living of the poor and weaker sections of the society. Accordingly, if population is to be effectively checked, not only the tempo of economic development should be speeded up but strategy of development should be such as will promote employment opportunities for the poor, especially landless labour, marginal and small farmers. It should be ensured that fruits of economic development should reach these poor people. For this land reform measures and income redistribution policies should also be effectively implemented. If the standards of living of the poor go up as a result of economic development, they will readily adopt small family norm.

POPULATION AND POVERTY

Population growth leads to the increase in poverty in developing countries in more than one way. First, rapid population growth swallows up a large part of annual increments in national income brought about by increase in investment or capital formation so that per capita income or level of welfare does not increase much. For example, as is seen from Table 12.1 that in India's Five Year Plans at least up to the 5th Five Year Plan (1974-79) a good part of the growth in national income was eatned by growth in population and therefore rise in per capita income or level of welfare did not go up significantly. This is because of lower growth in per capita income until 1980 that India did not succeed in making much progress in reduction of absolute poverty.

---

6 Ashish Bose, "New Directions in Family Planning Programme", *Asian Economist*, Vol. No. 889, May 23, 1978.

Population growth adversely affects the problem of poverty indirectly through lowering the rate of saving which does therefore permit higher rate of investment or capital accumulation. With lower rate of investment or capital accumulation rate of growth of national income or GDP remains lower which makes it difficult to make a large dent into the problem of poverty. It is generally believed that the stable solution to the problem of poverty requires stepping up rate of economic growth. Thus by lowering the rate of saving and investment, population growth is a great impediment to eradication of poverty in developing countries like India.

It is worth noting the findings of Coale and Hoover[7] in their important study of India's population problem in the fifties. According to Coale and Hoover, faster population growth affects the age structure of the population toward the very young and therefore causes the *dependency ratio* in families to rise. *The higher dependency ratio in the families tends to reduce their saving rate. The lower savings cause lower rate of investment which is an obstacle in the way of speeding up economic growth and reduction in the poverty problem.*

Further, Coale and Hoover, in their study of population growth and development, found that with rapid growth of population and labour force more resources need to be used for expansion of social expenditure on parks, hospitals roads, houses etc. and little resources are left for increase in capital per worker to raise labour productivity. This hinders higher growth in income per capita. A vicious circle of poverty operates in this regard. A rapid population growth lowers labour productivity which causes poverty, poverty causes high fertility rate which in turn causes high population growth rate. There is no wonder then that according to the poverty criteria fixed by Rangarajan Expert Committee 400 million people in India lived below the poverty line in 2011-12.

A similar argument of rapid population growth affecting our ability to raise the living standards of the people or to reduce poverty has been advanced by Prof. K. Sundaram of Delhi School of Economics. According to him, the *large increase* in the extra number of people due to rapid population growth (around 18.2 million extra population every year as per latest Population Census 2011) *requires resources for feeding and clothing even at the current low level* so that little is left for raising the living standards of the existing population. To quote him, "The size of increments to population is itself of some consequence. This is because the resource requirements of feeding and clothing even at the current low levels are such that the incremental population itself constrains the ability of the economy to raise the living standards of the existing population."[8]

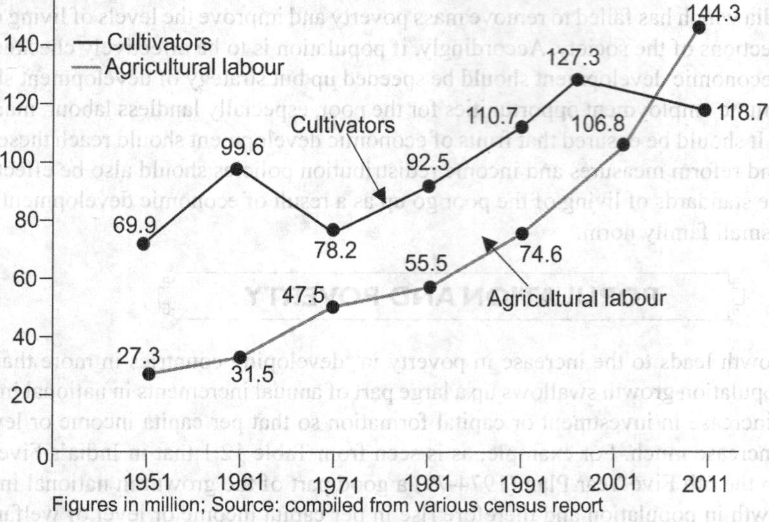

Fig. 12.1. *Falling numbers of cultivators and rising numbers of agricultural labour in India*

7 Coale and Hoover, *op.cit.*

8 K. Sundaram, *Demography and Development, 1951-2001*, A Paper presented at the Institute of Economic Growth, April 27, 1984.

That rapid population growth causes increase in poverty can also be known from its effect on agriculture. *Increase in population raises population pressure on arable land and reduces land-man ratio which causes lower productivity per person and leads to disguised unemployment and poverty.* Not only that, rapid growth in farming population in India has led to subdivision and fragmentation of land holdings which renders cultivation on tiny land-holdings unviable. Not able to meet their basic needs with cultivation of tiny land holdings, many cultivators sell their land and join the ranks of landless agricultural labourers. As a result, as is seen from Fig. 12.1, in India the ratio of cultivators in agriculture has been falling and that of agricultural labour has been increasing. According to Population Census of 2011, even the absolute number of cultivators in agriculture declined in 2011. Due to the increase in agricultural labour, many of them do not find work in agriculture for a good part of the year and therefore remain unemployed.

POPULATION AND ENVIRONMENT

Population growth raises concern over environment issues because it is thought that basic needs of growing population may not be adequately met by earth's natural resources resulting in fall in living standards of the people. This is because increasing population causes environmental degradation by making forest encroachment, deforestation and depletion of firewood. Increases in population cause over-exploitation of natural resources such as forests, water, fisheries and minerals at a rate far greater than their capacity to regenerate. Besides, population pressure on land compels us to cultivate arable land more intensively by using chemical inputs such as fertilizers, pesticides which cause soil degradation. Further, increase in population through its effect on deforestation by the rural and urban population for timber and fuel leads to the increase in carbon dioxide in the atmosphere and therefore causes air pollution. Thus the population impacts on environment primarily through the use and depletion of natural resources and is associated with environmental problems such as air and water pollution and loss of biodiversity and increased pressure on arable land. As an example of estimate of loss, Tata Energy Research Institute (TERI) estimates that economic losses due to soil degradation, diseases caused by pollution and forest degradation is between ₹ 1,00,000 and 4,50,000 crore every year and this does not include a series of other losses due to ecological destruction.[9]

Population increases cause over-exploitation of land and water resources and loss of biodiversity and forests and will therefore *endanger sustainability of agriculture and food security* in the country. According to Prof M.S. Swaminathan, a noted agriculture scientist, " *The capacity to support even the existing human and animal population has been exceeded in many parts of the world*"[10] and if population growth is not checked, it will endanger the attainment of food security. To quote him again, "In the recent years there has been considerable concern about human capacity to produce adequate food to meet the needs of the growing population and the increase in purchasing power resulting in higher consumption of animal products."[11]

It is manifest from above that rapidly increasing population in developing countries will lead to the over-exploitation and degradation of land and depletion of fisheries which will threaten the achievement of food security in the developing countries.

Besides, the growth of urban population in the absence of adequate infrastructure facilities has caused the **lack of clean water to drink** and given rise to **urban slums with the poor sanitation** which has increased the vulnerability of the people to several diseases. It follows from above that to meet the expanding needs of the developing countries, environment degradation must be halted. For

9 Quoted by Ashish Kothari in "Unsustainable Development, Unfulfilled Promises" in *Survey of Environment* 2000. *The Hindu.*, 2001.

10 M.S. Swaminathan, 'Agriculture: Route to an Evergreen Revolution' in ***Survey of Environment***. *2002 The Hindu*, p. 34.

11 *Ibid*, p. 33.

that purpose, reduction in population growth will greatly help in easing the intensification of many environmental problems.

As explained above, poverty in developing countries is also said to be responsible for environmental degradation. Poor people rely on natural resources more than the rich. For survival the rural poor are forced to cut forests for timber and fuel as well as graze animals on pasture lands more than the reproductive capacity of these natural resources. Besides, when the cultivable land becomes short relative to population, the poor are forced to make their subsistence by cultivating fragile land on hills and mountains resulting in soil erosion on a large scale. It is in such environment that poverty becomes a vicious circle. Poverty leads to land degradation and land degradation accelerates the process of impoverishment because the poor people depend directly on exploitation of natural resources on which property rights are not properly assigned.

Thus, though a large number of poor people earn a good deal of their livelihood from the unmarketed natural resources such as common grazing lands, forests from where food, fuel and building materials are gathered by them, the degradation and loss of such resources may harm the poor and result in perpetuation of their poverty.

APPENDIX 12A

DEMOGRAPHIC TRANSITION IN INDIA

Population in India has been growing at a fast rate since 1951. According to the Census of India 2001, the population in India crossed one billion mark and was estimated at 1,028 million as on March 1, 2001 and, according to Census 2011, on March 1, 2011, India's population was 1211 million. With this, India accounts for 16.7 per cent of the world population while it has a meagre 2.4 per cent of world surface area. It is now estimated that by 2050, India's population will cross that of Chine to become most populous country of the world with 17.2 per cent world population living there. This is because during 1990-2000, China's population has been growing at the rate of 1 per cent per annum, whereas India's population has been increasing in the this decade at the rate of nearly 2 per cent per annum and during 2001-2011 India's population increased at the rate of 1.6% per annum.

In Table 12A.1 we give the figures of Indian population which show that in 2011, population in India rose to 1211 million people as compared to the population of 361 million in 1951. That is, during 60 years we added 850 million people to our population, that is, our population increased more than three times during this period.

India's population growth during the 20th century can be classified into four phases:

1901–1921: Stagnant population

1921–1951: Steady growth

1951–1981: Rapid high growth

1981–2001: High growth with definite signs of slowing down.

Table 12A.1 Population Growth in India

Census year	Population (in million)	Increase during the decade (in million)	Decadal growth rate (%)	Annual Average growth rate (%)
1901	236	–	–	–
1911	252	+ 16	+ 5.7	0.56
1921	251	–1	– 0.3	– 0.03
1931	279	+ 28	+ 11.0	1.04
1941	319	+ 40	+ 14.2	1.33
1951	361	+ 42	+ 13.3	1.25
1961	439	+ 78	+ 21.5	1.96
1971	548	+ 109	+ 24.8	2.20
1981	683	+ 135	+ 24.7	2.22
1991	846	+ 163	+ 23.8	2.14
2001	1028	+ 184	+ 21.5	1.93
2011	1211	+183	+ 17.7	1.6

Source: Census of India 2001, Series 1 India, Paper 1 of 2001.
Note. Figures have been rounded off

It will be seen from Table 12A.1 that between 1901 and 1921, the population of India was almost stable on account of both high birth and death rates. Between 1901 and 1921 population increased by only 13 million in 20 years, that is, 0.65 million per year on average. Thus, during the period, Indian population growth was in the first stage of the theory of demographic transition.

After 1921, population started increasing at a relatively high rate. During the period 1921 to 1951, the population of India increased from 251 million in 1921 to 361 million in 1951, that is, 110 million in 30 years. This implies that during 1921-51 population of India increased annually at a moderate rate of 1.22 per cent. Therefore, in Indian population history year 1921 is generally called "*Great Divide*". During this period (1921-51) population of India increased as a result of fall in the death rate due to the improvement in medical services and success achieved in controlling epidemics like plague, cholera, smallpox etc. In this period therefore Indian population growth entered the second phase of the demographic transition.

After 1951, the Indian population started rising at a higher annual rate of nearly 2 per cent or more. This resulted from a drastic fall in the death rate from 27.4 per thousand during 1941-50 to 15.4 per cent during 1971-80, whereas birth rate fell only marginally from 40 per thousand in 1941-50 to 37.8 per thousand in 1971-80. With this, Indian population passed through the third phase of *explosive growth rate* (*i.e.*, a very high growth rate) in the process of demographic transition.

Table 12A.2. Birth and Death Rates Per 1000 Population (1901-2011)

Year	Birth Rate (per 1000)	Death Rate (per 1000)	Rate of natural increase (per 1000)
1901-10	48.1	42.6	5.5
1911-20	49.2	48.6	0.6
1921-30	46.2	36.3	9.9
1931-40	45.2	31.2	14.0
1941-50	39.9	27.4	12.5
1951-60	40.0	22.8	17.2
1961-70	41.2	17.8	23.4
1971-80	37.2	15.4	21.8
1981-90	33.0	12.6	20.4
1991	29.5	9.8	19.7
2000	25.8	8.5	17.3
2012	21.6	7.0	14.6

Source: Office of the Registrar General of India and Annual Report (2000-01) and 2011. *Economic Survey*, 2012-2013 and 2013-14.

After 1981, Indian population still grew at a high rate but it has shown definite signs of slowing down. Thus, whereas in 1971-81, population increased at the annual average rate of 2.22 per cent, its growth rate fell to 2.14 during 1981-91, and to 1.93 during 1991-2001 and further to 1.6 per cent during 2001-2011. This has occurred due to the birth rate also falling relatively more than before, while death rate continued its decline unabated. It will be seen from Table 12A.2 that birth rate fell from 37.2 per thousand in 1971-80 to 25.8 per cent in 2000 and death rate fell from 15.4 per thousand to 8.5 per thousand during the same period. Census Commissioner has called the fourth phase of the demographic transition during the period 1981-2001 as the "*High growth with definite signs of slowing down*".

Now, in the 21st century India has entered the *fifth phase of demographic transition* which is usually characterised by *rapidly declining birth rate* which will end with stable population. Census Commissioner raises this crucial question. "How long will this phase extend and when will India achieve a stable population ? The answer depends on the success of population control measures adopted by us. The National Population Policy (NPP) 2000 adopted by the Government of India states that "the long-term objective is to achieve a stable population by 2045 at a level consistent with the requirement of sustainable economic growth, social development and environment protection".

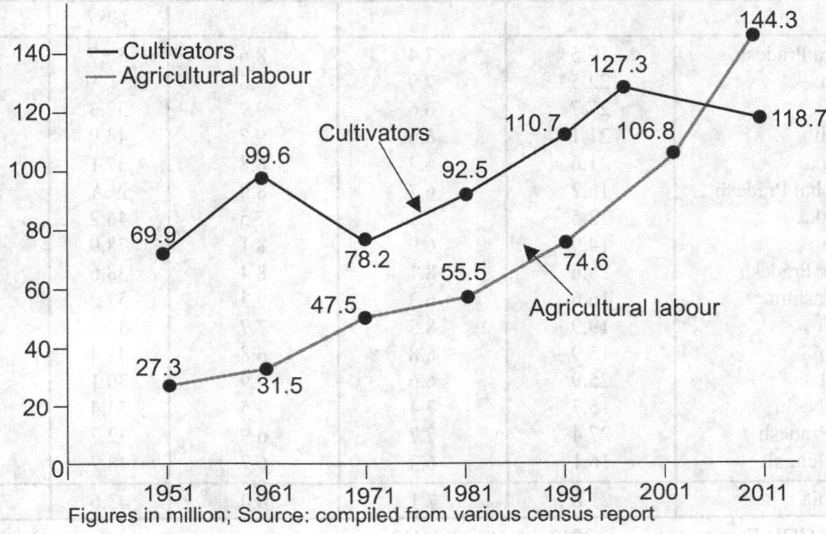

Fig. 12A.1. *Changes in birth and death rates in India*

Positive Demographic Trends in India

In a welcome development there is evidence to suggest that India's birth rate, death rate and natural population growth rate are on the decline. Recent staistics regarding population growth show that the overall birth rate in India dipped from 25.8 per thousand in 2000 to 21.6 per thousand in 2011. *In 2012, Kerala had the lowest birth rate of 14.9 per thousand followed* by Tamil Nadu (15.7), Punjab (16) and West Bengal (16). Death rate is lowest in West Bengal (6.3 per thousand) followed by Kerala, Maharashtra, Rajasthan, Gujarat and Haryana (all around 6.5 per cent). *Natural growth rate of population was lowest in Kerala (8 per thousand)* closely followed by Tamil Nadu (about 9 per thousand).

Fall in birth rates in various States implies that while coercive methods in the family planning programme failed to curb population growth, the people are now willingly reducing birth rate. This corroborates the economic theory of fertility described in Chapter 12 that education, particularly female literacy, the expansion in employment opportunities as well as growth in incomes of the people would reduce fertility by the families. We have shown in Table 12A.3 birth rate and death rates for the year 2012 and GDP growth rate during the period, 2005-06 to 2011-12 and literacy rates for 1981 and 2011 for various states of India. In the decade of 2001-2011 income of the families has increased and the fertility rate of women has declined. Performance of Punjab in reducing birth rate is particularly impressive as in it birth rate has declined to 15.7 per 1000 in 2012. On the other hand, the crude death rate in the concerned decade in case of all India has declined to 7.0 per 1000 in 2012. This shows that healthcare facilities are gradually becoming available to the public at large. But *what is truly a pleasant surprise* is that the so called BIMARU States are leading in the process of declining death rate. For example, there has been a decline in death rate by 23 per cent in the decade 2000-2012 in Madhya Pradesh and Rajasthan while Bihar has seen a reduction of death rate by 22 per cent and Uttar Pradesh by 20 per cent. This has led Dr. Montek Singh Ahluwalia, the former Deputy Chairman of the Planning Commission,to say that the *concept of BIMARU States in India is losing relevance*. The important thing to note is that it is the *higher growth in GDP per* capita and *increase in literacy rate* that has brought about this beneficial demographic change (see Table 12A.3).

Table 12A.3. Inter-State Comparison of Some Major States

State	Birth Rate (per 1000) 2012	Death Rate (per 1000) 2012	Average GDP Growth (2005-06-2011-12)	Literacy Rate (in per cent)	
				1981	*2011*
Andhra Pradesh	17.5	7.4	8.6	35.7	67.0
Assam	22.5	7.9	5.8	N.A	72,2
Bihar	27.7	6.6	9.9	32.3	61.8
Gujarat	21.1	6.6	9.7	44.9	78.0
Haryana	21.6	6.4	8.8	37.1	75.6
Himachal Pradesh	16.2	6.7	8.0	N.A	82.8
Karnatka	18.5	7.1	7.5	46.2	75.4
Kerala	14.9	6.9	8.1	78.9	94.0
Madhy Pradesh	26.6	8.1	8.4	38.6	69.3
Maharashtra	16.6	6.3	9.3	57.2	82.3
Odisha	19.9	8.5	7.7	33.6	72.9
Punjab	15.9	6.8	6.8	43.4	75.8
Rajasthan	25.9	6.6	7.9	30.1	66.1
Tamil Nadu	15.7	7.4	9.5	54.4	80.1
Uttar Pradesh	27.4	7.7	6.9	32.7	67.7
West Bengal	16.1	6.3	6.7	48.7	76.3
All India	21.8	7.1	8.0	43.6	73.0

Source: GOI, *Economic Survey 2013-14, Op. Cit.*, 113

Note: Literacy rate relates to the percentage of literate population to the population aged 7 years and above.

Malthus and Population Growth in India

It is generally believed that for labour-surplus developing countries such as India, Malthusian gloomy prognosis has come true. However, population in these countries has not changed in accordance with the Malthusian theory of population. According to Malthus, population would grow rapidly because of high and rising birth rate. But in India and other developing countries, it is not the rise in birth rate that has caused the population explosion but it is the fall in death rate brought about by medical improvements that is responsible for it. In fact, it will be seen from Table 12A.2 that between the periods 1911-20 and 1961-70, birth rate fell from 49.2 per thousand in 1911-20 to 41.2 per thousand in 1961-70 and to 21.6 per thousand in 2012. But as compared to the fall in birth rate, the death rate declined very rapidly; from 42.6 per thousand in the decade 1901-11, it declined to 17.8 per thousand in 1961-70 and to 7.0 per thousand in 2012. It is therefore clear that *population explosion in India is the result of sharp fall in the death rate rather than any rise in the birth rate.*

Moreover, Malthus thought that population would increase when the food supply or standard of living of the people rose above the minimum subsistence level. But this is not borne out by the actual experience of developing countries including India. Population in India and other labour-surplus economies have been increasing at an alarming rate without much rise in the levels of living of about 30 to 40 per cent of its people living below the poverty line. In other words, even while 30 to 40 per cent people of these countries are struggling below the absolute poverty line, the population of these countries has rapidly grown. Professor Hla Myint rightly says, "If the Malthusian theory has underrated the possibilities of technical improvements in food production, it has also underrated the medical improvements reducing death rates. *The possibility that even a population struggling at a minimum subsistence level could grow in the short run simply by medical improvements entirely unconnected with the general standard of life adds to the seriousness of the problem in the modern setting.*"[1]

1 Myint, Hla, The *Economics of the Developing Countries*, Hutchuison University Library, London, 1969. p. 37.

PART III

Modern Theories and Models of Economic Growth

- Harrod-Domar Model of Economic Growth
- Neoclassical Theory of Growth: Solow Model
- Meade's Neoclassical Model of Economic Growth
- Joan Robinson's Model of Growth
- New Theory of Economic Growth (Endogenous Growth Model)

CHAPTER 13

HARROD-DOMAR MODEL OF ECONOMIC GROWTH

Dual Effect of Investment: Income Effect and Capacity Effect

Keynes in his General Theory was concerned with the determination of income and employment in the short run. He explained that since in the short-run situation of developed capitalist economies aggregate demand was deficient in relation to the aggregate supply of output, the equilibrium will be established at less than full-employment level. Since the propensity to consume (and therefore saving propensity) is given and remains constant in the short run, if the amount of investment as determined by expected rate of profit and the market rate of interest is not equal to the amount of saving at the full-employment level of income, the economy will be in equilibrium at less than full capacity level (*i.e.*, less than employment level) of output. He did not go into the question of the long-run growth of the economy. In fact, he overlooked the effect of investment in a given period on the increase in productive capacity. However, *investment has a dual effect*. Firstly, investment increases aggregate demand and income of the people through the multiplier process, and secondly, it raises the productive capacity of the economy through the addition it makes to the stock of capital. Indeed, investment by very definition means the addition to the stock of capital. While Keynes took into account the demand effect of investment, he ignored the capacity effect of investment.

Harrod[1] and Domar[2] extended the Keynesian analysis of income and employment to long-run setting and therefore considered both the income and capacity effects of investment. Harrod and Domar models of economic growth explained at what rate investment should increase so that steady growth is possible in an advanced capitalist economy. In the growth models of Harrod and Domar, the rate of capital accumulation plays a crucial role in the determination of economic growth. The problem of present-day mature economies lies in averting both secular stagnation and secular inflation. It were the pioneer works of Harrod and Domar that set the ball rolling in regard to this issue, *i.e.*, the maintenance of steady growth in advanced industrialised countries. The *Harrod and Domar models seek to determine that unique rate at which investment and income must grow so that full-employment level is maintained over a long period of time, i.e., equilibrium growth is achieved.*

Harrod and Domar developed their models of steady growth quite separately, though Harrod published his theory earlier than Domar. Although their models of steady growth differ in details, yet the underlying basic idea is the same. Both of them assigned to capital accumulation a crucial role in the development process. But they emphasised the double role of the investment process, *viz.*, generating income (increasing demand) and adding to the productive capacity of the economy. The classical economists confined their attention to the capacity or supply side only, whereas the earlier Keynesian economists studied the problem of demand only whereas Harrod and Domar consider both sides.

1 R.F. Harrod, *Towards a Dynamic Economics*, Macmillan & Co., London, 1948.

2 E. Domar, "Capital Expansion, Rate of Growth and Employment", *Economica* Vol. 14, 1946.

They start with full-employment equilibrium level of income. According to them, to maintain full employment equilibrium, demand (total spending) generated by investment must be sufficient to be the additional output caused by this investment. To ensure steady growth with full employment the absolute amount of net investment must keep increasing and there must also be continuous growth of real national income. Because if demand and income did not increase while annual investment went on occurring, the additions made to the capital stock would remain unutilised and also employment could not be provided to the growing labour force which would result in unemployment of these two major resources. Obviously, such a situation is not conducive to steady economic growth.

DOMAR'S GROWTH MODEL

Capacity Effect of Investment

Let us first consider the supply side, that is, the capacity effect of investment. Increase in national output or national income of an economy during a period depends upon the increase in the stock of capital (which is represented by ΔK) during a period and the output-capital ratio or the productivity of capital. Assuming that both national income and the capital stock are measured in money, output-capital ratio can be written as $\Delta Y/ \Delta K$, where ΔY stands for the increase in the national income and ΔK for the increase in the stock of capital. Thus if ₹ 4 worth of capital goods is required to produce one rupee worth of real output, marginal output-capital ratio is equal to 1/4 or 0.25. Thus, the absolute increase in national income during a period (ΔY) can be obtained from increment in stock of capital ΔK multiplied by the output produced by a unit of capital $\left(i.e., \frac{\Delta Y}{\Delta K}\right)$. In symbolic terms we may express this as follows:-

$$\Delta Y = \Delta K . \frac{\Delta Y}{\Delta K} \qquad \ldots (1)$$

Now, change in capital stock (ΔK) is nothing else but investment. Therefore, following Domar in place of ΔK we can write I. The marginal output-capital ratio $\Delta Y/\Delta K$ which is assumed to be constant as well as equal to average output-capital ratio by Domar and Harrod, can be denoted by σ. Thus, as Domar puts it, growth in capacity-output can be written as under:

$$\Delta Y = I\,\sigma \qquad \ldots (2)$$

It may be noted that output-capital ratio (σ) is reciprocal of capital-output ratio *i.e.* $\left(\frac{\Delta K}{\Delta Y} \text{ or } \frac{K}{Y}\right)$. Let us give an example. If ₹ 500 crore is invested in a year and capital-output ratio is 4 (*i.e.* output-capital ratio will be 1/4), then growth in output in a year will be.

$$\Delta Y = 500 \times 1/4$$
$$= 125 \text{ crore}$$

Demand or Income Effect of Investment

Now, according to Domar, growth in capacity-output will be realised only if aggregate demand or income of the people increases by a sufficient amount. The increase in aggregate demand or income is explained by the Keynesian theory of multiplier. Domar has based his analysis of demand or income effect of investment on the Keynesian theory of multiplier and income determination. According to this, *increase in income (or aggregate demand) is given by the increase in investment (ΔI) and the size of multiplier*, *i.e.*, 1/s where s is the marginal propensity to save (assumed by Domar to be equal to the average propensity to save). Thus, according to income effect of investment,

$$\Delta Y = \frac{1}{s} . \Delta I \qquad \ldots (3)$$

Note that $\frac{1}{s}$ represents the size of investment multiplier.

The growth in income (ΔY) must be large enough to generate demand equal to capacity growth in output as explained above.

Domar's Growth Equation in Terms of Rates of Growth

It is greatly helpful to express the above growth equation in terms of *rates of growth* of income and capital. That is, growth in income and capital should be expressed as ratios of total income. For doing so we divide both sides of equation (1) above by Y and obtain :

$$\frac{\Delta Y}{Y} = \frac{\Delta K}{Y} \cdot \frac{\Delta Y}{\Delta K} \quad \ldots (4)$$

represents the rate of growth of income and is therefore written as simply G_Y. Besides, ΔK stands for increment in capital during a given time period and is nothing else but investment. Therefore, for ΔK in the equation (4) we can write I which represents investment. With these changes, we get the following equation :

$$G_y = \frac{I}{Y} \cdot \frac{\Delta Y}{\Delta K}$$

If it is further assumed that output-capital ratio remains constant, then the marginal output-capital ratio $\left(\frac{\Delta Y}{\Delta K}\right)$ will be equal to average output-capital ratio $\left(\frac{Y}{K}\right)$. With this assumption and also expressing output-capital ratio by σ we can write the above equation as follows :

$$G_y = \frac{I}{Y} \cdot \sigma \quad \ldots (5)$$

where G_y = Growth rate of output or income

$\frac{I}{Y}$ = Rate of investment as ratio of national income

σ = Output-capital ratio

From the growth equation (5) above, it is clear that, given the output-capital ratio, rate of growth of output depends upon the rate of investment; the greater the rate of investment, the greater the rate of growth of output or income. *To maintain full-employment equilibrium as the economy grows at a steady rate, rate of savings (S) must remain equal to rate of investment* (I). Therefore, in equation (5) we can write $\frac{S}{Y}$ for $\frac{I}{Y}$. By doing so and rewriting equation (5) we have

$$G_y = \frac{S}{Y} \cdot \sigma$$

Since $\frac{S}{Y}$ represents ratio of savings to national income, we can write it as s. With rewriting the above equation we have

$$G_y = s.\sigma \quad \ldots (6)$$

The above equation (6) represents the productive capacity effect of investment and saving and therefore represents the supply-side of the growth problem.

The Condition for Equilibrium Growth

To achieve and maintain equilibrium or balanced growth, aggregate demand (*i.e.*, aggregate expenditure) must increase at the rate which is large enough to absorb the increase in capacity-output. We have explained above (equation (3)) that aggregate demand or income increases at the rate $\frac{1}{s} . \Delta I$ where s is propensity to save and ΔI is the absolute increase in investment. On the other hand, as shown by equation (2) above, the increase in capacity output occurs at the rate of $I\sigma$ where I is the absolute rate of investment and σ is the output-capital ratio. Thus, *steady equilibrium growth rate will be achieved only if rate of growth of aggregate expenditure (demand or income) equals the rate of growth in capacity output.*

Thus, it follows that to *maintain full-employment equilibrium growth of output* the following condition must hold:

$$\frac{1}{s}.\Delta I = I\sigma$$

or $$\frac{\Delta I}{I} = s\sigma$$

where $\frac{\Delta I}{I}$ represents the rate of growth of investment.

As seen above in equation (6), rate of growth of income $\left(\frac{\Delta Y}{Y} \text{ or } G_y\right)$ is also equal to $s\sigma$, it follows that for equilibrium growth $G_y = \frac{\Delta Y}{Y} = \frac{\Delta I}{I} = s\sigma$.

If the above condition is not fulfilled, the economy would not move along the equilibrium growth path.

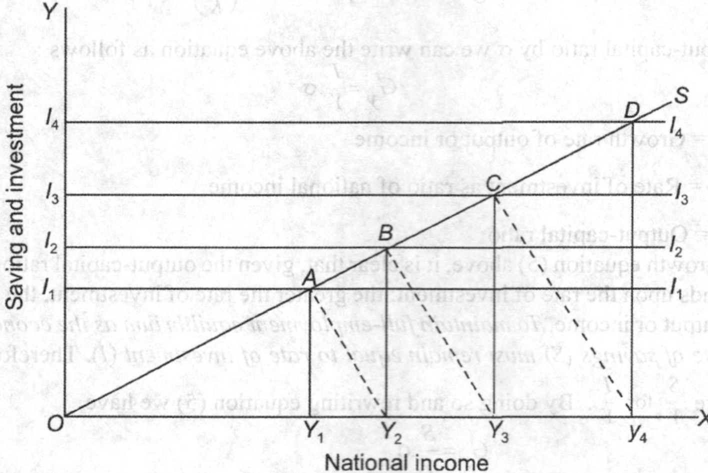

Fig. 13.1. *Harrod-Domar model of equilibrium growth*

Thus, the essential condition for maintaining a continuous equilibrium state of full employment is that investment and real income must both grow at a constant annual rate. This rate should be equal to the propensity to save (s) multiplied by output-capital ratio (σ) *i.e.*, $s\sigma$.

We can explain the model in geometrical terms with the help of Fig. 13.1 given above. Here real income is measured along the horizontal axis, while saving and investment (in real terms) are measured along the vertical axis. The saving function is represented by the line *OS* starting from the origin. Its slope is given by the marginal propensity to save (s) which is assumed to remain constant for a considerable period of time. The initial investment demand is represented by curve I_1I_1. This intersects the saving function *OS* at the point *A* so that the corresponding equilibrium level of income is Y_1. We assume that it corresponds to the full-employment level of national income.

Now, the new capital so created (represented by OI_1) will lead to the increase in productive capacity as determined by output-capital ratio. Given the output-capital ratio, investment OI_1 leads to Y_1Y_2 increase in output or income. As a result, national income will increase to Y_2. The ratio between the increase in income (ΔY or Y_1Y_2) and the increase in investment (OI_1) is given by the 'output-capital' ratio σ. But the new equilibrium level of income Y_2 will be realised or maintained only if the investment demand function shifts upward to I_2I_2 and intersects the saving function OS at the point B, which is vertically above Y_2.

However, as soon as the new capital equipment represented by the higher level OI_2 starts producing goods, capacity output or income will rise to Y_3 (indicating an increase by an amount σ times OI_2 over the previous level of income (Y_2). But the new level of income Y_3 will be maintained only if investment increases so much that the new investment demand curve I_3I_3 intersects the saving function OS at C. In this way, the process will continue so long as the investment increases by the appropriate amount in each period. The income would successively go on rising by an amount σ times the previous period's investment. And the investment in each period would rise by σ times the output-capital ratio. Thus, income would continue to grow at the steady rate of $s\sigma$.

It is evident from the basic equation $\frac{\Delta I}{I} = s\sigma$ that greater the saving rate(s), the greater will be the growth of investment needed to maintain the steady growth with full employment. Similarly, greater the value of (*i.e.*, the output-capital ratio), the greater should be the increase in income to avoid emergence of excess capacity. But greater income is possible only through greater investment. Hence, if income is to grow at a steady rate, investment must also grow at the annual steady rate given by $s\sigma$.

If, $\frac{\Delta I}{I} < s\sigma$, that is, if sufficient growth in investment does not take place, steady growth with full employment cannot be achieved. On the other hand, if today's investment is sufficient to achieve equilibrium growth with full employment, investment will have to be much more in the next period for generating sufficient increase in demand so as to utilise fully the expanded production capacity and to avoid the underutilisation of capital stock which will result in a fall in investment, and cause depression. In other words, "*the economy must, so to speak, run faster and faster to stay in the same place, otherwise it will slip downwards.*"[3]

HARROD'S GROWTH MODEL

Though Harrod's model of growth is similar to that of Domar, but it differs from the latter in details. Therefore we will explain below the essential features of Harrod's growth theory separately. In his essay "*Towards a Dynamic Economics*", Harrod put forward a theory which can be considered as truly dynamic. Explanation of secular trends is his main theme. He seeks to explain the secular causes of unemployment and inflation and the factors which determine the equilibrium and the actual rate of capital accumulation.

The classical economists considered economic development as a race between technological progress and capital accumulation on the one hand, and growing population and diminishing returns from land on the other. Harrod drops diminishing returns, regards technological progress and population growth as independent factors. In Harrod's analysis of economic growth there are three basic elements: (a) population growth, (b) output per head as determined by level of technique or inventions and (c) capital accumulation. Inventions may be neutral, *i.e.*, leave the capital coefficient unchanged, or capital-saving, *i.e.*, reducing the capital coefficient, or 'labour-saving' which will increase the capital-output ratio. It may be noted that capital-output ratio is the reciprocal of output-capital ratio (σ), the concept used by Domar. It is important to mention that Harrod uses the concept of incremental capital-output ratio, which is the reciprocal of marginal output-capital ratio (σ) of Domar's model.

3 Meier and Baldwin, *Economic Development*, 1966, p. 107.

While arriving at the behaviour of income as a response to entrepreneurial decisions regarding investment, Harrod makes two assumptions: (i) Saving in any period of time is a constant proportion *s* of the income received during that period, and (ii) the investment is proportional to the rate of increase of income. The second assumption is in fact the acceleration principle which states that the increase in output or income that occurs induces an increase in the stock of capital.

Harrod begins his analysis of growth by marrying together acceleration principle and the theory of investment multiplier. As in Domar's model, Harrod explains that growth rate $\left(G_Y \text{ or } \frac{\Delta Y}{Y}\right)$ depends on the rate of capital formation (or investment) and capital-output ratio which he defines as "*the value of the capital goods required for the production of a unit increment of output*". He put forward three growth equations. He takes saving as a fixed proportion of national output or income. Presenting a more elaborative analysis of growth than Domar, Harrod advanced three growth equations.

Harrod writes his first growth equation as follows:

$$G_y = \frac{s}{v} \quad \dots(1)$$

Where G_y is the rate of growth in a period $\left(\frac{\Delta Y}{Y}\right)$, s is the rate of saving (*i.e.* proportion of saving to national income $\left(\frac{s}{y}\right)$ and v is the capital-output ratio. It is important to note that capital-output ratio v in Harrod's growth equation (1) above is the one that is *actually obtained* from the extra capital accumulation (ΔK) and increase in production of goods and services in a year (ΔY). Harrod derives this growth equation as follows.

Following the Keynesian framework, Harrod takes that actual saving must be equal to actual investment. Further, since Harrod takes saving (S) as a constant proportion of national income (Y) in a period, we have

$$S = sY,$$

where s is propensity to save.

Investment (I or ΔK) in a period t depends on the rate of increase in production (or income), that is, ΔY (*or* $Y_t - Y_{t-1}$) and the actual capital-output ratio (v) . Thus we have

$$\Delta K \text{ or } I = v(Y_t - Y_{t-1})$$

Since in a period *actual* saving must be equal to *actual investment*, we have

$$v(Y_t - Y_{t-1}) = sY_t$$

Dividing both sides by Y we have

$$\frac{v(Y_t - Y_{t-1})}{Y_t} = s$$

or

$$\frac{(Y_t - Y_{t-1})}{Y_t} = \frac{s}{v}$$

Since $\frac{(Y_t - Y_{t-1})}{Y_t}$ represents actual growth of output or income, we can denote it by G_y. Thus

$$G_y = \frac{s}{v}$$

G_y is the growth of output or income which *actually* occurs in a period. The above growth equation is in fact a truism as it is always true by definition depending as it is on the accounting identity that actual investment equals actual savings of a period.

Warranted Rate of Growth

Harrod proposes a second growth equation which he calls a fundamental growth equation to describe *the equilibrium growth at a steady rate.* The warranted rate of growth is taken to be that rate of growth *which if it occurs will keep the entrepreneurs satisfied that they have produced neither more nor less than the right amount*. Being satisfied with the achievement of this growth rate, the entrepreneurs will maintain or perpetuate the same rate of growth. Warranted rate of growth is thus equilibrium rate of growth in the sense that producers, if they achieve it, will be induced to maintain it. The condition for warranted rate of growth is stated as under :

$$G_w = \frac{s}{v_r} \quad \ldots (2)$$

Harrod denotes capital-output ratio by the letter C, but following the modern practice we are using v for it.

G_w = "Warranted rate of growth", which is that rate of income growth of output or income. ($\Delta Y/Y$), which will keep entrepreneurs satisfied with the amount of investment they have actually made, *i.e.*, it is in fact the full-capacity rate of growth.

v_r = required incremental capital-output ratio to sustain the warranted rate of growth and is determined by the state of technology and the nature of goods constituting the increment in output.

s = average propensity to save.

The sort of entrepreneurial behaviour envisaged by Harrod means that to *maintain full employment, the desired (ex-ante) saving out of the full-employment income must be offset by an equal amount of desired investment*. But to induce this much investment, income must be growing.

In both the above equations (1) and (2) above s is the same because Harrod assumes that the saving intentions are always realised so that ex-ante savings are always equal to ex-post savings. Thus, Harrod is able to show that for dynamic equilibrium $G_w = \frac{s}{v_r}$.

It is important to note that v_r in growth equation (2) is different from v of the growth equation (1), As noted above, v in Harrod's growth equation (1) shows the increment in the amount of new capital installed during a period divided by the increase in output *actually* obtained from it during that period. It shows what has been actually produced with the addition to the capital stock in a period and *not whether producers are satisfied with the increase in output actually realised.* For example, if there are boom conditions in the economy and as a result the increase in capital installed during the period is fully utilised, actual capital-output ratio (v) will be lower. On the other hand, if there is a demand recession in the economy, the good amount of extra capital installed will not be utilised for production and consequently incremental capital-output ratio (v) will be higher.

But what determines the size of the required incremental capital-output ratio (v_r) which keeps entrepreneurs to perpetuate the growth rate. The size of the v_r is determined by technological conditions and the nature of goods comprising the increment of output. *This warranted rate of growth will be achieved if sufficient increase in income takes place during the growth process.*

The proportion of investment to income being fixed, an increase in income would mean that in the next period both income and investment must be higher. In such a situation the producers would like to perpetuate the rate of growth which they have already realised. *Under such circumstances the producers invest in the hope that they will be able to sell what they have planned to produce. In other words, the producers will desire to invest an amount required by* $G_w v_r$ *which will be equal in magnitude to s, i.e., the given proportional saving rate.*

Condition for Equilibrium Growth Rate in Harrod's Model

Now, what is the condition for equilibrium growth rate? *In Harrod's model, if incremental capital-output ratio (v) actually relalised happens to be equal to required capital-output ratio* (v_r), warranted by technological and other conditions, then the actual rate of growth, G_Y is equal to the equilibrium *warranted rate of growth (G_w), the rate which the circumstances of the economy warrants, the economy will be growing at the equilibrium rate ($G_y = G_w$).* It may be noted that actual rate of growth will be equal to the warranted rate of growth when investment is increasing at the rate high enough to generate adequate demand to ensure capacity growth rate (G_w).

Harrod lays down equilibrium condition for steady growth by saying that the actual rate of growth must be equal to the warranted rate of growth, i.e., the rate of increase in output or income should be just so much as to keep the entrepreneurs satisfied with the actual investment they have made. Thus for equilibrium growth rate $G_y = G_w$.

Thus, so long $v_r = v$, the producers would like to perpetuate a growth rate that is equal to the actual or realised rate. In other words, G_y (the actual growth rate) will be the same as that which the producers want to perpetuate, *i.e.*, G_w . But we have seen above that G_w stands for the rate of growth which when realised leaves the entrepreneurs in a state of mind that they shall be prepared to undertake a similar advance in the future. Furthermore, if the income increases at this rate it will continue to increase at this rate. This is how a steady growth rate is assured. Income will have to grow faster and faster, if the entrepreneurs are to be convinced that the higher investment was desirable. In this way, both income and investment will go on increasing from one period to the next. There is thus a cumulative equilibrium growth of income and investment.

Graphic Illustration of Harrod's Model

We can geometrically illustrate Harrod's model with the help of Fig. 13.2 given below. Here income is measured along the horizontal axis, while saving and investment are measured along the vertical axis. The line *OR* is drawn with a slope *s* (of the fundamental equation $G_w = \frac{S}{v_r}$) where *s* represents the saving function. The line *KA* represents the Harrodian investment function $I = v_r\ \Delta Y$ (*i.e.*, $v_r = \frac{I}{\Delta Y}$). For the sake of convenience we may write this function as $I_t = v_r\ (Y_t - Y_{t-1})$. This means that the investment will be zero if the current income (Y_t) is the same as the previous income (Y_{t-1}). As such the investment function line *KA* cuts the income-axis at *K* which corresponds to the previous period's income (Y_{t-1}). Further, the slope of the investment function *KA* is equal to v_r and this is greater than 45° on the assumption that $v_r > 1$.

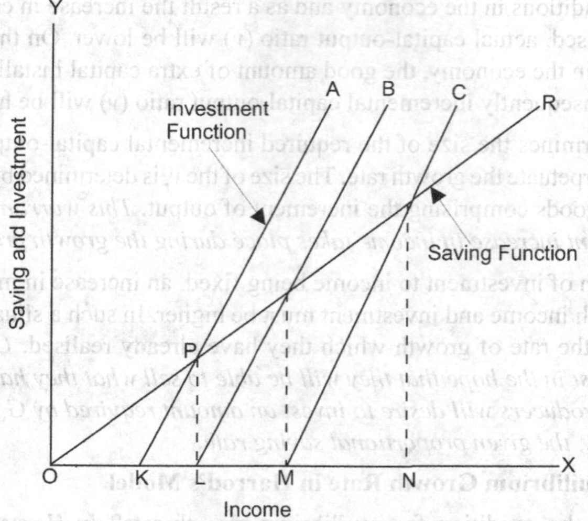

Fig. 13.2. *Graphical representation of warranted growth rate of Harrod's model*

From Fig. 13.2 given above, it can be seen that the saving-investment equilibrium in the current period is attained when the level of income is *OL*. And this level of income in the current period is more than the previous period's income level by an amount *KL*. Thus, the warranted rate of growth $G_w = \frac{\Delta Y}{Y} = \frac{Y_1 - Y_{t-1}}{Y_t}$ is given by $\frac{KL}{OL}$.

In the succeeding period $(t + 1)$, *OL* becomes the previous period's income and the investment function shifts to *LB*. So if v_r remains unchanged, *LB* will be parallel to *KA*. The new saving-investment equilibrium will be established where *LB* intersects *OR*. And this occurs at the income level of *OM*. As such the warranted rate of growth in the period $(t + 1)$ would be $\frac{LM}{OM}$. In the same way, the investment function of the period $(t + 2)$ will be given by the line *MC*, generating an equilibrium level of income *ON* and the corresponding warranted rate of growth of $\frac{MN}{ON}$.

Now, it may be observed that due to the properties of similar triangles $\frac{KL}{OL}, \frac{LM}{OM}, \frac{MN}{ON}$, are equal to each other. This implies that so long as the values of s and v_r remain unchanged, the warranted rate of growth takes place at an unchanged proportionate rate. However, *with the passage of time, the investment function goes on shifting successively to the right and the income would go on increasing at the warranted rate if the saving-investment equilibrium continues to be maintained in the successive periods.*

Natural Rate of Growth

Expansion, however, cannot go on indefinitely. The availability of labour and natural resources would put the limit. In other words, it is not necessary that the warranted rate of growth G_w (which in the equilibrium state is also equal to the actual rate of growth G_y) is the maximum attainable rate of growth. With this view in mind. Harrod introduces yet another rate of growth called the '*natural rate of growth*', G_n which is the maximum rate of growth allowed by the increases of macro variables like population growth, technological improvements, and growth in natural resources. In fact, G_n is the highest attainable growth rate which would bring about the fullest possible employment of the resources existing in the economy. This may be considered as the ceiling rate of growth. Joan Robiuson calls it the maximum feasible rate of growth. If *I* stands for growth rate of population (or labour force) and *t* for technological progress (*i.e.* rate of increase of productivity), then natural rate of growth can be written as

$$G_n = l + t$$

Hence, for the equilibrium growth rate at *full employment of all existing resources*, the following condition must be satisfied:

$$G_n = G_w = G_y$$

Any deviation from this path would bring about instability in the economy.

The Golden Age

The equality of three growth rates ($G_y = G_w = G_n$) ensures that economy is in moving or dynamic equilibrium. *This is also called balanced growth equilibrium. Joan Robinson describes the equality of these three growth rates as a golden age as its represents a very satisfactory and happy situation.* This is a happy situation because the equality of these three growth rates ($G_y = G_w = G_n$), will ensure steady equilibrium growth rate along with full unemployment of labour and without creating excess productive capacity. However, Joan Robinson has emphasised that the gold age, namely, the equality of three growth rates "*represents a mythical state of affairs not likely to obtain in any actual economy*"[4].

4 Joan Robinson, *The Accumulation of Capital*, London, 1956.

This is because the four key variables, namely, propensity to save (s), required capital-output ratio (v_r) of the warranted rate of growth, the rate of growth of population (l) and and rate of technological change (t) are determined quite independently of each other. While the warranted rate of growth (G_w) is determined by the value of s and v_r, the natural rate of growth is determined by rate of population growth (l) and the rate of technological progress (t). The golden age or balanced growth equilibrium of $G_y = G_w = G_n$ will occur only when the four variables, s, v, l and t have appropriate values. But this seems to be very unlikely to occur. It is only by chance that these four variables will have right or appropriate values to guarantee the golden age equilibrium.

Relevance of Harrod-Domar Growth Model for Developing Countries

Harrod and Domar models are closely similar to each other. As pointed out earlier, both these economists have sought to utilise the Keynesian framework, which was originally designed to tackle the short-term problems of a static economy to the dynamic problems associated with long-term sustained growth. Starting with an economy at full employment level, these economists have sought to provide answer to the following questions:

(*a*) How can a steady rate of growth be maintained at full employment level without inflation or deflation?

(*b*) Under what circumstances the rate of increase of income would be such as to save the economy from being entrapped in secular stagnation or secular inflation?

However, there are some limitations of applying Harrod-Domar models to the conditions of developing countries. First, to assume away the role of government is to disown the realities completely. In fact, due to the vast structural changes to be effected government in these economies must step in a big way to initiate and accelerate economic development as an efficient manager of the whole economy, lest we may slide down the slope. Besides, the assumption of an initial full-employment level of income is not valid for the developing countries; disguised unemployment pervades these underdeveloped economies, especially in the labour-surplus economies. It is a case of structural disequilibrium arising basically from the imbalance between labour and capital. Even if we make allowance for the entire savings to be invested, the growth of capital stock fails to match with the growth of labour force. Being based on fixed capital-output and capital-labour ratio, the Harrod and Domar models have only limited applicability to the developing world. Their peculiar problems demand a different solution from the one suggested by these models. To absorb the surplus labour force, there is a need to bring down both the capital-output and capital-labour ratios through reducing capital intensity. The Harrod-Domar models by assuming a constant capital coefficients rule out such a possibility.

Secondly, the usefulness of models based on the concept of capital-output ratio is of little operational significance in developing economies. Depending on the nature and degree of various shortages, bottlenecks and market imperfections, the productivity of invested capital is amenable to considerable fluctuations. It is indeed very difficult to have an accurate and valid estimate of a concept like capital-output ratio under such fluid conditions. Commenting in this regard, Prof. Hirschman[5] remarks that the predictive and operational significance of a model based on the concept of *capital-output ratio* is far less for an underdeveloped economy than for advanced economies. Models such as these, therefore, cannot explain the mechanism through which economic growth can get under way and could be carried forward in the present-day developing economies.

Thirdly, the Harrod-Domar growth variables are aggregative in nature and, therefore, fail to show the *sectorial interrelationship*. Besides, the processes of development of the developing economies are, as is being increasingly acknowledged, fundamentally linked with structural and institutional

5 Hirschman, *Strategy of Economic Development*, 1957.

changes. Their highly aggregative nature, comments Prof S. Chakravarty[6], 'prevents them from being used as a tool in detailed quantitative policy making and conceals many structural aspects of the problem of a steady rate of growth.'

Fourthly and very importantly, these models can at best offer counter-cyclical and counter-stagnation policy formulation. They are in no way any guide to industrialisation programming for growth which is the dire necessity of developing countries. For instance, in Harrod's model, the deviations between the actual, warranted and natural rates of growth indicate that the advanced economies are subject to cyclical fluctuations and secular stagnation. Harrod is of the view that chronic deflation is a far greater possibility in advanced countries on account of the fact that these countries save more than the investment can absorb. Domar has also presented a similar reasoning. He similarly maintains that the likelihood of effective demand falling short of productive capacity is more pronounced. Of course, even in developing countries, the problems of growth of effective demand falling short of growth in capacity output cannot be denied but the developing countries face more severe problems of low rate of savings and low productivity of investment.

Further, Harrod excludes autonomous investment as an explicit variable in his formulation of 'warranted' saving-investment equality. But the exclusion of autonomous investment as an important factor in determining growth in developing countries by Harrod in his growth model renders his concept of 'warranted' growth rate analytically inadequate for the purpose of developing countries. The apparent reason for this exclusion is to be partly found in Harrod's desire to make place for the acceleration principle in his growth model. He also ignored the role of public investment to which Keynes assigned a crucial role. But, autonomous investments, whether public or private, are of pivotal importance to the developing countries. Besides, Harrod-Domar growth models assume that propensity to save and the capital-output ratio are constant. But actually they are likely to change over the long-run. Further, if the proportion of factors can be changed as labour may be substituted for capital, then adjustment within the economy can be easily made and steady growth made possible without any rigid conditions.

In spite of the fact that these models are of limited applicability to the developing countries and fail to highlight the crucial issues involved in the development process of these economies they nevertheless are useful in fixing the overall targets of income, investment and savings and in checking the consistency of such targets. Prof. Kurihara states that "Harrod and Domar have made the essential nature of the growth mechanism operationally significant, for they stress saving ratio and the capital-output ratio (or its reciprocal) as measurable strategic variables to investigate and possibly to manipulate for a desired rate of growth. Because of the universal character of these strategic variables, the growth mechanism discussed by Harrod and Domar is applicable to all economic systems, albeit with the modification".[7]

An indirect use of these models has actually been made in some countries. For instance, in the First Five Year Plan of India, the rate of saving was planned to be raised through keeping the marginal rate of saving above the average rate of saving. And the current rate of capital formation and therefore growth of the economy was sought to be maximised through raising the marginal rate of saving. Thus, these models served to guide the planners in determining the growth rate of the Indian economy. Commenting on these models, Prof. S. Chakravarty remarks that "The great service that these models perform is to indicate very roughly the dimensions of the problem involved in raising the per capita income level in an underdeveloped country".[8] As noted above, Harrod-Domar model brings out the crucial role for the continuous growth of investment to ensure sustained growth at a steady rate. If investment is not growing sufficiently, the problem of deficient demand will emerge which will bring about recessionary condition even in a developing country. The demand recession

6 Sukhamoy Chakravarty, *The Logic of Investment Planning*, p. 43.

7 Ibid., p.185.

8 S. Chakravarty, *Op. cit.*

will result in rise in capital-output ratio due to the underutilisation of productive capacity. The Indian growth experience clearly brings out this fact. From the mid-sixties to the late seventies the Indian economy witnessed the problem of demand deficiency due to the fall in public investment resulting in lower industrial growth and increase in capital output-ratio. Again during 1997-2003 low industrial growth rate was achieved due to deficiency in demand resulting from stagnation in investment.

Further, Prof. Kurihara contends that though these models are "designed to indicate the conditions of progressive equilibrium for an advanced economy", yet he says these models are "important not only because they represent a stimulating attempt to dynamise and secularise Keynes's static short-run saving-investment theory, but also because they are capable of being modified so as to introduce fiscal policy parameters as explicit variables in the economic growth of an under-developed country".[9] He further writes, these growth models have this positive lesson for developing countries, that state should be allowed to play not only a stabilizing role but also a developmental role, if these economies are to industrialise more effectively and rapidly than the now industrialised economies did in conditions of *laissez faire*.[10]

It is evident from above that Harrod-Domar model states the equilibrium conditions for steady economic growth. Despite the fact that Harrod-Domar model was not intended to apply to the developing countries, it has nevertheless been extensively used for the growth problem of developing countries. The important aspect of the model has been that it emphasizes investment for accelerating rate of economic growth in developing countries. There are two issues in this regard. First, *whether it is the level of saving which restricts investment in developing countries* as Harrod-Domar formula explicitly implies and, second, as Cairncross[11] has argued, *it is the limited opportunities for profits that restrain the level of investment with saving levels adjusting to the scale of investment opportunities that exist.* Despite these reservations attempts have been made to answer such question as what rate of savings (and hence investment) is necessary to achieve a target growth rate given the assumed capital-output ratio.

Introducing Foreign Trade in Harrod-Domar Model

An important extension of the model is the introduction of foreign trade. This has been done by Bruton[12] who adjusts Harrod-Domar growth formula in the following way :

$$g = \frac{s}{v} + \frac{b}{v}$$

where g is growth rate, v is capital-output ratio and $b = \frac{\text{imports} - \text{exports}}{y}$

The implication of Bruton's formula is that imports can exceed exports (and therefore b in the above formula will be positive). This can take place if the developing country either accepts foreign aid or obtains funds by borrowing (*i.e.*, credit) or permit foreign investment to make up for the shortage of foreign exchange arising as a result of imports exceeding exports. Thus whatever be the form of capital transfers from the developed countries, they would enable additional investment to take place in the developing countries. Thus, the income-generating effect of additional investment would be the same as would occur from investment financed by domestic saving. Thus, the introduction of '*foreign sector*' in Harrod-Domar model shows how foreign aid, credit or private foreign investment can promote growth in developing countries.

However, the above particular view of introduction of foreign sector in Harrod-Domar model does not portray the full importance of foreign sector for the growth of developing countries. As a matter

9 K.K. Kurihara, *The Keynesian Theory of Development*, 1959. Ch.9. p.185.

10 *Ibid.*

11 A.K. Cairncross, *Factors in Economic Development*, George Allen and Unwin, 1962.

12 J. Bruton, "Growth Models and Underdeveloped Countries", *Journal of Political Economy*, Vol. 63, 1951.

of fact, the above adjusted growth formula implies that it will be equal to zero if balance of payments on current account is zero (*i.e.*, imports equal exports) and greater volumes of foreign trade will have no beneficial effect on economic growth of developing countries. Thus, according to this view, a country need not require much foreign exchange if it is pursuing *import-substituting* industrialization. Bruton challenged this viewpoint and argued that despite import-substituting industrialization adopted by several developing countries, they need to import raw materials, capital goods and intermediate products which they cannot manufacture within their countries and therefore they either need to expand their exports or get foreign aid, credit or permit foreign investment. It is worthwhile to note that similar argument for export-expansion in India was advanced by Dr. Manmohan Singh, former Prime Minister, in his Ph.D. thesis for Oxford University in the early 1960s. It was thus argued by him that even if domestic savings were sufficient for making the necessary payments for the *domestically produced* raw materials and other inputs but to procure foreign raw materials, capital goods and intermediate products a country needs foreign exchange which can be available if a country is able to either expand exports or obtain foreign aid, credit or foreign investment. This led to '*two- gap analysis*', domestic saving gap and foreign exchange gap which must be filled up to ensure steady economic growth. Thus it has been argued that domestic savings and transfer of foreign exchange (either through more foreign aid, credit or foreign investment) are not perfect substitutes of each other and that economic growth may be constrained by either *saving gap* or *foreign exchange gap*.

Chapter 14

Neoclassical Theory of Growth: Solow Model

Introduction

Having discussed Harrod-Domar growth model in the last chapter, we will discuss neoclassical growth theory in the present chapter. The neoclassical growth theory was developed in the late 1950s and 1960s of the twentieth century as a result of intensive research in the field of growth economics. The American economist, Robert Solow,[1] who won a Nobel Prize in Economics and the British economist, J. E. Meade[2], are the two well-known contributors to the neoclassical theory of growth. This neoclassical growth theory lays stress on capital accumulation and its related decision of saving as an important determinant of economic growth. Neoclassical growth model considered two factor production function with capital and labour as determinants of output. Besides, it added *exogenously determined factor, technology*, to the production function. Thus neoclassical growth model uses the following production function :

$$Y = AF(K, L) \qquad \ldots(1)$$

where Y is Gross Domestic Product (GDP), K is the stock of capital, L is the amount of unskilled labour and A is *exogenously* determined level of technology. Note that change in this exogenous variable, technology, will cause a shift in the production function.

There are two ways in which technology parameter A is incorporated in the production function. One popular way of incorporating the technology parameter in the production function is to assume that technology is *labour augmenting* and accordingly the production function is written as

$$Y = F(K, AL) \qquad \ldots(2)$$

Note that labour-augmenting technological change implies that it increases productivity of labour.

The second important way of incorporating the technology factor in the production function is to assume that technological progress augments all factors (both capital and labour in our production function) and not just augmenting labour. It is in this way that we have written the production function equation (1) above. To repeat, in this neoclassical approach production function is written as

$$Y = AF(K, L)$$

Considering in this way, *A represents total factor productivity* (that is, productivity of both factor inputs). When we empirically estimate production function specified in this way, then contribution of A to the growth in total output is called ***Solow residual*** which means that total factor productivity really measures the increase in output *which is not accounted for by changes in factors, capital and labour*.

Unlike the fixed proportion production function of Harrod-Domar model of economic growth, neoclassical growth model uses variable proportion production function, that is, it considers unlimited

1 Robert Solow, "A Contribution to the Theory of Economic Growth", *Quarterly Journal of Economics*, February 1956.

2 J. E. Meade, *Theory of Economic Growth.*

possibilities of substitution between capital and labour in the production process. That is why it is called neoclassical growth model as the earlier neoclassicals considered such a variable proportion production function. The second important departure made by neoclassical growth theory from Harrod-Domar growth model is that it assumes that *planned investment and saving are always equal* because of immediate adjustments in prices (including interest). With these assumptions, neoclassical growth theory focuses its attention on supply-side factors such as capital and technology for determining rate of economic growth of a country. Therefore, unlike Harrod-Domar growth model, it does not consider aggregate demand for goods limiting economic growth. Therefore, it is called '*classical*' along with '*neo*'. The growth of output in this model is achieved at least in the short run through higher rate of saving and therefore higher rate of capital formation, However, diminishing returns to capital limit economic growth in this model. Though the neoclassical growth model assumes *constant returns to scale which* exhibits *diminishing returns to capital and labour separately*.

We explain below how neoclassical growth model explains economic growth through capital accumulation (i.e., saving and investment) and how this growth process ends in *steady state equilibrium. By steady state equilibrium for the economy we mean that growth rate of output equals growth rate of labour force and growth rate of capital* $\left(i.e., \frac{\Delta Y}{Y} = \frac{\Delta L}{L} = \frac{\Delta K}{K}\right)$ *so that per capita income and per capita capital are no longer changing*. Note that for income per capita and capital per worker to remain constant in this steady state equilibrium when labour force is growing implies that *income and capital must be growing at the same rate as labour force*. Since growth in labour force (or population) is generally denoted by letter '*n*', in this steady state equilibrium, therefore, $\frac{\Delta Y}{Y} = \frac{\Delta K}{K} = \frac{\Delta N}{N} = n.$ Neoclassical growth theory explains the process of growth from any initial position to this steady state equilibrium.

Neoclassical Growth Theory: Production Function and Saving

As stated above, neoclassical growth theory uses following production function :

$$Y = AF(K, L) \qquad \ldots (1)$$

However, the neoclassical theory explains the growth process using the above production function in its intensive form, that is, in per capita terms. To obtain the above production function in per capita terms we divide both sides of the given production function by L, the number of labour force. Thus,

$$\frac{Y}{L} = AF\left(\frac{K}{L}, \frac{L}{L}\right)$$

$$= AF\left(\frac{K}{L}, 1\right) = AF\left(\frac{K}{L}\right) \qquad \ldots (2)$$

To begin with we assume that there is no technological progress. With this assumption then equation (2) is reduced to

$$\frac{Y}{L} = F\left(\frac{K}{L}\right) \qquad \ldots (3)$$

The equation (3) states that output per head $\left(\frac{Y}{L}\right)$ is a function of capital per head $\frac{K}{L}$. Writing y for $\frac{Y}{L}$ and k for $\frac{K}{L}$ equation (3) can be written as

$$y = f(k) \qquad \ldots (4)$$

Now, in Fig. 14.1 we represent the production function (4) in per capita terms. It will be noticed from Fig. 14.1 that as capital per capita (k) increases, output per head increases, that is, marginal product of labour is positive. But, as will be seen from Fig. 14.1, the slope of the production function curve decreases as capital per head increases. This implies that marginal product of capital diminishes. That is, the increase in capital per head causes output per head to increase but at a diminishing rate.

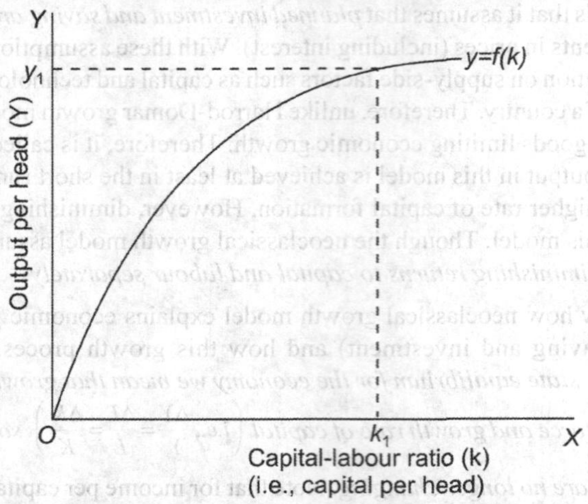

Fig. 14.1. *Production function relating output per head to capital per head*

It will be seen from Fig. 14.1 that at capital-labour ratio (*i.e.,* capital per worker) equal to k_1, output per head is y_1. Similarly, we can read from the production function curve $y = f(k)$ the output per head corresponding to any other capital per head.

Neoclassical Growth Theory: Fundamental Growth Equation

According to neoclassical theory, rate of saving plays an important role in the growth process of an economy. Like the Harrod-Domar model, neoclassical theory considers saving as a *constant fraction of income*. Thus,

$$S = sY \qquad \ldots (5)$$

where S = saving

Y = income

s = propensity to save

Since s is a constant fraction of income, average propensity to save is equal to marginal propensity to save. Further, since national income equals national product, we can also write equation(5) as

$$sY = sF(K, L)$$

As in neoclassical theory, planned investment is always equal to planned saving, *net addition to the stock of capital* is ΔK, which is the same thing as investment (I), can be obtained by deducting depreciation of capital stock during a period from the planned saving. Thus,

$$\Delta K = I = sY - D \qquad \ldots (6)$$

where ΔK = net addition to the stock of capital, I stands for investment and D for depreciation. *Depreciation occurs at a certain percentage of the existing capital stock*. The total depreciation (D) can be written as

$$D = dK$$

Substituting dK for D in equation (6) we have

$$\Delta K = sY - dK$$

or $$sY = \Delta K + dK \qquad \ldots (7)$$

Now dividing and multiplying the first term of the left-hand side of equation (7) by K we have

$$sY = K.\frac{\Delta K}{K} + dK \qquad ... (8)$$

We have seen above that *for the steady state equilibrium*, growth of capital $\left(\frac{\Delta K}{K}\right)$ must be equal to growth of labour force $\left(\frac{\Delta L}{L}\right)$, so that capital per worker and therefore income per head remains constant. If we denote growth rate of labour force $\left(\frac{\Delta L}{L}\right)$ by n, then in steady state $\frac{\Delta K}{K} = n.$ Substituting n for $\frac{\Delta K}{K}$ in equation (8) we have

$$sY = K.\, n + dK$$

or

$$sY = (n + d)\, K \qquad ... (9)$$

The above equation (9) is a fundamental growth equation of the neoclassical growth model and states the condition for the steady-state equilibrium growth rate when capital per worker and therefore income per capita remains constant even though population or labour force is growing. Thus, for steady-state growth equilibrium capital must be increasing equal to $(n + d)\, K$. Therefore $(n + d)\, K$ represents the *required investment* (or change in capital stock) which ensures steady state when capital and income must be growing at the same rate as labour force (or population)

The Growth Process

From the growth equation (9) it is evident that if planned saving *sY is greater than the required investment (i.e., (n + d) K) to keep per capita income constant, capital for worker will increase*. This increase in capital per worker will cause increase in productivity of worker. As a result, the economy will grow at higher rate than the steady-state equilibrium growth rate. However, this higher growth rate will not occur endlessly because diminishing returns to capital will bring it down to the steady rate of growth, though at a higher level of per capita income and capital per worker.

In order to graphically show the growth process, the growth equation is conventionally used in *intensive form*, that is, in per capita terms. In order to do so we divide both sides of equation (9) by L and have

$$\frac{sY}{L} = (n+d)\frac{K}{L}$$

where $\frac{Y}{L}$ represents income per capita and $\frac{K}{L}$ represents capital per worker (*i.e.* capital-labour ratio).

Writing y for $\frac{Y}{L}$ and k for $\frac{K}{L}$ we have

$$sy = (n + d)\, k \qquad ...(10)$$

The equation (10) represents fundamental neoclassical growth equation in per capita terms.

Growth Process and Steady Growth Rate. Fig. 14.2 shows the growth process that moves the economy over time from an initial position to the steady-state equilibrium growth rate. In this Fig. 14.2 along with per capita production function ($y = f(k)$) we have also drawn per capita saving function curve sy. Besides, we have drawn $(n + d)k$ curve which depicts required investment per worker to keep constant the level of capital per capita when population or labour force is growing at a given rate n.

In Fig. 14.2, $y = f(k)$ is per capita production function curve as in Fig. 14.1. Since per capita saving is a constant fraction of per capita output (*i.e.* income), the curve sy depicting per capita saving function is drawn below the per capita production function curve ($y = f(k)$) with the same shape.

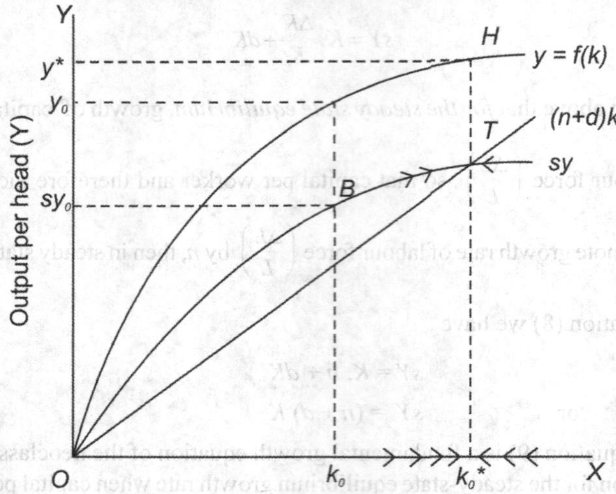

Fig. 14.2. *Neoclassical model: Growth process and steady-state equilibrium*

Another straight line curve labelled as $(n + d)k$, is drawn which depicts the *required investment* to keep capital per head (*i.e.*, capital-labour ratio) constant at various levels of capital per head.

Now, let us assume the current capital per head is k_0 at which per capita income (or output) is y_0 and per capita saving is sy_0. It will be seen from Fig. 14.2 that at capital per head k_0, per capita saving sy exceeds investment required to maintain capital per head equal to k_0 ($sy_0 > (n + d)k$). As a result, capital per head (k) will rise (as indicated by horizontal arrows) which will lead to increase in per capita income and the economy moves to the right. This adjustment process will continue so long as $sy > (n + d)\,k$. It will be seen that when the economy reaches at capital per head equal to k^* and per capita income equal to y^* corresponding to which saving curve sy interests the $(n + d)\,k$ curve at point T.

It will be noticed from Fig. 14.2 that the adjustment process comes to rest at capital per head equal to k^* because saving and investment corresponding to this state is equal to the investment required to maintain capital per head at k^*. Thus point T and its associated capital per head equal to k^* and income or output per head equal to y^* represent the steady-state equilibrium. It is worth noting that whether the economy is initially at the left or right of k^*, the adjustment process leads to the steady state at point T. It may however be noted that in steady-state equilibrium, the economy is growing at the same rate as labour force (that is, equal to n or $\Delta L/L$).

It will be seen from Fig. 14.2 that although growth of economy comes down to the steady growth rate, its levels of per capita capital and per capita income at point T are greater as compared to the initial state at point B.

An important economic implication of the above growth process visualised in neoclassical growth model is that ***different countries having same saving rate and population growth rate and access to the same technology will ultimately converge to same per capita income although this convergence process*** **may take different time in different countries.**

Impact of Increase in the Saving Rate

As has been explained above that in the steady state, both capital per head (k) and income per head (y) remain constant when economy is growing at the rate of growth of population or labour force (*i.e.*, n). In other words, in steady-state equilibrium $\Delta k = 0$ and $\Delta Y = 0$. It follows from this that steady-state growth rate or long-run growth rate which is equal to population or labour force growth rate n is not affected by changes in the saving rate. Changes in the saving rate affect only the *short-run growth rate* of the economy. This is an important implication of neoclassical growth model.

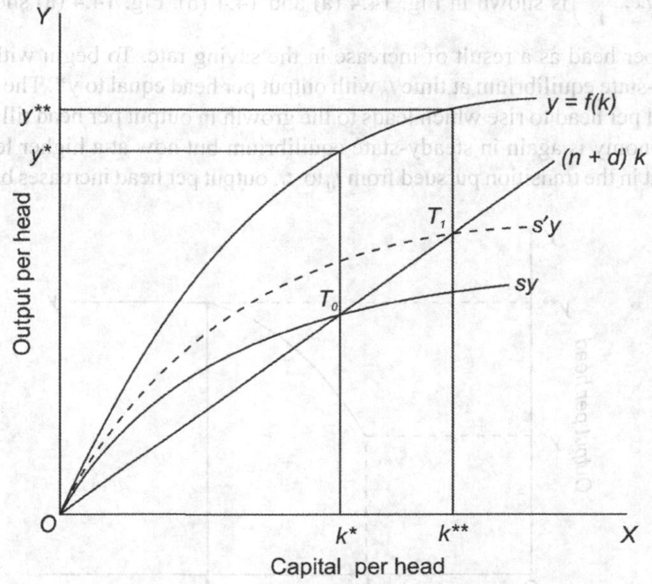

Fig. 14.3. *Impact of increase in saving rate*

Now an important question is why do we get this apparently incredible result from the neoclassical growth theory ? Impact of increase in the saving rate is illustrated in Fig. 14.3. It will be seen from this figure that initially with the saving curve sy, the economy is in steady state at point T_0 where the saving curve sy intersects required investment curve $(n + d)\ k$ with k^* as capital per head and y^* as income (output) per capita. Now suppose that saving rate increases, that is, individuals in the society decide to save a higher fraction of their income. As a result, saving curve shifts to the new higher position $s'y$ (dotted). This higher saving curve $s'y$ intersects the $(n + d)k$ curve at point T_1 which therefore represents the new steady state. We thus see that increase in saving rate moves the steady-state equilibrium to the right and causes both capital per head and income per head to rise to k^{**} and y^{**} respectively Note that in the new steady state the economy grows at the same rate as the growth rate of labour force (or population) which is denoted by n. It therefore follows that long-run growth rate of the economy remains unaffected by the increase in the saving rate though the steady state position has moved to the right.

Two points are worth noting here. First, though long-run growth rate of the economy remains the same as a result of increase in the saving rate, capital per head (k) and income per capita (y) have risen with the upward shift in the saving curve to $s'y$ and consequently the change in steady state from T_0 to T_1, capital per head has increased from k^* to k^{**} and income per head has risen from y* to y**.

However, it is important to note that *in the transition period or in the short run when the adjustment process is taking place from an initial steady state to a new steady state, a higher growth rate in per capita income is achieved.* Thus, in Fig. 14.3 when with the initial steady state point T_0, saving rate increases and saving curve shifts upward from sy to $s'y$, at the initial point T_0, planned saving or investment exceeds $(n + d)\ k$ which causes capital per head to rise in the short run resulting in a higher growth in per capita income than the growth rate in labour force (n) till the new steady state is reached.

The effect of increase in saving rate on growth of output or income per head (y) and growth rate of total output $\left(i.e., \frac{\Delta Y}{Y}\right)$ is shown in Fig. 14.4 (a) and 14.4 (b). Fig. 14.4 (a) shows the growth in output (income) per head as a result of increase in the saving rate. To begin with, the economy is initially in steady-state equilibrium at time t_0 with output per head equal to y*. The increase in saving rate causes capital per head to rise which leads to the growth in output per head till time t_1 is reached. At time t_1 the economy is again in steady-state equilibrium but now at a higher level y** of output per head. Note that in the transition pursued from t_0 to t_1, output per head increases but at a diminishing rate.

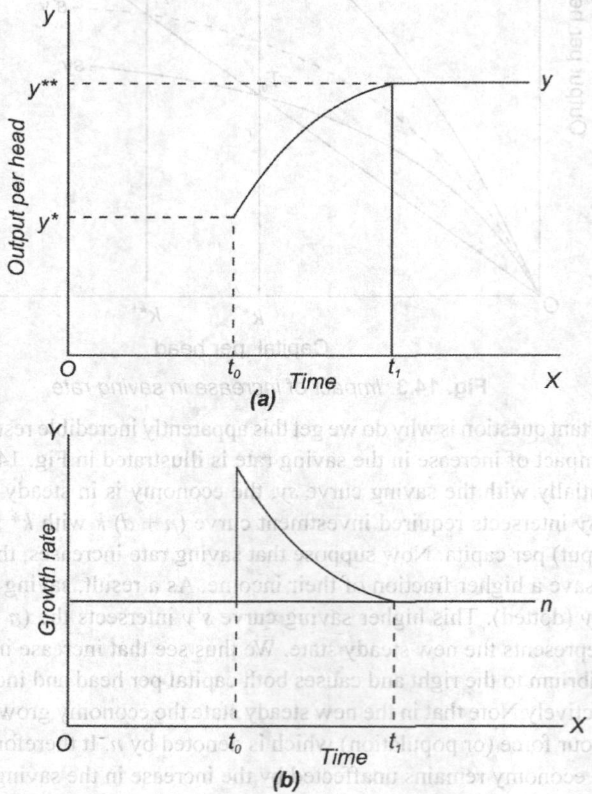

Fig. 14.4.

Fig. 14.4 (b) Illustrates the adjustment in growth rate of total output $\left(i.e., \frac{\Delta Y}{Y}\right)$. It will be seen from Fig. 14.4 (b) that starting from initial steady state at time t_0 the increase in saving rate and capital formation leads to growth rate in total output higher than the steady growth rate n in the period from t_0 to t_1 but in period t_1 it returns to the steady growth rate path n. It is thus evident that the higher saving rate leads to a higher growth rate in the short run only, *while long-run growth rate in output remains unaffected. The increase in the saving rate raises the growth rate of output in the short run due to faster growth in capital and therefore in output*. As more capital is accumulated, the growth rate decreases due to the diminishing returns to capital and eventually falls back to the population or labour force growth rate (n).

Effect of Increase in Population Growth Rate

For developing countries like India it is important to discuss the effect of increase in population growth rate on steady levels of capital per head (k) and output per head (y) and also on the steady-state rate of growth of aggregate output. Fig. 14.5 illustrates these effects of increase in population growth. An increase in population growth rate causes an upward shift in $(n + d)\, k$ line. Thus in Fig. 14.5, the increase in population growth rate from n to n' causes upward shifts of $(n + d)\, k$ to $(n' + d)\, k$ curve (dotted). It will be seen from Fig. 14.5 that the new $(n' + d)\, k$ curve cuts the given saving curve sy at point T' at which capital per head has decreased from k^*_1 to k^*_2 and output per capita has fallen from y^*_1 to y^*_2. This can be easily explained. Due to higher growth rate of population a given stock of capital is spread thinly over labour force which results in lower capital per head (*i.e.*, capital-labour ratio). Decrease in capital per head causes decline in per capita output. *This is an important result of neoclassical growth theory which shows that population growth in developing countries like India impedes growth in per capita income and therefore multiplies our efforts to raise living standards of the people.*

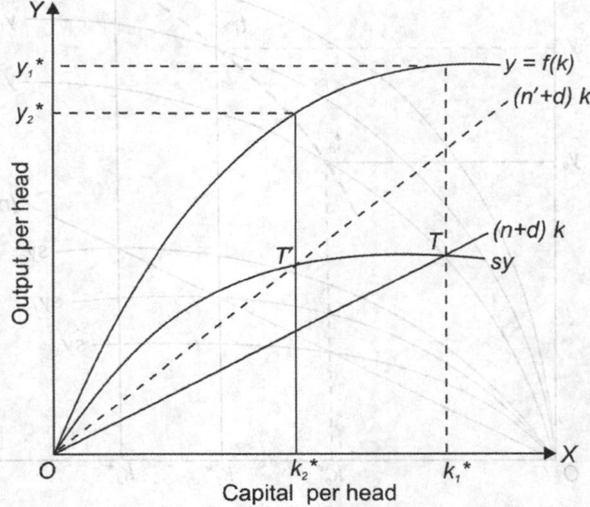

Fig. 14.5. *Effect of population growth rate on capital per head, output per head, and steady growth rate*

Fig. 14.5 also shows that higher growth rate of population raises the steady-state growth rate. It will be seen from this figure that increase in population growth rate from n to n' causes $(n + d)\, k$ curve to shift upward to the new position $(n' + d)\, k$ (dotted) which intersects the saving curve at new steady-state equilibrium point T'. The steady-state growth rate has therefore risen to n', that is, equal to the new growth rate of population. It may however be noted that higher steady rate of growth is not a desirable thing. As a matter of fact, *a higher steady growth means that to maintain a certain given capital-labour ratio and per capita income the economy has to save and invest more*. This implies that a higher rate of population acts as an obstacle to raise per capita income and therefore living standards of the people. Thus, this result provides a significant lesson for the developing countries like India, that is, if they want to achieve higher living standards for its people they should make efforts to control population growth rate.

Long-Run Growth and Technological Change

Let us now analyse the effect of technological change on long-run growth of an economy. It is important to note that *neoclassical growth theory considers technological change as an exogenous variable*. By exogenous technological change we mean it is determined outside the model, that is, it is independent of the values of other factors, capital and labour. That is why neoclassical production function is written as

$$Y = AF(K, L)$$

where A represents exogenous technological change and appears outside the bracket.

In the foregoing analysis of neoclassical growth theory for the sake of simplification we have assumed that the technological change is absent, that is, $\frac{\Delta A}{A} = 0$. However, by assuming zero technological change we ignored the important factor that determines long-term growth of the economy. We now consider the effect of exogenous technological improvement over time, that is, when $\frac{\Delta A}{A} > 0$ over time.

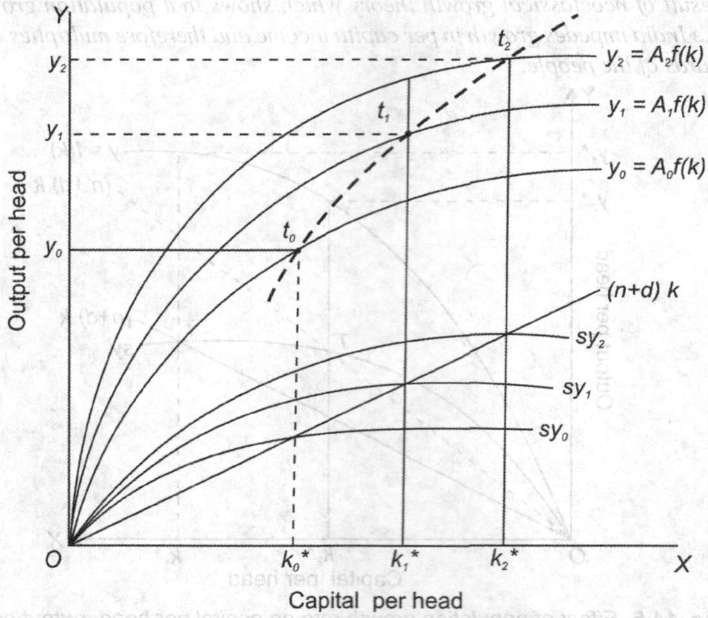

Fig. 14.6. *Growth in capital per head and output per head with exogenous technological change*

The production function (in per capita terms), namely, $y = Af(k)$ considered so far can be taken as a snapshot in a year in which A is treated to be equal to 1. Viewed in this way, if technology improves at the rate of 1 per cent per year, a snapshot taken a year later will be $y = 1.01\, f(k)$, 2 years later, $y = (1.01)^2 f(k)$ and so forth. As a result of this technological change production function will shift upward. In general, if technological improvement $\frac{\Delta A}{A}$ per year is taken to be equal to g per cent per year, then production function shifts upward at g per cent per year as shown in Fig. 14.6 where to begin with production function curve in period t_0 is $y_0 = A_0 f(k)$ corresponding to which saving curve is sy_0. With this, in steady-state equilibrium, capital per head is equal to k^*_0 and output (income) per head is y_0. With g per cent rate of technological progress in period t_1, production function shifts to $y_1 = A_1 f(k)$ and correspondingly saving curve shifts upward to sy_1. As a result, in period t_1, in new steady state equilibrium capital per head rises to k^*_1 and per capita output to y_1. With a further g per cent rate of technological progress in period t_2, production function curve shifts to a higher level, $y_2 = A_2 f(k)$ and associated saving curve shifts to sy_2. As a result, capital per head rises to k^*_2 and per capita output to y_2 in period t_2. We thus see that progress in technology over time causes growth of per capita output (income). With this, aggregate output will also increase over time as a result of technological progress.

The neoclassical growth theory has been successfully used to explain increase in per capita output and standard of living in the long term as a result, technological progress and capital accumulation.

Conclusion: Key Results of Solow's Neoclassical Model

Let us sum up the various key results of Solow's neoclassical growth model.

1. Neoclassical growth theory explains that output is a function of growth in factor inputs, especially capital and labour, and technological progress.
2. Contribution of increase in labour to the growth in output is the most important.
3. Growth rate of output in steady-state equilibrium is equal to the growth rate of population or labour force and *is exogenous of the saving rate, that is, it does not depend upon the rate of saving.*
4. Although saving rate does not determine the steady-state growth rate in output, it does cause *an increase in steady-state level of per capita income* (and therefore also total income) through raising capital per head.
5. Steady-state rate of growth of per capita income, that is, *long-run growth rate is determined by progress in technology.*
6. *If there is no technical progress, then output per capita will ultimately converge to steady-state level.*
7. A significant conclusion of neoclassical growth theory is that if the two countries have the same rate of saving and same rate of population growth and have access to the same technology (*i.e.* production function), their levels of per capita income will eventually converge, that is, they will ultimately become equal. In this context it is worthwhile to quote Dornbusch, Fischer and Startz. "*The poor countries are poor because they have a less capital but if they save at the same rate as rich countries, and have access to the same technology, they will eventually catch up.*[3]

SOURCES OF ECONOMIC GROWTH: PRODUCTION FUNCTION APPROACH

An important issue in growth economics is what contributions of different factors, namely, capital, labour and technology make to economic growth ? In other words, what is relative importance of these different factors as sources of economic growth. Robert Solow and Denison have attempted to study the relative importance of the various sources of economic growth by using the concept of production function. The rate of economic growth in an economy and differences in income levels of different countries and also their growth performance during a period can be explained in terms of the increase in these sources of economic growth.

It will be recalled that the *production function describes that the amount of total output produced depends on the amount of different factors used and the state of technology.*

The following production function has been used to measure the various sources of economic growth :

$$Y = AF(K, L) \qquad \ldots (1)$$

where Y = total national product

K = the quantity of physical capital used

L = the quantity of labour used

A = the state of technology

The production function equation (1) shows that increase in capital and labour and improvement in technology will lead to growth in national output.

3 Dornbusch, Fischer, Startz, *op. cit.* p. 61.

Growth Accounting and Total Factor Productivity

Note that improvement in technology causes output increases with the given factor supplies. In other words, advancement in technology leads to the increase in productivity of factors used. Therefore, improvement in technology is generally measured by growth in total factor productivity (TFP).

It will also be noticed from the production function equation (1) that technology (A) has been taken to be a multiplicative factor. This implies that progress in technology increases the marginal productivity of both capital and labour uniformly. Such technological change is generally referred to as neutral technological change. Besides, we measure the sources of economic growth with the above production function by assuming ***constant returns to scale***. Constant returns to scale implies that increase in inputs, that is, labour and capital, by a given percentage will lead to the same percentage increase in output. Further, the increase in improvement in technology (A) or what is also referred to as increase in total factor productivity causes a shift in the production function.

With the above assumptions it can be proved that the following factors represent the sources of economic growth :

or
$$\frac{\Delta Y}{Y} = \left(\theta \times \frac{\Delta K}{K}\right) + \left(1 - \theta \times \frac{\Delta L}{L}\right) \times \frac{\Delta A}{A} \qquad \ldots (2)$$

or Growth of Output = $\left(\begin{matrix}\text{Share of} \\ \text{Capital}\end{matrix} \times \begin{matrix}\text{Growth in} \\ \text{Capital}\end{matrix}\right) + \left(\begin{matrix}\text{Share of} \\ \text{Labour}\end{matrix} \times \begin{matrix}\text{Growth in} \\ \text{Labour}\end{matrix}\right)$ + Technical Progress (or Growth in Total Factor Productivity)

where θ denotes share of capital in national product, 1 – θ denotes share of labour in national product.

The above equation, which is generally referred to as *growth accounting equation*, shows the various sources of growth which are summarised below :

1. The contribution of increase in capital to the growth in output $\left(G \text{ or } \frac{\Delta Y}{Y}\right)$ is given by increase in $\left(\frac{\Delta K}{K}\right)$ capital multiplied by the share (θ) of capital in national product;
2. The increase in labour force contributes to rate of economic growth equal to the labour share (1 – θ) in national product multiplied by the growth in labour force $\left(\frac{\Delta L}{L}\right)$; and
3. The technological improvement $\frac{\Delta A}{A}$ which is measured by *the increase in total factor productivity also makes an important contribution to economic growth.* As mentioned above, technological progress leads to the increase in total factor productivity (TFP) which implies that with the given resources (*i.e.* capital and labour) more output can be produced.

Proof

We can formally prove the growth accounting equation mentioned above. In the production function equation (1) the change in output (ΔY) depends on changes in various inputs or factors — capital and labour ΔK and ΔL and change in technology. This can be written as under :

$$\Delta Y = F(KL)\,\Delta A + MP_k \times \Delta K + MP_L \times \Delta L \qquad \ldots (3)$$

where MP_k and MP_L represent marginal products of labour and capital respectively.

Dividing both sides of equation (3) by Y we have

$$\frac{\Delta Y}{Y} = \frac{F(K,L)\Delta A}{Y} + \frac{MP_K.\Delta K}{Y} + \frac{MP_L.\Delta L}{Y}$$

Since $Y = AF(K, L)$ we have

$$\frac{\Delta L}{Y} = \frac{F(K,L)\Delta A}{AF(K\,L)} + \frac{MP_K.\Delta K}{Y} + \frac{MP_L.\Delta L}{Y}$$

or $$\frac{\Delta Y}{Y} = \frac{\Delta A}{A} + \frac{MP_K.\Delta K}{Y} + \frac{MP_L.\Delta L}{Y} \qquad \ldots(4)$$

Now multiplying and dividing the second term of the right-hand side of equation (4) by K and also multiplying and dividing the third term of left-hand side of the equation by L we have

$$\frac{\Delta Y}{Y} = \frac{\Delta A}{A} + \frac{K.MP_K}{Y} \cdot \frac{\Delta K}{K} + \frac{L.MP_L}{Y} \cdot \frac{\Delta L}{L} \qquad \ldots(5)$$

Now, if rewards of factors of production are determined by marginal products of factors as actually is the case under perfect competition in neoclassical theory, then $\frac{K.MP_K}{Y}$ represents the share of capital in national product which we denote by θ and $\frac{L.MP_L}{Y}$ represents the share of labour in national product (Y) which we denote by $1 - \theta$, then substituting these in equation (5) we have:

$$\frac{\Delta Y}{Y} = \frac{\Delta A}{A} + \theta \frac{\Delta K}{K} + (1-\theta) \frac{\Delta L}{L}$$

The above is the same as growth accounting equation (2) which indicates the sources of growth of output.

Table 14.1. Source of Economic Growth

	Growth of Output %	Growth of Capital %	Growth of Labour %	Increase in total Factor Productivity %
United States				
1960–73	4.0	4.0	1.7	1.6
1973–90	2.5	3.4	2.1	0.0
Japan				
1960–73	10.0	10.6	1.3	5.9
1973–90	4.0	5.80	1.0	1.8
Europe				
1960–73	4.9	5.7	(–)10.1	3.2
1973–90	2.3	3.1	0.1	1.3

Source: Kuriharu, Shigehra, "*Causes of Declining Growth in Industrialized Countries in Policies for Long-run Economic Growth*". 1992.

In Table 14.1 we present the contributions made by capital, labour and total factor productivity (*i.e.,* technical improvement) in growth of output in the United States, Japan and the major countries of Europe in the two periods 1960-73 and 1973-90. It will be seen from the table that growth of capital and improvement in total factor productivity (*i.e*., technological progress) have been the important sources of economic growth, especially in case of economic growth in Japan and European countries. Table 14.1 further reveals that it is decline in total factor productivity (i.e. technological improvement) and in growth of capital that is responsible for slowdown of economic growth in the USA, Japan and European countries during the period 1973-90.

LIMITATIONS OF SOLOW'S NEOCLASSICAL GROWTH MODEL

Knowledge or Education is the Missing Factor. In the above growth accounting equation one factor, namely, knowledge or education, is missing which has been stressed among others by Nobel Laureate Prof. Amartya Sen as an important factor contributing to economic growth. It may be noted that increase in knowledge or education increases the productivity of workers by improving their productive skills and abilities. Besides, increased knowledge raises the productivity of capital and raises the return to investment in capital goods. Since investment in promotion of knowledge or education makes workers and machine more productive, the workforce equipped with knowledge and education is often called human capital which is regarded by modern economists as an important source of economic growth. Thus human capital or knowledge and education is the important missing factor in the growth equation of neoclassical economists, Solow and Denison. On including human capital as a separate factor which contributes to growth of output, the production function can be written as under.

$$Y = A\,F(K, L, H)$$

where H represents human capital which was omitted by Robert Solow in his growth accounting equation.

Ignores Economies of Scale as a Factor Contributing to Growth. Robert Solow in his study of sources of growth in real income also did not consider economies of scale as a factor contributing to growth. Solow assumed constraint returns to scale which implies if each factor in the production function increases by one per cent, output also increases by one per cent. However, some economists such as Denison and those associated with World Bank emphasise economies of scale or what is also called increasing returns to scale as a separate factor determining the rate of economic growth. In case of the United States Denison estimated that of 2.92 per cent annual growth in national income recorded during the period 1929–1982, 0.26 per cent was due to economies of scale. However, whether there are increasing returns to scale or constant returns to scale is an empirical matter for investigation.

Meade's Neoclassical Model of Economic Growth

Introduction

In his book, '*A Neoclassical Theory of Economic Growth*', Prof. J.E. Meade has put forward a model intended to explain the process of equilibrium growth (*i.e.*, the steady-state growth). In fact, the model attempts to analyse the manner in which the simplest type of classical system would behave under the conditions of equilibrium growth.

At the outset Prof. Meade states the three principal means whereby an economy can grow. They are :

(*i*) *Capital accumulation* resulting from the savings made out of current income. This brings about a growth in the stock of the 'capital instruments of production'.

(*ii*) *Growth of working population*, i.e., growth of labour force.

(*iii*) *Technical progress* which permits of growth in output through time out of a given amount of resources.

He then tries to examine the manner in which a classical economic system (*i.e.*, where perfect competition prevails) would behave if the three above mentioned factors were working simultaneously. To be more specific, Prof. Meade in his model analyses the manner in which a perfectly competitive economy would behave during a process of equilibrium growth when real capital is being accumulated, the labour force is growing and technical progress is occurring.

Assumptions of Meade's Model

1. A closed economy is assumed. That is, all types of economic and financial relationship *with other economies* are assumed away.
2. Complete *laissez-faire* is assumed to prevail in the economy and therefore there is no intervention by the government in the economy. Besides, the economy is working under the conditions of perfect competition.
3. The production in the economy is assumed to take place under the conditions of constant returns to scale. That is to say, if in a given state of technical knowledge all facators of production in an industry are increased by *x* per cent, then the output also increases by *x* per cent.
4. The economy is assumed to produce only two commodities, *viz*., a consumption good and a capital good. The consumption good satisfies all ultimate human needs of consumption. And the capital good is used to produce further the output of capital goods or consumption goods.
5. Machines are the only form which the capital is assumed to take. As such, the working capital in the form of goods in the process of production is assumed away.

6. *Besides machines, there are two other factors of production, viz., land and labour, and they are assumed to be in a state of full employment.*
7. There is assumed to be a constancy of the money price of consumption goods. That is, the cost of living index remains unchanged.
8. Like other neoclassical economists, in Meade's model production function is assumed to be such that the *substitution of one factor for another is possible*. In other words, in a given state of technical knowledge, it is possible to produce the consumption good or capital good by a more labour-intensive method or a more land-intensive method or by a more capital intensive method, depending upon the relative cheapness of labour, land or capital.
9. The substitutability between machines and labour, however, is assumed to be of a special type. It is assumed that all machines are alike (being regarded simply in terms of the tonnage of steel) and the *ratio of labour to machinery (i.e., of workers to tons of steel in stock) can be altered in any desired way, both in the short run and the long run.* Prof. Meade calls this as the assumption of perfect *malleability of machinery*.
10. It is also assumed that at *every moment of time, the production function for a unit of consumption good is the same as the production function for a unit of capital good.* The implication of this is that notwithstanding the state of technical knowledge, the cost-price of a machine is the same as the cost-price of a consumption good. Meade calls this as the assumption of *perfect substitutability in production between capital goods and consumption goods.*
11. Lastly, it is assumed that regardless of the length of time for which the existing machines had already been in sue, a certain percentage wears or tears out each year. For example, the existing stock of machines (measured in tons of steel) may require replacement to the extent of five per cent each year due to depreciation. Prof. Meade calls this as the assumption of *depreciation by evaporation.*

Meade's Formal Model

In the backdrop of the simplifying assumptions listed above, Prof. Meade tries to examine the system through time as the stock of machines increases, as the working population grows, and as productivity is raised by virtue of technical progress. However, the attention is concentrated only on the equilibrium growth of the system and not otherwise.

As a starting point of the model, Prof. Meade mentions four factors upon which the net output of the economy would depend. They are :

1. The net amount of the stock of machines which is available to the economy at a particular time. It is 'net' in the sense that from the existing stock of machines, the amount of depreciation has been deducted;
2. The amount of labour available for productive employment;
3. The amount of land or natural resources available for productive use in the economy; and
4. *The state of technical knowledge (which is assumed to improve through time).*

Now, the relationship between the net output and its above-mentioned determinants can be written in the form of a simple production function as follows:

$$Y = F(K, L, N, t)$$

where Y stands for the net output (or national income), K is the existing stock of machines, L is the amount of available labour force, N is the amount of land and t is the time which signifies technical progress as it (*i.e.*, technical progress) is supposed to occur merely with the passage of time and permits the increase in net output without any increase in K, L, or N.

As is clear from the production function, net output can increase in any one year due to the growth of K, L, N or t. But if it is assumed that the amount of land or natural resources available to the community remains unchanged (so that there is no change in land (to affect the level of net output Y), then the growth of net output will be entirely due to the growth of K, L, or t. We may, there-fore, express the total change in net output as equal to the sum of the changes in output arising from these three influences taken separately. That is:

$$\Delta Y = V\Delta K + W\Delta L + \Delta Y'$$

What this equation really means is that the annual increase in the net output (ΔY) is equal to the increase in the stock of machinery (ΔK) multiplied by *its marginal product* (V) plus the increase in the amount of labour (ΔL) multiplied by its marginal product (W) plus the increase in the rate of annual output due simply to technical progress ($\Delta Y'$).

Now, the *annual proportionate rate of growth of output* can be determined by dividing both sides of the above equation by Y and making some *meaningful adjustments*.

Thus, we have

$$\frac{\Delta Y}{Y} = \frac{VK}{Y}.\frac{\Delta K}{K} + \frac{WL}{Y}.\frac{\Delta L}{L} + \frac{\Delta Y'}{Y}$$

where,

$\frac{\Delta Y}{Y}$ = annual proportionate rate of growth of output,

$\frac{\Delta K}{K}$ = annual proportionate rate of growth of the stock of machinery,

$\frac{\Delta L}{L}$ = annual proportionate rate of growth in the working population, and

$\frac{\Delta Y'}{Y}$ = annual proportionate rate of growth of output due simply to technical progress.

Let us denote the above four proportionate rates of growth by the symbols y, k, l and r respectively. Further, let us call $\frac{VK}{Y}$, which is the proportionate share of capital in output as U and $\frac{WL}{Y}$, which is the proportionate share of labour in output as Q. Using these notations, we can rewrite the basic relationship in the following way:

$$y = Uk + Ql + r$$

This shows that the growth rate of output (y) is the weighted sum of the three other rates of growth. More specifically, the growth rate of output is the sum of the growth rate in the stock of machines (k) weighted by the marginal importance of machinery in the productive process (U) plus the growth rate of labour force (l) weighted by the marginal importance of labour in the productive process (Q) plus the growth rate of technical progress (r).

Now, to be able to gauge the real growth of the economy, we must express our basic relationship, *viz*, $y = Uk + Ql + r$ in such a way as to allow for the growth of population. Only then we can have a true index of the growth of real income per head. In other words, only when we *subtract the population growth from the income growth that we can get the growth in real income per head from our basic relationship*. For instance, if the income (y) increases by 10 per cent per annum and at the same time population (l) grows by 2 per cent per annum, then the real income per head will rise by $(y - l)$, *i.e.*, $10 - 2 = 8$ per cent per annum. Thus, subtracting the population growth (l) from the income growth (y) to get the real income per head, we can write the basic growth relationship in the following form:

$$y - l = Uk - (1 - Q)\, l + r$$

This equation tells us that the growth in real income per head ($y - l$) is the outcome of three factors – two of which tend to raise it, while the third works to decrease it. The factors which tend to raise the real income per head are : first, the growth in real capital (k) weighted by its proportional marginal product (U), and second, the rate of technical progress (r). On the other hand, the force which tends to depress the per capita real income is the growth rate of population (l) weighted by one minus the proportional marginal product of labour, *i.e.*, ($1 - Q$). This depressant factor, *viz*, ($1 - Q$) l is simply expressive of the familiar tendency for the diminishing returns to set in when increasing amounts of labour are applied on a given amount of land and capital equipment.

It can also be possible to incorporate the variable of savings in our basic growth relationship. We know that $U = \frac{VK}{Y}$ and $k = \frac{\Delta K}{K}$. Now, if S is the proportion of the net national income which is saved, then the total savings out of national income would be SY and this must be equal to ΔK, the addition to the stock of capital made thereof. Hence, we can write $k = \frac{SY}{K}$, where SY represents the amount of net real income which is added to the stock of machines through savings over the course of a year so that $Uk = \frac{VK}{Y} \cdot \frac{SY}{K} = VS$. We may, therefore, rewrite our basic growth equation in the following alternative way:

$$y - l = SV - (1 - Q)\, l + r$$

Changes in the Rate of Economic Growth

Having examined the main determinants of the rates of growth of real income per head, Prof. Meade proceeds to study the conditions under which the growth rates would tend, by itself, to rise or fall over time. More exactly, Prof. Meade, now, tries to answer the question : "Is growth likely to feed on itself and to become more and more rapid or is it likely to become less and less rapid and peter out as the economy develops ?"

To be able to pick out the factors crucial to the changes in the rate of economic growth, Prof. Meade concentrates on a limited number of relationships. And for that purpose, he assumed that the growth rates of population and technical knowledge (*i.e.*, l and r) in our basic growth relationship are given and constant—having been assumed to be determined by exogenous non-economic forces.

Once we grant that l and r are given and constant, it is evident from our basic growth equation, *viz.*, $y - l = SV - (1 - Q)l + r$, that whether with passage of time ($y - l$) will rise or fall would depend on the behaviour over time of V, S and Q. Now there are four major considerations which would govern the behaviour over time of V, S and Q. They are as follows:

First, if there is no technical progress and population growth, a rise in the rate of savings would cause the capital per head to increase with the resultant effect of lowering down the marginal product of capital (since there would be diminishing returns to a single factor of production). That is, V would fall. However, this decline in V would be lesser if the elasticity of substitution between machinery and other factors (labour and land) is greater.

Second, technical progress would cause V to rise over time. New technical knowledge and inventions would bring forth more profitable channels for new capital investment. So that, a given proportion of income saved would give rise to an increasing rate of growth in real income per head. As such, the rate of technical progress would tend to offset the depressing effect upon the level of V, caused by the diminishing returns to capital accumulation.

Third, the nature and extent of technical progress exerts a very important influence on the growth rate of real income per head over time. Whether or not the technical progress raises the marginal product of all factors simultaneously would depend on its nature. A rapid rate of neutral technical progress could indeed do so. However, as it is, the technical progress may be biased in favour or against a particular factor. And it may, therefore, make that factor more or less important at the margin over time.

Now, suppose that in an economy capital is being accumulated more rapidly than the growth of population. And if at the same time technical progress is biased in favour of capital relatively to labour then this will further go to raise the rate of growth of output per head with the passage of time. It is because, the nature of technical progress is such as to raise progressively the productivity of capital which by assumption is being accumulated rapidly. And the fact that technical progress is such as to diminish the relative importance of labour at the margin would be of no great consequences as by assumption the growth rate of population in the economy is quite low. Under these conditions, V would tend to rise and income per head over time would rise. And this, in turn, would raise S.

Fourth, a change in the distribution of income may cause the proportion of national income saved to rise or fall. Assume that : (*i*) savings out of profits are larger than out of wages, (*ii*) capital is being accumulated at a rate higher than that of population; (*iii*) there is a high elasticity of substitution between machinery and labour; and (*iv*) the technical progress is biased in favour of capital. Under these conditions, the income distribution would change towards larger profits so that there is a tendency for S to rise still further.

There are two valid reasons for one to expect a large proportion of national income going to profits than to wages under these circumstances. First, since the per head availability of machinery increases and because of the high elasticity of substitution between the two factors, neither the profit per machine would fall rapidly nor the real wage of workers rise rapidly. Second, the nature of technical progress being such as to raise the productivity of capital, the rate of profit would tend to rise relatively to the real wage rate. With these, therefore, following the change in income distribution towards larger profits, there will be a tendency for S to rise. As such, the element VS, in the determination of the rate of growth of the economy, will tend to rise with the passage of time.

In order to be able to appreciate the above mentioned set of four considerations, in so far as they influence the changes in the rate of growth over time, Prof. Meade considers the special case where population is constant (*i.e.*, $l = 0$). In this view, our basic growth relationship becomes :

$$y = VS + r$$

Evidently, in this situation, the rate of growth of real income depends upon capital accumulation (VS) and technical progress (r). Further, if the rate of technical progress (r) were constant, the growth rate of real income per head will depend simply upon whether VS will be rising or falling with the passing of time.

Now what are the factors which determine whether VS will be rising or falling through time? Prof. Meade, in fact, enumerates on the basis of an exercise,[1] the factors which, *with a constant population*, might cause VS to rise over time so that economic growth becomes self-sustaining and continually accelerating. They are :

(*i*) the prevalence of a high rate of technical progress,

(*ii*) the machine-using nature of technical progress,

(*iii*) initially a low proportion of savings out of income,[2]

(*iv*) a high elasticity of substitution between machinery on the one hand, and labour and land on the other,

(*v*) an increasing proportion of income saved as the real income rises, and

1 Sec. Meade, J.E., *A Neoclassical Theory of Economic Growth*, 1961, pp. 24.27.

2 This is because, the lower S is initially, the greater shall be the possibility of capital absorption with the progressive rise in S, and hence the strength of the diminishing returns to the single factor, machinery, will remain diluted for quite some time.

(*vi*) along with the change in income distribution in favour of profits brought about by (*ii*) and (*iv*) above–an especially large proportion of profits channelled to savings.

The State of Steady Economic Growth

Having examined the factors which, *with a constant population*, may condition economic growth in such a way that it feeds upon itself and continues to accelerate in speed, Prof. Meade proceeds to analyse the circumstances which would establish a path of steady-state economic growth. To do so, the assumption of constant population is given up. Rather we return to our original assumption that it is growing at a constant proportionate rate l. However, we continue to assume that the rate of technical progress is constant.

Now, the steady state of economic growth is that state wherein the growth rate in total output (y), as also the growth rate in income per head (y–l) is constant. In fact, with our assumption of a constant growth rate of population (l), the growth rate in income per head (y–l) will be constant only when the growth rate of total output (y) is constant.

Prof. Meade, then, shows that given the constant proportionate growth rate of population (l), and a constant rate of technical progress, the following conditions have to be met if a constant growth rate of total output, *i.e.*, a steady state of economic growth is to be achieved. These conditions are :

(*i*) all elasticities of substitution between the various factors must be equal to unity,

(*ii*) the technical progress must be neutral towards all factors, and

(*iii*) the proportions of savings out of profits, wages and rents are all constant.

The implication of the condition (*i*) is that if all the elasticities of substitution between our three factors—land, labour and machinery—are equal to one and if there are constant returns to scale, then no change whatsoever in the factor supplies would cause any change in the distribution of national income as between the three factors of production. Actually, any possible change in the relative amount of the factors of production would get compensated by the opposite changes in their relative rates of remuneration.

Condition (*ii*) simply states the definition of that type of technical progress which has no effect whatsoever upon the proportions of national income going to profits and wages.

The conditions (*i*) and (*ii*) taken together ensure that the proportions of national income going to profits (U), wages (Q), and rents (Z), would remain constant during the process of economic growth.

Now, since U is the proportion of profits out of the total national income Y, therefore, the total profits will be UY. And since S_v is the proportion of profits to national income saved, therefore, S_vUY represents the total savings out of profits. In the same way, S_wQY and S_gZY represent respectively the total savings out of wages and rents. But the aggregate savings in the economy are given by SY, where S represents the proportion of the total national income saved. As the aggregate savings of the economy must be equal to the sum of the savings out of profits, wages and rents, we, therefore, have

$$S = S_vV + S_wQ + S_gZ$$

With U, Q, Z, S_v, S_w, and S_g being all constants vide conditions (*i*), (*ii*) and (*iii*); it follows that S, the ratio of total savings to total national income, will also be constant. Actually, the above equation tells us that the ratio of total savings to total national income (S), is the sum of the constant proportions of savings out of profits, wages and rents (S_v, S_w and S_g), each respectively weighted by the constant proportions of the national income going to profits, wages and rents (U, Q and Z).

Let us now consider our basic growth relationship represented by the equation :

$$y = Uk + Ql + r$$

In this equation, we know l and r are constant by assumption. And also U and Q are constant vide conditions (*i*) and (*ii*). As such y will be constant only if k is constant.

Now, we know k, the growth rate of the capital stock, equals $\frac{SY}{K}$. But S, as shown already, is a constant. Hence, k will be constant only if $\frac{Y}{K}$, *i.e*, the ratio of annual national income to the value of the stock of capital, is constant. Again, $\frac{Y}{K}$ will be constant only if the rates of growth of Y and K are the same. That is to say, $\frac{Y}{K}$ will be constant only if $y = k$.

(**Note** that y and k represent rate of national income or output and capital respectively)

Thus, *we find that the growth rate of income will be constant only when the growth rate of capital stock is equal to the growth rate of the national income.*

In this view, therefore, the conditions under which the growth rate of income will be constant are simply given by the conditions under which the growth rate of capital stock equals the growth rate of the national income. *There would be some level of the growth rate of the capital stock which equalises the growth rate of national income with that of the capital stock.* Prof. Meade calls this as the ***critical growth rate*** of the capital stock. The equality between y and k would fail to be achieved if the growth rate of capital stock were more or less than this '*critical growth rate*'. Now, if we use 'a' to designate the 'critical growth rate', then we can write our basic relationship in the following way:

$$a = Ua + Ql + r$$

or

$$a = \frac{Ql + r}{1 - U}$$

That is, *if the growth rate of capital stock is* $\frac{Ql+r}{1-U}$, *then the growth rate of national income would also be* $\frac{Ql+r}{1-U}$ *and it would remain constant at this level.*[3]

Stability of the System

We have seen that the economy is in its state of steady growth so long as the rate of growth of capital stock k or $\frac{SY}{K}$ is at its critical or equilibrium level of $\frac{Ql+r}{1-U}$. But the growth rate of the capital stock will attain its critical level of $\frac{Ql+r}{1-U}$ if and only if the savings of the various recipients happen to be just and only just enough to make the existing stock of capital grow at the rate $\frac{Ql+r}{1-U}$. Now it remains to be seen whether the system can be stable in this state of steady growth level ? That is, if

3 Prof. Meade illustrates the whole argument with the help of numerical example. Supposes $Q = 1/2$, $l = 2\%$ and $U = 1/4$, then

$$a = \frac{(\frac{1}{2} \times 2) + 1}{1 - \frac{1}{4}} = \frac{2}{3/4} = 2 \times \frac{4}{3} = 2\frac{2}{3} \text{ which is the critical rate.}$$

With $2\frac{2}{3}$ as the critical rate, the equality of y and k can be seen to obtain from the basic relationship $y = Uk + Ql + r$. Putting the various values in it, we have, $y = (1/4 \times 2) + (1/2 \times 2) + 1 = 2\ .2/3$

Thus, y and k will have the value $2\frac{2}{3}$ in the steady state of economic growth. See Meade, *op. cit.*, pp. 33-34.

the growth rate of capital stock $\frac{SY}{K}$ were greater or lesser than the critical level, will certain forces set in, to bring back $\frac{SY}{K}$ to the equilibrium level given by $\frac{Ql+r}{1-U}$? It can be shown that the system would, indeed, be stable. Let us see how ?

Suppose first that, $\frac{SY}{K} > \frac{Ql+r}{1-U}$. In this case, it can be seen from our basic relationship $y = uk + Ql + r$, that if k or $\frac{SY}{K}$ is above the critical level 'a' by say an amount x, then the value of y will be raised above the critical level 'a' by only a fraction U of x. Therefore, in the case when the growth rate of capital stock exceeds the critical value, income will grow at a rate lesser than the growth rate of capital stock. In consequence thereof the savings will fall. This, in turn, would bring down the growth rate of capital. As such $\frac{SY}{K}$ would continue to decline till it reaches the critical level.

Similarly, if $\frac{SY}{K} > \frac{Ql+r}{1-U}$; the system would regain its equilibrium level. It is because, in this case, income would grow more rapidly than the capital stock with the result that savings would grow more rapidly than the capital stock. In consequences thereof, the rate of growth of the capital stock would rise till it reaches the critical level.

To sum up, *given that l and r are constant, all the elasticities of substitution between various factors are equal to unity, technical progress is neutral towards all factors and the proportion of savings out of profits, wages and rents are all constant, then the growth rates of national income and of the capital stock would both converge towards the constant level of* $\frac{Ql+r}{1-U}$.

Graphical Representation of the Model

The basic argument of Prof. Meade's model can be explained with the help of the geometrical construction shown in Fig. 15.1. In this diagram we measure the growth rate of the capital stock along the horizontal axis. And the growth rate of national income is measured along the vertical axis. The line *OAC* drawn through the origin with a slope *U*, represents the proportional share of capital in national income. The line *EFG*, drawn at a distance $Ql + r$ from the origin and parallel to the line *OAC*, represents the total growth rate of the national income. The 45° line *Ok* gives the growth rate of the capital stock.

If, to start with, the actual growth rate of the capital stock were *OB*, then the corresponding growth rate of national income would be *BF* (or *BA* + *FA*). In this, *BA represents that part of the growth rate of national income which is attributable to the accumulation of capital stock. And FA* (*= OE =* $Ql + r$) *would represent that part of the growth rate of national income which is on account of labour growth and technical progress.* But at the point *F*, *FB* > *FA*, *i.e*, the growth rate of national income is greater than the growth rate of the stock of capital or $y > k$. As such, k will start rising till finally the point *D on the horizontal axis* is reached. It is only then that the equality between y and k would be reached at the point *G* on the 45° line. That would represent the steady state of economic growth.

We can also derive the value y and k for '*steady growth rate*' from this diagram. Since $CD = Uk$ and $GD = k$, therefore, *GC* must be equal to $GD - CD$ or $k - Uk = (1 - U)k$.

i.e.,
$$GC = (1 - U)k$$

But $GC = OE = Ql + r$

$\therefore$ for equilibrium growth rate $(1 - U)\, k = Ql + r$

or $k = \dfrac{Ql + r}{1 - U}$, which is the value that y and k must have in the state of steady economic growth.

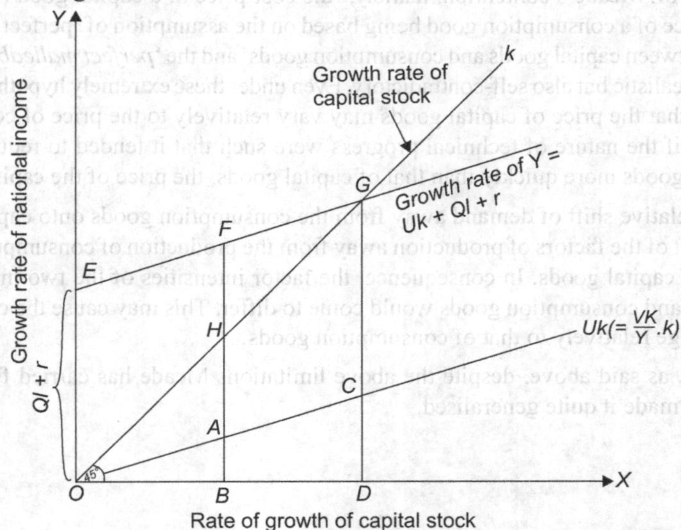

Fig. 15.1. *Meade's model of growth*

Critical Evaluation

Prof. Meade's model illustrates the manner in which the simplest form of neoclassical system with perfect competition and constant returns to scale would behave during the process of equilibrium growth. This in itself represents a major achievement as it enables the examination of the process of change in the variables of a simple neoclassical system over time. All the previous works had only attempted to compare two static positions of the neoclassical system. Having introduced the dynamic dimensions in the neoclassical system, Prof. Meade succeeds in bringing out the implications of the neoclassical analysis for economic growth in general and for steady state in particular.

By explaining a neoclassical system with perfect atomistic competition where capital is being simultaneously accumulated, working force is growing and technical progress is taking place, Prof. Meade provides a deep insight into the mechanism underlying the process of economic growth. The results so obtained in this model could well be modified by allowing for the effects of certain types of imperfect competition so as to bring them nearer to reality. Indeed, the main merit of Prof. Meade's model lies in the lucid manner in which his model demonstrates the simultaneous influence of capital accumulation, population growth and technical progress on the growth rate of national income and the standard of living over time.

Prof. Meade's exposition of steady state of economic growth is, in fact, a replica of Mrs. Joan Robinson's 'Golden Age'. But the merit of the former over the latter lies in the fact that it explains the same thing without having to make the unrealistic assumption of full employment of capital and labour. Mrs. Robinson's treatment of 'Golden Age' is tenable only under this assumption.

However, Prof. Meade's model captures but only a patch of reality and that too under rather limiting conditions. It completely neglects the influence of social, political and international factors in economic growth. A crucial weakness of Prof Meade's model stems from his assumption of the constant money prices of consumption goods as being ensured just through the operations of monetary policy. And that the adjustments in money wage rates ensure full employment. But it is quite unrealistic to assume that the easing or tightening of monetary conditions could, in fact, be carried out with all that foresight and precision as is called for by Prof. Meade's model. Mrs. Robinson, in fact, dubbed Meade's model as simply 'pseudo-casual.

Again, Prof. Meade's contention, namely, 'the cost-price of a capital good remaining the same as the cost price of a consumption good being based on the assumption of 'perfect· 'substitutability in production between capital goods and consumption goods' and the '*perfect malleability of machinery*', is not only unrealistic but also self-contradictory. Even under these extremely hypothetical assumptions, it is possible that the price of capital goods may vary relatively to the price of consumption goods. For instance, if the nature of technical progress were such that it tended to reduce the real cost of consumption goods more quickly than that of capital goods, the price of the capital goods may rise.

Also, a relative shift of demand away from the consumption goods onto capital goods[4]; would result in a shift of the factors of production away from the production of consumption goods onto the production of capital goods. In consequence, the factor intensities of the two industries producing capital goods and consumption goods would come to differ. This may cause the cost price of capital goods to change relatively to that of consumption goods.

However, as said above, despite the above limitations Meade has carried further neoclassical approach and made it quite generalised.

4 This could occur if, for example, with the rise in real incomes and standards of living a larger proportion of national income is saved so that the amount spent on capital goods would rise relatively to that on consumption goods.

Joan Robinson's Model of Growth

Introduction

Harrod and Domar extended the Keynesian analysis of income and employment to the long-run setting and therefore considered both the income and capacity effects of investment. Harrod and Domar models of economic growth explain at what rate investment should increase so that steady growth is possible in an advanced capitalist economy. In the growth models of Harrod and Domar, the rate of capital accumulation plays a crucial role in the determination of economic growth. Joan Robinson has further refined the model of capital accumulation in a private enterprise economy. *She relates investment with the rate of profit which in turn depends upon the distribution of income between wages and profits on the one hand and labour productivity and capital intensity on the other*. We shall explain below Joan Robinson's model of capital accumulation and growth which is suited to the labour-surplus conditions of less developed countries.

Assumptions of Joan Robinson's Model of Growth

In Joan Robinson's model of economic growth and capital accumulation the following assumptions are made:

(*i*) It is assumed that in a free private enterprise economy perfect competition prevails among producers and consumers of products. Further, the economy is a closed one, that is, it has no foreign trade with other countries.

(*ii*) There are only two factors of production, namely, labour and capital. Therefore, the entire national product is distributed among "entrepreneurs" and "workers". The entrepreneurs get profits (income from property) and workers obtain wages (the income from work).

(*iii*) State of technology remains the same, that is, no technological progress takes place.

(*iv*) Entrepreneurs save all their profits while workers spend all their wages on consumption and save nothing. Thus, it is only the entrepreneurs who do the savings and save all their profits.

(*v*) It is assumed that capital and labour are combined in a fixed proportion to produce a given level of output. In other words, technical coefficients of production are fixed.

(*vi*) Labour is the surplus factor, and entrepreneurs employ as much labour as they find it profitable.

Joan Robinson's Model: Output and Income Side of Capital Accumulation

Given the above assumptions, the net national income of the economy will consist of the total wage bill and the total profits. As such, the distribution of net national income among the entrepreneurs and workers is given by

$$pY = wN + \pi pK \qquad \ldots (1)$$

(National Income) = (Wage Bill + Profits)

Y = denotes net national output
N = denotes number of workers employed
K = denotes amount of capital stock used to produce the given national product Y
w = denotes money wage rate paid to the workers
π = denotes the gross rate of profit (inclusive of the interest rate)
p = denotes the average price level of output, both of output and stock of capital goods

From equation (1) above, we get

$$\pi pK = pY - wN$$

$$\pi = \frac{pY - wN}{pK}$$

Dividing both the numerator and the denominator by p, we get

$$\pi = \frac{Y - \frac{wN}{p}}{K}$$

Dividing the numerator and denominator by N, we get

$$\pi = \frac{\frac{Y}{N} - \frac{w}{p}}{K/N}$$

Now, in the above equation $\frac{Y}{N}$ implies labour productivity, and $\frac{K}{N}$ is capital-labour ratio and $\frac{w}{p}$ is the real wage rate.

Writing b for $\frac{Y}{N}$ and v for $\frac{K}{N}$ we have

$$\text{or} \qquad \pi = \frac{b - \frac{w}{p}}{v} \qquad \ldots (2)$$

where, $b = \frac{Y}{N}$, *i.e.*, the labour productivity

and $v = \frac{K}{N}$, *i.e*, the capital-labour ratio

The equation (2) shows that the profit rate is a function of the labour productivity b, real wage rate (w/p) and the capital-labour ratio (v). For maximising profits, the entrepreneurs will operate on these variables in conformity with the equation (2). The profit rate can be increased either with the increase in the labour productivity b or with the decrease in the real wage rate $\left(\frac{w}{p}\right)$ and decrease in the capital-labour ratio (v). The equation (2) shows that given the labour productivity (b) and capital-labour ratio (v), the rise in real wage rate (w/p) will reduce the profit rate and fall in the real wage rate will raise it.

Expenditure Side of Capital Accumulation

Now, the expenditure side of the economy is represented by the familiar Keynesian equilibrium condition, namely, national income equals the sum of consumption expenditure (C) and investment expenditure (I). Thus,

$$Y = C + I \qquad \ldots (3)$$

When aggregate expenditure ($C + I$) equals aggregate output (*i.e.*, Y), then intended saving must also be equal to intended investment (I). Therefore, at equilibrium level of national income;

$$S = I \quad \ldots (4)$$

where C, S and I have the usual meaning.

As mentioned above, Joan Robinson assumes that all profits made by entrepreneurs are saved and all wages earned by workers are consumed. Given this assumption

$$S = \pi K \quad \ldots (5)$$

All profits are, meant to be ploughed directly into investment. As such we can write the equation (4) in the following form:

$$S = \pi K = I \quad \ldots (6)$$

Writing ΔK (*i.e.*, increase in the stock of real capital) for I in the above equation we have

$$\Delta K = \pi K$$

or

$$\pi = \frac{\Delta K}{K}$$

This means that, given the assumptions made, rate of profit (π) is equal to the rate of investment expressed as a ratio of change in capital to the total stock of capital (K).

Equilibrium Growth

For getting the equilibrium, we simply have to juxtapose the income and expenditure sides expressed in (2) and (6) above respectively. Thus, the equilibrium condition is:

$$\pi = \frac{b - w/p}{v} = \frac{\Delta K}{K} \quad \ldots (7)$$

This equilibrium condition manifests a double-side relationship between the rate of profit and rate of accumulation. On the one hand, it tells us that the rate of accumulation going on in a particular situation determines the level of profits obtainable therefrom. It also shows the rate of profit which the entrepreneurs would expect on their investment. On the other hand, the equilibrium condition shows that the rate of profit itself governs the rate of accumulation. Anything that determines the rate of profit would also determine the rate of growth of capital. Thus in Joan Robinson's model of growth the urge to accumulate capital on the part of entrepreneurs determines the rate of economic growth. And the urge or desire of the entrepreneurs to accumulate capital depends on the expected rate of profit.

Accumulation and profit are, therefore, linked with each other in a circular way. "*If they have no profit, the entrepreneurs cannot accumulate and if they do not accumulate they have no profit.*[1] Thus, the basic mechanism underlying Mrs. Robinson's growth model is the desire of the firms to accumulate. And the urge to accumulate is dependent on the expected rate of profit.

Desired Rate of Accumulation

In a manner very much akin to that of Harrod's line of argument, Mrs. Robinson draws a distinction between the '*desired rate*' of accumulation (analogous to '*warranted rate*') and the *possible rate*' of accumulation (similar to '*natural rate*').

The *desired rate* of accumulation is that rate of accumulation which generates just that expectation of profit which is necessary to cause it to be maintained. In other words, it is that rate of accumulation which would make the firms feel satisfied with the economic conjuncture in which they find themselves.

To be able to appreciate the significance of this concept, it is necessary to know the relation

1 J. Robinson, *The Accumulation of Capital*, Book II, p. 76.

between "the rate of profit caused by the rate of accumulation and the rate of accumulation which that rate of profit will induce."[2] Mrs. Robinson makes use of the following diagram to bring out this distinction.[3]

The curve *A* depicts the rate of profit as a function of the rate of accumulation that gives rise to it. On the other hand, the curve *I* shows the rate of accumulation as a function of the rate of profit that induces it. The two curves are shown to intersect at the points *P* and *Q* in Fig. 16.1.

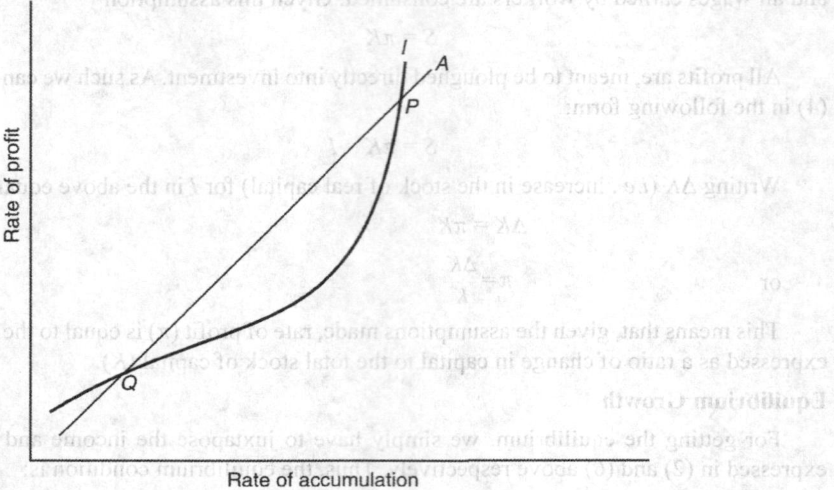

Fig. 16.1. *Desired rate of accumulation*

When the firms operate in the region lying to the right of the point *P*, the rate of accumulation that takes place in the economy exceeds than what is justified by the rate of profit that it entails. Such a situation may arise when the ratio of plant and equipment as between the basic and commodity sectors is unduly high. So that any further investment in the former is unlikely to be profitable. In the immediate future, therefore, this ratio is likely to fall and consequently the rate of accumulation would also fall.

If, however, the rate of accumulation that is taking place at present happens to be lower than the rate of profit that it entails, a situation quite converse of the one described above will be faced. In terms of the figure, if the firms are operating in the region bounded by the points *P* and *Q*, they shall tend to step up the rate of accumulation. This is likely to happen when the ratio of machinery as between the capital goods and the consumer goods sectors happens to be low, so that a higher proportion of current investment will tend to flow to the capital goods sector. This would result in increasing the rate of accumulation.

The lower point of intersection of the curves *I* and *A*, *i.e.*, the point *Q*, is indeed a crucial point. It is a point where the rate of accumulation is generating just that expectation of profit which is essential to cause it to be maintained. This is the '*desired rate*' of accumulation. It is desired in the sense that the firms feel contented in the situation in which they find themselves. Evidently, the '*desired rate*' of accumulation is quite analogous to Harrod's '*warranted rate*' of growth.

Possible Rate of Growth

I f the desired rate of accumulation continues unfailingly in the long nm without any disturbing influences, the economy will be said to develop under tranquil conditions. It is because under such

2 Joan Robinson, "Model of Accumulation" in *Growth Economics* (ed)., A,K. Sen, Penguine Series, 1970, p. 129.

3 *Ibid.*

conditions complete harmony in the growth process shall be achieved. The composition of the stock of productive capital will adjust completely in consonance with the requirements. In particular, the distribution of plants and machinery as between the basic and the commodity sectors shall be most appropriate and in keeping with the desired rate of accumulation. All in all, there shall be a steady proportionate growth in the physical stock of various kinds of plants on the one hand, and the working capital on the other. In sum, the system shall be in a sort of internal equilibrium.

But the pertinent question is : shall such internal equilibrium exhibiting tranquil conditions continue. to prevail uninterruptedly ? The answer is that it depends ! The unhindered continuance of the tranquil conditions is possible only if the desired rate of accumulation becomes so by virtue of the physical conditions of the economy. This leads us to the concept of '*possible rate*' of growth, which is the counterpart of Harrod's '*natural rate*' of growth. The '*possible rate*' of growth is that rate of growth which is made 'possible' by the physical conditions resulting from the growth of population and technical knowledge.

On the basis of the various possibilities arising out of the juxtaposition of the '*desired*' and '*possible*; rates of growth, Mrs. Robinson makes distinction between alternative types of equilibrium growth paths. She designates the various equilibrium growth paths as 'ages'. We now proceed to discuss them briefly.

GOLDEN AGES

The situation of smooth steady growth with full employment arising out of the equality of the '*desired*' and '*possible*' rates of accumulation has been designated by Mrs. Robinson as the 'golden age' equilibrium.

Assuming v to be constant under conditions of full employment, then from the equation $K/N = v$, we get

$$K = vN$$

$\therefore$
$$\Delta K = \Delta N\, v$$

or
$$\Delta N = \frac{\Delta K}{v}$$

or
$$\frac{\Delta N}{N} = \frac{\Delta K/v}{N} = \frac{\Delta K/v}{K/v}$$

or
$$\frac{\Delta N}{N} = \frac{\Delta K}{K} \qquad \ldots (8)$$

The equation (8) implies that if v is constant at the full-employment level, then labour and capital grow at the same rate.

This is the situation of '*golden age*' equilibrium. The equality between the desired and possible rates of accumulation coexists with full employment of labour and capital. Besides, both labour and capital grow at the same rate. The economy is thus on a tranquil steady growth path —"a steady rate of accumulation then rolls smoothly on its way."[4] There is harmony in all respects.

The entrepreneurs are in a state of equilibrium as their desired rate of accumulation is being realised. The wage-earners, on the other hand, are in an equilibrium state because there comes to prevail an overall harmony in the demand and supply of labour. In the Harrodian terminology, Mrs. Robinson's '*Golden Age*' is that state of the economy where the '*warranted rate*' gets equated to the '*natural rate*' and full employment is maintained throughout.

Stability of 'Golden Age' Equilibrium. If certain forces operate so as to disturb the 'golden age' equilibrium of the economy, equilibrating mechanism automatically comes into being to restore the equilibrium. Let us see how ?

4 Mrs. Robinson's Model of Accumulation, *Op. cit.*, p. 138.

The divergence from the 'golden age' equilibrium path will take place if:

$$(a) \quad \frac{\Delta N}{N} > \frac{\Delta K}{K}$$

$$\text{or} \quad (b) \quad \frac{\Delta N}{N} < \frac{\Delta K}{K}$$

In the first case, when $\frac{\Delta N}{N} > \frac{\Delta K}{K}$, the population will grow faster than the capital stock. This, therefore, signifies the situation of underemployment. With the prevalence of surplus labour, money wage rates get depressed. But if price level is to remain unchanged, the real wages will have to fall.

Now if real wages start falling, then as is clear from the basic equilibrium equation (*vii*), the rate of profit will rise gradually. As such, the rate of growth of capital accumulation will go on moving up till it catches up with the rate of growth of population. And the 'golden age' equilibrium would, thus, again be established. However, the equilibrium would fail to be restored if the money wages remain inflexible or if the price level falls in consonance with the fall in the money wages,

The second possibility for divergence from the '*golden age*' equilibrium occurs when $\frac{\Delta N}{N} < \frac{\Delta K}{K}$, *i.e*, the rate of population growth falls short of the growth rate of capital stock. Such a situation manifests a state of excess capital accumulation. It can be seen that under such circumstance, appropriate changes in the capital-labour ratio (v) or the labour productivity (b) can help to regain the '*golden age*' equilibrium. Another way is that the whole production function as such may be shifted up so that with the increase in capital accumulation, more and more labour gets absorbed in the production process. In any case, it is relatively easier to re-establish 'golden age' equilibrium when the divergence from that path stems from a slower growth of population than capital.

State of Economic Bliss. This is a special case of 'golden age' equilibrium. When the rate of accumulation is zero, profit rate is also zero and the entire output of the industry is drained out in the wage-stream, the consumption would be at its highest pedestal. It could be possible, says Mrs. Robinson, to maintain consumption at such a maximal level under the given technical conditions. This then is the 'state of economic bliss'.

Causes of Cyclical Fluctuations

So far we have discussed the stability conditions of the 'gold age' equilibrium. Let us now see as to how the emergence of cyclical fluctuations can be explained in Mrs. Robinson's 'golden age' equilibrium framework. Mrs. Robinson asserts that fluctuations would disturb the conditions of tranquil growth in the '*golden age*', if there occur certain random shocks or chance events, *viz*., the occurrence of a bout of exceptionally attractive innovations or a sudden burst of consumer expenditure and/or things like that. The manner in which the fluctuations get a pace and are maintained is explained below:

Any disturbance that pushes up the profit rate tends to raise the desired rate of accumulation. Consequent thereupon, the investment increases to prop up higher levels of accumulation New equipment gets installed. The result, therefore, is that the productive capacity of the economy moves ahead of the level of effective demand. This naturally leads to a decline in the profit expectations so that forces retarding fresh investments come into being. On the other hand, any chance disturbance that pushes down the profits tends to set in the downward movement.

Mrs. Robinson also mentions about a more radical type of cyclical instability that may sway the economy. When the expectations are influenced not only by the existing situation but also by the projection of the experiences of recent past, the system develops what is known as the '*inherent instability*'. The experience of a rise in profits in the immediate past would give rise to expectations of a further rise. Conversely, the recent past experience of a fall in the profits would bring expectations of a further fall.

Mrs. Robinson feels that under such exigencies, it would be difficult for the firms to settle down on any one perch of steady rate of accumulation. When, for instance, the profit rate is ascending, the firms are prone to pitch their desired rate of accumulation at a high level. However, the moment this desired rate of accumulable gets realised, the profits stop rising any further. As such the desired rate would no longer continue to be the desired one. A new rate of accumulation at a lower level would then be the one that is desired.

Such fluctuations are thus the outcome of the volatility of expectations. All this entails uncertainty which continually makes the firms to adopt self-contradictory policies. The net result is the emergence of an unsteady or disequilibrating rate of accumulation in relation to the desired rate. In consequence thereof, the path of growth also turns unstable. The point to be noted is that fluctuations of this type are endogenous to the system. They have not been generated by the entry of any random shock or chance event. What has happened in this case is that the system has become inherently unstable.

This part of Mrs. Robinson's exposition enables us to discover a common source of growth and fluctuations. *It is the fortuitous nature of expectations ·and enterprise in a system governed by profit that explains growth and fluctuations together*. This aspect of Mrs. Robinson's model is, therefore, particularly laudable in that it succeeds in coordinating the theories of cycles and growth.

Limping Golden Age

Under this limping golden age, steady rate of accumulation coexists with unemployment. It is just possible that sufficient capital stock with a composition quite appropriate to the desired rate of accumulation exists. But it may not be that enough in so far as the employment of the entire labour force is concerned. The steady rate of accumulation is taking place, but the conditions of full employment have not been achieved. Mrs. Robinson christens such a state of affairs as the '*limping golden age*'.

The intensity of the limp may be of different degrees depending on the rate of fall or rise in employability *vis-a-vis* the labour force. If the rise in the level of employment occurs at a rate smaller than that of labour force, unemployment would increase with time. The limp in this case is rather severe.

However, if the rise in the level of employment occurs at a rate greater than that of labour force, employment would increase more rapidly than the labour force. And, therefore, unemployment will shrink with time and the economy approaches full employment rather quickly. The limp here is thus mild and it tends to die away in the long run. As such, this age will only be a transient one.

Leaden Age

It, is in fact, a special case of a 'limping golden age' in which the degree of unemployment is increasing due to inadequate rate of accumulation. When there is a large proportion of unemployed workers in the economy, the level of living of all the workers will get reduced. Unless the real wages of the employed workers rise fast enough or else sufficient opportunities for self-employment arise, conditions of falling standards of living will continue. But it is quite unlikely that any of these possibilities would occur in practice. Real wages do not rise fast enough nor opportunities for self-employment crop up in large numbers.

The low rate of accumulation giving rise to the low standard of living may thus limit down the growth of numbers–a sort of Malthusian trap sets in. Assuming that there is no technical progress, a condition of 'golden age' may be forced upon the economy artificially. It is quite distinct from the true 'golden age' in that here a high ratio of non-employment keeps down the rate of growth of the labour force. If the standards of living had not fallen, growth of labour force would not have slided down so that the inadequate rate of accumulation would have expressed itself in increasing degrees of unemployment. Thus, under the leaden age, the rate of growth of labour force has been so leaden as to decline under the weight of increased misery stemming from an insufficient rate of accumulation.

Restrained Golden Age

This is an age of full employment but the '*desired rate*' of accumulation happens to exceed the '*possible rate*' determined by the rate of growth of labour force plus the rate of technological progress. The '*possible rate*' is kept down by factors such as financial stringency or monopsony in the labour market, so that the '*realised rate*' of growth is kept down to the level of the '*possible rate*'.

It may so happen that the stock of capital is appropriate to the desired rate of accumulation and the full employment has already been achieved. But it may fail to be realised on account of its being restrained by a stinted rate of growth of labour force and the rate of technical progress.

Bastard Golden Age

It denotes a situation where unemployment prevails but the real wages remain rigid downwards. As such, the rate of accumulation is prevented from increasing in the absence of technical progress. The ultimate cause of less than adequate growth of capital stock may lie in the existence of an '*inflation barrier*'.

For the rate of accumulation to be raised, it is necessary to lower down the real wages. But generally there is some level of minimum acceptable real wages so that when prices rise, some increase in money wages follows due to the attempts of the organised labour to resist the erosion of real wages through inflation below the minimum acceptable level. Thus, the realisation of the desired rate of accumulation would tend to be choked off. The attempts to raise the rate of accumulation would be arrested by the inflationary rise in money wages. This is the 'bastard golden age'.

Critical Appraisal of Robinson's Model

Mrs. Robinson's model represents a major step in enriching our understanding of the fundamental nature and process of capital accumulation in a capitalist economy. It also provides deep insight into the properties of equilibrium growth. It is worth mentioning that in Mrs. Robinson's model, all profits are saved and all wages are consumed. The Robinsonian model is essentially of the Harrod-Domar breed. This can be seen easily from the following relationships.

We have earlier shown that

$$\pi = \frac{Y - \frac{w}{p}N}{K}$$

Rearranging and dividing both sides of the equation by Y we have

or $$\frac{\pi K}{Y} = \frac{Y - \frac{w}{p}N}{Y}$$

or $$\frac{S}{Y} = \frac{Y - \frac{w}{p}N}{Y}, \quad [\because S = \pi K]$$

or $$\alpha = \frac{Y - \frac{w}{p}N}{Y}$$ [∵ in Domar's model, $\alpha = \frac{S}{Y}$ *i.e.*, ratio of saving to national income]

∴ $$\alpha\sigma = \left(\frac{Y}{K}\right)\left(\frac{Y - \frac{w}{p}N}{Y}\right)$$ [∵ σ in Domar's model represents capital productivity, *i.e.*, $\sigma = Y/K$]

or $$\alpha\sigma = \frac{\left(Y - \frac{w}{p}N\right)}{K}$$

As $\frac{Y - \frac{w}{p}N}{K}$ is the rate of profit on capital we have

$$\alpha\sigma = \pi$$

Again, in Harrod's model, capital-labour ratio, $C_r = 1/\sigma$ and $\alpha = s$

$$\therefore \quad \pi = \alpha\,\sigma = s.\frac{1}{C_r} = \frac{s}{C_r} = G_w$$

Thus $$\Delta K/K = \pi = \alpha\,\sigma = G_w$$

This shows that Mrs. Robinson's equilibrium condition is the same as that of Domar's stable rate of growth ($\alpha\,\sigma$) or Harrod's '*warranted rate*' of growth (G_w). However, Mrs. Robinson's model has an edge over the Harrod-Domar models in two respects. First, in the Harrod-Domar models, *capital accumulation is determined by the saving-income ratio and the capital productivity. But, Mrs. Robinson distinctly links capital accumulation with the profit-wage relation and the labour productivity*. This marks a big step forward in that she has brought growth theory closer to a market economy. Secondly, while in the Harrod-Domar models, the *prime-mobile of capital accumulation is capital itself*, in Mrs. Robinson's case, it is the labour. The latter is more realistic for labour is the ultimate source of all capital.

Synthesis between Value Theory and Distribution Theory. The chief merit of Mrs. Robinson's model lies in its successful synthesis of the classical value and distribution theory with the Keynesian saving-investment analysis into a single coherent stream of thought. The close connection between distribution and growth has been brought out exquisitely through the demonstration of mutual interdependence between *the effect of income distribution and the proportion of income saved on the one hand, and between the rate of profit and capital accumulation on the other*.

Problem of Measurement of Capital. Further, great credit goes to Mrs. Robinson for bringing to the fore the much neglected *problem of measurement and composition of capital*. She outrightly discards the dictum of homogeneity and malleability of capital stock. Her model demonstrates that a given set of machinery cannot by itself get adapted to more or less labour-intensive forms of production. In other words, *ex-post substitution is not possible. However, substitution is possible in the ex-ante sense, i.e.*, at the time when the choice of techniques is being made. Once the techniques are chosen and machines built, a particular technique gets permanently associated with them. The chosen technique is embodied in the machines and it will remain embodied throughout their lifetime. It is only in the long run when the existing machines get completely depreciated that they can be replaced by plants that embody a different technique.

Furthermore, the Robinsonian model provides a realistic meaning and significance of the '*steady-state growth' so as to analyse the various ingredients, properties and types of equilibrium growth process*. The idea of steady growth had been haunting economists since long. Cassel was the first to visualise it as a generalisation of stationary state, *i.e.*, a 'regularly progressing state' of the economy. Harrod introduced this concept in his comparative dynamic framework with a view to analyse the short-run instability implications arising from the divergence between the warranted and natural rates of growth. But it is not possible to employ the Harrodian concept of knife-edge equilibrium as a datum to compare different types of equilibrium growths. Besides, Harrod's steady growth does not take cognizance of the composition of the capital stock. As opposed to this, Mrs. Robinson's 'golden age' idea embodies the compositional aspects of capital stock. Also, it provides us with a device for comparing different types of equilibrium-growth paths. It plays the same role in comparative dynamic analysis as does the concept of stationary state in a comparative static setting. As such, Mrs. Robinson has perfected the analysis of comparative dynamics.

Above all, Mrs. Robinson's model has the merit of coordinating the theories of cycle and growth. While elucidating the idea of 'inherent instability' in the system, she successfully forges and organic link between fluctuations and growth. From her model one could say that the inherent tendency to oscillate is the cause and unsteady growth is the outcome.

Shortcomings of Robinson's Growth Model

However, Mrs. Robinson's model is not free from flaws. Some of the main drawbacks are as follows : First, Mrs. Robinson's model at best provides only a framework for studying the various forms of growth process. It cannot be used as a predictive model. If the economy is passing through a particular type of Robinsonian growth, we cannot predict on the basis of the model as to what possibly shall be the succeeding phase or type of growth. The different types of growth that have been analysed are left as '*isolated islands*' in her model. The inter-connecting straits have not been explored. Her each type of growth remains engulfed in a cassandra of darkness and no rays of light show the path leading to others.

Secondly, Mrs. Robinson contemplates that the prime variable of her model, *viz*., the rate of capital accumulation gets adjusted to the population growth via adjustments in wage rate, profit rate and labour productivity. This tantamounts to suggest redistribution of incomes through the media of relative factor prices. In our view it would be more practical and realistic to deploy fiscal and monetary measures for making adjustments in capital growth *vis-a-vis* population growth. Thus, Prof. K. Kurihara writes that "J. Robinson's chief contribution to Post-Keynesian growth economics seems to be that she has integrated classical value and distribution theory and modern Keynesian saving-investment theory into one coherent system. However, it is not capable of being modified so as to introduce fiscal and monetary policy parameters–unless labour productivity, the wage rate, the profit rate and the capital-labour ratio could be regarded as objects of practical policy–as they might be so regarded in a completely planned economy."[5]

Thirdly, in the Robinsonian model, State has been completely left out of the picture. It is, indeed, unrealistic and precarious to rely solely on the private entrepreneurs for the achievement of a stable growth of the economy in tune with the requirements of a growing population and rapidly changing technology.

Lastly, Mrs. Robinson's analysis of steady growth is carried out under the assumption of a given and constant technological horizon. Not only that it is a restrictive and unrealistic assumption, it also rattles the basic logicality of her analysis. For instance, under the given technical conditions when the rate of accumulation happens to be higher than what is required for achieving the '*golden age*' equilibrium, it will *ipso facto* alter the pace of technological progress. What is likely to happen in this case is that due to the pressure on the labour-supply, labour-saving innovations and inventions would be stimulated. Besides, there will be inducement for quick diffusion and introduction of labour-displacing technical improvements which had so far been held back due to an abundant and cheaper supply of labour. Capital accumulation, being the vehicle of technical progress, would, therefore, jeopardise the logical consistency of Robinson's model which assumes consistency of technical conditions.

Finally, an extension of the above-mentioned line of argument sledge-hammers another heroic assumption of Mrs. Robinson. Her model assumes that labour and capital are tethered together in a fixed proportion to produce a given level of output. Absence of substitutability of factors of production would make sense only under fixed and static technical conditions. But in a dynamic

5 K. Kurihara, *The Keynesian Theory of Economic Development*, p. 80.

setting where technical progress is inherent in the system, technical coefficients of production can no longer remain fixed.

Applicability of Robinson's Model of Growth to Developing Countries

We have explained above Joan Robinson's simple model of capital accumulation which she developed for capitalist economies dominated by free private enterprise. Joan Robinson has distinguished between *desired* and *possible* rate of capital accumulation and also presented the concepts of golden ages. Though Joan Robinson's model of capital accumulation is relevant for a free enterprise economy in which Government and planning have little role to play, it, however, has some significance for developing countries which have adopted the path of planned development of their economies in which both the private and public sectors coexist and undertake investment activities.

A significant factor which follows from Robinson's model and which is relevant for developing countries is that investment by private entrepreneurs depends upon the expected rate of profit; the greater the expected rate of profit, the greater the magnitude of investment that they will be induced to undertake. Therefore, whatever reduces the rate of profits, be it imposition of taxes by the Government, increase in the wages by trade unions, fall in the prices of the products will adversely affect investment and therefore rate of capital accumulation and growth. This explains demand side of capital accumulation.

Now take the supply-side of capital accumulation. The volume of investment that will be undertaken and therefore the rate of capital accumulation that will be achieved depends upon the available savings or surplus that will be made from the national income produced over and above the basic or productive consumption, that is:

$$I = f(S)$$

where I stands for investment and S for saving or surplus. This means that investment is a function of available actual surplus. Now if a part of this basic saving or economic surplus is used for either unproductive consumption by workers or by the capitalist class, rate of surplus actually used for investment will be lower and therefore the rate of capital accumulation will be lower to that extent. In terms of Joan Robinson's model where rate of profit has been identified with the rate of surplus by assuming that all profits are saved and all wages consumed, rate of profit (π) is given by the following equation:

$$\pi = \frac{b - \frac{w}{p}}{v}$$

where b is productivity of labour, $\frac{w}{p}$ is the real wage rate v is the capital-labour ratio.

It is evident from this growth equation that if wages (w) of labourers rise above the level of what is considered as productive consumption, the rate of profit or surplus (π) will be lower which will adversely affect the rate of capital accumulation and growth, productivity of labour (b) and capital-labour ratio (v) remaining the same.

Now, if the wages remain at the level of productive consumption but a part of surplus created by a worker which is equal to $b - \frac{w}{p}$ is appropriated by capitalist class as profits but spent on unproductive or luxury consumption, it will reduce the actual surplus or saving to be used for capital accumulation. Hence we conclude that *the lower the propensity of unproductive consumption both by the workers and capitalist class, the higher will be the rate of surplus (or profits) and higher the rate of accumulation.*

Another important conclusion for Robinson's model which is significant for the growth problem of developing countries is that *there exists an inverse relation between share of wages and the rate of profit*. This also follows from the growth equation of Joan Robinson and can be proved as under:

Multiplying the numerator and denominator by the number of workers (N), we get:

$$\pi = \frac{\left(b - \frac{w}{p}\right)}{\frac{K}{N}} = \frac{b\,N - \frac{w}{p}N}{K}$$

Number of workers multiplied by their productivity ($b.N$) will be equal to the real national income which can be written as Y. Further, number of workers multiplied by the real wage rate w/p will give us the total wages which can be written as W. Writing Y for $b.N$ and W for $\frac{w}{p}.N$ in the above equation, we get:

$$\pi = \frac{Y - W}{K}$$

Dividing the numerator and denominator of the right hand expression by Y we obtain

$$\pi = \frac{\frac{Y-W}{Y}}{\frac{K}{Y}} = \frac{Y-W}{Y}\cdot\frac{Y}{K}$$

$$\pi = \left(1 - \frac{W}{Y}\right)\cdot\frac{Y}{K}$$

It follows from above that given the income to capital ratio $\frac{Y}{K}$ (*i.e.* output-capital ratio), the rate of profit (π) depends upon the share of wages to national income $\frac{W}{Y}$. Thus, given the output-capital ratio, the greater the share of wages to national income (W/Y), the lower will be the rate of profit (π) which will adversely affect the inducement to invest and tend to lower the rate of capital accumulation.

But it should not be concluded from above that the rise in wages is not justified from the viewpoint of economic growth under any circumstances. If wages are below what might be regarded as basic or productive consumption which are essential for health and productivity, the rise in wages is likely to raise productivity and efficiency of labour which will cause real national income to rise. With this increase in national income through the rise in productivity of labour, rate of profit or surplus may not fall. Thus, when wages are below the level of productive consumption, as they are in developing countries, the increase in wages will not adversely affect the rate of profit and growth of the economy.

It is important to note that Joan Robinson's growth model assumes that all profits are saved and also productively invested. As has been mentioned above, all profits may not be saved and a good deal of them may be used for luxury consumption. Even if all profits are saved, they may not be productively invested. A good amount of profits may be dissipated on unproductive type of investment such as for buying gold, jewellery and real estate, building luxury houses, indulging in speculative activities, building inventories of goods, or *even building the productive capacity (i.e., capital stock) for the production of luxury consumption goods*. These unproductive forms of investment may generate some income and employment in developing countries. But, such unproductive investment will generate more inequalities of income and wealth which will militate against social justice.

In poor developing countries like India, investment can be regarded as productive if it is in the form of either addition to the capacity to produce basic consumption goods or what are now popularly called wage goods or if it is in the form of building capacity to produce those inputs, materials, instruments, machines which are used for producing basic consumption or wage goods such as foodgrains, sugar, edible oil, cloth, kerosene oil. The supply of wage goods is essential for the creation of employment opportunities in developing countries. Thus, it is the rise in productive investment which will expand the output of basic consumption goods and therefore employment and national income. Therefore, the growth of output of basic consumption goods depends upon the share of productive investment to total investment. We, therefore, conclude that *the higher the share of productive investment to the total investment, the greater the growth rate of basic consumption goods and of employment.*

It may be noted that Mrs. Robinson's model assumes away foreign trade. Autarky or absence of foreign trade in a world of reality is a completely non-existent phenomenon today. The foreign trade, indeed, plays a vital and propulsive role in the developing economies to bring about rapid economic development.

Above all, the main bastion of the Robinson's model, *viz.*, '*capitalist rules of the game*' will not ensure steady and rapid economic growth. In the developing countries there is undeniable an onus upon the State to help accelerate the process of development. The economic responsibility of government in these countries has been established. The fate of these countries cannot be left entirely to the whims and wishes of private entrepreneurs. It would be well-nigh difficult for these countries to match the rate of growth of population with that of capital accumulation under the banner of 'capitalist rules of the game'. The debated question today no longer concerns government intervention or not, but how much and how fast.

In fact, Mr. Robinson's model is itself a dictum against the 'capitalist rules of the game'. As Prof. Kurihara eloquently remarks,"*Joan Robinson's discussion of capital growth has the subtle effect of discrediting the whole idea of leaving so important a problem as economic growth to the capitalist rules of the game; for her model of laissez-faire growth demonstrates how precarious and insecure it is to entrust to private profit-makers the paramount task of achieving the stable growth of an economy consistent with the needs of a growing population and the possibility of advancing technology.*"[6]

Thus Mrs. Robinson's contribution to the theory of growth brings out clearly that the policy of *laissez faire* and completely free market will not ensure steady or sustained economic growth. Her model contains various elements which could be very helpful in showing these countries the path to steady growth. For instance, her model brings out cogently that the crux of the problem to achieve steady growth resides in population growth *vis-a-vis* capital accumulation.

Perhaps the only thing undisputed about the developing countries is the galloping growth of population as the chief hurdle in capital accumulation. With population growth rate being much above the rate of capital formation, these economies exhibit tendencies for increasing unemployment. This situation conforms to the Robinsonian case where $\frac{\Delta N}{N} > \frac{\Delta K}{K}$. As such the journey towards steady growth can be facilitated if the '*potential growth ratio*' as envisaged by Mrs. Robinson is determined on the basis of growth rate of labour force and of per capita output. The plans can thus be made more realistic and executed more efficiently to achieve the desired goals.

6 K.K. Kurihara, *op. cit.*, pp. 187-88.

CHAPTER 17

NEW THEORY OF ECONOMIC GROWTH (ENDOGENOUS GROWTH MODELS)

Neoclassical growth theory dominated the economic thinking for three decades (1955–1985), though it could not explain important facts about economic growth in various countries. By the late 1980s, the dissatisfaction with neoclassical growth theory to explain the real growth phenomenon increased so much that a need was greatly felt to propound a new theory of growth. *There are three basic difficulties with the neoclassical growth model*. First, neoclassical growth theory implies that increase in saving rate has only a temporary or short-run effect on rate of growth and it *does not affect the long-run rate of economic growth.* Secondly, neoclassical growth theory implies **convergence of growth rates.** That is, growth rates of countries whether having high or low saving rates will converge over time, though this convergence may be slow. This convergence implies that different countries with high and low saving rates but having same rate of population growth rate would over time achieve the same rate of growth in their national income in the long run $\left(i.e., \frac{\Delta Y}{Y} = \frac{\Delta N}{N}\right)$ while *growth rates in per capita income* $\left(\frac{\Delta y}{y}\right)$ *of these countries will tend to be equal to zero in long-run steady-state equilibrium.*

More importantly, neoclassical growth theory explained that long-run rate of economic growth depended on ***technological change which was considered as exogenous.*** By treating technological change as exogenous, neoclassical growth theory could not focus on the fundamental forces which determine long-run growth of nations. Furthermore, if there is free flow of technological knowledge between nations we should expect the rate of technological progress to converge and therefore cause long-run growth rates of different countries to converge. However, it was found in the real world that such convergence of long-run growth rates was not taking place or was occurring in case of only limited number of countries. Thus, ***neoclassical theory could not explain differences in growth rates of different countries nor it could explain greater proportion of economic growth observed in different countries.***

A basic concern of development economics is to explain why per capita incomes and growth rates differ among countries. Thus, the main motive of new growth theory is to explain differences in growth rates among countries and what are contributions of different factors to rates of growth observed in them.

ENDOGENOUS GROWTH MODELS

The new growth theory extends the neoclassical theory by making the *rate of technological progress as endogenous factor*. Therefore, new growth theory is also called *Endogenous Growth Theory* or *Endogenous Growth Model*. The new growth theory goes more deeply into ultimate sources of growth. Three different approaches have been adopted to make technological change as endogenous factor in determining economic growth.

Therefore, main feature of endogenous growth theory is to explain the growth of productivity and thereby the growth rate of output *endogenously*, that is, within the model itself and does not depend on *exogenous technological change* as is done by neoclassical Solow model. As we will see that the *important implication of endogenous growth theory is that, contrary to Solow's neoclassical theory, the long-run rate of economic growth depends on the rate of saving and investment* (It may be recalled that in Solow's neoclassical theory the long-run economic growth is determined by *exogenous* technological change which causes increase in productivity by shifting upward the production function). There are a number of endogenous growth models. We start explaining the simplest, endogenous growth model generally called AK Model.

AK Model

In AK Model it is assumed that the population or number of workers remains the same which implies that the growth rate of output per worker will be the growth rate of output of the economy AK Model is based on the following aggregate production function :

$$Y = AK \qquad \ldots (1)$$

where Y is aggregate output, K is total capital stock and A is a positive constant. It is noteworthy that in the capital stock K, both physical and human capital are included.

The above AK production function shows that an additional unit increase in capital K causes increase in output by A units irrespective of how much capital is used in production. Thus A measures marginal product of capital that does not depend on the rise of capital stock in the production function. Therefore, in the production function $y = AK$, implies that *marginal product of capital does not diminish* as more units of capital are added to increase production and instead remains constant. This is contrary to neoclassical growth theory of Solow in which marginal productivity of capital diminishes.

Now, an important question arises: What accounts for constant marginal productivity of capital for the economy as a whole when there is increase in capital stock ? A number of explanations have been given for this. The important explanation lays stress on the role of *human capital* which is included in the K term of above aggregate production function. By human capital economists mean the knowledge, skills and training of the people, especially the workers who are engaged in the production process of goods. Imparting knowledge, skills to the people is described as *investment in people* as it raises their productivity. Increases in physical capital alone, keeping human capital constant, will cause diminishing marginal productivity of capital. According to endogenous growth theory, as accumulation of physical capital takes place in the economy, its human capital also increases in the same proportion through the process what is called *learning by investment* so that each additional unit of physical capital works with the same quantity of human capital which ensures that marginal productivity of capital does not diminish. Thus, accumulation of capital brings about continuous growth of output.

In this AK model of endogenous growth theory, a second explanation of marginal productivity of capital remaining the same as capital accumulation takes place in the economy is based on the fact that in a *growing economy the firms have incentives to undertake investment in research and development (R&D) activities*. These R&D activities lead to the discovery of new production techniques and new products. With the use of new production techniques and increase in technical know-how as capital accumulation takes place in the economy marginal productivity of capital does not diminish that makes continuous economic growth possible. Having explained how production function, $Y = AK$ ensures constant marginal product of capital when we incorporate into the analysis the role of human capital and research and development activities, we are in a position to bring out the implications of AK model of endogenous growth theory. Let us assume that saving, S is a constant proportion, s of aggregate output Y which is equal to AK in the model. Thus $S = sY = sAK$. Since a closed economy investment must equal saving, we have

$$I = sAK \qquad \ldots (2)$$

Now, investment is *net addition to the stock of capital* (ΔK) *plus depreciation* (dK), *that is* $I = \Delta K + dK$ (Note that K is the stock of capital and d is the rate of depreciation). Substituting $I = \Delta K + dK$ in equation (2) above, we have

$$\Delta K + dK = sAK \qquad \ldots (3)$$

Dividing both sides of equation (3) by K, we have

$$\frac{\Delta K}{K} + d = sA$$

Now, taking d on the right side of the above we have

$$\frac{\Delta K}{K} = sA - d \qquad \ldots (4)$$

$\frac{\Delta K}{K}$ is the rate of growth of capital stock. Since output is assumed to be proportional to the capital stock, rate of growth of output $\left(\frac{\Delta Y}{Y}\right)$ will equal the rate of growth of capital stock $\left(\frac{\Delta K}{K}\right)$. Thus, the above equation (4) can be rewritten as

$$\frac{\Delta Y}{Y} = sA - d \qquad \ldots (5)$$

The above equation (5) of the *AK* model of endogenous growth theory shows that growth of output $\left(\frac{\Delta Y}{Y}\right)$ depends on the saving rate (s). The higher the saving rate, the higher the rate of long-run rate of growth of output. As it has been assumed that the number of workers remains the same over time, the rate of growth of output per worker will be equal to the rate of growth of output as given by the equation (5) above, that is, equal to $sA–d$. The rate of growth of output per worker also depends on the saving rate. The finding that long-run rate of growth of output depends on the saving rate is in a sharp contrast to Solow's neoclassical growth model in which rate of saving affects only the short-run growth rate and does not determine the long-run rate of growth of output. Commenting on the conclusion of endogenous growth model, A.B. Abel, B.S. Bernanke and D. Croushore write, "*Saving affects long-run growth in the endogenous growth framework because, in that framework, higher rates of saving and capital formation stimulates greater investment in human capital and R&D. The resulting increases in productivity help to spur long-run growth. In summary, in comparison to the Solow model, the endogenous growth model places greater emphasis on saving, human capital formation and R&D as sources of long-run growth.*"[1]

An important implication of endogenous growth model is that the Government can influence the long-run growth rate by taking suitable policies to raise saving rate of the economy.

Romer's Model of Endogenous Growth

In Romer's model, to incorporate endogenous technological change, the production function is modified as under:

$$Y_t = F(K_t, N_t, A_t) \qquad \ldots (1)$$

It will be seen from the equation (1) that the level of aggregate output depends on the quantities of capital (K_t), and labour (N_t) used in the production as well as on technology (A_t) *which is treated*

1 Andrew B. Abel, Ben S. Bernanke, and Dean Croushore, *Macroeconomics*, Pearson Education, 2011, p. 229.

as endogenous factor and therefore appears inside the production function as an endogenous input. However, the relationship between output and technology is not the same as between output and other inputs, capital and labour. This is because in Romer's model, the output of an individual firm not only depends on its *own* level of capital and labour but also on the *technology used by other firms whose benefits also accrue* to it. Looking at the relationship between output and technology in this way we can write production function of an individual firm denoted by the subscript *i* as under :

$$Y_{it} = F(K_{it}, N_{it}, A_t) \quad \ldots (2)$$

Note that in the production function in (2) above, the technology input subscript *t* appear along with subscript *i* because this technology may not be exclusive input of a firm, but may be copied or imitated from others. The technology is not assumed to progress exogenously *but to grow endogenously when more investment by firms takes place or may be the result of the efforts of labour*. In some models of endogenous technological change, more capital accumulation or investment by a firm promotes new inventions and improvements in machines (*i.e.*, capital goods) constituting the stock of capital through a process called *learning by doing*. In some other models of endogenous technological change, increase in labour inputs by firms also leads to the stock of technological knowledge as it is pointed out that increase in the use of labour input leads to the scope of learning and acquisition of new skills and discovering new better ways of doing things.

The *contribution of Paul Romer lies in explaining that the benefits of the new technology discovered and used by a firm will spill over to other firms in the economy.* Paul Romer,[2] one of the pioneers of endogenous growth theory has put forward the view that *investment is a source of technological progress*. He distinguishes between *private returns* to capital and *social returns* to capital. According to Romer, an individual firm does not capture all the benefits of increase in its stock of capital, as it also creates benefits which are *external to the firm*. Capital accumulation by a firm, that is, investment by a firm causes not only increase in new *machines* but also *new ways of doing things*.[3] These new better methods of doing things result either from deliberate investment in research and development and sometimes as accidental by-products of investment activity by a firm. These new methods and ideas of doing things can be easily copied by others who also get benefits from these new methods.

We can consider investment as a source of technical progress for various reasons. If investment simply consists of duplication of existing capital, then that investment does not lead to innovation or technological change. However, investment may lead to innovation as firms attempt to solve their problem, especially to raise their productivity. They will try to discover new methods or designs of machines which can raise productivity and for this purpose they will make investment. Such investment will lead to innovation or technical progress. For example, investment by car manufacturers in India has led to new designs and models of cars which are fuel-efficient and pollution-free. Thus their investment in research and development has led to new innovations or technical progress.

Furthermore, if investment by a firm is successful, the other firms will also try to adopt them with some modifications which suit their needs. Thus expansion in investment may represent a sequence of innovations with each innovation improving upon the previous innovation. Such a type of technological progress has been called **learning by watching**. Beneficial external effects resulting from learning by watching are key determinants of economic growth. Therefore, policies to increase investment should be adopted. It is due to the externalities that *social returns* to investment exceed private returns. The rapid and quicker increase in overall growth can be achieved through Government adopting proper policies to promote investment in research and development.

---

2 Paul Romer, *Increasing Returns and Long-Run Growth.*

3 For investment as a source of technical progress See M. Scott, "A New Theory of Endogenous Economic Growth", *Oxford Review of Economic Policy,* Winter 1992 and M. King and M Robson, Investment and Technical Progress, *Oxford Review of Economic Policy*, 1992.

This endogenous growth theory considers that whereas production function of a firm exhibits constant returns to scale *(i.e.,* constant returns to all factors) but there occur *external increasing returns to scale.* These external increasing returns are due to the endogenous technological improvements which result from (1) rate of investment, (2) size of the capital stock, and (3) *the stock of human capital.*

In the neoclassical model the increase in capital and labour will bring about increase in output proportionately, that is, constant return to labour and capital will occur. However, *in new endogenous growth theory increase in capital and labour will foster economy-wide technological progress,* that is, term A_t in the production function rises. This technological progress brings about extra expansion in output. Thus, *in the new growth theory, increase in capital and labour with endogenous technological advancement brings about increasing returns to scale.* "With increasing returns the changes in saving rate and therefore in the rate of capital formation can permanently affect the long-run equilibrium growth rate. This result contrasts the neoclassical growth theory in which the effect of changes in saving rate on the growth rate is temporary".[4]

Policy Implications. Endogenous growth model has important policy implications for the role of Government for accelerating economic growth. As just pointed out above, with endogenous technological change and therefore increasing returns to scale, the government policies that raise the saving rate and thereby the rate of capital formation can raise the long-run equilibrium growth rate of the economy. This shows Government can play an important role in accelerating economic growth.

Investment in Human Capital and Learning by Doing

In the above approach to endogenous technology the progress in technology is assumed to depend on growth of capital, that is, investment. New investment fosters innovations and improvements in machines and tools that also create external benefits and lead to increasing returns for the economy as a whole. In another important model of endogenous growth theory, *investment in human capital,* (that is, labour input) is also assumed to be the source of technological progress. Arrow introduced the concept of *learning by doing.* According to this, the greater the level of labour input, the greater is the scope for learning and acquiring of new skills. An endogenous growth model which lays stress on the accumulation of human capital has been developed by Lucas.[5] According to Lucas' model, labour can be devoted either to production goods or to the accumulation of human capital, that is, acquiring of new skills and knowledge. Acquiring of new skills and knowledge will not only make a worker more productive but also increase the productivity of capital and other workers in the economy. Each new knowledge or skill makes the next idea possible and so the knowledge can grow indefinitely. Let e be the proportion of labour input directly devoted to production and H be the human capital, then the Cobb-Douglas type production function can be stated as under:

$$Y = AK^{a}(H.eL)^{1-a}$$

where the technology coefficient $A = H^{b}$ represents the external effect of human capital (H) on productivity of capital (K) and labour (eL). Since human capital (H) is a function of labour input, output per worker can be obtained as a function of capital and labour according to this approach, as with the earlier one of investment in physical capital. Though each firm faces constant returns to scale, there are increasing returns to the economy as a whole.

Policy Implications of New Growth Theory

New growth theory with its emphasis on endogenous technological change has important policy implications which in some important respects differ from the neoclassical growth theory. First. whereas neoclassical theory predicts that growth rates of different countries with same rates of saving and population growth and with access to the same technology will converge, *in the endogenous growth theory there is no force leading to the convergence of growth rates of different countries with*

4 Richard T. Froyan, *Macroeconomics, Theory and Policy*, Pearson Education, 8th edition, 2005, p. 108.

5 R. Lucas. "On the Mechanics of Economic Development", *Journal of Monetary Economics*, 22 (1988). pp. 3–42.

closed economies.[6] This is because of *the possibility of sustained long-term growth resulting from increasing returns to scale* which was not accounted for in the neoclassical theory. Growth rates of different countries in new endogenous growth theory will remain constant or differ depending on their saving rates and technological levels. This is because of large differences in investment in human capital, research and development and increasing returns or external benefits accruing from them.

Furthermore, new growth theory emphasises that higher saving rate will ensure a higher long-run economic growth but there is no any mechanism working which ensures that per capita income in poor countries will catch up with those of the rich countries with similar saving rates.[7] The external increasing returns to the accumulation of capital, both physical and human, implies that rate of return on capital in capital-abundant rich countries will not fall in the developed rich countries relative to the poor less-developed countries. As a matter of fact, it is possible that due to endogenous technological improvement, rate of return to capital in capital– abundant rich countries exceeds that of capital-scarce countries and as a result capital may not flow from rich to poor countries. It is noteworthy that "potentially high rates of return on investment offered by developing countries with low capital ratios are greatly eroded by lower levels of complementary investments in human capital (education), infrastructure or research and development (R & D).[8]

Endogenous Growth Theory and Developing Countries

In sharp contrast to the policy implications derived by some from neoclassical theory, important implication of endogenous growth theory is that because individual firms do not capture full benefits from the positive externalities created by their own investments, the free market will lead to the accumulation of less than optimal level of complementary capital[9]. This will cause lower rate of economic growth in them. Lastly, because of the externalities created by investment, the new endogenous theory of growth envisages greater role of Government in improving the efficiency of resource allocation and promoting investment to raise rate of economic growth in the developing countries. The Government can directly adopt policies to raise the rate of saving and also make more investment in human capital (*i.e.*, education and healthcare) which promote private investment and generate increasing returns to scale. Though in many respects endogenous growth theory is a mere extension of neoclassical theory of growth, it however, makes a departure from the neoclassical policy of free market and passive role of Government, To quote Todaro, "*In contrast to neoclassical counter revolution theories, models of endogenous growth suggest an active role for public policy in promoting economic development through direct and indirect investment in human capital formation and the encouragement of foreign private investment in knowledge-intensive industries such as computer software and telecommunications.*"[10]

Lastly, it may be noted that endogenous growth theory, like the neoclassical theory, focuses on supply-side factors determining economic growth and *totally neglects role of adequate growth in effective demand* for sustained long-run growth of the economy. As has been recently seen that in both the developed and the developing countries lack of effective demand due to sluggish investment, decline in exports and, in countries like India, due to monsoon–dependent decline in agricultural growth rate may come about. As a result of lack of effective demand recession occurs in the economy which slows down the short-run economic growth which may ultimately affect long-term growth rate. For instance, for the first time after the Second World War, the Japanese economy which achieved very high growth rates in the past has experienced recessionary conditions and a very slow growth rate

6 An important empirical study by Robert Barrow "*Determinants of Economic Growth : A Cross-Country Empirical Study*", finds no evidence of convergence of growth rates.

7 Michael Todaro, *Economic Development,* Addison-Wesley, 6th' edition, 1997, *pp* 92–93.

8 *Ibid*, p. 93.

9 Todaro, *op. cit.* p. 93.

10 Todaro, *Economic Development*, Pearson Education (Singapore), 8th edition, p. 148.

for more than a decade now. This growth experience of the Japanese economy cannot be explained by new endogenous growth theory.

Further, it has been pointed out that endogenous growth theory assumes that there is either a single sector of production or that all sectors are symmetrical. This ignores the importance of growth-generating reallocation of labour and capital among the sectors for bringing about structural change in developing countries.[11] Besides, economic growth in developing countries often faces obstructions arising from lack of adequate infrastructure, poor institutional framework, imperfect financial and money markets. To remove these obstructions is important for accelerating economic growth but are overlooked by the new endogenous growth theory and therefore it has limited applications for the developing countries.

Furthermore, there may be *lack of incentives* due to uncertainly of profit prospects to make investment which may be responsible for slowdown in economic growth in developing countries. This important factor has not been taken into account by the new endogenous growth theory. For example, India is presently facing slowdown in economic growth because of lack of incentives on the part of private sector to make more investment as they find bleak profit outlook.

11 See Syed Nawab Haider Naqvi, "The Significance of Development Economics, *World Development*, 24 (1996). p. 977

PART IV

Theories of Economic Development: Classical, Marx, Schumpeter

- Classical Theories of Economic Development: Adam Smith and Ricardo
- Malthus's Theory of Economic Development
- Marx's Theory of Capitalist Development
- Schumpeter's Theory of Development

CHAPTER

18

CLASSICAL THEORIES OF ECONOMIC DEVELOPMENT: ADAM SMITH AND RICARDO

The theory of economic development started with classical economists of the eighteenth and nineteenth centuries. Adam Smith, David Ricardo, Malthus, James Mill, Karl Marx, and Joseph Schumpeter were all interested in issues of economic development and explained what determines economic growth. All of them also explain how capitalist or free market economies reach the *stationary state* when further economic growth ceases to occur. The classical economists lived at a time when Europe was going through a process of rapid industrialisation. Therefore, their views regarding development are of great interest for developing economies which want to get rid of poverty and raise the standards of living of their people. In the present chapter we will explain theories of economic development of Adam Smith and David Ricardo. In the next three chapters we will explain and evaluate the theories of development of Malthus, Karl Marx and Joseph Schumpeter.

ADAM SMITH'S THEORY OF ECONOMIC DEVELOPMENT

Adam Smith is known as father of economics. We get his ideas about economic development from his well-known book, **"An Enquiry into the Nature and Causes of Wealth of Nations"** (1976) which has tremendously influenced the thinking about economic growth and development. We briefly explain below his ideas about economic development. We will study below that he advocated the policy of **laissez faire,** that is, non-intervention of Government in economic activities of the individuals. He laid stress on individual freedom in conducting their economic affairs without any obstructions and restrictions by the Government. He advocated free trade among nations of the world and urged that all restrictions on foreign trade should be removed to promote international specialisation so as to increase the incomes of the nations. **The crucial aspects of development theory as propounded by Adam Smith are (1) division of labour and (2) capital accumulation.** Productivity of labour increases through division of labour. The two factors that facilitate the use of more division of labour are capital accumulation and size of market. We explain below these factors in detail.

Division of Labour. A very important contribution made by Adam Smith to the analysis of the factors that bring about expansion of output is the division of labour. His treatment of this aspect of production is classic. He pointed out that there was a natural tendency among human beings "to truck, barter, and exchange one thing for another."[1] Among the benefits of division of labour he refers to increase in *dexterity, saving in time, and invention of better machines and appliances*. But Adam Smith points out that the degree of division of labour is limited by the extent of the market. Division

1 Adam Smith, *An Inquiry into the Nature and Causes of the Wealth of Nations,* ed. Edwin Cannan, 1937, p. 13.

of labour is profitable only if there is adequate market for the goods produced. He, thus, emphasised the expansion of international trade, which widens market for goods.

One of the most significant contributions to economics by Adam Smith was to introduce the idea of ***increasing returns*** caused by division of labour. He thought the gain from by division of labour or specialisation was a basic feature of social economy otherwise everyone, like Robinson Crusoe, will produce everything they want for themselves. Thus Thirwall writes, "*It is the notion of increasing returns, based on division of labour that lay at the heart of Adam Smith's optimistic vision of economic progress as a self-generating process, in contrast to later classical economists who believed that economies would end up in a stationary state owing to diminishing returns in agriculture.*"[2]

Given the crucial significance of increasing returns based on division of labour, productivity of labour rises with the increase in the size of market. Along with division of labour it is acceleration of investment or capital accumulation that leads to the increase in growth of output and living standards of people. It is worth noting that Adam Smith expressed the view that industry generally permitted greater scope for division of labour or specialisation than agriculture and, therefore, in rich developed countries industrialisation had taken place to a greater extent.

Another importants related notion put forward by Adam Smith was that '*division of labour is limited by the size of market*'. If the extent of market is small, it will not be profitable to produce on a large scale which requires to introduce a higher degree of division of labour or specialisation. This is because if size of market for a good (*i.e.,* the magnitude of demand for it) is quite small, it will not be profitable to introduce a higher degree of division of labour along with the use of large capital stock. In the absence of adequate demand, only a little degree of division of labour or specialisation can be used and a good deal of capital stock is likely to remain underutilised. It is in this context that he advocated for *free international trade* which leads to the increase in the extent of market for goods and makes their production on a large scale profitable and induces the capitalist class to accumulate more capital.

Accumulation of Capital. As a means of economic development, Adam Smith gave an important place to saving and accumulation of capital. To quote his words, "*Capitalists are increased by parsimony and diminished by prodigality and misconduct...parsimony and not industry is the immediate cause of the increase of capital. Industry indeed provides the subject which parsimony accumulates.* But whatever industry might acquire, if parsimony did not save and store up, the capital would never be greater."[3] Here is a clear guideline and suggestion to the developing countries. Their greatest obstacle to economic development is the deficiency of capital. In this respect they are caught up in a vicious circle of poverty. Productivity of people is low because the capital stock is small; capital stock is small because savings of the people are small and savings are low because incomes of the people are small due to the their low productivity. The way out of the vicious circle, according to Smith, is if capitalist class saves most of their profits and invest in capital accumulation for accelerating economic growth. Thus, according to Adam Smith, saving of the society is increased by '*parsimony*' (*i.e.,* habit of frugality) of the capitalists. In fact, Adam Smith assumed that capitalist class behaves in such a manner and save a very large proportion of their profits.

Besides, capital accumulation, according to Smith, facilitates a greater degree of division of labour which causes productivity of labour to rise. Without capital accumulation the extent of division of labour cannot be increased much. Increase in capital formation leads to the production of different types of specialised equipment which are operated by different classes of workers who are skilled

---

2 A.P. Thirlwall, "*Growth and Development with Special Reference to Developing Economies*" (New York: Palgrave Macmillan, 7th edition, 2003), p. 127.

3 Adam Smith, *op. cit.,* p. 94.

and specialised in various tasks. Thus, capital accumulation along with division of labour leads to the increase in industrial output and employment.

Development Process is Cumulative

Adam Smith points out that the development process once started gathers momentum and becomes cumulative, that is, it feeds upon itself. This happens in the following ways. First, increase in saving causes more accumulation of capital which in turn facilitates a great degree of division of labour and thereby raising productivity of labour and levels of incomes of the people. Second, the higher incomes due to the capital accumulation and a higher degree of division of labour leads to the increase in the size of market or demand for goods. This expansion in demand for goods causes increase in national output and income which brings about more saving and further investment and capital accumulation. In this way spiral of economic growth rises higher and higher. Third, the increase in size of market and availability of capital induces improvement in technology.

This cumulative process of development provides a cheerful note for the developing countries. That is, if they start the development process in right earnest they can be sure of further and rapid economic development and can catch up with the presently advanced developed countries.

Sequence of Development

According to Adam Smith, the natural course of development is first agriculture, then industry and finally commerce. Agriculture creates a surplus and increases the purchasing power of the people which generates demand for industrial products. It also supplies raw materials for industries. Agricultural growth thus provides a base for industrial development.

Stationary State. Through his belief in increasing returns based on the increase in the extent of division of labour. Adam Smith was optimistic about economic growth in future. In fact, he emphasized the cumulative and self-propelling nature of development process. However, *he also pointed out that there is limit to the economic development which ultimately lands a free market economy in a stationary state* in which further capital accumulation ceases to take place and therefore there is no more growth of the economy. This happens because of two reasons. First, there is a *limited amount of natural resources at the disposal of the economy* and after passing through a phase of growth a point is reached when they are fully utilised and do not permit further growth of output.

The second factor responsible for occurrence of stationary state is *fall in profits* which reduces inducement to invest further. *Profits tend to fall as a result of competition among the capitalists, i.e., investors.* This results in decrease in demand for more capital accumulation. With slackening of capital accumulation demand for labour decreases resulting in decline in wages. Thus, after a significant economic growth, *stationary state* of the economy is reached where further capital accumulation ceases and profits fall to a low level and with the further increase in population wages become equal to the subsistence level.

Policy of Laissez-faire

As an instrument of economic development, Adam Smith was a strong champion of the policy of *laissez-faire* or allowing economic freedom to every individual not hampered in any manner by State action. He believed that "there is a set of rules of rights or justice, and perhaps even of morality in general, which are, or may be known by all men by the help either of 'reason' or of a moral sense." He was thus a strong believer in 'natural reason' guiding human affairs and he regarded State interference not only superfluous but positively harmful to economic progress. Guided by enlightened self-interest, each individual was capable of promoting his own well-being and while promoting his own interests he promotes the welfare of the whole society in the process. It is, therefore, according to Adam Smith, the production by individuals is led as if by the 'invisible hand', to promote social welfare. Thus, though individual capitalists produce goods to make profits for them but in doing so they promote social welfare though it was no part of their intention. As a matter of policy, therefore, Adam Smith advocated the removal of all restrictions on trade, choice of occupation and the use of property by individuals.

Critical Evaluation of Adam Smith's Theory of Development

The great influence of Adam Smith on subsequent thinkers can be traced in the pattern he set for later discussion on development problems. The emphasis he laid on the accumulation of capital as fundamental to the development process finds a place in subsequent theories of development. His idea of stationary state is also taken up and repeated in later writings on the subject. The policy of *laissez-faire* advocated by him is emphasised in the theories propounded by later classical writers. Similarly, his view that development was gradual and cumulative process was adopted by subsequent economists.

One of Smith's significant contributions to the theory of development has been to introduce into economics the concept of *increasing returns* based on the division of labour. According to him, the gains from division of labour or specialisation is the basis of a social economy as without it man's productivity will be very low. His model represents *optimistic view of development* in contrast to the pessimistic views of later classical economists such as Ricardo and Malthus and to Marx A.P. Thirlwall rightly writes, "It is the notion of increasing returns, based on the division of labour that lay at the heart of his optimistic version of economic progress as a self-generating process in contrast to later classical economists who believed that economies would end up in a stationary state owing to diminishing returns to agriculture and also in contrast to Marx who believed that capitalism would collapse through its own contradictions."[4] Increasing returns implies rising labour productivity and higher per capita income while diminishing returns means fall in labour productivity and therefore per capita income which set a limit to the growth of output and employment.

The most important contribution of Smith to the theory of economic development is his emphasis on capital accumulation and division of labour as the factors that determine economic growth of a country and further that capital accumulation or *investment depends on savings out of profit generated by growth of industry and agriculture*. This is very much relevant to the growth problem of present-day developing countries which requires acceleration of investment and capital formation.

Besides, Smith's emphasis on division of labour for raising productivity of labour is a highly significant contribution to economic thought and to the theory of development. He uses the term 'Division of Labour' in a wider sense which incorporates technological progress though he does not say so explicitly. He also rightly pointed out that division of labour provides greater scope for capital accumulation and the use of machinery in the complex production processes in the production of commodities that result in higher labour productivity. It is worth mentioning that Smith's vision of development as a cumulative interactive process based on the division of labour and increasing returns remained neglected for a long time until an American economist, Allyn Young, revived it in 1928 in his important paper entitled. "Increasing Returns and Economic Progress".[5] It may be noted that unlike Marshall, Young was not simply concerned with the factors that raise productivity or cost-reduction *within an individual industry* as it expands but explained the increase in productivities in *interrelated industries of the economy as a whole*. Therefore, the notion of increasing returns put forward by Young is sometimes called *macroeconomies of scale*.

4 A.P. Thirlwall, *Growth and Development (with Special Reference to Developing Economies)*, New York: Palgrave Macmillan, 7th edition, p. 129.

5 Allyn Young, "*Increasing Returns and Economic Progress,*" 1928.

Finally, it goes to the credit of Smith that he explained the gains from international trade based on specialisation by various countries on the basis of greater efficiency in the production of different goods and then trade with each other. That is, he extended his division of labour to the international level. He advocated free trade as it would increase the size of market for goods produced by different countries to reap benefits of higher degree of division of labour.

Relevance of Adam Smith's Theory to Developing Countries

Adam Smith based his theory of development on the socio-economic conditions prevailing at his time in Europe. It was a period when the seeds of industrialisation had already been dispersed in the economy. Industrial revolution was in its inception. Smith's views on development are, therefore, an answer to the questions posed by the problems of economic transition from a pre-industrial to an industrial England. Basically, he, like all other classicals, regarded that economic welfare of the society was roughly proportional to the volume of output and level of economic activity.[6] The society was regarded to be composed of two classes—the capitalists and the labourers. The wages being at the subsistence level, the labouring class was incapable of saving. Only the capitalists were able to save. The institution of private property, social attitudes and existence of perfect competition were considered congenial to economic growth. He believed in political liberalism and the philosophy of *laissez-faire.* He wanted that government should perform only those functions which individuals cannot. In his view the forces of competition were powerful enough to establish an optimum equilibrium in a society.

Division of labour symbolises the core of Smith's theory of development. It in turn depends on the '*size of the subsistence fund with which to maintain labour, i.e.,* on the amount of savings'. As such, division of labour has got to be preceded by capital accumulation. Further, 'capitals are increased by parsimony and diminished by prodigality and misconduct'. *Division of labour is also dependent on the extent of market.* So Smith favoured a widening of market through greater freedom of exchange. Now, given adequate size of market, and sufficient amount of capital accumulation, division of labour would make its sway in pushing up the level of productivity. As such, with increased incomes, greater saving would be forthcoming. This goes to improve further the degree of specialisation. The development proceeds ahead and becomes cumulative. Thus, in his theory, the economy grows like a tree in a steady and continuous way. It is this approach which forms the crux of Smith's theory of development.

It is against this background that we have to estimate the relevance of Adam Smith's theory to the socio-economic environment of presently developing countries. This theory has only limited relevance to the developing countries because of the following reasons. The size of market in these countries is quite small so that the effective demand for goods is low. Consequently, the inducement to invest is low. The size of market in turn depends on the level of income. Thus, the volume of production could be increased only if people's incomes increased. Again this can be possible only if productivity is increased. But productivity depends to a large extent on the degree to which capital is employed in the productive process. However, in the developing economies, small size of the market keeps productivity and hence income at a low level. This results in a small capacity to save and invest. This in turn reinforces the forces keeping the extent of market small.

Besides, the policy implications of Smith's theory are quite inapplicable to the developing economies. His policy recommendations of *laissez-faire*, free trade and harmony of interests are unsuitable in the context of the development of developing economies. As it is, the market economy of developing economies has been distorted due to the emergence of various kinds of monopolistic elements. The monopolists inhibit technological progress on account of the fear that innovations might result into a devaluation of their investments in capital in their existing business.

6 Hla Myint, *Theories of Welfare Economics*, 1948, pp. 84-88.

In a free market competitive economy where prices perform parametric functions, the entrepreneurs have to submit themselves to the losses resulting from innovations, because there is no way out to counteract these innovations. But when monopoly in any of its forms exists, the prices lose their parametric functions and the possibilities of free entry of new firms into the industry becomes less effective, so that the tendency to resist the devaluation of the capital invested becomes stronger and stronger. This becomes a drag on technological progress.

The monopolists assume market powers to fix higher prices and obtain larger profits as compared to competitors. This not only accentuates economic inequality but also distorts the consumers' preferences through sales promotion techniques. It is on these grounds that the governments of the developing economies have opted to intervene and exercise control on such undesirable forms of business activities. Besides, factors such as the loss of flexibility of wage rates, the unpredictable instability of demand and growth of mass production have all added to the impracticability of Smithian advice of *laissez-faire*. Even if competition was sought to be restored, there is no surety that efficiency in production would necessarily be increased. This is because of following reasons:

First, competitive prices generally fail to include *social costs*. As such, the possibility of a divergence between marginal social net product and marginal net private product in a competitive economy cannot be ruled out. The magnitude of this divergence might be so great that it becomes the responsibility of the government to intervene to make the desired adjustments.

Second, competition may also fail to achieve maximum social welfare. Demand price does not reflect relative urgency of demands or wants of different persons in an environment of inequality. As such, an allocation of resources sought to be determined by demand price that is offered for consumer goods may in fact give rise to distortions in the economy. In view of these arguments, we find that government intervention is desirable, be it monopoly or competition.

Apart from the above-mentioned reasons, there are certain special grounds for the developing countries to necessitate greater intervention in the economic affairs by the government. It is only through rigorous and systematic planning and judicious government intervention that these economies can be lifted up from the depths of stagnation. The developing countries are confronted with the collosal problems of (*a*) acute inadequacy of capital resources in relation to their requirements, (*b*) open and disguised unemployment of a vast chunk of population and (*c*) low *per capita* productivity of the working force. These stupendous problems cannot be surmounted unless the government steps in a big way to take positive steps to transform the traditional economies into the industrial ones.

Further, due to the ill-bred structure of the industry in the developing countries, the capacity to produce capital goods falls short of the availability of savings. What it really means is that even when the economy's belt is tightened so as to extract larger savings, capital formation cannot be correspondingly increased to the same extent. This is because there is immobility of resources, plants and equipment are primitive and obsolete and there is huge capital wastage involved due to rapid depreciation. It is only the government which can undertake huge investments in plants and equipment and ensure mobility of resources for increasing capital formation through increased savings.

Besides, there is the *need for building infrastructures* and social overheads like roads, transport, communications, river valley projects, power, schools, hospitals and things like that. They involve huge investments with long gestation periods. The returns are uncertain and long delayed. As such, no private entrepreneur would come forward to undertake investments in these. Government must step in to provide these basic facilities. Furthermore, the developing countries are greatly ill-placed on account of their being consumption-oriented. Due to the widespread poverty, the marginal propensity to consume of people is very high and thus the savings are very low. However, in case of a developing economy, the consumption would increase not only due to an increase in income but also due to the rise in the propensity to consume because the working of demonstration effect, both domestic and international. As such, it becomes incumbent for the government to take special measures to mobilise savings to step up capital formation.

The upshot of the discussion is that the government must play a positive role in accelerating the process of economic development in developing economies. It is, of course, very much true that the government machinery in developing countries is not that competent to bring about the desired rate of growth. But this should in no way be taken to mean that the government intervention has to be limited or eliminated. What is actually required is that the efficiency of the government be increased so that it can play its desired role to achieve the warranted rate of growth. Nevertheless, some of the crucial variables of Smith's model are as valid in the developing countries as they were for the economies that formed the basis of his theory of development. Capital accumulation and technology (*i.e.* division of labour) that played the strategic role in his model, are even today recognised as the key variables in the process of economic progress of the developing countries.

Further, for economies which are just on the threshold of take-off, Smith's prescriptions in terms of division of labour, extension of the market, rational distribution of national income, anti-usury and anti-monopoly laws, furtherance of the interests of agriculturists, industrialists and those engaged in commerce by a proactive, promotional and developmental role of government, provide a comprehensive theory of economic development. But it should always be kept in mind that this was a theory mainly formulated in the context of England with a view to tackle the problems involved in the process of transition from a pre-industrial to an industrial state. We should, therefore, not hope to get proper and direct solution to all the problems of development which are posed by the development and industrialisation of developing countries owing to the tremendous difference in the circumstances in the two cases.

RICARDO'S THEORY OF ECONOMIC DEVELOPMENT

Although Ricardo drew heavily on Adam Smith's writings, yet he was the first economist who presented the classical thought in a consistent body of economic analysis, presented in a vigorous form. His ideas are embodied in his book, *The Principles of Political Economy and Taxation* (1817) and the many letters that he addressed to contemporary economists. The Ricardian theory of rent is well known; but there are also ideas contained in his writings which throw light on the development process and we shall briefly explain them below.

Role of Agriculture and Diminishing Returns to Labour

Like that of Smith in Ricardo's model growth and development depends on capital accumulation. And capital accumulation depends on reinvestment of profits. But the profits earned by the capitalists depends on the growth of agricultural output, especially food, or what is now generally called wage goods. However, the important fact which was emphasised by Ricardo was diminishing returns which occur as more doses of labour (equipped with some tools and equipment) are used in agriculture. As we shall see below, it is diminishing returns in agriculture that causes food prices to rise and result in rise of wages of workers which squeeze profits and ultimately lands the economy into stationary state. According to Ricardo, there are three agents of production that participate in the process of growth of output. The capitalist hires labour and land and plays a key role in the process of economic development. Ricardo uses the term capitalist in the sense the modern economists use the term *entrepreneur*. In the Ricardian model capitalist undertakes production, pays rent to the landlords and wages to the workers employed for the production work and what remains is his profits.

Besides diminishing returns to labour in agriculture, the other fact emphasised by Ricardo, like other classical economists, is that wages were determined by *minimum subsistence level of the workers*. Whenever during the growth process wages rise above the subsistence level, population increases and brings them to the level of subsistence. On the other hand, wages cannot fall below the subsistence level because below it workers cannot survive.

Ricardian Growth Model

Let us now explain Ricardian model of growth in detail. Ricardo makes two-sector analysis of the economy. He draws distinction between an agricultural sector and industrial sector. He assumes that agriculture is subject to law of diminishing returns while industry is subject to constant returns. Further, Ricardo regarded real wages to be fixed in terms of corn, *i.e.*, the product of the agricultural sector. Labour when supplied with corn (wage goods), *i.e.*, circulating capital and also some fixed capital (tools and equipment) to produce more than its subsistence and the difference between the output and subsistence wages is the surplus produced by the labourers which is shared between the capitalists, the owners of capital, and the landlords, the owners of the lands.

Let us first take the agricultural sector which, according to Ricardo, is subject to diminishing returns. As more and more doses of labour and capital are employed, marginal product of labour and capital would diminish. The capitalist employer will employ labour to the extent that he just meets the expenses of production on the margin. The intra-marginal doses of labour employed would produce surplus over the expenses incurred on them, which is the source of capital, that is, the *wage fund* that will be used for employing labour in future for further production. The greater the volume of saving out of the surplus, the faster will be the rate of capital accumulation and more rapid the growth of output and employment.

Graphically, the growth of agricultural output and employment of labour in Ricardian model is depicted in Fig. 18.1. In this figure marginal productivity of labour is depicted on the *Y*-axis and the amount of labour employment on the *X*-axis. The curve *MP* is the marginal productivity curve which will remain fixed as it is assumed that land is fixed and no technological progress occurs. If *OB* is the expenses on a dose of a labour and capital, then *OL* labour would be employed. It will be seen from Fig. 18.1 that the employment of *OL* labour produces the total output equal to *OQHL*. The total expenses of production incurred on capital and labour are equal to *OBEL*. It is thus clear that labour produces surplus over costs of cultivation incurred on labour and capital. The surplus is equal to *BQHE*. *This surplus represents the rent which will be obtained by the landlords, the owners of the*

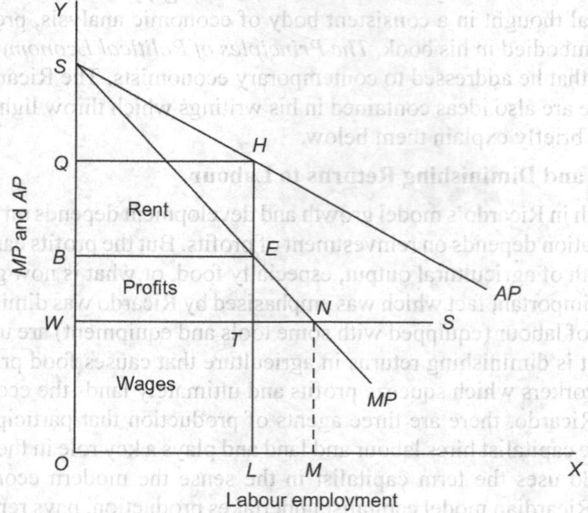

Fig. 18.1. *Ricardo's model of growth: agricultural sector*

land. If *OW* represents the minimum level of subsistence wage which will be paid to the workers, then *OWTL* would be the share of labour (*i.e.*, total wages bill) in the agricultural output produced. The remaining agricultural output equal to *WTEB* will be the profits made by the capitalist farmers.

According to Ricardo, surplus (*i.e.*, profits) of capitalist farmers will be saved and reinvested. As a result of reinvestment both the output and employment will increase. *Since the land for the society as a whole is fixed, marginal product curve of labour (equipped with certain tools) will remain unchanged.* Due to diminishing returns, with the increase in more and more of employment of labour its marginal product, (*MP*) will go on falling till it becomes equal to *minimum subsistence level of wages OW* (that is, at point *N* on *MP* curve in Fig. 18.1. As a result of marginal product of labour being equal to minimum subsistence wages *OW*, *profits will disappear* and rent of landlords will increase. With this total agricultural output equal to the area *OSNM* (that is the area under *MP* curve up to point *M*) will be distributed between wages and rent, profits having been fallen to zero. Ricardo thought that the landlords who receive rent do not save and consume all their incomes.

It may be noted that *in equilibrium*, according to Ricardo, rate of profit in agriculture must equal the rate of profit in industry. During the development process as profit rate in agriculture falls capital will be shifted to industry. As we will see below, with the increase in capital accumulation in industry profits will decline in industry as a result of rise in wages due to rise in food prices caused by diminishing returns in agriculture.

Ricardo's Model: Growth of the Industrial Sector

It should be noted that the foodgrain surpluses generated in agriculture are essential to employ labour in the industrial sector. It is in the industrial sector that stock of fixed capital plays an important role in the growth of output and employment, while in agriculture it is the amount of land which is of crucial significance. While the land as a whole is fixed and diminishing returns ultimately occur when more doses of labour and capital are used, increase in the stock of fixed industrial capital on the other hand is possible since it is made by man. But workers engaged in building up of capital stock must be paid in real terms, *i.e*., in foodgrains and other wage goods, or corn as Ricardo called it. As the *stock of capital increases in the industrial sector marginal productivity curve of labour in the industry sector will shift upward implying that more labour will be employed at the minimum subsistence level of wages through the process of capital widening.*

It is again worth emphasising that in the short run real wages may rise above the minimum subsistence level, but this will lead to the increase in population and labour force, so that as long as foodgrains are available at the same price, the minimum subsistence level in money terms will remain constant and supply of labour will be perfectly elastic at the minimum subsistence level in money form. However, if the prices of foodgrains rise due to the operation of diminishing returns in agriculture, the wages in the industrial sector will rise. But, the wage rate in terms of corn or wage goods will remain the same and the labour supply will be perfectly elastic at this rate due to the growth in population and labour force.

But *availability of wage-goods surpluses proves a constraint on the growth of industrial sector*. If sufficient food surpluses are not forthcoming and demand for them increases as a result of the growth in labour employment brought about by the expansion of stock of industrial capital, the prices of foodgrains will rise. The increase in the prices of foodgrains will raise the subsistence wage rate in terms of money which will reduce the surplus of the capitalists. Since Ricardo and others assumed that agriculture was subject to diminishing returns, the prices of foodgrains will rise as cultivation on land is increased both extensively and intensively. Therefore, as a result of the rise in the prices of the foodgrains and thereby the rise of the wages of labourers will reduce the surplus or profits made by the capitalists in the industrial sector. The rate of profit expressed as ratio of net revenue earned on the capital will go on declining till it becomes zero. When the rate of profit becomes zero, further capital accumulation in the industrial sector will cease and in this way a stationary state will be reached. Before the stationary state is reached, the level of output and employment of labour force during any given period in the industrial sector will depend on the stock of given fixed capital (and therefore the marginal productivity curve of labour) on the one hand and the wage goods supply forthcoming from the agricultural sector on the other.

We depict the growth of output and employment in the industrial sector in Fig. 18.2. In this figure labour employment is measured along the *X*-axis and marginal product of labour is measured along the *Y*-axis, Along the *Y*-axis and below the origin the stock of capital is measured. To start with, suppose OK_1 is the stock of industrial capital and corresponding to this the marginal productivity curve of labour is M_1P_1. Suppose OW is the minimum subsistence level of wages in real terms. With OW as the wage rate, OL_1 labour force would be employed. At OL_1, the marginal product of labour is equal to the given wage rate of OW, the total wage bill will be equal to $OWEL_1$ and WEM_1 will be the profits or net revenue earned by the capitalists. According to Ricardo, a good part of this net revenue or profits earned by the capitalists will be reinvested in the expansion of capital equipment. This reinvestment of the profits will result in the expansion of the capital stock. The expansion in the stock of capital will shift the marginal productivity curve of labour upward to the position M_2P_2. Now, if the subsistence wage rate remains at the level OW, OL_2 labourers will be employed and the profits will now increase to WFM_2. In this way, the profits will continue to be reinvested and stock of capital will go on expanding, resulting in the shift of the marginal productivity curve of workers and the increase in labour employment and output.

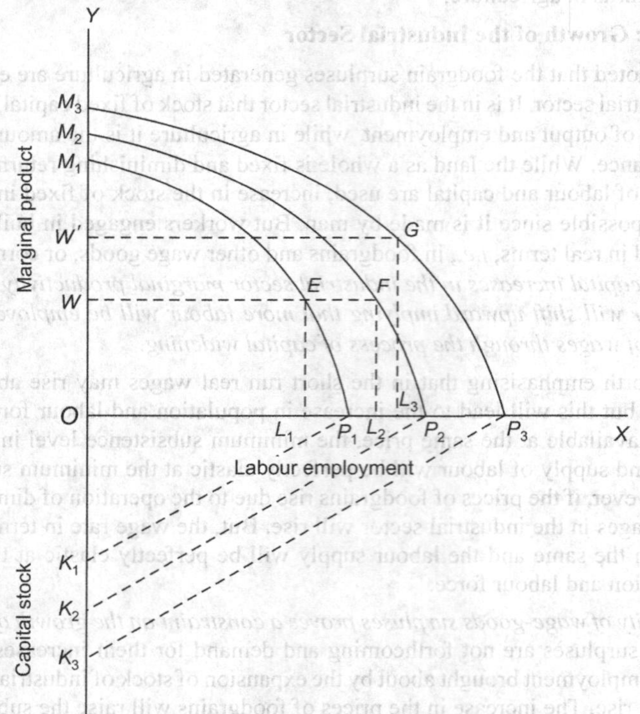

Fig. 18.2. *Ricardo's growth model: the industrial sector*

However, according to Ricardo, the industrial sector cannot go on expanding indefinitely. As according to him, agriculture is subject to diminishing returns, the increase in industrial output and employment and the resultant rise in the demand for foodgrains will cause the prices of foodgrains to rise. The rise in prices of foodgrains will bring about the increase in the wage rate in the industrial sector. If the wage rate rises to OW' when the capital stock is OK_3, OL_3 labour force would be employed and the net revenue or profits of the capitalist would be reduced to $M_3W'G$. Thus, the occurrence of diminishing returns in agriculture and the consequent rise in the prices of foodgrains and the rise in wage rate, the rate of profits made by capitalists will go on declining till it becomes zero. When the rate of profit is reduced to zero, further expansion in the stock of industrial capital ceases to occur. As a result of this, the whole growth process of increase in output and labour employment will stop.

From the above, it is thus clear that in Ricardo's model the growth of output and employment depends on capital accumulation on the one hand, and the available supplies of foodgrains or wage goods on the other which are constrained by the operation of diminusting returns in agriculture.

Stationary State

Ricardo shows how the rate of profit goes on falling as more and more capital is accumulated and invested. As the rate of profit falls, the accumulation of capital also slows down. The economy reaches the stationary state when rate of profit is too low to provide any incentive for any business enterprise. After the initial rise in wages as economy grows forward, the wages are brought down to the subsistence level by the pressure of population. At this stage, the rents are high. The real wage rate is at its minimum and population growth slackens. The rate of profit falls to near zero and further expansion of capital ceases. These are all the symptoms of a stationary state.

Given the crucial importance of capital accumulation in Ricardo's model of growth, anything that discourages investment will adversely affect capital accumulation and economic growth. Ricardo was therefore against imposing any levies, taxes and tariffs on inputs which raises the cost of production and lowers profits and thus serves as disincentive to make investment. That is why he emphasised imports of cheap food by abolishing corn laws in England at that time and thought that imports of cheap food would delay the reaching of stationary state indefinitely by holding down wages in terms of food. To quote him, "A country could go on for an indefinite time increasing its wealth and production for the only obstacle to this increase would be scarcity, and consequent high value of food and other raw produce. Let these be supplied from abroad in exchange for manufactured goods and it is difficult to say where the limit is at which you would cease to accumulate wealth and to derive profits from its employment."[7]

Such has been the appeal of Ricardo's growth model that Arthur Lewis based his view of development in **"Economic Development with Unlimited Supplies of Labour"** for developing economy with dualistic structure on Ricardo's model of growth. However, instead of assuming wages for the modern capitalist sector remaining equal to the minimum subsistence level based on Malthusian law of population *Lewis considered perfectly elastic supply of labour to the modern capitalist sector due to the existence of disguised unemployment prevailing in the traditional sector* (*i.e., agriculture*). He assumed that wages would stay at the given level until all disguisedly unemployed labour in agriculture is absorbed in the modern industrial sector.

Critical Evaluation of Ricardo's Model

We have seen above that Ricardo, like other classical economists, emphasised the wage goods as determinants of growth of output and employment in an economy. In the growth of output and employment, they ignored the role of aggregate effective demand despite the protest by Malthus. Their neglect of effective demand as a factor affecting growth of income and employment flowed from their belief in Say's Law. However, in the context of developing countries, his emphasis on wage goods as determinant of income and employment is quite right. In developing countries like India, the cause of mass unemployment and disguised unemployment is to be found in the lack of fixed capital and other cooperating factors and the supplies of the wage goods on the other and not in the lack of aggregate demand. Therefore, a solution to the unemployment problem in labour-surplus developing countries lies in the accumulation of fixed capital as well as the expansion of wage goods supply in the economy. Keynesian remedy of curing unemployment through the increase in aggregate

7 David Ricardo, *Principles of Political Economy and Taxation.*

demand by expansionary fiscal policy financed by creating new money will not solve the problem of unemployment and disguised unemployment in developing countries.

It is worth emphasising that Ricardo rightly pointed out that the growth of output and employment in the industrial sector depends upon the availability of wage goods. That the availability of foodgrain surpluses or wage-goods serves as a constraint on the growth of industrial output and employment has now been well recognised. In the Second and Third Five Year Plans of India and in the Soviet industrialisation, especially higher priority to basic and heavy industries, brought about rise in prices of foodgrains and the deceleration in the industrial sector. However, it may be pointed out that the contention of Ricardo that agriculture is subject to the law of diminishing returns that will ultimately raise the prices of foodgrains and reduce the profits in the industrial sector which will ultimately result in the occurrence of the stationary state, is too pessimistic and unwarranted. In their analysis of the growth process, they underestimated the role of technological progress in raising production which can suspend the operation of the law of diminishing returns. The increase in agricultural productivity due to technological progress can prevent the rise in prices of foodgrains and therefore the reaching of the stationary state. In actual practice, in today's developed countries, agricultural revolution took place along with the industrial revolution. In this regard, the gloomy prognosis of classical economists has not come true as far as capitalist developed countries are concerned.

A drawback in Ricardo's theory of development is that it regarded all increase in the stock of fixed capital as increasing labour employment. In other words, it ignored the *labour-displacing effect* of capital equipment in which improved technology is embodied. Actually, much of technological progress made in advanced developed countries has been of capital-intensive nature. It has tended to displace labour. Therefore, the technology evolved and developed in advanced countries does not suit the factor-endowment conditions of developing countries with surplus labour and scarce capital. Therefore, in developing countries, to accelerate economic growth and employment generation emphasis has to be put not only on the expansion of fixed capital but also on the right choice of technology which is labour-using rather than labour-saving.

Ricardo was also not right in ignoring the effective demand in determining growth of income and employment. Despite warning by Malthus, Ricardo thought that development process would not be constrained by lack of effective demand as he believed in Say's Law that supply creates its own demand. The main hurdle in the development process, according to him, is the rise in wages due to diminishing returns in agriculture. Ricardo thus writes, "There is no limit to demand—no limit to the employment of capital while it yields any profit, and that however abundant capital may become, there is no other adequate reason for a fall in profit but a rise in wages."[8] As has been emphasised by Keynes, there is nothing in the working of the capitalist economic system which would always ensure adequate effective demand so as to maintain full employment and ensure steady growth. According to Keynes, in a modern monetary economy, the saving and investment activities have been separated from each other. The investment may not be equal to the savings done at the level of full employment. Hence full employment and steady growth may not be maintained.

Ricardo's contribution to economic analysis and theory of economic development is regarded as outstanding and his view are widely shared by other classical economists. As in the case of other classical economists, his analysis of the economy relates to a long period of time as distinguished from a short period analysis. He regards the economy as dynamic and ever-changing. It grows till it ultimately reaches a stationary state. In the development process, Ricardo focuses his attention on the major variables like capital accumulation, population growth and trends in profits. He studies interrelations among these variables and then draws conclusions about their behaviour. His analysis

8 Ricardo, *op. cit.*

of the relative shares in the national income of the various agents of production such as rent, wages and profits is indeed thought-provoking.

It must, however, be said that although he refines and extends the classical theory of development, yet the main points in his analysis are haphazardly scattered in his book *'The Principles of Political Economy'*. His predictions regarding the advent of stationary state have not turned out to be true, nor are about the changes in relative shares of the various agents of production borne out by history. The two fundamental principles in his model of economic development, *viz.*, the principles of population and the law of diminishing returns, are only partially correct. All the same, it has to be admitted that he made a significant contribution to the theory of economic growth.

RELEVANCE OF RICARDO'S THEORY OF GROWTH TO DEVELOPING COUNTRIES

The Ricardian theory of development as we have seen in his analysis is based upon two fundamental principles, *viz*., principle of diminishing returns and the principle of population growth. Ricardo like Smith realises that a high rate of capital accumulation is necessary for economic growth. He considers profits as the primary source of accumulation, although among the secondary sources he includes rent and wages (when they are high enough to generate a surplus over subsistence). Further, in the Ricardian system, there is an organic relation between agricultural development and economic growth. In this context Ricardo attacks the landlords' interests, as they are opposed to agricultural improvements. The fertility of soil, he says, falls as the margin is extended (as a result of increasing population). As such the rate of profit will fall in the absence of agricultural improvements and free trade.

Ricardo points out that the normal progress of the economy is towards stationary state. The gloomy forecast of the ultimate advent of a stationary state as envisaged by Ricardo has been falsified by history. The rapid economic strides by capitalist economies in many parts of the world in the past and the squeezing gulf between the capitalists and the labourers following a steady betterment in their economic status, all go to disprove Ricardo's dismal picture about the future of capitalism.

The two fundamental principles—the principle of diminishing returns and the principle of population on which Ricardo based his theory of economic development—have partially, if not completely, been negated in the developing countries of today. With improved techniques and technical know-how, it has been possible to effectively check the tendency towards diminishing returns to set in. In the same way, his views on population growth have been disproved for it cannot explain the changes in population in the developing countries. There is no tendency towards subsistence wages. Not only that, Ricardo's conjectures about the relative share of labour, capitalists and landlords have not been proved to be correct.

Nevertheless, Ricardo's emphasis on the role of agriculture in accumulation of the various methods of savings, including taxation of rent as an important element, entrepreneurial ability, specialisation of labour, attack on landlordism, the role of labour productivity which could be increased either through organisational or technological changes and the importance of the National Bank (Ricardo being the first to conceive of a Central Bank) still remain the policies of direct relevance to the developing economies.

CHAPTER 19

MALTHUS'S THEORY OF ECONOMIC DEVELOPMENT

The students of economics generally remember Robert Malthus as the propounder of his famous Theory of Population. But it is well to remember that Malthus had also some important things to say about economic development and it is refreshing to note that in several ways he anticipated the later economists like Keynes and Kaleeki. Also, the Malthusian version of economic growth represents in several respects a refinement of the general classical theory. He recognised, more than did the other classical economists, the importance of a distinct and systematic theory of economic growth. Book II of his "*Principles of Political Economy*" deals with the "Progress of Wealth" where he says: "*There is scarcely any inquiry more curious or, from its importance more worthy of our attention, than that which traces the causes which practically check the progress of wealth in different countries.*"[1]

The problem of development, according to Malthus, lies in explaining why the *actual* gross national product (actual riches) should differ from the *potential* gross national product (power of producing riches). He thus points out the way in which the potentialities of economic development in a country should be realised. This can be done by larger production and fairer distribution.

Malthus contends that the process of *economic growth is not automatic.* Rather a conscious, deliberate efforts are needed to bring it about. For instance, Malthus explains that *mere increase in population cannot by itself lead to economic development unless there is increase in effective demand.* (This is anticipation of the Keynesian doctrine). He says: "A man whose only possession is his labour has, or has not, an effective demand for produce according as he is, or is not, in demand by those who have the disposal of the produce."[2] He rejects Say's Law which says "supply creates its own demand" and that savings are automatically invested and constitute a demand for capital goods. Malthus's important contribution is in showing that savings in the sense of not consuming is a mere negative act and instead of creating more demand it will lead to a decline in effective demand. Only savings which are furnished by increased gains and are invested create an effective demand. Thus, according to him, "abstinence on the part of capitalists, far from accelerating economic growth, will in itself retard it."[3] Hence, Malthus brings out an important fact that in an advanced economy consumption, saving and investment all should expand simultaneously.

Role of Capital

Malthus attaches great importance to the accumulation of capital for economic development. He regards capital as indispensable to development. According to him, "no permanent and continued increase of wealth can take place without a continued increase of capital." Besides, Malthus underlined

1 T. R. Malthus, *Principles of Political Economy* (Augustus Kelly, reprint of Second Edition, New York, 1951), p. 300.

2 *Ibid.,* p. 310.

3 *Ibid.,* p. 311.

the **importance of foreign trade** for speeding up economic growth. Foreign trade provides incentives for investing, since it leads to the extension of the market for the goods produced and for greater division of labour resulting in increased output.

There is another important fact brought out by Malthusian analysis of economic growth, namely, the **structured change** that takes place in the process of economic development *i.e.,* a decline in the relative importance of agriculture as the economy moves forward. We know that economic development in developing countries is regarded as synonymous with the development of industries. Naturally, agriculture is eclipsed by the speedier development of industries. As a means for expanding agricultural output, Malthus suggested land reforms.

Of far greater importance than what has been pointed out above, is the *anticipation by Malthus of the theory of 'dualism'* as applied to underdeveloped economies. He envisaged the economy as consisting of the two major sectors, *viz.,* the agricultural sector and the industrial sector. His analysis of the interrelation between these two sectors is quite interesting and enlightening. The law of increasing returns operated in the industrial sector, whereas the agricultural sector was subject to the law of diminishing returns, the rate of technological progress being responsible for this difference.

Malthus brings out an important truth that when *one of these sectors lags behind, it retards the development of the other sector.* We know how in India the failure on the agricultural front was responsible for the slow rate of growth. "*The development of the industrial sector of underdeveloped countries is limited by the poverty of the agricultural sector.*" This is due to the fact that the lack of purchasing power in the rural masses reduces effective demand in the economy and retards its growth.

Assessment of Malthus's Contributions

There is no doubt that Malthus made a valuable contribution to the theory of economic growth. His repudiation of Say's Law and emphasising the importance of effective demand and its relation to saving and investment are indeed noteworthy for their modern touch. A great deal of what he wrote on the subject is applicable to an underdeveloped economy, especially relating to the theory of dualism.

It has been pointed out by the critics of Malthus's theory of economic development, he concentrates on explaining the factors which hinder growth rather than the factors that promote economic progress. However, some elements of his theory make positive contribution to the growth process. For example, he considers production and distribution as the two grand elements of economic growth. *The distribution of production is as important as production itself for sustained economic growth.* He also gives importance to capital accumulation in bringing about economic growth. At the same time he emphasises that the capital accumulation will choke off if it is not possible for the additional goods to find consumers. That is, he points to the significance of effective demand for sustained accumulation of capital. Increase in effective demand, according to him, is as important as increase in production. Therefore, unlike Adam Snuth, he thinks that excessive parsimony will reduce aggregate demand leading to widespread depression and unemployment. He recommends a more egalitarian system of distribution in order to increase effective demand. He also recognizes the importance of non-economic factors in economic growth.

Though Malthus is more well-known for his theory of population than his contribution to growth economics, his emphasis on fair distribution of production and effective demand makes his theory of development distinct from that of other classical economists, such as Adam Snuth and David Ricardo. According to his population theory, population increases so rapidly as to outstrip the food supply due to the operation of law of diminishing returns which has largely been falsified owing to the rapid increase in agricultural productivity yet it is very helpful in probing the problem facing the labour-surplus developing countries of today.

Relevance of Malthus's Theory to Developing Countries

Malthus's theory of development is negative in the sense that he concentrates his attention on the causes which hinder growth rather than the causes which promote economic progress. However, some elements making positive contribution to growth process are discernible in his *Principles of Political Economy.* Malthus considers production and distribution as the two grand elements of economic progress. The distribution of production is as important as production itself for the furtherance of economic progress. He also fully realises the significance of capital accumulation in economic growth. At the same time he makes the important point that the accumulation of capital will choke off if it is not possible for the additional goods to find consumers. Herein are contained the seeds of the significance of effective demand.

Increase in effective demand, according to Malthus, is as important as the increase in production. Excessive parsimony decreases the effective demand leading to widespread depression and unemployment. He recommends a more egalitarian system of distribution in order to increase effective demand. Malthus also duly recognizes the importance of non-economic factors. Above all, Malthus is more well known for his theory of population than his contribution to growth economics. He held the view that population increases so rapidly as to outstrip the food supply due to the operation of the law of diminishing returns.

Malthus's contribution to economic growth contains several elements that are relevant to the developing economies. His emphasis on both production and distribution, capital accumulation and the creation of congenial non-economic factors is as valid today as was in his time. Though his theory of population has largely been falsified owing to the rapid increase in agricultural productivity, yet it is very helpful in probing the problems facing the overpopulated developing countries of today.

CHAPTER

20

MARX'S THEORY OF CAPITALIST DEVELOPMENT

Karl Marx presented his theory of development in his now famous book **Das Kapital** (1867). There are many similarities between his theory and Ricardo's theory of development but he drew quite different implications. Basic similarity between Marx and Classicals (including Ricardo) is that *capital accumulation is prime mover* of *economic growth*. The other basic assumption of Marx and Ricardo is that supply curve of labour to the modern industrial sector is perfectly elastic at the minimum subsistence level. However, the reason given for the determination of wages at the subsistence level is quite different. White Ricardo believed in the Malthusian Law of Population to assume that wage rate will remain stable at minimum subsistence level; if as a result of development, wage rate rises above minimum subsistence level, population will increase bringing down the wage rate to the minimum subsistence level. On the other hand, wage rate cannot go below the minimum subsistence level as workers would not survive at that level which will lower the population growth rate causing wage rate to rise to the minimum subsistence level. Marx rejected Malthus's law of population and explained the determination of wage rate at the minimum subsistence level with the help of his notion of *reserve army of labour* (that is, unemployed labour force). We will explain this below.

Why Do Wages Remain at the Subsistence Level: Marxist View

According to Marx, the forces at work in a capitalist economic system bring about the increase in the rate of exploitation of labour. The basic force at work is the competition among the capitalists to the *increase in the rate of surplus value* what Marx called rate of exploitation and thereby enlarge their profits share relative to wages share. Now the question is how the capitalists are able to do this. First thing to understand in this connection is that Marx, like Ricardo, believed that the market wage rate tended to be equal to the minimum subsistence level in the long tun. In other words, wage rate, according to Marx, cannot rise above the subsistence level except in the very short run.

However, reason given by Marx for the existence of the minimum subsistence wages is different from what Ricardo thought it to be. According to Ricardo, it was the increase in population above the subsistence level that kept the wages tied to the minimum subsistence level. *In Marx's analysis, it is the prevailing excess of labour supply over the demand for labour that prevents the wages from rising above the minimum subsistence level*. Because of the continuous increase in labour supply over demand, there comes to exist a large amount of unemployed workers which Marx called "*the reserve army of labour*." It is therefore the existence of reserve army of labour (*i.e.,* the unemployed) that prevents the wages from going above the minimum subsistence level.

Now, why does supply of labour remain excess relative to demand for it. "Marx assumed that as capitalist enterprise progresses at the expense of pre-capitalistic enterprise more labourers are released through the disappearance of the handicraft units than are absorbed in the capitalist sector owing to the difference in productivity per head between the two sectors. As long as the growth of capitalist enterprise is at the cost of a shrinkage of pre-capitalist enterprise the increase in the supply of wage-labour tends to run ahead of the increase in the demand for wage labour.[1] Thus, as long as the reserve army of labour exists wage rate in the industrial sector will be prevented from rising above the subsistence level.

Concept of Marx's Theory of Surplus Value

Marx's concept of surplus value plays an important role in his theory of capitalist development. It is therefore proper for us to explain his concept of surplus value and how it is related to profits earned by the capitalist-entrepreneur and exploitation of the workers which leads to the class struggle in the economy.

The Marxian analysis of capitalism rests on the *labour theory of value,* which Marx took over from Adam Smith and Ricardo. According to Marx's labour theory of value, the value of a commodity is determined by the labour time necessary for its production. *It is the labour alone that is the ultimate source of all value.* According to Marx, equipment and raw materials do not create value; they merely transfer their own value to the value of the final product. On the other hand, labour creates more value than the value of labour power expended on the production of goods and services. In other words, it is the unique characteristic of labour power that it creates more value than its own value. The value of labour power is determined by the cost of reproduction of labour, that is, by the value of goods and services that are required to maintain the labourers at the minimum subsistence level. In other words, the value of labour power, that is, the own cost of labour, means the minimum subsistence wages which are just sufficient to keep the labourers living and intact.

Labour theory of value and the concept of value of labour power as being equal to the minimum subsistence level are crucial in Marxian theory because they form the basis of Marx's *theory of surplus value* which in turn explains the distribution of aggregate income into wages and profits in a capitalist economy.[2] Since labour creates more value product than its own cost or value of labour power, that is, more than the minimum subsistence output, the surplus emerges which is expropriated by the capitalists who happen to own the material means of production such as capital equipment, land and raw materials with which labour is employed to produce goods and services. *This surplus value represents profits of the capitalists.* According to Marx, the surplus value or profits which are created by labour over and above the value of their subsistence requirements are unjustifiably expropriated by the capitalist class. In other words, the surplus value or profits extracted from labour by the capitalists represents the *exploitation of labour.*

It is through the ownership of material means of production that the capitalists are able to exploit the labour class and extract surplus value from it. Thus the share of profits in the total value of output depends upon the magnitude of surplus value extracted from it. Prof. Patterson rightly remarks, "*The notion of surplus value is crucial to the Marxian theory of income distribution; surplus value is the source of profits and thus the amount of surplus that can be expropriated by the capitalist class will determine the relative share of profits in the income total.*"[3]

In the Marxian analysis, the total value of output is composed of three elements. Firstly, it consists of the value of the capital and raw materials consumed in the production of goods and services. Marx calls this as *constant capital* which is written as *C*. Secondly, the total value of output contains the value of labour power used in the production of goods and services, that is, total wages in terms of minimum subsistence wages paid to the workers. Marx calls this as *variable capital* which is written

1 Kaldor, "Alternative Theories of Distribution," *Review of Economic Studies,* Vol. 23, pp. 83, 100.

2 It should be noted that Marx considers two classes—workers, and capitalists—between which total income is to be distributed. He regards profits as the income of the property owning class. Therefore, rent from land is included in his profits.

3 Wallace, C. Patterson, *Income, Employment and Economic Growth* (New York, 1962), p. 432.

as V. Thirdly, the total value of output contains the *surplus value* which is created by the labourers over and above the value of their labour power and which, as seen above, is bagged by the capitalist class as profits. Thus,

$$\text{Total value output} = \text{constant capital} + \text{variable capital} + \text{surplus value}$$
$$= C + V + S$$

C, as said above, stands for capital consumption. It should be noted that in case of the whole economy C will contain only the consumption of fixed capital, since raw materials are intermediate products and their value will be included in the value of final goods produced. If we subtract the value of C from the total output, we get the *net* output which will consist of value of the labour power or variable capital (V) and the surplus value (S). V and S are wages share and profits share respectively in the net output. Thus

$$\text{Net output} = V + S$$

If Y stands for net national output, then

$$Y = V + S$$

or $\quad$ Surplus value, $(S) = Y - V$

That is, surplus value (S) is equal to net national income minus the variable capital (*i.e.*, wages). The *rate of surplus value* or what Marx called '*degree of exploitation*' is given by the ratio $\frac{S}{V}$

It is this rate of surplus value $\frac{S}{V}$ which represents the ratio of profits share to the wages share in the national income. A rise in this ratio means the increase in the rate of exploitation and hence increase in the profits share relative to wages share in the national income.

However, the *rate of profit* in Marx's theory is given by the ratio of surplus value (S) to the *total capital*, that is, variable capital (V) + constant capital (C). Thus rate of profit (p) is given by

$$p = \frac{S}{V + C} \qquad \text{...(1)}$$

We further elaborate it by dividing the numerator and denominator in equation (1) by variable capital, V. In doing so we have

$$\text{rate of profit } (p) = \frac{\frac{S}{V}}{\frac{V + C}{V}}$$

$$= \frac{\frac{S}{V}}{1 + \frac{C}{V}} \qquad \text{...(2)}$$

where $\frac{C}{V}$, that is, ratio of constant capital to the variable capital was called by Marx as '*organic composition of capital*' which in modern terminology is called *capital-labour ratio* or simply *capital intensity*. From equation (2) above it follows that with economic development as technology becomes more capital-intensive, the organic composition of capital (that is, capital-labour ratio) $\frac{C}{Y}$ rises through time and rate of profit (p) falls unless rate of surplus value $\left(\frac{S}{V}\right)$ rises. However, Marx expected that rate of profit can be kept high by increasing the surplus value. Only when a large accumulation of capital has taken place and as a consequence reserve army of labour is exhausted, wages will go up resulting in decline in profit. Even then the capitalists try to keep wages down by substituting more capital for labour. This will, on the one hand, lead to the 'immiseration of workers' causing social upheaval and on the other hand, would raise the '*organic composition of capital*' $\left(\frac{C}{V}\right)$ which will lower the ratio of profit.

Capital Accumulation, Technological Progress and Economic Growth

Unlike other classical economists Marx considered technological change rather than profits as the primer driver of economic growth in capitalist economies. According to him, technological changes in each stage of a country's economic development determines not only the economic situation but also the production relations in a society. Thus, according to him, the hand mill created the feudal landlord and steam mill the capitalist.

Marx explained his theory of development with his assumption that labour supply is perfectly elastic at the subsistence wages. The capitalist engages workers for the production of goods and these workers create surplus value which is reinvested to increase capital accumulation. But Marx believed that capital accumulation along with technological progress increases labour productivity and brings about economic growth. But Marx regarded technological progress as being *labour-saving* and *capital-using.* At the time of writing *Das Kapital,* technological change dominated the capital-intensive innovations such as steamship, machines run by diesel engine, railroads, heavy chemicals. Thus, according to Marx, with further economic development there was tendency for capital per worker to rise. With wages remaining sticky at subsistence level, the more surplus value is created by workers which is invested in new capital goods.

The growth of factory system of industrial production with the establishment of capitalist mode of production brought about the destruction of handicrafts, that is, the simple commodity production by craftsmen and artisans. This is because the craftsmen could not compete with the goods produced with the aid of machines. This led to the decline of simple commodity production of handicrafts by craftsmen. With the destruction of handicrafts, capitalist mode of production became the dominant mode of production.

The change from small-scale production of handicrafts by craftsmen to large-scale industrial production with the aid of machines in a factory system was, without doubt, a big stride forward in the development of the productive forces. Machines proved to be powerful means by which man could tame the forces of nature. Machines also lightened labour of workers and considerably raised their productivity. With further inventions and development of science and technology, the machines became bigger and more sophisticated. *The exploitation of the workers and plunder of colonies by the capitalist class and consequently concentration of wealth in its hand enabled this class to invest more and more in machines and factories*. This ensured a higher rate of capital formation and industrial growth in the Western European countries.

It is worthwhile to note that at that time the propensity of the capitalist class was not so much 'to consume' but 'to accumulate'. *The function of the capitalist, according to Marx, is to 'accumulate and it is primarily because capitalist system offered stimulus to accumulation of capital that Marx recognized the historical role performed by it in the development of the Western economies. Having high propensity to save the capitalist class invested the surplus value extracted from the workers.* 'To accumulate' was passion with the capitalists in the earlier phases of capitalism. This generated a higher rate of capital formation and consequently of economic growth. To quote Marx. "Frantically bent upon the expansion of value, he (the capitalist) relentlessly drives human beings to production for productions's sake, thus bringing about a development of social productivity and the creation of those material conditions of production which can alone form the real basis of a higher type of society... only as the personification of capital is the capitalist respectable."[4] Consequently, rapid accumulation of capital brought about unprecedented economic growth in the Western countries. It is because of economic growth achieved under capitalism that Western European countries and the U.S. have become *affluent* nations today.

Rising Exploitation of Labour with Capitalist Development

Now, the wages being fixed at the minimum subsistence level, the measures which bring about the increase in the output of labour will raise the rate of exploitation and therefore the profits of the capitalists. According to Marx, the capitalists who own the material means of production *compete with each other* to increase the rate of exploitation (S/V) which is the same thing as the increase in profits share relative to wages share. Thus, Professor Patterson remarks. "*In the Marxian theory competition takes the form of a struggle among the owners of the material instruments of production to increase the rate of exploitation or, and this comes to the same thing, the non-wage share in the income total.*"[5]

Now, there are three ways of increasing the surplus value or rate of exploitation. In the first place, this can be done by *lengthening the working day.* When the workers are forced to work for a larger number of hours in a day than before, the total output increases and, given the wages paid to them, the surplus value expropriated by the capitalists and therefore the rate of exploitation increases. Secondly, the surplus value or rate of exploitation may be raised by *increasing the intensity of labour,* that is, forcing the workers to do greater amount of work while keeping the working day constant. However, the extent to which the surplus value can be increased in these two ways is very limited. The third and, according to Marx, a major way in which the capitalist can increase the surplus value is *raising the physical productivity of workers through technical progress.* Technical progress involves the improvement in techniques of production. Workers working with better and improved techniques produce more than before while working the same number of hours in a day and with same intensity and as a result the total output produced by them increases. With wages remaining constant at the minimum subsistence level, the difference between total output and the subsistence output as a result of technical progress increases and hence the surplus value or rate of exploitation rises.

Technological Progress and Capital Accumulation

But technical progress can be achieved only if there is capital accumulation. As a result, the competition among the capitalists seeking to increase the surplus value forces them to accumulate capital, that is, to make investment. But in the Marxian scheme, as has been pointed out by Kaldor, *capital accumulation or investment activity is not motivated by the lure of profit, but it is the necessity forced on them by the competitive struggle among the capitalists.*

We thus see that as technical progress and capital accumulation proceed apace and capitalist economic system develops, the surplus value extracted from the workers or rate of their exploitation will increase as a result of the competitive struggle among the capitalists. Consequently, with the development of capitalist economic system, the relative share of wages (labour's share) in the national income will fall and the relative share of profits (capitalist's share) will rise. Therefore, the

4 Karl Marx, *Capital,* Vol. I, p. 651. It should be noted that the preference of capitalists for accumulation over consumption of wealth can be said to be true only of the earlier phases of capitalism, it is not true of modern capitalism. Now, with the technical progress the luxury goods such as cars, refrigerators, televisions, washing machines, decorative materials for houses have increasingly become available and modern capitalists spend quite a lot of their profits on these luxury consumer goods. Describing the modern capitalist system, Prof. A.K. Gupta writes. "*The modern capitalist knows how to spend and what to spend on. Far from being the 'puritan' that his ancestors used to be he now indulges conspicuously in luxury consumption*" in *Economics of Austerity,* Oxford University Press, 1975, p. 6.

5 Patterson, *op. cit,* p. 433.

development of the capitalist economy involves the steady worsening of the living conditions of the working classes. This has been called by Marx as **"the immiseration of the proletariat" or "the law of increasing misery of the working classes."** According to this law, technical progress and capital accumulation in a capitalist society and consequently the growth in the national income must lead to the fall in the relative share of wages in the national income and the rise in the relative share of profits.

It is thus clear that about the changes in the relative share with development of the capitalist system Marx reaches a conclusion which is diametrically opposed to the conclusion of Ricardo who thought that with the development of the capitalist economy, relative share of wages will increase and the relative share of profits will decline. Professor Patterson rightly points out that in the Marxian macroeconomic model of income distribution "*the fundamental cause of decline in the relative share of wages is technical progress, the fruits of which entirely go to the owners of the physical instruments of production. The alleged increasing misery of the working class does not come from any decline in the level of real wages, since their 'misery' does not increase in any absolute sense; it is the result instead of the failure of real wages to advance along with gains in productivity. This is the heart of Marx's theory of distribution.*"[6]

Graphic Illustration of Marxian Model of Development

Marxian model of economic development is illustrated in Fig. 20.1 through demand and supply curves of modern economics. It represents the labour-market in the modern capitalist sector. Note that demand curve of labour represents marginal product (*MP*) of labour as more labour is employed. In Fig. 20.1, the vertical axis represents the wage rate in the modern capitalist sector. $\overline{W}$ represents the subsistence level of wages and as per Marx's theory labour-supply curve *LS* is perfectly elastic at this subsistence wage level $\overline{W}$ over a long range of expansion in labour employment. With a given initial stock of capital (K_1), labour demand curve is given by $D_1 D_1$ which cuts labour-supply curve *LS* at point E_1 and determines OL_1 level of labour employment at the subsistence wage level $\overline{W}$. If $\overline{W}R_1$ represents the number of workers seeking employment at the subsistence wage $\overline{W}$, then out of

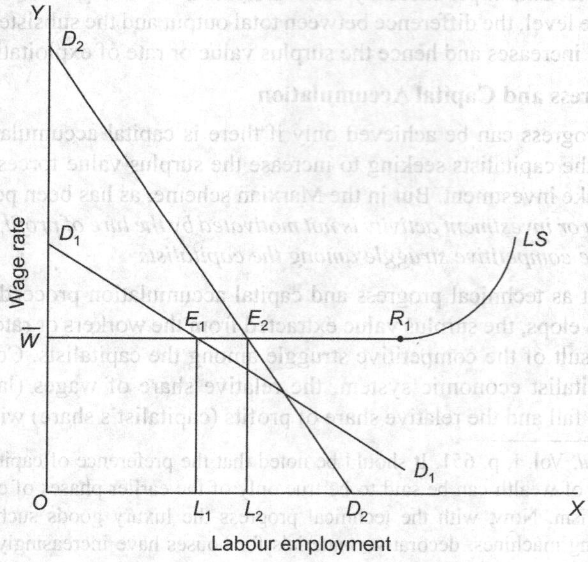

Fig. 20.1. *Marx's model of capitalist development*

6 *Op. cit.*, p. 434.

this, with the given initial capital stock and demand for labour $D_1 D_1$, $\overline{W}E_1$ (= OL_1) will be employed and E_1 R_1 will constitute reserve army of labour (*i.e.,* unemployed workers). The area OL_1 E_1 $\overline{W}$ is total wages earned by workers where $\overline{W}$ E_1 D_1 represents the surplus value extracted by the capitalists from workers. This surplus value will be reinvested. This will promote capital accumulation over time. However, Marxian theory of capital accumulation is not of the type of *capital widening* in which investment is made in the same type of capital goods. In his theory technological progress takes place along with capital accumulation and the *new capital goods or machines in which investment is made embody new and more productive labour-saving technology*. As a result, labour employment grows much slowly than growth of output. In Fig. 20.1 the effect of labour-saving bias of new technology embodied in the new machines or capital goods is represented by the change in labour demand curve to a *more steep curve* D_2 D_2 which cuts the initial labour demand curve D_1 D_1 from above at point E_2 and determines labour employment equal to OL_2. Thus with the use of new capital goods embodying new labour-saving technology while there is a large increase in output from OL_1 E_1 D_1 (= ΣMP_s) with labour employment OL_1 to the output OL_2 E_2 D_2 with labour employment OL_2. On comparing we find that the increase in labour employment is much less than the growth in output.

Thus wage remaining fixed at the subsistence level $\overline{W}$, the capital accumulation embodying labour-saving new and improved technology would create higher surplus value for further investment and growth. Besides, use of labour-saving technology will create unemployment while labour force is growing. As a result, according to Marx, *reserve army of labour will never be exhausted.* Thus Yujiro Hayami and Yoshisa Godo, "Marx envisioned that, with the ability of the modern capitalist productive system to ruin traditional self-employed producers together with the labour-saving bias in industrial technology, *the industrial reserve army will never be exhausted,* high rates of profit and capital accumulation in the capitalist economy are guaranteed by maintenance of low wage rates under the pressure of the ever-existing reserve army."[7]

The process of capitalist development with rapid capital accumulation and use of labour-saving technology necessarily involves rapid increase in income inequalities as in his model wages remain at the subsistence level and technological unemployment prevails on a large scale due to slow growth of employment opportunities. This increasing inequalities will create conflict between the working class and capitalist class. This will, according to Marx, lead to violent revolution in which capitalism will be eliminated and in its place socialism based on public ownership of property will come into existence.

INNER CONTRADICTIONS OF CAPITALISM AND ITS COLLAPSE

Class Struggle and Increasing Misery of the Workers

Though capitalism brings about unprecedented riches and affluence to the Western countries, it also contains, according to Marx, inner contradictions which would ultimately cause its collapse. It is due to the basic inner contradictions that class struggle becomes more intense with the development of capitalist mode of production. Capitalist mode of production, according to Marx, is based upon the exploitation of the working class. As a result, under capitalism there is a clash of interests between the 'haves'—the capitalists— and the 'have-nots'—the proletariat. This gives rise to class struggle between the two. In order to compete successfully with each other, each capitalist tries to raise the surplus value and the rate of exploitation of the workers. He tries to do this by lowering the real wages, increasing the working hours and increasing the intensity of work by the workers. This makes the life of the workers quite miserable. The *increasing misery of the working classes will prompt them to revolt against the capitalist system and ultimately overthrow it through revolution.*

7 Yujiro Hayami and Yoshihisa Godo, *Development Economics* (New Delhi. 2005), Oxford University Press, Third edition, p. 129.

Emergence of Under-Consumption, that is, Over-Production. Another related form of inner contradictions exists in the capitalist mode of production which also causes its downfall. This form of contradiction leads to under-consumption or what is also called over-production, that is, lack of demand for goods which, according to Marx, causes periodic depressions and economic crises. In order to increase the surplus value, capitalists introduce new machines embodying higher technology. This raises, in Marxian terms, the organic composition of capital, which in modern terminology means capital-labour ratio. The rise in capital-labour ratio and the technological displacement of labour in handicrafts as a result of the use of technically superior new machines causes the reserve army of unemployed to increase. This mounting unemployment of labour also enables the capitalists to keep the wages of labour at the bare subsistence level and appropriates all gains in labour productivity. *The low level of employment as well as low wages of labour creates meagre incomes or purchasing power for the workers who constitute a majority in the society. This creates the problem of lack of effective demand for goods or what is called by Marx as under-consumption.* As a result, the goods produced on a mass scale by the capitalists cannot be sold. This results in depression or economic crisis. According to Marx, as the capitalist system gains maturity, these depressions or economic crises will go on increasing in intensity and will ultimately bring about its collapse.

Cut-Throat Competition

It follows from above that Marx attempts to explain how capitalism itself will generate conditions which will bring about its end and replace it by socialism. For a time, he says, capitalism will flourish. The capitalists will become richer and richer, but will at the same time become fewer and fewer, the bigger whale swallowing up the smaller fish on account of the cut-throat competition among them, Production will expand resulting in scramble for markets abroad. This will lead to imperialist wars, one war followed by another and more terrible than the preceding one till capitalism perishes in the conflict through workers overthrowing the system through revolution.

Thus, the law of capitalistic production itself will result in expropriation of the capitalists when capital is centralised. "Along with the constantly diminishing number of the capitalists who usurp and monopolise all gains in production, grows the mass of misery and exploitation of working classes. But with this grows the revolt of the working class, a class which will increase in numbers. The time will come when the monopoly of capital will become a fetter upon the capitalist mode of production. Then the knell of capitalist private property will sound. The expropriators will be expropriated. Colonialism and imperialism can lend only temporary respite by supplying cheap raw materials and market for the manufactured goods. But they will also give rise to colonial and imperialist wars resulting in mutual destruction of the capitalist powers.

Thus, according to Marx, capitalism will collapse on account of the growing conflict between labour and capital. Then a new economic and social order represented by socialism will be established, in which private property will disappear and the State will wither away.

Falling Rate of Profit and Collapse of Capitalism

Although Marx concluded that the *relative share* of profits will increase with the development of capitalistic economic system as a result of technical progress and capital accumulation, he, however, following Ricardo, took the view that with capital accumulation the *rate of profit* will be falling.[8] It should therefore be carefully noted that in view of Marx, whereas *relative share* of profits increases, the *rate of profit* declines as the capitalist economy develops. This looks like a contradiction but Marx

8 Kaldor, *op. cit.*

proved their co-existence.[9] But unlike Ricardo, Marx did not explain the falling rate of profit on the basis of operation of diminishing returns. He explained this tendency of declining rate of profit on the basis of the increase in what he called the *"organic composition of capital"*. Organic composition of capital is the ratio of constant capital (C) to the total capital ($C + V$). Thus organic composition of capital is $\frac{C}{C+V}$. Now, the rate of profit is equal to the ratio of surplus value (S) to the total capital ($C + V$) employed, that is, rate of profit is equal to $\frac{S}{C+V}$.

Let P stand for the rate of profit. We then have the following relationship:

$$P = \frac{S}{C+V}$$

$$P = \frac{S}{V} \cdot \frac{V}{C+V}$$

$\frac{V}{C+V}$ is the ratio of variable capital to the total capital. If we subtract $\frac{C}{C+V}$ from 1, we will get the ratio of variable capital to the total capital $\left(\text{or } \frac{V}{C+V}\right)$ because the total capital is equal to $C + V$. Therefore,

$$P = \frac{S}{V}\left(1 - \frac{C}{C+V}\right)$$

where $\frac{C}{C+V}$ is organic composition of capital.

From the above equation it follows that if the S/V (the rate of exploitation) remains constant, the rate of profit will decline if $\frac{C}{C+V}$, *i.e.*, organic composition of capital increases. Thus while bolding that relative share of profits will increase, Marx also took the stand that the rate of profit will decline in the capitalist economy as a result of capital accumulation and consequent increase in the organic composition of capital. In the modern terminology we can say that Marx was of the view that as more capital is accumulated and capital-output ratio rises in the productive processes or, in other words, as more capital-intensive production techniques are employed, the rate of profit will fall.

CRITICAL EVALUATION OF THE MARXIAN ANALYSIS OF CAPITALISM

Marxian theory has been criticised on several grounds. Marx has proved to be a bad prophet. Predictions which he made on the basis of his theory have not come true and the actual events have not taken the Marxian line. Marx had predicted that relative share of wages in the national income would fall and the economic conditions of the workers would deteriorate. All this has not come true. Empirical research has found that share of wages in the national income has remained constant in the Western capitalist countries instead of falling as predicted by Marx. The workers have obtained a due share from the increases in physical productivities brought about by the technical progress and capital accumulation in the capitalist countries. As a result, in absolute terms the living conditions of the workers have greatly improved so that they have now become less revolutionary.

Besides, there has not been found any tendency for the falling rate of profit. On the basis of the falling rate of profit and the concentration of purchasing power in the hands of the few, Marx predicted that the capitalist economies would have periodic crises and ultimately the system would

9 It has been pointed by several authors that falling rate of profit does not necessarily follow from Marxian theory but Marx definitely held the view and tried to prove that there was a tendency of the falling rate of profit. Moreover, Marx employed this tendency of falling rate of profit to explain the ultimate collapse of the capitalist system.

collapse. Actual events have falsified this gloomy forecast of Marx. Of course, there has been trade cycles in these economies but in spite of these short-run fluctuations capitalist economies have made phenomenal progress in the last 200 years or so, so that they have now become affluent countries. Prof, Patterson rightly remarks, "*Marx thought the capitalistic system would be increasingly wrecked by crises of greater and greater severity until finally it would collapse amid an uprising of the working class that would usher in the era of Communism. Marx proved to be a bad prophet concerning not only the behaviour of the wage share in the national income, but also the long-term development of capitalism.*[10]

Further, there is a great theoretical flaw in Marx's contention of falling rate of profit with the increase in organic composition of capital. Several authors[11] have pointed out that law of the falling rate of profit cannot really be derived from the law of the increasing organic composition of capital. Since Marx believes that the real wages of the workers remain fixed at the subsistence level, then as a result of increase in organic composition of capital due to capital accumulation and technical progress, the output per head will greatly increase and, given the real wages constant at the subsistence level, the surplus value (*i.e.,* the profits) earned by the capitalists will greatly increase and will secure a rising rate of profit.

Lastly, Marx's theory of income distribution under capitalism is based upon the labour theory of value which is not acceptable to the modern economists. Marx's analysis of surplus value or exploitation of labour is directly based upon his contention that all value is created by labour and capital merely transfers his own value to the value of the commodity. Capital adds greatly to the productivity of the process and does create a good deal of value. To deny this is to show one's prejudice. Therefore, Marx's thesis that value of a commodity is determined by the necessary labour time required to produce it is quite obsolete and not acceptable to the modern economists. Thus when labour theory of value is wrong, the theory of surplus value and exploitation based upon it falls to the ground.

One of the successful predictions of Marx was that the process of capitalist development leads to the increase in inequalities of income distribution and concentration of wealth in few hands. As seen above, incomes of workers are reduced relative to the profits made by the capitalists by the use of the labour-saving nature of new technology in the modern industrial sector. This is borne out by the experience of developing countries like India where ever since the initiation of economic reforms based on the Washington Consensus of liberalisation, privatisation and globalisation, income inequalities have greatly risen. Where the rich have become very rich, the reduction in poverty is far less. In developing countries where trade movement is weak, labour is ruthlessly exploited.

Besides, it goes to the credit of Marx by pointing out in his model that capital accumulation and technological improvement are drivers of economic growth. While classical economists emphasised rapid capital accumulation for accelerating economic growth, they underestimated the role of technological progress in sustaining economic growth. Marx, on the other band, laid stress on both capital accumulation and technological progress in determining growth of output. In fact, as explained above, Marx visualised the accumulation of new capital goods (*i.e.,* machines) embodying new improved technology. This is highly relevant for developing countries which aim at accelerating economic growth. However, for generation of adequate employments opportunities, efforts should be made that the new technology used is *labour-using* rather than *labour-displacing.*

Further, Marx's model gives an important insight into the problem of unemployment faced by developing countries (including India). The developing countries like India have achieved rapid industrial growth through large increase in capital accumulation but growth of labour employment in the modern industrial sector has been very slow while, on the other band, increase in labour force has been high due to rapid population growth. This can be explained by Marx's view of the use of labour-saving technological change which lowers the employment potential of capital accumulation. Thus,

10 Patterson, *op. cit.*, p. 435.

11 Joan Robinson, *An Essay in Marxian Economics,* pp. 75-82, and N. Kaldor, *Alternative Theories of Distribution.*

Hayami and Godo write: "Many developing economies have attempted to achieve rapid development by concentrating investment in the modern industrial sector. In some cases significant success in the growth of industrial production has been recorded. However, increases in employment have typically been much slower than output growth owing to concentration of investment in modern machinery and equipment embodying labour-saving technologies developed in high-income countries. On the other hand, the rate of increase in the labour force has been high under explosive population growth. Where labour absorption in agriculture reaches its saturation point under the rapidly closing land frontiers, labour tends to be pushed from rural to urban areas. The swollen urban population beyond limited employment in the modern industrial sector of high capital intensity has accumulated as lumpen proletariat in urban slums."[12]

A shortcoming of Marx's model is that he neglected the possibility of food shortage or lack of wage goods leading to the increase in cost of living of the people causing rise in wage rate. At the higher wage rate demand for labour will decline. Marx's neglect of food problem or wage goods availability has been explained by some by pointing out that Marx was primarily dealing with England which could get cheap supply of food and raw materials from overseas. But this cannot be the case of present-day developing countries in which supply of wage goods acts as a constraint on the industrial growth.

It is evident from above that despite several shortcomings in Marx's model, especially the fall in profit rate due to rise increase in organic composition of capital (*i.e.,* rise in capital-labour ratio), Marx provided important insights into the growth of the capitalist economy which is generally called these days free market economy. Besides, it is Marx who brings out the contradiction in the capitalistic system, *viz.,* reduction in labour costs, which is intended to raise profits, reduces workers' consumption and lowers the rate of profit. "Technological progress is a treadmill for capitalists—they must run faster just to stand still for technological progress must always keep one step ahead of the rate of capital accumulation."[13] Marx emphasised the *rate* of profit and not the *level* of profits, as determining the capitalists' investment.

Marx also fully appreciated the capacity of the capitalist system for economic development. Schumpeter says: "Nobody had then a fuller conception of the size and power of the capitalist engine for the future...Marx said repeatedly that it was the historical task and privilege of capitalist society to create a productive apparatus that will be adequate for the requirements of a higher form of human civilisation."[14] Though Marx predicted that increasing misery of workers and consequent social upheaval will result in collapse of the capitalist system but, according to him, this would occur only after a good deal of economic development had been achieved.

RELEVANCE OF MARXIAN THEORY OF CAPITALIST DEVELOPMENT FOR DEVELOPING COUNTRIES

The Marxian model is reflective of the socio-economic conditions following industrial revolution in Europe. He saw in capitalistic order the seeds of its own doom and suggested the course it was bound to adopt. At the outset it needs to be pointed out that the parameters in the growth models of earlier writers become the dependent variables in the Marxian framework. The cultural, political and social institutions were regarded as given by the earlier writers. But Marx conceived them as superstructures determined by the *methods of production.* The socio-economic and political conditions are regarded by him as reflective of the forces of production. They in course of time generate tensions and contradictions which ultimately give way to revolution. The post-revolution institutions and attitudes, then, reflect the new conditions of production.

12 Y. Hayami and Y. Godo, *op. cit.* p. 130.

13 Benjamin Higgins, *Economic Development: Principles, Problems and Policies,* 1961, p. 116.

14 Joseph Schumpeter, *History of Economic Analysis,* p. 537.

Marx, in his sole preoccupation and enthusiasm about the socialistic revolution in the system of production that obtained in the European countries in his times, failed to pay much attention to the problems of economic development of the developing countries. In this regard Alfred Bonne remarks that "Apart from a few allusions remarkable for their determinist note with regard to obtaining prospects for economic development in regions like Western Asia or India, no special attention is given to the problems of change in underdeveloped countries."[15]

The Marxian concept of under-consumption *prima facie* appears to have relevance to the conditions prevailing in the developing economies. With the prevalence of low levels of consumption in the developing economies, one is likely to think that the Marxian conviction of crisis in industrial economy applies to the problems of these countries as well. But this is not correct. The main cause of under-consumption in a capitalist economy in the Marxian sense is attributable to the developed system of capitalistic productive forces and the limited purchasing power of the working class. On the other hand, under-consumption in case of underdeveloped economies refers to nutritional standards below which consumption levels have fallen in these countries. The low level of productive capacity stands in the way of the consumption level of the people in these countries. Such an under-consumption arises mainly due to the low levels of output arising from the underdeveloped productive potential. In contrast, the level of this potential is highly developed in case of capitalist production.

In the same way, Marxian notion of an industrial reserve army does not represent a true picture of the surplus labour in the underdeveloped economies. According to him, the root cause of a reserve army was the introduction of technological improvements or the slow pace of capital accumulation. In developing economies the surplus labour assumes the nature of disguised underemployment, which is mainly attributable to socio-demographic factors such as traditions of work-sharing by joint family structural obstacles, falling mortality rate, etc. The system of extended joint families keeps the rural masses tied to their farms and obstructs the movement of disguisedly underemployed to industrial employments.

As such, genesis of disguised employment does not lie in technological innovations or a decline in profits due to rise in wages above the subsistence level as is assumed by Marx for the creation of his 'reserve army'. In this context Marxism fails to offer any solution to this labour surplus problem which has assumed serious proportions in many developing economies.

According to Marx, capitalistic development involved two important characteristics, *viz.*, accumulation of capital and technological improvement. Stagnating underdeveloped economies, he contends, result from the absence of both of these factors. However, it is now well known that this dual criteria—endless capital accumulation and technological change—does not apply to the presently stagnating economies. They operate on entirely different lines than what Marx envisaged for them. They have a social system which is tradition-ridden, lack in technical skill and entrepreneurial ability, possess inefficient administration and are bogged down by immobility of factors of production and structural imbalances. The Marxian analysis in its entirety cannot, therefore, be transplanted to developing economies. A separate analytical scaffolding and policy framework is required to solve their problems.

To say all this is not to completely belittle Marxian theory in so far as its relevance to developing countries is concerned. There are, in fact, certain features of developing economies that closely approximate the conditions that Marx predicted for advanced countries.[16] They may provide certain threads of relevance of his theory to these economies, provided, of course, that they are viewed in a somewhat different setting. For instance, the existence of wage levels close to the subsistence margin resulting in excessive exploitation of labour, the sharply defined class structure with increasing income inequalities and the evidence of increasing misery in some cases are a pointer towards the need for employing a development strategy that is more *inclusive*.

15 Alfred Bonne, *Studies in Economic Development*, p. 245.

16 B. Higgins, *Economics of Development*, pp. 120-121.

However, in reality the increasing awareness of such conditions in the developing countries has resulted not in the pure Marxian socialism but a greater role of State in economic development. In an increasing number of developing countries, the State has come to play a more active role in the economic affairs. Many of them have adopted the system of mixed economies. The State has increasingly stepped in to regulate the wages and conditions of workers. The income inequalities have also been sought to be reduced through land ceilings, taxation and other suitable means.

Above all, in his attempt at discovering the laws of motion of capitalism, Marx provided a theoretical construct known as the *'Departmental Schema'* which is as significant and valid to the developing countries embarking upon the path of planned economic development as it was for market-oriented capitalistic economies. In fact, the applicability of Marxian Departmental Schema has assumed special relevance and significance for the developing economies of today in view of their aspirations to develop themselves and attain maximum welfare in a relatively short span of time.

The crucial problem in the developing countries is the transformation of the *'potential economic surplus'* into an *'actual economic surplus'* and its acceleration.[17] Marxian idea of departmentalisation of the economy into two sectors (*i.e.,* capital-goods sector and the consumer-goods sector) is helpful in achieving this end more quickly. By adopting a classification of Department I and Department II, it gives, in fact, a method of inter-industry transformation. It is generic in application, being applicable to underdeveloped and developing countries alike.

Marx categorises the economy into two departments : Department I (capital-goods sector) and Department II (consumer-goods). Representing the constant capital being employed in Department I and Department II by C_1 and C_2 respectively; the variable capital by V_1 and V_2; the corresponding surplus values by S_1 and S_2 and the values of the two Departments by W_1 and W_2, he states the following formula for describing the total production in each Department:

$$C_1 + V_1 + S_1 = W_1 \quad \text{...(1)}$$

$$C_2 + V_2 + S_2 = W_2 \quad \text{...(2)}$$

For *Simple Reproduction, i.e.,* for merely keeping the growth rate of the economy at a constant level with the same stock of capital year after year, Marx points out that the total amount of constant capital used up, *i.e.,* $(C_1 + C_2)$ must be equal to the total output of the Department I, *i.e.,* $(C_1 + V_1 + S_1)$. And the total consumption (both of workers and the capitalists) must be equal to the total output of the Department II $(C_2 + V_2 + S_2)$.

For economic growth to pick up speed, it is necessary that the Department I should be so rearranged as to become a source of high-yielding economic surplus. This accordingly calls for structural and technological reorganisation. The institutional factors that hinder reinvestment of profits and hence capital accumulation have to be thrashed out quickly. The economic transformation of Department II to make it a surplus-yielding sector involves a still more difficult task to be accomplished. Perhaps the most important and desired step in this direction would be the implementation of a planned programme of land reforms with a view to provide land to the tiller. This has to be achieved through an appropriate system of land ceilings and the redistribution of the surplus land above the maximum fixed limit in the shortest possible time. Though in the initial years of planning in India, great importance was given to the land reforms laws regarding ceiling on land holdings and reforms in the tenancy system, but unfortunately in the present emphasis on privatisation and liberalisation no actions have been taken to implement them.

---

17 Baran, P. A., *Political Economy of Growth,* London, p. 57. He defines *'potential economic surplus'* as the difference between output that could be produced in a given natural and technical conditions and the essential consumption. On the other hand, *'actual economic surplus'*, according to him, is the difference between the economy's *actual output* and its *actual current consumption.*

Such a programme is expected to go a long way in increasing production by allowing an intensification of agricultural operations, reducing disguised unemployment, increasing employment opportunities, better and more effective utilization of the limited State funds for agricultural development, elimination of middlemen, and the promotion of cooperative and joint systems of farming.

In this way the elasticity of accumulation in relation to agricultural incomes can be considerably increased, thus putting the subsistence sector on a surplus-yielding path. In essence, it means transformation of sector I into II, and this implies the rendering of less developed economies to an increasing application of Marxian '*Departmental Schema*'. Thus, we find the adoption of the Marxian '*Departmental Schema*' with a view to reorganise the Department I and the transformation of Department II would greatly facilitate and quicken the pace of transformation of a primitive, stagnant and exploitative system into a more progressive and dynamic one. It may be noted that in the developing economies Department I has to play the most crucial role. The pace of economic development is governed by the surplus generated by Department I. A high magnitude of such a surplus over and above the replacement needs of the economy is necessary for the realisation of an accelerated economic growth.

In fact, the planning bodies of the various underdeveloped countries such as India, Burma, Ghana and U.A.R. have been greatly influenced in their plan formulation by the Marxian '*Departmental Schema*'. The Mahalanobis model of growth which formed the basis of India's Second Five Year Plan employed a growth strategy based basically on the Marxian '*Departmental Schema*'. In consonance with the Marxian '*Departmental Schema*', it emphasised the growth of producer-goods sector (*i.e.,* Department I) in relation to the consumer-goods sector (*i.e.,* Department II); the need of a greater role of government in matters of basic allocation decisions in order to regulate private and public sectors; the urgency of making investment decisions to increase their social effectiveness, adoption of necessary organisational and structural changes and the necessity of long-term planning to achieve sustained growth.

Hence, we find that the Marxian formulation of *Departmental Schema* is of pivotal importance to the developing economies struggling to generate surplus for economic development. The undeniable practical significance of this Schema lies in the fact that it paves the way for realisation of the twin objectives of providing simultaneously for a high rate of growth as well as employment in the developing economies. The applicability of Marxian Schema to the underdeveloped countries also highlights the urgency for the institutional and technological transformation with due emphasis on the development of Department I—*i.e.,* the sector producing the mother of the means of production for the long-run substained growth.

CHAPTER 21

SCHUMPETER'S THEORY OF DEVELOPMENT

Schumpeter's Production Function

Schumpeter's theory of development assigns paramount role to the entrepreneur and innovations introduced by him in the process of economic development. According to Schumpeter, the process of production is marked by a combination of material and immaterial productive forces. The material productive forces arise from the original factors of production, *viz*., land and labour, etc., while the immaterial set of productive forces are conditioned by the '*technical facts*' and '*facts of social organization*'. The Schumpeterian production function can, therefore, be written as

$$Q = f(k, r, l, u, v) \qquad ...(1)$$

where Q stands for the output, k for the Schumpeterian concept of "produced means of production", r for natural resources, l for the employed labour force. The symbol u represents the society's fund of technical knowledge and v represents the facts of social organization, *i.e*., the socio-cultural milieu within which the economy operates.

The above function shows that the rate of growth of the output depends upon the rate of growth of productive factors, the rate of growth of technology and the rate of growth of investment friendly socio-cultural environment. Schempeter held that the alterations in the supply of productive factors can only bring about gradual, continuous and slow evolution of the economic system. On the other hand, the impact of technological and social change call for spontaneous, discontinuous change in the channels of output flow. Thus taking into account these two types of distinct influences Schumpeter distinguished two components in the dynamic evolution of the economy : (*a*) the "*growth component*" which brings about gradual, continuous and slow evolution due to the changes in the factor availability, (*b*) *the* "*development component*" which brings about spontaneous and discontinuous change in the channels of output flow due to changes in the technical and social environments.

Schumpeter regarded land to be constant. The growth component will, therefore, include only the effects of changes in population and of increase in the producer goods. But Schumpeter further maintains that there does not exist any *a priori* relationship between the changes in population and the changes in the flow of goods and services. In other words, Schumpeter considers the population growth to be exogenously determined. Now, the *increase in producer goods results from a positive rate of net savings*.

The *major part of savings and accumulations are attributed by Schumpeter to profits*. But, according to him, the profits can arise if innovations such as new techniques of production are employed or if new product is introduced. Hence ultimately it is the change in the technical knowledge (*i.e*., variable u) which is responsible for any change in the stock of producer goods, *i.e*., the rate of capital accumulation directly depends on the rate of technical change.

Regarding the historical development, *Schumpeter subscribed to Marx's mateialistic interpretation of history* and he maintained that the economic state of people emerges only from the preceding total situation. However, the most important point of Schumpeter's theory is that the expansion of output depends upon the history of technological development. In simple words, we can say, according to Schumpeter, *the growth of output is geared to the rate of innovations*. No doubt, Schumpeter holds that the trend of economic growth shall be fixed by the exogenous variable of population growth, yet according to him, the process of economic development is synonymous with discontinuous technical change, *i.e.*, innovations. *The agent which brings about innovations is called by Schumpeter as entrepreneur*. Thus, entrepreneur becomes the pivot of Schumpeter's model.

Role of Entrepreneur as an Innovator

In economic development as outlined by Schumpeter, the entrepreneur plays a key role. The credit for innovations and the outburst of economic activity goes entirely to the entrepreneur. Innovation consists in (*i*) *introduction of a new good, (ii) introduction of a new method of production, (iii) the opening of a new market, (iv) the discovery of a new source of supply of raw materials or semi-manufactured goods, and (v) introduction of a new organisation in an industry*.

In a world characterised by a high degree of risk and uncertainty, only businessmen of exceptional ability and daring will be able to undertake innovations and launch enterprises and exploit opportunities for profit. But *these entrepreneurs are not only lured by profit but are also motivated with a desire to found a dynasty in the business world or a desire for conquests in the competitive world or have the joy of creating*. Thus, in the Schumpeterian analysis, the role of the entrepreneur is a determining factor of the rate of economic growth. In his absence the growth rate is bound to be slow.

The supply of entrepreneurs depends not only on the rate of profits (which is obvious) but also on the favourable social climate. They will appear and continue only in a society which honours them, where prestige is attached to them and the social rewards or recognition they are able to earn. In short, the conditions or social values in which they have to operate must be favourable. *The rate of profit is an unfailing thermometer of the favourable climate. Any tendency to squeeze profits, increase taxes, intensify welfare programmes, strengthening of the trade union movement or measures of redistribution of income will deteriorate the climate for investment and so for economic development*.

Development Cycle: The Circular Flow and the Process of Creative Destruction

Schumpeter's starting point in the "circular flow" is a stationary equilibrium in which there is no investment, population growth is at a standstill position and there is full employment. But there are numerous opportunities in business which the entrepreneurs are quick to exploit and innovations are undertaken. The success of the original innovators attracts 'swarmlike' many others who follow them. Economic activity becomes more and more brisk and the boom gathers momentum with the result that prices and money incomes rise. There is then the secondary economic wave '*imitative investment*' superimposed upon the earlier one, *i.e.*, '*innovational investment*'.

But soon follows the process of *creative destruction*. The boom gives way to slump or recession. Completion of innovations brings in a large supply of goods which cannot be marketed at profitable price. There are forced bankruptcies since the banks call back loans. The repayment of bank loans accentuates deflationary forces. Business risks scare away the prospective entrepreneurs. In this unfavourable climate, the innovational activity comes to a halt. After this painful process of adjustment in which weak enterprises are liquidated, the businessmen find conditions again ripe for a further spurt of entrepreneurial activity. The economic activity is resumed at a higher equilibrium. This is how the circle of development process is completed. There is a new wave of innovations and the development cycle repeats itself.

Role of Credit

Another new point introduced by Schumpeter in this analysis of economic development is the important role that credit plays in economic development. It is not the saving out of current income which supplies funds for investment, but the credit creation by the banking system. The classical and the neoclassical economists thought in terms of given supply of money or the supply coming forth to match the increased supply of goods and services, so that the price level is not affected. To them "money is a mere veil which tends to hide the behaviour of the basic forces at work". *But Schumpeter makes credit creation an integral part of the development. process.* In this analysis the entrepreneurs expand their business merely by borrowing from banks who will lend not because some persons have made savings and deposited in the banks. But the banks just create credit themselves to accommodate the business borrowers. This pushes up the prices. "*Thus credit-creating facilities tend to free investors from the voluntary abstinence routine of the savers. Forced savings become an important means of capital accumulation.*"[1]

Two points are worth mentioning in regard to Schumpeter's analysis of development process in a capitalist society. In the first place, the *dominance of the entrepreneur or the producer limits and reduces correspondingly the sovereignty of the consumer*. The producer does not passively produce the goods as dictated by consumers' tastes and preferences. By his dynamic role, through high pressure of salesmanship, he attempts and succeeds farily in changing even the tastes of consumers or in creating in them new wants and desires. This again emphasises the crucial role of the entrepreneur in giving new directions and dimensions to the development process. Secondly, unlike the neoclassical economists who believed that the process of economic development was gradual and harmonious, *Schumpeterian analysis brings out the uneven and disharmonious nature of economic growth*. It proceeds by spurts and leaps and bounds. "*The essence of development is a discontinuous disturbance of the circular flow*." This disturbance appears in the form of innovations. This arises from the fact that the world is dynamic and not static. In the static world rational calculations are possible and reasonable forecasting is feasible, but the dynamic world is full of risk and uncertainty mainly arising from the innovational activity of the entrepreneur who is able to exploit new investment horizons.

Capitalism: Its Potentialities and its Degeneration

The classical economists were depressed by the inexorable law of diminishing returns and the irresistible growth of population. Schumpeter does not share their pessimism. He also does not believe in the inherent tendency towards a maldistribution of incomes resulting in ever-recurring severe crises as Marx did. Nor does he agree with the stagnationists that there is persistent lack of investment opportunities together with institutional rigidities making for an equilibrium at less than full employment. *Schumpeter, on the other hand, has faith in the capacity of the capitalist system in attaining ever increasing levels of national output and income. He is prepared to admit, however, that there might be temporary setbacks.*

Although Schumpeter has infinite faith in the potentialities of capitalism, but he also believes in a Marxian fashion that the very success of capitalism will breed the germs of its ultimate degeneration which will pave the way for socialism. In Schumpeter's view, it is not failure of capitalism which will spell its doom, but its very success that would result in killing the goose that lays the golden egg. He thus says: "*The actual and prospective performance of the capitalist system is such as to negative the idea of its break-down under the weight of economic failure, but ... its very success undermines the social institutions which protect it, and inevitably create conditions in which it will not be able to live and which strongly point to socialism as the heir apparent.*"[2] In other words, it is not the economic barriers but social factors which will undermine capitalism.

1. Meier and Baldwin, *Economic Development* D, 1966, pp. 90-91.
2. Joseph Schumpeter, *Theory of Economic Development*, p. 64.

According to Schumpeter, the economic and social foundations of capitalism will crumble on account of (*a*) the decay of the entrepreneurial function, (*b*) the destruction of the institutional framework, and (*c*) the distintegration of the protecting political framework. The entrepreneurs make their business grow so big that innovation itself becomes a routine and is in the charge of salaried persons and technological progress now becomes the province of specialists; marketing and administration become automatic. "*Innovation thus degenerates into a depersonalised routine activity carried on in big business through a bureaucracy of highly trained managers.*"

This is how the entrepreneurial function is rendered obsolete. *The concentration of business and the growth of monopolies destroy the institution of private property and freedom of contract.* Whereas 'bigness' contributes to more rapid economic progress, it also weakens the concepts of private property and freedom of contract. In a big business corporation, the proprietary interest is replaced by shareholders, big and small, none of whom is particularly interested in the business. The part that the proprietor used to play is now played by professional salaried managers.

The social class that used to protect capitalism also loses its political power which is captured by a new group of politicians who are ill-equipped to rule and unwilling to support the established trade and industry. They adopt policies inimical to capitalists' interest. This is what we are witnessing in India. The common people and many politicians are now positively hostile to big business like the Birlas, Tatas and Ambanis. The intellectuals who derived freedom and power from capitalism now lead the anti-capitalist groups. The educated unemployed is another group of 'have-nots' against the capitalist class of 'haves'. Labour also organises itself for fight against capital and the intellectuals supply the leadership. All these new forces lead to the gradual degeneration of capitalism and strengthen the movement towards socialism. Capitalism cannot function in this new atmosphere.

Apart from differences in emphasis, three major differences may be noted between the Classical School of Marx and the Schumpeterian analysis: (*a*) *Schumpeter introduces interest rate as a determinant of savings which is an important factor in economic development*; (*b*) *He separates the autonomous investment from the induced investment and emphasises innovations as the factor affecting autonomous investment; and* (*c*) *He regards entrepreneurship as the vital force which shapes an economy.*

Evaluation of Schumpeter's Theory of Development

Schumpeter has been a great 'theorist' whose writings contain brilliant thoughts and a deep insight into the working of an economy. However, his analysis of the entrepreneurial innovations is not applicable to modern conditions in which the act of invention and innovation is carried on not by individual entrepreneurs but by large corporations as a routine affair. It is not possible to identify entrepreneurs who introduced many actual innovations. He himself recognises the tendency towards obsolescence of the entrepreneur.

It has been pointed out by critics that *what Schumpeter gives is the theory of business cycles and not an analysis of economic development*. Even Schumpeter's analysis of business cycles can be accepted only with some modifications to suit modern economic conditions. *According to Shumpeter, crisis in capitalism is brought about by maladjustment caused by waves of innovations*. But big businesses in modern times can absorb these waves and produce steadier and larger expansion of the total output. Further, the main cause of business cycles is fluctuations in aggregate demand as pointed out by J.M. Keynes.

The assumption that innovations are financed by borrowing from credit creation by the banks is also not very realistic. It is a well-known fact that most of the bank loans are short-term loans whereas the implementation of innovations requires long-term finances. *The long-term projects are financed by retained profits or by the issue of shares and debentures by the companies concerned.*

Schumpeter's socio-economic analysis of the capitalist process is also not fully convincing. He seems to overemphasise the influence of economic factors on social culture. It is not one-way link between rationalism in economic matters and rationalism in other fields, social and political. Not many would agree that capitalism was about to crumble and socialism was round the corner. Capitalism in countries like the U.K. and the U.S.A. which were its traditional homes too strongly established themselves to yield place to socialism. Only, we can say with him that the nature of capitalism has changed. There is no doubt that the political strata protecting the old type capitalism are weakening and the traditional entrepreneurship too is becoming obsolete, as Schumpeter said. But it does not mean that capitalism is about to collapse and socialism is coming. On the contrary, it is socialism that collapsed in eighties of the 20th century. In both Soviet Russia and Republic of China socialism came to end and in its place free-market economy came into existence. Meier and Baldwin rightly write: "Although Schumpeter's analysis is provocative, it seems one-sided and overemphasised. To recognise that history involves perpetual change is quite different from concluding that a socialist form of society will emerge from an equally inevitable decomposition of capitalist society."[3]

Relevance of Schumpeter's Theory for Developing Countries

The conditions obtaining in Western Europe and America after the First World War presented a capitalist system in full swing, wherein the innovator acted as the initiator and controller of economic development. Schumpeter's observant eye got the clue to formulate a theory of development presenting a unified view of the whole economic process. Schumpeter viewed "development" as a distinct phenomenon which, he says, "is spontaneous and discontinuous change in the channels of flow, disturbance of equilibrium, which forever alters and displaces the equilibrium state previously existing."[4] This springs from changes in the economic life due to endogenous factors (initiated from within) and not exogenous factors which are forced upon it. Explaining his contention further, he holds that "Should it turn out that there are no such changes arising in the economic system itself, and that the phenomenon that we call economic development is in practice simply founded upon the fact that the data change and the economy continuously adapts itself to them, then we should say that there is no economic development."[5] This concept wherein endogenous changes in the economy act as the sole *prime mobile* of development restricts the relevance of Schumpeter's theory to the growth problems of developing economies.

Rigid and outmoded socio-economic institutions, low saving potential and laggard technology are completely incapable to generate developmental impulses from "within" in the underdeveloped countries. They have to take recourse to imported capital, technology and skill to initiate and propel their developmental wheels. For instance, India made a big stride forward in growth and it has sought foreign capital to help in its economic development. It has also gone for foreign collaboration in terms of loan, equipment, skill and technical know-how. Since factors from 'without' are responsible for initiating and operating development projects, they cannot, according to Schumpeter, be regarded as embodiments of India's genuine process of economic development. This contention of Schumpeter is unsustainable and unconvincing.

It cannot be gainsaid that every such plant has generated a developmental wave in the Indian Economy. Thus, Alfred Bonne remarks, "Exclusion from Schumpeter's definition would not make the new plant cease to be a case of development, having in view precisely those goods which are the essential objectives of development activities in economically backward countries."[6] In this view, therefore, Schumpeter's theory of development is incongruent with the conditions prevailing in the developing world.

3 Meier and Baldwin, *op. cit.*, p. 101.
4 J. A. Schumpeter, *The Theory of Economic Development*.
5 *Ibid.*, p. 63.
6 Alfred Bonne, *op. cit.*, p. 250.

Further, Schumpeter's preoccupation with only the endogenous factors and his insistence on development as embodying only the spontaneous and discontinuous changes makes him oblivious of the role of population growth as an economic force in the developmental process. He regarded population as exogenously determined and held that there does not exist any deterministic *a priori* relationship between population growth and variations in the flow of goods and services. But it is precisely the excessive population pressure that is responsible for revolutionising the methods and techniques of agricultural production in the presently overpopulated developing countries. In fact, some of the post-Keynesian theories regard population growth as a stimulant for autonomous investment. By failing to take proper cognisance of one of the most vital phenomena operating in the presently underdeveloped economies, Schumpeter rendered his theory almost ineffectual to such countries.

Further, the existence of a business elite, *i.e.*, the entrepreneurial class, is fundamental to Schumpeter's theory of economic development. The carrying out of innovations and using new production functions is the prerogative of this elite group of private entrepreneurs. However, there are serious doubts about the effectiveness of this social group in the development of the developing countries. The contemporary history of economic development of these countries provides ample evidence to reveal that it is not only the private entrepreneurial class, but also the national governments that are responsible for preparing and launching programmes of industrialisation.

With the development process of these countries being rapidly imbued with the socialistic hues, their governments have increasingly assumed the role of a national entrepreneur. Not the innovations of the private entrepreneur but the "government action and mass impulses today seem to be the most characteristic motive forces of economic development."[7] So much so that even in the private sector of these economies the entrepreneurs cannot fulfil their functions without the active and substantial assistance from the government and semi-public bodies. Moved by such an un-Schumpeterian economic landscape in the developing countries, Prof. Gunnar Myrdal remarks that "it represents, indeed, an attempt at a complete reversal of what once happened in the now developed countries as described by the Schumpeterian model."[8]

In developing economies, a number of factors such as the outmoded socio-economic institutional framework, tradition-ridden investment horizon and unreliable attitude for undertaking of new ventures, have all contributed in denigrating the pivotal role assigned to the Schumpeterian entrepreneur in his functional aspects. The governments of these countries under such conditions cannot afford to remain an idle and passive spectator. It is incumbent for them to come forward and become the herald of industrialization by playing the role of a unified national entrepreneur.

Furthermore, the governments of the developing countries are committed to the rapid creation of '*social overheads*' or what is now called *infrastructure* in order to fulfil the popular demand for higher standards of living. The private capital fails to come forward because of the lumpy nature of such investments and the long gestation periods involved. On the other hand, an agency like the government has sufficient means to mobilize the capital resources of the economy through various fiscal and monetary measures and by borrowing from abroad. The very exigency of the situation in the developing economies compel their governments to shoulder the responsibility of initiating and steering the gigantic task of economic development. Thus, the Schumpeterian model of development which assigns the primary and central role to the private entrepreneur and only a secondary and passive function for the government is a misfit to the conditions obtaining in the developing countries.

---

7 Henry C. Wallich, "Some Notes Towards A Theory of Derived Development," in Aggarwal and Singh (ed.), *op. cit.* pp. 193-202.

8 Gunnar Myrdal, *Economic Theory and Underdeveloped Region*, London, 1957, p. 80.

Besides, the entrepreneurial innovation so pivotal to the working of Schumpeter's model has no significance to the process of development in the developing countries. Henry C. Wallich[9] and H.W. Singer[10] have held that due to the *demonstration effect* on an international plane, the businessmen in the developing countries are prone to import and assimilate the already known technology and methods of production from the developed countries rather than undergo the risks of innovating anew (some of which in any case may prove to be abortive). Hence the development process in the developing countries is increasingly becoming a process of *derived development*, being based on assimilation of existing innovations made elsewhere rather than on the Schumpeterian type of indigenous innovations.

In the Schumpeterian model, by its very nature and approach, inflationary pressures are bound to operate as the development process gathers momentum. The entrepreneurs' innovational activity being financed by the credit-creating banking system, credit-creation assumes a vital role in his model. The creation of credit leads to a rise in purchasing power of the community without a corresponding increase in production. Increased purchasing power results in an increased demand for production services and consumer goods. The increased demand coupled with the increased volume of money in circulation results in a general price rise.

But in the consumption-oriented development process of a developing economy, the inflationary tendencies are very powerful, persistent and cumulative in nature. "It is not only development and associated investment that are responsible for inflationary tendencies, but the entire social climate of demand-oriented economy."[11] They become a serious drag on the development process itself. Thus, the production-oriented Schumpeterian vision of development process fails to realise the hurdles like secular inflation that characterise the consumption-oriented development of the developing economies. What in fact is needed is a totally different framework of analysis and theory that is realistic to the circumstances of these economies.

However, certain aspects of Schumpeter's model retain universality of application. Irrespective of the type of economy and its stage of development, the importance of innovations as one of the major factors in economic development remains unassailable. 'Technological possibilities are an uncharted sea', and in this Apollo age, we can safely assume that the developing countries can hardly afford to remain mere imitators and assimilators. Even if mere transfer of ready-made and proven techniques of production is sought, there remains the problem of adaptation of foreign technology in the domestic economy. It calls for a certain amount of pioneering spirit and entrepreneurial skill in so far it is new to the country in which it is to be adapted. Further, the risks of transplanting such technology in underdeveloped economics would be considerable. Hence the entrepreneurs in these countries should possess at least some of the basic qualities of the Schumpeterian entrepreneur.[12]

From the point of view of successful development in developing countries Schumpeter's theory highlights the urgency of bringing about drastic transformation of the tradition-ridden socio-economic institutions and reshaping of the inimical attitudes to develop a favourable climate for the growth of entrepreneurship. Adequate entrepreneurship is one of the prerequisites for sparking off a take-off stage in these countries.

Further, once the process of industrialisation sets apace in the developing countries, Schumpeter's theory can undoubtedly throw considerable light on the problems associated with the long-run increase in productivity. It shall also provide clues to the problem of absorption of 'surplus labour' in gainful empolyment as a result of innovations. In this way Schumpeter's theory of development can provide some valuable lessons to the countries for avoiding waste and extra hardships that are liable to attend an unplanned and uncoordinated development.

---

9 Henry C. Wallich, *op. cit.*, pp. 189-204.

10 Singer, H.W., "Obstacles to Economic Development," *Social Research*, Vol. XX, 1953, pp. 19-31.

11 Henry C. Wallich, *op. cit.*, p. 203.

12 Rimmer Douglas, "Schumpeter and Underdeveloped Countries," *Quarterly Journal of Economics* August, 1961, pp. 422-50.

PART V

Various Approaches and Strategies of Development

- Lewis's Model of Development with Unlimited Labour Supply
- 'Big Push' Strategy of Economic Development: Rosenstein-Rodan Approach
- Balanced and Unbalanced Growth Strategies
- 'Critical Minimum Effort' Theory and Strategy
- Dualism and Development: Boeke's Social Dualism
- Dualism and Development: Technological Dualism
- Mahalanobis Growth Model and Heavy-Industry Strategy of Development
- Wage-Goods Model and Strategy of Development

CHAPTER

22

Lewis's Model of Development with Unlimited Labour Supply

An eminent development economist, Arthur Lewis, put forward his model of "*Economic Development with Unlimited Supplies of Labour*"[1] which envisages the capital accumulation in the modern industrial sector so as to draw labour from the subsistence agricultural sector. Lewis model has been somewhat modified and extended by Fei and Ranis[2] but the essence of the two models is the same. Both the models (that is, one by Lewis and the other modified one by Fei-Ranis) assume the existence of surplus labour in the economy, the main component of which is the enormous disguised unemployment in agriculture. Further, they visualise '*dual economic structure*' with manufacturing, mines and plantations representing the modern sector, the salient features of which are the use of reproducible capital, production for market and for the profit, employing labour on wage-payment basis and modern methods of industrial organisation. On the other hand, agriculture represents the subsistence or traditional sector using non-reproducible land on self-employment basis and producing mainly for self-consumption with inferior techniques of production and containing surplus labour in the form of disguised unemployment. As a result, the productivity or output per head in the modern sector is much higher than that in agriculture. Though the marginal productivity in agriculture over a wide range is taken to be zero, the average productivity is assumed to be positive and equal to the bare subsistence level.

Lewis's Model of Development with Surplus Labour

In the labour-surplus models of Lewis and Fei-Ranis, the wage rate in the modern industrial sector is determined by the average productivity in the agriculture. To this average productivity is added a margin (Lewis fixes this margin at 30%) which is required for furnishing an incentive for labourers to transfer themselves from the countryside to the urban industries as well as for meeting the higher cost of urban living. In this setting, the model shows how the expansion in the industrial investment and production or, in other words, capital accumulation outside agriculture will generate sufficient employment opportunities so as to absorb all the surplus labour from agriculture and elsewhere.

The process of expansion and capital accumulation in the modern sector and the absorption of labour by it is explained by Fig. 22.1 *OS* represents the real wages which a worker would be getting in the subsistence sector, that is, *OS* is the average product per worker in the subsistence sector. *OW* is the wage rate fixed in the modern sector which is greater than *OS* (*i.e.*, average product in agriculture) by 30%. So long as surplus labour exists in the economy any amount of labour will be available to the modern sector at the given wage rate *OW*, which will remain constant. With a given initial amount of industrial capital, the demand for labour is given by the marginal productivity

1 Authur Lewis. "Economic Development with Unlimited Supplies of Labour," *Manchester School*, 22, May 1954.

2 C.H. Fei and Gustav Ranis, *Development of the Labour Surplus Economy*, Irwin, 1964

curve MP_1. On the basis of the principle of profit maximisation, at the wage rate OW, the modern sector will employ OL_1 labour at which marginal product of labour equals the given wage rate OW. With this the total share of labour, *i.e.*, wage in the modern sector, will be OWQ_1L_1 and WQ_1D will be the capitalists' surplus. Now, Lewis assumes that all wages are consumed and all profits saved and invested

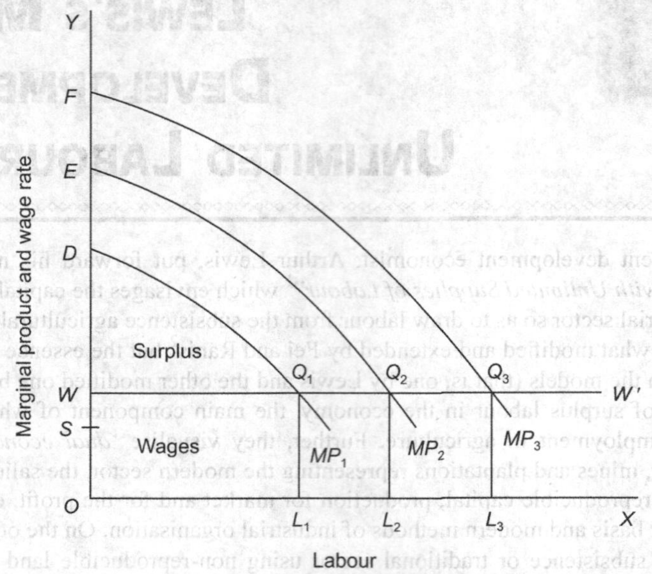

Fig. 22.1. *Capital expansion and growth in labour employment*

Reinvestment of Capitalists Surplus (Profits)

When the capitalists will reinvest their profits for setting up new factories or expanding the old ones, the stock of capital assets in the modern sector will increase. As a result of the increase in the stock of industrial capital, the demand for labour or magrinal productivity curve of labour will shift outward, for instance from MP_1 to MP_2 in our diagram. With MP_2 as the new demand curve for labour and the wage rate remaining constant at OW, amount of labour OL_2 will be employed in the modern sectpr. In this new equilibrium situation profit or surplus accruing to the capitalist class will rise to WQ_2E which is larger than the previous WQ_1D. The new surplus or profits of WQ_2E will be further invested with the result that capital stock will increase and the demand or marginal productivity curve for labour will further shift upward, say to MP_3 position. When the demand curve for labour is MP_3 employment of labour will rise to OL_3. In this way, the profits earned will go on being reinvested and the expansion of the modern sector will go on absorbing surplus labour from the subsistence sector until all the labour surplus is fully absorbed in productive employment.

It is worth mentioning that in Lewis model, the rate of accumulation of industrial capital and, therefore, the absorption of surplus labour depends upon the distribution of income. *With the aid of classical assumption that all wages are consumed and all profits saved, Lewis shows that the share of profits and therefore rate of saving and investment will rise continuously in the modern sector and capital will continue to be expanded until all the surplus labour has been absorbed.* Rising share of profits serves as an incentive to reinvest them in building industrial *capacity as well as a source of savings to finance it.*

Profit as the Main Source of Capital Formation

It is clear from the above analysis of Lewis's model with unlimited supply of labour that profits constitute the main source of capital formation. The greater the share of profits in national income, the greater the rate of savings and capital accumulation. Thus with the expansion of the modern or capitalist sector, the rate of saving and investment as percentage of national income will continuously rise. As a result, rate of capital accumulation will also increase relative to national income. It is of course assumed that all profits or a greater part of the profits is saved and automatically invested.

It is also evident from above that share of capitalists' profit depends on the share of the capitalist sector in the national product. As the capitalist or modern sector expands, the share of profits in national product will rise. This rise in the share of profits in national product is due to the assumption of the model that wage rate remains constant and prices of the products produced by the capitalist sector do not fall with the expansion in output. To quote Lewis himself, *"If unlimited supplies of labour are available at constant real wage rate, and if any part of the profits is reinvested in productive capacity, profits will grow continuously relative to the national income."*[3]

Credit-financed Money – Another Source of Capital Formation

Furthermore, profits are not the only source of capital formation in the Lewis model. It is equally possible to create capital through credit-financed money. Prof. Lewis holds that in an economy marked by scarcity of capital and abundance of the resources, credit creation would have the same effect on capital accumulation as do the more respectable means of profits. In both cases, the ultimate result would be the increase in output and employment.

However, capital formation resulting from a net increase in the money supply would necessarily be accompanied by an inflationary rise in prices. But this is only a temporary phase – a short-lived phenomenon. When the surplus labour gets employed in the capitalist sector for purposes of capital formation and is paid out of the created money, the immediate effect would be the rise in prices. What happens is that while the purchasing power in the hands of workers immediately increases, the output of the consumer goods remains constant for a time. However, the moment the newly formed capital created by credit money is put to use, the output of consumption goods would also rise. Therefore, after a time-lag, the output of consumer goods catches up with the increased purchasing power, and thus the prices start taking the downturn.

Besides, the inflationary process would also be made to die away through another mechanism that operates simultaneously. With the monetary expansion, not only the output and employment rise, but also the profits. As the profits increase relative to national income, so will do the savings. Therefore, the volume of investment being financed out of created money would go on diminishing with the increase in voluntary savings. In the ultimate analysis, the seeds of inflation would be completely killed when the voluntary savings catch up with the 'inflated level of investment'. Once the equilibrium is restored, new investments, made thereafter, could be financed without having to fall back upon bank credit. With the savings growing into equilibrium with investment, the rise in prices is bound eventually to peter out.

Introducing Technical Progress. What about the role of technical progress in the type of economic expansion proposed in the Lewis model? Prof. Lewis contends that for the purposes of his analysis, the growth of technical knowledge and the growth of productive capital can be taken to work in the same direction – *i.e.*, to increase profits and wage employment. He argues that to be able to apply new technical knowledge, we ought to have new investments. If the new technical knowledge is capital-saving, it could be regarded as equivalent to an increment in capital. And if it happens to be labour-saving, it could be regarded as equivalent to an increment in the marginal productivity of labour. In effect, therefore, both cases would produce the same result—an outward shift in the marginal productivity schedule. As such, *Prof. Lewis in his model, takes the growth of knowledge and the growth of productive capital to be essentially a 'single phenomenon'*.

However, the growth of technical knowledge in the subsistence sector is going to be a different kettle of fish. Its effect would be to raise the level of wages. As such, the capitalists' surplus would

3 Arthur Lewis, *op. cit.*

be reduced. It is, thus, that the capitalists have a profound and direct interest in holding down the productivity of labour in the subsistence sector.

Tapering off of the Expansionary Process

Now, if there is no hitch in the process of expansion and things go on smoothly, the capitalist sector will continue to expand till it has completely absorbed the surplus labour. Then comes the stage where capital accumulation has matched the excess supply of labour. Thereafter, the supply of labour ceases to be perfectly elastic. As a result, *real wages, instead of remaining constant, start rising. Also, the share of profits in the national income ceases to show any further rise*. And, thus, investment rather than growing relative to the national income comes almost to a standstill.

However, the expansion process may come to a halt much before the surplus labour has completely been absorbed. Prof. Lewis suggests three ways whereby the expansionary process might be halted before its natural conclusion. These are :

(*a*) The expansion of the capitalist sector may be rapid enough, so that the absolute population in the subsistence sector is greatly reduced, without, of course, affecting the total product. As a result, the average productivity of labour in the subsistence sector will rise. Consequently, the level of subsistence earnings (*S*) and the capitalist wage (*W*), are raised thereby reducing the volume of capitalists' surplus. However, *this shall not be if the growth of population happens to be greater than the rate of growth of the capitalist sector*.

(*b*) Technical progress may occur in the subsistence sector and may, therefore, raise the productivity there. This will, in turn, be reflected in a rise in the level of subsistence earnings (*S*) and the capitalist wage (*W*). The result, again, would be the squeezing of the capitalist surplus.

(*c*) *The terms of trade may turn against the capitalist sector due to a rise in the prices of raw materials and food.* This is very likely to happen, especially where the modern capitalist sector produces no food products. Now, as the capitalist sector expands, the demand for food will increase. As such, the food prices must rise in terms of the prices of the products of capitalist sector. In other words, the terms of trade would become unfavourable to the capitalist sector. But if the real income of the worker is to be kept constant, the capitalist wage (*W*) must rise (and so also the subsistence earnings (*S*)). The effect is that the capitalists' surplus is reduced.

However, if none of these methods operate or do so only mildly, the capital accumulation will continue to take place. And the modern capitalist sector will continue expanding till the whole surplus labour is absorbed. In any case, the process of expansion cannot proceed indefinitely as wage rate in the modern industrial sector will rise, profits (or capitalist surplus) will decline and as a result capital accumulation will decline and ultimately bringing the growth process to a halt.

A Critical Appraisal of Lewis's Model

The validity and usefulness of the labour-surplus model of Lewis for developing countries like India depend of course on the extent to which their underlying assumptions are valid for the economies in question. We are here not interested in validity of all the assumptions, explicitly or implicitly, made in this model. In our view the basic premise of this model is wrong and that makes it unrealistic and irrelevant for framing a suitable development strategy to solve the problem of surplus labour and unemployment. The basic premise of the model is that industrial growth can generate adequate employment opportunities so as to draw away all the surplus labour from agriculture in an labour developing country like India where population is currently increasing at the annual rate of around 1.6 per cent. This premise has been proved to be a myth in the light of generation of little employment opportunities in the organised industrial sector during over sixty years of economic development in India, Latin American and African countries.

For instance, in the 30 years (1951-81) of industrial development in India during which fairly good rates of industrial production had been achieved, the organised industrial employment increased by only 3 million which was too meagre to make any significant impact on the urban unemployment situation, far from providing a solution to the labour-surplus problem in agriculture. Thus, the generation of adequate employment opportunities and as a result the absorption of surplus labour from agriculture in the expanding industrial sector has not proceeded as predicted by the Lewis model.

In may be pointed out here that migration of some workers from the rural to the urban areas in India has occurred as shown by the slight increase in the degree of urbanisation noticed in the various censuses but these immigrants to the urban areas have not been absorbed into the modern high-productivity employment, as envisaged by Lewis and Fei-Ranis. This is evident from the statistical data about meagre increase in employment in the organised sector. These immigrants to the urban areas have been mainly employed in petty trade, domestic service and casual work in which the disguised unemployment and poverty exist as acutely as in agriculture. Thus, as things stand, the traditional sector of the economy is simply moving from the countryside into the cities in apparent contrast to the Lewis model.

Lewis Model Neglects the Importance of Labour Absorption in Agriculture. A grave weakness of the models of Lewis and Fei-Ranis is that they have ignored the generation of productive employment in agriculture. No doubt, Lewis in his later writings and Fei-Ranis in their modified and extended version of Lewis model have envisaged an important role for agricultural development so as to sustain industrial growth and capital accumulation. But they visualise such an agricultural development strategy that will *release labour force from agriculture* rather than absorbing them in agriculture. Thus to quote Fei and Ranis: "*In such a dualistic setting the heart of the development problem lies in the gradual shifting of the economy's centre of gravity from the agricultural to the industrial sector through labour reallocation.* In this process each sector is called upon to perform a special role: productivity in the agricultural sector must rise sufficiently so that *smaller fraction of the total population can support the entire economy* with food and raw materials, thus enabling agricultural workers to be released; simultaneously, the industrial sector must expand sufficiently to provide employment opportunities for the released workers ... *labour reallocation must be rapid enough to swamp massive population increases if the economy's centre of gravity is to be shifted over time.*"[4]

We have shown above that employment potential of organised industrial sector is so little that labour reallocation between agriculture and industry and "smaller fraction of the total population being employed in agriculture" is just not possible in labour-surplus developing countries like India. Indeed, a good amount of employment opportunities can be generated in agriculture itself by capital accumulation in agriculture, adopting proper agricultural technologies and making appropriate institutional reforms in the pattern of land ownership.

Even about the African countries most of which do not suffer from the Malthusian problem of overpopulation but are currently faced with acute urban unemployment (especially of what is known as "*Unemployment of School Leavers*" majority of which have migrated from the villages to the urban areas) the expert opinion has veered round to the view of seeking solution of labour-surplus problem within agriculture. Thus Sara S. Berry remarks about the African experience: "*Most students of the problem of rising African urban unemployment agree that the solution to the problem lies in raising incomes and employment opportunities in agriculture so as to ensure a new market equilibrium with more people productively employed in agriculture.*"[5]

4 Fei and Ranis, *op. cit.*

5 Sara S. Berry, "Economic Development with Surplus Labour : Further Complications Suggested by Contemporary African Experience," *Oxford-Economic Papers*, June 1970.

Assumption of adequate labour-absorptive capacity of the modern industrial sector. Another related shortcoming of development models of Lewis, Fei and Ranis is their assumption that the growth of industrial employment (in absolute amount) will be greater than the growth in labour force (which in India at present is of the order of about 12 million people per year). Because only then the organised industrial sector can absorb surplus labour from agriculture. The employment potential of industrial sector is so little that far from withdrawing labour currently employed in agriculture, it does not seem to be possible for the organised industries and services, on the basis of existing capital-intensive technologies, even to absorb the new entrants to the labour force.

An important drawback of the Lewis model is that it has neglected the importance of agricultural growth in sustaining capital formation in the modern industrial sector. When as a result of the expansion of capitalist modern sector, transfer of labour from agriculture to industry through agricultural development to meet the additional demand for foodgrains, prices of foodgrains will rise. With the rise in prices of foodgrains wages of industrial labour will increase. Rise in wages will lower the share of profits in the industrial product which in turn will slow down or even choke off the process of capital accumulation and economic development. Thus, if no allowance is made for agricultural growth, the expansion of modern sector and capital accumulation is bound to be halted. Thus, neglect of agriculture in the development strategy pursued in India since the Second Plan virtually resulted in stagnation in the industrial sector, during the period 1966-1979.

The Assumption of Constant Real Wage Rate in the Modern Sector. The assumption of *constant* real wages to be paid by the urban industrial sector until the entire labour surplus in agriculture has been drawn away by the expanding industrial sector is quite unrealistic. The actual experience has revealed a striking feature that in the urban labour markets where trade unions play a crucial role in wage determination, there has been a tendency for the urban wages to rise substantially over time, both in absolute terms and relative to average real wages even in the presence of rising levels of urban open unemployment. The rise in wages, as explained above, seriously impairs the development process of the modern sector.

It neglects the labour-saving nature of technological progress. A serious lacuna of the Lewis model from the viewpoint of employment creation is its neglect of the labour-saving nature of technological progress. It is assumed in the model, though implicitly, that rate of employment creation and therefore of labour transfer from agriculture to the modern urban sector will not be proportional to the rate of capital accumulation in the industrial sector. Accordingly, the greater the rate of growth of capital formation in the modern sector, the greater the creation of employment opportunities in it. *But if capital accumulation is accomplished by labour-saving technological change, that is , if the profit made by the capitalists are reinvested in more mechanised labour-saving capital equipment rather than in existing types of capital, then employment in the industrial sector may not increase at all.*

The Lewis model has been reproduced in Fig. 22.2. with a modification that profits made are reinvested in labour-saving capital equipment due to the technological change that has taken place. As a result of this, marginal productivity curve does not shift uniformly outward but crosses the original marginal productivity curve from above. It is evident from Fig. 22.2 that with the constant wage rate *OW*, the employment of labour does not increase even though marginal productivity curve has shifted to the right.

It will be observed from Fig. 22.2 that though employment of labour and total wage (*OWQL*) have remained the same, the total output has increased substantially, the area *OEQL* is much greater than the area *ODQL*. This illustration points to the fact that while the industrial output and profits of the capitalist class can increase, the employment and incomes of labour class remain unchanged. Although GNP has increased, labouring class has not received any benefit from it. It is not just theoretical illustration but has been actually borne out by the experience of industrial development of several developing countries. This experience shows that while industrial output has significantly increased, employment has lagged far behind.

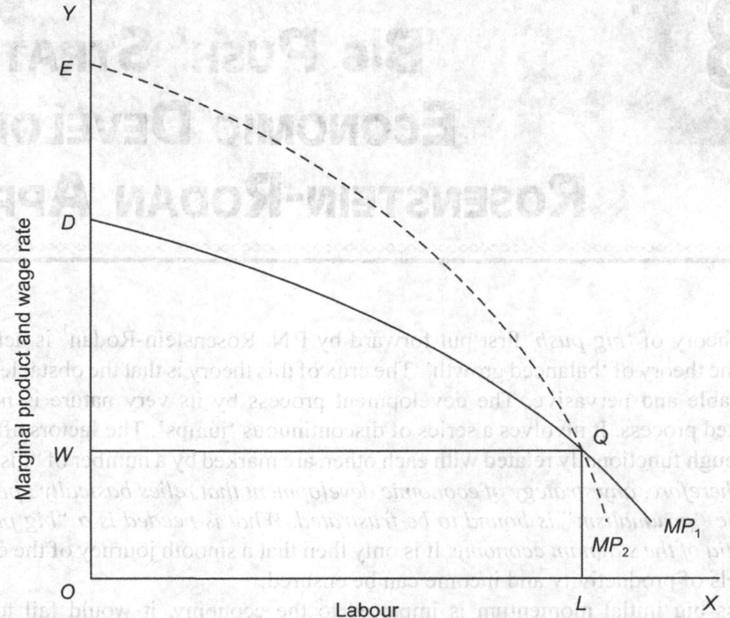

Fig. 22.2. *Capital expansion with labour-saving technological change*

Lewis Model Ignores the Problem of Aggregate Demand. A serious factor which can slow down or even halt the expansionary process in the Lewis model is the problem of deficiency of aggregate demand. Lawis assumes, though implicitly, that no matter how much is produced by the capitalist or modern sector, it will find a market. Either the whole increment in output will be demanded by the people in the modern sector itself or it will be exported. But to think that entire expansion in output will be disposed of in this manner is not valid. This is because a good part of the demand for industrial products comes from the agricultural sector. If agricultural productivity and therefore incomes of the farming population do not increase, the problem of shortage of aggregate demand will emerge which will choke off the growth process in the capitalist industrial sector. However, once an allowance is made for the increase in agricultural productivity through a priority to agricultural development, the basic foundations of the Lewis model crumble down. This is because a rise in agricultural productivity in Lewis model will mean a rise in wage rate in the modern capitalist sector. The rise in the wage rate will reduce the captalists' profits which in turn will bring about a premature halting of the expansionary process.

Conclusion

Despite several limitations and drawbacks, the Lewis model retains a high degree of analytical value. It clearly points out the role of capital accumulation in raising the level of output and employment in labour-surplus developing countries. The model makes a systematic and penetrating analysis of the growth problem of dual economies and brings out some of crucial importance of such factors as profits and wages rates in the modern sector for determinating the rate of capital accumulation and economic growth. It underlines the importance of inter-sectoral relationship (*i.e.*, the relationship between agriculture and the modern industrial sector) in the growth process of a dual economy.

Chapter 23

'Big Push' Strategy of Economic Development: Rosenstein-Rodan Approach

The theory of '*big push*' first put forward by P.N. Rosenstein-Rodan[1] is actually a stringent variant of the theory of 'balanced growth'. The crux of this theory is that the obstacles of development are formidable and pervasive. The development process by its very nature is not a smooth and uninterrupted process. It involves a series of discontinuous 'jumps'. The factors affecting economic growth, though functionally related with each other, are marked by a number of "discontinuities" and "hump." *Therefore, any strategy of economic development that relies basically upon the philosophy of economic "gradualism" is bound to be frustrated. What is needed is a "big push" to undo the initial inertia of the stagnant economy*. It is only then that a smooth journey of the economy towards higher levels of productivity and income can be ensured.

Unless big initial momentum is imparted to the economy, it would fail to achieve a self-generating and cumulative growth. A certain minimum of initial speed is essential if at all the race is to be run. A big thrust of a certain minimum size is needed in order to overcome the various discontinuities and indivisibilities in the economy and offset the diseconomies of scale that may arise once development begins. According to Rosenstein-Rodan, marginal increments in investment in unrelated individual spots of the economy would be like sprinkling here and there a few drops of water in a desert. Sizable lump of investment injected all at once can alone make a difference.

Rationale for the Big Push

The basic rationale of the 'Big Push' like the 'Balanced Growth' theory is based upon the idea of '*external economies*.' In the theory of welfare economics, external economies are defined as those unpaid benefits which go to third parties. *The private costs and prices of products fail to reflect these*. And the market prices have to be corrected if an account of these external economies is to be taken. However, the concept of external economies has a different connotation in growth theory. Here, they are pecuniary in nature and get transmitted through the price system.[2]

To explain the emergence of such external economies and their transmission, let us consider two industries *A* and *B*. If the industry *A* expands in order to overcome the technical indivisibilities, it shall derive certain *internal economies*. This may result in the lowering of the price for the product of the industry *A*. Now if the industry *B* uses *A*'s output as an input, the benefits of *A*'s internal economies shall then be passed on to the industry *B* in the form of pecuniary *external economies*. Thus, "the profits of industry *B* created by the lower prices of product. *A* call for investment and expansion in industry *B*, one result of which will be an increase in industry *B*'s demand for industry *A*'s product. This in turn will give rise to profits and call for further investment and expansion of industry *A*."[3]

1 P. N. Rosenstein-Rodan, "Notes on the Theory of 'Big Push", *M.I.T. CIS*, March, 1957.
2 T. Scitovsky, "Two Concepts of External Economies", in Aggarwal and Singh, *op. cit*.
3 P. N. Rosenstein-Rodan, *op. cit*.

Following such a line of argument, Prof. Rosenstein-Rodan contends that the importance of external economies is one of the chief points of difference between the static theory and a theory of growth. In the static allocative theory there is no such importance of the external economies. "*In the theory of growth however*," remarks Prof. Rodan, "*external economies abound because given the inherent imperfection of the investment market, imperfect knowledge and risks, pecuniary and technological external economies have a similarly disturbing effect on the path towards equilibrium.*"

Now, the basic contention of the "big push" theory is that such a mutually beneficial way of output expansions is not likely to occur unless the initial obstacles are overcome. There are "non-appropriabilities" or "indivisibilities" of different kinds which if not removed through a "big push" will not permit the emergence and transmission of 'external economies' – which lie at the back of a self-generating development process. Associated with the removal of each set of indivisibilities is a stream of external economies. A 'bit by bit' approach to development would not enable the economy to cross over certain indivisible economic obstacles to development. What is required is a vigorous effort to jump over these obstacles. As such, for the economy to be successfully launched on the path of self-generating growth a "big push" in the form of a minimum size of investment programme is necessary. In essence, therefore, an *all-or-nothing* approach to development is stressed in big-push approach to development.

Requirements for Big Push

The hallmark of the 'big-push' approach *lies in the reaping of external economies through the simultaneous installation of a host of technically interdependent industries*. But before that could become possible, we have to overcome the economic indivisibilities by moving forward by a certain "minimum indivisible step". This can be realised through the injection of an initial big dose of a certain size of investment.

Prof. Rodan distinguishes three kinds of indivisibilities and externalities with a view to specify the areas where big push needs to be applied. They are:

(*i*) Indivisibilities in the production function, *i.e.*, lumpiness of capital, especially in the creation of social overhead capital.

(*ii*) Indivisibility of demand, *i.e.*, compelmentarity of demand.

(*iii*) Indivisibility of savings, *i.e.*, kink in the supply of savings.

Let us study each of these individually so as to bring out their importance in providing a self-generating stimulus to the development process.

I. Indivisibilities in the Production Function

Prof. Rodan argues that it is possible to generate enormous *pecuniary external economies* by overcoming the 'indivisibilities of inputs, processes and outputs.' The emergence of such externalities would bring about a wide range of increasing returns. To corroborate his contention he cites the case of United States. He feels that the fall in the capital-output ratio in U.S.A. from 4:1 to 3:1 over the last eighty years was chiefly due to the increasing returns made possible by the levelling down of production indivisibilities.

The most important case of indivisibilities and external economies on the supply side resides in the *social overhead capital* which is now called *infrastructure*. The most important effect of jumping over this indivisibility is the "investment opportunities created in other industries". Social overhead capital consists of all the basic industries such as transport, power, communications, and such other public utilities.

The construction of these infrastructures involves 'lumpy' capital investments. And the capital-output ratio in the social overheads is considerably higher than in other industries. Moreover, these services are only indirectly productive and involve long gestation periods. Besides, their "minimum feasible size" is large enough. As such it is well-nigh difficult to avoid excess capacity in these, at least in the initial periods. Above all, there is a "minimum industry mix of public utilities" that must be required to divert at least 30 to 40 per cent of their total investment in the creation of social overhead capital.

In this view, therefore, it is possible to distinguish four types of indivisibilities of creating social overhead capital. They are:

(*a*) *Indivisibility of time*. The creation of social overhead capital must precede other directly productive industries so that it is irreversible or indivisible in time.

(*b*) *Indivisibility of durability*. The infrastructures generally last long. The overhead capital with lesser durability is either technically not feasible or is very poor in efficiency.

(*c*) *Indivisibility of long gestation periods*. The investments in social overhead capital, by all counts, involve a highly protracted period of time for their fruition as compared with investments in other directly productive channels.

(*d*) *Indivisibility of an irreducible industry mix of public utilities*. Social overhead capital must grow collectively. There is an irreducibly minimum industry mix of different public utilities that have to be created all at one stroke.

As it is impossible to import the infrastructures, they have got to be produced domestically. And because of the existence of above mentioned indivisibilities, it is necessary to make 'lumpy' investments in them. And their creation is a precondition to the investments in directly productive and other quick-yielding productive activities. Only then the way for a self-generating economy can be paved. Thus the absence of adequate social overhead capital constitutes the most important bottleneck in the development of developing countries.

II. Indivisibility of Demand

This refers to the complementarity of demand arising from the diversity of human wants. The very fact that there is an indivisibility of complementarity of demand requires simultaneous setting up of interrelated industries in countries to initiate and accelerate the process of development.

Indivisibility of demand generates interdependencies in investment decisions. As such, if each investment project was undertaken independently, it is in most cases likely to flop down. This is because individual investment projects generally have "high risks because of uncertainty as to whether their products will find a market," This point can be clarified with the help of the following well known example given by Rosenstein-Rodan for a closed economy.

To start with, let us suppose that 100 disguisedly unemployed workers in an underdeveloped country were withdrawn and employed in a shoe factory. The wages of the newly employed workers would provide an additional income to them. Now, if they spend all their newly received purchasing power on the shoes, an adequate market for the shoe industry would be ensured. As a result, the industry would succeed and survive. But the fact is that human beings having diversity of wants cannot simply afford to survive simply by the consumption of shoes and nothing else. As such, they will not spend all their earnings on the purchase of shoes. The market for the shoe industry will, therefore, remain limited as before. Therefore, the incentives to invest will be adversely affected. As a result, the shoe factory investment project might end in a fiasco.

Now let us make a somewhat different assumption to see how an atmosphere congenial to the undertaking of investments can occur. Suppose that instead of only 100 workers being engaged in the shoe factory, 10,000 workers are put to work in 100 different factories producing a variety of consumer goods. These new factories provide larger employment and thus purchasing power to their workers. There is an increase in the total volume of purchasing power and the total size of the market. This is because the "*new producers would be each other's customers*". In a way, what has happened is that due to the complementarity of demand, the risk of limitedness of market is greatly reduced. The result is that the incentives to invest are increased. "*Thus provided that the total volume of employment and purchasing power is increased by a minimum indivisible step, each factory will have enough market to reach full capacity production and the point of minimum cost per unit.*"

We, therefore, find that the indivisibility of demand requires the simultaneous production of a "bundle" of large number of wage goods on which the newly employed workers could spend their income. That alone would ensure adequate market for the product of each producer. In terms of investment the implication is that "*unless there is assurance that the necessary complementary investments will occur, any single investment project may be considered too risky to be undertaken at all.*"

This, as Prof. Higgins[4] remarks, results into an *indivisibility in the decision-making* process. A large-scale investment programme based on complementarity of demand undertaken as a unit may bring forth large increases in national income. But each of the individual investment projects undertaken singly may not fructify at all. The essence of the whole analysis is that a high minimum quantum of investment in interdependent industries is needed to overcome the indivisibility of demand and hence that of decision-making. That, according to the big push theory, is the only reliable way of overcoming the smallness of the market size and low inducement to invest in the developing economies.

III. Indivisibility in the Supply of Savings

A high minimum package of investment cannot be undertaken without an adequate supply of savings. But it is not possible to have such high volume of savings in underdeveloped countries due to an extremely low price and high income elasticities of the supply of savings. The savings are low primarily because incomes are low. This, thus, constitutes the third indivisibility. "The way out of the vicious circle," remarks Rosenstein-Rodan, "is to have *first* an increase in income ... and to provide mechanisms which assure that in every *second* stage the marginal rate of savings will be very much higher than the average rate of savings." The Smithian advice that '*frugality is a virtue and prodigality a vice*' has to be adapted to a situation of growing income." But in the ultimate analysis the initial big increase in income has got to be provided through an initial big increase in investment.

The existence of the three indivisibilities outlined above make it abundantly clear that the solution to all these lies in a high minimum quantum of investment. Thus, a big push through a minimum indivisible step forward in the form of a high minimum quantity of investment could alone make it possible to jump over the economic obstacles to development in the underdeveloped countries.

Lastly, Resenstein-Rodan consider the role of international trade *vis-a-vis* the strategy of big push in generating a self-sustaining process of development. In this regard he is of the view that international trade cannot be a substitute for "big push." The provision of some of the needed wage goods through imports can at best help in narrowing down the range of fields which call for a 'big push'. The historical experience provided by the nineteenth century corroborates Rosenstein-Rodan's conclusion that international trade cannot by itself obviate the need for 'big push' altogether.

Once the process of development by an initial application of 'big push' is underway, its sequel course would tend to follow simultaneously three sets of balanced growth relations. They are :

(*i*) A balance between the social overhead capital and the directly productive activities (in both the consumer and capital goods sectors).

(*ii*) A vertical balance between capital goods and consumer goods (including the intermediate goods).

(*iii*) Lastly, there should be the horizontal balance between various consumer goods industries due to complementary nature of expanding consumer demand.

4 B. Higgins, *Economic Development*, 1961, p. 387.

The Need for Balanced Growth of Centralised Planning

The mutual benefits arising from the external economies for industrialisation cannot be included in the cost calculations of entrepreneurs to the fullest possible extent without recourse to some sort of centralized '*balanced growth*' planning. This is because of a number of reasons. First, due to the imperfections in the market, the free market price system does not adequately give proper signal to the private investors for the future possibilities of expansion in complementary industries. Second, in developing countries due to the imperfections of knowledge and risks, the response of the private entrepreneurs to any given price signal is quite imperfect and unsatisfactory. Thus, due to the failure to take advantage of the external economies to the fullest extent, investments which may be profitable in terms of '*social marginal net product*' remain unprofitable in terms of '*private marginal net product*'. In this view, therefore, there is a need for an integrated investment scheme to be carried out in complementary industries. The best way to do that would be to carry out the investment programme under the direction of some centralised planning authority. An individual entrepreneur in a developing country cannot hope to have all the necessary data which the central planning authority can draw upon.

The crash programme of investment envisaged by the 'big-push' theory cannot by its very nature be made just at random. It has to take into consideration the various balances – horizontal as well as vertical. Only then could the achievement of self-generating, cumulative and harmonious growth of the economy is possible. For this what is necessary is a unified dicision-making process. "Allocation of capital," remarks Prof. Higgins,[5] "on the basis of individual estimates of short-run returns on various marginal investment projects is the very process by which the underdeveloped countries got where they are. The basic reason for government action to promote development is that each of a set of individual private investment decisions may seem unattractive in itself, whereas a large scale investment program undertaken as a unit may yield substantial increase in national income." Prof. Rosenstein-Rodan's theory is essentially a theory of development and thus helps us to examine the path towards development rather than restricting itself simply to the study of conditions at the point of equilibrium. The theory highlights the inefficiency of price system of signalling the desirable directions for investment. It is big-push investment through a centralised planning that could put the developing countries on an self-generating development process.

Evaluation of Rosenstein's Big Push Strategy

However, Prof. Rosenstein-Rodan's all-or-nothing approach is not perfect in itself in all respects. It suffers from a number of lacunae. Some of these are discussed below.

First, the main implication of the 'big-push' theory is State intervention and centralised planning. It is argued that due to imperfections of market the free price system fails to register and thus communicate properly the economic events, much less their future course. But the pertinent question involved here is: will the prevailing circumstances of the developing countries warrant a conclusion to the contrary? The actual fact of the matter is that the current institutional and administrative set-up of the government machinery of the the poor developing countries is too weak to cope with the dictates of the 'big push' theory. It is, therefore, quite doubtful whether the government sponsored brand of communication system about the future events would at all be more effective than the free price mechanism.

The governments of developing countries may somehow manage to draw up their initial integrated economic plans. But they are bound to be faced with tremendous difficulties in the execution of these plans. In any comprehensive programme comprising a complex set of related projects, delays and continued revision of the original time-bound schedules are inevitable. "The greater the interdependence", remarks Prof. Myint,[6] "between the different components of the plan, the greater the repercussions of an unexpected or an unavoidable change in one part of the plan on the rest and the greater the need to keep the different parts of the plans continually revised in the

5 B. Higgins, *op. cit.*, p. 387.
6 H. Myint, *op. cit.*, 1967, p. 120.

light of the latest information available." These are indeed formidable hurdles for the developing countries to cross.

Besides, on account of the poor and incompetent institutional set-ups of the developing countries, there is bound to be insufficient knowledge about the local conditions and an "inefficient feedback of this vital local knowledge from different parts of the country to the central planning machinery." Mere improvement in the standard type of statistical information would not remedy all this.

Above all, the process of unified decision-making and coordination becomes all the more difficult in mixed economies like India. This is so because not unoften, the public and private sectors rather than being complementary are in fact competitive with each other. Thus, it may so happen that the "private enterprise is inhibited by uncertainties not only about the general economic situation but also about the future intention of the government regulations."

Thus, it is quite clear that the application of a 'big push' programme in the developing countries with their weak and incompetent institutional and administrative machinery is likely to die its own death. In fact, as Prof. Myint remarks, it can be compared to "*an attempt to impose a complete and brand new 'second floor' on the weak and imperfectly developed one floor economy of these countries.*"[7]

Secondly, the chief plank on which the 'big push' theory is founded is the emergence of a wide range of external economies. Prof. Viner has shown that international trade can provide much more external economies than does the domestic investments. However, the developing countries being primarily primary producing countries, engage a large part of their total investment for their exports and marginal import substitutes, the field where the external economies are found to be very negligible.

Thirdly, the 'big push' theory concentrates mainly on the industrial sector – *viz*., capital goods, consumer goods and social overhead capital. The manufacturing sector is considered inherently to be a better vehicle of economic growth. But in the developing countries, the most dominant sector is composed of agricultural and primary production. For a balanced growth of the economy, agriculture also requires a corresponding 'big push'. Any neglect of the agricultural sector in these countries is bound to jeopardise the 'big push' effort.

Fourthly, the major part of the 'lumpy' investments involved in the 'all-or-nothing' approach is called for by the 'technical indivisibilities' embodied in the creation of social overhead capital. Not only is the quantum of investment enormously 'lumpy' but also the capital-output ratio high in the provision of social overhead services than in other directions. Thus, due to the inherent capital scarcity in the developing countries, it is really a matter of dubious wisdom to require these countries to overstrain their meagre resources in the provision of a complete outfit of infrastructures.

The 'big push' theory recommends a 'starting from scratch' concerted action in the creation of social overheads. This is on the implicit assumption that these services are totally non-existent in these economies. However, for most of these countries, remarks Prof. Myint, "*the practical question is not whether to have a completely new outfit of these services starting from scratch but how to extend and improve the existing facilities.*"

Further, the 'big push' theory by its very nature requires the 'lumpy' investments in different social overheads to be made simultaneously and once for all. With the very long gestation periods usually associated with such investments, there are bound to be inflationary pressures in the economy due to the shortage of consumption goods. In an inflationary atmosphere, the process of construction of the social overheads is bound to be a protracted one. In this light it would be better to spread the infrastructure-building activity over a period of time through phasing and changing the time dimension of the projects. This requires selection of a suitable economic size of the social overhead investments.

7 *Ibid*., p. 118.

CHAPTER 24

BALANCED AND UNBALANCED GROWTH STRATEGIES

In the nineteen fifties and sixties there were among the development specialists the two major schools of thought regarding the strategy of economic development that should be adopted in developing countries. On the one side, there are economists like Ragnar Nurkse and Rosenstein-Rodan who are of the view that the strategy of investment should be so designed as to ensure a balanced development of the various sectors of the economy. They, therefore, advocate simultaneous investment in a number of industries so that there is a balanced growth of different industries. Economists, like H.W. Singer and A.O. Hirschman, on the other side, believe that for rapid economic growth there should be concentration of investment in certain strategic industries rather than an even distribution of investment among the various industries. In other words, in the view of these latter economists, unbalanced growth is more conducive to economic development than a balanced one. We may now consider both these views at some length.

STRATEGY OF BALANCED GROWTH

In an earlier chapter, we explained how the underdeveloped countries were caught up in a *vicious circle of poverty*. We also pointed out how difficult it was to break this vicious circle. We explained there how the vicious circle of poverty operates both on supply and demand sides of capital formation. Nurkse put forward the doctrine of balanced growth in order to break the vicious circle of poverty on the demand side of capital formation. It will be useful to have again a cursory look at this vicious circle.

In an underdeveloped country, the level of per capita income is low which means that the people's purchasing power is low. Owing to small incomes and low purchasing power their demand for consumer goods is low. As a result of low demand for goods, the inducement for investment is less and capital equipment per capita (*i.e.*, per worker) is small. Since the amount of capital per capita is small, productivity per worker is low. Low per capita productivity means low per capita income, *i.e.*, poverty. This completes the vicious circle of poverty. In a poor country, the size of the market for goods is small so that sufficient opportunities for profitable investment in industries are lacking. According to Nurkse, this is the main reason for lack of inducement to invest which we discuss presently.

Size of Market and Inducement to Invest

Investment means the expenditure on the making and installation of capital goods, *e.g.*, construction of factories and the making of machines and their installation in industries. Obviously, an entrepreneur will be induced to invest in factories, machinery, etc., if he expects sufficient return on his investment. Businessmen invest only from a motive of earning a profit. It is the expectations of profits which is a fundamental factor influencing the amount of investment in a country at a given time. In a poor country, the low level of investment is due to low expectations of making profits because of less demand for goods or a small size of the market.

Let us understand clearly why there is less inducement to invest in a poor country. It is easily understandable that, in developing countries, there is great need for capital for economic development. Many people are too poor even to have two square meals a day or clothing to cover their bodies. Hence, there is an urgent need for large-scale production of consumer goods, but it cannot be done without the production and use of capital goods in large quantities. The establishment and expansion of industries require investment. The need for capital can be great but the inducement to invest can be weak. The level of investment depends not on the need for capital but on the inducement to invest in the form of attraction to earn profit from the capital invested. Without reasonable expectations of making profits, much capital will not flow into investment.

The quantity of profitable investment in a country depends on the size of the market. Adam Smith said, "*Division of labour is limited by the size of the market*." Nurkse says in the same manner that inducement to invest depends on the size of the market, that is, on the level of demand. The small size of the market or the low level of demand for the products concerned discourages the entrepreneurs from investment in industries.

This will be clear from an illustration. In a modern dairy, milking, filling up bottles and their loading all these operations are done with the aid of automatic machinery. Will the installation of such a machinery in every small Indian town be profitable for individual entrepreneurs? Obviously, it will not be profitable. Per capita income being low in India, the demand for milk in each town will be too small to make the full use of such automatic machinery. Such costly plant and machinery will remain mostly idle and there will be work for such a machinery only for a few hours during a week. This means a great waste of valuable capital asset. Which entrepreneur will dare start such a business? As an inducement to invest, the entrepreneurs should be sure that the capital equipment will be profitably employed. This will be possible only if the machinery can be kept in continuous use, and this cannot be done unless there is sufficient demand for the product made by this machinery.

Take another example. Suppose a cloth of a special design is very attractive and it can fetch a very high price. But it will not be economical to install a big machine to make a cloth of a special design, because owing to its high price and low incomes of the people, there will not be sufficient demand for this type of cloth, *i.e.*, the market will be too small. In America, the cars are cheap but they are very expensive in India. What is the reason? The one reason is that the demand for cars in India as compared with that in America is so small that manufacturers of cars cannot be induced to make them in large quantities which would have made them cheap on account of the economies of scale. Examples can be miltiplied. The conclusion is clear that inducement to invest depends on the size of the market or the purchasing power of the people.

It may be clearly understood that in the developing countries, according to Nurkse, *demand for consumer goods cannot be increased merely by the expansion of money supply in the country. The real demand will increase only if there is increase in the productivity per worker and as a result thereof there is increase in the real per capita income*. But mere expansion of money supply and thus putting more money into people's pockets demand for goods increases which will result in inflation or higher prices, but not increase in the real effective demand and expansion in the capacity to produce goods.

Similarly, the demand for goods or the size of the market cannot be large merely because size of a country is big or its population is large. If the purchasing power of the people is low because of their extreme poverty, the demand for goods in that country will be small or the size of the market will be small even though the country is big in size or its population is large. Mere more people without having purchasing power will not create real demand. Further, in poor countries, where the people's purchasing power is low on account of low per capita income, the demand for goods, and hence the size of the market, cannot be increased by high pressure salesmanship and vigorous advertising campaigns. There should be enough people to buy them. Thus, it is clear that, in the underdeveloped countries, the demand for goods, or the size of the market, cannot be increased by increasing money supply, or by increase in population or by greater salesmanship and advertisement or the large size of the country. *The size of the market can be increased only by increasing productivity.* As Nurkse puts it, *"The crucial determinant of the size of the market is productivity."*[1] Increase in productivity will increase people's incomes and hence their purchasing power.

The level of people's income in any country can be raised and consequently their purchasing power can be increased by increasing productivity and aggregate output or, in other words, by increasing productive employment. A situation of higher productivity, the greater employment and incomes and high purchasing power of the people will provide a profitable field for investment. It may be said that the size of the market can be enlarged by lowering the price of the products. But, according to Nurkse this is no solution of the problem. The real solution of the problem is only an increase in productivity of the people by raising productive employment. Only as a result of increase in productivity, there is increase in income and increase in purchasing power which will increase demand and enlarge the size of the market.

Say's Law propounded by classical economists, which we have studied earlier, tells us that production or supply creates its own demand. But this law cannot be accepted in the sense that the production of cloth creates its own demand because the workers engaged in the making of cloth will not spend their entire earnings on the purchase of cloth. In the same way, production of shoes cannot create its own demand. The reason lies in the variety of man's wants. But, according to Nurkse, Say's Law can be applied to the developing countries if investment is made simultaneously in a large number of industries in a way that incomes of a large number of workers engaged in these industries will increase. This will create demand for goods produced by one another. In other words, if investment is made simultaneously in a number of industries and production is increased, the supply will create its own demand. Say's Law will hold good in such a situation.

Thus in Nurkse's view, investment in a particular industry and the resultant production or supply cannot create its own demand but simultaneous investment in a number of industries can. As Nurkse puts it, "*An increase in production over a wide range of consumables, so proportioned as to correspond with the pattern of consumer's preferences, does create its own demand.*"[2]

Nurksian Strategy of Balanced Growth

We have explained above how, in the developing countries, the small size of the market or the limited demand for goods acts as a hindrance in the way of their economic growth or capital formation. When an entrepreneur wants to set up a factory or install plant and machinery, he makes sure whether there is enough demand for the goods he proposes to manufacture and whether the investment will be profitable. We have seen above that owing to low demand for industrial goods investment is discouraged because of low profitability. That is why the vicious circle of poverty operates on the demand side of capital formation. The people in the developing countries are poor and their per capita income is low. This keeps the demand limited and size of the market small. Since the market is small, the entrepreneurs are discouraged from investment in plant and machinery in which only large-scale production is possible and economical.

The result is that capital formation in the country is discouraged. Nurkse points out that owing to lack of capital, productivity is low and since productivity per worker is low, the per capita

1 Ragnar Nurkse, *Problems of Capital Formation in Underdeveloped Countries*, p. 8.
2 Nurkse, *op. cit.*, p. 12.

income is low which means there is poverty. This is how the vicious circle of poverty operates in the developing countries. According to Nurkse, it is the vicious circle operating in the developing countries which stands in the way of their capital formation and economic development and, accordingly, if this vicious circle can be broken, capital accumulation will take place and economic development will follow. The operation of the vicious circle can also be described thus : Inducement to invest depends ultimately upon demand, *i.e.*, the size of the market. And the size of the market in turn depends upon productivity because the capacity to buy is ultimately based on the capacity to produce. Productivity, in its turn, largely depends on the use of capital. But, for an entrepreneur, the small size of the market will limit the use of capital so that productivity will remain low, thus keeping the size of the market small. The vicious circle will then repeat itself. This *vicious circle of poverty, according to Nurkse, can be broken by a simultaneous investment in a large number of industries, i.e., by a balanced economic growth.*

We have explained above how Say's Law cannot be helpful in developing countries if investment is made only in one industry. The output of any single industry newly set up with capital equipment cannot create its own demand. Human wants being diverse, the people engaged in the new industry will not wish to spend all their income on their own product. Nurkse gives the example of shoe industry. Suppose a shoe manufacturing industry is set up. If in the rest of the economy, nothing happens to increase productivity and employment, and hence the buying power of the people, the market for the additional output of shoes is likely to be deficient. People outside the shoe industry will not give up the consumption of essential food, clothing, etc., to create a sufficient demand for shoes every year. The supply of shoes is likely to outrun demand, and if investment is confined only to one particular industry, it cannot prove profitable.

But if investment is made simultaneously in a large number of industries, it will provide work for a large number of people producing diverse commodities. It will increase their income and they will be in a position to buy the consumer goods made by one another. This is how supply can create its own demand (as Say's Law asserts) through the strategy of balanced growth. The workers employed in different industries become customers of one another's goods and demand is increased or the size of the market is enlarged. The expansion of one industry helps in the expansion of others and there is all-round growth. This is how the difficulty arising from small size of the market is overcome and the obstacle in the way of economic growth cleared. In Nurkse's words, "The difficulty caused by the small size of the market relates to individual investment incentives in any single line of production taken by itself. At least in principle, the difficulty vanishes in the case of different industries. Here is an escape from the deadlock; here the result is an overall enlargement of the market. *People working with more and better tools in a number of complementary projects become each other's customers. Most industries catering for mass consumption are complementary in the sense that they provide a market for, and thus support, each other. This basic complementarity stems in the last analysis from the diversity of human wants. The case for balanced growth rests on the need for a balanced diet.*"[3]

Taken separately, a number of industries may be unprofitable so that the private profit motive would not suffice to induce investment in these industries. However, undertaken together in a synchronized manner, a balanced increase in production would enlarge the size of the market for each firm or industry so that "synchronized undertaking" would become profitable. *This wave of capital investment in a number of different industries is called by Nurkse as "balanced growth."*

In this way, in Nurkse's view, through balanced growth the hindrance to economic growth owing to the small size of the market is removed. The aggregate demand is increased as a result of simultaneous investment in a large number of industries, because the incomes go up and productivity levels of persons employed in different industries go up. Hence, the underdevelopment equilibrium

3 Nurkse, *op. cit.*, p. 11.

trap and the vicious circle of poverty can be broken by balanced growth. If once this circle is broken, then, since there is circular connection, this circle will turn from poverty to balanced growth and to all-round development of the economy. In this way, the circle can be given beneficial form.

Now the question arises: Which industries should be selected for investment? The answer is to be found in the above solution offered by Nurkse. Investment should be made simultaneously in such industries the manufactured products of which are in accordance with the wants of the consumers, that is, on which the persons engaged in different industries would spend their incomes. There should be investment in a large number of complementary industries in the sense that persons employed in them become each other's customers. Only by a simultaneous investment in such industries, production or supply will create its own demand.

Then the question is : How is it to be made sure that simultaneous investment in a large number of industries is actually made? Nurkse answers that, if in the country there are dynamic and constructive entrepreneurs and industrialists, they can be induced to make investment simultaneously in different industries. If there is lack of such entrepreneurs, then the government cant take the work of balanced growth in its own hands. That is, the government can itself make simultaneous investment in several industries and can thus increase people's incomes and productivity. As a result of investment in several industries, it will be possible to increase the use of capital goods in large quantities which will raise the level of productivity and there will be a large increase in the aggregate output of consumer goods and services. As a result of this, the level of national income will rise which will help to raise the standards of living of the people. In this way, the poverty of the people will be eliminated. What is needed to remove the poverty of the people is to launch an attack on the various sectors of the economy simultaneously. This will remove the obstacle arising from limited demand or small size of the market. With this, inducement to invest will increase.

External Economies and Balanced Growth

It will be proper to refer in this connection to *external economies*. When one industry creates demand for another, it will be profitable to the other industry. When one industry benefits from the growth of another industry, then we say that external economies are available from one industry to another. We have seen above that it proves profitable to make investment in complementary industries, because people engaged in such industries become one another's customers or create demand for one another. It is clear, therefore that the *doctrine of balanced growth is based on the concept of external economies*.

It should, however, noted that here we do not use the term "external economies' in the sense in which Marshall used it. By 'external economies' Marshall meant those economies which arise from the localisation of a certain industry in a particular place and these economies are enjoyed by *each firm* in the industry by the establishment of numerous *other firms* there. But in development economics, by *external economies we mean those benefits which accrue to the* ***industries*** *by the establishment of* ***new other industries*** *or the expansion of the other existing industries*. We have seen above how, according to Nurkse's doctrine of balanced growth, these benefits accrue to the other industries by the establishment of other new industries or the expansion of old industries through simultaneous investment in such industries in the form of increased demand or extension of the market. In fact, *the increasing returns which arise from the process of economic growth, are mainly due to the creation of external economies in the form of extension of the market or increase in demand and not due to the external economies mentioned by Marshall such as technical information from the journals, improvement in the technical skill of labour, development in the means of communication and transport, etc. which arise from the expansion of a particular industry in a particular place*.

Nurkse has also not made clear in his doctrine of balanced growth whether investment should be made in capital goods industries and social overhead capital like transport and communications to promote balanced growth. Actually, Nurkse has suggested investment in consumer goods industries.

But how will the machinery and capital equipment required in these industries be obtained ? If they are not to be imported from abroad, they will have to be produced in the country and for that purpose investment will have to be made in their production.

A Critique of Balanced Growth Doctrine

Prof. Hans Singer and Albert Hirschman, eminent American economists, have criticized Nurkse's doctrine of balanced growth. They contend that what is needed is not balanced growth, but a strategy of judiciously-planned unbalanced growth. According to Singer, balanced growth cannot solve the problem of the developing countries, nor do they have sufficient resources to achieve balanced growth. Singer[4] maintains that balanced growth doctrine might be better expressed as follows: "As hundred flowers may grow whereas a single flower would wither away for lack of nourishment." But where are the resources to grow hundred flowers? Singer argues that the slogan "stop thinking piecemeal and start thinking big" is a sound advice for the poor developing countries but he also feels that there are "several areas of doubt" about the balanced growth theory in its Nurksian form.

First, if the balanced growth doctrine is interpreted to advise the developing countries to embark on a large and varied package of industrial investment with no attention to agricultural productivity, it can lead to trouble. Balanced growth strategy of Nurkse, as of earlier 'Big-Push Strategy' of Rosenstein-Rodan *underestimetes the role of agriculture* in economic development of developing countries. India in the Second and Third Five Year Plans followed Mahalanobis' strategy of industrialsation with relative neglect of agriculture which led to shortage of food supply and balance of payments problems resulting in foreign exchange crises.

Further, the big push in the form of simultaneous investment in a large number of industries requires a huge amount of resources/costs. At the initial stages of development, as the income grows with new industrial investment and employment, the relatively greater demand would be created for food and other agricultural goods. In order to sustain industrial investment, the agricultural productivity would have to be greatly raised. Thus, the big push in the industries must be accompanied by a big push in agriculture as well, if the country is not to run short of foodstuffs and agricultural raw materials during the transition to an industrialised society.

But serious doubts arise about the saving capacity of developing countries to follow the balanced growth path. According to Marcus Fleming, "Whereas the balanced growth doctrine assumes that the relationship between industries is for the most part complementary, the limitation of factor supply assures that the relationship is for the most part competitive."[5] Singer adds : "*The resources required for carrying out the policy of balanced growth...are of such an order of magnitude that a country disposing of such resources would in fact not be underdeveloped.*"[6]

Further, Furtado (1954)[7] has made an important point that investment in large-scale industrial sector as envisajed in *Nurksian balanced growth strategy is associated with capital-intensive production technologies used in the advanced industrialised countries*. According to him, there are more labour-intensive technologies which are viable for production in small-scale industries and are not constrained by small size of the market or lack of demand for their products. In fact, the balanced growth doctrine, like the big-push strategy, took for granted the appropriateness of capital-intensive production techniques. In so doing they underplayed the lower rate of saving and lack of adequate financial resources and other factors of production in the developing countries. Further, as has been pointed out by Fleming[8] that if a particular factor is in short supply, expansion of one industry far

4 H.W. Singer, *Economic Progress in Underdeveloped Countries*.

5 Marcus Fleming, "External Economies and Balanced Growth," printed in Agarwala and Singh, *Economics of Underdevelopment*, Oxford University Press.

6 *Op. cit.*

7 C. Furtado, "Capital Formation and Economic Development, 1954" in Agarwala and Singh (eds.), *Economic Development and Underdevelopment*, 1958.

8 Marcus Fleming, 1955 *op. cit.*

from creating external economies to the benefit of other industries is likely to push up the price of that factor and thereby creating *external diseconomies* to the disadvantage of other industries.

Investment may be of whatever type, it necessarily induces some additional investment and some other productive activities. According to Singer, the *expansion of social overhead capital and the growth of consumer goods industries and improvement of production techniques in them to raise productivity cannot take place simultaneously, because the developing countries have only limited capabilities of making use of their resources*. In the developing countries, not only are the resources and the capabilities to bring about balanced growth lacking but, according to Hirschman, balanced growth is not even desirable. His view is that if economic growth is to be accelerated, it will have to brought about by unbalanced growth. If we promote growth by creating imbalances in the economy, the growth will be acclerated, because it will produce such incentives and pressures which will encourage overall development in the private sector. "*The balanced growth doctrine is premature rather than wrong*." Singer concludes, "*It is applicable to a subsequent stage of self-sustained growth rather than to the breaking of a deadlock*." For launching growth "it may well be a better development strategy to concentrate available resources on those types of investment which help to make the economic system more elastic, more capable of expansion under the stimulus of expanded market and expanding demand". He mentions investments in social overhead capital and removal of special bottlenecks as examples of such "strategic" investment.

The fundamental trouble with the balanced growth doctrine, according to Singer, is its failure to come to grips with the true problem of developing countries, the shortage of resources. "Think Big" is a sound advice to underdeveloped countries, but "Act Big" is unwise counsel, if it spurs them to attempt more than their resources permit. Moreover, the balanced growth doctrine assumes that a developing country starts from scratch. In reality, every developing country starts from a position that reflects previous investment and previous development. Thus, at any point of time, there are some highly desirable investment programmes which are not in themselves balanced investment packages but which represent unbalanced investment to complement the existing imbalances.

There is another great lacuna in Nurkse's balanced growth doctrine. Nurkse considers investment in only final consumer goods industries. But these final goods industries require capital goods such as machinery and other equipment. How will these capital goods required by final industries for their production would be obtained if they are not to be imported from abroed? They will have to be produced in the country and for them adequate investment will have to be made which will require more resources for investment. Besides, the expansion of production in final industries also require social overhead capital such as power, steel, transport and communication to foster balanced growth. Nurkse did not show adequate recognition of interrelationship of industries from the supply-side viewpoint. The industrial growth is constrained both by the demand and supply-side factors. In the initial stages of industrialisation, tackling supply-side constraints is more important and relevant than the demand side. As regards demand for industrial goods acting as a constraint, Paul Streeten[9] rightly writers, "In so far as balanced growth is concerned, with the creation of markets through complementary investment projects and the inducement to invest by providing complementary markets for final goods, it stresses a problem which is rarely serious in the countries of the region. Final markets can often quite easily be created without recourse to balanced growth by import restrictions and less easily by export expansion."

Another weakness of balanced growth argument, as pointed out by Hirschman, is lack of recognition by Nurkse that *industries have both backward and forward linkages*. Because of the limited availability of resources investment in those industries be given higher priority which have maximum linkage effects. The industries with maximum linkage effects are the leading sectors which ought to be given higher priority in order to ensure smooth and sustained growth.

9 Paul Streeten, "Balanced versus Unbalanced Growth," *The Economic Weekly*, April 20, 1963, pp. 669-71.

What remains of the doctrine of balanced growth is its emphasis on complementarity of final goods as they create demand for each other's products. Besides, the importance of balanced growth lies in the fact that it brings out that level of demand may act as a constraint for industrial growth of the economy. India's growth experience shows that industrial deceleration during 1965-66 to 1978-79 was primarily caused by lack of demand caused by decline in public sector investment and exhaustion of possibilities of further import substitution.

HIRSCHMAN'S STRATEGY OF UNBALANCED GROWTH

Professor Albert Hirschman in his book, "*Strategy of Economic Development*," carried Singer's idea further and contended that deliberate unbalancing of an economy, in accordance with a predetermined strategy, was the best way of achieving rapid economic growth. Like Singer, he argues that balanced growth theory requires huge amounts of precisely those abilities which have been identified as likely to be very limited in supply in the poor developing countries. He characterises the balanced growth doctrine as *"the application to underdevelopment of a therapy originally devised for an underemployment situation" by J.M. Keynes. In an advanced country, during depression, "industries, machines, managers, and workers as well as the consumption habits" are all present, while in poor developing countries this is obviously not so.*

As a developing country is incapable of financing and managing simultaneously a balanced "investment package" in industry and the needed investment in agriculture, in order to give a big push to lift an underdeveloped economy from a position of stagnation, *Hrishman prescribes big push in strategic selected industries or sectors of the economy*. After all, he points out, the industrialised countries did not get to where they are now through "balanced growth." True, if you compare the economy of the United States in 1950 with the situation in 1850, you will find that many things have grown, but not everything grew at the same rate throughout the whole century. *Development has proceeded "with growth being communicated from the leading sectors of the economy to the followers, from one industry to another; from one firm to another*."[10]

According to Professor Hirschman, the real scarcity in developing countries is not the resources themselves "but the ability to bring them into play." He divides the initial investment into two related activities : (*a*) *directly productive activities* (*DPA*) and (*b*) *social overhead capital* (*SOC*). A poor developing country may follow the method of unbalanced growth by undertaking initial investment either in social overhead capital or the directly productive activities. Whichever the type of investment, it will yield an 'extra dividend' of induced decisions resulting in additional investment and output. He contends that social overhead capital, and directly productive activities cannot be expanded simultaneously because of the limited ability to utilise resources. Thus, the planning problem is to determine the sequence of expansion that will maximize induced decision-making. Balanced growth (of social overhead capital and directly productive activities) is not only unattainable in most developing countries, it may also not be desirable. The rate of growth is likely to be faster with crucial imbalances precisely because of "the incentives and pressures" it sets up.

Hirschman's Illustration of Balanced and Unbalanced Growth Paths

Now, should we choose 'development via excess capacity of *SOC* or 'development via shortage of *SOC*? According to Hirschman, the sequence of development which is vigorously self-propelling should be adopted. We may explain the rationale behind this contention with the help of Hirschman's diagram as shown in Fig. 24.1. In this diagram, the units of investment in *SOC* are measured along the vertical axis, while the unit of investment in *DPA* are measured along the horizontal axis. The curves, *I, II, III* are the isoquants, reflecting the different combinations of *SOC* and *DPA* that result in the same gross national products at a given time. As we move successively from curve *I* to *II* to *III*, we reach a higher level of gross national product. For the sake of analytical simplicity, the curves

10 Albert Hirschman, *Strategy of Economic Development*, pp. 63-64 (italics added).

have been drawn in such a way that their optimal points lie on the 45° line. In fact, this line gives the locus of balanced growth of *DPA* and *SOC*. Assuming that balanced growth of *SOC* and *DPA* is not possible because of the inherent limited ability of the poor developing countries to utilise resources, we have to determine that sequence of development which maximises induced decision-making.

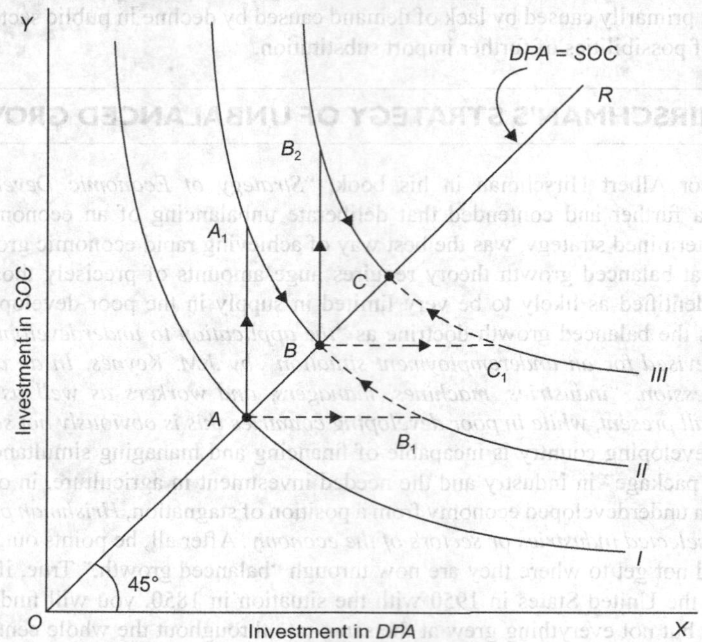

Fig. 24.1. *Balanced and unbalanced growth paths*

Let us first consider the *sequence of development via excess capacity of SOC*. The path of development assumed by the economy would then be given by the heavy lines $A \rightarrow A_1 \rightarrow B \rightarrow B_2 \rightarrow C$. Starting from *A*, the increase in *SOC* to A_1 invites increase in *DPA* till the balance is achieved at *B*. With the increased gross national product, the government may undertake further investment in *SOC* to B_2. This in turn will induce the *DPA* to increase to the point *C*.

If, on the other hand, the economy adopts the *sequence of development via shortage of SOC*, the course followed by the economy would be the one shown by the dotted lines AB_1BC_1C. In this case to start with, we increase *DPA* from *A* to B_1. To restore balance, this will be followed by the increase in *SOC* from B_1 to *B*. If there is a further increase in *DPA* to C_1, *SOC* will have to follow suit until balance is restored at *C*.

It needs to be noted that unbalanced growth via both the paths yields an "extra dividend" of "induced easy-to-take, or compelled decisions resulting in additional investment and output". However, the *sequence of development via excess capacity of SOC is what Hirschman calls "self-propelling" in the sense that it is more continuous and smooth.* The second path, *i.e.*, 'development via shortage of *SOC*, lacks this attribute since it may take some time for the political pressure to be generated so that the adjustment in *SOC* is delayed. And thus the *DPA* cost of producing an amount of output is pushed up. In Hirschman's terminology, the 'development via excess *SOC* is basically a *permissive sequence*, while the development via shortage of *SOC* is essentially a *compulsive sequence*.'

Having demonstrated the virtues of strategic imbalances, we are left with the problem of discovering what kind of imbalance is likely to be most effective. Any particular investment project may have both ***"forward linkage"*** (that is, it may encourage investment in subsequent stages of production) and ***"backward linkage"*** (that is, it may encourage investment in *earlier stages* of production). The task is to find the *projects with maximum* "*total linkage*." The projects, with the maximum total linkage, will vary from country to country and from time to time and can be discovered only by empirical studies of the "input-output tables".

In determining the sequence of projects, planning authorities should also give attention to the alteration of "*pressure-creating" and "pressure-relieving" investment*. In countries with vigorously expanding private enterprise sectors, the government's function can be largely limited to "pressure-relieving." As private investment takes place, shortages and bottlenecks will appear in transport, public utilities, education, and other activities traditionally assigned (in whole or in part) to public enterprises in such societies. Government ought not to feel "restless and slighted" when confined" to this "induced role."

Where expansion through private investment is not assured, the government's role must be more active. For example, it might build an iron and steel industry. "It is interesting to note," says Hirschman, *"that the industry with the highest combined linkage score is iron and steel. Perhaps the underdeveloped countries are not foolish and exclusively prestige-motivated in attributing prime importance to this industry, because of the high total linkage effects of iron and steel industry*." The building of it by the government will lead to a spurt of investment and production in a variety of fields both in the stages before and after this industry. In this way, it accelerates economic growth. The investment in iron and steel industry will reveal deficiencies in the preceding and succeeding sectors of industry that the government must fill up. To remove these deficiencies and obstacles, further investment will be stimulated. When these deficiencies are filled up, further private investment will take place, and so the process of growth goes on.

The foregoing discussion leads us to the conclusion that according to Hirschman, the balanced growth doctrine is neither attainable nor desirable. On the other hand, for rapid economic development the developing countries should rely largely on **judiciously-planned unbalanced growth.** In fact, under the Mahalanobis strategy of development, India followed this course.

A Critique of Unbalanced Growth Strategy

The strategy of unbalanced growth has come in for severe criticism. First, it has been pointed out that unbalanced growth strategy is based on wrong assumption that only factor constraining economic growth is the *scarcity of decision-making ability* in respect of investment. According to it, all that is needed for accelerating growth in less developed countries is to provide *inducements and incentives* to private enterprise to undertake investment projects. Once this is done, supply of financial resources will adequately flow into investment projects. This is not a realistic assumption to make in the context of the developing economies. In the developing countries supply of financial resources is scarce due to low rate of saving and this hampers economic growth. Hirschman paid little attention to overcome this bottleneck to accelerate growth. Thus, *not only the supply of physical resources are limited but also the availability of financial resources for funding the developmental projects is scarce*.

Hirschman's unbalanced growth strategy has also been criticised on the ground that *it will generate inflationary pressures in the economy*. Whether more investment is undertaken in social overhead capital (*SOC*) or directly productive activities (*DPO*) incomes of the people will rise which will lead to the increased demand for consumer goods, especially foodgrains. If sufficient investment in agriculture and other consumer goods industries is not made, it will cause rise in prices as was actually witnessed in India during the Second and Third Five Year Plans.

Thirdly, it has been pointed out that in case response from private enterprises to the inducements and pressure created by unbalanced growth strategy is not adequate, imbalances will be created in the economy without causing expansion in the other linked sectors *resulting in excess capacity in some industries or sectors*. This excess capacity represents waste of resources.

Lastly, it has been pointed out by Paul Streeten that unbalanced growth strategy *neglects the possibility of resistances* for adjustment to imbalances created by the unbalanced growth strategy. These resistances to growth may occur in a variety of forms. There may come into existence monopolies which have vested interests in restricting expansion in output. In the background of imbalances and shortages private enterprises which are interested in making quick profits will be more willing to raise prices of products rather than expanding their quantities. As Paul Streeten emphasises "*The theory of unbalanced growth concentrates on stimuli to expansion and tends to neglect or minimise resistances caused by unbalanced growth.*"[11]

We however conclude that despite some shortcomings in the unbalanced growth strategy, laying stress on the decision-making ability for accelerating economic growth and on the need for building up social overhead capital, Hirschman has made a valuable contribution to development economics.

An important weakness of Hirschman's doctrine of unbalanced growth, like that of Nurkse's balanced growth approach is that be does not consider the role of supply limitations. Hirschman lays stress on decision-making for accelerating investment. He thinks that supplies of inputs and physical resources will be forthcoming with relative ease once lack of decision to undertake investment or expand production can be tackled; Hirschman seems to think that supplies of resources are not a constraint and emphasises the scarcity of decision-making in developing countries. Paul Streeten rightly writes, "The contrast drawn by unbalanced growth doctrine between scarcity of resources and scarcity of decision-making can be misleading. Those who stress resources say that decisions will be taken as soon as resources are available; those who stress decision-making say that resources will flow freely as soon as adequate inducements to take decisions are provided. While the former group of experts out on missions advocate high taxation in order to "set resources free", the latter recommends low taxation in order to "encourage enterprise."[12]

Another important shortcoming of Hirschman's unbalanced growth doctrine, like Nurkse's balanced growth doctrine, is that planning is required to implement his strategy. In unbalanced growth strategy planning is required "as much at *restricting* supplies in certain directions as at expanding them in others. The policy package presupposes a choice of allocating limited supplies ... and in response to certain stimuli the most important uses combined with inducements to make decisions of all kinds (not only investment decisions)."

Hirschman has underestimated the difficulties and problems faced in the implementation of unbalanced growth. All investments create imbalances because of rigidities, indivisibilities, sluggishness of response both of supply and of demand and because of miscalculations. Free working of market will be unable to overcome these difficulties. These problems can only be solved if economic planning is adopted to coordinate and make required adjustments so that smooth and sleady growth is possible. In the words of Paul Streeten, "There will be, in any case, plenty of difficulties in meeting many urgent requirements whether of workers, technicians, managers, machines, semi-manufactured products, raw materials or power and transport facilities and in finding markets permitting full utilization of equipment. *Market forces will be too weak or powerless to bring about required adjustments and unless coordinated planning of much more than investment is called out*, the investment projects *will turn out to be wasteful and will be abandoned*."[13]

Although Hirschman's unbalanced growth doctrine is not without flaws, his emphasis on ability to take decision and the need for incentives for investment if economic growth is to be accelerated. He rightly lays stress on right attitudes and institutions for bringing about economic growth. More importantly, Hirschman's analysis of backward and forward linkages is an important contribution to the theory of economic development.

11 Paul Streeten, "Balanced and Unbalanced Growth," printed in G. Meier, *Leading Issues in Economic Development*, Oxford University Press, 1995.

12 Paul Streeten, *op*. cit.

13 Paul Streeten, *op. cit.*

'Critical Minimum Effort' Theory and Strategy

The 'big push' theory as we have seen in an earlier chapter advocated a massive all-or-nothing development programme in order to break through the 'inter-locking vicious circle' in which the developing countries find themselves deeply entrenched. Based essentially upon the same general thesis regarding underdevelopment, Nelson[1] and Leibenstein[2] have proposed a slightly different version of the 'all-or-nothing' approach to development.

Prof. Rosenstein-Rodan's big-push theory stressed the phenomena of low purchasing power, small size of market size, indivisibilities, and the interdependence of capital investments in the underdeveloped countries. As a result, in order to avail of internal economies of scale and the external economies arising from complementarity of investments, a large-enough minimum quantum of investment was advocated. However, Professors Nelson and Leibenstein arrive at almost similar conclusion by emphasising certain different elements of the vicious circle.

According to them, the chief villain of the piece resides in the population growth. Holding that there is direct relationship between the growth rate of per capita income and that of the population, they argue that the latter tends to offset any small increases in the former that may occur. The economy is thereby "trapped" in a low-level equilibrium. Any small and fragmentary increases in per capita income are swallowed up by the population growth induced by it. It is only when the development effort of a 'critical minimum' size is made that the resulting large and viable increases in per capita income would enable the economy to free itself from the bonds of population trap. Once it does, it will be well set on the path of self-sustained growth. Since the analyses of Nelson and Leibenstein are fundamentally very similar, we choose to describe the more comprehensive and popular version as given by Leibenstein.

LEIBENSTEIN'S CRITICAL MINIMUM EFFORT THESIS

The Two Basic Propositions

There are two basic propositions underlying the 'critical minimum effort' thesis. These are:

(1) The first proposition is the argument that the underdeveloped countries are poor because they have low capacity to save and invest. With their low per capita income, the magnitude of savings remains low. As a result, the rate of investment is very small resulting thereby in an almost negligible rate of growth of the national income.

1 R.R. Nelson, "A Theory of the Low-Level Equilibrium Trap," *Economic Review*, 1956, pp. 894-908.

2 Harvey Leibenstein, *Economic Backwardness and Economic Growth*.

In this view, therefore, it is contended that if the per capita income is made to rise above a certain minimum level, a rising proportion of total income would be saved and invested. This will push up the rate of growth of national income.

(2) The second proposition is a recognition of the fact that population growth is the main obstacle to economic growth of developing countries.

Prof. Harvey Leibenstein holds the view that the population growth is a function of the level of per capita income. He argues that the developing countries possess a subsistence structure and are thus entrapped in a '*Malthusian underemployment equilibrium*'. He bases his view on the observed relationship between the per capita income and the fertility rate. With a rise in per capita income above the subsistence level, the mortality rate tends to fall without any commensurate reduction in the fertility rate. This gives rise to a high growth rate of population which tends to swallow up whatever small increases in per capita income occur. But this mechanism can work up to a point only. Beyond a certain limit, the increase in the per capita income tends to lower down the fertility rates as well. The population growth rate is contained and a momentum to the process of growth is therefore provided.

Prof. Leibenstein has sought to base his contention on Dumont's '*Social capillarity*' thesis. The realisation by the people that the opportunities for rising socially are far greater with the *decrease* in the number of children is the motive force behind people's desire to limit their family sizes and thus attain higher levels of per capital income. Furthermore, with the rise in per capita income, the urge to have more children to supplement the parental incomes is very much diluted.

Three Stages of Demographic Evolution of a Society

On this showing Prof. Leibenstein recognises three stages in the economico-demographic evolution of a society. They are :

(*a*) To start with when the per capita incomes are very low, the utility of having more children tends to outweigh the costs of rearing them. What happens is that due to a very high mortality rate, a large number of new children need to be constantly added in order to maintain the existing size of the population. The burden of having more children is, however, sought to be relieved by engaging them in work at premature ages.

(*b*) With the initial increases in per capita incomes, *the mortality rate shows a decline* in the next stage. However, the *fertility rate lags behind* because it takes some time for the social institutions and attitudes to undergo a change. Now with reduced mortality, more children will survive up to the productive age. As such, their contribution to production as a proportion of their maintenance costs tends to increase.

But Prof. Leibenstein holds that there is a biologically determined upper limit to the population growth rate. In fact, he says that the growth rate of population cannot be higher than 3.4% per annum.

(*c*) As further increases in per capita income occur, the significance of children as potential contributors to their parental incomes substantially declines. At the same time there is an increasing awareness of the benefits of having fewer children in order to rise up in the socio-economic ladder. Thus, an attitude favourable to the limiting of family sizes is induced. Consequently this stage (*i.e.*, the third stage) is marked by lowness of both the birth and death rates, thereby tending to keep population more or less constant.

The Growth-Inhibiting Tendencies

Prof. Leibenstein holds that underdeveloped countries are 'trapped' in the *low-level income equilibrium* as characterised by the first and second stages. There are also other 'growth-inhibiting' and 'income-depressing' tendencies operating in the underdeveloped countries which all the more keep them to the low-level income equilibrium trap. These other tendencies which reinforce the backwardness of underdeveloped countries are as follows:

(*i*) *The prevalence of 'zero-sum' entrepreneurial activities*. The activities in which majority of the entrepreneurs of the underdeveloped countries are engaged are quite inert in respect of raising the national income. Such activities include "non-trading activities in order to secure for their interest a greater monopolistic position, increased political power, more prestige, etc." They also include trading activities such as the speculative pursuits which rather than utilizing savings productively, tend to waste the scarce entrepreneurial resources or do not add to the aggregate resources. Above all, the 'zero-sum activities' are characterised by those activities which "do use up net savings, but the investments involved are in the enterprises of such a nature that their social value is either zero, or their social value is very much lower than their private value."

It is thus only the '***positive-sum activities***,' according to Leibenstein, which can result in the growth of national income. But for the 'positive-sum' activities to be undertaken by the entrepreneurs, the essential condition is the anticipation of making profits. But anticipation of making profits is a *sine qua non* of growth in national income. Thus, even when a handful of entrepreneurs engage themselves in 'positive-sum activities', they would gradually tend to switch over to 'zero-sum activities' in the absence of any net growth in the national income. The precondition for the flourishing of the 'positive-sum activities' is the *creation of a congenial investment climate*. And this may not be possible to be attained by random piecemeal efforts. What is required is a concerted big developmental effort of a "critical minimum size".

(*ii*) *Conservative attitude*. In the underdeveloped countries there is also the gravitational pull exerted by the conservativeness of the attitudes towards change. Both the organised and unorganised labour are tradition-bound and opposed to change. For development to occur it is necessary that these pulls of conservatism are weakened to the maximum.

(*iii*) *New ideas and knowledge not adopted*. Further, in the underdeveloped countries there is aversion to the adoption of new ideas and knowledge. The society is engulfed by old ideas and out-of-date knowledge. A climate conductive to the imbibing of new knowledge and idea is one of the basic prerequisites for the economy to march progressively on the road to economic development.

(*iv*) *Conspicuous consumption*. Further, there is a huge amount of wastage of scarce resources in conspicuous consumption. Such unproductive expenditures obtain a high priority on the agenda of both the private and public consumption. Hardly any viable expenditure is made in productive directions. The result is the formation of both the physical and human capital which remain at a low ebb. For higher rate of capital accumulation to occur, it is necessary to plug these leakages.

(*v*) *High Capital-Output Ratio*. Above all, there is the bottleneck posed by the prevalence of a high capital-output ratio. The rapid population growth tends to accentuate this problem reducing the per capita availability of capital.

All these 'growth-inhibiting' tendencies taken together with the fact that there are internal diseconomies of scale because of inherent indivisibilities of the factors of production and external diseconomies arising from the phenomenon of internal tendencies to consume to keep the economy shackled in a vicious circle. It is necessary, therefore, for the underdeveloped countries to resort to a big endeavour of a 'critical minimum size' in order to overcome these depressing forces.

The Incoming-Increasing Forces

Leibenstein holds that it is possible to overcome this difficulty by creating an economic environment favourable to the flourishing of 'income-increasing' forces or what he calls the '**growth agents**' (*i.e.*, the entrepreneur, the saver, the investor and the innovators). But, this cannot occur all by itself. The necessary, though not a sufficient, condition for the economy to cultivate an atomosphere of economic progress lies in securing a sufficiently high initial increase in income.

The initial increase in income could accrue through any one or a combination of a number of appropriate methods. For instance, this may be made possible either by importation of a large amount of foreign capital or through technological breakthrough or emigration of labour. Whatever be the method applied, if the initial increase in income is large enough it would by itself induce a decrease in the population growth. The result is that after a point further increases in per capita income become easier. The time interval that would elapse before a stage of self-sustained growth is reached depends *inter alia* chiefly upon the rate of growth of population, the initial capital-labour ratio and the magnitude and momentum of the initial increase in income. Thus *the slower the population growth, more favourable the capital-labour ratio and larger the size of the initial increase in income, the more quickly would a stage be reached after which the further growth in per capita income becomes easier*.

However, the fact remains that more strenuous and momentous is the initial effort, the quicker and easier it would be for the attainment of subsequent higher levels of per capita income. The very fact that there is a biologically determined maximum rate of growth of population between 3 and 4% annually, the size of the critical minimum effort required to break through the low-level equilibrium trap cannot in any case be of utopian magnitude. Given the urge and the necessity of achieving self-sustained growth, the underdeveloped countries can manage to put in such an effort.

Creation of Conditions Conducive to Sustained Growth

Once the economy is able to cross over the population barrier as a result of the critical minimum effort, an atmosphere conducive to self-generating growth would be created. While the 'zero-sum activities' get nipped, the 'positive-sum activities' would be spurred. There is therefore, an increase in the saving and investment in the economy. This, in turn, would unleash a number of forces that ensure a socio-economic climate quite congenial to sustained growth. Among these the following factors are worth mentioning:

(*i*) Activation and expansion of the growth agents.
(*ii*) A decline in the capital-output ratio.
(*iii*) Stimulus to factors permitting social and economic mobility.
(*iv*) A decline in the magnitude and effectiveness of the 'growth-inhibiting' forces.
(*v*) Promotion of the division of labour with the expansion of the secondary and tertiary activities.
(*vi*) Creation of an atmosphere conducive to economic and social improvement that eventually leads to a reduction in fertility rates.

Thus, *it is evident that an underdeveloped country can jump over its 'low-equilibrium trap' by the application of a 'critical minimum' effort in the form of big doses of investment'*. However, the necessary condition for the success of the operation lies in the fact that the resulting 'income-increasing' forces should outweigh the 'income-depressing' forces.

Diagrammatic Illustration of Leibenstein's Thesis

We can explain Leibenstein's thesis with the help of Fig. 25.1. Here all the '*income-increasing' forces* are represented by the curve X_tX_t. On the other hand, the curve Z_tZ_t indicates all the '*income-depressing' forces*. The 45° line has been drawn to measure the induced increases and decreases in per capita income. For instance, corresponding to the per capita income level X_1 the 'income-increasing' forces are given by *af*, while the 'income-depressing' forces amount to *bf*. Point *E* is the initial point of low level equilibrium with *Oe* as the per capita income (vertical axis) where the income-increasing and income depressing forces are in balance.

Now, let us suppose that the initial investment effort is of such a magnitude as to raise the per capita income level from the initial low-level equilibrium *e* to *m* (shown on the vertical axis).

This would induce 'income-increasing' forces of a magnitude given by *af*. On the other hand, the 'income-depressing' forces associated with the new level of per capita income are *given by bf*. And since the 'income-depressing' forces outweigh the 'income-increasing' forces, the economy will slip down along the path *abcd* shown by arrows till finally it again settles at its original low-level equilibrium trap point *E*. Similarly, any investment programme that entails a *rise* in per capita income *less than that given by ek* is going to meet the same fate.

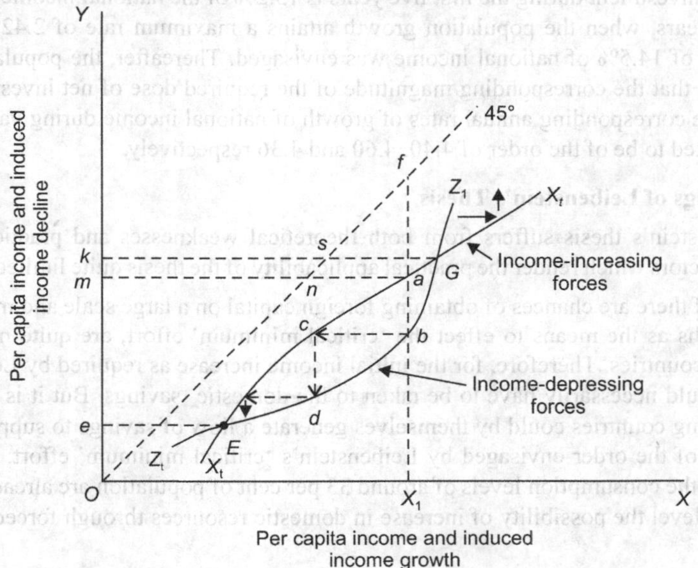

Fig. 25.1 *Critical minimum effort*

The economy can climb up the path of sustained growth only if the investment programme is of such a magnitude as to ensure a rise in per capita income at least to the level *Ok*. With this per capita income will rise by *sG*. Thus, *if the initial income gain is sufficient enough to raise the per capita income level to Ok, the 'income-increasing' forces will outweight the 'income-depressing' forces*. As a result' the path of continued expansion of the economy would be ensured. This can be shown in the figure by the upwardly directed arrows emanating from *G*. As such, the size of the 'critical minimum' effort in this case is given by an investment that will raise the per capita income to at least the level of *Ok*.

Thus, the crux of Leibenstein's thesis is the application of a 'critical minimum' effort such as described above. Only then can the economy overcome the population barrier and free itself from the gravitational pulls of the 'low-level equilibrium trap'. If the magnitude of the investment effort falls short of the 'critical minimum', the economy is bound to slip down to be entrapped again in the old low-level equilibrium.

Phasing the 'Critical Minimum Effort'. One of the most creditable features of Leibenstein's approach is that *it is not necessary to apply the 'critical minimum' effort all at once.* Indeed, Prof. Leibenstein contends that it is quite possible and effective to split up the 'critical minimum' effort into a series of smaller efforts. However, the applications of the smaller efforts (constituting the 'critical minimum') have to be optimally timed.

Magnitude of the 'Critical Minimum Effort'

Prof. Leibenstein has also tried to estimate the magnitude of the critical minimum effort in terms of the quantum of investment required. Considering an underdeveloped country with a starting population of one million, he bases his calculations on the fertility and mortality rates actually prevailing in the poor developing countries. He makes several projections about the 'critical minimum' size of investment on the basis of different assumptions. However, the projection most appropriate for countries like India is the one which assumes an annual rate of growth of population of 2.03 per cent and a capital-output ratio of 3:1.

On the basis of the above-stated assumptions, Prof. Leibenstein estimated that the required quantum of investment during the first five years is 13.2% of the national income. In the succeeding 25th–30th years, when the population growth attains a maximum rate of 2.42%, net investment of the order of 14.5% of national income was envisaged. Thereafter, the population growth starts declining so that the corresponding magnitude of the required dose of net investment was fixed at 13.08%. The corresponding annual rates of growth of national income during various periods have been estimated to be of the order of 4.40, 4.60 and 4.36 respectively.

Shortcomings of Leibenstein's Thesis

Leibenstein's thesis suffers from both theoretical weaknesses and practical lacunae. Some important factors which render the practical applicability of the thesis quite limited are the following:

First, if there are chances of obtaining foreign capital on a large scale and major technological breakthroughs as the means to effect the 'critical minimum' effort, are quite meagre in the poor developing countries. Therefore, for the initial income increase as required by Leibenstein's thesis, recourse would necessarily have to be taken to the domestic savings. But it is quite difficult that the developing countries could by themselves generate a flow of savings to support an investment programme of the order envisaged by Leibenstein's 'critical minimum' effort. In economies like India where the consumption levels of around 33 per cent of population are already at an almost the subsistence level the possibility of increase in domestic resources through forced savings is at best limited.

Secondly, the population problem in poor developing countries is not as simple and straight as has been conceived by Leibenstein. The contention that the changes in population growth are a direct consequence of the changes in per capita income level is open to serious objections. In particular, Leibenstein's view that moderate increases in per capita income reinforce population growth but beyond a certain stage it tends to decelerate is a dubious hypothesis.

Actually, the rise in population growth in the initial stages is not the outcome of moderate increases in per capita income. By and large, it is due to the improvements in medical and public health measures. And the availability of improved medical and public health facilities are in no way dependent upon any prior increases in per capita income. The fact is that even the most backward countries today have an easy access to all the known life-saving drugs and techniques which can be transported from abroad.

In the same way, the view that the decline in fertility is attributable simply to increases in per capita income above the critical minimum thesis is also unsustainable. Actually, fertility rate is more a function of the socio-cultural factors than anything else. Rise in per capita income above the 'critical minimum' level alone cannot be depended upon for attaining the desired change. Of course, it is true that an improvement in economic conditions may be a precursor to the creation of a socio-cultural fabric favourable to family delimitation. But this need not always be the case.

CHAPTER

26

DUALISM AND DEVELOPMENT: BOEKE'S SOCIAL DUALISM

A common feature of the poor developing economies is their dualistic character. While certain parts of these economies have to some extent been exposed to the influence of modernization, their dominant segment belongs to the backward indigenous economy. *The coexistence of such contrasting economic and social organisations—a relatively modern money economy and the traditional indigenous economy is a fundamental aspect of the growth process of the developing countries.*

Any growth strategy for these countries must take cognisance of their dualistic character. For that, it is necessary to analyse the basic features, causes and consequences of dualism. It is only then possible to determine the possible effects of the dualistic character of these economies on their development.

One of the earliest attempts to diagnose the causes underlying the dualistic character of underdeveloped countries and its implications for their developmental process was made by J.H. Boeke,[1] a Dutch economist. He developed his theory called 'social dualism' on the basis of his studies of Indonesian development experience. His theory is a distinctive theory in the sense that it is applicable only to the underdeveloped countries—for it emphasises the contrasting social organisations and cultural patterns embedded in the overall framework of their underdevelopment.

According to Boeke, any society can be described in the economic sense by three characteristics. These are:

(*i*) The social spirit.

(*ii*) The organisational forms.

(*iii*) The techniques dominating it.

The type or form of a given social system is determined by the form, extent and interrelationship between the above basic characteristics of the society. When a single uniform social system pervades the entire society, it is homogeneous in Boeke's sense. However, a *society may be marked by the simultaneous coexistence of two or more social systems. As such, there could be a dual or plural society*. Each one of these concurrently prevailing systems is markedly differentiated from the other in good many respects. And each of these comes to dominate a segment of the society.

Prof. Boeke concentrates his attention on dualism and expresses the view that it is a "form of disintegration, (which) came into existence with the appearance of capitalism in pre-capitalistic

1 J.H. Boeke, "*Economics and Economic Policy of Dual Societies*, 1953," '*Three Forms of Disintegration in Dual Societies,*' Indonesia, April, 1954 and 'Western Influence on the Growth of Eastern Population,' *Economics International,* May, 1954.

countries."[2] Reserving the term 'dualism' to such a phenomenon he offers its formal definition. *"Social dualism," he holds, "is the clashing of an imported social system with an indigenous social system of another style. Most frequently the imported social system is high capitalism. But it may be socialism or communism just as well or a blending of them."*[3]

Thus, one of the two social systems in a dualistic economy will necessarily have been imported from abroad. It is this imported western system that is an advanced one, while the other—the one indigenous to the country—is generally the pre-capitalist agricultural system. The western capitalistic system gains ground in the overall matrix of the traditional pre-capitalistic agrarian community. Boeke calls the indigenous social system as the *'eastern' or the 'pre-capitalistic' sector*. On the other hand, he christens the imported system as the *'western' or the 'capitalistic' sector* of the dualistic economies. The basic contention of Boeke is that dualism is the product of the clash between the East and West. He in this regard quotes the famous phrase of Rudyard Kipling: "East is East and West is West and the twain shall never meet."

CHARACTERISTIC FEATURES OF SOCIAL DUALISM

Boeke argues that the coexistence of two markedly different social systems gives rise to certain distinct economic features which are peculiar to all dualistic economies. They are:

(1) The 'eastern' or the 'pre-capitalist' indigenous sector of the dualistic economies is marked by '*limited needs.*' In this sector, the fulfilment of the basic needs makes people feel fully contented. In contrast, the 'western' or the 'capitalist' sector of these economies is the one where people have '*unlimited needs*'. The realisation of basic needs does not end their wants. Their wants are ever increasing and being continually stimulated by the '*demonstration effect.*'

(2) As a consequence of their limited needs, the '*eastern sector*' *is characterised by the backward sloping supply curves of effort and risk-taking*. People do not wish to make additional effort beyond what is utmost necessary for the realisation of their basic needs. Once they are able to earn an amount that is adequate enough to provide them with their basic requirements, they have no inherent desire to work any further. Thus, "when wages are raised the manager of the estate risks that less work will be done; if three acres of land are enough to supply the needs of the household, a cultivator will not till six."

One the other hand, the 'western sector' is characterised by a normal upward sloping supply curve of effort. This is because people here have constant desire to move up from one standard of living to the higher one. Therefore, they are always on the lookout for additional income. And they won't mind putting in extra effort to eke out larger earnings. But the extent to which extra effort is put would vary according to the quantum and intensity of the desire to realise the new wants.

(3) Further, the commodities in the 'eastern sector' are not evaluated on the basis of '*value-in-use*' but on the '*prestige value*'. This economic aberration stems from the fact that people here are influenced largely by the social rather than economic needs. "If the Madurese values his bull ten times as much as his cow," remarks Boeke, "this is not because the former is ten times as useful to him in his business as the latter, but because the bull increases his prestige at the bull races."[4]

(4) There is almost the *total absence of 'profit motive' in the 'eastern sector'*. The profits from speculative activities, however, hold attraction for them. But, "these profits lack every element of that regularity and continuity which characterizes the idea of income."[5]

2 Boeke, *Three Forms, op. cit.*, p. 282.

3 Boeke, *Economics, op. cit.*, p. 4.

4 Boeke, *Economics,* pp. 37-38.

5 *Ibid.*, p. 41.

(5) 'Professional trading' is conspicuous by its absence in the 'eastern sector'. There may be an exchange of goods at personal levels. But by and large trading as a profession is almost unknown for people are ignorant of the market.

(6) Also the industry in the 'eastern sector' is not investment-minded. There is so to say an "*aversion to capital*" owing to some sort of "conscious dislike of investing capital and the risks attending this." Besides, the industry in the 'eastern sector' lacks initiative, drive, discipline and organisational capabilities. In contrast, the industry of the 'western sector' possesses these business qualities.

(7) The labour too, in the 'eastern sector', is unorganised and unskilled. They happen to be quite "passive, silent and casual." Another dominant characteristic of the labour of the 'eastern sector' it that it lacks mobility. People have strong affinity to remain in the village community. As such, autonomous intra, and inter-country migrations are not at all possible. These may perhaps occur through government intervention. As a consequence of the immobility of labour, the wage structure in the 'eastern sector' is marked by sharp differentials. This is particularly so as between the 'eastern' and the 'western' sectors.

(8) Technological progress along the western lines has yet to see the light of the day in the 'eastern sector' of the dualistic economies. In fact, Boeke argues that : "There is no question of the eastern producer adapting himself to the western example technologically, economically or socially."

(9) Another outstanding feature of distinction Boeke contends is that while "*export is the great objective*" *of foreign trade in the 'eastern sector,'* it is "only the means which makes import possible" in the 'western sector'.

(10) Boeke also holds that in a dual economy, urban development flourishes at the expense of the rural life. What he actually means by this is that in the wake of urbanization, there occurs a progressive fall in the rural population and income. Boeke also holds that in the absence of free competition for land, the rents in the 'eastern sector' depend on the "landowners' need for money."

(11) Above all, the 'eastern society' is guided by "fatalism and resignation" as opposed to 'western industry' which is moulded by common-sense and reason.

In the backdrop of the above markedly distinct features of the dual societies, the western economic theory becomes completely otiose for these economies. Boeke argues that the western economic theory is based on "unlimited wants, a money economy, and many-sided corporative organisations." And none of these features is exhibited by the eastern societies. Thus, while western theory was developed basically to explain the capitalistic society, but the typical eastern village is pre-capitalistic. In particular, Boeke is highly skeptical of any effort to explain the distribution of income or the allocation of resources on the basis of the marginal productivity theory. For such a theory to be applicable, the basic prerequisite is the free mobility of resources in the economy. And it is precisely the immobility of resources which distinguishes an 'eastern society' from its western counterpart. Boeke sounds the note of warning by saying that, "we shall do well not to try to transplant the tender, delicate, hot house plants of western theory to tropical soil, where an early death awaits them."[6]

POLICY IMPLICATIONS OF THE THEORY OF SOCIAL DUALISM

The dismal socio-economic panorama revealed by the dualistic economies led Boeke to hold very pessimistic views on policy. He saw no hope of bringing about rapid development of these economies on the western pattern. In fact, he maintained that "any effort to develop them along Western lines can only hasten their retrogression and decay."

6 Boeke, *Economics,* p. 143.

The fact of dualism led Boeke to draw two policy conclusions: "first, that as a rule one policy for whole country is not possible and, second, that what is beneficial for one section of society may be harmful for the other."[7] Any effort to effect improvements in the pre-capitalistic agriculture of dualistic economies, on the western pattern, will not only fizzle out but also cause retrogression. Unless the mental attitudes of the farmers undergo a basic change, the attempts to westernize the eastern agriculture will be frustrated. There is, in fact, the dilemma: *If the modernisation of agricultrual techniques succeeds in improving productivity, the increased wealth would bring in its wake further growth of population. On the other hand, if the modern techniques fail, the consequences would be tremendous indebtedness.*

In this respect, therefore, Boeke is of the view that the existing agricultural system should not be disturbed. He is of the firm view that the existing system of agricultural production is "perfectly adapted to the environment," so that the agricultural methods "could hardly be improved upon."[8] Almost totally identical views are held by Boeke in regard to the industrial production. The eastern production in the industrial field as compared with their western counterparts is conducted on entirely different lines. There is no scope of the western technology being filtered down into the eastern modes of industrial production. Actually, Boeke maintains that the imitation of western technology by the eastern producers would tend to destroy their competitive qualities. Boeke seeks to corroborate his views on the basis of the Indonesian experience. The attempts at using the western technology dealt a death blow to small industry in Indonesia. The goal of self-sufficiency had thus been made all the more difficult and farther than it otherwise would have been.

In line with his pessimistic approach, Boeke held similar views with regard to the problem of unemployment. He recognises five types of unemployment in the underdeveloped countries: "seasonal, casual, unemployment of regular labourers, unemployment of the urban white collar workers and unemployment among the Eurasians". Boeke maintains that there is not much that the government can do to eliminate any of these types of unemployment. This is because, he believes, to deal with them "would entail a financial burden far beyond the governments' means."[9]

Above all, Prof. Boeke holds that limited wants stand in the way of economic development of any kind. Whether it is the increased production of foodstuffs or the industrial goods, the result would be the same, *i.e.,* supply overshooting the demand. Consequently, there would occur a glut of commodities in the market leading to a fall in prices and ultimately to depression.

The foregoing discussion shows that no *positive* policy formulation is given by Boeke. However, one can discern from his views that he favoured a small scale and slow process of industrialization "adapted to a dualistic" framework. The agricultural development should also be a gradual process based on the dualistic fabric of these societies. Further, the native people have to undertake the responsibility of the entire developmental process. New leaders must strive for the goal of economic progress with "faith, charity, and patience, angelic patience."[10] But the sphere of action must be a small and the time slow.

APPRAISAL OF BOEKE'S THEORY OF SOCIAL DUALISM

Boeke's theory of 'social dualism' provides basic insight into the structure of the underdeveloped economies. Practically all these countries are segregated into two sharply differentiated sectors. The coexistence of a backward indigenous sector with an advanced exchange sector, is the main consideration upon which any realistic theory of development of the underdeveloped countries should be based. In fact, the major parts of economic development policy have to be directed against the

7 Boeke, "*Three Forms*", p. 289.

8 Boeke, "*Economics*", p. 31.

9 *Ibid,* pp. 318-19.

10 Boeke, "*Western Influence*", *op. cit.,* p. 369.

prevalence of such a dualism. To the extent Boeke spotlighted on this crucial aspect of the development of underdeveloped regions, he deserves all praise. However, *Boeke focussed his analysis on dualism through the wrong mirror. Though dualism is an undeniable fact in the underdeveloped countries, yet the explanation given by Boeke that it primarily stems from the nature of society is not a very convincing one*. Rather than to be a purely sociological phenomenon, it also has its roots in the economic and technological matrices. In this light, Benjamin Higgins makes a scathing attack on Boeke's theory of 'social dualism'. Following are the chief grounds of attack:

First, it *is erroneous to think that people in underdeveloped countries have fixed or static wants*. The case of Indonesia, on the basis of which Boeke held his views, is itself an example to the contrary. In less developed counties as Benjamin Higgins points out, the marginal propensities to consume and import are high. The fact is that the people, be they urbanites or ruralites, have multiple and varied wants. Thus, "any 'windfall', occurring initially through increased exports, is quickly spent on imported semi-luxuries unless vigorous import and exchange controls are applied to prevent it."[11]. This phenomenon is not peculiar to Indonesia alone. Virtually all the underdeveloped countries have clamped stringent import and exchange controls. Besides, it is a matter of common observation that when farmers' pockets bulge—following a bumper harvest—there follows a swelling stream of orders for semi-luxuries, *viz*., transistors, radios, watches, scooters and bicycles, etc. The 'Green Revolution' in India brought with it a large demand for transistors and things like that. Thus, *Boeke's contention that the wants of people in the underdeveloped countries are limited is not borne out by the actual facts.*

Secondly, having shown that the wants of people in underdeveloped countries are not really limited, the *basic justification for the backward-sloping supply curve of efforts and risk also does not hold*. However, the basic tragedy is the absence of a mechanism to realise these wants. "*To turn these wants*," remarks Higgins, "*into a wellspring of economic growth, the people must be shown the connection between satisfaction of their wants and their willingness to work, save, and take risks—a difficult but not impossible task.*"[12] Besides, the backward-falling supply curve of effort is not peculiarly an eastern phenomenon. The recent economic history of developed countries provides several examples to the contrary. For instance, a backward-sloping supply curve of effort was all too evident in Australia and USA in the immediate post-War period. Benjamin Higgins, therefore, opines that the "*backward-sloping supply curve is not exclusively a feature of eastern societies, but appears in any society which stagnates (or slows down) long enough to weaken the 'demonstration effect' provided by people moving from one standard of living to another, as a result of their own extra effort, directed specifically towards earning additional income*."[13]

Thirdly, Boeke's contention that technological progress along the western lines in eastern production is not possible is not borne out by facts. "*Considering the growing number of enterprises*," remarks Higgins, "*efficiently organised and operated by Orientals, along western lines, it is difficult to share Boeke's pessimism regarding possibilities of technological progress in eastern industry.*" Assimilation of the already developed technology of advanced countries by the developing countries is now an established fact of the growth process of these countries.

Fourthly, Boeke's view that the eastern labour is characteristically "unorganised, passive, silent and casual" is unacceptable. The contemporary experience in this regard points to the contrary. The emergence of strong trade unionism, not only in the field of large-scale primary production, *viz.*, plantations in rubber, tea and coffee, but also large-scale modern industries in the developing countries is too hard a fact to be denied.

Fifthly, it is difficult to accept Boeke's contention that the eastern people are inherently immobile. In fact, the mushroom growth of the urban centres with their attendant malaise of congestion, insufficient

11 Benjamin Higgins, *Economic Development: Principles, Problems and Policies,* 1961, p. 282.

12 *op. cit.*, p. 286.

13 Quoted in Bauer and Yamey, *The Economics of Underdeveloped Countries,* 1957, p. 123.

basic amenities and increasing unemployment are the consequences of large-scale migration from the villages to the towns. The attractions of the urban life such as cinemas, cafes, shops, libraries have always held attraction for the rural people. Thus, it is quite inadmissible to hold that the labour in the underdeveloped countries is inherently less mobile than that of the western countries.

Sixthly, Boeke's view regarding complete absence of profit seeking is not sustainable. There is lot of evidence showing that the people of underdeveloped countries are not that oblivious to the 'opportunities for making profit and the willingness to seize them'. "*There is available a great volume of evidence*" claims Prof. Bauer,[14] "(*which*) *illustrates prompt and sensitive response to small differences in prices.*" The entrepreneurial acumen and other business qualities are very much there in the underdeveloped countries. Thus, remarks Prof. Bauer[15] in this regard, "the Indian is perhaps all else an entrepreneur, a businessman always looking for new means of turning a penny."

Seventhly, Boeke takes the one-eyed view by holding that the phenomenon of dualism is confined only to the eastern economies. Indeed, at one point, Boeke himself suggested that dualism existed in underdeveloped countries of Latin America. Besides, dualism is not a special feature of the underdeveloped economies alone. To some degree, it exists in almost every economy in the sense that any economy can be divided on the basis of the differences in the technological advance experienced by different regions. In this sense even the most advanced economies such as that of U.S.A., and Canada could be categorised as dual.

Eighthly, Boeke's view that the characteristics of '*preference for speculative profits over long-term investment in productive enterprises*' is typical of eastern societies alone, smacks of lopsidedness. Such attitudes are not peculiar to the people of underdeveloped countries alone. These are to be found in the Western economies as well. The fact is that whenever the inflationary pressures persist for a long time, people in the western economies start preferring investments in quick profit-yielding speculative activities rather than in long-term projects. Thus, remarks Prof. Higgins[16], that the "conscious dislike of investing capital in long-term projects and of risk attending this" prevails everywhere.

Further, Boeke's view that people value goods in terms of the prestige associated with them rather than according to their use-value, is also not exclusively an eastern phenomenon. It is very much there in the western economies too. Had it not been the case, there was no necessity for Veblen to coin the term '*conspicuous consumption*' to refer to such a behaviour of the American society.

Ninthly, Boeke ignores one of the most conspicuous and stark realities of the underdeveloped countries, *viz.*, the *prevalence on a vast scale of disguised unemployment.* Any theory meant to be applicable specially to the underdeveloped economies must take account of this phenomenon. Besides, his contention that the five types of unemployment, which he recognised, are "beyond the reach of government help" is quite implausible in the present-day conditions. It has been realised the world over that the government can play a significant and effective role in mitigating the unemployment problem in both the developed and developing countries.

Finally, Boeke's contention that the western economic theory is completely irrelevant to the 'eastern societies' is also not wholly valid. While counselling against the use of "the tender, delicate, hot house plants of western theory" for underdeveloped countries, it seems, Boeke had in his mind the neoclassical theory. But this economic theory is applicable in many ways to even the western world.

However, the fact remains that some branches of the contemporary western economic theory, especially the theory underlying monetary and fiscal policy as also policies directed towards the elimination of disequilibrium in the balance of payment, is equally useful to the underdeveloped countries. Of course, it is necessary to choose the right institutional assumptions. "Thus although it

14 P.T. Bauer, *Economic Analysis and Policy in Underdeveloped Countries,* 1957, pp. 21-24.

15 Quoted in Bauer and Yamey, *The Economics of Underdeveloped Countries,* 1957, p. 123.

16 B. Higgins, *op. cit.,* p. 286.

is necessary to take account of differences in institutional framework and of cultural pattern", says Benjamin Higgins, "*economic behaviour is much the same in underdeveloped as in advanced countries*."

In conclusion, we might say that although "there can be no question about the phenomenon of dualism," as a distinguishing feature of underdeveloped countries, yet "Boeke looked in the wrong place for his explanation." of backwardness of less developed countries. The proper explanation of dualism rather than to be a sociological one, is to be found in economic and technological terms. This theory of technological dualism has been put forward by Benjamin Higgins. In the next chapter we will critically examine this theory of technological dualism.

CHAPTER

27

DUALISM AND DEVELOPMENT: TECHNOLOGICAL DUALISM

One of the most significant consequences of dualistic development is to be found in the pattern of employment. The fact that the unemployment problem has assumed alarming proportions in the developing countries is indicative of some sort of fundamental disproportionality in the production relations inherent in dualistic development. Boeke's exposition of social dualism did not recognise any such thing.

However, in recent times increasing number of writers have attempted to explain the unemployment problems of developing countries in terms of what has come to be known as '*technological dualism*'. The chief exponent of this theory is Benjamin Higgins. This theory incorporates the problem of factor proportions in the production of commodities.

It is held that the chief cause of rather inelastic productive employment opportunities in the developing countries is not the deficient effective demand. Rather it is due to the technologically dualistic nature of these economies. The fundamentally different production functions and factor endowments in the advanced and the backward indigenous sectors of the economy are responsible for generating an ever-increasing volume of unemployment. Therefore, the unemployment associated with dualistic development is structural or technological in nature.

Higgins's Theory of Technological Dualism

Higgins explains his theory of technological dualism on the basis of a model in which there are two commodities, two factors of production and two sectors, *viz*., the modern and traditional sectors. The dichotomy between the two sectors is sharply defined chiefly on the basis of the distinctly different factor endowments and production functions attributable to each of these.

The traditional rural sector is engaged primarily in peasant agriculture and the handicrafts or very small-scale industries. However, the most distinctive feature of this sector is the flexibility in the techniques of production. The products can be produced with a wide range of alternative input-mix. With the possibility of easy substitutability between capital and labour, a wide spectrum of techniques could be employed in production of this sector. They range from the wooden plough to the modern tractor and from the sickle to the harvestor. As such, the chief characteristic of the production function in the traditional sector is the prevalence of *variable technical coefficients of production.*

Associated with the phenomenon of fairly wide range of technical substitutability is pro-labour factor endowments, *i.e.,* while labour is abundant, capital is the relatively scarce factor of production. The result is that labour-intensive techniques are chosen in the traditional sector for the production of commodities. As distinct from this, we have the modern sector consisting of large-scale industries, oil fields, mines and plantations. The main feature of this sector is the use of *fixed technical coefficients of production.* That is, the elasticity of substitution between the factors of production is almost zero. With the almost total absence of technical substitution, the production of a particular commodity in the modern sector requires a particular technique and none else to be adopted. And the production process is capital-intensive in nature. The production function of the modern sector can be diagrammatically represented in Fig. 27.1, given below:

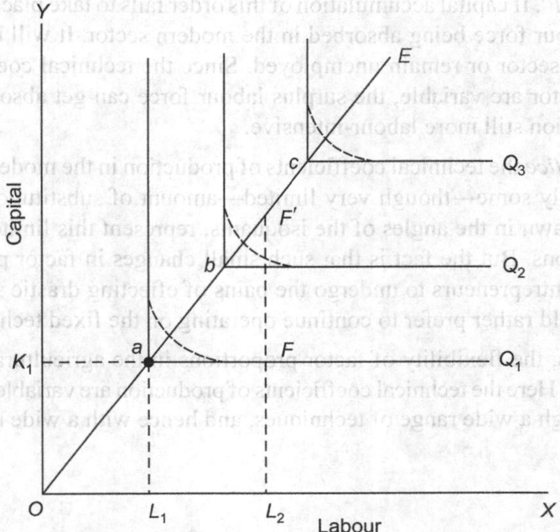

Fig. 27.1. *The modern industrial sector*

Here the units of labour (L) are measured along the horizontal axis and those of capital (K) are represented along the vertical axis. The curves Q_1, Q_2, Q_3 are the isoquants depicting different levels of output. The rectangular shape of the isoquants indicates that the different levels of output can be produced only by a unique combination of the factors capital (K) and labour (L). For instance, the output level Q_1 could be attained only by combining capital and labour in the amounts OK_1 and OL_1, respectively.

Thus, the points *a, b* and *c* around which the isoquants turn about perpendicularly, represent the fixed combinations of capital (K) and labour (L), that are required to produce the output levels Q_1, Q_2 and Q_3 respectively. In such a production function no matter what the relative factor prices are, the factor proportions remain fixed.

The expansion path of output is given by *OE*—obtained by joining the points, *a, b* and *c*. It shows that the output can be increased by increasing the factor inputs K and L, in the proportion given by the slope of the line *OE*. The slope of the expansion path *OE,* as is clear from Fig. 27.1, gives a relatively capital-intensive factor ratio. In other words, a greater quantum of capital relative to labour is required to produce a given level of output.

Now, given the fixed capital-labour ratio as obtaining in the production process and given the factor endowments, the question is, will the factors be simultaneously fully utilized? The simultaneous full utilization of factors will be possible only when the proportions in which they are available is exactly equal to the fixed capital-labour ratio—as given by the expansion path *OE.* However, if there is a deviation in the factor proportionality—as between the actual factor endowment and that necessitated by the productive process, at least one of the factors would be less than fully utilized.

Let us suppose that the actual factor endowment is represented by a point such as *F,* situated to the right of the expansion path *OE*. That is OK_1 amount of capital and OL_2 units of labour are available in this sector. But to produce the output level given by the isoquant Q_1, we need OK_1 units of capital and only OL_1 number of labour. Thus, L_1L_2 number of labour will remain surplus, no matter how favourable is the relative price of labour *vis-a-vis* capital. As production in this sector depends on the basis of fixed technical coefficients, this *surplus labour will remain unemployed.*

The only way to eliminate the unemployment of L_1L_2 units of labour, is to increase the capital stock by the amount FF'. If capital accumulation of this order fails to take place, there is no possibility of that redundant labour force being absorbed in the modern sector. It will have either to fall back upon the agricultural sector or remain unemployed. Since the technical coefficients of production in the agricultural sector are variable, the surplus labour force can get absorbed there, making the techniques of production still more labour-intensive.

However, *in practice* the technical coefficients of production in the modern sector are not all that fixed. There is possibly some—though very limited—amount of substitution between the factors. The dotted curves, drawn in the angles of the isoquants, represent this limited degree of flexibility in the factor proportions. But the fact is that such small changes in factor proportions would hold no attraction for the entrepreneurs to undergo the pains of effecting drastic shifts in the production techniques. They would rather prefer to continue operating on the fixed techniques of production.

In contrast to this, the flexibility of factor proportions in the agricultural sector is depicted by Fig. 27.2, given below. Here the technical coefficients of production are variable, a given level of output can be obtained through a wide range of techniques, and hence with a wide range of combinations

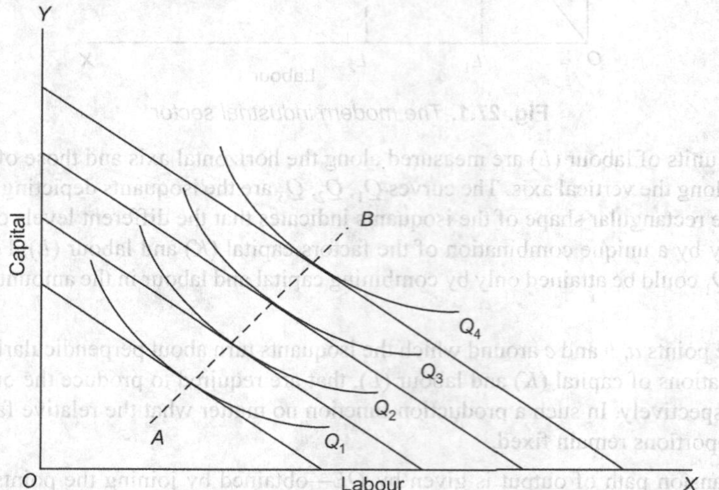

Fig. 27.2. *The agricultural sector*

of labour and capital. Thus, the factor proportions being actually used would be in consonance with its given factor endowments. And, therefore, the techniques employed in this sector would depend on the prevailing relative prices of labour and capital.

Technological Dualism and the Aggravation of Unemployment Problem

With the two sectors possessing typical and distinctly different configurations of the production functions, it is now easy to trace as to how technological dualism has aggravated the problem of unemployment and disguised unemployment in developing countries. Generally, the modern sector in these economies experienced a rather quick expansion, especially with the inflow of foreign capital and enterprise. As a sequel to this economic expansion, there also occurred in this sector rapid growth of population. In fact, the rate of population growth tended to outstrip the rate of capital accumulation.

But with its capital-intensive techniques and fixed coefficients of production, it was not possible for the modern sector to generate adequate employment opportunities commensurate with the growth of population. The consequence was that labour became a surplus factor in this sector. The only course open to this redundant labour was to shift to the traditional agricultural sector.

The redundant labour so released by the modern sector goes to increase the supply of labour in the traditional agricultural sector. In the initial stages, it may be possible to bring more land under cultivation to engage the excess supply of labour. However, eventually the inelastic supply of land exhausts all possibilities of extending cultivation. Meanwhile, the redundant labour continues pouring into the traditional sector. Now, the technical coefficients of production being variable in this sector, the entire additional labour is absorbed. But all this is at the expense of reduction in the capital intensity of the production process. It becomes ever more labour-intensive. Eventually, highly labour-intensive cultivation extends to all the available land. As such, the marginal productivity of labour declines to zero or even below that, the result being the emergence of disguised unemployment on a substantial scale.

Thus, continued growth of population striking against limited capital stock gives rise to surplus of labour. There then comes the stream of unproductive workers who appear to be employed but, in fact, they constitute the ranks of disguisedly unemployed, for they add virtually nothing to the output.

Under such conditions, there is no reason for the farmers to seek to apply labour-saving innovations, even if it is granted that they know about them and have resources to finance them. This apart, even the incentive on the part of labour itself to put in increased efforts is not to be found on account of the surplus supply of labour. The result is that productivity and earnings of labour and their well-being remain low as ever.

Further, it is held that the *nature of technical progress is such that, even in the long run, it does not alleviate the problem of unemployment.* In the modern sector, the technical progress has tended to be capital-using thus accentuating the unemployment problem. On the other hand, until recently, that is prior to green revolution there was little technical progress in the traditional sector, on account of the lack of complementary inputs and the smallness of the scale of operations. Besides, the problem of disguised unemployment tends to be all the more accentuated on account of the artificially bolstered up wages as a result of trade unionism or by government policy. Such a phenomenon of industrial wages outstripping the productivity further stimulates the adoption of labour-saving techniques. So that the capacity of the industrial sector to absorb population growth is all the more undermined. All these factors continue to reinforce and perpetuate the problem of disguised unemployment in the developing countries.

Evaluation of Higgins's Technological Dualism

Higgins's theory of technological dualism definitely marks a march over Boeke's sociological dualism. It brings out elegantly the underlying cause of the historical increase of underemployment in the traditional and agricultural sectors of underdeveloped countries. However, Higgins's contention that production in the modern sector is invariably carried on with fixed technical coefficients is contestable. In some sectors of the industrial sector such as textiles, leather and leather products, electronics and sugar, there is a good scope for variability of factor proportions. Even in these cases in countries like India, capital-intensive technologies have been used. This is partly due to the factor price distortions, that is, while price of scarce capital has been lower but wages of abundant factor higher relative to their availabilities. In 1971, a prominent development economist, Gustav Ranis wrote, "The Koreans and the Taiwanese.....are showing a wide range of technological choice in textiles, in electronics and in plywood industries, during the last decade. What the Japanese were doing relative to British and American machinery in the nineteenth country, the Koreans and Taiwanese are now doing relative to the Japanese as well as the American technology. They produce the same quality textiles or plywood or transistors with three to four times as much labour input per unit of capital. The sub-contracting which can be so important a feature of labour-saving technological change is being used increasingly at an international level as exemplified by the export-bonded processing schemes in both Korea and Taiwan[1]".

It follows from the examples of Japan, South Korea and Taiwan that factor proportions in the production of manufactured products are not so rigid as has been made out by the theory of technological dualism. Contrary to the factor endowments of developing countries, for the use of capital-intensive technologies in the modern sectors, advanced developed countries are to blame because the tendencies of foreign private investors as well as official policy of the developed countries with respect to foreign aid often encourage the adoption of capital-intensive technologies in the recipient countries.[2] Further, multinationed corporations which play an important role in the industrial development of the developing countries are unlikely to spend much time in investigating alternative technologies which are more labour-intensive and better suited to the labour-surplus conditions of developing countries. They prefer to instal plants of their mother countries which embody highly capital-intensive technologies.

Besides, the *practice of tying foreign aid to* developing countries by the donor countries to purchase capital-intensive capital equipment from them promotes the use of capital-intensive technologies. Further it has been found that the producers in the developing countries often attach prestige value to installing modern capital-intensive equipment of latest technology imported from the developed countries. They themselves are not interested in investigating through R & D activities the labour-using technologies that are more suited to the factor endowments of the developing countries. Further, Gustav Ranis rightly writes, "Even if we concede that there are absolutely no technological choices, there is still the question of changes in *output-mix* (*i.e.,* the production of various products) which should make it possible to adjust one's production structure in line of factor endowment."[3]

1 Gustav Ranis, "Output and Employment in the Seventies: Conflict or Complements" in R.G. Ridker and H. Lubell, *Employment and Unemployment Problems of the Near East and South Asia*, Vol. 1, Vikas, 1971.

2 Gustav Ranis, *op. cit*.

3 Gustav Ranis, *op. cit*.

CHAPTER 28

MAHALANOBIS GROWTH MODEL AND HEAVY-INDUSTRY STRATEGY OF DEVELOPMENT

Having discussed Harrod-Domar model of growth and neoclassical and new theories of economic growth in the previous chapters, we proceed to discuss two alternative strategies of development which have been the subjects of a good deal of controversy in India. One is the strategy of development which accords top priority to basic and heavy industries. This basic heavy industry model of development was put forward by a renowned statistician, late Professor P.C. Mahalanobis who was friend and adviser to late Prime Minister Jawaharlal Nehru and who was one time member of the Planning Commission. At the time of the formulation of the Second Five Year Plan, Prof. Mahalanobis prepared a growth model with which he showed that to achieve a rapid long-term rate of growth it would be essential to devote a major part of the investment outlay to building of basic heavy industries. Mahalanobis strategy of development emphasising basic heavy industries which was adopted first of all in the Second Plan also continued to hold the stage in Indian planning right up to the Fifth Plan which was terminated by the Janata Party Government in March 1978, a year before its full term of five years.

In critique of the Mahalanobis heavy industry development strategy, Professors Vakil and Brahmanand of Bombay University put forward a *wage-goods model of development* and suggested a development strategy which accorded a top priority to agriculture and other wage-goods industries in sharp contrast to the Mahalanobis heavy industry biased strategy of development. In the present chapter we shall critically examine the heavy industry biased strategy of development and in the next chapter we shall discuss wage-goods model of development.

Mahalanobis Model of Growth

It will be useful to explain first Mahalanobis model of growth which provided a rationale for the heavy industry biased development strategy. An important point to note is that Mahalanobis identifies the rate of growth of investment in the economy not with rate of growth of savings as is usually considered by the economists but with rate of growth of output in the capital goods sector within the economy. The growth of capital goods sector in turn depends upon the proportions of total investment allocated to the capital goods sector and output-capital ratio in the capital goods sector. Given the output-capital ratio in capital goods sector (*i.e.* heavy industries), he proves that if the proportion of total investment allocated to the capital goods is relatively greater, the rate of growth of output of capital goods will be greater and hence, given the Mahalanobis assumption, the future rate of growth of investment in the economy will be greater. Now, the greater the rate of investment, the greater will be the long-term rate of growth. We thus see that with the rate of growth of output of capital goods industries. Mahalanobis shows that the proportion of total investment resources allocated to the capital goods industries, for each year is the most important factor determining the long-term rate of growth of national income. Let us represent his two-sector model in the mathematical form.

In his basic two-sector model Mahalanobis divides the economy into two sectors—the sector C produces consumer goods and sector K produces capital goods.

Let

t_0 = Initial rate of investment.

λ_k and λ_c = Proportions of total investment allocated to capital goods and consumer goods sectors respectively.

Therefore $\lambda_k + \lambda_c = 1$

β_k and β_c = Marginal output-capital ratio in the capital goods and consumer goods sectors respectively. In other words, they represent ratio of increment of income to investment in the sector K and sector C respectively.

Y_0, C_0, I_0 = The national income, consumption and investment in the base period.

Y_t, C_t, I_t = The national income, consumption and investment respectively in period t.

In Mahalanobis model, the net investment in any period can be divided into two components; the one $\lambda_k I_t$, going to capital goods sector K and $\lambda_c I_t$ going to consumer goods sector C. Therefore it follows that,

$$I_t = \lambda_k I_t + \lambda_c I_t$$

Let ΔI_t stands for increase in investment (*i.e.*, addition to the stock of capital goods) and ΔC_t for increase in consumer goods in any period t depend on the net investment in the previous period t–1. Now, given the output-capital ratios, β_k and β_c of the capital goods and consumer goods sectors respectively, the relationship between investment and the resultant increment in output in capital goods can be worked out as follows:

$$\Delta I_t = \beta_k \lambda_k I_{t-1} \text{ or } I_t - I_{t-1} = \beta_k \lambda_k I_{t-1} \quad \ldots (1)$$

This implies that the increase in investment in period t is equal to the increment in output of capital goods. The increase in output of capital goods ($\beta_K \lambda_K I_{t-1}$) in period t is given by investment in period I_{t-1} multiplied by the proportion of it going to capital goods sector (λ_k) and the output-capital ratio (β_K) in the capital goods sector.

It is clear from above that Mahalanobis takes into account only the physical aspect of investment and makes it dependent on the proportion of investment allocated to capital goods sector λ_k and output-capital ratio β_k in the capital goods sector.

Similar to equation (1) we can also write:

$$\Delta C_t = \beta_c \lambda_c I_{t-1}$$

$$C_t - C_{t-1} = \beta_c \lambda_c I_{t-1} \quad \ldots (2)$$

and also

$$\Delta I_{t-1} = \beta_k \lambda_k I_{t-2}$$

Now, income in a period t is the sum of consumption and investment, therefore:-

$$Y_t = I_t + C_t$$

$$Y_t = \beta_k \lambda_k I_{t-1} + \beta_c \lambda_c I_{t-1}$$

By further manipulation, Mahalanobis derives the following formula:

$$Y_t = Y_0 \left[1 + \alpha_0 \frac{\beta_c \lambda_c + \beta_k \lambda_k}{\lambda_k + \beta_k} (1 + \lambda_k \beta_k)^{t-1} \right] \quad \ldots (3)$$

where α_0 is the initial rate of investment expressed as percentage of income. that is,

$$\alpha_0 = \frac{I_0}{Y_0}$$

Rationale of Mahalanobis Growth Model

It is worth noting that Mahalanobis recognises that output-capital ratio β_c in the consumer goods sector is greater than the output-capital ratio β_k in the capital goods sector. If this is the case, then it apparently implies that growth of output or income will be greater if more investment is made in the consumer goods sector. But in this case the higher rate of growth of income will be only in the short run. As growth equation (3) above shows that after a critical range of time, the larger the investment allocated to capital goods industries, (λ_k), *i.e.*, the higher will be growth in output or income. Elaborating this point Prof. Raj states, "The *logic here is the same as the more common proposition that a higher rate of investment* (*i.e., a larger proportion of the productive factors used for accumulation*) *would result in a smaller volume of output being available for consumption in the short run but that over a longer period, it would result in higher rate of growth of consumption; the difference is that the choice is here stated as between investment in capital goods and investment in consumer goods industries*."[1]

The rationale of Mahalanobis growth model and development strategy can be expressed in simple words without mathematical language. According to Mahalanobis, rate of economic growth depends upon the capital formation or real investment. The greater the rate of capital formation, the greater the rate of economic growth. The rate of capital formation in an economy, according to Mahalanobis, depends upon the capacity of the economy to produce capital goods. Thus, according to him, given a closed economy, the rate of real capital formation depends not upon the savings of the economy but on the capacity to produce capital goods. Even if the rate of savings was substantially raised in order to accelerate the rate of capital formation, it would be futile, for required capital goods would not be there if there is a lack of capacity to produce capital goods. Of course, this is based on *closed economy* assumption.

Thus, according to him, if large investment is not made in the basic heavy industries producing capital goods, the country will for ever remain dependent on foreign countries for the imports of steel and capital goods like machinery for real capital formation. Since it is not possible for India to earn sufficient foreign exchange by increasing exports, the capital goods cannot be imported in sufficient quantities owing to foreign exchange constraint. The result will be that the rate of real capital formation and the rate of economic growth in the country will remain low. Thus, Mahalanobis was of the opinion that without adequate investment in basic heavy industries, it would not be possible to achieve rapid self-reliant economic growth. Therefore, according to him, to achieve rapid economic growth and self-reliance, it would be necessary to give the highest priority to basic capital goods industries in the development strategy of a plan.

Employment Generation in Mahalanobis Model. It is necessary in this connection to mention Prof. Mahalanobis' views on increasing employment opportunities and to achieve a stage of full employment. According to him, productive employment can be increased only by increasing the production of capital goods like steel, electricity, machinery, fertilizers, etc. Whether it is increase in employment in the industrial sector or in the agricultural sector, it cannot be achieved without increasing the output of capital goods. To quote him, "*The only way of eliminating unemployment in India is to build up a sufficiently large stock of capital which will enable all unemployed persons being absorbed into productive capacity. Increasing the rate of investment is, therefore, the only fundamental remedy for unemployment in India.*"[2] Thus, in Prof. Mahalanobis' opinion, not only to achieve the objective of rapid economic growth but also to achieve the goal of full employment, it is necessary to accord high priority to capital goods industries in the development strategy.

Import-Substituting Industrialisation. Mahalanobis' emphasis on basic heavy industries was also due to his objective of meeting the requirements of higher rate of capital accumulation from

1 K.N. Raj, "Growth Models in Indian Planning", *The Indian Economic Review*, Feb. 1961. Reprinted in C.D. Wadhwa, *Some Problems of India's Economic Policy*, Tata Publishing Co. Ltd., Bombay.

2 P.C. Mahalanobis, "The Approach of Operational Research to Planning in India". *Sankhya*, Vol. 16., December 1953.

within the economy and therefore enabling the economy to stop imports of foreign capital equipment and machines. To quote him, "The proper strategy would be to bring about a rapid development of the industries producing investment goods in the beginning by increasing appreciably the proportion of investment in the basic heavy industries. As the capacity to manufacture both heavy and light machinery and other capital goods increases, the capacity to invest by using domestically produced capital goods would also increase steadily and India would become more and more independent of the imports of foreign machinery and capital."[3] In fact, Mahalanobis growth model advocates import-substitution type of industrial development strategy.

It is important to note that Mahalanobis assumed though implicitly that export earnings of India cannot be sufficiently increased. If this assumption is not valid, as has been pointed out by several critics, then he could not justifiably identify rate of investment in the economy with the domestic output of capital goods. If exports of a country can be adequately raised, the various capital goods can be imported in exchange for exports. In that case rate of investment or rate of capital accumulation in the economy can be stepped up without giving high priority to the basic heavy industries provided the exports can be adequately increased. Thus, the assumption of stagnant exports is crucial in the Mahalanobis growth model for providing the rationale for a general shift in the investment pattern to the domestic production of capital goods.

Mahalanobis Growth Model and Development Strategy in India's Five Year Plans

As pointed out above, Mahalanobis heavy industry first strategy of development was put into actual practice in India's Five Year Plans beginning from the Second Plan. India started planned development of its economy in 1951 when First Five Year Plan was started. However, the Five Year Plan did not propose any explicit strategy of development; it took over several projects which had been worked out earlier and some of them were already in the process of being carried out. It laid emphasis on stepping up the rate of saving and therefore investment and growth by maintaining the marginal rate of saving at a substantially higher level than the average rate of saving. Although it did not present any explicit formulation of development strategy regarding the pattern of investment, its emphasis was on agriculture, irrigation, power and transport aimed at creating the base for more rapid industrialisation of the economy in the future.

The Second Five Year Plan, based as it was on Mahalanobis growth model, proposed an explicit strategy of development which gave top priority to basic heavy industries. Not only the objectives of rapid rate of economic growth and employment generation but also the aim of self-reliant and self-generating economy were sought to be achieved by *"the building up of economic and social overheads, exploration and development of minerals and the promotion of basic industries like steel, machine building, coal and heavy chemicals."*[4] Identifying underdevelopment with dependence on agriculture and thinking industrial growth especially the development of heavy industries, as the core of development underlied the approach and strategy of the Second Five Year Plan. To quote from Second Plan again, "Low or static standards of living, underemployment and unemployment, and to a certain extent even the gap between the average incomes and the highest incomes are all manifestations of the basic underdevelopment which characterises an economy depending mainly on agriculture. Rapid industrialisation and diversification of the economy is thus the core of development. But *if industrialisation is to be rapid enough, the country must aim at developing basic industries and industries which make machines to make the machines needed for further development.*"[5]

It is clear from above that in the Second Plan there was clear shift of priorities from agriculture to industries and within industries to basic heavy industries. As mentioned above, the logic of Mahalanobis in emphasizing heavy industries was that the growth of basic heavy industries will

3 *Ibid*, p. 22.
4 Government of India, Planning Commission, *Second Five Year Plan*, 1956, p. 24.
5 *Ibid*, p. 25.

enable the economy to accelerate the rate of capital formation and therefore economic growth. In fact, he identified the rate of growth of investment in the economy with the rate of growth of output in the capital goods (sector) industries within the economy.

Mahalanobis' Four-Sector Model. Mahalanobis realised that the basic heavy industries being capital-intensive will not ensure rapid expansion of employment opportunities and to bring the employment aspect into sharp focus he put forward a four-sector growth model in which he kept heavy industry sector (*i.e. K*-sector) intact but divided the *C*-sector (*i.e.,* consumption goods sector) into three sub-sectors : C_1, C_2, and C_3 (sector C_1 represented factory enterprises using mechanised techniques and producing consumer goods; Sector C_2 represented the household and small-scale enterprises also producing consumer goods and Sector C_3 represented provision of services). It was sector C_2 representing households and small-scale industries which in Mahalanobis' four-sector model was visualised to ensure the increased supply of consumer goods to meet their rising demand for them and also to ensure, being labour-intensive, expansion of employment opportunities. In keeping with this approach, Second Five Year Plan put restrictions on the growth of capacity in factory enterprises engaged in commodity production. However, since for these household or cottage enterprises, adequate resources were not provided, nor any effort was made to improve their productivity, they could neither fulfil their target of production of consumer goods nor of generating enough employment opportunities.[6]

In the Third Plan (1961–66) also the strategy of Second Plan was continued as is clear from the following: "In the Third Plan, as in the Second, the development of basic industries such as steel, fuel and power and machine building and chemical industries is fundamental to rapid economic growth. These industries largely determine the pace at which the economy can become self-reliant and self-generating."[7] Though, "to achieve self-sufficiency in foodgrains and increase agricultural production to meet the requirements of industry and exports" was stated to be one of the objectives of the Third Plan, actual allocation of resources between agriculture and other sectors did not exhibit any difference from that of the Second Plan. Therefore, the concern for food and agriculture in the Third Plan appears to be mere verbal and was not built into the strategy of development.

The Fourth Five Year Plan (1969–74) which was prepared under the Deputy Chairmanship of Late Prof. D.R.Gadgil, tried to give new shape to the planning strategy and emphasis was sought to be placed on the common man, the weaker sections and the less privileged. However, the Fourth Plan slightly raised the allocation of Public Sector outlay to agriculture and irrigation to about 23 per cent as against 20 per cent in the Second Plan and the Third Plan, and a good deal of hang over of the heavy industry biased strategy still prevailed in this Plan too.

Despite all talk of *Garibi Hatao* and direct attack on poverty which preceded the formulation of the Fifth Plan, in the Fifth Plan allocation of public sector investment to agriculture and irrigation was once again reduced to about 20 per cent and the same old heavy industry bias prevailed in the Fifth Plan's development strategy.

Critical Evaluation of Mahalanobis Heavy-Industry Strategy of Development

Mahalanobis' 'heavy industry first' strategy of development has come in for severe criticism right from the time of formulation of the Second Plan. First, **a serious mistake in Mahalanobis model is that he identified investment with saving**. That indicates lack of knowledge of economics. Economists have been emphasizing especially in the context of developing countries that increase in the rate of investment is governed by the increase in the rate of savings. If planned investment is not matched by savings, then inflationary gap will emerge which will cause prices to rise. It is

6 See Amlan Datta, *Strategy of Economic Development*, 1973. In the spinning of cotton, main emphasis was on Ambar Charkha. Ambar Charkha experiment failed because productivity and earning capacity per person engaged in it was found to be too low.

7 Government of India, Planning Commission, *Third Five Year Plan,* 1961, p. 50.

bad economics to identify investment with savings. Savings in an economy are determined by behavioural characteristics of the decision-making units such as households, the corporate sector and the Government. Saving by the households depends upon the propensity to consume which in turn depends upon various subjective and objective factors. Savings by the corporate sector depend upon the policies regarding depreciation, distribution of dividends and undistributed profits. Savings of the Government are governed by its policies regarding taxation and consumption expenditure, efficiency and profitability of public enterprises. Thus, when the planning authority allocates relatively more resources to heavy capital goods industries, as is envisaged in Mahalanobis growth model, it will lead to more physical investment or growth of capital stock. But there is no guarantee that savings, governed as they are by various behavioural characteristics of decision-making units, will rise to the level of planned investment. Therefore, by envisaging higher rate of physical investment without considering how savings of the community could be raised to the planned investment, Mahalanobis model contained built-in inflationary potential. Therefore, being unmatched by savings to fulfil the investment targets of the plan, recourse in actual practice had to be made to deficit financing. No wonder that due to the existence of inflationary gap in India's Five Year Plans prices began to rise from the very beginning of the Second Plan so much so that during the Fourth Plan period (1969–74) rate of inflation assumed serious proportion reaching as high as about 30% during 1973-74, the last year of the Fourth Plan.

A crucial weakness of Mahalanobis heavy industry strategy of development was pointed out by Professors Vakil and Brahmananda. They criticised heavy industry strategy in their now well known joint work, "*Planning for an Expanding Economy*." According to them, growth of national income and employment is determined by the supply of wage goods. They pointed out that when disguised unemployed are employed in productive work on the wage basis, the demand for wage goods will increase and unless the adequate amount of wage goods are not available, the disguised unemployed and openly unemployed cannot be put to work on the wage basis. According to them, there exists a *wage-goods gap* in underdeveloped countries like India and the basic cause of unemployment and disguised unemployment in them is the existence of this wage-goods gap. Wage goods act as a constraint on the growth of industrialisation and non-agricultural growth. Thus, in the determination of growth of income and employment, while Mahalanobis emphasised '*fixed capital*', Brahmananda and Vakil laid stress on the wage goods which are also called '*circulating capital*'. As mentioned earlier, Vakil and Brahmananda put forward a growth model in which wage goods played a key role. Accordingly, they suggested a developed strategy in which top priority was given to agriculture which produces most important form of wage goods, *i.e.*, foodgrains. We shall discuss in detail the views of Professors Vakil and Brahmananda regarding the growth of income and employment in the next chapter. We shall also critically examine their wage-goods model of development in the next chapter.

There is no doubt that **Mahalanobis "heavy industry" strategy overlooked the importance of agriculture or wage goods in the growth process of the economy**. This manifested itself in the rapid rise of prices from the very beginning of the Second Plan. While a relatively large investment in the basic industries resulted in the creation of money incomes and consequently in a large increase in demand for wage goods, the supply of wage goods did not adequately increase due to the continued neglect of agriculture in India's planning strategy. This caused imbalance between demand for and supply of wage goods which has been responsible for inflationary situation in the Indian economy. The continued neglect of wage goods in the development strategy of Indian Plans, right up to the Fifth Plan, is quite surprising since, as pointed out above, this weakness of the strategy was pointed out by Professors Vakil and Brahmananda at the time of the formulation of the Second Plan.

The larger allocation of resources to the basic heavy industries deprived agriculture (including irrigation) and rural industries of enough resources required for their growth. It is now well known as brought out by Professor Lipton, B.S. Minhas that India's Five Year Plans beginning from the Second Plan, based as they were on Mahalanobis growth model with its emphasis on heavy industries, suffered from '*relative neglect of agriculture*'. The view that there has been relative neglect of agriculture in Indian Plans has been forcefully and effectively expressed and provided by Professor Michael Lipton. He writes: "We have seen that neither allocations of public money, nor incentives to the movement of persons and other resources, have favoured agricultural development; that 70 per cent of the workers get less than 35 per cent of investment finance and a far smaller share of human skills. Several types of pressures on opinion and policy have combined to bias the allocation of cash, effort, personnel and research away from rural needs."[8]

Like Professor Lipton, B.S. Minhas also holds as similar view about relative neglect of agriculture in Indian Planning. He thus states, "In practical terms the most unfortunate consequences of our adherence to this philosophy of development has been the appalling neglect of agriculture and rural development."[9] Before Lipton and Minhas, Professors C.N. Vakil and P.R. Brahmananda, as mentioned above, have been consistently expressing the view about the low priority assigned to agriculture since the beginning of Second Plan. Recently, C.H. Hanumantha Rao has also deplored the neglect of agriculture in the strategy of Indian Plans. He writes, "*The failure of the present strategy to step up public investment for agricultural development has accentuated the problem of unemployment in rural areas*."

A serious failure of Mahalanobis development strategy with its emphasis on basic heavy industries is that **it failed to generate adequate amount of employment opportunities.** Pattern of industrialization has been based on capital-intensive technology imported from abroad and has been oriented towards urban large-scale industries. If the emphasis were on rural-oriented industrialization promoting cottage and small-scale industries, using intermediate technologies, the problem of surplus labour and unemployment would not have been as acute as it is now. Besides this, attention was not paid to absorb labour in the agricultural sector, and the agricultural development strategy that could absorb more labour in productive employment was not adopted. Necessary technological and institutional changes for designing such an agricultural strategy required to create more employment were not in actual practice made. Many land reform measures, apart from abolition of big Zamindars and Jagirdars, remained mostly on paper. Legislations regarding tenancy reforms and ceiling on land holdings were not actually enforced and implemented. Being highly capital-intensive the basic heavy industries have themselves created very little employment opportunities.

It is no doubt true that certain products of heavy industries such as fertilizers, steel, cement, etc. are certainly required for the growth of agriculture, especially in the context of new agricultural technology and should, therefore, be produced, but Mahalanobis strategy envisaged achievement of self-sufficiency all along the line, involving production of highly sophisticated machines to make machines. This *autarchic* nature of Mahalanobis development strategy has been rightly criticised. B.S. Minhas rightly writes, "*The logic of the Heavy Industry First Strategy in India sprouted from a number of philosophical riddles. One important conundrum runs as follows: should you import food, or import fertilisers to produce food at home? Rather than import fertilisers, should you not import fertiliser materials and machinery in order to make fertilisers at home? But why import fertiliser machinery? Should you not import machines to make; fertiliser machinery at home? On and on goes the riddle.*"[10]

In view of the limited resources available for investment, the inclusion of highly capital-intensive industries producing machines and mother machines, exhaust a great deal of resources, leaving relatively little for agriculture and rural industries which contain large employment potential. Therefore, in our view, in initial stages of development some intermediate products, machines, and capital goods

8 M. Lipton, "Strategy for Agriculture: Urban Bias and Rural Planning", Printed in P. Streeman and M. Lipton (ed.), *The Crisis of Indian Planning*, Oxford University Press, 1960, p. 130.

9 B.S. Minhas, *Self-Reliance and India's Planning Strategy*, Indian Statistical Institute (Discussion Paper No. 138), March 1976, p. 14.

10 B.S. Minhas, *op.cit.*, p. 12.

should be imported if they are urgently needed for some industries, even if in their case, we possess comparative advantage in the dynamic context.

However, it needs to be emphasised again that the form of capital is crucial for employment generation. What is required is the small and simple types of machines and tools which are required for the growth of agriculture and small-scale rural industries. Further, the production of those types of capital goods such as fertilizers, pesticides, cement which will help in raising agricultural production and employment need to be expanded. Some large-scale industries, if their large size is necessary in view of technological considerations, should play a supporting role to the development of agriculture and rural industries. Thus, *the strategy of growth in India should be reoriented so that agriculture and rural industries constitute the main thrust of the development effort.*

From the foregoing analysis, it follows that if the mounting unemployment problem is to be tackled, the strategy of development adopted need to be revised and modified. In the new strategy, agriculture has to play a key role in generating enough employment opportunities for a long time to come. The fact that 68 per cent of the Indian labour force and majority of the unemployed and underemployed reside in the rural areas and further that the employment potential of the industries of large-scale type is very little, the promotion of agricultural and rural development must be made the springboard and the leading sector for generating productive employment for millions. Therefore, *the strategy for agricultural development should be such as will absorb productively the largest possible number of workers*.

Another weakness of the "heavy industry first" strategy and development was that it chose pattern of investment with *higher capital-output ratio*. In basic heavy industries capital-output ratio was admittedly high and in agriculture and related activities, capital-output ratio was low. Thus, the highest priority to basic heavy industries and low priority to agriculture in the pattern of investment meant the choice of high macro-value of incremental capital-output ratio (ICOR). As has been made clear in earlier chapters that if a higher growth rate is desired, given the initial value of a rate of saving and annual increments therein over the projected period, then the criterion should be to choose a pattern of investment with a lower macro-value of capital-output ratio. In the case of India, this would have implied a high priority to be given to agricultural and related sectors over a long period of time. Therefore, the choice of the pattern of investment containing a high priority to basic heavy industries and low priority to agriculture meant a low rate of economic growth. As has been pointed out above, Mahalanobis and others supporting his strategy contended that their strategy would ensure high rate of growth in the long run. But in actual practice even after 25 years (1956-80) Mahalanobis development strategy of 1955–56 failed to ensure more than 3.5 per cent average annual rate of growth. In the meantime people suffered a lot due to the inflation generated by the strategy and the non-availability of requisite amount of essential consumer goods.

Mahalanobis heavy industry strategy suffers from another weakness in that it heavily depends upon foreign exchange requirements. Though the strategy assumed that exports from the Indian economy could not be sufficiently increased, it required a large amount of foreign exchange resources to establish a network of heavy capital goods industries which required the imports of capital equipment and machinery on a large scale from other countries. For a self-contained growth model framed in the context of a closed economy or stagnant exports, this was an inner contradiction. This also had two evil effects. Because of the low priority to agriculture and consumer goods industries which had export potentials, export could not rise much, and secondly, due to the highest priority to heavy capital goods industries large imports of capital equipment and materials had to be made. Such was the large requirement of foreign exchange to import capital equipment that despite the liberal foreign aid received from countries, especially the U.S.A., the country had to face a serious foreign exchange crisis.

It was said in the defence of the heavy industry strategy that it would ultimately help in substituting imports of heavy industrial products such as steel, cement, various kinds of machines, fertilizers etc. This implies that import substitution when accomplished would enable the economy to dispense with foreign aid. However, it was said that in the meantime aid was required to import equipment and materials to set up heavy capital goods industries. Thus it was claimed that the heavy industry strategy envisaged getting "*aid to end aid*".

However, the fact remains that far from moving the economy towards self-reliance, the heavy industry strategy increased the dependence on foreign aid. Because of low priority to agriculture in the strategy, production of foodgrains did not increase adequately and as a result the imbalance between population and foodgrains further increased during the planning period. In order to correct this imbalance foodgrains had to be imported on a large scale from other countries. Whereas the imports of foodgrains into India during the First Plan period were of the order of 12 million tones, it rose to 17 million tonnes in the Second Plan period. The situation worsened in the Third Plan period as the implementation of heavy industry strategy further proceeded and 26 million tonnes of foodgrains were imported during the Third Plan period. During the three years of plan-holiday period (1966–69), the imports of foodgrains jumped to 25 million tonnes in *three* years period. In the Fourth Plan period in which hangover of the heavy industry strategy persisted, foodgrains imports continued unabated with the exception of the year 1972. During the six years period 1970-76, 26.4 million tonnes of foodgrains were imported.[11]

It is thus clear that the imbalance between foodgrains and population was the direct result of the neglect of agriculture in India's 'heavy industry first strategy'. Thus the most distressing effect of the strategy was that the country came to be dependent on even foodgrains. But for the imports of foodgrains under PL 480 and liberal foreign aid which was made available, India could not have been able to implement the Mahalanobis strategy for its inner contradictions and its inappropriateness to the Indian reality would have come to the surface much earlier. The situation in the beginning of the Fifth Plan, *i.e.,* in 1974, was that India's large foreign exchange resources were being used to meet the needs of current consumption (*i.e.*, to import foodgrains) rather than to import capital equipment and materials to sustain *new investment* or capital accumulation. Thus for stepping up the rate of capital accumulation and therefore economic growth we came to be dependent on all the three types of commodities, (i) capital equipment, (ii) raw materials, and (iii) foodgrains. Thus, despite the objective of achieving self-reliance, the strategy adopted drove the economy away from it. The philosophy of "*aid to end aid*" proved to be myth.

Heavy industry strategy has also been criticised for its *ignoring the relevance of the principle of comparative advantage* and the gains to be obtained from specialisation in some selected fields. As mentioned before, Mahalanobis formulated his growth model on the assumption that exports could not be expanded sufficiently. With the help of his model he showed that it is through the adoption of the strategy of substituting imports by domestic production of heavy industry products such as steel, fertilizers, various kinds of machines and machines to make machines, heavy chemicals that high long-term rate of growth could be achieved. Thus Mahalanobis strategy involved industrialisation of import-substitution type. The question whether the new heavy industries would have a comparative advantage or not was not considered as a relevant consideration. The reckless pursuit of import substitution all along the line and accordingly setting up of all basic heavy industries such as steel, fertilizers, heavy chemicals, machine building and also industries which make machines to make machines (*i.e.*, industries producing mother machines), and so on without considering whether we had comparative advantage in their production. If we had comparative advantage in *some* basic heavy industries we should have concentrated our resources and enjoyed advantages of quick specialisation in selected lines rather than *thinly* spreading our resources on all types of basic heavy industries

11 Government of India, *Economic Survey*, 1977-78, p. 69.

irrespective of whether we have comparative advantage or not in them caused misuse of scarce investment resources. As seen above, as a result of this strategy of all-round import substitution to build basic heavy industries we came to be dependent on imports from the rest of the world than we ever were or needed to be.

It may also be pointed out that in the Mahalanobis heavy industry strategy alternative policy of development of industries which had large export potential was not at all given any consideration. That supplies of some capital goods could be procured from abroad by development of export industries was ruled out. In this connection it was pointed out by the followers of Mahalanobis that the expansion of India's exports would mean the decline in its terms of trade. In our view, the contention that the increase in India's exports would necessarily mean decline in terms of trade was not justified. In fact, up to 1972 (*i.e.,* before the oil crisis) the terms of trade had been in India's favour. It may be pointed out that declining terms of trade argument was advanced by supporters of Mahalanobis strategy only after the Mahalanobis model had been accepted and put into actual practice.

Finally, it may be noted that for achieving high long-term rate of economic growth Mahalanobis and later Raj and Sen[12] and Gautam Mathur[13] have laid the greatest stress upon high magnitude of the ratio of incremental ploughback of heavy industry products to the expansion of heavy industries sector itself as compared to all other sectors. This pattern of industrialisation, according to them, would automatically raise the saving-income ratio and generate a high rate of economic growth in the long run. However this argument is full of deficiencies and infirmities. The all-round development of heavy industry sector and the highest ratio of ploughback of heavy industry products to the heavy industry sector involves, given the scarcity of resources, not only the appalling neglect of agriculture and rural development but also the neglect of the development of export industries and thereby enjoying the benefits of specialisation.

12 K.N. Raj and A.K. Sen, "Alternative Patterns of Growth under Conditions of Export Earnings", *Oxford Economic Papers*, Feb. 1961.

13 Gautam Mathur, *Planning for Steady Growth*, Oxford University Press, 1965.

CHAPTER

29

WAGE-GOODS MODEL AND STRATEGY OF DEVELOPMENT

As stated in the previous chapter, an alternative model of development was developed by Vakil and Brahmananda. Professors Vakil and Brahmananda adapted and modified classical theory of growth of income and employment in the context of today's developing countries characterised by disguised unemployment. In sharp contrast to Mahalanobis model which emphasised the role of fixed capital, Vakil and Brahmananda laid stress on wage goods or what they called liquid capital in determining the growth of employment and income. In conformity with their emphasis on wage goods or liquid capital in their model they propounded a strategy of development which accorded the highest priority to wage-goods industries, especially agriculture, in allocation of investment resources. In the present chapter we shall explain here their wage-goods model and development strategy only briefly.

Wage-Goods Model

As in their old work, '*Planning for an Expanding Economy*' written in 1956, Vakil and Brahmananda attribute the prevailing poverty and unemployment to the existence of **wage-goods gap.** They, however, later defined their wage-goods gap with reference to the magnitude of poverty rather than with reference to magnitude of disguised unemployment as they did in their old work. Admittedly, poverty and unemployment are the two most pressing problems facing the underdeveloped countries today. Poverty is defined as living by households below minimum level of subsistence or real income.

According to Vakil and Brahmananda, to remove this poverty it is essential to increase the aggregate supply of wage goods. Unless and until the wage-goods gap is bridged, poverty will not be eliminated. In an article published in 1976, Dr. Brahmananda explained the causes of poverty in the following terms: "Poverty in 1975-76 could have been eliminated if the aggregate supply position in regard to basic wage-goods was higher, let us say, about 25% to 30%, and poverty would not raise its ugly head, if from 1975-76 onwards, each year our aggregate supplies of these goods would be growing at the same rate as our population would be growing. Thus, *there is a basic wage-goods. gap in the economy which explains poverty*."[1]

Components of Wage Goods

It is useful to note what are the components of wage goods whose output expansion is stressed in the wage-goods strategy. According to Brahmananda, they are: (1) Foodgrains; Cereals, Pulses, (2) Milk and Milk Products (3) Edible oils, (4) Fish, Eggs and Meat, (5) Sugar and Sugar Products, (6) Fruits and Vegetables, (7) Spices, (8) Tea, (9) Coffee, (10) Cloth, (11) Matches, (12) Soap, (13) Salt, (14) Kerosene.

In addition to the above wage goods which are of the nature of private consumption goods, there are goods or services which fulfil minimum needs of the people and are generally provided at the collective level. These are "drugs for common use, medical and hospital facilities, minimum

1 P. R. Brahmananda, "How Well have We Planned", *The Illustrated Weekly of India*, October 24, 1976.

educational and library facilities, minimum utility services like water, electricity, roads etc., recreational services and facilities." Besides these, there may be other wage goods in different regions depending upon the conventional and physiological-cum-nutritional requirements of workers.

Now, the question arises as to why there is a deficiency of wage goods in the economy. This is due to the fact that the capital stock or productive capacity designed and directed to produce wage goods is deficient. To eliminate poverty capital stock designed for the production of wage goods needs to be expanded. It may be noted that overall capital stock may be adequate but the capital stock in the specific form of productive capacity to produce basic consumer goods may be deficient. This is because all types of capital stocks cannot be used for the production of wage goods. For instance, steel plants and machine making factories cannot be utilized for producing wage goods such as foodgrains, kerosene oil, cloth, sugar, etc. In this connection economists generally draw distinction between capital in "putty" form and "clay' form. While *putty capital* is generalised form of capital which is capable of being used to manufacture all types of goods, that is, *capital goods*, *luxury goods and basic wage goods, capital in a clay form* is suited to the production of specific goods for which it is designed. Thus, according to Dr. Brahmananda, "*So long as capital is in a putty, all-purpose suited form, it can be directed towards creation of any sort of specific capacity built when once putty capital becomes capital goods in the form of factories, projects like mills, machinery, plants, mining and power stations and transport networks, it partakes "the nature of clay, fit for a particular purpose.*" [2]

It is only the stock of wage goods and the raw materials and accessories used in the production of these wage goods that represents putty capital or generalised capital because "*if stocks of wage goods exist, labour power can be purchased and deployed for whatever specific capacities are needed in the country.*"[3] We can represent the argument of Brahmananda in the following type of production process:

Wage goods → Labour employment → Capital → Wage goods

This means that if wage goods are somehow made available, they can be used to employ labour for producing capital. If the new capital is designed to manufacture wage goods, the growth process can be started which will become cumulative and self-sustaining. The general argument of most modern economists is that for providing productive employment to the workers and to raise their productive efficiency and thereby accelerate the rate of economic growth, it is the deficiency of cooperating factors such as capital equipment, machines, cement, etc. which stand in the way. Vakil and Brahmananda hold this generally held view as quite fallacious since, according to them, this is based upon the assumption that adequate quantities of wage goods are already available. Thus Vakil and Brahmananda lay greater stress on wage goods (*i.e.*, liquid or circulating capital) than fixed capital in the growth process of the economy and for eradication of poverty and unemployment. "If only sufficient quantities of real liquid capital were available, the labour force can be diverted towards the manufacture of the tools and other equipment."[4]

It follows from above that, according to Vakil and Brahmananda, for removal of poverty, promotion of economic growth or capital accumulation alone is not enough. "*The way out of poverty is, therefore, to pay immediate attention to making good the capital gap in respect of wage-goods capacity. This, in its turn, would imply drastic alteration in the pattern of investment in the economy.*" [5]

Disguised Unemployment and Wage-Goods Model

Not only does the removal of poverty but also the eradication of disguised unemployment requires the need for the expansion of basic wage goods. We will explain in a later chapter how Vakil and Brahmananda visualise saving potential in the form of wage goods in the disguised unemployment. They take it granted that a huge amount of disguised unemployment exists in Indian agriculture and to

2 P. R. Brahmananda, *op. cit.,* p. 31.

3 *Ibid*, p.33.

4 Vakil and Brahmananda, *Planning for an Expanding Economy*, *op.cit.*, p. 250.

5 P. R. Brahmananda, 1976, *op.cit.*, p.35.

eradicate it they propose a strategy of withdrawing the disguised unemployment from agriculture and using the wage goods surplus left behind by them. They recognise that there will be *leakage* of wage goods in the process of withdrawal of disguised unemployed. They propounded in this connection a *consumption multiplier* or *wage goods multiplier*. In their scheme the disguised unemployed can be productively employed in capital construction works provided the additional supplies of wage goods are made available. They will produce those kinds of capital goods which will be used for manufacturing wage goods. In this way productive capacity designed for the production of wage goods will increase which will set in motion a cumulative process of growth in employment and output.

As a matter of fact, according to them, poverty and disguised unemployment are not two different problems; they are the two aspects of the same problem. Further, the solution of the problem of poverty as well as of disguised unemployment lies in raising the supply of wage goods. To quote Brahmananda, "Granted the existence of disguised unemployment, its eradication becomes conditional upon additional supplies of wage goods; for their employment in full-bodied productive capacity would create additional demand for such goods, unless the system is able to procure these wage goods additional employment will not be stabilised. Additional supply of wage goods leading to an improvement in per capita real income in terms of wage goods and/or in the real wage rate is the mechanism by means of which unemployment gets eradicated. Poverty in terms of inadequate supplies of wage goods is the barrier to full employment or fuller employment. In fact, there are no two problems like poverty and unemployment; there is only one problem—inadequate supply of wage goods."[6]

In the wage-goods model of Vakil and Brahmananda "*the rate of growth of real income is determined by the proportion of savings to income and the portion of such savings devoted to the expansion of the wage goods sector*." It follows, therefore, that in order to accelerate the increase in the capital stock (or productive capacity) designed and directed to produce wage goods the proportion of saving to national income must be raised. Given the capital-output ratio, the greater the rate of saving, the greater will be the rate of investment or capital accumulation. To raise the proportion of saving to national income, Vakil and Brahmananda[7] recommended an increase in the rate of interest especially on bank deposits, fiscal incentives to those who are in a position to save and check on inflation or rising prices as they reduce the value of money and adversely affect the propensity to save. But, according to wage-goods model, to achieve faster rate of growth of employment and real income increase in the rate of saving is not enough. The pattern of investment must also be oriented towards building of capital stock designed for the production of wage goods rather than building capital stock in the form of heavy industries.

Wage-Goods Strategy Further Developed and Modified

In recent years Brahmananda has further developed and modified his wage goods model and development strategy thereof. He now calls his strategy as the "*Extended Wage Goods Strategy*" for he now includes in his priority sector what he calls '*integrated wage goods complex*' not only the wage goods but also those capital goods which are required for the production of wage goods. To quote him, "Since not all capital goods (machinery and plant, tools and raw materials) are directly and/or indirectly but necessarily involved in the production process of wage goods, priority in development of capital goods has to be assigned to those capital goods whose supply (and/or production) leads to the production of wage goods."

It is therefore clear that Prof. Brahmananda later realised the importance of capital goods and modified his model in the light of the criticism levelled against his earlier model that it was based on simple type of production process which considered that only labour is required for production

6 P. R. Brahmananda, 1976, *op.cit.*, p.35.

7 C. N. Vakil, *Growth with Stability*, Dr. Gadgil Memorial Lectures, Oct. 9, 1977.

of wage goods or capital goods. Thus, the modification made by him is in the right direction and makes his model more consistent and realistic. In order that not only the growing population but also the existing unemployed and disguised unemployed are provided with employment, the extended wage-goods strategy suggests that the integrated wage goods complex (that is, basic wage goods and capital goods required for their production) should grow at a much higher rate than population. Accordingly, in the development strategy a very high priority must be accorded to the investment in wage goods complex.

Real Income Multiplier. Besides in the wage-goods model, real income *multiplier* plays a significant role in the process of economic growth. It may, however, be noted that Vakil-Brahmananda's concept of consumption multiplier has undergone some change in recent years. While their old concept of consumption multiplier expounded in their earlier work "*Planning for an Expanding Economy*" was defined with particular reference to the removal of disguised unemployed from agriculture they have now put forward a concept of multiplier which relates the increase in the supply of wage goods to the increase in real income. In a later econometric study, Dr. Brahmananda found that ₹ 100 *worth of increase in the supply of wage goods leads to an increase in real domestic product (national income) equivalent to more than ₹ 300. There is a stable multiplier.*"[8] This has, therefore, been called consumption-real income multiplier and is an important factor in the determination of the magnitude of real income in the economy. This multiplier works on account of the fact that net productivity or output per unit of labour employed far exceeds the amount of wage goods consumed per unit of labour. The surplus of wage goods so obtained can be further used to provide more labour employment to yield more output. "There is thus a multiplier process in regard to supply of output, the value of the multiplier being dependent upon the fractional excess of the net output efficiency of labour over and above the portion contributing to meeting the wage goods requirements of performance of labour."[9]

Let us briefly state the wage-goods model of development

1. The poverty and unemployment exist because there is a wage-goods gap.
2. It follows from first proposition that for solving the problem of poverty and unemployment, expansion in the supply of wage goods is required.
3. To secure a rapid increase in the supply of wage goods, capital stock (or productive capacity) designed for the production of wage goods must be expanded. In other words; agriculture, other wage goods industries and capital goods needed for production in them must be given topmost priority in the investment pattern.
4. To enlarge the capacity to produce wage goods, proportion of saving to national income should be raised and a relatively high proportion of national saving should be invested in wage goods complex.
5. The importance of increase in the capacity to produce wage goods is enhanced because of the working of consumption-real income multiplier.

Arguments in Favour of Wage-Goods Strategy

Many arguments have been given in defence of wage-goods model as compared to Mahalanobis' Heavy Industries model of growth. Firstly, given the investment resources, rate of economic growth will be faster if a high priority is given to the wage goods sector in the pattern of investment. This is because capital-output ratio is much lower in wage goods industries, especially agriculture, than in basic heavy industries sector. It has been contended by Dr. Brahmananda that within the framework of heavy industries model we cannot achieve a growth rate higher than 4% given the saving and investment rate of about 15% because of the high capital-output ratio in the heavy industries.

8 P. R. Brahmananda, *Determinants. of Real National Income and Prices Level in India*. University of Bombay.

9 Vakil and Brahmananda, 1956, *op.cit*., p. 215.

But, according to him, if we make a shift to wage-goods model, the achievement of a higher growth rate becomes possible because of lower capital-output ratio in wage goods sector.

Secondly, the implementation of the wage-goods model will not involve much foreign exchange requirements both for building the wage goods capacity and for current purposes of using the capacity to produce wage goods. As a result, as compared to the Mahalanobis heavy industry strategy, the balance of payments gap in 'wage-goods bias' development strategy would be quite negligible.

Further, another merit of wage-goods model of development which was pointed out was that the wage-goods industries such as agriculture, cotton textile, sugar had a large export potential. Their products tend to have a large foreign demand. Thus, with the expansion of exports on the one hand and low import requirements on the other, the wage-goods strategy will result in net earning of adequate amount of foreign exchange which can be utilised for importing capital equipment required for building capital goods base needed for producing capital goods and materials for the expansion of industrial and agricultural sectors. In this way the adoption of wage-goods model will ensure the attainment of self-reliance in a short time.

Thirdly, the most important advantage of wage-goods model is that the high rate of growth of the agriculture and the related sectors under it would provide potentially increasing amount of wage goods or circulating capital. The expansion in supplies of wage-goods or circulating capital will enable us to provide employment to the open and disguised unemployed and will thus help in solving the problems of poverty and unemployment. Fourthly, as the majority of the new workers getting employment following the implementation of the wage-goods strategy will be drawn from the poverty-stricken households, the wage-goods strategy will have a good income redistribution effect. It was thus claimed by Dr. Brahmananda that the wage goods strategy put forth by him would promote economic growth with social justice.

Lastly, the expansion of wage-goods sector, that is, agriculture will generate a large demand for the products of manufacturing industries. This will ensure rapid industrial development with proper linkage with agriculture. The manufacturing industries would obtain foodgrains and raw materials from agriculture and in turn would feed latter with inputs and industrial consumer goods. It is here worth mentioning that Vakil and Brahmananda, like Ragnar Nurkse, believed that disguised unemployment in labour-surplus developing countries contained saving potential in the form of wage goods. By withdrawing the disguised unemployed people from agriculture, some amount of"wage goods can be released for providing productive employment in the creation of capital assets (that is, in the investment sector). But Vakil and Brahmananda thought that the surplus of wage goods so released would not be sufficient to provide employment to all the potentially available labour force. Therefore, they also emphasised an increase in the production of wage goods, especially foodgrains, so as to fill in the wage-goods gap and thus to achieve full-employment conditions.

The most important kind of wage goods are foodgrains which are the product of agriculture and for which income elasticity of demand in the less developed countries is very high. Therefore, the approach to unemployment which visualises wage goods gap as the cause of unemployment assigns a paramount role to agricultural development in the strategy of growth so that food surpluses are made available to the newly employed workers outside agriculture. That the growth in non-agricultural employment through creating capital assets under rural works programme or through the development of manufacturing industries (including the capital goods industries) depends upon the marketable food surpluses has long been recognised in development economics. Development experience of Western capitalist countries as well as of socialist Russia shows that for growth of industrial employment, availability of food surpluses is an essential prerequisite, though the methods of mobilising food surpluses have been different in the capitalist and socialist countries. Whereas in today's Western developed countries such as U.K., U.S.A. and France, required food surpluses were obtained through agricultural growth by adopting capitalist mode of production, in Soviet Russia collectivisation of agriculture helped a good deal in extracting food surplus for growth in industrial employment.[10]

The Critical Evaluation of Wage-Goods Strategy

That the growth of non-agricultural sector depends on the availability of foodgrains or wage goods is quite obvious. When people are employed in rural public works and in industries producing capital goods and consumer goods outside agriculture, there will be need for food to feed them. If food is not made available to them directly or through market mechanism, their employment cannot be sustained. It may be asked even when unemployed they must be consuming food to make their living possible and therefore no extra food would be required when they are given employment. That is, whether employed or unemployed people must consume food in order to live. However, when employed and paid wages for their work, they would definitely increase their demand for food, income elasticity of demand for food being quite high in underdeveloped countries. If more food is not forthcoming pressure of demand would push up prices of foodgrains which will result in the redistribution of foodgrains. It is thus clear that the supply of foodgrains is an important bottleneck in the way of expansion of employment outside agriculture. Thus, Prof. Vakil and Brahmananda's stress on wage goods as an important factor in determining employment outside agriculture is quite proper.

If b stands for food output per person employed in agriculture, w for consumption of food per person in agriculture, then food surplus per man employed in agriculture will be $(b-w)$ and if E_1 is the total number of persons employed in agriculture, then the total food surplus will be $(b-w)\ E_1$. Now, the magnitude of this $(b-w)\ E_2$ will determine the generation of employment opportunities outside agriculture. If we designate employment outside agriculture by E_2 then we can express employment outside agriculture in the following functional form:

$$E_2 = f(b - w)E_1$$

In other words, viewed in this way, employment outside agriculture depends upon the food surplus in the agricultural sector. And the food surplus in agriculture depends upon the productivity per head (b) in agriculture and the consumption per head of the persons E_1 engaged in it. If productivity per head (b) in agriculture is increased substantially, opportunities of wage-employment outside agriculture can be expanded rapidly.

However, the assertion by Vakil and Brahmananda that the growth in employment solely and exclusively depends upon the supply of wage goods and that the capital goods (that is, heavy industry products) play no important role in the creation of employment opportunities is open to question. Under adequate organisation and entrepreneurial ability as well as optimum institutional forms, two important bottlenecks, namely, capital goods bottleneck and wage goods bottleneck, are faced in creating opportunities for productive employment. For expansion in productive employment both these bottlenecks have to be overcome and to emphasise the breaking of one bottleneck, while making no attempt to tackle the other, is an unrealistic approach to the employment problem. Wage goods are required to meet the demands of the newly employed people, but if some people are to be. employed in productive activities in the very first instance, they are required to be equipped with some capital goods. Further, for the production of wage goods themselves, capital goods are required. That is, labour is to be equipped with capital goods to produce wage goods.'[11] Professor Dantwala rightly

10 M. M. Dobb, *Soviet Economic Development since* 1917. See also his *Economic Growth* and *Underdeveloped Countries,* 1963, p. 49.

11 This does not mean that capital goods industries should get high priority in the pattern of investment. What has been emphasised is that to make the employment productive, labour is required to be equipped with capital. Besides, for generation of employment opportunities, form of capital is as important as its amount. Whether capital goods needed for growth of industries or for the growth of agriculture to be given higher priority, depends upon whether industry or agriculture constitutes the main thrust of the development strategy.

points out that, *"it is a mistake to consider capital goods and wage goods as exclusive and unrelated categories. Anyone who studies the composition of inputs needed for transformation of traditional agriculture should be able to appreciate the interconnection between the two."*[12]

Thus, development strategy for rapid expansion of employment has to be such as will envisage the increase in production of both wage goods and capital goods. Thus, to talk of wage goods *versus* capital goods is a false issue and an unrealistic approach to the problem of employment since both are needed to generate employment; capital goods are required to make the employment productive and wage goods are needed to feed the workers provided with new employment, that is, to sustain their employment. To say this, however, does not imply that all capital goods industries should be necessarily developed at home and given higher priority in the allocation of resources. Which specific capital goods should be produced at home and which be imported from abroad should be decided on the basis of resource endowments and comparative advantage conceived in the dynamic context.

Further, it needs to be emphasised again that crucial factor in the generation of employment opportunities is the production and use of appropriate types of capital which aid labour in production rather than displace it. Thus, the use of appropriate technology for production is as important as the accumulation of capital if employment opportunities are to be increased and poverty eradicated. In other words, form of capital is as important as its amount. Moreover, in view of the limited employment potential of large-scale industries using capital-intensive technology, if a development strategy is to generate sufficient employment opportunities, agriculture and rural industries must play a leading role and be given higher priority in the pattern of investment, for it is in the agriculture and rural industries that vast employment potential exists. Industries should play a supporting role to the development of agriculture, *i.e.*, industry should produce such capital goods and other inputs such as fertilizers, cement, pesticides that are required for the growth of agriculture. Thus, whereas, in the development designs of Western countries as well as of Soviet Russia, agriculture played a supporting role to urban industrialisation, in India with surplus labour industrialisation must serve the needs of agricultural growth. Thus, if for generation of employment opportunities agriculture is to constitute the main thrust, it is the basic and capital goods needed for the expansion of agriculture such as irrigation facilities, fertilisers, HYV, improvement and development of land that need to be given a high priority.

However, the wage-goods approach to employment, as enunciated by Vakil and Brahmananda, has not considered the creation of employment opportunities in wage-goods industries themselves, especially in agriculture. Emphasis on agricultural development in wage-goods approach has been laid for increasing the supply of wage goods so that they can be used for employment generation in non-wage goods sector, especially the rural public works or accumulation of capital. Professors Vakil and Brahmanada in their proposed growth strategy had visualised withdrawing disguised unemployed from agriculture rather than creating employment opportunities in agriculture itself. That the problem of unemployment and underemployment or disguised unemployment in agriculture can be solved through agricultural growth itself, if proper strategy for agricultural development is adopted, was ignored by them. In our view, in over-populated and agriculturally backward developing countries like India, agriculture can still absorb more labour if appropriate technological and institutional changes are brought about. Thus, agriculture is to be given high priority not only because it will yield wage goods which are badly needed for the expansion of non-agricultural employment but also because it is agriculture which, if proper strategy is adopted, contains immense potential for the absorption of labour in productive employment. Therefore, a great weakness of the strategy proposed by Vakil and Brahmananda is that it ignores the need for bringing about appropriate technological and institutional changes to generate enough employment opportunities in the agricultural sector itself.

12 M. L. Datwala, Approaches to Growth and Employment, *Economic and Political Weekly*, December 1972.

Further, Vakil and Brahmananda's strategy of employing labour in public works or in constructing other forms of capital is based upon a simple production process which assumes that labour alone can produce capital goods. This is far from the prevailing situation in the real world. Labour with bare hands can do little. Extra capital equipment and materials are required to employ labour in capital creating works. This necessitates a more elaborate approach to the growth of employment in developing economies. involving proper balance between wage goods, labour employment, capital goods and materials.

PART VI

Sectoral Aspects of Economic Development

- Agriculture, Productivity and Economic Development
- New Technology and Sustainable Agriculture
- Land Reforms: Farm Size, Productivity and Efficiency
- Rationale and Pattern of Industrialisation
- Choice of Techniques and Appropriate Technology in Developing Countries
- Infrastructure and its Importance

Chapter 30

Agriculture, Productivity and Economic Development

ROLE OF AGRICULTURE IN ECONOMIC DEVELOPMENT

Agriculture plays a vital role in economic development of developing countries. Even in most of the presently developed countries agricultural revolution preceded industrial revolution. The role of agriculture in economic development is crucial because a majority of the population of developing countries make their living from agriculture. Besides, quite a large number of the poor, especially small and marginal farmers, landless agricultural labour eke out their subsistence from agriculture and their incomes can be increased through raising agricultural productivity. Therefore, to eradicate rural poverty agricultural productivity and production have to be increased so as to fulfil their basic needs. Moreover, contrary to popular perception, for increasing employment opportunities and absorbing labour productively there is need for rapid growth of agriculture.

Besides, there are important linkages between agriculture and industry and, as shall be explained in detail below, agriculture contributes to industrial growth by providing food to the workers employed in industries. Industrial growth will be held back if enough food is not available to feed the growing workforce in industries. We explain below the role of agriculture in detail and point out in what ways agriculture can contribute to economic growth of a country. Agriculture's contribution to economic development has been classified into four categories: (1) Product contribution; (2) Factor contribution; (3) Market contribution and (4) Foreign exchange contribution.

1. Product Contribution: Most of the developing countries depend on their own agriculture to provide food to be consumed by their population. However, there are few exceptions. Some countries such as Malaysia, South Saudi Arabia have large exports based on natural resources which enable them to earn enough foreign exchange to import their food requirements for their people. But most developing countries do not have necessary foreign exchange earnings to import foodgrains to feed their people and therefore have to rely on their own agriculture to produce enough food to meet the consumption needs of their people. Farmers in these developing countries have to produce food over and above their subsistence needs so as to provide necessary food to their urban population. If the industrial and services sectors have to grow, the food requirements of the workforce employed in them have to be met by the marketable surplus of the farmers. As the industrial and services sectors develop further, the agricultural productivity and production must also rise to sustain the industrial development by feeding the increasing industrial workforce.

If with industrial development, productivity of agriculture does not rise sufficiently and imports of foodgrains are not possible due to non-availability of sufficient foreign exchange, the *terms of trade will turn heavily against the industrial sector* and as several models of growth point out the growth process will eventually stop because industrial production will become unprofitable.

As of result, the economy will reach a stationary state. Besides, according to Rostow's model of economic growth, prior to take-off stage of economic development there must be agricultural revolution. As a matter of fact, why Britain was the first country to have industrial revolution is the fact that Britain had an agricultural revolution. Abolition of serfdom and enclosure movement led to the significant increase in agricultural productivity which enabled agriculture to provide enough food to feed its increasing industrial workforce.

It is here worth mentioning the concept of *marketable surplus*. The marketable surplus is the difference between the agricultural output and the subsistence needs of the farmers producing it. This marketable surplus must be extracted from the agricultural population to be used for the expansion of the industrial sector.

If agricultural productivity does not rise the marketable surplus for industrial growth has been obtained by some countries through coercion as was the case in Japan at the time of Meiji Restoration (1869) when through compulsory taxation marketable surplus was extracted from the farmers. More conspicuously, marketable surplus was forcefully collected from *kulaks* (small class of rich landowners) in 1920-21 during Stalin's Collectivisation Scheme.

2. Factor Contribution: Another contribution of agriculture to economic development is that it provides two important factors — labour and capital — for industrial growth. The size of agricultural sector in developing countries is quite large as around 60 per cent of their population is engaged in it and therefore it can release a significant amount of labour to be employed in the industrial and other non-farm sectors. However, agriculture can release labour for industrial development if its productivity rises. In Lewis' "*Model of Development with Unlimited, Supplies of Labour*," mobilisation of surplus labour (*i.e.*, disguisedly unemployed) in agriculture for expansion of modern industrial sector and capital accumulation has to be made for employment in expanding industries. The smaller the wages of labour, the lower will be the cost of industrial sector which will bring large profits to the industrialists which can be ploughed back for further industrial development and capital accumulation. But as coercion is ruled out in democratic countries like India, the release of labour from agriculture for use in industrial sector can be achieved if there is rise in agricultural productively and therefore the increase in marketable surplus. Thus, it is through increase in agricultural productivity as a result of green revolution technology since the mid-sixties of the last century that has been used for generating agricultural marketable surplus for industrial growth by the developing countries of South-East Asia by using cheap labour from agriculture.

Source of Capital: Agriculture can also be a major source of saving or capital for industrial growth of developing countries. Even, in poor developing countries, as income from agriculture is unequally distributed, rural people with high incomes can invest their savings for industrial development. In Britain at the time of industrial revolution rich landlords voluntarily invested some of their savings in growing industries. Besides, small farmers can deposit their small savings in banks operating in the rural areas and then these banks can provide loans to the industrialists for investment purposes.

The government can also extract savings from the farmers by taxing the agricultural sector. In Japan a tax on agriculture was levied to mobilise savings for capital accumulation. In India land revenue from agriculture has been a negligible source of State income. A committee headed by late Dr K.N. Raj recommended '*Agricultural Holding Tax*' to mobilise savings from agriculture for economic development. Since taxing agriculture is a State subject, no State has levied agricultural holding tax or agricultural income tax because no party can turn farmers who are voters against it. Therefore, in India agriculture remains undertaxed. However, with the expansion of branches of nationalised banks farmers are voluntarily depositing their savings in these banks, which the banks can lend for industrial growth of the country.

3. Market Contribution: The market contribution of agriculture means the demand for industrial products. In the earlier stages of development when urban sector is very small and markets for exports have not yet been found, agricultural sector of developing countries is a major source of demand or market for industrial products. The farmers often produce cash crops such as sugar, jute, cotton and from their sales they obtain money incomes which they can spend on industrial goods. Besides, the farmers who have marketable surplus of foodgrains (cereals and pulses) sell them in the market from which they get money incomes which also become a source of demand for industrial goods. Unless the market or demand for industrial products expands, rate of industrial growth cannot be high. In India it has been found that whenever there is sluggish or negative agricultural growth, there is stagnation in the industrial sector due to lack of demand for the industrial products. The increase in agricultural productivity and production causes increase in the home market for manufactured goods and services and thereby speeds up rate of economic development. According to *World Development Report* of the year 1979, "*a stagnant rural economy with low purchasing power holds back industrial growth in many developing countries.*"

In fact, there is interrelationship between agriculture and industries. Not only is agriculture a source of demand for various industrial products but it also supplies food and raw materials (such as sugarcane, jute, cotton, oilseeds etc.) to industries. Besides, various agro-based industries such as rice-husking, sugar manufacturing, oil-crushing, handloom weaving also depend on agriculture for the raw material supplies. Therefore, if agricultural growth is sluggish, these agro-based industries would not get their required supplies of raw materials.

The household studies of the currently developed economies indicate that in the earlier stages of development industrial revolution took place in the countries that had already experienced substantial increase in agricultural production. On the other hand, developing countries which have neglected agriculture (as India in the Second and Third Five Year Plans) and allocated bulk of their investment resources to the industrial sector soon found themselves with problems of food shortage, inflation and balance of payments difficulties. Thus Jean Waelbroeck and Irma Adelman write: "*In the absence of increase in agricultural productivity, countries quickly find themselves in the balance of payments problems as they find themselves compelled to import food in order to avoid upsurge in real wages that would jeopardise their industrial programme.*"[1]

It follows from above that rapidly growing agricultural sector is a precondition for rapid industrial growth. This has however implication for pricing of agricultural products relative to the industrial goods, that is, *terms of trade* between agriculture and industry. Lower agricultural prices are good for industry as it would get cheaper food and raw material, which would lower its cost of production and raise its profitability. On the other hand, low agricultural prices are bad for the farmers because they reduce their incomes and therefore their buying power to purchase industrial goods. Besides, lower agricultural prices would serve as disincentive to raise agricultural productivity. Therefore, there is need to strike a balance in terms of trade between agriculture and industry so that agricultural prices are not too high so that they should not make industrial production unprofitable. The agricultural prices should also not be too low so as to provide incentives to the farmers to increase agricultural production.

In the early fifties some economists were of the view that farmers do not respond positively to higher agricultural prices as they aim at earning fixed incomes. With higher agricultural prices the farmers, according to this view, produce and supply less agricultural output. That is, according to this viewpoint, there was backward bending supply curve of agricultural output. Thus, according to this viewpoint for raising agricultural production, agricultural prices should be kept at low levels.

---

1 Jean Waelbroeck and Irma Adelman, '*Agricultural Development-Led Industrialisation in Global Perspective*,' paper presented at International Economic Association of World Congress, 1986, New Delhi.

This view did tremendous harm to the agriculture as it was based on wrong premises and the implementation of this view by some developing countries stood in the way of achieving a higher growth of agricultural output. The empirical evidence now clearly shows *that farmers respond positively to higher agricultural prices*. Even in case of India recently (2012-13, 2013-14) when minimum support prices (MSP) of wheat and rice were raised by the Government, farmers responded positively and not only they increased production of wheat and rice but also exported them on a large scale in the years 2012-13 and 2013-14. With this India became the world's largest exporter of rice which no one even dreamed of.[2] That the farmers respond positively to incentive prices is also shown by the fact that the farmers in India and other developing countries adopted the green revolution technology (*i.e.,* use of HYV of seeds along with fertilizers and pesticides) when higher prices of foodgrains were offered to them as incentives.

4. Foreign Exchange Contribution: The exports of agricultural products can also be a source of foreign exchange earnings. In the initial stages of development when industrial sector has not yet developed much, agriculture is a source of foreign exchange earnings from its exports of primary goods.

The developing countries in the early stages of economic development often experience shortage of foreign exchange or what has been called '*foreign exchange gap*' to meet the requirements of imports for industrial development. By contributing to foreign exchange earnings, it enables the developing countries to have access to imported goods needed for industrial growth which cannot be produced at home or can be produced at a higher opportunity cost. Thus agriculture can make significant contribution to economic development by earning foreign exchange required for importing industrial raw materials and capital goods required for expanding industries. The lack of foreign exchange acts as a great constraint on the growth process. Thus, in India as in the Second and Third Five Year Plans (period 1956-1966), agriculture was relatively neglected in allocation of investment resources, the growth process came to a halt as even food could be imported and also in the absence of availability of enough foreign exchange earnings, it experienced balance of payments problems and it became difficult to import even necessary inputs for industrial growth.

5. Agriculture and Poverty Alleviation: A majority of poor people live in rural areas. Even after 60 years of independence around 40% of population in the rural areas of India live below the poverty line and a majority of them consists of small and marginal farmers, landless agricultural labourers, Scheduled Casts and Tribes. It has been shown, among others, by Montek Singh Ahluwalia, the former Deputy Chairman of Indian Planning Commission, that *poverty declines with agricultural growth*.[3]

In any strategy of eradication of poverty agricultural growth plays an important role. Agricultural growth raises the productivities and incomes of small and marginal farmers, and raises and employment and wages of agricultural workers. With this, it helps to reduce poverty and disguised unemployment. Besides, increase in agricultural productivity leads to lower food prices and keeps inflation under control which also contribute to lowering of poverty.

6. Contribution of Agriculture to Employment Generation. In major growth models for labour-surplus developing countries, prominent among them are 'Lewis' model of growth with unlimited supply of labour,' Mahalanobis' growth model of assigning higher priority to basic and heavy industries visualised withdrawal of surplus labour from agriculture to be employed in the expanding industrial sector. However, the empirical evidence shows that far from withdrawing surplus labour from agriculture, the modern industrial sector being highly capital-intensive generates very little employment opportunities which are not enough even to employ all the openly unemployed persons in the urban areas.

2 See Ashok Gulati, "The Cereal Wonder," *The Economic Times*, April, 24, 2014.

3 See Montek Singh Ahluwalia, "Rural Poverty and Agricultural Performance in India," *Journal of Development Studies*, 14 : 13, 1978, pp. 298-323.

It has been found that agricultural growth has a good employment potential provided a proper strategy of agricultural growth is pursued.[4] The new agricultural technology represented by the use of HYV seeds, fertilizers, pesticides along with use of optimum quantity of irrigation water leads to the expansion in agricultural employment. The use of these inputs of high-yielding technology enables the farmers to adopt *multiple cropping* which has a large employment potential. What is needed is the increase in capital investment for expansion of irrigation facilities and other infrastructure for agriculture so that farmers throughout India can draw benefits from the new high-yielding technology. The widespread diffusion of new high-yielding technology in the rural economy of India will raise agricultural productivity as well as employment. However, to realise the full employment potential of agricultural growth, reckless mechanisation of agriculture should be avoided. Besides, to increase employment in agriculture, lands reforms such as tenancy reforms and distribution of land through imposition of ceilings on landholdings should be effectively implimented as small farmers employ more labour, have larger cropping intensity and higher productivity.

Irma Adelman and Jean Waelbroeck[5] have put forward a strategy called '*Agricultural Development- Led Industrialisation Strategy*' *simply called ADLI Strategy* in which they have argued for allocating a greater share of investments to the agricultural sector to improve agricultural productivity and achieve a more rapid growth. To quote them, "With current initial conditions and in the present low-growth world environment, an "*Agricultural Development-Led Industrialisation* (*ADLI*) *Strategy*" leads to higher rates of economic growth, better income distribution, more rapid industrialisation and a stronger balance of payments than continuation of purely export-led growth strategy. The main reasons for the favourable result of ADLI strategy are that: (1) the strong domestic linkages of agriculture with manufacturing, through both the demand and the input sides, lead to high domestic demand multipliers for agricultural output; (2) investment in agriculture is less import-intensive and more labour-intensive than investment in industry and so is agricultural production; (3) the rate of return to investment in agriculture is high, equal or be exceeding that of investment in industry."[6]

AGRICULTURAL PRODUCTIVITY

For the agriculture to produce enough food for the growing population and generate adequate demand for the products of growing industries in a developing economy, agriculture must produce surplus of production over its subsistence needs. Agricultural production is a function of sown area and productivity per hectare. Since there is not much scope for increase in net sown area, productivity in agriculture must increase if it has to produce marketable surplus of foodgrains. Further, in a reaction to the failure of industrialisation to solve the problems of poverty and unemployment, some economists as Irma Adelman, John Mellor have laid stress on giving higher priority to the development of agriculture and raising its productivity. Table 30.1 gives figures of agricultural productivity per worker as measured by value added per worker in 2000 US dollar and land productivity as measured by cereal yield in terms of kilograms per hectare in both developed and developing countries for the years 1990 and 2009. It will be seen from the table that agricultural productivity (both per worker and yield per hectare) differs quite substantially across countries. For example, agricultural productivity per worker was 468 in India and 525 in China whereas it was 49,512 in the United States and 26,370 in the United Kingdom. In least developed countries of Sub-Saharan Africa agricultural productivity per worker was 318 in 2000 US dollars in 2009. It will be further observed from Table 30.1 that in

4. John Mellor, *The New Economics of Growth* and H. L. Ahuja, *Development Strategy in a Labour Surplus Economy*, Unpublished Ph. D. Thesis, Delhi University, 1982.
5. Jean Waelbroeck and Irma Adelman, *Agricultural Development-Led Industrialisation in Global Perspective*, Paper presented at International Economic Association of World Congress, December 1-6, 1986, New Delhi.
6. *Ibid.*

the developed countries there has been larger increase in productivity per worker between 1990 and 2009 as compared to the developing countries.

Similarly, it will be seen from Table 30.1 that there are large *differences in agricultural land productivity* (*i.e.,* yield per hectare) between developed and developing countries. It will he seen from Table 30.1 that whereas cereal yield per hectare measured in kilograms per hectare was 2,473 in India, 5,460 in China and 5,920 in Japan, it was 7,238 in the US and 7,008 in the United Kingdom in the year 2009.

The above figures reveal that agricultural productivity in developing countries after several years of gaining independence is quite disappointing and consequent lack of marketable surplus of agriculture is impeding overall economic development of the developing countries

Table 30.1. Agricultural Productivity in Developed and Developing Countries

Country	Agricultural Productivity (value added per worker in 2000 US $)		Cereal Yield (kilograms per hectare)	
	1990	2009	1990	2009
Developed Countries				
United States	18,523	49,512	4,755	7,238
United Kingdom	21,400	26,370	6,171	7,008
France	21,423	58,070	6,083	7,460
Japan	20,934	52,062	5,846	5,920
Sweden	23,307	51,057	4,964	5,086
Euro area	11,982	26,730	4,490	5,822
Developing Countries				
Brazil	1,625	3,760	1,755	3,526
Mexico	2,275	3,364	2,424	3,111
Russian Federation	1,917	3,031	1,743	2,270
China	263	525	4,323	5,460
Nigeria	NA	NA	1,148	1,598
Sri Lanka	678	926	2,965	3,722
Indonesia	512	734	3,800	4,813
Malaysia	3,850	6,529	2,740	3,750
India	362	468	1,891	2,473
Bangladesh	251	435	2,491	3.890
Pakistan	739	903	1,766	2,803
Sub-Saharan Africa	304	318	1,033	1,302

Source: World Bank, *World Development Indicators, 2011*, pp. 134-136.

Factors Responsible for Low Agricultural Productivity in Developing Countries

There are a number of factors that are obstructing the increase in agricultural productivity in developing countries. They are: (1) excessive pressure of population on land resulting in lowering of *land-labour ratio*; (2) geographical factors such as climate and terrain of a country; (3) lack of irrigation facilities and dependence on the uncertain rainfall; (4) limited adoption of new green revolution technology; (5) *urban bias* in development strategies adopted in various developing countries; (6) *lack of access to credit* for farmers; and (7) inefficient land-tenure system which acts as a disincentive for farmers to raise productivity.

We explain below in detail the above factors responsible for low agricultural productivity in developing countries. We also discuss the issues concerning agricultural productivity with special reference to India.

1. **Decline in Land-Labour Ratio as a Result of Increase in Demographic Pressure:** Agricultural productivity per worker is affected by land-labour ratio. In a country like India with increase in population since 1951 and lack of adequate employment opportunities outside agriculture, the population pressure on agriculture has been increasing that has resulted in sharp decline in land-labour ratio. The increase in population pressure on agricultural land has resulted in excessive sub-division and fragmentation of land holdings that has caused decline in the size of operational holdings. Thus 83 per cent of operational holdings are less than 2 hectares and average size of holding is 1.23 hectare. Obviously this decline in cultivated land per person would lower the agricultural productivity per worker engaged in agriculture. In this case of lower land-labour ratio, agricultural productivity per person can be raised with small application of capital in the form of increase in irrigation facilities and use of fertilisers.

On the other hand, it may be noted that in developing countries of Latin America and Africa, there has not been population pressure on land and as a result in these countries the *opposite situation of high ratio of land to labour* is found. In this situation there is not enough labour to ensure optimum utilisation of land. In this case high ratio of land to labour, agricultural productivity per person can be raised by using larger doses of capital for labour to work with, that is, in this case deficiency of labour can be made up by using more labour (even having higher degree of mechanisation of agriculture).

2. **Geographical Factors:** The geographical factors such as climate and terrain determine to a large extent what agricultural goods can be produced, the amount of land available for cultivation and the fertility of soil. Elaborating the importance of geographical factors, Thirwall writes, "*To some extent the application of capital to land can compensate the natural forces but there are obvious limits. Mountains cannot be easily flattened or deserts readily watered. This is the concept of geographic determinism which can be advanced as hypothesis of underdevelopment*."[7] Thus, various hilly parts of Himachal Pradesh, Uttarakhand, and Jammu and Kashmir, it is difficult to raise agricultural crops due to difficult terrain and floods that often occur in these regions. Similarly, in desert region of Rajasthan, it is difficult to raise agricultural productivity due to scarcity of rainfall.

3. **Lack of Irrigation Facilities:** Water is an essential input for agricultural production. In the absence of adequate rainfall with good spatial distribution, irrigation is a prime determinant of agricultural productivity. Around 40 per cent of cultivated area in India is cultivated, the remaining 60 per cent is rain-fed. Productivity is much higher on the irrigated land compared to non-irrigated area. Irrigation makes double cropping or even multiple cropping possible which leads to the increase in both output and employment.

It is also well known that in India even when irrigation facilities are available they are not fully utilised. For instance, in 1999-2000, 94.73 million hectares of land had irrigation potential but actually 84.70 million hectares were utilised. The costs of irrigation are also rising and small farmers who lack resources and have no access to institutional credit are unable to make full use of irrigation facilities.

4. **Capital Formation in Agriculture:** Capital formation in agriculture is one of the key determinants of agricultural productivity. Unfortunately in the initial years of planning in India, that is, in Second and Third Five Year Plans, capital formation in agriculture was neglected since following Mahalanobis' strategy of development the resources were concentrated on basic heavy industries. It is therefore not surprising that there was slower growth in agricultural production and productivity in the 1950s and 1960s. After 1970s, there was pick-up in gross fixed capital formation (GFCF) in agriculture in order to raise food production. However, after the mid-1980s, there has been declining trend in gross fixed capital formation (GFCF) in agriculture in the public sector as a percentage of

7 A.P. Thirlwall, *Economic Development*, 9th edition, p. 188.

GDP in agriculture. It will be seen from Table 30.2 that in the post-1980-84 period while there is a *declining trend in public sector capital formation there is rising trend in private sector fixed capital formation* but in almost two decades (1984-2002), the total gross fixed capital formation in agriculture as a percentage of GDP in agriculture declined which had an adverse effect on agricultural growth and productivity. It may however be noted that a good part of private sector fixed capital formation which increased during the post-1984 period relative to fixed capital formation by the public sector was in *mechanisation of agriculture* which prevented labour-absorption in agriculture.

Table 30.2. Private and Public Sector Capital Formation, and Subsidies (as percentage of GDP - Agriculture)

	1975-79	1980-84	1985-89	1990-94	1995-99	2000-02
1. Gross Fixed Capital Formation (GFCF) in Agriculture: **Private Sector**	3.64	3.89	3.87	4.48	4.49	4.89
2. Gross Fixed Capital Formation (GFCF) in Agriculture: **Public Sector**	3.95	4.08	2.90	2.07	1.75	1.54
3. Gross Fixed Capital Formation in Agriculture-**Total**	7.59	7.97	6.76	6.55	6.24	6.43
4. Subsidies to Agriculture Sector	2.58	3.51	4.79	4.99	5.41	6.06

Source: Ramesh Chand and Pramod Kumar, "**Determinants of Capital Formation and Agricultural Growth: Some New Explanation,**" Research Paper of Agricultural Economics Unit, Institute of Economic Growth, Delhi

It is worthwhile to note an important fact from Table 30.2 that in the post-1980-81 period whereas there is declining tendency in fixed capital formation is agriculture by the public sector, subsidies by the public sector shows the increasing trend as percentage of GDP in agriculture. GDP in agriculture is affected by capital formation as well as subsidies. It has been found that *long-term return* from capital formation is more than double the return from subsidies. Divesting one per cent resources from subsidies to public investment raises output by more than two per cent. As there is a trade-off between resources going into subsidies and resources available for public investment, diverting resources from subsidies to public sector capital formation is highly desirable to ensure rapid growth in GDP agriculture."[8]

5. **Use of New Technology:** It had been found by Schultz that under the traditional agriculture, resources were efficiently used and therefore given the land tenure system and other institutional structure, agricultural productivity could not be increased through any change in resource use in traditional agriculture.[9] Therefore, in the mid-sixties, a new agricultural technology was evolved by the discovery of new high-yielding varieties (HYV) of seeds which were obtained through cross of dwarf Mexican varieties with local varieties first in case of wheat and then in case of rice. The new high-yielding varieties (HYV) of seeds raise yield per hectare when used in optimum ratio with fertilizers and irrigation or assured rain-water. This new technology was therefore called *bio-chemical technology or new seed-fertilizer technology*. The use of new technology led to the increase in output through increase in yield per hectare. The use of new technology *does not involve change in the existing resource use* but an upward shift in the production function. After the mid-sixties adoption of the new seed-fertilizer technology along with the provision of incentive prices for agricultural output, made countries like India *self-sufficient in food*. The new technology raised the profitability of investment for the farmers which led to its widespread use by farmers.

Though *new seed-fertilizer technology is size-neutral, it is not resource-neutral*. Therefore, in

8 Ramesh Chand and Pramod Kumar, *op. cit.*

9 T.W. Schultz, *Transforming Traditional Agriculture*, Yale University Press, 1964, New Haven.

the earlier years of green revolution the large farmers who had enough resources to buy new seeds, fertilizers and pesticides adopted the new technology to a greater extent than small farmers. However, in course of time when the institutional credit for small farmers improved significantly and with improved extension services, the use of new high-yielding technology among small farmers caught up with the large farms. It is worth mentioning that as the new technology raised the per acre yield and profitability of investment for the farmers, it led to the increase in investment or capital formation in agriculture both by the private and public sectors. This increase in investment or capital formation in agriculture had a favourable effect on the agricultural productivity.

6. **Inefficient Land Tenure System:** Land tenure system has a significant effect on agricultural productivity. Zamindari system that prevailed in India before independence was not conducive to higher agricultural productivity. Actual cultivator under it was highly exploited as a major part of output was bagged by the Zamindar and other intermediaries. As a result, the actual tiller of the soil lacked the incentive to work hard, nor had he means to make improvements and investment in agriculture. Having no ownership rights of land, he had no access to credit. On the other hand, Zamindar or landlord was absentee landlord and was merely interested in collecting rent from the tenants. Consequently, agricultural productivity per hectare was low. After independence Zamindari system was abolished and tenants were brought in direct contact with the State. This had a favourable effect on yield per hectare.

Besides, tenancy system that prevails in India provides no incentive to raise agricultural productivity. Tenants can be evicted at the will of landowners and have thus *no security of tenure*. This discourages them to make investment in agriculture or make other improvements. Besides, rents charged by landowners are very high. In case of sharecropping a significant part of output, generally 50%, is bagged by the landowner. Thus sharecroppers lack incentive to use adequate labour and other inputs to maximise output. Thus *sharecropping is said to be inefficient*.

An important land tenancy reform in India for which laws were enacted was to *confer ownership rights to the tenants*. This has the most favourable effect on the agricultural productivity as being owners, the former tenants have *the incentives to use labour and other inputs to the extent that maximises agricultural production*. With ownership rights over the land, they gain adequate access to institutional credit. With this they can buy inputs of new technology such as HYV seeds, fertilizers, pesticides and thereby raise their productivity. However, except in West Bengal and Kerala where Leftist parties ruled for a long time, this important reform remains unimplemented.

7. **Lack of Access to Credit:** The farmers require credit for buying fertilizers, new HYV seeds, pesticides, construction of wells and buying pumps, payment of irrigation charges. Though banks and other financial institutions have been asked to give liberal loans to the farmers, but the farmers are unable to fulfil the requirements of banks for obtaining credit for them. As a result, small farmers have to depend on village money lenders for fulfilment of their credit needs. But the village money landers exploit them by charging higher interest rates. Burden of debt on them has been increasing. Unable to get credit at lower rates of interest, small farmers do not buy inputs of high-yielding new technology. This causes lower productivity in agriculture.

Chapter 31

New Technology and Sustainable Agriculture

NEW HIGH-YIELDING TECHNOLOGY

New technology or popularly known as Green Revolution technology was adopted to *produce adequate food* to meet the needs of growing population of developing countries like India. Besides, new agricultural technology was adopted to promote agricultural growth to generate more employment opportunities and to reduce poverty in the rural sector of the economy.

The basic features of new agricultural strategy are the following:

1. **Use of New HYV Seeds**: The important element of new agricultural strategy, which has been adopted since 1966-67, is the discovery and use of new hybrid seeds which are high-yielding varieties, briefly called HYV. The important characteristic of these high-yielding varieties of seeds is that they convert soil nutrients into *grains* rather than *leaf growth*. This enables the plant to produce higher yields.

2. **Use of Appropriate Amount of Fertilizers**: The use of HYV seeds could not produce higher yields without the use of appropriate quantity of fertilizers. Natural soil nutrients can be increased by the use of fertilisers. Therefore, HYV seeds increase agricultural production greatly if they are used along with the appropriate dose of fertilizers.

3. **Irrigation-Water, Effect of Water Control and Water Management**: The fertilizers require the use of water for yielding higher output. Therefore, the HYV seeds and fertilizers are used where the adequate water supply is available. Therefore, the HYV seeds, fertilizers and water are used as a package to get higher agricultural productivity.

It may be noted that fertilizers can be absorbed by plants as well as seeds. Therefore, effective weeding is required to prevent wasteful use of fertilizers. The new varieties of seeds produce dwarf-size plants which are likely to be submerged in water. Therefore, use of HYV seeds require more effective water control and better drainage.

4. **Use of Pesticides:** Further, the new varieties of seeds are more prone to local pests and diseases than the traditional varieties. Therefore, they require the use of pesticides to prevent the damage to crops from the pests and diseases. Thus, the use of pesticides along with HYV seeds and fertilizers are called *bio-chemical inputs* for raising yield per acre.

5. **Multiple-Cropping:** Another important feature of new technology is that the new HYV seeds mature more quickly than the traditional varieties. This enables the farmers to practise multiple-cropping in a year. Multiple-cropping means growing more than one crop on an area in a year. This leads to greater outputs as well as more employment. The use of new biological-chemical innovation (HYV seeds, fertilizers, pesticides) and double cropping increase yield per hectare. They are therefore called *land-augmenting or land-saving innovations*.

Thus it follows from above that the basic feature of new agricultural strategy is the application of a number of *biological-chemical inputs* — HYV seeds, fertilizers, pesticides, irrigation water which are complementary to each other and lead to higher yield per hectare. The new seeds were first discovered in case of wheat when Mexican wheat was modified to suit Indian conditions and later new high-yielding varieties were found in case of rice, maize and of some other crops. An important feature of these new inputs is that fertilizers, pesticides, pumps and tubewells for irrigation are of manufacturing origin and require more capital. That is why the *new green revolution technology is relatively more capital-intensive than the traditional technology*.

It may be further noted that to provide incentives to the farmers to adopt the new technology, the fertilizers have been heavily subsidized and even electricity used for running pumpsets and tube-wells are heavily subsidised so that farmers can use irrigation water at cheap rates. But in case of India the use of new technology has raised yield per acre substantially and in view of the practically no scope for increase in net such area, enabled India to achieve food self-sufficiency. Not only that, we are now (years 2012-13 and 2013-14) have become exporters of wheat and rice and earning foreign exchange.

SUSTAINABLE AGRICULTURAL DEVELOPMENT

While striving for faster agricultural growth to meet the food requirements of growing population one must pay attention to the sustainability of agricultural growth. *Economists use the term sustainable development that ensures the balance between economic growth on the one hand and conservation of natural resources and protection of environment on the other. Sustainable agricultural development thus refers to meeting the needs of present generation without compromising the needs of the future generation*. The adoption of a technology to generate higher agricultural growth and to ensure food security to the people will be unsustainable if it leads to the degradation of land and depletion of other natural resources. There is a need to devise a strategy of agricultural growth which effectively reconciles the objective of rapid growth of agriculture with the conservation of land and forests and protection of environment. It is worth mentioning that capacity to produce and quality of life of future generations depend on the natural resource base (including land) and quality of environment *i.e.*, the quality of land, water and air. Therefore, degradation of land and over-exploitation of other natural resources such as water and forests and pollution of the environment will though raise the short-term agricultural growth and provide food security to the present generation but will have adverse effects on future growth and quality of life of future generations. Such a process of agricultural growth will therefore be unsustainable.

Though the new agricultural technology which involves the use of fertilizers, pesticides and irrigation water has enabled us to increase yield per hectare and generate higher agricultural growth, but has certain undesirable effects on the ecology and environment such as land, water, forests and the atmosphere which are essential for sustainable agricultural growth. Expressing concerns about these adverse effects of green revolution technology, Dr. M.S. Swaminathen, an agricultural scientist who made an important contribution to the adoption of green revolution technology in India writes, "The indicators used to measure unsustainability of food security are: land degradation and salination, extent of forest cover, groundwater depletion and the measure of crop rotation. In all these parameters, Punjab and Haryana occupy a low position. The rice-wheat rotation has led to the displacement of grain and fodder legumes capable of enriching soil fertility. What is happening now is best described as land and water mining and not farming"[1].

What steps are required to put agriculture on the path of sustainable growth where increases in crop production and productivity are not accompanied by ecological damages? In the words of Swaminathan again "Agriculture in most d2eveloping countries is not just a food producing machines

1 M.S. Swaminathan, "Agricultural Route to an Evergreen Revolution" in *Survey of Environment 2002, The Hindu.*

but is the backbone of the livelihood security system."[2] We explain below the measures that should be adopted to prevent damages to the agricultural ecology and environment and therefore to ensure sustainable *soil health, to prevent land degradation and to raise agricultural productivity.*

Soil is one of the basic natural resources that support life on earth and this resource is under threat in India from soil erosion due to natural factors compounded by the excessive use of fertilizers and deforestation which causes floods. The soil ecosystem is a living *self-balancing system* and excessive use of chemical fertilizers disturbs the balance often causing long-term damage to the soil.

Chemical fertilizers, especially urea, are highly subsidised and the fertilizer subsidy has grown enormously in the last over four decades of the adoption of new agricultural strategy: These heavy subsidies on some fertilizers which has resulted in *severe depletion of micronutrients and degradation of soil* in many parts of the country. Chemical fertilizers should be used with great care and in combination with other means of using organic sources to replenish the soil. What is needed is to rejuvenate the soil and restore soil health through addition of organic matter in large quantities. The use of organic manures will gradually bring down the dependence on chemical fertilizers. However, the use of organic manures is discouraged because they receive no subsidy while urea fertilizer is heavily subsidised. Thus price distortion is the important factor discouraging the shift from the use of urea to the organic manure.

For sustainable agriculture the *best practices of soil fertility management* need to be adopted which include generation of biomass for bulk addition of organic matter in the soil to maintain proper soil health through degeneration of biomass through sole cropping/intercropping/bund cropping of green manure crops, especially of farm and household waste through the use of intensive nutrient recycling methods such as composting, production of bio fertilizers at regional and local levels. Besides, there is need for the adoption of biodynamic farming methods and crop rotation to enrich the soil.

Rational Use of Land for Sustainable Agriculture

Land is a fixed resource and its availability in India on per capita basis is relatively low compared with most countries. It is therefore of paramount importance that for sustainable agricultural growth, rational and proper use of land is made. Besides, India's population is likely to continue to grow till at least 2040 whereas the landmass may actually shrink with the increased coastal erosion and flooding due to climate change. In these circumstances rational and planned use of landmass must be an issue that needs the highest priority in our strategy of agricultural development.

It may be noted that diversion of land from agricultural to non-agricultural uses is inevitable in any development process since industries must expand and greater urbanisation must occur. This will involve in the long run the shift of population from agriculture to non-agriculture, that is, industries and services. This will require increase in marketable surplus of food and other essential goods. The need for more marketable surplus to accomplish the shift from agriculture to non-agriculture is therefore possible by increase in agricultural productivity if soil fertility is maintained and the rational use of land is made.

The Optimum Use of Water and Sustainable Agricultural Development

Water is another key natural resource in a fixed supply and its availability in India is now at a level which is just about equal to demand on an average. For the spread of new agricultural technology throughout the country to accelerate agricultural growth the availability of water is essential. At present the availability of water in some areas of India is greater than the demand for it but there are other areas in which there is acute scarcity of water. While intensive use of ground water resources made a great contribution to the green revolution, today in large parts of West, Central and South India there is man-made crisis of ***falling water tables***. Economic growth at 8 per cent and 9 per cent in a year will only be possible if water requirements of growing GDP are to be met."[3]

2 *Ibid.*
3 Government of India, *The Twelfth Five Year Plan.*

Extensive studies made by some economists suggest that given the current rate of use of water, total demand for water by 2031 is likely to the 50 per cent higher than today. This gap has to be bridged by taking steps to augment availability of water through *additional storage and ground water retention*. The rest of the deficit has to be bridged *through greater water-use efficiency*. Fortunately, there is a large scope for improving water use in our economy. Agriculture consumes around 50 per cent of our available water resources at present and its water use efficiency is among the lowest in the world. Expressing concern over this inefficiency of water use, the Planning Commission writes, "Absence of rational pricing for canal water, combined with free or very *cheap power for agricultural practices which are extremely wasteful, cheap power has encouraged excess drawal of ground water leading to falling of water tables in large parts of the country.*"[4]

However, man-made crisis of falling water tables is forcing some changes as farmers are beginning to recognise the need to adopt technologies that economise on water. "The agricultural strategy to be adopted in the future must break new ground in bringing *sustainable management of our acquifiers* to the forefront of policy making. Although efforts are being made for recharging of ground water resources these are yet to show sustained result across most parts of the country. An acquifier mapping programme would enable more informed participatory management and better alignment of cropping pattern to water availability across the country. This must be combined with massive ground water recharge programme by integrating reformulated MGNREGS with programmes of watershed development scheme and restoration of water bodies."[5]

Sustainable agriculture in most developing countries is not just a food producing machine but is the backbone of livelihood security system. Degradation, diversion of arable land and the depletion and pollutions of water resources result in the loss of rural households. Sustained agricultural development represent best safety net against poverty, hunger and unemployment. Unsustainable land and water use and forests will lead not only to the food insecurity of the people but also adversely affect the rural people. Food security has the following two major aspects:

1. Availability of food which depends on the production of food in turn depends on agricultural productivity
2. Access to food which depends on the purchasing power of the people earned through performing various economic activities.

It follows from above that sustainable agriculture is a guarantee for ensuring food security to the people of a country. Hence, according to Dr. M.S. Swaminathan, "The future of food security depends on the conservation and care of arable land through attention to soil health and replenishment of fertility and the conservation and careful management of all water sources so that more crops can be produced. Improvement of production in perpetuity without associated social or ecological harm is vital to safeguard food security. This is the phenomenon I have christened *evergreen revolution.*"[6]

4 Planning Commission, *Twelfth Five Year Plan.*
5 Planning Commission, *Twelfth Five Year Plan.*
6 M.S. Swaminathan, *op. cit.*

CHAPTER

32

LAND REFORMS: FARM SIZE, PRODUCTIVITY AND EFFICIENCY

Importance of Land Reforms

After abolition of Zamindari system which involves several intermediaries between the State and the tenant or actual tiller of the soil, there are two types of land reforms that have important bearing on production and employment in agriculture. These are **(a)** redistribution of land through imposition of ceilings on land holdings, and **(b)** reforms in the tenancy system. The purpose of reform of redistribution of land through imposition of ceilings on land holdings was to bring about equitable distribution of scarce agriculture land among poor rural households consisting of small and marginal farmers and landless agricultural labour. The principle of equity is the guiding principle of redistribution of land through imposition of ceilings on land holdings. Besides, as shall be explained in detail later, the creation of small farms through the redistribution of land als leads to the increase in productivity and employment in agriculture and thereby helps to solve the problems of poverty and unemployment in developing countries like India.

The tenancy reforms include the fixation of fair rent, guaranteeing security of tenure and conferment of ownership rights to the self-cultivating tenants and sharecroppers. The land reforms in India were emphasized in India's Second Five Year Plan wherein it was stated that the objectives of these reforms are "*firstly, to remove the impediments upon agricultural production as arise from the character of agrarian structure and, secondly, to create conditions for evolving as speedily as may be possible an agrarian economy with high levels of efficiency and productivity.*"[1]

It follow from above that land reforms are important both from the social and economic viewpoints. From the social point of view redistribution of land and creation of small farms is important for promoting not only equity or distributive justice but also for increasing efficiency and productivity of agriculture. The rural poor constitute a significant segment of the population. Giving them any assets must therefore help them to earn some income from the assets. Recent studies have found that more equitable distribution of wealth (including land) can promote efficiency.[2] With more assets the poor are able to get more credit and better insurance coverage which induces them to make more investment. This leads to the rise in productivity of land. Reforms in the tenancy system would remove disincentives on the part of tenants to put in more labour and other inputs to increase output as well as to undertake long-term investment in land.

In what follows we will first discuss the relationship between farm size and agricultural productivity. The inverse relationship between farm size and productivity implies that land reforms

1 Planning Commission, *Second Five Year Plan*, 1956, p. 178.

2 (*a*) Galor, O. and J. Zeira, "Income Distribution and Macroeconomics," *Review of Economic Studies*, 60, 1993, pp. 35-52, and

(*b*) Banerjee A. and A. Newman, Occupational Choice and the Process of Development *Journal of Political Economy*, 101, 1993, pp. 274-98.

could raise productivity by breaking less productive large farms into several more productive small farms. After discussing farm size and productivity relationship we will discuss the efficiency and productivity of tenancy, especially sharecropping. If productivity under sharecropping is lower than the owner-cultivated farms, then conferment of ownership rights to the sharecroppers will increase productivity and efficiency in agriculture.

FARM SIZE AND PRODUCTIVITY

The relationship between farm size and agricultural productivity per hectare has been a great controversial issue of the Indian agriculture as case for redistribution of land from large landowners to small farmers and landless agricultural labour depends on it. With the publication of ***Farm Management Studies*** in the mid-nineteen fifties and early 1960s it was found that there existed *inverse* relation between farm size and productivity of land, that is, productivity per hectare was higher on small farms as compared to the large farms. This gave rise to the controversy about the proper explanation of this inverse or negative relation between the farm size and productivity or yield per hectare. Amartye Sen.[3] argued that small farms employ family labour and due to the existence of large-scale unemployment in the economy, the opportunity cost of labour for the small farms was zero and therefore they would apply labour to the point where marginal product of labour is zero and in this way small farms using family labour would *maximise production*. On the other hand, according to Sen, large farms generally employ hired labour and would use labour to the extent where value of marginal product of labour is equal to the market wage rate. This is illustrated in Fig. 32.1 where *MP* is the value of marginal product (*VMP*) of labour. Now, the small farms using family labour will apply OL_2 amount of labour at which value of marginal product is zero and the total output is maximised to *OMP* which equals the whole area under the *VMP* curve up to L_2. On the other hand, large farms using hired labour will apply labour equal to OL_1 at which value of marginal product of labour (*VMP*) is equal to the market wage rate *OW*.

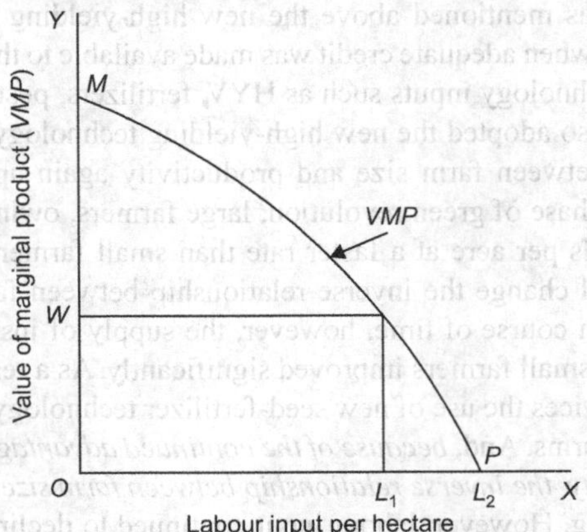

Fig. 32.1. *Use of labour by a capitalist large farm and small farm using family labour*

In this way the large farms will maximise their surplus or profit. It will thus be seen that large farms using hired labour will apply less labour as compared to small farms using family labour. As a result, according to Sen, with the given technology, productivity per hectare on small farms will be more as compared to the large farms using hired labour.

Krishna Bhardwaj in her important study using Farm Management data of nineteene fifties found that the *higher productivity per acre on small farms was due to higher cropping intensity*[4] on *them*

3 Amartya Sen, "An Aspect of Indian Agriculture," *Economic Weekly*, Annual Number, February, 1962.

4 Krishna Bhardwaj, "*Production Conditions in Indian Agriculture*," Cambridge University Press, 1974.

as well as the cropping pattern with more valued crops being grown by small farms. A. M. Khusro[5] attributed the higher productivity of small farms to the superior soil fertility of the small farms.

Ashok Rudra[6] challenged the validity of the inverse relation between farm size and productivity and on the basis of empirical study asserted that there existed no such negative relationship between productivity and size of farm. However, Rudra related ***output per acre of gross cropped area with farm size*** and, therefore, his findings were criticized among others by Krishna Bhardwaj and Hanumanth Rao who pointed out that gross cropped area subsumed the effect of cropping intensity which was negatively correlated with farm size. Thus, according to them, Rudra's study did not disprove the inverse relation between productivity per hectare and the size of operational holding. G.R. Saini who made a comprehensive study of the relation between farm size and productivity per hectare using disaggregated farm management data of nineteen fifties of several districts of India concluded, "By and large inverse relation between farm size and productivity is a *confirmed phenomenon* in Indian agriculture and its statistically validity adequately established."[7]

Surprisingly, however, the negative relationship between farm size and productivity did not remain inverse for a long time when after 1965 the new high-yielding technology of using HYV seeds along with fertilizers came to be used in Indian agriculture. In the early years of green revolution in Indian agriculture the relationship between farm size and productivity got reversed and turned positive.[8] This is because in the early years of post-green revolution period, it was mainly big farmers having adequate resources to buy new inputs (HYV seeds, fertilizers, pesticides) adopted the new technology to a much large extent than the *small farmers who* lacked the resources to buy the new inputs. Thus the adoption of new high-yielding technology by large farmers in the early years of green revolution to a much greater extent more than offset the advantage of small farms applying larger human labour per hectare and having greater cropping intensity. From this it follows that it is not the farm size as such but other factors such as human labour, new technology inputs such as HYV, fertilizers that are responsible for the level of productivity of a farm.

As a matter of fact, as mentioned above the new high-yielding technology is *size neutral*. Therefore, after a time lag when adequate credit was made available to the small farmers by financial institutions to buy new technology inputs such as HYV, fertilizers, pesticides along with improved extension services, they also adopted the new high-yielding technology to almost the same extent, the inverse relationship between farm size and productivity again appeared. Thus Hanumantha Rao writes. "In the early phase of green revolution, large farmers, owing to better access to capital resources stepped up yields per acre at a faster rate than small farmers. Because of this, in areas experiencing technological change the inverse relationship between farm size and for output per acre began to disappear. In course of time, however, the supply of institutional credit for the less developed regions and for small farmers improved significantly. As a result of this and also because of improved extension services the use of new seed-fertilizer technology among small farms caught up with that among large farms. And, *because of the continued advantage of the small farms have in respect of cropping intensity, the inverse relationship between farm size and output per net* cropped area has started reappearing. However, labour input continued to decline sharply with the increase in size of holding."[9]

---

5 A.M. Khusro, Economics of Land Reforms and Farm Size in India, Macmillan, Delhi 1973.

6 Ashok Rudra, Farm Size and Yield Per Acre, *Economic and Political Weekly*, Special Number July, 1968.

7 G.R. Saini, *Farm Size, Resoure-Use Efficiency and Income Distribution* , Allied Publishers, 1979, p. 109.

8 See Hanumantha Rao, *Technological Change and Distribution of Gains in Indian Agriculture*, Macmillan Company of India, Delhi, 1975.

9 Hanumantha Rao, '*Technological Change in Indian Agriculture, Emerging Trends'*, Presidential Address delivered at the 49th Annual (Golden Jubilee) Conference of the Indian Society of Agricultural Economics, December 4, 1989.

Thus, the above view confirms our view that the farm size as such (that is, farm size net of other inputs) does not affect the agricultural productivity. To confirm this empirically the present author in his unpublished Ph.D. thesis[10] submitted to the University of Delhi in 1982, instead of farm size as a single independent factor determining agricultural productivity per hectare estimated the following functions containing a number of relevant variables as independent factors that affect agricultural productivity. Note that our data belong to the early phase of post-green revolution period.

$$\text{Log } X = B_0 + B_1 \log FS + B_2 \log CI + B_4 \log Ht + B_5 Ig + B_6 \log HL + B_7 D_1$$

where X denotes agricultural productivity per hectare, FS is farm size measured by net sown area (NSA) in hectares, HT high-yielding technology (that is, expenditure on HYV seeds + fertilizers + pesticides), HL is human labour, CI stands for cropping intensity(*i.e* GCA/NSA × 100). IG is expenditure on irrigation, D_1 is tractor dummy that is estimated for Ferouzepur district of Punjab only.

The above log-linear production function was estimated and the results obtained are given in Table 32.1.

Table 32.1. Farm Size and Productivity

Centre and Year	Constant Term (Log)	Size of Farm (FS)	Cropping Intensity (CI)	High-Yielding Technology (HT)	Irrigation@ (IG)	Human Labour (HL)	Tractor Dummy D_1	R^2	F-Value
Ferozepur 1969-70 (n = 129)	1.65 (3.73)	0.05 (0.80)	0.38 (1.78)	0.21 (6.27)	–	0.17 (1.69)	0.005 (0.19)	0.41	14.46
Muzaffar-nagar 1968-69 (n = 144)	2.53 (11.62)	0.038 (1.09)	0.17 (1.85)	0.13 (4.84)	–	0.24 (4.26)	–	0.42	13.48
Thanjavur 1969-70 III (n = 139)	1.94 (6.80)	0.05 (1.18)	0.18 (1.45)	0.21 (6.28)	0.11 (2.49)	0.07 (0.82)	–	0.44	20.99
W. Bengal 1972-73 IV (n = 355)	1.67 (11.16)	0.09 (1.16)	0.67 (5.95)	HYV: 0.005 (1.87) F: 0.04 (2. 93)	0.02 (4. 47)	0.44 (7.39)	–	0.52	63.79

Note: Figures in parentheses are t-values. Note that the value of R^2 is relatively small because of the use of per hectare data.

@ Note that the variable of irrigation in Ferozepur and Muzaffarnagar was dropped as it was highly correlated with cropping intensity. The effect of irrigation on productivity is captured by cropping intensity.

n = Number of observations.

HYV = Percentage of gross area under high-yielding varieties.

F = Expenditure on fertilizers per hectare.

The results obtained from the above function given in Table 32.1 indicate that *partial elasticity of output per hectare with respect to size of farm* is not found to be significant by conventional statistical standards in all the four centres. This clearly shows that *size of the farm as such* does not appear to have any impact on productivity. As will be seen from Table 32.1, it is other factors, namely, high-yielding technology, cropping intensity, irrigation and human labour that increases productivity. The coefficient of tractor dummy is quite insignificant showing that the use of tractors does not increase productivity.

10 H. L. Ahuja, *Development Strategy in a Labour-Surplus Economy with Special Reference to India,* Delhi School of Economics, Delhi University, 1982.

In case of West Bengal, the coefficients of 'ara under HYV' and expenditure on fertilizers (F) are very small though satistically quite significant. This is due to high correlation with cropping intensity, the coefficient of which captures some of their effects. Besides, data limitation did not permit us to combine the use of HYV and fertilizers (F) to find out their combined effect.

Thus in the conventional way of estimating the simple log-linear relationship between farm size and productivity, the coefficient of farm size *subsumes* some effect of other factors that determine productivity. In the mid-fifties when traditional technology was in use both on small and large farms, productivity on small farms was higher as compared to that on large farms because of the greater use of labour input per hectare as well as greater cropping intensity on the small farms. But in the post-green revolution period, the use of fertilizers and HYV and in some centres availability of irrigation (due to installation of tubewells and pump-sets by large farmers) was greater on large farms which tended to offset the advantage of greater labour input and higher cropping intensity of small farms. As a result, *the negative relationship between farm size (gross of other factors) and productivity either weakened or no longer applied in the post-green revolution period.* With regard to the effects of land redistribution on output and employment we must also note (*i*) that differential access to credit facilities enjoyed by large farmers at present would cease to exist if the land is redistributed because in that case, there would be no big farmers, (*ii*) that the greater cropping intensity and labour use on small farms would tend to increase output.

Hence the conclusion that land redistribution would not only increase employment but would also tend to increase output because of the use of greater labour input and the higher cropping intensity. This would hold even if the output augmenting factors such as fertilizers, high-yielding varieties, irrigation are kept constant. Of course, if along with redistribution of land suitable institutional reforms are also made in the financial institutions supplying credit and in the administrative machinery distributing fertilizers, HYV etc. so that all farmers get these additional modern inputs in appropriate quantities, output per acre on small farms would increase further which in turn would further raise employment.

As mentioned above, the small farms have been found to increase both employment and output per hectare because of their well known feature of higher cropping intensity.

TENANCY REFORMS, AGRICULTURAL PRODUCTIVITY AND EFFICIENCY

It has been mentioned above that reforms in the tenancy system would remove disincentives on the part of tenants to put in more labour and other inputs as well as undertake long-term investment for improvement of land. We propose to explain how the reforms in tenancy system would affect agricultural productivity and efficiency.

When a farmer gets land on rent, his production decisions will be determined to a great extent by the rent contracts made with the landowners. In this connection two types of rental arrangements are noteworthy:

(*i*) **Fixed Rent System:** Under this system a fixed amount whether in kind or cash is paid by the tenant to the landlord.

(*ii*) **Share-cropping Tenancy:** Under this system a certain share of the crops, generally 50%, is paid to the landlord.

Of the above two, crop-sharing tenancy has come in for heavy attack on account of its adverse effect on agricultural output and resource use efficiency. Under fixed rent tenancy the landlord regardless of the amount of output he produces, that is, after paying a fixed sum, the fixed-rent tenant would retain 100 per cent of extra output that he produces. As will be seen below, the fixed rent tenant, like the owner-cultivator, has the incentive to maximise surplus over cost and accordingly will put in more labour and other inputs.

In contrast, as will be explained in detail below, since the share-cropper has to pay to the landlord 50% share of any extra output he produces he would have no incentive to put in labour which maximises overall surplus over cost but will employ labour and other inputs which maximises *his share of surplus over cost. This is however subject to the condition that the labour supply or work effort supplied by the sharecropper cannot be monitored and controlled by the landlord.* The decision of the sharecropper is illustrated in Fig. 32.2 where on the *X*-axis the amount of labour applied is measured and along the *Y*-axis marginal product of labour is measured. *VMP* measures the value of marginal product of labour and due to the operation of law of diminishing returns is stopping downwards. If 50% is the share of output that a sharecropper has to pay to the land owner, then marginal return to his labour will be *half* of the marginal product a labour Therefore, in Fig. 32.2 1/2 *VMP* curve represents marginal return to his labour. *OW* is the market wage rate of labour which represents opportunity cost to the sharecropper. Explaining the cost of labour for sharecroppers equal to market wage rate *OW*, Debraj Ray writes: "Labour *is costly to the tenant. Labour does have other uses. For instance, part of labour may be hired by the tenant for a wage. Even if this is not the case, the tenant could work as a labourer on somebody else's plot or might have some land of his own on which he wishes to devote part of his labour.*"[11]

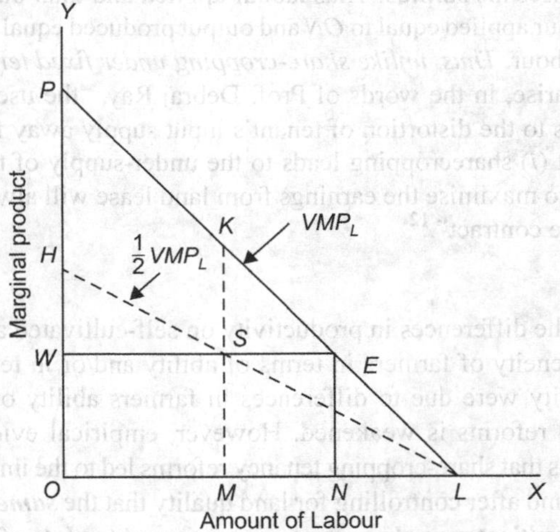

Fig. 32.2. *Tenancy, resource use and productivity*

Now consider Fig. 32.2. A landowner who cultivates his land using hired labour will equate value of marginal product (VMP) of labour with market wage rate *OW* and apply *ON* amount of labour to ***maximise his surplus over cost*** (Note that labour cost is the only cost incurred by the landowner). With the use of *ON* amount of labour the total output is given by the area *OPEN* and the total wage cost is *OWEN* and therefore surplus earned by the landowner is given by the area *WPE*.

Now consider the case of a sharecropper who pays 50 percent (or one-haf) of output to the landlord as rent. For him, as explained above, the marginal return of his labour is given by the curve *HL* which is $\frac{1}{2}$ *VMP* at every extra unit of labour applied. Therefore, *HL* or $\frac{1}{2}$ *VMP* curve would be vertically halfway from the marginal product *PL* of labour. As explained above, for the sharecropper the opportunit unity cost of labour is also the market wage rate *OW*. However, in order to maximise his own return the sharecropper will equate his marginal return (*i.e.,* $\frac{1}{2}$ VMP) with the given market

11 Debraj Ray, *Development Economics*, Oxford University Press.

wage rate $OW\ \frac{1}{2}$ by applying *OM* labour and thereby maximise his net total return (*WHS*). Note that total output produced by the share cropper is given by *OPKM* but he gives half of it to the landlord as rent.

It will be seen from Fig. 32.2 that *share-cropper produces MKEN less output* than the landlord using hired labour for cultivation of his land. It is therefore sad *that because of the incentive problem share-cropping leads to inefficiency* in use of labour as he *undersupplies labour* and therefore produces less output compared to owner cultivator using hired labour.

Tenant with a Fixed Rent Contract. Now, how much labour will be applied and output produced by a tenant who pays a fixed sum to the landlord no matter how much output is produced by him? Since the tenant with a fixed rent contract after paying the fixed amount obtains the whole of extra output produced by him, he has the incentive to apply labour so much that maximises total economic surplus. As the alternative for the fixed rent tenants is to work on other farms at the market wage rate *OW*, he will apply labour to the extent at which value of marginal product (VMP) equals the wage rate as this maximises his surplus. Thus labour applied and total output produced under fixed tenancy is the same (labour applied equal to *ON* and output produced equal to *OPEN*) as under owner-cultivator using hired labour. *Thus, unlike share-cropping under fixed tenancy there is efficiency in resource use*. To summarise, in the words of Prof. Debraj Ray, "the use of contracts other than a fixed rent contract, leads to the distortion of tenant's input supply away from the efficient level. In particular it appears that (*i*) sharecropping leads to the under-supply of the tenant's inputs and (*ii*) rational landlord trying to maximise the earnings from land lease will always prefer a suitable fixed rent contract to any share contract".[12]

Empirical Evidence

Some thought that the differences in productivity on self-cultivated and share-tenancy reforms were due to the heterogeneity of farmers in terms of ability and/or in terms of soil fertility. If the differences in productivity were due to differences in farmers ability or quality of soil, then the efficiency case for land reforms is weakened. However, empirical evidence proves this wrong. Empirical evidence shows that share-cropping tenancy reforms led to the improvement of productivity. For example, Shaben found after controlling for land quality that the ***same farmer puts in less effort in plots of land that he cultivates as share-cropper compared to plots of land that he cultivates as owner-cultivator***.[13] Similarly, an empirical study to test the effect of tenancy reforms on productivity by A.V. Banerjee, P.J. Gertler and M. Ghatak studied thoroughly the data from West Bengal *after* the tenancy reforms were implemented by the government of the Leftist parties, which was elected in 1977, found that tenancy reforms improved agricultural productivity under these reforms, which were called ***Operation Barga***, under which registered tenants with the Department of Land Revenue would be entitled to permanent and inheritable tenure on the land they sharecropped as long as they paid the landlord 25 per cent of output as rent.[14]

The present author in his Ph.D. dissertation submitted to Delhi university in 1982 econometrically tested the effect of sharecropping tenancy on employment and output per hectare using Farm Management Data of West Bengal covering six districts (24 Parganas (North), Nadia, Murshidabad, Hoogly, Burdwan and Birbhum) for the year 1972-73, that is, before the land reform of 'Operation Bagra.' The variable of share cropping intensity was measured as percentage of leased in area (LIA)

12 Debraj Ray, *op. cit.*, p. 428.

13 R.A, Shaban, "Testing Between Alternative Models of Sharecropping," *Journal of Political Economy*, 95, 1987, pp. 893-920.

14 A.V. Banerjee, P.G. Gertler, and M Ghatak, "Empowerment and Efficiency: Efficiency and Tenancy Reforms in West Bengal," *Journal of Political Economy*, 110 (2), 2002, pp. 239-80.

to the net sown own (NSA), that is, LIA/NSA. The higher LIA/NSA, the greater the degree of share-cropping intensity. Since farm size, the use of HYV and fertlizers, cropping intensity also affect employment and output, it is imperative to isolate their effects from the effect of share-cropping on farmer's *own labour employment.*[15] It is worth mentioning that though irrigation is a crucial factor in determining agricultural employment and output, but as it is highly correlated with cropping intensity, the use of *HYV* and fertilizers, its effect is subsumed by these other factors.[16] To test the impact of share-cropping on employment and output per hectare, the following two regression equations were estimated:

1. $\log HL = \beta_0 + \beta_1(LIA/NSA) + \beta_2 FS + \beta_3 \log CI + \beta_4 \log HYV + \beta_5 \log F$
2. $\log x = \beta_0 + \beta_1 \log (LIA/NSA) + \beta_2 \log FS + \beta_3 \log CI + \beta_4 \log HYV + \beta_5 \log F.$

where HL = employment (man-days) per hectare of net shown area

LIA/NSA = percentage of net sown area leased in and is a measure of share-cropping intensity

FS = farm size, that is, net shown area of the farm (in hectares)

HYV = area under *HYV*

FS = Expenditure on fertilizers per hectare

x = output per hectare

The following estimates of *B* coefficients of regression equation (1) with log *HL* as the dependent variable were obtained:

$$\log HL = \underset{(3.90)}{0.80} - \underset{(2.64)}{0.047} (LIA/NSA) - \underset{(7.22)}{0.24} FS + \underset{(8.68)}{0.78} (CI) + \underset{(5.63)}{0.018} HYV + \underset{(1.20)}{0.004} F$$

$R^2 = 50$, F = 68.59

(**Note:** figure in brackets are *t*-values)

It will be seen from the above that the coefficient of share-cropping variable (*i.e., LIA/NSA*) is negative and statistically quite significant which shows share-cropper will use his labour input (HL) less as compared to the owner-cultivators, the effects of other employment determining factors having been isolated. Further note that the cropping intensity (CI), HYV and fertilizers have positive effect on employment per hectare. Cropping intensity has a very large effect on employment.

Effect of Share-cropping on Productivity

We now turn to show the impact of share-cropping tenancy on productivity per hectare in West Bengal (for the Year 1972-73) by estimating the equation 2 above with log *x* (log of output per hectare as the dependent variable). The following estimates of β-coefficient, were obtained:

$$\log x = \underset{2.71}{0.68} - \underset{(1.92)}{0.0237} (LIA/NSA) - \underset{(0.46)}{0.021} FS + \underset{(9.27)}{1.02} CI + \underset{(3.30)}{0.01}(HYV) + \underset{(6.26)}{0.06} F, \quad R^2 = 45, \quad F.\ \text{value} = 47.6$$

It will be seen from the estimates that cropping intensity (CI), the use of high-yielding varieties of seeds (*HYV*) and fertilizers (*F*) have a positive effect on agricultural productivity per hectare. But the crop-sharing tenancy as measured by LIA/NSA has a *negative effect* on productivity per hectare and its coefficient is statistically significant. This shows sharecropping adversely affects agricultural productivity per hectare. As mentioned above, irrigation was not included in the final estimation of

15 The data of 355 farms spread over the five districts of West Bengal was taken from the State level '*Study of Farm Management and Cost of Production*' by the State Directorate of Education, for Year 1972-73.

16 In fact, some authors use cropping intensity as a proxy variable for irrigation.

the regression as it was highly correlated with cropping intensity, the use of *HYV* and fertilizers and, therefore, its effect is subsumed in these other variables.

It is evident from the above that the reasoning advanced by Amartya Sen (1975)[17] and R.A. Shaban[18] that share-cropper uses less of its own labour and other inputs and therefore producers less output per hectare as compared it to the owner cultivator has proved to be correct in case of West Bengal where share-cropping tenancy predominantly prevailed before the land reforms of the leftist Government after 1977.

We may add to the reasonings why productivity under cropshare tenancy is lower. *Share-croppers lack risk-bearing capacity and are also not able to get credit to finance its needs of required inputs, especially for the adoption of high-yielding technology if costs are not shared by the landlord.*[19] Besides, share tenants lack security of tenure and this may also leads to lower investment in the improvement of land. This may render their land of poor quality incapable of producing more.

17 Amartya Sen, *Employment, Technology and Development*, Oxford University Press, Delhi 1975.

18 R.A. Shaban, Testing between Alternative Models of Share-cropping, *Journal of Political Economy*, 1987.

19 See J.E. Stiglitz, "Incentives and Risk sharing in Sharecropping" *Review of Economic Studies* 41, 1974.

CHAPTER

33

RATIONALE AND PATTERN OF INDUSTRIALISATION

RATIONALE OF INDUSTRIALISATION

The term industrialisation denotes the expansion of manufacturing by factories that use machines and non-human sources of energy (such as electricity, oil) and employ wage labour. The industrial sector includes mining, manufacturing and construction). In general modern industries are large-scale, capital-intensive, use wage labour and are urban based. This is however definition of large-scale industries which are different from small-scale industries which are relatively more labour-intensive and use simple tools and light machines for producing goods and being small can be set up in small towns and villages. We will explain the role of small-scale industries in a separate chapter. Therefore, at present we are concerned with rationale for and role of large-scale industries in the growth of developing countries.

The need for industrialisation arises because, according to Engel's law of consumption, *as income levels increase the people spend a relatively less on food and tend to spend more on industrial goods*. That is, whereas demand for industrial goods is income-elastic, the demand for food is income-inelastic. Textiles (cloth and jute), vanaspati (vegetable oils), refined sugar, chemicals (including drugs and pharmaceuticals), tea, scooters, three wheelers, cars, paper, detergents, basic metals including steel are some examples of manufactured products. Besides there are capital goods such as machines which are either meant for producing machines that are used for producing consumer goods or for producing machines to make further machines.

In their comparative study of different countries of the world Kuznets[1] (1957) and Chenery[2] (1960) and Chenery and Syrquin[3] (1973) arrived at the conclusion that for the countries to grow there must be *structural transformation* which involves shift in resource allocation from primary to secondary activities mainly manufacturing. Kuznets (1957) in his empirical study showed that expression path as the developing countries of the world grow was first towards the industry and then services. The similarity of structural shift is based on the assumptions that composition of consumer demand varies in a similar fashion with rising income and all countries have access to international trade, capital inflow and technology.

Nicholas Kaldor[4] (1967) in his important study discovers that driving force behind economic growth rests upon growth in the manufacturing sector. He finds that there is a close positive

1 Kuznets, S. Quantitative Aspects of Economic Growth of Nations, *Economic Development and Structural Change*, 5,1957.

2 Chenery, H. B., "Pattern of Industrial Growth," *The American Economic Review*, 50, 1960.

3 Chenery, H. B. and M. Syrquin, *Pattern of Development*, 1950-1970 (New York: Oxford University Press, 1975).

4 Kaldor, Nicholas (1967), *Strategic Factors in Economic Development*, Cornel University Press, Itacha, 1967.

association between growth in manufacturing output and overall growth of the economy. He attributes this association to the fact that productivity expands faster in manufacturing sector than in others because *the former operates under increasing returns to scale* and this expression in productivity in manufacturing sector helps expansion in other sectors of the economy. In fact, according to Kaldor, *the industrial sector is the engine of economic growth.*

Until recently, the *industrialisation and economic development were treated synonymous with one another*. This is because England where industrial revolution took place first of all became rich and prosperous as a result of it. This industrial revolution in England was the result of a series of innovations including the steam power. Later other European countries of France, Germany also became rich through industrial revolution followed by the United States which ultimately emerged as the richest country of the world through industrialisation. In the early twentieth century, Japan, also got developed through rapid industrial growth.

Having known the prosperity and richness gained through industrialisation by the developed countries many poor developing countries such as India, Pakistan, Indonesia and Malaysia after gaining independence from the colonial rule opted for industrialisation of the basically agricultural economies to develop and raise the living standards of their people. Besides, through industrilisation they planned to end *their dependence* on the developed countries for their needs of industrial goods.

It is worthwhile to note that since *in industries productivity is much higher than in agriculture*, industrialisation was considered as an instrument for *creating employment at higher productivity levels for supplies of labours from agriculture* and as a result raising per capita income. Significantly, it was thought that industrialisation would induce necessary and desirable changes in social and cultural attitudes through the modernising impact of developed countries's organisational methods and techniques.

Besides, following the findings of Nurkse[5], Prebisch[6] and Singer[7] that internationally terms of trade for exports of primary goods by developing countries would deteriorate they gave priority to industrialisation for bringing about rapid economic growth and ***also alleviating the balance of payments problem***. Industrialisation, it was argued, would diversify the economy and reduce excessive dependence on the exports of a few primary commodities, the prices of which were subject to long-run secular deterioration. Furthermore, the demand for primary goods fluctuates heavily in the international markets and therefore causes a lot of economic instability in the developing countries dependent on the exports of primary goods.

For stepping up the rate of growth in developing countries the debate between balanced growth doctrine of Ragnar Nurkse and unbalanced growth approach of Hirschman was concerned about the proper strategy of industrialisation. Similarly, the dual economy model of *Development with Unlimited Supplies of Labour* of Arthur Lewis focussed on how surplus labour and food could be transferred for the expansion of modern industrial sector. The idea behind this transfer of labour from agriculture to the modern industrial sector was key to raise productivity and per capita income of the dominantly agranan economies. Besides, it was emphasised that the use of cheap labour from agriculture to modern industries would yield high profits which could be ploughed back for further capital accumulations. In fact, industrialisation and capital accumulation required for accelerating economic growth were considered to be one and the same thing in the early development literature.

5 Ragnar Nurkse, *Problems of Capital Formation in Underdeveloped Countries,* Oxford University Press, 1953.

6 Raul Prebisch, *The Economic Development of Latin American and Some of its Problems,* U.N, New York, 1949.

7 Hans Singer, 'The Distribution of Gains between, Investing and Borrowing Countries', *American Economic Review*, May, 1950.

Import-Substituting Industrialisation Vs Exports-Led Growth Strategies

Before gaining independence from the colonial rule, the developing countries exported primary goods and raw materials for industries of developed countries in return for the finished industrial products. As mentioned above, the terms of trade in this trade regime were heavily against the developing countries exporting primary goods and they were thus exploited. Therefore, after independence the developing countries such as India and of Latin America adopted import *substituting industrialisation* strategy under which goods that were previously being imported began to the produced at home. Some other countries such as South Korea, Taiwan, Hong Kong adopted strategy of *export-substitution* under which instead of exporting primary goods they developed the industries whose products they exported and this is popularly called *exported-led growth strategy*. Both the import-substituting and export-substitution strategies have been prompted by the desire to industrialise to raise per capita income and living standards of their people.

Industrial Vs Agricultural Growth

It is worth mentioning that industrial and agricultural growth are viewed as conflicting objectives. However, if properly understood the two are complementary to each other. Agriculture provides market for manufactured products, satisfies the need for food for the labour employed in the growing industrial sector, releases labour and capital for industrial growth and earns foreign exchange required for importing machinery and raw materials for industries. Industry in turn supplies the machines (such as tractors, threshers, pumps for irrigation and other inputs such as fertilisers, pesticides) required for modernisation of the agricultural sector. Industries also supply consumer goods demanded by the rural population and provide market for agricultural goods for processing them to produce finished goods such as refined sugar, cotton and woollen cloth, jute manufactures. etc.

It follows from above that what is needed is the balanced growth of industry and agriculture. If any development strategy ignores agriculture it will soon land itself into troubles. For example, in the Second Five Year Plan based on Mahalanobis' growth model which gave high priority to basic heavy industries and neglected agriculture faced problems of rising inflation on the one hand and shortage of foreign exchange to make necessary exports for industrial growth on the other. Thus Paul Baran correctly writes, There can be no question as to whether development should proceed through industrialisation or through improvement of agriculture. It can take place only by a *simultaneous efforts in both directions,* the investment policy has to place its main accent on the development of industry ... lifting agriculture at the same time high enough to support the industrialisation process ... so as to be able eventually to turn around and give agriculture a major boost with the help of the expanded resources of industrial production".[8]

However, it may be noted that after about two and a half decade of industrialisation (1950-75) it was found *that rapid growth of manufacturing output had not been matched by an equally rapid growth of employment in majority of developing countries*. It was initially believed that the growth of industrial sector would generate adequate employment opportunities to absorb surplus labour drawn from agriculture and further that benefits of rapid industrial growth would trickle down to the poor *resulting in alleviation of poverty problem* in the developing countries. But this did not happen The rapid industrial growth did not generate much employment opportunities, nor it could make much contribution to the alleviation of poverty in the developing countries. For this the use of capital-intensive technologies in the modern industrial sector was held responsible. In the mid-1970s the problem of choice of techniques and the use of appropriate technology become an issue of intense debate among economists for tackling the problems of unemployment and poverty. In this connection the issue of large-scale *vs.* small-scale industries also became a matter of debate

8 Baran P.A., *The Political Economy of Growth*, Monthly Press Review, New York, 1957, pp. 282-83.

among the economists. We will explain in a later chapter the issues of choice of techniques and small-scale *vs* large-scale industries from the viewpoint of economic growth and employment generation.

Linkages of Industry with Other Sectors

Those who advocate for giving priority to industrialisation suggest that the industry has linkages with other sectors and therefore industrial growth stimulates investment in other sectors of the economy as well. The pattern of industrial development in which consumer goods are developed first followed by producer goods industries which supply capital goods for other industries points to important linkages within the industrial sector. Besides, industrial growth generates demand for transport, telecommunication, power generation and other infrastructure and therefore stimulates output and employment in these services and infrastructure sectors. Industry's requirements for supporting service, infrastructure and labour leads to rapid ***urbanisation*** which is an important characteristic of economic development.

Albert Herichman's strategy of unbalanced growth discussed in an earlier chapter suggests that the rapid growth of one or few industries leads to the development of other industries which have linkages with initially growing industries. *Linkages can be backward or forward.* For example, the growth of textile industry causes increase in investment of cotton or dyestuffs which are important inputs used in the textile industry and represents backward linkages. On the other hand, the development of textile industry stimulates production in a user industry such as clothing (*i.e.* making of ready-made shirts, trousers, woollen fabrics etc) which in the absence of textiles would not be developed is an example of forward linkages. Thus the strategy of unbalanced growth suggests that for rapid industrial growth priority should be given to these industries which have maximum backward and forward linkages.

PATTERN OF INDUSTRIALISATION

Patterns of industrial development in developing countries have been the result of whether they have pursued strategy of import-substitution or export-substitution (*i.e.* export-led growth). We explain below the pattern of industrialisation of India and Brazil which adopted initially import-substitution strategy. We will then explain the pattern of industrialisation of south Korea which followed the path of export-led growth.

In India in the first phase of economic development (1951 to 1964-1965) industrial pattern was determined by Mahalanobis' strategy of development which assigned higher priority to basic heavy industries. The economic growth in this phase was expected to take place through modern industrialisation. In accordance with Mahalanobis' strategy of development during the Second and Third Five Year Plans (1956-1965), the public sector made large investments in basic heavy industries such as steel, fertilizers, coal, power and capital goods to make machines and machine tools, heavy electricals etc. Besides, during this phase public sector heavily invested in building infrastructure such as roads, communication and railways. Although planning in this first phase sought to encourage the cottage and small-scale industries as a means of providing employment and increasing the supplies of consumer goods as a part of plan strategy but neither enough resources were allocated to the small-scale industries nor much success was actually achieved in their development.

The industrial growth in this first phase please of industrialisation was the result of Mahalanobis' basic heavy industries biased strategy along with the ***import-substitution policy*** under which capital goods such as electrical machinery, machine tools and also the capacity to produce basic intermediate goods such as steel, fertilizer, coal were expanded to substitute ***in the long run*** the imports of these commodities. Besides, the consumer goods production which was largely in the private sector and were being imported was planned to be produced domestically. For this purpose import restrictions, both through imposition of heavy tariffs on imported goods and fixation of quotas for them, were imposed. In this phase quite a high industrial compound growth of around 8 per cent per annum was achieved.

It will be seen from Table 33.1 that in the pattern of industrialisation emerged in India in the first phase of economic development (from 1959-60 to 1965-66) the basic goods (such as steel, fertilizers) grew at the rate of 11 per cent per annum, capital goods grew at the rate of 15.4 per cent per annum and consumer goods by 4.7 per cent (Durable consumer goods grew at the rate of 11.5 per cent and non-durable consumer goods at the rate of 4.2 per cent in the period, 1559-60 to 1905-66).

Table 33.1. Annual Growth Rate in NVA from 1959-60 to 1965-66, 1966-67 to 1979-80, as per Use-Based Classification

Type of Organised Industry	1959-60 to 1965-66	1966-67 to 1979-80
Total Organised sector	8.0	5.7
1. Basic goods	11.0	5.9
2. Intermediate goods	5.7	4.5
3. Capital goods	15.4	6.6
4. Consumer goods	4.7	5.0
(*a*) Durable	11.5	4.8
(*b*) Non-Durable	4.2	5.0

Source: I.J. Ahluwalia, *Industrial Growth in India: Stagnation Since Mid-Sixties.*

This pattern of industrial growth in India is along expected lines as the growth strategy pursued in the first phase of economic development gave high priority to basic heavy industries which include basic, intermediate and capital goods industries. Import-substitution was also much higher in case of durable consumer goods and therefore they registered a high annual growth rate of 11.5 per cent in the period 1959-60 to 1965-66.

Change in the pattern of industrialisation are better revealed from Table 33.2 where we have shown the share of various industrial segments as per use-based classification. From this Table 33.2 it will be seen that share of capital goods in the industrial value added increased from 4.7 per cent in 1956 to 11.8 per cent in 1960 and then to 15.5 per cent in 1970, to 16.4 per cent in 1980 and further to 23.7 per cent in 1990. The share of basics goods increased relatively moderately from 22.3 per cent in 1956 to 25.1 per cent in 1960, to 32.3 % in 1970, and further to 39.4 per cent in 1980 and 38.4 per cent in 1980. It is important to observe from Table 33.2 the share of consumer goods in the industrial value added declined from 48.4 per cent in 1956 to 20.5 per cent in 1990. It is worth mentioning that a greater part of change in industrial pattern in favour of capital and basic goods industries was achieved by 1965-66, that is, by the end of the Third Plan period.

Table 33.2. Changes in Shares in Industrial Value Added

Type of Industries	1956	1960	1970	1980	1990
Basic goods	22.3	25.1	32.3	39.4	38.4
Intermediate goods	24.6	25.9	20.9	17.5	17.5
Capital goods	4.7	11.8	15.5	16.4	23.7
Consumer goods	48.4	37.2	31.5	23.7	20.5
(*a*) Non- Durables	–	31.6	28.1	21.1	–
(*b*) Durables	–	5.7	3.4	2.6	–
Industry	100.0	100.0	100.0	100.0	100.0

Source: Sandesara, *Industrial Policy and Planning: 1947-1991*, Delhi, 1992 Sage Table, 3.2.

Decelerations in Industrial Growth Rate in India during 1965-66 to 1978-79

In the second phase covering the period from 1966-67 to 1979-80 there was deceleration of industrial growth in India as will be seen from Table 33.1 the industrial growth rate in the organised sector slowed down to 5.7 per cent in the period 1966-67 to 1979-80 from 8.0 per cent during the period 1965-66 to 1965-66. It will be further seen that the decline in growth rate in case of capital goods and basic goods was much higher. The growth rate in capital goods fell from 15.4 per cent during the period 1959-60 to 1965-66 to 66 per cent during the period from 1966-67 to 1979-80 and in case of basic industries, the growth rate declined from 11.0 per cent during the period 1959-60 to 1965-66 to 5.9 per cent in 1966-67 to 1979-80. Iswar J Ahluwalia is her important work, '*Industrial Growth in India: Stagnation Since the Mid-Sixties*' (1985) concluded that the following factors contributed to the observed deceleration in industrial growth rate:

(*a*) slowdown in public investment and as a result the emergence of inadequate infrastructure environment;

(*b*) poor management of the infrastructure;

(*c*) the decline in agricultural incomes and the resulting slowdown in demand for industrial products; and.

(*d*) restrictive industrial and foreign trade policies leading to high-cost industrial structure.

The other important factor said to be responsible for deceleration in industrial growth was slowing down of import substitution. The pursuance of the strategy of import-substituting industrialisation stimulated industrial growth during 1956-65-1965-66. But the process of import-substitution slowed down after 1966 causing slow growth is industries enjoying protection. Besides, slowdown in public sector investment after 1966 resulted in not only the decline in infrastructure facilities that not only adversely affected the supply side of industrial goods but also caused decline in demand for goods through the reverse working of multiplier. Prof. K.L Krishna of Delhi School of Economics after examining the various studies inferred that *demand constraints were more important than supply constraints in causing deceleration in industrial growth rate during the period 1965-66 to 1979-80.*[9]

It is worthwhile to note that in 1980s industrial growth rate picked up following the increase in public sector investment and better performance of the agricultural sector. Both of them led to the increase is demand for industrial goods. Therefore, Prof. K.L. Krishna writes, "*Empirical evidence suggests that the explanations for the resurgence of growth in 1980s are similar to those for the deceleration after the mid-sixties.*"[10]

Export-orientation of India's industrialisation in the 1990s

India adopted the strategy of import-substituting industrialisation in the fifties and sixties because of what is now called *export-pessimism* which characterised the thinking of most development economists at that time. Our former Prime Minister Dr. Manmohan Singh was perhaps the first economist who on the basis of his empirical findings about India's export-potential argued that it was necessary to stimulate exports to meet at least the requirements of imported raw materials and capital equipment needed for India's industrial growth.

As explained above, the import-substituting industrialisation was carried too far in India resulting in higher unit costs of production and was one of the important factor responsible for deceleration of industrial growth from 1965-66 to 1978-79. As a result, in the eighties the need was felt to give export-orientation to India's industrial growth and some steps were taken to promote exports and facilitate imports of essential inputs and capital goods needed for industrial growth, especially the growth of export-industries.

9 K. L. Krishna, Industrial Growth and Diversification, in Uma Kapida (ed.), *Indian Economy Since Independence* 1999-2000 edition. p. 494.

10 *Ibid*, p. 501.

However, the severe balance of payment crisis of 1991 forced us to make drastic reforms in industrial and trade policy. The policy of import liberalisation for export promotion was emphasised and adopted. The steps were taken to expand exports by removing anti-export bias of the earlier years. Various incentives such as cheap credit to exports, duty draw back scheme, the policy of the abolition of MAT (Minimum Alternative Tax) on the industrial units located in Export zones were given. For liberalising imports, import-licensing was abolished and quantitative restrictions on imports were removed. Further, a significant step towards import-liberalisation has been drastic reduction in tariffs on imports on the advice of IMF and World Bank. Thus protection to domestic industries provided under the import-substitution policy was ended with the removal of quantitative restrictions and drastic reduction in tariffs on imports. However, the empirical evidence shows that removal or reduction of protection promotes efficiency and productivity of domestic industries as they have to face competition from the cheap foreign products.

Pattern of Industrialisation: Import-Substitution Strategy in Brazil

Like India, Brazil, a Latin American country, adopted a strategy of import-substitution but with a difference. While India started with import-substitution of capital goods, *Brazil followed the pattern of import-substitution of consumer goods.* Brazil's import-substitution policy was prompted by its desire to industrialise rapidly and it believed that without protection of its consumer goods industries the higher industrial growth rate could not be achieved. Like India, Brazil has a large domestic market so that it could successfully pursue import-substitution pattern of industrialisation. In case of Brazil, import-substitution policy was producing at home consumer goods, especially consumer durables. According to the estimates of Debraj Ray, in case of Brazil "over the period 1949-64 import-substitution was responsible for about a quarter of total demand growth in manufacturing using much of it in consumer goods".[11]

For a brief period from mid-1960s to mid-1970s Brazil followed a policy of export promotion but it again reverted back to its policy of import substitution but this time with a difference. After the mid-1970s it stated pursuing the policy of import-substation of capital goods. As a result, its imports of capital goods relative to total imports declined sharply. It is worth mentioning that, contrary to that of India and South Korea, *Brazil followed a liberal policy of foreign investment with multinational companies playing an important role in the production and export of goods.*

Export-oriented Pattern of Industrial Growth in South Korea

After gaining freedom from colonial rule South Korea achieved a remarkable success achieving a high economic growth in 1960s. During the first two Five Year Plans, 1962-71, the annual GDP growth rate in South Korea was remarkably high at 9 per cent followed by a still higher GDP growth per annum during the pursed 1972-79. However, South Korea achieved an exceptionally high growth rate in exports. During the first two Five Year Plans (1962-71) exports registered a very heavy growth rate of 40 per cent per annum on an average followed by somewhat lower but still quite a high growth rate of 28 per cent per annum between 1972 and 1979. It is also worthwhile to mention that its exports were not of primary products (*i.e.*, agricultural goods and minerals) in which it is generally believed that underdeveloped countries have comparative advantage *but of industrial goods and heavy manufactures*. South Korea specialised in exports of manufactures such as consumer electronics and motor vehicles and recently in high technology which recorded an extraordinary high growth rate. The national export-led industrialisation strategy adopted by South Korea favoured the promotion of exports that required *increasingly* sophisticated skills and technology. The government gave strong financial incentives to firms for upgradation of skills and technologies to be used in industrial production. Another important feature of South Korea's successful industrial export promotion is that in the beginning many export industries began as infant industries and therefore required

11 Debraj Ray, *Development Economics*, Oxford University Press, 1998, p. 675.

protection which was provided by the government. But with their growth through enhanced skills and technologies, the industries did not remain infant and could compete with firms of developed countries. With its export-orientation industrialisation South Korea cought up with the developed countries and is now classified by the World Bank as a 'high-income country' with PPP per capita income greater than $ 20,000 in 2006 and in respect of human development index (HDI) its ranking was 26th among more than 180 countries. Thus, the development experience of South Korea is a highly success growth story. It is therefore said *that South Korea followed export-led growth strategy* instead of import-substituting industrialisation of India and Brazil.

Besides, until recently it was believed that South Korea's high GDP growth and export-led growth was achieved through free market and free foreign trade policy. However recently it has been contested and has been pointed out that in the acceleration of economic growth and expansion of exports, government played a significant role in South Korea. The government provided incentives to the exporters in the form of lower direct taxes on exports earnings, assigning priority in providing import licences to import necessary raw materials and preferential interest rates charged on the credit to exporters. Thus, in the remarkable expansion of exports of South Korea there was significant involvement of Government intervention. Therefore, it cannot be said that the rapid growth of GDP and exports of South Korea represents the case of successful performance of mechanism of free market and free trade.

CHAPTER 34

Choice of Techniques and Appropriate Technology in Developing Countries

A choice between alternative techniques of production is a major problem in the planning for developing countries. This is because a particular choice of technique of production affects not only the magnitude of employment but also the rate of economic growth. Several alternative techniques of production are available to produce a commodity and these differ with regard to the amount of capital being used with a unit of labour for production. In other words, the various techniques differ with regard to capital intensity which is generally measured by the magnitude of capital-labour ratio (*K/L*). Thus, the higher the capital intensity, the more quantity of capital as compared to labour will be used to produce a given level of output. On the other hand, the lower the capital intensity, more employment for labour will be created. Thus, the lower capital intensity implies the higher labour intensity. Therefore, in labour-surplus developing countries, it is generally believed that for rapid growth of employment labour-intensive techniques (*i.e.* less capital-intensive techniques) should be preferred.

Factor Price Ratio and Choice of Technique

In economic theory based on the perfect competition model where the factor prices are given and constant for a firm and factor proportions are variable, the choice of a technique or capital-labour combination is easily made by a firm which aims to minimise cost for a given level of output

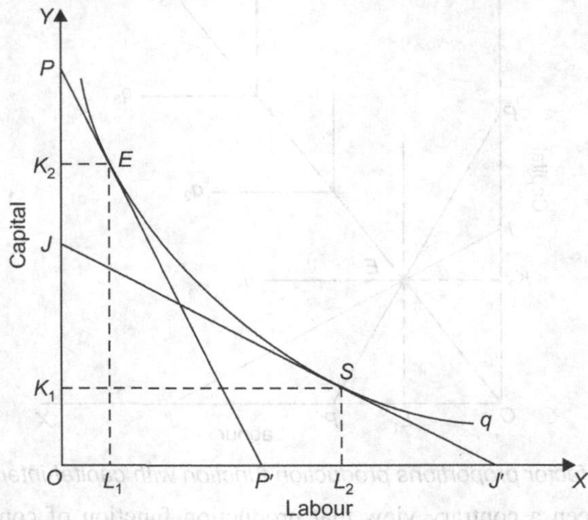

Fig. 34.1. *Factor prices and choice of techniques*

through equating relative prices of factors to their relative marginal products. In a developing country where labour is abundant and capital is scarce, price of labour (*i.e.*, wages) should be low and price of capital (generally measured by rate of interest or user cost of capital) should be high.

In Fig. 34.1 where an isoquant representing a given level of output has been drawn with amount of labour measured on the *X*-axis and amount of capital measured on the *Y*-axis. A factor price line, often called iso-cost line *JJ'* has been drawn which in Fig. 34.1 represents the lower price (wages) of labour and higher price of capital which is in accordance with the factor endowments of a labour-surplus developing economy. The firm which aims to minimize cost for a given level of output (*q* in our Fig. 34.1) will choose a factor combination point *S* at which the iso-cost line *JJ'* is tangent to the isoquant *q* and will use OL_2 amount of labour and OK_1 amount of capital and represents a labour-intensive technique.

However, it has been found that in developing countries due to *factor-price distortions*, which make labour relatively more expensive and capital relatively cheaper, the actual iso-cost line instead of being more flat as *JJ'* is steeper as shown by *PP'*. With *PP'* as the iso-cost line showing relatively more expensive labour and cheaper capital a firm on isoquant *q* will choose factor combination *E* which represents a capital-intensive technology and uses OL_1 of labour and OK_2 of capital. Thus in a labour-surplus economy, labour-intensive technique may not be actually chosen by a cost-minimizing firm because of the existence of distortions of factor prices from their true scarcity values.

Now, the question arises why in labour-surplus developing countries factor prices are distorted? The pressure of trade unions of labour for higher wages, minimum wage legislation fixing wage at higher level make labour costlier on the one hand and lower interest rates fixed either by the government if interest rates are administered by it or by cheap credit policy followed by the Central Bank make capital relatively cheaper. Further, liberal investment allowance (*i.e.,* tax break) on capital investment also lowers the cost of capital and encourages the use of more capital. Besides, *overvalued exchange rate* makes the import of capital equipment cheaper.

Therefore, in order to ensure the use of labour-intensive or less capital-intensive techniques in order to maximise employment of labour it has been suggested that *factor prices must be set right*, that is, labour should be made cheaper and capital relatively more expensive.

In our above analysis, it has been assumed that *there exits a high degree of elasticity of substitutions* between factors and if factor prices are set right, labour-intensive technologies will be used.

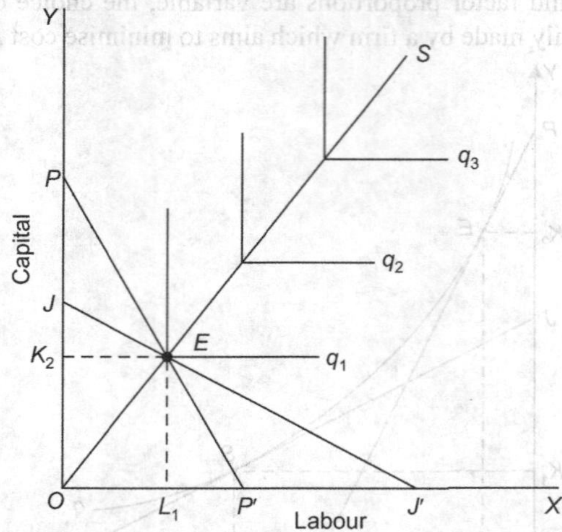

Fig. 34.2. *Rigid factor proportions production function with capital-intensive technology*

However, there has been a contrary view that production function of commodities is such that shows the existence of rigid *factor proportions*[1] for the production of industrial goods in which the choices of techniques are few and of a relatively capital-intensive variety. The extreme case of

1 R.S. Eckaus, "The Factor Proportions Problem in Underdeveloped Areas," *American Economic **Review***, Vol. 45, 1955.

rigid factor proportions production function is shown in Fig. 34.2 where for production of output q_1 of a commodity, a larger quantity of capital Ok_2 and relatively smaller quantity L_1 is used. With a factor-price ratio line *PP'*, the equilibrium to produce q_1 of the commodity is reached at point *E* which represents capital-intensive technique. In this case even if factor prices are set right and labour is made cheaper and capital costlier so that factor price line (*i.e.*, iso-cost line) changes to *JJ'*, to produce output q_1 of the commodity the same factor ratio, K_2 of capital and L_1 of labour will be used in equilibrium,. In such a fixed-proportion factor production function as the economy expands along the expansion path *OS*, the growth of labour employment will be very small. We conclude that if production function is rigid or nearly rigid, then correction of factor price distortions will not ensure the choice of a labour-intensive technique of production and faster rate of growth of employment as the economy grows. However, the empirical findings do not support the existence of rigid factor proportions production function. It has been found that although the elasticity of substitution is not very high as shown by the isoquant *q* in Fig. 34.1, but it is around 0.5 which implies that if labour is made cheaper by reducing wage rate and capital is made costlier, labour will be substituted for capital and, as a result, a relatively more labour-intensive technique will be used. Thus correction of factor-price distortions will ensure higher rate of growth of employment of labour as the economy expands.

Choice of Techniques: Maximum Reinvestible Surplus Criterion

The maximum reinvestible surplus criterion has been put forward by Galenson and Leibenstein.[2] In their view the choice of technique in planning for developing countries is not to be decided from the point of view of private profit maximisation or private cost minimisation. In it choice of capital intensity has to be decided keeping in view the problem of mass unemployment and the need for rapid economic growth to raise levels of living of the people. The problem is made difficult because the achievement of the twin objectives of reducing unemployment and promoting rapid economic growth through a choice of technique clash with each other at least in the short run. For the optimum choice of technique of production or capital intensity two alternative criteria have been compared by Galenson and Leibenstein. They are the *maximum output and maximum reinvestible surplus criteria.*

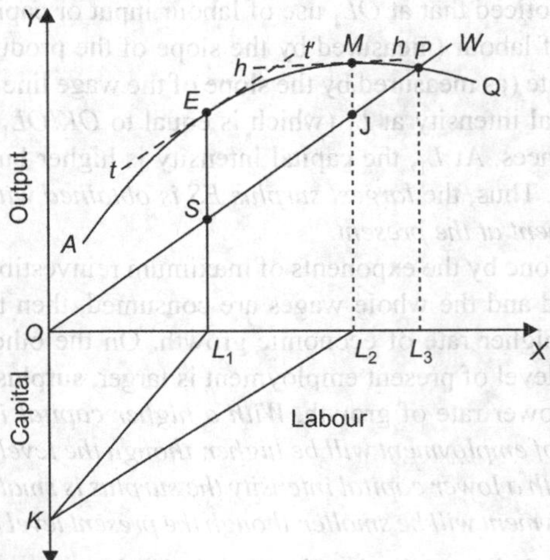

Fig. 34.3. *Maximum reinvestible surplus and choice of techniques*

To explain these criteria let us take a single product model in which two factors, capital and labour, are used to produce a commodity. We further assume that there is a given amount of capital

2 W. Galenson and H. Leibenstein, "Investment Criteria, Productivity and Economic Development," *Quarterly Journal of Economics,* Vol. 69-1955.

but the form it takes varies depending on the technique it embodies. *With a given amount of capital, output of the commodity becomes a function of labour*. We represent this production function and explain the two alternative criteria with the help of Amartya Sen's diagram.[3]

In this Fig. 34.3 along the *X*-axis, labour input is measured and along the *Y*-axis (upward from the origin) output is measured and also on the *Y*-axis (downward from the origin) amount of capital is measured. *OK* is the given amount of capital available which takes different forms according to different degree of capital intensity. The line *OW* measures the wage bill, given a wage rate equal to the slope of the wage line *OW*. It should be noted that with the increase in labour employed, given the stock of capital *OK*, capital-labour ratio falls (or labour-capital ratio increases). Thus, as we use more labour input, capital intensity will fall as we move rightward along the line *OX*. It should be further noted that, given the wage rate, as more labour is used total wage bill will be increasing. Thus with OL_1 labour employed L_1S is the wage bill and with OL_2 labour employed L_2J is the total wage bill. With capital stock equal to *OK*, output is a function of labour which is given by the production function curve *AQ*. In drawing this production function we have assumed that as more labour is used with a given capital stock there occurs diminishing returns to labour and ultimately with increasing labour intensity, total output declines, so that a certain labour-capital ratio corresponds to maximum output.

We are now in a position to explain the choice of technique on the basis of maximum output and maximum reinvestible surplus criteria. If *the planner wants to choose capital intensity (i.e., technique of production) to maximise output*, then he will choose point L_2 where output is maximum (at OL_2 marginal product of labour is equal to zero). With the given capital stock *OK*, capital intensity chosen will be equal to the slope of the line L_2K, *i.e.* OK/OL_2. With the choice of capital intensity, (*i.e.*, capital labour ratio, OK/OL_2), OL_2 labour is employed. If maximisation of employment in the present is desired, then, obviously, capital-intensity OK/OL_2 is the optimum choice. However, *maximisation of present employment may not yield a satisfactory rate of growth*. The surplus of output over total wage bill at OL_2 level of employment is *MJ* which is not the largest. If the maximum of surplus over wage bill is required, then the *capital intensity (or in other words, employment of labour with the given capital stock) at which the wage rate equals the marginal product of labour should be chosen*. From Fig. 34.3 it will be noticed that at OL_1 use of labour input or capital intensity represented by L_1, the marginal product of labour (measured by the slope of the production function curve *AQ* at point *E*) equals the wage rate (as measured by the slope of the wage line *OW*). The surplus of output over the wage bill at capital intensity at L_1 (which is equal to OK/OL_1) is *ES* which is the largest under the given circumstances. At L_1, the capital intensity is higher but employment smaller than with capital intensity at L_2. Thus, the *largest surplus ES is obtained with a higher capital intensity and lower labour employment at the present.*

If it is assumed, as is done by the exponents of maximum reinvestible surplus criterion, that the whole surplus is reinvested and the whole wages are consumed, then this larger surplus on being reinvested would yield a higher rate of economic growth. On the other hand, with lower capital intensity at L_2, though the level of present employment is larger, surplus *MJ* is smaller which when reinvested would yield a lower rate of growth. *With a higher capital intensity and higher rate of growth, the rate of growth of employment will be higher, though the level of present employment will be less. On the contrary, with a lower capital intensity the surplus is smaller and concurrently rate of growth of output and employment will be smaller, though the present level of employment will be large.*

Thus the choice of capital intensity implies the choice between the higher levels of present employment and output on the one hand and the higher rates of growth of employment and output on the other. Thus, it is argued *if you are interested in maximising the current level of employment (and production) choose a lower capital-intensive technique such as the one represented by L_2. On the other hand, if you want a higher rate of growth of employment and output choose a higher capital-intensive technique such as the one represented by L_1.* Thus we find that there *is a conflict between*

3 Amartya Sen, *Choice of Techniques*, Oxford University Press, 1962.

maximising present employment (or consumption) and maximising rate of growth of output and employment. Galenson and Leibenstein's maximum reinvestible surplus criterion has been criticised for its assumption that all profits are saved and reinvested and all wages are consumed. It has been pointed out that capitalists consume a lot of profits earned by them as they indulge in conspicuous consumption. Further, they point out that all wages may not be consumed and workers do save from their wages. In case of State enterprises it has been pointed out that due to their inefficiency, they may not generate much surplus and if they have some surplus they may be spent by the government for their current consumption expenditure. Furthermore, in case of multinational corporate companies (MNCs), operating in developing countries they are likely to repatriate their profits (i.e., surplus) to their home countries rather than reinvesting them in the developing countries. A more important critique of maximum reinvestment criterion is that it is best to raise necessary savings or surplus through the use of appropriate fiscal and monetary measures rather than using choice of technique for the purpose. Further, it is unrealistic on the part of Galenson and Leibenstein to assume that the wage rate is constant whatever technique of production is chosen. In this connection it may be noted that MNCs using capital intensive techniques in their production process are likely to pay higher wages to their workers which will reduce the reinvestible surplus and promote higher consumption on the part of their workers.

Lastly, Galenson and Leibenstein ignore the role of other factors such as the availability of raw materials, skilled labour and foreign exchange to import capital goods required by the investment plan.

Amartya Sen's Time Series Criterion for Choice of Technique

Amartya sen also propounded surplus maximisation criterion but he improved upon Galenson and Leibenstein by introducing time horizon and social welfare function in deciding about choice of technique by the Planning Authority or government. To resolve the above conflict or dilemma, in choosing between present consumption and future consumption, Prof. Sen in his famous work, '*Choice of Techniques*' has proposed what is called *Time Series Criterion*. According to it, choice of technique depends upon the time horizon of output or employment generation, the time preference and social welfare function. To make an optimum choice of technique, alternative time series of employment and output following the adoption of different techniques have to be obtained. This is illustrated in Fig. 34.4. Let the vertical axis measure labour-employment and output of consumer

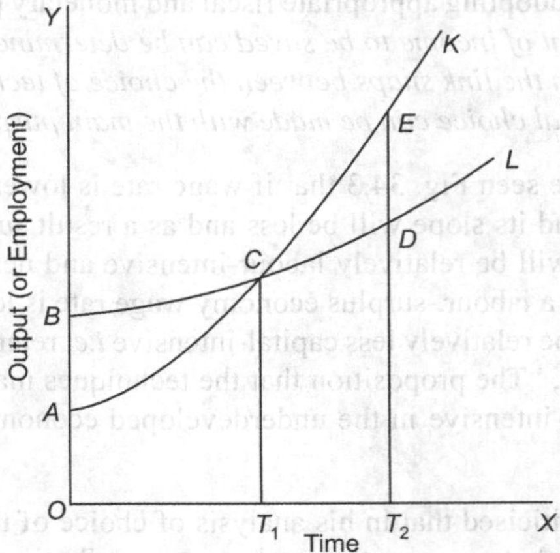

Fig. 34.4. *Amartya Sen's criterion of choice of technique*

goods and the horizontal axis measure time. The more steep curve *AK* represents growth of output or employment over time with using capital-intensive technique *K* whereas the less steep curve *BL* shows the growth of output and employment over time with adopting labour-intensive technique of production *L*.

Till time T_1, labour-intensive technique generates more output and employment as compared with the capital-intensive technique. But, since the growth of output or employment is greater in case of capital-intensive technique due to its yielding larger surplus and reinvestment, beyond time T_1 output or employment is greater in case of capital-intensive technique K. And on account of higher growth of output and employment the capital-intensive technique fully compensates for the *initial loss of output* (*or employment*) by the time T_2. Note that the ares *CED* equals the area *ABC* in Fig. 34.4). It is evident from Fig. 34.4 that after time T_2, the society would have higher levels of output and employment by choosing capital-intensive technique. Thus though the choice of labour-intensive technique yields higher levels of output and employment *in the present,* it yields lower rate of growth due to smaller reinvestible surplus. On the basis of this time series criterion, Amartya Sen argues that if social welfare function of a society is such that it is prepared to wait up to time T_2 (say, thirty years) output and employment sacrificed at present could be fully compensated and after T_2, the society would enjoy higher levels of consumption and employment by choosing capital-intensive technique. However, if social welfare function is such that society prefers present output (consumption) and employment to future consumption and employment, then it may choose labour-intensive technique.

Many of the criticisms levelled against Galenson and Leibenstein's maximum reinvestible criterion also apply to Sen's time-criterion for choice of technique as it is also based on maximisation of surplus. As mentioned above, this criterion depends on a particular choice of technique to generate more saving or surplus for investment to bring about higher rate of growth of output and employment. As has been stated above, in his analysis Sen assumes that a higher proportion of profits is saved than that from wages (in the extreme case it is assumed that all profits are saved and all wages are consumed). The critics have pointed out that this is not true. In fact a lot of profits are consumed instead of being saved and further that employees do save a part of their wages or salaries.

Furthermore, it is assumed by Sen that wage rates do not depend on technique. In fact, as with capital-intensive technique productivity of workers is higher, their wages will also be higher and this will lower the surplus made on using capital-intensive technique. Sen has also been criticised that saving or surplus for investment can be increased by the choice of capital-intensive technique alone. Rather than depending on choice of technique, in a planned economy saving can be increased by the government through adopting appropriate fiscal and monetary policies. In a later article Sen concedes, *"The total amount of income to be saved can be determined by the planner in any way he likes ... if this is true then the link snaps between the choice of technique and the proportion of income saved. Then technical choice can be made with the main purpose of maximising output."*[4]

Furthermore, as well be seen Fig. 34.3 that if wage rate is lower, then the wage line will lie below the wage line *OW* and its slope will be less and as a result surplus maximising technique will to the right of L_1 and will be relatively labour-intensive and nearer to the maximum output point. Given the fact that in a labour.-surplus economy wage rate is lower, it follows that surplus-maximising technique will be relatively less capital-intensive *i.e.* relatively labour-intensive. Even Sen in his later work writes, "The proposition that the techniques maximising output would tend to be relatively less capital-intensive in the underdeveloped economies compared with those in the advanced economies."[5]

Lastly, Sen has been criticised that in his analysis of choice of technique his emphasis is on raising saving and assumes that consumption makes no contribution to future, growth. It is now well recognised that level of consumption demand or growth in demand plays an important role for sustained growth of the economy.

4 Amartya Sen, "Choice of Technology: A Critical Survey of a Class of Debates,", in G. M. Meir, *Leading Issues in Economic Development*, 1975.

5 Amartya Sen, *Ibid.*

CONFLICT BETWEEN MAXIMISING EMPLOYMENT AND MAXIMISING PRODUCTION

When new projects for investment are planned, there is likely to be greater scope for varying the amount of labour employment. For example, a given amount of resources may be invested in either handlooms or automatic looms which employ quite different amounts of labour. It may, however, be noted that a given amount of new investment in labour-intensive and capital-intensive techniques may result in different levels of output; labour intensive techniques may yield less output as compared with capital-intensive techniques. Thus, while the labour-intensive techniques are characterised by *higher labour-output ratios*, it is not necessary that all such techniques have *lower capital-output ratio*. For instance, it is worthwhile to note that Amartya Sen has shown that the labour-intensive technique of Ambar Charkha has higher capital-output ratios than the factory methods. Dhar and Lydall have also found that some labour-intensive small-scale industries have higher capital-output ratios. Hence, a *conflict between output and employment arises*. However, the decision whether output should be sacrificed or employment will depend upon the social welfare function. Given the extent of unemployment and underemployment and the glaring disparities of income we feel that some output is worth sacrificing for more employment. Provision of employment is by far the most important way of raising the people above the poverty line and of ensuring widespread sharing in the fruits of economic development. In addition, employment gives an individual a sense of participation in socially gainful activity and prevents the feeling of being not wanted which has a great demoralising effect. Indeed, as has been remarked by Barbra Ward, "*of all the evils worthlessness is the worst*."

It should however be noted that *all labour-intensive techniques do not have higher capital-output ratio* and therefore in their case conflict does not arise between maximizing employment and maximising production. In fact, in many labour-intensive techniques and small-scale industries, capital-output ratio is lower than the corresponding large-scale industries. Hence a case for encouraging such industries in developing countries like India.

Conflict between Maximising Current Employment and Maximising Rate of Growth of Production and Employment

Conflict which generally arises relates to the *maximisation of current employment and maximisation of rate of growth of production and employment.* As seen above, from Sen's analysis of choice of techniques, maximisation of output-employment in the current period will not lead to the higher rate of economic growth of both output and employment. This question is of particular importance in respect of (a) allocation of resources for investment between capital goods and consumer goods and (b) the choice between labour-intensive and capital-intensive techniques.

Maximising rate of growth of production now at the cost of present employment makes it possible to use extra output produced for generating more employment in the future. It is worth noting that more output (*i.e.*, more reinvestible surplus) is useful not only for its own sake but enables the planners to generate more employment opportunities in the future. Thus, a conflict (and therefore inter-temporal trade-off) arises between *more employment now and more employment tomorrow.*

Let us explain how conflict arises in the two cases mentioned above. Allocation of more resources to the production of investment goods by sacrificing some employment in the present (that is, if extra output is in the form of capital goods such as machines etc.) will enable us to provide employment to more men in the future. Similarly, if extra production is in the form of more wage goods– liquid capital as they are sometimes called– it enables the planners to create more jobs in the future as the availability of wage goods limits the opportunities for creation of employment opportunities.

On the contrary, raising employment now means sacrificing not only some production in the current period but also lowering the rate of growth of employment. Thus with the allocation of resources to the consumer goods industries ensuring more employment now, level of employment at some future date would be lower than would have been possible if more allocation of resources to capital goods industries in the present was preferred.

Turning to the conflict between current employment and the rate growth of employment arising out of the choice of techniques of production, Galenson and Leibenstein, Sen and others have shown that the choice of labour-intensive techniques, though maximises employment in the current period, will reduce the share of profits (or invertible surplus) as compared to wages. And the reduction in profits will adversely affect the rate of saving and investment and therefore the growth of output and employment. On the contrary, if capital-intensive techniques are chosen, they may yield less employment (and output) in the present but they will yield more surplus or profits as compared to wages. Therefore, the choice of capital-intensive techniques will ensure higher rate of growth and therefore more employment in the future. Here, the conflict or trade-off involved does not arise between current output and current employment. Instead, there is intertemporal trade-off, that is, more employment *now* or more employment *tomorrow*. It means that some more unemployment in the present may be tolerated for the sake of generating more invertible surpluses (profits) so that higher growth rate is achieved and more employment opportunities are provided in the future.

But the above argument regarding capital-intensive techniques yielding more employment in the future is based on the crucial assumption that a major part of profits is reinvested and most of wages are consumed.[6] Besides, account should also be taken of the fact that increase in consumption of the poor and unemployed will generate demand for basic wage goods which are produced with much more labour-intensive techniques as compared to those used in the production of goods demanded by the rich. Thus only a part of any increased income going to the rich will be saved and the part that will be spent would generate less employment than a similar amount of spending by the poor. In view of these, the use of capital-intensive techniques will not necessarily promote more rapid growth of employment and output.

APPROPRIATE OR INTERMEDIATE TECHNOLOGY

As has been stated above, the growth of organised or large-scale industries with modern capital-intensive technology yields only meagre employment opportunities. Therefore, in order to create adequate employment opportunities through industrial growth, there is a need for developing and adopting an '*intermediate technology*' which requires less capital per work place without loss of efficiency. Besides, to prevent excessive urbanisation and concentration and to arrest the tendency for mass migration into the urban areas, there is need for adoping a *strategy for rural industrialisation*, based on small-scale manufacturing using intermediate technology dispersed throughout the countryside to increase rural employment and income. Dr. E.F. Schumacher, the advocate of the adoption of intermediate technology, rightly says, "*It is surely an astonishing error to assume that the technology developed in the West is necessarily appropriate to the developing countries. Granted that their technological backwardness is an important reason for their poverty: granted too, that their traditional methods of production, in their present condition of decay, lack essential viability: it by no means follows that the technology of the richest countries is necessarily suitable for the advancement of the poor*. It must never be forgotten that modern technology is the product of the countries which are 'long' in capital and 'short' in labour, and that its main purpose, abundantly demonstrated by the trend towards automation, is to substitute machines for men. How could this technology fit in

6 Generally, models concerning this aspect of development assume that all profits are saved and all wages are consumed. On the contrary, an ILO Report on Columbia found that "*Notwithstanding the extreme degree of economic inequality that has prevailed in Columbia total personal savings appear to be quite low*".

the conditions of countries which suffer from a surplus of labour and a shortage of machines?"[7] He further remarks *that "technology devised primarily for the purpose of saving labour should be inappropriate in a country troubled with a vast labour surplus could hardly be called surprising"*.[8]

It is worth noting here that research in India, after making proper cost and price calculations, has already discovered intermediate technologies for producing some thirty types of such goods as agricultural implements, processed foods and consumer goods which are actually cheaper and more efficient than those produced by the advanced machinery.[9] It should be further noted that the evolving of intermediate technologies for various industries does not imply discovery of altogether new principles of science and engineering. What is required is the application of the basic principles of modern science and engineering to evolve the production techniques which conform to the factor endowments of the labour-surplus economies. These appropriate or intermediate technologies may be obtained by scaling down advanced techniques by adapting them so as to make them more labour intensive, or by scaling up handicrafts techniques with the introduction of new tools and simple machines and thus improving economic efficiency of these techniques while maintaining their labour-intensity. In this process of adaptation product design itself will also have to be modified and standardised. Further, entirely new appropriate technologies have also to be evolved from the applications of the basic principles of modern science and engineering so as to suit the labour-surplus conditions of developing countries. For that, a good deal of research and development is required to be undertaken.

It may be noted again that Japan's remarkable adaptability has been reflected not only in agricultural techniques but also in the extent to which it has organised its new industries efficiently on a cottage industry basis. Here, as in agriculture, Japan's production methods are especially well-suited to the conditions of labour-abundant economies. Lastly, it may be noted that recently, four East Asian countries, namely, South Korea, Taiwan, Hong-Kong and Singapore, which have achieved remarkably higher growth rates and are therefore called *Asian Tigers followed labour-intensive path of economic growth*. That is, they used relatively much more labour in their industrial development than India.

---

7 "Industrialisation through Intermediate Technology", a paper presented by Dr. Schumacher to the Cambridge Conference on Industrialisation in Developing Countries in September 1964. Published in Ronald Robbinon, *Developing the Third World: The Experience of the Nineteen-Sixties* (Cambridge University Press, 1971), pp. 88-89.

8 *Ibid.*, p. 97.

9 Small Industry Extension Training Institute (Hyderabad, India), *Appropriate Technologies for Indian Industries*, pp. 11-12.

CHAPTER 35

INFRASTRUCTURE AND ITS IMPORTANCE

The infrastructure is important for faster economic growth and alleviation of poverty in the country. The adequate infrastructure in the form of road and railway transport system, ports, power, airports and their efficient working is also needed for *integration* of the Indian economy with other economies of the world. The following are the important constituents of infrastructure:

1. Power and the source of its production such as coal and oil;
2. Roads and road transport;
3. Railways;
4. Communication, especially telecommunication;
5. Ports and airports; and
6. For agriculture, irrigation constitutes the important infrastructure.

A distinguishing feature of infrastructure is that while the demand-supply gap in case of other factors can be met by importing some of them, *the deficiency of infrastructure can not be made up through imports*. Because location-based the need for relevant infrastructure facility can be met through development of its capacity in the domestic economy. For example, you cannot import power facility, roads, ports or railways as they have to be built up in the domestic economy.

IMPORTANT FEATURES OF INFRASTRUCTURE

It is worthwhile to mention some distinctive features of infrastructure: First, the building of infrastructure require *large and lumpy investment* and they contribute to output, after a long time, that is their gestation period is quite long. Second, due to large overhead capital and lumpy investment, the *significant economies of scale* are found in most of them. Due to the significant economies of scale found in many infrastructure services, they have the characteristics of natural money. The third important feature of infrastructure facilities is they create *externalities*. For example, building of rural roads will benefit agriculture as the farmers are able to sell their products in towns where they can get remunerative prices. Besides, they can get some inputs such as fertilizers, pesticides and other industrial products at relatively cheaper prices as their transport costs decline due to improved transportation. Power plants generate both positive and negative externalities. The construction of power plants producers electricity which is used for industrial helps production and commercial use and thereby helps in acceleration of economic growth. Power plants also producers *negative externalities* in the form of emission of pollutants, especially CO_2.

The above features of infrastructure means that *competitive market system* will not be able to achieve a socially optimal level of infrastructural services in most of the cases. Besides, as mentioned above, in many of infrastructural facilities, there are significant economies of scale and therefore they have the features natural monopoly. In other words, we find market failure to achieve their socially optimal level. Therefore, these infrastructural facilities are either built and run by the government an public sector enterprises or if private sector is permitted to make investment in them and run them, they need to be regulated by the government, so that they should not exploit the consumers. For example, the distribution of electricity which is an infrastructural service is being provided by two power Companies of Tata and Reliance in different regions of delhi, the electricity rates and other charges are being regulated by an authority appointed by the government. Similarly, in telecommunication, which is another infrastructural service, various companies such as Airtel, Vodaphone, Idea, MTNL are providing this service of wireless telephony (*i.e.*, mobile service) are being regulated by TRAI.

IMPORTANCE OF INFRASTRUCTURE

It needs to be emphasized that good quality infrastructure is important not only for faster economic growth but also to ensure inclusive growth. By inclusive growth we mean that benefits of growth are shared by the majority of the people of a country. Thus the inclusive growth will lead to the alleviation of poverty and reduction in income inequality in the country. For example, micro, small and medium enterprises (MSME) are dispersed throughout the economy and production by them and their growth require access to quality and reliable infrastructure services to *compete efficiently* with large-scale enterprises which can often build some of their own infrastructure such as installing their own small power plants or generators. Besides, large-scale firms can even locate themselves near ports and near transport hubs where required infrastructure is available. Small enterprises, on the other hand, are dispersed widely in the economy and have to rely on the availability of the general infrastructure facilities. Thus, by building up general infrastructure facilities helps the small enterprises to compete successfully with large-scale industries and being labour-intensive generate large employment opportunities for the workers. This will help to alleviate the poverty in developing countries.

The expansion in infrastructure facilities such as irrigation, rural electrification, roads and road transport will promote agricultural growth and setting up of agro-processing industries. These general infrastructure facilities will help farmers and owners of processing industries to get their requirements of raw materials, fertilizers and other inputs at cheap rate and also help them to bring their products to the markets which are located in big towns and cities. Thus, according to Thirwal, "For poor farmers improved infrastructure will reduce their input cost and increase agricultural production and reduce traders' monopoly by improving their access to markets. Nearly two-thirds of African farmers are cut off from national and world markets because of poor infrastructure and market access better transport means greater access to public resources including schools, hospitals and other health facilities".[1]

It follows from above that the expansion of infrastructure facilities will ensure sustained growth of employment in agriculture and small-scale rural industries and bring prosperity in the rural areas and in this way ensure inclusive growth. Besides, this will also help to prevent the mass exodus of the rural people to urban areas where they cause problems of urban congestion, growth of slums and acute housing shortage.

Lack of adequate infrastructure not only holds lack economic development, it also causes additional costs in terms of time, effort and money of the people for accessing essential social services such as healthcare and education. Emphasizing the importance of adequate infrastructure, authors of Economic Survey of India for the Year 2013-14 quite rightly write, "*Rural economic growth in recent years has put enormous pressure on existing infrastructure particularly on transport, energy and communication. Unless it is significantly improved infrastructure will continue to be a bottleneck for*

1 A.P. Thirlwall, *Economic Growth and Development*, Palgrave Macmillan, 9th Edition, p. 242.

growth and obstacle to poverty reduction. In other words, the challenge to ensure strong, sustainable and balanced development through integration of the economy with environmentally sustainable development of infrastructure.[2]

It may be noted that with large investment in infrastructure during the last decade (2003-04 to 2013-14) India has become the second fastest growing economy of the world but in the two years (2012- March 2014) economic growth slowed down and this has been mainly due to the stalled infrastructure projects which held back economic development. It is therefore urgently needed that infrastructure projects be given environment clearance quickly and investment in them be speeded up if the Indian economy is to be brought back on the fast growth trajectory.

As mentioned above, the availability of good quality infrastructure raises productivity levels in the economy and brings down costs of the enterprises. Besides, *the availability of adequate infrastructure helps to expand trade not only within a country by improving transport facilities but also promote foreign trade through improvement of ports and airports*. It also helps to diversify production by the firms as they are able to get the required supplies of raw materials and other inputs from the places where these are available in abundance. Furthermore, with improved infrastructure the firms can produce goods in accordance with the demands of the people of different regions and countries.

According to World Bank estimates, in the year 2008 developing countries made investment of around $ 500 billion a year in new infrastructure—transport, power, water, sanitation, telecommunication, irrigation and so on equal to 20 per cent of GDP but the need for infrastructure investment is still large. In developing countries one billion people still lack access to clean water, two billion people lack access to sanitation and electric power and adequate transport facilities are still lacking in developing countries.[3]

Having discussed the importance of infrastructure in general, we now discuss below the importance of sector-specific infrastructure for economic growth of a country.

Power or Energy

Power or energy is a crucial input into all economic activities and therefore rapid economic growth is possible only if adequate power is made available everywhere. It is essential not only for growth of industry, agriculture and commercial business but also for household-lighting. In India, the percentage of households having electricity connection has increased from 56 in 2001 to 67 in 2011. Thus even now about 33 per cent of households have no electricity connection.[4] Besides, for achieving rapid economic growth on sustainable basis, there is need for rise in productivity. The rise in labour productivity ultimately requires greater use of electric power which is obtained from primary sources such as coal, oil and gas. Consumption of energy by the various countries of the world varies significantly. The United States and other developed countries use or consume much higher energy per capita as compared to the developing countries such as India. We give in Table 35.1 the data of per capita consumption or use of energy for some selected developing and developed countries along with their per capita income for the year 2009. It will be seen from the table that per capita energy use in 2009 in USA was 7503 kilograms of oil equivalent while in India it was only 545, that is, *energy use per capita in the USA is 15 times higher* as compared to India. No wonder that the per capita income of the USA was 45,640 PPP $ as compared to India's 3,280 PPP $, that is, about 15 times higher than that of India. In fact, the data in the table shows that *there is a very high degree of positive correlation between per capita energy use and per capita income of a country*.

---

2 GOI, *Economic Survey, 2013-14*, p. 207.
3 See *World Development Report*, 2011.
4 GOI, *Twelfth Five Year Plan*, Vol. 1.

Table 35.1. Energy Use 'Per Capita and Income Per Capita in Some Developing and Developed Countries

Country	Income Per Capita in PPP $ 2009	Use of Energy in Kilograms of Oil Equivalent in 2009
Developing Countries		
India	3,280	545
Brazil	10,160	1,295
China	6,890	1,598
Indonesia	3,720	874
Sri Lanka	4,720	443
Pakistan	2,680	499
Bangladesh	1,550	175
Developed countries		
USA	45,640	7,503
UK	35,860	3,395
Canada	37,280	8,008
France	33,950	4,279
Germany		4,083
Australia	38,510	6,071
Japan	33,440	3,803
Korea Republic	27,240	4,669

Source: World Bank, *World Development Indicators*, 2011.

That is, the greater the energy use per capita of a country, the higher the per capita income and productivity levels of a country. This shows the importance of increasing energy production for economic growth.

In case of India, according to the Twelfth Plan projections, total energy production will reach around 670 million tonnes of oil equivalent (MTOE) by 2016-17 and 844 MTOE by 2021-22. This will meet around 70 per cent of expected energy consumption of the Indian economy, the balance will be met through imports. Thus, even through the domestic production of energy in India is projected to increase significantly, *dependence on imports will continue to remain high*, particularly for crude oil where nearly 78 per cent of the demand will have to be met through imports by the end of the 12th Plan (*i.e.* by March 2017). Further, it is estimated by the Planning Commission that the import dependence for coal, liquified natural gas (LNG) and crude oil taken together in the terminal year (2016-17) of the 12th Plan is likely to remain at the 11th Plan level of 36 per cent. It is worthwhile to note that the potential for energy generation depends upon a country's natural resource endowments and the technology used to harness them. India has both *non-renewable energy resources* (such as coal, lignite, petroleum and natural gas) and *renewable* energy sources (such as hydro, wind, solar, biomass).

Twelfth Plan Target: The Eleventh Five Year Plan (2007-12) added 55,000 MW of additional power generating capacity and the Twelfth Plan (2012-17) aims to add another 88,000 MW generating capacity. This large increase in the additional capacity is not impossible but actual delivery of power depends critically on solving serious fuel availability problems that arise relating to coal and natural gas. Uncertainties about fuel availability would seriously dampen investment activity in this sector, especially since about half of the generating capacity is expected to come from the private sector and they will not be able to obtain the required finance if fuel supply issues are not resolved.

Road Transport

Road transport is another important infrastructure which is essential for movement of goods, raw materials and fuel. The availability of transport expands the market for agricultural and industrial products and thereby enables the producers to produce on a large scale and reap the benefits of the economies of scale.

Besides, transport development helps to open up more regions and resources for production. Some parts of a country may have abundant forests and reserves of mineral resources but they remain unexploited for production because they are remote and inaccessible through means of transport. There is thus a need for linking these backward regions with building of roads and railways so that their untapped mineral and forest resources be utilised for production. India has one of the largest road networks in the world spread over around 49 lakh kilometres. It comprises national highways, expressways, state highways, district roads with length details given in Table 35.2. In the last few years there has been some progress in the development of *national highways* and in rural roads but much more needs to the done.

Table 35.2. Road Network in India (as in May 2014)

Type of Road	Length (in km)
National Highways and Expressways	92,851
State Highways	142,687
Other Roads	4,629,482

Source: GOI, *Economic Survey*, 2013-14

The National Highways (NHs) with a total length of 92,851 km serve as the arterial network of the country. The development of National Highways is the responsibility of the Central Government which has been mandated to upgrade and strengthen a total of 54,478 km of NHs, through various phases of the National Highways Development Project (NHDP). A total length of around 22,000 km has been completed till March 2014. There are some difficulties in the way of developing national highways due to acquisition of land from the owners from which national highways have to pass through.

In India a special effort is needed to speed up road connectivity in Jammu and Kashmir. North East, and other special category States. A good start had been made in the development of roads in North East in the Eleventh Five Year Plan and is proposed to be pursued with greater vigour in the 12th Plan in which enhanced connectivity of North East has been given a high priority. Furthermore, the construction of roads and upgradation of national highways (NHs) in the districts affected by *Left-Wing extremism* in Andhra Pradesh, Bihar, Chhattisgarh, Jharkhand, Madhya Pradesh, Odisha and Uttar Pradesh have been taken up for inclusive growth of these areas.

Railways

Railways is an important infrastructure as a means of transport whose expansion and efficient working is required for rapid growth of the economy. The demands of a growing economy such as ours require railways to expand its freight network, increase its ability to carry larger weight per wagon and the efficiency of the rail system for faster delivery. Besides, the railway require to improve the reach and quality of its passenger services. To meet the growing demand for carrying goods and passengers the current focus of Indian Railway should be the creation of additional capacity, modernisation of its existing network, improvement in asset utilisation and productivity. Besides, it should pay attention to modernisation of its rolling stock and maintenance practices to bring about overall improvement in the quality of its services.

It may be further noted that the Indian Railways is expected to generate its internal resources for its expansion and modernisation. The broad objective of Indian Railways should be to develop a strategy to be a part of an effective multi-modal transport system and to ensure an environment-friendly and economically-efficient transport system.

Airports

Airport development is a basic infrastructure requirement for international connectivity, especially because the demand for air travel is projected to grow rapidly in India. There had been a significant progress of airport development in the Eleventh Plan period with the development of four new airports at Bangalore, Hyderabad, Delhi and Mumbai under public-private participation (PPP) mode. To expand airport infrastructure in India, modernisation of airport infrastructure in metro and non-metro cities and construction of greenfield airports are under consideration of the government. Development of 35 non-metro airports which have been identified based on regional connectivity, development of regional hubs, etc has been undertaken by Airports Authority of India (AAI). Out of 35 metros airports work has been completed in 33 metros and in the remaining two airports of Vadodra and Khajuraho work is in progress.

Ports

Ports are another important infrastructure for *international trade connectivity*. It is mainly through these that the goods are exported to other countries and the goods and raw materials are imported. Without efficient ports it is not possible to expand foreign trade. In the Eleventh Plan period (2007-12) some problems were faced for expansion of the Indian ports because several issues had to be resolved for the proposed public-private participation (PPP) in this connection. These have now been resolved and it is expected that in the next five years there will be significant progress in this area. As regards minor ports which come under State governments, there has been good progress in the Eleventh Plan period.

During 2013-14 major and non-major ports in India handled a total cargo of 980 million tonnes reflecting increase of 5.0 per cent over 2012-13. This can mainly be attributed to an increase of 1.8 per cent in the cargo handled at major ports. In contrast, traffic at non-major ports increased at around 9.6 per cent during 2013-14 as compared to 9.8 per cent in 2012-13.

Telecommunications

Telecommunications occupy an important place in the modern economy. E-commerce and E-governance require the efficiency of telecommunication services. The companies like Amazon, Flipkart, Snapdeal are engaged in E-commerce to for sale of goods. They work through mobiles and internet network. Besides, many BPO companies are providing outsourcing services through telecommunication. Without the efficient telecommunication system, the business through E-commerce and BPO is not possible. Telecommunications and the associated increase in Internet connectivity is a productivity enhancing development and India is well based to benefit from this.

Telecommunications in India have seen impressive expansion and large investment in the past several years with a tele-intensity increasing from 26.2 per cent in 2008 to 78.7 per cent in 2012. The expansion of telecommunications in India has been led by private sector whose market share (in terms of number of connections) increased from 73.5 per cent in 2008 to 86.3 per cent in 2012. However, due to arbitrariness and irregularities in the allocation of 2G Spectrum in 2008, 2G licences and associated spectrum were cancelled by the Supreme Court in 2011 and ordered for reallocation of the spectrum through auction. The new auction of 2G spectrum was completed by January 2013.

There is a very large scope for further expansion in the telecommunications, especially with the introduction of 3G and 4 G services. Besides, recently in july 2015, Prime minister has launched *Digital India* scheme to promote the role of telecom. In India a large number of companies providing telecom services have come into being. Business firms and even farmers can sign up for a telecom service which provides information through SMS or E-mail about market prices and other prevailing market conditions. This will help them to take optimal decisions regarding their business. Banks are also providing their customers, through SMS or E-mail, the status of their deposits and withdrawal. Besides, the banks are providing through E-mail the information regarding investment avenues open to them.

Keeping in view the role of an efficient telecom network in E-commerce and E-governance and delivery of public services provisions for state-of-art IT facilities in the country need to be put in place. Issues requiring attention include the policy for better spectrum management, strengthening a national fibreoptic network, network mobile number possibility and rural telephony.

EVALUATION OF THE PERFORMANCE OF INFRASTRUCTURAL SERVICES

Whether in the public sector or regulated private sector the performance of infrastructural services has been quite poor. In many developing countries, the majority of the population, does not have access to the electricity and until recently in telephone services. After over 50 years of independence, in India the adequate pucca rural roads had not been built and natural highways were in very bad shape and not properly built and maintained lack of good ports and ports in India affected foreign trade of the country. It is only since 2001 that the work of building rural roads, highways, good ports and airports has been started in the 10th, 11th and 12th Five Year Plan.

In the case of electricity, the quality of service has been quite poor. There has been quite often fluctuations in voltages and often supply-cuts even in capital city of Delhi. In UP, Haryana and other states there are interruptions of supply for many hours compelling big companies to install their own big generators. Besides, State Electricity Boards which are usually responsible for distribution of electricity are running heavy losses. Prices charged by them even do not cover variable costs of supply, let alone contributing to overhead costs.

Similarly, until recently before the extensive use of mobile-phone wireless technology, telephone connections were very few and were a luxury consumer service rather than an essential productive service required to link markets, producers and consumers. Besides, one has to wait for many years to get telephone connection. However in the last 12 years, regarding telephone service things have improved a lot in India, especially with the widespread use of mobile telephone service. Likewise, in India, the performance of railways port and airport services has been quite inefficient and poor and need drastic reforms to be undertaken to improve their services.

To conclude, Prof. T.N. Srinivasan is right in saying that, "the said performance of enterprises providing infrastructural services has been a factor in the poor performance of many developing countries including India. Thus the case for reforming the infrastructural sectors is very strong, both for improving their own performance and for removing the drag of an unreformed and poorly performing infrastructure sector on the realisation of potential benefits of reforms in other sectors.[5]

5 T. N. Srinivasan, Eight *lectures on India's Economic Reforms* (New Delhi; 2000, Oxford University Press), p. 53.

Appendix 35A

Efficiency of Small-Scale vs Large-Scale Industries

There has been a good deal of controversy regarding efficiency of small-scale industries as compared to the large-scale industries. How should efficiency be measured is also not without controversy. Whether efficiency should be judged by cost per unit of output or output per unit of fixed capital (*i.e.*, *Y*/*K*) or the amount of output per unit of labour (*i.e.*, *Y*/*L*). It is well known that while *large-scale industries are capital-intensive* [that is, they use more *fixed capital per employee* (*i.e.* higher *K*/*L*)]. On the other hand, small-scale industries are *labour-intensive*, that is, they employ more labour per unit of capital or per unit of output.

However, before discussing these issues it is appropriate to explain the *economies of scale*. In microeconomic theory long-run average cost (LAC) is generally to be of U-shape, that is, as output is expanded in the beginning it falls due to the economies of scale and after a point it starts rising due to the diseconomies of scale. The point at which the long-run average cost is minimum is called the *minimum efficiency scale.* The size of plants beyond the minimum efficiency scale are not built.

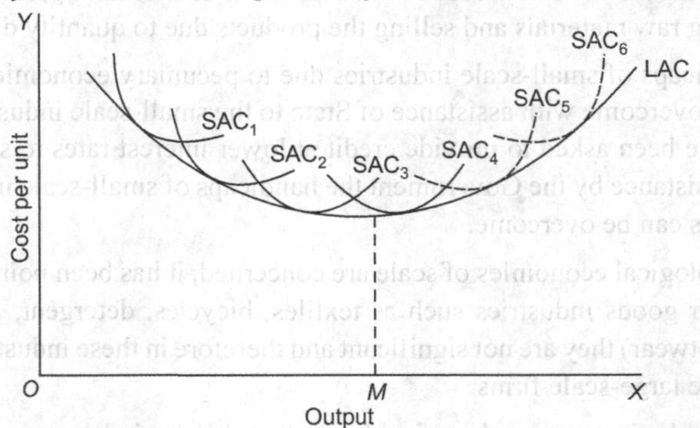

Fig. 35A.1. *Long-run average cost curve and minimum efficiency scale*

It will be seen from Fig. 35A.1 that up to output level *OM* cost per unit of output falls with the increase is scale of output until output level *OM* is reached (that is, up to the minimum efficient scale of output with plant represented by short-run average cost curve SAC_4.) Note that *minimum efficiency scale is reached beyond which long-run average cost ceases to decline*. It is evident that small-scale firm producing with plant size, for example, represented by SAC_1 can produce at a higher average cost compared to the firm of large-scale producing with plant size SAC_4. Generally, no plant larger than the size of SAC_4 will be built and therefore they are shown by dots. As mentioned above, long- run average cost falls up to size of output *OM* because economies of scale occur with increase in the scale of plant and production with it. Mathematically, economies of scale can be represented by the following cost function:

$$C = AQ^{\alpha}$$

where C is total cost, Q is output, A is a constant and α is the *scale coefficient* or *cost elasticity*.

The above cost function shows that as scale or size of output increases the total cost (C) of an optimally designed plant rises less than proportionately, that is, scale coefficient (α) which also represents cost elasticity is less than one ($\alpha < 1$). This means if cost per unit of output is the criterion of efficiency, the large-scale industrial enterprise will be more efficient.

There are several factors or which account for economies of scale that cause decline in long-run average cost. First, the greater the division of labour and specialisation takes place as the size of output is increased. Second, installation of more efficient and specialised machinery as scale of output is expanded. Further, large-scale firms get cheap finance an they are able to get funds at lower interest rate as compared to the small-scale firms. Further, large-scale industrial firms get raw materials and other inputs at cheaper rater as they are given quantity discounts. Besides, economies are also enjoyed by the large-scale firms on account of transport cost and marketing cost, as overheard expenses per unit of output declines on the transportation and marketing products on a large scale.

Dr. J.C. Sandesara, an expert in the field of development of small-scale industries, points out that while "*large industry has often access to cheap capital and small industry to cheap labour* and these respective advantages and handicaps may keep the *cost-scale in balance, so that small industry may not suffer from any special handicap.*[1] Besides, in producing a new product there is a lot of risk involved. Setting up small-scale industries will be suited for it as this will minimise risk.

The distinction has been drawn between two types of economies of scale: ***technological and pecuniary economies***. The greater division of labour and specialisation and use of technologically superior machinery for production at a large scale are technological economies of large-scale manufacturing firms which lead to lower cost per unit of output. In this respect large-scale firms have definite advantage over the small-scale industries. On the other hand, *pecuniary economies* enjoyed by the large-scale firms are the lower cost of finance, lower cost of transportation and lower cost of marketing for buying raw materials and selling the products due to quantity discounts.

In case of handicaps of small-scale industries due to pecuniary economies it has been pointed out that they can be overcome with assistance of State to the small-scale industries. For example, in India, the banks have been asked to provide credit at lower interest rates to small-scale industries. Thus with proper assistance by the Government the handicaps of small-scale industries arising from pecuniary economies can be overcome.

As far as technological economies of scale are concerned, it has been pointed out that in a good number of consumer goods industries such as textiles, bicycles, detergent, footwear, leather and leather products (footwear) they are not significant and therefore in these industries small-scale firms can compete with the large-scale firms.

Generally, technological economies of scale are found in basic heavy industries such as steel, heavy chemicals, fertilizers, etc and capital goods industries such as machine tools, power generating plants, electrical machinery, machines to make machines and durable consumer goods such as automobiles. In such industries, large-scale firms can operate with greater efficiency.

Efficiency in Terms of Output Per Unit of Capital

In some industries, as seen above, large-scale industrial enterprises are efficient in terms of cost per unit of output due to their enjoying economies of scale. However, *lower cost per unit of output is not the only criterion* of efficiency. In developing countries such as India, capital is scarce and labour is abundant. Therefore efficiency in the use of resources requires that the industrial units which

1 J.C. Sandesara, "Small-scale Industrialisation: The Indian Experience," printed in Uma Kapila, *Indian Economy since Independence*, Academic Foundation.

economise the use of scarce capital and use more the abundant factor labour. In this respect small-scale units are more efficient than large industrial units. Take first the case of the use of capital. If the objective is maximisation of output (or income), then the technique which maximises *output per unit of capital* (that is, which has greater output-capital ratio (Y/K) should be preferred. It has been pointed out that a number of small industries have a *higher output-capital ratio* (Y/K) as compared to the competing large-scale industries though the latter have a lower cost per unit of output. Consider Table 35A.1 where we have given the data of fixed capital per employee (*i.e.* capital-labour ratio, K/L), output (*i.e.*, value added) per employee, that is, productivity [Y/L] of labour and output (*i.e.*, value added) per unit of fixed capital (*i.e.*, Y/K ratio), that is, productivity of capital in case of India.

Table 35A.1. Capital Per Employee and Output Per Unit of Employee and Fixed Capital (in Rupees)

Year	Type of Industry	Fixed Capital per Employee (K/L)	Value added per unit of Employee (Y/L)	Value added per unit of Fixed Capital (Y/K)
1965	Small	2,018	2,359	1.17
	Medium	4,044	3,815	0.94
	Large	17,753	5,217	0.29
1974-75	Small	3,706	4,790	1.29
	Medium	7,935	8,785	1.11
	Large	30,536	13,736	0.43
1978-79	Small	16,582	7,051	0.43
	Medium	27,610	12,512	0.45
	Large	68,166	15,903	0.23

Source: Compiled from data of Annual Survey of Industries, 1965, 1974-75 and 1978-79.

It will be seen from the 3rd column of Table 35A.1 that fixed capital per employee (*i.e.*, capital -labour ratio) is much higher in large-scale industries as compared to the small and medium scale industrial units. This shows that *large-scale industrial units are highly capital-intensive* in nature. Since fixed capital used per employee is higher in large-scale industries, value added per employee (*i.e.* productivity of labour as seen from col. 4) is also greater in them.

However, the *important fact is revealed in column 5 of the table which shows value added per unit, of fixed capital* (*i.e.*, output-capital ratio) which indicates that the *productivity of capital is much higher in case of small scale industrial units* as compared to the medium and large-scale industries. From this it follows that if *the objective is to maximise output* (or value added) per unit of fixed capital, then small-scale industries using more labour-intensive techniques should be preferred.

Recent reports of *Annual Survey of Industries* of India classify various industries from the viewpoint of *capital investment per unit* into tiny industrial units, small-scale units and large industrial units. The data for the year 1994-95 reveal that in large industrial units with value of plant and equipment of 50 lakh, and above with capital per employee (*i.e.*, K/L ratio) equal to 5.89 lakh,

Table 35A.2. Capital-labour Ratio and Output per unit of Employee in various Types of Industries (in rupees)

Gross Value of Plant and Machinery	Capital Per Employee (K/L)	Value added per unit of Employee (Y/L)	Value added per unit of Capital (Y/K)
Tiny units (upto ₹ 5 lakh) small-scale units	33,620	25,683	0.79
(From 5 lakh to 50 lakh)	104,526	64,148	0.61
large industrial units (50 lakh and above)	5,89,523	1,61,371	0.27

Source: Annual Survey of Industries, 1994-95.

value added per unit capital (*i.e.*, *Y/K* ratio) is only ₹ 0.27 as compared to ₹ 0.79 of tiny industrial units (with value of plant and machinery per employee less than ₹ 5 lakhs) and ₹ 0.61 of small-scale industrial units (with value of plant and machinery between ₹ 5 lakh and ₹ 50 lakh) in 1994-95. This clearly shows that in tiny and small scale industries output per unit of capital employed (*i.e.*, productivity of capital) is much higher as compared to large-scale industrial units.

It has been argued by Galenson-Leibenstein[2] and Amartya Sen[3] that criterion of low capital-labour ratio is better only from the viewpoint of maximisation output in the short run, but it may not lead to the maximisation of output in the long run. It is argued that for achieving higher rate of economic growth in the long run, what is required is maximisation of reinvestible surplus which is ploughed back into further investment. But, according to them, labour-intensive small-scale industries do not yield much reinvestible surplus and therefore do not lead to higher investment and economic growth in the long run.

On the other hand, large-scale industries using capital-intensive techniques yield large investible surplus which can be used for further investment to achieve higher rate of economic growth. Thus, according to them, there is conflict between the *maximisation of employment and income in the short run* and *maximisation of growth of output and employment*. However, this has not been found to be true in case of India. As seen above, from the empirical data furnished by *Annual Survey of Industries*, output-capital ratio is higher in case of small and medium enterprises. Moreover, given the fact that small-scale industries pay lower wages than paid by large-scale industries using highly capital-intensive techniques, the higher output-capital ratio in them will ensure large reinvestible surplus and therefore higher rate of growth of output and employment.

Besides generating more employment, small-scale industries have a *short gestation period* and yield quick returns in the form of output and help to check inflationary pressures which are generally created in the process of economic development. Moreover, small-scale industries using labour-intensive techniques or lower capital-intensive techniques require little foreign capital and technology and use local resources and skills. As a result, they *have lower foreign exchange component*. Saving of foreign exchange is of vital importance for the developing countries which are prone to suffer from balance of payments difficulties. Furthermore, in developing countries like India small-scale industries have *substantial export potential* and thereby help to earn foreign exchange.

Besides, the small-scale industries being less capital intensive can be easily set up in small towns and therefore help to bring about *decentralisation of industries* and promote the objective of balanced *regional development*. On the other hand, large-scale industries have a tendency to concentrate in the big towns and cities where required infrastructure facilities are available for them. Further, by providing remunerative employment in the rural areas and small towns the *small-scale industries will relieve congestion in overcrowded urban centres and thus prevent environment pollution*. Further, small-scale industries can also help sustain agricultural growth in the rural areas through the *development of agro-processing industries* and providing resources such as repair and service workshops.

It may however be pointed out that *modern small and medium enterprises* (MSME) cannot be easily set up in the rural areas but they can be set up in the small towns. It needs to be emphasised that development of traditional and modern small and medium enterprises require adequate infrastructure such as availability of power, good roads and transport facilities. The good roads and transport facilities will connect villages and small towns with big urban centres for getting the supplies of raw materials and for marketing of their products.

It is evident from above that small-scale industries can play an important role in the development of the developing countries.

---

2 W. Galenson and H. Leibenstein, "Investment Criteria, Productivity and Economic Development," *Quarterly Journal of Economies*, 1955.

3 Amartya Sen, *Choice of Technique,* Oxford University Press.

PART VII

International Aspects of Economic Development

- Static and Dynamic Gains from International Trade
- International Trade as an 'Engine of Economic Growth'
- Myrdal, Prebisch-Singer Thesis vs Free Trade
- Primary Export-Led Growth
- Manufacturing Export-Led Growth Model
- Dual Gap Analysis
- Foreign Trade Strategy: Import Substitution vs Export Orientation with Special Reference to India
- Balance of Payments Problems of Developing Countries
- Theory of Protection and Tariff
- Post-GATT International Economic Order and WTO

Static and Dynamic Gains from International Trade

International trade confers a good deal of benefits on the trading countries. According to the comparative cost theory, if different countries specialise on the basis of comparative costs of commodities, it would enable them to make optimum use of their resources and thereby add to their output, income and welfare of their people. Gains from trade are broadly divided into two types:

(*i*) Static Gains

(*ii*) Dynamic Gains.

Static gains from trade refer to the increase in production or welfare of the people of the trading countries as a result of the optimum allocation of their given factor-endowments, if they pecialise on the basis of their comparative costs. On the other hand, dynamic gains refer to the contributions which foreign trade makes to the overall economic growth of the trading countries. We shall explain below in detail these two types of gains.

STATIC GAINS FROM TRADE

As stated above, static gains from trade are measured by the increase in the utility or level of welfare when there is opening of trade between the countries. Note that in modern economics increase in utility or welfare is measured through indifference curves. When as a result of foreign trade, a country moves from a lower indifference curve to a higher one, it implies that the welfare of the people has increased. To show the static gains from trade, let us take an example. Suppose two commodities, cloth and wheat, are produced in two countries, India and U.S.A., before they enter into trade. Their production possibility and indifference curves for cloth and wheat are shown in Figs. 36.1 and 36.2. It will be seen from Fig. 36.1 that before trade India would be in equilibrium at point *F* (*i.e.*, producing and consuming at point *F*) where the price line *pp*′ is tangent to both production possibility curve *AB* and indifference curve IC_1. The slope of the price line *pp*′ shows the price ratio (or cost ratio) of the two commodities in India.

India can gain if international price ratio (*i.e.*, terms of trade) is different from the domestic price ratio represented by *pp*′. Suppose the terms of trade settled are such that we get *tt* as the terms of trade line showing the price ratio at which goods can be exchanged between India and the U.S.A. Now, with *tt*′ as the given terms of trade line (*i.e.*, new price ratio line), India would produce at point *R* at which the terms of trade line *tt* is tangent to her production possibility curve. It will be seen from Fig. 36.1 that at point *R*, India will produce more of cloth in which it has comparative advantage and less of wheat than at *F*. Though India will produce at point *R* on her production possibility curve, where the terms of trade line *tt*′ is tangent to her production possibility curve *AB*, it will not consume or use the quantities of wheat and cloth, represented by the point *R*. Given the new price ratio represented by the terms of trade line *tt'* the consumption of the goods will depend upon the pattern of demand of the country. To incorporate this factor we have drawn social indifference curves IC_1, IC_2 of the country. These social indifference curves represent the demands for the two goods, or, in other words, the scale of preferences between the two goods of the Indian society.

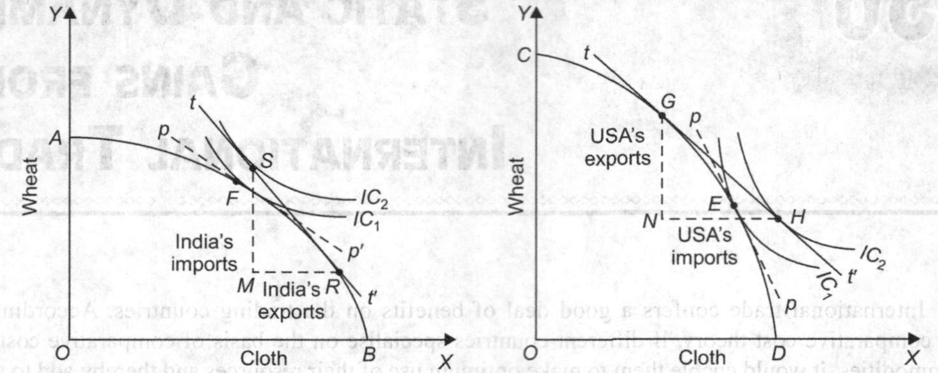

Fig. 36.1. *Static gains from trade: India* **Fig. 36.2.** *Static gains from trade: U.S.A.*

It will be seen from Fig. 36.1 that the terms of trade line *tt'* is tangent to the social indifference curve IC_2 of India at point *S*. Therefore, after trade India will consume the quantities of cloth and wheat as represented by point *S*. It is therefore clear that as a result of reallocation of resources and specialising, and producing more of cloth and less of wheat by India and trading with the US she has been able to shift from point *F* on indifference curve IC_1 to the point S on higher indifference curve IC_2. This is the gain obtained from specialisation through reallocation of resources and trade and implies that trade enables India to increase her consumption beyond her production possibility curve. (It will be seen that point *S* lies beyond the production possibility curve *AB* of India).

It is also worth noting that when specialisation and trade occur, the quantities of the two goods consumed by a country will differ from the quantities of the two goods produced by her without specialisation and reallocation of resources. In Fig. 36.1 whereas India produces the quantities of two goods represented by point *R*, it will consume the quantities of the two goods represented by the point *S*. The difference arises due to exports and imports of goods. In Fig. 36.1, while India will export *MR* quantity of cloth, she will import *MS* quantity of wheat.

Now consider the position of U.S.A. which is depicted in Fig. 36.2. Given its factor endowments *CD* is the production possibility curve between wheat and cloth of the U.S.A. It is evident from the production possibility curve *CD* that the factor endowments of the U.S.A. are more favourable for the production of wheat. It will also be seen from Fig. 36.2 that before trade the U.S.A. will produce and consume at point *E* on her production possibility curve *CD* where the domestic price ratio line *pp* and indifference curve IC_1 are tangent to it. The USA will gain from trade if it can sell at a different price ratio from *pp'*. Suppose the terms of trade line is *tt'*. With this terms of trade line *tt'* the U.S.A. will produce at point *G* on her production possibility curve *CD*. She will now produce more of wheat in which she has comparative advantage and less of cloth than before. On the other hand, given the price ratio as represented by the terms of trade line *tt'* the U.S.A. will consume the quantities of the two goods given by the point *H* where the terms of trade line is tangent to her indifference curve IC_2. Welfare of its people has increased. It is therefore clear that through reallocation of resources between the two goods and specialisation in the production of wheat and consequently trade with India has enabled the U.S.A. to shift from her lower indifference curve IC_1 to her higher indifference curve IC_2. This is the gain which she obtains from trade.

By comparing the production and consumption points of the U.S.A. it will be observed that the U.S.A. will export *NG* amount of wheat and import *NH* amount of cloth.

It is worth remembering that while in case of constant opportunity cost *each country attains complete specialisation*, that is, it produces one of the two goods after trade, in case of *present increasing opportunity* cost specialisation is not complete. In case of increasing opportunity cost as shown in Fig. 36.1 and Fig. 36.2 a country produces only a relatively large amount of the good in which it has comparative advantage.

DYNAMIC GAINS FROM TRADE: INTERNATIONAL TRADE AND ECONOMIC GROWTH

We have seen above in the discussion of comparative cost theory that specialisation followed by international trade makes it possible for the countries to have more of both commodities than before. This additional production of commodities is the gain which flows from specialisation to different countries in the production of different goods and then trading with each other. Specialisation by different countries in the production of different goods according to their comparative efficiency and resource endowments brings about an increase in the total world production by increasing the level of their productivity. However, these gains from specialisation and trade made possible by reallocation of the given resources along a given production possibility curve are **one-time event** and are therefore called **static gains from trade.** Empirical evidence shows that such gains are quite small, less than one per cent of GDP of the trading countries. However, in addition to static gains there are dynamic gains from trade. These *dynamic gains from trade refer to the gains from* trade that accrue to the countries over time because trade induces economic growth of a country and brings increase in efficiency in the use of resources by a country. It is this trade that makes possible the division and specialisation of labour on which higher productivity of different countries is so largely based. If the various countries could not exchange the products of their specialised labour, each of them would have to be self-sufficient (*i.e.*, each of them would have to produce all goods it requires, even those which it could not produce efficiently) with the result that their productivity and standard of living will go down. Thus according to Professor Haberler, "*International division of labour and international trade, which enable every country to specialise and to export those things which it can produce cheaper in exchange for what others can provide at a lower cost, have been and still are one of the basic factors promoting economic well-being and increasing national income of every participating country.*"

We thus see that the main gain from specialisation and trade is the increase in national production, income and consumption of the participating countries. But the *above explanation of gains from trade in terms of comparative cost theory deals only with static gains from trade, that is, the gains which accrue to a country from specialisation brought about by reallocation of a given amount of resources.*

As pointed out above, the importance of and gain from international trade follows from the theory of comparative cost. Specialisation by different countries according to their production efficiency and factor endowments *ensures optimum use and allocation of resources* of the countries. Differences in production possibilities and costs of production of various products between different countries of the world are so great that tremendous gain in terms of additional output and income accrues to the world community from international specialisation and trade. For instance, the relative differences in cost of production of industrial products and food and raw materials between developed and developing countries are almost infinite in the sense that either type of these countries cannot produce what they buy from the other.

But the theory of comparative cost is static. It indicates only those gains which accrue to the trading countries as a result of the differences in *given costs* of production and *given production possibilities* of various products at *a given point of time*. As pointed out above, besides the static gains indicated by comparative cost theory, international trade bestows very important indirect gains and benefits, which are generally described as *dynamic gains*, upon the participating countries. These dynamic gains also promote economic growth in the participating countries. It is worth noting that both developed and developing countries have obtained benefits from trade. The international trade has contributed a good deal to the economic development of underdeveloped countries. To quote Professor Haberler again, "If we were to estimate the contribution of international trade to economic development especially of the underdeveloped countries solely by the static gains from trade in any given year on the usual assumption of *given production capabilities*, we would indeed grossly underrate the importance of trade. For over and above the direct static gains dwelt upon by the traditional theory of comparative cost, trade bestows very important indirect benefits upon the participating countries".[1]

Dennis Robertson described foreign trade as "*an engine of growth.*" With greater income and production made possible by specialisation and trade, *greater savings and investment become possible* and as a result higher rate of economic growth can be achieved. Through promotion of exports, a developing country *can earn valuable foreign exchange* which it can use for the imports of capital equipment and raw materials which are so essential for economic development. Therefore, Professor Haberler argues that since international trade raises the level of income, it also promotes economic development. He thus remarks : "What is good for the national income and the standard of living is, at least potentially, also good for economic development; for the greater the volume of output the greater can be the rate of growth—provided the people individually or collectively have the urge to save and to invest and economically to develop. The higher the level of output, the easier it is to escape the 'vicious circle of poverty' and to 'take off into self-sustained growth' to use the jargon of modern development theory. Hence, *if trade raises the level of income, it also promotes economic development.*"[2]

Explaining the dynamic or growth benefits, Sawyer and Sprinkle write, "A country engaging in international trade uses its resources more efficiently. Businesses in search of profits will naturally move resources such as labour and capital ... into industries with a comparative advantage. The resources employed in the industry with a comparative advantage can produce more output which leads to a higher real GDP. A higher real GDP tends to lead to more saving and therefore more investment. The additional investment in plant and equipment usually leads to a higher rate of economic growth .... In a roundabout way gains from international trade grow larger over time. What is happening is that economies that are more open grow faster than the closed economies, everything else equal."[3]

Another trade benefit which accrues to the countries (even small countries) is the **economies of scale** which occur in some industries which lower unit cost of production when these industries expand. Economies of scale or what are called increasing returns to scale imply that as an industry expands, its unit cost of production falls. Highlighting the significance of increasing returns to scale of trade, Sawyer and Sprinkle write, "there may be even greater benefits from trade for small countries.... For industries subject to increasing returns to scale, free trade may allow an industry in a small country an opportunity to expand its production and lower its unit cost. This reduction in cost makes the industry more efficient and allows it to compete in the world markets. Imagine the loss of opportunities for producers in small countries such as Belgium, the Netherlands and Denmark if they did not have free access to the European countries."[4]

Similarly, the Canadian economy benefited a lot from its trade with large US economy. The free access to Canadian firms in the US and Mexican markets under the North Atlantic Free Trade

1 G. Haberler, *International Trade and Economic Development*.

2 *Op. cit.*

3 W. Charles Sawyer and Richard L, Sprinkle, *International Economics,* Prentice Hall of India, 2003, New Delhi p. 44.

4 Sawyer and Sprinkle, *Ibid.*

Agreement (NAFTA) permitted Canadian firms to expand and lower unit costs making their industries more efficient leading to the increase in their output.

Another important gain from trade is the effect on competitive forces and prices of developing countries when they open up to the world economy. The opening up of the developing countries such as India is to enhance competition in the domestic market which ensures lower prices in the domestic market. For example, in India under economic reforms initiated since 1991, the Indian economy was opened up and in view of competition from imports to survive and expand the big Indian firms were forced to reduce their prices as their monopoly power ended by the entry of foreign products at cheap rates. Even Maruti Company which enjoyed a high degree of monopoly power in the Indian car industry had to improve its quality and fix prices of its models at reasonable levels. Thus opening up of the Indian economy led to the increase in quality of goods as well as lower prices. This caused increase in production of goods not only for the domestic economy but also for exporting them to other countries.

Further, through foreign trade, developing countries get material means of production such as capital equipment, machinery and raw materials which are so essential for economic growth of these countries. There has been rapid technological progress in the developed countries. This advanced and superior technology is incorporated or embodied in various types of capital goods. It is thus clear that developing countries derive tremendous gains from technological progress in the developed countries through the imports of capital goods such as machinery, transport equipment, vehicles, power generation equipment, road building machinery, medicines, chemicals. It is worth mentioning here that the pattern of import trade of the developing countries has changed in the last several years and now consists of greater quantity of various forms of capital goods and less of textiles.

Furthermore, even more important than the importation of capital goods is the transmission of technical know-how, skills, managerial talents., entrepreneurship through foreign trade. When the developing countries come to have trade relationship with the developed countries, they also often import technical know-how, with all their skills, managers, etc., from them. With this they are also able to develop their own technical know-how, managerial and entrepreneurial ability. The growth of technical know-how, skill and managerial ability is an important requisite for economic development of developing countries. Professor Haberler rightly says: "The late-comers and successors in the process of development and industrialization have always had the great advantage that they could learn from the experiences, from the successes as well as from the failures and mistakes of the pioneers and forerunners... Today the developing countries have a tremendous, constantly growing store of technical know-how to draw from. True, simple adoption of methods, developed for the conditions of the developed countries, is often not possible. The adaptation is surely much easier than the first creation... Trade is the most important vehicle for the transmission of technological know-how... Today there are a dozen industrial centres in Europe, the U.S., Canada, Japan and Russia which are ready to sell machinery as well as engineering advice and know-how."[5]

For further details of dynamic gains from trade, see next Chapter 37 regarding '*Trade as an Engine of Economic Growth*.

5 G. Haberler, *International Trade and Economic Development*.

CHAPTER 37

INTERNATIONAL TRADE AS AN 'ENGINE OF ECONOMIC GROWTH'

The classical and neoclassical economists believed that international trade played a vital role in accelerating economic growth of the countries. In fact they called international trade as an '*engine of economic growth*'. The contribution of trade to economic growth, according to them, is determined partly from static and partly from dynamic gains that flow from foreign trade. International trade permits all countries to specialise through reallocation of resources in the production of those goods in which they have comparative advantage and trading with each other will provide them the greater quantity of goods than they could obtain if they do not open up to foreign trade. Specialization and trading will enable them to consume more goods than they could produce. Commenting on the significance of international trade in increasing welfare of the people Meier writes, "More generally, classical economists considered comparative advantage as determining the pattern of trade. Not the use of surplus resources but *resource reallocation* allowed trade to benefit a country by producing a more efficient international allocation of resources. Without any increase in resources or technological change, *every trading country is able to enjoy a higher real income* by increasing production according to its comparative advantage and trading. The exports have instrumental significance as the intermediate goods used for the "indirect production" of imports; *exports allow the country to "buy" imports* on more favourable terms than if produced directly at home. The gain from trade is on the import side; and it is significant that the gains are mutually realised by all the trading countries"[1]

Gains from Trade and Terms of Trade

Of course, the gains from trade to the countries specialising in production of different goods and trading with each other depend on ***terms of trade***, that is, rate of exchange of goods between any two countries trading with each other. To quote Walter Elkan, "The size of these static gains will depend on the rate of exchange which is such as to produce gains so that in the extreme one could conceive of a situation in which even though a country had a comparative advantage in the production of a good, trade would not take place because the rate of exchange nullified any gains that might have been derived from it."[2]

Thus static gains from trade can accrue to a trading country if its terms of trade are favourable. It is worth noting that *role of trade depending on comparative advantage assumes* that the country has a given amount of resources and that *they are fully employed*. It is through reallocation of resources from goods in the production of which they are relatively inefficient to the production of goods in which they have greater efficiency. This implies that through reallocation of resources *they move from one point to another on a given production possibility frontier*.

1 Gerald M. Meier, "Trade as an 'Engine of Growth'–Note" in *Leading Issues in Economic Development* (New York : Oxford University Press, 1984) 4th edition, pp. 489-90.

2 Walter Elkan, *An Introduction to Development Economics* (Penguin Modern Economic Texts, 1973) p. 40.

Further, Classical economists, especially Adam Smith, emphasised the role of trade in utilising fully the country's resources, *if they are initially lying idle and unemployed.* When such a country enters into foreign trade, it opens up the possibility of a 'vent for surplus', that is, using the surplus resources for producing for exports which it can exchange for imports which it cannot produce at home for which it has an unsatisfied demand. This 'vent for surplus' implies that a country would be moving from a point *within* the given production possibility frontier to a point on it. This too is a 'static gain'. We explain this below in detail.

Trade as Vent for Surplus and Economic Growth

According to Hla Myint, it is export expansion of the type of "vent for surplus" that occurred in south East Asia and African countries rather than resource reallocation of given resources towards production for primary exports on the basis of comparative advantage. To quote him, "The export expansion of peasant products, particularly South East Asia and from Uganda and West Africa, took place not so much through the reallocation of given and fully employed resources from the domestic to the export sector as through bringing hitherto underutilised land and labour in the subsistence economy into export production."[3] Thus 'vent for surplus' theory assumes more realistically that "a previously isolated country about to enter international trade possesses a surplus productive capacity. In this exports can be raised without reducing domestic production by utilising the surplus productive capacity."[4]

Hla Myint explained the growth of countries of South East Asia and Africa through *'primary exports as an engine of growth'* in the colonial period on the basis of 'vent for surplus'. However, in our view the gain from trade between the colonies and the coloniser countries went mostly to the latter. Further, as Hla Myint has pointed out that growth in underdeveloped colonies remained confined to the export sector and did not spread to the rest of their economies. It is worth quoting Gills, Perkins, Roemer and Snodgrass, "When underutilised land or labour was 'vented' as a result of colonisation, as was typical during the nineteenth century, the gains from trade were often purchased at high cost to indigenous population. Land which may have been idle or utilised at low productivity was frequently alienated from its occupiers, whether these were American Indians, the Kikuyu and other peoples of East Africa or Javanese farmers. Colonisers also used taxation and coercion to keep plantations and mines supplied with low-cost labour in many parts of Africa and Asia, and especially in British India, the movement along a production frontier toward greater production for export resulted in cheap imports to compete with traditional handicraft industries, displacing artisans and workers. The question about colonisation is whether the distribution of gains from trade favoured native populations enough to compensate them for the losses they bore, and whether colonial economies propelled indigenous people toward development or retarded their eventual progress."[5] Thus while evaluating gains from entering into foreign trade much depends on who gains and who loses.

According to Myint, the contribution of Western entrepreneurs to development of colonies was mainly in the development of transport and communication and development of new mineral resources. "In underdeveloped countries", he writes, "the surplus labour existed ..... because in the subsistence economies with poor transport and little specialisation, each self-sufficient economic unit could not find any market outlet to dispose of its potential surplus and therefore no incentive to produce more than its requirements. Here then we have a form of Smith's *unproductive labour* locked up in a semi-idle state in the underdeveloped economy of a country isolated from outside economic contacts. In most peasant economies this surplus labour was mobilised, however, not by the money wage system of employment but by peasant economic units with their employment of 'family' labour moving *en bloc* into the money economy and export production."[6]

---

3 Hla Myint, *Economic Theory and the Underdeveloped Economies,* Oxford University Press, 1971.

4 Higgins, *Economic Development* (Indian Edition, Central Book Depot, Allahabad), 1963, p. 148.

5 M. Gills, D. H. Perkins, M. Roemer and Donald R. Snodgrass. *Economics of Development* (New York : W. N. Norton & Co., 3rd edition, 1983), p. 414.

6 Hla Myint, "The Classical Theory of International Trade and Underdeveloped Countries", *The Economic Journal*, June, 1958.

TRADE AS AN ENGINE OF ECONOMIC GROWTH: DYNAMIC GAINS

Mention may be made here of dynamic gains which result from a greater degree of degree of division of labour and specialisation when a country is opened to world trade resulting in rise in productivity of their resources and permits a country to reap the benefits of economies of scale. They are dynamic in the sense that unlike static gains which accrue to a nation as a result of reallocation of resources to the production of goods in which a country has a comparative advantage, dynamic gains cause an outward shift in the production possibility frontier. Explaining these dynamic effects which he calls indirect effect. J. S. Mill, a classical economist, writes, "The tendency of every extension of the market improves the process of production. A country which produces for a larger market than its own can introduce a more extended division of labour and make greater use of machinery and is *more likely to make innovations and improvements in the processes of production.*"[7]

Besides, classical economists thought that increase in exports and consequent rise in incomes of the people engaged in the export sector *will generate demand for the products of other sectors giving boost to them*. Thus the gains from export will spread to other sectors of the economy through what Keynes later called multiplier effect and lead to what has been called ***export-led growth***. Furthermore, for growth of underdeveloped countries J. S. Mill. emphasised the **'educative effect'** of trade. Thus J. S. Mill writes, "The opening of foreign trade by making them acquainted with new objects .... by instilling new ideas and breaking the chain of habits .... and tends to create in them new wants, increased ambition and greater thought for the future."[8]

To sum up, according to Meier, the gains from trade on development from the viewpoint of underdeveloped countries are mainly of three types : (1) those that widen the market, induce innovations and raise productivity; (2) those that promote saving and capital formation; and (3) those that have an eductive effect in instilling new wants and tastes and in transferring technology, skills and entrepreneurship. The emphasis is on the supply side of the development process."[9]

Trade as an Engine of Economic Growth: Historical Experience

We have explained above the view of traditional theory about the role international trade can play in development of advanced developed countries and poor underdeveloped countries. We will now spell out that historical experience shows that the traditional theory has been mainly proved correct *except its conclusion about the gains the poor underdeveloped countries would derive from international trade by specialising in exports of primary goods*.

In the eighteenth century Britain had the industrial revolution through technological breakthrough. Joseph E. Stiglitz and Charlton write: "There were many social, political and geographical factors that caused the Industrial Revolution, but Britain's trade with her neighbours and colonies played a decisive role in fuelling the new industrial activity and spreading prosperity in other countries. Before long British cities became the workshops of the world importing vast quantities of food and raw materials and exporting manufactured goods to America, Asia and Africa."[10] Thus international trade proved to be engine of economic growth for Britain.

Similarly, Japan under the Meiji rulers in the early twentieth century achieved rapid industrial growth in which, among other things, trading with other countries made an important contribution to its rapid growth. To quote Stiglitz and Charlton again, "It is hard to imagine the Meiji industrialisation

7 John Stuart Mill, *Principles of Political Economy*, London, 1948.

8 J. S. Mill, quoted by Meier, in *Leading Issues in Economic Development* (Oxford University Press, Fourth Edition, 1983), p. 490.

9 See Gerald M. Meier, *op. cit*, 4th edition, 1983, p. 450.

10 Joseph E. Stiglitz and Andrew Charlton, *Fair Trade for All* (New York: Oxford University Press, 2005). p. 11.

occurring if Japan had not been able to import vast quantities of machinery, transport equipment, and other capital goods from the West in exchange for exports of cheap cloth, toys and other labour-intensive consumer products. And this trade would have been impossible if it were not for the steady flow of food and cheap raw materials arriving in Japan from its colonies in Taiwan and Korea".[11]

Similarly, international trade played a crucial role in the industrial development in North America and Austria. English capital opened up mines and plantations and built railroads in America, Canada and Australia. This led to the development of these countries and as these countries opened up they provided expanding markets for the products of Europe which led to the rapid growth in European countries.

Like classical economists, Marx thought that international trade prevented the occurrence of diminishing returns in Europe. However, Marx emphasised exploitation of the colonies by the colonial powers. He thought governments of England and France worked in the interests of the capitalists of their countries. In trade relations terms of trade were determined to the disadvantage of the underdeveloped colonies. Marx maintained that the form of trade that took place between the industrialised developed countries and underdeveloped countries made it possible for the advanced countries to retain profits from trade.

However, the classical and neoclassical theories of free trade were proved correct as rubber plantations of Malaya developed, coffee plantations of Brazil registered rapid growth, Australia's sheep flock and Argentina's cattle herd grew, Indonesian oil reserves were developed by Dutch, Artesian wells were sunk in Sahara by the French. English capital developed mines and plantations, and built railroads in India and its other colonies and their products were taken away to feed their manufactured industries. Besides, India, Brazil and Burma provided expanding markets to the British products. Although trade with Britain contributed to the development of mines, plantations, railroads and to some extent agriculture, *its benefits were however derived more by Great Britain due to the unfavourable terms of trade for the underdeveloped colonies*. Besides, the imports of cheap manufactured products from Britain did not permit the industrialisation of the underdeveloped colonies. In fact, there was a decline of handicraft industries as a result of cheap imports from Britain.

Though in the nineteenth century the free trade and capital movements contributed a good deal to the industrial growth of the nations of Western Europe and, during this period, the countries of Western Europe, North America and Australia became rich, the *underdeveloped countries remained poor despite some growth in the primary sector*. As has been pointed out by Myint,[12] the *growth of the export sector in underdeveloped countries could not transmit growth to the rest of their economies*. Importantly, stagnation of the underdeveloped countries from 1913 to 1939 occurred because of strangled international trade due to various restrictions that were imposed by the developed countries and worldwide depression and World Wars.

Many economic historians believe that "*in the 19th century international trade acted as an engine of growth not only in that it contributed to a more efficient allocation of resources within countries but also because it transmitted growth from one part of the world to another*. The demand for Europe, and for Britain in particular, for new materials brought prosperity to such countries as Canada, Argentina, South Africa, Australia and New Zealand. As the demand for their commodities increased, investment in these countries also increased. Trade was therefore mutually profitable".[13] However, all economists would not agree to this view of trade under colonial rule. Marx's prediction about disastrous effects of colonialism on underdeveloped countries seems to be substantially correct as despite growth of primary exports, they remained in a state of backwardness and poverty.

---

11 Stiglitz and Charlton, *op. cit.*, p. 12.

12 See Hla Myint, *The Economics of Developing Countries* (London : Hutchunson & Co Publishers Ltd, 3rd edition, 1967)

13 A. P. Thirlwall, *op. cit.*, p. 632.

It is evident from above that *whereas for industrialised developed countries international trade proved to be an engine of growth, for underdeveloped countries under the colonial rule exports of primary products in exchange for industrial goods from developed countries did not lead to the overall growth of their countries. In fact they remained backward and poor.*

Trade after the Post-Second World War Period

The situation significantly changed after the post- Second World War period with the attainment of independence from the colonial rule by the underdeveloped countries. Now they were free to make their own choices. Having been suffered from the exports of primary products for the exchange of manufactured goods India and Latin American countries adopted *import-substitution policy* to accelerate their industrial growth. On the other hand, Korea and East Asian countries such as Taiwan, Malaysia, Indonesia, Hong Kong and Singapore adopted export-substitution policy and accordingly developed their industries and exported manufactured products instead of relying exclusively on exports of primary products. They also succeeded in achieving rapid industrial growth. The growth of East Asian countries during the period from mid-sixties to mid-nineties was so high that they were called *Asian Tigers*.

The success of *export-led growth strategy* in East Asia began with *Japan which within a few decades after World War II through its rapid growth became the second largest economy of the world.* It achieved sustained growth through export promotion of manufactured products. Japan's success was followed by South Korea successfully. Again East Asian countries such as Taiwan, Hong Kong, Singapore, Thailand, Indonesia and Malaysia which are generally called *Asian Tigers* achieved a higher economic growth through international trade by promoting their exports of industrial products. After 1991 India also gave importance to the expansion of exports in the economic reforms and structural adjustment policy initiated in 1991. India's export of software services also grew rapidly.

Since 1950 there has been liberalisation of world trade on a large scale, first under GATT established in 1947 and then under WTO which replaced GATT in 1995. Barriers to trade such as tariffs and non-tariff barriers and quantitative restrictions such as quota, licenses were brought down significantly to promote world trade. However, Doha Round talks to address to the problems of developing countries under the auspices of WTO have not succeeded so far to help in growth and poverty eradication in the developing countries. The developed countries of the US and EU which have been the strong advocates of free trade have adopted a selfish and duplicitous attitude towards trading with developing countries. Mentioning about this selfish attitude of the developed countries, Stiglitz and Charlton write, "They have negotiated the reduction of tariffs and elimination of subsidies for the goods in which they have a comparative advantage, but are more reluctant to open up their own markets and to eliminate their own subsidies in other areas where the developing countries have an advantage. As a result *we now have an international trade regime which, in many ways is disadvantageous to the developing countries*. In a world in which many see global poverty — by some estimates there are more than 2 billion living on less than a dollar a day — as the world's most pressing problem, this is especially disturbing. It seems obvious that if the developed countries truly wanted to promote developments in Doha Round they would have reduced their tariffs and subsidies on the goods of interest to the developing countries."[14]

14 Stiglitz and Charlton, *op. cit.*, pp. 12-13.

Appendix 37A
Trade as a Vent for Surplus

With regard to gains from trade, it is worth explaining 'Vent for surplus' theory of trade put forward by Adam Smith. According Adam Smith's vent for surplus theory an important gain from trade is the provision of outlet for surplus commodities which in the absence of foreign trade would remain outsold and thereby resources of a country will be wasted. When a country is shut off from world trade it might have substantial resources that might remain idle or unutilised for lack of demand for the goods which they can produce. In the absence of market for those goods which can be efficiently produced with the idle resources, these resources might be used in relatively unproductive or inefficient ways. Foreign trade enables the countries to put their idle resources to produce the goods for which there is demand in foreign countries. Adam Smith laid stress on the importance of foreign trade as a vent for surplus and as a means for widening the market for goods. Further, in exchange for the goods producted by the idle resources they can import goods from abroad for which there is demand in the country and satisfy the wants of its people and thus increase their welfare. To quote Adam Smith, "*Foreign trade carriers out the surplus part of the produce* of their land and labour for which there is no demand among them and brings back in return for it something else which may satisfy a part of their wants and increase their employment."[1]

Vent for Surplus Distinguished from Gains from Comparative Advantage

The gains from trade arising from 'vent for surplus' should be distinguished from gains arising from comparative advantage or cost. This can be explained with the help of production possibility curve shown in Fig. 37A.1 where the case of a land-abundant and capital-scarce developing country is represented. If in the absence of foreign trade all factors are fully utilised, the developing country will be at point, say at a point *A,* on its given production possibility curve *PP'* where it is tangent to the domestic price ratio line *JJ'*. In this case no resources will be lying unutilised. Now, foreign trade would occur if world terms of trade showing relative prices of the two goods in the world market are favourable for a country say as represented by terms of trade line *tt'*. As per comparative cost theory, the country will reallocate resources between the two goods and moves from point *E* to *A* on the given production possibility curve *PP'*, producing greater quantity of land-intensive good in which it has a comparative advantage. At point *A* on the production possibility curve land is being more intensively utilised in the sense that more of agricultural commodity (say wheat) is produced by shifting towards its production. However, its consumption point will be determined at point *H* on an indifference curve IC_2 where terms of trade line *tt'* is tangent to it. Thus, in accordance with comparative cost theory the developing country will gain from trade as it reaches at a higher indifference curve IC_2.

---

1 Adam Smith, *Wealth of Nations,* 1976.

However, *vent for surplus theory is different as it assumes* a country with idle or unutilised resources in the absence of foreign trade. This was the case of underdeveloped countries in the *eighteenth and nineteenth century* when in the absence of foreign trade these countries had idle or

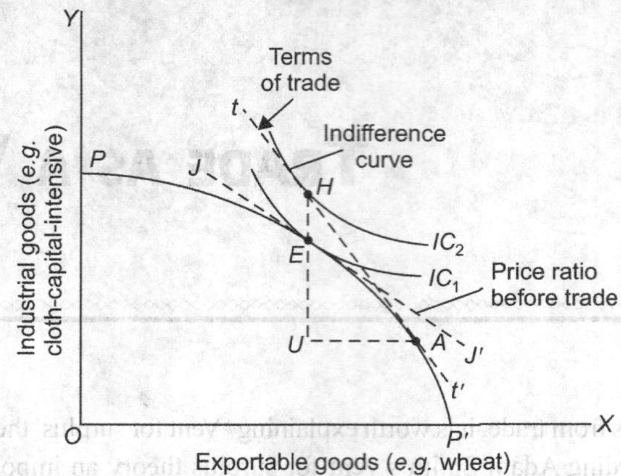

Fig. 37A.1. *Trade gain from vent for surplus*

unutilised resources. In this case without trade, the underdeveloped country's situation will lie within the production possibility curve such as point *U* in Fig. 37A.1. In this case the country will gain substantially from foreign trade as it will enable it to fully utilise its idle resources to produce more of both the products or produce one product without reducing the production of the other and move to a point on the production possibility curve where resources are fully utilised. If there is external demand for land-intensive products such as wheat, rice when the economy opens up to foreign trade by utilising its land resources fully, it can move to point *A* on the production possibility curve *PP'*. As seen in Fig. 37A.1, while it can expand its production to point *A*, given the world terms of trade by the line *tt'*, its consumption equilibrium will be at *H* on indifference curve IC_2 which represents a higher level of welfare.

Vent for Surplus and Economic Growth

Thus by providing outlet (*i.e.,* vent) for land-intensive products foreign trade leads to the expansion in output in this case. It is important to note that expansion in production from point *U* within the production possibility curve to point *A* on the production possibility curve would represent gain from trade if surplus export resources have no alternative uses and cannot be put to domestic uses. Explaining this A.P. Thirlwall writes, "If there is gain, this implies that the 'surplus' export resources have no alternative uses and cannot be switched to the domestic use. This may not be as unreasonable an assumption as it sounds, bearing in mind the country's resource endowments in relation to its population size and tastes of the community. Mines and fishing grounds, for example, have no alternative uses and the marginal utility of consuming their products would soon become zero if demand was confined to domestic consumption alone."[2]

Such gains arising from utilising idle resources for production of goods to meet foreign demand were obtained by several countries in the nineteenth century. For example, in the 19th century the U.S. and Canada had abundant land in relation to their endowment of labour and capital. Since much of land in these countries was lying unutilised, both countries produced at points *within* their production possibility curve such as point *U* in Fig. 37A.1. As a result of foreign trade, Britain which had a demand for wheat and cotton, the U.S. and Canada utilised their idle land for production of wheat and cotton and exported them to Britain and imported from it manufactured goods which they could not produce as efficiently as Britain. Thus, vent or outlet furnished by foreign trade with Britain increased the welfare of the people of the U.S. and Canada.

2 A.P. Thirlwall, *Growth and Development, with Special Reference to Developing Countries* (New York, Palgrave Macmillan, 2003) 7th edition, p, 631.

The above trade theory of vent for surplus also applies to the underdeveloped countries where much of land and mining were lying idle. Consequent to trade with the developed countries such as Britain, France and other industrialised countries, they by utilising the idle land and mineral resources exported wheat, rice and several minerals to them and imported from them manufactured goods such as cloth. Thus they also derived gain from trade with the developed countries. Applying Adam Smith's theory of vent for surplus Hla Myint[3] explains that when parts of Asia and Africa came under colonial rule, the foreign trade with European countries enabled these underdeveloped Asian and African countries to utilise their abundant resources and expanded their production of cocoa, palm oil for export and imported industrial products. This led to the development of underdeveloped countries and they gained from trade.

However, the gain from trade by underdeveloped countries of Asia and Africa as a result of colonisation, particularly in the nineteenth century, ultimately came at a heavy cost to the underdeveloped countries. Thus, Gills, Perkins, Roamer and Snodgrass in their joint work write, "When underutilised land or labour was 'vented' as a result of colonisation as was typical during the nineteenth century, the gains from trade were often purchased at high cost to the indegenous population. Land which may have been idle or utilised at low productivity was frequently alienated from its occupiers, whether these were American Indians, Kikuyu and other peoples of East Africa or Javanese farmers. Colonizers also used taxation and coercion to keep plantation and mines supplied with low cost labour in many parts of Africa and Asia. And especially in British India, the movement along a production frontier toward greater production for export often resulted in cheap imports to compete with traditional handicraft industries, displacing artisans and workers. The question about colonisation is whether the distribution of gains from trade favoured native populations enough to compensate them for the losses they bore and whether colonial economies propelled indigenous people toward development or retarded their eventual progress."[4] Thus, when evaluation of static and dynamic gain from foreign trade is made the crucial question to be answered is 'who gains and who loses'? As explained above, according to 'vent for surplus' theory when as a result of trade a country moves from inside the production possibility curve to a point on the production possibility curve by utilising its idle resources it shows a gain from trade or increase in welfare of the people provided the surplus resources to be used for exports have no alternative uses and cannot be put to any alternative domestic use.

According to Thirlwall,[5] 'vent for surplus' therefore provides a better explanation for expansion in exports of many underdeveloped countries in the nineteenth century. He gives four reasons for this. First, if there had been no unutilised resources, the process of expansion of production could not have been continued for a long time in the nineteenth century. Second, while comparative cost theory cannot explain the trade between two countries when both have similar resource endowment, one develops a major export sector while the other does not. 'Vent for surplus' theory explains that the countries which have unutilised resources in relation to their population (and therefore size of domestic demand) can utilise its idle resources for expansion of production of goods for export to those which have demand for them. Third, as A.P. Thirlwall writes, 'Vent for surplus' is a much more plausible explanation for *the start of trade*. It is difficult to believe that small-scale peasant farmers with

3 Hla Myint, "Classical Theory of International, Trade and Underdeveloped Countries," *Economic Journal* (1959), pp. 317-37.

4 M. Gills, D.H. Perkins, M. Roamer and Donald R. Snodgrass, *Economics of Development* (New York, W.N. Norton & Company, 1983), p. 414.

5 A.P Thirlwall, *Growth and Development, with Special Reference to Developing Countries* (New York: Palgrave Macmillan, 2003).

no surplus would eventually and instinctively start specialising according to the law of comparative advantage in anticipation of reaching a higher consumption possibility curve."[6]

Fourth, foreign trade permits to import of capital goods that are more productive than the domestic resources and as a result import of more efficient capital goods, leads to the lower overall capital-output ratio. This has a beneficial effect on the underdeveloped economy as it will relieve domestic supply bottlenecks and lead to the expansion in output and therefore higher growth rate.

In the end it may be noted that in the nineteenth century, under the colonial rule in the underdeveloped countries of Asia and Africa, there was expansion in output of agricultural goods (such as foodstuffs and industrial raw materials), products of mines and of plantations in which the colonial supers were interested. However, as has been pointed out by Hla Myint[7] *expansion in exports confined to these products and it did not transmit growth to the other sectors of the economy*. On the other hand, exports of primary product led to the imports of manufactured goods from the industrialised developed countries which resulted in the decline in handicraft industries. This caused increase in unemployment in underdeveloped countries. Besides, as pointed out above, gains from trade by underdeveloped countries depends much on the *terms of trade* with the industrialised developed countries.

6 A.P. Thirlwall, *op. cit.* p. 631.
7 Hla Myint, *The Economies of Developing Countries.*

CHAPTER 38

Myrdal, Prebisch-Singer Thesis vs Free Trade

The theory that free trade between the developed and developing countries will promote growth of the developing countries was challenged by three noted economists, Gunnar Myrdal, Raul Prebisch and Hans Singer. According to the comparative cost theory, if various countries specialise in the production of goods in accordance with their comparative costs of production free trade between the developed countries specialising in the production of manufactured goods and the underdeveloped countries specialising in production of primary goods will benefit both of them. Besides, Heckscher-Ohlin theory shows that with specialisation by countries in accordance with their factor endowments (which determine the comparative costs of production of different goods) will tend to equalise the factor prices (*e.g.* wages of labour and rate of interest on capital) between developed and developing countries. Gunnar Myrdal challenged this and argued that far from tending to become equal free international trade between developing countries specialising in the production of manufactured goods and underdeveloped countries specialising in the production of primary goods would start a cumulative process which will tend to move the factor prices away from equality. He showed that free trade between developed and developing countries would have a backwash effect on the growth of developing countries which would perpetuate their underdevelopment.

Similarly, Raul Prebisch and Hans Singer argued that free trade between developed countries specialising in the production of manufactured goods and developing countries specialising in the production of primary goods would lead to the *deterioration of terms of trade* for the developing countries. As a result, the industrialised countries will not benefit from free trade. Thus, Myrdal, Prebisch and Singer urged upon the developing countries to *industrialise* their countries if they want to have rapid economic growth to raise the living standards of their people.

MYRDAL'S THESIS OF INTERNATIONAL TRADE: BACKWASH EFFECT

Myrdal put forward the contrary thesis about the effects of free trade on the underdeveloped countries. On the basis of traditional trade theory based on comparative cost and factor endowments the effects of trade between developed and developing countries will be to make marginal productivity of factors (labour and capital) and therefore factor prices (wages and return on capital) to become equal. Thus, according to traditional theory trade transmits growth to developing countries. Myrdal challenged this proposition and points out that factors are completely different from the predictions of traditional theory. Myrdal has argued that actually far from causing movement towards equality, *free international trade sets up a cumulative process away from equilibrium in factor prices*. This cumulative causation causes a growing disparity between the developed and developing countries. To quote Myrdal, "In the normal case there is no such tendency towards automatic self-stabilisation in the social system. The system is not by itself moving towards any sort of balance between forces that are constantly on the move away from such a situation. In the normal case a change does not call forth countervailing changes but instead supporting changes which move the system in the same direction (that is, towards the benefits of the developed countries having initial advantages) as the first change and much further. Because of such circular causation a social disequilibrium tends to become cumulative and often gathers speed at accelerating rate."[1]

Myrdal contends that the actual facts regarding the effects of trade are quite different from the predictions of comparative cost theory and as a matter of fact disparities between developed and developing countries have widened instead of levelling out international disparities of income as a result of trade. Myrdal explains this phenomenon by two types of effect of trade between developed and developing countries – *backwash effect and spread effect*. Myrdal gives several examples of backwash effect. *Backwash effect is the unfavourable effect of foreign trade on the developing countries*. Myrdal shows that with the opening of trade between the developed and developing countries, the traditional comparative cost theory and Heckscher-Ohlin's factor endowments theory shows that under certain restrictive conditions free international trade of goods and services is perfect substitute for complete mobility of factors and therefore tends to equalise not only the prices of goods but also the prices of factors such as wages of labour, interest on capital between developed and developing countries. This is in accordance with *Samuelson's factor equalisation theorem* which states that under some restrictive assumptions wages and profits in the countries that trade with each other tend to be equal.[2]

According to Myrdal, in actual practice, the equalisation of factor prices does not happen. This is because, according to him, international trade leads to the *cumulative causation process* which tends to counteract the tendency towards equalisation in factor prices. This is because opening of trade between developed and developing countries also causes migration of *human capital*, that is, educated and highly skilled manpower, and entrepreneurs to the developed countries. As a result, demand for labour in poor developing countries decreases which prevents wages to rise despite migration of labour to the developed countries. On the other hand, in the developed countries immigration of human capital and entrepreneurs will cause increase in demand for labour and for goods and services leading to higher wages and higher growth of output in these developed countries. Besides, because of these changes in demand initial wage discrepancy is likely to persist if not widen. Thus, according to Myrdal, once development differences appear, there is set in motion a chain of cumulative expansion in favoured regions and this has unfavourable effect which is called *backwash effect* by Myrdal on the other regions causing differences in general to persist or even diverge"[3]

Furthermore, capital movements and terms of trade also play a part in cumulative causation to prevent the developing countries to grow and cause persistence of their underdevelopment. In a free market economy, capital, like labour, moves to the regions and countries where rate of return on capital is higher. Now, according to Myrdal, it is the developed countries where return on capital is higher because of buoyant demand for goods and services as they have initial advantage, capital flows into them. In fact, capital, labour and entrepreneurs migrate together to the developed regions or countries having initial advantages. If production is subject to increasing returns the regions or countries where rapid growth of factor supplies (*i.e.,* supplies of labour and capital) take place will gain greater comparative advantage over the relatively lagging underdeveloped nations containing handicrafts and small-scale industries. This will cause increase in real incomes of countries experiencing rapid growth at the expense of the poor underdeveloped countries. With this the free trade between developed and underdeveloped countries will tend to favour the former causing greater disparities of income between them. This is what Myrdal called backwash effect. Thus because of backwash

1 Gunnar Myrdal, *Economic Theory and Underdevelopment Regions* (London, Packworth, 1957), pp 28-29.

2 P.A. Samuelson, "International Trade and Equalisation of Factor Prices," *Economic Journal*, June 1948, pp. 163-184.

3 A.P. Thirlwall, *Growth and Development* (Palgrave Macmillan, 2003, 7th edition, p. 26.

effect free trade far from transmitting growth to the poor underdeveloped countries is responsible for their underdevelopment and poverty. Thus, free trade favours the developed countries and works to the disadvantage of the poor underdeveloped countries.

In addition to the backwash effect, Myrdal also mentions *spread effects* of trade between developed and developing countries. These spread effects or what is called *trickle down effects* consist mainly of increased demand for underdeveloped countries' products and *diffusion of knowledge and technology* of developed countries in the underdeveloped ones. However, *in Myrdal's view these spread effects are weaker than the backwash effect.* As a result, the developing countries do not receive much benefits from trade with developed nations and therefore there is persistance of underdevelopment and poverty in them. Thus, through the means of labour migration and capital movements, income inequalities between developed and underdeveloped countries have widened as a result of free trade between them.

Further, like Prebisch and Singer, Myrdal thinks that through trade with developed countries, the underdeveloped countries have been forced into producing mainly primary products which have low price and income elasticities of demand. This causes *worsening of terms of trade* for the underdeveloped countries and worked against economies from deriving benefits from trade in their growth process. Besides, free trade between them gave rise to the problems of balance of payments and foreign exchange for the underdeveloped countries. Further, *reduction in efficiency wage* (that is, money wage of labour relative to its productivity) in the rapidly growing developed countries has provided a competitive advantage to the developed countries, especially in the production of manufactured products. This further discourages industrial growth in the developing countries whose products cannot compete with those of the developed countries.

To sumup, according to Myrdal's thesis, because of backwash effect of free trade with developed countries on the growth of underdeveloped countries, the latter remain poor and backward.

A Critical Evaluation

Myrdal's hypothesis that free international trade would not benefit the underdeveloped countries was supported on the basis of empirical grounds by Raul Prebisch[4] and H. Singer who argued that in the long run, the terms of trade have a tendency to move against the primary producers and since most underdeveloped countries are primary producers, it is in their long-term interest to industrialise and use tariffs to protect their industries.

However, given free mobility of factors and free trade Myrdal's hypothesis appears to be valid in the context of interregional differences in economic development and incomes *within* a country but it does not adequately explain the *international differences in income.* Contrary to Myrdal's thesis, East Asian countries which were underdeveloped and poor by international standards a few decades before and adopted export-orientation model of growth registered high rates of growth that resulted in rapid rise in their per capita income which narrowed down their differences in per capita incomes with the developed countries.

Further, recently both China and India have opened up their economies to foreign trade and foreign investment by completely removing quantitative restrictions and drastically reducing tariffs. Both have benefited from foreign trade and investment. Growth in their exports of goods and service has contributed to their economic growth. In post-reform period when we have abandoned import substitution policy in favour of export-promotion policy, rate of India's economic growth rose to 6 per cent between 1992 and 2003 and 8 per cent from 2004 to 2011 whereas growth of the developed countries such as the US, UK and France had been only 2 to 3 per cent. This has worked to narrow down the difference between India and the developed countries such as US and UK. This shows that

4 Prebisch, R., *The Economic Development of Latin America and its Principal Problems*, U.N, 1950, pp. 45-46.

Myrdal's thesis that free trade between developed and developing countries would have unfavourable effect on the underdeveloped countries is not valid. In fact China and India are *two main drivers of economic growth of the world* economy. Though India may sometimes experience problems of balance of payments but its growth records in the last two decades (1992-2012) is far better than those of the developed countries. This is quite contrary to Myrdal's hypothesis. However, it may be noted that both India and China after 1980 have diversified their exports and do not rely on the exports of primary goods but are exporting many manufactured products.

PREBISCH-SINGER DOCTRINE

An important thesis was propounded by Raul Prebisch who pointed out the *deterioration of average terms of trade* of primary products produced and exported by underdeveloped Latin American countries and the industrial products produced and exported by the developed countries between 1876 and 1938 at the rate of 0.9 per cent per annum. He therefore emphasized that deterioration of terms of trade for Latin American countries. Likewise Hans Singer in 1949 suggested deteriorating terms of trade of primary goods producing underdeveloped countries at the rate of 0.64 per cent per annum during the same period (*i.e.* 1876 to 1938). Therefore, the long-term tendency of deteriorating terms of trade of countries producing primary products and raw materials has been called *Prebisch-Singer thesis*. This thesis prompted various underdeveloped countries to go in for industrialisation of their economies instead of concentrating on producing primary goods and industrial raw materials to sell them to the developed industrialised countries. India also in Second Five Year Plan adopted for import-substituting industrialisation. Before Prebisch and Singer[5] analysis of deteriorating terms of trade between industrialised and primary producing underdeveloped countries, the underdeveloped countries of Latin America and Asia were advised to specialise in the production of food products and industrial raw materials and export them to the developed countries in exchange for imports of industrial products from them. Thus, Prebisch writes: "Under this Nineteenth Century scheme Latin America as a part of periphery of the world economic system its specific task was to produce food and raw materials for the industrialised countries and this scheme did not consider industrialisation of newer countries."[6]

Prebisch emphasized that according to the accepted doctrine it was to the advantage of under-developed countries of Latin America and Asia to specialise in the production of primary products such as food and raw materials and to share in the benefit of technological progress throught international exchange with the industrial countries. Further, *according to this* viewpoint, due to their lesser efficiency in the production of industrial goods underdeveloped countries will be losing their advantage of international specialisation and exchange. Prebisch challenged this viewpoint that it was not in the interest of underdeveloped countries to industrialise themselves. He argued that "*industrialisation of Latin America was not incompatible with the efficient development of primary products.*"[7]

Using the UN data Prebisch pointed out that price of manufactured products produced by the industrialised countries rose relative to the primary products of underdeveloped countries (*i.e.*, countries of periphery). From this empirical evidence he concluded that there was a long-term tendency for the decline in terms of trade of underdeveloped countries producing only primary products and exporting then a good part of them. Thus, according to him, the decline in terms of trade for the peripheral (*i.e.* underdeveloped) countries while industrial countries which Prebisch called 'centre countries' get the whole benefits of the technological progress in their industries with not much benefits of technological progress accruing to the underdeveloped countries. To put in a nutshell,

5 Prebisch writing for UN Economic Commission for Asia and the Far East in its report "*The Economic Development of Latin America and Some of its Problems*" (New York, 1949) pp. 1-3.

6 Prebisch, *op.cit*.

7 Prebisch in "Report of UN Economic Commission for Asia and the Far East," *op cit*. pp. 8-9.

Prebisch argued that there was a tendency for secular decline in terms of trade for underdeveloped countries producing and exporting primary products. Therefore, it is in their long-term interest to industrialise and use tariffs to protect them from foreign competition.[8]

For the deterioration of terms of trade of primary producing underdeveloped countries the main reason given by Prebisch was that the advantages of technological progress accrue mainly to industrialised developed countries such as UK which he called 'centre countries'. When these is improvement in technology in the manufacturing industries, the periphery countries expected to gain from it on account of fall in the prices of their imports. But, according to Prebisch, this does not happen in actual practice because manufacturing industries operated under imperfectly competitive conditions which enabled producers of the developed countries to prevent price from falling and thus they succeeded in increasing their profits as a result of technological progress which increases productivity and lowers cost per unit of output. In the industrialised developed countries labour market is dominated by trade unions which also succeed in getting a share from rise in production as a result of technological progress by getting their wages raised. Elaborating Prebisch's view Walter Elkan writes, "The proceeds of improved methods of production are alleged to accrue in part to capitalists in the form of higher profits and in part to the trade unions in the form of higher wages. The consumer has no share in it, and since the only way that the primary producing countries could benefit is through lower prices of their imports, their gain is zero."[9]

On the other hand, when technical progress in production occurs in primary producing underdeveloped countries, the industrial countries are able to gain from it. This is because primary producers work in conditions of competitive markets, both domestically and externally. Therefore, when due to technical progress in production of primary products their prices fall, its benefits accrue to the consumers of the industrialised countries who import the food and raw materials from the primary producing underdeveloped countries.

Prebisch gives further reason for deterioration of terms of trade of primary producing underdeveloped countries. He points out that in the US, the income elasticity of demand for primary products is 0.66, that is, 1 per cent increase in GDP of the US is associated with only 0.66 per cent increase in demand for primary products while in Latin America income elasticity of demand for manufactured goods is 1.58 (that is, 1 per cent increase in GDP of Latin America is associated with 1.58 per cent increase in demand for manufacture). This is due to the operation of **Engel's Law of Consumption** according to which as income rises the proportion of it spent on food falls while that on manufactures increases. Since the industrialised countries such as the US imports food from Latin America while Latin America imports manufactures and exports food, the terms of trade decline for Latin American countries. Besides, for other primary products such as industrial raw materials exported by periphery countries increase in demand has been restrained by the development, of synthetic substitutes such as nylon for natural silk, plastic for natural rubber and synthetic material for jute and hemp have been developed which have worked to lower demand by 'centre' countries for natural raw materials. This has also led to the decline in terms of trade for primary producing underdeveloped countries.

Singer's View of Terms of Trade

Hans Singer, who was in UN Department of Economic Affairs in the early 1950s, expressed similar views regarding deterioration of terms of trade for the underdeveloped countries as Raul Prebisch. However, unlike Prebisch, Singer considers foreign trade as a crucial factor for development

8 See R Prebisch, *The Economic Development of Latin America and some of its Principal Problems*, UN, 1950, pp. 46-47.

9 Walter Elkan, *An Introduction to Development Economics*, Penguin Books, 1973, p. 46.

of underdeveloped countries.[10] According to him, underdeveloped countries derive considerable benefits from foreign trade and therefore foreign trade significantly contributes to their national income. Underdeveloped countries have a small surplus of income over their subsistence needs and this surplus is the main source of capital formation. It is this export surplus, however small it may be, is used to buy raw materials and capital goods which they require for their industrialisation.

But he emphasises that production facilities set up in underdeveloped countries for exports in many cases were largely the result of foreign investment in plantations such as tea plantations of Ceylon, the oil wells of Iran, copper mines of Chile. Though these investment facilities were located in underdeveloped countries, the major benefits from them accrue to the developed countries from which foreign investment came from. To quote him, "In many cases the productive facilities for export from underdeveloped countries which were so largely a result of foreign investment never became part of internal economic structure of those underdeveloped countries themselves except in the purely geographical and physical sense. Economically speaking, they were really an outpost of the economies of the more developed investing countries. The main secondary multiplier effects .... from investment took place not where the investment was physically or geographically located but they took place from where investment came from. I would rather suggest that if the proper economic test of investment is the multiplier effect in the form of cumulative additions to income, employment, capital, technical knowledge and growth of external economies, then a good deal of investment in underdeveloped countries which we used to consider as "foreign" should in fact be considered as domestic investment on the part of the industrialised countries".[11]

From above it is evident that, according to Singer, foreign investment that occurred in underdeveloped countries prior to 1950 in fact largely benefited the developed industrialised countries and might have been harmful to the underdeveloped countries. Thus, foreign investment in the tea plantations of Ceylon and oil wells of Iran, the copper mines of Chile and the cocoa industry of Gold Coast were developed by foreign investors whose products were used as raw materials for the processing industries of the developed world. The underdeveloped countries had become specialised in plantations and agriculture whose products, food and raw materials were exported to provide the means of producing manufactured products in industrialised developed countries.[12]

Singer emphasised the industrialisation of underdeveloped countries because it not only causes expansion in immediate industrial products and creates externalities for the development of other industries but also leads to the increase in general development of education, skill, way of life, inventiveness, habits, store of technology, creation of new demand. All these ensure rapid economic development. It is precisely for these reasons, according to Singer, "why manufacturing industries are so universally desired by the underdeveloped countries, namely, that they *provide growing points* for increased technical knowledge, urban education, dynamism and resilience that goes with urban civilisation as well as the direct Marshallian external economies".[13]

Deterioration of Terms of Trade

In addition to the adverse effects of foreign investment on underdeveloped countries, Singer, like Prebisch, also points out the deterioration of terms of trade of underdeveloped countries. Relying on the same data as Prebisch, he points out that benefits of technical progress in industrialised countries accrue to their producers in the form of higher incomes whereas the gain of technical progress that occur in primary production in underdeveloped countries are enjoyed by the consumers of industrialised developed countries in the form of lower prices of food and industrial raw materials produced in the

10 Hans Singer, "The Distribution of Gains between Investing and Borrowing Countries," *American Economic Review*, Papers and Proceedings, May 1950.

11 Hans Singer, *op. cit.*, 1950 p. 473.

12 Singer, *op. cit.*, p. 474.

13 Singer, *op. cit*,, p. 476.

underdeveloped countries. To quote him, "The developed countries had the best of both the worlds, both as consumers of primary commodities and as producers of manufactured articles whereas the underdeveloped countries had the worst of both the worlds as consumers of manufactures and producers of raw materials".[14]

Singer further says that economic fluctuations in developed countries also impede economic growth of underdeveloped countries by delaying the required structural changes in them. These structural changes require capital goods for industrialisation but perverse terms of trade do not enable them to buy needed capital goods to buy them for industrialising their economies. It is worth quoting Singer on this issue. He writes, "The purpose of foreign investment and foreign trade ought perhaps be redefined as producing gradual changes in the structure of comparative advantage and of comparative endowment of the different countries rather than to develop a world trading system based on existing comparative advantage and existing distribution of environment. This perhaps is the real significance of the present movement towards giving technical assistance to underdeveloped countries not necessarily linked with actual trade or investment. *The emphasis on technical assistance may be interpreted as a recognition that the present structure of comparative advantage and endowment is not such that it should be considered as a permanent basis for a future international division of labour.*"[15]

A Critical Evaluation of Prebisch-Singer Doctrine

Prebisch Singer thesis has been challenged on various empirical and theoretical growth. First, the data of terms of trade between Great Britain and underdeveloped countries during the period 1870-1938 on the basis of which it was concluded that terms of trade improved for Great Britain and deteriorated for underdeveloped countries is not correctly interpreted. It has been pointed out that Britain's trade data as traditionally measured exports are valued at f.o.b. and imports at c.i.f.[16] It has been pointed out that during the period in question ocean freight rates declined sharply so that improvement in terms of trade of Great Britain during the period was partly the result of fall in ocean rates rather than the lower prices paid to the exporters of underdeveloped countries. This was however a controversial issue and was not finally resolved.

Secondly, it has been said that 69 per cent imports of Great Britain came from the other developed countries of Europe, North America, Australia and New Zealand and not from underdeveloped countries. Therefore, it was pointed out that improvements in terms of trade of Great Britain had been at the expense of underdeveloped countries.

Thirdly, it has been said that deterioration of '*net barter terms of trade*', that is, ratio of prices of exports to prices of imports (*Px/Py*) does not necessarily make a country worse off if it takes place as a result of technical progress causing improvement in productivity. In this regard Prof. Walter Elkan writes, "If evidence is required we have only to remember that fall of wheat prices in the course of *opening up of highly productive virgin land* which enabled American farmers to conquer the markets of Europe and to prosper in consequence. Similarly, Gold Coast cocoa farmers were able to create for themselves much higher incomes by entering the world markets at *a lower* cost than their competitors ..... *The mistake is to confuse the static terms of trade with the dynamic gains from trade*".[17]

Further, it has been pointed out that there has been a *basic problem in comparing prices over a period of time* to estimate 'net barter terms' because the goods sold at these prices undergo changes over a long period of time. While there has been no significant changes in primary products of 1880s from those traded sixty years later, the manufactured goods had significantly changed over the period.

14 H. Singer, *op. cit.*, p. 479.

15 *Ibid*, p. 484. (Italics added).

16 f.o.b. stands for '*free on board*' in which expenses on *carriage and insurance* are not included in the valuation while c.i.f. stands for *cost, insurance and freight* which means expenses on freight and insurance are included in valuation of imports.

17 Walter Elkan, *op. cit.*, p. 48.

Thus, it has been pointed out that the model of Ford car of 1900 was quite different from the model sold 40 years later. Similarly, machines produced and traded in 1938 were much more efficient and technically superior from those produced, say, in 1980s. Besides, the entire composition of exports had changed a good deal, and new products such as car and radios came to be exported which were not even produced in 1980s.

It has been seen from above that Prebisch-Singer thesis has been criticised on several grounds. It may however be noted that their thesis has not been conclusively proved by the analysis of statistics up to 1938 on the basis of which they propounded their thesis in the mid-nineteen fifties which really mattered in the mid-1950s and 1960s when many underdeveloped countries got independence from colonial powers their thesis of deterioration of terms of trade of primary producing countries appeared to be true and therefore it was quite right for Prebisch and Singer to urge upon underdeveloped countries not to rely on primary products exports for their development but also to industrialise themselves. It is important to note that during and immediately after the Second World War the terms of trade had moved in favour of countries producing primary products and this reached the peak following the outbreak of Korean War in 1980s. But since the mid-1950s net barter terms of trade turned against underdeveloped poor countries producing and exporting primary products (if exports of oil are excluded) though the extent of deterioration varied from country to country and from time to time.[18]

Haberler's Critique. Prof. G. Haberler, who has laid stress on dynamic gains from trade, also criticised Prebisch-Singer's view regarding deterioration of terms of trade of developing countries. He denies the validity of Prebisch-Singer view regarding terms of trade. He writes, "To my mind the alleged historical facts lack proof, their explanation is faulty, reckless and the policy conclusions irresponsible to put it mildly...... Can anyone seriously maintain that the long-term change in the terms of trade is the same for agricultural exporters (Argentina, Uruguay) mining commodities (Bolivia), (*c*) coffee exporters (Brazil), (*d*) petroleum exporters (Venezuela)".[19] According to Haberler, even if it was true that terms of trade of underdeveloped countries deteriorated in the period considered by Prebisch and Singer, it was wrong to conclude that this deterioration would likely to continue in future. For drawing such conclusion would require some kind of theory which Prebisch and Singer did not provide. In addition, Haberler questioned the validity of Prebisch-Singer thesis that prices of manufactured products were kept high by monopolistic behaviour of producers and trade unions of labour. He says that it is true that industrial growth in developed countries rising wages was associated with *constant or rising prices* of manufactured products. According to him, "This may be quite unjust for fixed income receivers but there is no evidence that it has changed relative prices between industry and agriculture or between finished goods and raw materials".[20]

Further, Haberler does not agree to the explanation of deterioration of terms of trade of underdevelopment countries on the basic of Engel's law of consumption. Though Haberler admits that Engel's law is one of crucial laws of economics but be is of the view that through it applies to food in general but not in case of every type of food. Besides, he asserts that Engel's law does not apply to primary raw materials which formed important components of exports of undeveloped countries for the period considered by Prebisch and Singer. That is, rise in incomes by no means leads to the decline in demand for raw materials by industries in developed countries as was assumed by Prebisch and Singer.

To sum up, Haberler maintains that "the theory of secular deterioration of terms of trade of the underdeveloped countries is completely unfounded and the policy recommendations based on it

18 See Walter Elkan, *op. cit.*, p. 69.

19 Harberler, "Critical Observations on Some Current Notions in the Theory of Economic Development (1957), quoted by Benjamin Higgins, *Economic Development*, (1963) p. 372.

20 Quoted by Benjamin Higgins, *op. cit.*, p 374.

are devoid of any solid bases".[21] However, in the opinion of Benjamin Higgins what Haberler has demonstrated is that Prebisch-Singer hypothesis is not necessarily true. According to him, Haberler definitely proved that the thesis could never be right. As is often the case in economics, the discussion up to this point leads to the conclusion, "it depends".[22]

Conclusion: Our Comments

It is evident from above that movements of terms of trade in the post-Second World War is also a controversial issue. It has been asserted by some that '*income terms of trade*' which takes into account both change in *prices* as well as *volume of* exports and imports improved for underdeveloped countries since the Korean boom. From this it is concluded that *underdeveloped countries exporting primary products gained from trade although less than that of developed countries*.[23] It may however be noted that to say that developing countries gained less as compared to the developed countries is quite different from Prebisch-Singer hypothesis that developing countries exporting primary products became worse off as a result of trade with industrialised developed countries.

It is evident from above that no firm conclusion can be drawn about the changes in long-term terms of trade of primary exporting underdeveloped countries since the post-Second World War period. This prompted some economists to enquire into making comparison of *total proceeds of exports* of developing and developed countries on the basis of empirical data. On the findings of such empirical studies Elkan Walter concludes that while total world exports have increased vastly since the Second World War, the exports of primary products have increased much more slowly than the exports of manufactures and also the export increase of primary products from low income countries has been even smaller than the increase from developed countries".[24] This proves Singer's thesis that to increase their export earnings the underdeveloped countries should not rely on exports of primary products alone but to industrialise themselves along with continuing exporting primary products.

Further, apart from the issue of long-term terms of trade of underdeveloped countries producing primary products, it is often pointed out that in the short run demand for primary products is highly unstable. Demand for them is inelastic in the short rum and subject to great variations caused by cyclical fluctuations in the industrialised developed countries who buy the primary products. On the other hand, short-run supply of primary products is quite inelastic and also subject to changes brought about by vagaries of nature as in case of India changes in monsoon often bring drought conditions in Indian agriculture and affect the output or supply of primary products. The short-run instability in agriculture also strengthens the case for industrialisation of developing countries for sustained growth and not to rely alone on production and exports of food, raw materials, and mineral products. This shows that despite the controversial issue of long-term terms of trade, for the sustained growth developing countries must industrialise to raise the living standards of their people while continuing to develop their agriculture to meet the needs of their growing population and also to export to make adequate export earnings. This proves the validity of the crucial point made by Prebisch and Singer.

21 Quoted by Benjamin Higgins, *op. cit.*, p, 373.

22 Benjamin Higgins, *op. cit.*, p. 373.

23 T. Wilson, R.P. Sinha, and J.R Castree, "The Income Terms of Trade of Developed and Developing Countries." *Economic Journal*, 1969, Vol. 79, pp. 813-832.

24 Walter Elkan, *op. cit.*, p. 50.

Primary Export-Led Growth

We have explained in a previous chapter the gains from trade, both static and dynamic. On the basis of his comparative cost theory Ricardo explained that a country will gain from trade if it specialises through reallocation of resources in the production of those goods in which it has a comparative advantage and exports them to other countries in exchange for imports of goods in which other countries have comparative advantage. Adam Smith laid stress on '*vent for surplus*' and explained that when a country has idle or unutilised resources it will gain from trade and develop if it opens up to foreign trade and utilise its idle or unutilised resources to produce goods for exports for which there is demand by other countries. Beside, he explained that *opening up to foreign trade* leads to widening of markets for goods which makes it possible to use greater division of labour and large-scale production and therefore a country opening up to foreign trade enjoys economies of scale. The gains explained by both Ricardo and Adam Smith are static gains and involve a movement from either one point of production possibility curve to another or a point *inside* a production possibility curve to a point on it.

Now, an important question which arises from above is *whether an expansion of the exports can lead to a process of export-induced overall growth of the economy. This is what export-led growth means and involves the expansion of exports leading to the growth of other sectors of the economy as well*. That is, export-led growth implies that expansion in exports is not merely confined to the growth of export sector itself but it stimulates growth in other sector of the economy so that there is widespread development of the economy. *Thus, in such a case exports will act as an engine of growth.*

Two types of export-led growth patterns can be distinguished:

(1) *Primary export-led growth,* and

(2) *Manufacturing export-led growth.*

In what follows we will discuss both types of export-led growth models.

PRIMARY EXPORT-LED GROWTH

Before 1950 it was widely believed that by following the traditional comparative costs theory the underdeveloped countries could achieve rapid growth, if they specialise in the production of those goods in which they have comparative advantage, that is, by allocating resources to food, industrial raw materials and other primary goods and exporting them and thereby raise their per capita income and undergo structural change to take place as a consequence. Following the comparative cost principle, the United States, Canada and Australia by exporting food and raw materials in the nineteenth century had become developed and rich countries. Thus, to begin with they had primary export-led growth. Argentina also had gone quite far in the primary export-led growth. Some underdeveloped countries such as Colombia, Mexico, Ghana, Nigeria, Malaysia and the Philippines also achieved large expansion in exports leading to the structural changes and propelled growth to the significant parts of their economies. Now, how do we explain this primary export-led growth in these countries. Broadly speaking, the following factors account for the primary export-led growth in these countries:

(1) Efficient allocation of existing resources;

(2) Inflow of foreign capital; and

(3) Linkage effects.

We explain these below.

(1) Efficient Allocation of Resources: When a country which is isolated from other countries is opened to trading with other countries of the world, as explained above, it will specialise in the production of those goods in which it has a comparative advantage and therefore reallocates its existing resources more to the production of those goods which will be exported. By doing so it will move along its given production possibility curve. In exchange for the exports, it will get imports. In this way it will be able to get more goods for consumption. As a result, its welfare will increase. Some of these imports may be machines and other capital goods which may be used for production in other sectors of the economy, leading to their growth. In this way expansion in primary exports through improved allocation of resources leads to widespread growth of the economy.

Besides, as Adam Smith pointed out in his 'vent for surplus' theory, if before trade the country has idle resources, it can gain substantially from trade by utilising *idle* resources for producing goods for primary exports for which there is demand in foreign countries and in exchange can obtain imports. In such a case of utilising idle resources for production of exports, the country moves from *within its production possibility frontier to a point on it*. In this case trade and exports of primary goods may stimulate the economy by utilising its idle resources for production so that its resources are fully utilised so that more of many goods are produced which ensures widespread growth of the economy.

The above explanation of primary export-led growth can be applied to the development of several countries in the nineteenth century. In the nineteenth century, the United States and Canada had surplus land relative to the supplies of labour and capital. Much of their land was lying unutilised so that both countries worked within the production possibility frontier and could produce more some primary goods without reduction in the output of others. British demand for wheat and cotton enabled the US and Canada to bring this idle land into production for growing wheat and cotton for export and imported manufactured goods in exchange for goods which at that time they could not produce as efficiently as Britain.

Besides, Hla Myint[1] has explained that when various countries of Africa and Asia came under the colonial rule and these countries were opened up to world trade, they used their surplus land and labour more intensively to produce tropical products such as rice, palm oil, cocoa for exporting them to obtain industrial goods in return. However, as explained in the previous chapter, these underdeveloped countries did not gain much from trade with colonial powers as the terms of trade were not favourable for them. In case of India, as mentioned earlier, the imports of cheap factory-made manufactured products in return for exports of primary products such as foodstuffs, minerals and plantation products had a *backwash effect* in the form of decline in handicraft industries displacing artisans and labour. Thus, while in case of India, foreign trade in the British period induced growth in agriculture, mines and plantations, it acted as a barrier to its industrial growth.

(2) Inflow of Foreign Capital: Once it was known that profitable opportunities existed in tropical agriculture and development of mines and plantations, foreign investment was attracted to the

1 Hla Myint, "The Classical Theory of International Trade and Underdeveloped Countries", *Economic Journal*, 1959.

country. Besides, if the export of the commodity was found to be subject to large *economies of scale* in production, this required a large foreign investment to establish the enterprise. Foreign investment came in underdeveloped countries to produce those goods in which they had a comparative advantage. Thus, inflows of foreign investment in minerals exporting countries as well as of development of plantations to export unprocessed tea, rubber, coffee. Even to procure wheat and rice grown in agriculture, foreign investment came to develop railroads. Thus, Standard Oil in Venezuela, British Petroleum in Iran, Anacoda in Chile, Alcoa in Jamaica, Lever Brothers and Firestone in West Africa and United Fruit in Central America are some examples of foreign companies which invested capital in underdeveloped countries, *mainly in extraction of minerals from mines and development of planations*. Wherever there was shortage of domestic labour, foreign investors *brought in migrant labour* to do work in mines and planations as in the case of Southern West Africa, Malaysia and Sri Lanka. It is important to note that foreign investment and migrant labour were normally employed for production for export in 'new lands' of America and Australia in the nineteenth century.

The impact of role of foreign investment in exports sectors such as for development of mines and plantations in underdeveloped countries is a controversial issue. When local labour is used for extracting minerals and development of planations they are paid money wages which is generally spent on other goods, especially foodstuff and cloth, giving boost to the agriculture and cloth producing industries. The foreign investment in some areas for export production may open up new profitable avenues for investment in related industries such as processing of agricultural products before being exported and these related industries may be left to the local investors to undertake investment in them. These new opportunities for investment may lead to the increase in savings of the country and also attracting foreign investment. In this way *foreign investment has some multiplier effect,* however small it may be.

Foreign investment in building railroads in India did lead to the development of agriculture in some of its regions for procuring wheat for exports by foreign capital. This contributed to the development of agriculture in these regions. Railroads and railways had beneficial external effects on the Indian economy as improved transportation in the country. It may however be noted that most of the profits made by foreign investors were sent back to their home countries rather than using them for local investment. Besides, local labour had been paid very low wage, merely sufficient for their subsistence. However, the dominant view among economists is that foreign investment in export sectors benefited the underdeveloping countries on the whole and contributed to their economic growth. Commenting on it some development economists write, "Thus the expansion of potential markets for primary products can lead to the expanded supplies of foreign investment, domestic saving, labour and skilled manpower. Not only does trade help an economy move toward production frontier and then along it, but trade can also expand the frontier outward enabling the economy to produce more of all goods."[2]

The spread effect of producing any export depends on the nature of the export good. The main determinant in this regard is how the value added by export of a good is distributed between payments for local residents and the payment made to the foreign factors of production. For example, in case of copper mining a relatively greater part of value added went to the foreign investors and therefore it adds less purchasing power to the domestic population and therefore had a lower stimulating effect on the local economy.

(3) Linkage Effect: The concept of export-led growth implies that expansion of exports gives stimulus to other industries which would not grow in the absence of export expansion. The important factor that determines the stimulus to other industries that is provided by the growth in exports is the amount of *forward and backward linkage* effects that are likely to provide stimulus to the development

2 M. Gills, D.H. Perkins, M. Roemer, D.R., *Snodgrass, Economics of Development* (New York: W.W. Norton and Company, 1983), pp. 414-15.

of other local activities in the economy. Prof. Hirschman coined the phrases of *forward and back ward linkages* for the stimuli that are given by an industry to other industries in the economy.[3]

Many primary goods exports give rise to forward linkage in the form of *processing* that must be done before exporting the products as in the case of sugar, rice, vegetable oil because processing them is technically feasible or profitable only immediately after harvesting them. The other example of forward linkage is found in case of some metal products whose costs are greatly reduced by smelting the metal before exporting them.

Backward linkage of production of an industry occurs *when the needed inputs are supplied at lower cost when a given exporting industry expands its production.* Backward linkages are particularly important when the using industry becomes so large that *production in inputs supplying industries achieve economies of scale* which reduce the cost of production. The lower cost per unit of input-supplying industry enables it to sell it at cheaper cost to the using industry. Its chief example is the growth of wheat industry in North America in the nineteenth century that created a larger demand especially for railway rolling stock and farm equipment which led to the establishment of industries producing them in the United States. Another such important example is the rapid expansion of fish-meal industry in Peru in the 1950s and 1960s. This led to significant increase in the fishing boats and processing equipment. Michael Roemer in his important study points out that in the nineteen fifties and sixties in Peru boat-making industry became highly efficient to produce for export *fishing craft* to other countries and also Peru's processing equipment industry registered a sharp and efficient growth that enabled it to supply capital equipment to a wide variety of food processing industries.[4]

Though in agriculture backward linkage is generally weak but modernisation of agriculture such as through green revolution technology, may lead to the large increase in the use of inputs such as fertilizers, pesticides, pump sets, barbed wire that is likely to the growth of local industries producing these inputs. In mining also backward linkage is very weak and the equipment required for it is of a highly specialised nature and is therefore usually imported.[5] Further, the strength of spread effect depends on the extent the production for export *introduces new methods of products or skills that can be used in other sectors or activities*.

Linkage effect also occurs through increase in demand for consumer goods by the residents whose income increases as a result of production for export. This consumption-demand linkage is present to a larger extent if a larger labour-force is employed and is paid higher wages than received by them previously. This raises the demand for clothing, processed foodstuffs, footwear etc. which are produced on a large scale in underdeveloped countries. This gives a boost to the development of consumer good industries in the underdeveloped economies. Thus, it has rightly been pointed out that in "North American wheat industry with its extensive endowment of land, high labour productivity, and egalitarian income distribution based on family farms successfully stimulated consumer goods industries. Neither plantation agriculture in Africa with *its large labour force but low wages* nor mining industries which pay high wages but *employ relatively few workers*, are able to generate adequate demand to stimulate local consumer goods industries."[6]

Provision of Physical Infrastructure

The availability of physical infrastructure such as power, roads, railroads, ports, etc built for exporting primary products from India in the later 19th and early 20th century and in the United States in the 19th century also helped in the growth of manufacturing industries by lowering costs.

3 Albert O. Hirschman, *The Strategy of Economic Development* (New Haven Yale University Press, 1958), Chapter 6.

4 Michael Roemer, *Fishing for Growth, Export-Led Development in Peru* 1950-67 (Cambridge, Mass., Harward University Press. 1970).

5 See R. E. Baldwin, *Economic Development and Export Growth: A Study of Northern Rhodesca*, 1920-60, University of California Press, 1966.

6 M. Gills, D.H. Perkins, M. Roemer, D.R. Snodgrass, *op. cit.*, pp. 415-416.

Besides, building of road and rail and ports network for export of cocoa and timber in Ghana, tea in India, copper in South Africa had also stimulating effect on domestic manufacturing industries.

Primary Export-Led Growth and Underdeveloped Countries

Contrary to the effect of exports on stimulating growth in the presently developed countries such as the US, Canada and Australia, the expansion of primary exports in the underdeveloped countries prior to 1950 did not transmit growth to the other sectors of the economy failed to achieve widespread development in these countries. As a result, many countries of Asia and Africa which experienced rapid growth of primary exports remained poor and underdeveloped as export expansion in these countries did not transmit growth to the rest of the economy. Thus Meier writes, "In most cases, after a country was exposed to the world economy, its exports grew markedly in volume and in variety. Yet, despite their secular rise, *exports in many countries* did not act as a key propulsive sector, propelling the rest of the economy forward. Although the classical belief that development can be transmitted through trade has been confirmed by the experience of some countries that are now among the richest in the world. *Trade has not had a similar stimulating effect for countries that have remained underdeveloped.*"[7]

Now the question arises why expansion in exports of underdeveloped countries of Asia and Africa failed to stimulate growth in the other sectors of these countries. Some attribute it to the *development of their export sector by foreign capital* that led to the growth of a *dual economy* in which production had export-biased and the pattern of resources allocation by the foreign capital was such that prevented economic development of other sectors. Mines and plantations were developed by foreign capital under colonisation. Colonisers also often used taxation and coercion to keep plantations and mines supplied with cheap labour in many parts of Asia and Africa, especially India under the British rule. Besides, the trade policy adopted under the British rule was such that encouraged cheap imports of British manufactured goods produced with the minerals and raw materials exported by the British capitalists. The cheap imports of industrial products from Britain led to the decline of handicraft industries in India, displacing artisans and workers. British policy was in favour of their own capitalist class and was not interested in the overall industrial growth of India. They used India as market for sale of industrial goods and source of supply of food, raw materials, minerals and plantation products to promote their industrial growth. Thus, from foreign trade India did not gain much and its growth of exports during the colonial rule did not stimulate growth of the other sectors of the economy.

Thus, the foreign investment in agriculture, mines and plantations led to the development of '*enclaves of development*' which failed to transmit growth to the other sectors of the economy. Not only in case of India but also many other countries, especially in Asia and Africa, which developed as a result of foreign capital induced growth of exports, this did not lead to widespread growth of their economies.

Another factor that is said to be responsible for impeding growth in developing countries from expansion of trade or exports is what has been called *demonstration effect*. The higher consumption standards of the developed countries raised the propensity to consume of underdeveloped countries and thereby reduced their saving rate. The lower saving rate led to the smaller investment rate that acted to lower growth in the underdeveloped countries and nullified the growth-augmenting effect of expansion in exports of primary products. However, against this it has been contended by some economists that international demonstrative effect also works to increase incentives to *supply more work effort and other productive services*. In our view this favourable demonstration effect has been quite weak compared to the adverse demonstration effect. An important reason given for inadequate growth of primary exports is *sluggish demand growth* for primary products of the underdeveloped countries by the industrialised developed countries. Ragnar Nurkse had pointed out *structural shifts* in

7 Gerald M. Meier, *Leading Issues in Economic Development*, Oxford University Press, Fourth Edition, 1984, p. 503.(italics added).

the demand pattern in the developed countries that caused slower growth in exports of primary goods of the underdeveloped economies.[8] In accordance with the well-known Engel's Law of Consumption the *demand for* staple foods and beverages in the industrialised developed countries grew more slowly than their income. For the industrialised countries it was estimated that income elasticity of demand for foodstuffs was less than 0.5. As a result, their imports of foodstuffs lagged behind their income growth. Besides, technological changes in the manufacturing sector worked to lower the demand for primary raw materials as producers attempted to reduce the wastage in the use of raw material products and also to increase the yield of finished products from a given quantity of raw materials. Thus, as a result of improvement in technology metal cans began to use less tin, modern looms wasted less cotton yarn, saw mills began to turn wood shavings into boards and so forth.

However, it may be noted that such gloomy prospects for expansion of primary exports may not hold good in case of all primary goods and all primary-exporting countries. Many of the materials which were hardly there at the beginning of the 20th century became prominent exports after 1950 and registered substantial growth. Thus, the demand for petroleum, rubber, copper, aluminium, newsprint, plywood, vegetable oils and soybean products recorded high growth and led to the substantial increase in their exports by developing countries as a result of earlier technological development. Countries of Malaysia, Jamaica, Liberia, Jordon, Keyna, Ivory Coast and Thailand experienced a rapid growth of traditional exports.

What follows from above is not the primary exports of developing countries will register high growth in future but demand for some commodities will rise substantially and the countries producing them will gain substantially and the countries producing them would achieve rapid growth in their exports. But for the developing countries as a whole prospects for rapid growth in exports of primary products as a result of the operation of the factors discussed above are quite bleak. To conclude, "With slower growth in industrial countries, the impact of Engel's law and materials-saving innovations, it seems unlikely that developed countries will import enough tropical foods and raw materials to fuel an era of rapid development for the Third World during the rest of this century."[9]

Another important factor that has acted to dampen the positive effect of expansion of exports of primary products as emphasised by Prebisch and Singer is the *deterioration of terms of trade* of the underdeveloped countries. Though this has been challenged by some but the dominant view is that in the nineteenth century terms of trade between primary goods-exporting countries and manufactured goods-exporting countries declined for the underdeveloped countries. This prevented the export-expansion from stimulating the growth in other sectors of underdeveloped countries of Asia and Africa.

According to Meier, a more important explanation why export-led growth occurred in some countries but not in others is "*to distinguish the differential effects of the integrative process by focusing on the stimuli in different countries from their exports and on the different response mechanism within the exporting countries*".[10] He argued that in the underdeveloped countries where export-led growth did not occur techniques of production in the export sector was the same as already in use in other sector or the expansion of export sector took place by widening of the production function without any change in the production technology. To quote him, "If the introduction or expansion of export crops involves simple methods of production that do not differ markedly from the traditional techniques already used in subsistence agriculture, the stimulus to development will clearly be less than if the growth in exports entailed the introduction of new skills and more productive re-combinations of factors of production".[11]

---

8 Ragnar Nurkse, *Equilibrium Growth in the World Economy* (Cambridge, Mass. : Harward University Press, 1961) Ch. 10.

9 M. Gills, D.H. Perkins, H. Roemer and D.R. Snodgrass, *op. cit*, p. 419.

10 G.M. Meier, *Leading Issues in Economic Development*, 4th edition, 1984, p. 505.

11 *Ibid*, p. 506.

Weak Linkages: The export sector may grow rapidly, yet it still fails to induce widespread development of the economy if linkages of the export sector are quite weak and ineffective. As pointed out by Hla Myint in case of underdeveloped countries the growth of exports of planation industry and most of the mining industries did not transmit growth to the other sectors of the economy remained only *enclaves*, isolated from the rest of the economy as a result of ineffective linkages, both forward and backward, in underdeveloped countries. Generally, neither backward linkages to suppliers of production materials nor consumption linkages worked to stimulate overall growth of underdeveloped countries. Of course, in some cases railroads and ports built for the mines helped the growth of other industries by lowering costs and inducing investment. Further, with the exception of planation agriculture in Colonial Africa, the linkages of agricultural export sectors have been quite ineffective to stimulate growth in other sectors of the underdeveloped countries.

As mentioned above, it is due to the weak linkage effect or non-operation of spread effect from the growing export-sector that led to the development of *dual economy* in the underdeveloped countries such as India with labour abundance. Gills, Perkins, Roemer and Snodgrass rightly point out that, "The high wages typically paid in capital-intensive petroleum and mining sectors which often provide high wage standards for union bargaining and government minimum wages in other sectors. As wages rise, the prospects for development based on abundant low-cost labour diminish. The dualistic structure is perpetuated, with a small but relatively high income workforce in modern employment and a large low-productivity workforce of farmers and marginal urban workers, the latter mostly in casual employment and petty services".[12]

12 M. Gills, D.H. Perkins, M. Roemer, D.R. Snodgrass, *op. cit.*, p. 426.

CHAPTER 40

MANUFACTURING EXPORT-LED GROWTH MODEL

After the Second World War many underdeveloped countries attained freedom from the colonial rule. They were now free to decide about the appropriate trade strategy. They had suffered from the exports of primary goods in exchange for manufactured goods. Besides, the findings of eminent economists, such as Raul Prebisch and Hans Singer showed that exports of primary goods were income inelastic and therefore their expansion would cause deterioration in terms of trade for underdeveloped countries. Therefore, many developing countries, especially India and Latin American countries (with the exception of Brazil), adopted *import-substituting industrialisation strategy*. Indian planners in the 1950s thought that there was little possibility of expansion of primary exports and therefore Mahalanobis growth model which emphasised the role of basic heavy industries and capital goods industries for indusrial development formed the basis of India's Second Five Year Plan (1956-61). Mahalanobis growth model was based on export-pessimism and assumed a closed economy and laid stress on the import-substituting industrialisation with a higher priority to basic heavy industries and capital goods industries in the resource allocation in the public sector while the development of consumer goods was left to the private sector which were protected by imposing high rates of tariff and quantitative restrictions on their imports. On the other hand, Latin American countries from the very beginning opted for import-substitution of consumer goods industries and imported capital goods for their development.

With the initiation of economic reforms in 1991 India started giving export orientation to its strategy of industrial growth. However, before India, from the mid-nineteen sixties onwards East Asian countries of South Korea, Taiwan, Singapore, Hong Kong and even China in nineteen eighties adopted manufacturing export-led growth strategy to promote their development.

Reasons for the Adoption of Manufacturing Export-Led Growth Model

Now, what are the reasons which prompted the adoption of manufacturing export-led growth model? First reason is the traditional comparative cost theory according to which it benefits the countries if they produce and speciabse in the production of those goods in which they have comparative advantage and export a major part of them and import the goods from other countries which can produce them comparatively more efficiently. In this way they can raise the living standards of their people. This emphasis on specialisation on the basis of comparative costs was supported by Hecksher and Ohlin theorem according to which there is **difference in factor andowments** of different countries. For example, some countries are labour-abundant and some, especially rich developed countries, are capital-abundant countries. Therefore, according to Hecksher-Ohlin theorem, the developing countries which are abundant in low-skilled labour can produce labour-intensive goods comparatively at a lower cost and rich developed countries which have abundant high-skilled labour and capital would benefit from concentrating on the production of capital-intensive goods which they can produce at a comparatively lower cost per unit.

Another important reason for adopting manufacturing export-led growth strategy by developing countries was the realisation that expansion in exports of manufactured goods by them can overcome the small size of the domestic market (*i.e.*, low leval of aggregate demand) for industrial goods. The third reason for giving up export-pessimism was that various countries (including India) was that with adoption of strategy of import-substituting industrialisation various developing countries experienced trade deficit and balance of payments difficulties without giving a push to the expansion of their exports of goods to pay for imports of raw materials and capital goods which were essential for their industrial growth.

Modern manufacturing industries are capital-intensive and require large-scale production enjoying economies of scale. This requires a larger market to sell the manufactured products. The growth of exports as a result of opening the economy to foreign trade ensures wider market for goods and services and greater division of labour. This raises the productivity of resources through growth of specialised skills and introduction of specialised techniques and capital equipment in the export sector. Therefore, international trade causes increase in capital accumulation and technological progress and raises the productivity of labour and other resources. As Hla Myint points out, "*The increase in productivity in the export sector and the rising real incomes they generate also spread to the rest of the economy resulting in export-led growth by the manufacturing sector*."[1]

Success of Manufacturing Export-Led Growth in Japan, South Korea and East Asian Countries

The success of export-led growth began with Japan which through growth of exports and its spread effect on Japanese economy became within few decades after the Second World War the second largest economy of the world. It achieved a high rate of sustained economic growth never witnessed before and was therefore called '*Japanese Miracle*' Again, South Korea also achieved rapid growth both in income and employment by recording rapid growth in exports of products of labour-intensive industries whose benefits accrued widely in the South Korean population.

Then, the success of Japan and South Korea from export-led growth was followed by East Asian Countries of Taiwan, Hong Kong, Singapore and then by Thailand, Indonesia and Malayisia since the mid-sixties to mid-nineties. These East Asian countries achieved a growth record unmatched by the other developing countries. Their rapid development experience through *expansion of exports* has therefore been called *'East Asian Miracle'*.

Now, an important question that has been raised is what has caused rapid growth of the East Asian countries by adopting an export-led growth strategy or which is also *outward-looking development strategy.* Bhagwati[2] and Krueger[3] have attributed the high growth of the East Asian countries to removal of restrictions on trade and emphasizing international competitiveness or more generally through adopting export-oriented strategy of development. The contention of Bhagwati and Kruger has been that it is the policy of free trade and export-orientation of these countries based on comparative advantage that generated high growth of their GDP. Arthur Young,[4] explaining the reasons for higher growth of East Asian countries, pointed out that increase in *total factor productivity (TFP) made only a modest contribution to higher growth achieved by East Asian countries and it was the usual*

1 See Hla Myint, *Economic Theory and Underdeveloped Countries* (Hutchinson University Press, 3rd Edition, 1971), p. 41.

2 Jagdish Bhagwati, "The Miracle That Did Happen : Understanding East Asian Crisis" in *Comparative Perspective*, Keynote Speech delivered on 3 May 1986, at Conference on the Subject.

3 A Krueger, 'Asian Trade and Growth Lessons' "*American Economic Review*", Vol. 80 1990, pp. 850-72.

4 Young, A., "The Tyranny of Numbers: Confronting the Statistical Realilies of East Asian Growth Experience", *Quarterly Journal of Economics*, Vol. 110, 1990, pp 641-80.

high rate of capital accumulation and greater use of labour that accounted for high GDP growth rates achieved by East Asian countries. However, some economists, prominent among them is Paul Krugman, expressed the view that since high rates of capital accumulation or investment in East-Asian countries was debt-driven, it was therefore unsustainble.[5] Their prediction proved to be correct as GDP growth in East Asian countries slowed down after 1995 and they faced a serious crisis due to difficulties of repayment of debt.

Now, expansion of exports of manufactured products did not have stimulating effect on the growth of other sectors of some developing economies. Some countries as India and Latin American countries influenced by Nurkse and Raul Prebisch's writings about the bleak prospects for exports of underdeveloped countries deliberately adopted import-substituting industrialisation strategy. As noted above, for the *export sector to have a more stimulating effect on the widespread growth of underdeveloped countries it is necessary that export sector should not remain an 'enclave' separate from the rest of the economy.* Instead, integrated process of development should be built up so that stimuli from the export sector diffuse to the rest of the economy and create response in other industries of the economy. G.M. Meier rightly writers, "A more convincing explanation of export-led development has occurred in some countries but not in others would therefore distinguish effects of the integrative process by focussing on the varying strength of the stimuli in different countries from their exports and on the different response mechanism within the exporting countries".[6]

Different manufacturing exports will provide different stimuli to the other industries or sectors depending on the technological characteristics of their production. The nature of production functions of goods being exported determines the extent of other secondary changes in the rest of the economy. If the production of goods being exported have different input coefficients, there will be different rates of learning and different linkage effects through which it will induce growth in other industries. The extent of processing goods for exports will create *important external economies* by way of increasing the **learning process.** If the goods for export use modern methods in their production they will benefit other activities and industries through the spread of technical knowledge, training of labour, demonstration of new production techniques that might be adopted and used in other industries in the economy. Besides, the use of modern methods in export sector promotes organisational and supervisory skills in the economy which promote widespread growth of the economy. In contrast, if the export sector uses same techniques as being already used in other sectors of the economy, it will have negligible spread effect on the growth in other sectors of the economy. On this issue, to quote Meier again, *"More favourable linkages may stem from exports that require skilled labour than from those using unskilled labour. The influence of skill requirements may operate in various ways: greater incentives for capital formation may be provided through education; on-the-job training in the export sector may be disseminated at little real cost through the movement of workers into other sectors or occupations; skilled workers may be source of entrepreneurship; skilled workers may save more of their wage-incomes than the unskilled workers".*[7]

Demand Linkages

Apart from affecting supply-side factors by increase in exports, the nature of production function of goods to be exported determines the distribution of income which in turn determines the demand pattern of goods and increases the employment opportunities in the economy. If in the production of the export-commodity capital-intensive techniques are used, share of profit relative to those of wages will be higher which will cause inequalities in income distribution. The recipients of profits have lower marginal propensity to consume and therefore not only direct demand effect will be small but also demand pattern and therefore resource allocation in favour of luxury goods will take

5 Paul Krugman, "The Myth of Asia's Miracle" *Foreign Affairs*, Vol. 73, pp. 62-75.

6 G. M. Meier, *Leading Issues in Economic Development*, 4th edition, p. 505.

7 G. M. Meier, *op. cit.*, p. 506.

place, some of which may be imported and thereby affecting the foreign exchange situation. On the other band, as in case of South Korea and Japan if in the production of export commodity labour-intensive techniques are used, this will not only cause more growth of employment but also generate greater demand for domestic goods. Both these effects will lead to the increase in both income and employment. Meier therefore writes, "If the internal distribution of the export income favours groups with a higher propensity to consume domestic goods than to imports, the resultant, distribution of income will be more effective in raising demand for home produced goods and to the extent that these home produced goods are labour-intensive, there will be more of an impact on employment. In contrast, if income is distributed to those who have a higher propensity to import, leakages through consumption of imported goods will be greater. If income increments go to those who are likely to save large portions, the export sector may also make a greater contribution to the financing of growth in other sectors."[8]

Furthermore, if production of export commodity is subject to *large economies of scale*, this will require a greater amount of financing for setting up enterprises for which borrowing of foreign capital or investment by foreigners will be needed. This will have a dual effect. One, foreign investment will have a multiplier effect on increases in output and employment in the domestic economy. Second, this may lead to the outflows of profits made by foreigners instead of further reinvestment of profits in the domestic economy. Therefore, net effect of foreign investment requires assessment of its costs and benefits and this will also depend on the nature of export sector in which foreign investment takes place. Besides, as has been recently witnessed, the spillover effect of exports will also depend on the *instability in export receipts* as a result of fluctuations in world trade and global economic environment. This instability in exports will have repercussions on the domestic economy affecting steady growth of income and employment and also causes fluctuations in foreign exchange rate. Meier sums up the factors determining the stimulating effect of integrating process (that is, exports and imports of goods and services and also flows of capital) on the domestic economy in the following way:

*"We would normally expect the stimulating forces of integrating process to be stronger under the following conditions: the higher the growth rate of the export sector, the greater the direct impact of the export sector on employment and personal income, the more the expansion of exports has a "**learning effect**" in terms of increasing productivity and instilling new skills, the more the export sector is supplied through domestic inputs instead of imports, the more the distribution of export income favours those with a marginal propensity to consume for domestic goods instead of imports, the more productive is the investment resulting from any saving of export income, the more extensive are the externalities and linkages* connected with the export sector, and the more stable are the export receipts that are retained at home. Some exports fulfil these conditions more readily than others and countries specialising on these exports will enjoy greater opportunities for development".[9]

Even the stronger stimulus from the exports sector does not guarantee the transmission of growth by it to the other sectors of the economy as this transmission mechanism depends upon other conditions in the economy. The weak propelling force of exports in developing countries depends not only on weak stimulus of particular export sector but also on a number of other factors such as *lack of adequate infrastructure*, skilled labour and education in the domestic economy that hinders the transmission of benefits to the rest of the economy even when the stimulus of export base may be strong.

Now, we have to explain on what factors the strength of the response or diffusing mechanism in the domestic economy to the stimulus from export base depends. These factors are as follows.

1. The extent of market imperfections (that is, the existence of monopolies, oligopolies and other forms of imperfect competition in the domestic economy, the less the imperfections,

8 G. M. Meier, *op. cit.*, p. 507.
9 *Ibid.*

the greater the transmission of expansion in exports to increase growth in the rest of the economy.

2. The non-economic impediments, as explained above, in the general environment of the economy. The smaller these impediments, the greater the diffusing growth effect of stimulus of exports.
3. The *extent of developed infrastructure* in the domestic economy. The greater the availability of developed infrastructure in the domestic economy, the greater the spread effect on growth of stimulus from exports.
4. The extent of *development of human resources* (*i.e*., skills and education of the workforce) which determines the learning rate of the economy.
5. The *existence of price distortions* that reduce the efficiency of resource allocation and therefore affects the spread effect on the growth from stimulus of export base.
6. *The greater the existence of entrepreneurs in the economy and capacity to bear risk on their part*. The greater the supply of entrepreneurs and greater the capacity to bear risk, the greater the response to the stimulus of exports in terms of transmitting growth to other industries in the economy.
7. *The mobilisation of surplus over consumption in the form of taxation and saving*. The greater the surplus, over-consumption and taxes, the greater the amount of funds auoilable for investment which are needed for growth in other sectors of the economy in response to the stimulus from exports.

The above factors determine the economic fundamentals. If these are strong, the various sectors (such as agriculture, various industries and services) of the economy will respond more in generating growth of output to the stimulus provided by exports.

Many developing countries were pessimistic about the possibility of expanding exports rapidly. Japan, South Korea and later East Asian countries and recently China have proved that manufacturing export-led growth is possible. Now, since 1991 when economic reforms were initiated, India too has given up *export-pessimism* and relying exclusively on import-substitution industrialisation. India's exports in the last 15 years have been growing at a rapid rate and have also shown good spread effects within the Indian economy. As a result of several policy initiatives by the Government, the share of manufactured products in our exports has substantially increased while that of traditional exports consisting of primary products (*i.e*. agricultural and mineral products) have declined. Thus "it is important that the less developed countries pursue policies that will ensure that they specialise as much as they can in *exports with the highest growth prospects*. To do this, a country must have the capacity to reallocate resources ..... to exports of goods for which demand may be rising rapidly. Of special significance is the country's potential for taking advantage of new export opportunities in manufactured goods. The exports of manufactured commodities may play a strategic role in transmitting development to some poor countries that have a favourable factor endowments and can gain a comparative advantage by utilissing labour-intensive methods".[10]

10 G. M. Meier, *op. cit.*, p. 509.

Dual Gap Analysis

Dual Gap Analysis

Dual gap analysis which is also called **two gap analysis** was made in the context of foreign aid or foreign borrowing of capital by developing countries required for achieving rapid economic growth. The question raised was what constrains acceleration of investment which is required to achieve a certain target growth rate of economic growth in the developing countries. The first important factor mentioned in this connection is the domestic saving rate in the country on which investment depends. Therefore, Harrod-Domar model which was generally used for development planning laid stress on the saving rate (and therefore investment) and capital-outquit ratio, as the two factors that determine economic growth. Thus, according to Harrod-Domar model,

$$g = \frac{s}{k}$$

where g is the growth rate of GDP, s the saving rate of the economy (*i.e.*, ratio of saving to national income) and k is the capital-output ratio. Capital-output ratio (which is the reciprocal of output-capital ratio) in this model is taken as given and rate of investment and therefore rate of economic growth depends on the domestic saving rate of the economy.

However, Harrod-Domar model was a closed economy model and foreign trade was not incorporated in it. However, every developing country even if it followed import-substitution development strategy needed imports of certain capital goods and raw materials which they could not manufacture themselves and required them for their industrialisation. Therefore, in Harrod-Domar model foreign trade was to be introduced so as to explain the role of foreign exchange required to import capital and intermediate goods and raw materials needed for industrial growth. Accordingly, the extension of Harrod-Domar model was made by adding the term for foreign trade balance (namely, imports minus exports) as per cent of national income. The extended Harrod-Domar model was written as:

$$g = \frac{s}{k} + \frac{b}{k}$$

$$\text{where } b = \frac{\text{Imports} - \text{Exports}}{\text{National Income}}$$

The significance of this extended version of Harrod-Domar model was that the growth of exports of developing countries was limited, imports could exceed exports only if foreign aid (both grants and concessional loans) or private foreign investment was available to enable the developing countries to get the required foreign exchange for importing capital goods and industrial raw materials so that more investment than domestic saving can occur to achieve target growth rate. However, *even if domestic saving could be raised to achieve the required investment for attaining target growth rate, the foreign exchange needed to import essential capital goods and raw materials would not be there as the domestic savings and foreign exchange (provided by foreign aid and foreign investment) are not perfect substitutes of one another*. Thus, the higher domestic saving would not make up the deficiency of foreign exchange to import the required capital goods and industrial raw materials more than value of exports. For example, for imports of capital goods and industrial raw materials we require dollars and not rupees. And the dollars can be obtained by either increasing exports or through foreign aid or foreign investment. This implies foreign exchange gap or bottleneck as distinct from saving gap to achieve the desired growth rate. Since it was not possible for the developing countries in the initial stages of development to achieve sufficient growth in exports (except the oil producing Arab countries), foreign exchange gap was faced by them. It was therefore pointed out that to meet the foreign exchange gap, foreign aid or foreign investment was needed to help them achieve the desired rate of economic growth in the fifties and sixties of the 20th century.

Now, it is important to note that in view of lack of substitutability between domestic saving and foreign exchange resources *economic growth could be constrained by whatever factor, domestic saving or foreign exchange reserves*, is the most binding factor. Foreign capital (both in the form of foreign aid or borrowed funds) can play an important role in supplementing domestic resources in order to relieve both domestic saving constraint and foreign exchange constraint. Therefore, this was called *dual gap analysis* of foreign assistance by Chenery and Strout.[1] It was argued by them that the most developing countries either face lack of domestic saving to finance the required investment to achieve the desired rate of economic growth or shortage of foreign exchange required to import necessary capital goods and raw materials for industrialisation. Besides, as mentioned above, it was generally assumed by the exponents of two-gap analysis that the two gaps were unequal in size and were independent of each other, that is, there did not exist any substitutability between domestic saving and foreign exchange. We explain below these two gaps in some detail.

Saving Gap or Saving Constraint

The implication of the dual gap analysis that either of the two gaps will be binding for any developing country at any particular point of time. The saving gap is said to be binding or dominant when domestic savings are inadequate to support the desired rate of economic growth though it has adequate foreign exchange earnings for importing the necessary capital goods and raw materials.

Given the assumption of full employment or capacity output, the shortage of saving can be viewed as *lack of productive resources* such as manpower or other productive resources in the economy for being used for increasing investment to achieve higher growth rate, though the adequate foreign exchange resources are available and are not being used fully. In such a situation saving-gap constraint implies that the excess foreign exchange might be used for importing luxury consumer goods rather than capital goods and industrial raw materials for bringing about higher industrial growth rate. Todaro and Smith therefore rightly say, "If, for example, the savings gap is dominant, this would indicate that the economy is operating at full employment and not using all of its foreign exchange earnings. It may have enough foreign exchange to purchase additional capital goods from abroad but there is not enough excess domestic labout or other productive resources to carry out additional investment projects ... As a result, 'excess' foreign exchange, including foreign aid, might be spent on the importation of luxury consumption goods. Such a country is said to have a *shortage of productive resources* which from a different viewpoint can be regarded as a shortage in saving."[2] Thus, in such a case a developing economy is said to be *incapable of absorbing foreign exchange* for purposes of economic growth.

1. Hollis B. Chenery and Alam M. Strout, "Economic Development and Foreign Assistance," *American Economic Review*, 56, September, 1966.
2. Michael P. Todaro and Stephen C. Smith, *Economic Development*, 7th edition, Pearson Education, Delhi-110092, pp. 634-35.

It is worth mentioning that such a saving gap was faced by oil-exporting countries of Middle East in the 1970s when they suddenly had a flush of petro-dollars due to rise in oil prices by OPEC. These petro-dollars were spent by these countries for importing luxury consumer goods rather than using them for additional domestic investment. However, in later years they realised the importance of their petro-dollars which they started using for buying capital goods and hiring manpower from abroad. In this way they were able to overcome their domestic saving gap by using their foreign exchange earnings. This means saving gap countries do not need foreign aid to increase their investment for attaining higher growth rate.

Foreign Exchange Gap

On the contrary the saving-gap countries, the countries facing foreign exchange gap cannot overcome it by using their excess domestic saving. Therefore, for them foreign exchange gap is binding for achieving a desired rate of economic growth. In their case foreign exchange resources are inadequate for supporting higher rate of economic growth that is permitted by their domestic saving rate. Most of the developing countries are assumed to fall in this category as they face a situation where the foreign exchange gap is binding. These countries have enough domestic saving or productive resources such as labour and other inputs but lack adequate foreign exchange resources to import capital and intermediate goods, such as machines, oil, certain industrial raw materials which they cannot produce themselves. In such a situation due to lack of complementary foreign exchange resources, a certain part of domestic savings may remain unutilised. The availability of domestic savings or resources would permit them to undertake new investment projects if they receive foreign capital inflows through foreign aid or through FDI and FIIs so that they can import new capital and intermediate goods (including oil and petroleum products). In the two years 2011-12 and 2012-13 India faced such a situation of foreign exchange because there was a large deficit on current account of balance of payments of more than 4% of GDP. If we had got adequate foreign capital inflows, it would have been possible to fill in the foreign exchange gap. As the surplus on foreign capital account was inadequate we used foreign exchange reserves held by RBI to finance the foreign exchange gap.

It is important to mention here a confusion which usually arises because in national income accounting of an open economy such as ours saving-investment gap is said to be equal to import-export gap (*i.e.*, current account balance). If this were so, then question arises where does the problem lie? We state below the national income account identity of an open economy.

$$Y = C + I + X - M \quad \text{...(1)}$$

where Y stands for national income, C for consumption, I for investment, X for exports and M for imports. (Note that both exports and imports include both goods and services).

$$Y - C = I + X - M$$

Since $Y - C$ = national saving (S)

Therefore, $S = I + X - M$

or $I - S = M - X \quad \text{...(2)}$

Thus the above equation (2) shows that saving-investment gap equals import-export gap. How does it happen? As a matter of fact, the above national income identity is only in accounting or *ex-post* sense and not in *ex-ante* or intended sense. Despite the trade deficit (or current account deficit) this identity will hold good. This is because import-export gap is somehow financed either by foreign capital inflows which may occur either through commercial borrowing or foreign assestance or private capital inflows through FDI and FIIs or ultimately by withdrawal from accumulated foreign exchange reserves of the past years held by the Central Bank of a country. Thus, the real problem remains how to relieve foreign exchange gap to undertake necessary additional investment which requires import of capital goods and raw materials. In fact, it was in this context that dual gap theory was used to show the crucial importance of foreign aid and other forms of capital flows to finance a deficit in the current account balance of payments (that is, the excess of imports of goods and services over their exports).

A Critical Appraisal of Dual Gap Theory

Two-gap theory was put forward to bring out the crucial role of foreign assistance to relieve foreign exchange gap faced by developing countries. Of course foreign aid has been helpful for accelerating economic growth in developing countries but it has been often tied to development projects in which donor countries were interested. It has been rightly asserted by Bruton[3] that even developing countries which pursued import-substitution development strategy such as India needed foreign exchange to import capital goods, intermediate goods and industrial raw materials for the development of their basic heavy industries as all of them could not produce them at home and in view of the limited possibilities of increasing exports needed foreign assistance not only to supplement their domestic saving but also to fill up their foreign exchange gap. However, in our view dual gap analysis overemphasized the lack of substitutability between saving and foreign exchange. As has been mentioned above, the oil-rich Arab countries used their own foreign exchange resources to buy both manpower and capital goods from abroad to relieve their shortage of domestic savings. Further, if you can cut down consumption of some goods which have export potential (and therefore save more) the foreign exchange earnings from exports so made can be used to import capital goods and raw materials for their development. The dual gap model underplayed the export potential of developing countries. Therefore, after the mid-seventies of the last century, the emphasis was shifted from "*aid*" to "*foreign trade*," Many countries such as Japan, South Korea, Taiwan and Singapore by adopting export-led growth strategies succeeded in achieving higher economic growth without much foreign aid.

In India too after 1991 when economic reforms have been made stress has been laid on export-orientation of our development strategy rather than import-substitution and we have succeeded a lot as our exports have registered quite a satisfactory growth rate in the post-reforms period. As a result, our current account deficit has been quite small (1 to 2.5 per cent of GDP), except for a few years which was easily met by private capital inflows through foreign direct investment (FDI) and foreign institutional investors (FIIs). Our recent problem of large current account deficit (CAD) for the years 2011-12 and 2012-13 arose because of our dependence on imported oil and petroleum products whose prices sharply rose and our exports in these years have not been growing adequately due to sluggish growth in the US and recession in European countries. Besides, our excessive demand for gold has led to the increase in its imports adding to our current account deficit, But once the US economy recovers and European crisis is over, our exports will rise resulting in reduction in of our current account deficit to a comfortable level. This shows that *foreign trade* (*i.e.*, higher export growth rate) and not *foreign aid* can help relieve foreign exchange constraint on our economic growth. In fact in the last two decades the role of foreign assistance in financing India's development has been only marginal.

Further, the two-gap model laid stress on foreign aid *i.e.* grants and loans at concessional rates of interest from developed countries. In the last over two decades (1991-2015) instead of foreign aid, the foreign capital inflows in the form of direct private investment (FDI) and FIIs have become more important as a source of foreign exchange. Despite the financial instability caused by them, the private capital inflows can play an important role in promoting economic growth. India is a favourable destination for private capital inflows. Moreover, these *private capital inflows are not-debt creating* and therefore do not lead to the increase in external debt burden.

However, if a country finances its development programme through borrowing from abroad (even foreign assistance at concessional rates of interest), it leads to the problem of *indebtedness*. The problem of indebtedness had been actually faced by developing countries and recently by Eurozone countries. This leads to the problem of paying back the foreign debt and also servicing it. While describing foreign exchange gap and the need for foreign aid, dual gap models overlooked the problem raised by indebtedness caused by foreign aid.

3. Henry Bruton, *A Reconsideration of Import Substitution.*

CHAPTER 42

Foreign Trade Strategy: Import Substitution vs Export Orientation with Special Reference to India

Trade policy plays an important role in achieving the objectives of rapid economic growth and self-reliance. We have explained in a previous chapter both static and dynamic gains from trade with other countries. It is on the basis of these static and dynamic gains of trade that case for free trade or liberalisation of trade has been built. When a country specialises on the basis of its comparative cost or production efficiency and export and import accordingly, it enables it to make optimum use and allocation of its resources. As a result, output, income and welfare of its people increase. These gains emanating from trade through improved allocation of given resources of a country are generally described as static gains. Thus, Professor Haberler writes, "International division of labour and international trade which enable every country to specialise and to export those things which it can produce in exchange for what others can provide at a lower cost have been and still are one of the basic factors promoting economic well-being and increasing national income of every participating country."[1]

However, importance of trade is not confined to static gains flowing from improved allocation of the given resources. Foreign trade also promotes economic growth of a country. It is the beneficial effect of trade on economic growth that is described as dynamic gains. D.H. Robertson described foreign trade as **"an engine of growth".** With grate income and production made possible by specialisation and trade, greater savings and investment become possible and as a result higher rate of economic growth can be achieved. Through promotion of exports, a developing country can earn valuable foreign exchange which it can use for imports of capital equipment and raw materials which are so essential for economic growth. To quote Haberler again, "The higher the level of output, the easier it is to escape the 'vicious circle' of poverty and to 'take off into self-sustained growth' to use the jargon of modern development theory. Hence, if trade raises the level of income, it also promotes economic development."[2] Elaborating how trade promotes growth he emphasises the following factors:

1. Through foreign trade developing countries can get material resources such as capital equipment, machinery and raw materials which are so essential for industrial growth.
2. The developing countries through trade can import and use superior technology which has been invented in advanced developed countries and is embodied in the machines, capital equipment which they import.
3. Foreign trade enables the transmission of technical know-how, skills, managerial talents to the developing countries.

---

1 G. Haberler, *International Trade and Economic Development.*

2 G. Haberler, *op. cit.*

India's Trade Strategy of Import Substitution

As we began our planning for development, the two options were open to us with regard to our foreign trade policy. First, we should lay stress on export promotion in our strategy of development for accelerating economic growth. The second option was to adopt import substitution as a major element of our trade policy. Note that the second policy of import substitution does not emphasise the role of foreign trade for accelerating economic growth. In fact, the policy of import-substitution was adopted in view of the perceived bleak prospects of raising India's exports. When exports could not be increased substantially, we could not pay for imports on a large scale. Therefore, India's strategy of industrialisation was based on substitution of imports rather than export-oriented trade policy. The policy of import substitution for promoting growth was also thought to be quite feasible in view of India's vast domestic market.

It is clear from above that India adopted the policy of import–substitution because of what is now called *export-pessimism*. In fact, in the nineteen fifties and sixties export pessimism characterised the thinking of most development economists. For example, Raul Prebisch postulated that the terms of trade of developing countries have a tendency to deteriorate over time regardless of the policies of developing countries. Prebisch's postulate was based on three grounds. First, demand for primary products which underdeveloped countries were exporting were income-inelastic. Second, technological progress that was taking place in developed countries was of the nature that saved the use of raw materials which underdeveloped countries were exporting. Third, because of the prevailing monopolies in the manufacturing industries of the developed countries, the prices of their manufactured products were relatively higher than the prices of primary and agricultural products whose production and sale were being done under competitive conditions. Thus, according to Prebisch, export expansion by developing countries was quite unprofitable.

Similarly, R. Nurkse, another pioneer in development economics, believed that for the newly emerging countries like India foreign trade could no longer serve as 'engine of growth'. Nurkse's export pessimism arose from his belief that foriegn market could not absorb imports on a sufficient scale as developing countries accelerated their process of economic growth. In view of this external environment, Nurkse concluded that in order to accelerate growth developing countries should undertake a balanced pattern of investment in a number of different industries so that they can generate mutual demand for each other's product leading to the expansion in size of home market. To quote Nurkse, "When developing countries face difficulties in exporting both traditional and new exports, import-substitution strategy may be adopted by them as an escape route from stagnation."[3] Nurkse further writes, "International trade cannot now be an effective engine of 'economic growth' and in the strategy of growth, underdeveloped countries have of necessity to lay emphasis on 'balanced growth' – a coordinated development of local industries in accordance with the growth and structure of domestic demand."[4]

It is interesting to note here that our former Prime Minister, Dr. Manmohan Singh, was perhaps the first economist who challenged this export pessimism of early development economists, especially in the context of India. On the basis of his empirical findings about the export potential of the Indian economy, he concluded that it was not easy to meet the increase in import requirements in raising the rate of economic growth by any other means but export promotion. Arguing the case for export-promotion policy of development he writes, "*Whatever the development strategy, the function of international trade as a supplier of 'material means indispensable for development' is likely to retain its importance for most underdeveloped countries in their quest for higher rates of economic growth...Imports, however, have to be paid for either by current export earnings or by withdrawal from reserves of foreign exchange or by fresh capital inflows. The withdrawal from reserves is not*

3 R. Nurkse, *Patterns of Trade and Development,* Wicksell Lectures, 1989.
4 R. Nurkse, *op. cit.*

unlimited process,..capital inflows ultimately lead to higher service charges and repayment obligations. In the long run, therefore, the import capacity of an economy and its ability to utilise the above mentioned benefits of international trade is crucially dependent on its export capacity."[5]

But Dr. Manmohan Singh not only highlighted the need for export promotion for accelerating economic growth but with his empirical study he demonstrated in India's case that export promotion to meet the growing needs for imports was in fact possible and that the stagnation of India's exports during 1951-61 was partly a consequence of faulty Indian economic policies. Commenting on Dr. Manmohan Singh's work, Prof. Amartya Sen writes, "Rapid increase in exports would be impossible if export pessimism prevailing at that time was well-grounded." And Professor Sen himself answers that "with its very careful and painstaking empirical arguments, Dr. Manmohan Singh demonstrated that it was not so well grounded after all."[6]

Empirically, the export pessimism of the nineteen fifties (Post-War Period) has been proved to be untrue and unjustified. World trade in the nineteen fifties and sixties grew faster than world income. Several developing countries used export promotion as a means of attaining a fast economic growth. In the early 1960s Japan was the shining example of using export promotion strategy to achieve a fast rate of economic growth, beginning from a state of underdevelopment. Japanese growth experience is often described as **Japanese miracle.**[7] In the later period, other success stories of achieving high growth through outward-looking strategy of development have been of Asian countries of South Korea Taiwan, China, Thailand, Singapore and Hong Kong. Owing to their rapid economic growth in nineteen seventies and eighties they have been called **'Asian Tigers.** It is also worth mentioning that the expansion in exports of developing countries which have used export promotion as a strategy of growth has not been confined to primary products such as fuel and agricultural products (food, agricultural raw materials). As a matter of fact, there has been significant change in the composition of exports of developing countries towards manufacturers.

It may be noted that in the nineteen fifties and early sixties free trade was opposed on political grounds also. Fears were expressed that through free trade industrial developed countries would acquire political domination, as happened in case of India. East India Company of Britain which came to India for trading acquired political domination. It may however be noted such fears of political domination through trade have now receded in the present political context. In fact, the *protectionist sentiment is now stronger in the developed countries* such as US and EU. There is now huge cry in USA for protecting American jobs by banning outsourcing of business services (BPO) to India.

The success in export promotion accelerates economic growth of a country. The emergence of Japan and Germany and recently China as major economic powers has shown that their success in export expansion made them economically more independent and strong. On the other hand, developing countries like India which followed import-substitution strategy had to face recurrent balance of payments crises and the persistence of huge external debt problem which made them more dependent on developed countries and international institutions such as IMF and World Bank.

As mentioned above, for at least up to 1980, India adopted a trade strategy of import substitution. The choice of this policy was based on export pessimism which led the Indian planners to believe that export earnings of India cannot be increased. The choice of this inward-looking strategy was further strengthened by the vast size of Indian domestic market To implement this trade policy of import

5 Manmohan Singh, *India's Export Trends and Prospects for Self-Sustained Growth*, Oxford : Clarendon Press, 1964, pp. 3-4.

6 Amartya Sen, "Theory and Practice of Development" published in *India & Economic Reforms and Development* , Essays in honour of Manmohan Singh, Isher Judge Ahluwalia and I.M.D. Little, (ed.), Delhi, Oxford University Press, p. 28.

7 Jagdish Bhagwati, "Export Promoting Trade Strategy: Issues and Evidence," *The World Bank Research Observer*, Vol, 3. No.1.

substitution the imports of several commodities into India were banned and quantitative restrictions on some other commodities were imposed. Besides, to give protection to the domestic industries, customs duties were levied on a number of commodities to discourage their imports by raising their prices. The customs duties levied in India on certain commodities were as high as 200 per cent or 150 per cent which were one of the highest in the world. In addition to these, the import-licensing was used so as to regulate the quantities of some essential goods and raw materials that could be imported and accordingly licences for import quotas were issued by the Government. A scheme of import-licensing in case of certain commodities was introduced under which imports were permitted to the extent that domestic production fell short of domestic demand. Further, stringent foreign exchange regulations were introduced and foreign exchange was released to the holders of import licences for importing specific commodities.

It may be noted that India's policy of import substitution was indiscriminate and also continued for quite a long period. This is unlike some other countries such as Japan and South Korea which adopted import substitution only for some period of time and that too in case of selected commodities for which they had potential comparative advantage.

Results of Import-Substitution Policy

However, it may be noted that policy of import substitution contributed significantly to industrial growth between 1956-66. But several weaknesses of the policy of import substitution became evident during the course of time. First, the policy-makers underestimated the possibilities of expansion in exports. As in the path-breaking study about the trends in exports, Dr. Manmohan Singh[8] found that a lot of export possibilities was lost due to faulty trade policies. As a result, India's share of world exports declined from about 2 per cent in 1951 to about 0.53 per cent in 1992.

Second, policy of import substitution underestimated the import intensity of import substitution process itself. Growth of import-substituting industries required large quantities of imports of capital goods, machines, raw materials etc. As a consequence, whereas imports increased substantially there was no adequate growth in exports resulting in balance of payments problems. In 1966 we had to devalue the rupee to promote exports and discourage imports in order to solve balance of payments problem. However, 1966 devaluation did not succeed in improving the trade deficit.

It may be noted that deficit in balance of payments which arose mainly due to import-substitution policy forced Indian policy-makers to make some changes in attitude towards exports. Accordingly, in the Third Plan period (1961-66) and the Fourth Plan period (1969-74) several export promotion measures (including devaluation of 1966) were taken. However, as has been correctly pointed out by C. Rangarajan that "Until the end of 1970s, exports *were primarily regarded as a source of foreign exchange rather than as an efficient means of allocating resources. Import substitution remained the basic premise of the development strategy.*"[9]

Since import-substituting industrialisation was pursued regardless of comparative cost considerations, inefficiencies crept into the system resulting in the Indian economy becoming increasingly high-cost economy. This high cost and inefficiency in production was an important reason for poor export performance despite the various incentives and concessions given by the Government for export promotion.

Trade Liberalisation in the 1980s

In the early 1980s because of the deficits in balance of payments export-promotion measures "acquired great urgency". In the eighties, especially in the later half of eighties, a more *liberal trade policy* was adopted to promote exports on the one hand and to provide for imports of capital goods and technology so as to enable India to obtain benefits from international trade. It needs to

8 Manmohan Singh, *op. cit*.

9 C. Rangarajan, *India's Balance of Payments : The Emerging Dimensions*, Gobind Ballabh Pant Lecture, January 1994 (italics added).

be emphasised that liberalisation of trade policy in the 1980s was in view of the mounting deficits in balance of payments as a consequence of pure import-substitution policy followed earlier. In 1981 IMF had also advised India to use export promotion and not export restrictions as the strategy for reducing deficit in balance of payments. The following measures were taken for export promotion and liberalisation of imports in the 1980s:

First, incentives scheme to promote exports was launched which provided for imports of raw materials, machinery and capital equipment and accessories against exports. This schemes we called Replenishment (Rep.) Scheme which was later replaced by **Exim Scripts.** Exim scripts equivalent to the 30 per cent value of their exports were given to the exporters. These exim scripts could be even sold in the market at premium. Exim scripts entitled exporters to import a certain amount of materials and machinery for expanding exports. Thus, **'import liberalisation for export promotion'** became the focus of trade policy.

Secondly, fiscal concessions for export promotion were given. The important fiscal concession was the introduction of *'duty drawback scheme'* under which taxes paid on materials used in the manufacture of goods for export were refunded. Besides, a good proportion of profits or income earned from exports was exempted from income tax. Further, a 5-year tax holiday was provided to the units set up in Special Exporting Zones (SEZ) for financing exports. Further, liberal credit facilities at concessional rates of interest were given by the commercial banks to exporters.

Thirdly, in the later half of 1980s the '*exchange entitlement*' scheme was introduced to enable exporters to utilize a part of their foreign exchange earnings for the purpose of market development. Further, **Cash Compensatory Scheme** for providing cash assistance to the exporters was started. Under this scheme cash assistance was given to the exporters to compensate them for the taxes paid by them on the imported inputs used by them for the production of exported goods. This was in fact a form of export subsidy paid for providing incentives to the exporters.

Lastly, in the later half of 1980s quota system in case of several commodities was replaced by tariffs. This liberalised imports therefore provided revenue to Government.

INDIA'S TRADE STRATEGY SINCE 1991: IMPORT LIBERALISATION AND EXPORT ORIENTATION

There was a severe economic crisis in 1991. This economic crisis had its root in persistent deficits in balance of payments in the last several years. Gulf war of 1990 added to the problem as it resulted in shooting up of oil prices which required enhanced spending in terms of foreign exchange. By March 1991, current account deficit in balance of payments reached a record level of about 10 billion US dollars or over 3 per cent of our GDP. Exports were declining. Foreign borrowing in last several years raised the ratio of short-term debit to foreign exchange reserves to an extremely high level of 146.5 per cent. Foreign debit reserve ratio rose to a peak of 35.5 per cent. As a result, our foreign exchange reserves dwindled to a meagre amount which was hardly adequate to meet only a few weeks imports. A default on payments for the first time in our history became a distinct possibility in June 1991. Foreign capital was flying from India. No one was willing to lend us any more.

The severe economic crisis of 1991 forced us to make drastic reforms in trade policy. Fortunately, Dr. Manmohan Singh was appointed as Finance Minister. Since then many far-reaching reforms in trade policy have been undertaken. Though some liberalisation of trade policy was undertaken in the 1980s, a truly liberalised trade policy was adopted from 1991 onwards.

The liberalisation of trade policy in India is characterised by two important features:

1. Import liberalisation and
2. Export orientation of trade policy.

This new trade policy has accelerated India's transition to a globally oriented economy by stimulating exports and facilitating imports of essential inputs and capital goods. Steps were taken to promote exports by removing anti-export bias in the earlier policy. This policy of import liberalisation and export-orientation was in fact the policy that was recommended by IMF and World Bank to solve the balance of payments problem facing the developing countries and to accelerate rate of economic growth. We explain below this trade policy in some detail.

Import Liberalisation in Economic Reforms of 1991

The first important reform in India's trade policy has been the elimination of quantitative restrictions in a phased manner on most of intermediate and capital goods since 1991. Secondly, prior to 1991 imports were regulated by means of a positive list of a freely importable items. Instead, since 1992 as a part of trade policy reforms only a *short negative list of imports* is subject to regulations by Government. Other goods can be imported, subject of course to payment of duty.

Abolition of Licensing. Prior to 1991 a large number of goods were subject to import-licensing restrictions. Now, most of the items of imports have been put on Open General Licence (OGL). That is, for their imports prior approval or licence from any authority is not required. Thus, *Licence -Permit Raj* regarding imports has been done away with.

Tariff Reduction. An important step towards import liberalisation has been reduction in import duties to eliminate protection given to domestic industries from foreign competition. The maximum import duty which was as high as around 150 per cent was reduced to 110 per cent in 1992-93. This was further reduced to 85 per cent in 1993-94, to 65 per cent in 1994-95 and to 50 per cent in 1995-96. In 2004-05 average customs duty had been reduced to 20 per cent only.

Empirical evidence shows reduction in protection increases efficiency and productivity in the domestic industries as it exposes them to foreign competition.

Liberalisation of Imports of Gold and Silver. Another significant import liberalisation has been that imports of gold and silver have been liberalised. This has helped in preventing smuggling of these metals.

Critique of Import Liberalisation

It may be noted that fears were expressed about import liberalisation both by certain politicians and economists, especially with Leftist leanings. They contended that import liberalisation would kill domestic industries as they would not be able to compete with the cheap foreign products. This would lead to closure of a large number of industrial units, especially small-scale industries. Besides, they claimed that large-scale imports would require substantial foreign exchange resources. Thus, according to them, import liberalisation would worsen the balance of payments problem rather than solving it. Even a reputed economist, Dr. Bimal Jalan, a former Governor of Reserve Bank of India, expressed reservations about the policy of import liberalisation and pointed out that it would be highly risky for the Indian economy. Writing in 1991, he says, "Given the balance of payments constraints operating now, and the financing options currently available, import-liberalisation as strategy does not seem to be a feasible option over the next few years. This pragmatic view is not dependent on the theoretical validity (or otherwise) of the liberalisation argument. By implication, import liberalisation would have the effect of raising, even in the short run, the ratio of import to GDP. This may not be undesirable in itself, but it would require larger inflows of external capital in the next few years and this is not available *on appropriate terms*. Past experience shows that further commercial borrowing to finance import liberalisation . . . would also be undesirable, given the high level of external debt. In this situation, import liberalisation would be unduly risky and could lead to a repetition of the unfortunate experiences of several other developing countries."[10]

However, as shall be explained later, in actual experience, these fears about import-liberalisation leading to adverse consequences have not proved to be true.

EXPORT ORIENTATION OF INDIA'S TRADE POLICY

Along with import liberalisation, export-orientation was also given to India's trade policy pursued since 1991. In other words, for the first time greater emphasis was placed on export promotion in our trade policy by *removing anti-export* bias of our earlier policy. Some economists describe it as **outward-looking strategy** which was adopted since 1991 in place of **inward-looking strategy** of import substitution followed earlier. We explain below the various export-promotion measures taken to give export orientation to trade policy.

1. Reduction in Customs Duties to end Anti-Export Bias. As mentioned above, prior to 1991 customs duties of India were the highest in the world and were levied to promote import substitution. These very high customs duties provided a high degree of protection to domestic industries. In actual practice, the high degree of protection lowers efficiency and is not conducive to optimum use and allocation of resources. In the absence of competition from imported products, the prices of domestic goods were high and this served to induce import substitution but worked against promotion for exports. Since prices of products in international markets were lower, it was not profitable to produce for export. Therefore, to remove this anti-export bias and promote the growth of exports, customs duties were reduced and in 2004-05, average rate of customs duties has been reduced to 20 per cent.

2. Devaluation of Rupee. Another important step to promote exports was devaluation of rupee by 20 per cent in July 1991. Devaluation lowered the prices of our exports and gave an important boost to them. Prior to 1991 rupee currency was overvalued and to ensure growth in exports to make some foreign exchange earnings, export subsidy in the form of cash compensatory allowance was provided to exporters. Therefore, along with devaluation cash compensation allowance was withdrawn.

Market-Determined Exchange Rate: Convertibility of Rupee. After two years of reforms in 1993, exchange rate of rupee was made market determined, that is, exchange rate of rupee with foreign currencies was left to be determined by demand for and supply of rupee and other currencies. This implies that rupee can appreciate or depreciate in terms of other currencies every day depending on demand and supply conditions. This flexible exchange rate works to some extent to correct disequilibrium in the balance of payments. However, it is worth mentioning that exchange rate though determined by demand for and supply of foreign exchange can be influenced by RBI through buying and selling of dollars and other foreign currencies in the foreign exchange market. Therefore, present exchange rate system is more correctly described as **managed float.**

It may be noted that over a period of time since 1993, exchange rate of rupee has declined, that is, rupee has depreciated. This has tended to promote exports and discourage imports. In addition to the introduction of market-determined exchange rate rupee has been made convertible on current account of balance of payments, that is, importers can now get their rupees converted into dollars and exporters can sell their dollars for rupees at market-determined exchange rate. Thus, convertibility of rupee has facilitated imports and exports and has contributed to the globalisation of the Indian economy.

3. Liberalisation of Control over Exports. Through continuous review and revisions during the last 20 years controls on exports has been liberalised to the extent that now *all goods may be exported without any restriction except the few items* mentioned in the negative list of exports. The items in the negative list of exports are regulated because of strategic considerations, environmental and ecological grounds, essential domestic requirements, employment generation and on account of socio-cultural heritage.

10 Bimal Jalan, *India's Economic Crisis: The Way Ahead,* Oxford University Press, 1991.

4. **Duty-free Import of Capital Goods for Use in Production for Exports.** A significant export-promoting measure is that capital goods meant to be used for production of exportable products can be imported free of customs duty. There are two windows to fulfil export obligation on FOB (free on board) and NFE (net foreign exchange) basis.

5. **Advance Licences for Imports Against Exports.** Advance licences which are used to import specified raw materials without payment of any customs duty against confirmed export order and/or letter of credit have been made transferable after export obligation has been fulfilled.

6. **Exemption from Tax and Credit Subsidies.** Profits or incomes from exports are *completely exempt from income tax*. Besides, exporters are provided preferential access to credit from banks. Concessional rates of interest are charged for pre-ship and post-ship credit to exporters.

7. **The Duty Drawback Scheme.** In this important scheme of providing incentives to exporters customs duty and excise duty paid on inputs which are used for production of exports are reimbursed to exporters.

8. **Incentive to Exports of Services.** In an attempt to provide massive thrust to export of services EXIM Policy 2003-04 has introduced duty-free import facility for the service sector units having a minimum foreign exchange earning of ₹ 10 lakh. The scheme is likely to provide a major boost to export of services like healthcare, entertainment, professional services and tourism.

9. Small-scale industries (SSI) reservations have been withdrawn from a large number of items so that large-scale producers can produce these items cheaply and export them.

Case for Export Orientation of India's Development Strategy

The export orientation of trade policy (or outward-looking growth strategy) is believed to have many advantages and is regarded as superior to import-substitution policy. We explain some of these advantages below.

First, it has been pointed out that export-oriented trade policy is conducive to *more efficient use and allocation of resources*. Jagdish Bhagwati[11] has emphasized the efficiency gain of export promoting trade strategy. He is of view that export orientation and import liberlisation trade strategy will ensure domestic resource allocation closer to efficient production of goods in accordance with comparative cost of a country. According to him, such a trade strategy will not lead to rent-seeking unproductive activities.

An important advantage of export-oriented strategy arises from *economies of scale* which can be reaped more effectively. As a result, cost per unit of output rises which will tend to lower prices of exports. Lower export prices will help in significant expansion in exports and enable us to earn more foreign exchange. As export demand or market size for a good expands this will lead to economies of scale. With adequate size of market even small-scale and medium enterprises can set up plants of optimum size to enjoy the economies of scale.

Export-oriented trade policy makes substantial contribution to economic growth by *relaxing the foreign exchange constraints.* Export-promoting trade policy places emphasis on industries geared towards earning foreign exchange. This helps to keep the balance of payments in equilibrium. It has been found that import-substitution trade strategy generally causes shortage of foreign exchange and leads to the balance of payments problem, as happened in case of India in 1991. Shortage of foreign exchange and balance of payments problem lower rate of economic growth.

On the other hand, export-oriented trade policy does not have to face the problem of shortage of foreign exchange and is therefore conducive to higher rate of economic growth. Further, a significant merit of export-oriented trade policy is that *it will help to achieve self-reliance, that is, self-sustained*

11 Jagdish Bhagwati, "Export-Promoting Trade Strategy : Issues and Evidence," *The World Bank Research Observer* Vol. 3, No. 1.

growth of the Indian economy. As a matter of fact, import-substitution strategy was adopted in India with the belief that through it we will achieve self-reliance. But the policy underestimated the import intensity of import-substitution process. Import-substitution strategy substantially increased our import requirements for equipment and raw materials. This necessitated a large amount of foreign exchange which could not be earned sufficiently through exports. Thus, far from helping to do away with foreign assistance, import-substitution, strategy increased our dependence on foreign capital inflows.

Export-oriented trade policy coupled with liberalised foreign investment will enable us to earn adequate foreign exchange to solve our balance of payments problem and ensure self-sustained economic growth. Above all, several studies have found a highly positive relation between growth of national income and expansion in export. However, as Balassa has pointed out that for relation between export orientation and economic growth initial conditions matter a lot. These initial conditions include resource endowment, expansion opportunities of trade, stock of technical knowledge. No doubt, these initial conditions are important for determining economic growth. However, trade policy is certainly important for providing incentives for expansion of exports for availing of the opportunities thrown up by international trade. This will lead to the optimum use and allocation of material resources which will stimulate economic growth.

CHAPTER 43

BALANCE OF PAYMENTS PROBLEMS OF DEVELOPING COUNTRIES

As a country is increasingly integrated into the world, its financial transactions with the rest of the world increase. These transactions involve not only imports and exports of goods and services between countries but also capital flows among them. These capital flows are in the form of foreign aid and loans and foreign private investment in the form of portfolio investment by foreign institutional investors and foreign direct investment. *The balance of payments of a country is a systematic record of all economic transactions of residents of a country with the rest of the world during a given period of time*. The main aim of preparing balance of payments accounts is to present an account of all receipts and payments of an open economy on account of goods and services exported and flows of capital received by residents of a country and payments for goods imported, services received and capital transferred to the residents of the other countries of the world. This balance of payments may be in surplus or negative. In case of balance of payments being in surplus, a country will be buying assets in other countries and these will be net capital outflow. On the other hand, balance of payment of a country for a year may be in deficit and, in this country, the foreigners will be buying new assets in it. The main purpose of keeping the balance of payments account is to know the external financial position of a country which helps the government to frame its foreign trade and payments policies and also to adjust its monetory and fiscal policies so that economic growth with external balance is possible.

Today no country in the globalized world can be fully insulated from what happens in the world economy. In 2008 global financial crisis which started in the US impacted several countries of the world including the Indian economy causing a drop in growth, higher deficit in the current account deficit of the balance of payments. Trading of goods and services of developing countries can lead to severe balance of payments difficulties which can act on constraint on their economic growth. In what follows we first explain the meaning and composition of balance of payments of a country. We will then explain the factors that determine balance of payments situation of a developing country, with special reference to India, and the factors that cause deficit or disequilibrium in a country's balance of payments.

Two types of balance of payments of a country are distinguished: (1) Balance of payments on current account and (2) Balance of payments on capital Account. We explain below these two concepts of balance of payments of a country.

Balance of Payments on Current Account

Balance of payments on current account is more comprehensive in scope than *balance of trade*. While balance of trade is concerned only with exports and imports of merchandise goods only, the balance of payments on *current account is a wider concept* and includes not only *traditing of goods but also other foreign transactions such as trade in services, investment income and unilateral transfers (i.e., transfer payments)*. A country, say India, has to make payments to the other countries not only for its imports of merchandise but also for services of banking, insurance and shipping rendered by other countries to India . It has to pay further the expenditure of Indians tourists in foreign countries, interest on loans obtained by India from other countries and such international organizations as the I.M.F., I.B.R.D., etc. These are debit items for India. Since these are *debt terms* for India these transactions involve payments to be made to the foreign countries.

In the same way, the foreign countries import goods from India for which they make payments to India. These are *credit terms* for India and therefore it receives payments from foreigners.

Table 43.1. India's Balance of Payment on Current Account **(in Billions US $)**

S.No.	Item	2009-10	2010-11	2011-12	2012-13	2013-14
1.	Exports	182.2	256.2	309.8	306.6	318.6
2.	Imports	300.6	383.5	499.5	502.3	466.2
3.	**Trade Balance**	– 118.4	– 127.3	– 189.9	– 195.7	– 147.6
		(– 8.6)	(– 7.8)	(– 10.1)	(– 10.6)	N.A
4.	**Invisibles (Net)**	79.9	79.3	111.6	105.5	115.2
	(*i*) Non-Factor Services	35.7	44.1	64.1	64.9	72.9
	(*ii*) Investment Income	– 8.0	– 17.9	– 16.0	–21.5	–23.0
	(*iii*) Private Transfers	52.3	53.1	63.5	64.0	65.3
5.	**Goods and Services Balance**	– 83.0	– 83.2	– 125.7	– 130.7	N.A
6.	**Current Account Balance (Net)**	– 38.4	– 48.1	– 78.2	– 88.2	– 32.4
		(– 2.8)	(– 2.7)	(– 4.2)	(– 4.7)	(– 1.7)

Source: RBI

Note: *Figures in brackets show per cent of GDP at market prices*.

To illustrate the various credit and debit items included in the current account balance we show them in Table 43.1 for five years, 2009-2014. In the first row of this we give the data of merchandise exports (a credit item) and in the second row we give the data of merchandise imports (a debit item). The difference between merchandise exports and imports gives us *trade balance of goods* shown in the third row. India's trade balance is generally *negative* as its imports exceed its exports.

The next row shows invisible items. They are called *invisible* items as they are not recorded at the ports and airports at which goods are exported and imported. In invisibles first item is the services (*non-factor services*) such as charges of services of shipping, insurance, banking etc rendered by the Indian residents to the foreigners **net** of charges of such services rendered by the foreigners to the Indian residents. The second item included in invisibles is investment income in the form of interest and dividends from the residents of a country **net** of the similar incomes paid to the foreigners. The third item in the invisibles is *net private transfers* which include gifts, donations and *remittances* by Indian immigrants from abroad.

It is worth noting that invisible part of the balance of payments on the current account is generally. found to be in surplus in case of India as shown in the fourth row. Therefore, in case of India, the surplus in the invisible account offsets a good part of deficit in trade balance and as a result the deficit on current account balance (CAD) becomes smaller than the trade balance.

In the fifth row we give the balance on account of *both goods and services* (*i.e.,* non-factor services). Note that in Goods and Services balance, investment income (*i.e.*, item 4) (*ii*) and private transfers (*i.e.*, item 4) (*iii*) are not included because though they are treated as invisible items, they do not form parts of services.

Lastly, in row 6 we give current account balance which consists of trade balance and whole of invisibles (*i.e.*, row 4).

It will be seen from Table 43.1 that in all the five years (2009-14) there is deficit in current account balance (CAD) of India. This current account deficit is financed by surplus in the capital account balance or by using some funds from the foreign exchange reserves held by the Reserve Bank of India.

Balance of Payments on Capital Account

The second part of the balance of payments is balance on capital account which relates to foreign capital receipts and payment of debts and claims, that is, capital inflows. If there is deficit on current account, then there should be surplus on capital account for the total balance of payments to be in equilibrium. To explain the various items in the capital accounts, we give India's balance of payments on capital account in Table 43.2 for the five years 2009-14. Important items are *borrowings from foreign countries* and lending funds to other countries. This takes two forms: (*i*) *External assistance* which means aid from foreign countries at *concessional* rates of interest; (*ii*) *External commercial borrowings* under which the Indian Government and the private sector borrow funds from world money markets at the market rates of interest. (*iii*) *The non-resident deposits* are another important item in capital account. These are the deposits made by non-resident Indians (NRI) who keep their surplus funds with Indian banks. (*iv*) Another important item in balance of payments on capital account is *private foreign investment* by foreign companies in India. There are two types of foreign investment. First is *portfolio investment* under which foreign institutional investors (FIIs) *purchase shares and bonds* of Indian companies. The second is *foreign direct investment* (FDI) under which foreign companies set up plants and factories on their own or in collaboration with the Indian companies.

Table 43.2. India's Balance of Payments On Capital Account **(in Billion US $)**

S.No.		Item	2009-10	2010-11	2011-12	2012-13	2013-14
1.		External Assistance (Net)	2.9	4.94	2.3	0.98	1.0
2.		Commercial Borrowings (Net)	2.8	12.16	10.3	8.5	11.8
3.		Non-Resident Deposits (Net)	2.9	3.14	11.9	14.8	38.9
4.		Foreign Investment (Net) of which	50.4	42.13	39.2	46.7	26.4
	(*i*)	FDI net	18.0	11.83	22.1	19.8	21.6
	(*ii*)	Portfolio Investment (Net)	32.4	30.3	17.2	26.9	4.8
	(*iii*)	Other capital flows (Net)	– 13.1	– 10.48	– 7.0	–5.1	–10.8
5.		**Capital Account Total (Net)**	**51.6***	**63.74***	**67.8***	91.9*	47.9
6.		Use of Exchange Reserves*	– 13.4*	(– 13.1)*	(–12.8)*	(–3.8*)	(–15.5)

* Also includes errors and omissions

Source: RBI Annual Report 2012-13 and 2013-14. Use of foreign exchange reserves (-indicates increase of *reserves*, and + indicates decrease of reserves on BOP basis.

The data of various items given in Table 43.2 is *net* basis, that is, for example, external assistance *received* minus the external assistance *given* by India to some other countries. Capital inflows in the capital account can be classified into ***debt creating*** and ***non-debt creating***. Foreign investment (both direct and portfolio) represents non-debt creating capital inflows, whereas external assistance (*i.e.*, concessional loans taken from abroad), external commercial borrowing (ECB) and non-resident deposits are debt-creating capital inflows.

It will be seen from Table 43.2 that for all the five years there is surplus on capital account. This surplus on capital account is used to finance the deficit on current account. Since for these years current account deficit is larger, it is not fully financed by the surplus on capital account. To meet this shortage, some funds from foreign exchange reserves are withdrawn for this purpose. The last row in the capital account is therefore the use of foreign exchange reserves to bridge the deficit.

It is worth mentioning that private capital flows (both private foreign direct investment (FDI) and portfolio investment by FIIs are driven by pull factors such as economic fundamentals of recipient countries and push factors such as economic policies of source countries. It is worth emphasizing that to the extent that current account deficit is financed through capital surplus, it would be better if it is financed through stable and growth-enhancing foreign direct investment (FDI) rather than portfolio capital inflows as the latter are volatile and leave the country in a *short time* causing instability in the share market and exchange rate of rupee.

Distinction Between Current Account and Capital Account

The distinction between the current account and capital account of the balance of payment may be noted. The current account deals with payment for *currently produced goods and services,* that is, GDP. It also includes interest earned or paid on claims and also gifts and donations. *The capital account, on the other hand, deals with capital receipts and payments of debts and claims.* The current account of the balance of payments affects the level of national income directly. For instance, when India sells its currently produced goods and services to foreign countries, the producers of those goods get income from abroad. In other words, current account receipts have the effect of increasing the flow of income in the country. On the other hand, when India imports goods and services from foreign countries and pays them money, capital flows out to foreign countries. Thus, current account payments to foreigners involve reduction of the flow of income within the country and constitute a leakage. Thus, the current account of the balance of payments has a direct effect on the level of income in a country. The capital account, however, does not have such a *direct effect on the level of income;* it *influences the volume of assets which a country holds and debts it has to pay.*

Determinants of Balance of Payments

There are several variables which determine the balance of payments position of a country, *viz.,* national income at home and abroad, the prices of goods and factors, the supply of money, the rate of interest, etc., all of which determine exports, imports, and demand and supply of foreign currency. At the back of these variables lie the supply factors, the state of technology, tastes, distribution of income, economic conditions, the state of expectations, etc. If there is a change in any of these variables and there are no appropriate changes in other variables, disequilibrium will be the result.

The *main cause of disequilibrium in the balance of payment arises from imbalance between exports and imports of goods and services,* that is, deficit or surplus in balance of payments. When for one reason or another exports of goods and services of a country are smaller than their imports, disequilibrium in the balance of payments is the likely result. Exports may be small due to the lack of exportable surplus which in turn results from low production or the exports may be small because of the higher costs and prices of exportable goods and severe competition in the world markets. Important causes of lower exports are higher rate of inflation or rising prices in the country or over-valued exchange rate. When the prices of goods are high in the country, its exports are discouraged and imports encouraged. If it is not matched by other items in the balance of payments, disequilibrium emerges.

The globalization of the economy has an important consequence with regard to capital flows into the economy and influences the balance of payments. Suppose India faces given prices of its imports and a given demand for its exports of goods and services. Under these circumstances , if domestic rate of interest is higher as compared to what exists abroad, then given the mobility of capital, capital will flow into the Indian economy to a very large extent. This principle can be expressed as follows.

$$BP = NX(Y_d, Y_f, R) + CF(I_f - I_d)$$

where BP = balance of payments, NX is net exports of goods and services (*i.e.*, exports–imports which is also called trade balance, CF stands for surplus in the capital account of the balance of payments, that is, capita flows.

The above equation reveals that trade balance (NX) is a function of level of domestic income (Y_d) and foreign income (Y_f) and real rate of exchange (R). The amount of exports being given, an increase in the domestic income due to higher industrial growth or appreciation in real exchange rate of rupee will adversely affect the trade balance (NX) by increasing imports. On the other hand, depreciation in exchange rate of rupee will encourage exports and lower imports and is likely to improve the balance of payments. $I_f - I_d$ in the equation measures net foreign investment, *i.e.*, net capital inflows which are influenced by rate of interest. Further , the above equation shows that higher interest rate in India as compared to that in the foreign countries such as the United States will cause large capital inflows into India.

Equilibrium in the Balance of Payments

It is important to know what do we mean by equilibrium in the balance of payments. The idea of equilibrium in the balance of payments is based on the concepts of *autonomous items* and *accommodating items* in the balance of payments.

The autonomous items in the balance of payments are those items which cannot be influenced or changed so easily or quickly by the Government and they are determined by some basic factors. In this concept of basic balance, besides the items in the current account, *the long-term capital movements* both on private and Government accounts contained in the capital-account balance of payments are regarded as autonomous. On the other hand, in the capital account *short-term capital movements* such as borrowing from IMF or Central Bank of other countries, drawings from SDR with IMF, use of foreign exchange reserves of a country are transitory and *accommodating in nature* and are therefore excluded from the concept of balance of equilibrium. The recourse has to be made to these accommodating items (also called *compensatory items*) so as to ensure equality between payments and receipts of foreign exchange. Changes in the compensatory items are made so as to offset the surplus or deficit in the autonomous items. Thus, "*when autonomous movements cancel out over some appropriate time period and there is no need for compensatory movements, the balance of payments is in equilibrium.*[1] *Note that the equilibrium is a state of balance which can be sustained without intervention by the Government or the Central Bank of a country.*

The concept of equilibrium in the balance of payments can be represented by the following equations:

$$(X - M) + LTC = 0$$

where X stands for exports including invisible items,

M stands for imports including invisible items,

LTC stands for long-term capital movements, that is, autonomous capital flows.

If $(X - M)$ is positive (*i.e.*, $X > M$), then for balance of payments to be in equilibrium, LTC will be negative and equal to $(X - M)$. This implies that there will be *net capital outflow*. On the other hand, if $M > X$, then for the balance of payments to be in equilibrium LTC must be positive (that is, there will be *net capital inflow* to offset the deficit in current account).

When excluding these accommodating items there is neither deficit nor surplus in the overall balance of payments, it is said to be in equilibrium. When in this sense, there is either deficit or surplus, the balance of payments is said to be in disequilibrium. The deficit in balance of payments can be financed by drawings from the IMF, use of SDRs, drawings from the reserves of foreign currencies and aid received from abroad.

1. C. P. Kindleberger, *International Economics*, p. 311.

It follows from above that when the balance of payments of a country is in equilibrium, the demand for the domestic currency is equal to its supply. The demand and supply situation is thus neither favourable nor unfavourable. If the balance of payments moves against a country, adjustments must be made by encouraging exports of goods, services or other forms of exports, or by discouraging imports of all kinds. No country can have a permanently unfavourable (*i.e.*, deficit) balance of payment. Total liabilities and total assets of a nations, as of individuals, must balance in the long run.

Equilibrium in the balance of payments is therefore a sign of the soundness of the economy. However, the disequilibrium may arise either for the short or for long periods. A continued disequilibrium indicates that the country is heading towards economic and financial bankruptcy which will make its growth unsustainable. Therefore, steps should be taken in time to correct this disequilibrium.

Financing and Reducing Balance of Payments Deficits

We have seen above that India like many other developing countries has been facing deficit in current balance. Though a part of this deficit has been financed by surplus on capital account, there still remains a deficit in the combined current and capital account balance *which is financed by drawing down on foreign monetary reserves held by the RBI*. These foreign monetary reserves consist of gold, reserves of some hot currencies such as US Dollar, Pound Sterling, Euro, Japanese Yen and SDR (Special Drawing Rights) with IMF. However, the foreign monetary (or exchange) reserves of a country are not unlimited. It the combined balance of payments on current and capital accounts continue to be deficit for several years, the foreign exchange reserves will soon be exhausted which will put severe strains on the developing economy and greatly affect its ability to import capital goods and raw materials required for its industrial growth. This limited capacity to import will hurt their economic growth and create foreign exchange crisis. Such a crisis situation in balance of payments actually happened in India in 1991 when foreign exchange reserves declined to such a small quantity that they were sufficient to finance only 15 day imports. With such a weak financial situation no one was willing to lend international money (*i.e.,* US Dollars, British Pounds) to India. This forced India to pledge a good amount of gold to Bank of England and Bank of Japan to get necessary foreign exchange to make essential imports required for industrial growth. For some least developed countries with limited foreign exchange reserves which have to import food to feed their hungary population, the deficit in balance of payments poses a great danger to the lives of the millions of the poor people.

To overcome their problems of deficit on combined current and capital accounts, for the developing countries various policy alternatives are available which we explain below.

1. **Expanding Exports and Restricting Imports**: Depending on their ability, the developing countries faced with balance of payments deficit can expand their exports of primary or manufactured goods to eliminate or reduce the deficit. Alternatively, they can reduce imports by adopting the policy of import substitution to produce domestically some of the manufactured goods that are being imported. To restrict imports, the developing countries can levy tariffs on imports and fix physical quotas of imports of some goods. In the next chapter we will explain how through imposition of tariffs and quotas imports of some goods can be reduced and the domestic industries given protection.

The second way in which exports can be expanded and imports reduced to tackle the problem of deficit in balance of payments is the devaluation (or allowing to depreciate their currencies) . It has been noticed that the currencies of the developing countries are often overvalued and their devaluation or depreciation will lower the prices of their exports and raise the prices of their imports. This will help to expand exports and lower imports and thereby will tend reduce deficit in current account deficit. In fact, IMF agrees to give loans to the developing countries to meet the deficit in their balance of payments on the condition of their adopting stabilisation policies and one important measure of them is the devaluation of their currencies by the developing countries.

2. **Structural Adjustment Reforms:** The other important measure is the restrictive fiscal and monetary policies recommended by the World Bank to provide a permanent solution of the balance of payment deficit. Under these structural adjustment reforms, the developing countries have to reduce fiscal deficit by taking some *austerity* measures. This implies reducing government expenditure, drastically reducing subsidies, reducing direct taxes to promote private investment. Besides, structural adjustment reforms also include reduction in tariffs on imports to open up the economy to free foreign trade and to encourage foreign private investment, both direct and portfolio. It is worth mentioning that all these structural adjustment and stabilisation measures were taken by India while carrying out economic reforms since 1991 as their compliance was part of the conditionalities for getting aid from IMF and World Bank to bail India out of balance of payments crisis. However, as we will discuss in a later chapter, promoting private direct foreign investment has wider implications from the viewpoint of development of the developing countries than mere transfer of financial or capital resources.

Lastly, the developing countries can reduce the detrimental effect of chronic balance of payments deficit by building up the stock of official monetary reserves which include gold, reserves of US Dollars, British Pounds and Special Drawing Rights (SDR) with IMF, which are also known as "**paper gold**'. In 1970, to supplement the limited stock of gold and US dollars and facilitate international payments, IMF was authorised to create special drawing rights of the countries which can be used by the member countries. On certain financial strength and deposits of gold and dollars with the IMF, the different countries were allotted certain amounts of SDRs. They work in the similar way as paper money is used in a domestic economy for making payments for goods and services and settlement of debt. In recent years India has been accumulating more SDRs. Besides, the Reserve Bank of India has purchased quite a large amount of gold from IMF. This has enabled India to make necessary payments to foreign countries so as to prevent detrimental impact of larger deficit in balance of payments as was faced by India in 1991.

CHAPTER 44

THEORY OF PROTECTION AND TARIFF

Introduction

In this chapter we shall explain theory of protection which is a highly important issue in foreign trade. The foreign trade policy has been the subject of heated discussion since the time of Adam Smith who advocated for free trade and recommended that tariffs should be removed to avail of the advantages of free trade. Even today, economists are divided over this question of foreign trade policy. Various arguments have been given for and against free trade. If the policy of protection of domestic industries is adopted, the question is whether for this purpose tariffs should be imposed on imports or quantitative restrictions through quota and licensing be applied. In India certain political parties and groups have been demanding a policy of '*Swadeshi*' which in essence means that domestic industries should be protected against low-priced imports of goods from abroad, that is, free foreign trade should not be allowed.

Besides Adam Smith, the other famous classical economist, David Ricardo, in his famous work "*On the Principles of Political Economy and Taxation*" also defended free trade to promote efficiency and productivity in the economy. We have seen in a previous chapter that Adam Smith and the other earlier economists thought that it pays a country to specialise in the production of those goods which it can produce more cheaply than any other country and import those goods which it can obtain at less cost or price than it would cost to produce them at home. This means they should specialise according to absolute cost advantage. However, Ricardo put forward the 'Theory of Comparative Cost' where he demonstrated that to obtain benefits from trade it is not necessary that countries should produce those goods for which their absolute cost of production is the lowest. He proved that it could pay a country to import a good even though it could produce that good at a lower cost, if its cost is relatively lower in the production of some other good. Ricardo's theory of trade rests on the idea of relative efficiency or comparative cost.

Despite the classical arguments for free trade to promote efficiency and well-being of the people, various countries have been following the protectionist policies which militate against free trade. By imposing heavy tariff duties on imports of goods or fixing quotas of imports they have prevented free trade to take place between countries. Several arguments have been given in favour of protection. We explain below the various arguments given in favour of protection.

CASE FOR PROTECTION

Despite gains from free trade, many arguments have been given against free trade and in favour of protection. By protection we mean in order to safeguard the domestic industries from low-priced imports some barriers against import of foreign goods are imposed. Some arguments given in defence of protection are irrational and invalid, whereas some are valid. We critically examine below various arguments given in favour of protection (*i.e.*, against free foreign trade). Protection has been defended on the basis of nationalistic feeling. It has been said that patriotism requires that people of a country should buy products of their domestic industries rather than foreign products. In the USA there has been a campaign '*Be American, buy American*' appealing people to buy American goods instead of imported foreign products. Similarly, in India the campaign of '*Swadeshi*' appeals to the patriotic feeling of the Indian people that we should protect our indigenous industries and impose barriers on imports of foreign goods or provide subsidies to our industries. However, this argument is misplaced and invalid. Those policy-makers who yield to such arguments deny the people of a country the gains from trade such as rise in productive efficiency and greater well-being, stimulus to growth through higher capital formation and spread of superior technology. The policy of protection in the name of nationalism or *swadeshi* is actually contrary to our national interests because it promotes inefficiency and prevents rapid economic growth. However, in defence of protection important economic arguments have been given which we will critically examine below.

Employment Argument

An important argument for protection is that it will lead to increase in domestic employment or at least preserves present domestic employment. It is often believed that imports of goods from abroad reduce domestic employment. Therefore, if instead of imports we produce those goods at home, employment in the country will increase. Besides, as prices of imported goods are lower, the domestic producers would not be able to compete with them and may be competed out of the market. This will destroy even present jobs in the domestic industries. It is therefore concluded that protection of domestic industries will lead to their expansion and therefore employment in them will increase.

In our view employment argument for protection is not logical and valid. This argument ignores the adverse effects of protection on our industries. An important economic principle is that exports must pay for imports. If imports are restricted by imposing barriers, the exports cannot remain unaffected. For example, many raw materials and capital goods are imported to be used in domestic industries which export goods. If imports are restricted, exports will therefore fall. This will lead to the decline in employment in export industries which will offset the increase in employment in the import-substituting industries.

Further, when you restrict imports to protect domestic industries so that they should expand, other countries are likely to retaliate and will impose restrictions on our exports which are imported by them. This too will reduce exports and cause reduction in employment in export industries. Thus net effect on employment of restricting imports for providing protection to domestic industries may not be positive.

Infant Industry Argument

A powerful argument given in support of protection, especially in the context of developing countries, is that infant industries should be provided protection from the competition of low-priced imports of the mature and well-established industries of the industrialised developed countries. Shortly after American Revolution, Alexander Hamilton argued that British industrial supremacy was due to its early start over American infant industries. He pointed out that these infant American industries required temporary protection for some time so that they should grow and achieve production efficiency and economies of scale before they could successfully compete with low-cost British goods. He thus argued that temporary protection of infant American industries was necessary for industrial development of America.

Similarly, the infant industry argument has been advanced for protecting infant industries of the developing countries from competition of the low-cost firms of the industrialised developed countries. It has been argued that, given some time, these infant industries will grow and will be able to benefit from the economies of scale and learn the techniques necessary to lower their cost of production. As a result, over a period of time their cost per unit will go down and these industries will therefore be in a position to compete with the foreign imports. Therefore, for some time they should be protected otherwise they would be destroyed by foreign competition.

However, there are some lacunae in infant industry argument. First, it is assumed that protected infant industries will make efforts to lower cost when provided protection. However, actual experience shows that it is more likely that protected industries lose incentives to become efficient and lower cost. It is said "*once an infant, always an infant*." Secondly, even if an industry makes efforts to improve productivity and lower cost per unit when it is provided protection, it has been assumed in the argument that the Government is the best judge as to which industries will prove to be capable of competing low-priced foreign goods. It has been asserted in defence of free trade that selection of industries which will acquire competitive strength can be done better by private market mechanism. It is pointed out that when opening up the economy to foreign competition the domestic industries would try to increase their efficiency. As a result, only those industries will survive which are efficient and produce at a lower cost. Therefore, it is better if the domestic industries are left to foreign competition and in this way they will have incentives to improve productivity to escape from losses. Only those domestic industries will survive and operate which are efficient and produce at a low cost per unit.

Indian automobile industry is a shining example of an industry not making any efforts to become efficient even after given protection for more than three decades. Before the setting up of Maruti Udyog with Japanese collaboration, Indian car industry was fully protected by heavy duties on imports of cars. The two domestic firms producing Ambassador and Fiat cars did not make any efforts to improve their efficiency, nor did they bring out any better models of their cars. It is only after 1991 following the policy of liberalisation that new foreign firms such as Daewoo of South Korea, General Motors of the U.S. have come in India and are producing new models and at relatively low prices. Even Maruti is now trying to improve its efficiency further and brought out new models of Maruti such as Aristo and Esteem.

However, it may be noted that in developing countries the Government is in a better position to protect certain industries such as steel and cement *which lead to an expansion of the infrastructure of the developing economies*. This is because these industries create external economies and the private firms will not be compensated for creating these external benefits.

Anti-Dumping Argument

The other important argument for protection is that foreign producers compete unfairly by dumping the goods in another country. Dumping is a form of price discrimination when producers of a country sell goods in another country at lower prices than those charged at home. Of course, consumers in a country in which foreign goods are dumped are beneficiaries, the industries of that country suffer as they are unable to compete with the '*dumped goods*'. Besides, there is more harmful '*predatory dumping*' which implies that foreign firms try to sell goods in other countries even below their cost to establish a worldwide monopoly by driving competitors out of the market. Once the local industries are competed out, they raise prices to obtain monopoly profits.

There is a lot of evidence that firms of USA and Japan often indulge in dumping of their goods in other countries to eliminate competition. But, in our view, instead of providing protection to domestic industries through tariff or non-tariff barriers, it will be a better policy to enact laws against dumping. Dumping should be prohibited by law declaring it illegal. In India such a law has been enacted but is not being properly implemented.

Correcting Balance of Payments Deficit

Correcting deficit in balance of payments is also mentioned as justification for imposing tariffs to restrict imports or fixing of quotas of imports. This appears to be a valid argument for providing protection. Due to rising imports of raw materials and capital equipment for their industrial development, the developing countries often face deficit in their balance of payments. Because of the protectionist policies by the developed countries, their exports have not been increasing. To finance the deficit in their balance of payments, they often borrow from abroad. This ultimately leads to increase in their burden of debt which leads to foreign exchange crisis. This happened in case of India when it borrowed heavily from abroad during the nineteen eighties to finance its industrial growth which resulted in balance of payments crisis in 1990-1991. This too happened in case of East Asian countries some of whom also grew through foreign borrowing and landed themselves in foreign exchange crisis. Therefore, many economists have argued that developing countries adopt protectionist policies to achieve sustained growth. However, in our view the solution for fundamental disequilibrium in the balance of payments lies in the adoption of suitable adjustments in exchange rate, appropriate fiscal and monetary policies to lower domestic prices so as to encourage exports. The deficit in balance of payments can be reduced by ensuring rapid growth in exports of a country.

Conclusion

We have critically examined the various arguments in favour of protection. Some of them are valid, others appear to be misplaced. Some people consider trade as a ***'zero sum game'***, that is, in trading if one gains, the other loses. This has given rise to the doctrine of exploitation. For example, it is believed by some that the developing countries like India are exploited by the developed countries such as the USA, Japan and Britain. That is, the developing countries are net losers in trading with the developed countries. However, in our view, this is wrong thinking. No trade can occur without expectations of gain. India would not have entered into trade relations with USA if it did not expect to gain from it. Trade occurs between two countries if it benefits both the trading partners, the developed and the developing countries. Therefore, in our view world trade should be promoted by lifting barriers put up by various countries based on wrong notions about effects of free trade. Some countries such as USA and Japan have resorted to protectionist measures as a retaliation against foreign countries who restrict imports into their countries. The retaliatory actions of imposing trade barriers have done great harm to the expansion of world trade. New international organisation WTO (World Trade Organisation) which has replaced earlier GATT has framed rules which every country should observe so that barriers to trade be removed and world trade be promoted without doing any injustice to the member countries. It may be noted that retaliatory activities of restricting imports from foreign countries generally lead to the depression in the economies of the world as it happened during the worldwide depression of 1930s. The retaliatory activities may cause another global depression.

TARIFF AND PROTECTION

Tariff is an important means of protecting domestic industries against competition from the low prices of imported products. The rates of the tariffs are not so high as to completely prohibit imports into the country. Rise in prices of imported products as a result of imposing tariffs, foreign producers lose their competitive strength. There are two main reasons advanced for protection of domestic industries from imports by developing countries. First, the developing countries which adopted import-substituting industrialisation of their economies require to replace the imports by producing the goods at home. This requires the protection of their infant industries which had higher unit cost of production. It was pointed out that once the infant domestic industries have recorded sufficient growth, they will be able to enjoy the economies of scale and also gain through learning by doing, their unit cost of production will fall and enable them to compete with the imported foreign products. In the mean time they need protection from imports by the imposition of tariffs. The imposition of tariffs on the imported products raises their prices and thereby provides protection to the domestic industries producing those products.

It is worth mentioning that most of the developed countries registered industrial growth by protecting their industries through levying tariffs. Once having been industrially developed they become champions of free trade. However, even now, when agreement has been made about reduction of tariffs, they prevent the entry of labour-intensive manufactured products of developing countries through one way or the other. It has been pointed out by Todaro and Smith that "WTO rules eliminated many formal barriers but many implicit barriers remain. Anti-dumping investigations increased significantly, reaching a peak in 1999 and the United States was the largest user of these protectionist measures. Although the number of new investigations declined in the early years of the new century, they remained an important weapon in the protectionist arsenal. Countervailing duty impositions are also on the rise. Regional trading agreements, including the North American Free Trade Agreement (NAFTA) and the EU may also have the effect of discriminating and the EU may also have the effect of discriminating against exports from non-member developing countries."[1] Thus, the protectionist measures still being adopted by the US and EU further induce the developing countries to protect their industries from unfair foreign competition.

Second, it has been argued that, since many developing countries face difficulties of balance of payments, they have to restrict imports to reduce their current account deficit (CAD). For example, in India due to heavy imports, its current account deficit has exceeded 4 per cent of GDP in some years. As foreign capital flows are very volatile, sometimes it becomes difficult to finance the deficit and recourse has therefore to be made to use foreign exchange reserves held by the Reserve Bank of India to finance it. As the foreign exchange reserves with the RBI are limited, they cannot be a permanent solution of the deficit in balance of payments.

In view of the balance of payments difficulties faced by the developing countries, they raise tariffs to reduce imports and thereby improve the balance of payments situation. Thus, in case of developing countries, "Although initial costs of production may be higher than former import prices, the economic rationale put forward for the establishment of import-substituting manufacturing operations is either that industry will be able to reap the benefits of large-scale production and lower costs (the so called *infant industry* argument for tariff protection) or that the *balance of payments will be improved* as fewer consumer goods are imported"[2].

Diagrammatic Illustration of How Tariff Can be Used for Protection

We now explain how tariff can be used to protect an industry. Let us take a product, computers, in which India does not have a comparative advantage. The protective effect of levying tariff on the import of computers from the US can be illustrated through simple demand and supply curves of computers in India. In Fig. 44.1, we have drawn domestic demand curve D_d and supply curve S_d of computers in India. These domestic demand and supply curves of computers intersect at point *E*. In the absence of foreign trade in computers, the domestic price P_3 is determined at which quantity OQ_3 of computers is produced and sold in India.

Now, suppose India opens up to world trade where the price P_1 prevails. Since India's market for computers is quite small relative to the total world market, it will take the world price P_1 as given for it and therefore can buy computers as much as it likes at the world price P_1. As a result, with free trade the consumers of India will buy the quantity Q_5 at price P_1 as indicated by the domestic demand curve D_d. Note that as compared to the quantity Q_3 in case of no trade, with free trade quantity purchased by the domestic consumers has risen to Q_5 at the lower world price P_1. However, the domestic producers of computers will supply only the quantity Q_1 at world price P_1. The remaining supply of the computer Q_1Q_5 (= *GH*) will be imported at world price P_1. Thus, with free trade the domestic producers of computers will be adversely affected.

Now suppose to protect its domestic computer industry Indian Government imposes a tariff '*t*' on the imports of computers. Suppose with this tariff the price of imported computers rises from P_1 to P_2. At this higher imported price P_2, the quantity demanded by the domestic consumers will fall

1 Todaro and Smith, *op.cit.*, (10th edition), p. 623.

2 Todaro and Smith, *op.cit.*, p. 624.

to Q_4 and the quantity supplied by the domestic producers of computers will increase to Q_2 and the remaining quantity demanded equal to Q_2Q_4 ($= RT$) will be imported. Thus, with the imposition of tariff the domestic producers have gained as their production has increased to Q_2. However, with imposition of tariff the consumers have suffered a loss of consumer surplus equal to the total area P_1HTP_2 which consists of areas $a + b + c + e$. With the imposition of tariff equal to P_1P_2 the Government has earned the revenue equal to the rectangular *shaded* area *JKTR* which it can use for other purposes.

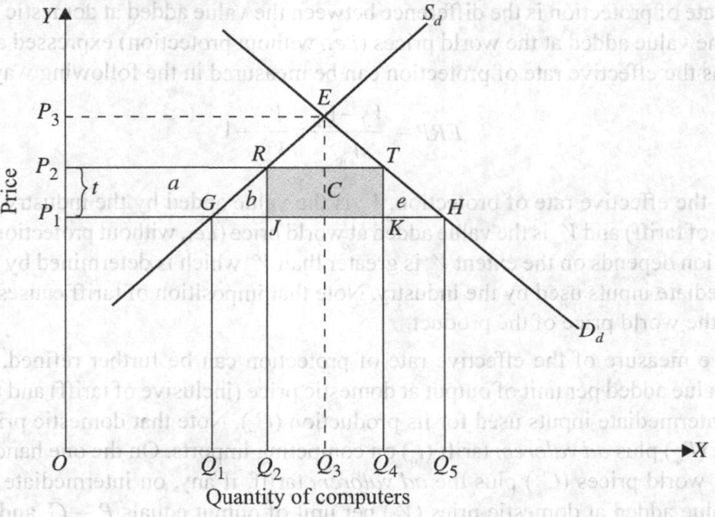

Fig. 44.1. *Protection by tariff*

It may be further noted that if Government raises tariff on computers equal to P_1P_3, the imports will fall to zero and the whole quantity demanded at price P_3 will be met by the domestic producers of computers. But with such a prohibitive tariff though the domestic computer industry has got full protection, the consumers have suffered a great loss of welfare as a result of protection they have now been deprived of purchasing imported cheaper computers.

EFFECTIVE RATE OF PROTECTION

To what extent the imposition of a tariff on an industry's product provides protection to it requires a proper measure. The rate of tariff imposed on a commodity raises the price of the commodity and therefore the percentage by which the domestic price rises as a result of levying tariff represents the *nominal rate of tariff*. The nominal rate of tariff is therefor defined as

$$t_0 = \frac{P_t - P}{P}$$

where P_t is the domestic price inclusive of tariff (*i.e.*, with protection) and P is the price without tariff (*i.e.*, under free trade).

For example, if a particular model of a car has domestic price inclusive of tariff equal to ₹ 5 lakh and its import price at the entry at port (*i.e.*, CIF or cost, plus insurance plus freight) is ₹ 4 lakh, then nominal rate of tariff (t) would be $\frac{5-4}{4} = \frac{1}{4} = 0.25$. However, nominal rate of tariff does not correctly reflect the extent of protection to an industry. To find the actual degree of protection one must not only consider the tariff on the final product but also the tariff, if any, on the intermediate inputs that the industry uses to produce the final product. This implies that for measuring actual or effective protection received by an industry we should consider value added by an industry. Note that the value added by an industry equals the sum of wages, interest, rent and depreciation allowance payable by the firms in the industry. Effective rate of protection of an industry is the extent (*i.e.*, percentage) by which value added by an industry at the domestic price as a result of protection (*i.e.*, inclusive of tariff) exceeds the value added if the industry had got no tariff protection from the foreign imported product and had to face unrestricted competition in the free world market. In other words, the effective rate of protection is the difference between the value added at domestic prices inclusive of tariff and the value added at the world prices (*i.e.*, without protection) expressed as percentage of the latter. Thus the effective rate of protection can be measured in the following way:

$$ERP = \frac{V_d - V_w}{V_w} = \frac{V_a}{V_w} - 1 \qquad \ldots (1)$$

where *ERP* is the effective rate of protection, V_d is the value added by the industry with protection (*i.e.*, inclusive of tariff) and V_w is the value added at world price (*i.e.*, without protection). The effective rate of protection depends on the extent V_d is greater than V_w which is determined by the rate of tariff on the intermediate inputs used by the industry. Note that imposition of tariff causes domestic price to rise above the world price of the product.

The above measure of the effective rate of protection can be further refined. The difference between the value added per unit of output at domestic price (inclusive of tariff) and the cost per unit of output of intermediate inputs used for its production (C_d). Note that domestic price (P_d) is equal to world price (P_w) plus *ad valorem* tariff (t_0) on competing imports. On the one hand, domestic cost equals cost at world prices (C_w) plus the *ad valorem* tariff, if any, on intermediate material inputs (t_i), that is, value added at domestic pries (V_d) per unit of output equals $P_d - C_d$ and value added at world prices equals $P_w - C_w$. Given these expressions effective rate of protection given in equation (1) can be rewritten as

$$ERP = \frac{P_d - C_d}{P_w - C_w} - 1 \qquad \ldots (2)$$

As we are considering *ad valorem* tariff (which is percentage of world price, $P_d = P_w + P_w t_0 = P_w (1 + t_0)$. Likewise $C_d = C_w + C_w t_i = C_w(1 + t_i)$ where t_0 is the tariff on the finished product and t_i is the tariff on intermediate materials input. With this the effective rate of protection given in equation (2) above can be written as:

$$ERP = \frac{P_w(1+t_0) - C_w(1+t_i)}{P_w - C_w} - 1$$

$$= \frac{P_w + P_w t_0 - C_w - C_w t_i}{P_w - C_w} - 1$$

$$= \frac{P_w - C_w + P_w t_0 - C_w t_i}{P_w - C_w} - 1$$

$$= 1 + \frac{P_w t_0 - C_w t_i}{P_w - C_w} - 1$$

$$ERP = \frac{P_w t_0 - C_w t_i}{P_w - C_w} \qquad \ldots (3)$$

Thus, the effective rate of protection depends on the following factors :

1. The nominal rate of tariff on the finished product (t_0);
2. The world price (P_w) of finished product and the world price of material inputs (C_w);
3. The nominal rate of tariff (t_i) on the imported intermediate material inputs of the finished product; and
4. The value added at world prices,that is, $P_w - C_w$.

We now give a numerical example of calculating effective rate of protection by giving some examples using equation (3) above. Suppose that $150 worth of cloth valued at world prices will need $ 100 of imported material inputs such as cotton and dyes valued at world prices. In this case the value added by cloth is equal to $ 150 – 100 = $ 50 at world prices. Now, if Government levies import duty (*i.e.*, tariff) of 20% on *both* the competitive imports of the finished cloth and material inputs of cotton and dyes, then the effective rate of protection is :

$$ERP = \frac{P_w t_0 - C_w t_i}{P_w - C_w}$$

$$= \frac{(150 \times 0.20) - (100 \times 0.20)}{150 - 100}$$

$$= \frac{30 - 20}{50} = \frac{10}{50} = 0.20 \text{ , } i.e., \text{ } 20\%$$

It follows from above that if *the uniform nominal rate of tariff is levied on both the final product and the material inputs, the effective rate of protection (ERP) will equal the nominal rate of tariff.*

However, in order to protect investment in an industry, the Government levies 20% tariff on the import of computers (*i.e.*, final product) and no tariff on the imports of material inputs used in the production of computers, then

$$\text{ERP} = \frac{150(0.20) - 100(0)}{150 - 100}$$

$$= \frac{30}{50} = 0.6, \text{ } i.e., \text{ } 60\%$$

Thus in this case effective rate of protection is 60 per cent, that is, 3 times the nominal rate of tariff of 20% on the final product.

Take the third example. Suppose that on the imported computer the import duty is 30 per cent whereas the import duty on its material inputs is 20 per cent, then

$$ERP = \frac{150(0.30) - 100(0.20)}{150 - 100}$$

$$= \frac{45 - 20}{50} = \frac{25}{50} = 0.5 \text{ or } 50\%$$

It follows from the last two examples that the modest nominal protective tariff rate of 20% and 30% on the final product provides much higher, 3 times and 2.5 times respectively, of effective rate of protection. The higher effective rate of protection to an industry encourages business men to invest more in the industry as it yields much higher value added which not only gives them more profits but also enables them to pay higher wages, interest and rent. This ensures the faster development of the domestic industry of the country which will enable it to substitute imports.

It is also worthwhile to note that the effective rate of protection is generally greater than nominal rate of tariff. But *if nominal rate of tariff on the competing imports of material inputs is greater than that on the finished product, then the effective rate of protection will be negative*. However, this form of tariff structure is unlikely to exist in the real world. In actual practice, the consumer goods industries in the developing countries are highly protected to ensure import-substituting industrialisation. The capital goods in the developing countries get less degree of protection because high tariffs on capital goods discourage investment in the developing countries. Thus, in actual practice the performance of most of the developing countries is quite disappointing. Their poor performance in respect of industrial growth is attributed to some extent the high effective rates of protection provided to the final consumer goods and less effective protection to the intermediate and capital goods industries. This has resulted in more allocation of scarce resources to inefficient production of highly protected final consumer goods by the developing countries with the development of indigenous capital and intermediate goods industries remaining underdeveloped. This has caused rise in costs of production of domestic consumer goods industries.

Protection and Quotas

Import quotas are another instrument used to check free trade. Import quotas refer to the maximum quantities of goods which may be permitted to be imported during any period of time. They are also referred to as *quantitative restrictions* on imports. Quotas are more effective method of reducing trade than tariffs. A given commodity may be imported in a relatively large quantity despite high tariffs but low quotas totally stop the imports of a commodity beyond the fixed quota of the commodity. Since international negotiations to reduce trade barriers have tended to focus on tariffs, the various countries have resorted to non-tariff barriers to free trade. We discuss below the effects of quotas.

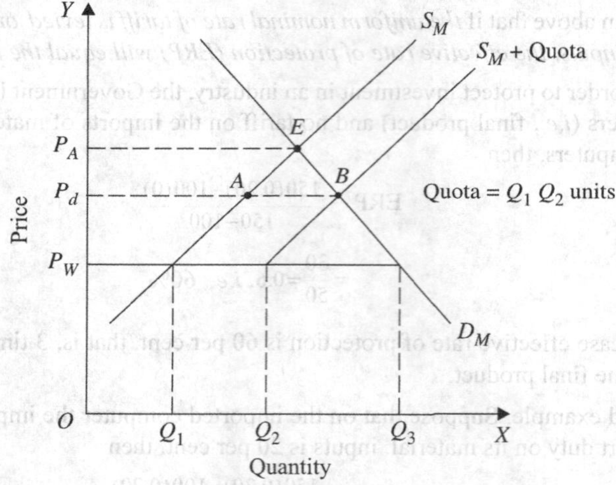

Fig. 44.2. *Protection through quota*

Since quota limits the imports of a commodity, it reduces supply of a commodity in a country as compared to the case with a free trade. Like tariffs, quotas raise the prices of imported goods and encourage domestic production of those goods. But in case of quotas, the government does not collect any revenue. Quotas may be imposed against imports from all countries or used against the imports of only a few countries.

Economic effects of quota are graphically shown in Fig. 44.2 where *DM* and *SM* are domestic demand and supply curves of a commodity respectively. In the absence of trade, price of the commodity in the country is P_A. Suppose the world price of the product is P_w. Under free trade, at price P_w of the commodity the domestic producers of the country will produce OQ_1 quantity but as domestic demand of the product at price P_w is OQ_3, the quantity Q_1Q_3 represents the imports at the world price

P_w. Now assume that the Government imposes a quota and fixes the quantity of the product equal to Q_1Q_2 to be imported. With this the total supply of the product in the domestic market will be away from the domestic supply S_M equal to the distance $Q_1\,Q_2$. Incorporating the quota equal to $Q_1\,Q_2$, we draw a new supply curve S_M + Quota, which lies to the right of the domestic supply curve S_M in the absence of trade. It will be seen from Fig. 44.2 that interaction of the supply curve (S_M + Quota) with the domestic demand curve D_M determines price P_d which is higher than the world price P_w. It will be seen from Fig. 44.2 that difference *AB* between demand and domestic supply at price P_d is exactly equal to the fixed quota of Q_1Q_2 quantity of imports. It is thus dear that, like tariffs, fixation of quota has served to protect the domestic industry and raise price. It will therefore have same effects as we have explained in case of tariff. It may however be noted that, unlike tariff, in case of quota Government would not collect any revenue.

Post-GATT International Economic Order and WTO

GATT (General Agreement on Tariffs and Trade)

During the period of Great Depression (1929-33) and the Second World War various countries imposed high tariffs on the imports to protect domestic industries. They followed what is called '*Beggar Thy Neighbour*' policy. The high tariffs resulted in large shrinking of world trade bringing about loss of efficiency in resource use in the world economy. As a reaction against the devastation caused by high tariffs during the thirties and Second World War period, the General Agreement on Tariffs and Trade (GATT) was established in 1947 after the Second World War. GATT aimed at liberalisation of trade between countries through multilateral trading system and sought to promote trade between various countries by *reducing tariffs significantly*. GATT organised various rounds of negotiations between member countries that led to reduction of tariffs. As a result, not only trade between countries increased but world GNP also significantly rose after 1947.

In one of the negotiations carried out by GATT, Kenedy Round, which began in early, 1960s member countries agreed to make large reduction in tariffs starting from 1967. Another Round Tokyo Round, resulted in further cuts in tariffs in 1979.

In the latest round under GATT, **Uruguay Round**, negotiations started in 1986 and concluded in 1994. After several years of negotiations comprehensive agreement was reached on a set of proposals which is popularly called **Dunkel Draft** as it was prepared by Arthur Dunkel who was then Director General of GATT. In this agreement 40 per cent reduction in tariffs was reached. This sought to promote world trade significantly. Besides, Uruguay Round of talks established a world body called WTO (World Trade Organisation) to achieve further liberalisation of free trade among countries. WTO came into existence in January 1995. WTO replaced GATT . The objective of WTO is to ensure efficiency in use of world resources and specialisation of various countries in accordance with their comparative advantage.

An important step in global commercial policy in setting up of World Trade Organisation (WTO) is a very important trade organisation to promote free trade among different countries. Protection has harmful effects on economic growth and consumer welfare. Bretton Woods Conference held in 1944 which recommended the setting up of International Monetary Fund (IMF) and World Bank (WB) also recommended the establishment of an International Trade Organisation (ITO) to promote free trade among nations. However, while IMF and World Bank were established in 1946, agreement to set up International Trade Organisation could not be finally reached because the US Congress did not ratify the agreement. Instead, a less formal organisation called GATT (General Agreement on Tariffs and Trade) was set up to guide the international trading system based on rules and principles agreed between the member countries. However, it was found to be weak and ineffective although it succeeded in achieving its objective of promoting world trade to some extent by bringing down the level of tariffs on manufactured products imposed by the developed countries. The process of liberalisation of trade, however, suffered a setback since 1974. Although the process of reducing tariff barriers continued, non-tariff barriers (NTBs) were substantially increased by various countries including the developed countries. Strangely enough, it was found that while the developed countries were adopting non-tariff barriers such as quantitative restrictions to protect their industries, the developing countries were liberalising their trade by reducing tariff on the imports from the developed countries.

WORLD TRADE ORGANISATION (WTO)

WTO started with 125 countries. But seven more States including China and Russia were admitted later on as members. Members range from the top four world trade powers—the United States, the European Union, Japan and Canada—to the increasingly influential emerging developing economies of Asia such as India and China to some of the world's poorest countries, like Bangladesh, Guinea.

The objective of WTO agreements is to *establish* a *multilateral trading system* in order to promote free and fair trade among nations. Dunkel Act on which WTO has been founded is wedded to liberalisation of trade based on comparative costs. Accordingly, this provides for a multilateral framework for trade not only in industrial and agricultural goods but also in services. It also seeks to protect *trade related intellectual property rights (TRIPS)*. By committing the member countries to give Most Favoured Nation (MFN) treatment to all trading partners, it has sought to discourage bilateral trading so as to encourage multilateral trading system.

At present there are 148 member countries of WTO and includes both developed and developing countries of the world.

It is important to note a significant difference between GATT and WTO. Under GATT, a member country could lodge a trade complaint against any other member country. GATT investigated the matter to find out whether the complaint was genuine. However, if investigations by GATT found that complaint was valid, it has no power to enforce its decision. As a result GATT's findings were generally ignored by the offending country. However, under WTO, a country can file a trade complaint against another country of violating a WTO rule, its dispute redressal authority would investigate the matter and give its verdict within 6 months and its decision would be legally binding on the offending country to accept it and act accordingly. If the offending country continues to violate, the complainant will be legally entitled to retaliate. Besides, the country that found to be guilty of violating WTO rule, can be penalised by imposing restrictions on its exports.

WTO is officially defined as the legal and institutional foundation of the *multilateral trade system*. Unlike GATT, the WTO is a permanent organisation created by international treaty ratified by the governments and legislatures of member States. As the principal international body concerned with solving trade problems between countries and providing a forum for multilateral trade negotiations, it has global status similar to that of the International Monetary Fund and the World Bank.

But unlike them, it is not a United Nations agency although it has a 'cooperative relationship' with the United Nations. Its underlying documents are a General Agreement consisting of a 38-article code aimed at ensuring open and fair trade in goods, services, agricultural produce and textiles and 500 pages of specific agreements reached at the Uruguay Round.

Salient Features of WTO

The following fundamental principles have been provided for the functioning of WTO as a multiple trading system :

(a) Market Access Commitment. WTO agreements which seek to establish multilateral trading system require the member countries to undertake market access commitment on reciprocity basis. In fact, market access is ensured by abolishing non-tariff barriers as well as by reducing tariffs. The understanding on market access requires that member countries will cut tariffs on industrial goods and agricultural products by about 37 per cent. In order to provide market access for the products of developing countries to the USA, USA agreed to cut down farm subsidies. The developing countries are also required to reduce agricultural subsidies to the level of 10 per cent of the value of agricultural produce.

In the area of trade in services, market access has been ensured by giving foreign service suppliers the same treatment as domestic service suppliers.

(b) Decision at the Ministerial Level Meeting. Another feature of WTO agreement is that it has upgraded decision-making at the ministerial level. Important decisions regarding trade related matters are to be taken at the Ministerial level meetings. Ministerial level meetings have now been incorporated in the legal structure of WTO.

(c) Wider Range of Issues. Another important feature of WTO is that it wil deal with not only issues and disputes relating to trade in goods but also the whole range of issues concerning trade in services and intellectual property rights.

(d) Multilateral Trading System. The most important features of WTO is that it seeks to establish just and fair multilateral system of international trade wherein the developed countries, the developing countries, and the least developing countries all have equal opportunities for market access of their products in foreign countries and wherein in discriminatory trade barriers and unjust Government support to exports by different countries have to be eliminated.

WTO AGREEMENTS AND LIBERALISATION

We discuss below various WTO agreements which seek to promote liberalisation of trade.

(1) Liberalisation of trade in manufactures
(2) Liberalisation of agricultural trade
(3) General Agreement on trade in services (GATS)
(4) Trade related Intellectual Property Rights (TRIPS)
(5) Trade related Investment Measures (TRIMS).

Liberalisation of Trade in Manufactures: Agreement on Tariff Bindings and Tariff Reduction

The main agreements with regard to trade liberalisation in manufactures are:

Firstly, the provision for expansion of tariff bindings which prevent the developed countries from increasing tariff rates in future beyond a particular level. Tariff bindings cover 99 per cent of imports. Secondly, the agreement provides for reduction in tariff rates by the developed countries by 40 per cent from 6.2 to 3.7 per cent. Thirdly, the agreement provides for expansion of duty-free access from 20 to 43 per cent of their imports by the developed countries.

It is however important to note that gain to the developing countries from tariff reduction by the developed countries is not very significant. The average reduction of tariffs on their imports to the developed countries is estimated at 30 per cent and in case of labour-intensive industrial products such as textiles, clothing, leather goods and certain processed primary products such as fish products which are regarded as sensitive, the reduction in tariffs is less than even the average reduction of 30 per cent.

On the other hand, the offers of tariff cuts on imports of manufactures by the developing countries are estimated at about one-third of the average tariff reduction by the whole world. The expansion of tariff bindings which prevent the developing countries from increasing tariffs in future represent significant gains for the developed countries.

Agreement on Agriculture

To achieve liberalisation of agricultural trade, agreement on agriculture was also reached during multinational trade negotiations resulting in the establishment of WTO in 1995. Agreement on agriculture was highly significant as agriculture was a highly protected sector in the developed countries. This distorted world prices of agricultural products as it prevented the developing countries to realise the benefits of their comparative advantage. As a result, exports of developing countries could not increase significantly. Agreement on agriculture includes the following conditions :

(a) **Tariffication.** It was agreed that existing non-tariff barriers imposed by the member countries would by replaced by suitable tariffs which would provide almost the same level of protection. This is called tariffication.

(b) **Tariff Bindings.** The agreement on agriculture also required that developed countries would reduce their tariff bindings by an average of 36 per cent within six years from 1995. The developing countries were required to reduce tariffs by an average 24 per cent over a period of 10 years, while the least developed countries are not required to make any commitment regarding reduction of tariffs on their farm products.

The developing countries were permitted to indicate only their maximum bindings. For example, India declared maximum bindings of 100 per cent on farm products and 300 per cent on edible oils.

(c) **Subsidies and Domestic Support Policies.** Reduction in agricultural subsidies and domestic support prices is another important aspect of agreement on agriculture. The developed countries such as USA and the countries of East European Union (EU) maintain high level of agricultural subsidies and other domestic support programmes to protect their farmers and prevent imports from the developing countries. As a result, exports of farm products of the developing countries suffer a lot. *WTO agreement on agriculture requires that subsidies on farm products should not exceed 10 per cent of the value of agricultural production.*

Besides, it was agreed that product-specific subsidies, non-product specific subsidies on fertilizers, irrigation, power and seeds etc were also not to exceed 10 per cent of the value of agricultural output. Agreement on agriculture also provided that countries with closed agricultural markets will have to import agricultural commodities to the extent of 3 per cent of their domestic consumption, going up to 5 per cent over six years. However, developing countries which were facing balance of payments problems were exempted from this rule of compulsory imports.

Agreement on agriculture also provides that countries are free either to give patents on agricultural products or to evolve an effective *sui generis* (*i.e.* special) system of protection for plant breeder rights. It implies freedom of multiplication and exchange of indigeneously produced seeds or plants in the country. In other words, the farmers are free to retain seeds from their own harvests for their uses and exchange with each other. The only exception is seeds evolved genetically through the tools of high-tech biotechnology. The patent fee would be payable if the seed or plant varieties bought are genetically superior to and more productive than the local varieties. Thus, the farmers will have to pay a patent fee on branded seeds or plant varieties imported from developed countries. The commercial sale of such seeds would be affected by patents.

GATS (General Agreement on Trade in Services)

The General Agreement on Trade in Services (GATS) has been one of the major achievements of Uruguay Round of negotiations which now forms part of WTO legal framework. GATS covers all service sectors including financial services, telecommunications, transport, tourism, audio-visual and professional services. GATS requires some basic obligations to be fulfilled by all member countries of WTO with regard to international trade in services. GATS applies to services provided by service suppliers of one country and sold to consumers of another country (for example, tourism). It also applies to services provided by the commercial presence of a supplier of one country in the territory of another (for example, bank of a country providing banking service in another country). It is equally applicable to services supplied by companies of one country in the territory of another. However, GATS shall not cover services provided by the government which are not supplied on a commercial basis.

GATS requires countries to provide most favoured nation treatment (MFN) to all member countries. It implies that equally favourable treatment is to be accorded to service suppliers of all member foreign countries. GATS also requires that member countries should have transparency in their trade in services. This implies that each country should promptly publish all its relevant law and regulations pertaining to services including international agreements pertaining to trade in services to which the country is a signatory. Besides, each member country shall provide all information sought by any other member country relating to any service covered by GATS. Further, the countries are required to accord foreign service suppliers the same treatment as domestic service suppliers.

The countries may be exempted from GATS if they face balance of payments difficulties. They may also be exempted from GATS for national security reason as well as for purposes of protecting public order. The GATS requires that the countries would provide market access to foreign service suppliers. Hence, they would not impose restrictions on the number of service suppliers, total value of service transactions, the total number of service operations, joint ventures through which service may be supplied and the participation of foreign capital. The GATS has excluded labour movement from its purview. It allows countries to apply immigration laws to regulate the entry of persons into their territories. Countries are specifically allowed to apply visa requirements selectively to some countries and not to others.

TRIPS (Trade Related Intellectual Property Rights) Agreement

One of the most controversial agreements of Uruguay Round of negotiations relates to Trade-Related Intellectual Property Rights or briefly known as TRIPS. The agreement regarding TRIPS requires member countries to provide patent protection to all products or processes in all fields of technology. This protection is granted subject to the following three conditions :

(1) The product or the process is a new one

(2) It contains an inventive step

(3) It is capable of industrial application for 20 years from the grant of the patent.

TRIPS agreement covers the following seven intellectual properties:

(*i*) Patents
(*ii*) Copyrights and other related rights
(*iii*) Geographical indications
(*iv*) Industrial designs
(*v*) Trade marks
(*vi*) Layout designs of integrated circuits
(*vii*) Undisclosed information including trade secrets.

Patents shall be available without discrimination as to the place of invention, the field of technology and whether products are imported or locally produced. The patent-holder would enjoy exclusive marketing rights for a particular period. Anybody else seeking to manufacture and sell the product would have to establish that there has been no violation of the patent-holder's rights. The term of patent under the new regime would be 20 years from the date of the filling of the application.

Since the patent would be available for products or processes, it would be possible in chemical-based products like drugs and pharmaceuticals, agro-chemicals, alloys and food products to take patents for new products for 20 years and process patents thereafter for another 20 years. The countries which do not have product patent in certain areas (in India, agriculture and horticulture, technologies relating to atomic energy and chemical-based products like chemicals, alloys, drugs and pharmaceuticals, agro-chemicals, food products and so on are exempt from product patents) are given 10 years transition period for the introduction of product patents.

The countries are free to give patents or adopt an effective *sui generis* system of protection for plant breeder rights enshrined in the International Union for Protection of New Plant Varieties (IUPOV) convention.

A period of five years was given to implement the provisions of the TRIPS agreement. In respect of copyrights and related rights India is a signatory to the Berne convention. Likewise, in respect of layout designs and integrated circuits India is signatory to Washington Treaty whose main obligations have also been incorporated in the TRIPS.

TRIMS (Trade related Investment Measures) Agreement

TRIMS agreement refers to conditions or restrictions imposed on foreign investors. This agreement requires that investment regulations by member countries have to give same treatment to domestic products and imports. The TRIMS agreement specifically forbids imposing restrictions on operations of an enterprise which result in protecting domestic products and making imports disadvantageous. The foreign trade related restrictions on investment by foreign enterprises were generally imposed by developing countries including India. The following conditions which favour domestic production were prohibited under TRIMS agreement :

1. **Local content requirement.** That is, foreign enterprises must use a certain amount of locally produced inputs in production of products.
2. **Trade balancing requirement.** That is, imports by a foreign enterprise shall not exceed a certain proportion of exports by it.
3. Trade and foreign exchange balancing requirements.
4. **Domestic sales requirement.** This requires an enterprise to sell a certain proportion of its output locally.

However, it was agreed that subsidies applicable solely to domestic enterprises and government procurement policy in favour of domestic producers will not violate the TRIMS agreement. Thus, under TRIMS agreement, investment regulations have to accord same treatment to domestic products and imports. The TRIMS agreement requires removal of quantitative restrictions on imports and exports. However, exemptions are allowed if a country is suffering from balance of payments problems.

The industrialised countries were required to eliminate conditions covered under TRIMS by July 1, 1997. Developing countries were required to do so by 2000 and least developed countries were required to eliminate them by 2002.

India notified the TRIMS required by it before 2000. It notified two TRIMS conditions (1) relating to local content requirements in the production of certain pharmaceutical products and (2) dividend balancing requirements in the case of investment in 22 categories of consumer items. These were to be eliminated by 1-1-2000. The developing countries, including India, requested for extension of transition period for the elimination of the notified TRIMS. In view of the failures of the Seattle Ministerial Conference and Cancun conference no final decision was taken on this request of the developing countries.

INDIA'S ROLE IN WTO TALKS

India has consistently taken the stand that the launch of any new round of talks depends on a full convergence of views amongst the entire WTO membership on the scope and framework for such negotiations. Our more urgent task is to resolve the concerns of developing countries on implementation of the Uruguay Round agreements. We are against calls for new commitments from the developing world for achieving symmetry and equity in the existing agreements. It is in favour of 'non-trade' issues to be permanently kept off the negotiating table.

Incorporating Livelihood Clause. Ensuring food and livelihood security is critical, particularly for a large agrarian economy like India. India's proposal in ongoing negotiations includes suggestions like allowing developing countries to maintain appropriate level of tariff bindings, commensurate with their developmental needs and the prevailing distortions in international markets. We are also seeking a separate safeguard mechanism including provision for imposition of quantitative restrictions under specified circumstances, particularly in case of a surge in imports or decline in prices; exemptions for developing countries from obligations to provide minimum market access; exemptions of all measures taken by developing countries for poverty alleviation, rural development and rural employment.

Our immediate priority is that the agreements reached earlier with the developing countries should be implemented so as to correct inherent imbalances in some of the Uruguay Round agreements. Sincere and meaningful implementation of commitments undertaken by developed countries and operationalisation of all special and differential treatment clauses for developing countries in the various agreements be made.

Indian also strongly favours extension of higher levels of protection to the geographical indications for products like Basmati rice, Darjeeling tea, and Alphonso mangoes at par with that provided to wines and spirits under the Trade-Related Aspects of Intellectual Property Rights (TRIPS) agreement. In the TRIMS (Agreement on Trade-Related Investment Measures) review we want flexibility for developing countries in adopting appropriate domestic policy while permitting foreign investment.

Developed Countries' Demand and Singapore Issues. Developed countries are pushing for a comprehensive agenda like ***rules on investment, environment, competition policy, trade facilitation, transparency in government procurement, labour standards*** etc. They are pressing for incorporating non-trade issues of environment and labour standards. Using as an excuse that production of products in developing countries is not being done under proper environment and labour standards they can ban the imports of their products or impose other non-tariff restrictions. The developing countries are opposed to these non-trade issues.

WTO and Indian Agriculture and Farmers

Some critics of WTO have expressed the fears that Indian farmers are threatened by the WTO. There is however no adverse impact. India has bound its tariff to the extent of 100 per cent for primary agricultural products, 150 per cent for processed agricultural products and 300 per cent for edible oils. A few agricultural products had been bound historically at low levels but these bindings have been raised following the Article XXVIII negotiations held in this regard.

It has also been possible to maintain without hindrance the domestic policy instruments for promotion of agriculture or for targeted supply of food grains. Domestic policy measures like the operation of minimum support price, public distribution system as well as provision of input subsidies to agriculture have not in any way been constrained by the WTO agreement. Certain provisions in the Agreement on Agriculture (AoA) also give us flexibility to provide support for research, pest and disease control, marketing and promotion services, infrastructure development, payments for relief from natural disasters, payments under the regional assistance programmes for disadvantaged regions and payments under environmental programmes. Indian farmers now need to take advantage of the opportunity provided by the AoA, by addressing productivity issues and making their products more competitive globally.

WTO and Indian Industries

Indian industry has had to face greater competition in the wake of globalisation. But it has successfully competed, as can be inferred from the fact that there has been no particular surge in imports. In fact, as per the provisional data for 2000-01 our non-oil imports declined by 14 per cent while our exports rose by over 20 per cent in the same period. A close watch is also being kept to ensure that Indian industry does not have to face unfair competition from dumped or subsidised imports of other countries.

As for drug prices, safeguards are provided like compulsory licensing, price controls, and parallel imports which should help address this concern. It must also be recognised that the prices of medicines are influenced by several factors including the level of competition, size of market, purchasing capacity etc. The issue of affordable access to treatment for AIDS, which has gathered international attention in recent months, is hopefully a pointer in the right direction. The TRIPS agreement should not be allowed to hinder the efforts of developing countries to provide affordable access to medicines.

The apex Indian organisations representing various industries are sincerely working towards ensuring a gainful transition with least disadvantage into the global economy. The government also has to strive to improve infrastructure and provide a facilitating environment for inducing acceleration in trade. Developed countries have been putting pressures on inclusion of non-trade issues such as labour standards, environment protection, human rights, rules on investment, competition policy in the WTO agreements. This is because by asserting that particular developing countries are not observing and implementing the rules in regard to the non-trade issues so that the developed countries can ban the imports of some goods in their countries, as the USA has been trying to do so from time to time. We are against any inclusion of non-trade issues that are directed in the long run at enforcing protectionist measures, particularly against developing countries.

INDIA'S GAIN FROM WTO

Now more than a decade has passed when India joined WTO from the very beginning in Jan. 1, 1995. India has benefited from joining WTO, despite the failures of two ministerial level conferences at Seattle and Cancun. We explain below the gains India has achieved by joining WTO.

Exports and Imports. According to the recent estimates. India's exports have almost doubled in less than a decade. With exports going up from $26.33 billion in 1994-1995 when India joined WTO to $51.7 billion in 2002-03. Besides, India's share in total world exports of goods and commercial services increased from 0.6 in 1995 to 0.86 in 2001 whereas its total world imports of goods and commercial services increased from 0.78 in 1995 to 0.99 per cent during the same period.

Exports of Textiles and Clothing. According to a WTO agreement known as Multi-Fibre Agreement (MFA) entire quotas in textile and clothing trade will come to end from January 1, 2005. Till now WTO agreement has required the member countries to phase out their existing quotas by Dec. 31, 2004. It has further restrained them from expanding the size of quotas annually. These measures have helped India to increase its market access for its textile and clothing products. With effect from January 1, 2005, the entire textiles and clothing trade would get integrated into the multilateral trade framework of WTO. According to recent report (Feb. 2004), after China, India is largest gainer from the end of quotas and the consequent free trade in textiles and clothing. It is estimated that export market of $500 billion in garments alone with employment potential of 30 million jobs will be up for grabs from which India can get a good share.

Five years ago, Indian economists feared the country's fabrics sector would be steam-rollered by China. But recent reforms in the industry have given hope. India could see apparel exports rise between 40-100 per cent ($6.7 billion in 2001). A target of $50 billion in textile and clothing exports by 2010 is no longer a pipe dream.

Gain in Exports of Software Services. Further, thanks to WTO agreement on free trade in services, India has become a world leader in software services which are contributing a lot to foreign exchange earnings and employment generation for Indians.

A Good Deal of Earnings from BPO. BPO (Business Processing Outsourcing Services) from USA and UK are coming to India which have enabled us to earn not only foreign exchange but also to generate a large number of employment opportunities for educated Indian youth. Recently, there is resentment in the USA against BPO to India and other countries because it is causing loss of jobs in the USA and UK. But BPO to India and other developing countries are in accordance with the comparative advantage principle and raises profits of American companies which on being used for further investment will generate more employment opportunities in the USA

India's Demand from Industrialised Countries about Agricultural Subsidies and Movement of Labour. In its negotiating proposal, India has demanded substantial reduction in tariffs, elimination of trade-distorting domestic support and export subsidies in developed countries. The movement of professionals (*i.e.*, labour) from developing countries is constrained by a number of factors such as lack of specific sectorial commitments, lack of mutual recognition of qualifications, lack of transparency in administration of visa regimes, discriminatory practices in use of Economic Needs Test and social security contributions. India has, therefore, sought liberalisation of movement of professionals through removal of these constraints and submitted a paper for discussion at the ongoing negotiations.

WTO: DOHA ROUND NEGOTIATIONS

Failure of Doha Round WTO Negotiations at Cancun

From Sept. 10 to 14, 2003 trade ministers of developed and developing countries met for the next stage of talks on multilateral trading system. In a ministerial meeting of WTO held at Doha, in Qatar, in November 2001 which was attended by 142 countries it was recognised that there were inequities of Uruguay Round of negotiations. In this meeting it was decided to start a new round of global trade negotiations and complete it within 3 years. The major issues on which the fresh negotiations were to be conducted related to trade liberalisation, through reduction in tariffs and non-tariff barriers between countries; particularly regarding agricultural commodities and trade between developed and developing countries. Reduction of Government's procurement practices and support to farmers, general rules regarding trade in services, revision of TRIPS agreement especially patent protection of drugs. Doha Round of talks has been called Doha Development Round talks as its main purpose was to promote economic development of developing countries through trade liberalisation. It was expected that the developing countries would get a just and fair global trading system at the conclusion of Cancun meeting. But these hopes were not fulfilled and Cancun meeting ended in a failure. At Cancun, a group of 21 developing countries led by India, Brazil and China frustrated the attempts of US-European Union Combine to pressurise the developing countries to accept the agenda that suited them most and was against the interests of the developing countries. Draft declaration prepared by WTO allowed the developed countries to maintain or keep domestic subsidies and support for their agriculture and farmers and avoided eliminating export subsidies and credit concessions on their exports, especially on farm products and textiles. On the other hand, draft declaration sought even stiffer tariff cuts by developing countries. In this way, developing countries were badly treated with regard to market access of their products to the developed countries. All these were not acceptable to the developing countries including India. African countries who are badly hit by the subsidies and domestic support on the farm products by the developed countries walked out of the meeting. As a result, Cancun meeting ended without adopting any declaration. The lesson from the failure of Cancun meeting is that unless the developed countries look beyond their own interests and try to evolve multilateral trading system which is just and fair to the developing countries talks cannot succeed.

WTO'S HONG KONG DECLARATION AND DEVELOPING COUNTRIES

After failures at Seattle and Cancun, the ministerial meeting in Hong Kong in December 2005 negotiated trade liberalisation to conclude Doha Round on Development. In Nov. 2001 in the Ministerial meeting at Doha the developed countries (the US and EU) and developing countries, it was agreed to start new round of talks to *promote development through trade liberalisation*. Hence the name '*Doha Round on Development*'. The two successive ministerial meetings at Seattle and Cancun failed to arrive at an agreement acceptable to the LDCs and developing countries. It may be noted that Uruguay Round of 1994 resulted in setting up of WTO in Jan. 1995. It may be further noted that the agenda of Uruguay Round as well as its outcome discriminated against developing countries. The trade negotiations of Doha Round are meant to remove this discrimination against the developing countries[1]. During the negotiations developed countries have been raising irrelevant issues so as to protect their agriculture and textiles industry through tariffs and non-tariff barriers (NTB) so as to prevent free and fair trade from the viewpoint of developing countries.

On the other hand, at the conclusion of Uruguay Round, the developed countries succeeded in extracting an agreement regarding the *inclusion of services and intellectual property rights* – the two issues which concern them most. In return for this agreement on services and intellectual property rights, they agreed to *eliminate* over a period of 10 years high tariff and non-tariff barriers on textiles, agricultural products, sugar – the products which are of special interest for developing countries. However, the developed countries did not fulfil promise on one protest or the other. Commenting on this duplicity on the part of developed countries, Stiglitz writes, "When the Uruguay Round began there was a grand bargain to expand the trade agenda to include services and intellectual property rights—the two issues which are of particular concern to developed countries. In return *developed countries were to make major concessions on agriculture*—the livelihood of the vast majority of people in developing countries — and textile quota, the only trade area (besides sugar) in which quantitative restrictions persist. In the end developed countries got what they wanted, and developing countries were told to be patient : eventually the developed countries would fulfil their part of the deal. *Even as the rich countries urged developing countries to make quick adjustments, they claimed that they needed a decade to make the transition to a quota-free textile regime*. In truth they were buying time; they did nothing for a decade and when the quota finally ended last January (*i.e.*, Jan. 2005) they pleaded they were still not prepared and thus concluded a three-year extension with China."[2]

Hong Kong Conference was meant to negotiate trade issues relating to agriculture, non-agriculture services and intellectual property rights so as to achieve trade liberalisation for promoting economic development. *The problem with regard to agriculture is that the developed countries, the US and EU, provide export subsidies and also give financial support on a large scale to their agriculture resulting in cheapening of their agricultural products. This distorts trade between the countries as it prevents market access in developed countries for products of developing countries which have comparative advantage in their production.* Developing countries discovered that their gains from trade with developed countries were far less than they were made out to be and LDCs (Least Developed Countries) felt that they were actually worse off by agreeing in Uruguay Round of talks resulting in establishment WTO. Thus developed countries lost their credibility.

With the above background the Ministerial Conference at Hong Kong adopted a declaration which called for conclusion in 2006 of trade negotiations launched at Doha in Nov. 2001. This Hong Kong declaration established time frame and targets in specific areas of trade liberalisation. The following agreement which addresses some of the concerns of developing countries related to agriculture was reached.

1. First, it was resolved to complete Doha Round on Development in 2006 and conclude negotiations for liberalisation of trade between members of WTO.

2. **Elimination of Agricultural Export Subsidies.** The agreement was reached in Hong Kong that export subsidies given by the developed countries will be eliminated by the year 2013 in a phased manner. While the earlier proposal was to phase these export subsidies by 2010, the EU, the

1 See Joseph E Stiglitz, *Fair Trade for All : How Trade Can Promote Development*, Oxford University Press, 2006.

2 Joseph Stiglitz, "The Development Round that Wasn't," *The Economic Times*, December 15, 2005.

largest provider of export subsidies, sought a longer phase-out period. Thus, the agreed end-date of 2013 gives the EU a level of comfort of phasing out its export subsidies as a part of its next phase of reforms of the *common agricultural policy* (CAP). This is an achievement of the developing countries as it was contended by its earlier Trade Commissioner of WTO, Pascal Lamy, that Doha declaration had not mandated elimination of export subsidies in the developed countries. It may be noted further that *under the agreement developing countries like India will continue to have the right to provide marketing and transport subsidies on agricultural exports for 5 years beyond the date for elimination of all forms of subsidies*.

Agricultural Tariffs. To increase market access in the developed countries for the agricultural products of developing countries, the Hong Kong declaration has agreed to banding approach suggested by the group G-20 of developing countries, According to this approach, agricultural tariffs have been put in four bands ranging from the lower to the high level, with the provision that tariff in the higher band will be subject to deeper cuts. The extent of cut in agricultural tariffs in each band is yet to be agreed upon in future negotiations. The higher cuts in tariffs in the higher bands will greatly bring down the agricultural tariffs of the developed countries and will therefore improve market access for agricultural exports of the developing countries in the developed industrialised economies. However, it will also mean substantial reduction in agricultural tariffs of developing countries such as India who have higher tariff bindings. India's tariff bindings for agricultural products are in the range of 100 to 150 per cent and will therefore require reduction of about 35 per cent which is quite large.

However, in the Hong Kong declaration, the developing countries have been provided some special safeguards in connection with the cuts in agricultural tariffs. Firstly, the developing countries have been given the flexibility to self-designate an appropriate number of tariff lines as special products (SPs). However, the self-designation of a number of tariff lines as special products will require the satisfaction of some criteria such as needs of food security, livelihood security and rural development.

Secondly, under Hong Kong agreement on agriculture (AoA) the developing countries were also entitled to adopt Special Safeguard Mechanism (SSM) based on import quantities and price triggers. This means under special safeguard mechanism, developing countries can raise their tariff on imports of agricultural products in the event of a sudden increase in imports or fall in prices of imports. However, they are not allowed to reintroduce quantitative restrictions (QRs) which both the developed and developing countries have already eliminated

Domestic Support for Agriculture. In Hong Kong declaration developed countries agreed to the proposal of G-20 (*i.e.*, the group of developing countries including India and Brazil) for reduction of trade-distorting agricultural subsidies with higher linear cuts in higher bands. However, the extent of reduction in these subsidies were left for future negotiations. It may be noted that Blue Box and Green Box agricultural subsidies have been excluded from the scope of reduction. But there is a provision for review of the criteria of the Green Box subsidies in which most of the EU domestic subsidies are included.

In Doha Round on Development it was agreed to reduce the minimum level of support (*de minimis*) to agriculture allowed to be exempted from reduction for both developed and developing countries. Developing countries were entitled to a 10 per cent of the value of total production for providing domestic support to agriculture. In Hong Kong it was agreed that those developing countries whose domestic support to agriculture was below 10 per cent of the value of production and therefore no commitment to reduce them will be exempt from reductions in *de minimis* as well as overall trade-distorting agricultural subsidies.

Under the Hong Kong agreement export subsidies on cotton will be eliminated by developed countries in 2006 and trade-distorting domestic subsidies on agricultural products were to be reduced drastically over a storter period of time.

Non-Agricultural Market Access (NAMA). The Hong Kong declaration provided for the reduction or elimination of tariffs including peak levels of tariffs, high levels of tariffs and tariff escalation on non-agricultural goods, particularly on the products of exports which are of great interest for the developing countries. In this context of market access for non-agricultural products it has been agreed to apply Swiss formula. According to this formula, deeper cuts in tariff rates on a line-by-line basis have to be made by countries levying higher tariffs. How larger will be the cut in tariff levels will depend on the coefficients to be agreed.

However, in Hong Kong declaration the provision for *special and differential treatment (S&DT) and less than full reciprocity* for developing countries had been included. According to this provision, a certain proportion of tariff lines of the developing countries may be subjected to tariff cuts lower than that permitted by applying Swiss formula and a certain percentage of the tariff lines of these countries may be kept unbound (that is, without any binding for tariff reduction). Thus flexibilities granted under S&DT include the longer implementation period as well as applying less than Swiss formula cuts or no cuts for a specified list of tariff lines as unbound. These have been declared as an integral part of the modalities for negotiations under NAMA. On the sectoral initiatives, India and most of the developing countries have emphasized that formula approach should be the main modality for negotiations and sectoral initiative can only be a voluntary exercise.

Services. In the Hong Kong declaration it was also decided to achieve a higher level of liberalisation of trade in services and towards that negotiations would be intensified. New date lines were fixed for submission of revised offer and draft schedules of commitments by the member countries. These negotiations on trade in services will be conducted in accordance with principle of GATS and the Guidelines and Procedures for the Negotiations on Trade in Services. According to GATS and these guidelines, the developing countries were required to liberalise the service sectors and modes of supply of their own choice and determine the extent of liberalisation.

India is particularly concerned with liberalisation of trade in services as it wants to increase its access to the markets of developed countries for the services such as ITES (Information Technology Enabled Services) in which it has a comparative advantage. In services, India submitted its revised offer in August 2005. Eleven service sectors and 94 sub-sectors were covered in the revised offer.

It is thus clear that with regard to services much depends on revised services offer by the member countries and the future negotiations.

Market Access for LDCs. An important feature of Hong Kong declaration is that it was decided to provide *duty-free and quota-free* market access for all LDCs (Least Developed Countries) products to all developed countries. The developing countries which are in a position to provide such access to LDCs are expected to do so.

Agreement on TRIPS. On December 6, 2005, the General Council of WTO adopted the amendment to the *TRIPS to address public health concerns of developing countries which was reaffirmed by Hong Kong Declaration. This amendment enables manufacturing and export of pharmaceutical products under compulsory licence to countries with limited or no manufacturing capacities in the pharmaceutical sectors*. On Trips, CBD (Convention of Bio-Diversity) on relationship and protection of traditional knowledge, India along with a number of other developing countries which are rich in bio-diversity proposed that the Trips Agreement of WTO should be amended to provide for : (i) disclosure of source of the traditional knowledge used in the invention; (ii) disclosure of evidence of prior informed consent under the relevant national regime; and (iii) disclosure of evidence of benefit sharing under the relevant national regime. With this amendment the use of India's natural herbs such as Neem, Arjuna, Ashavagandha and others for preparing medicines and also certain plant varieties such as Basmati rice will get protection from the use by multinational companies.

WTO Negotiations and India

In Hong Kong India made some modest gains in the field of agriculture, industrial products and

TRIPS. A good number of issues concerning liberalisation of global trade were yet to be resolved. However, much depends on future negotiations during which several issues, particularly regarding market access for industrial goods and services were to be resolved. Whether in these future negotiations, developed countries will adopt an attitude which ensures fair and free trade from the viewpoint of LDCs and developing countries. Already *the developed countries propose to link lower farm subsidies by them to greater market access for non-agricultural goods in the developing countries*. This is against the letter and spirit of Hong Kong Declaration. And it is these kinds of tactics of the developed countries that Joseph Stiglitz predicted and thought that due to this Doha Round on Development will collapse. This issue and other ones were to be resolved in a meeting of group G-6 (to be held in mid-March 2006) to which India along with Brazil had been invited. The other members invited in this meeting of G-6 were the US, European Union (EU), Japan and Australia.

After the suspension in negotiations during July 2006 due to the wide differences in the positions of WTO members, especially on agricultural domestic support and market access, there was a resumption of negotiations on Nov. 16, 2006, and again on Feb. 7, 2007, in Geneva on the suggestions that the framework of negotiations, inclusiveness and the progress made so far be preserved and attempt should be made to arrive at an outcome that strikes a balance between development of the developing countries and interests of the developed countries. However, due to difference in the positions of USA and European Union on the one hand and the developing countries including India, China, Brazil on the other no final agreement could be reached.

During the negotiations while safeguarding the interests of India's poor agricultural producers remains paramount for India, making gains in services negotiations where it is a demander is no less important. In the case of industrial tariffs, India's growth and development concerns need to be addressed along with other developing countries.

In our view it must be made clear to the developed countries that the artificiality of prices arising out of the substantial domestic agricultural subsidies provided by the developed countries must be dealt with firmly if we are to make any headway towards fair trade in agriculture. Developing countries have a right to use the flexibilities provided in Hong Kong declaration to protect their small and medium enterprises and their infant industries like automobiles. Therefore, in future trade negotiations no compromise be made on flexibilities in connection with agriculture and industrial products granted to the developing countries in Hong Kong declaration.

Trade Facilitation Agreement at Doha Round Negotiations

An important issue of Doha Round Negotiations relates to the agreement on trade facilitation for easing of customs procedures and movement of goods between countries. A draft of agreement on trade facilitation was worked out by WTO members on December 14, 2009. The draft text was revised six times in 2010 through discussions in the meetings of negotiating group on trade facilitation. India has been actively participating in these meetings and has given a few proposals regarding trade facilitations on which agreement could not be reached. Developing countries do not want to change their trade procedures but expect others to do so. Least developed countries, in general, do not want to undertake amy binding commitment. Capacity constraint and lack of resources are two major factors that prevent developing countries (and least developed countries) from taking on binding commitment regarding trade facilitation. However, there were general indications that developed countries might not invest in building infrastructure in these countries, although the July 2004 Framework Agreement clearly linked commitments by developing countries to provide support and assistance for infrastructure development by the developed countries. It is important that this linkage is respected, especially by the developed countries, before any agreement on trade facilitation is finalised.

Besides, before final agreement on trade facilitation is reached, it needs a solution where it does not have to compromise on its *minimum support price* (*MSP*) for agricultural products which is the most critical requirement for India's *food security policy*. Therefore, India is pushing for a change in rules to ensure its grain document programme and minimum support price for rice and wheat are not affected by subsidy cap of 10 per cent of the value of production which has been fixed by WTO. The exemption from this 10 per cent of the value of production of these crops is valid only up to 2017. That is, beyond 2017, the value of India's procurement of these products at the minimum support prices would not exceed this ceiling of 10 per cent of the value of production and therefore this would affect India's food security programme as with future rise in procurement prices would breach this 10 per cent subsidy cap. This violation would invite penalty on India under WTO agreement. Therefore, India is insisting that its food security concerns must be addressed before international agreement on easing of trade procedures is reached.

Bali Agreement. Negotiations on trade facilitation went on for years. This trade facilitation will help large exporters such as the US, EU and China. In Bali in 2013 WTO members agreed to finalise the trade facilitation agreement by July 31, 2014. Unfortunately despite food security concerns having not been addressed along with finalising trade facilitation agreement, India's then UPA government agreed for trade signing this agreement by July 31, 2014. When the Negotiating Group (which included India) meeting was held in the last week of July 2014, there was NDA government which refused to sign the agreement saying that its food security concern should be first addressed. As a result, there was deadlock in negotiations on trade facilitation agreement.

PART VIII

Resource Allocation: Choice and Pattern of Investment

- Investment Criteria: Minimum Capital-Output and Social Investment Criteria
- Alternative Investment Criteria
- Cost-Benefit Analysis and Project Evaluation

CHAPTER 46

INVESTMENT CRITERIA: MINIMUM CAPITAL-OUTPUT AND SOCIAL INVESTMENT CRITERIA

NEED FOR INVESTMENT CRITERIA

How to allocate investment resources among competing industries or projects is a central issue facing all economies. However, the allocation of resources in developing countries assumes a great significance as capital is very scarce while the needs and aspirations of the people are very large. There is need for investment in agriculture to produce more food grains to feed the rapidly increasing population and more cash crops to fulfil the needs of raw materials for industrial growth. We require to invest in capital goods producing industries, in basic goods industries such as iron and steel, fertilizers, in numerous consumes goods industries and above all in infrastructure such as power, roads, highways, ports and airports. Besides, more investment is required to be made in education and health which are now regarded as important drivers of growth. Given that resources are scarce, how much resources be allocated to each of these uses is a very difficult problem. No developing country can afford to take a leap in the dark and utilise its resources in a haphazard manner. As a general rule it can be stated that *we must make an optimum use of our economic resources*. But the problem is how precisely to do it. It is necessary therefore to lay down certain criteria which should guide the allocation of scarce resources for planned economic development. What priorities should be given to various industries and projects so that not only rapid economic growth is achieved but also other objectives of planning are fulfilled. It is the pattern of investment allocation among different uses that will determine whether the pace of economic growth as well as its direction are such as we desire.

It may also be pointed out that the investment criteria will vary according to the objectives of development envisaged in the plan. There are several objectives that can be kept in view by the planners of a developing economy. The proper choice of criteria for investment allocation depends on the preference of the planners for achieving particular objectives. Thus, the planners may seek to raise the *present* level of standard of living (*i.e.,* level of consumption) or maximise the rate of growth of the economy to achieve a higher level of consumption in future. The other objective may be to give higher priority to reduce the levels of poverty and unemployment which implies the choice of techniques and industries which have higher labour intensity.

It may be further noted that alternative criteria will affect economic growth differently. One type of investment may maximize total output over one period and another over a different time period. It is not therefore possible to have a criterion of investment capable of application in all periods. This is due to the fact that no economy is static. In a dynamic economy situations change calling for a change in investment strategy.

Marginal Rule of Resource Allocation. Microeconomic theory tells us that in a perfective competitive market economy resources are efficiently or optimally allocated and used. Under conditions of perfect competition in both the product and factor markets marginal products of factors are equated in all their uses and as a result total output is maximum. This is known as the *marginal rule of resource allocation* and its fulfilment implies the achievement of *efficiency* or what is also called *Pareto optimality*, which ensures maximum social welfare with the given resources of the economy.

Now the question arises if the marginal rule of resource allocation leads to the achievement of efficiency, investment resources in a planned economy should be allocated to different industries, projects or uses in a way that marginal product of capital in different uses is equated to maximise total output, then why there is need for some other criteria to guide allocation of resources in a planned developing economy. The important reason for this is that marginal rule of resource allocation is *static* and is concerned with the maximisation of the *present level* of output or welfare with the given resources, while for developing countries we need the criteria which should ensure rapid growth of output and employment so as to maximise output and consumption over a long period. The second reason for developing countries to adopt investment criteria other than the marginal rule is that the concept of efficiency or Pareto optimality ignores a number of factors that affect welfare of the society. Owing to a large number of imperfections in market and the existence of structural disequilibrium in the developing economies, the *market prices of factors and goods* on which the concept of Pareto efficiency is based *do not truly reflect the social costs and benefits of production.* Therefore, in developing countries the marginal rule of resource allocation for achievement of efficiency in resource allocation cannot be applied unless market prices are corrected so that they reflect social costs and benefits.

Let us explain in some detail why market prices do not reflect true social costs and benefits. The first important reason for this is that some projects, especially relating to infrastructure, generate *external economies* which are not taken into account by private enterprises in determination of their costs and prices. As a result, when external economies exist, social benefits will exceed the private benefits. Unless some corrections are made for these external economies, social optimum or efficiency in resource allocation will not be achieved by applying the above mentioned marginal rule. The second reason for the divergence of market prices from the social values of goods and factors is the existence of imperfections in the market such as monopolies, oligopolies and monopolistic competitions in both goods and factor markets and therefore the market prices determined under these conditions depart from the valuation of goods and services from the viewpoint of maximising social welfare. Emphasizing the imperfections causing failure of market prices goods and factors to reflect their social values, Thirlwall writes: "If perfect competition does not prevail in the factor markets, the prices of these factors will not reflect their opportunity costs to the society so that employing factors up to the point where their marginal product equals their price will not produce a social optimum. Idle resources such as labour will be overvalued and scarce resources such as capital and foreign exchange will be undervalued and market prices must therefore be corrected to reflect the value of these resources to the society."[1]

Thirdly, the real world is dynamic and the present prices of goods and factors may not prevail in the future and therefore the optimum choice of investment among industries or uses on the basis of present prices of goods and factors may not ensure social optimum in the future.

Last but more important reason for non-applicability of the marginal rule to optimum resource allocation in developing countries is its assumption that the prevailing income distribution is optimal and is not adversely affected whatever pattern of resource allocation is chosen. If the pattern of investment chosen leads to the increase in income distribution, the output may be maximised but social welfare will be diminished. The concept of efficiency or social welfare maximisation is based on the assumption that prevailing income distribution is optimal. If the choice of a particular pattern of resource allocation affects the income distribution adversely and renders a large part of labour

1 Thirlwall, A.P., *Growth and Development with Special Reference to Developing Countries* (New York: Palgrave Macmillan, 2003), Seventh Edition, p. 362.

force unemployed and poor represents a change for the worse. Guided by these concerns the Eleventh and Twelfth Five Years Plans of India, the objective is not just higher rate of economic growth but *inclusive growth* which means that benefits of growth should be widely shared in the society and poverty and unemployment be reduced. The achievement of efficiency as implied by Pareto optimality would not ensure this.

For the above reasons, there has been a long debate among economists about the appropriate criteria of investment allocation among different industries or projects for developing countries. The various criteria that have been suggested in this regard differ mainly in respect of what developing countries should seek to maximise, especially whether the *present* level of output or consumption should be maximised or rate of growth be maximised so as to achieve higher level of *future consumption*. (We will discuss the issue of *present* consumption and *future* consumption in detail later in this chapter.) Besides, as explained above, the difference about the appropriate investment criteria in developing countries also relates to the *objectives of planned development* in developing countries.

It may be further noted that various criteria were concerned with the *allocation of capital* as capital was considered as an important *scarce resource* in developing countries. However, some earlier writers on the subject considered *foreign exchange* resources as crucial scarce resource and proposed criterion that ensures balance of payments problem may not arise.

Furthermore, the investment criteria refer to the *pattern of investment* and to *choice of techniques*. In our earlier chapter, we discuss various criteria with regard to the *choice of techniques* in developing countries. In the present chapter we are concerned with the choice of investment criteria about what should be the appropriate pattern of investment in developing countries. However, some criteria, especially Galenson and Leibenstein maximising reinvestment surplus criterion, apply both to the choice of *appropriate pattern of investment* and *appropriate choice of techniques*, but the two should not be confused.

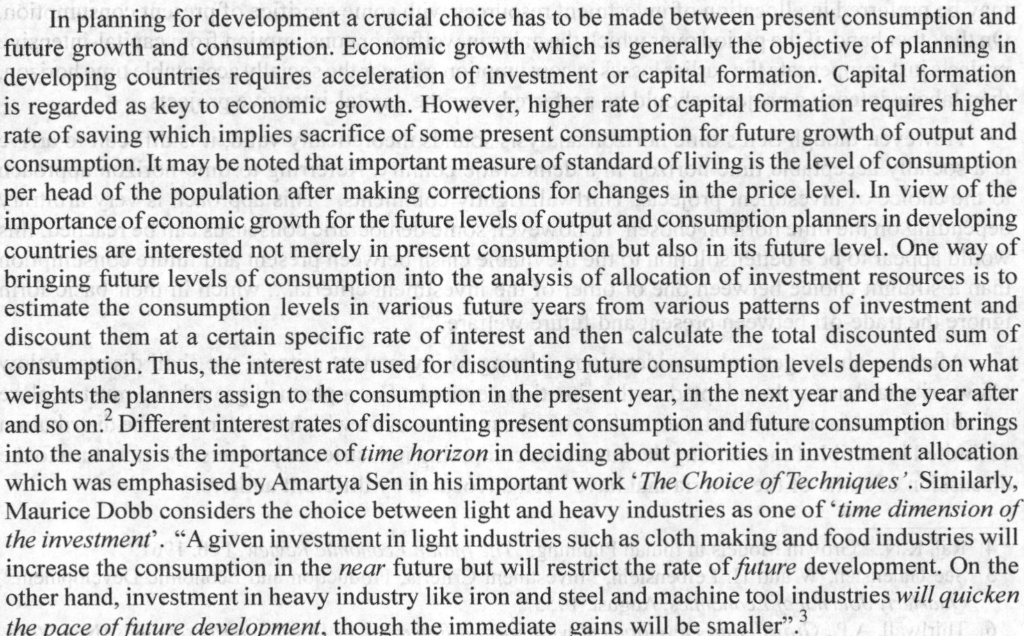

PRESENT CONSUMPTION VS FUTURE GROWTH

In planning for development a crucial choice has to be made between present consumption and future growth and consumption. Economic growth which is generally the objective of planning in developing countries requires acceleration of investment or capital formation. Capital formation is regarded as key to economic growth. However, higher rate of capital formation requires higher rate of saving which implies sacrifice of some present consumption for future growth of output and consumption. It may be noted that important measure of standard of living is the level of consumption per head of the population after making corrections for changes in the price level. In view of the importance of economic growth for the future levels of output and consumption planners in developing countries are interested not merely in present consumption but also in its future level. One way of bringing future levels of consumption into the analysis of allocation of investment resources is to estimate the consumption levels in various future years from various patterns of investment and discount them at a certain specific rate of interest and then calculate the total discounted sum of consumption. Thus, the interest rate used for discounting future consumption levels depends on what weights the planners assign to the consumption in the present year, in the next year and the year after and so on.[2] Different interest rates of discounting present consumption and future consumption brings into the analysis the importance of *time horizon* in deciding about priorities in investment allocation which was emphasised by Amartya Sen in his important work '*The Choice of Techniques*'. Similarly, Maurice Dobb considers the choice between light and heavy industries as one of '*time dimension of the investment*'. "A given investment in light industries such as cloth making and food industries will increase the consumption in the *near* future but will restrict the rate of *future* development. On the other hand, investment in heavy industry like iron and steel and machine tool industries *will quicken the pace of future development*, though the immediate gains will be smaller".[3]

2 See Amartya Sen, "The Flow of Financial Resources", UN Conference on Trade in December, 1971, reprinted in G. Meier (ed), *Leading Issues in Economic Development*, 4th edition.

3 Maurice Dobb, *Some Aspects of Economic Development*, p. 50.

Present consumption vs future growth of output and consumption has been a matter of serious debate in connection with Mahalanobis growth model which formed the basis of the Second and Third Five Year Plans of India. Mahalanobis model gave a high priority to capital-intensive basic heavy industries such as iron and steel, fertilizers, machine tools and other capital goods industries) and lower priority to light consumer goods industries and agriculture. As mentioned in quotation from Maurice Dobb above, in favour of basic heavy industries it was argued that though in the present they imply lower consumption level but as they bring about higher growth rate, in the future they will cause higher levels of output and consumption. Defending Mahalanobis, Dr K.N. Raj writes, "The logic here is the same as the more common proposition that a higher rate of investment (*i.e.,* a larger proportion of productive factors used for capital accumulation) would result in a smaller volume of output being available for consumption in the short run but that over a long period it would result in higher level of growth of consumption; *the difference is that the choice here is stated as between investment in capital goods and investment in consumer goods industries*".[4]

It is noteworthy that Galenson and Leibenstein in their proposed investment criteria, which will be discussed in detail later, argued that to maximise the rate of growth of output investment resources should be allocated to industries and projects that yield the maximum rate of surplus per worker. The surplus is difference between output and wages ($Y–W$) and they showed that the rate of surplus per worker employed is the maximum in capital-intensive industries and projects "which will bring about higher rate of economic growth and higher level of consumption over a long period time.[5] Thus, according to them, some present consumption has to be sacrificed for having more consumption in future. However, in our view, this involves the relative evaluation of present and future consumption and on this will depend the choice of investment allocation among industries and projects. Amartya Sen has rightly pointed out that the choice of techniques and also of industries and projects *must be evaluated* with respect to a fixed *time horizon* acceptable to the society. If in case of those capital intensive projects the actual time period it takes for the future growth in consumption to offset the loss of present consumption is *less than* that of the fixed time horizon acceptable to the society, then they may be preferred in allocation of investment resources with some sacrifice of present consumption. On the other hand, if the period over which the gains in welfare or consumption from capital-intensive projects just compensate the earlier losses in consumption *exceeds* the socially acceptable time horizon, then labour-intensive projects should be preferred over the capital-intensive projects.

However, though Sen's time horizon analysis sounds theoretically valid, it is difficult to arrive at a socially acceptable time horizon in a democratic country. Referring to time-horizon approach to the choice of investment projects, Thirlwall rightly comments, "This approach is very arbitrary depending on the time horizon chosen. If, however, some democratic consensus can be reached, this would appear to be a better solution to the inevitable clash between present and future consumption than a straight choice between one or other of the investment criteria.... which in their basic form ignore the trade-off between present and future welfare."[6]

After the above general considerations relating to investment criteria, we shall discuss below a few criteria that can be adopted as the situation demands. For a planned growth we must explore suitable criteria for investment, *i.e.*, to discover the main bases on which to determine the distribution of limited investible funds among the numerous competing industries or projects. We now turn to the discussion of some of the criteria that have been advocated by different authors.

4 Raj, K.N., "Growth Models in Indian Planning," *The Indian Economic Review*, Feb. 1961.
5 See Galensten, W and H. Leibenstein, "Investment Criteria, Production and Economic Development," *Quarterly Journal of Economics*, August, 1955.
6 Thirlwall, A.P., *Growth and Development with Special Reference to Developing Economies* (New York: Palgrave Macmillan), Seventh edition, 2003, p. 368.

MINIMUM CAPITAL-OUTPUT RATIO CRITERION

We have already discussed capital-output ratio in a previous chapter. The investment criterion that has often been advocated by some economists is that of capital-output ratio. That is, for choosing among investment projects and for determining priorities, capital-output ratios of different investment projects be compared. Those investment projects (or their technical forms) should be selected that minimize the capital-output ratio. If capital-output ratio of investment in project *A* (3: 1) is less than the capital-output ratio of investment project *B* (5: 1), then, in developmental planning, investment project *A* must get priority over investment project *B*.

It may be noted that similar criterion known as '*the highest rate of turnover criterion*' has been put forward by J.J. Polak[7] and N.S. Buchanan. Rate of turnover means "ratio of output to capital investment" or simply output-capital ratio, that is , reverse of capital-output ratio. Under this the objective in the choice of allocation of investment is to maximise the rate of turnover, that is, maximise $\frac{\Delta O}{I}$ where Δ indicates flow of output resulting from invetsment in a year. Note that when rate turnover ratio $\left(\frac{\Delta O}{I}\right)$ is maximum, capital-output ratio, which can be written as $\frac{I}{\Delta O}$ will be minimum. Thus, when rate of turnover is maximised, capital-output ratio is minimised. Further, the rate of turnover indicates productivity of capital. Elaborating the highest rate of turnover criterion, Prof. N.S. Buchanan writes: "*If investment funds are limited, the wise policy, in the absence of special considerations, would be to undertake first those investment having a high value of annual product relative to the investment*."[8] That is, investment projects with a higher rate of turnover should be given preference. In other words, capital-output ratio is to be minimised in order to maximise ratio of output to capital investment.

The importance of lower capital-output ratio was brought out by Harrod-Domar model of growth according to which $g = \frac{s}{v}$ where *g* is rate of growth *s* is rate of saving [*i.e.*, ratio of total saving (*S*) to national income (*Y*)] and *v* capital-output ratio. According to this, the lower the rate of capital-output ratio, the higher the rate of growth. It was thought that one could also use the capital-output ratio as the basis for choice of investment projects in development planning and in this connection refinement in the capital-output ratio was made. A criterion for investment choice was made in terms of incremental capital-output ratio (ICOR). Incremental capital-output ratio implies marginal capital-output ratio. It was argued that those investment projects be chosen for which ICOR was lower.

The underlying assumption of this criterion is that projects in which capital investment is to be made are substitutes of each other. If every project is a substitute of every other, there is strong reason of preferring industries or projects with a lower marginal ratio of capital to net output. The classic case of substitutability is provided by the problem of choosing between alternative techniques to produce the same commodity. Various examples can be given of it. Additional foodgrains production can be obtained either from constructing major irrigation works or by building minor irrigation works or by producing and using more fertilizers. Electricity can be produced either by thermal projects or by hydel projects. Further, more cloth can be produced either in the small-scale industries sector or large-scale industries sector.

Critical Evaluation

The capital-output ratio criteria has been subjected to several important criticisms. It suffers from all subject shortcomings of a static criterion which ignores the important factor of time dimension. It

7 J.J. Polak, "Balance of Payments Problems of Countries: Reconstructing with the help of Foreign Loans", *Quarterly Journal of Economics*, Feb., 1943.

8 N.S. Buchanan, *International and Domestic Welfare*, New York, 1945.

has been alleged that it is difficult to measure capital-output ratio or ICOR. The incremental capital-output ratio is generally measured by the investment divided by the flow of output from that investment over a year. But the lives of projects are different. Some projects with a higher capital-output ratio go on yielding output for a longer time period, while the projects with a lower capital-output ratio has a shorter life time. Therefore, when time period over which projects go on yielding output in future is different it is difficult to make a choice. Attempt has been made to overcome this problem by finding out the present discounted value of output in future years of projects. However, what rate of discount rate is used for this purpose is a matter of controversy.

The minimum capital output ratio criterion suffers from another drawback. It is maintained that the economic world is not an abode of perfect or very high substitutability between various investment projects. For example, the allocation of investment between agriculture and industry or between consumption goods and investment goods cannot be adjudged on the basis of capital-output ratio, since the degree of substitutability between these products is very limited. Agricultural products and industrial products are complementary rather than substitutes.

Furthermore, it has been pointed out that some projects may have a higher productivity of capital than others, (that is, a lower capital-output ratio) because of the higher efficiency of cooperating factors used with capital, but there is no surety that these cooperating factors will be sufficiently available in the future. Thus, the projections of output from investment projects with lower capital-output ratios may not actually materialise due to the short supply of the cooperating factors used along with capital to produce output. Further, since the actual world is dynamic where technology is changing rapidly projects with lower capital-output ratios in the present may not remain so in the long run.

The important drawback of the minimum capital-output ratio is that choice of industries on this basis leads to the investment in light consumer goods industries such as cotton cloth, leather goods, food-processing industries (*e.g.,* sugar) etc. which have lower capital-output ratio at the cost of basic heavy industries such as iron and steel, fertilizers, power generating projects, machine tool industries which have higher capital intensity. However, as has been pointed out by Galenson and Leibenstein, the rate of investable surplus is lower in light consumer goods industries and therefore rate of *growth of output in the long run will be lower* if higher priority is assigned to them in the allocation of resources. It is noteworthy that Dr K.N. Raj and Amartya Sen[9] defended Mahalanobis strategy of giving higher priority to basic heavy industries arguing that it would ensure higher rate of growth in the long run which will lead to greater consumption in future. Thus, in India it has been strongly argued that what should be compared in choosing among investment projects is not their capital-output ratios, but their contribution to economic growth in future. The goal of developmental policy is not the maximum output at a point of time but a maximum rate of growth over time.

Furthermore, as has been rightly pointed out by Thirlwall that in the minimum capital-output criterion. "There is no explicit discussion either of how the flow of output should be measured at market prices or at prices adjusted to measure the social valuation of goods and factors of production. The concern with measuring costs and benefits from society's point of view has led to the use of social marginal product while change in output is measured as the change in value added to society".[10]

Lastly, capital-output ratio may be one of the criteria when substitutes are involved, but is not the sole consideration. There are many other considerations too, such as the labour-investment ratio and the effect of investment allocation among projects on income distribution. In a developing country like India, where greater employment and better distribution of income and wealth are also the cherished goals of the Five Year Plans, these other considerations of investment projects are of paramount importance.

9 See K.N. Raj, "Growth Models in Indian Planning," *The Indian Economic Review*, Feb 1961

10 Thirlwall, A.P., *Economic Growth and Development* (New York: Palgrave Macmillan, 2003), 7th edition, p. 364.

THE SOCIAL MARGINAL PRODUCTIVITY (SMP) CRITERION

A more general criterion to guide allocation of investment to different projects or industries is the social marginal productivity (SMP) criterion. It was put forward by A.E. Kahn[11] and was further improved and extended by Hollis B Chenery.[12] It is based on the conventional marginal productivity approach with a difference that it emphasises productivity of investment from a *social point of view* rather than from the viewpoint of private enterprise. According to A.E. Kahn, the allocation of *limited investment resources* among different industries or projects should be such as to ensure *maximum social returns or national product*, rather than achieving maximum return to the private investors. The maximum national product will be achieved from the limited investment *resources when* marginal social product (SMP) of investment in different industries or projects are equalised. Kahn emphasises that marginal social product does not mean what an investment would yield to the private investor but what it contributes to the social or national product. To quote Kahn, "The correct criterion for obtaining the maximum return from limited resources is social marginal productivity, taking into account the *total net contribution of marginal unit* to *national product*, and not merely that portion of the contribution (or its costs) which may accrue to the private investor."[13]

The private marginal productivity of investment can be written as

$$MP = \frac{R - C}{K}$$

where MP is private marginal productivity of investment, R is the discounted stream of future returns, C is the discounted stream of future costs and K stands for capital funds. Now, in Kahn's criterion social marginal productivity of investment is found by adding net external economies to the above private marginal product to obtain social marginal product.

Thus $$SMP = \frac{R - C + E}{K} \qquad ...(1)$$

where E is the discounted stream of future net external economies.

It may be noted that it is the addition of net externalities (E) that accounts for the difference between the private and social benefits. According to *Kahn's investment criterion for obtaining maximum social or national output, marginal social products (SMP) of investment in different industries or projects be equalised.*

Extension and Improvement made by Chenery. Chenery extended Kahn's social marginal productivity criterion by including in it the impact of investment projects on the balance of payments to find the socially optimum investment pattern. Two aspects of his extension of Kahn's criterion are noteworthy. First, it includes the *ranking* of different investment projects according to their effect on their national income, balance of payments and the costs of the domestic and imported materials used in production. The second aspect is the actual *number* of investment projects from which to choose. It will depend on the costs of projects and the availability of investment funds.

Given the above considerations, the social marginal productivity is obtained from the *increase in the social value added* (*i.e.*, $X + E$) minus costs incurred on labour, materials (both domestic and imported) and overhead costs expressed as a ratio of total investment funds (K). With this we write social marginal product (SMP) of investment as per Chenery's criterion. Thus

$$SMP = \frac{X + E - (L + M + O)}{K} \qquad ...(2)$$

11 A.E. Kahn, "Investment Criteria in Development Programmes", *Quarterly Journal of Economics*, Feb., 1951, pp. 38-61, reprinted in A.N. Aggarwal and S.P. Singh (ed.), *Accelerating Investment in Developing Economies*, 1969, pp. 131-157.

12 Hollis B. Chenery, "The Application of Investment Criteria", *Quarterly Journal of Economics*, Feb., 1963. pp. 76-96, reprinted in A.N.' Aggarwal and S.P. Singh (ed.), *op. cit.*, pp. 158-181.

13 A. K. Kahn, *op. cit.*

where X is increased *market value* of output and E is the addition to value of output due to net external economies, while L is labour costs, M is costs incurred in both domestic and imported materials and O is overhead costs and K is total capital investment made. Further, the combined $X + E$ can be represented by V and the combined costs $L + M + O$ can be written as C. With this social marginal product (SMP) in equation (3) can be written as

$$SMP = \frac{V - C}{K}. \quad \ldots(3)$$

Now, an important contribution of Chenery has been to include the effect of investment projects on balance of payments. Some investment projects require imported materials for which foreign exchange is needed. Similarly, the products of the investment projects may be exported which earn foreign exchange. (X stands for national product and for external economies). Chenery adds the term $\frac{B_r}{K}$ to the above Kahn's measure of social marginal product (SMP) in equation (3) to show the impact of balance of payment on social marginal productivity (SMP) of an investment project. To do so we have

$$SMP = \frac{V - C}{K} + \frac{B_r}{K}. \quad \ldots(4)$$

If r equals zero, the term $\frac{B_r}{K}$ will also be zero which implies balance of payments is in equilibrium and therefore demand for foreign exchange equals its supply. If r is positive it implies a surplus in balance of payments and if r is negative it means a deficit in balance of payments. Actually, r in Chenery's formulation is taken to represent the investment in national income that could be considered as equivalent to one unit improvement in the balance of payments under the given conditions. It could, therefore, be regarded "*as a premium attached to foreign exchange earning or saving*". And it could be measured in terms of the average overvaluation of the national currency at the prevailing rate of exchange.[14]

To sum up, *according to this criterion, those investments should be made in which social marginal productivity is the highest.* Those who advocate social marginal productivity as the main investment criterion have also deduced several corollaries as practical guides to investment policy. Some of these are: (1) a given volume of investment should be allocated in a manner that maximizes the ratio of current output to investment, *i.e.*, capital-output ratio be minimized; (2) those investment projects should be selected that will maximize the ratio of labour to investment so as to maximise the growth of employment; and (3) to reduce pressures on the balance of payments, investment should be allocated in a manner that will maximize the ratio of export goods to investment.

Merits of SMP Criterion

Social marginal productivity criterion of investment is very useful as it shows the effect of investment projects on the total value of social product as compared to the marginal rule, that is, equating marginal productivities of investment in different projects which is based on profitability from the viewpoints of private investors. Further, as improved by Chenery social marginal productivity (SMP) criterion also incorporates the impact of investment projects on balance of payments which is highly significant as developing countries often face the balance of payments problem.

Furthermore, by considering the effects of external economies and diseconomies on the value of national product and costs, social *marginal* productivity criterion a significant part of social benefits and costs of various investment projects are taken into account.

Thus, the social marginal productivity criterion which aims to achieve *maximum social returns* from limited investment resources makes a significant improvement over the minimum capital-output

14 Of course, account has to be taken of "the expected effect on imports and exports of the whole investment programme and also the balance of payments position at the beginning". Vide, Chenery, in Aggarwal and Singh, *op. cit.*, p. 163.

ratio criterion. By including the effect of pattern investment on balance of payments, Chenery has made it very useful tool of project evaluation.

A Critical Evaluation

Despite the merits of social marginal productivity criterion, its application in actual world is, however, likely to be difficult. This is because development is a dynamic process which involves change in the size and quality of population, tastes and pattern of demand, technological knowledge and social and institutional factors. The criterion of social marginal productivity must therefore be interpreted within the total dynamic complex. To do this, one must make value judgments regarding the various social objectives, some of which can be conflicting.

Suppose an economy is at a stage when investment in agriculture is likely to be most productive and will provide maximum employment to rural labour. Even then it does not follow that priority to investment in agriculture is decided for ever. This is because, as the economy grows, in accordance with Engel's law of consumption, the demand for industrial products increases relativity to foodgrains and to meet this demand allocation of investment resources has to be raised. With further growth, the *demand for services* increases relatively more as compared to the demands for agricultural and industrial goods. This calls for higher allocation of resources to services.

Secondly, different patterns of investment are likely to result in different distribution of income. But by not incorporating in the SMP criterion, the effects of investment on income distribution, Chenery ignores a very important aspect of economic development. Investment affects welfare not only through the economic growth it achieves but also how it affects income distribution in a society. For example, if a pattern of investment chosen on the basis of SMP criterion maximises total output or income but at the same time involves a more unequal distribution of income than would another project do, should it be preferred? Answers to questions like this involve value judgements and different individuals may reach different conclusions. The social marginal productivity of project will alone not be a sufficient guide to investment.

Like the capital-output criterion, the social marginal productivity criterion is also ambiguous as a guide to social investment decisions, *when the shape of income stream over time is considered.* To determine the most productive investment projects, future yields of capital assets must be discounted to their present values, and these discounted values compared with their present costs. Investment decisions will differ according to the shape of the future income stream which is desired. For instance, from the standpoint of having a maximum increase in national output during the next five years, one type of investment, say, cotton textile production, might be the best. From the standpoint of having the highest national output 15 years hence, investment in some other direction, say steel production, might be better. Conflicting conclusions will also emerge if we want to maximise level of consumption over different periods of time, say immediately or later. One project may raise consumption level in the short run and another prove to be more fruitful in this direction in the long run. It is therefore not easy to decide which project to choose. Thus even though there may be an agreement on a general principle, it will be difficult to take an investment decision in actual practice in a dynamic world.

Further, the SMP criterion *evaluates various investment projects independent of one another,* and *ignores the structural linkages* among various investment projects through supply of inputs and sale of output. For appropriate and consistent resource allocation requires input-output analysis which takes into account these linkages between various industries. But these linkages between industries do not find any place in SMP criterion. In this connection special mention may be made of lack of infrastructures facilities in the fields of power, transport, communication (especially telecommunication), roads and highways, iron and steel which serve as a constraint on the growth of other industries and therefore by not taking into account the important linkage of investment in various industries with adequate investment in the growth of infrastructural facilities SMP criterion cannot ensure rapid and sustained growth of gross national product (GDP). Thus one should evaluate not a particular investment project but a package of projects if SMP criterion is to ensure appropriate pattern of investment.

CHAPTER

47

ALTERNATIVE INVESTMENT CRITERIA

In the previous chapter, we have critically examined *'Minimum Capital-Output Ratio'* and *'Social Marginal Productivity Criterion'*. There are some other investment criteria, namely, *'Marginal Reinvestment Quotient Criterion, 'Growing Points Criterion'* and *'Social Costs and Benefits Criterion'*. The choice of investment priorities has to be determined in the light of objectives of development and also the preference between the present consumption and future growth of the economy. A change in the emphasis on some objectives will lead to the change in the allocation of investment resources. For instance if there is widespread unemployment in the economy, the larger investment expenditure may be directed toward the development of labour-intensive small scale industries. On the other hand, if the objective is to achieve the higher rate of growth of the economy, then capital-intensive basic and capital goods industries will be given higher priority as was dine by P. C. Mahalanobis in his basic heavy industry strategy of development for the Second. Five Year Plan of India. Recently, following the studies of Prof. Amartya Sen the human resources such as education and health for expanding capabilities of the people and thereby to achieve higher growth are being given higher priority in investment allocation by the developing countries. In what follows we critically examine 'Marginal Reinvestment Quotient Criterion put forward by Galenson and Leibenstein and 'Growing Points Criterion. 'Social Costs-Benefits Criterion' will be discussed in the next chapter.

MARGINAL REINVESTMENT QUOTIENT CRITERION

Marginal reinvestment quotient criterion has been suggested by Galenson and Leibenstein[1] which seeks to maximise investible surplus per worker so that it can be reinvested to maximise rate of growth of the economy. It aims at maximising per capita income and consumption at some future point of time rather than maximise the income or consumption at the present. For this purpose the rate of savings or surplus should be maximised so that the rate of reinvestment can be maximised. Hence, each unit of investment should be chosen "that will give each worker greater productive power than any other alternative."

This criterion assumes that profits are largely saved and reinvested and that wages are largely spent on consumption. Actually, according to the advocates of this criterion, the amount available for reinvestment is determined by *'net productivity per worker minus consumption per worker'*, called the marginal reinvestment quotient. The formula given for the rate of reinvestment is as follows:

$$r = \frac{p - ew}{c}$$

1 W. Galenson and H. Leibenstein, "Investment Criteria, Productivity and Economic Development", *Quarterly Journal of Economics*, August 1955. pp. 348-70, reprinted in A.N. Aggarwal and S.P. Singh (ed.), *Op. cit.* pp. 182-207.

where, r = rate of investment

p = net output per machine;

e = the number of workers per machine;

w = real wage rate;

c = cost per machine, (*i.e.*, c is the cost of investment made in machine)

To maximise the flow of investment that is created by a unit of investment today, it is recommended that the capital resources should be so allocated among the alternative uses that the marginal per capita reinvestment quotient is the same in different alternatives. The application of the law of equi-marginal return will bring about an optimal utilisation of scarce capital resources.

According to this criterion, capital-intensive projects should be undertaken in developing countries even though capital is scarce because in this way output per capita will be maximised. Maximisation of reinvestible surplus in the present is required so that each additional unit of labour is equipped with maximum possible capital so that output per worker is maximised to achieve the highest possible growth rate. This criterion implies the allocation of investment resources to the projects with a much higher capital-intensity than if the aim was to maximise consumption in the present. The greater capital intensity, given the wage rate, ensures higher profits which when reinvested will bring about higher growth rate. With higher growth rate at some future point, higher consumption per capita will be achieved. The focus of Galenson and Leibenstein is the choice of projects or industries that causes higher rate of capital accumulation on which rate of economic growth depends. Elaborating Galenson-Leibenstein criterion, Thirlwall writes, "It is designed to take account of the influence of projects on the rate of capital formation, or to put it another way, to take account of the choice of projects on the distribution of income between savers and spenders. The economic basis of the approach is the belief that the level of *per capita* output is largely determined by the capital-labour ratio and the amount of capital per worker must largely depend on the level of profits (the surplus over wages) stemming from the original investment."[2]

It may by noted that Galenson and Leibenstein argued against the labour-abundant countries specialising in labour-intensive industries in line with their comparative cost on the ground that labour-intensive industries would yield lower 'reinvestment quotient'. Their criterion favours-capital intensive industries because it will not be necessary to pay more wages and as a result will generate more surplus or profits over wages and thereby will ensure higher rate of investment. According to them, if labour-intensive industries are given higher priority, more wage employment will be created, more additional wages will be paid which will be consumed, there will be less surplus or saving and investment. Therefore, Galenson and Leibenstein recommend strategy of development which favour capital-intensive basic heavy industries such as iron and steel, fertilizers, machine toots, power generating and other capital-producing industries as they have a higher 'reinvestment quotient' or those which maximise *productivity per worker minus consumption.*

It is worthwhile to give an example which Galenson and Leibenstein give in their article mentioned above. They explain that, given certain assumptions, an amount of employment generated over a period of time by an initial investment of ₹ 1,200 in various kinds of cotton textile *machinery*. They say that if this sum of funds is invested in handlooms *i.e.*, cottage industries, it would initially generate employment for 35 persons and since there will be *no margin for reinvestment* (almost all output being paid as wages), there will be no growth even after 25 years and the amount of employment provided will still be thirty-five. On the other hand, if the same amount of funds (*i.e.*, ₹ 1,200) is invested in a large-scale modern mill, it will initially create employment for 5 workers but because it will yield large surplus for further reinvestment and growth, the extra employment generated will exceed 35 after 15 years.

2 A.P. Thirlwall, *Growth and Development with Special Reference to Developing Economies*, New York: Palgrave Macmillan, 4th edition, p. 366.

It is noteworthy that similar logic was used by the supporters of basic heavy industry strategy of development proposed by P C. Mahalanobis. Thus, to quote Dr. K. N. Raj, "The logic here is the same as the more common proposition that a higher rate of investment, *i.e.*, a larger proportion of productive factors used for capital formation would result in a smaller volume of output being available for consumption in the short run but that over a long period, it would result in higher level of growth of consumption; the difference is that the choice is here stated as between investment in capital goods and consumer goods industries."[3]

It follows from above that Galenson-Leibenstein criterion does not give much priority to *present* consumption and welfare and focuses on accumulating capital for greater output and consumption in future. The application of this criterion leads to the choice of highly capital-intensive projects and larger sacrifice of present consumption. Galenson and Leibenstein implicitly assume that the *gain in future* output and consumption will more than offset the consumption losses in the initial periods. The capital-intensive projects are advocated also on the ground that they will provide training to the workforce and experience to management and these are the things that the developing countries lack the most.

Critical Evaluation

However, this Galenson-Leibenstein criterion suffers from some serious objections. First, it is not necessarily always true that the most capital-intensive techniques ensure highest rate of reinvestment. Increased capital intensity while raising labour productivity, also raises the cost of capital. So that the rate of reinvestment will increase only if the rise in labour productivity is more than the increase in capital cost.

Second, this criterion is based on the assumption that all wages are consumed and all profits are reinvested. But, it is quite likely that as with higher capital intensity, the productivity of workers will be greater which will prompt them to get their wages increased. This will make the workers better off than before and will thus able to contribute to savings. Similarly, it is unlikely that the whole profits would saved and reinvested.

Third, it has been assumed that the proportion of consumption national income remains unchanged over time. But it is unlikely to be so. The consumption of the community will normally increase with the increase in employment. So the volume of investible surplus will decline unless, of course, with additional employment, the increase in output is more than the increase in consumption.

Fourth, increase in capital intensity of production is likely to render some labour unemployed. And the unemployed labour has got to be provided with something to survive. There is thus the social cost of unemployment which the authors have neglected.[4]

Fifth, the *criterion values future income and consumption more than the present income and consumption*. That would mean overstraining the present generation for the comforts of the future generation. What is required is a proper balance between the present and future income and consumption.

Sixth, the criterion is suggestive of a greater emphasis on the capital goods sector to the neglect of the consumer goods sector. But this is fraught with serious socio-economic consequences. There may be social unrest due to inflation resulting from the scarcity of essential consumer goods. This happened during the Second and Third Five Year plan periods.

Lastly, the application of this criterion is likely to produce some undesirable social effects: It will accentuate inequalities in income and wealth in the community, because the capitalists will gain at the expense of the wage earners.

3 Raj, K. N., "Growth Models in Indians Planning, *The Indian Economic Review*, Feb. 1961.

4 Hans Neisser, "Investment Criteria, Productivity and Economic Development: Comment", *Quarterly Journal of Economics*, Nov. 1955, pp. 644-45.

Growing Points Criterion

It has generally come to be accepted that the basic consideration in selecting industries for development in an underdeveloped economy is the prospect of external economies. Allyn Young drew attention to this important consideration in 1928, and Rosenstein-Rodan in 1943 made out a strong case for developing those industries which would create conditions favourable to the growth of other industries. *Some enterprises may promote economic development more by indirect contribution to the output of the economy than by their own direct contribution.* Investment in infrastructure projects has a high potential for development. For example, the development of transport, roads and highways or of sources of fuel and power influence both the costs and the market possibilities of diverse manufacturing industries or investment in iron and steel and engineering industries increase the growth potentiality of industry in general.

From the standpoint of supply, it thus emerges that one of the requirements of investments should be that *it creates additional external economies*. From this point of view, it will be better to direct investment so as to bring about and promote horizontal and vertical integration of the process of production and introduce a more effective and fruitful division of labour. Investment should be in such directions as to help the industries avail themselves jointly of facilities like pool of technical skill, a common source of raw materials or better utilisation of social overheads. In this manner, the economy will move nearer to an optimum increase in national output.

On the demand side, when considering particular industries, one cannot assume that supply will create its own demand. There must be markets for the commodities produced. Where are the potential markets in the poor countries? Investment should be made in those industries which would have a readily available demand. The demand for building and construction is likely to be high, since poor countries are deficient in roads, railways, houses and public utilities. Investment in export industries for which there is a foreign demand is another attractive area, and import substituting industries provide still another potential choice of investment.

Giving Higher Priority to Industries with Greatest 'Total Linkages'

It is important to refer here the unbalanced growth strategy of Hirschman[5] who favoured unbalanced growth and pointed out that economic growth cannot be accelerated by an even distribution of investment among various sectors or industries. He, on the other hand, strongly feels that investment priority should be given to strategically selected industries—industries which have the greatest '*total linkage*'. The establishment of any industry may encourage investment in both the succeeding and preceding stages of production. That is to say, the setting up of a particular industry may produce both the '*forward' and 'backward' linkages*. In this view, therefore, investment should first be made in those industries or sectors which have the greatest 'total linkage'.

The same industries need not necessarily be the industries with greatest 'total linkage' effect in all countries. For any country, the industries with the highest potential of total linkage can be determined from the input-output tables of the economy. The building of such projects or industries as have the highest linkage effects would produce a spurt of investment over a variety of other fields. The crux of this approach, therefore, lies in directing investment in judiciously selecting industries that have the highest 'total linkage' score.

These considerations of external economies, total linkages, and of available market demand, may be summarised by saying that investment should be directed to 'growing points' in the economy. In the initial stages of economic development, it is highly useful to concentrate on certain focal points which seem to have the promise of more rapid growth. These focal points refer to those projects the products of which have a readily available demand and which provide significant external economies to other existing firms and industries and greater linkages or they will generate demand for supplementary

5 Hirschman, A.O., *The Strategy of Economic Development*, Yale University Press, 1918.

products and services. From these focal areas a chain reaction usually starts that gradually spreads chain to the remaining areas of the economy. Thus even an unbalanced process of initial economic growth has every possibility of ultimately merging into the broader requirement of balanced growth.

Employment Absorption Criterion

It is well known that in the developing but overpopulated countries, labour supply is abundant and cheap. There is large-scale unemployment or underemployment, especially in the agricultural sector in the form of disguised unemployment. Hence, it is suggested such investments should be undertaken which are capital-saving and labour-absorbing. In other words, such industries should be given higher priority which are labour-intensive. Besides providing more employment, such labour-intensive industries and techniques will raise the level of consumption because the newly employed labour will spend most of their incomes on consumption. Higher propensity to consume will stimulate further investment which will accelerate economic growth. Also, such techniques will be conducive to a high degree of economic equality by rising the level of incomes of the working class people.

But the defect of such labour-techniques is that they do not necessarily maximise the national output. Labour-intensive techniques are not as productive as the capital-intensive techniques. Low labour productivity may be perpetuated. Besides, the quality of the end-products suffers. However, for a country suffering from widespread unemployment, a very suitable criterion of investment is that investment, should be made in those industries which have a high employment potential. Investment will also depend on the type of unemployment it is sought to cure. If unemployment among the educated classes is more rampant, then it will be necessary to create employment opportunities specially for this class of people by opening more schools, expanding facilities for teachers' training and developing small industries which the educated people may be able to manage. If, on the other hand, it is a case of disguised unemployment among the rural masses, then it will be necessary not only to employ them in the urban areas by opening there suitable avenues of employment but also absorbing them in agriculture by increasing capital formation especially expansion of irrigation, in it and undertaking land reforms to raise productivity and cropping intensity in agriculture. Setting up suitable agro-processing industries in close proximity to the rural areas can be very helpful. Rural development programmes may be intensified to absorb surplus labour in productive employment.

Conclusion

From the above analysis of the various investment criteria, it is clear that we cannot lay down dogmatically the criterion or criteria which should guide us in undertaking investment. There are so many considerations influencing investment that one would easily lose one's way in the maze of numerous investment criteria. In this possible confusion it is best to bear in mind the economic situation at the time and the principal objective or objectives that are desired to be achieved. The investment must accord with their objectives. Of the criteria mentioned above one or the other will determine investment as the situation demands or according to the objective kept in view. The latest investment criterion which has gained much popularity in recent years is of '*Social Cost-Benefit Criterion*' which we will discuss in the next chapter.

CHAPTER

48

COST-BENEFIT ANALYSIS AND PROJECT EVALUATION

Cost-Benefit Analysis: Meaning and Approach

While taking business decisions the private firms being driven mainly by profit motive take into account only the internal direct effects (that is, cash flows accruing to them and the costs they have to incur) and *do not take the longer and wider view of their activities from the social point of view*. But public enterprises and non-profit institutions have to take a broader social repercussion of their resource allocation and investment decisions. That is, they take into account both internal (direct) and external (indirect) effects of their business decisions. An analytical model called cost-benefit analysis is used to analyse the wider impact of resource allocation and investment decisions. Properly understood, it is *Social Cost-Benefit Analysis* of investment projects though the word '*social*' is often omitted. Thus in social cost-benefit analysis, we estimate both the *direct* and *indirect* costs of a project to the society and *both the direct and indirect benefits to it*. These indirect costs and indirect benefits are often called **externalities**. Thus social cost and benefit analysis in addition to the direct costs and benefits take into account the externalities of an investment project.

Therefore, *cost-benefit analysis is especially used for analysing the desirability of public sector investment projects and programmes and is a counterpart of capital budgeting technique which is used to evaluate an investment project by a private enterprise*. Explaining the essence of cost-benefit analysis Prest and Turvey who are the pioneers of the technique of cost-benefit analysis write, "*Cost-benefit analysis is a practical way of assessing the desirability of projects where it is important to take a long view (in the sense of looking at repercussions in the distant future as well as the nearer future) and a wider view (in the sense of allowing for side-effects of many kinds and many persons, industries, regions, etc.), i.e., it implies the enumeration and evaluation of all relevant costs and benefits*."[1] It is important to note that in estimating social costs of a project **market prices of resources** are not used as they are generally distorted; they are distorted due to the imposition of taxes by the Government or due to the market imperfections or monopoly power of the resource owners. Instead, in social cost-benefit analysis **shadow prices** which reflect the opportunity costs or true scarcity values of the resources are used.

It is worth noting that public sector enterprises and non-profit institutions face the same problem of resource allocation and investment as the private sector. But in deciding about them while the public sector enterprises take a wider view and consider both internal and external effects (*i.e.*, externalities) of their decisions, the private sector, guided by profit considerations alone, adopts a narrow view and takes into account only internal effects of their business decisions, disregarding the external effects which may be harmful or beneficial. Thus in cost-benefit analysis we are not concerned only with internal benefits and internal costs of an investment project to be undertaken.

1 Prest and Turvey, *Economic Journal*, December, 1975.

Instead the cost-benefit analysis enumerates and evaluates *all social benefits and all social costs of a project or expenditure programme in contrast to the capital budgeting technique used by private firms which take into account only their private costs and private benefits to judge the desirability of an investment project*. Thus, to quote Todaro and Smith, "The need for social cost-benefit analysis arises because the normal yardstick of commercial profitability that guides the investment decisions of private investors may not be appropriate guide for public investment decisions. Private enterprises are interested in maximising private profits and therefore normally *take into account only the variables that affect net profit receipts and expenditure*. Both receipts and benefits are valued at *prevailing market prices* for inputs and outputs."[2]

According to the social cost-benefit analysis, the actual revenue or receipts from a project do not truly reflect the social benefits from a project nor the expenditure incurred on the inputs valued at market prices used as the true social costs. Besides, in calculation of social costs and benefits, the Government or planner takes into account the **external effects** (both external economies and diseconomies) of the public investment projects whereas private enterprise will ignore them in its evaluation of a project.

It follows from above that divergence of social costs and benefits from private costs and benefits, the investment decisions based on private costs and benefits would lead to inappropriate **decisions** which will therefore not maximise social welfare. Further, the approach of social cost-benefit analysis thinks that social costs and benefits can be arrived at by making suitable adjustments in market prices. Besides, since benefits from an investment project accrue mostly in the future years and costs are also incurred for a long period in future, it is *discounted social benefits* and *discounted social costs* that are compared to decide about the desirability of a project. However, for discounting social costs and benefits of an investment project, it is **social discount rate** that is used to obtain the net present value rather than market rate of interest.

The Use of Cost-Benefit Analysis

As mentioned above, the technique of cost-benefit analysis is particularly used when *a long and wider view* of the effects of a particular project or expenditure programme is needed. As in case of capital budgeting by private firms cost-benefit analysis is generally used in case when the economic effects of a project or an investment expenditure programme or policy change *accrue in future years*. However, unlike the capital budgeting by private firms, the cost-benefit analysis attempts to estimate all direct economic effects as well as indirect spill-over effects.

Cost-benefit analysis is used to assess whether a particular project or specific public expenditure programme should be accepted or rejected. In order to do so, benefits, both direct and indirect, of the project or specific public expenditure programme and similarly the costs to be incurred on the project over the years are estimated. Then the present value of both the benefits and costs over the future years are estimated using an **appropriate discount rate from social points of view**. It follows from above that cost-benefit analysis is a method of evaluating public projects and investment programmes for making decisions regarding the desirability of the projects to be undertaken. Accordingly, it is used to assess big public investment schemes such as building dams and airports, controlling diseases (for example, malaria control programme), planning for defence and safety, and spending for health, education and research.

Cost-Benefit Criterion

Having calculated the present values of both benefits and costs at a given social discount rate, then the two are compared. If using the given social discount rate *present value of benefits from a project (or other investment programme) exceeds the present value of costs, the said project or investment*

2 Michael P. Todaro and Stephen C. Smith, *Economic Development*, Pearson Education Ltd. Tenth Edition 2012, p. 535 (italics added).

programme is accepted for being undertaken. On the other hand, if present value of benefits is less than the present value of costs, the proposed project or investment programme is economically inefficient and should be rejected.

Besides being used to evaluate the economic justification of the entire investment project, the cost-benefit analysis is used to determine whether the size of project under implementation be increased and if so to what extent. Such decision is usually made by using traditional marginal analysis be estimating additional benefits from the proposed increase in size and additional costs to be made. Thus the objective of public sector decisions-making whether it is building of an airport or regulating a public utility (such as electricity generation and distribution) is wider than maximising private profits which guides private sector decision. *In making a decision the Government or public enterprise has not only to consider benefits that accrue as revenue to the enterprise but also the external benefits (beneficial externalities) that accrue to other members of the society.* Likewise, the cost-benefit analysis considers not only the costs that are paid by the enterprise but also the costs (*including environment pollution*) it inflicts on others by its activity.

General Steps in Making Cost-Benefit Analysis

There are no simple rules or steps which government or any public authority should follow to undertake cost-benefit analysis. Through cost-benefit analysis we seek to find **social profitability** of a project. In the calculation of social profitability we need to measure both social benefits and social costs taking into account both direct social costs and benefits (that is, the real costs of inputs used directly in the project, and real benefits in the form of real value of outputs obtained directly from it) and indirect costs (*e.g.* external diseconomies) and indirect benefits (*e.g.* the creation of employment opportunities). The social profitability is judged by the difference between social benefits (both direct and indirect) and social costs (both direct and indirect). The whole process of calculating social profitability or social cots and benefits can be divided into the following four steps:

1. Specifying Social Objective Function: The first step in making cost-benefit analysis is to **specify the social objective function** that has to be maximised. In this objective function the **weights** are to be assigned to different benefits (*e.g.* increase in per capita consumption, increase, in employment, desired income distribution). These weights will reflect the importance given to the various benefits of the project.

2. Identifying Various Benefits and Costs: The second step in cost-benefit analysis is to identify and enumerate all benefits and costs, both direct and indirect, of investment projects. The direct benefits of a project can be measured by the extra quantity of goods and services produced if the project is undertaken compared to the conditions without it. Thus, the direct benefits of an irrigation project is the quantity of extra crop produced net of extra costs in the form of more labour, seeds and equipment used as compared to the non-irrigated land. On the other hand, direct costs include capital costs incurred on capital equipment, machines installed, land acquired to undertake and implement the project and the operating and maintenance costs incurred over the life span of the project.

In addition to the direct effects of an investment project, there are invariably *indirect or external effects*. These indirect or external beneficial effects are classified into two types, (1) *real or technological and* (2) *the pecuniary effects*. The real external benefits may include reduction in costs to be incurred on other Government programmes. For example, the construction of an irrigation dam may lead to reduction in flooding and soil erosion which would reduce the Government outlay on flood control and anti-soil erosion programmes. Such real indirect benefits are counted in cost-benefit studies.

On the other hand, *indirect* (*external*) ***pecuniary*** *benefits* are not generally included in the enumeration of benefits and costs in a cost-benefit study. These external pecuniary benefits accrue in the form of increased volume of business or increase in land values as a consequence of undertaking a project. Thus the areas in Delhi which fall near Metro railway routes have caused increase in land values in these areas. Besides, the shops and restaurants which exist in the areas surrounding the metro lines have found increase in the volume of their business. These indirect or external pecuniary benefits are distributional and not counted in cost benefit studies of Metro-railways.

Similarly, indirect multiplier effects and induced investment effects which result from Government investment projects are also generally not counted (except in some special circumstances) since they would occur whether investment made is by the public sector or private sector. For example, if the objective of Government investment programme is regional development, undertaking a local investment project may induce local investment, create multiplier effect on generation of income and employment resulting in reduction of regional unemployment. Since regional development forms a part of the social objective function to be maximised, some include them in their cost-benefit studies of regional investment programme.

3. Evaluation of Social Benefits and Costs: The third step in the social cost-benefit analysis is to measure social values of benefits, that is, outputs (both goods and services) produced by the project and social costs of inputs used in the project.

For evaluation of outputs of goods and services their *shadow prices* (also called *accounting prices*) are used instead of their market prices. *Shadow prices are used to measure social values of outputs since there is divergence of market prices from their true social values.* We will explain later in detail the various reasons for the divergence of market values of outputs and inputs from their true social values. In fact, the greater the divergence between the shadow prices and market prices, the greater the need for social cost-benefit analysis for deciding about public investment.

Similarly, in cost-benefit analysis costs are also measured using **shadow prices** of inputs or factors used in the project. It is noteworthy that **shadow prices of inputs or factors are their opportunity costs or the values** foregone by the factors and resources used for the initial capital investment and production during the life period of the project. This is because resources have to by withdrawn from other activities to the implementation of the proposed project.[3] For example, if for undertaking an irrigation project, 50 per cent of required labour is withdrawn from the ranks of unemployed labour force. The soical opportunity cost of such labour is zero and ought to be calculated as such in cost-benefit analysis though the workers employed will be paid market wages. The same holds in case of *idle land* used for a project. With no alternative use, the opportunity cost of idle land is zero. This is so despite the fact that Government has actually to pay compensation to the landowners for acquiring this idle land. This compensation will affect only the distribution of benefits from the project for use of land and not the social cost of the project.

All the benefits and costs (both internal and external) over the life span of the project have to discounted to obtain their present values. In this connection a difficult decision has also to be made about **appropriate social discount rate** with which future benefits and costs are discounted to find their present values.

Another important issue in the calculation of social benefits and costs is in what **common unit of account** (also called **numeraire**) social benefits and social costs are measured and expressed, especially when a country has trade relations with other countries of the world and, therefore, needs to sell and buy abroad. This common unit is required to make domestic and foreign goods comparable. There are two main approaches to find the common unit of account. The first approach is **UNIDO approach** and the second is **Little-Mirrlees** approach.

In the UNIDO approach benefits and costs are measured at **domestic market prices** using consumption as **numeraire**. Besides, in this approach adjustments are made for the divergence of market prices from social values by using shadow prices of goods and factors. Furthermore, to make the domestic and foreign resources comparable, **shadow exchange rate** is used.[4]

3 E.J. Mishan, *Cost Benefit Analysis.*

4 For knowing the details of this approach Sea Partha Das Gupta, Stephen Margin and Amartya Sen, *UNIDO Guide lines for Project Evaluation* (New York: United Nationa Industrial Development Organisation, 1972).

In the Little-Mirrlees approach benefits and costs of projects are measured at **world prices** so that they should depict the opportunity costs of outputs and inputs. The use of world prices for measuring benefits and costs helps in avoiding the use of shadow exchange rate. Further, **in Little-Mirrlees approach, instead of consumption public saving** in foreign exchange is used as **numeraire**. That is, benefits and costs in this approach are evaluated in terms of foreign exchange equivalent. However, this does not mean that project accounts are kept in foreign currency but only that in the project appraisal report values are recorded in terms of foreign exchange equivalent so as to estimate how much foreign exchange is earned by the project.

It may be noted that in both UNIDO and Mirrlees approaches some problems of measurement are faced.

4. **Finding Social Discount Rate**: In the cost-benefit analysis the next step is to choose an appropriate social discount rate. Since benefits from an investment project are reaped mostly in the future years and costs are also incurred for a long period in future, it is **discounted social benefits** and **discounted social costs** that are compared to decide about the social desirability of a project. For this a social discount rate is required. The private enterprises in their calculation of commercial profitability **market rate** of **interest** is used to discount the future benefits and costs. However, for social profitability of the public sector investment, market rate of interest is not appropriate for discounting future social benefits and costs.

Now why social rate of discount differs from market rate of interest? The private individuals hope to live only a certain number of years and therefore discount the future at a higher rate which is reflected in the market rate of interest. On the other hand, since the planners or the government in developing countries would like to take a longer view and give greater importance to the consumption and welfare of the future generations, they will use a lower discount rate for discounting a stream of future social benefits and costs, both evaluated using shadow prices. Thus, Todaro and Smith write, "Social discount rate may differ from market rates of interest **depending on subjective evaluation placed on future net benefits**; the higher the future benefits and costs are valued in the government's planning scheme–for example, if government also represents future unborn citizens, the lower the social discount rate will be"[5]

5. **Decision Criteria to Choose a Project:** Finally, it has to be decided whether an investment project should be accepted for investment by the government or rejected. For this a decision criterion is required. The most commonly used criterion is **net present value (NPV) criterion**. To use this criterion we have to find the net present value of the proposed project by using the following formula

$$\text{NPV} = \sum_{t=0}^{n}\left(\frac{V_t - C_t}{1+r_t}\right) - K_o\,.$$

where V_t is the stream of social benefits measured by using shadow prices of goods produced, C_t is the social cost of inputs measured by their shadow prices (*i.e.,* opportunity costs), r_t is the social rate of discount and K_o is the social cost of investment in the project.

Now, an investment project is economically profitable from the viewpoint of the society if the net present value (NPV) of the project using social rate of discount is positive (*i.e.,* exceeds zero). In other words, the proposed investment project should be accepted for investment if the present value (PV) of the project exceeds the social cost of initial capital investment (K_o) of the present.

Internal Rate of Return Approach

It is noteworthy that net present value (NPV) is highly sensitive to social rate of discount chosen to find the net present value. Therefore, an alternative criterion of internal rate of return is used to accept or reject a project. The internal rate of return method is also based on present value of net

5 Todaro and Smith, *op.* cit, (10th ed.), p. 541 (italics added).

cash flows generated by a project over its life period. *Internal Rate of Return (IRR) is the rate of discount that equates the present value of net cash flows equal to the initial investment cost of the project.* If $R_1, R_2, R_3, \ldots, R_n$ represent the net cash flows associated with a project which have an initial investment cost equal to C_0, Internal rate of return (IRR) is calculated by setting.

$$\frac{R_1}{(1+r)} + \frac{R_2}{(1+r)^2} + \frac{R_3}{(1+r)^3} + \ldots + \frac{R_n}{(1+r)^n} = C_0$$

or

$$\sum_{t=1}^{n} \frac{R_t}{(1+r)^t} = C_0$$

Solving for r, we get the internal rate of return.

It may however be noted that for social cost-benefit analysis, the initial cost of the project and return in the form of value added by the production of goods and services by the project over a number of years are calculated using *shadow prices of goods and resources.*

Decision Rule: According to internal rate of return (IRR) method, *if the internal rate of return (r) of a capital project is greater than the cost of capital, investment in the project should be made.* If the internal rate of return (r) is less than the cost of capital, the project should be rejected. When the internal rate of return from a project exceeds the cost of capital, it will increase the value of the firm and is, therefore, worthwhile to make investment in the project. For instance, if the use of funds costs 12 per cent per annum (that is, cost of capital is 12 per cent per annum) to a society and if internal rate of return from the project is 15 per cent, the project should be accepted for investment.

It may however be noted that it is not easy to calculate internal rate of return when the life of a project exceeds one year. Fortunately, these days electronic calculators are available with which we can easily calculate internal rate of return from the data. Further, calculations of present values and internal rate of return can be done using personal computers through simple computer programmes such as *Lotus 1-2-3 or Microsoft Excel*.

Choice Among Several Investment Projects. The method of internal rate of return can also be used to make a choice among several projects. This issue is faced when a firm has limited funds for making investment. To decide about choosing among alternative investment projects on the basis of the criterion of internal rate of return, internal rates of return (IRR) are calculated from the cash flows of various available projects. Then, in terms of the magnitudes of internal rate of return of the various projects can be given rank-ordering from the highest rate of return to the lowest rate of return. Then investment funds should be employed to those projects which yield highest possible rates of return from the given limited available funds.

SHADOW PRICES AND PROJECT EVALUATION

In free market economies allocation of resources among different projects is made through market mechanism and is based on market prices of goods produced by the projects and market prices of factors used in them. However, in developing countries there are many imperfections in the markets for goods and factors and therefore market prices of goods and factors do not reflect their true social benefits and social costs of various investment projects. It is the distortions in goods and factor markets that cause divergence of market prices of goods and resources from their real social values and costs. Therefore, for proper evaluation of various investment projects require their social cost- benefits analysis. Thus, for optimum allocation of investible resources among competing projects require adjustment or correction of market prices of goods and factors so that they should reflect their true social costs and benefits. Therefore, in evaluation of investment projects, economists use **shadow prices** of factors or resources and goods. Little and Mirrlees who have made significant contribution to social cost-benefit analysis of projects write, "The whole point of shadow prices is indeed that **it**

shall correspond more closely to the realities of economic scarcity and strength of economic needs than will guess as to what future prices will actually be."[6] E.J. Mishan in his theory of 'social costs and benefits' gives a simple and general definition of shadow prices. He writes, "A shadow or accounting price is the price the economists attribute to a good or a factor that is **more appropriate rate for** the purpose of economic calculation than its existing price, if any."[7]

But what is more apriate for economic appraisal of investment projects is a subject of severe controversy. Many economists define shadow prices in terms of opportunity cost of a factor or good. Thus, G. Meier writes: "Shadow prices are determined by the interaction of the fundamental policy objectives and the *basic resource availabilities*. If a particular resource is very scarce (that is, many alternative uses are competing for that resource), then its shadow price or opportunity cost (the foregone benefit in the next best alternative that must be sacrificed) will tend to be high. If the supply of this resource were greater, its opportunity cost (or shadow price) will be lower .... in less developed countries, imperfect markets may cause a divergence between market and shadow prices. Such divergences are thought to be particularly severe in the markets for three important resources: labour, capital, and foreign exchange."[8]

A private firm while evaluating the projects for investment will attempt to maximise possible future profits from its given resources. Its appraisal of various projects is based on **market** prices of goods and resources and therefore evaluation of projects for the purpose of investment in it is called **'Commercial Project Appraisal'**. On the other hand, the government or planner in a developing economy is concerned with maximising its social objective function and is therefore concerned with social costs and benefits and therefore its appraisal of projects is based on shadow prices (or opportunity costs) which truly reflect the social costs and benefits of the projects. Therefore, the project appraisal by the government or planner based on shadow prices reflecting real social costs and benefits is called **'Economic Appraisal of the Projects'**. Project appraisal through opportunity costs or shadow prices is an important tool to allocate investment resources optimally in developing countries.

Opportunity Costs as Shadow Prices

Let us explain in some detail the relevance of the concept of opportunity cost in economic appraisal of the projects. When any project uses goods and resources, it deprives them to others. For examples, a project to construct a dam, it will use saving that could otherwise be invested in textile industry or in building rural roads. Similarly, as decision to invest in the expansion of cotton textile industry will need more cotton for its production and this cotton could have been exported to earn foreign exchange. Likewise, labour used for the construction of a dawn might have been employed in the textile industry. It is thus obvious that goods and resources used in one project can be used in alternative projects in the economy. The **concept of opportunity cost implies the value of net benefits of these resources in alternative projects that have to be sacrificed for their use in a particular project**. The shadow prices reflect the opportunity costs of factors or resources used in any investment, project. Three important resources whose shadow prices need to be explained in detail are: labour, capital and foreign exchange. We explain them below.

Opportunity Cost of Labour. In a developing economy with a dual economic structure, there exists surplus labour in agriculture. For an industrial project if labour is withdrawn from agriculture, the opportunity cost of labour is the loss of output in agriculture as a result of withdrawing an additional worker from it and employing him in the industrial, project. Since it is assumed by many economists

6 J.M.D. Little and Mirrlees, "Social cost Benefit Analysis, Project Appraisal and Planning for Developing Countries" In M.G. Meier, *Leading Issues in Economic Development*, 4th edition, 1984.

7 E.J. Mishan, **Cost-Benefit Analysis** 1971.

8 Gerrd M. Meier, 'General Rationale of Project Appraisal - Note' in "*Leading Issues in Economic Development*" edited by him, 4th Edition, p. 640.

that there prevails underemployment and disguised unemployment in agriculture, marginal product of a worker in agriculture, is very low or even zero. On the other hand, when a worker withdrawn from agriculture, is employed in the industry, he will get a market wage rate equal to his marginal productivity in the industry which is much higher than the loss of output in agriculture caused by his withdrawal from it. Thus the **opportunity cost of labour or its shadow wage rate employed in the industrial** project in a labour-surplus developing economy is very low if not zero. This implies that social cost of labour in the industrial project will be much lower than the market wage rate. This will result in greater net social benefits over cost and will go in favour of the project being selected for investment.

Shadow Exchange Rate. The other important example of shadow price relates to the foreign exchange rate. In general, in the developing countries the **shadow exchange rate** tends to be higher than the official exchange rate of domestic currency. This is the result of imposition of high tariffs and quotas on the imports of goods in the developing countries and the avoidance by them to devalue their currencies despite the rise in domestic prices of goods in them due to rapid inflation. This overvaluation of domestic currency discriminates against the export sector that earns more foreign exchange and favours the import substituting industrial projects. To put it in general terms, the higher shadow exchange rate of a domestic currency will tend to raise the **net** cash flows of projects that earn more foreign exchange than they use and those import-substituting projects that save more foreign exchange than they use. *In terms of net discounted cash flows from projects, the use of lower shadow exchange rate for evaluation of the projects will yield a higher net present value of the project and therefore will be preferred for investment*.

Social Discount Rate. The social discount rate, according to one view, should be to take the **marginal rate of return on private capital** as a measure of opportunity cost considering that investment in a public sector project must earn at least the rate of return earned by the private sector which is to be replaced by the public sector investment projects. This gives the social discount rate of 10 to 15 per cent for most of developing countries. In view of the present author, though this approach considers capital as a scarce factor, it yields a higher discount rate and is advocated on the ground that public and private sectors compete for funds and therefore public investment must yield benefits at least equal to the rate of return earned by the private investor which is replaced by the public sector in a planned mixed economy, However, this is not good as the public sector should not aim at maximising rate of return but should pursue maximisation of social welfare.

The second approach to measure social discount rate at which the government or planner whishes to discount the future benefits is determined by the rate at which the marginal utility of public saving declines. This shadow or accounting rate of interest should equal the rate of return on public money. This gives a lower discount rate but involves a higher shadow price or social cost of investment in a project. However, in actual practice, the social discount rate is determined by trial and error method so that its value is such that it does approve more projects that are beyond the investment budget of the government or the planning authority.

It follows from above that finding an appropriate social discount rate is a very ticklish and difficult task. One thing is certain that social rate of discount should measure **social time preference** for current and future consumption and **therefore depends on the subjective evaluation placed on future net benefits** by the government or the planner. Thus Todaro and Smith write, "Social discount rates may differ from market rates of interest (normally used by private investors to calculate the profitability of investments) depending on the subjective evaluation placed on future net benefits. The higher the *future* benefits and costs are valued in the government planning scheme 'for example, if government also represents future unborn citizens, the lower the social discount rate will be."[9]

9 Todaro and Smith, *op.cit*., p. 541.

Decision Rule Regarding Project Selection. To decide whether a public project should be selected or rejected: the **net present value** (NPV) of stream of future benefits and costs of the project is calculated using the shadow prices of resources and social discount rate as given by the following formula:

$$\text{NPV} = \sum_{t=0}^{n} \frac{B_t - C_t}{(1+r)^t}.$$

Where B_t is the future estimated benefits and C_t is the estimated future costs both using shadow prices, r is the social discount rate and n is the number of years representing the life of the project. (Note that C_t above includes the cost of initial investment in the project.) If the net present value (NPV) of the project is positive, it should be accepted for public investment and if its net present value is zero or negative, it should be rejected.

Implementation of Shadow Price in the Real Economy

Now, an important issue is how to implement the shadow prices in the real economy where both the public and private enterprises work. The evaluation of projects on the basis of shadow prices and undertaking those projects that pass the net present value criterion poses a difficult problem for its actual implementation. This is because shadow prices exist only on paper and are used only for evaluating the social desirability of projects. In the real economy, a public or private enterprise which actually undertakes a project has to pay market prices for the resources used by it. Therefore, to be financially viable, it must earn profit at market prices. This makes the implementation of shadow prices difficult in actual practice. For example, if the government or a planning authority in a labour-surplus developing country has found a cotton textile industrial project as a desirable one on the basis of cost-benefits analysis using **low** shadow wage rate. However, whether a public or private enterprise which executes the project will have to pay higher market wage rate to the workers rather than **low** shadow wages which were merely used to judge the economic desirability of the project for maximum absorption of labour in the industry. But the payment of higher market wage rate to the workers may cause the enterprise to suffer losses. Of course, a private enterprise will never undertake such a project however economically desirable it may be on the basis of social cost-benefit analysis. However, if the government wants the project to be undertaken as it generates more employment for labour, it will have to compensate the enterprise. The effective way of compensating the enterprise will be to give a **wage subsidy** equal to the difference between the shadow wage rate and market wage rate that the enterprise actually pays. The payment of wage subsidy to the enterprise will make the project commercially sound and will therefore provide incentive to the enterprise to undertake it.

It follows from above that the projects that are approved on the basis of social cost-benefit analysis using shadow prices require payment of **subsidies** by the government. It is this reasoning that lies behind the payment of subsidies on the fertilizers, petroleum products by the government in India as they are sold to the people at prices cheaper than the market prices.

IMPORTANCE OF COST-BENEFIT ANALYSIS

Social cost-benefit analysis is highly significant for development planning in developing countries. The significant benefit of cost-benefit analysis is that it can guide investment decisions, especially for the public sector. Given the constraint of resources, on the basis of cost-benefit analysis, the Government can choose the most beneficial among them. The Government can use the social cost-benefit analysis even for evaluating the effects of private investment projects. This helps the Government for formulating its policies to either support or discourage private investment. The Government can support private investment projects by providing subsidies or provide financial support through financial institutions. The Government can discourage them by imposing taxes if the social costs exceed social benefits of the private investment.

The significance of cost-benefit analysis can be better recognized when we consider that alternative method of resource allocation is market mechanism which uses **market prices** of goods and services which do not reflect true social benefits and costs of investment projects. As mentioned above, social cost-benefit analysis takes into account wider and broader social benefits and costs incorporating both the direct and indirect effects of an investment. To quote Thirwall, "*The technique of cost-benefit analysis is recommended for the appraisal of publicly financed projects in order to allocate resources in a way that is most profitable to the society, recognising that the market prices of goods and factors of production do not necessarily reflect their social values and costs respectively and given that the society is concerned with the future level of consumption as well as the present, the level of current saving may be suboptimal.*"[10]

Ensuring Optimal Use of Scare Resources. Planning in developing countries requires a lot of investment in infrastructure and heavy projects such as building of highways, airports, irrigation dams and canals, steel plants and communication network. These projects have indirect beneficial effects which are crucial for acceleration of economic growth and generation of employment opportunities. However, these investment projects require not only financial resources which are scarce in developing countries but also foreign exchange, skilled or technically trained manpower, a lot of energy resources (such as coal, petroleum oil). The desirability of the investment of these investment projects relating to infrastructure and basic heavy industries cannot be analysed on the basis of market prices of goods and factors. Hence cost-benefit analysis which uses **shadow prices reflecting opportunities costs or true scarcity values of resources** used in investment projects is essential for optimum use of scarce resources in development planning.

Importance for Planning. Cost-benefit analysis is of vital importance in economic planning for growth and employment generation in developing countries. It is on the basis of cost-benefit analysis that those investment projects are chosen in a five year plan which help in achieving the objectives of the plan. Since through cost-benefit analysis different investment projects are ranked in accordance with their contribution to the plan objectives relating to GDP growth and employment generation, priorities can be assigned which projects be undertaken in a plan period. Little and Mirrlees consider the appraisal of various investment projects on the basis of cost-benefit analysis as a *sine quo non* economic planning for development.[11]

Besides, cost-benefit analysis helps in promoting social interest rather than any sectional or group interest. If the projects are selected on the basis of social cost-benefit analysis, it becomes difficult for any vested interests or groups of the people to oppose them if they do not suit their narrow interests.[12]

10 A.P. Thirlwall, *Growth and Development with Special Reference to Developing Economies*, Macmillan, 2004, 7th edition, pp. 373-374.

11 I.M.D. Little and Mirrlees, "*Manual of Industrial Projects in Developing Countries*", OECD, 1969.

12 See Stephen A Marglin, *Public Investment Criteria*, George Allen & Unwin, London, 1973.

PART IX

Macroeconomic Policies and Development

- Monetary Policy in Developing Countries
- Role of Fiscal Policy and Taxation in Economic Development
- Role of Fiscal Policy: Government Borrowing for Financing Development
- Financing Development Through Money Creation: Inflationary Financing
- External Resources: Foreign Aid
- Foreign Direct Investment and Role of Multinational Corporations in Developing Countries
- IMF and World Bank Directed Macroeconomic Policies for Developing Countries

CHAPTER 49

MONETARY POLICY IN DEVELOPING COUNTRIES

Monetary policy is concerned with the measures taken to regulate the supply of money, the cost and availability of credit in the economy. Further, it also deals with the distribution of credit between uses and users and also with both the lending and borrowing rates of interest of the banks. In developed countries, the monetary policy has been usefully used for overcoming depression and inflation as an anti-cyclical policy. However, in developing countries, it has to play a significant role in promoting economic growth with price stability. As Prof. R. Prebisch writes, "The time has come to formulate a monetary policy which meets the requirements of economic development, which fits into its framework perfectly." Further, along with encouraging economic growth, the monetary policy has also to ensure price stability, because the excessive inflation not only adversely affects distribution of income but also hinders economic growth.

It is important to understand the distinction between *objectives* or *goals*, *targets* and *instruments* of monetary policy. Whereas **goals** of monetary policy refer to its objectives which, as mentioned above, may be price stability, full employment, exchange rate stability or economic growth, ***targets*** *refer to the variables such as supply of money or bank credit, interest rates which are sought to be changed through the instruments of monetary policy so as to attain these objectives.* The various instruments of monetary policy are changes in the supply of currency, variations in bank rate and other interest rates, open market operations, selective credit controls, and variations in cash reserve requirements of banks.

Objectives of Monetary Policy

Before explaining in detail the monetary instruments undertaken by the central bank to regulate credit and growth of money supply, it is important to explain the objectives of monetary policy pursued by RBI which is India's central bank in formulation of its policy. Since monetary policy is one instrument of economic policy, its objectives cannot be different from those of overall economic policy. The three important objectives of monetary policy are:

1. ensuring *price stability,* that is, containing inflation.
2. to encourage *economic* growth.
3. to ensure *stability of exchange rate of the rupee,* that is, exchange rate of rupee with the US dollar, pound sterling and other foreign currencies.

Let us explain below these objectives in some detail.

Price Stability or Control of Inflation. It may be noted that each instrument of economic policy is better suited to achieve a particular objective. Monetary policy is better suited to the achievement of price stability, that is, containing inflation. To quote C. Rangarajan, a former Governor of Reserve Bank of India, "Faced with multiple objectives that are equally relevant and desirable, there is always the problem of assigning to each instrument the most appropriate target or objective. Of the various objectives, *price stability is perhaps the one that can be pursued most effectively by monetary policy.* In a developing country like ours, acceleration of investment activity in the context of supply shocks in the agricultural sector tends to be accompanied by pressures on prices and, therefore, monetary policy has much to contribute in the short-run management."[1]

Thus, achieving price stability has remained the dominant objective of monetary policy of Reserve Bank of India. It may however be noted that price stability does not mean absolutely no change in price level at all. In a developing economy, like ours, where structural changes take place during the process of economic growth, some changes in relative prices do occur that generally put upward pressure on prices. Therefore, some changes in price level or, in other words, a certain rate of inflation is inevitable in a developing economy. Thus, *price stability actually means reasonable rate of inflation.* A high degree of inflation has adverse effects on the economy. First, inflation raises the cost of living of the people and hurts the poor most. Therefore, inflation has been described as enemy No. 1 of the poor. Inflation sends many people below the poverty line. Secondly, inflation makes exports costlier and, therefore, discourages them. On the other hand, due to higher prices at home people are induced to import goods to a large extent. Thus, inflation has an adverse effect on the balance of payments. Thirdly, when due to a higher rate of inflation value of money is rapidly falling, people do not have much incentives to save. This lowers the rate of saving on which investment and economic growth depend. Fourthly, a high rate of inflation encourages businessmen to invest in the unproductive assets such as gold, jewellery, real estate, etc.

An expert committee on monetary reforms headed by late Prof. S. Chakravarty suggested 4 per cent rate of inflation as a reasonable rate of inflation and recommended that monetary policy by RBI should be so formulated that ensures that rate of inflation does not exceed 4 per cent per annum.

Economic Growth. Promoting economic growth is another important objective of the monetary policy in developing countries. In the past Reserve Bank has been criticised that it pursued the objective of achieving price stability and neglected the objective of promoting economic growth. *Monetary policy can promote economic growth through ensuring adequate availability of credit and lower cost of credit.* There are two types of credit requirements of businesses. First, they have to finance their requirements of working capital and for importing needed raw materials and machines from abroad. Secondly, they need credit for financing investment in projects for building fixed capital. Easy availability of credit at low interest rate stimulates investment and thereby quickens economic growth.

However, during the seventies, eighties and the first half of nineties, Reserve Bank followed a tight monetary policy under which cash reserve ratio (CRR) and statutory liquidity ratio (SLR) were continually raised to restrict the availability of credit for private sector. Besides, lending rates of interest were kept at high levels which discouraged *private* investment. This tight monetary policy worked against promoting growth. However, in the opinion of Prof. Rangarajan, there is no conflict between the objectives of price stability and growth. Price stability, according to him, is a means to ensure economic growth. To quote him, "*It is price stability which provides the appropriate environment under which growth can occur and social justice can be ensured.*"[2] In our opinion, this may be true in the long run but *in the short run there exists trade-off between growth and inflation.* To ensure higher economic growth the adequate expansion of money supply and greater availability of credit at a lower rate of interest is needed. But large expansion in money supply and bank credit

1. C. Rangarajan, "*Issues in Monetary Management*" printed in *Indian Economy: Essays on Money and Finance,* 1998, p. 6.
2. C. Rangarajan, *"The Changing Context of Monetary Policy"*, Address at 31st Convocation of the Indian Statistical Institute, March 31, 1997.

leads to the increase in aggregate demand which tends to cause a higher rate of inflation. This raises the issue of what is *acceptable trade-off* between growth and inflation, that is, what rate of inflation is acceptable to promote growth through appropriate monetary policy. The Expert Committee on Monetary Policy headed by late Prof. Chakravarty suggested a target of 4 per cent as "the acceptable rise in prices". According to it, the growth of money supply and availability of credit should be so regulated that rate of inflation does not exceed 4 per cent per annum. However, C. Rangarajan, former Governor of Reserve Bank, fixed a higher target, namely, 5 to 6 per cent rate of inflation in the context of objective of achieving 6 to 7 per cent rate of economic growth.[3]

It may be noted that in the context of the openness of the economy and floating exchange rate system, as is the case of the Indian economy today, the objective of achieving higher rate of economic growth through monetary measures may also conflict with objective of exchange rate stability, that is, value of rupee in terms of the U.S dollar and other foreign currencies. Whereas prevention of the depreciation of rupee requires tightening of monetary policy, that is, raising of interest rate and reducing liquidity of the banking system so that banks restrict their credit supply, the promotion of growth objective requires lower lending rates of interest and greater availability of credit for encouraging private investment. It is this dilemma of conflicting objectives of achieving higher economic growth rate or price stability which is generally faced in India and other developing countries.

Exchange Rate Stability. Until 1991, India followed fixed exchange rate system and only occasionally devalued the rupee with the permission of IMF. The policies of floating exchange rate and increasing openness and globalisation of the Indian economy, adopted since 1991, have made the exchange rate of rupee quite volatile. The changes in capital inflows and capital outflows and changes in demand for and supply of foreign exchange, particularly US dollar, arising from the imports and exports cause great fluctuations in the foreign exchange rate of rupee. In order to prevent large depreciation and appreciation of foreign exchange rate Reserve Bank has to take suitable monetary measures to ensure foreign exchange rate stability. Owing to the fixed exchange rate system prior to 1991 the concern about foreign exchange rate had not played a significant role in the formulation of monetary policy.

Today, the exchange rate of rupee is determined by demand for and supply of foreign exchange (say, US dollar). When there is mismatch between demand for and supply of foreign exchange, external value of rupee changes. For instance, from August 2011 to December 2012 depreciation of rupee as against US dollar had been caused by the increase in demand for dollars from (1) the corporate sector for financing their imports, (2) Foreign Institutional Investors (FII) who wanted to take out their dollars from India (*i.e.*, capital outflow) to the US had risen and (3) increase in demand for US dollar by the Indian banks on the instructions of the public sector undertakings for financing necessary imports from abroad. Since export earnings and capital inflows which determine the supply of dollars had not risen adequately, mismatch between dollars and supply of dollars had arisen causing the depreciation of rupee as against the U.S dollar.

Thus when there is large current account deficit (CAD) that exceeds comfortable level (which in Indian situation is estimated at 2.5 per cent of GDP as it can be financed by normal capital inflows), it tends to depreciate the Indian rupee. In 2011-12, there was current account deficit (CAD) of 4.2 per cent and for 2012-13 the current account deficit (CAD) was around 5 per cent of GDP. This is too high current account deficit which put downward pressure on the exchange rate of rupee. The depreciation of rupee raises the costs of imports which adds to the inflationary pressures in the Indian economy. Therefore, reducing current account deficit (CAD) to the comfortable level is not only essential for exchange rate stability but also for controlling inflation and achieving price stability. According to D. Subbarao, the then Governor of RBI, the widening of current account deficit in India during the last two years (2011-12 and 2012-13) emerged as a major constraint on easing of monetary policy

3 *Op. cit.*

because causing lower lending interest rates and larger availability of funds with banks will lead to more imports which will add to the current account deficit.

To arrest the fall in value of rupee Reserve Bank raises the bank rate and repo rate and thus sends signals to the banks to raise their lending rates. The higher interest rates will discourage FIIs to invest abroad or send their capital funds back to the US or their home countries. The Reserve Bank can also raise the *cash reserve ratio* (CRR) of the banks to reduce liquidity in the banking system. With higher lending interest rates and reduction in availability of credit, corporate borrowing from the banks will be discouraged *which will reduce the demand for US dollars* and tend to prevent the fall in value of the rupee.

A more effective way to prevent the depreciation in value of rupee is to release dollars from its foreign exchange reserves and sell in the foreign exchange market. This will increase the supply of dollars in the foreign exchange market and will correct the imbalance between demand for and supply of US dollars. This will therefore help in stabilising the exchange rate of the rupee.

It is clear from above that in the context of flexible exchange rate system, RBI can intervene to prevent the volatility in the exchange rate of rupee.

ROLE OF MONETARY POLICY IN ECONOMIC GROWTH

Economic growth implies the expansion in productive capacity or capital stock in the economy so that increases in real national output or income are attained. As is well known, economic growth can be speeded up by accelerating the rate of savings and investment in the economy. This requires the following steps:

(*a*) Increase in the aggregate rate of savings in the economy;

(*b*) Mobilisation of these savings so that they are made available for the purpose of investment and production;

(*c*) Increase in the rate of investment; and

(*d*) Allocation of investment funds for productive purposes and priority sectors of the economy.

Proper monetary policy can help in producing favourable effects on the above requirements of economic growth. We explain below the appropriate monetary policy to promote growth in developing countries.

Monetary Policy and Savings

Several monetary measures can be adopted to raise the aggregate rate of saving. First, a high interest rate policy can promote savings. In the fifties and sixties of the 20th century, it was widely believed that interest rate reflected the price of capital and since capital was scarce in developing countries, the real interest rates should be kept at higher levels to promote saving so that capital accumulation is speeded up. However, this argument in favour of higher real interest rates in developing countries was based upon the belief that *savings were positively elastic or sensitive to the interest rate*.

It is worthwhile to mention an opposite viewpoint regarding interest rate policy which has gained large support in recent years. According to this view (emphasised by Keynes in his monetary theory), rate of interest represents the cost of investment, and lower the lending rate of interest, the greater will be inducement to invest. However, Keynes was of the view that investment was not much sensitive or elastic to lower rate of interest and easy or cheap monetary policy was ineffective to revive the economy from depression. Dr. K.N. Raj argued that *since investment is an important factor determining economic growth in developing countries, it should be promoted by lowering the interest rates*. However, this is not fully correct. This is because whereas inducement to invest may be promoted by lowering the interest rates, the adequate amount of savings or resources needed to finance larger investment may not be forthcoming at lower interest rates. Further, a low interest rate policy in developing countries like India is likely to promote more investment in inventories and luxury consumer goods such as cars, air conditioners, luxury houses rather than that in fixed capital goods.

In our view therefore in a developing economy *a reasonably positive real interest rate policy* should be pursued to provide incentives for more savings so that large sources are made available for investment in fixed capital stock. If monetary policy in a developing country is to promote economic growth it must aim at raising the rate of saving. It may be recalled that *real rate of interest is nominal rate of interest minus rate of inflation.* In our view, real rate of interest should be positive and preferably should not be allowed to fall below 5 per cent per annum, if it is to provide reasonable rate of return on savings. Therefore, with the rise in rate of inflation nominal rate of interest should also be raised to keep incentives for saving intact. It may be noted that in recent years (2011-12 and 2012-13) in India low deposit rates offered to the public by banks have prompted the people to invest their savings in unproductive assets such as gold, jewellery and real estate. *This led to the fall in financial saving* required for productive investment. This led the Finance Minister, Mr. Chidambaram, in his budget for 2013-14 to announce issuing of **inflation-indexed bonds** on which nominal interest rate will automatically rise with the increase in inflation rate.

Besides, the monetary policy can play a strategic role in increasing national savings by promoting the expansion of banking facilities and other financial intermediaries in the developing countries, especially in their rural areas. With more bank branches in under-banked and underdeveloped regions, the people who consume away their surplus incomes will be induced to save them in the form of bank deposits which are quite safe as a store of value. The commercial banking encourages thrift or propensity to save by offering a return on savings in the form of interest rate on bank deposits. It also induces more savings by providing outlets for mutual funds which can be equity linked and other saving schemes for fruitful investment of the savings by the people who would have otherwise put them to unproductive or wasteful uses such as buying land, real estate, gold and jewellery. But to tap and raise savings sufficiently and to prevent its unproductive use, banks and other financial institutions need to be numerous and dispersed throughout the economy in both the urban and rural areas. Speaking from the development experience of various countries, Prof. Lewis, a development economist, has emphasised that the volume of savings depends partly upon how widespread banking and other financial institutions are. To quote him, *"If the saving institutions are placed under the individual's nose, people save more than if the nearest saving institutions is some distance away."*[4]

Thus growth in saving in the form of bank deposits will be greater, if a reasonable real rate of interest policy is pursued. Similarly, with the expansion of other financial institutions, the people will feel induced to save more for buying financial assets. It is generally agreed that the rapid expansion of banking facilities after the nationalisation of major commercial banks in 1969 promoted by the Reserve Bank of India has contributed considerably to the growth of aggregate savings. While the aggregate saving rate has gone up from 16.5 per cent in 1969-70 to 22.7 per cent in 1982-83, bank deposits, which accounted for 8.7 per cent of total domestic savings in 1969-70, accounted for 22.5 per cent of these savings in 1982-83. The number of commercial banks' offices increased from 8,262 in July 1969 to 44,521 in 1984 and to 62,350 in 1995. Although it is difficult to establish a precise quantitative relationship between expansion of bank branches and savings in the form of bank deposits, its significant contribution to the promotion of savings cannot be denied. Therefore, the future branch expansion policy must fully take into account the untapped saving potential of under-banked and underdeveloped regions.

It may be noted that in order to facilitate mobilisation of an increasing proportion of savings by the banking system, it is essential to maintain a reasonable price stability. Dr. Manmohan Singh, when he was Governor of Reserve Bank of India, pointed out, "*It is only under conditions of reasonable price stability that people will have less attraction for savings in the form of physical*

4 Arthur Lewis, *Theory of Economic Growth,* George Allen and Unwin, 1960.

assets such as gold, real estate and excessive accumulation of inventories." Further, if banks are to mobilise adequate amount of savings in the form of bank deposits, interest rates on bank deposits must remain positive in real terms. That is, the rate of interest be maintained at a higher level than the rate of inflation. If through excessive rise in prices real rate of interest becomes negative, people will be discouraged to save.

Monetary Policy and Investment

Monetary policy has an important role to play in boosting up the level of investment by making available savings or resources mobilised by banks for purposes of investment and production. The banks fulfil this task by offering bank credit for investment to business and industry.

Cost of Credit. It may be noted that Keynesian theory of monetary policy emphasises that the effect of a change in the supply of money on the level of production and investment operates through the changes in the rate of interest. The increase in the supply of money by the monetary authority will cause the market rate of interest to fall. At lower rate of interest, the entrepreneurs will be induced to invest more. Accordingly, Keynesian monetary theory has been described as "*cost of credit*" theory. However, Keynes himself and several economists after him believed that this effect of changes in money supply on investment which operates through rate of interest is not very vigorous. It has been asserted that investment in fixed capital is interest inelastic. That is why Keynes did not have much faith in the effectiveness of monetary policy and instead emphasised the role of fiscal policy in influencing the level of economic activity. However, it is now generally believed by the economists that since interest is an important cost of investment, *investment demand is fairly interest elastic.* Therefore, to promote investment, the easy monetary policy should be adopted.

It may be noted that in the post-economic reforms period from 1996 to 2003 easy or low interest rate policy was adopted to promote private investment so as to revive the industrial sector whose growth slowed down from 1996-97 to 2002-03. Following the soft-interest rate policy of Reserve Bank of India prime lending rates of interest of commercial banks, which varied between 15 and 16 per cent prior to 1996, were reduced over a period of time to 9 to 10 per cent in 2003. Again when in September 2008 global financial crisis occurred as a result of bust of housing bubble in the US, there was worldwide (including India) economic slowdown, Reserve Bank of India in October 2008 reduced its repo interest rate from 9 per cent in July 2008 to 7 per cent in October 2008 and further to 4.75 per cent on March 4, 2009, to promote private investment so as to prevent sharp economic slowdown in India.

However, the soft interest rate policy does not always, especially during recession, achieve much success in stimulating private investment. This is because when there are sluggish demand conditions, the existing fixed capital is underutilised, it is not profitable to make more investment for expanding fixed capital stock, private enterprises are therefore not willing to make further investment despite lower interest rates. It is for such economic conditions that it has been said that *'you can bring the horse to water but you cannot make it drink'*. Therefore, in our view, the favourable effect of lower interest rate on investment has been exaggerated. As Keynes emphasised, it is the *prospective yield from investment* which plays a crucial role in determining investment. Unless the private business class *expects* to earn sufficient profits, they will not increase their investment. Unless the expectations of the business class about profit making are raised or what Keynes called *'animal spirits'* of entrepreneurs are revived, investment will not increase. The profit expectations can be raised by government increasing its expenditure, especially on infrastructural projects which through its multiplier will raise the aggregate demand for goods and services. Besides, through its fiscal policy the government can provide liberal depreciation allowance against taxation. This will raise the internal rate of return. However, the profit expectations of businessmen depend on the demand for goods produced by the capital assets they plan to invest. Thus, "the only way in which businessmen can be persuaded to invest more is if they genuinely believe that the *demand for the output of the assets will be there* when they have been acquired..... Consequently, the best way of increasing prospective yield is to increase demand either by increasing consumption or by increasing government expenditure"[5].

Availability of Credit. It is noteworthy that in the recent times monetary theory emphasises the **credit-availability effect on investment** of the changes in the supply of money. According to this, an increase in the supply of money causing expansion in the reserve money with the banks directly enlarges the availability of bank credit for investment purposes and thereby raises the level of investment in the economy. On the contrary, contraction in money supply will directly reduce the availability of credit and hence tend to decrease investment in the economy. The credit availability of banks can be increased by RBI by lowering cash reserve ratio (CRR) and statutory liquidity ratio (SLR) of banks. Note that statutory liquidity ratio (SLR) of the banks is the proportion of their deposits which the banks have to invest in government securities. The reduction in CRR and SLR release resources for the banks to lend to private businessmen for investment.

Further, in this context it is noteworthy that in developing countries, government or public investment plays a crucial role in the development of their economies. Therefore, monetary policy requires to promote not only private but also public investment by making available adequate amount of credit for it.

Monetary Policy and Private Investment. If the private sector plays an important role in the development process, as it does in India after economic reforms undertaken since 1991, monetary policy has also to ensure that the needs for bank credit for investment and production in the private sector are fully met. The banks must provide adequate bank credit to meet at least essential working capital requirements of industry and agriculture. Both large-scale and medium industries require funds for investment in fixed capital, working capital and for maintaining inventories. Subject to appropriate norms fixed for inventory holdings, the credit needs of the private sector should be met if existing capacities in the private sector are to be fully used and also more productive capacity is to be built up. In India banks have been asked by the Reserve Bank of India to give specific percentage of loans at concessional rates of interest to some priority sectors such as agriculture and small and medium enterprises.

Monetary Policy and Public Investment. Let us first explain the promotion of the public investment through monetary policy. Monetary policy has to ensure that the banking system contributes to the financing of the planned public investment. For this, a good part of bank deposits mobilised by the banks should be invested in Government and other approved securities so that the government should be able to finance its planned investment, especially in infrastructure. At present in India, there is lack of infrastructure such as power, roads, highways, ports, irrigation facilities which is obstructing economic growth. Besides, when industry faces demand recession, public investment is an ideal tool to develop infrastructure and to increase the demand for industrial products through the operation of multiplier. This will stimulate private investment. Therefore, in our view, policy of raising public investment will *crowd in* private investment rather than *crowding it out.* In India a new technique of monetary policy has been designed to secure larger resources from the banking system for financing public investment. This technique has been described as Statutory Liquidity Ratio (SLR). According to this, *in addition to cash reserve requirements* banks in India are required to keep a minimum proportion of their total demand and time deposits in the form of specified liquid assets. And the most important specified liquid asset for this purpose is the investment in government and other securities. To raise the lendable resources of the banks, cash reserve ratio of the banks must be kept at low level.

Allocation of Investment Funds

Mobilisation of savings alone would not do. Proper canalisation of these into suitable directions of investment is or perhaps more important than mobilisation itself. The monetary policy should restrict the growth of wasteful lines of investment which are inimical to economic growth. It should

5 Stonier and Hague, *A Textbook of Economic Theory*, 5th edition, Pearson Education, Ltd. 1980, p. 539.

be able to direct investment in productive channels. In this regard, the monetary policy has to play a selective or qualitative role in so far as it is possible through its operations to *discriminate between productive and unproductive outlays. It should give a fillip to the former and stint* the growth of the latter. Further, it has to be so designed as to influence the specific sectors and industries which are most significant to affect the growth of the economy. In fact, the particularised application of credit can greatly activise the process of economic growth. Therefore, it is necessary to operate the *selective credit rationing with a view to influence the pattern of investment.* However, in the gamut of monetary policy, there are selective credit control measures of both general and specific nature. In the general category, measures such as voluntary credit restriction and moral suasion are included. In the category of specific measures there exist measures to control credit institutions.

For the purpose of regulating the individual credit institutions, the method of varying the reserve requirements is quite effective. On the other hand, in order to divert the financial resources into desired channels, the method of **credit rationing** should be used by the Central Bank. This may be done by fixation of a ceiling on the aggregate portfolio of the commercial banks, thereby making it incumbent that loans and advances do not exceed the fixed ceiling. Alternatively, it may be done by directly allocating funds that can be granted and used. Besides, policies such as the selective rediscount policy, prior deposit requirement policy and the fixation of deposit requirement policy can also be adopted to achieve similar goals. However, it may be pointed out that the potency of credit planning depends upon the extent of the area over which it operates. The developing economies must strive for an extension of credit planning over wider areas.

Credit control measures such as noted above promote growth by directing the stream of domestic savings into the desired lines of investment. Measures such as lengthening the periods of repayment, lowering of margin requirements, providing rediscounting facilities at rates below the bank rate, provision of special loans by commercial banks to be used for specific purposes or the setting up of special investment institutions such as Industrial Development Bank can provide the required inducement to channelise savings in the desired directions. In the indirect sense, these measures may prove conducive to growth in two ways. First, the qualitative credit control measures prevent the savings from being wasted in unproductive channels. Through their application it becomes possible to deny or discourage certain lines of investment that are inimical to the growth of the economy. However, the extent to which such measures can help providing resources for investment in the desired directions depends on the extent to which the flow of credit towards the undesirable channels can be prevented.

Secondly, such measures may go a long way in galvanising the process of growth by restraining inflation and its adverse effects. When inflationary tendencies set in, generally the bank advances to businessmen tend to rise. In this way, certain undesirable and unproductive enterprises may grow and flourish. For instance, activities such as speculative demand for building up inventories, accumulation of precious metals for purchase of foreign exchange and real estate get a fillip. Growth of these and such other unproductive activities can be held in check by raising the margin requirements for the blackballed collaterals. Further, the monetary authority can fix a ceiling by holding the loans and advances of the value of the collateral. Thus, it *serves the dual purpose of curbing inflation and protecting certain essential productive forms of investment from being restricted.*

In the context of the planned development of the underdeveloped countries, the use of methods of selective credit controls and credit rationing is not only necessary but also essential. They greatly widen the horizons of development along predetermined and desired directions. They are not only helpful in preventing inflation but also *act as a positive means of directing the process of economic development on the desired lines.* Furthermore, the policy of selective credit controls is especially suited to the needs of underdeveloped countries where the orthodox monetary techniques have limited applicability. As it is, the structure of these economies is not very conducive to the general methods of credit control.

The huge investment expenditure made by the government in the public sector in its endeavour to accelerate the process of growth is not amenable to control by the monetary authority. The monetary authority is, in fact, subversive to the wishes of the government in the matter of providing resources for development. Further, in order to help government borrowings, the bank rate policy of the Reserve Bank tends to become more or less inflexible. Besides, for the sake of supporting government loans, the institutions such as SEBI (Stock Exchange Board of India) is also required to stabilise the securities market.

MONETARY POLICY TO CONTROL INFLATION IN DEVELOPING COUNTRIES

The developing countries are prone to the emergence of inflationary pressures in the economy. This is because in developing countries the government often spends more to raise public investment and as a result often experience fiscal deficit which they finance (1) by *borrowing* by issuing bonds (which are generally purchased by banks, insurance companies, mutual funds, pension funds etc.) and (2) *by creating new printed money.* They result in *excess demand conditions* in the economy and therefore generate inflation. Monetary policy is an important tool of demand management in the economy and therefore of checking inflation. In what follows, we explain the role and limitations of monetary policy in controlling with special reference to India.

Monetary policy refers to the adoption of suitable policy regarding *interest rate and* the *availability of credit.* Monetary policy is important measure for reducing aggregate demand to control inflation. As an instrument of demand management, monetary policy can work in two ways. First, it can affect the *cost of credit* and second, it can influence the *credit availability* for private business firms. Let us first consider the cost of credit. The higher the rate of interest, the greater the cost of borrowing from the banks by the business firms. As anti-inflationary measure, the rate of interest has to be raised to discourage businessmen to borrow more so that less bank credit is created. The cheap credit policy (*i.e.,* lower interest rates) is recommended on the ground that lower rate of interest will promote more private investment which is an important factor determining economic growth. Keeping in view this consideration, cheap money policy was adopted in India up to 1972 and accordingly bank rate was kept low.

The dear money policy (that is, *higher interest rate policy*) has often been used in India to curb the inflationary pressures in the Indian economy. In India, bank rate has not been generally used to check inflation. Instruments like *repo rate* and *reverse repo rate* have often been used to manage aggregate demand. Repo rate is the interest rate at which Reserve Bank of India lends funds to the commercial banks *for a short period.* To curb inflation *repo rate* is raised. Hike in repo rate raises the cost of funds for the banks which will, if they do not have excess reserves, raise their *lending rates.* The higher lending rates will lower the demand for bank credit for investment and for purchases of cars (auto loans) and housing (housing loans). Under these circumstances to mobilise funds banks raise their deposit rates. The higher rate of interest on saving and fixed deposits will induce more savings by the households and help in cutting down aggregate consumption expenditure. Besides, higher rates of interest will discourage more investment in inventories and consumer durables and will help in reducing aggregate demand.

However, rise in repo rate will lead to the decline in credit growth if ***monetary transmission mechanism*** works. This will happen only if banks are short of liquid funds. If the banks have excess liquid reserves with them they would not raise their lending rates when the RBI raises repo rate. Therefore, for monetary transmission mechanism to work liquidity with the banks must be curtailed. This can be done by the RBI by raising cash reserve ratio (CRR) and by *open market operation* through sale of government securities.

It is noteworthy that a recent monetary theory emphasizes that it is changes in the ***credit availability*** rather than ***cost of credit*** (*i.e.,* rate of interest) that is a more effective instrument of regulating aggregate demand. There are several methods by which credit availability can be reduced. Firstly, it is through *open market operations* that the central bank of a country can reduce the availability of credit in the economy. Under open market operations, the Reserve Bank sells government securities. Those, especially banks, who buy these securities will make payment for them in terms of cash reserves. With their reduced cash reserves, their capacity to lend money to the business firms will be curtailed. This will tend to reduce the supply of credit or loanable funds by the banks which in turn would tend to reduce aggregate demand.

However, in the past in India open market operations did not play a significant role as an instrument of credit control to fight against inflationary situation. This was because market for government securities was narrow as well as captive. However, with financial reforms this is no more the situation. At present RBI often uses open market operations to influence liquidity of the banking system. General public do not buy more than a fraction of government securities. It is the institutions such as commercial banks, LIC, GIC and Provident Funds which are required by law to invest a certain proportion of their funds in buying government securities. The RBI can reduce the liquidity with the banks by selling government securities to them through open market operations.

In India, it is the ***cash reserve ratio*** **(CRR)** which can be effectively used to curb inflation. By law banks have to keep a certain proportion of cash money as reserves against their demand and time deposits. This is called ***cash reserve ratio***. To reduce liquidity with the banks and thereby to contract credit availability Reserve Bank can raise this ratio. In recent years to squeeze credit for checking inflation, cash reserve ratio in India has been raised from time to time.

Statutory Liquidity Ratio (SLR). Another instrument with Reserve Bank of India for affecting credit availability is the statutory liquidity ratio. In addition to CRR, banks have to keep a certain minimum proportion of their deposits in the form of specified liquid assets. And the most important specified liquid asset for this purpose is the government securities. To mop up extra liquid assets with banks which may lead to undue expansion in credit availability for the business class, the Reserve Bank has often raised statutory liquidity ratio.

Limitations of Tight Monetary Policy

However, tight monetary policy for controlling inflation is not without its limitations. First, monetary transmission mechanism may be weak and raising of short-term interest rates by the RBI may not actually lead to the restriction of bank credit. This can happen when the banks may have surplus liquidity (*i.e.,* cash reserves) with them and therefore they may not follow tight monetary policy and raise their lending rates. As a result, supply of credit by banks will not be restricted. Secondly, if the economic environment is such that boom conditions prevail in the economy and aggregate demand for products is quite high, demand for credit may not be much affected by higher lending rates. As emphasized by J.M. Keynes, investment is determined more by marginal efficiency of capital (that is, expected rate of return) rather than rate of interest. Thirdly, at present in India corporate firms are more easily able to borrow from foreign capital markets (*i.e.,* external commercial borrowing, ECB) especially when rates of interest in the US, European zone and Japan are extremely low. Therefore, unless this debt-capital inflow (*i.e.,* ECB) is checked RBI's monetary policy may not be effective to check the supply of credit to control inflation in the economy.

Thirdly, when the stock market prices are rising and aggregate demand is quite high, the corporate sector is able to raise funds itself more easily from the capital market. This will also offset the impact of tight monetary policy of the RBI to control inflation. Fourthly, if adequate internal funds are available with the corporate firms as a result of *retained profit earnings* by the companies they can use them to finance their expansion plans and thereby add to the aggregate expenditure or demand. This will also nullify the tight monetary policy of the RBI to curb inflation.

It may be noted that in recent years to control inflation the Reserve Bank of India raised its *repo rate* 13 times from March 2010 to November 2011 (from 4.75% in March 2010 to 8.50% in November 2011) but inflation as measured by the WPI remained at an elevated level. It was estimated at 10 per cent (YoY) in September 2011, 9.73% in October 2011 and 9.11 per cent in November 2011. After November 2011, WPI inflation declined because of dip in food inflation due partly to the base effect and partly to easing of supply position of some food articles. Thus tight monetary policy failed to check inflation despite 3.75 percentage points increase in repo rate. The RBI explained failure of its tight monetary policy to curb inflation by blaming the *large fiscal deficit* of the government in 2011-12. Due to large fiscal deficit, aggregate demand was increasing which was feeding inflation in the Indian economy. According to the RBI, unless fiscal deficit is brought down by the government, tight monetary policy alone will not succeed in checking inflation. Besides, the RBI *blamed supply-side factors* responsible for food inflation which has contributed to overall rise in WPI inflation.

Lastly, if inflation in the economy has originated from the **supply-side factors,** for example, if production of foodgrains and other essential food articles such as milk, vegetables, fruits etc. in a year declines or does not increase adequately to meet the growing demand for them due to certain supply-side bottlenecks, this will cause the demand-supply imbalances leading to the rise in inflation. Such supply-side inflation cannot be checked by raising interest rates under the tight monetary policy. This happened in 2009-10 when due to the shortage of monsoon rainfall, drop in agricultural production was expected, inflationary pressures emerged in the Indian economy raising food inflation to around 20 per cent in December 2009. This food inflation continued to prevail at double digit level till November 2010. Tight monetary policy which is aimed at management of aggregate demand rather than augmentation of supply is ineffective in tackling this supply-side inflation as in case of food inflation in 2010. Likewise, in 2010-11 and 2011-12 *shortage of protein-based food* products such as pulses, milk, fruits and vegetables, eggs, meat and fish contributed a good deal to the persistence of food inflation. It is only after October 2011 when there was a drop in food inflation, the WPI inflation also declined. Similarly, supply-side inflation arises when prices of petroleum products rise which is passed on to the domestic consumers and cannot be tackled with use of tight monetary policy. In addition to fuel, if output growth in *core industries* such as steel, cement, coal declined as they did during 2011-12 in India, they create supply-side bottlenecks in various industries leading to supply-side inflation.

Now to control food inflation what is required is to take long-term measures to augment supply of foodgrains and other food articles by raising agricultural productivity by undertaking appropriate technological changes and land reform measures. In the short run to control food inflation what is needed is to release food stocks through public distribution system (PDS) which should be properly monitored to check black market. Besides, to control rise in food prices in the short run release of food stocks for sale in the open market should be made. However, this presupposes enough food stocks with the government. Further, to check food inflation, foodgrains, pulses, oilseeds and other feed articles in short supply can be imported.

It may however be noted that when inflationary expectations arise as a result of emergence of shortage of supply of some essential commodities, there is tendency on the part of traders to hoard stocks of goods in short supply for speculative purposes. To discourage such speculative hoarding of goods in short supply monetary policy of high interest rates can be helpful. Besides, as explained above, selective credit controls of monetary policy can also be used to check excessive hoarding.

THE POLICY OF QUANTITATIVE EASING (QE) AND DEVELOPING COUNTRIES

We have explained above the conventional monetary policy to bring stability in the economy. Now, in 2008 there was a severe economic crisis caused by bursting of housing buble. Prior to

2008, when the prices of houses were rising the Americans had made excessive investment in houses financed by sub-prime housing loans given on a large scale by the American banks at a low rates of interests. The American banks sold these sub-prime mortgaged housing loans to other financial institutions which converted them into securities that were traded in the market. Now in 2007-08 when the prices of houses declined sharply, the people who had got the sub-prime housing loans from the banks started defaulting on paying interest and the principal amount. This caused serious financial crisis as the prices of securities based on sub-prime mortgage housing loans fell almost to zero. As a result, the banks and financial institutions such as Lehman Brothers, Citi Bank which had made large investment in them came to the brink of bankruptcy. In July 2008, Lehman brothers declared itself bankrupt. This caused great panic which ultimately result in severe recession in the US economy which had world-wide repercussion. The recession in the US economy was so severe that its growth rate came down to almost zero and unemployment shot up to 10 per cent of labour force.

It is to tackle such severe recessionary conditions the non-conventional monetary policy of quantitative easing (QE) was adopted by the Federal Reserve (which is the Central Bank of the US). The interest rates were then so low that the conventional monetary policy of lowering interest rates had lost its ability to stimulate the economy. Therefore, non-conventional monetary policy of quantitative easing (QE) was adopted by the Federal Reserve keeping near zero rate of interest under the quantitative easing (QE) the Federal Reserve purchased bonds (both treasury bonds and private corporate bonds) and other financial assets on a large scale and to purchase them created new money. In this way, the Federal Reserve pumped a large liquidity (*i.e.*, cash) in the banking system and has continued this policy for several years now since 2008, though the scale of purchase of bonds has slowed down in recent years.

Now, selling bonds and other financial assets to Federal Reserve and getting a lot of cash allowed American Commercial banks to provide loans to business firms and investors at low rate of interest to make more investment and thus increasing spending in the economy. It was hoped that more investment and spending would help the economy to get out of recession. Thus, quantitative easing (QE) was expected to stimulate the US economy and recover from recessionary conditions.

It may be noted that with the Federal Reserve purchasing bonds from the market on a large scale, their supply in the market was reduced which drived up the bond prices. Higher bond prices mean the yield from them declined and therefore investors were discouraged to buy them. The investors or business firms which got loans from the banks not only invested some money in building new factories or expanding their existing capacities but also used them to buy back their own stock or shares with the intention to shore up their prices. Since return on more investment in the US was very low, a good amount of US dollars created through quantitative easing also flowed into the emerging economies, especially India and China where returns from investment in shares and bonds were quite high. The inflows of capital (*i.e.*, US dollars) in India and China caused share prices in these countries to shoot up. In this way, American foreign institutional investors (FIls) made a good amount of profits in investing in India and China.

With the policy of pumping a lot of liquidity in the banks which gave liberal loans at very low interest rates has succeeded in reviving the American economy whose annual GDP growth has on average reached 2.5 per cent and unemployment rate has also declined to 5 per cent labour force (June 2015). However, the recovery of the American economy is fragile. The Federal Reserve has quite often decided to withdraw completely the quantitative easing policy and raise of interest but each time it has postponed the implementation of its decision. It may be noted that when quantitative easing (QE) policy is completely withdrawn and rates of interest raised by the Federal Reserve, there will be outflows of capital (*i.e.*, dollars) by FIIs from India. When this happens the share prices in India will fall sharply, the Indian rupee would depreciate and thus creating a lot of economic instability in the Indian economy. This economic instability will also be seen in other emerging economies.

CHAPTER 50

ROLE OF FISCAL POLICY AND TAXATION IN ECONOMIC DEVELOPMENT

Introduction

The most important instrument of government intervention in the economy today is that of fiscal or budgetary policy. Fiscal policy refers to the taxation, expenditure and borrowing by the government. The economists now hold that government intervention through fiscal policy is essential in the matter of overcoming recession or inflation as well as of promoting and accelerating economic growth. Monetary policy alone will not do. There is no doubt that the government budgetary or fiscal policy must be sound, keeping in view the needs and requirements of a developing economy.

The main problem faced by the capitalist economies is economic instability prevailing in them. This instability is reflected in the periodic occurrence of trade cycles which are a general phenomenon in the free-market capitalist economies. Thanks to J.M. Keynes, an eminent British economist, whose theory helped to understand the basic reason of the fluctuations in economic activity or trade cycles in the capitalist economies. It is Keynes's theory which has a profound effect on fiscal policy pursued to avoid economic fluctuations. Now, governments have learned to take suitable fiscal measures beforehand to correct the impending depression or severe inflation. Therefore, the severity of economic instability in the advanced capitalist economies has declined due to the adoption, by governments, of fiscal measures suggested by J.M. Keynes.

During a recession or depression fiscal policy should help in increasing demand. For this purpose, the government can increase its expenditure and spend more on public works. This will provide employment to more people. The government can also increase its expenditure on subsidies to producers of consumer goods so as to increase consumption spending. Similarly, the government can lower its tax rates so as to stimulate consumption and investment. Thus, a budget deficit during a depression helps greatly in removing unemployment. On the other hand, during periods of inflation, there is too much of demand and hence the government should reduce its own expenditure and curb private spending by increasing taxes. Thus in periods of inflation, we should have surplus budgets. Therefore, there is no inherent superiority in a balanced or a surplus budget. It all depends on the prevailing economic situation. This view of public finance is called as ***functional finance*** because, according to this view, public revenue and expenditure of the government are not to be considered as being governed solely by the requirements of government finances but by the requirements of attaining and maintaining full employment and price stability.

Objectives of Fiscal Policy in Developing Countries

In developing countries, taxation, the government expenditure, taxation and borrowing have to play a very important role in accelerating economic development. In fact, fiscal policy is a powerful instrument in the hands of the government by means of which it can achieve the objectives of development. There are several peculiar characteristics of a developing country which necessitate the adoption of a special fiscal policy which ensures a rapid economic growth. There are vast and diverse resources, human and material, which are lying underutilised. Such countries have weak infrastructure, *i.e.,* they lack adequate means of transport and communications, roads, ports, highways, irrigation and power. They also lack technical know-how. Their population is increasing at an explosive rate which necessitates rapid economic development to meet the requirements of the rapidly-growing population. Above all, these countries suffer from deficiency of capital. They are caught up in a vicious circle of poverty. In order to overcome these handicaps, a suitable fiscal and taxation policy is called for.

In developing countries like India, budget has to play a more important role. The developing countries face a more difficult problem of how to generate a higher economic growth so as to tackle the problems of poverty and unemployment. Therefore, fiscal policy has to play a special role of promoting economic growth in the developing countries like India so as to tackle the twin problems of poverty and unemployment. Besides, India has been facing the problem of *inflation* from time to time. Inflation adversely affects economic growth and hurts the poor most. Therefore, besides accelerating economic growth, fiscal policy has to control inflation and thus to ensure price stability. Besides, fiscal policy has to reduce large inequalities of income distribution and to ensure just distribution of fruits of economic growth. Thus the fiscal policy in a developing country such as ours has to *"strike a fine balance among three mutually reinforcing objectives of growth, stability and equity"*. Further, for developing countries mere economic growth is not enough; the budgetary policies should be so designed as to ensure removal of poverty and unemployment. Therefore, the function of fiscal policy is not only to raise resources for development and to achieve optimum allocation of resources, but also to promote fair distribution of income and expansion in employment opportunities. This is the functional view of public finance in the context of the developing countries.

The principal objectives of fiscal policy in a developing economy are:

1. to mobilise resources for economic growth, especially for the public sector;
2. to promote economic growth in the private sector by providing incentives to save and invest;
3. to restrain inflationary forces in the economy in order to ensure price stability; and
4. to ensure equitable distribution of income and wealth so that fruits of economic growth are fairly distributed, that is, to achieve *inclusive growth.*

In developing economies, the government has to play a very active role in promoting economic development and fiscal policy is the instrument that the state must use. Hence the great importance of public finance in developing countries desirous of rapid economic development. In a democratic society, there is an inherent dislike for direct (physical) controls and regulation by the state. The entrepreneurs would not like to be ordered about to produce this or that, how much to produce or where to produce. Fiscal incentives in the form of tax concessions, rebates or subsidies are, therefore, preferable. Similarly, the consumers would not like to be told directly to curtail their consumption or to consume this and not to consume that. Taxation of articles whose consumption is to be discouraged is therefore preferable. Hence, a democratic state must rely on indirect methods of control and regulation and this is done through fiscal and monetary policies. Thus, in democratic countries, fiscal policy is a powerful and least undesirable weapon on which the states can rely for promoting economic development.

Capital formation is of strategic importance in the matter of rapid economic development and the developing economies suffer from capital deficiency. It is, therefore, necessary to achieve a higher ratio of savings to national income. In early days of capitalism, payment of low wages and the existence of inequalities of income helped capital formation in the present-day developed countries. But no democratic country can adopt this method in modern times; the effort rather is to raise wages and reduce inequalities of income and wealth. Under a regime of socialist dictatorship, capital formation was brought about by ruthlessly curtailing consumption and keeping down the standards of living. But in modern democracies with every adult person having a right to cast vote, very low levels of living for a long time is not feasible. Hence *the state must rely on instruments of fiscal policy to mobilise resources for economic development*. Taxation can be used to raise collective savings for public investment and also at the same time to promote private investment. A well-conceived scheme of taxation is an important way of raising ratio of savings to national income which is one of the crucial determinants of the rate of economic growth. As Nurkse says, "*Public finance assumes a new significance in the face of the problem of capital formation in underdeveloped countries*."[1]

On the expenditure side, there is positive need for public investment, especially in those branches of economic activity where the private investments are not easily attracted, for example, the development of power resources, means of transport and communications, basic heavy industries, education and research. Such investments are very often the very foundations of rapid economic advance. Thus, fiscal policy is of crucial importance in accelerating the pace of development in developing countries.

We explain below in detail how fiscal policy measures can be used to achieve the objectives of economic growth, more equal distribution of income and price stability in the developing countries.

Taxation and Resource Mobilisation for Economic Development

As mentioned above, capital formation is an important determinant of economic growth. For accelerating the rate of capital formation, saving and investment rate in the economy has to be stepped up. For this purpose, savings have to be mobilised and channelled into productive investment. Due to the severe limitations of alternative ways of mobilising resources for economic growth such as government borrowing and money financing, the role of taxation in performing this task assumes greater importance. Fiscal policy, if properly designed, is an efficient and equitable way of mobilising resources for augmenting public investment. Through it not only collective public savings can be raised for financing public investment but also at the same time private savings and investment can be encouraged. In fact, *taxation may be the most effective means of increasing the total volume of saving and investment in developing countries where the propensity to consume is normally high.* Further, the fiscal policy can be so devised that not only the objective of rapid capital accumulation or growth, but also other objectives of economic policy such as equitable distribution of income and wealth, price stability and promotion of employment opportunities can be achieved.

In what follows we shall explain how taxation can be used to mobilise resources for economic development.

Taxation is an important instrument of fiscal policy which can be used for mobilising resources for capital formation in the public sector. To raise ratio of savings to national income and thereby raise resources for development, *it is necessary that marginal saving rate be kept higher than the average saving rate.* By imposition of direct progressive taxes on income and profits and higher rates of indirect taxes such as excise duties and sales tax on luxury goods for which income elasticity of demand is higher, the marginal saving rate can be made higher than the average saving rate. This will cause a continuous increase in the saving rate of the economy. An important merit of taxation is that it is not only a good instrument of resource mobilisation for development but it also cuts down demand for consumer goods and thereby helps in checking inflation. Whereas direct taxes on income, profits and wealth reduce the disposable incomes of the people and thereby tend to reduce aggregate demand in the economy, indirect taxes directly discourage the consumption of the goods on which they are levied by raising their prices.

Direct Taxes and Mobilisation of Resources

Now the question arises what should be the taxation structure of a developing economy which will mobilise the potential economic surplus to the maximum, that is, what kinds of taxes be levied, how much progressive should be their rates and what should be the exemptions and concessions in various taxes. This is, however, a highly controversial issue. It has been suggested that an appropriate

1 Ragnar Nurkse, *Problems of Capital Formation in Underdeveloped Countries.*

tax which would mobilise resources or mop up economic surplus is the progressive income tax. *In India and other developing countries income has been regarded as a good base for direct taxation.* And the imposition of highly progressive income tax not only mops up relatively greater amount of resources but also tends to reduce inequalities of income. However, a progressive income tax with high marginal rates of taxes adversely affects private saving and investment and also raises the propensity to evade the tax. In view of this, two proposals have been put forward to make the income tax both as an effective instrument of resource mobilisation for the public sector and of providing incentives to save and invest. First, Prof. Kaldor of Cambridge University, who in 1956 was invited by the Government of India to suggest reforms in the Indian tax system for mobilising resources for development, suggested that whereas the *marginal rate of income tax be reduced to, say, 45 to 50 per cent,* expenditure tax be levied to discourage the people belonging to upper income brackets from dissipating their income in conspicuous consumption. According to him, this will also reduce the tendency to evade income tax on the one hand and promote private savings on the other. The second proposal to reform the income tax put forward by others is that whereas marginal rates of income tax may be kept high but some *exemptions for approved forms of saving and investment be allowed to the individuals.* This will channel individual savings along desired lines and at the same time mobilise resources for development.

Recently supply-side economics has pointed out that increase in income tax rate beyond a point will lead to the reduction in tax revenue. In this connection, the concept of *Laffer curve* has been suggested. Thus, according to a Laffer curve concept put forward by an American economist, Arthur Laffer, raising income tax rate beyond a point will yield lower tax revenue. This is because *higher income tax rates adversely affect incentives to work, save and invest* and are therefore counter-productive. Thus higher income tax rates beyond a certain point causes reduction in supply of labour and capital and lead to lower national income and tax revenue.

A Laffer curve is shown in Fig. 50.1 where along the *X*-axis income tax rate is measured and along the *Y*-axis tax revenue is measured. It will be seen from this figure that as rate of income tax is increased, in the beginning tax revenue rises but after the tax rate t_3, further increases in tax rate yields lower tax revenue. At tax rate t_3, tax revenue $t_3 H$ is maximum. Empirical studies have found that tax rate in the range of 30 to 35 per cent is optimal from the viewpoint of maximum tax revenue.

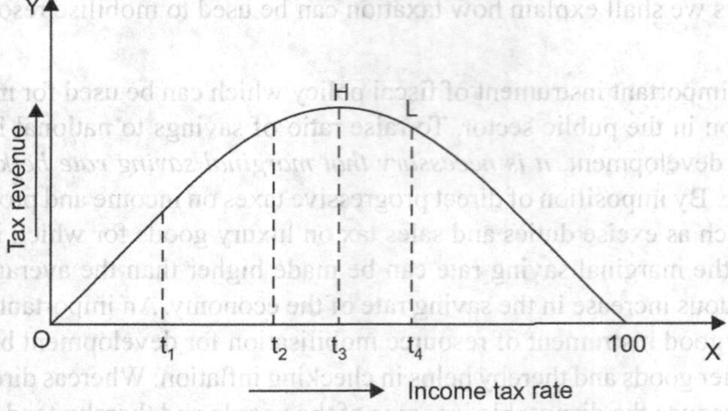

Fig. 50.1. *Laffer curve depicting relationship between tax rate and tax revenue*

Apart from the income tax on individuals and companies, the *imposition of other direct taxes such as capital gains tax, wealth tax, gift tax, and estate duty* is also needed to mobilise sufficient resources for capital formation. Unlike income tax, these capital taxes do not have any adverse effect on incentives to save and invest.[2] They are also important instruments of reducing inequalities of income and wealth. Because of these advantages, Professor Kaldor in his report on taxation reforms in India recommended the imposition of these capital taxes and this recommendation was accepted

2 I.S. Gulati, *Capital Taxation in India,* Orient Longman, 1957.

and the annual wealth tax and gift tax were levied in 1957 with estate duty having been already introduced in 1954.

Agricultural Taxation and Resource Mobilisation. A good part of national income in India and other developing countries originates in the agricultural sector which has substantial economic surplus which can be tapped for capital formation. This economic surplus mainly goes to rich farmers, landlords, merchants and other intermediaries and, in the absence of suitable taxation on agriculture, is used for conspicuous consumption and for investing in unproductive activities such as buying gold, jewellery, real estate. Thus, according to Professor Kaldor, "*the taxation of agriculture by one means or another has a critical role to play in the acceleration of economic development.*"[3] Further, owing to economic growth in general and agricultural development in particular income of the agricultural class and therefore economic surplus enormously increases and therefore needs to be mopped up for further development. Besides, the agricultural sector has to be taxed not only because it has a potential surplus but also to *achieve maximum utilisation of land through devising a system of land taxation which would penalise poor use of good land.* In this regard, a progressive land tax "the effective rates of taxation of which vary with the total value of landholdings of the family unit" may be suitable one. Besides this, progressive agricultural income tax with appropriate exemption may be levied to tap resources from affluent sections of the agricultural sector.

It may be noted that as compared to the non-agricultural sector, agricultural sector in India and other developing countries is quite under-taxed. Land revenue which was at one time the greatest source of revenue for government has now become an insignificant yielder of revenue. In the context of India, Agricultural Taxation Committee under the chairmanship of Dr. K.N. Raj recommended Agricultural Holdings Tax (AHT) which was to be imposed at a progressive rate on the rateable value of an agricultural holding of ₹ 5000 and above. It was expected to yield annually ₹ 200 crore. However, Agricultural Holdings Tax was found to be difficult to assess and administer. In our view, a *graded surcharge on the existing land revenue* will be far easier to assess and administer and make land revenue a more elastic source of revenue. However, it may be noted that in India agricultural taxation is a State subject and there is lack of political will on the part of the State Governments to raise the level of land taxation in a country. But if sufficient resources are to be mobilised for development, the level of agricultural taxation has to be raised.

Role of Direct Taxation in Promoting Private Saving and Investment

It is worth mentioning that in a mixed economy such as ours, *there is need to raise not only the public savings and investment but also to promote private saving and investment* so that the overall rate of saving and investment in the economy is stepped up. This implies that taxation measures should not impair incentives to save and invest of the people. Therefore, a developing economy encounters a crucial dilemma in augmenting larger resources for public investment on the one hand and to promote private savings and investment on the other. Thus, according to Prof. Heller, "*Tax Policy faces a basic dilemma in its role as an instrument of capital formation for economic development.* On the one hand, high levels of taxes are necessary to finance that part of the development which falls in the government share and to mobilise for investment the private resources that might otherwise be dissipated. On the other hand, the lower the taxes, the greater will be the inducement to private investment... The dilemma is worsened by the fact that those taxes which are most effective in capturing a large share of the gains for further capital formation are the ones most likely to affect the returns from private investment. The *only way to overcome the dilemma may be to combine high rates of taxation in general, with preferential treatment for categories of desired development activity.*"

However, as Kaldor pointed out in his recommendations for tax reforms in India, very high rates of income tax cause evasion of the tax and also discourage incentive to save and invest. Besides,

3 N. Kaldor, "The Role of Taxation in Economic Development," in E.A.G. Robinson (ed.), *Problems in Economic Development,* 1965, p. 177.

according to Laffer Curve concept, on which supply-side economics is based, if rate of income tax is raised beyond a point (above the range of 30 to 35%), revenue from income tax decreases. This has been confirmed by the Indian experience as under the economic reforms initiated since 1991, marginal rate of personal income tax has been reduced to 30 per cent and this has led to substantial increase in tax revenue from both personal income tax and corporate income tax. Therefore, *the policy of moderate direct taxes with preferential treatment for some desired forms of saving and investment is ideal one for resource mobilisation for economic growth.*

Thus, while the policy of moderate rates of taxation on income and profit may be adopted but even with this private saving and investment can be promoted through preferential treatment of them. Besides the adoption of moderate rate of income tax, private savings can be promoted in several other ways. First, interest on several types of private savings such as bank deposits, investment in units of Unit Trust of India, National Savings Certificates, mutual funds, pension funds, equity linked saving schemes (ELSS) and other approved forms of saving be substantially exempted from taxation. This will encourage private savings through raising the rate of return on savings as the savers would earn interest income free of income tax. Secondly, voluntary savings in certain selective lines such as voluntary contributions to provident fund, life insurance premium, certain specific schemes of UTI and National Savings Certificates be substantially exempted from income tax. This will also stimulate private savings by raising the rate of return on these savings. For, people will not only earn rate of interest or dividend but will save a good amount of income tax on these approved forms of savings. Thirdly, some economists have suggested that if progressivity in tax rates is avoided (that is, if rates of income taxes do not increase much with the increase in income) private saving and investment will be boosted up. However, this is based upon a questionable assumption that richer people in countries like India have high propensity to save. In view of the present author, the lower marginal rates of taxes will place more disposable income in the hands of higher income brackets which will tend to raise their conspicuous consumption, especially when goods catering to their frivolous wants are available in abundance these days through both domestic production and imports. As mentioned above, this is reinforced by the *international demonstration effect* which exercises a strong influence on the consumption behaviour of the richer sections of the Indian society. However, too high marginal rates of income will encourage tax evasion. Therefore, in order to ensure tax compliance on the one hand and to achieve equity in distribution of tax burden, marginal tax rates should be moderately high.

Besides private savings, private investment can be directly encouraged through taxation. Firstly, in order to stimulate private investment, the *retained profits* which are reinvested by the business firms instead of distributing them among the shareholders can be exempted from taxation or taxed at preferential rates. Secondly, to boost private investment *liberal depreciation and investment allowances* may also be allowed to the business firms which will be used for purposes of investment in new plant, equipment and machinery. Further, "subsidies on investment can also be provided by the government which generally prove to be a very effective way of promoting private investment".

Another important fiscal method of stimulating private investment in developing countries is *granting of tax holidays or relief from tax on the profits of new enterprises* for some specified period of time. Further, indirect taxes can also be manipulated in a variety of ways to promote private investment in certain selected fields of industrial activity. Thus exemption or lowering of sales tax or excise duties on some domestically produced important raw materials or lowering of import duties on raw materials and capital goods from abroad can provide a boost to private investment. Likewise, reduction of export duties may also bring about a healthy effect on investment outlook.

It needs to be stressed that various incentives to promote private savings and investment will prove effective only if they are kept as simple, certain and stable as possible. A complicated scheme of incentives with frequent and arbitrary changes is likely to defeat the very purpose of these incentive schemes. Prof. Prest rightly points out, *"If the main purpose of investment incentives is to raise the long-term level of investment rather than offset cyclical downturns and this clearly is the case in underdeveloped countries ... the emphasis should be on the* ***stability of these tax arrangements rather than their variability.***"[4]

It is important to note that private investment depends upon several factors such as size of the market, cost of inputs, availability of infrastructural facilities such as power, coal, oil, transport, availability of technical know-how. Tax incentives will prove effective only if conditions regarding these other factors are not unfavourable. Further, *unless there is an efficient and competent system of tax administration, it is very likely that incentives become tax loopholes.* The businessmen in the developing countries tend to take advantage of these tax exemptions on bogus basis without fulfilling and carrying out the underlying intent of such concessions. An honest and efficient administrative machinery, therefore, remains the basic precondition for the purposeful use of incentives.[5]

Merits of Direct Taxes for Resource Mobilisation

As seen above, as an instrument of resource mobilisation for development direct taxes enjoy several advantages:

1. They raise resources in a non-inflationary way. Indeed, they tend to check inflation by curtailing consumption demand.
2. They help to reduce inequalities of income and wealth.
3. They discourage conspicuous and non-essential consumption and thereby enlarge economic surplus. But the direct taxation of agricultural and non-agricultural sectors has its own limits. In India there is a great potential for raising resources through direct taxes. At present about 4 crore people out of 125 crore population pay income tax. As economic growth takes place incomes of the people increase and as a result their taxable capacity also increases. There is a considerable evasion of income tax and corporation tax in India. If this evasion is checked more resources can be raised. Yield from other direct taxes such as wealth tax, gift tax is quite meagre due to very small coverage, low rates and considerable evasion of them. Therefore, more revenue from these taxes can also be obtained by making suitable reforms in them.

How much tax revenue in developing countries can be raised depends on two factors: (1) *taxable capacity* of the country and (2) *tax effort* made by the country. The tax efforts mean the policy measures are taken by the government to raise revenue so that taxable capacity is fully used. The taxable capacity of an economy depends on the level of its per capita income the distribution of income among the people. The higher the per capita income and greater the inequalities in income distribution, the larger will be the taxable capacity of the country. Besides, taxable capacity depends on the degree of urbanisation and the size of the industrial sector, the importance of foreign trade in the economy of the country.

The tax effort depends on the fiscal measures such as income tax, capital gains tax, wealth tax, gift tax, estate duty taken by a country to raise tax revenue. The data regarding tax revenue collected by the government in developing countries on an average are around 20 per cent of GDP as against 31 to 37 per cent of GDP in the developed countries.[6] It is worth mentioning that India lags far behind in regard to tax efforts made as tax revenue as a percentage of GDP is equal to 10 per cent only.[7] In the developing countries the scope for increasing tax revenues is very limited because a large proportion of the population earns a very low income and falls outside the purview of the tax system. Besides, many exemptions and rebates given by the government in the direct taxes lower the tax base and the

---

4 A.R. Prest, "Fiscal Measures and Capital Accumulation" in Agarwala and Singh (ed.), *Accelerating Investment in Developing Countries,* Oxford University Press.

5 A.R. Prest. *op. cit., p.* 445.

6 See World Bank, *World Development Indicators*, 2011.

7 GOI, *Economic Survey*, 2013-14.

collection of tax revenue. In developing countries, less than 30 per cent of population is subject to income tax as compared to 70 per cent of population in the developed countries.

Therefore, there is a good deal of scope for raising tax revenue through undertaking reforms. An important object of tax system in the developing countries is to promote saving so that capital formation is accelerated. The high marginal tax rates, as explained above in the Laffer curve concept, often discourage work effort and also to the extent that high marginal tax rates fall on those groups having high marginal propensity to save, the saving rate may fall as marginal tax rate is increased. Besides, several exemptions in personal income tax given by the government are misused by the persons to evade and avoid income tax and wealth tax.

Likewise, corporate income tax which is a tax on profits of corporate companies is full of several exemptions and rebates given apparently for promoting social objectives are misused by the corporates to illegally reduce their tax liability. For example, in India though corporate income tax rate was 33 per cent including surcharges, then according to the estimate of the Finance Ministry actually on an average the companies actually pay only 20 per cent tax on their profits or income. This is because of various exemptions in the corporate tax system. Even then in his budget for 2015-16, the new Finance Minister, Mr. Arun Jaitly has reduced the corporate tax rate to 25 per cent in a phased manner subject to withdrawal of some exemptions. In our view, this will further reduce the actual income tax rate paid by the companies.

This reduction in corporate income tax rate has been done to woo foreign investors to make investment in India. In our view, this is quite inequitable and unjust as individuals have to pay marginal income tax rate of 33 per cent (including surcharge) on their earned income of more than 10 lakh per annum, the corporates have to pay only 25 per cent. This shows that far from making tax system equitable and buoyant the government is making it more inequitable. Wages and salary earners are being discriminated against vis-a-vis the owners of property and capital. The equity demands that the tax system for both individuals and companies should be such as discourages luxury consumption and makes it difficult to evade and avoid taxes. This will also cause savings to increase.

Besides, the tax reforms are needed for effective taxation of wealth as the ownership of wealth bestows the owners with an inherent taxable capacity regardless of the income it yields. Strangely, instead of making it more effective by plugging its loopholes the Finance Minister in the budget for 2015-16 has abolished the wealth tax and has instead levied 2 per cent surcharge on income of above rupees two crore per annum. Due to large scale evasion of income tax, this move will not serve the end of justice and equity in taxation. A.P. Thirwall, a renowned development economist, has suggested the following four tax reforms in developing countries:[8]

"1. That overall income (including capital gains) be aggregated and taxed in the same way at a progressive rate but not exceeding a maximum marginal rate of, say, 50 per cent. Marginal rates above this level may not discourage incentive but may also be counter-productive by encouraging evasion and avoidance.

2. The institution of progressive personal expenditure tax levied on rich individuals who reach the maximum marginal rate of income tax.

3. The institution of wealth tax.

4. The institution of a gift tax."

However, the above proposals of tax reforms are exactly those recommended N. Kaldor in case of India.

Role of Indirect Taxes in Resource Mobilisation

As a result of limitations of direct taxes, developing countries have resorted to extensive use of indirect taxes. *In India, almost all commodities have been brought within the net of indirect taxes such as excise duties and sales tax. Besides, there are customs duties* (*i.e., taxes on imports and exports*). Indirect taxation is an important source of development funds in a developing country. In the last six

8 A.P. Thirlwall, *The Economics of Development,* 9th edition, pp. 419-20.

decades of planned development, revenue from several indirect taxes has been rising as a percentage of total revenue as well as of national income. It has been found that indirect taxes are better suited to the conditions obtaining in developing countries for reducing current consumption and mobilising resources for development. This is because in such countries quite a large proportion of national income tends to be diverted to current consumption instead of being saved and productively invested. The average propensity to consume in such countries is much higher than is the case in advanced countries. Indirect taxes which reduce consumption must thus play a more important part. They will raise the rate of savings which are so essential for economic growth. *"High rates of taxes on commodities with a high income elasticity of demand are quite effective in siphoning a substantial proportion of increase in output into the resources of the public sector needed for development financing and a stiff rate of commodity taxes on luxury articles tends to introduce an element of progressiveness in an otherwise predominantly regressive tax structure in developing countries."*[9]

But in order to make sure that the resources raised through commodity taxes are adequate, it will be necessary to extend their coverage to include some articles of mass consumption. In the poor countries, it is not possible to exempt entirely goods of general and necessary consumption, because they are the only goods that provide a base broad enough to assure an adequate amount of resources. The rates of two important indirect taxes, namely, excise duties and customs duties which yielded increasingly greater revenue for government before 1991 had to be reduced under economic reforms initiated since 1991. To promote free trade customs duties had to be reduced as a part of agreement under WTO. Excise duty had to be reduced so that domestic industries could compete with imports from abroad after the adoption of liberal foreign trade policy. However, to compensate for the loss in revenue due to reduction in customs duties and excise duty, new ***service*** **tax** (which is an indirect tax) has been imposed. Service tax which now covers more than 100 services has become a good source of tax revenue. In the financial years 2012-13 and 2013-14 service tax yielded ₹ 132,601 and ₹ 154,630 crore respectively. Besides, in the States sales tax has been replaced by value added tax (VAT) which is also yielding more revenue.

Limitations. But there are some limitations of raising resources through indirect taxes. First, they lead to *cost-push inflation*. The burden of indirect taxes is passed on to the consumers in the form of higher prices charged from them. In India excise duties on sugar, cloth, kerosene oil, petrol etc., have raised the prices and have contributed a good deal to cost-push inflation witnessed in last several years. Secondly, levying of customs duties on imports of capital goods, raw materials used for industrial production have accelerated cost-push inflation in the Indian economy. Thirdly, imposition of customs duties on imports of goods also protects inefficiency in domestic industries. This also contributes to high-cost production and promotes inefficiency. Lastly, indirect taxes are ***regressive*** in nature; both the rich and poor have to pay the same rate on the taxed commodities. The regressive character of indirect taxes has been attempted to be reduced by imposing higher rates of excise and customs duties on luxury items and smaller rates of duties on goods of mass consumption. However, the need for mobilising greater resources has forced the Finance Ministers to levy higher indirect taxes even on articles of mass consumption.

Reforms in the Indirect Tax System: Goods and Services Tax (GST)

An important reform in the indirect tax system is the introduction of goods and service tax (GST). GST will replace all multistage sales or value added taxes such as CENVAT and service tax levied by the Centre and the sales tax, value added tax (VAT), entertainment tax, luxury tax levied by the States. *This is the comprehensive tax on goods and services*. The introduction of GST will not only simplify the indirect tax system in the country but will also yield more revenue for the government. The significant reason of complexity of the present indirect tax system is related to the existence of various exemptions and multiple rates of CENVAT on various commodities and different rates of

9 R.N. Tripathy, *Public Finance in Developing Countries,* 1966, p. 200.

sales tax or VAT levied by the States. Since GST is a tax on consumption, it will promote saving. Besides, it will reduce the incidence of evasion.

The starting base of Central excise duty or CENVAT is narrow and is further eroded by a variety of area-specific and conditional and unconditional exemptions. Therefore, the introduction of comprehensive single GST would be appropriate for deepening indirect tax system in India.

It has been decided that rate of GST will be 16%. Therefore, imposition of GST will lead to lowering of prices of goods. This is because a good with 8% excise duty and 12 per cent VAT will face a total tax rate of 20%. Under single GST it will fall to 16% given that rate of GST is fixed at 16%.

It has now been decided that GST will apply from April 2016. It is now widely recognised that GST will be a major milestone for indirect tax reform in India. By replacing all existing indirect taxes, the GST will create a national market as it will eliminate the cascading effects of multiple layers of taxation all over the country and facilitate movements of goods and services across State borders. Besides, it will align taxation of imports and exports correctly. This will improve the competitiveness of production and exports from India. The single GST will also improve tax collection as it will end the long-standing distortions of differential treatment of manufacturing goods and services and uniform removal of exemptions.

CHAPTER 51

ROLE OF FISCAL POLICY: GOVERNMENT BORROWING FOR FINANCING DEVELOPMENT

Government borrowing is another fiscal method by which resources may be mobilised for economic development. In developing economies, the governments resort to borrowing in order to finance schemes of economic development. Government or what is also called public borrowing becomes necessary because taxation alone cannot provide sufficient funds for economic development. Besides, too heavy taxation has an adverse effect on private saving and investment. It may be noted that when government increases its expenditure, it often results in budget deficit which is also fiscal deficit. This fiscal deficit can be financed in two ways. First, by borrowing by the government from the market and this borrowing leads to the increase in public debt. Borrowing as a means to finance the fiscal deficit is therefore called **debt-financing of budget deficit.** Second, budget or fiscal deficit can be financed by ***printing new money*** and therefore it is called **money financing of fiscal deficit.** The debt-financing of budget deficit will be discussed in the present chapter and money financing of fiscal deficit will be discussed in the next chapter.

How much resources should be mobilised through borrowing and creation of money by the government depends on whether or not the funds so obtained are used for productive purposes which generates higher growth in GDP. In our view, in a developing economy such as ours, a fine balance needs to be struck between how much resources have to be raised through taxation, borrowing (*i.e.*, debt financing) and newly created money.

GOVERNMENT BORROWING OR DEBT-FINANCING OF BUDGET DEFICIT

A popular method of financing budget deficit is borrowing by the government which issues bonds and sells them to the public. Generally, sale of interest-bearing bonds to the public is indirect through financial intermediaries such as banks. Banks buy the bonds floated by the government with the currency deposits of the public. Therefore, borrowing by the government for financing of budget deficit is also known as ***bond-financing of budget deficit***. With the borrowed money in this way the government is able to expand its expenditure but at the same time it adds to public debt which has both short-run and long-run consequences. It may also be noted that budget deficit also comes about when taxes are reduced, keeping government expenditure constant. This type of budget deficit can also be financed through borrowing by selling bonds to the banks or public. The government has not only to pay annually interest on borrowed funds but has to pay back also the principal sum borrowed for which it may levy higher taxes in future.[1]

The Keynesians have emphasised the expansionary effect of debt financing of government expenditure. **In the Keynesian model with a fixed price level, the increase in government**

1 R. Dornbusch, S. Fischer, & R. Startz, *Macroeconomics,* Tata-McGraw Hill, 8th edition, p. 476.

expenditure through use of borrowed money causes an upward shift in aggregate expenditure ($C+I+G$) curve. If the economy is working at less than full-employment level of national income so that output gap exists in the economy, the increase in debt-financed government expenditure will bring about expansion in output or income. With the increase in income at the given tax rate, tax revenue collected will rise which will over time reduce the budget deficit or even ultimately eliminate it so that budget becomes balanced. This can also be illustrated through *IS-LM* model in Fig. 51.1 where *IS* and *LM* curves are drawn, given the money supply in the economy. Y^* is the full-employment level of output. Initially, the equilibrium is at income level Y_0. Now, with increase in government expenditure through borrowing *IS* curve shifts to the right from IS_0 to IS_1 with *LM* curve remaining the same. As a result, as will be seen from Fig. 51.1, national income increases to Y_1. This will bring about increase in tax revenue collected by the government and over time budget deficit will be reduced or even eliminated. It will be seen from Fig. 51.1 that though interest rate also rises but it does not fully offset the expansionary effect of increase in government expenditure so that there is net expansionary effect of debt-financed increase in government expenditure.

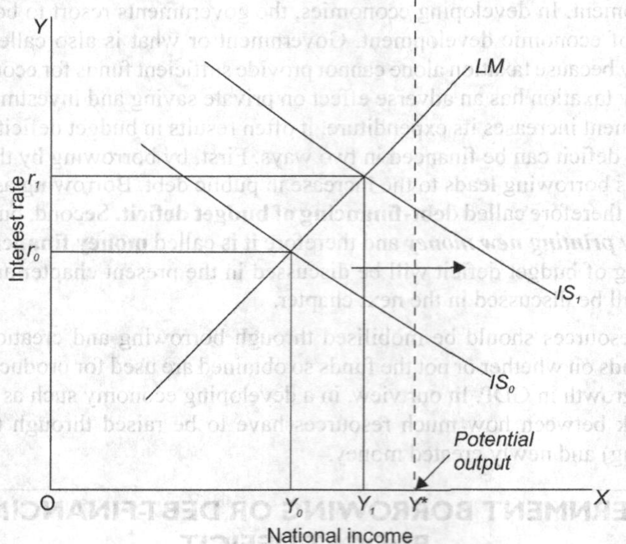

Fig. 51.1. *Expansionary effect of increase in government expenditure by borrowing: IS-LM curves approach*

However, critics have pointed out that debt-financed government expenditure is largely offset by the ***crowding-out effect*** of debt financing on private investment. The crowding-out effect on private investment takes place in a variety of ways. First, it has been pointed out that government's borrowing funds to finance budget deficit will lead to the increase in demand for lendable funds which will cause the rate of interest to rise. The rise in interest rate will cause private investment to decline. Thus debt-financed increase in government expenditure crowds out private investment. According to this view, due to crowding-out effect on private investment net expansionary effect of increase in government expenditure is negligible. On the other hand, the society will have to bear the burden of increase in public debt as a result of debt-financed expansion in government expenditure. If budget deficit arises due to reduction in taxes, keeping government expenditure constant, this will also lead to rise in interest rate and will therefore cause crowding-out effect on private investment. This happens because reduction in taxes stimulates consumption expenditure of the people which reduces savings. The decline in savings causes interest rate to rise resulting in fall in private investment.

Wealth Effect of Government Borrowing (*i.e.,* Debt-Financing)

In our above analysis, we have not taken into account the wealth effect of debt financing. When the government issues bonds to finance its budget deficit, it creates private wealth. This is because bonds are considered as wealth by the people. Patinkin and Friedman in their models include wealth in their money demand function. That is, according to them, demand from money depends on the real value of wealth, apart from other factors. If this wealth effect of bond-financing of budget deficit

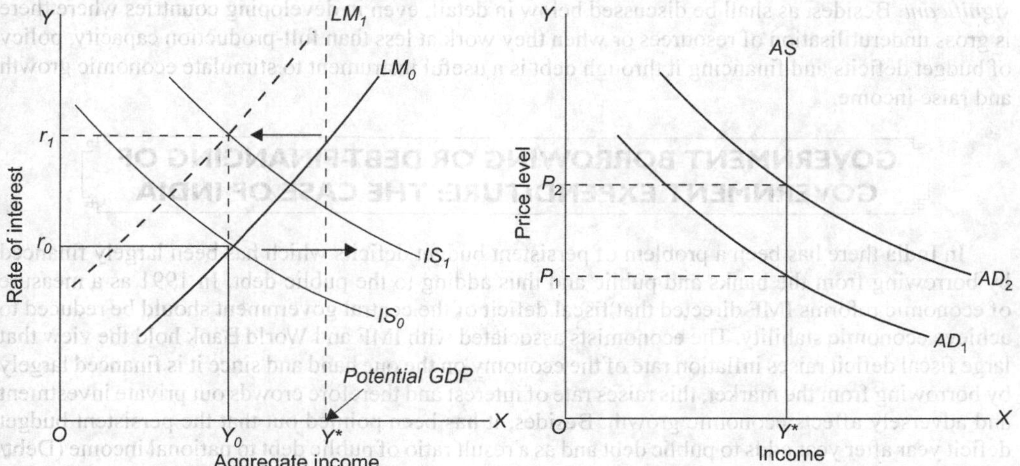

Fig. 51.2. *Borrowing for financing budget deficit with wealth effect of bonds sold by the government*

Fig. 51.3. *Rise in price level offsets the expansionary effect of debt financing of budget deficit*

is recognised, then it exercises an important influence on the dynamic behaviour of the economy. When through borrowing for financing budget deficit more bonds are issued and sold by the government, the wealth of the people increases which will raise the demand for money. *The increase in demand for money, money supply remaining the same, causes a leftward shift in the LM curve,* for instance, from LM_0 to LM_1 in Fig. 51.2. (Note that, on the contrary, financing of government expenditure through creation of printed money, *LM* curve will shift to the right.) Thus, while with the increase in government expenditure *IS* curve shifts to the right to the new position IS_1 which tends to raise aggregate income, the wealth effect of bonds issued to finance the deficit causes leftward shift in the *LM* curve which tends to raise rate of interest and thereby crowds out private investment. According to Friedman, the wealth effect is quite substantial so that it completely offsets the expansionary effect of increase in government expenditure. In Fig. 51.2, initially the equilibrium is at Y_0 level of income. With bond-financed increase in government expenditure *IS* curve shifts from IS_0 to IS_1 and due to wealth effect *LM* curve shifts leftward to LM_1. It will be seen that interest rate rises from r_0 to r_1 with no net effect on the level of income which remains unchanged at Y_0. Due to rise in interest, private investment declines so much that it completely offsets the expansionary effect of debt-financed budget deficit. As a result, budget deficit persists and debt goes on accumulating and becomes unsustainable.

In the above analysis of crowding-out effect of debt-financing, it is assumed that price level remains fixed. However, when the aggregate supply function is vertical as is the case when the economy is working at full capacity output (*i.e.,* full-employment level), increase in aggregate demand (*AD*) brought about by increase in government expenditure through borrowing will result in rise in price level, equilibrium level of income remains unchanged as shown through *AS-AD* model in Fig. 51.3. Since income remains unchanged, tax-revenue will not increase and therefore budget deficit persists and debt will go on accumulating and over time become unsustainable.

Conclusion: We have seen above that expansionary effect of borrowing to finance budget deficit has been challenged on the ground of its crowding-out effect. However, in our view, the crowding-out effect of debt financing has been blown out of all proportions. As a matter of fact, crowding-out effect of debt financing of budget deficit is negligible, especially when the economy is working at less than full-employment level of income. Generally, budget deficit and its financing through floating of bonds is recommended to overcome depression when there is underemployment equilibrium and therefore output gap exists. *Empirical evidence also shows that wealth effect of sale of bonds is not significant*. Besides, as shall be discussed below in detail, even in developing countries where there is gross underutilisation of resources or when they work at less than full-production capacity, policy of budget deficits and financing it through debt is a useful instrument to stimulate economic growth and raise income.

GOVERNMENT BORROWING OR DEBT-FINANCING OF GOVERNMENT EXPENDITURE: THE CASE OF INDIA

In India there has been a problem of persistent budget deficits which has been largely financed by borrowing from the banks and public and thus adding to the public debt. In 1991 as a measure of economic reforms IMF directed that fiscal deficit of the central government should be reduced to achieve economic stability. The economists associated with IMF and World Bank hold the view that large fiscal deficit raises inflation rate of the economy on the one hand and since it is financed largely by borrowing from the market, this raises rate of interest and therefore crowds out private investment and adversely affects economic growth. Besides, it has been pointed out that the persistent budget deficit year after year adds to public debt and as a result ratio of public debt to national income (Debt/GDP ratio) will greatly increase which will land the country in debt trap.[2]

In view of the above, it is appropriate to discuss the above issues relating to borrowing for financing budget deficit and thereby to increase its developmental expenditure in the light of the recent Indian experience. It is worth mentioning that from 1997 to 2002-03 the Indian economy experienced slowdown in economic growth due to lack of aggregate demand resulting mainly from the fall in public investment and poor performance in agriculture. In this situation, *output gap* in the Indian economy emerged as the existing production capacity was not fully utilised. Besides, there has been lack of infrastructure facilities which stands in the way of raising private investment. Again in 2008-09 there was slowdown in the Indian economy due to global financial crisis (2007-09) leading to a sharp fall in Indian export which is now an important component of aggregate demand.

With their focus on reducing fiscal deficit the government reduced its capital expenditure (*i.e.,* investment expenditure) because it failed to curb its consumption expenditure and subsidies. Thus, Mihir Rakshit, a leading Indian macroeconomist, rightly states, "With their focus on fiscal deficit, policy makers seem to think that what matters primarily is curbing government expenditure ... irrespective of changes in their composition. The period 1995-2000 was marked by 9.6 per cent and 12.6 per cent growth in government consumption and subsidies respectively, but public accumulation grew at snail's pace of 1.9 per cent and its two crucial constituents, namely, investment in agriculture and infrastructure, actually declined by 5.6 per cent and 0.2 per cent respectively".[3]

The consequences of borrowing to finance budget deficit in the case of India depends on whether or not output gap exists due to lack of demand and infrastructural facilities. If the output gap exists, then increase in government expenditure on consumption and subsidies will raise aggregate demand and help in utilising more fully the existing production capacity and over time will cause private investment to rise. But this will not raise public saving and public investment and therefore will not

2 For this view, see Shankar Acharya, former Chief Economic Advisor, who puts forward this view in a forceful manner in "*How Fiscal Deficit Hurts Economic Growth.*" We have explained in detail this main-stream view in the next chapter.

3 Mihir Rakshit, "*Some Macroeconomics of India's Reforms Experience*" in Kaushik Basu (ed.), *India's Emerging Economy,* Oxford University Press, 2004, p, 104.

result in much higher growth of the economy. This may also raise ratio of public debt to GDP since due to slow growth in GDP, tax collection will not appreciably rise. Mihir Rakshit aptly points out that, "The Indian economy since 1997[4] has also been characterised by output gap, high fiscal deficit and growing debt/GDP ratio. The mainstream view in India is that despite the output gap fiscal deficits crowd out private investment and are unsustainable."[5]

The mainstream view of borrowing for financing fiscal deficit is not correct and has been rightly challenged by some prominent Indian economists such as Mihir Rakshit, V.N. Pandit and Prabhat Patnaik, among others. *Under the circumstances when there exists output gap and underutilisation of production capacity, the increase in government expenditure, especially of investment nature, will crowd in private investment and speed up rate of economic growth.* To quote Mihir Rakshit, "Contrary to widespread perception among commentators *budget deficits associated with closing the output gap in fact crowds in private investment*… crowding in will be much more pronounced in countries like India where government's infrastructural investment favourably affects private investment even while projects are being executed: the fact that highways are being built in some areas or that it will soon have abundant supply of power, communication facilities is likely to induce private investors to start setting up new units and expanding existing ones even in the short run."[6]

When there is outgap in a developing economy such as India, even increase in government's consumption expenditure will crowd in private investment through the former's demand effect. But, as has been pointed out by Dr. Mihir Rakshit, crowding-in effect of government's investment expenditure will be greater because it expands the infrastructural facilities (*i.e.,* supply-side factors) badly needed for increase in private investment.

In our view, the expansionary effect of government's investment expenditure and also its crowding-in effect on private investment in a developing country like India is not confined to the situation when output gap and underutilisation of capital stock exists due to demand deficiency but also when such an economy functions at its normal capacity. Besides, even in normal times, government borrowing to finance its investment expenditure which brings about rapid economic growth, budget deficits and debt/GDP ratio over time can be reduced. **An important rule of public finance, which is sometimes described as a golden rule, is that if borrowed money by the government is used for investment or developmental purposes, it leads to growth in GDP or national income.** Given the tax rate, this increase in income will ensure collection of more tax revenue possible. As a result, fiscal deficit will be reduced and debt/GDP ratio will decline. This has actually happened in India.

As a matter of fact, long ago (in 1994) E.D. Domar had stated the **condition for sustainability of persistent budget deficits** and consequently of mounting public debt. According to Domar, debt-financed fiscal deficits *are sustainable if growth rate exceeds the rate of interest.* This is because economic growth means increase in income or GDP from which annual interest payments can be made and if growth in income exceeds the rate of interest, the part of increase in income may be used for retiring public debt. In this way with the growth of the economy fiscal deficit and debt/GDP ratio can be reduced. Elaborating Domar's condition, Mihir Rakshit writes, "According to Domar, if the government finances part of its expenditure (amounting to a given fraction of full-employment output) through borrowing, in a growing economy public debt and the government interest outgo as proportion of GDP will be stable in the long run provided the growth rate exceeds the interest rate. The implication is that when this condition is satisfied, maintenance of full employment through debt financing of budget deficit does not erode fiscal viability or produce a debt trap."[7]

4 Mihir Rakshit describes the situation that prevailed during 1997–2002-03 when there was a lot of underutilisation of productive capacity due to lack of aggregate demand.

5 "Budget Deficit: Sustainability, Solvency and Optimality," printed in Amaresh Bagchi, *Readings in Public Finance*, Oxford University Press, 2005, pp. 342-343.

6 Mihir Rakshit, *op. cit.,* p. 345.

7 Mihir Rakshit, *op. cit.* (2005), p. 340.

In case of India's macrodynamics the viability and sustainability can be explained through the following equation:

$$Y = C(Y_d) + I_v(Y_1 - Y_{t-1}) + I_g + G \quad ...(1)$$

where Y stands for national income (*i.e.*, GDP_{FC}), Y_d for disposable income, C for consumption which depends on disposable income (Y_d), I_v for private investment which depends on change in national income (Y), I_g for government's investment expenditure, and G for government's consumption expenditure

Now, $Y_d = Y - T$ where T stands for tax revenue. If t is the rate of income tax, then $T = tY$. Thus

$$Y_d = Y - tY = (1 - t)\,Y \quad ...(2)$$

Since budget deficit (*BD*) in our simple model is the difference between government total expenditure on consumption (G) and investment (I_g) and the tax revenue collected, we have

$$BD = (I_g + G) - tY \quad ...(3)$$

Now substituting $(1 - t)Y$ for Y_d in equation (1) above we have

$$Y = C[(1 - t)Y] + I_v(Y_1 - Y_{t-1}) + I_g + G \quad ...(4)$$

The viability and sustainability of government borrowing for financing fiscal deficits in a growing economy must be based on the magnitude of government investment expenditure (I_g) in the total expenditure ($I_g + G$). Suppose the economy is working at the full capacity output, and government increases its investment expenditure, say, on infrastructure and finances the budget deficit through incurring debt. This increase in government investment expenditure will raise income through both demand effect and capacity effect and will therefore stimulate private investment which depends on change in income (*i.e.*, $Y_1 - Y_{t-1}$). This increase in both government and private investment will over time cause rapid growth in income which in turn will result in more tax revenue. Thus, in this way budget deficit will be reduced with favourable effect on public debt/GDP ratio, if rate of growth in income (GDP) exceeds rate of interest.

It is thus clear that sustainability of fiscal deficit and public debt depends on ***shifting the composition of government expenditure towards investment***. To quote Mihir Rakshit, "Budgetary viability requires an improvement in revenue balances in the medium term and the long run public investment in agriculture aided by crowding-in effect raises agricultural productivity and acts as a stimulant to a rural economy, brings down poverty and *enables the government to reduce over time expenditure on food or fertilizer subsidies and poverty alleviation measures.* An increase in government investment in rural and urban infrastructural facilities through increased revenue receipts and decreased subsidies will strengthen budgetary position not only in the medium term and the long run but in the short run as well."[8] It is interesting to note that when with effect from year 2003 the government investment expenditure in India has been raised, tax revenue collection has significantly risen and also fiscal deficit, revenue deficit and debt/GDP ratio also declined. Besides, private investment went up (*i.e.*, crowded in) rather than crowding out by increase in debt-financed increase in government expenditure.

Thus, in the 1990s when the focus in our strategy was to reduce fiscal deficit, no matter reducing capital expenditure of the government for this purpose, the Indian economy experienced slowdown in growth and our fiscal situation worsened. On the other hand, when from March 2003 we shifted the focus toward increase in government investment expenditure on power, ports, highways, rural roads in a big way, private investment also crowded in, generated higher economic growth which resulted in lower fiscal deficits and lower debt/GDP ratio.

Nowadays, the Central Government borrows mostly from the market through sale of its bonds of different maturities carrying different rates of interest by RBI.

8 Mihir Rakshit, *op. cit.*, 2005, p. 105.

Public Borrowing Generates Additional Productive Capacity. The funds raised by public borrowing can be utilised for building up economic infrastructure for the economy through schemes for the development of irrigation, transport, power and communication. They can help also in building up of the agricultural and industrial base of the economy. All such investments facilitate further economic growth. There is no doubt, therefore, that the public borrowing plays a very useful and important role in accelerating economic growth of developing economies. Public debt promotes saving and investment, the two most crucial determinants of economic growth.

But there are three problems concerning government borrowing. First, government borrowing leads to increase is public debt whose burden falls on future generations who have to pay higher taxes to the government for paying back the borrowed funds. Besides, every year the government has to pay interest on the borrowed funds and these annual interest payments which are very large due to accumulated large public debt generally cause large deficit in revenue account of the government budget. As a result, a large chunk of new borrowings every year are used to make interest payments. Thirdly, borrowing by the government from the market leads to increase in demand for loanable funds and *causes rise in interest* rate. At a higher interest rate private investment falls. Thus it is often asserted that *Government borrowing crowds out private investment.* However, when the Central Bank through its accommodating monetary policy expands the money supply to ensure ample liquidity in the banking system, the banks can make adequate funds available for meeting the demand for funds for the corporate sector.

However, government borrowing has often been used to finance its current or consumption expenditure as there has been *large revenue deficit* year after year with the result that financing of capital expenditure through government borrowing has been very small. This does not promote growth of the economy. The *golden rule of government borrowing* is that it should be used for financing investment or productive projects so that it yields returns which can be used to pay interest on the borrowed funds as well as pay back the principal amount. In this way, government borrowing would not involve any burden on future generations and instead higher economic growth will occur which will benefit the future generations.

Another problem of government borrowing to finance large fiscal deficit is that it causes large increase in government expenditure which leads to *excess demand conditions* in the immediate future which cause inflation in the economy. Therefore, financial prudence requires that fiscal deficit should be of reasonable degree and the funds borrowed by the government should be used for investment and productive purposes so that inflationary pressures can be contained.

Obstacles. But there exist a number of obstacles which hinder the success of borrowing policy in developing countries. The resources of the organised financial market may be too inadequate to fulfil the needs of both the private and public sectors. Further, in the financial market the competition for funds between the government and the private sector will raise rate of interest and this will have a highly disincentive effect on the expansion of investment in the private sector. More borrowing by the government leads to the rise in market rates of interest. The higher interest rates tend to reduce private investment. Therefore, it is often asserted that the *higher borrowing target by the government 'crowds out' private investment.* In India the rates of interest on loans (on bonds or securities) of government have been raised quite substantially. Since banks and others prefer to invest in government securities because they are safe (*i.e.,* riskless), this has reduced funds for private investment. However, in our view, this can be avoided if RBI through its monetary measures ensures adequate availability of funds available with the banks so that rate of interest does not rise when investors borrow from the market.

For the success of government's borrowing policy, it is necessary that financial institutions be developed and extended into the rural areas of the economy in order to inculcate the habit of thrift in the population and to mobilise for productive purposes the amount of savings originating in this sector. Besides, for the mobilisation of savings it will be necessary to check and regulate the diversion of savings into unproductive investment such as real estate, gold and jewellery and inventory accumulation.

Suitable techniques of borrowing must also be devised. For example, bonds issued by the government should be adjusted to the preferences of the general public; bonds of large denomination and long maturity may be offered to the institutional investors, whereas those of small denomination and short maturity may be reserved for the non-institutional public. If properly devised and conducted small savings campaign can mobilise a sizable amount of resources. Further, the mobilisation of the hoardings of gold and jewellery through government borrowing programmes constitutes a highly desirable source of resource mobilisation. In this connection the anouncement by the Finance Minister in his budget for 2015-16 to issue gold bonds is a welcome step in this direction.

CHAPTER

52

FINANCING DEVELOPMENT THROUGH MONEY CREATION: INFLATIONARY FINANCING

The government normally finances its expenditure through receipts from taxes, both direct and indirect. When government expenditure increases and it finds it difficult to raise more resources from taxation, it resorts to borrowing from the public or printing money to finance its expenditure. Increase in rates of income and other taxes not only adversely affects incentives to work more, save and invest more but also promotes tax evasion. Further, as Laffer curve concept shows, increase in rate of a tax beyond a point causes revenue from taxes to decline. Thus, there are limits to increasing revenue from taxes to finance the increased expenditure of the government. As a result, when government finds it difficult to raise adequate resources to finance its increased development expenditure fully through normal taxes, it faces a resource constraint resulting in *budget deficit* which in recent years is often called fiscal deficit. Thus government budget constraint *refers to the limit placed on the government expenditure by the extent it can raise resources through taxation, borrowing from the market (i.e., through sale of its bonds) and using printed money*. The government has to make a choice between the magnitude of borrowing from the market and the magnitude of using printed money to finance its budget deficit.

The general form of government budget equation is:

$$G = T + \Delta B + \Delta M \qquad ...(1)$$

where G stands for government expenditure (including subsidies and interest payments on past debt), T is tax revenue, ΔB is the new borrowing from the market (through sale of bonds or securities) and ΔM is the new printed money issued to finance government expenditure. According to the budget constraint equation (1), government expenditure in a year can be financed by tax revenue (T), new borrowing (ΔB) by the government from the market (both within and outside the country) through sale of its bonds, and by creating new high powered money (ΔM). The government budget constraint can be rewritten as

$$G - T = \Delta B + \Delta M \qquad ...(2)$$

where $G - T$ represents fiscal deficit that must be financed by new borrowing (ΔB) by the government through sale of bonds and through creation of new high powered money (ΔM).

The fiscal deficit can be financed by the government either by *printing money* by the government or by borrowing through sale of bonds to the public (which includes banks, insurance companies, mutual funds and other financial institutions). Thus, it is through sale of bonds that the government borrows from the market which adds to the government debt. The government has to pay interest annually on its debt and has also to pay back the principal sum borrowed at the maturity of bonds or securities. Besides, borrowing by the government leads to the rise in interest rate which crowds out private investment. On the other hand, if government finances its budget deficit by using printed money, it can lead to inflation. Thus, due to budget constraint the government has to make a difficult choice between borrowing from the market or using printed money to finance its budget deficit. Financing through the use of printed money is also called **money financing**. We have discussed in the previous chapter, Financing of Government Development Expenditure Through Borrowing. In the present chapter, we will explain financing budget deficit or investment expenditure through creation of new money.

Before explaining how creation of new money can be used for financing investment or budget deficit by the government to accelerate economic growth, we will explain broadly the Keynesian and quantity theory approaches to *prior savings, investment* and *inflation*. Both these approaches suggest that *subject to some limits* created money can be used to finance development.

PRIOR SAVINGS, INFLATION AND INVESTMENT

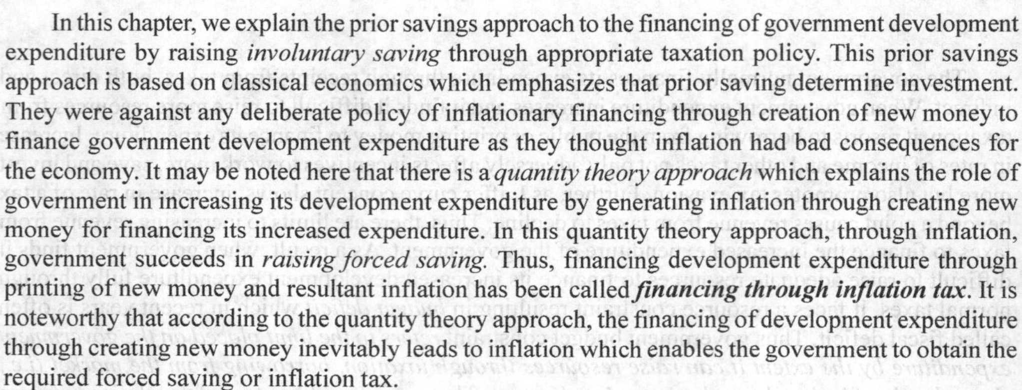

In this chapter, we explain the prior savings approach to the financing of government development expenditure by raising *involuntary saving* through appropriate taxation policy. This prior savings approach is based on classical economics which emphasizes that prior saving determine investment. They were against any deliberate policy of inflationary financing through creation of new money to finance government development expenditure as they thought inflation had bad consequences for the economy. It may be noted here that there is a *quantity theory approach* which explains the role of government in increasing its development expenditure by generating inflation through creating new money for financing its increased expenditure. In this quantity theory approach, through inflation, government succeeds in *raising forced saving.* Thus, financing development expenditure through printing of new money and resultant inflation has been called ***financing through inflation tax***. It is noteworthy that according to the quantity theory approach, the financing of development expenditure through creating new money inevitably leads to inflation which enables the government to obtain the required forced saving or inflation tax.

The Keynesian Approach. The Keynesian approach also departs from 'prior savings approach' to financing of investment expenditure and considers that *it is investment that determines saving* and not the other way round. According to this it happens in two ways. First, as explained below, when resources are unemployed due to deficiency of aggregate demand, the increase in investment by the government through creating new money will cause fuller utilisation of resources and thereby increase in output and income. At higher levels of income, given the propensity to save, more will be saved. Thus, as opposed to prior savings approach, it is increase in investment that has generated larger savings for its funding. The second way in which the Keynesian approach explains the higher investment causing larger savings is that when there prevails full employment increase in investment causes *income redistribution from the wage-earning workers with lower propensity to save to the profit earners with higher propensity to save as a result of inflation* and thus cause larger saving. Therefore in the Keynesian model, investment is not constrained by prior savings but by inflation rate acceptable to the workers. Consumption is reduced through cut in real wages as a result of income redistribution through the medium of inflation. Thus, Thirwall writes, "At full employment, inflation is the inevitable result of the Keynesian approach to development. In contrast to classical and neoclassical theory, Keynesian theory specifies independent saving and investment functions and allows price changes in response to excess demand in the goods market to raise saving by redistributing income. Inflation is the means by which resources are redistributed between consumption and investment. In Keynesian model, investment is not constrained by saving but the inflation rate willing to be tolerated by wage earners who have had their real wages cut."[1]

As in the developing countries in the normal times there does not exist underutilization of productive capacity in the consumer goods industries due to deficiency of aggregate demand, the

1 A.P. Thirlwall, *Economics of Development,* Palgrave Macmillan, 9th edition, 2011, p. 421.

situation is similar to that of full employment of the Keynesian theory. In such a situation, both the Keynesian and quantity theory approaches to financing of development involve inflation. It is through the means of inflation that resources are released from consumption to be used for investment. In this respect both these approaches differ from the prior savings approach which involves no inflation. Explaining the importance of difference of the Keynesian and quantity theory approach from prior savings approach. Thirlwall writes, "In the prior savings approach the resources released for investment come from voluntary and involuntary savings and no inflation is involved. In the Keynesian and quantity theory approaches the resources are partly released through the process of inflation by income redistribution from classes with low propensity to save to those with higher propensities to save, and by inflation as a 'tax' on money."[2]

How New Money is Created

Before explaining how creation of new money is used by government for financing investment for promoting development of the economy, it will be useful to explain how new money is created. When government's investment expenditure increases and it cannot be fully financed by tax revenue, the government's budget becomes deficit. This budget deficit or what is these days called ***fiscal deficit*** has to be somehow financed.

There are two possible links between budget deficit and growth of money supply. First, the budgetary deficit that is financed by borrowing by the government from the market reduces the supply of lendable resources for the private sector in the short run, and, as we saw in the previous chapter, this causes market interest rate to rise. Higher market interest leads to decline in private investment. In this way, *budget deficit financed by borrowing crowds out private investment. If the Central Bank is following the policy of targeting interest rate, then to prevent the interest rate from rising it will increase the money supply. To do so the Central Bank will buy a part of the securities or bonds issued by the government. This is generally called* ***accommodating the deficit***.

Note that in some countries, such as the USA, the Central Bank, *i.e.*, Federal Reserve enjoys independence from the government. Therefore, it can decide independently whether to buy a part of the bonds or securities floated by the government. The Central Bank prints money notes against these government securities or bonds held by it as an asset. In this way, budget deficit leads to the growth of money and possibly causes inflation. The *second way by which the budget deficit leads to growth in money stock* is the deliberate policy of the *government of financing the budget deficit through the use of printing high powered money by virtue of its sovereign right of creating money. In this method, the government itself may print new money or in some countries by the Central Bank as in India where the Central Bank is a nationalised bank* without having any independence from the government. In India the Central government when it wants to finance the budget deficit through printed money just issues its securities or bonds and the Reserve Bank prints new money notes and credits them in government account which the government can use for spending to finance the deficit.[3]

Thus when Central Bank on its own buys government bonds or securities to accommodate the budget deficit so that its crowding-out effect on private investment does not take place, there is growth of money stock in the economy. Alternatively, when the government follows a deliberate policy of printing high powered money to finance its fiscal deficit it leads to growth in money supply in the economy. As we shall discuss below when money stock grows at a greater rate than the increase in output, it may lead to inflation. Thus risk of inflation acts as a constraint on printing money to finance budget deficit.

---

2 A.P. Thirlwall, *op. cit*, p. 392.

3 Note that State governments in India do not have the power to print new money.

FINANCING OF DEVELOPMENT THROUGH MONEY CREATION

As stated above, the government can finance its deficit and meet its increased expenditure by printing high powered money. The revenue raised through printing of money is also called ***seigniorage***. When government finances its budget deficit through printing money, money supply in the economy increases. There are two views regarding the effect of increase in money supply on inflation. According to the Keynesian view, when money supply is increased in times of depression when both productive capacity and labour are lying idle or unemployed due to deficiency of aggregate demand, price level is not likely to rise much and the effect of increase in money supply is to raise output or income. The increase in real income, given the rate of taxation, will bring about increase in revenue from taxation, which will *tend to reduce budget deficit in the short run.* However, if the economy is operating at or near full employment, printing money to finance the deficit will cause inflation. Printing money to raise revenue for financing the budget deficit that has arisen as a result of increase in government's investment expenditure without being matched by extra taxation to raise revenue causes inflation which is like an *inflation tax*. This is because the government is able to get resources through printed money which causes inflation and *reduces the real value of the holdings of money by the public.*

Let us first explain the Keynesian model with a fixed price level when the economy is in recession due to demand deficiency and a lot of unemployment of resources prevails. The tax function can be written as

$$T = t(Y)$$

where t is the rate of tax and Y is real income and T is the total tax revenue. If G is government expenditure, then budget deficit (BD) is given by

$$BD = G - t(Y) \qquad \text{...(1)}$$

If $G - t(Y) = 0$, budget deficit will be zero and therefore the budget will be a balanced one. If $G - t(Y) > 0$, there will be budget deficit.

If the overnment finances its deficit through money creation, then the short-run macro equilibrium in simple *IS-LM* model is shown in Fig. 52.1 where *IS* and *LM* curves of the economy intersect at point E and determine equilibrium income Y_0 and equilibrium interest rate r_0.

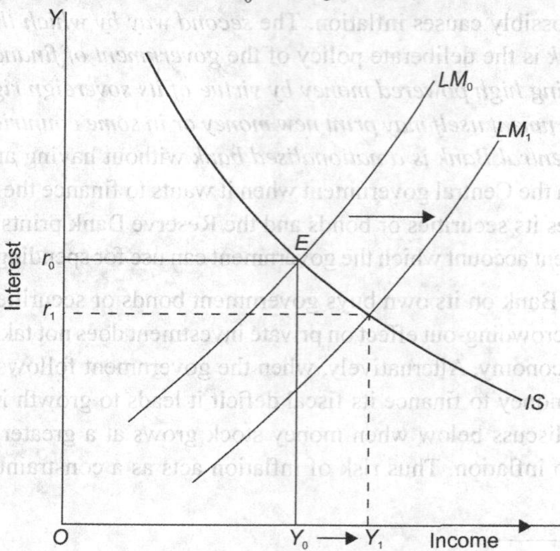

Fig. 52.1. *IS-LM model; The effect of budget deficit financed by printing money*

Suppose in this equilibrium the government has a budget deficit so that $G - t(Y) > 0$. Further, government finances this budget deficit through creating high powered money. As a result, money supply in the economy increases and *LM* curve shifts to the right to the new position LM_1. With this, as will be seen from the figure, level of equilibrium income increases to Y_1 and rate of interest falls to r_1. Since we are assuming an economy with a depression, when unutilised productive capacity exists due to deficiency of aggregate demand, increase in demand brought about by expansion in money supply will not cause any rise in price level.

In the above model of an economy representing the period of recession price level remains unchanged as more money is created to finance budget deficit. In an important contribution. Fischer and Easterly explain the condition for *non-inflationary printing of money.* They write, *"The amount of revenue that the government can expect to obtain from the printing of money is determined by the demand for base or high powered money in the economy, the real rate of growth of the economy and the elasticity of demand for real balances with respect to inflation and income."*[4] Further, assuming income elasticity of demand equal to unity and currency to GNP ratio equal to 0.13, they conclude that "for every one percentage point that GNP increases, the government can obtain 0.13 percentage points of GNP in revenue through the printing of money that just meets the increased demand for real balances. With an annual economic growth rate of 6.5 per cent of GNP the government should be able to obtain nearly 0.9 per cent of GNP for financing the budget deficit through the non-inflationary printing of money, increasing the high powered money stock at an annual rate of 6.5 per cent".[5] If rate of growth of money exceeds this and, given a stable demand function for currency, inflation will result.

Printed Money and the Inflation Tax

It follows from above that if the economy is operating at full-employment level of GNP or if growth rate of money due to persistent budget deficits over time is in excess of rate of growth of GNP, inflation will come about. It has been pointed out by some economists that *inflationary financing through the creation of high powered money is an alternative to explicit taxation.* Though in most of the industrialised economies (including the United States) the creation of high-powered money or inflationary financing of budget deficits is only a minor source of revenue, in other countries (including India), the creation of high powered money has been a significant source of raising revenue to finance government expenditure. *Before March 1997, in India the creation of new money to finance the budget deficit was called '**deficit financing**,' which has been a significant source of revenue for the Central Government in the sixties, seventies and eighties of the last century.* Though, as explained above, it is not entirely correct that financing government expenditure through creation of high powered money necessarily leads to inflation, in the quantity theory approach every creation of high-powered money has been called **inflationary**.

Why is the creation of high powered money that causes inflation is called *inflation tax* and is an alternative to explicit taxation as a source of financing government expenditure? When government uses printed money to finance its deficit year after year, it uses it to pay for the goods and services it buys. Thus in this process the government gets the resources to buy goods and services and as a result, money balances with the people increase, a part of which they will save and the rest they will spend on goods and services. However, due to inflation *real value of money balances* held by the people decreases. That is, with their given money balances, people can buy fewer goods and services due to inflation. Thus, when the government finances its budget deficit through creation of new high powered money and in the process causes inflation, the purchasing power of old money balances held by the public falls. Hence, *inflation caused by creation of new money is like a tax on holding money. Though, apparently people do not pay inflation tax, but since their old money balances can*

4 Stanley Fischer and William Easterly, "Economics of the Government Budget Constraint," *World Bank Research Observer,* Vol. 5, No. 2, July 1990, pp 127-42.

5 Fischer and Easterly, *op. cit.*

buy fewer goods and services due to inflation, they in fact bear the burden of inflation in terms of decline in their purchasing power. To conclude in the words of Dornbusch and Fischer, ***"Inflation acts just like a tax because people are forced to spend less than their income and pay the difference to the government....*** The government thus can spend more resources, and the public less just as if the government had raised taxes to finance extra spending. When the government finances its deficit by issuing new printed money which the public adds to its holdings of nominal balances to maintain the real value of money balances constant, we say the government is financing itself through the *inflation tax.*"[6]

We can even estimate the revenue raised through inflation tax as under :

Inflation tax revenue = *Inflation tax* × *real monetary base*

Note that monetary base is the amount of the high powered money. It may be mentioned that in the 1980s the inflation rate due to excess creation of high powered money in the Latin American countries was very high and therefore the revenue raised through inflation tax was very high.[7] In fact, some Latin American countries experienced *hyperinflation*. Thus, during 1983-1988 average annual inflation rate in Argentina was 359 per cent, in Bolivia 1,797 per cent, Brazil 341 per cent, Mexico 87 per cent and Peru 382 per cent.

Inflation Tax Revenue

In the Latin American countries, the governments raised large revenues due to high inflation rates caused by creation of large amount of printed money due to budget deficits year after year. From the above equation, it is evident that inflation tax revenue of the government depends on the inflation rate and real money base. When the inflation rate is zero, inflation tax

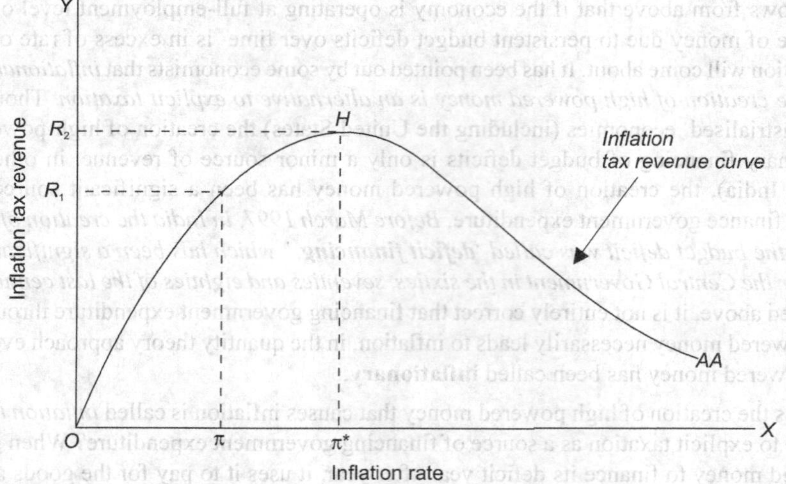

Fig. 52.2. *Inflation tax revenue*

revenue obtained by the government will also be zero. As the *inflation rate rises, the revenue obtained by the government through inflation tax increases.* But as the inflation rate rises, the people tend to reduce their holdings of the real money balances as the purchasing power of money holdings declines. As a result, as the inflation rate rises the public holds less currency and banks hold less excess reserves with them. With this the real money balances with the public and banks decline so much that inflation tax revenue collected by the government declines after a point.

---

6 Rudiger Dornbusch, Stanley Fischer and Richard Startz, *Macroeconomics*, Tata McGraw Hill, 8th edition, p. 436.

7 *Ibid*, p. 437.

The change in the tax revenue received by the government as the inflation rate rises is shown by *AA* curve in Fig. 52.2. Initially, in the economy there is no budget deficit and therefore no printing of money, inflation rate is zero, inflation tax revenue received by the government is also zero and the economy's situation lies at the point of origin. Now suppose the government reduces taxes, keeping its expenditure constant, budget deficit emerges which is financed by printing high powered money and suppose the resulting inflation rate is π at which the government collects tax revenue equal to OR_1. But as the inflation rate further rises as a result of increase in printed money, the tax revenue collected increases until inflation rate π^* is reached. At inflation rate π^* brought about by a certain amount of increase in printed money, the tax revenue collected by the government is OR_2. Beyond this growth in printed money and rise in inflation rate greater than π^*, tax revenue collected declines because real money balances with the public and banks decline, as explained above. Thus OR_2 is the maximum of tax revenue raised by the government through inflation tax and the corresponding inflation rate is π^*.

In the developed industrialised countries where the real money base is relatively small, the government collects a small amount of inflation tax revenue. For example, in the United States where money base is only about 6 per cent of GDP the government raises revenue through inflation tax equal to only 0.3 per cent of GDP corresponding to 5 per cent rate of inflation.[8] However, some developing countries such as Argentina, Brazil, Mexico, Peru have collected 3.5 per cent to 5.2 per cent of their GDP as inflation tax revenue.[9] But for this they had to pay a heavy price in terms of a very high rate of inflation. Dornbusch, Fischer and Startz comment, *"In countries in which the banking system is less developed and in which people hold large amounts of currency, the government obtains more revenue from inflation and is more likely to give much weight to the revenue aspects of inflation in setting policy.* Under conditions of high inflation in which the conventional tax system breaks down, the inflation tax revenue may be the government's last resort to keep paying its bills. But whenever the inflation tax is used on a large scale, inflation invariably becomes extreme."[10]

Evaluation of Inflation Tax Revenue

The above view of inflation tax revenue is based on the assumption that every increase in printed money causes inflation. In our view this is not correct. When the economy is working much below its full production capacity due to deficiency of aggregate demand as it happens at times of recession or depression, then more printed money can be created by the government to finance its projects. The increase in demand resulting from this will help in fuller utilisation of idle production capacity and will also generate employment for unemployed labour. This will not lead to inflation as output of goods and services will increase in this case to meet the increased demand. This case was analysed by J.M. Keynes who advocated for the adoption of budget deficit to overcome depression and financing it through printed money without causing inflation. It is only when there exists full employment in the economy that financing government expenditure through printed money causes inflation.

Similarly, in developing countries like India where growth in GDP is taking place annually and also the economy is getting increasingly monetised, the demand for money is increasing. Therefore, since GDP is growing and the economy is getting monetised, the reasonable increase in money supply to meet the increase in demand for it will not generate inflation. Besides, in developing countries like India a huge amount of natural and human resources are lying unutilised or underutilised, investment expenditure by creating a reasonable amount of new money to finance it for utilising these underutilised resources will lead to the increase in productive capacity of the economy and is therefore less likely to cause much inflation. Further, if newly created money is used to invest in quick-yielding projects such as small irrigation works, anti-soil erosion projects, the danger of inflation will not be much

8 Dornbusch, Fischer, and Startz, *op. cit*., *p*. 438.
9 *Ibid*, p. 438.
10 *op. cit.* p. 439.

there. Besides, if under the development plans, efforts are made to help the farmers to increase agricultural production, especially of foodgrains, by providing them with HYV seeds, fertilizers and irrigation facilities in time and in adequate quantities, then the supply of agricultural goods will increase to match the reasonable amount of newly created money. To the extent we are able to increase agricultural production we can safely use created money without generating much inflation. Since the income elasticity of demand for foodgrains is very high in the developing countries like India, the incomes generated by government investment expenditure are mostly directed to the purchase of foodgrains. Therefore, if we increase the production of foodgrains and other essential consumer goods, a reasonable increase in created money will not cause much inflation.

It is worth repeating that danger of increase in newly created money generating inflationary pressures depends on the *quality of government expenditure.* If newly created money is used for productive investment expenditure, or what is called capital expenditure, it will lead to the expansion in productive capacity which will increase the supply of output of goods in the future which will bring down the inflation rate in the long run. However, if newly created money is used to finance subsidies or current revenue deficit of the government, it is likely to cause inflation.

It follows from above that within limits, the increase in created money can play a useful role in financing productive investment expenditure of the government. *It is inflationary only if safe limit is crossed.* Thus, *to a reasonable extent* depending on the quality of public expenditure, new money can be used to finance development in developing countries. However, in India, prior to 1991 the excessive use of newly printed money which was then called ***deficit financing*** for financing of various Five Year Plans, was made and therefore it led to high inflation rate in the Indian economy. Therefore, under the Stabilisation and Structural Adjust Reforms since 1991, IMF and World Bank laid the condition of upper limit of fiscal deficit of 3% of GDP. It is up to this 3% of GDP the government could borrow from the market and use creation of new money. However, this could not be achieved in actual practice due to global financial crisis of 2008 and therefore new road map for achieving 3 per cent target has been planned.

In our above analysis of quantity theory approach to development, by ensuring *'forced saving'* or treating inflation as a tax *inflation has been treated as beneficial.* The present author does not agree with this viewpoint of inflation as beneficial. In fact it is now widely recognised that, far from encouraging savings and generating higher rate of economic growth, inflation slows down the rate of capital accumulation. There are several reasons responsible for this. First, as seen above, when due to rapid inflation value of money is declining, people will not like to keep money with themselves and will, therefore, be eager to spend it before its value goes down heavily. This raises their consumption demand and therefore lowers their saving. Besides, people find that the rapid inflation will erode the real value of their savings. This discourages them to save. Thus, *inflation or rapid rise in prices serves as a disincentive to save.* Further, as a consequence of the rise in prices, a relatively greater part of the income of the people is spent on consumption to maintain their level of living and therefore little is left to be saved. Thus, not only does inflation reduce the willingness to save, it also slashes their ability to save.

Secondly, *inflation or rising prices lead to unproductive form of investment* in gold, jewellery, real estate, construction of houses etc. These unproductive forms of wealth do not add to the productive capacity of the economy and are quite useless from the viewpoint of economic growth. Thus, inflation may lead to more investment but much of this is of unproductive type. In this way, economic surplus is frittered away in unproductive investment.

Thirdly, a highly undesirable consequence of inflation, especially in developing countries, is that *it accentuates the problem of poverty in these countries.* It is often said inflation is enemy number one of the poor people. Due to rising prices poor people are not able to meet their basic needs and maintain minimum subsistence level of consumption. Thus inflation sends many people to live below the poverty line with the result that the number of people living below the poverty line increases. Besides, due to inflation, consumption of a large number of poor people is reduced much below what may be regarded as *productive consumption,* that is, essential consumption required to maintain health and productive efficiency. In India, rapid inflation in recent years is as much responsible for the mounting number of people below the poverty line as the lack of employment opportunities.

Fourthly, *inflation adversely affects balance of payments* and thereby hampers economic growth, especially in the developing countries. When prices of domestic goods rise due to inflation, they cannot compete abroad and as a consequence exports of a country are discouraged. On the other hand, when domestic prices rise relatively to prices of foreign goods, imports of foreign goods increase. Thus, falling exports and rising imports create disequilibrium in the balance of payments which may, in the long run, result in a foreign exchange crisis. The shortage of foreign exchange prevents the country to import even essential materials and capital goods needed for industrial growth of the economy. The Indian experience during 1988-92 when foreign exchange reserves declined to abysmally low level and created an economic crisis in the country, shows the validity of this argument.

There is no agreement among economists whether or not moderate or mild inflation encourages saving and therefore ensures higher rate of capital accumulation and economic growth. However, there is complete unanimity that a very rapid inflation or what is often called hyperinflation discourages saving and hinders economic growth. However, barring the special case of hyperinflation, whether or not saving is encouraged by inflation depends on whether there exists *wage lag.*[11] While there is sufficient evidence in the industrialised countries such as the U.S.A., Great Britain, France etc., about the existence of wage lag in the period before World War II, in the period after this there is no solid evidence of it. In the present, wages quickly catch up with the rising prices. Indeed, there is evidence in some developed countries that the share of profits in national income has declined and that of wages has gone up during the post-World War II period. Therefore, "To the extent that rate of long-run economic growth depends on the rate of capital accumulation, a major basis for the conclusion that inflation promotes rapid economic growth is undermined given that *wages no longer lag during inflation as they apparently did in time of past.*"[12]

However, it may be noted that in the developing countries like India labour is mostly unorganised and trade unions of labour are not strong and further there is a lack of information which causes wages lagging behind prices during periods of inflation. This itself will cause greater proportion of national income going to profits and other business incomes which should ensure higher saving rate. However, in India, businessmen are prone to make unproductive investment in speculative activities, gold, jewellery, real estate and palatial houses whose prices rise rapidly during periods of inflation. Such kind of investment is not only counter-productive and anti-growth but is repugnant to social justice as it further accentuates inequalities in the distribution of income and wealth.

It follows from above that rising prices as a goal of menetary policy are full of disastrous consequences for the economy and the people and therefore cannot be recommended as a desirable goal for the economic policy. Rising prices often get out of hand and hyperinflation might set in which will shake the confidence of the people in the monetary and fiscal system of the country.

---

11 See D. Felix, "Profit Inflation and Industrial Growth," *Quarterly Journal of Economics,* August 1956, pp. 441-63 and E.J. Hamilton, "Prices as a Factor in Business Growth," *Journal of Economic History,* December 1952, pp. 325-49.

12 E. Shapiro, *Macroeconomic Analysis,* Fourth Edition, 1978, p. 443.

EXTERNAL RESOURCES: FOREIGN AID

In the previous two chapters, we have discussed how resources for investment and economic growth can be mobilised through taxation and internal borrowing by the government. In the present chapter, we will explain external resources for accelerating economic growth and solve the problems of poverty and unemployment. Foreign capital in developing countries come in four forms:

(*a*) **Foreign aid** (*i.e.*, borrowing at concessional rates of interest from foreign governments and international institutions such as International Monetary Fund (IMF) and World Bank;

(*b*) **External commercial borrowing** (*i.e.*, borrowing from International Financing Institutions at commercial rates (*i.e.*, ECB);

(*c*) **Private Portfolio investment** (*i.e.*, buying of shares and debentures of domestic companies by foreign investors); and

(*d*) **Foreign Direct Investment (FDI)** which means direct investment in plant, equipment of industries either on their own or in collaboration with the domestic private companies.

We will explain foreign aid and external commercial borrowing in the present chapter and the other two external resources in the next chapter.

ROLE OF FOREIGN AID IN ECONOMIC DEVELOPMENT

According to many economists foreign aid can play a useful role in breaking the vicious circle of poverty that operates in an underdeveloped country. There is a great urge among the people of developing countries to break this vicious circle and to accelerate the rate of economic growth so as to raise their living standards. The high rate of economic growth, however, requires high rate of investment. But being poor their own savings are too low to permit them to undertake sufficiently high rate of investment required to get the economy out of low-level equilibrium. Thus there exists a ***saving gap*** which shows inability of a developing country to raise its saving rate to the level of required investment so that target rate of economic growth is reached and low-level equilibrium is overcome. The foreign assistance can play a critical role by *supplementing the domestic savings* and thereby ensure the desired rate of investment. Without foreign aid, the rate of investment, governed as it will be by the domestic saving, will be lower and, therefore, it may not be possible for a developing economy to get out of low-level equilibrium. Thus without foreign aid the growth rate will be lower and the economy may remain caught up in the vicious circle of poverty. If required foreign assistance is not forthcoming and developing economy persists in raising the rate of investment beyond domestic saving, then it will have to make recourse to excessive deficit financing, that is, financing growth through creation of new money, which will bring about inflation with all its attendant evils. It, therefore, follows that for achieving high growth rate and stability in prices, foreign aid can play a useful role in raising the rate of investment by filling the saving gap.

Secondly, developing countries face another problem for speeding up the rate of economic growth. This is the problem of ***foreign exchange gap*** or what is also called ***balance of payments constraint***. To accelerate economic growth, especially industrialisation, the developing countries need to import raw materials, machinery and other capital goods on a large scale from the developed countries. This is because in developing countries basic heavy industries which manufacture capital goods such as machinery and intermediate products such as fertilizers, iron and steel, cement etc. are not there. On the other hand, the possibilities of expanding exports such as raw materials and agricultural products of the developing countries to the developed countries also do not exist adequately.[1] This is firstly because income elasticity of consumer demand for many agricultural products in developed countries is very low. Secondly, in developed countries there has been a change in industrial structure in favour of heavy industries which need very small amount of imported raw materials. This discourages the exports of raw materials from developing countries. Thirdly, there is a rising share of services in the total output of developed countries and as is well known production of services does not require much imported raw materials and agricultural products as compared to the manufacturing industries. Fourthly, developed countries have developed synthetic raw materials which substitute the raw materials imported from developing countries. In the fifth place, the developed countries have started introducing several economies in the use of raw materials, for instance, through reprocessing of scraps. The last but not the least, developed countries are hindering the exports from developing countries by adopting *protectionist policies.*

It follows from above that the large need for imported capital equipment and material on the one hand and small foreign exchange earnings due to bleak export prospects on the other, developing countries face a very serious problem of foreign exchange gap. As a result of large imports and small exports, balance of payments of several developing countries has been thrown into disequilibrium. The foreign aid can play a critical role in overcoming the shortage of foreign exchange to finance needed imports of capital and intermediate products and can thus overcome the balance of payments constraint faced by the developing countries.

It follows from above that the need for foreign aid to developing countries has been brought out in terms of ***dual gap analysis–saving*** **gap and foreign exchange gap**.[2] The significance of these two gaps emerging in a country which impede development efforts is that they can be filled by foreign aid. To conclude the argument of the last few paras: "*Foreign aid can permit a country either (a) to invest more than it is able to save domestically or (b) to import more than it is capable of financing by its own exports. In so far as these constraints really do limit economic development, then aid clearly does help promote growth in developing world.*"[3]

It is also worth noting that foreign aid itself will *further increase* the domestic savings of developing countries. With the receipt of foreign aid, as the rate of investment increases and the process of economic growth is accelerated and real incomes rise, additional domestic savings will be generated. If this process goes on for some time and domestic savings increase to a sufficient extent, the saving gap will be eliminated and the developing countries will be capable of achieving economic growth in a self-sustaining manner. Keeping this in view, many economists have argued that foreign assistance enables developing countries to achieve *'take off into self-sustained growth'* in a shorter time.

The importance of foreign aid also lies in the fact that along with it *technical* know-how, that is, high-level technical personnel are also obtained which are in scarce supply in developing countries. By providing technical know-how or expertise, foreign aid helps in building modern industrial structure.

1 See R. Nurkse, "Patterns of Trade and Development" and A.K. Cairncross, "Trade and Development," both in J.D. Theberge (ed.), *Economics of Trade and Development.*

2 See especially H.B. Chenery and A.M. Strout, "Foreign Assistance and Economic Development," *American Economic Review*, September 1966, pp. 679-733.

3 Richard T.Gill, *Economic Development: Past and Present,* 3rd Ed. 1975, p. 110.

The foreign technical know-how educates and trains the indigenous people in various industrial arts and processes so that in course of time developing countries can set up and run modern industries on their own and do away with foreign technical assistance. This will help in ultimately achieving self-reliance. As is well known, for setting up and running for sometime steel plants, engineering industries, oil exploration, India obtained not only foreign financial aid but also technical assistance. This helped a good deal in building a network of modern heavy industries as well as in training the Indian engineers and technicians. This has accelerated the technological progress of the Indian economy.

Foreign aid contributes to economic growth in the form of realisation of ***external economies*** flowing from the basic heavy industries such as steel, fertilizers and from economic infrastructure such as means of transport and communication, railways, hydroelectric projects supplying power and irrigation, developed through the receipt of foreign assistance. The development of basic industries and economic infrastructure induces growth in *other sectors* of the economy including agriculture. Thus foreign aid acts as a catalyst in stimulating economic growth and helps in transforming the economy structurally. As is well known, India has received a good amount of foreign aid in setting up steel plants, engineering industries, fertilizer industry and hydroelectric projects. The development of these has undoubtedly contributed to the growth of the Indian economy as a whole though creating external economies.

Case Against Foreign Aid

But some economists do not regard foreign aid as conducive to economic growth in developing countries. They are of the view that foreign aid does not help but hinders economic growth. They, therefore, suggest that developing countries should try to do away with foreign aid and achieve economic self-reliance as soon as possible.

In the first place, it is argued that the country obtaining foreign assistance cannot pursue an independent political and economic policy and various sorts of political pressures are put by the donor countries. These donor countries while giving assistance generally try to influence the investment priorities of the recipient countries. It is further argued that as a result of foreign aid dependence on other countries for financial resources, foreign machinery, equipment and raw material increases. If foreign assistance is suspended or stopped for one reason or the other, it creates difficulties for developing countries and a lot of uncertainty prevails in the formulation and implementation of development plans. For instance, in 1965 and 1971 during war with Pakistan, America suspended aid to India and this had an adverse effect on the implementation of the Indian Five Year Plans.

Another argument against foreign aid is that it makes the developing country complacent in raising the rate of saving and domestic investment. When there is easy access to the foreign aid, the government does not make much efforts to raise the domestic rate of saving and investment. If the foreign aid were not available, the governments in developing countries would have made much larger efforts to raise the domestic rate of saving and investment. Thus, foreign aid instead of being supplement becomes substitute of the domestic saving and investment. If this be the case, foreign aid will not help in raising the rate of economic growth. Thus, Nurkse states, "*It is nearly always possible to some extent to substitute foreign funds for domestic saving so that the country's consumption is increased or no addition is made to the rate of accumulation.* This can happen even if each foreign loan is earmarked for a specific production project. If the inflow of capital is accompanied by a relaxation of domestic saving efforts there may be no change in the total rate of capital formation. Strong and persistent pressures in this direction are set up by ..... the high and the rising propensity to consume which is induced in the poor countries by the great and growing discrepancies in per capita income and consumption standards."[4] Without the increase in domestic saving and investment, it is argued, self-sustained economic growth cannot be attained. This is why some economists regard foreign aid as *anti-growth.*

4. Ragnar Nurkse, *Problems of Capital Formation in Underdeveloped Countries,* Basil Blackwell, 1958, pp. 991-92.

Another disadvantage of foreign aid is that when foreign aid is easily available, the country does not make efforts to promote exports and substitute imports. In the absence of foreign aid the government and the people of the country would have tried their utmost to promote exports and substitute imports. Thus some economists regard foreign aid as *anti-export promotion* and *anti-import substitution measure.*

There are disadvantages of tied aid which is the dominant form of aid received by developing countries. About 75% of the foreign aid which India has got so far, is of the form of tied aid. In the tied form of foreign aid, a country has to buy machines, equipment and raw materials from the countries which provides aid. Since India has obtained much of the foreign assistance from the United States, it has spent the aid so received on importing machines, equipment, raw materials, etc., from America. But American machines, equipment, and raw materials are comparatively much costlier than those of other countries. Therefore, as a result of tied aid India has been forced to get machines and other materials at very high prices. Owing to this, cost of production of the products of the industries set up with the imported equipment and machinery obtained through foreign assistance is high and this raises the prices of these products. Besides contributing to the general rise in prices in the country, this has discouraged our exports because, due to higher prices, our products are competed away in the international markets.

Another disadvantage of the foreign aid is that *it raises the burden of the public debt* because much of the foreign assistance is in the form of loans rather than grants. We have to pay interest every year on them and when these loans mature we have to return the principal amount borrowed. Thus foreign aid adds to the burden of the country which creates difficulties of the future years. India had to pay ₹ 1032 crore and ₹ 1115 crore in the years 1983-84 and 1984-85 respectively to other countries as debt services charges. This is a huge sum which has an adverse effect on our balance of payments situation.

Foreign aid is further criticised on the ground that it is mostly concentrated on the development of modern sector and as a result it has increased the gap between the rich and the poor and has thus worsened income inequalities.[5] Workers who have been employed in industrial enterprises set up with foreign assistance are paid higher wages due to the higher capital intensity and their higher productivity. On the other hand, workers employed in traditional sector have not benefited from foreign aid. As a result of this, it is alleged that foreign aid has further widened *urban-rural or modern sector-traditional sector gap.*

In the light of these various disadvantages of foreign aid it is suggested by some economists that developing countries should do away with foreign aid forthwith. It is argued *by* them that *developing countries like India should expand trade rather than get aid and try to achieve self-reliance in the long run.* While the objective of achieving self-reliance in the long run is quite laudable, in the short run it is neither feasible nor desirable if tempo of economic growth is to be maintained. Therefore, in the opinion of the present author the totally negative attitude to the foreign aid is not warranted. In spite of uncertainty it creates, and political pressures and rising burden of public debt it involved, foreign assistance has in fact contributed to the economic growth of developing countries and in the *New International Economic Order* for which the developing countries are now seeking both trade with and aid from the developed countries. It is only through aid that some real wealth and resources can be transferred from the rich countries to the poor countries of the Third World. It hardly needs to be stressed that foreign aid can make net contribution to economic growth of developing countries only if it does not lead to relaxation of efforts to raise domestic savings and investment. Further, to get full benefits from aid every effort should be made to utilise it properly and optimally and not frittered away in senseless projects.

5. See K. Griffin and J.L. Enos, "Foreign Assistance: Objectives and Consequences," *Economic Development and Cultural Change,* April 1970, pp. 133-327.

CHAPTER 54

Foreign Direct Investment and Role of Multinational Corporations in Developing Countries

After the Second World War, the developing countries are making concerted efforts to achieve rapid economic growth so as to alleviate problems of poverty and unemployment. Besides, there has been rapid growth of international trade. The developing countries like India have been facing the problem of shortage of capital. To meet this shortage, capital flows from the developed countries to the developing countries in the last two decades have substantially increased.

Immediately after the Second World War, capital flows were largely in the form of *foreign aid* from the governments of the developed countries and international institutions such as IMF and World Bank to the governments of the developing countries. In the last three decades the capital flows in the form of foreign aid on government to government basis have dried up, whereas aid from IMF and World Bank is based on certain conditionalities of undertaking some structural economic reforms which the developing countries often find difficult to implement to the entire satisfaction of these institutions. Besides, the capital needs of the developing countries are so large that IMF and World Bank alone cannot meet them. Therefore, there is a great need for ***capital flows on private account*** on a large scale. Fortunately, capital flows on private account have substantially increased in the last two decades. These capital flows on private account are of the following two types:

1. Foreign Portfolio Investment
2. Foreign Direct Investment (FDI)

We discuss below the roles of the above two types of capital flows briefly.

FOREIGN PORTFOLIO INVESTMENT

This is important type of capital flow under which foreign institutions such as banks, insurance companies, companies managing mutual funds and pension funds purchase stocks and bonds of companies of other countries in the secondary markets (*i.e.*, stock markets). They get returns in the form of capital gains and yearly payable dividends but do not exercise any direct control in running these companies. Pension funds, mutual funds and insurance companies have been very active in moving portfolio capital in the last three decades because restrictions on foreign equity investment by various countries have been reduced or removed in recent years allowing pension and mutual funds and insurance companies to diversify their portfolio in order to reduce risk. Besides, the growth of portfolio foreign capital in the last three decades has also been due to the policies of liberalisation followed by the developing countries. In India following the adoption of policy of liberalisation the flow of portfolio capital was permitted in 1991. Consequently, foreign portfolio capital flows have come to India in large amounts in the last thirty years (1995-2015).

However, Mexico has been the chief beneficiary of portfolio capital flows. Portfolio capital flows now account for one-third of net capital flows to the developing countries.

Advantages and Disadvantages of Portfolio Capital Flows

Benefits and costs of portfolio capital flows have been a subject of severe controversy. Private foreign portfolio investment in stocks, equities and bonds has been made by foreign investors in order to get higher return or higher interest on their investment and also to diversify their portfolio in order to reduce risk. Thus, Prof. Todaro rightly writes, "*From the investor's point of view, investing in the stock markets of emerging countries permits them to increase their returns while diversifying their risks*."[1]

In the early 1990s, the return on the portfolio investment in the so called '*emerging*' developing countries was quite high, for instance, it was 39 per cent during 1988-93 in Latin America which is main recipient of portfolio capital flows. But the high returns were marred by *high volatility* of stock markets of these countries. Many mutual fund based US companies which were lured by high returns had to suffer heavy losses when there was collapse of Mexican stock market following 35% devaluation of Mexican currency in December 1994. The experience of these heavy losses resulted in drastic fall in portfolio capital flows in 1995 not only in Mexico but also in other developing countries. In fact, there was net capital outflows from the developing countries for some months.

From the perspective of developing countries private portfolio capital flows are generally considered as a welcome means for raising capital for private domestic companies. However, it has been argued whether it is prudent to rely on large and volatile private capital flows as they have a destabilising influence in both the financial markets and in the overall economy. It has been pointed out that when the developing countries run into trouble, the portfolio capital flows disappear in few days as happened in case of Mexico in 1995 and recently in South East Asian countries in 1997-98. However, it may be noted that a developing country should not cover up its structural weakness by obtaining private capital flows. If they want to ensure that these private portfolio capital flows continue occurring year after year on a sustained basis, they should manage the foreign exchange rates efficiently by controlling deficits on current account and also keeping adequate reserves of foreign exchange so that their currencies should not remain overvalued which might lead to severe long-term consequences.

From above it follows that private portfolio capital flows are welcome as they provide needed finance for developing countries and also bring in required foreign exchange. However, one should not consider them as substitutes for making structural changes in these economies such as maintaining exchange rate at the right level, controlling deficits in balance of payments, checking rate of inflation and adoption of proper monetary policy which should ensure relatively higher interest rates. We agree with Prof. Todaro who while commenting on portfolio capital flows writes, "*Like multinational corporations, portfolio investors are not in the development business. If developed country interest rates rise or expected Third World profit rates decline, foreign speculators will withdraw their 'investments' as quickly as they brought them in. What LDCs need is true long-run economic investment (plants, equipment, physical and social infrastructure etc.) and not speculative equity capital.*"[2]

FOREIGN DIRECT INVESTMENT (FDI)

The foreign direct investment (FDI) is the investment in the construction of physical capital such as building factories and infrastructure (*i.e.*, power, telecom, ports etc.) in the capital-importing country. It may be done in several ways. Companies or corporations may be specially set up for the purpose in the capital-exporting country to carry out trade and industry in a developing country. This

1 Michael P. Todaro, *Economic Development*, 6th edition, p. 544.
2 *Op. cit.*, p. 545.

is how the East India Company operated in India or railways were constructed in India. The head office is in the investing country and the operations are in the developing country. Another method is that an already existing corporation spreads out its business in another country by establishing branches. Thus, many foreign companies producing cars, colour TVs have set up branches in India and are producing these items in India. There is another way open to the foreign entrepreneur, that is, to form companies and register them in the borrowing country without having any connection in the lending country. When India adopted protection, it became profitable, and quite fashionable too, for the foreign entrepreneurs to set up so called "*India Limited*," to jump over the tariff wall and to avail themselves of the various concessions which the government extended to national concerns. These were in fact disguised branches of the foreign firms. The Indian match industry, for instance, is dominated by Swedish concerns. There is still another possibility which is now becoming common in India, *viz.*, of joint ventures or joint participation. The foreign firms start industrial concerns in collaboration with Indian firms. This form of foreign investment has some special advantages. The standing and reputation of foreign firms inspire confidence in the domestic and foreign capital. The long experience and efficient techniques are placed at the disposal of the domestic companies. It avoids evils of absentee ownership; it provides full opportunities for developing local skills, and also a large proportion of profits is retained in the country. It is also advantageous to the foreign investor. He is able to ward off in this manner any danger of discriminatory treatment by the government. A developing country lacks capital for development and it requires foreign capital.

Merits of Foreign Direct Investment (FDI)

Several advantages can be claimed for foreign direct investment (FDI).

1. Such investment does not burden the tax payer since no interest at fixed rate is to be paid as in the case of foreign borrowing. The foreign investor is compensated by the profit he gets.

2. In private investment, the investor is actuated by the profit motive; hence the business operations are subjected to careful calculations. This is a guarantee that the capital resources are most efficiently employed and are not frittered away in some reckless investment as may happen in the case of borrowing.

3. Direct investment by foreign companies introduces, in the developing country, new technology, modern skills, innovations and new ideas. This is a great gain because the developing countries are backward in technology and skills. The local entrepreneurs take a clue and start similar concerns. The Indian cotton textile industry was inspired by the Indian jute industry established by British entrepreneurs. Thus, direct foreign investment serves as an instrument for transferring modern technology to the developing countries.

4. Another advantage is that a part of the profit is ploughed back into business and is not drained off from the country as it happens in the case of portfolio investment. The profits are invested either in modernisation and expansion of existing concerns or for establishing ancillary or subsidiary concerns in related fields. There is thus a continuing advantage for the developing country.

5. Foreign direct investments are most likely to flow into export industries. By increasing exports and reducing imports, it will improve balance of payments of the developing country. It has a specially favourable effect on balance of payments position during recession because direct investment is serviced by dividends which are related to profits and not by fixed interest charges as in the case of loans. This flexibility of pressure on the balance of payments is of great advantage. It is worth mentioning that China in the last decades has industrially developed rapidly through foreign multinational firms to make investment in China to produce manufactured goods for exports. As a result, there has been unprecedented growth in industrial output and employment and as a result China has emerged as the fastest growing economy of the world. However, the latest trends show that in 2014-2015 and 2015-16, due to slowdown in world trade growth and protectionist policies of the developed countries, China's *overall* growth has fallen to 7% y-o-y as compared to over 9 per cent in the previous several years.

6. Even otherwise flexible return on direct investment is a great advantage as compared with rigid interest and amortization requirements associated with public foreign loans.

7. Direct foreign investment induces domestic investment also either in the form of joint participation or in local ancillary industries. Thus, foreign capital activates otherwise inert domestic capital. The domestic capital sheds off its shyness and enters into fields opened by direct foreign investment.

8. The direct foreign investment makes a real addition to the productive capacity of the capital-importing country. There is no question of foreign capital coming in this form being used for unproductive purposes. In the case of other types of foreign borrowings, there is nothing to prevent them from being utilised unproductively.

9. Another important advantage of direct foreign investment is that it can be induced to be invested in infrastructure such as power, telecom, development of ports which is an obstacle to accelerating economic growth in the developing countries. Such direct foreign investment enables the developing countries to overcome supply-side bottlenecks which will spur domestic investment. It should be mentioned that in recent times the Indian government has been wooing foreign investors to invest in the infrastructure sector. The foreign companies have the resources, technology and technical know-how to start productive ventures in the infrastructure.

10. The capital that comes through foreign direct investment has a distinct advantage over portfolio investment. While foreign institutional investors can sell their shares and take capital out of the developing countries in a very short time and thus destabilise these economies as recently happened during East Asia Crisis, it is not easy to close down foreign concerns established through direct investments. Foreign Direct Investment (FDI) enters the developing economies to build factories and these factories (*i.e.*, physical capital) stay even if the investors decide to sell out later to domestic buyers.

The direct foreign investment (DFI) is opposed on the ground that it seeks to establish ***'financial imperialism'***. It leads to political domination and economic exploitation. That is why foreign capital was so unpopular in India. The strength of this objection really rests on the nature of political set-up. A free democratic country of the continental size such as India need not entertain such fears.

In order to promote private foreign direct investment, it is necessary both for the lending and borrowing countries to remove the impediments to free flow of capital and to grant the necessary facilities. The borrowing country should guarantee immunity from nationalisation and repatriation of profits. The crux of the problem is to assure higher returns and minimum risk. At present investment is deterred by political and social instability, uncertainty about the jurisdiction of courts, exchange controls and currency inconvertibility, controls on capital issues, fear of discriminatory legislation and fear of nationalisation, the practice of shutting out some industrial fields for foreign investors, employment of nationals in superior posts etc. Among the measures to minimise risks and allay fears may be mentioned investment treaties, government guarantees, tax incentives, joint ventures, relaxation of restrictions and granting of concessions. In short, the investment climate must be made most favourable by ensuring the following:

(*i*) Political stability and freedom from external aggression.

(*ii*) Security of life and property.

(*iii*) Availability of opportunities for earning profits.

(*iv*) Prompt payment for fair compensation and its remittance to the country of origin in the event of compulsory acquisition of a foreign enterprise.

(*v*) Facilities for the remittance of profits, dividends, interest, etc.

(*vi*) Facilities for the immigration and employment of foreign technical and administrative personnel.

(*vii*) A system of taxation that does not impose an excess burden on private foreign enterprise.

(*viii*) Freedom from double taxation.

(*ix*) A general spirit of friendliness for foreign investors.

The Department of Commerce of the United States mentions certain factors which stand in the way of private investment of American capital. These are uncertainty created by the present political situation, the policies and practices with respect to foreign investment, the relatively low level of economic infrastructure and the lack of trained labour, and the limited knowledge of the developing countries on the part of American businessmen. The particular impediments mentioned in the case of India are the nature of India's screening policy shutting out foreign investment in certain spheres and controls on imports, exports and foreign exchange and the absence of a double taxation agreement, obligation to employ and train Indian labour. India also offers some special inducements, *e.g.*, special tax exemptions, increased depreciation allowance and other benefits available to domestic industry, guarantee of exchange facilities for profit remittances, capital repatriation and import of essential requirements, government assistance in the acquisition of land, transport facilities, etc., the right to hold controlling interest. This compares quite favourably with many other countries. But there are still some countries with more attraction in the form of higher returns and better guarantees and they can absorb a substantial supply of foreign U.S. capital.

However, in the opinion of the present author direct foreign investment in the field of infrastructure in India may not be as much as expected because infrastructure projects relating to power, telecom, ports are of the nature of public utilities and, therefore, the price of their end-product (for example, electricity charges) has to be controlled which may not yield sufficient profits to attract foreign investment.

NDA's 'Make in India' Policy

As part of structural economic reforms initiated in India from 1991 under the former Prime Minister, Dr. Manmohan Singh, there was *liberalisation of foreign investment policy*. To attract foreign investment, it was decided to grant automatic permission to private foreign investors to hold equity up to 51 per cent of total equity shares in high priority industries. The priority sector included power generation and petroleum refining. The government also gave a guarantee of 16 per cent return on foreign investment in priority sectors. As a result, foreign direct investment started coming into India and after 2003, it picked up but foreign direct investment into India was much less than that in China and some other developing countries. Now, after coming into power in 2014, NDA Government headed Mr. Modi has proposed a new scheme called '***Make in India***'. For this scheme, foreign investors have been invited to make large-scale investment in India for producing *manufacturing goods in India and mainly export them abroad*, just like China did three decades before. In this way, it is thought industrial growth of output and employment will rise rapidly and overall growth of the economy will greatly pick up. Modi Government intends to solve the problem of unemployment in this way.

To 'make in India' scheme success, foreign investment norms in India have been greatly liberalised, land acquisition bill is being passed so that land for setting up industrial projects by foreigners be procured. In the budget for 2015-16, corporate income tax has been reduced from 30 per cent to 25 per cent in a phased manner in the five-year period. This will raise the return on foreign capital invested. No retrospective taxation has been promised to woo foreign investor. Minimum Alternative Tax (MAT) on the earnings of FIIs has been abolished with effect from 2015-16 so as to prevent them flowing out.

In the view of the present author the timing of '*Make for India*' is wrong as at present expansion in world trade has slowed down. The recovery in the US from 2008 crisis is fragile, Europe too is not yet developing and facing the problem of burden of external debt. It is due to these reasons that China's industrial growth has slowed down. India's exports are also falling. How then in the present context under 'Make in India' by foreigners to export them would succeed. In our view, what is important is to launch a scheme of '*Make for India*', India's domestic product is quite large. What is needed is a well-designed development strategy which *use labour-intensive technologies to produce mass consumer goods* and essential capital goods needed for them. Scarce resources should be discouraged to be used for manufacturing big luxury cars, colour TVs, Smart Mobiles etc. if growth with social justice in India is to be achieved.

ROLE OF MULTINATIONAL CORPORATIONS (MNCs)

Multinational corporations are those large firms which are incorporated in one country but which own, control or manage production and distribution facilities in several countries. Therefore, these multinational corporations are also known as *transnational corporations.* They transact business in a large number of countries and often operate in diversified business activities. The movements of private foreign capital take place through the medium of these multinational corporations. Thus multinational corporations are important source of foreign direct investment (FDI). Besides, it is through multinational corporations that modern high technology is transferred to the developing countries.

The important question about multinational corporations is why they exist. *The multinational corporations exist because they are highly efficient. Their efficiencies in production and distribution of goods and services arise from internalising certain activities rather than contracting them out to other firms.*[3] Managing a firm involves which production and distribution activities it will perform itself and which activities it will contract out to *other firms and individuals*. In addition to this basic issue, a big firm may decide to set up and operate business units in other countries to benefit from *advantages of location.* For examples, it has been found that giant American and European firms set up production units to explore and refine oil in Middle East countries because oil is found there. Similarly, to take advantages of lower labour costs, and not strict environmental standards, multinational corporate firms set up production units in developing countries.

Alternative Methods of Foreign Investment by Multinational Companies

In order to increase their profitability many giant firms find it necessary to go in for horizontal and vertical integration. For this purpose, they find it profitable to set up their production or distribution units outside their home country. The firms that sell abroad the products produced in the home country or the products produced abroad to sell in the home country must decide how to manage and control their assets in other countries. In this regard, there are three methods of foreign investment by multinational firms among which they have to choose which mode of control over their assets they adopt. There are three main modes of foreign investment.

1. Agreement with Local Firms for Sale of MNCs Products. A multinational firm can enter into an agreement with local firms for exporting the product produced by it in the home country to them for sale in their countries. In this case, a multinational firm allows the foreign firms to sell its product in the foreign markets and control all aspects of sale operations.

2. Setting up of Subsidiaries. The second mode for investment abroad by a multinational firm is to set up a *wholly owned subsidiary* to operate in the foreign country. In this case, a multinational firm has complete control over its business operations ranging from the production of its product or service to its sale to the ultimate use or consumers. A subsidiary of a multinational corporation in a particular country is set up under the Companies Act of that country. Such subsidiary firm benefits

3 See Ronald Coase, "The Nature of the Firm", *Economica*, Nov. 1937, pp. 368-405.

from the managerial skills, financial resources, and international reputation of their parent company. However, it enjoys some independence from the parent company.

3. Branches of Multinational Corporation. Instead of establishing its subsidiaries, multinational corporations can set up their branches in other countries. Being branches they are not legally independent business unit but are linked with their parent company.

4. Foreign Collaboration or Joint Ventures. Thirdly, the multinational corporations set up joint ventures with foreign firms to either produce its product jointly with local companies of foreign countries for sale of the product in the foreign markets. A multinational firm may set up its business operation in collaboration with foreign local firms *to obtain raw materials* not available in the home country. More often, to reduce its overall production costs multinational companies set up joint ventures with local foreign firms to manufacture inputs or sub-components in foreign markets to produce the final product in the home country.

Some of the world's largest multinational corporations are given below.

Table 54.1. World's Some Important Non-Financial Multinational Corporations

S.No.	International corporation	Parent country	Industry of operation
1.	General Electric	United States	Electronics
2.	Exxon Mobil Corporation	United States	Petroleum (exploring, refining and distributing)
3.	Royal Dutch Shell Group	Netherlands/UK	-do-
4.	General Motors	United States	Motor Vehicles
5.	Ford Motor Co.	United States	Motor Vehicles
6.	Toyota Motor Co.	Japan	Motor Vehicles
7.	IBM	United States	Computers
8.	BP	United Kingdom	Petroleum (Exp/Ref./Distt.)
9.	Nesle SA	Switzerland	Food/Beverages
10.	Nippon Oil Co.	Japan	Petroleum/Expl., Ref./Distt.
11.	Sieman AG	Germany	Electronics
12.	BMW AG	Germany	Motors Vehicles
13.	ABB	Switzerland	Electrical equipment
14.	Sony Corporation	Japan	Electronics
15.	Seagram	Canada	Food/Beverages
16.	Aventis	France	Pharmaceuticals/Chemicals
17.	Roche Group	Switzerland	Pharmaceuticals
18.	Honda Motor Co.	Japan	Motor Vehicles
19.	Phillips Electronics	Netherlands	Electronics
20.	Hewlett-Packard	United States	Electronics/Computers

Role of Multinational Corporations in the Indian Economy

Prior to 1991, multinational companies did not play much role in the Indian economy. In the pre-reform period the Indian economy was dominated by public enterprises. To prevent concentration of economic power the Industrial Policy 1956 did not allow the private firms to grow in size beyond a point. By definition multinational companies are quite big and operate in several countries. While multinational companies played a significant role in the promotion of growth and trade in South-East Asian countries they did not play much role in the Indian economy where import-substitution development strategy was followed. Since 1991 with the adoption of industrial policy of liberalisation and privatisation role of private foreign capital has been recognised as important for rapid growth of the Indian economy. Since source of bulk of foreign capital and investment are multinational corporations, they have been allowed to operate in the Indian economy subject to some regulations. The following are the important reasons for this change in policy towards multinational companies in the post-reform period.

1. Promotion of Foreign Investment. In the recent years, external assistance to developing countries has been declining. This is because the donor developed countries have not been willing to part with a larger proportion of their GDP as assistance to developing countries. MNCs can bridge the gap between the requirements of foreign capital for increasing foreign investment in India. The liberalised foreign investment pursued since 1991 allows MNCs to make investment in India subject to different ceilings fixed for different industries or projects. However, in some industries 100 per cent export-oriented units (EOUs) can be set up. It may be noted, like domestic investment, foreign investment has also a multiplier effect on income and employment in a country. For example, the effect of Suzuki firm's investment in Maruti Udyog manufacturing cars is not confined to income and employment for the workers and employees of Maruti Udyog but goes beyond that. Many workers are employed in dealer firms who sell Maruti cars. Moreover, many intermediate goods are supplied by Indian suppliers to Maruti Udyog and for this many workers are employed by them to manufacture various parts and components used in Maruti cars. Thus their incomes also go up by investment by a Japanese multinational in Maruti Udyog Limited in India.

2. Non-Debt Creating Capital Inflows. In pre-reform period in India when foreign direct investment by MNCs was discouraged, we relied heavily on ***external commercial borrowing*** (ECB) which was of debt-creating capital inflows. This raised the burden of external debt and debt service payments reached the alarming figure of 35 per cent of our current account receipts. This created doubts about our ability to fulfil our debt obligations and there was a flight of capital from India and this resulted in balance of payments crisis in 1991. As direct foreign investment by multinational corporations represents non-debt creating capital inflows we can avoid the liability of debt-servicing payments. Moreover, the advantage of investment by MNCs lies in the fact that servicing of non-debt capital begins only when the MNC firm reaches the stage of making profits to repatriate. Thus, MNCs can play an important role in reducing stress and strains on India's balance of payments (BOP).

3. Technology Transfer. Another important role of multinational corporations is that they transfer high sophisticated technology to developing countries which are essential for raising productivity of working class and enable them to start new productive ventures requiring high technology. Whenever, multinational firms set up their subsidiary production units or joint-venture units, they not only import new equipment and machinery embodying new technology but also skills and technical know-how to use the new equipment and machinery. As a result, the Indian workers and engineers come to know of new superior technology and the way to use it. In India, the corporate sector spends only few resources on Research and Development (R&D). It is the giant multinational corporate firms (MNCs) which spend a lot on the development of new technologies which can greatly benefit the developing countries by transferring the new technology developed by them. Therefore, MNCs can play an important role in the technological upgradation of the Indian economy.

4. Promotion of Exports. With extensive links all over the world and producing products efficiently and therefore with lower costs multinationals can play a significant role in promoting exports of a country in which they invest. For example, the rapid expansion in China's exports in recent years is due to the large investment made by multinationals in various fields of Chinese industry. Historically in India, multinationals made large investment in plantations whose products they exported. In recent years, Japanese automobile company Suzuki made a large investment in Maruti Udyog with a joint collaboration with Government of India. Maruti cars are not only being sold in the Indian domestic market but are exported in a large number to the foreign countries.

As a matter of fact, until recently, when giving permission to a multinational firm for investment in India, government granted the permission subject to the condition that the concerned multinational company would export the product so as to earn foreign exchange for India. However, in case of Pepsi, a famous cold drink multinational company, while for getting a product license in 1961 to produce Pepsi Cola in India it agreed to export a certain proportion of its product, but later it expressed its inability to do so. Instead, it ultimately agreed to export things other than what it produced such as tea.

5. Investment in Infrastructure. With a large command over financial resources and their superior ability to raise resources both globally and inside India it is said that multinational corporations could invest in infrastructure such as power projects, modernisation of airports and ports, telecommunication. The investment in infrastructure will give a boost to industrial growth and help in creating income and employment in the Indian economy. The external economies generated by investment in infrastructure by MNCs will therefore *crowd* in investment by the indigenous private sector and will therefore stimulate economic growth.

In view of above, even Common Minimum Programme of the UPA government provided that foreign direct investment (FDI) would be encouraged and actively sought, especially in areas of (*a*) infrastructure, (*b*) high technology, (*c*) exports and (*d*) where domestic assets and employment are created on a significant scale.

A Critique of Multinational Corporations

In recent years, foreign direct investment through multinational corporations has vastly increased in India and other developing countries. This vast increase in investment by multinational corporations in recent years is prompted by factors: (1) the liberalisation of industrial policy giving greater role to the private sector, (2) opening up of the economy and liberalisation of foreign trade and capital inflows. In this economic environment multinational corporations which are in search for global profits are induced to make investment in developing countries. As explained above, foreign direct investment by multinational firms bring many benefits to the recipient countries but there are many potential dangers and disadvantages from the viewpoint of economic growth and employment generation. Therefore, role of multinational corporations in India and other developing countries has been criticised on several grounds. We discuss below some of the criticisms levelled against multinational corporations.

1. Capturing Markets. First, it is alleged that multinational corporations invest their capital and locate their manufacturing units on their own or in collaboration with local firms in order *to sell their products and capture the domestic markets of the countries where they invest and operate*. With their vast resources and competitive strength, they can weed out their competitive firms. For example, in India if corporate multinational firms are allowed to sell or produce the products presently produced by small and medium enterprises, the latter would not be able to compete and therefore would be thrown out of business. This will lead to reduction in employment opportunities in the country.

2. Use of Capital-intensive Techniques. It has been seen that increasing capital intensity in modern manufacturing sector is responsible for slow growth of employment opportunities in India's industrial sector. These capital-intensive techniques may be imported by large domestic firms but presently they are being increasingly used by multinational corporations which bring their technology when they invest in India. Emphasising this factor, Thirwall rightly writes, "*In this case the technology may be inappropriate not because there is not a spectrum of technology or inappropriate selection is made but because the technology available is circumscribed by the global profit maximising motives of multinational companies investing in the less-developed country concerned.*"[4]

3. Encouragement to Inessential Consumption. The investment by multinational companies leads to overall increase in investment in India but it is alleged that they encourage conspicuous

4 A.P. Thirlwall, *Growth and Development,* Palgrave, Macmillan, Seventh Edition, 2003, p. 435.

consumption in the economy. These companies cater to the wants of the already well-to-do people. For example, in India very expensive cars (such as City Honda, Hyundai's Accent, Mercedes, Audi, etc.), the air conditioners, costly laptops, washing machines, expensive fridges, and Plasma TVs are being produced/sold by multinational companies. Such goods are quite inappropriate for a poor country like India. Besides, their consumption has a demonstration effect on the consumption of others. This tends to raise the propensity to consume and adversely affects the increase in savings of the country.

4. Import of Obsolete Technology. Another criticism of MNCs is based on the ground that they import obsolete machines and technology. As mentioned above, some of the imported technologies are inappropriate to the conditions of Indian economy. It is alleged that India has been made a dumping ground for obsolete technology. Moreover, the multinational corporations do not undertake Research and Development (R&D) in India to promote local technologies suited to the Indian factor-endowment conditions. Instead, they concentrate R & D activity at their headquarters.

5. Setting up Environment-Polluting Industries. It has been found that investment by multinational corporations in developing countries such as India is usually made for capturing domestic markets rather than for export promotion. Moreover, in order to evade strict environment control measures in their home countries they set up polluting industrial units in India. A classic example of this is a highly polluting chemical plant set up in Bhopal resulting in gas tragedy when thousands of people were either killed or made handicapped due to severe ailments. "With the tightening of environmental measures in the such countries, there is a tendency among the MNCs to locate the polluting industries in the poor countries, where environmental legislation is non-existent or is not properly implemented, as exemplified in the Bhopal gas tragedy."[5]

6. Volatility in Exchange Rate. Another major consequence of liberalised foreign investment by multinational corporations is its impact on the foreign exchange rate of the host country. Foreign capital inflows affect the foreign exchange rate of the Indian rupee. A large capital inflows through foreign investment brings about increase in the supply of foreign exchange, say, of US dollars. With demand for foreign exchange being given, increase in supply of foreign exchange will lead to the appreciation of exchange rate of rupee. This appreciation of the Indian rupee will discourage exports and encourage imports causing deficit in balance of trade. For example, in India in the fiscal years 2004-05 and 2005-06, there was large capital inflows by FII (giant financial multinationals) in the Indian economy to take advantage of higher interest rates here and cause further boom in the Indian capital market.

On the other hand, when interest rates rise in the parent countries of these multinationals or rates of return from capital markets go up or when there is loss of confidence in the host country about its capacity to make payments of its debt as happened in case of South-East Asia in the late nineties, there is large outflow of capital by multinational companies resulting in the crisis and huge depreciation of their exchange rate. Thus, capital inflows and outflows by multinationals have been responsible for large volatility of exchange rate.

Then there is the question of ***repatriation of profits*** by the multinationals. Though a part of profit is reinvested by the multinational companies in the host country, a large amount of profits is remitted to their own parent countries. This has a potential disadvantage for the developing countries, especially when they are facing foreign exchange problem. Commenting on this Thirlwall writes "FDI has the potential disadvantage even when compared with loan finance, that there may be outflow of profits that lasts much longer.[6]

---

5 Biplab Dasgupta, *Globalisation : India's Adjustment Experience,* Sage Publications, New Delhi, 2005, p. 81.

6. A.P. Thirlwall, *op. cit.*

Transfer Pricing and Evasion of Local Taxes. Multinational corporations are usually vertically integrated. The production of a commodity by a multinational firm comprises various phases in its production, the components used in the production of a final commodity may be produced in its parent country or in its affiliates in other countries. *Transfer pricing refers to the prices a vertically integrated multinational firm charges for its components or parts used for the production of the final commodity, say in India.* These prices of components or parts are not real prices as determined by demand for and supply of them. They are arbitrarily fixed by the companies so that they have to pay less taxes in India. They artificially inflate the transfer prices for intermediate products (i.e., components) produced in their parent country or their overseas affiliates so as to show lower profits earned in India. As a result, they succeed in evading corporate income tax.

Conclusion. We have seen above foreign investment by multinational companies have both advantages and disadvantages. Therefore, they need regulation and should be permitted in selected sectors and also subject to a cap on their investment in particular fields. If objective of economic growth with stability and social justice is to be achieved, there should not be complete open door policy for them.

It is true that multinational corporations take risk in making investment in India, they bring capital and foreign exchange which are non-debt creating, they generally promote technology and can help in raising exports. But they must be regulated so that they serve these goals. They should be allowed to invest in infrastructure, high-technology areas, and in industries whose products they can export and if they help in generating net employment opportunities. We agree with Colman and Nixon who write :

"*Transnational corporations cannot be directly blamed for lack of development (or the direction development is taking) within less developed countries. Their prime objective is global profit maximisation and their actions are aimed at achieving that objective, not developing the host less developed country. If the technology and products that they introduce are inappropriate, if their actions exacerbate regional and social inequalities, if they weaken the balance of payments position, in the last resort it is up to the government of less developed country to pursue policies which will eliminate the causes of these problems.*"[7]

---

7. D. Colman, and F Nixon, *Economics of Change in Less Developed Countries*, Oxford University Press, 1978.

CHAPTER 55

IMF AND WORLD BANK DIRECTED MACROECONOMIC POLICIES FOR DEVELOPING COUNTRIES

The role of IMF has been to help the countries including the developing countries to help them when they face balance of payments problem and give them short-term structural adjustment facility (SAF) for this purpose. Many developing countries borrowed heavily from abroad and total foreign debt became too large that was beyond their capacity to pay. They approach IMF for help. When balance of payments disequilibrium is chronic, short-term solutions are not possible and therefore desirable structural reforms have to be undertaken. On the other hand, World Bank is an international agency to provide development assistance to the countries.

From the mid –1980s, several developing countries faced serious problems of balance of payments difficulties, slowdown in economic growth, huge fiscal deficits resulting in high rates of inflation. IMF and World Bank were started with a basic belief that problems and policies of one country are important for the rest of the world. But experts at IMF and World Bank saw merits in liberalisation, privatisation, greater efficiency of function of goods and factor market and capital markets. They advocated for trade liberalisation and thus for abolition of licence, drastic reduction in tariffs. To check inflation they try reducing government expenditure (what are called 'austerity measures'), drastic cut in fiscal deficit so that aggregate demand declines. They held that public sector is quite inefficient and therefore its role in the economy should be minimised. Besides, they advised devaluation of their currencies and adoption of steps to facilitate foreign direct investment to promote economic growth. These reforms in the economic system are generally called '*Structural Adjustment Reforms*', as they seek to change the basic structure of the functioning of the economy *situation in India in 1991*.

Situation in India in 1991

Like many other developing countries, India in early 1991 faced a serious economic crisis. Fiscal deficit of the Centre and States combined went up to more than 12 per cent of GDP with the result that inflation rate shot up to around 13 y-o-y.

Balance of Payments Crisis. In the external sector, *the huge deficits in the balance of payments due to the rising imports and sluggish exports persisted for a long time and, to meet this deficit, the government resorted to commercial borrowing from abroad at higher market rates of interest*. As a result of persistent deficits on the current account, the foreign exchange reserves declined to a very small sum in June 1991 which could last for payments for necessary imports only for about few weeks. This compelled the Government to approach IMF (International Monetary Fund) for loans to make necessary payments and enhance the foreign exchange reserves.

Though the annual growth of national income *during the eighties* went up to over 5 per cent and of the industrial sector to 8 per cent, which was considered to be a good performance, but due to macroeconomic imbalances which emerged in the economy they could no longer be sustained any more. In the external sector, the situation became so worse in 1991 that India came to the brink of default. To avoid the default and to win over the confidence of international business community, the government had to sell a part of its gold reserves and a certain amount of gold was even pledged with Bank of England to obtain the foreign exchange reserves to meet its obligations. Further, it had to approach the IMF for loans to tide over the foreign exchange crisis.

Excessive Government Controls over Private Sector. Besides, excessive government regulation and control over the private sector proved to be counter-productive. The following drawbacks of excessive regulation of the private sector were emphasised and case for liberalisation of private sector was built up, especially by Jagdish Bhagwati and T.N. Srinivasan, the two economists associated with World Bank and International Monetary Fund. The following arguments were given in favour of deregulation of the private sector and assigning to it a greater role in economic growth of the Indian economy.

The industrial licensing and controls had degenerated into arbitrary bureaucratic controls on the allocation of resources in competing industries. The licences were issued to make investment in those industries which bureaucrats chose in tune with the policies they administered. This licensing system replaced the efficient market system of resource allocation by personal system of resource allocation. Thus excessive regulation of the private sector, according to the advocates of economic reforms, had resulted in the sub-optimal resource allocation in industries. Hence, there was a need for liberalisation.

Washington Consensus, Development Policy and Structural Adjustment Reforms

Before explaining the economic reforms initiated in 1991 under the pressure of IMF and World Bank, it may be mentioned that these reforms mainly constituted what is now labelled as *Washington Consensus*. This consensus was formulated by John Williamson, with the other officials of World Bank, IMF and key US government agencies. This consensus contains 10 elements of development policy which were suggested to promote economic growth in the developing countries and also help them solve their problems of indebtedness, balance of payments difficulties and high rate of inflation. *It is noteworthy that this Washington Consensus followed a free market approach to development and, contrary to the views of many development economists, it did not emphasise elimination of poverty and reducing inequalities to achieve real development, as it is now widely understood.* The Washington Consensus and fiscal and structural reforms it envisages views that poverty will be automatically removed if rapid economic growth is achieved. Its message is 'take care of growth, poverty will take care of itself'. Economic policy reforms by IMF-World Bank are in fact a 'standard blueprint', a sort of 'same size fit all' regardless of their special problems.

Let us list below the various elements of Washington Consensus.

1. **Fiscal Adjustment.** This means that developing countries should take steps to reduce fiscal deficit through curtailing government expenditure by drastically reducing explicit and implicit subsidies provided by the government of developing countries.

2. **Tax Reforms.** It was suggested that tax rates should be cut substantially to promote saving and private investment. This will promote investment and ensure a higher rate of economic growth. This was in line with supply-side economics. In fact, Jagdish Bhagwati and T.N. Srinivasan invoked *Laffer Curve* concept of supply-side economics to argue that reduction in rates of taxes would cause not only greater private saving and investment but will lead to greater revenue for the government.

Besides, it was suggested to broaden the tax base by withdrawing exemptions and plugging the loopholes in taxes.

3. **Deregulation.** This was most significant policy measure under which it was recommended that industrial licensing controls be abolished but also such measures as Monopolistic and Restrictive Trade Practices Commission (MRTPC) and FERA (Foreign Exchange Regulation Act) be done away with so that private sector should grow without any obstructions.

4. **Privatisation.** This is another significant measure of development policy under which it was proposed that there should be disinvestment of public sector enterprises and accordingly either they should be sold outrightly to the private sector or government stake should be reduced and its shares sold or transferred to private enterprises.

5. **Trade Liberalisation.** Under this, it was suggested that tariffs on imports should be drastically reduced *to promote free trade*. Besides, all quantitative restrictions on imports were also to be eliminated to permit free trade.

6. **Competitive Exchange Rate.** Under this, it was recommended that developing countries like India should devalue their over-valued currencies and ultimately adopt flexible exchange rate system. Besides, it was suggested to make the currency convertible so that obstacles to growth of free trade and capital mobility be removed.

7. **Removal of Barriers to Foreign Investment.** It was stressed that economic growth in developing countries could be accelerated through larger foreign direct investment (FDI). Therefore, all barriers put up by developing countries should be eliminated to attract foreign investment in their countries. To facilitate foreign investment it was also suggested to adopt *Convertibility of currency on current account as well as on capital account.*

8. **Financial Reforms.** They involve reforms in the banking and insurance system and also in capital market.

9. **Protection of Property Rights.** According to this, suitable legislative measures should be taken to protect property rights. Besides, labour law should be amended so that it becomes easy for *private enterprise to enter and exit* the industries. In this, *freedom to exit* was emphasised and it was recommended that labour laws be made flexible so that it should be easy to retrench workers.

10. **Redirection of Public Sector Investment.** Lastly, it was emphasised that public sector investment should be redirected towards education, health and infrastructure only and also leave these and other fields open to private sector operation.

IMPLEMENTATION OF STRUCTURAL ADJUSTMENT REFORMS IN INDIA

However, to evolve a long-term solution to promote price stability, to bring about equilibrium in balance of payments and, above all, to ensure higher rate of economic growth, the elected Congress government with Dr. Manmohan Singh as Finance Minister adopted in 1991 what is popularly called *New Economic Policy* on the advice of IMF and World Bank. According to this policy, the government was to prune down its expenditure so as to *reduce budget deficits for achieving price stability. But more important element of new economic policy is the adoption of what are called Structural Adjustment Reforms* which sought to change the nature of Indian economic system by ultimately establishing *a predominantly free market economy*. Under this structural adjustment programme, the role of public sector in economic development had been diluted and that of private sector enhanced and expanded.

It may be noted that the policy of free-market economy also got strong stimulus due to the collapse of socialist system in Soviet Russia, China and other centrally planned socialist economies in Eastern Europe. Accordingly, under the new economic policy, the idea of the predominant role of the public sector was abandoned and the private sector was given a greater role in promoting economic growth through competition and efficiency. Instead of being directed by the planning and licensing, the private sector was now to be governed by the market forces, that is, by the free play of demand and supply of commodities and factors. We describe below the new economic reforms undertaken in India since 1991 under the *New Economic Policy* or *Structural Adjustment Programme.*

However it is worth noting that it is generally believed that Dr. Manmohan Singh formulated these reforms. This is quite wrong. As has been seen above that these reforms were proposed by IMF and World Bank and they used them as '*conditionalities*' for giving aid. They asked 'devalue the rupee', he devalued it; they asked cut tariffs for trade liberalisation, he did so and so on.

Dereservation of Industries of the Public Sector

The new industrial policy 1991 was adopted under which far-reaching structural reforms have been initiated to lift excess direct controls and regulations on industries and to ensure a free market-oriented economic system. The list of industries reserved for the public sector has been pruned. Now, only 6 industries remain reserved for the public sector. Among the industries reserved earlier for the public sector were many core industries like iron and steel, electricity, air transport, ship building, heavy machinery industries such as heavy chemical plants and telecommunication cables and instruments. The new industrial policy of 1991 threw open all these industries for the private sector for investment and growth. Thus the new policy indicates the government's intention to invite a greater degree of participation by the private sector in important areas of the economy. The six industries which continue to be reserved for the public sector are in areas where security and strategic considerations predominate. According to the new policy, the resources in the public sector will now be used for the development of strategic, high-technology industries and essential infrastructure areas and for social sectors such as education, public health and poverty alleviation programmes.

Liberalisation: Abolition of Industrial Licensing System

Until 1991 the Indian industrial sector had functioned under a system of tight controls and regulations represented by industrial licensing which meant to allocate the scarce resources towards building the industrial base of the economy. By the year 1991, the Indian industrial economy had a quite wide and diversified base, the new policy abolished all industrial licensing irrespective of the level of investment except for 15 industries for which licence was still required. These industries are those which are essential for security and safety purposes and for protection of environment. For granting of licence for even these 15 industries procedure has been greatly simplified. For getting licences only certain locational guidelines are to be fulfilled so that polluting industries should not cluster around the major urban centres. Besides, restrictions by Monopolistic and Restrictive Act Trade Practices (MRTPA) for expansion of big firms were also relaxed.

Privatisation of Public Sector Enterprises

An important aspect of new industrial policy of the government is that it should not operate commercial enterprises. With that end in view the government decided to disinvest the public enterprises. The government can sell its enterprises completely to the private sector or disinvest a part of its equity capital held by it to the private sector companies or in the open market. Therefore *this policy of public sector disinvestment has also been called the policy of privatisation.* Through disinvestment or privatisation, the government can mop up a good amount of resources which can be used for various purposes. The released resources can be used to restructure and strengthen the public sector enterprises which are potentially viable. These resources can also be used to pay back a part of public debt. These resources can also be used to finance budget deficits.

What are the reasons for the policy of privatisation or public sector disinvestment? First, resources available with the government are scarce. The government needs resources to reduce its budget deficit. The government urgently requires resources to make investment in infrastructure, education, public health and for poverty alleviation programmes. Resources released through disinvestment can be used for investment in these crucial sectors. Second, a good number of existing public enterprises are working inefficiently and incurring huge losses.

Accordingly, as part of the economic reforms policy, the government started reforms in public sector enterprises. The main elements of government policy towards Public Sector Enterprises (PSU) are:

1. Disinvestment of government equity in all *non-strategic* public sector undertakings (PSU) to 26 per cent or lower if necessary.

2. Those public sector enterprises which are potentially viable have to be restructured and revived.

3. Those public sector undertakings (PSU) which cannot be revived would be closed down.

Table 55.1. Disinvestment of Public Sector Undertakings in India Since 1991

Year	*Target (₹ Crore)*	*Actual Receipts (₹ Crore)*
1991-92	2,500	3,038
1992-93	2,500	1,913
1993-94	3,500	NIL
1994-95	4,000	4,843
1995-96	7,000	168
1996-97	5,000	380
1997-98	4,800	910
1998-99	5,000	5,371
1999-2000	10,000	1,860
2000-01	10,000	1,871
2001-02	12,000	5,632
2002-03	12,000	3,348
2003-04	14,500	15,547
2004-05	4,000	2765
2005-06	no target	1568
2007-08	no target	2367
2008-09	no target	546
2009-10	no target	1120
2010-11	40,000	13,854
2012-13	30,000	NA

Source: GOI, *Economic Surveys*, 2003-04, 2005-06, 2006-07 and 2007-08, 2008-09, 2009-10, 2010-11 and 2011-12.

The government has now evolved a fair, transparent and equitable procedure for disinvestment in selected public sector enterprises. The achievement made with regard to disinvestment of Public Sector Undertakings which started in 1991-92 with the sale of minority stakes in some public sector undertakings are given in Table 55.1.

Globalisation

The following measures for globalisation of the Indian economy were taken.

Welcoming Private Foreign Investment and Foreign Technology. Till 1991, foreign investment and import of foreign technology was regulated tightly in India. In the case of foreign technology agreements sought by Indian firms as well as foreign investment, it was necessary to obtain specific prior approval from the government for each project. This involved delays and hampered business decision-making in the import of technology by Indian firms. Under the new economic policy for a selected list of high technology and high investment priority industries, firms receive *automatic approval* to make foreign technology agreements within certain guidelines. This policy measure is expected to remove the delay and uncertainty which earlier clouded the relationships between Indian and foreign firms.

Further, the government has *liberalised its policy regarding foreign investment*. To attract private foreign investment, it has been decided to grant *automatic permission to private foreign investors to invest up to 51 per cent of the total equity shares in 34 high priority industries if certain norms are fulfilled.* This facility will be available to those firms which are able to finance their capital equipment imports through their foreign equity. This is a major departure from the previous policies which required case-by-case approval of foreign investment normally limited to 40 per cent equity participation. The priority sector includes power generation and petroleum refining. Further, the government has given a guarantee of 16 per cent return on foreign investment in priority sectors. There is also proposal to allow automatic clearance for foreign *financial* and technical collaboration with Indian firms.

Trade Liberalisation. In a bid to open up the economy, under the new economic policy *quantitative restrictions*, that is, import licensing for imports of goods have been removed. Further, to promote competitiveness, efficiency and globalisation of the Indian economy import duties have been reduced to 20 per cent (excluding agricultural and dairy products) with effect from January 9, 2004. The new thinking is that with the cheapening of imported goods, the Indian firms will try to increase their efficiency and reduce costs so that their products can compete with the foreign products. In this way, they will be able to expand their exports.

Currency Convertibility and Floating of Indian Rupee. Another major step taken towards liberalisation of the Indian economy has been to make the Indian rupee fully convertible on current account since March 1993. This implies that for the purpose of foreign trade and travel you can convert the rupees into dollars and dollars into rupees in the foreign exchange market at the market determined exchange rate. That is, the foreign exchange rate of rupee is now not fixed but liable to change as demand for and supply of foreign exchange change. In July 1991, the Indian rupee was devalued by about 20 per cent. But now rupee has been made flexible whose price is determined by demand and supply. The Indian rupee can depreciate or appreciate depending upon demand and supply conditions.

STRUCTURAL ECONOMIC REFORMS

It is evident from the reforms introduced in the Indian economy that from a planned economy it has moved towards a free-market economy. Though we still have mixed economy with both the public and private sectors coexisting but the role of private sector which is governed by market forces has been greatly increased and that of the public sector greatly diluted. So we now have a mixed economy with greater orientation towards a free market and private sector.

Now, 25 years have passed when we initiated economic reforms in 1991 laying greater emphasis on liberalisation and privatisation. Now, the pertinent question is whether these economic reforms have ensured higher and sustained economic growth which the supporters of these reforms argued they would, whether these reforms have led to a higher growth rate and to the greater reduction of poverty and unemployment which was expected of them. The answer to these questions is a mixed one. Foreign exchange reserves which had gone too low in 1991 due to profligacy of the late 1980s and temporary oil shock of first Iraq (Kuwait) war in 1990, have substantially increased in the post-reform period.

Foreign Exchange Reserves and Balance of Payments. Foreign exchange reserves are now, in August 2013, at around 285 billion US dollars. In 2007-08, our growth in export was 29.0 per cent and in the later half of 2008-09 due to global financial crisis our export started falling and for the whole year 2008-09 there was 13.6 per cent growth rate in exports and due to global slowdown in 2009-10 there was negative growth in exports to the extent of 3.5 per cent. But in 2010-11 and 2011-12 exports registered substantial growth of 40.5 and 21.3 per cent respectively but again there is negative growth of exports (– 4.9 per cent) in 2012-13.

Following the adoption of export-oriented strategy in place of import-substitution strategy, exports on an average have grown at a higher rate in the post-reforms period. An important achievement in this regard has been that India has become a leading country in *software exports*. India's software exports rose from near zero in 1991 to 17 billion US dollars in 2004-05. Foreign investment in India which was barely US $ 1 million in 1990-91 rose to $ 33 billion in 2011-12. But a serious problem which has risen recently is of *large current account deficit* (CAD) due to import liberalisation of economic reforms. Current account deficit (CAD) was within comfortable zone until 2010-11, it was 1.5% of GDP in 2007-08, 2.3% in 2008-09, –2.8 per cent in 2009-10 and 2010-11 but worsened thereafter. In 2011-12 it was estimated at –4.2 per cent of GDP and in 2012-13 CAD rose to 4.8% of GDP. This had been due to imports of large quantity of **gold** and our dependence on foreign supply of crude oil. Therefore, many persons said we were back to the state of crisis of 1991. However, Dr. Manmohan Singh refuted this by saying that in 1991 our foreign reserves were sufficient for only 15 days of imports and we had to pledge gold with central banks of England and Japan to obtain US dollars and UK pound sterlings to escape from defaulting on paying our foreign debt. According to him, in August 2013 we had $ 285 billion foreign exchange reserves which were sufficient to cover 7 months of imports.

But whatever Dr. Manmohan Singh says, the high magnitude of our current account deficit poses a serious challenge. There are two ways to solve this problem. First, we must expand our export and restrict imports by raising customs duty on imports, especially which are of luxury types. We have already raised the duty on gold to 10% which will help to bring down the imports of gold. Second, we must attract *foreign direct investment* (FDI) which is a stable source of foreign funds and reduce our dependence on portfolio investment by foreign investment institutions (FIls). In July 2013 to solve our current account deficit and to prevent the depreciation of the rupee Government had raised the **caps** of foreign direct investment in various sections such as telecom, power, oil refineries etc and made their entry easier by permitting a proportion of their investment through '*automatic route*'. The present author is of the view that these steps may take a long time and therefore we may approach IMF again to bail out.

Control of Inflation. Another achievement of economic reforms *in the initial stages* was that inflation rate had been controlled. The inflation rate as measured by change in Whole Sale Price Index (WPI) which reached a peak of over 15 per cent in August 1991 was brought down to 4.5 per cent in 1997-98. The inflation rate as measured by WPI (1999-2000 = 100) varied somewhat since then but it had been small on an average till 2008-09. Annual rate of inflation as measured by WPI (1999-2000 = 100) was 7.1 per cent in 2000-01, 3.6 % in 2003-04, 6.5% in 2004-05 and 5.4% in 2006-07. It was about 4% in 2007-08. However, inflation rate flared up in 2008-09 when year-on-year WPI inflation rate started rising from March 2008 and crossed 9% mark in June 2008 and 11% in August 2008 and reached a peak level of 12.63% in mid-Sept. 2008 and after it started falling and was estimated at 8.1 per cent during 2008-09. It further fell to 3.8 per cent during 2009-10.

However, WPI inflation flared up again during 2010-11 and was estimated at 9.6% in 2010-11 and 9.4 per cent in 2011-12 and in Aug. 2012 it was at around 8 per cent despite tightening of monetary policy by RBI in the last three years. The inflation regarding consumer price index (CPI-IW) was estimated at 9.1% in 2008-09, 12.4 per cent in 2009-10, 10.4 per cent in 2010-11 and 9.1 per cent in 2011-12. It crossed 11 per cent in August 2012. Thus, inflation at present is a matter of serious concern. However, it may be noted that current inflation rate is not due to economic reforms undertaken since 1991. It is the result of both demand and supply-side pressures working in the Indian economy. Government's inability to reduce large fiscal deficit and to increase the supply of essential goods (especially food times) are responsible for current inflation.

WPI inflation has been brought down to zero per cent in March 2015 but CPI (IW) inflation was still at 5.5 per cent y-o-y basis in March 2015.

Economic Growth. A significant achievement of economic reforms has been that rate of economic growth on an average rose to 6.1 per cent per annum during 1992-2002 as compared to the previous decade of 1980's when GDP grew at 5.6 per cent per annum (See Table 55.2).

After 2003-04 rate of economic growth rose further to 8% to 9% with the exception of year 2008-09 when there was 6.7% growth rate due to global financial crisis.

It will be seen from Table 55.2 that growth rate of industry where major reforms have been undertaken was estimated to be lower at 6.4 per cent per annum in the immediate post-reforms period during 1992-93-2000-01 (even omitting the year 1991-92) as compared to 7.1 per cent achieved in the pre-reform decade 1981-82-1990-91. The industrial growth rate was still lower at 4.6 per cent per annum during the five years period of Ninth Plan, 1997-98-2000-02. The overall growth rate in GDP during the post-reforms period has been 7.2 per cent which is higher than that of pre-reforms period.

Table 55.2. Average Annual Growth Rate

	1981-82 to 1990-91	1992-93 to 2000-01	1997-98 9th Plan	2002-07 10th Plan	2007-08	2008-09	2009-10	2010-2011	2011-2012	2012-2013
Agriculture	3.6	3.2	2.0	2.5	2.5	0.1	1.0	7.0	3.6	1.9
Industry	7.1	6.4	4.6	8.9	9.0	4.5	8.3	7.9	2.7	1.2
Services	6.7	7.8	8.1	9.3	10.2	10.9	10.0	9.4	7.9	6.8
GDP (factor cost)	5.6	6.1	5.5	7.8	9.3	6.7	8.6	9.3	6.2	5

Source: 1. Dr. Shankar Acharya, Growth has slowed, *Economic Times*, 22 May, 2001

2. GOI *Economic Surveys* 2007-08, 2008-09, 2009-10, 2010-11, 2011-12, and 2012-13

However, industrial growth rate picked up to 8.9 in the 10th Plan period 2002-07. It is important to note that overall higher growth rate of 7.2% per annum in 1992-93 to 2011-12 was achieved due to higher growth rate (7.8%) achieved in services. As has been pointed out by Dr. Shankar Acharya[1] the higher growth rate in both industry and services was due to large increase in government administration services where as a result of 5th Pay Commission large increases in salaries to the Government employees (including army) were given which pulled up the overall growth rate. However, during the 9th Plan period (1992-98 to 2002) and 10th Plan period (2002-07) growth rate in services has been quite high, 8.1 % and 9.3% respectively. *In fact, services have been the important driving force of economic growth in India in the last 20 years.*[2]

From 2003 to 2011-12 onward, industry also achieved appreciable growth rate of 8.9% per cent in the 10th Plan period (2002-07) and 9 per cent in 2007-08. Leaving the year 2008-09 when industrial growth rate fell to 4.5 per cent it picked up to 8.3 per cent in 2009-10 and 7.9 per cent in 2010-11. However, during 2011-12, it fell to 2.8% and during 2012-13, industrial growth further fell to 1.2 per cent only due to adverse global conditions created by slow growth in the US and stagnation in European countries due to Eurozone crisis. Even overall GDP growth in 2011-12 has fallen to 6.2 per cent as against the original target of 9 per cent for this year. Even industrial growth during 2012-13 as stated above has fallen to 1.2 per cent due to the above mentioned factors which are still operating to lower economic growth rate of India. However, it is agriculture which has registered a low growth in the last decade; agriculture grew at the rate of only 2 per cent per annum in the 9th Plan period (1997-98 to 2002) and 2.5 per cent per annum in the 10th Plan period (2002-07).This is mainly because in the post-reform period investment in agriculture has been very low.

A significant achievement of economic reforms has been a higher overall rate of economic growth in the post-reform period. *A high overall growth rate of 6.2 per cent was achieved during 1991-2003, and about 7.8 per cent growth in GDP in the five years (2002-07) of 10th Plan. India has become one of the fastest growing economies of the world.* In fact in the three years period (2005-08) annual average growth had been over 9 per cent which is quite a high rate of growth. However, the benefits of

1 Shankar Acharya, "Macroeconomic Management in the Nineties", *EPW*, April 2002.

2 Shankar Acharya, '*India Rising, 2004-05 Outlook*, April 4, 2005.

this high growth rate had not trickled down much to the poor. Therefore, the Eleventh Plan laid stress on **inclusive growth** along with the target growth of 9 per cent during the plan period. However, in the 11th Plan period (2007-12) India succeeded in achieving average 8 per cent growth rate despite global financial crisis of 2007-09 which affected India also.

As stated above, quite a *dismal performance* in the post-reform period has been witnessed in respect of agricultural growth. Agricultural growth has greatly decelerated after mid-1990s. Agriculture which had grown at 3.2 per cent per annum from 1980 to 1996 deteriorated to 2.0 per cent during the 9th plan (1997-2002). In the five years (2002-07) of the 10th Plan agricultural growth was estimated at 2.5 per cent per annum[3] against the target of 4 per cent per annum. This shows whatever the objectives, in actual investment effort and implementation of programmes, agriculture, especially irrigation, has been grossly neglected.

It may be noted that **for the last three years (2011-12, 2012-13 and 2013-14) Indian economy has been in crisis,** its GDP growth rate has fallen drastically. In 2011-12 its GDP growth was 6.2 per cent and in 2012-13, it fell to 5 per cent – the lowest in a decade. For 2013-14 also an NCAER research study shows that GDP growth rate will most likely not be greater than 5 per cent. *Lack of infrastructure is a key constraint* which as a result of **policy paralysis** on the part of government is holding down growth rate. Growth of exports which is now an important part of our GDP has been sluggish partly because of policy paralysis and partly due to recession in the US and European countries. Sentiments of investors have been quite subdued because of policy uncertainty of the government and dear monetary policy of the RBI which had to be adopted to fight inflation and widening current account deficit (CAD) which was 4.2 per cent in 2011-12 and 4.8 per cent of GDP in 2012-13. On the one hand, lack of infrastructure and the delays in environment clearances of projects have held up various investment projects and adversely caused uncertainty in the minds of investors. Further, due to lavish unproductive expenditure aimed at getting votes in the future parliamentary elections has resulted in macroeconomic imbalances in the economy which has resulted in large fiscal deficit of the central government which was 5.7 per cent in 2011-12 and 4.8% in 2012-13 creating the problem of inflation and widening of current account deficit (CAD) which has caused among other factors fast depreciation of rupee. Our dependence on volatile capital flows brought in by FIIs to meet current account deficit and spur economic growth is now creating problems. The large outflows of capital by FIIs have caused sharp depreciation of rupee.

Employment and Unemployment: Jobless Growth

But a more dismal performance of the Indian economy has been in respect of growth of employment opportunities. The growth of employment in the organised sector (consisting of industrial and services sectors, both public and private sectors) of the Indian economy has been negative in the last 15 years since 1991. In fact in April 2010 about 40 million jobless persons were registered with

Table 55.3. Rate of Growth of Employment in the Organised Sector in India

(Per cent per annum)

	1983-94	1994-2008	2010/09	2011/10
Public Sector	1.53	–0.65	0.4	1.8
Private Sector	0.44	1.75	4.5	5.6
Total Organised Sector	1.20	0.05	1.9	1.0

Source: GOI *Economic Survey*, 2012-13, p. 275

the employment exchanges. It will be seen from Table 55.3 that in the post-reforms period 1994-2008 while rate of growth of employment in the public sector was negative (–0.65% per annum), in the organised private sector employment increased at the rate of 1.75 per cent per annum. The increase in employment in the total organised sector was only 0.05 per cent per annum in 1994-2008 whereas in the pre-reforms period (1983-1994) the growth of employment in total organised sector was 1.20 per cent per annum. Thus *Economic Survey* 2014-15 states that a cause for concern is

3 Planning Commission, *Tenth Plan: Mid-Term Appraisal Report*, 2005.

the deceleration in the compound annual growth of employment during 2004-05 to 2011-12 to only 0.5 per cent as against 2.9 per cent annual growth in labour force during the same period.[4] This has been due to the *decline in employment elasticity of growth of output*. Thus, the policy of economic reforms, namely, *liberalisation, privatisation and globalisation,* failed to generate higher growth of employment despite the achievement of higher average GDP growth of around 8 per cent per annum in the period, 2004-05 to 2011-12.

The generation of fewer employment opportunities in the post-reforms period knocks out the argument advanced by pro-reforms economists that higher economic growth by itself will generate enough employment opportunities. The dismal performance in respect of employment growth is due to three factors. First, capital-intensive technologies have been used in the organised sector which have tended to displace labour rather than absorbing it in productive employment. Secondly, no attention has been paid to the implementation of land reforms and improvement of the credit delivery system in agriculture. Thirdly, investment in agriculture, especially in irrigation, has been neglected.

The contention of the Indian Planning Commission and many economists that economic growth generates sufficient employment opportunities has further proved to be wrong by special employment and unemployment survey carried out by NSSO in 2011-12. This survey shows dramatic drip in employment generation. According to it, on the basis of *usual principal and subsidiary status* the proportion of population gainfully employed declined in 2011-12 compared to 2009-10. In 2009-10, 36.5 per cent of population was gainfully employed for the better part of the year. By 2011-12, the proportion of population employed declined to 35.4 per cent. Accordingly, *unemployment rate as per usual principal and subsidiary status went up from 2.5 per cent to 2.7 per cent*. Further, the survey reveals that the share of employed men remained roughly constant between 2009 and 2011, women's employment dropped from 18 per cent to 16 per cent. This may appear a small decline but translated into real numbers, the crisis in employment is starkly revealed. In rural areas about 90 lakh women lost their jobs in the two years period. This would have been catastrophic but for the fact that in urban areas about 35 lakh new women got jobs in these two years.

However, unemployment rate on the daily status basis fell from 6.6 per cent in 2009-10 to 5.6 per cent in 2011-12. This is due to a large number of mandays of employment created under Mahatma Gandhi National Rural Unemployment Guarantee Scheme (MGNREGS) which was implemented on a large scale in these two years. It is now a common knowledge that employment created in this scheme is of very low quality and does not create any durable assets. Thus, fall in daily status unemployment rate does not show creation of productive employment. It is important to note that dismal performance of employment generation in these years 2009-10, 2010-11 and 2011-12 has been despite a relatively higher GDP growth; 8.6 per cent in 2009-10, 9.3 per cent in 2010-11 and 6.2 per cent in 2011-12.

It is worth mentioning that this higher growth in employment has been registered in the unorganised and informal sector where productivity of labour is quite low. As seen from Table 55.3 the growth of employment in the organised sector has been negligible (0.05 per cent) per annum in the post-reforms period (1994-2008).

The low growth of employment was expected. As mentioned above, the chief drawback of New Economic Policy has been that it involves the use of labour-saving modern technology, the competition from the imported products to be faced by the domestic industries, and public sector disinvestment on a large scale. The use of capital-intensive technology not only displaces labour already employed but also lowers the growth of employment from the new investment and capital accumulation. Besides, due to the greater role assigned to the private sector, big business houses, foreign capital (MNCs) the already existing inequalities will further increase. This is against the objective of social justice which has been the cherished goal of the Indian planning.

4 GOI, *Economic Survey* 2014-15, p 135.

Poverty Reduction and Economic Reforms

The impact of economic reforms on poverty in India is a highly controversial issue. The critics point out that the economic reforms aimed at liberalisation, privatisation and globalisation of the Indian economy has slowed down the reduction in poverty ratio (*i.e.*, the percentage of population living below the poverty line) despite a higher rate of economic growth achieved in the post-reform period. On the basis of uniform recall period (that is, 30 days recall period for all items included in the consumption basket for estimating poverty ratio), the poverty at all India level fell from 36 per cent in 1993-94 to 27.8 per cent in 2004-05, that is, about 0.79 per cent per annum fall in the poverty ratio in this period. This is much lower than the fall in poverty ratio (on URP basis) which declined from 51.3 per cent in 1977-78 to 38.9 per cent in 1987-88, that is, about 1.24 per cent annual fall in poverty ratio in these 10 years of pre-reform period.

According to critics several factors are responsible for the existence of poverty in India despite over 60 years of planned development. First, there had been slow growth of productive employment opportunities relative to population growth resulting in increase in unemployment which on daily status basis, as mentioned above, rose from 6.1 per cent in 1993-94 to 7.3 per cent in 1999-2000 and further to 8.2 per cent in 2004-05. Secondly, due to liberalisation of cheap imports of capital goods abroad, the small and medium enterprises (SME) could not compete with them resulting in their closure and decrease in employment opportunities. Thirdly, in the post-reform period the rate of investment in agriculture has been significantly reduced. As a result, there has been a low rate of growth of employment in agriculture in the post-reform period. This caused a relative reduction in the supply of wage goods, especially foodgrains which increased the problem of hunger and malnutrition in various vulnerable sections of population in various parts of the country. It was expected that higher rate of growth will ensure greater reduction in poverty. However, this did not happen as benefits of economic growth have not trickled down to poor.

The debate on poverty flared up when the Planning Commission released the data on poverty estimates for the 66th round of NSS for the year 2009-10. These poverty estimates were based on the *new poverty line* norm suggested by an expert committee headed by late Prof. Suresh Tendulkar which submitted its report in 2009. The committee deviated from the calorie intake as norm for poverty estimates and included in their poverty line poverty indices for health and education. Thus contrary to popular belief, the poverty line was higher in Tendulkar committee approach. Therefore, to compare the estimates for 2009-10, poverty estimates were prepared afresh on the basis of new poverty line suggested by Tendulkar committee approach. The poverty line in 2009-10 was fixed at ₹ 4,298 per month for a family in urban areas and ₹ 3,364 per month for a family in rural areas. *According to estimates on the basis of new poverty line, the people living below the poverty line fell to 29.8% of its population in 2009-10 from 37.2% in 2004-05.* That is, poverty declined by 1.5 percentage points per annum between 2004-05 and 2009-10. It is the fastest decline in poverty compared to the earlier periods. The several economists and social scientists challenged the new poverty norm and the significant fall in the poverty ratio keeping in view that 2009-10 was one of the worst drought year. However, the Planning Commission attributed it to high rate of economic growth and government intervention by way of starting special anti-poverty schemes such as MGNREGA on a large scale during 2009-10. The critics also raised the question regarding whether a person can live or survive with the meagre amount of money expenditure fixed as poverty line norm by the Tendulkar committee. The criticism of poverty estimates was so severe that government appointed a new expert committee headed by C. Rangarajan to suggest appropriate methodology for fixing poverty line norm and prepare estimates of poverty in India on the basis of new norm.

However, to estimate poverty new special survey for the year 2011-12 was ordered on the basis of Tendulkar committee methodology because 2009-10 as the drought year poverty estimates for it did not present true picture about poverty. The result of this survey was released by the Planning Commission in June 2013. Adjusted for price change, *on the basis of Tendulkar committee methodology, poverty line for 2011-12 was fixed at ₹ 27.20 for rural areas and ₹ 33.40 for urban areas. On the basis of these poverty norms, Planning Commission estimated that poverty ratio for India declined from 37.2 per cent in 2004-05 to 21.9 per cent of population in 2011-12, a decline of 15.3% in just seven years*. This means poverty declined at the rate of 2.2 per cent a year between 2004-05 and 2011-12 compared to 0.74 per cent a year between 1993-94 and 2004-05. According to this the number of population declined from 400 million in 2004-05 to 270 million in 2011-12, that is, 137 million persons were lifted out of poverty. This was described as a big achievement of economic reforms carried out by UPA government and as a result higher economic growth of around 8 per cent was achieved during these years.

After both Congress and opposition leaders debunked expenditure of ₹ 27 per person per day for rural areas and ₹ 33 per person per day for urban areas as a benchmark, the government said the line had not been cast in stone. *"The poverty line is being reassessed. The Rangarajan committee is doing just that. In any case, the line is not linked to pro-poor programmes like rural job guarantee or food security"*.

The problem for the government lies in the perception that ₹ 27 and ₹ 33 seem embarrassingly low consumption limits, particularly in the context of persistent high inflation rates. The politically incorrect figures mean the government is unable to admit that incomes have risen and absolute or extreme poverty has declined. Wary of being seen as callous in an election year the government is set to revise the poverty line but in the process it will dent its claim that 137 million people were brought above the below poverty line since the UPA government took over. Upward revision of the poverty line will send millions of people back into poverty in terms of head-count ratio. This is not a comfortable prospect of any government.

Adverse Effects of Globalisation

Economic reforms undertaken since 1991 brought about globalisation of the Indian economy as under them the Indian economy was opened up. Trade liberalisation occurred following removal of quantitative restrictions on imports and large reduction in tariffs. Reforms also led to the free flow of foreign capital. This benefited India as its exports increased at a higher rate in the initial years and balance of payments on current account improved. Further foreign investment in India contributed to a higher growth rate achieved in the post-reform period. However, globalisation is not without dangers. These benefits of globalisation were proved to be only temporary.

Foreign Exchange Rate Volatility. The adverse effect of globalisation has been clearly seen in the two years, 2007 and 2008, and recently since May 2013. First, the free flow of portfolio capital has created a lot of volatility in exchange rate of rupee. Due to large capital inflows the value of rupee which was around ₹ 46 to a US dollar in end-March 2004, appreciated to ₹ 44.27 to a US dollar in end-March 2006 and further to ₹ 39.4 to a dollar in January 2008. However, most often due to capital outflows there has been depreciation of rupee. Recently, after May 2013, there has been a sharp depreciation of rupee which has been triggered by the announcement of governor of US Reserve System that it would start relaxing its ***Quantitative Easing*** (*QE*) Programme from September 2013 onwards due to the signs of revival of the US economy. As a result of this it was feared that current account deficit (CAD) would further widen and India's paying capacity will be adversely affected. This also contributed to the capital outflows by FIIs. First, they pulled out from debit market and then from equity market. As a result of these, rupee depreciated sharply, the value of rupee which was around ₹ 56 to a US dollar in the early June, 2013 first declined to ₹ 60 to a US dollar in the end of June 2003, and then to ₹ 61.21 to a US dollar on 8th July 2013 and then to ₹ 68.8 to a dollar on 28th August 2011.

Global Financial Crisis. However, when financial crisis in the US which was triggered by defaults of subprime-housing loans given by American banks and other financial institutions in the US deepened in 2008, creating liquidity crunch in the American economy, capital outflows started occurring from India. The flight of capital from India led to depreciation of Indian rupee. To meet liquidity requirements in their parent country, foreign financial institutions (FII) started selling shares of Indian corporate companies and got rupee receipts converted into US dollars which they repatriated to their parent country. These outflows of dollars led to the increase in demand for US dollars in the foreign exchange market which caused the depreciation of Indian rupee. The depreciation of rupee will make our imports, especially crude oil, costlier and can adversely affect our balance of payments. The higher prices of imported products, especially capital goods and metals, will tend to raise inflation rate in India.

From August 2011 there was again outflow of capital due to uncertainty caused by worsening of sovereign debt crises of European countries and slowdown of the US economy. The capital outflows led to a large depreciation of rupee from September 2011. The Indian rupee which was around ₹ 44 to a US dollar in August 2011 fell to nearly ₹ 52 to a US dollar on November 2011 and further to ₹ 53 to a US dollar in mid-December 2011. From January to March 2012 value of the Indian rupee remained within range of ₹ 51 to 52 to a US dollar.

The sharp depreciation of rupee is harmful for the Indian economy. To prevent excessive depreciation of the Indian rupee, the RBI uses its foreign exchange reserves to sell US dollars in the foreign exchange market. As a result, there is decline in foreign exchange reserves which are needed to cover imports of goods and services needed for industrial growth and to pay interest on the foreign debt every year. Further, lack of adequate foreign exchange reserves with the RBI leads to the loss of confidence of the foreign investors about the ability of the country to pay back the loans. Besides, weakening of the rupee is likely to cause losses to the foreign investors who repatriate their profits to their home countries. This discourages inflows of foreign direct investment needed for economic growth of the country.

It is thus evident that capital outflows and consequent depreciation of rupee causes a lot of macroeconomic instability in the economy. Therefore, RBI intervenes in the foreign exchange market to check the sharp depreciation of rupee through sale of US dollars in the foreign exchange market. Besides, it takes other measures to encourage capital flows into the Indian economy. It relaxed the norms for external commercial borrowing (ECB) so that the Indian companies directly borrow foreign money from abroad rather than through foreign exchange market. RBI also raised the interest rate cap on NRI deposits of foreign exchange in our banks. Further, it eased the conditions for foreign direct investment (FDI) to encourage more capital inflows through this route. These measures help in increasing capital inflows and prevent excessive depreciation of the rupee.

It is evident from above that globalisation with its free capital flows causes a lot of volatility in exchange rate which has adversely affected the Indian economy. Besides, volatility in exchange rate, financial crisis in the US affected our stock market and banking system. The financial crisis in the second half of 2007 following the defaults in sub-prime housing loans given by the American banks and other financial institutions resulted in the collapse of the banking system and crash in American stock markets. This caused liquidity crunch in America and affected credit flow in the economy. The effects of this financial crisis were not only confined to America but also spilled over to other countries not only of Europe but also of Asia (including India) as they were integrated with America. As a result of this world-wide financial crisis global meltdown occurred. Under pressure of redemption of securities of investment banks and other financial institutions, foreign institutional investors started selling shares in the Indian stock market and repatriating dollars to their parent countries. These outflows of dollars also led to the liquidity crunch in the Indian banking system which affected credit flow for investment in the Indian economy. The recessionary conditions in the United States and global meltdown caused by the financial crisis also adversely affected the growth of our exports. The lower exports and costlier imports affected our current account balance of payments.

Besides, the aggressive selling of shares by FIIs which held substantial stock in the Indian corporate companies resulted in crash in Dalal Street, Sensex of Bombay Stock Exchange which reached the peak of 20827 on January 11, 2,008 fell to 15,976 in May 2008, to 13,531 on September 15, 2008 and went below 10,000 mark on 17-10-2008. It reached a three year low of 8,000 in the last week of October 2008. This caused huge losses to the Indian investors and washed away the vast amount of their wealth. Even the share prices of banks (both of public and private sectors) registered a sharp decline. The negative wealth effect of the fall in the value of shares has affected the investment spending and demand of the investor class which adversely affect our industrial growth. Again since May 2013, the decision to unwind the *Quantitative Easing* (QE) by the US Federal Reserve System has triggered capital outflows from India resulting in sharp depreciation of rupee.

We have seen above that due to the globalisation of the Indian economy the bad effects of financial crisis originated in the United States have spilled over to the Indian economy.

Impact of Globalisation on Economic Growth

In the year 2008-09 global financial crisis affected the Indian economy as it reduced the growth of our exports and caused capital outflows from the Indian economy as due to uncertain global conditions capital flows went to the safe destination of government bonds of the US which is considered as quite safe investment. As a result of this, investment or gross domestic capital formation (GDCF) in India fell to 34.3 per cent of GDP bringing down the growth rate to 6.7 per cent in 2008-09. As a result of various fiscal and monetary stimulus measures by the government investment rate as per cent of GDP rose to 36.6 per cent in 2009-10 and 35.1 per cent in 2010-11 which caused higher GDP growth rate of 8.4 per cent in both these years. But in 2011-12, the global environment again changed. The deepening financial crisis in European countries, especially Greece and Spain, slow growth in the US and Japanese nuclear disaster resulted in a sharp global slowdown during 2011-12. As this happened quickly after the global recession of 2008-09 when the economies of the US and Europe had not yet fully recovered from the previous crisis, it was difficult to deal with Eurozone crisis. Much of the fiscal and monetary policies to revive and stimulate the earlier recession of 2008-09 had not yet been fully withdrawn that threat of new global meltdown had to be faced. Thanks to India's rapid growth over the last two decades and its increasing integration with the world it could no longer be impervious to global developments. Not surprisingly the Indian economy was adversely affected and its GDP growth fell to 6.5 per cent in 2011-12, the lowest in nine years since 2003. Further, even for the year 2012-13, RBI has forecast 6.5 per cent growth rate of GDP.

Besides adverse global environment, domestic factors also contributed to slowdown in economic growth in 2011-12 and 2012-13. The persistent inflation in the last three years required to control inflation by tightening monetary policy (*i.e.,* raising interest rate and checking excessive growth in liquidity in the banking system by the RBI) raised the borrowing costs of the private corporate sector which forced them to defer various investment projects. This resulted in lower *investment in fixed capital assets* and as a result as per cent of GDP it fell to 32.3 per cent in 2010-11 and further to 30 per cent in 2011-12. Further, policy paralysis caused by various scams and corruption charges on Ministers and top bureaucrats and hurdles put by various coalition partners of the government stalled the process of economic reforms.

Market Failures and Role of Government

The supporters of economic reforms who argued for diluting the role of public sector or government as it does not ensure efficiency in production laid great stress on '*Government failures*' in promoting economic growth. They however turned a blind eye to the *market failures*. To quote an eminent American economist, Dr. Joseph Stiglitz, who won Nobel Prize in economics in recent years, "*Market failures are a fact of life, as are government failures. New liberal ideologies assume perfect markets, perfect information, and a host of other things which even the best performing market economies cannot satisfy.*" He therefore forcefully argues for a *balanced approach to government* and *markets recognising* that both are important and complementary. This means both public sector and private sector should play complementary roles in bringing about economic growth. Due to market failures we cannot rely on private sector alone to bring about sustained economic growth and adequate expansion in employment opportunities.

We are not arguing here that we should go back to '*licence-permit Raj*". What we are stating is that (1) markets need to be regulated effectively by the government if the objective of growth with equity is to be realised. Stock market scam of 1992 prompted by Harshad Mehta and the recent stock market scam of 2001 engineered by Ketan Parikh and recent (2008) the Indian stock market crash triggered by financial crisis in the US caused by defaults of sub-prime housing loans there and collapse of the American banking system are shining examples of the absence of effective regulation of the market by the government which is playing havoc with the economy. Again UTI fiasco of July 2001 suspending the sale and repurchase of US 64 units has showed that activities of mutual funds be effectively regulated and not left to the free working of markets. The recent financial crisis in the US which has spilled over to the European and Asian countries (*including India) has clearly shown that free markets economy is not self-correcting*. It is due to the failure of market system to correct itself that even in the capitalist America President Bush had planned 700 billion dollars to bail out the US economy. The US government *announced buying of CDO securities and also equity shares of the banks and other financial institutions* to solve their liquidity problem. This implies a part ownership by the government of banks and other financial institutions. This means free market or capitalist system cannot be relied upon for smooth functioning of an economy and the government has to play an important role to avoid and overcome recession in the economy.

Further, apart from regulation of markets and private sector, what is needed in the context of the Indian economy is the *paramount role of government in stepping up public sector investment in infrastructure* if sustained rate of higher growth rate is to be achieved. Government role is also crucial for *adequate investment in social sectors such as education, healthcare and poverty alleviation programmes* which are generally neglected by the private sector. For the purpose of poverty alleviation, undertaking of rural public works to utilise not only accumulated food stocks but also to generate employment opportunities for the poor and unemployed is of paramount importance for which the government should increase its expenditure. For the purpose of investment in infrastructure and social sectors (education and healthcare) and expenditure on employment schemes for the poor it should not hesitate to incur fiscal deficit. In this way, if fiscal deficit increases, it should do so and does not follow unthinkingly IMF inspired policy of reducing fiscal deficit under all circumstances.

In our view reduction in fiscal deficit should not be elevated to a *dogma*. What is relevant is that government *should spend its borrowing for investment purposes*, especially infrastructure, and on development of human capital, education and healthcare. What is needed is that government should not borrow for consumption purposes. Prof. Amartya Sen rightly writes that *the success of liberalisation and closer integration with the world economy* may be severely impaired by India's backwardness in basic education, *elementary healthcare, gender inequality and limitations of land reforms*.[5] While Manmohan Singh did initiate the correction of governmental *over-activity* in some fields, the need to correct the governmental *under-activity* in other areas has not really been addressed. Further, referring to the higher growth rate in some East Asian countries which have received high growth rate with considerable equality, he writes, "These countries all share some conditions that are particularly favourable to widespread participation of the population in economic change. *The relevant features include high rates of literacy, a fair degree of female empowerment, and quite radical land reforms*. Can we expect in India results similar to those that the more socially egalitrian countries have achieved, given that half the Indian population (and two-thirds of the women) are still

5 Amartya Sen, "Theory and Practice of Development", in *India's Economic Reforms and Development, Essays for Manmohan Singh*, ed. by Isher Judge Ahluwalia and I.M.D. Little, Oxford University Press, 1998, p. 83.

illiterate, that female empowerment is very little achieved in most parts of India, that credit is very hard to secure by the rural poor, and that land reforms remain only partially and unevenly expected? Should we not have expected more in the direction of breaking the terrible neglect of these concerns, on which the basic capabilities of the Indian masses depend?"[6]

6 *Ibid*, p. 84.

PART X

Environment and Development

- Environment, Economy and Economic Development
- Environment Use and Degradation: The Problem of Market Failures
- Pollution Control
- Sustainable Development and Climate Change

CHAPTER

56

ENVIRONMENT, ECONOMY AND ECONOMIC DEVELOPMENT

In recent years there has been growing concern about degradation and pollution of environment and climate change as they impact on future development of both the developing and developed countries. In 1992, representatives of over 150 countries met at Rio in Brazil to discuss the environmental issues and their implications for future development of the world. This meeting at Rio is called the **'Earth summit'** or the **United Nations Conference on Environment and Development** (UNCED). This conference clearly spelled out the linkages between natural environment and development and put forward the concept of **"sustainable development".** This has produced greater awareness about environmental issues and facilitated the cooperation between different countries to reduce environmental degradation, particularly to reduce emission of greenhouse gases (GHG) such as carbon dioxide to prevent adverse climate change, that is, global warming in future which, if not prevented, will have disastrous consequences for the welfare and development of the population, both in developing and developed countries.

In recent years economists have increasingly become interested in environmental economics which is concerned with how economic activities of producers and consumers affect the environment in which we live and explain the policies to improve the quality of life of the present and future generation. Environmental issues are more important for developing countries where poverty prevails on a large scale and acceleration of economic growth is urgently needed.

The conflict between economic growth and environment is sharper today than ever before, particularly in developing countries like India with fast growing population and mass poverty. The developing countries are making strenuous efforts to balance their need for rapid economic growth with the environmental concerns for keeping their natural base intact. In India, as in other developing countries, the adoption of development strategy based primarily on large-scale industrialisation, energy-intensive technologies and biochemical-based agricultural technology, which ignored indigenous development paradigm based on locally self-sufficient technologies, has led to environmental degradation. In this chapter, we shall explain various environmental issues and the adverse impact of climate change and explain the need for sustainable development.

In a recent conference of State Environment Ministers held in August 2009, Prime Minister Manmohan Singh said that the ecological crisis that confronts the country has led to **'alarming situation'.** He urged upon the State governments to control environment pollution, clean rivers and fight climate change. This statement highlights the fact that India's growth is increasingly taking place at the cost of its environment. This shows that we have not been taking adequate measures to ensure sustainable development. To stop further decline in our natural resources and protect environment from pollution stringent regulations and incentives are needed. But, as the PM has said, due to rampant corruption prevailing in the bureaucracy the rules regarding the use of our natural resources and protection of environment have been flouted with impunity. There are numerous instances when the Ministry of Environment and Forests has flouted all norms to give clearance to dubious projects at the cost of environment and communities that depend on it.

Economy-Environment Linkages (Relations)

Modern economics is not only concerned with financial matters but also with several unpriced services and resources which natural environment provides us. In environmental economics how economic activity and policy affect the environment in which we live and also how environment supports economic activities. It is of great importance to explain how the economy and environment are interlinked. The environment supports economic activity by man in four ways: it provides life support, supplies natural resources for production and consumption, absorbs waste products and supplies amenity services. The economy works from *inside the environmental system* and its activities affect the environment and the latter also affects the economy. The economy is a system consisting of producing firms, consumers and the market system where interaction between the producers and consumers takes place. The purpose of economy is to produce goods and services to satisfy consumer wants. For the production of goods and services, the economy uses made-made capital, labour and natural resources (such as coal, oil (petroleum and diesel), CNG gas), minerals and metals, etc from environment. There are two types of resources–renewable and non-renewable. *The renewable resources such as forests and fisheries are those whose quantity can be increased when they are depleted.* For example, when, there is deforestation by cutting trees, new trees can be planted to make up the deficiency. Similarly, new fisheries can be developed. On the other hand, the *non-renewable resources are those whose exhausion as a result of their use cannot be made up.* Coal, iron ore, crude oil are examples of non-renewable resources as they cannot be produced by man. They are also called exhaustible resources.

It may be noted that resource inputs are transformed by the economy into outputs. For example, wood through a production process is converted into paper and crude oil is refined to produce petrol.

How the economy is related to the environment is depicted in. Fig. 56.1. The environment in Fig. 56.1 is represented by the whole big circle. Note that the environment means all natural resources such as land, ecosystem (*i.e.,* flora and fauna), all mineral and metal deposits under the land surface, world's oceans and atmosphere and natural climate. The economy is shown inside the environment system in which it works. As mentioned above, in the economy the firms produce goods and services

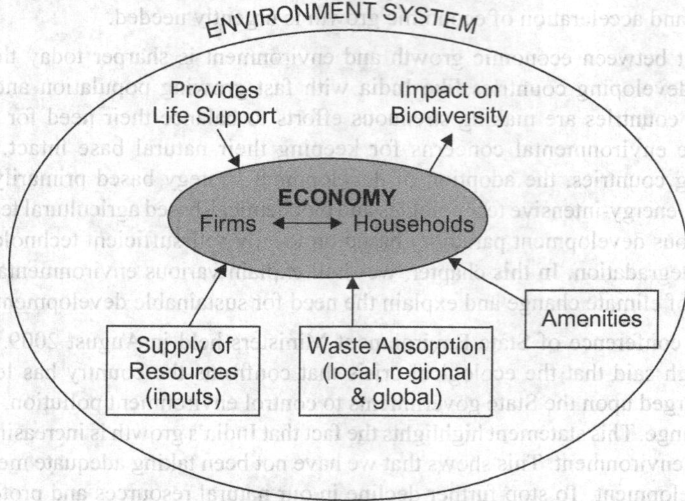

Fig. 56.1. *Economy–environment linkages or relations*

with the use of natural resources, man-made capital and labour to satisfy the consumption wants of the households. There are many relations between the environment and the economy. First, by providing a *biological, chemical and physical system* that makes it possible for human beings to live. The environment system that includes the air and atmosphere, rivers, the fertility of the soil and biodiversity (*i.e.,* various types of plant and animal life) on which life of households depends. They are essential and necessary for their existence. If there is any large reduction in these conditions provided by the environment system, there will be highly devastating effect on human life. This life-support function of the environment system is shown by the arrow towards the economy in the upper part of Fig. 56.1.

Second, the environment provides raw materials and energy resources such as minerals, metals, food, wood and cotton for production and use by the firms and households in the economy,. As mentioned above these natural resources may be renewable or non-renewable. Some non-renewable resources must be preserved for future generations and in this regard efforts should be made to find their man-made substitutes. For example, to save coal, solar energy can be used.

Besides, even renewable resources can be used in a sustainable manner. For example, to ensure deforestation should not result in desertification, new trees be planted to make up the loss of trees. The use of renewable resources is shown in Fig. 56.1. by the opposite *flow of resources from the economy to the environment*. As regards non-renewable resources such as coal and crude oil, their use causes permanent reduction in their stock.

Third important function of the environment is to *absorb the waste products* such as carbon dioxide (CO_2) which originate from the production processes of the firms, from power plants or the consumption activities of the households which generate garbage for collection and disposal. Thus, the environment is used as a **waste sink**. Wastes may be in a variety of basic forms such as solid, air and water-borne. It is important to note that environment has a limited assimilative capacity to absorb these wastes or to dispose of them safely, that is, to transform them into some harmless substances. For example, carbon dioxide gas which is responsible for global warming is captured through growth of forests and a part is absorbed by oceans. Deforestation on a large scale and limited ability of oceans to absorb the carbon dioxide have caused the increase in global warming. In this context, it is worth mentioning that the global warming in the Indian Ocean has disturbed the weather system in the Indian sub-continent and weakened monsoon in India on which a majority of farmers depend for their livelihood, Consequently, it has been suggested that to prevent the rise in global warming carbon dioxide emissions have to be reduced and alternative means of capturing these CO_2 emission have to be followed. Besides, we need to take measures *to adapt to climate change*. Fourth, the environment provides the people with direct source of *amenity* services such as *natural scenic beauty* which give pleasure and happiness to them. The beauty of Kashmir Valley and of parts of Kerala of India are a source of greater happiness and therefore attract a large number of tourists. These amenity services, though *they are not essential for the existence of life,* are a source of enjoyment, a sort of luxury for the people.

It may be noted that different parts of the environment system may perform more than one function. For example, "the oceans are important in determining the life-support system provided by the global and microclimates; they are sources of many minerals and other resources; they assimilate many different wastes and they provide the space and opportunity for marine pastimes"[1]. Further, the functions of environment may be competitive or complementary. For example, the excessive deposit of wastes in the oceans will reduce their capacity to provide habitat for fish stock. Environment functions may be complementary as the forestry policy of planting more trees can ensure sustainable way of reducing soil erosion (promoting a life support function), a source of timber (a function of natural resource supply) and absorbing carbon dioxide from the atmosphere (*i.e.,* a waste absorbtion function).

1 A.P. Thirlwall, *Economic Development,* Palgrave, Macmillan, Ninth Edition, 2011, p. 354.

From our above analysis, it is evident that the economy has important relations with the environment.

Economic development, especially industrialisation, is associated with the *increase in consumption* of energy which in the modern times is mostly derived from fossil fuels (petrol, diesel, coal). Before the modern industrial era, we used biomass for cooking and space heating and other economic activities were performed using muscle power of human labour and that of animals reared and domesticated by man for carrying out the various productive activities. But the industrialisation along with rapid growth of population has necessitated the greater increase in consumption of energy which could no longer be adequately supplied by human and animal muscle power. As a result, to produce goods and and services to meet the increasing consumption for them required the use of energy to be derived from fossil fuels. It is worth noting that even electricity is generated with the use of coal in thermal power plants or water in the hydel projects.

It is the energy derived from fossil fuels in the industrial development that creates external diseconomies in the form of *pollution* of air and water and involves the *use of natural resources* such as forests, minerals and water. Thus rapid industrialisation in developed countries has resulted in the emission of large-scale carbon dioxide and other green house gases which has adversely affected our environment and created global warming with the disastrous consequences for the future generation. Mr. Rajendra K. Pachauri who with his team of environmentalists got Nobel Prize writes, *"Modern technology and innovation have alleviated the drudgery and distress that humans faced in the past....* But in this melee of rapid growth and development, fuelled by increasing consumption of modern fuels, *we have also imposed negative externalities on our global commons, particularly on the earth's atmosphere which has now almost 400 parts per million of carbon dioxide as opposed to 280 million parts in the pre-industrial period."*[2]

Further, a key aspect of our economic development in the past is marked by total indifference to the use of key natural resources of the earth. This has led to unsustainable and inefficient increase in the growth of output of goods and services to meet the basic increases in consumption of the present generation at the cost of future generations. If this process of increases in consumption and growth continues, this will end in full exploitation of fossil fuels, the main source of energy today. When this happens the process of economic development will cease and the economies will reach stagnation. Therefore, *there is paramount need for use of renewable energy such as solar energy.* To quote Mr. Pachauri again' "the natural wealth of the planet and ability to use it for welfare is directly the gift of the sun, a reality that most of us seldom reflect on. We are living in a world where people believe that age of fossil fuels must inevitably come to a close and the future undeniably lies in the widespread use of renewable forms of energy"[3].

In this context it is important to mention the theme of Rio-12 Earth Summit held in June 2012 at Rio which was to suggest measures to achieve the objective of green economy. *"A green economy is the one that results in improved human well-being and social equity while significantly reducing environmental risks and ecological scarcities. Growth in a it green economy is driven by investments that reduce pressures on the environment and the services it provides us while enhancing the energy and resource efficiency."*[4]

While developed countries which experienced unprecedented growth in the last more than a century there are several developing countries where a lot of population live in poverty and misery. It is the developed countries which have contributed most to the present level of environmental pollution and global warming. Therefore, they ought to help the poor developing countries with adequate funds and needed technology transfer and achieve sustainable development.

---

2 Rajendra K. Pachauri, "Let Us Connect with Nature's Marvels," *Times of India* (Sunday Issue), June 15, 2013.

3 Rajendra K. Pachauri, *op. cit.*

4 Janez Potocnik, "Prosperity for Many or Misery for All", in *Economic Times*, 21 June, 2012.

SOURCES OF POLLUTION AND ENVIRONMENT DEGRADATION

We now explain below the various sources of pollution and environment degradation. They must be checked if the objective of sustainable development has to be achieved.

Industrialisation, Urbanisation and Environment

Industrialisation of the economy and urban development go together. In the post-Independence period, especially since the beginning of the Second Five Year Plan (1956–61) high priority has been accorded to industrialisation to achieve the goals of rapid growth of output and employment. New industrial factories and plants have been set up in the towns and cities or near to them. This industrialisation and urban development may bring about rise in material levels of living but they also cause environmental degradation, especially the pollution of air and water and creation of hazardous wastes. Across the world in both the developed and developing countries air and water pollution are being considered as a matter of serious concern as they not only cause harm to the health of the present population but endanger future generation also by causing global warming with disastrous consequences.

It is worth mentioning that urbanisation, that is, the growth of the urban population has been increasing at a faster rate than industrial growth causing not only air and water pollution but also putting increased stress on the existing water supplies and sanitation facilities which create health hazards for the urban population. The governments of developing countries are generally unable to cope with the vastly increased needs for clean water and sanitation facilities resulting from rapid growth of urban population. Urban population has been increasing not only at the rate of natural population growth but also through rural-urban migration induced by industrialisation. Thus the lack of clean water and sanitation has led to several diseases from which urban people suffer resulting in their poor health, Besides, due to poor housing facilities the growth of urban population has led to the growth of slums without clean water and hygienic conditions.

Let us understand the Indian urban scene as unfolded by the census 2001. Between 1991 and 2001, the number of towns and cities increased from 3,696 to 4,368. The total urban population in India rose to 285 million in 2001. Of this 108 million, that is, nearly 40 per cent, lived in 35 cities with a population of one million or more each. Such a large increase in urban population has led to the growth of slums with acute scarcity of clean drinking water and poor sanitation facilities. Apart from growth of slums, industrialisations and urbanisation has led to the problems of air and water pollution and piles of hazardous wastes which we discuss below in some detail. Though these problems exist both in the developed and developing countries but they are often more serious and acute in developing countries. It is worth mentioning that it is consumption of energy from fossil fuels such as petroleum, coal and gas in various urban activities such as industrial production, vehicular traffic that is the basic source of pollution. In this early stage of industrialisation, as we find today in the case of developing countries, as the share of industry in domestic product increases, it results in energy consumption faster than the growth in national product. If a developing country gives a higher priority to basic heavy and chemical industries, as was the case in India in the second, third and fourth Five Year Plans, consumption of energy takes place at a higher rate resulting in higher degree of pollution.

Air Pollution and Urban Development. Two main urban activities, namely, industrial production and vehicular traffic are the principal man-made sources of air pollution as energy is consumed. Therefore, as more industrial growth takes place in developing countries, it results in more air pollution. Industries emit smoke containing carbon dioxide, carbon monoxide, methane gas in the atmosphere causing air pollution. This air pollution is quite harmful for human beings as it causes tuberculosis, asthma, and other respiratory diseases and, according to World Development Report 1992, causes 3 to 7 lakh premature deaths annually. Besides, respiratory diseases adversely affect health of the people and reduce their productivity and working capacity. The people have to spend a lot of money for treatment of the ill-effects of toxic emissions by the factories which represents social cost which is ignored by the private entrepreneurs in their cost-profit accounting.

Since anti-pollution regulations are quite weak in developing countries, the emission of toxic gases and pollution of water have been increasing enormously resulting from increased energy consumption in the industrial sector.

Vehicular Traffic and Environment. Besides industrial production, toxic gases are also emitted from vehicles plying in the urban areas. Motor vehicles cause both air and noise pollution. Motor vehicles such as cars, buses, trucks, scooters and bikes emit pollutants such as carbon monoxide, hydrocarbon and nitrogen oxide which cause immense damage to the health of the human beings. At present (2009) more than 1.5 million registered motor vehicles are there in Delhi alone and about 150,000 are being added every year. These emit around 1000 tonnes of toxic gases into Delhi's atmosphere every day. In other metropolitan cities, Mumbai, Kolkata, Chennai, Bangalore air pollution due to vehicular transport is also enormous.

In recent years under pressure of High Courts and Supreme Court which have delivered judgements for improvement of environment some success has been achieved towards the use of lead-free fuels, better emission standards for cars and buses plying in the city roads. As a result, new models of cars with more fuel efficiency and lower emission levels have come in the market. In Delhi DTC buses and three-wheelers have been using less toxic CNG gas instead of diesel and petrol. Similarly, government has taken some measures to reduce emission of **lead** by vehicular traffic. It has been found that dangerous level of lead in the blood of young children exposes them to the various health problems including neurological deficiencies. Elevated levels of lead in the atmosphere expose even adults to higher blood pressure, higher risk of heart attack and stroke.

Water Pollution and Urban Development. Water pollution is another major environment problem in urban areas. Water is contaminated mostly from wastes of expanding industries in the urban areas. In the towns and cities where industrial growth is taking place, rivers become polluted with toxic chemicals and heavy metals such as lead and mercury thrown into them by expanding industries and mining activities. The rivers like Ganga and Yamuna have become highly polluted over time. It is very difficult to remove pollutants from drinking water with standard purification facilities. Therefore, special measures and instruments are being used to clear rivers from pollutants. As a result, not only there is scarcity of safe drinking water for human beings, even the capacity of rivers to support aquatic life has decreased.

Not only surface water near towns and cities has been contaminated over the years but also ground water has been polluted through seepage of chemical wastes, heavy metals and other hazardous wastes created by industries and thrown into rivers and drains. Water pollution is a very serious problem in the urban areas, especially is cities like Delhi, Mumbai and Kolkata, especially for the urban poor who live in slums with no proper facilities for clean drinking water and sanitation, It is mainly these urban poor who bear the direct impact of water-borne diseases which are responsible for a large number of deaths, especially of children. According to **World Development Report 1992,** in the year 1990 one billion people in developing countries had no access to clean water and 1.7 billion lacked access to proper sanitation. After two decades of development now in 2009 the number of population without access to clean water and proper sanitation must have increased substantially despite good rate of economic growth achieved during this period.

Rural and Agricultural Development and Environment

About 75 per cent of India's population live in rural areas. Agriculture is the main occupation of rural people. Population in India has been increasing at the rate of 1.90 per cent per annum. Adequate food production is needed to feed the teeming millions. In recent years there has been considerable debate about the need to ensure food security for the rising population Food security, as is now generally understood, refers not only to the adequate food production but also sufficient increase in purchasing power of the people for having access to the consumption of required food and animal products. An eminent agricultural scientist, Dr M.S. Swaminathan, writes, *"The future of food security depends on the conservation and care of arable land through attention on soil health and replenishment of fertility and the conservation and careful management of all water sources so that more crops can be produced. Improvement of production in perpetuity without associated social or ecological harm is vital to safeguard food security."*[5]

Land degradation is the chief environment problem in rural areas. **Land degradation occurs through soil erosion, salinisation of soil, and waterlogging.** The land degradation lowers agricultural production and adversely affects the fertility or productivity of the soil. Reduction in agricultural production and productivity threatens the livelihood of the rural people. To quote Dr Swaminathan aganin, "Land degradation, diversion of arable land and the depletion and pollution of water resources result in the loss of rural livelihood. This triggers unplanned migration of the rural poor to towns and cities resulting in the proliferation of urban slums."[6]

It is worth mentioning that degraded land belongs either to the poor farm households or it is common property which has been overused and overgrazed. To ensure food security and livelihood to the rural population land and water resources ought to be protected from degradation and pollution. Land degradation of various forms in the regions of both the irrigated agriculture and rain-fed agriculture is causing serious threats to sustainability of agricultural growth. A serous problem that affects the sustainability of rain-fed agriculture is the **top–soil erosion** which occurs as a result of rain water draining away the top soil of the land and thereby lowers its fertility. It has been estimated that 6 billion tons of soil in India are eroded from Indian crop land each year. The soil erosion adversely affects agricultural growth and achievement of food security.[7]

Though land degradation due to soil erosion is taking place gradually, farmers do not take effective measures to prevent or halt the process of soil erosion, Kerr and Sanghi[8] observe that the most important factor responsible for farmers not adopting the recommended practices to control soil erosion is **due to their perception** about soil erosion and other forms of land degradation It is therefore important that government should integrate the use of technologies for preventing land degradation with its programme and strategy of agricultural growth.

Deforestation: Another important factor causing land degradation is deforestation, that is, cutting of trees for fuel and timber. A good deal of deforestation has also been due to commercial logging. Forests are highly useful for protecting environment. Trees of forests during the process of photosynthesis absorb carbon dioxide from atmosphere and give out oxygen. Thus, deforestation reduces CO_2 in the atmosphere that prevents the increase in temperature of the earth surface. Therefore, deforestation (*i.e.*, cutting of trees) for fuel and timber and for extending cultivation for agricultural crops leads to the increase in CO_2 in the atmosphere which is responsible for global warming. Besides, deforestation causes floods waterlogging and soil erosion in the local areas and thereby leads to land degradation.

Overgrazing on Common Land. The other factor causing land degradation is **overgrazing on common land** and intensification of agriculture through use of excess irrigation water and chemicals such as fertilizers and pesticides. According to a global survey conducted by the UN. Environmental Programme, land degradation during five decades (1945-95) was of the order of 2 billion hectares of total cultivable land area of the world. Of this 80 per cent of degraded area was located in Asia, Africa and Latin America. According to this global survey, 30 per cent of land degradation was caused by deforestation ,7 per cent by over-exploitation for getting fodder and fuel, 35 per cent by overgrazing,

5 M.S. Swaminathan, 'Agriculture : Route to an Evergreen Revolution', in *Hindu Survey of Environment,* 2002 p. 34.

6 *Op. cit*, p. 35.

7 See V.V Naryana and Ram Babu, "Estimation of Soil Erosion in India' in *Journal of Irrigation and Drainage Engineering,* ASCE, 109(4), pp 419-33.

8 Kerr T.M. and V. Sanghi, "Indigenous Soil and Water Conservation in India's Semi-Arid Tropics," *Gatekeepers,* Series 34, 1992, International Institute of Environment and Development.

28 per cent by agricultural production activities and only 1 per cent by industrialisation. Though agricultural growth with the use of modern agricultural technology such as the use of excess irrigation water, chemical inputs has played a part in causing land degradation, the main factor responsible for land degradation is over-exploitation of natural resources by poverty-driven population.

Water Scarcity. Another important environmental problem facing India is the **decline in underground water resources.** A recent release **'State of the Environment Report'** says that the amount of water being used in India from underground sources is estimated to be 45 per cent more than what natural system can replenish. A National Aeronautics and Space Administration study released in August 2009 found that ground water levels in northern India–Punjab, Haryana and Rajasthan–are declining at an alarming rate as much as one foot per year over the last decade. Its reason is that water is being pumped and consumed by human activities, mainly for irrigation, faster than aquifiers can be replenished by natural processes. The problem of water shortage therefore poses a serious threat to the sustained agricultural growth. Therefore, it is necessary to ensure scientific delivery and usage of water for irrigation besides encouraging the development and use of drought-resistant seeds and change in cropping pattern where necessary. The use of **drip irrigation** should be encouraged as in this water is delivered in measured doses through slender pipes close to the plant, thereby avoiding waste from spillovers and is being used successfully in some countries where water is scarce. Besides, water-intensive crops like sugur cane and rice ought to be confined to the areas where these crops are grown traditionally because of availability of enough water.

India depends on ground water reserves for most of its agricultural and domestic water requirement. Hence there is increased stress on ground water reservoirs. Urban and rural **rain water harvesting** therefore should be explored fully. Check dams can be thought of as an alternative to mega dam projects to provide local water support. In our view the way to stop environment degradation in the rural areas is not to curb the use of modern green revolution technology for fear of its defects but efforts should be made to overcome its defects through undertaking new scientific research.

Lack of Clean Water and Sanitation Facilities. Another important environmental problem faced by rural population, especially the rural poor, arises due to lack of clean drinking water and sanitation. These greatly contribute to many water-borne diseases such as typhoid, cholera, amoebic infections, bacillary dysentery and diarrhea which account for 80 per cent of all diseases that prevail in developing countries and account for a large number of child deaths each year. Apart from responsible for deaths in rural areas these diseases lower the **health** of the people which in modern economic theory is considered as **human capital** and its deterioration in the rural areas lowers productivity and economic growth.

Similarly, air pollution in the rural areas which arises due to greater dependence on **biomass fuels** such as wood, straw, manure that is closely related to the poverty of the rural population impacts their health. About the harmful effects of air pollution due to greater dependence on biomass fuel, Todaro and Smith write, "The burning of biomass fuels for cooking and boiling of water creates dangerously high levels of indoor pollution to which 400 million to 700 million people, mostly women and children, are exposed each year. Smoke and fumes from indoor stoves are believed to contribute significantly to up to 4.3 million childhood deaths each year from respiratory diseases and to an ever-larger number of chronic respiratory illness."[9]

Population and Environment

Concerns over environment issues arise because it is thought that population may increase to a level whose needs cannot be met by earth's resources resulting in fall in the living standards of the people. This is because increasing population causes environmental degradation. Increases in population causes over-exploitation of natural resources such as forests, water, fisheries and minerals at a rate far greater than their capacity to regenerate. Besides, population pressure on land compels us to cultivate arable land more intensively by using chemical inputs such as fertilizers, pesticides which

9 Todaro and Smith, *op.cit*, 10th Edition, 2012, p. 491.

cause soil degradation. Further, increase in population through its effect on deforestation by the rural and urban population for timber and fuel leads to the increase in carbon dioxide in the atmosphere and therefore causes air pollution. Thus *the population impacts on environment primarily through the use and depletion of natural resources and is associated with environmental problems such as air and water pollution and loss of biodiversity and increased pressure on arable land.* As an example of estimate of loss, Tata Energy Research Institute (TERI) estimates that economic losses due to soil degradation, diseases caused by pollution and forest degradation is between ₹. 1,00,000 and 4,50,000 crore every year and this does not include a series of other losses due to ecological destruction.[10]

As explained above, population is linked with environment in three main ways: (1) space for living, (2) a stock of supply of resources such as food, energy, water and minerals and (3) as a sink for absorption of wastes. Traditional debate on population and environment had focused on the use of environment as a resource supply. Neomalthusians led by Club of Rome predicted that continued growth of population and consumption by them would exhaust natural resources and reduce per capita food availability resulting in disastrous consequences for mankind. However, critics pointed out that human beings are quite inventive and therefore will find new technologies to increase the productivity of resources to prevent the catastrophic consequences. The immediate link of increasing population is its effect on the supporting capacity of land. The present emphasis on '*population dividend*' ignores that further increases in India's population will adversely affect population-supporting capacity of land. So far we have through the use of new HYV seeds and fertilizers (*i.e.,* inputs of green revolution) have succeeded in preventing the fall in population-supporting capacity the Indian land. It is worth while to note that as productivity on irrigated land is much higher than on non-irrigated land (that is, irrigation is land augmenting), the expansion in irrigation will greatly help in population-supporting capacity of land.

Per capita availability of land in India has been declining over the years due to the increase in population without corresponding increase in the land area. Similarly, per capita availability of forest in India has also been falling due to the growth in population; it declined from a level of 0.113 hectares per capita in 1950 to 0.078 hectares per capita in 1992-93 and this process of reduction in per capita forest has been going on. As mentioned above, due to increase in production of some crops such as wheat and rice witnessed in the green revolution it has been possible to increase the total food gains availability. However, productivity of crops cannot keep on increasing indefinitely. Therefore, it is imperative that steps should be taken to control the further increase in population.

The rapid population is an important factor responsible for poverty in developing countries such as India. Even after 68 years of independence, about 30 per cent of the Indian population (269 million people) lived below poverty line in 2011-12 (Tendulkar Committee estimates). What is required not only to eliminate poverty by meeting the basic needs of the poor but this should occur as a result of *sustainable development* so that the level of living of the future generations is taken care of and environment degradation is prevented. A world in which poverty is endemic will always be prone to the ecological and other catastrophes.

It is worthwhile to note that tribals and village women are most affected by environment destruction. In villages in India every morning we see the poor rural women travel a long distance to collect fuel, fodder and water. Collecting fuel and water carrying are extremely strenuous activity undertaken by the poor village women and consuming a lot of their time, particularly in the hilly areas and in the arid and semi-arid parts of the country.

Population increases cause over-exploitation of land and water resources and loss of biodiversity and forests and therefore will endanger sustainability of agriculture and food security in the country.

---

10 Quoted by Ashish Kothari, "Unsustainable Development, Unfulfilled Promises" in "Survey of Environment," *The Hindu,* 2002.

According to Prof M.S. Swaminathan, a noted agriculture scientist, "*The capacity to support even the existing human and animal population has been exceeded in many parts of the world*"[11] and if population growth is not checked, it will endanger the attainment of food security. He further adds, "In the recent years there has been considerable concern about human capacity to produce adequate food to meet the needs of the growing population and the increase in purchasing power resulting in higher consumption of animal products."[12]

It is manifest from above that rapidly increasing population in developing countries will lead to the over-exploitation and degradation of land and depletion of fisheries which will threaten the achievement of food security in the developing countries.

Besides, the growth of urban population in the absence of adequate infrastructure facilities has caused the **lack of clean water to drink** and given rise to **slums with poor sanitation** which has increased the vulnerability of the people to several diseases. It follows from above that to meet the expanding needs of the developing countries, environment degradation must be halted. For that purpose, reduction in population growth will greatly help in easing the intensification of many environmental problems.

Poverty and Environment

Poverty in developing countries is also said to be responsible for environmental degradation. Poor people rely on natural resources more than the rich. For survival the rural poor are forced to cut forests for timber and fuel as well as graze animals on pasture lands more than the reproductive capacity of these natural resources. Besides, when the cultivable land becomes short relative to population, the poor are forced to make their subsistence by cultivating fragile land on hills and mountains resulting in soil erosion on a large scale. It is in such environment that poverty becomes a vicious circle. Poverty leads to land degradation and land degradation accelerates the process of impoverishment because the poor people depend directly on exploitation of natural resources on which property rights are not properly assigned. Moreover, poverty results in malnutrition and reduces poor people's capacity to do work. Thus poverty is both a cause and effect of environment degradation.

With growing population the poor encroach upon large remote areas of forests and grasslands for their livelihood. If there are strict regulations to prevent such encroachment, it is opposed with stiff resistance by the poor, especially in tribal areas.

The solution to the poverty problem of these teeming millions lies in land reforms, generation of more employment opportunities and improvement in productivity of arable land already in use, for example, shifting the poor from poor resource-based to modern science-based agriculture. This is what has been sought to be achieved through green revolution technology.

However, the green revolution has been criticised for environmental reasons, especially the use of fertilizers and pesticides that increase soil salinity. Besides, ample use of irrigation in green revolution technology without adequate drainage facilitiess results in soil degradation through salinity and waterlogging. Adequate and appropriate steps should be taken to make the green revolution technology clean and environment-friendly. There can be no two opinions that major efforts must be made to overcome these defects through development of **less poisonous chemicals,** pest and insect control with reduced chemical application and improved drainage facilities. However, if the efforts to develop modern technology were abandoned because of these defects, employment and income-earning opportunities for marginal farmers and agricultural labourer would continue to be reduced under population pressure. As a result, many would be forced to push cultivation frontiers into ecologically fragile lands resulting in increased incidence of food and soil erosion[13].

---

11 M.S. Swaminathan, "Agriculture : Route to an Evergreen Revolution" in the "Survey of Environment. *2002,*" *The Hindu.*, p. 34.

12 *Ibid*, p. 33.

13 Yujiro Hayami and Yoshihisa Godo, *Development Economics*. Oxford University Press, 3rd ed, 2005, p. 227.

Chapter 57

Environment Use and Degradation: The Problem of Market Failures

Neoclassical economists think that the market system works efficiently in the allocation of resources and thus achieves maximum social welfare. However, in regard to the use of environmental resources, market system does not function efficiently and this requires intervention by the government to correct market failures and ensure efficient use of environmental resources of the society. Markets fail when private individuals working in unregulated market economy fail to achieve efficiency in the use and allocation of resources. It is worth mentioning that *market failures occur when there are no definite property rights over resources or goods by the private individuals or firms*. In the absence of well-defined property rights over the environmental resources free market cannot work to achieve efficient allocation of resources. Market failures occur in case of the existence of *externalities*, in which case the productive activity by an individual affects *other individuals* whose welfare is not considered by the individuals while doing the productive activity. In case of *public goods* also market fails to achieve efficiency. A *public good is that from which all get benefits but no one can be excluded from enjoying benefits from it if he does not pay for it*. Thus "market failure comes about when people cannot define property rights clearly. Markets fail when we cannot transfer rights freely, we cannot exclude others from using the good. Under these conditions, free market does not lead to socially desirable outcome. We either produce too much of bad good like pollution or too few of goods things like open space. Since everyone 'owns' the right to clean air and good climate and biodiversity, nobody owns the right and therefore it is impossible for a market to exist so that people can trade freely".[1]

There are four types of market failure: externalities, public goods, asymmetric information between sellers and buyers of goods or services and common property. We explain these below in some detail.

EXTERNALITIES

Externalities is the most important case of market failure and one most directly relevant to the use of environmental resources. Externalities refer to the beneficial and detrimental effects of the economic activity of an agent (a firm or a consumer or industry) on others. To be more precise, when an economic agent through his activity benefits others for which he does not receive any payment, there exist beneficial or positive externalities. On the other hand, detrimental or negative *externalities occur* when the activity of an economic agent harms others for which it is not required to pay. It is

1 Nick Hanley, Jason F. Shogren and Ben. White, *Introduction to Environmental Economics*, Oxford University Press, 2001, p. 16.

important, to note that when there are individual property rights over goods, services and factors of production, the markets function efficiently (that is, allocate resources optimally). This is because when there is a complete set of individual property rights, the market exercises control over their activities to ensure optimum consumption and production of goods or services or use of a factor as they require payment to be made to the owner. However, when externalities occur and there are no individual property rights on goods, services or factors, market will not ensure optimum or socially desirable output due to the non-payment for the benefits or harms created for others. In case of positive externalities less will be produced and in case of negative (*i.e.*, detrimental) externalities more of a good is produced than is socially desirable.

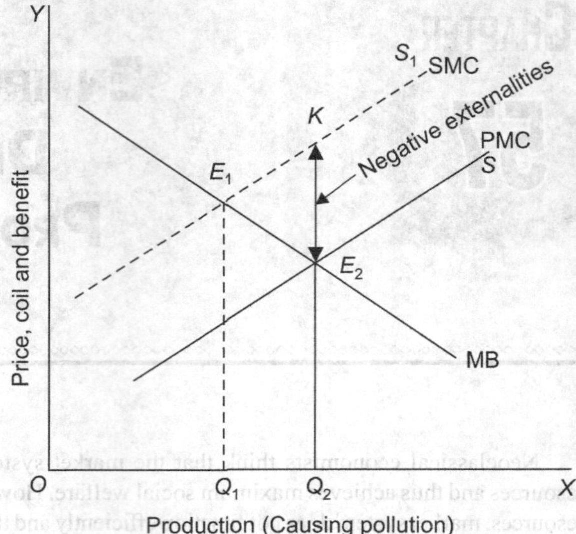

Fig. 57.1. *In the presence negative externalities more output is produced than is socially desirable*

Let us give an example of how negative externalities lead to more than socially desirable output. The chief example the negative externalities occurs in case of electricity producing firm which pollutes air which harm others but they are not paid for this by] the firm. Note that *no one has individual property rights over the air* which is provided by the environment. Therefore, the firm can extend its production to the level which maximises its profits or benefits for the industry: In the case of a firm, which pollutes air and does not pay those who suffer as a result of pollution, *marginal private cost (MPC)* will be smaller than the *social marginal cost (SMC)* as the latter will also include negative externalities of pollution. How, in this case, more of output of good will be produced than is socially desirable? This is illustrated in Fig. 57.1 where MB is marginal benefit curve of the firm whose production pollutes the air and is sloping downward. This is because this marginal benefit curve depends on the demand curve of the product of the firm. As the firm produces and sells more of its product, *its price falls.* This price is the benefit for the firm. Therefore, as it produces more, its marginal benefit (MB) declines. On the other hand, as more is produced by the firm its private marginal cost (PMC) will rise in accordance with the principle of diminishing returns of traditional microeconomic theory, and rising private marginal cost (PMC) of the firm will cause the private marginal cost curve of the firm to slope upward as shown in Fig. 57.1 by PMC. As explained above, *the firm does not take into account the harms done to others* especially those living in the surrounding areas of air pollution generated by it. The question is how it is allowed to pollute the air to extend its production to the level beyond what is socially desirable? This is because, as mentioned above, no one has the ownership rights over the air which is supplied by the environment (*i.e.*, air is environmental good). It will be seen from Fig. 57.1 that considering only its private marginal cost the firm will equate private marginal cost (PMC) with its marginal benefit (MB) and produce output OQ_2 to maximize its profits.

Now, if negative externalities represented by creation of air pollution, which inflicts costs on others, are taken the account, we will add to private marginal cost, these negative externalities to get *social marginal cost* (SMC) curve which lies above the *private marginal cost* (PMC) curve. The socially desirable output which represents optimum allocation of resources is equal to OQ_1 at which social marginal cost (SMC) equals marginal benefits (MB). Thus, by producing OQ_2 output, the firm in case of the existence of negative externalities produces more than what is socially optimum output level OQ_1.

Another important example of negative external economies is found in case of a firm discharging its toxic effluent into the water of a lake which is used by the fishermen to catch fishes to make their living. The toxic effluent in the lake kills many fishes which reduces the number of fishes captured by the fishermen and thus harms them. The harms done to the fishermen by the firm dumping its toxic product into lake do not enter into the calculations of the polluting firm. As no one has ownership right over water of lake, the firm produces more product than is socially desirable. In this case also *social marginal cost* (SMC) curve will be above the *private marginal cost* (PMC).

PUBLIC GOODS AND MARKET FAILURES

Market failure also arises in the supply of goods known as public goods. Public good is one from which everybody benefits from it even when he does not pay for it. There are two features of a public good. First, it *is non-rival in consumption*. Second, in case of a public good even those who have not paid for it, *cannot be excluded* from enjoying its consumption. A non-rival in consumption implies that consumption of a public good by one individual does not exclude its consumption by others. Public street lighting, television signals, parks, flood control project, pollution control project, lighthouse in the sea are some examples of public goods. Thus, when public street lighting is provided in a colony everyone living will benefit from it, even those who have not paid for it. Similarly, all persons of a city can benefit from the television signals and enjoy the programme telecast. The enjoyment provided by a park, if there is free access to it, can be obtained by all who visit it. Public street lighting, parks, television signals and such other goods are non-rival goods as their consumption by one individual does not exclude its consumption by others. That is, the consumption of a non-rival good by an individual does not reduce its amount available for others to consume.

Non-Excludiability

The other essential characteristic of a public good is non-excludiability in distribution of their consumption benefits. This non-exclusive nature of a public good implies that *it is difficult if not impossible to exclude those from consuming them* who are not willing to pay for them. In case of private rival goods such as shirts, cars, Pepsi Cola, apples those who do not pay for them can be easily prevented from consuming them or receiving benefits from them because the producer or seller simply does not provide them these goods, if they do not pay price for them. On the contrary, in case of public goods, either it is not possible or it is very costly to prevent those people from consuming them who do not pay for these goods. We will explain later that it is due to the feature of non-excludiability of public goods that accounts for the failure of market in case of these goods to ensure economic efficiency.

For example, national defence is a public good and is provided to all members of a society and its benefits are available to all equally irrespective of whether some people pay for it or not. It is difficult if not impossible to exclude those people from receiving benefits of security provided by national defence system who do not pay for it. Likewise, if a lighthouse is constructed in a sea, it provides light for all the ships whether any one of them pays for it or not and it is not possible to prevent those who do not pay from receiving light from the lighthouse. This inability to exclude those who do not pay from receiving benefits also applies in case of other public goods such as television signals, pollution control project to provide clear air, flood control projects, parks etc.

Free-Rider's Problem in Case of Public Goods and Market Failure

It is easy to show how non-excludiability of a public good can lead to the market failure, that is, failure of market to achieve pareto efficiency. As explained above, non-excludiability of public goods arises because producers are not able to prevent those from consuming these or enjoying benefits from these who do not pay their share of cost. There is a problem called a *free-rider's problem* which states that because people cannot be excluded from consuming public goods or enjoying benefits from them, there is incentive for persons in these situations to free ride and try to enjoy benefits from reduced pollution, parks, television signals, lighthouse without paying for them. These persons want to get something for nothing and rely on others to make payment for public goods whose benefits they will also automatically get.

Due to this free-rider problem or inability of the producers of public goods to prevent those who do not pay from receiving benefits from them, that a profit-maximising firm will either not produce a public good or produce too little of it. This creates economic inefficiency or Pareto non-optimality. Let us take an example of this free-rider's problem in case of public goods leading to economic inefficiency. Suppose the construction of a dam to check floods which cause a lot of damage in a city is required. This dam when built will protect equally all people of the city from the damages due to floods. However, some people of the city would not like to pay for the dam with the hope that others would pay for it and they because of non-excludiability would also enjoy its benefits. But in view of this incentive to free ride, adequate revenue to cover costs of building the dam cannot be provided, and therefore, no private entrepreneur would consider it worthwhile to construct the dam to control floods. Similarly, the production of other public goods such as lighthouse, television signals, pollution abatement projects would not be extended to the socially desirable level in view of the non-excludiability and incentive to free ride.

COMMON PROPERTY RESOURCES

Common property resources are the resources to which everyone has *free access*, that is, anyone can use the property without making any payment. Parks, rivers, ocean, fisheries, public roads and highways are examples of common property resources. For example, anyone can have a free entry into the India Gate parks in Delhi and enjoy there. However, *each person's use of common property reduces its value to others and thus creates* ***negative externality***. We explain this below.

Since people do not have to pay for the use of common property resources, they tend to be overused or overexploited. For example, parks with free entry often become overcrowded which results in lowering of enjoyment of parks by everybody. Further, the use of rivers, Ganga and Yamuna, in India is quite free and have become so much polluted because factories dump their waste products into them without paying any cost. Even people in general throw all sorts of their wastes (even dead bodies, and their remains) into these rivers. Similarly, costless use of public common land for grazing of cattle, or hunting results in overuse of these common property resources. **This *overuse* of common property resources where there is free access to them is often referred to as the tragedy of commons.** This is also called the *common problem*.

An important common property resource is fisheries in which no fee is charged for catching fishes from them. Each fisherman wants to catch fish before others do the fishing. *This results in overfishing which may ultimately* lead to the destruction of stock of fish in the fisheries for use in future years.

It is worth noting that ***lack of property rights over the common resources*** *leads to their overuse. Fishermen when they have costless access to the use of common property resources have incentive to catch more fish than they would if the fisheries were private property, whose owner would charge fee or price for catching fishes by fishermen.* Suppose now each fishery has been given exclusive private property right to a lake where fishes are caught by fishermen. Now, since there exist well-defined property rights, there are no externalities. Therefore, each owner of lake would not allow overfishing in any year so as to maintain the stock (*i.e.*, the number) of fish for the future years.

On the other hand, most *ocean fisheries* are common property to which fishermen have free access. As in case of private manufacturers who create external diseconomy by polluting air or water, fishermen operating in ocean fisheries take into account only their *private costs*. Thus in calculating their costs they include in them the cost of boats, other complementary equipment, a crew etc. *They do not take into account the costs they impose on future generation as their fishing in the present leads to the decrease in the stock of fish in the ocean in the future years.* Thus Professor Perloff writes, "The fewer fish there are, the harder it is to catch any, so reducing the population of fish today raises the cost of catching fish in the future. As a result, fishers do not forego fishing now to leave fish for the future. *The social cost is the private cost plus the externality cost from reduced future population of fish*."[2] It may be emphasised again that it is the lack of clearly defined property rights of fisheries that leads to overfishing. Fishermen have an incentive to catch more fish than they would if the fishery was private property.

Roads and Highways. Let us take another case of common property resources: roads and highways. Everyone has access to them for driving their cars and other vehicles. Since owner of a car has no exclusive right to use the highway on which he drives, he cannot exclude others from driving on the same highway and must share it with others. This leads to the too many drivers using the highway for driving their vehicles which leads to congestion and often jams (*i.e.*, a negative externality). This slows down driving on the highway. Thus this is another example of overuse of the common property resource.

Diagrammatic Illustration of Overuse of Common Property Resources

Let us illustrate diagrammatically *how in case of common property resources, there is overuse of them which is often referred to as 'tragedy of commons'*. Let us take the case of a lake which is the common property of nearby town and this lake is used for fishing. Every fisherman has free (*i.e.*, costless) access to catch fishes from the lake and then sell it in the market. But by catching fish from the lake, fishermen reduce the population of fish in the lake and thereby raise the cost of catching fishes for others. That is, by catching fishes from the lake, fishermen create external diseconomy for other fishermen.

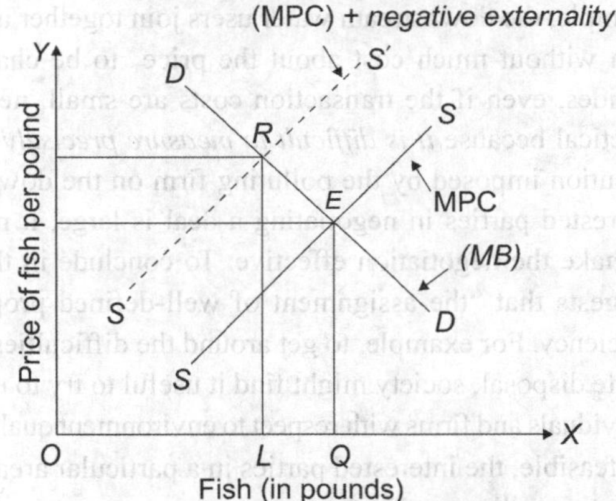

Fig. 57.2. *Overuse of common property resources*

In Fig. 57.2 we have drawn a demand curve *DD* for fish (in pounds) in the market which reflect consumer's marginal benefits (MB) from fish and *SS* is the market supply curve of fish based on marginal private cost (MPC) of fishermen. If there is free access to lake, the number of fish caught and supplied in the market is *OQ* pounds. Since fishermen do not take into account the negative externality they create, the fishermen's marginal private costs (therefore the supply curve *SS* based on them) will be less than the marginal social cost (MSC). Therefore, the supply curve *S′S′* representing the marginal social costs intersects the market demand curve (*i.e.*, marginal benefit curve) at point *R* and thus determine the *OL* quantity of fish caught and sold. (Note that the marginal social cost (MSC) equals marginal private cost (MPC) plus the negative externality created). Thus *OL* quantity of fish (in pounds) is the *socially optimum* output. But as fishermen do not take into account the external diseconomy or social marginal cost and operate on the basis of their marginal private cost (MPC), they catch more fish equal to *OQ* which thus *leads to the overuse of the fishery*. This is therefore called *tragedy of commons*.

---

2 Jeffrey M. Perloff, *Microeconomics*, Addison-Wesley, 1998, p. 679.

Assigning Property Rights for Common Property Resources: Coase Theorem

We have explained above that common property resources tend to be overused and therefore there is economically inefficient use of them. R. Coase,[3] a Nobel Prize winner of 1991, has proposed a solution for this problem to ensure economically efficient use of common property resources. According to Coase, if costs of negotiating between the parties is quite small, the parties that create negative externality and the victims of their activity negotiate, they can arrive at a price which properly takes into account the negative external effect and thus ensures economic efficiency in the use of common property resources. For example, if *downstream water users* are assigned the property right *to obtain water of a particular quality*, a firm that wants to pollute the stream will be prepared to give compensation to them (*i.e.*, to downstream water users who have been given rights to obtain water of certain specified quality). *Since the firm will now have to give compensation to the downstream water users, it will not find it worthwhile to pollute the stream beyond the economically efficient point*. This is the gist of Coase theorem and its importance lies in its suggestion that assignment of well-defined property rights might help to promote economic efficiency.

It may be emphasised that Coase theorem assumes that transaction costs, that is, costs of negotiating and contracting by the interested parties are very small. For instance, in our above example, the downstream water users join together and then effectively negotiate with the polluting firm without much cost about the price to be charged from the latter for polluting the stream. Besides, even if the transaction costs are small, negotiations with the polluting firm may not be practical because *it is difficult to measure precisely the external cost* (*i.e.*, negative externality) of pollution imposed by the polluting firm on the downstream water users. Further, if the number of interested parties in negotiating a deal is large, it may not be possible to get unanimity required to make the negotiation effective. To conclude in the words of Edwin Mansfield, Coase theorem suggests that "the assignment of well-defined property rights might help to promote economic efficiency. For example, to get around the difficulties caused by external diseconomies arising from waste disposal, society might find it useful to try to establish more unambiguous property rights for individuals and firms with respect to environment quality. Then, assuming that the relevant negotiations are feasible, the interested parties in a particular area might try to negotiate to determine how much pollution will occur."[4]

3 R. Coase, *The Problem of Social Choice*.

4 Edwin Mansfield, *Microeconomics*, Seventh Edition, 1991, p. 472.

CHAPTER

58

POLLUTION CONTROL

The World Health Organisation's (WHOs) latest finding that air pollution is the world's biggest environmental health risk should be of particular concern to India, given that its air pollution is among the world's worst. Of the 20 most polluted cities, 13 are said to be in India. Delhi has the dubious distinction of being the most polluted city of the world. In India, there is also acute problem of water pollution. The two big rivers, namely, Ganges and Yamuna are highly polluted and need to by cleaned. In big cities like Delhi, Bombay and Calcutta there is problem of disposal of garbage. The sewage and garbage problem makes these cities quite dirty.

Whether wastes or pollutants are gaseous, liquid or solid, they impose costs upon the society. If the emitter is not controlled or charged from polluting the environment and his wastes are disposed of without any cost to him, the polluter is induced to pollute a great deal. The harms done by pollution are now well known. Pollution causes many diseases and affects health and quality of life of the people. It is due to air pollution that, according to WHO, 40 per cent of children of Delhi have weak lungs. Therefore, need has been felt for the government to control and abate the pollution to promote the well-being of the people.

Both production and consumption activities of the people cause pollution of rivers. The controlling and abatement of pollution require costs to the society. A society has limited resources; allocation of resources for reduction or abatement of pollution will mean they will have to withdraw from other resources, that is, resources devoted to control and abatement of pollution have opportunity cost. In view of the costs to be incurred on pollution control and abatement, achieving zero pollution is not socially desirable. It is due to the cost factor that a pertinent question is: what level of pollution a society should accept. Thus Stephen Smith in his recent book writes, "Pollution is harmful and undesirable and a civilised society should be willing to fend the resources to eliminate it entirely … Achieving a cleaner environment has a cost in terms of the resources used to install and operate pollution control equipment… Some of these costs are likely to rise sharply, the more vigorously we try to "control pollution."[1]

Costs and Benefits of Pollution Control

Economists use cost-benefit analysis to the question as to what extent pollution be reduced. Economists evaluate costs and benefits of each additional one thousand rupees spent on pollution control. Does extra pollution abatement have benefits that are greater or less than its costs? The costs of pollution control and abatement include costs of pollution control equipment and benefits include the effects on improvement of health of the people and the quality of life. It may however

1 Stephen Smith, *Environmental Economics, A Very Shot Introduction*, 2011, Oxford University Press, p 14.

be noted that it is difficult to measure precisely all the costs and benefits of pollution control but a good approximate measurement of the costs and benefits can be made. However, in case of pollution control, not only monetary costs incurred and benefits obtained but all costs and benefits, monetary and non-monetary, are considered while evaluating the programme of pollution control. Effects on health and quality of life are as much important in the analysis of pollution control as the costs of the firms of installing equipment to remove pollutants from their emission or costs to local municipal authorities of disposal of sewage and garbage. However, for economic analysis of pollution control to be comprehensive use of money as measure of value of such things as effects on health and quality of life. To quote Stephen Smith again, "Most of the energies of environmental economists have gone into devising ways to value fully and comprehensively those effects which lie outside market mechanism".[2]

It is important to emphasize, as mentioned above, that the **issue is not 'pollution or no pollution' but how much pollution** is to be reduced. Zero pollution sounds ideal but, as mentioned above, it costs the society to reduce it. If achievement of zero pollution or 100% purity were costless, then there will be no problem for bringing an immediate end to all pollution. But the cost of achieving zero pollution is quite prohibitive. Therefore, there exists trade-off between pollution abatement on the one hand and cost incurred on it on the other. If more pollution abatement is required to be achieved, more costs for this will have to be incurred. In view of the costs to be incurred on reduction of pollution we require what is called **optimal pollution or socially desirable pollution.**

It is also worth noting that social benefits of successively higher degrees of pollution control also vary. In fact increasingly pollution-free environment will yield decreasing marginal social benefits (in terms of **avoided marginal environmental damage** (MED). Now, the question may be asked as to why people tolerate some pollution. However, while a lot of benefits may be realised from removing first more deadly pollutants but as environment becomes increasingly clean from pollution, people become more tolerant of removing minor effluents. For example, people will not be prepared at all to swim in a sewer but a large number of them would be prepared to swim in relatively cleaner rivers like Ganges and Yamuna.

That there is degree of purity of environment and more costs have to be incurred if greater abatement of pollution is desired. Consider the case of environment pollution by a factory whose chimney is emitting smoke and other pollutants into the neighbouring environment. Pollution abatement can be achieved by installing equipment called filters which remove some proportion of effluents but if greater and more effective removal of pollutants is required, then more advanced and costlier filters are to be installed. Thus, more pollution-free environment is achieved by incurring higher costs. Thus successively increasing marginal cost on installing more advanced filters has to be incurred if greater abatement (*i.e.*, reduction) of pollution is required. In other words, marginal social cost (MSC) of achieving greater abatement of pollution rises upward. This is shown in Fig. 58.1 where on the horizontal axis we measure pollution abatement (that is, percentage of pollution removed) and on the vertical axis we measure cost or benefit in terms of rupees. As explained above, marginal social cost (MSC) slopes upward as more abatement of pollution is attempted, that is, additional cost incurred on achieving an extra percentage of pollution eliminated increases. *Note that marginal social cost (MSC) curve drawn includes only the additional cost of an extra percentage of pollution eliminated and does not include any private marginal cost of production* (*PMC*). Pollution is a negative externality which a private firm will not take into account in its cost calculations and therefore can be imposed by the government to control pollution.

2 Stephen Smith, *op. cit.*, p. 16.

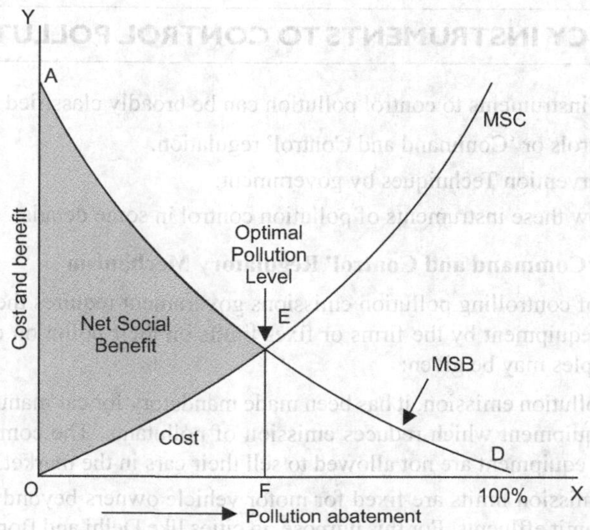

Fig. 58.1. *Optimum pollution level and pollution abatement*

On the other hand, *downward–sloping marginal social benefit curve* (MSB) *of pollution abatement* has been drawn. This decreasing marginal social benefit curve (MSB) depicts the fact that increasing abatement of pollution yields decreasing marginal social benefit in terms of cleaner environment as we approach toward the right to zero pollution (*i.e.,* 100 per cent pollution-free environment). That is, while on the one hand more pollution abatement yields decreasing marginal social benefit (in terms of avoidance of damage done by pollution), more pollution abatement causes marginal social cost (MSC) to rise on the other. It will be seen from Fig. 58.1 the two curves of marginal social benefit (MSB) and marginal social cost (MSC) intersect at point *E* and determine *OF* as the optimum pollution level. Before we reach this optimum or socially desirable pollution level, each additional percentage of pollution is socially justified in the sense of marginal social benefit obtained an extra percentage of pollution abatement is greater than the marginal social cost (MSB > MSC) resulting in the net benefit to the society.

But pushing pollution abatement beyond the point where MSC equals MSB will mean cost of extra pollution abatement will exceed extra social benefit gained resulting in reduction in social welfare. Thus, "Achieving zero pollution is virtually impossible. Maximising social welfare requires that MSB = MSC at point *E* (in our Fig. 58.1). To extend abatement beyond the optimal level would waste resources because further reduction in pollution costs more than they are worth."[3] It will be seen from Fig. 58.1 that at the pollution abatement level *OF*, the two curves of MSC and MSB representing marginal social cost and marginal social benefit cut each other at point *E* corresponding to pollution abatement level *OF*. Thus *OF* is the optimal level of pollution abatement. The total social benefits from this pollution abatement equal to *OF* is equal to the area *OAEF* under the social marginal benefit curve MSB, up to the optimal level point *F*. On the other hand, total social cost of this optimal pollution level *OF* is given by the area, *OEF* under the marginal social cost curve, MSC. Thus, the net social benefit over social cost, is given by the triangular area *OAE.* It will be further seen that if pollution abatement is carried out beyond point *F*, MSC > MSB resulting in some loss of welfare. It is worthwhile to note that optimal pollution level will vary for different regions and industries depending upon their benefits and costs of pollution abatement.

3 Ralph T. Byrns and Gerald W. Stone, *Microeconomics,* 6th edition, Harper Collins College Publishers, New York, 1995, p. 437.

POLICY INSTRUMENTS TO CONTROL POLLUTION

The methods or instruments to control pollution can be broadly classified into two categories:

1. Direct Controls or 'Command and Control' regulation.
2. Market Intervention Techniques by government.

We explain below these instruments of pollution control in some details.

Direct Controls or 'Command and Control' Regulatory Mechanism

In this method of controlling pollution emissions government requires the use of certain types of pollution control equipment by the firms or fixes limits on their pollution emission in a period. The following examples may be given:

1. To check pollution emission, it has been made mandatory for car manufacturing companies to install equipment which reduces emission of pollutants. The companies which do not install such equipment are not allowed to sell their cars in the market.
2. Pollution emission limits are fixed for motor vehicle owners beyond which their vehicles should not emit effluents. For this purpose, in cities like Delhi and Bombay, vehicle owners are required to get their cars and other vehicles checked for pollution emission level. They are to produce '*pollution under control*' certificate when checked.
3. Recently, in Delhi National Green Tribunal (NGT) has prescribed that no diesel vehicles of more than 10 years old can ply on the roads of Delhi.
4. The use of coloured polythene bags (which are harmful for health) for storing things has been banned in Delhi. In their place bags made of cloth and jute are allowed for carrying goods.
5. Companies producing mineral water, cold drinks such as Pepsi and Coca Cola are mandatorily required to install equipment to remove pesticides from their drinks before bottling them for sale in the market.
6. Recently, in June 2015, the sale of Maggi made by a multinational company, Nestle, has been banned as it contained lead beyond the permissible limit.
7. In European countries to check "*acid rain*" it is required from new power stations to make use of particular pollution abatement technology, namely, installation of FGD scrubbers.

   Similarly, to check air pollution transport buses in Delhi and other big cities are required to use CNG instead of diesel or petrol.
8. Limits may be placed on effluent emission from particular sources such as industrial firms for a specified period of time. For example, in the US Environment Protection Agency's National Pollution Discharge Elimination System (NPDES) regulates emission of organic and toxic effluents to lakes and rivers from the industrial factories and local municipal bodies by issuing permits which prescribe both average daily discharge limits over a specified period of time and maximum daily limit. The Indian rivers of Ganges and Yamuna have become too dirty because there exists no control over releasing toxic discharges by factories and municipal bodies of the cities and big towns near them.

It is often said that direct, controls or 'Command and Control' instruments for controlling emissions is difficult to implement. Costs have to be incurred on checking and monitoring these controls We agree with Stephen Smith, "Where Command-and-Control regulation sets limit on pollutant concentration in effluent flows, it may be possible to achieve a good level of compliance through occasional, unannounced checks on pollution level, so long as these are backed up with sufficiently severe sanctions for those plants found to be exceeding the limits set. On the other hand, a limit on total monthly or annual emissions may require a completely different approach to monitoring, based on continuous recording of effluent flow through chimney or discharge pipe has in the past been costly and difficult, but recent technological advances may be widening the scope for this approach."[4]

Pollution Control through Market Mechanism

The government can control pollution emission through intervention in market mechanism by imposing taxs or providing subsidies. It is worth noting that market mechanism approach to control pollution attempts to **internalise** the costs of pollution, which is a negative externality, to ensure that the polluter pays the costs of polluting the environment. This is done through inposition of indirect tax on specific type of polluting activity such as using carbon-based fuels. In this to achieve a socially efficient output, *rate of indirect tax equal to the marginal external cost* (*in the form of pollution emission*) caused by a polluting enterprise is imposed. This is illustrated in Fig. 58.2 where on the horizontal axis, output of a polluting industry is measured and on the vertical axis, the price of the product is measured.

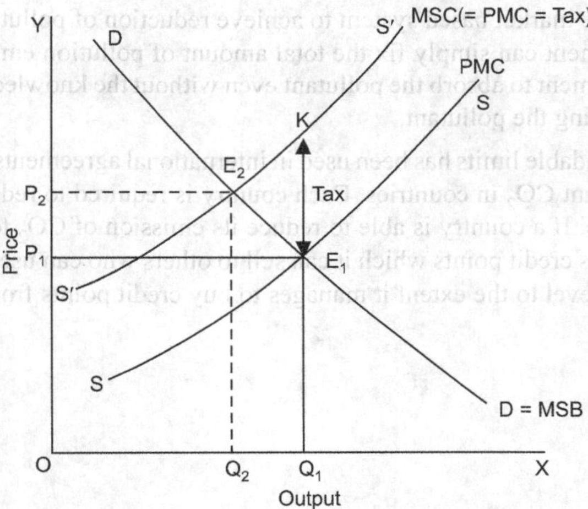

Fig. 58.2. *Imposition of an indirect tax to reduce pollution*

In this Fig. 58.2, the demand curve *DD* depicts marginal social benefit (MSB) of output. PMC is the supply curve of the product depending on private marginal cost only. In the absence of any tax, the industry will produce output OQ_1 where demand curve (MSB) cuts supply curve PMC and determines profit maximising output OQ_1 and price of the product equal to OP_1.

Now since the industry is a polluting one emitting effluents and harming others (that is, inflicting costs on others by creating pollution whose cost is not being taken into its cost calculations by producers of the industry. The government can impose an indirect tax, say excise duty **equal to the value of environment pollution or damage** done by the industry. When we add this tax to the private marginal cost we get the new supply curve *S′S′* which reflects the social marginal cost (SMC = PMC + Tax) curve which lies above the PMC curve. The social marginal cost curve (SMC) cuts the given demand curve which depicts marginal social benefit (MSB) at new point E_2 and determine lower output level OQ_2 and higher price OP_2. The lower quantity of polluting industry implies less emission of pollution. It is worthwhile to note that firms themselves have reduced output following the imposition of an indirect tax as they have taken into account the imposed indirect tax as an additional cost. This is what is said that by imposing indirect tax on the polluting industry implies that government works through market mechanism to influence the behaviour of the firms. In this way, the government *internalises* the cost of pollution by the firms.

4 Stephen Smith, *op. cit*, p. 41.

Issuing Tradable Permits

A policy measure which has gained much popularity in recent years is the issuing of tradable permits to control pollution. Under this measure, a maximum level of emission of a given pollutant is set for a factory and the firm is issued a permit to emit the pollutant up to this level. If a firm emits less pollutant than the permitted amount it is given *credit points* for the difference. The firm can use these credit points for use in its other factory or it can sell them to others. The total emission of pollution by the firm itself and sale of its saved credit points must not exceed the permitted level for which it has been given permit. Let us give an example of two firms *A* and *B* which are presently creating 15 units of pollutants each. Now to reduce emission of pollutant by 6 units a limit of 12 units of emission of the given pollutant **for each firm** is fixed and the permit of the same amount is issued to them. Now, if the firm *A* manages to reduce its emission of the pollutant to 9 units instead of 12 it will be given 3 credit points which the firm can sell to the firm *B*. Therefore, the firm *B* can emit 15 units of pollutant; 12 units of its own permit and 3 units of credit points purchased by the firm *A*.

The main merit of tradable points is that it combines the simple method of Command-and-Control (CAC) method with the market based system to achieve reduction of pollution to the optimal level. Under this the government can simply fix the total amount of pollution emission depending on the capacity of the environment to absorb the pollutant even without the knowledge of costs and benefits of business firms emitting the pollutant.

The principle of tradable limits has been used in international agreements such as Kyoto Protocol for reduction of pollutant CO_2 in countries. Each country is required to reduce its emission of CO_2 by a certain percentage. If a country is able to reduce its emission of CO_2 to less than its permitted discharge, it can earn its credit points which it can sell to others who can use them to emit more CO_2 beyond the permitted level to the extent it manages to buy credit points from others. This has been called *carbon trading*.

CHAPTER

59

SUSTAINABLE DEVELOPMENT AND CLIMATE CHANGE

SUSTAINABLE DEVELOPMENT: MEANING AND CONDITIONS

Economists have used the term **sustainable development** in an attempt to clarify the balance between economic growth on the one hand and conservation and protection of environment on the other. Sustainable development refers to **"meeting the needs of the present generation without compromising the needs of future generation"**[1] Thus economic growth will be sustainable if the stock of capital assets including land remains constant or increases over time. Though the stock of natural resources are a part of capital assets of a society, they are only limited substitutes of other types of capital assets. It may however be noted that future economic development and quality of life crucially depends on the natural resource base and quality of the environment, *i.e.*, the quality of land, water and air. To destroy and over-exploit the natural resources indiscriminatly and pollute the environment will though raise the short-term growth rate and living standards of the people will have adverse effect on the long-term future growth and the quality of life of the future generations as the latter will have smaller natural resource base and poor quality of environment.

It is therefore necessary that while deciding about growth environmental issues should be factored in. For instance, loss or preservation of important environmental resources should be taken into account while preparing estimates of growth and wellbeing of the people. Alternatively, economic policy makers may opt for framing a growth strategy of **no net loss of environmental assets** so as to ensure sustainable development. In this latter case if environmental resources are destroyed or depleted in one area, an equal or greater amount of environmental resources are replenished or regenerated elsewhere so that future economic growth is not adversely affected.

Pearce and Warford[2] have put forward a view which takes into account preservation of environment for sustainability of growth. In the overall capital stock they include not only the man-made physical capital (such as machines, factories, roads) but also human capital (education, skills, healthcare) and environmental capital (such as forests, water resources, climate, arable land, soil quality). According to Pearson and Warford, sustainable development implies that overall capital stock, as defined above, does not decrease in the growth process. In this regard, they point out that the sustainable measure of net national product (NNP*) can be obtained as the amount that is consumed during the growth process without any decrease in the overall capital stock during a year. Thus according to Pearce and Warford the condition for sustainable development can be written as :

$$NNI^* = GNI - D_m - D_n$$

---

1 Michael P. Todaro and Stephen C. Smith, *Economic Development,* 8th edition, 2003, Pearson Education (Singapore): p.471.

2 David W. Pearce and Jeremy J. Warford, *World without End: Economic Environment and Sustainable Development: A Summary* (Washington DC: World Bank, 1993).

where NNI* is sustainable level of national income, GNI is gross national income, D_m is depreciation of manufactured capital assets, and D_n is the depreciation of environmental capital resource. It is only when the above condition is fulfilled, NNI* will remain constant as the growth of GNI will make up the loss due to depreciation of manufactured capital assets, and use of environmental resources.

Michael Todaro and Stephen Smith have proposed a better measure of sustainable development, which though difficult to calculate provides a better indicator of sustainable development. They write the condition for sustainable development as under :

$$NNP^* = GNP - D_m - D_n - R - A$$

where NNP* stands for sustainable net national product which does not diminish over the course of a year

where

GNP stands for gross national product

D_m stands for depreciation of man-made physical capital stock

D_n stands for decrease in money value of destruction of capital over the course of a year.

R is the expenditure required to replenish environmental capital (forests, fisheries etc.) destroyed during a year.

A is the expenditure required to prevent destruction of environmental capital such as air, water, soil quality etc.

In the context of rising consumption standards both in the developing and developed countries along with rapid growth of population in developing countries achievement of the goal of sustainable development is a major challenge facing the world today. It is evident that meeting the consumption needs of future generations when the world population is estimated to increase by an additional 2 billion by 2050 require substantial changes in consumption and production pattern.

Rio Conference held in 1992 where 150 countries participated was an important milestone in defining the concept of "sustainable development". This was spelled out in considerable detail in agenda 21, which set out general principles for sustainable development and framed blueprint for conservation and use of forests and suggested important steps that are required to be taken to generate an environmentally stable and sustainable planet.

Over the last two decades there has been increased awareness about the need for preventing environmental degradation, checking pollution and averting global warming as a result of climate change but not significant practical steps have been taken in this regard and more world conferences on environment and climate change have taken place since 1992. These conferences were expected to resolve the issues eoncering environmental pollution and climate change between the developing and developed countries. The difficult problem is that the development and technological path pursued by the western developed countries is highly energy-intensive and exploits huge quantities of natural resources and leaves a highly degraded environment with emission of greenhouse gases (GHG) in the atmosphere. It is this path that developing countries are also following for their economic and social development which is quite unsustainable and leads to a large-scale pollution and ecological degradation.

To ensure sustainable development in the world today both the developed and developing countries have to take appropriate environment-friendly steps, especially by the developed ones as they have in the past through reckless industrialisation and use of energy-intensive technology, emitted greenhouse gases to a larger extent. A noted Indian environmentalist, Sunita Narain, rightly writes, "*The process of ecological globalisation is driven by the fact that levels of production and consumption have reached a stage where what one does in one's country can have major impact on neighbouring countries or even on the rest of the world. Even simple things like using a refrigerator or an air-conditioner can today destroy the world's ozone layer, running an automobile or cutting a tree without planting another one can destabilize the world's climate. And, using a persistent organic compound like DDT can mean life threatening pollution for human beings and other life forms in the remote polar regions of the world as these compounds are slowly but steadily carried to these regions by the world's oceanic currents and air streams. Never before have human beings needed to learn to live in 'one world' as now.*"[3]

Sustainable Development and Climate Change in the Indian Context

The key environmental challenges in India have been sharper in the past two decades. The State of the Environment Report by the MoEF clubs the issues under five key challenges faced by India, which are climate change, food security, water security, energy security, and managing urbanization. Climate change is impacting the natural ecosystems and is expected to have substantial adverse effects in India, mainly on agriculture on which 50 per cent of the population still depends for livelihood, water storage in the Himalayan glaciers which are the source of major rivers and groundwater recharge, sea-level rise, and threats to a long coastline and habitations. Climate change will also cause increased frequency of extreme events such as floods and droughts. These in turn will impact India's food security problems and water security. As per the Second National Communication submitted by India to the UNFCCC, it is projected that the annual mean surface air temperature rise by the end of the century ranges from 3.5°C to 4.3°C whereas the sea level along the Indian coast has been rising at the rate of about 1.3 mm/year on an average. These climate change projections are likely to impact human health, agriculture, water resources, natural ecosystems, and biodiversity.

Wary of the threats imposed by climate change and pressures on natural resources, sustainability and environment are increasingly taking centre stage in the Indian policy domain. India has been part of 94 multilateral environmental agreements. *India has also voluntarily agreed to reduce its emission intensity of its GDP by 20-26 per cent over 2005 levels by 2020, and emissions from the agriculture sector would not form part of the assessment of its emissions intensity*. Indian economy is already moving along a lower carbon and sustainable path in terms of declining carbon intensity of its GDP which is expected to fall further through lower carbon strategies. It is estimated that India's per capita emission in 2031 will still be lower than the global per capita emission in 2005 (in 2031, India's per capita GHG emission will be under 4 tonnes of carbon dioxide equivalent (CO_2 eq.) which is lower than the global per capita emissions of 4.22 tonnnes of CO_2 eq. in 2005). Along with the national efforts in different sectors, India also recognizes that rural areas are equally prone to stress and pressures from natural resource exploitation. In this context, schemes for rural development and livelihood programmes are very relevant. A vast majority of the works under the Mahatma Gandhi National Rural Employment Guarantee Scheme (MGNREGS) are linked to land, soil, and water. There are also programmes for non-timber forest produce-based livelihood, promotion of organic and low-chemical agriculture, and increased soil health and fertility to sustain agriculture-based livelihoods. These schemes help mobilize and develop capacities of community institutions to utilize natural resources in a sustainable manner and their potential can be further developed.

Together with efforts to incorporate sustainability in the rural development process, India is increasingly making efforts to *integrate the three pillars of sustainable development into its national policy space*. In fact, environment protection is enshrined in our Constitution (Articles 48A and 51A[g]). Various policy measures are being implemented across the domains of forestry, pollution

3 Sunita Narain, "Southern Challenges: Need for One Version," in *The Hindu*, "Survey of Environment," 2002, p. 13.

control, water management, clean energy, and marine and coastal environment. Some of these are policies like Joint Forest Management, Green Rating for Integrate Habitat Assessment, Coastal Zone Regulation Zone, eco labelling and energy efficiency labelling, fuel efficiency standards etc. Over a period of time, a stable organizational structure has been developed for environment protection. *The country has been making fast progress in increasing its renewable energy capacity and has displayed the fastest expansion rate of investment of any large renewables market in the world in 2011, with a 62 per cent increase to $12 billion (Frankfurt School of Finance and Management 'Global Trends in Renewable Energy Investment 2012'*). The Twelfth Five Year Plan with a prominent focus on sustainability makes provision and provides for many more opportunities like these.

Economic development without environmental considerations can cause serious environmental damage, in turn impairing the quality of life of present and future generations. Such environmental degradation imposes a cost on the society and needs to be explicitly factored into economic planning, with necessary remedial measures incorporated. The challenge of sustainable development thus requires integration of the country's quest for economic development with its environmental concerns. Environment management in India has, over the years, recognized these sustainable development concerns. The National Environment Policy 2006 has attempted to mainstream environmental concerns in all our developmental activities. It underlines that '*while conservation of environmental resources is necessary to secure livelihoods and well-being of all, the most secure basis for conservation is to ensure that people dependent on particular resources obtain better livelihoods from the fact of conservation, than from degradation of the resource*'. The Government of India, through its various policies, has been factoring ecological concerns into the development process so that economic development can be achieved without critically damaging the environment. The strong sustainable development agenda followed by India incorporates rigorous environmental safeguards for infrastructure projects, strengthening of the environmental governance system, revitalizing of regulatory institutions, focusing on river conservation, and efforts for improvements in air and water quality, on a continuous basis.

Our environmental standards are set through Government policies aimed at a development process that is environmentally sustainable and ensures well-being of the people. The broad objectives of our environmental policies and programmes are:

1. Conservation of flora, fauna, forests, and wildlife;
2. Prevention and control of pollution;
3. Afforestation and regeneration of degraded areas; and
4. Protection of the environment.

As a country, India has been in the forefront of *preserving biodiversity, sustainable management of forests, reducing emissions intensity of the economy*, and following sustainable consumption and production patterns. Specifically, India has been following a development path that takes into consideration the needs of the present generation without compromising the ability of future generations to meet their needs. Suitable attention has been given to protecting and conserving critical ecological systems and resources and invaluable natural and man-made heritage, which are essential for life-support, livelihoods, economic growth, and a broad conception of human well-being. Moreover, the effort has been to ensure equitable access to environmental resources and quality for all sections of society, in particular to ensure that poor communities which are most dependent on environmental resources for their livelihoods are assured secure access to these resources.

Sustainable Development and Poverty Eradication

Working on the *social and economic pillars of sustainable development policies, programmes and targeted schemes have been introduced to eradicate poverty*. This is done either through a direct focus on economic indicators like employment generation, youth mobilization, and building up assets of the poor, or indirectly through social indicators of human development with emphasis on health, education, and women's empowerment. Many parameters on this front have shown improvement. The poverty head-count ratio declined by 15.3 percentage points from 37.2% in 2004-05 to 21.9% in 2011-12, maternal mortality rate (MMR) dropped from 301 per 100,000 live births in 2001-03 to 212 in 2007-09; literacy rates have been constantly rising and are estimated to be 82.14 per cent for men and 66.46 per cent for women as per the 2011 Census of India. However, India is still not on target to meet some key Millennium Development Goals (MDGs) by 2015.

Over the years arguments in favour of looking beyond the conventional measure of GDP and taking into account the environmental damage caused by production of goods and services have received attention. An expert group under the chairmanship of Prof Sir Partha Dasgupta has been set up to develop a framework for '*Green National Accounts*' for India. In fact, the Central Statistics Organisation (CSO) under the Ministry of Statistics & Programme Implementation (MOSPI) has been publishing comprehensive environment statistics since 1997. The process of putting in place a system for *natural resources accounting was initiated by* MOSPI way back in 2002.

Despite all these efforts, the challenges that confront us on the environmental front continue to be harsh and complex. Increasing population, urbanization, and growing demand for water and land resources have severely impacted the quality and availability of water and soil resources. Rising energy needs is another area of concern. Besides, rapid growth will require corresponding growth in energy supply. Presently a large share of our energy demand is met through coal and oil and this trend will continue, given the unprecedented surge in energy demand and resource constraints. Energy issues have become more complex with existing energy shortage and rise in energy prices. There is considerable scope for increasing efficiency in the use of energy and water in India together with other development indicators like infant mortality rate, maternal mortality rate (MMR), sanitation facilities, and public health services. Economic instruments, regulatory measures, and market mechanisms can play an important role in helping to achieve development and growth in a sustainable manner.

THE UNITED NATIONS CONFERENCE ON SUSTAINABLE DEVELOPMENT (UNCSD), RIO +20, 2012

Recognising the well-founded concerns on the need to redress environmental problems, there have been global calls for cooperation, action, and innovation. World leaders in 2012 continued to engage and deliberate in international forums dedicated to climate and environment and also in forums like the G-20 where sustainable development and climate change were an integral part of the discussions. Ambition or goal setting to reach targets, provision of finance and technology for developing countries, and institutions and mechanisms for capacity building were the common threads of negotiations running through all these forums. One such event in 2012 was the United Nations Conference on Sustainable Development (UNCSD) which was held at Rio in Brazil in June 2012. This is also known as Rio + 20 Conference since the first United Nations Conference on Environment and Development was held at Rio in Brazil in 1992. Therefore, the name Rio + 20. It was attended by the heads of states of the member countries.

The objective of the Rio+20 Conference was to secure renewed political commitment for sustainable development, review progress made and identify implementation gaps, and assess new and emerging challenges since the UNCSD held 20 years ago in Rio in 1992. Towards this end, the Conference had two themes, viz, (a) *green economy* in the context of sustainable development and poverty eradication, and (b) *institutional framework for sustainable development*. The most significant outcomes of the Rio Summit have been the ***restoration of the principles of equity and of common but differentiated responsibilities (CBDR) in the global environmental discourse***

and placing poverty eradication at the centre of the global development agenda. The outcome also ensures the required domestic policy space to countries on a green economy **and launched four processes or mechanisms,** *i.e.* developing sustainable development goals (SDGs), financing strategy, technology transfer, and defining the format and organizational aspects of the proposed high-level political forum to follow up on the implementation of sustainable development.

Equity or 'Fairness' as an issue received attention. It is a matter of satisfaction and achievement for India that the Rio outcome document reaffirms equity and the principle of common but differencial responsibility (CBDR) among other Rio principles. India together with other developing countries played an instrumental role in this. CBDR is especially important for developing countries, as it *implies that while all countries should take sustainable development actions, the developed countries have to take the leading role in environmental protection*, as they have contributed the most to environmental problems. Also they should support developing countries with finance and technology in their sustainable development efforts. *India has always held that the eradication of poverty should be the over-arching goal of sustainable development*. This was given due recognition in the deliberations at the Rio Summit and in the outcome document.

On the issue of Green economy, the outcome document affirms that there are different approaches, visions, models, and tools available to each country, in accordance with its national circumstances and priorities, for achieving sustainable development. *It identifies green economy in the context of sustainable development and poverty eradications as one of the important tools for achieving sustainable development* but specifies that while it could provide options for policy-making, it should not be a rigid set of rules. The outcome document clearly states what green economy policies should result in and what they should not. It is a matter of satisfaction that the document firmly rejects prescriptive policies, unilateral measures, and trade barriers as well as unwarranted conditionality of official developmental assistance in this context.

The Rio+20 Conference will also be remembered for kick-starting the process on developing sustainable development goals (SDG). The SDGs would address and incorporate in a balanced way, all the three dimensions of sustainable development and their inter-linkages. The SDGs would be universal, global, and voluntary. Since the SDGs are expected to become a part of the post-2015 UN development agenda, they would hopefully guide the international community towards inclusive sustainable development.

From India's point of view, SDGs need to bring together development and environment into a single set of targets. The fault line, as ever in global conferences, is the inappropriate balance between environment and development. Developing countries do not want any bindings on their efforts towards poverty eradication or any agreement that comes with such a price tag. Therefore, we could also view the SDGs and the post-2015 agenda as an opportunity for revisiting and fine-tuning the *millennium development goals* (MDGs) framework and sustainable regaining focus on developmental issues. India and many developing countries are slow or offtrack in achieving targets under some of the MDGs, which have concrete areas of overlap between environment and development. This is another reason why these MDGs should continue to be a part of the post-2015 global policy architecture.

The Rio Summit did not lead to any specific commitments on the finance and technology front. The developed countries, having obligations and responsibilities, need to commit to provision of adequate public funds to provide assistance including transfer of technology and capacity building to developing countries.

ENVIRONMENT ACCOUNTING

In recent years the economists have realised that in national income accounting two aspects or costs of producing GDP need to be incorporated in estimating GDP or national income so that it should truly reflect welfare of the people. These real costs are of two types. First, *when producing GDP firms pollute the air and water which adversely affects the welfare of the people*. Thus, it has been found that while producing goods the firms pollute the river water by dumping their wastes in local rivers. Similarly, the factories in the urban areas using oil and coal emit smoke and gas that pollute the air which harms those who live in the surrounding area. Therefore, ***in estimating real GDP or national income the costs of environmental damage caused by environment degradation and pollution of air and water by the firms in the production process of goods must be subtracted to arrive at what has been called green GDP or green GNP.***

Another important aspect of producing GDP which requires adjustment for calculating green GDP is **depletion of natural resources** such as oil, forests, coal and natural gas. Conventional national income accounting does not take into account the depletion of natural resources. For example, when oil drilling machines pump out oil from an underground field, it leads to the depletion of the non-renewable resources but no deduction is made to account for the *depletion of reserves* in national income accounting. In fact, the depletion of natural resources should be treated as a type of *negative inventory investment* which if accounted for in national income accounting would tend to lower the GDP estimates, other things remaining the same. Likewise, measuring the true cost of timber from cutting trees of the forests which causes not only destruction of forests–a natural resource–but also soil erosion. The damage caused by cutting trees and thereby destroying forests and causing soil erosion be assessed and accordingly proper deduction be made on this count in estimation of real GDP. In this connection the loss due to destruction of forests can be better understood from the damage and devastation caused by floods and landslides in May 2013 in Uttarakhand in India which was the result of cutting of trees in the forests nearby the rivers passing through them. It follows from above that "*in ideal accounting system, the economic costs of environment degradation would be subtracted in the calculation of a firm's contribution to output and all activities that improve the environment because they provide real economic benefits to the people be added to output*."

In the measurement of national income or GNP environment accounting must be incorporated. This is because, as explained above, the use of environment affects human welfare in any development policy that arises to promote growth and living standards, not only the increase in GNP be assessed but also whether valuable environment is preserved in the development process. Therefore, in any calculation of real GNP and economic growth, the use and preservation of environmental resources must also be taken into account. Todaro and Smith rightly emphasize that "future growth and overall quality of life are critically dependent on the quality of the environment. The natural resource base of a country and the quality of its air, water, and land represent a common heritage for all generations. To destroy that endowment indiscriminately in the pursuit of short-term economic growth penalizes both and, especially, future generations. *It is therefore important that development policy makers incorporate some form of* **environmental accounting** into their decisions.[4]

Methods of Incorporating Environmental Accounting

There are three methods of incorporating environmental accounting in national income accounts. One method has been suggested by Nordhan and Tobin (1972) who calculated national income accounts which incorporated environmental effects of economic activities so that better measure of economic welfare was obtained. It is worthwhile to note that when environmental accounting is incorporated in national income accounts, rate of growth of national income declines. The early estimates of decline in rate of growth of GNP when environmental accounting is incorporated were

4 Todaro and Smith, *op. cit*, 10th Edition, 2012, p. 485.

as high as 12 to 17 per cent. However, recent estimates of World Bank in this regard show that loss of rate of economic growth when environment accounting included is not so high.

The second method of accounting for environmental damage for growth of GNP is based on the weak view of sustainable development, namely, that the level of national capital should be maintained, that is, not reduced. In this approach, magnitude of national saving in monetary terms is calculated and also the depreciation of all types of capital, manufactured capital and natural capital, is also calculated in monetary terms. Then the two are compared. If the depreciation of all types of capital exceeds the national saving, it means national income will not remain constant which indicates unsustainable development.

The third approach to environmental accounting in national income accounts is conducted in physical rather than in monetary terms. In this approach environment accounts are divided in different environment sectors such as forest resources, mineral and coal reserves and separate estimates of their use over a period of time are made. The effect of human activities of production and consumption on environment are then calculated in physical terms. On the one hand, the estimates of the use or consumption of natural resources are made and, on the other, the estimates of the discovery of new mineral and energy resource are also made and the net effect on environment of human activity is assessed.

However, as pointed out by Thirwal, The three methods of accounting for the environment are not substitutes. The monetary approach of the first two methods requires the calculation of physical resources. Physical environmental accounts are useful for considering ecological and environmental issues. Monetary environmental accounts are useful as they reduce all effects to a common measure a net figure for the use of environment."[5]

In this regard some western economists have pointed out that some developing countries in their attempt to speed up economic growth and raising their GDP as rapidly as possible have over-exploited the natural resources and caused a good deal of environment pollution and natural resources degradation, they therefore suggest that costs of environment pollution and natural resource degradation are incorporated in their estimates of growth of GDP and their growth policies need to be modified. However, in our view this is not entirely correct to blame the developing countries who want higher GDP growth rate to reduce poverty in their countries. As a matter of fact, it is the developed countries which in the past for achieving rapid industrial growth have contributed a lot to the emission or harmful gases such as carbon dioxide that have significantly contributed to the global warming affecting the welfare of the people of developing countries. As a matter of fact, they should not only provide financial assistance to the developing countries for the harm done to the global environment in their growth process in the past but also transfer technology that ensures protection of environment from the growth processes in poor developing countries.

However, apart from what the developed countries say, it needs to be emphasized that India needs **green growth,** that is, growth in green GDP so as to ensure environment sustainability and thereby to promote the welfare not only of the current generation but also of future generations. India's quest for growth with the objective to pull out millions of its people from poverty is a necessary and legitimate pursuit. But so is the pursuit of clean and safe environmental and conservation of natural resources. No growth process can afford to neglect the environment consequences of economic activity, or allow unsustainable depletion and deterioration of natural resources. For the last over one decade (2003-14) India is the second fastest growing economy in the world, next only to China. The growth cannot take place without additional energy. The Indian economy heavily depends on coal and hydropower to meet its energy needs and the growth of each of these energy sources involves the issue of protection of environment and depletion of its natural resources. Therefore, the pursuit of our growth objective has to be reconciled with the objective of protection of environment.

5 A P. Thirlwall, *Economics of Development,* Palgrave, Macmillan, 9th edition, 2011, p. 367.

Unfortunately, the experience of growth in many countries and our own experience suggests that environmental pollution and unsustainable depletion and deterioration of natural resources occur due to laxity in environment monitoring. This has to be avoided in the future to achieve clean and sustainable growth. Therefore, we have to explore the sources and practices that use less of the polluting agents and more of clean sources of energy such as solar energy and nuclear energy. A good start has already been made in India in both these alternative sources of energy.

If growth of green GDP is adoped to be pursued, then the growth will promote welfare of the people and protect them from health hazards. For such growth to occur, environmental and ecological consequences of growth activities must be taken into account. The current estimates of growth based on GDP and national income as conventionally measured do not reflect a true and genuine growth in the sense of green and sustainable growth. Therefore, we conclude that a green economy will make growth more inclusive and sustainable. Neglecting the ecological consequences of growth adversely affects the welfare of the people in the long run.

CLIMATE CHANGE; ISSUES: CAUSES AND EFFECTS

Climate Change: The Issue

The climate change has become one of the most important environmental issues that confronts the human beings both in the developed and developing countries. The issue is that the various economic activities by the people, especially the burning of fossil fuels such as coal, petroleum, natural gas in various productive activities, is likely to disturb the planet's heat and radiation balance. It will lead to an increase in earth's temperature (*i.e.,* warmer climate) in the next 50 years which would have disatrous consequences not only for the quality of life (*i.e.,* clean environment) of the people but also for economic development. Climate change has therefore become a global issue and negotiations among the countries, both developed and developing, are going on to mitigate global warming through reduction in emission of greenhouse gases such as carbaon dioxide (CO_2) and thereby save the humanity.

What is climate change?

Now, what is climate change ? 'Climate change' means a change of climate which is attributed directly or indirectly to human activity that alters the composition of the global atmosphere and which is in addition to natural climate variability observed over comparable time periods. Increasing levels of fossil fuel burning and land use changes have emitted, and are continuing to emit, greenhouse gases (mainly carbon dioxide (CO_2), methane, and nitrous oxide) into the earth's atmosphere. This increasing level of emissions of greenhouse gases has caused a rise in the amount of heat from the sun trapped in the earth's atmosphere, heat that would normally be radiated back into space. This has led to the **greenhouse effect**, resulting in climate change. The major characteristics of climate change are rise in average global temperature, ice cap melting, changes in precipitation, and increase in ocean temperature. The efforts needed to *address the climate change problem include greenhouse gas emissions on the one hand and building of capacities to cope with the adverse impacts of climate change on various sectors of the society and economy on the other*. Scientists who have been working on the subject for a long time point out that greenhouse gases (GHGs) such as carbon dioxide in the atmosphere trap the incoming heat from the sun and thereby leads to the increase in earth's temperature which is often referred to as **global warming.** Besides carbon dioxide, other greenhouse gases are methane, nitrous oxide and water vapour. This climate change is likey to cause adverse change in weather patterns and extreme events such as cyclones, hurricanes, floods, rise in sea level. How to **reduce the emission of greenhouse gases** and also to **adapt to the changes in climate** are the issues that confront the humanity.

Why does carbon dioxide concentration in the atmosphere increase ? Though human beings also emit carbon dioxide while they breathe, the most important source of carbon dioxide emission is **burning of fossil fuels** such as coal, oil, gas during the process of industrial production. As most of the industrual growth has taken place in the developed countries such as the USA, Europe and Japan over the last more than a century, it is they who have contributed most to the increase in carbon dioxide concentration in the atmosphere. It is the unsustainable consumption pattern of the rich developed countries that is responsible for much of the emission of carbon dioxide and other greenhouse gases by burning fossil fuels. While 25 per cent of world population live in these rich industrialised countries, they emit more than 70 per cent of total global carbon dioxide emission[15]. In per capita terms disparities in emission of carbon are also very large. Thus, while a citizen of USA on an average emits more than 5.5 tonnes carbon per year, an Indian citizen emits only 0.25 tonnes of carbon per year.[6]

It may be noted that though the developed countries emit more carbon dioxide and other greenhouse gases (GHGs) into the atmosphere, it is not only their local atmosphere that gets polluted, but the whole **global atmosphere** is adversely affected. The air and winds know no national boundaries; the emission of toxic gases into the air by one nation easily travels to the whole global atmosphere. Thus, there is climate change for India and other developing countries though it is the rich industrialised nations of the USA, European countries and Japan which have contributed most to the concentration of greenhouse gases (GHGs) in the atmosphere. Similarly, the flow of sea water knows no national boundaries and therefore rise in sea level as a result of climate change will affect the people of coastal areas of many countries. Therefore, global cooperation and efforts are required to mitigate climate change.

The Size of the World Greenhouse Gas Emission Problem

According to the Fourth Assessment Report of the Inter-Governmental Panel on Climate Change (IPCC 2007), over the century, atmospheric concentrations of carbon dioxide increased from a pre-industrial value of 278 parts per million to 379 parts per million in 2005, and the average global temperature rose by 0.74°C. Projections indicate that global warming will continue and accelerate. Thus climate change represents additional stress on ecological and socio-economic systems that are already facing tremendous pressure due to rapid economic development. With climate change, the type, frequency, and intensity of extreme events, floods, and droughts are expected to increase. Hence addressing climate change is a major challenge in terms of policies and resources needed to address it at domestic and international levels.

While the worldwide emissions of GHGs have increased since 1945, with the largest increases taking place in carbon dioxide (CO_2) emissions, scientists attribute the global problem of climate change not only to the current GHG emissions but also to the stock of historical GHG emissions. Most of the countries, particularly the industrialized countries, having large current emissions, are also the largest historic emitters and the principal contributors to climate change. A relatively small number of such countries are responsible for the largest chunk of the stock of global GHG emissions. The industrialized countries with the largest total emissions also rank among those with the highest per capita emissions. Per capita emissions are generally higher in wealthier countries. Global Greenhouse Gas (GHG) emissions have risen sharply since 1945. As per a working paper published by the World Resources Institute, total GHGs were estimated at 44,153 MtCO_2 equivalent (million metric tons) in 2005. As CO_2 is the predominant GHG, an analysis of its emissions across

6 Jyoti K. Parikh and Kirti Parikh, "Climate Change: India's Perceptions, Position, Policies and Possibilities," in *Climate Change and Development*, *OECD*, 2002, p. 5.

G-20 countries in per captia terms in 2009, compared to 2005, presents an interesting picture which can be seen from Fig. 59.1. Although the G-20 is referred to as a group, there are stark disparities on the ground between member countries in terms of incomes, stages of development as well as respective per capita CO_2 emissions. In 2005, the USA had the highest CO_2 emissions in metric tons per capita at 19.7, followed by Australia (18.0). The lowest per capita emitters in 2005 were Brazil (1.9), Indonesia (1.5), and India (1.2) who continued to be the bottom three in 2009 as well. In 2009, Australia ranked first within the G-20 followed by the USA.

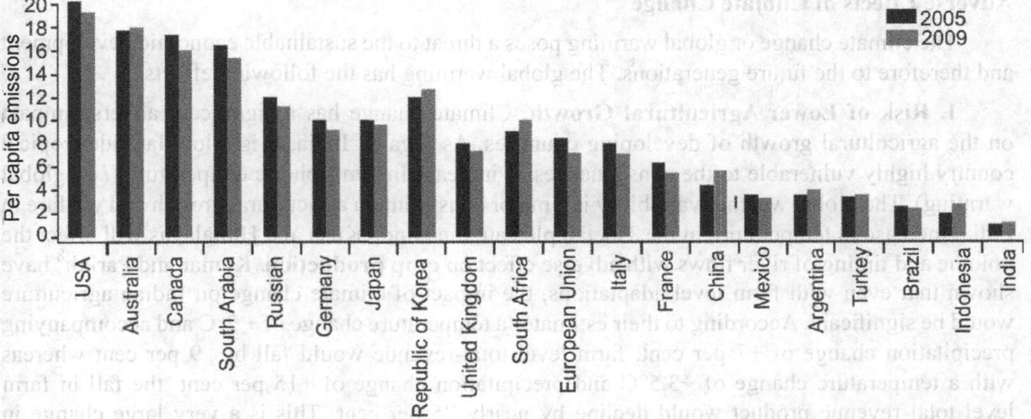

Fig. 59.1 *Per capita CO_2 emission of G-20 countries in 2005 and 2009*

India is a country which will be severely impacted by climate change. This puts additional hurdles in its developmental path in addition to the challenges of poverty eradication and growing population. The projected impacts of climate change cut across water resources, forests, agriculture, and health. With a large agrarian population, India is vulnerable to changes in weather parameters. Further, rainfall, variability and melting of glaciers will impact replenishment of rivers, thereby affecting availability of water in river basins and watersheds. In India, most of the rivers flowing in the northern regions are dependent on snow and glacial melt, thus climate change threatens the perennial nature of these rivers. This has huge implications for agriculture and allied activities and resultant livelihoods. This is a serious concern for an economy that is tied to its natural resource base along its developmental path.

Why should India be concerned about climate change?

India is deeply concerned about climate change because it will have substantial adverse effects on the Indian people. As will be explained later in detail, climate change or global warming will (1) lower agriculture production (2) raise sea level leading to submergence of coastal areas, and (3) increase the frequencies of extreme events such as cyclones, hurricanes, floods. These are long-term issues. Negotiations at the global level are taking place to reduce global warming. India must play an active role in negotiations so that agreement about the extent of global level reduction in emission of greenhouse gases is reached and just and fair distribution of individual countries' contribution to it.

Since the developed countries have made substantial contribution to the concentration of CO_2 and other greenhouse gases (GHGs), they have to accept greater responsibility in reducing emission of these gases in future. Besides, they have to give financial and technical support to the developing countries for reduction of emission of GHGs.

It is worth mentioning here that **India's main energy source is coal which is highly polluting.** With the threat of climate change India is being urged by developed countries to change its energy strategy based on coal and instead use other energy sources such as oil, natural gas, nuclear energy which are more expensive. Thus immediate important issue facing India and other developing countries is to reach an agreement with the developed countries so that we have more freedom to decide which type of energy source we use, how we generate power, how to reduce methane emissions by agricultural practices or forestry and so on. Negotiations are important for us as a means to reduce or postpone future vulnerability by getting the developed countries to reduce their emissions"[7]

Adverse Effects of Climate Change

The climate change or global warming poses a threat to the sustainable economic development and therefore to the future generations. The global warming has the following effects:

1. Risk of Lower Agricultural Growth. Climate change has a significant adverse impact on the agricultural growth of developing countries. As regards India, it is a low latitude tropical country highly vulnerable to the consequences of increase in atmospheric temperature (*i.e.,* global warming). The global weather variability is a major constraint on agricultural growth and welfare in India. Increase in temperature in the Tibetan plateau, the Hindu Kush and Himalayas will affect the volume and timing of river flows with adverse effect on **crop production.** Kumar and Parikh[8] have shown that even with farm level adaptations, the impact of climate change on Indian agriculture would be significant. According to their estimates a temperature change of + 2°C and accompanying precipitation change of +7 per cent, farm level total-revenue would fall by 9 per cent whereas with a temperature change of +3.5°C and precipitation change of +15 per cent the fall in farm level total revenue product would decline by nearly 25 per cent. This is a very large change in agricultural production which can cause much hardship for the Indian people, especially the poor. These estimates reveal that even 2°C increase in temperature will be quite substantial for India.

2. Rise in Sea Level. There is a great risk of rise in sea level as a result of global warming. It is expected that a large coastal area will be submerged with the rise in sea level. This will cause large-scale emigration from the coastal settlements. These climate migrants, often called climate refugees, will create problems for India for their settlement and cause much human hardship. The Ganges-Brahmaputra delta of India has been perceived to be exceptionally vulnerable area as water level in this area will rise submerging most of the land. Early signs of the potential impact can already be seen in the Sunderbans and Bangladesh. In view of this India faces a serious prospect of climate migrants.

According to the estimates of Asian Development Bank (ADB) made in 1995, if there is one metre rise in sea level today, it would displace 7 million people in India. With one metre rise in sea level 35 per cent of land in Bangladesh would be submerged. The cost of building a wall along the coastal line to prevent submerging is quite enormous.

3. Risk of Extreme Events. As a result of climate change extreme events like cyclones, hurricanes will more frequently occur causing a lot of human misery in terms of both death and loss of livelihood of the people. For example, in Andhra Pradesh in India the cyclone of 1996 and again of 2009 caused deaths of more than 1000 people. Further, it caused loss of large property owned by the people, especially the poor.

4. Climate Change and Economic Growth. Climate change is intimately linked to the process of economic growth and development. Since greenhouse gases (GHGs) are generated by burning fossil fuels for energy use for industrial production and vehicular transport, industrial factories, power plants, automobiles generate CO_2 and other greenhouse gases. The reduction in their emission will mean lower GDP and economic growth and consequently rise in poverty. Therefore, in developing

7 Jyoti Parikh and Kirti Parikh, *op cit.* p., 6.

8 See Kumar, K.S. Kavi and Jyoti Parikh, "Socio-Economic Impacts of Climate Change on Indian Agriculture," *International Review of Environment Strategies,* 2(2), 2001.

countries where absolute poverty still prevails on a large scale and the need for sustained economic growth is therefore very necessary, it is very difficult for them to reduce emission of GHGs to achieve the global target. Thus, in case of developing countries the larger reduction in GHGs will come at the expense of economic growth.

On the other hand, the rich developed countries which contributed most to CO_2 and other GHG emissions in the past and where absolute poverty has been largely eliminated are in a better position to reduce emission of these gases. Besides, they have both the finance and technology to mitigate climate change.

Murthy, Panda and Parikh[9] have shown that reduction in CO_2 emission in developing countries imposes costs in terms of lower GDP and higher degree of poverty. Using a multisectoral and intertemporal model they have estimated the effect of reduction of CO_2 emission on GDP and incidence of poverty in developing countries. Their estimates show that in India reduction of emission of CO_2 over the period of 30 years (taking the year 2000 as baseline) and using annual emission target will lead to a fall in GDP by 4 per cent and increase in the number of poor by 17.5 per cent. Therefore, in view of this an important problem faced in this regard in democratic countries like India is to get public support for this reduction in CO_2 emission. While the cost will be borne by the present generation in the immediate period, the benefits of climate change will accrue to the future generations. Anand Patwardhan rightly poses this problem when he writes :

"Any serious attempt to cut emission will have clear and immediate costs but the benefits may not appear for a long time. To the extent that the benefits may be disasters that did not happen, they may never be obvious that the costs will be. As the debate develops **much of it is being cast in terms of the restraint that** the present generation owes to future generations."[10]

Mitigating Climate Change to Ensure Sustainable Development

As seen above, climate change or global warming has disastrous consequences. The global negotiations are going on to reach an agreement regarding emission of greenhouse gases by the developed and developing countries as per certain time framework. However, realising that it is in our own interest, India has been for quite some time pursuing environment-friendly policies and taken steps to reduce emission of GHGs through reduction in energy consumption. It is worth noting that India is committed to eradication of poverty. This requires stepping up rate of economic growth (*i.e.* increase in GDP). Therefore, emphases of high economic growth to reduce poverty results in higher energy consumption which is likely to adversely affect elimate change. Given this constraint the following steps have been taken in India to mitigate climate change:

1. Promoting energy conservation and efficiency
2. Promotion of renewable energy sources
3. Reduction of air pollution
4. Afforestation and wasteland development
5. Fuel substitution policies

We discuss these policies below in some detail.

Energy Conservation and Efficiency. In India energy conservation and greater efficiency in energy use play an important role in national policy to reduce GHG emissions. It has been estimated by Jyoti Parikh and Kirti Parikh that power sector is the highest direct CO_2 emission in India (48%) followed by transport sector, *i.e.* road, railways, air transport (10%), iron and steel (10%). Increase in the use of coal and electricity is estimated to result in significant reduction in CO_2 emission. Nag

9 Murthy, NS, Manoj Panda and Jyoti Parikh, "Economic Growth, Energy Demand and Carbon Dioxide Emission in India, 1999-2020 in *Environment and Development Economics*, Vol 2, 2009.

10 Anand Patwardhan, "Global Warming and India," *Seminar,* 486, Feb. 2000, pp. 63-69.

and Jyoti Parikh[11] have found that *greater efficiency in energy* use has been actually achieved in India as a result of government efforts.

Production of Non-Commercial Energy Sources. Apart from energy conservation and increase in efficiency in energy use, the steps have also been taken in India by Ministry of Nn-Conventional Energy Sources to develop and exploit non-conventional energy sources which are clean and renewable. Various renewable sources, namely, wind farms, micro-hydroelectric plants, biomas and cogeneration power plants, biomass gasfiers system and solar photovoltaic system of aggregate installed capacity of 2302 MW was planned to set up by the end of the Eigth Plan in 1997 and this was planned to rise to 6500 MW by the end of Ninth Plan (1997-2002).

According to data furnished by Jyoti Parikh and Kirit Parikh, about 2.6 million family size biogass plants and 25 million improved cooking gas stoves that use less fuelwood and 43,0000 solar cookers had been cumulatively installed by the end of Eighth Plan. The expected energy savings from these non-commercial energy sources amounts to 12 to 15 per cent in total wood consumption which is quite significant.

Reduction of Air Pollution. Measures taken by the Government to increase efficiency in use of fossil fuels has led to dual benefits. First, they have succeeded to a great extent in reducing local area pollution. Secondly, they have achieved abatement in GHGs emission. Pollution levels have been prescribed for vehicles in cities like Delhi to reduce urban pollution. Thus by providing for more energy efficiency in vehicles attempt has been made to reduce air pollution. This regulation of pollution has also resulted in higher fuel quality. It is estimated that pollution control measures for vehicular traffic will cause reduction of GHS in the range of 10 to 15 per cent by 2015 by which time the current stock of vehicles would be largely replaced.

Afforestation and Wasteland Development. Afforestation and wasteland development can contribute significantly to reduction in emission of CO_2 if proper policy is adopted and enforced. Biomass is widely used in India for various purposes such as fuel, timber and feedstock. This causes degradation of forests and as a result degradation of soil. Recently, Government has initiated programme for afforestation and wasteland development. This programmne is meant not only to halt deforestation but also plant more trees to increase green cover. Under this programme various agencies spend about ₹ 50 billion every year on wasteland development. If we succeed in our efforts to achieve the targets of afforestation and wasteland development there will be significant decline in India's emission of CO_2. Afforestation and regreening of wasteland is also desirable to arrest land degradation, to improve soil fertility, to provide renewable source of fuel and timber and non-timber forest products which provide livelihood to the millions of poor people.

Coal Substitution. In India till recently coal was the main source of commercial energy. After the policy of liberalisation initiated in 1991, the use of oil and natural gas has been increasingly made in sectors where its use was not permitted earlier. That is, the use of oil and gas has increasingly substituted coal since 1991. For example, power plants now use natural gas instead of coal. Similarly, fertilizer plants no longer use coal for its production and instead use other fuels. The use of coal in railways has been completely stopped.

Increases in Energy Efficiency

Due to import liberalisation strong competition from imports has induced the private firms including joint ventures producing consumer goods such as cars, televisions, refrigerators, air conditioners, consumer appliances to become more fuel efficient as price of electricity has been raised by removing subsidy on it.

---

11 Nag, Barnali and Jyoti Parikh Indicators of Carbon Emission Intensity from Commercial Energy Use in India, *Energy Economics* Vol. 22, pp. 441-461.

INDIA'S GREENHOUSE EMISSIONS AND THEIR IMPACT

Although India ranks in the top five in terms of GHG emissions, the *per capita emissions* are much lower compared to those of the developed countries, even if the historical emissions are excluded. Its high level of emissions is due to large populace, geographical size, and large economy. The most recent data available for India are the assessment carried out by the Indian Network for Climate Change Assessment (INCCA) in May 2010. The key results of the assessment are that the total net GHG emissions from India in 2007 were 1727.71 million tons of CO_2 equivalent (eq.), of which carbon dioxide emissions were 1221.76 million tons; methane 20.56 million tons; and nitrous

Table 59.1. A Comparison of GHG Emissions by Sector between 1994 and 2007

(in million tons of CO_2 equivalent)

	1994	2007	CAGR (per cent)
Electricity	355.03 (28.4)	719.30 (37.8)	5.6
Transport	80.28 (6.4)	142.04 (7.5)	4.5
Residential	78.89 (6.3)	137.84 (7.2)	4.4
Other Energy	78.93 (6.3)	100.87 (5.3)	1.9
Cement	60.87 (4.9)	129.92 (6.8)	6.0
Iron and Steel	90.53 (7.2)	117.32 (6.2)	2.0
Other Industry	125.41 (10.0)	165.31 (8.7)	2.2
Agriculture	344.48 (27.6)	334.41 (17.6)	-0.2
Waste	23.23 (1.9)	57.73 (3.0)	7.3
Total without LULUCF	1251.95	1904.73	3.3
LULUCF	14.29	-177.03	
Total with LULUCF	**1228.54**	**1727.71**	**2.9**

Note: Figures in brackets indicate percentage emissions from each sector with respect to total GHG emissions without LULUCF (*Labour use, land use change and forestry*) in 1994 and 2007 respectively.

Source: GOI, *Economic Survey,* 2010-11.

oxide 0.24 million tons. In 1994, the total net GHG emissions for India were 1228.54 million tons of CO_2 eq. This represents a compounded annual growth rate of 2.9 per cent during the period 1994 to 2007 (See Table 59.2). GHG emissions from the energy, industry, agriculture, and waste sectors in 2007 constituted 58 per cent, 22 per cent, 17 per cent, and 3 per cent of the net CO_2 eq. emissions respectively. India's per capita CO_2 eq. emissions including land use, land use change, and forestry (LULUCF) were 1.5 tons per capita in 2007.

Impacts of Climate Change in India

Climate change has enormous implications for the natural resources and livelihoods of the people. It will have wide-ranging effects on the environmental and socio-economic and related sectors. Various studies indicate that the key sectors in India such as the agriculture, water, natural ecosystem, biodiversity, and health are vulnerable to climate change. This is happening precisely at a time when it is confronted with huge development imperatives. The Indian Network for Climate Change Assessment (INCCA) released a report in November 2010 on assessment of the impact of climate change on key sectors and regions of India in the 2030s. The assessment covers four key sectors of the Indian economy, namely, agriculture, water, natural ecosystems and biodiversity, and health in four climate sensitive regions, namely, the Himalayan region, the Western Ghats, the Coastal Area, and the North-east region. The report warns of impacts such as sea-level rise, increase in cyclonic intensity, reduced crop yield in rainfed crops, stress on livestock, reduction in milk productivity, increased flooding, and spread of malaria. This calls for urgency of action in reducing vulnerability to adverse impacts of climate change and enhancing adaptive capacity through sector-specific interventions and efforts.

India's Policies to Tackle Climate Change

India's total CO_2 emissions are about 4 per cent of total global CO_2 emissions and the energy intensity of India's output has been falling with improvements in energy efficiency, autonomous technological changes, and economical use of energy. India's climate modelling studies show that even with 8-9 per cent gross domestic product (GDP) growth every year for the next decade or two, its per capita emissions will be around 3-3.5 tonnes of CO_2 eq. by 2030, as compared to the present 1-1.2 tonnes. These are well below developed country averages by any estimation. India's determination in addressing climate change is evident from the fact that an indicative target of increasing energy efficiency by 20 per cent by 2016-17 was included in the Eleventh Five Year Plan. This has now been supplemented with the domestic mitigation goal of reducing emissions intensity of the GDP by 20-25 per cent of the 2005 level by 2020 through proactive policies.

The resources for the measures required to achieve this objective will need to be mobilized from various sources including the national planning process. Studies in respect of a low carbon strategy for development aimed at ensuring inclusive growth are being conducted with the aim of including this as one of the key pillars in the Twelfth Five Year Plan. Second, India is taking conscious steps to diversify the energy fuel mix such as setting up of 20,000 MW of solar power-generating capacity by 2022, doubling the present share of 3 per cent of nuclear power in the energy mix over the next decade, putting in place a major market-based programme to stimulate energy efficiency, imposing clean energy cess on coal for funding research and development (R&D) of clean energy technologies even though coal will continue to play a key role in our future energy strategy, and aggressively expanding the use of natural gas in power production. Third, India has been pursuing aggressive strategies for forestry and coastal management to increase the quality and quantity of forest cover and has launched a major new programme on coastal zone management to address the adaptation challenges facing over 300 million people in our country who live in vulnerable areas near our coast.

As part of its international obligations under the United Nations Framework Convention on Climate Change (UNFCCC) India periodically prepares the National Communication (NATCOM) that gives an inventory of the GHG emissions in India, assesses the vulnerability and impacts, and makes appropriate recommendations regarding social, economic and technological measures for addressing climate change. The First NATCOM was presented to the UNFCCC in 2004. The Government's NATCOM II was presented to the UNFCCC in 2011. Preparation of NATCOM is an exercise of high scientific rigour based on an extensive network of research and scientific institutions in India and draws upon expertise and excellence from different institutions. India has set up an elaborate Indian Network for Comprehensive Climate Change Assessment of some 250 scientists and 120 research institutions to assist in this work. This Network has already published India's GHG inventory for the year 2007 and a 4 × 4 assessment of climate change impacts on four key sectors and four key regions of the country for the 2030s, a time frame for which decisive interventions can be made now. This network is expected to put in place a programme for measuring, monitoring, and modelling the impact of black carbon which could have climate change and public health impacts.

India's strategy for *enhancing its adaptive capacity to climate* variability is reflected in many of its social and economic development programmes. For developing countries like India, adaptation ultimately boils down to assisting the vulnerable population during exigencies and empowering them to build their lives and cope with uncertainties in the long run. Several of India's social-sector schemes, with their emphasis on livelihood security and welfare of the weaker sections, aim to do just that. India implements a series of Central sector and centrally sponsored schemes under different Ministries/Departments aimed at achieving social and economic development. Many of these schemes contain elements (objectives and targets) that are decidedly geared to adaptation. In other words, there is substantial adaptaion orientation in many of the sectoral schemes currently under operation. An exercise has been carried out to measure the expenditure on adaptation-related programmes with critical adaptation components: (*a*) crop improvement and research, (*b*) poverty alleviation and livelihood preservation, (*c*) drought proofing and flood control, (*d*) risk financing, (*e*) forest conservation, (*f*) health, and (*g*) rural education and infrastructure. It has been found that India's expenditure on these *adaptation oriented schemes* has increased from 1.45 per cent of GDP in the year 2000-01 to 2.84 per cent during 2009-10. This is a fairly impressive level of spending and is an obvious reflection of the multiplicity of economic and social welfare.

India announced a **National Action Plan on Climate Change** (NAPCC) in June 2008 which incorporates its vision of sustainable development and the steps it must take to realize it. The NAPCC is coordinated by the Ministry of Environment and Forests and implemented through the nodal Ministries and is aimed at advancing relevant actions in specific sectors/areas. Eight national missions in the areas of solar energy, enhanced energy efficiency, sustainable agriculture, sustainable habitat, water, Himalayan ecosystem, increasing the forest cover, and strategic knowledge for climate change form the core of NAPCC. State Governments are also preparing, under the advice of the Central Government, State Action Plans aimed at creating institutional and programme-oriented capacities to address climate change. These, together with the National Missions, will enhance climate change-related actions in the public and private domains.

COST OF ENVIRONMENT DAMAGE IN INDIA: WORLD BANK STUDY IN 2009

On the request of Government of India World Bank carried out a study of cost of environment damage in India whose report was brought out in July 2013. According to this study outdoor air pollution in urban areas by itself claims 1.09 lakh lives of adults and 7,513 lives of chilldren below 5 years, annually. The study revealed that the annual cost of environmental degradation in India is about ₹ 3.75 lakh crore, which is equivalent to 5.7 of the country's GDP in 2009. However, the report says, India can make green growth a reality by putting in place strategies to reduce the damage at a minimal cost of 0.02% to 0.04% of its average annual GDP growth rate. The World Bank has brought out how urban growth centres are choking and claims that outdoor and indoor air pollution have the maximum share of this annual burden on India's economy. According to the estimates of the Bank, outdoor air pollution accounts for 29% of this, followed by indoor air pollution (23%), cropland degradation (19%), water supply and sanitation (14%), pasture (11%) and forest degradation (4%). This is shown in the following Table 59.2.

Table 59.2. In 2009, India's Environmental Degradation Cost is Pegged ₹ 3.75 Trillion Annually Cost of Degradation

Environmental Categories	₹ Billion	% age of Total Damage
Outdoor Air Pollution	1,100	29
Indoor Air Pollution	870	23
Croplands Degradation	703	19
Water Supply, Sanitation & Hygiene	540	14
Pastures Degradation	405	11
Forest Degradation	133	4
Total Environmental Damage	**3.75 lakh crore**	

Besides, according to World Bank study environmental degradation and diseases are responsible for 22.8% of *child mortality* in India. As will be seen from Table 59.3, 0.4% of child mortality was due to outdoor air pollution, 9.8 per cent was due to Indoor air pollution and 12.6% of children's death was caused by polluted water supply, poor sanitation and hygiene

Table 59.3. Estimated Share of Child Mortality because of Pollution

Cause	% share of Child Mortality due to Pollution
Outdoor Air Pollution	0.4
Indoor Air Pollution	9.8
Inadequate Water Supply, Sanitation and Hygiene	12.6
Total	22.8

Cost of Environmental Degradation in Some Other Countries

It may be noted that the cost of environmental degradation on health related outdoor and indoor air pollution, sanitation and hygiene and cost of natural resource damages as per cent of GDP in India is lower as compared to some other countries such as China, Ghana, Nigeria and Pakistan as will be noticed from the following table.

Table 59.4. Cost of Environmental Degradation
(Health & Natural Resources Damage) % of GDP

Ghana	9.6			India	5.7
Tajikistan	9.5	Nigeria	7.7	Bangladesh	4.0
China	9.0	Pakistan	7.4	Nepal	3.5

It will be seen that cost of environment degradation as per cent GDP was 9 per cent in China, 9.6 per cent in Ghana, 7.4 per cent in Pakistan, 4.0 per cent in Bangladesh and 3.5% in Nepal as against 5.7 % GDP in India.

PART XI

Planning and Development

- Rationale and Need for Planning in Developing Countries
- Review of Planning in India: 1951 to 1991
- Economic Crisis of 1991 and Review of Planning in Post-Reforms Period (1992-2012)
- Twelfth Five Year Plan (2012-17): A Critical Review
- The Indian Growth Miracle

CHAPTER

60

RATIONALE AND NEED FOR PLANNING IN DEVELOPING COUNTRIES

Most of the developing countries were under colonial rule prior to 1950. They were greatly exploited by the colonial powers. For instance, India, which was once quite prosperous, became underdeveloped and poor during the British rule. Its handicrafts could not compete with the cheap imported industrial products, and as a result the artisans and workers employed in them were rendered unemployed. To make their meagre living they also sought employment in agriculture. With this too many people came to be employed in agriculture than required resulting in disguised unemployment on a large scale. On attaining freedom from colonial rule, they adopted economic planning as a means of developing their economies. That is, instead of relying on market mechanism to bring about optimum allocation of resources and bring about economic growth and development, the State through proper economic planning has to play an important role in the following ways:

Correct Market Imperfections

The markets in developing countries are characterised by widespread imperfections. The product markets are *characterised by widespread imperfections. The product markets are characterised by monopolies, oligopoly and other forms of imperfect markets*. Under these market forms, firms have a lot of market power to influence price by restricting their output. The exercise of this markets power is more common when the firms enjoy increasing returns to scale. Prices in these market do not reflect their social values and are set above the marginal cost of production and therefore lead to less than socially optimum output. There is need for government to regulate the prices of goods, especially those of essential products such as drugs, milk, soaps, washing powder, cement, steel, petroleum products such as petrol, diesel, LPG etc. Besides, the Competition Commission should ensure that mergers do not lead to the emergence of monopolies or formation of cartels.

Further, *imperfect factor markets* prevail in developing countries due to which factor prices determined do not reflect the social opportunity cost. Under the pressure of trade unions, labour is overvalued and paid higher wages than its productivity. On the other hand, to provide incentives to investors, capital is undervalued compared to its scarcity value by providing various tax breaks, lower interest rate policy of the Central Bank of the developing countries. The overvaluation of labour and undervaluation of capital lead to the use of capital-intensive techniques of production which cause increase in unemployment of labour. Likewise, foreign exchange rate of the national currency of a developing country may be overvalued which discourages exports and encourages imports and causes difficulties of balance of payments of a country.

It is evident from above that imperfections in product, factor and foreign exchange markets of developing countries would lead to economic inefficiency or pareto non-optimality and would therefore be unable to achieve maximum social value. There is therefore a case *for the role of State and planning by it to remove these factors of price distortions* if the goal of economic efficiency is to be achieved.

Ensure Benefits of Positive Externalities on Resource Allocation and Economic Growth

Even when perfect competition prevails in the markets, there is no guarantee that social optimum levels of certain important goods *which generate substantial positive externalities* would be produced. The most important examples of such goods are education and healthcare facilities which have substantial positive externalities and *should be provided below their cost of production or even free*. It is the State which can provide them in *adequate quantities through proper planning*. The private sector, guided as it is by profit motive, would not produce them free or below their cost of production. It is quite well known that so called public schools in India not only charge high tuition fees from the students but also huge capitation fees from them for admission. The engineering and medical institutes run by private sector trusts demand several lakhs of rupees as capitation fee for admission in them. Obviously, the general public or common men cannot get their children admitted in these private institutions for education. Likewise, in private hospitals such as Apollo, Fortis, Max charges are so high that only the rich can get treatment in them while common man is deprived of proper treatment to maintain his health. *Because of generating positive externalities education and health services have a high social value which is not reflected in market prices*. In modern economic thinking education and health services are called ***human capital*** because of their crucial importance for economic growth but the private sector guided by market forces does not make adequate investment in these sectors.

Therefore, to accelerate economic growth and provide social justice, it is of paramount importance that the State through planning should make adequate investment in them. The planning by state in these manpower resources (*i.e.*, education and health) will not only quicken the process of economic growth but will also help in eradicating poverty. Todaro and Smith write, "*Because such goods, as education and health services, must be valued at a price below their cost or even free, the private sector has no incentive to produce them. Thus the government often be responsible for providing these goods in order to ensure a minimum of welfare. In view of the population growth and poverty that characterise many developing countries it is likely that public sector activity in this area will continue to expand.*"[1]

Besides social capital represented by education and health services, the ***physical infrastructure*** such as power generation, coal and gas, transport facilities (including roads and highways), posts and telegraphs also create positive externalities and their short supplies are a major bottleneck to accelerate economic growth. The private sector driven by market forces has no incentive to make adequate investment in them as much of their benefits *accrue to others*. Therefore, it is now well recognised that planning in developing countries should make adequate investment in them to achieve higher rate of economic growth.

To Correct Market Failure due to Imperfect Information

Another important market imperfection in developing countries is *lack of information and the presence of uncertainty* that are faced by both producers and consumers. Joseph E. Stiglitz rightly emphasises that even if markets are competitive, *they are almost never efficient when information is imperfect or asymmetric*. By asymmetric information it is meant that of the two parties in the market while one party has complete information about the good, service or financial security which is being sold, the other party lacks the necessary information about this. Writing about the financial crisis arising out of bursting of housing bubble in 2008, he says that investors in the tainted securities did not have the same information about the quality of the securities as the banks or investment institutions issuing them. According to Stiglitz, this asymmetric information played a crucial role in bringing about financial crisis in the U.S. in 2008 when the sub-priming housing bubble burst.

1 Todaro & Smith, *Economic Development*, Pearson Education, Asia (Singapore) Pvt., Ltd. Eighth Edition, 2003, p. 700.

Stiglitz also brings out flaws in so called ***rational expectations model*** of Lucas according to which investors are rational and their behaviour will ensure stability in the market. Referring to the financial crisis of 2008 in the U.S. he writes, "A long line of research has shown that even using the models of the so called '*rational expectations*' school of economics, markets might not behave stably and that there can be price bubbles. *The crisis of 2008 has indeed provided ample evidence that expectations are far from rational*, but the flaws in the rational expectations line of reasoning, namely, hidden assumption such as that all investors have the same information had been exposed well before the crisis."[2]

He further adds, "Just as the crisis has *reinvigorated thinking about the need for regulations*, so it has given new impetus to the exploration of alternative strands of thought that would provide better insights into how our complex economic system functions."[3] Similarly, speaking about the situations prevailing in developing countries Todaro and Smith write, "*In many developing countries producers are often unsure about the size of local market, the presence of other producers, and the availability of inputs, both domestic and imported. Consumers may be unsure about the quality and availability of products and their substitutes. Moreover, in contrast to their counterparts in developed countries, producers and consumers usually lack the tools to ferret out this information because little is done by way of marketing. Under such circumstances profit and utility maximising behaviour may be based on wrong information and hence does not lead to an efficient allocation of resources*. Planning by the government may attempt to provide this information or may decide to intervene in the market by guiding producers and consumers."[4]

Accelerating Capital Formation and Economic Growth

Further, market not only fails to attain efficiency in allocating current resources at a given point of time. It may not however ***operate efficiently in allocating resources over time***, that is, it may not *ensure adequate rate of investment* which is required to bring about rapid capital accumulation so as to raise the productive capacity and consumption in the future. This also shows the importance of planning for allocating resources over time. Capital formation is a prerequisite for economic growth. Though there are large inequalities in income distribution in developing countries that should ensure higher rate of private saving, but due to the conspicuous consumption by the rich and the working of its demonstration effect on the upper middle class and middle class people, the private saving rate determined by market mechanism is not large enough to meet the needs of higher rate of investment or capital formation. Therefore, it is through appropriate fiscal and monetary policy measures that can raise the total saving and capital accumulation to accelerate economic growth. In this connection, investment in infrastructure, both physical and social, is of crucial importance. Private sector, driven by profit motive, as explained earlier, may have neither any incentive nor sufficient funds to make adequate investment in them.

Further, it is important to note that economic development is a ***process of structural change.*** The market may perform well in allocating resources at the margin by developing some industries further and allow others to decline but is generally ineffective in structural transformation of the developing economy that requires a broad and long-term view of the growth process. Therefore, active role in making a desired structural change of the economy is essential. Todaro and Smith rightly write, "*The market may be ineffective in producing large discontinuous change in the economic structure, changes that may be crucial to the country's long-term development. The government may therefore have to intervene in sectors crucial to the country's development to ensure that they change over time and flourish.*"[5]

2 Joseph E. Stiglitz (co-authored by George Aberlop), "Let A Hundred Theories Bloom", *The Economic Times,* August 2012 (italics added).

3 *Ibid.*

4 Todaro and Smith, *op.cit.*, p. 700.

5 *Op.cit.*

It is evident from above that due to widespread imperfections and the special requirements for eradicating absolute poverty and chronic unemployment and bringing about structural changes the market mechanism fails to deliver and therefore active government intervention is needed to achieve the desired results. Besides, as seen above, the free working of market mechanism without regulation by the government may produce income distribution that is highly unequal that can pose dangers to the social and economic stability. However, this should not mean that government should do everything and put stringent controls on the private sector and on the working of market mechanism. In fact as there are market failures, there are government failures too. What is needed is the ***judicious mix of roles of private sector and government*** to bring about not only rapid economic growth but also to ensure equitable distribution of income and eradication of poverty and unemployment. To conclude in the words of Professors Todaro and Smith, "No Central Planning agency is capable of regulating the vast array of different goods and services, nor this would be desirable. Rather it means greater and more effective *cooperation between the public and private sectors*. It also means that governments must seek to determine in which areas the market can most efficiently operate and in which areas the governments itself can achieve the best results given its own limited human resources. This *public sector-private sector* partnership through a proactive government industrial policy is a key lesson of the success stories of South Korea, Taiwan and Singapore."[6]

Accelerating Industrial Development

There were two main features of economic policy of the developing countries, especially India, that emphasised the role of planning and intervention by the State in the development process of the economy until 1980. First, to accelerate economic and industrial growth economists and planners recognised that raising the rate of saving and investment was essential to accelerate the rate of economic growth. It was thought that the private sector on its own would not be able to achieve a higher rate of saving and investment required to break the vicious circle of poverty. Therefore, the State had to intervene to raise resources through its fiscal and monetary policy and thus increase the rate of saving and investment. This made the planning and the expansion of the public sector essential to accelerate economic growth.

Secondly, the strategy of development adopted in India's Second and Third Five Year Plans laid stress on the industrialisation with an emphasis on the development of basic heavy industries and capital goods industries. This implied allocating a higher proportion of invisible resources to capital goods industries than to consumer goods industries. Private sector which is driven by profit motive could not be expected to allocate sufficient resources to the growth of capital goods industries. Therefore, the role of planning and the public sector was considered essential for rapid growth of basic heavy industries.

Latin American countries such as Brazil and Mexico after gaining freedom from colonial rule also adopted import-substituting industrialisation to bring about rapid economic growth. They gave higher priority to the development of consumer goods industries instead of capital-goods industries. But to bring about industrial development they did not rely on market and the private sector but the State and planning played a crucial role in their economic growth.

Similarly, South Korea, Taiwan, Hong-Kong and Singapore instead of import-substituting industrialisation adopted *export-led industrial growth strategy.* Contrary to popular perception the State played an important role in facilitating and promoting exports by the private sector.

Promoting Agricultural Growth

Though priority was given to rapid industrialisation to bring about structural transformation of their economies, developing countries (including India) did not entirely neglect agriculture. Unlike in the communist countries in the 1950s, the agriculture was left to the private sector for developing

6 *Ibid.*

it. However, in India land reforms were undertaken to protect tenants from eviction and fixed fair rents to be charged by the landlords from them. Attempts were also made in India to redistribute land after fixing ceilings on land holdings.

But rapid growth of agriculture itself requires a good deal of State intervention and planning. The land reforms in agriculture, supply of adequate credit to farmers, development of infrastructure such as irrigation, power, roads were necessary where planning and the State could play an important role.

Regulation of Market and Private Sector by the State

There is another important aspect of the role of State and planning in the development of the Indian economy which dominated economic thinking in the pre-reform period. Though the private sector was given an important role to play in the framework of mixed economy, to achieve optimal allocation of resources among different industries according to plan priorities, economic activities in the private sector were required to be regulated by the State. Further, to achieve other objectives of planning such as restraining the concentration of economic power in a few big business houses, the private sector was subjected to industrial licensing controls. To quote C. Rangarajan, the former Governor of the Reserve Bank of India, "*While the private sector was given space to operate in keeping with the concept of a mixed economy, in the field of industry particularly the decisions of the private sector were circumscribed by the licensing mechanism. Hence, while foreign trade was subject to controls because of the strategy of import substitution, industrial production and investment were subject to control because of the need to direct resources according to plan priorities.*"[7]

Role of Planning and State in the Post-Reforms Period of Liberalisation and Privatisation

The crisis of 1991 which was the result of fiscal imbalances and balance of payments difficulties proved to be a turning point in Indian planning and economic policy pursued for accelerating economic growth. On the recommendations of IMF and World Bank a drastic change in India (and also in other developing countries) was made in economic policy. Under this the policy of liberalisation and privatisation was adopted to quicken the pace of economic growth and achieve economic stability. A permanent question has been raised whether in this regime of liberalisation and privatisation, there was any useful role for planning and State to play in the development of the Indian economy. In the review of earlier economic policy, public sector was found to be inefficient. Far from generating resources for investment, it became burden on the national exchequer. Private sector was crippled by various direct bureaucratic controls which prevented its growth. In response to these, policy of economic liberalisation and privatisation was adopted. Licensing was abolished except in case of few industries. In the new economic policy, the exclusive role of public sector was confined to a few strategic industries. All other industries were thrown open for production and investment by the private sectors. However, even in this regime of liberalisation and privatisation planning by the State has an important role, though somewhat different one from that envisaged earlier. We explain below the role of planning and the State in the post-reform period.

Tackling the Problems of Poverty and Unemployment. Despite higher GDP growth in the 1980s, India faced the acute problem of poverty and unemployment. The planning and State intervention is needed to tackle the problems of poverty and unemployment. Since the beginning of the seventies the Indian planners realised, especially in the Fifth, Sixth and Seventh Five Year Plans, that even if growth rate of GDP was raised to 5 to 6 per cent per annum, it was not possible to make a significant dent on the problems of mass poverty and unemployment prevailing in the Indian economy. It was realised that benefits of economic growth did not trickle down to the poor. Others are of the view that even if the poor get benefits from growth by way of more employment opportunities generated by it, mere economic growth is not enough to eradicate poverty and unemployment. Therefore, role of planning and State is

7 C. Rangarajan, *Indian Planning: Objectives, Strategy and Instrumentality*, Paper presented at the Conference on Planning and Economic Policy in India, at the ISI, Calcutta, June 1993.

necessary to start and implement special employment schemes such as Food for Work Programme and Employment Guarantee Schemes to help the poor and weaker sections of the society.

Planning has to play an important role in poverty alleviation and employment generation. Poverty exists because the poor people and downtrodden have little asset endowments with which to engage themselves in productive activities to earn sufficient incomes. Lack of adequate number of jobs on wage basis is another important cause of poverty and unemployment. It is through planning that the assets for the poor can be built. For example, adequate credit supply to the poor farmers is necessary if they have to make improvements in their land, build irrigation facilities and other assets to increase their productivity. Private sector and market mechanism cannot be expected to build and provide assets to the poor.

Besides, due to various factor price distortions such as relatively low price of capital due to various fiscal concessions, overvalued exchange rate of rupee, private sector has a tendency to use more capital-intensive techniques and therefore will not create sufficient employment opportunities. It is due to increasing capital-intensity of the production processes that employment elasticity of output in the industrial and agricultural sectors of the Indian economy has greatly fallen in the last two decades. This has significantly reduced the employment potential of the Indian economy. Planning and State intervention is needed to provide disincentives to the use of capital-intensive techniques and to give incentives to use labour-intensive techniques of production.

Further, plans can provide for special anti-poverty schemes and special employment programmes for the poor and unemployed. Anti-poverty programmes such as Food for Work Programme, Employment Guarantee Programme to provide one person of a household living below the poverty line employment for 100 days in a year will be of great help for the poor and unemployed. If the poor and unemployed are used to build *durable assets*, it will enhance the productivity of the economy. It is through planned actions by State that such anti-poverty programmes can be effectively implemented.

Building Physical Infrastructure. It is now well known that private sector is least interested in building physical infrastructure such as power, communication, roads, ports, highways as private benefits are less than social benefits in their case. This is because building of infrastructure generates *external economies*. It is now well recognised that economic growth is impeded by the lack of these infrastructural facilities. Past experience also shows that except in the field of telecommunication, private sector in India does not feel attracted to make adequate investment in the infrastructure projects. Therefore, to achieve 8 per cent annual growth rate in GDP on a sustained basis, which is the new goal set for the Indian economy, public investment in economic infrastructure in the framework of a well-designed plan is of paramount importance.

Investment in Agriculture. Whereas economic reforms initiated since 1991 had a focus on accelerating industrial growth through liberalisation and privatisation, investment in agriculture was neglected. Much of the resources of the government were spent on providing subsidies to farmers. As a result, capital formation in agriculture has substantially slowed down since the early nineties. The average rate of agricultural growth has been extremely low in the last one decade and a half. This has worsened the employment opportunities in agriculture and in some States, especially Andhra Pradesh, Karnataka and Odisha, several farmers have committed suicide. Agriculture needs adequate investment for which access to credit to farmers at low interest rates is needed. Besides, to enhance the productivity in agriculture investment in irrigation is essential. Only the State in a planned framework can make adequate investment in expanding irrigation facilities and in undertaking flood control projects.

Creating Social Infrastructure and Promoting Human Development. The first and foremost, planning is needed even after the policy of liberalisation and privatisation for creating the social infrastructure and for human development which are of crucial importance for promoting economic development. We need to build schools, colleges, hospitals, institutions of technical education and scientific research. We have to impart skills to the youth so that they can be employed in productive activities. These can be built better through planning by the State. Private sector participation in creation of social structure and human development is not capable of taking care of the entire needs of the society, particularly of the poor and weaker sections of the society. Market mechanism which is driven by private profit motive will not be able to bring an equilibrium between the 'need' and 'supply' in this regard. Therefore, planning in this area will remain important.

Regional Balanced Development. Planning in developing countries is also necessary to remove large disparities in development between regions. The removal of the regional disparities in economic development requires flow of investible resources across regions. With greater freedom and choice of location that is now available to the private sector, it is more likely that some States would be able to attract more private investment than others. As a matter of fact, the past experience has shown that market forces do not work in a way to achieve regional balance in economic development. Therefore, planning is needed to manage the flow of resources across regions for rapid removal of regional disparities. For this plan formulation has to ensure that public investment in infrastructure must be reoriented in favour of the less well-off States. At present plans do provide for special area programmes such as the Hill Area Development Plan, Tribal Area Plan, Plans for Development of North East area and Jammu and Kashmir. While these programmes help in development of basic infrastructure in these areas, the backlog of development is large. Therefore, considerable planned efforts and resources are needed for integration of such backward regions into the mainstream of development process in the country.

It may be further noted that the focus regarding the issue of backwardness and regional balance has traditionally been on industrialisation. The evidence, however, suggests that reduction in regional disparities, particularly in average standards of living, may be better achieved through greater focus on agriculture and other rural activities. For this plan formulation should be such that provides for increasing the productivity of agriculture in backward areas. Besides, planned efforts are needed to improve connectivity of these areas in terms of transport and communication with the rest of the country.

Protecting Environment and Ecology. Finally, there are areas such as protection of environment, forests and ecology in which markets cannot play an efficient allocative role. The intervention of the State is essential to regulate private sector operations and working of market mechanism in respect of activities which adversely affect environment, forests and ecology of the economy. Similarly, working of market mechanism works in a way that leads to the excessive depletion of scarce natural resources like rare minerals, land and water. This harms the prospects of sustainable growth. Proper planning for their optimal use is therefore necessary. In this regard, the observations of India's Eighth Five Year Plan are worth quoting: "*Market mechanism is never adequate for protecting environment, forests and ecology. Nor is it adequate in giving guidance about the use of scarce resources like rare minerals, land and water. A long-term perspective, and hence planning, is needed in these areas*."[8]

Allocation of Resources among States. India is a federal State. Both the Centre and States have distinct areas of operation. Investment for development requires resources. Resources from certain taxes levied by the Centre are distributed among the States by the Finance Commission which is appointed every five years to review the situation. Non-tax resources are allocated among the States by the Planning Commission according to their developmental needs and projects submitted by them in this regard.

8 Planning Commission, *Eighth Five Year Plan.*

MARKET-FRIENDLY NEW ECONOMIC REFORMS IN DEVELOPING COUNTRIES SINCE 1980

Since 1980s there has been a *neoclassical counter-revolution* in economic policy in both the developed countries such as United States, Britain, Canada, West Germany and developing countries of Latin America and Asian countries such as India, Pakistan, Bangladesh. Under this there has been a change from public ownership of enterprises in various sectors of the economy to dismantling of public ownership, and also to the dilution of the role of government and public sector in the economy. As a result, market economy has been allowed to work freely without much controls by government over it. Besides, under this new policy framework, *supply-side macroeconomic policies* have been given dominant role in promoting economic growth in place of *demand-management policies* adopted under the influence of J.M. Keynes.

Many developing countries (including India) after independence did not completely do away with market system of production, exchange and distribution by private sector on the basis of profit motive. In fact, India and also some other developing countries adopted '*mixed economy model*' where both the public and private sectors were allowed to work and grow in their respective fields. In India, Industrial Policy Resolution of 1956 demarcated the respective fields in which the public and private sectors were conceived to work and grow with crucial sectors such as basic heavy industries, power generation, making arms and ammunition, atomic energy having been reserved for the public sector. Almost all consumer goods industries were left to the private sector for production, exchange and distribution on the basis of free play of market forces. However, the centralised planning and public sector was given a dominant role in providing or producing goods, especially in which private sector was not attracted to invest. In India for almost four decades from 1950 to 1990 this mixed economy system of coexistence of public and private sectors *with public sector occupying commanding heights of the economy prevailed.*

However, the actual experience with the mixed economy model though seemed to work well for some time, it had its shortcomings too. Economic growth rate in India in the first four Five Year Plans (1951-1974) was on an average 3.5 per cent per annum which was hardly sufficient to make dent into the problems of poverty and unemployment in view of rapid population growth of around 2 per cent per annum and requirement of 1 per cent of GDP for increase in investment per year in the economy. As a result, the magnitudes of poverty and unemployment remained very high. Given a very modest poverty line (₹ 49.1 per capita per month for rural India and ₹ 56.6 per capita per month at 1973-74 prices), 54.9 per cent of population was found to be living below the poverty line in 1973 which fell to 51.36 per cent of population in 1977-78 and to around 40 per cent in 1983 for All India (both rural and urban areas put together). Likewise, in India in 1983 a high 9 per cent of labour force was found to be unemployed on daily status basis.

However, as a result of relaxation of certain industrial controls over the private sector and adoption of some measures to promote exports during the eighties and pickup in public sector investment in the later part of the eighties, the growth rate of GDP rose to 5.6 per cent per annum during the eighties. However, the period of eighties in India was characterised by large-scale borrowing from abroad which led to the large increase in India's foreign debt and its annual service charges. This ultimately resulted in balance of payments crisis in 1990-91 and sharp rise in inflation rate in India. Thus in the overall period of four decades (1951-91) reliance on centralised planning and important role given to the public sector for accelerating economic growth seemed to be not successful. It was realised that as there are market failures, there are government failures too. Thus due to apparent failures of economic planning and the macroeconomic imbalances as reflected in balance of payments crisis on the one hand and high inflation on the other in India and other developing countries, the role of government and planning in economic growth began to be called into question. This called for revision of the role of government and planning in economic development.

Why Market-Friendly New Economic Reforms were Adopted?

Due to failures of Government in the late eighties it was felt that importance given to the public sector in the strategy of industrial development and stiff controls over the working and expansion of the private sector were obstructing economic growth and *promoting inefficiency*. Further, in 1991, India experienced serious problems of a *high rate of inflation* on the one hand and *huge deficit in the balance of payments* on the other. To overcome these problems some economists such as I.M.D. Little, Jagdish Bhagwati, Bela Balassa who had been advisors of World Bank and IMF argued for the adoption of the policy of economic liberalisation by India and other developing countries to promote growth, check inflation and solve the problem of balance of payments. They advocated that *free markets and greater role of private sector (including foreign investors) would ensure efficiency by encouraging competition.*

As explained above, the experiment of a mixed economy as described in the Industrial Policy Resolution of 1956 and later amendments made in it wherein public sector was given a prominent role in industrial development of the Indian economy seemed to be a success in the beginning. It was through public sector investment that a lot of infrastructure such as irrigation, transport, power was developed. Many basic and basic heavy industries such as steel, fertilizers, machine-making industries were built by the public sector. But during the eighties several shortcomings of the working of public sector were observed. First, the *public sector which was expected to generate adequate resources* for the growth of the economy not only failed to do so but *in fact was incurring huge losses* which raised the expenditure of the government. The losses of the public sector were said to be due to the inefficiency of the public sector enterprises. Secondly, the *problem of macroeconomic imbalances*, both in the internal and external sectors, emerged and assumed serious proportions in 1990-91. The huge budget deficits of the government and expansion in money supply led to the serious problem of inflation.

On the external front, higher commercial borrowing from abroad at higher rates of interest resulted in the serious problem of persistent deficit in the balance of payments. This caused a *sharp decline in the foreign exchange reserves*. The foreign exchange reserves fell to such a meagre amount that it could meet the payments for imports only for 15 days. This compelled the Government to approach IMF and World Bank for necessary help to tide over the foreign exchange crisis. IMF and World Bank agreed to help only if policy of economic liberalisation was adopted and accordingly greater role be assigned to the private sector in boosting industrial investment and production in a competitive environment. *It was believed that market competition would ensure efficiency and stimulate economic growth*. The objective of new industrial policy based on liberalisation, privatisation and globalisation was to improve the efficiency of the economic system by eliminating the regulatory mechanism that involved various licences and permits which reduced competition in the market and planning in the late eighties switched back to the market system which led to the policy of liberalisation and privatization in many developing countries under the guidance and direction of World Bank and IMF. Dr. C. Rangarajan, Chairman of the Advisory Council to the Prime Minister of India, writes, "*The thrust of the new economic policy was towards creating competitive environment in the economy as a means to improving the productivity and efficiency of the system. This is to be achieved by removing the barriers to entry and restrictions on growth of the firm. While the industrial policy seeks to bring about a greater competitive environment domestically, the trade policy seeks to improve international competitiveness subject to the protection offered by tariffs which are coming down.*"[9]

We explain below these structural adjustment reforms, with special reference to India. After independence, India avoided the extremes of both capitalism and socialism and opted for a mixed economy where planning and the public sector played an important role in the economic development of the country. The experiment of a mixed economy as evolved in India seemed to be a success in

9 C. Rangarajan, "Growth and Challenges, Survey of Indian Industry 2011", *The Hindu*, pp. 9-10.

the beginning but during the seventies and eighties several shortcomings of its working had been noticed.

Inefficient Working of Public Enterprises. First, the public sector which was expected to generate adequate resources for the growth of the economy not only failed to do so but in fact was incurring huge losses which raised the expenditure of the government. The losses of the public sector were said to be due to the *inefficiency in the working of public enterprises*. Secondly, the problem of *macroeconomic imbalances*, both in the internal and external sectors, emerged and assumed serious proportions in 1990-91. The huge deficits in the successive budgets of the government due to internal imbalance of Government expenditure and revenue led to the creation of more money supply which created the serious problem of rising prices, so much so that rate of inflation went up to about 17 per cent per annum during August 1991. This compelled the newly elected Congress government to reduce government expenditure and fiscal deficit for stabilising prices.

Balance of Payments Crisis. In the external sector, *the huge deficits in the balance of payments due to the rising imports and sluggish exports persisted for a long time and, to meet this deficit, the government resorted to commercial borrowing from abroad at higher market rates of interest*. As a result of persistent deficits on the current account, the foreign exchange reserves declined to a very small sum in June 1991 which could last for payments for necessary imports only for about few weeks. This compelled the government to approach IMF (International Monetary Fund) for loans to make necessary payments and enhance the foreign exchange reserves.

Thirdly, though the annual growth of national income *during the eighties* went up to over 5 per cent and of the industrial sector to 8 per cent, which was considered to be a good performance, but due to macroeconomic imbalances which emerged in the economy they could no longer be sustained any more. In the external sector, the situation became so worse in 1991 that India came to the brink of default. To avoid the default and to win over the confidence of international business community, the government had to sell a part of its gold reserves and a certain amount of gold was even pledged with Bank of England to obtain the foreign exchange reserves to meet its obligations. Further, it had to approach the IMF for loans to tide over the foreign exchange crisis.

Excessive Government Controls over Private Sector. Besides, excessive government regulation and control over the private sector proved to be counter-productive. The following drawbacks of excessive regulation of the private sector were emphasised and case for liberalisation of private sector was built up, especially by Jagdish Bhagwati and T.N. Srinivasan, the two economists associated with World Bank and International Monetary Fund. The following arguments were given in favour of deregulation of the private sector and assigning to it a greater role in economic growth of the Indian economy:

1. The industrial licensing and controls had degenerated into arbitrary bureaucratic controls on the allocation of resources in competing industries. The licences were issued to make investment in those industries which bureaucrats chose in tune with the policies they administered. This licensing system replaced the efficient market system of resource allocation by personal system of resource allocation. Thus excessive regulation of the private sector, according to the advocates of economic reforms, had resulted in the suboptimal resource allocation in industries. Hence, there was a need for liberalisation.

2. The industrial licensing system had stifled private initiative and enterprise because this system had left no scope for private initiatives in investment planning and investment decisions. In fact, the industrial licensing system did not allow the competitive economic environment to operate. As a result of this, the entrepreneurs had become attuned to secure *monopoly rent*, rather than to earn profits through enterprise and skills. Jagdish Bhagwati and T.N. Srinivasan identified licensing and control regime as the causative factor responsible for low productivity and high capital-output ratio.

Hence, industrial liberalisation became an imperative condition for the growth of forces of competition to ensure high efficiency and productivity in Indian industries.

3. Under the regime of licensing, the industrial units which tried to increase output by making full utilisation of *installed capacity* were penalised on the ground that their production exceeded the *licensed capacity* even if goods produced were much needed and were in short supply. Hence, industrial liberalisation became essential from the point of view of promoting industrial growth by the creation of additional productive capacity and its optimal utilisation.

4. The industrial licensing policy had failed to achieve its objectives of balanced regional industrial development and prevention of concentration of economic power. In fact, during licensing regime, the regional industrial imbalances and concentration of economic power had got intensified. Hence, there was a strong case for scrapping licensing system and switching over to market system.

WASHINGTON CONSENSUS AND REFORMS

Before explaining the economic reforms initiated in 1991 under the pressure of IMF and World Bank, it may be mentioned that these reforms mainly constituted what is now labelled as *Washington Consensus*. This consensus was formulated by John Williamson, with the other officials of World Bank, IMF and key US government agencies. This consensus contains 10 elements of development policy which were suggested to promote economic growth in the developing countries and also help them solve their problems of indebtedness, balance of payments difficulties and high rate of inflation. It is noteworthy that this Washington Consensus followed a free market approach to development and, contrary to the views of many development economists, it did not emphasise elimination of poverty and reducing inequalities to achieve real development, as it is now widely understood. The Washington Consensus and fiscal and structural reforms it envisages views that poverty will be automatically removed if rapid economic growth is achieved. Its message is 'take care of growth, poverty will take care of itself'.

Various Reforms Under Market-Friendly New Economic Policy: Liberalisation, Privatisation and Globalisation

However, to evolve a long-term solution to promote price stability, to bring about equilibrium in balance of payments and, above all, to ensure higher rate of economic growth, the newly elected Congress Government with Dr. Manmohan Singh as Finance Minister adopted in 1991 what is popularly called *New Economic Policy* on the advice of IMF and World Bank. According to this policy, the government was to prune down its expenditure so as to *reduce budget deficits for achieving price stability. But more important element of new economic policy is the adoption of what are called Structural Adjustment Reforms* which sought to change the nature of Indian economic system by ultimately establishing *a free market economy*. Under this structural adjustment programme, the role of public sector in economic development had been diluted and that of private sector enhanced and expanded.

It may be noted that the policy of free-market economy also got strong stimulus due to the collapse of socialist system in Soviet Russia and other centrally planned socialist economies in Eastern Europe. Accordingly, under the new economic policy, the idea of the predominant role of the public sector was abandoned and the private sector was given a greater role in promoting economic growth through competition and efficiency. Instead of being directed by the planning and licensing, the private sector would now be governed by the market forces, that is, by the free play of demand and supply of commodities and factors. We describe below the new economic reforms undertaken in India since 1991 under the *New Economic Policy* or *Structural Adjustment Programme*.

Dereservation of Industries of the Public Sector. The new industrial policy 1991 has been adopted under which far-reaching structural reforms have been initiated to lift excess direct controls and regulations on industries and to ensure a free market-oriented economic system. The list of industries reserved for the public sector has been pruned. Now, only 6 industries remain reserved for the public sector. Among the industries reserved earlier for the public sector were many core industries like iron and steel, electricity, air transport, shipbuilding, heavy machinery industries such as heavy chemical plants and telecommunication cables and instruments. The new industrial policy of 1991 threw open all these industries for the private sector for investment and growth. Thus the new policy indicates the government's intention to invite a greater degree of participation by the private sector in important areas of the economy. The six industries which continue to be reserved for the public sector are in areas where security and strategic considerations predominate. According to the new policy, the resources in the public sector will now be used for the development of strategic, high-technology industries and essential infrastructure areas and for social sectors such as education, public health and poverty alleviation programmes.

Liberalisation: Abolition of Industrial Licensing System. Until 1991 the Indian industrial sector had functioned under a system of tight controls and regulations represented by industrial licensing which meant to allocate the scarce resources towards building the industrial base of the economy. By the year 1991, the Indian industrial economy had a quite wide and diversified base, the new policy abolished all industrial licensing irrespective of the level of investment except for 15 industries for which licence was still required. These industries are those which are essential for security and safety purposes and for protection of environment. For granting of licence for even these 15 industries procedure has been greatly simplified. For getting licences only certain locational guidelines are to be fulfilled so that polluting industries should not cluster around the major urban centres. Besides, restrictions by Monopolistic and Restrictive Trade Practices Act (MRTPA) for expansion of big firms were also relaxed.

Privatisation of Public Sector Enterprises. An important aspect of new industrial policy of the Government is that it should not operate commercial enterprises. With that end in view the Government decided to disinvest the public enterprises. The government can sell its enterprises completely to the private sector or disinvest a part of its equity capital held by it to the private sector companies or in the open market. Therefore *this policy of public sector disinvestment has also been called the policy of privatisation.* Through disinvestment or privatisation, the government can mop up a good amount of resources which can be used for various purposes. The released resources can be used to restructure and strengthen the public sector enterprises which are potentially viable. These resources can also be used to pay back a part of public debt. These resources can also be used to finance budget deficits.

What are the reasons for the policy of privatisation or public sector disinvestment ? First, resources available with the Government are scarce. The government needs resources to reduce its budget deficit. The Government urgently requires resources to make investment in infrastructure, education, public health and for poverty alleviation programmes. Resources released through disinvestment can be used for investment in these crucial sectors. Secondly, a good number of existing public enterprises are working inefficiently and incurring huge losses.

Accordingly, as part of the economic reforms policy, the government started reforms in public sector enterprises. The main elements of Government policy towards public sector enterprises (PSU) are:

(1) Disinvestment of Government equity in all non-strategic public sector undertakings (PSU) to 26 per cent or lower if necessary.

(2) Those public sector enterprises which are potentially viable have to be restructured and revived.

(3) Those public sector undertakings (PSU) which cannot be revived would be closed down.

Globalisation. The following measures for globalisation of the Indian economy were taken :

Welcoming Private Foreign Investment and Foreign Technology. Till 1991, foreign investment and import of foreign technology was regulated tightly in India. In the case of foreign technology agreements sought by Indian firms as well as foreign investment, it was necessary to obtain specific prior approval from the government for each project. This involved delays and hampered business decision-making in the import of technology by Indian firms. Under the new economic policy for a selected list of high technology and high investment priority industries, firms receive *automatic approval* to make foreign technology agreements within certain guidelines. This policy measure is expected to remove the delay and uncertainty which earlier clouded the relationships between Indian and foreign firms.

Further, the government has *liberalised its policy regarding foreign investment.* To attract private foreign investment, it has been decided to grant *automatic permission to private foreign investors to invest up to 51 per cent of the total equity shares in 34 high priority industries if certain norms are fulfilled.* This facility will be available to those firms which are able to finance their capital equipment imports through their foreign equity. This is a major departure from the previous policies which required case-by-case approval of foreign investment normally limited to 40 per cent equity participation. The priority sector includes power generation and petroleum refining. Further, the government has given a guarantee of 16 per cent return on foreign investment in priority sectors. There is also a proposal to allow automatic clearance for foreign *financial* and technical collaboration with Indian firms.

Trade Liberalisation. In a bid to open up the economy, under the new economic policy *quantitative restrictions*, that is, import licensing for imports of goods have been removed. Further, to promote competitiveness, efficiency and globalisation of the Indian economy import duties have been reduced to 20 per cent (excluding agricultural and dairy products) with effect from January 9, 2004. The new thinking is that with the cheapening of imported goods, the Indian firms will try to increase their efficiency and reduce costs so that their products can compete with the foreign products. In this way they will be able to expand their exports.

Currency Convertibility and Floating of Indian Rupee. Another major step taken towards liberalisation of the Indian economy has been to make the Indian rupee fully convertible on current account since March 1993. This implies that for the purpose of foreign trade and travel you can convert the rupees into dollars and dollars into rupees in the foreign exchange market at the market determined exchange rate. That is, the foreign exchange rate of rupee is now not fixed but liable to change as demand for and supply of foreign exchange change. In July 1991, the Indian rupee was devalued by about 20 per cent. But now with market-determined exchange rate, the Indian rupee can depreciate or appreciate depending upon demand and supply conditions.

It is evident from the reforms introduced in the Indian economy that from a planned economy it has moved towards a free-market economy. Though we still have mixed economy with both the public and private sectors coexisting but the role of private sector which is governed by market forces has been greatly increased and that of the public sector greatly diluted. So we now have a mixed economy with greater orientation towards a free market and private sector.

More than two decades have passed when we initiated economic reforms in 1991 laying greater emphasis on liberalisation and privatisation. Now, the pertinent question is whether these economic reforms have ensured higher and sustained economic growth which the supporters of these reforms argued that they would, whether these reforms have led to a higher growth rate and to the greater reduction of poverty and unemployment which was expected of them.

Emergence of Market Failures. Now, from 2008 onwards as a result of financial crisis which shattered the U.S. and European countries and through the greater integration of the world economy through trade and international capital flows the developing countries (including India) could not remain unaffected. Financial crisis in the US occurred because banks and other financial institutions in their financial market operations clubbed sub-prime housing loans securities into the new derivatives in a non-transparent manner and sold them in the market. This whole financial market system collapsed when people started defaulting in paying their housing loans. In India as in other developing countries, which adopted the free market system under directions of World Bank and IMF which insisted on the adoption of policy of liberalisation, privatisation, globalisation as a precondition to bail them out of the balance of payments crisis and tough fiscal situation have witnessed again in recent years the failures of market system to ensure growth with stability. The most important reason is that in developing countries markets are characterised by widespread imperfections due to which they failed to work with efficiency and rationality. Joseph E. Stiglitz argues that "*markets are not necessarily either efficient or stable or that our economy is not well described by the standard model of competitive equilibrium used by a majority of economists*".[10]

10 Joseph E. Stiglitz, 'Let A Hundred Theories Bloom', *The Economic Times*, Aug. 2012.

CHAPTER

61

REVIEW OF PLANNING IN INDIA: 1951 TO 1991

At the time of independence India was a backward underdeveloped country. There was a lot of exploitation of India during the British colonial rule. This made Indian people very poor. The aim of freedom struggle was not mere gaining political freedom from the British rule but also to attain economic freedom for the Indian people. Economic freedom implies the removal of mass poverty that prevailed in India. At the time of independence there was deficiency of good entrepreneurs who could use the natural resource endowment of India for economic development. To improve living standards of the people, it was necessary to accelerate rate of economic growth. It was thought that the private sector lacked the necessary resources and the proper mindset to bring about rapid economic growth. Inspired by the Russian experience, planning as an instrument of economic development was adopted. The Planning Commission was set up to prepare five year plans which would indicate directions in which the Indian economy should move. Resources were to be allocated both at the Centre and in the States according to the plan priorities decided in a five year plan.

The basic objective of Indian planning has been acceleration of economic growth so as to raise the living standards of the people. Further, various five year plans also gave high priority to generation of employment opportunities, reduction of income inequalities and removal of poverty. In what follows we will explain the role of planning in India and then explain the development strategies adopted in various plans to achieve the objectives.

Development planning in India from 1951 to 1991 can be divided into the following two phases:

1. ***The Slow Growth Phase of 1950-51 to 1980-81***
2. ***The High Growth phase of 1980s.***

The first phase of slow growth covers the development plans from the First Five Year Plan (1951-56) to the Fifth Five Year Plan (1974-79). The high growth phase covers the plan periods of the Sixth Plan (1980-85) and Seventh Plan (1985-91). We critically review below the development strategies and growth models adopted in these five plans.

It is important to note that planning in India was initiated under the leadership of Pandit Jawaharlal Nehru, the first Prime Minister of India. Being a fabian socialist, Nehru believed in bringing about growth with equal distribution of income within the framework of a parliamentary democracy under which people enjoy fundamental rights not only to life and liberty but also to the ownership of property. With this, the objectives of India's five year plans were not only to achieve higher rate of economic growth but also to reduce inequalities of income and wealth and to check concentration of economic power in a few private hands.

Development Strategy of the First Five Year Plan (1951-56)

The First Five Year Plan is generally considered as a mere collection of various investment projects started earlier rather than based on a well thought-out strategy of planned development. However, this is not fully correct as First Five Year Plan was based on simple, aggregative Harrod-Domar growth model. According to Harrod-Domar growth model, rate of GDP growth depends on rates of saving and investment on the one hand and capital-output ratio on the other. In accordance with this, the target of achieving the growth rate was fixed on the basis of increasing the rates of saving and investment in the five-year plan period. Let us briefly explain how Harrod-Domar growth model explains that the rate of growth is a function of rate of saving or investment and capital-output ratio.

According to Harrod-Domar growth model, increase in national output or national income of an economy during a period depends upon the increase in the stock of capital (which is written as ΔK) during a period and the output-capital ratio or the productivity of capital. Assuming that both national income and the capital stock are measured in money, output-capital ratio can be written as $\Delta Y/\Delta K$, where ΔY stands for the increase in the national income and ΔK for the increase in the stock of capital. Thus if ₹ 4 worth of capital goods is required to produce one rupee worth of real output, incremental output-capital ratio $\left(\frac{\Delta Y}{\Delta K}\right)$ is equal to 1/4 or 0.25. Thus, the absolute increase in national income during a period (ΔY) can be obtained from increment in stock of capital ΔK multiplied by the output produced by a unit of capital $\left(i.e., \frac{\Delta Y}{\Delta K}\right)$. In symbolic terms we may express this as follows:

$$\Delta Y = \Delta K . \frac{\Delta Y}{\Delta K} \quad \ldots (1)$$

Now, change in capital stock (ΔK) is nothing else but investment. Therefore, following Domar in place of ΔK we can write I. The marginal output-capital ratio $\Delta Y/\Delta K$ which is assumed to be constant as well as equal to average output-capital ratio $\left(\frac{Y}{K}\right)$ by Domar and Harrod, can be denoted by σ. Thus, as Domar puts it, growth in capacity-output can be written as under:

$$\Delta Y = I\sigma \quad \ldots (2)$$

It may be noted that output-capital ratio (σ) is reciprocal of capital-output ratio *i.e.*, $\sigma = \frac{1}{v}$.

where v stands for capital-output ratio. Thus, increase in national income (ΔY) can be written as:

$$\Delta Y = \frac{I}{v}$$

Let us give an example. If ₹ 500 crore is invested in a year and capital-output ratio is 4, then growth in output in a year will be

$$\Delta Y = 500 \times 1/4$$
$$= 125 \text{ crore}$$

Domar's Growth Equation in Terms of Rates of Growth

It is greatly helpful to express the above growth equation in terms of *rates of growth of income and capital*. That is, growth in income and capital should be expressed as ratios of total income. For doing so we divide both sides of equation (1) above by Y and obtain:

$$\frac{\Delta Y}{Y} = \frac{\Delta K}{Y} . \frac{\Delta Y}{\Delta K} \quad \ldots (3)$$

$\frac{\Delta Y}{Y}$ represents the rate of growth of income and is therefore written as simply G_y. Besides, ΔK stands for increment in capital during a given time period and is nothing else but investment. Therefore, for ΔK in the equation (3) we can write I which represents investment. With these changes, we get the following equation:

$$G_y = \frac{I}{Y} \cdot \frac{\Delta Y}{\Delta K}$$

If it is further assumed that output-capital ratio remains constant, then the marginal output-capital ratio $\left(\frac{\Delta Y}{\Delta K}\right)$ will be equal to average output-capital ratio $\left(\frac{Y}{K}\right)$. With this assumption and also expressing output-capital ratio by σ we can write the above equation as follows:

$$G_y = \frac{I}{Y} . \sigma \qquad \ldots (4)$$

where G_y = Growth rate of output or income

$\frac{I}{Y}$ = Rate of investment as ratio of national income

σ = Output-capital ratio

From the growth equation (4) above, it is clear that, given the output-capital ratio, rate of growth of output depends upon the rate of investment; the greater the rate of investment, the greater the rate of growth of output or income. *To maintain full utilisation of the increasing capital stock as the economy grows the rate of savings (S) must remain equal to rate of investment* (*I*). Therefore, in equation (4) we can write $\frac{S}{Y}$ for $\frac{I}{Y}$. By doing so and rewriting equation (4) we have

$$G_y = \frac{S}{Y} \sigma$$

Since, $\frac{S}{Y}$ represents ratio of savings to national income, we can write it as s. With rewriting the above equation we have,

$$G_y = s.\sigma = \frac{s}{v} \qquad \ldots (5)$$

The above equation (5) represents the productive capacity effect of investment and saving and therefore represents the supply side of the growth problem.

With the above Harrod-Domar growth formula, the First Five Year Plan laid stress on raising the rate of saving in the economy so as to increase rate of investment or capital formation to achieve higher rate of growth of the Indian economy. To increase the rate of saving of the economy through appropriate fiscal and monetary policies, marginal rate of saving be kept higher than the average rate of saving. With this over time, the higher rate of saving will be achieved and in this way higher rate of investment and growth will become possible. In this regard Prof. Kurihara rightly states that, "Harrod and Domar have made the essential nature of growth mechanism operationally significant, for they-lay stress on saving ratio and the capital-output ratio (or its reciprocal) as measurable strategic variable to investigate and possible to manipulate for a desired rate of growth." [1]

Development Strategy in India's Second Five Year Plan

In the Second Five Year Plan strategy which continued practically till the Fourth Plan period (1969-74) it was visualised that basic constraints on development was the acute deficiency of physical capital which was responsible for small productive capacity of the Indian economy. It was further thought that the rate of capital formation depended on the domestic rate of saving which could be raised by the adoption of proper fiscal and monetary policies. However, Mahalanobis, author of the

1 K.K. Kurihara, *The Keynesian Theory of Development*, 1959, pp. 153-154.

Second Five Year Plan's development strategy, asserted that even if domestic rate of saving could be increased, the non-availability of the domestic capacity to produce capital goods would prevent the transformation of these savings into real productive investment. Note that real investment occurs when savings are spent on purchasing capital goods such as machinery and equipment. The alternative to the expansion of domestic capacity to produce capital goods would be importing capital goods to ensure sustained increase in the rate of real investment.

Mahalanobis ruled out import of capital goods on grounds of lack of foreign exchange earnings from exports. He argued that if large investment was not made in basic heavy industries producing capital goods, the country would ever remain dependent on foreign countries for the import of steel and capital goods. Since it was not possible for India to earn sufficient foreign exchange by increasing exports, the capital goods could not be imported in sufficient quantities owing to foreign exchange constraint. The result will be that the rate of real capital formation and rate of economic growth in the country would remain low. Thus, Mahalanobis was of the opinion that without adequate investment in basic heavy industries, it would not be possible to achieve rapid self-reliant economic growth. According to Mahalanobis, "*The proper strategy would be to bring about a rapid development of the industries producing investment goods in the beginning by increasing appreciably the proportion of investment in basic heavy industries. As the capacity to manufacture both heavy and light machinery and other capital goods increases, the capacity to invest in home produced capital goods would also increase steadily and India would become more and more independent of imports of foreign machinery and capital.*"[2]

Further, according to Mahalanobis, productive employment can be created only by increasing the production of capital goods. To quote him, "*The only way of eliminating unemployment in India is to build up a sufficiently large stock of capital which will enable all unemployed persons being absorbed in productive activity. Increasing the rate of investment is therefore the only fundamental remedy for unemployment in India.*"[3]

Another important element of development strategy adopted in India's earlier Five Year Plans was their emphasis on modern industrialisation, especially of import-substitution type. It was generally believed that industrialisation would generate sufficient employment opportunities which would cause surplus labour currently unemployed in agriculture to be shifted to more productive employment in industries. The underlying assumption was that agriculture was subject to diminishing returns and could not absorb unemployed labour productively whereas industries operated according to increasing returns to scale.

Thus, identifying underdevelopment with dependence on agriculture and thinking industrial growth especially the development of heavy industries as the core of development underlined the approach and strategy of the Second Five Year Plan. To quote from Second Plan again, "Low or static standards of living, underemployment and unemployment, and to a certain extent even the gap between the average income and the highest income are all manifestations of the basic underdevelopment which characterises an economy depending mainly on agriculture. Rapid industrialisation and diversification of the economy is thus the core of development. But *if industrialisation is to be rapid enough, the country must aim at developing basic industries and industries which make machines to make the machines needed for further development.*"[4]

It is clear from above that in the Second Plan there was a clear shift of priorities from agriculture to industries and within industries to basic heavy industries. As mentioned above, the logic of Mahalanobis in emphasising heavy industries was that the growth of basic heavy industries would

2 P.C. Mahalanobis, "The Approach of Operational Research to Planning in India", *Sankhya*, Vol. 16, Dec. 1953.

3 Mahalanobis, *op. cit.*, p. 22.

4 Government of India, Planning Commission, *Second Five Year Plan*, 1956.

enable the economy to accelerate the rate of capital formation and therefore economic growth. In fact, he identified the rate of growth of investment in the economy with the rate of growth of output in the capital goods sector of the economy.

Mahalanobis' Four-Sector Growth Model and Employment Generation. Mahalanobis realised that the basic heavy industries being capital-intensive would not ensure rapid expansion of employment opportunities and to bring the employment aspect into sharp focus he put forward a four-sector growth model in which he kept heavy industry sector (*i.e.*, K-sector) intact but divided the C-sector (*i.e.*, consumption goods sector) into three sub-sectors : C_1, C_2, and C_3 (sector C_1 represented factory enterprises using mechanised techniques and producing consumer goods; sector C_2 represented the household and small-scale enterprises also producing consumer goods, and sector C_3 represented provision of services). It was sector C_2 representing households and small-scale industries which in Mahalanobis' four-sector model was visualised to ensure the increased supply of consumer goods to meet the rising demand for them and also to ensure, being labour-intensive, expansion of employment opportunities. In keeping with this approach, Second Five Year Plan put restrictions on the growth of capacity in factory enterprises engaged in commodity production. However, since for these household or cottage enterprises adequate resources were not provided, nor any effort was made to improve their productivity, they could neither fulfil their targets of production of consumer goods nor of generating enough employment opportunities.[5]

Vital Role of the Public Sector. Lastly, the other important element of development strategy pursued in India's Five Year Plans (which continued up to the end of 1980s) was the vital role given to the public sector in economic development of the Indian economy. This was based on the assumption that if private sector and market mechanism were relied upon for development of industries there would be more investment in consumer goods industries catering to the needs of upper income groups while adequate investment in the sectors essential for rapid growth of the economy would not be forthcoming.

In the **Third Plan (1961-66)** also the strategy of Second Plan was continued as is clear from the following: "In the Third Plan, as in the Second, the development of basic industries such as steel, fuel and power and machine building and chemical industries is fundamental to rapid economic growth. These industries largely determine the pace at which the economy can become self-reliant and self-generating."[6] Though, "to achieve self-sufficiency in foodgrains and increase in agricultural production to meet the requirements of industry and exports"[7] was stated to be one of the objectives of the Third Plan, actual allocation of resources between agriculture and other sectors did not exhibit any significant difference from that of the Second Plan. Therefore, the concern for food and agriculture in the Third Plan appears to be mere verbal and was not built into the strategy of development.

Planning Strategy of the Fourth Five Year Plan (1969-74)

The Fourth Five Year Plan (1969-74) which was prepared under the Deputy Chairmanship of Late Prof. D.R. Gadgil, tried to give a new shape to the planning strategy and emphasis was sought to be placed on the common man, the weaker sections and the less privileged. The Fourth Plan slightly raised the allocation of public sector outlay to agriculture and irrigation to about 23 per cent as against 20 per cent in the Second Plan and the Third Plan. However, a good deal of hangover of the heavy industry biased strategy still prevailed in this plan too.

Thus, the development strategy pursued till the end of the Third Plan was *growth-oriented,* though objectives of increasing employment and reducing income inequalities were mentioned

5 Amlan Datta, *Strategy of Economic Development,* 1973. In the spinning of cotton, main emphasis was on Ambar Charkha. Ambar Charkha experiment failed because productivity and earning capacity per person engaged in it was found to be too low.

6 Government of India, Planning Commission, *Third Five Year Plan,* 1961, p.50.

7 *Ibid,* p. 48.

but never seriously pursued and implemented. However, the situation changed dramatically in the mid-sixties. The two wars, one with China in 1962 and the second with Pakistan in 1965, compelled us to increase defence expenditure. During this time foreign aid situation also became unfavourable resulting in foreign exchange crisis. The devaluation of rupee in June 1966 also did not improve the foreign exchange situation. The situation became more grim with the successive two droughts that hit the country in 1966 and 1967.

Worsening economic situation and growing concerns for national security highlighted the two shortcomings of the development strategy adopted in the Second and Third Five Year Plans. They were (1) *relative neglect of agriculture* resulting in the acute food problem for the country, (2) *crucial dependence on foreign aid* which could not be relied upon for accelerating growth in the future plans. This highlighted the importance of pursuing the *objective of self-reliance* which implied reducing the dependence on foreign aid.

In the later half of the sixties, resource situation for the public sector became difficult and uncertain. This resulted in the suspension of planning for three-year period (1966-69). This three-year period (1966-69) is therefore called *period of plan holiday.* Due to non-availability of adequate funds, public sector investment was reduced from the mid-sixties onwards.

Thus, in the Fourth Five Year Plan resource allocation to agriculture was increased to achieve self- sufficiency in foodgrains. Besides, new strategy of agricultural development, initiated earlier in 1966-67, was pursued more vigorously during the Fourth Plan period. The new strategy of agricultural development which involved the use of high-yielding varieties (HYV) of seeds, fertilizers, pesticides with appropriate quantity of water was introduced in a few selected districts of the country where assured irrigation facilities were available.

Second, in the Fourth Plan relatively more importance was given to export promotion than before along with the policy of import substitution which was continued. Though the new agricultural development strategy proved to be successful and production of foodgrains, especially wheat, grew at a satisfactory rate, the growth scenario remained dim due to slackening of public sector investment which started in the mid-sixties and continued up till mid-seventies. Average growth in net national product (NNP) achieved during the Fourth Plan was only 3.3 per cent per annum. As a result of *cut-back in public investment, problem of deficiency of aggregate demand emerged* which resulted in slowing down of industrial growth during 1966 to 1978-79. It is important to note that in first four Five Year Plans of India it was never visualised that in the Indian economy level of aggregate demand could possibly be a constraint on the growth process.

Development Strategy in the Fifth Five Year Plan (1974–79)

Besides, in the early seventies, it was realised that growth-oriented development strategy adopted in the first over two decades of planned development (1951-74) had not succeeded in alleviating poverty. Statistical evidence revealed that about 321 million people lived below the poverty line in 1973-74 and unemployment problem was mounting. At this time political situation in the country became uncertain with Congress Party losing election in some States. Further, while preparing the Fifth Five Year Plan it was recognised that trickle down effect of economic growth on the poor and unemployed was not working. Thus, in "***Towards an Approach to Fifth Five Year Plan***" it was stated that "*Economic growth by itself would not lead to the solution of the problem of poverty and unemployment in the foreseeable future*". Therefore, Fifth Plan formulated a programme of making a '*direct attack on poverty*' which visualised special employment such as *Jawahar Rozgar Yojana,* for providing wage employment to the poor and IRDP (Integrated Rural Development Programme) for providing self-employment to the poor. Except for these anti-poverty schemes Fifth Plan was not much different from the earlier Five Year Plans. These anti-poverty schemes were merely added to the Fifth Five Year Plan without integrating them with the growth programmes.

But while formulating Fifth Plan (1974-79) the new Planning Minister, Mr. D.P. Dhar, took charge of preparing the final draft. According to the **Approach to Fifth Plan** on which the final draft was made, "*The strategy for elimination of poverty ... rested on two major factors, a rising rate of growth of domestic product combined with declining rate of population growth*". This latter approach was indeed a combination of old planning strategy with emphasis on economic growth though increase in employment was considered to be a desirable objective. Thus *employment orientation* was not actually given to the planning strategy in the Fifth Five Year Plan. For achieving a higher rate of economic growth Fifth Plan draft was also based on a wrong assumption of incremental capital-output ratio (ICOR) of 3.4 whereas in the previous plan it was actually found to be equal to 4.3.

However, during the period of Fifth Plan (1974-79), the emergency was declared in the country and Prime Minister's 20-Point Programme was given more importance over the implementation of Fifth Plan projects and policies. The Fifth Plan could not be completed as in March 1977, Janata Government came to power and terminated the Fifth Plan in March 1978.

INDIA'S ECONOMIC PERFORMANCE IN THE FIRST THREE DECADES (1951-81) OF DEVELOPMENT PLANNING

The development strategy pursued in the first three decades of planning (1951-81) has both successes and failures in achieving the objectives and targets. The Indian economy witnessed a profound structural transformation during this period. We became wholly self-sufficient in foodgrains and most other agricultural commodities. Food production grew at a rate faster than that of population. As a result of industrial growth during the first three decades of the Indian industry planning (1950-80) became capable of meeting nearly 100 per cent of our requirements of consumer goods and about 85 per cent of our annual demand for capital goods. The strong base of future industrial growth rate was laid as a result of significant development of basic and heavy industries.

Table 61.1. Economic Growth in the Planning Period (1951 to 1981)

Years	Average annual growth rates (%)			
	GDP at Factor Cost (at 1993-94 Prices)	Agriculture and related activities	Industrial Sector (Manufacturing and related activities)	Tertiary Sector (Services)
1950-51 to 1960-61	3.85	2.8	6.2	4.2
1960-61 to 1970-71	3.4	2.1	5.4	4.5
1970-71 to 1980-81	3.6	1.9	4.3	4.5

Source: Calculated from the data given in GOI, *Economic Surveys*, for the years 2001-02, 2002-03 and 2003-04 and T.N. Srinivasan and Suresh D. Tendulkar, *Reintegrating India with the World Economy*, p.26 (Table 62.1)

We succeeded in building up a vast reservoir of technical and managerial skills. For three decades, 1951-81, the average annual growth rate of real GDP was 3.6 per cent against a virtual stagnation in real GDP during the first half of the 20th century. However, as compared to international standards the Indian growth rate in the first three decades was quite low. As will be seen from Table 61.1, annual growth rate in GDP was 3.85% during 1951-61, 3.4% during 1961-71 and 3.6% in 1971-81. Further, as is seen from Table 61.1, **growth rate in GDP was pulled down in the decades of sixties and seventies as compared to the fifties by slowdown in both industrial and agricultural growth rates.**

Table 61.2. Overall GDP Growth, Saving and Investment Rates and Incremental Capital-Output Ratios in the Indian Economy (1951-1981)

Period	GDP growth rate in plan period at 1993-94 prices	Saving Rate (% of GDP)	Investment Rate (% of GDP)	ICOR	Current Account Deficit* (% of GDP)
First Plan (1951-1955-56)	3.85	10.28	10.64	3.83	0.36
Second Plan (1956-57 to 1960-61)	3.38	11.73	14.50	5.63	2.77
Third Plan (1961-62 to 1965-66)	2.84	13.21	15.46	5.4	2.25
Plan Period (1966-67 to 1970-71)	4.66	14.35	15.98	3.4	1.63
Plan Period (1971-72 to 1975-76)	3.08	17.98	17.88	5.8	0.6
Plan Period (1976-77 to 1980-81)	3.20	21.65	21.46	6.7	–0.19

* Current account deficit indicates *foreign savings used.*

Source: CSO, *National Accounts Statistics* and Plan Documents and T.N. Srinivasan and Tendulkar, op. cit..

It may be further noted that there was a *significant deceleration in industrial growth rate from mid-sixties to mid-seventies (1965-76)* due to decline in public sector investment. With population growing at the rate of 2.25 per cent per annum, per capita income increased at the rate about 1.5 per cent per year during the period (1951-81). However, as we will see below during the decade of eighties (1981-1991) growth rate in per capita income accelerated due to higher growth in GDP and also due to decline in growth rate of population.

Increase in Saving Rate and Capital Formation: 1951 to 1980

Rates of gross saving and capital formation as a per cent of GDP which are important determinants of economic growth showed upward trends with some fluctuations during the period 1951-80. Both rates increased from around 8 per cent in 1950-51 to 13 per cent in 1955-56, the beginning of the second Five Year Plan. Thus the two rates remained in balance during this period (see Table 61.2). However, from 1956 to 1965-66, the gap between the two emerged; gross domestic saving (GDS) falling short of gross domestic capital formulation (GDCF). Besides, the two rates fluctuated a good deal during the decade of 1956-1965. The deficit of gross domestic saving and gross domestic capital formation (GDCF), *i.e.*, gross domestic investment during this decade, was met mostly by obtaining concessional foreign assistance with net capital inflow as percentage of GDFC being equal to 2.12 during 1956-60 and 2.26 during 1961-65.

Table 61.3. Rate of GDS, GDCF and Rate of Growth GDP$_{FC}$ from 1951 to 1980

Period	GDS at current market prices as % of GDP$_{FC}$	GDCF at current market prices as % of GDP$_{FC}$	Net Capital Inflow (+) as % of GDP$_{FC}$ (at current prices)	Rate of growth of GDP$_{FC}$ at1993-94 prices
1951-55	8.74	8.96	0.22	3.85
1956-60	11.10	13.22	2.12	3.38
1961-65	11.96	14.22	2.26	5.00
1966-70	13.18	15.00	1.82	2.90
1971-73	14.67	15.50	0.83	1.90
1974-80	18.60	18.46	–0.14	3.40

Source: T.N. Srinivasan and Suresh Tendulkar, *Reintegrating India with World Economy* OUP, 2003, p. 26

As will be seen from Table 61.3, during the periods 1966-70 and 1971-73, annual rate of gross domestic capital formation (GDCF) increased to 15 per cent of GDP in 1966-70 and to 15.50 per cent of GDP in 1971-73. This was largely financed by domestic saving which increased only little. The average annual rate of gross domestic saving rose from about 13.2 per cent during 1966-70 to 14.7 per cent during 1971-73. It is mainly due to stagnation of gross capital formation during 1966-70 and 1971-73 that average annual rate of growth of GDP during this period fell to 2.9 per cent per annum during 1966-70 and 1.9 per cent during 1971-73 (See Table 61.3). It may be further noted that after war with Pakistan in 1965 on Kashmir issue and then in 1971 on Bangladesh issue, India could not get much foreign aid. As a result, *capital inflow* during this period declined which also accounted for low rate of capital formation. From the mid-seventies public sector investment was raised which resulted in higher average rate of capital formation (18.5 per cent of GDP) during 1974-80 and this was fully financed by domestic saving which shot up to 18.6 per cent per annum during this period.

A Critical Evaluation of Planning in the First Three Decades (1951-81)

The first three decades of planning in India (1951-81) was characterised by lower rate of economic growth at around 3.6 per cent per annum on an average. There are mainly two explanations for this. First, Late Prof Sukhamoy Chakravarty attributed it to the gross inefficiency of public sector enterprises which were given a crucial role in economic development during this plan period.[8] According to him, there were many areas of public sector production such as transport, steel, fertilizers where gross inefficiency prevailed and this accounted for low productivity and lower growth rate. Further, according to him, *in Indian planning adequate growth of aggregate demand was taken for granted* and it was due to the decline in aggregate demand caused by decrease in public sector investment from mid-sixties to late seventies that caused underutilisation of productive capacity and raised incremental capital-output ratio (ICOR) and led to lower growth of output.[9]

It is important to note that it is only from mid-eighties when industrial policy was liberalised somewhat and private sector was given relatively greater role that economic growth rate picked up and overall GDP growth rate of 5.6 per cent was achieved in the decade of 1981-91.

Prof. T.N. Srinivasan and Prof Suresh Tendulkar attributed lower growth rate in the first phase of pre-reform period (*i.e.,* before 1981) to the **import-substitution strategy** (which is also called first phase of **inward-oriented strategy)** ***and inadequate attention paid to expanding exports to generate higher growth of output.*** To quote them, "*India's inward-orientation has had significant economic costs to lower overall growth and stagnating living standards. Japan's rapid export growth was associated with very rapid GDP growth and improvement in living standards.*"[10]

Further, Srinivasan and Tendulkar hold Mahalanobis' strategy with its emphasis on basic heavy and capital goods industries and import-substitution industrialisation responsible for lower growth of GDP and the high incidence of poverty. Thus they write, "Indian economic performance under this development strategy was poor. For three decades until 1980-81 the average annual rate of growth of real GDP was 3.75 per cent. With the population growing at nearly 2.25 per cent a year income per head grew at about 1.50 per cent. *With such a low rate of growth, it is no surprise that there was little reduction in poverty*—the proportion of population with consumption below a very modest poverty line fluctuated at around an average of more than 50 per cent. *The economy was insulated from world markets*—India's share of world merchandise exports declined from about 2.2 per cent in 1948 to 0.5 per cent in the early eighties.[11]

The other drawback of planning in the first four decades has been that industrialisation to which a large chunk of resources were allocated failed *to generate adequate employment opportunities* and the goal of transformation of occupational structure by transfer of population from agriculture to organised industries and services remained unfulfilled. The occupational structure remained almost unchanged, Besides, rate of unemployment increased as the increase in employment opportunities could not keep pace with the growth of labour force. No wonder that the change in plan strategy was called for.

---

8 Sukhamoy Chakravarty, *Development Planning: The Indian Experience,* 1987, p. 28.

9 Sukhamoy Chakravarty, "Development Strategies in the Eighties" in *Economic and Political Weekly,* 1984.

10 T.N. Srinivasan and Suresh D. Tendulkar, "*Reintegrating India with the World Economy,* Oxford University Press, 2003, p.12.

11 Srinivasan and Tendulkar, *op. cit.* p. 8.

No Reduction in Poverty. In the first three decades (1951-81) of planned development in India the rate of economic growth was not high enough to make a significant dent on the problem of poverty. The proportion of population with level of consumption below a very modest poverty line fluctuated between 50 and 58 per cent of population during the fifties, sixties and seventies (that is, in the first three decades of planning). These estimates clearly show that in the first three decades of planning (1951-81) economic growth did not have any impact on the poverty problem in India. This is because of not only slow rate of economic growth during this period but also the benefits of whatever economic growth occurred did not trickle down to the poor. As we shall discuss later that it is only in the eighties and nineties when annual rate of economic growth rate accelerated to around 5.6 per cent and 6 per cent respectively and special employment schemes were started on a large scale that there was a significant decline in the incidence of poverty.

Table 61.4. Trends in Poverty in India in Three Decades of Planned Development (1951-80)

Period	Percentage of Population below the poverty line (HCR)			Number of Poor (in millions)		
	Rural	Urban	All India	Rural	Urban	Total
1951-55	54.77	42.70	52.66	170.6	28.1	198.7
1965-66	53.96	47.06	52.74	184.6	34.8	219.5
1961-65	48.59	45.46	48.02	183.0	38.6	221.6
1966-70	60.44	50.90	58.60	251.0	50.7	301.7
1973-74	56.4	49.0	54.9	261	60	321
1977-78	53.1	45.2	51.3	264	68	329

Source: *Planning Commission* for the data from 1973-74 onwards and from 1951-55 to 1966-70. Gaurav Datt, *Poverty in India, 1951-92, Trends and Decomposition,* World Bank Study 1996. Gaurav Datt's estimates are comparable with Planning Commission data as he uses the same indices for estimating poverty from the data of earlier NSS.

Note: Poverty line used to measure Head-Count Ratio (HCR) of poverty was ₹ 49.1 **per capita per month** (rural) and ₹ 56.6 **per capita per month** (urban) in **1973-74. Consumer Price Index** for agricultural labourers (rural) and **Consumer Price Index** for industrial workers (urban) have been used to estimate the poverty line according to the prices prevailing in each year.

PHASE OF HIGH GROWTH RATE OF THE DECADE OF THE 1980S

The 1980s made an important break in the changes in economic policy and growth performance of the Indian economy. The decade of the 1980s emerged out of a three-decade-ong low growth phase (1951-1981). The decade of the 1980s covered the two Five Year Plans, the Sixth Five Year Plan (1980-85) and the Seventh Five Year Plan (1985-90). Let us first briefly explain the broad strategy of development followed in these two plans.

The Development Strategy in the Sixth Five Year Plan (1980-85)

It may be noted that there were *two* Sixth Five Year Plans. One Sixth Five Year Plan for the period 1978-83 was prepared by Janata Government but it could not be completed as Janata government collapsed and failed to win the new election held in December 1979. The Congress Government again came to power in 1980 and formulated new Sixth Five Year Plan for the period 1980-85. The development strategy of Sixth Plan (1980-85) laid emphasis on promotion of efficiency in resource use and improvement in productivity to achieve 5.2 per cent growth in GDP. Besides, the infrastructure sector was given the topmost priority in the allocation of resources. Further, in the Sixth Plan *employment generation and poverty eradication* were given high priority. In this additional employment opportunities for 46 million persons were planned to be generated during the plan period through IRDS (Integrated Rural Development Scheme), NREP (National Rural Employment Programme) and RLEP (Rural Landless Employment Programme) schemes. The Sixth Plan aimed at reducing the percentage of people below the poverty line to 30 per cent of population.

The infrastructure sector was given the topmost priority in the development strategy of the Sixth Plan whereas, like the earlier plans, agriculture, rural development and special employment programme received allocation of about 13 per cent of total outlay.

The Seventh Plan (1985-90) Strategy

The Seventh Plan's strategy of development was to improve the utilisation of existing productive capacities rather than creating new capacities. It sought to secure more output out of productive assets that had been built up in the previous years. Besides, the plan strategy laid emphasis on a direct attack on the problems of poverty and unemployment by providing a greater outlay on special employment schemes rather than relying on 'trickle -down' effect of economic growth. The other important aspect of development strategy of the Seventh Plan was that it planned for a non-inflationary growth process by laying greater emphases on the production and supply of *mass consumption goods* like foodgrains, edible oils, sugar, cooking fuel and textiles. Thus, the strategy of development for the Seventh Plan accorded a higher priority to wage goods. Another *important change in the policy regime during the Seventh Plan period (1985-90) was that process of liberalisation was initiated.* In the industrial policy resolution of 1956 amendments were made under which licensing procedures were somewhat relaxed and liberalised, and the existing capacities were allowed to be used liberally by diversification through broad-banding. Besides, measures were taken to give greater role to the private sector in economic development.

It is worthwhile to mention that Bhagwati and Desia in their important work '*India: Planning for Industrialisation*' published in 1970 strongly advocated the case for domestic and external liberalisation of the Indian economy to accelerate economic growth. Besides, Bhagwati and T.N. Srinivasan in their important work '*Foreign Trade Regime in Economic Development*', published in 1976 made a strong case for relaxation of controls on India's external sector and liberalisation of the Indian economy and give greater role to the private sector to accelerate economic growth.

In the eighties of the 20th century, two Five Year Plans, the Sixth Plan (1980-85) and Seventh Plan (1985-90), were launched. In the Sixth Plan period (1980-85) and Seventh Plan period (1985-90), average annual growth rate of 5.6 per cent and 5.8 per cent respectively was recorded. This higher growth rate in national income also resulted in a higher growth rate in per capita income of 3.2 per cent and 3.6 per cent in the Sixth Plan and Seventh Plan periods respectively. Favourable result of this higher growth rate in both national income and per capita income was the decline in the ratio of people living below the poverty line. As will be seen from Table 61.5 percentage of population living below the poverty line (All India) which was 51.3 in 1977-78 fell to 44.5 in 1983 and further to 38.9 in 1987-88 and 36.3 in 1993-94.

Table 61.5. Rate of GDS, GDCF and Rate of GDPF growth in the Decade of 1980s

Period	GDS at Current Market Prices as % of GDP_{FC}	GDCF at Current Market Prices as % of GDP_{FC}	Net Capital Inflow as % of GDP at Current Prices	Rate of Growth of GDP_{FC} at 1993-94 prices
1981-1985	18.36	19.70	1.34	5.66
1985-1990	20.26	22.60	2.34	5.84
1990-1991	23.10	26.30	3.20	5.30

Source: Srinivasan and Tendulkar, *Reintegrating India in the World Economy*, OUP, 2002

Now, the question is what caused this acceleration in growth rate in the late seventies and the eighties. The *important factor causing this acceleration in growth rate in the late seventies and early eighties was the increase in public sector investment which remained sluggish earlier since the mid-sixties.* Among other factors bringing about higher growth rate is the *liberalisation measures* of removal of some restrictions and relaxation of licensing procedures by making amendments through industrial policy statements of July 1980 and December 1985. In these industrial policy statements certain changes were made in the industrial licensing policies and procedures which were designed to facilitate capacity expansion in the private sector and create competitive environment. In the later half of eighties (1985-90), contrary to the Mahalanobis strategy of growth, export promotion was given relatively more importance than import substitution which led to higher growth rates of exports of 9.4 per cent, 24.1 per cent, 15.6 per cent, and 18.9 per cent in 1986-87, 1987-88, 1988-89 and 1989-90 respectively which speeded up the overall growth rate of the Indian economy during the later half of eighties.

As will be seen from Table 63.1, from the mid-seventies public sector investment was raised which resulted in higher average rate of capital formation (18.5 per cent of GDP) during 1974-80 and this was fully financed by domestic saving which shot up to 18.6 per cent per annum during this period. It will be seen from Table 61.2 that in the first half of the eighties (1981-85), average annual rate of GDCF as per cent of GDP picked up to 19.7 percent and in the second half (1986-90) of eighties to 22.6 per cent of GDP_{FC}. As a result, annual average growth rate of GDP rose to 5.6 per cent during 1986-90) and to 5.8 per cent during 1986-90. However, in the second half of the eighties (1986-90) annual rate of gross domestic saving (GDS) as per cent of GDP_{FC} was 20.26 resulting in capital inflow of 2.34 per cent of GDP_{FC} which was mostly in the form of commercial borrowing from abroad. This led to a sharp increase in external foreign debt which put pressure on our balance of payments. In 1990-91, the gap between GDS and GDCF widened and resulted in capital inflow of 3.2 per cent of GDP_{FC} causing foreign exchange crisis.

But, as mentioned above, *the higher growth rate achieved in the eighties was not sustainable as public sector investment was increased by incurring higher doses of deficit financing leading to higher rates of inflation in the economy and through commercial borrowing on a large scale from abroad which significantly raised external public debt.* External public debt servicing consumed a large part of our export earnings. This created foreign exchange crisis in 1990-91 which brought India to the brink of default.

Table 61.6. Trends in Poverty in India in the 1980s

	Percentage of Population below the Poverty Line (HCR)			Number of Poor (in millions)		
Period	Rural	Urban	All India	Rural	Urban	Total
1977-78	53.1	45.2	51.3	264	68	329
1983	45.7	40.8	44.5	252	71	323
1987-88	39.1	38.2	38.9	232	75	307
1993-94	37.3	32.4	36.3	244	76	320

Source: Gaurav Datt, *Poverty in India, 1951-92, Trends and Decomposition,* World Bank Study 1996. Gaurav Datt's estimates are comparable with Planning Commission data as he uses the same indices for estimating poverty from the data of earlier NSS.

Notes: Poverty line used to estimate the percentage of population living below the line is ₹49.1 **per capita per month** (rural) and ₹56.6 **per capita per month** (urban) in **1973-74. Consumer Price Index** for agricultural labourers (rural) and **Consumer Price Index** for industrial workers (urban) have been used to estimate the poverty line according to the prices prevailing in each year.

Since capital-intensive technologies were used in the growth process of both industrial and agricultural sectors, the employment opportunities increased but not large enough to absorb even annual growth of labour force in productive employment. As a result, backlog of unemployment went on increasing with each successive Five Year Plan. At the end of Fourth Plan period (1973-74) unemployment was estimated at 9 per cent of labour force on current daily basis.

In contrast to the planning in the first three decades. (1951-80), in the decade of eighties growth rate picked up to 5.6 per cent due to revival of public sector investment and along with expansionary fiscal policy financed by commercial borrowing mainly from abroad which proved to be quite unsustainable as it led to balance of payments crisis of 1991. Explaining the debt-driven unsustainable consequences of policy of fiscal expansionism during the 1980s, Srinivasan and Tendulkar write, "*The current account deficit rose to a record 3.2 per cent of GDP in 1990 and debt-service payments amounted to as much as 35.3 per cent of current foreign exchange receipts*. Foreign exchange reserves were down to a level barely enough to finance imports for two and a half month. Short-term deposits amounted to a dangerously high level of 146.5 per cent of foreign exchange reserves by the end of March 1991. The rate of inflation soared exceeding 10 per cent in 1990. Expectations of an immediate devaluation of the rupee led to withdrawal of deposits by non-resident Indians. A spectre of default on short-term loans and downgrading of India credit rating loomed. Such was the nature of crisis that it compelled India to go in for structural reforms.

Now, the important question arises what caused the change in economic policy and strategy in the 1980s. First, as explained above, the GDP growth rate in the Indian economy got stuck at 3.6 per cent per annum under the controlled regime where public sector was dominant. This slow growth rate was not enough to raise the standards of living of the population which was during that period increasing at an explosive annual growth rate of 2.25 per cent. As a result, the population below the poverty line remained above 50 per cent which posed threat to social stability.

Two major changes in the world economy also prompted thinking about change in economic policy and relaxing controls over the private sector in the interest of accelerating economic growth. The first important change was the breakdown of the Bretton Woods system of fixed exchange rates when in 1972, the US government decided to delink the US dollar from gold. This resulted in the beginning of floating exchange rate which caused sharp fluctuations in foreign exchange rates of currencies of the major trading partners. The second important international factor that caused change in India's economic policy in the 1980s was the steep hike in oil prices first in 1973 and again in 1979 which raised the energy costs of oil-importing countries. Commenting on this Professors and Suresh D. Tendulkar and T.N. Bhawani write, "*With chronic foreign exchange shortages and almost total dependence on oil imports to meet the growing energy needs, both the events faced India's reluctant entry into the world economy. While fluctuating exchange rates and steep hikes in energy destabilized the growth process in many other developing countries, paradoxically they proved a blessing in disguise rather than a disaster for the Indian policy makers*".[12]

The above changes in the international economy forced the Indian government to make departure from the earlier economic policy and moved towards liberalisation and relaxed controls over the private sector and to give somewhat export-orientation to the Indian economy. Industrial policy resolution of July 1980 assigned relatively greater role to the private sector so as to achieve optimum utilisation of the installed capacity and maximum production and higher levels of productivity. This was needed to ensure the urgency of bringing about rapid economic growth. The second important change in the Industrial policy statement of July 1980 was to launch a drive to increase the efficiency of the public sector through a time bound programme of improving the working of the public sector. This was considered essential for reviving the faith of the people in the public sector.

It is important to note that for acceleration of GDP growth in the 1980s, stimulus came from the domestic demand rather than increase in share of India's exports.[13] Further, the domestic market expansion during the 1980s was due to relatively growth rate of 4.4 per cent in agriculture and allied activities and sharp rise in fiscal deficit of the Centre and States combined from 6.3 per cent of GDP in 1981-82 to 9.4 per cent in 1990-91.

---

12 Suresh D. Tendulkar and T.N. Bhavani, *Understanding Reforms: Post-1991 India*, Oxford University Press, New Delhi, 2007, pp. 66-67.

13 See Tendulkar and Bhavani, *op.cit.*, p. 70.

CHAPTER 62

ECONOMIC CRISIS OF 1991 AND REVIEW OF PLANNING IN POST-REFORMS PERIOD (1992-2012)

1991 Crisis and Macroeconomic Imbalances

During the whole of the eighties public sector faced a financial crunch as its expenditure on defence, food, fertilizers and imports increased tremendously giving rise to huge budget deficits of the Government. The Government resorted to commercial borrowing from abroad which resulted in heavy debt burden and increased debt service charges. This caused great balance of payments crisis in 1990-91. This crisis compelled us to adopt fiscal stabilisation and structural adjustment programme of World Bank and IMF.

As mentioned above, the intervention by the government was essential to initiate the process of economic development and thereby to break the vicious circle of poverty. As a result, public sector made investment in a big way in basic heavy industries and in irrigation. However, during the seventies and eighties several shortcomings of the working of public sector were noticed.

First, the public sector which was expected to generate adequate resources for the growth of the economy not only failed to do so but in fact was incurring huge losses which raised the expenditure of the Government. The losses of the public sector were said to be due to the *inefficiency in the working of public enterprises.* Secondly, the problem of *macroeconomic imbalances*, both in the internal and external sectors, emerged and assumed serious proportions in 1990-91. The huge deficits in the successive budgets of the government due to the internal imbalance of Government expenditure and revenue led to the creation of more money supply which created the serious problem of rising prices, so much so that annual rate of inflation went up to about 17 per cent during August 1991. This compelled the newly elected Congress Government to adopt fiscal policy to reduce budgetary deficits for stabilising prices.

In the external sector, the huge deficits in the balance of payments due to the rising imports and sluggish exports persisted in the eighties and, to meet this deficit, the Government resorted to commercial borrowing from abroad at higher market rates of interest. As a result of persistent deficits on the current account, the foreign exchange reserves declined to a very small sum in June 1991 which were sufficient for payments for necessary imports only for a few weeks. This compelled the government to approach IMF (International Monetary Fund) for loans to make necessary payments and enhance the foreign exchange reserves.

Thirdly, though the annual growth of national income during the eighties went up to 5.9 per cent and growth rate of the industrial sector to 8 per cent, which was considered to be a good performance, it was feared that due to macroeconomic imbalances which emerged in the economy they would not be sustained any more. In the external sector, the situation became so worse in 1991 that India came to the brink of default. To avoid the default and to win over the confidence of international business community, the Government had to sell a part of its gold reserves and a certain amount of gold was even pledged to obtain the foreign exchange reserves to meet its obligations. Further, it had to approach the IMF for loans to tide over the foreign exchange crisis.

New Economic Policy of Structural Adjustment

However, to evolve a long-term solution to achieve higher rate of economic growth with price stability, to bring about equilibrium in balance of payments the newly elected Congress Government with Dr. Manmohan Singh as Finance Minister adopted what is popularly called *New Economic Policy* on the advice of IMF and World Bank. According to this policy, the Government pruned down its expenditure so as to *reduce fiscal deficit for achieving price stability. But more important element of new economic policy was the adoption of what are called* ***Structural Adjustment Reforms*** which sought to change the nature of Indian economic system by ultimately establishing *a free market economy*. Thus, the economic crisis of 1991 provided an opportunity for the Government to undertake major economic reforms aimed at removing restrictive control on the domestic industrial production and investment and foreign trade. Thus Professors T.N. Srinivasan and S. Tendulkar write, "*The reforms indeed heralded a major change in the country's development strategy. India gradually abandoned the use of quantitative controls in economic management in favour of market-based instruments. There was a decisive move away from inward orientation and toward greater integration with the global economy. Finally, the reforms signalled a shift away from an overstretched, over-extended, rigid and inefficient public sector and toward greater reliance on the private sector.*"[1]

Under this structural adjustment programme, the role of public sector in economic development has been diluted and that of private sector enhanced and expanded. It may be noted that the policy of free-market economy also got strong stimulus due to the collapse of socialist system in Soviet Russia and other centrally planned socialist economies in Eastern Europe. Accordingly, under the new economic policy initiated in 1991 the idea of the predominant role of the public sector was abandoned and the private sector was given a greater role in promoting economic growth through competition and efficiency. Instead of being directed by the planning and licensing, the private sector was to be governed by the market forces. Besides, there has been liberalisation of imports as tariffs have been drastically cut down. Foreign private investment has been given greater importance and incentives have been provided to attract them. Further, instead of import-substitution, now greater emphasis has been laid on the expansion of exports to achieve growth with self-reliance. In the post-reform period four Five Year Plans have been launched.

Indicative Planning. As far as the role of the private sector is concerned under the present policy of economic liberalisation it is regulated through *indicative planning*. Under the indicative planning, Planning Commission has to outline the broad directions in which the economy should be growing. To conclude, the planning has to (a) provide vision of the future, (b) construct medium term economic projections for the entire economy, (c) evolve a system of information pooling and dissemination, (d) identify areas of development where the economy has strengths or where the country needs to build up strengths, (e) evolve *appropriate policy measures* to achieve the desired goals.

Thus, despite a more deregulated environment as it exists today in India, planning has a useful role to play, especially in policy formulation, to achieve the national goals and objectives.

EIGHTH PLAN AND ITS DEVELOPMENT STRATEGY

Eighth Plan which was to start from April 1990 was deferred because of political uncertainty. Finally, when, in June 1991, Congress Government came back to power, Indian economy was in the grip of economic crisis due to balance of payments difficulties. Due to this economic crisis, as mentioned above, the whole approach to economic policy went a sea change. When the final version of Eighth Plan covering the period 1992-97 was formulated in accordance with the new economic policy it laid emphasis on liberalisation, privatisation and globalisation of the Indian economy. The role of public sector, which played a vital role in development strategies of earlier plans, was greatly

1 T. N. Srinivasan and Suresh D. Tendulkar, *Reintegrating India in the World Economy*, Oxford University Press, 2002.

restricted. The Eighth Five Year Plan visualised the role of public sector in the following terms.

1. The public sector should make investment only in infrastructure such as power, communication, irrigation, and transport where private sector investment is not likely to come forth to an adequate extent within reasonable time perspective. In line with new Industrial Policy of 1991, the public sector was to withdraw from the areas where no public purpose was served by its presence. Thus *public sector disinvestment* was planned to be accelerated. The licensing and other physical controls over the private sector were abolished. The private sector was allowed to invest in those industries which were previously the exclusive concern of the public sector.

2. Public enterprises were expected to accept the principle of market economy as the main operating principle unless the commodities and services that were produced and distributed by them were specifically required for protecting the poorest in the society.

Indicative Planning. In line with the policy of liberalisation and privatisation the Eighth Plan mentioned that planning in India would be increasingly *indicative*. The main purpose of indicative planning is to improve the information available to private enterprises so that they can make optimal decisions regarding investment and production. This information is provided through making forecasts or projections of GDP, demands for various goods, consumer spending, balance of payments, money supply, inflationary trends and other macro aggregates. However, such projections of various macro-aggregates are not regarded as targets as would be the case under centralised planning. Private enterprises face a lot of uncertainties regarding future due to lack of information. Indicative planning is regarded as a way of providing information to the private enterprises. Besides, by using various fiscal and monetary instruments, the government could encourage industries which have a bright future and discourage industries which have no future. Thus, through indicative plans efforts are made to identify so called *'sun-rise' industries* and *'sun-set'* industries.

Promoting Competition. The major thrust of the Eighth Plan was to create a more competitive environment as a means to improving the productivity and efficiency of the system. This was sought to be achieved by removing the barriers to entry and restrictions on the growth of firms in the private sector.

Export-oriented Growth Strategy. Another important element of the growth strategy of the Eighth Plan was that it laid greater emphasis on the growth of exports to accelerate rate of economic growth and to achieve self-reliance. Thus, export pessimism of earlier plans was abandoned and it set a target of achieving 13.6 per cent annual growth rate in exports as against the target of 8.4 per cent annual growth in imports.

Realising that investment was a major driving force of economic growth, the Eighth Plan planned an average saving rate of 21.6 per cent of GDP and a foreign saving rate (that is, current account deficit) of 1.4 per cent of GDP, and fixed investment rate of 23 per cent of GDP. With the assumed incremental capital-output ratio (ICOR) of 4.1, it was expected to achieve average annual growth rate of 5.6 per cent during the Eighth Plan period (1992-97). However, in the Eighth Plan higher growth rate of 6.7 per cent per annum was actually achieved. Actual investment rate achieved was 23.3 with 3.5 as incremental capital-output ratio (ICOR).

PLANNING STRATEGY IN THE NINTH PLAN (1997-2002)

In the development strategy adopted in the Ninth Plan, private sector was given a greater role in raising rate of growth and creating employment opportunities in the economy. It was thought that vigorous private sector operating in the macroeconomic environment of competition and free markets would be able to make efficient use of scarce resources. However, the role of government and public sector in providing healthcare, education and safe drinking water, especially in rural areas, was emphasised, since it was believed that private sector would not adequately invest in these social sectors.

In the Ninth Plan a high priority was also given to public investment in economic infrastructure such as power, roads, posts, telecommunications and transport. The higher growth will take place only if adequate infrastructure was available. It was thought that private investment will also rise if infrastructure facilities were available. Further, it was laid down that economic infrastructure in the form of irrigation, rural roads, promotion of agricultural research and creation of organised agricultural markets were quite necessary if broad-based agricultural growth was to be achieved. Besides, exports of agricultural products were planned to be promoted to raise the incomes of the farmers. Like the strategy pursued in the Eighth Plan, ***export-led growth strategy*** was given importance in the Ninth Plan as well. Export orientation was given to the strategy so as to achieve not only self-reliance but also more rapid economic growth. To open up our industrial economy to international competition, phased reduction in import tariffs was to be carried out. However, to protect Indian industries against foreign competition, anti-dumping measures were planned to be strengthened.

It was stressed that in the Ninth Plan there was no need for retaining majority stake in public sector undertakings except for those that are in the strategic spheres where national security concerns were involved. The resources mobilised from public sector disinvestment in non-strategic enterprises were to be used for much needed investment in social sector, especially health and education. Finally, for keeping inflation under check the need for reduction of *fiscal deficit* of both the Centre and States was emphasised. This was to be achieved through greater tax collection, reduction in subsidies and non-plan expenditure. Besides, subsidies were to the targeted to specific groups who needed help from Government.

In the Ninth Plan (1997-2002), the target of achieving 7 per cent growth rate per annum was fixed which was later revised to 6.5 per cent in view of lower rate of growth actually achieved in the first year (1997-98) of the plan. To achieve this growth rate annual investment rate of 28.2 per cent was planned and incremental capital-output ratio (ICOR) of 4 was assumed.

Rate of growth of GDP actually achieved in the Ninth Plan was 5.5 per cent per annum as against the target of 6.5 per cent. The lower growth of GDP relative to target was due to lower actual growth rate of 2.5 per cent per annum in agriculture as against the target of 3.9 per cent and sharp fall in growth rate of manufacturing which registered 3 per cent annual growth rate as against the target of 8.2 per cent. The lower industrial growth rate in the Ninth Plan was mainly due to demand recession for industry caused by fall in public sector investment and poor performance of agriculture. Another important failure of the Ninth Plan was that it could not generate employment for 50 million persons as per the target fixed. As a matter of fact, it has been found that unemployment rate on current daily status basis which was 7.32 per cent in 1999-2000 went up during the plan period and the backlog of unemployment reached the alarming figure of about 35 million persons at the end of the Ninth Plan.[2]

OBJECTIVES AND DEVELOPMENT STRATEGY OF THE TENTH FIVE YEAR PLAN (2002-07)

Objectives and Targets

The Tenth Five Year Plan which covers the period 2002-07 had set an *ambitious growth target of 8 per cent per annum*. In recognising that economic growth cannot be the only objective of a national plan, the Tenth Plan had also set the targets for a few other aspects of human development.

Reduction in Poverty. First, it envisaged to reduce poverty ratio from 26.1 in 2000 to 21 per cent of population by the year 2007. Second, overall literacy rate (of 7 years +) is to be increased

2 See Planning Commission, *Tenth Five Year Plan* (2002-07), Vol 1, p. 24.

from 65 per cent of population in 2000 to 75 per cent by the end of 2007.

Employment Generation. A significant objective of Tenth Five Year plan was to generate 50 million jobs[3] over the five year period (2002-07) of the Tenth Plan, that is, creation of **one crore jobs** every year. This was a very ambitious objective and doubts had been raised about its feasibility. This is significant because no measures had been suggested in the Tenth Plan to make process of economic growth more labour-intensive.

Balanced Development of States. The Tenth Plan laid stress on the importance of balanced development of all States and included a State-wise break-up of broad development targets including targets for growth rates and social development consistent with national targets.

Equity and Social Justice. The Tenth Plan also emphasised the goal of achieving equity and social justice. It had been pointed out that rigidities in the Indian economy make poverty-reducing effects of economic growth ineffective. In this regard various poverty alleviation and employment generation programmes such as the Swarnajayanti Gram Swarozgar Yojana (SGSY), Sampoorna Grameen Rozgar Yojana (SGRY), Antyodaya Anna Yojana, drinking water supply projects and housing projects for the poor had been included for effective implementation. These programmes were expected to help reduce poverty and generate gainful employment opportunities.

Development Strategy of the Tenth Plan

Redefining the Role of Government. The development strategy adopted in the Tenth Plan provides for redefining the role of Government in the context of the emergence of a strong and vibrant private sector. Accordingly, the larger participation of private sector in raising investment and bringing about higher economic growth rate was provided for in the plan. Besides, the role of public sector for development of infrastructure such as investment in the development of highways, ports, telecommunication, irrigation, transport facilities was emphasised. Further, the role of Government's fiscal and monetary policies in directing private investment and raising resources for public investment in infrastructure had been given due importance.

Improving Quality of Life. Economic development does not merely mean higher rate of growth in Gross Domestic Product (GDP). Ultimately, economic development means improvement in the *quality of life* of the people. *The strategy of the Tenth Five Year Plan laid stress on the greater access to basic social services such as education, health, availability of drinking water and improvement in basic sanitation.* In respect of these the Tenth Plan fixed specific targets which were planned to be achieved during the Tenth Plan period. These targets were:

1. Universal access to primary education by 2007.
2. Increase in literacy of the people to 75 per cent of the population by 2007.
3. Reduction of infant mortality rate to 45 per 1000 live births by the end of the Tenth Plan (*i.e.,* 2007).
4. Reduction of maternal mortality ratio to 2 per 1000 live births by 2007.
5. To improve ecology increase in forest and tree cover to 25 per cent by 2007 had been planned.
6. Access to potable drinking water was to be ensured to the people in all villages by the year 2012.
7. Provision for cleaning all major polluted rivers by the year 2007 had been made.

To achieve the above targets adequate amount of resources had been allocated to the social sectors.

Emphasis on Agricultural Development. Another important element of the development strategy of the Tenth Plan was to accelerate agricultural growth. It was pointed out that higher

3 Planning Commission, *Mid-Term Appraisal of the 10th Plan.*

agricultural growth would benefit the rural poor. In this respect stress was laid on the *diversification of agriculture* which means farmers should increasingly take to horticulture, fisheries, vegetables apart from growing of crops.

Employment Generation and Services Sector. Besides, the development strategy of the Tenth Plan was to ensure rapid growth of those sectors which would generate more opportunities for gainful employment. For generation of more employment opportunities role of the services sector was specially highlighted. In this connection mention may be made of such services as construction, tourism, IT enabled services, computer software, transport trade and hotels. However, it was rightly pointed out that rapid growth of services sector was dependent on higher industrial growth. Therefore, the two could not be promoted in isolation.

Special Anti-Poverty Programmes. Lastly, as in the previous Five Year Plans, it was recognised in the Tenth Plan that higher economic growth rate alone was not enough to generate employment opportunities for 50 million workers during the Tenth Plan period. Therefore to reduce poverty ratio to 21 per cent of population by 2007, special anti-poverty programmes were planned to supplement the growth efforts to reduce the poverty ratio.

Growth Target and Macroeconomic Parameters

The target of 8 per cent average annual growth rate for the period 2002-07 was considered to be feasible as it was thought that scope for improvements in efficiency in both public and private sectors was very large which would ensure reduction in incremental capital-output ratio (ICOR) from 4.53 during the Ninth Plan to 3.58 in the Tenth Plan. In this regard for utilising the idle capital stock in the economy, the Tenth Plan laid emphasis on completion of ongoing projects and privatisation of public enterprises, especially those which were working below capacity.

Table 62.1. Macro Parameters for the Tenth Plan

	Ninth Plan (1997-2002) (Actuals)	Tenth Plan (2002-07) (Target)	Tenth Plan 2002-07 (Actuals: Average)
Gross Domestic Saving rate (% of GDP_{mp}) at current market prices	23.6	26.84	30.8
Investment rate (% of GDP_{mp})	24.3	28.41	32.0
Current account deficit of balance of payments (% of GDP_{mp})	0.7	– 1.57	1.3
ICOR	4.4	3.58	4.0
GDP_{mp} growth rate (% per annum)	5.5	8.0	7.5

Source: *11th Five Year Plan Documents and Economic Survey,* 2007-08, pp.7 and 8.

The achievement of Tenth Plan target of 8 per cent annual growth rate of GDP depended crucially on the expected reduction in incremental capital-output ratio (ICOR) from then estimated 4.53 during the Ninth Plan to 3.58 in the Tenth Plan. The investment required to achieve this growth target had been estimated to be 28.4 per cent of GDP. This means a sharp acceleration in the investment rate from 24.4 per cent in the base year to 32.3 per cent in the terminal year (2006-07). For achieving this increase in investment, foreign savings (*i.e.,* current account deficit in balance of payments) equal to 1.57 per cent of GDP_{mp} was estimated.

The total outlay envisaged for the Tenth Plan was ₹ 19,68,815 crore for both Central and State plans. Fiscal and revenue deficits had been projected at 4.7 per cent and 2.9 per cent of GDP respectively. It was emphasised that both the Central and State Governments had to take appropriate fiscal measures to achieve the plan targets. The fiscal policy measures suggested by the Planning Commission were effective enforcement of income tax administration, elimination of exemptions under corporation tax, moving towards a single excise duty rate, expansion in the coverage of service tax, implementation of recommendations of the Expenditure Reforms Commission, better targeting of food subsidy so as to reduce expenditure on food subsidy, reduction in the paybill of Central Government, reduction in staff strength, reduction in Government borrowings to reduce interest rate burden. At the State level, implementation of VAT (value added tax) and raising of user charges on power supply were suggested to increase financial resources for plan projects.

Achievements in the Tenth Plan. As will be seen from Table 62.1, the targets of economic growth and its related macro-variables were substantially achieved. It was estimated that average annual growth rate in the Tenth Plan period (2002-07) was 7.5% as against the target of 8%, investment rate rose to 32 per cent of GDP as against target of 28.41. However, the average agricultural growth rate per annum was 2.1 per cent as against the target of 4 per cent. Further, unemployment rate on current daily status basis for the economy rose from 7.3 per cent in 1999-2000 to 8.3 per cent in 2004-05.

Evaluation of Achievements of Tenth Five Year Plan

In the 10th Plan, the Indian economy made significant progress in terms of GDP growth. As against a target of 8 per cent annual average growth in GDP, the actual growth rate achieved has been estimated at 7.5 per cent, that is, the target of 10th Plan was substantially achieved and was much higher than the growth rate of 5.5 per cent achieved during the 9th Plan period. This higher growth rate during the 10th Plan period had been possible due to higher rate of domestic saving and investment and reduction in capital-output ratio in the 10th Plan period. The gross domestic saving rate and investment rate which were 23.1 and 23.8 per cent in the 9th Plan rose to 30.8 and 32 per cent on an average in the 10th Plan period respectively. Besides, incremental capital-output ratio (ICOR) improved from 4.4 in the 9th Plan period to 4.0 in the 10th Plan period. Thus we succeeded in achieving substantially growth targets in the 10th Plan period. This has inspired the Planning Commission to set a target of average growth rate of 9 per cent per annum in the 11th Plan period.

Increase in Foreign Exchange Reserves. Another significant achievement of 10th Plan was large increase in foreign exchange reserves. It will be remembered that economic crisis of 1991 occurred as a result of drastic fall in foreign exchange reserves. The substantial increase in foreign exchange reserves was the result of continuing economic reforms initiated in 1991. The increase in foreign exchange reserves had been possible because of increase in capital inflows due to foreign institutional investment (FII), foreign direct investment (FDI) and non-resident Indian (NRI) deposits. Foreign exchange reserves which crossed 100 billion US dollars in December 2003 reached the level of about 165 billion US dollars at the end of March 2007.

However, it is worth noting that in the capital inflows the proportion of FDI which enhances productive capacity were low as compared to FII inflows which were invested in highly speculative activities, especially shares of Indian companies and are very volatile.

In view of the above as compared to the 9th Plan, the pace of growth of the Indian economy accelerated with improvement in major macroeconomic fundamentals.

Lower Growth Rate of Agriculture. A great failure of 10th Plan was its dismal performance regarding growth rate of agriculture. As against the target of 4 per cent annual growth rate in agriculture, the estimate of actual annual growth rate in agriculture was estimated at 2.1 per cent for 10th Plan period. Thus the objective of the 10th Plan miserably failed to achieve a reversal of declining trend in the growth rate of agriculture and to eventually take it to 4 per cent per annum. It is important to note that rise in inflation rate during 2006-07 and after had been fuelled by supply-side constraints posed by lower growth rate in agriculture.

Failure to Reduce Poverty as per the Target. An important failure of 10th Plan was that it did not achieve the targeted reduction in poverty ratio. It was planned in the 10th Plan period that higher rate of economic growth envisaged in the 10th Plan and introduction of employment guarantee scheme would help in reducing poverty ratio to 19.2 per cent in 2006-07 as against 26.1 per cent in 1999-2000. However, the 61st Round of NSS finds that on the basis of uniform recall period of 30 days, poverty ratio was 27.5 per cent in 2004-05 as against 36.0 per cent in 1993-94. This means in the years of post-reform period 1993-94 to 2004-05 there was a reduction in poverty by 8.5 percentage points which works out to be 0.74 per cent per annum. The higher growth in GDP of 7.8 per cent during the 10th Plan did not result in greater reduction in poverty ratio. In absolute number about 302 million persons were found to be below the poverty line in 2004-05. The data also reveal that 55.4 per cent of total poor living below the poverty line were concentrated in five States of Uttar Pradesh, Bihar, Maharashtra, West Bengal and Odisha.

Dismal Performance Regarding Reduction in Unemployment. In the 10th Plan the target of reducing daily status unemployment rate to a level of 5.11 per cent was fixed. The 61st Round of NSS revealed that daily-status unemployment rate which was 6.1 and 7.3 per cent in 1993-94 and 1999-2000 respectively rose to 8.3 per cent in 2004-05. *Rural unemployment on daily status* basis rose from 7.2 per cent in 1999-2000 to 9.1 per cent in 2004-05 whereas *daily status urban unemployment* rose from 7.2 per cent in 1999-2000 to 8.8 per cent in 2004-05. A matter of serious concern is that this had been associated with a sharp increase in unemployment from 9.3 per cent in 1993-94 to 15.3 per cent in 2004-05 among agricultural labour households which represent poorests sections of the society.

Besides, it is worth noting that in the organised sector there had not been any *net* increase in employment opportunities despite a very fast rate of its growth. Actually it was in the unorganised sector where labour productivity was very low that employment of labour increased. The dismal performance on employment front was a great failure of development strategy of the 10th Plan.

It follows from above that though in the 10th Plan objectives of GDP growth rate, increase in domestic saving and investment rates, expansion of capital flows and foreign exchange inflows were achieved, the important objectives of significant reduction in poverty and unemployment remained unfulfilled.

REVIEW OF THE ELEVENTH FIVE YEAR PLAN

The Approach Paper of the Eleventh Plan proposed faster and more inclusive growth in the five-year period (2007-12). According to the *Approach to the 11th Plan*, though annual growth in GDP in the 10th Plan period rose to 7.5 per cent as against 5.5 per cent in the 9th Plan, it failed to be sufficiently inclusive. The failure to achieve inclusive growth implies that all sections of the population were not benefited from higher growth rate achieved. The employment in the organised sector did not increase despite faster growth in GDP. The percentage of population below the poverty line declined but only at a slower pace. Malnutrition levels though declined but still continued to be very high. Too many people still lacked access to basic services such as health, education, clean drinking water and sanitation facilities without which they cannot gain a share in the benefits of economic growth.

Despite the above observations, *Approach to the 11th Plan*, as in the past, emphasised the achievement of rapid growth in GDP. Thus, according to it, "*Rapid growth is an essential part of our strategy for two reasons: Firstly, it is only in a rapidly growing economy that we can expect to sufficiently raise the incomes of the mass of our population to bring about a general improvement in living conditions. Secondly, rapid growth is necessary to generate the resources needed to provide basic services to all*."[4]

---

4 Planning Commission, *Approach to the 11th Plan.*

Objectives of the 11th Plan (2007-12)

1. Faster Economic Growth and Related Targets. The foremost objective of the 11th Plan was to achieve a higher annual growth rate of 9 per cent over the 11th Plan period. With population growing at 1.6 per cent per year 9 per cent growth in GDP would double the real per capita income in 10 years. The approach document envisaged achievement of higher growth rate by increasing investment rate to 36.7 per cent. It assumed capital-output ratio of 4.1. Though investment target of 36.7 per cent GDP had already been crossed in the year 2007-08, the 11th Plan target of rate of growth of GDP was revised downward to 7 per cent due to impact of *global financial crisis*.

To achieve higher rate of investment for generating 9 per cent growth rate, the 11th Plan envisaged increasing the domestic saving rate to 34.8 per cent of GDP and foreign saving to 1.88 per cent of GDP. Further, with overall objective of attaining 9 per cent growth in GDP, the target for agricultural growth was fixed at 4 per cent per annum, for industry at 10.11 per cent and for services at 9.11 per cent per annum. As will be seen from Table 62.2, compared with actual growth rate (2.5%) of agriculture

Table 62.2. Macroeconomic Targets of the 11th Plan and its Achievements

Indicator	10th Plan (Actuals Average)	11th Plan (Targets)	11th Plan (Actual)
(A) Growth Rate GDP at market prices (%)	7.5	9.0	8
1. Agriculture and Allied Sectors	2.1	4.0	3.7
2. Industry	8.9	10.11	7.2
3. Services	9.3	9.11	9.7
(B) Investment Rate (GDCF) (as % of GDP) of which	32.0	36.7	38.2 (36.4)
1. Public Sector	6.9	8.0	–
2. Private Sector	22.9	28.7	
(C) Gross Domestic Saving Rate (% of GDP)	30.8	34.8	33.5
(D) Current Account Deficit (% of GDP), that is, foreign savings	1.3	–1.88	2.7
(E) Government Fiscal Deficit (both Centre and States Combined (as % of GDP)	8.0	6.0	–

Source: (1) Planning Commission, *11th Five Year Plan,* 2007.
(2) GOI, *Economic Survey* 2008-09, 2009-10, 2010-11.

attained in the 10th Plan period target for agricultural growth in the Eleventh Five Year Plan was substantially increased to 4 per cent per annum but for industry there was small increase from 8.6 per cent in the 10th Plan to 10.11 per cent and for services from 9.3 per cent achieved in the 10th Plan to 9.11 per cent in the 11th Plan.

Inclusive Growth: As mentioned above, *Approach to the 11th Plan* laid emphasis on achieving inclusive growth. Inclusive growth means that benefits of economic growth should accrue to all sections of the population. In fact, this is a new term for equitable growth or growth with equity. Thus, the *Approach Paper of 11th Plan states, "The higher growth rate must be combined* with *policies that will ensure that per capita income growth is broad-based benefiting all sections of the population, especially those who have thus far remained deprived*"[5]. For achieving the objective of inclusive growth, *Approach Paper* of 11th Plan lays stress on (1) faster agricultural growth, (2) faster generation of employment opportunities, (3) reduction in poverty ratio, and (4) the expansion of education, health

5 *op. cit.*, p. 97

and other essential services. Thus, according to 11th Plan Approach Paper, "*The structure of growth should also be such as to promote a widespread of benefits. Doubling agricultural GDP growth rate to around 4 per cent is particularly important in this respect*. This must be combined to promote rapid growth in *non-agricultural employment* so as to create 58 *million jobs* in the 11th Plan period. If these objectives are achieved the percentage of poverty can be reduced by 10 percentage points by the end of the Plan period."[6]

Expansion in Education. Besides faster agricultural growth and employment generation, the provision of good quality education was considered very important for attaining inclusive growth. Thus 11th Plan Approach Paper states: "*Education is the most critical input for empowering people with skills and knowledge and for giving them access to productive employment in the future. The 11th Plan should ensure that we move towards raising public spending on education to 6% of GDP.... It must fulfil the constitutional obligation of providing free and compulsory elementary education of good quality to all children up to age 14.*"[7]

For promoting education the following measures were suggested by the 11th Plan:

1. Though the enrolment for education of children of the age of 6 to 14 years will be completed by 2007, the 11th Plan envisages that children *must complete* 8 years of schooling and this poses a great challenge. To ensure this drop-out rate in primary school education for both boys and girls of all social groups must be reduced sharply from 52.2 % in 2003-04 to 20% by 2011-12.

2. Literacy rate for persons of age 7 years and above was planned to be raised to 85 per cent by 2011-12. Besides, the *gender gap* in literacy was to be reduced by 10 percentage points.

3. To expand higher education so that the percentage of youth in the relevant age group receiving higher education was to be raised from the present 10 per cent to 15 per cent by the end of 11th Plan.

Promotion of Health. As regards promoting health of the people, the following targets had been fixed:

1. It was planned to reduce *infant mortality rate* to 28 per cent and maternal mortality rate to 1 per 1000 live births.

2. The target of reduction in total *fertility rate* to 2.1 per cent by 2011-12 had been fixed so as to reduce population growth rate.

3. It was planned to provide clean drinking water facilities to all people in the country by the year 2009.

4. It was planned to reduce malnutrition among children of age group 0–3 years to half its present level.

Development of Infrastructure. For the development of infrastructure the following measures were planned to be undertaken:

1. It was planned to ensure connection to all villages and to all households below poverty line (BPL) by 2011-12.

2. It was proposed to ensure all-weather road connections to all habitations with a population of 1000 persons and above (500 and above for hilly areas) by the year 2009.

3. To connect every village by telephone and provide broad-band connectivity to all villages by 2012.

4. It was planned to provide homestead sites to all by the end of 11th Plan and to speed up the pace of housing construction for the poor so as to cover all the poor by 2016-17.

---

6 *op. cit.*, p. 57

7 *op. cit.*, p.57

Population, Labour Force and Employment Generation

Another important aspect of the 11th Plan was its estimates of growth of population, labour force and employment generation during the plan period. On the basis of its estimates of population growth and participation rate, as will be seen from Table 62.3, Planning Commission estimated that population of India would increase from 1,092 million in 2004-05 to 1,208 million in 2011-12 and labour force from about 420 million in 2004-05 to 439 million in 2006-07 and to 483.6 million in 2011-12, *i.e.*, 45 million during the plan period (2007-12). It will be seen from Table 62.3 that employment opportunities for 58 million persons (460-402 = 58) were estimated to be generated during the plan period (2007-2008). On this basis it was calculated that the number of persons unemployed would decline from 36.7 million in 2006-07 to 23.3 million in 2011-12. As a result, daily status unemployment rate as per cent of labour force would fall from 8.36 per cent in 2006-07 to 4.83 per cent in 2011-12.

However, according to National Sample Survey daily status unemployment rate was actually found to be 5.6 per cent in 2011-12 as against 8.2 per cent in 2004-05.

Table 62.3. Population, Labour Force and Employment: Estimates of 11th Plan

	2004-05	2006-07	2011-12
1. Population (in million)	1092.8	1128.1	1208
2. Labour force (in million)	419.6	438.9	483.6
3. Employment opportunities (in million)	384.9	402.2	460.3
4. Unemployed (in million)	34.7	36.7	23.3
5. Unemployment Rate (%) on Daily Status Basis	8.28	8.36	4.83

Source: Planning Commission, *Eleventh Five Year Plan,* 2007-08.

Critical Evaluation of the Eleventh Plan

The Eleventh Five Year Plan sets for itself highly ambitious objectives and targets. It not only aimed at achieving faster economic growth of 9 per cent per annum but also inclusive growth which was expected to ensures rapid reduction in poverty and unemployment and broad-based improvement in the quality of life of the people, especially of the poor. Though the targets of financial outlay, saving and investment rate were achieved, objectives of higher economic growth (*i.e.*, 9 per cent per annum), employment generation for 58 million person years during the period 2004-05 to 2011-12 were not achieved. There were several factors responsible for this. First, take the objective of achieving economic growth at the rate of 9 per cent per annum. In the first year (2007-08) of the 11th Plan, growth in GDP_{MP} of 8.7 per cent had been achieved. However in the year 2008-09, due to global meltdown, especially serious financial crisis in the USA, our growth in exports was seriously affected was seriously affected. There was also decrease in capital inflows, especially foreign direct investment (FDI). Rupee depreciated increasing our cost of imports which adversely affected our balance of payments. Growth rate in 2008-09 declined to 7.7 per cent. However, the *annual rate of economic growth actually achieved for five years of Eleventh Plan period was 8 per cent which is the highest achieved in any Five Year Plan of India.*

As regards the employment generation for 58 million persons on current daily status basis during 2007-12, it was too high an objective to be achieved, keeping in view the past record. There were no any specific measures suggested in the 11th Plan which would have ensured rapid absorption of surplus labour in gainful employment. Whatever new employment opportunities (net) were created, they happened to be in the unorganised informal sector in which how much employment generated is of productive or gainful type is anybody's guess. In fact in the post-reforms period there had been net *decrease* in employment in the organised sector (public and private sectors taken together) . During the post-reform period (1994-2008) whereas there had been a low positive growth of employment (0.58% per annum) in the private sector, there was negative growth of employment in the public sector resulting in net decrease in employment in the organised sector. Now, why there has been slow growth of employment opportunities in India.

First, due to the tendency on the part of industries to use capital-intensive technologies, sufficient new employment opportunities are not likely to be created. As a result, unemployment will increase. Second, most of the poor live in rural areas and are dependent on agriculture. It is necessary that land reforms should be undertaken so that landless labour and small farmers possess land to generate self-employment and also in case of tenant farmers to ensure security of tenancy at reasonable rate of rent. Besides, the farmers must get loans from banks and other institutions at lower rate of interest as recommended by National Commission on Farmers headed by Dr. M.S. Swaminathan which recommended interest on farm loans be reduced to 4 per cent to promote agricultural investment and production. Further, the Eleventh Plan neglected the issue of land reforms and peasant agriculture and instead pleaded for contract farming which is capital-intensive and not labour-intensive. Further, 11th Plan did not propose any concrete measures to create employment opportunities in agriculture. In view of all these achieving inclusive growth was an unrealistic objective.

Decline in Poverty

The biggest achievement of the 11th plan was a large reduction in the incidence of poverty during the plan period. As per Tendulkar Committee estimates the percentage of population living below the poverty line declined from 37.2 per cent in 2004-05 to 21.9 per cent in 2011-12. That is, more than 2 percentage points decrease every year during the period, 2004-05 to 2011-12 whereas it had declined by 0.74 percentage point each year during 1993-94 to 2004-05. However, the absolute number of people living below the poverty line was estimated at 2.70 million in 2011-12 which is quite large.

Regardless of the impact of the global financial crisis on India, the *fact remains that some of the challenges that India faces are of a continuing nature*. These *inter alia include eradicating poverty, improving its physical and social infrastructure, education and creating productive employment opportunities*. In consonance with the commitment to ensure faster social development and achieving an inclusive pattern of growth, the government continued its focus on several initiatives and programmes towards that end.

Some of the *major social sector initiatives for achieving inclusive growth and faster social sector development and* to remove economic and social disparities in the Eleventh Five Year Plan included the Bharat Nirman Programme, Mid-Day Meal Scheme, National Rural Health Mission, Jawaharlal Nehru National Urban Renewal Mission and the National Rural Employment Guarantee Scheme (NREGS). Central support for the social programmes continued to supplement efforts made by the States.

A major achievement of the 11th Plan was starting of Mahatma Gandhi National Rural Employment Guarantee Scheme (MGNREGS). Under MGNREGS, over four crore households were provided employment in 2008-09. This is a significant jump over the 3.39 crore households covered under the scheme during 2007-08. Out of the 215.63 crore person-days of employment created under the scheme during this period, 29 per cent and 25 per cent were in favour of SC and ST population respectively. 48 per cent of the total person-days of employment created went in favour of women. The agriculture debt waiver and relief scheme implemented during the year was able to restore institutional credit to farmers and helped to support demand and revive investment in the rural and agricultural sectors.

CHAPTER 63

TWELFTH FIVE YEAR PLAN (2012-17): A CRITICAL REVIEW

Before explaining the approach and strategy of the Twelfth Five Year Plan, it may be mentioned that it was prepared during the regime of earlier UPA government when Dr. Montek Singh Ahluwalia was its Vice-Chairman. However, the new NDA government did not scrap it but continued with it. It may be noted further that the name of the Planning commission has now been changed to *Niti Aayog* and Dr. Panagariya has been appointed its Vice Chairman.

The Twelfth Plan commenced at a time when the global economy was going through a second financial crisis precipitated by the sovereign debt crisis of Eurozone which arose in the last year of the Eleventh Plan. This crisis affected all countries including India. As a result, India's GDP growth rate slowed down to 6.7 per cent in the year (2011-12) of the Eleventh Plan. Slowdown in economic growth continued in the first year (2012-13) of the 12th Plan when rate of GDP growth fell to 5.1 per cent. *The Twelfth Plan emphasised that our first priority was to bring the economy back to rapid growth while at the same time ensuring that growth is both inclusive and sustainable*.

At the very start of the 12th Plan, the Indian economy faced macroeconomic imbalances. First, fiscal deficit increased sharply after 2008 as a result of global financial crisis. Fiscal deficit of the Central Government rose to 6 per cent of GDP in 2008-09 but again declined to 5.7 per cent of GDP in 2011-12. With reduction in plan expenditure by ₹ 90,000 crore, Finance Minister was able to bring down fiscal deficit to 4.8 per cent of GDP in 2012-13. In the first year of the 12th Plan 4.8 per cent of GDP as fiscal deficit is still very high. The second macroeconomic imbalance had been the widening of current account deficit of our balance of payments which rose to 4.7 per cent of GDP in 2012-13.

In view of the above, the Twelfth Plan proposed a **two-pronged strategy** focusing initially on the need to bring the macroeconomic imbalances under control and to reverse the slowdown in economic growth, while also pushing for structural reforms in many areas that were crucial for maintaining medium-term GDP growth rate.

APPROACH AND DEVELOPMENT STRATEGY OF THE TWELFTH PLAN

As the earlier Five Year Plans, in the Twelfth Five Year Plan the Planning Commission says that the *growth of an economy depends on capacity of the economy to maintain high rate of investment while ensuring productive use of capital*. This is nothing new as it follows from Harrod-Domar growth model on which our first Five Year Plan (1951-56) was based. The higher rate of investment depends on the ability to financing the investment, which in turn depends on the domestic saving and the external funds available for investment in the economy. In the Twelfth Plan, following the policy of liberalisation and privatisation, private sector investment has been given a prominent role in economic development. The rate of private investment depended on investor's expectations and the ability of entrepreneurs to mobilise necessary finance for their investment. This requires the existence of dynamic entrepreneurs and managerial class capable of taking risks in the competitive economy opened up to the global pressures.

The Twelfth Plan (2012-17) was prepared when the Indian economy was passing through a period of great uncertainty. The global financial crisis of 2008 slowed down the growth of the world economy in the next few years and new Eurozone crisis which emerged when European countries of Greece, Cyprus, Portugal could not pay back their sovereign loans and came to the brink of declaring them bankrupt. As a result, our exports suffered and current account deficit went up to 4.2 per cent and 4.7 per cent of GDP in 2011-12 and 2012-13 respectively. Besides, due to appearing of scams in 2G spectrum allotment and coal allotment and cancellation of these allotments by supreme court of India created a *policy paralysis* in the economy. Delay in environment clearances of a large number of investment projects adversely affected investment sentiments of the entrepreneurial class. Further, high rate of inflation in the Indian economy came to prevail in the Indian economy. All these factors led to the decline in rate of saving and investment in the economy which lowered the GDP growth rate in the year (2011-12) of the Eleventh Five Year Plan to 5.1 per cent. As a result of this economic uncertainty, as we will see later, Planning Commission presented the three alternative scenarios for the 12th Five Year Plan.

For the formulation of development strategy of a Five Year Plan one has to consider the complexities of development challenges facing the economy and recognise the changes that are taking place in the domestic economy as well as in the world. With the understanding of the ground reality, the planning Commission, emphasizes that in the 12th Five Year Plan for the formulation of an appropriate strategy one needs to identify the *critical leverage points where government action could have the maximum impact*. The focus must be on identifying the critical leverage points where the government action could have the maximum impact. The focus must be on identifying the strategic leverage points where the successful action could trigger many supportive reactions rather than fixing everything everywhere."[1] This is quite a vague statement about to what fields or projects government would give priority in its investment in the 12th Five Year Plan.

Second, the Planning commission states that in the 12th Five Year Plan both government and the private sector will jointly make efforts to enable the country to move forward. However, strangely enough, the planning commission relies more on private sector to bring about inclusive growth rather than spell out policies in detail how the government itself will plan to achieve inclusive growth. Thus it states that, "*Much of the inclusive growth we hope to achieve depends on the investment in the private sector which accounts for 70 per cent of total investment*. This includes not only the organised corporate sector but also Micro, small and medium enterprises (MSMEs)."[2]

Thirdly, the 12th Plan emphasises that along with the increase in outlay on government programmes there is *need for improved implementation of the programmes*. For this it lays stress on capacity building and *governance reforms*, including system change that will increase accountability of the public sector.

Having explained its basic vision and aspirations which drive the Plan, the Planning commission explains the following three dimensions of its vision and approach of the 12th Plan.

1. Faster, sustainable and more inclusive growth.

2. Development of capabilities–both human and institutional – to achieve the vision.

3. Focus on the challenge of managing our natural resources rationally so as to ensure that growth is consistent with environment sustainability.

1 Planning Commission, *Twelfth Five Year Plan,* p. 2.
2 *Ibid.*

We explain below in brief these aspects of development strategy.

Faster GDP Growth

Twelfth Plan lays stress on achieving rapid GDP growth and set a target of achieving 8 per cent average annual growth during its period, 2012-17. According to it, rapid GDP growth is a necessary condition because *it ensures an expansion in productive capacity* of the economy without which broad-based improvement in living standards of the people is not possible. For example, it points out that growth of agriculture will increase the opportunity for a large part of the population (including small farmers and landless labourers) to improve their incomes. Similarly, the growth of Micro, Small and Medium Enterprises (MSME) will generate higher incomes and larger employment opportunities to the people engaged in them.

Secondly, the faster GDP growth is required because without it the growth process will not be *sufficiently inclusive* as it will directly raise the incomes and living standards of a large section of people. Thirdly, according to it, rapid growth of GDP is important as it will generate large revenue for the government which can be used to finance critical anti-poverty programmes of employment creation such as MGNREGA and also to finance such schemes as Pradhan Mantri Gram Sadak Yojana (PMGSY), Sarv Siksha Abhiyan, Mid-Day Meals (MDMs) and National Rural Health Mission.

Inclusive Growth

The Twelfth Plan emphasises that growth must not only be rapid, it must be inclusive and sustainable. It points out that *inclusiveness of economic growth has a number of aspects such as reduction in poverty by uplifting the poor from below the poverty line, generating more employment opportunities so that incomes of a large section of the population increase*. Secondly, inclusive growth involves improvements in living standards of all socio-economic groups in the society, especially marginalised groups such as Scheduled Castes (SCs), Scheduled Tribes (STs), other backward classes (OBCs) and minorities so that they should get fair share of the benefits of growth.

Another aspect of inclusiveness in economic growth relates to the *balanced development of all regions and States of the country*. This requires accelerating growth not only in the States that are lagging behind but also rapid growth of backward regions or districts which may not share the general improvement in living standards experienced elsewhere. Many of these backward districts have unique characteristics including high concentration of tribal population for which special growth schemes are required.

Furthermore, inclusive growth requires *removal of gender based inequalities*, discrimination of all forms of violence against girls and women so as to enable women to gain from general improvement in standards of living in the society and become equal partners in economic progress. While addressing the 57th National Development Council (NDC), the former Prime Minister, Dr. Manmohan Singh, said, "*Gender inequality is an aspect which deserves special attention. Women and girls represent half the population and our society has not been fair to this half. Their socio-economic status is improving but gaps persist . . . . . There cannot be meaningful development without the active participation of half of the population and this participation simply cannot take place if their security and safety are not assured.*"[3]

Environment Sustainability

Besides laying stress on faster and more inclusive growth, the Twelfth Plan states that economic growth must also be consistent with sustainability of our environment. Thus, according to it, "No development process can afford to neglect the environment consequences of economic activity or allow unsustainable depletion and deterioration of natural resources."[4] It may be noted that development cannot take place without additional energy and the energy requirements of development will have to

3 Quoted in the *Twelfth Five Year Plan*, p. 6.

4 *Twelfth Five Year Plan*, p. 8.

be reconciled with the objective of protection of environment. The Indian economy depends heavily on coal and hydropower to meet its energy needs and development of each of these energy sources involves potential trade-off with conservation of forests and the objective of avoiding displacement of the people.

GDP GROWTH AND ITS SECTORAL PATTERN

The Twelfth Plan sets a target of average annual 8 per cent GDP growth over the five year plan period, 2012-17. This overall growth rate is to be achieved with target growth rates of 4 per cent in agriculture, 7.6 per cent in industry (which comprises mining and quarrying, manufacturing, electricity, gas and water supply and construction) and 9 per cent in services. Sector-wise break-up of growth targets in the five year plan period (2012-13 to 2016-17) along with the average growth rates achieved in the Eleventh Plan period is given in Table 63.1.

The Twelfth Plan sets a target of average annual 8 per cent growth rate in the five-year period of 2012-17 which equal to the actual average growth rate achieved in the 11th Plan period. Since in the first three years of the 12th Plan (2012-13, 2013-14 and 2014-15), the actual rate of economic growth achieved is around 6.4 per cent it requireds a very sharp acceleration in growth rate to 10 per cent in the later two years to achieve an average annual growth rate of 8 per cent. This seems to be quite non-feasible. Therefore, the Deputy Chairman of the Planning Commission, Dr. Montek Singh Ahluwalia, talked about revising the growth rate target. Thus, to achieve the whole 12th Plan growth targets were quite uncertain, when its first three years are already over. It may be noted that in the 12th Plan, *Planning Commission recognised that though faster economic growth was necessary but not a sufficient condition for raising the living standards of the people as a whole*. This is of course true but

Table 63.1. Annual Growth of GDP by Industry of Origin at Constant (2004-05) Prices

Sector	*11th Plan*	*Twelfth Plan Period*					
	Average	2012-13	2013-14	2014-15	2015-16	2016-17	Average
1. Agriculture, Forestry and Fishing	3.6	2.0	4.5	4.5	4.5	4.5	4.0
2. Mining and Quarrying	3.2	1.0	5.0	7.0	7.0	8.5	5.7
3. Manufacturing	7.7	2.2	6.0	8.5	9.5	9.5	7.1
4. Electricity, Gas and Water Supply	6.1	5.2	7.5	8.0	8.0	8.0	7.3
5. Construction	7.7	8.0	8.0	8.5	10.0	11.0	9.1
6. Trade, Hotels, Restaurants	8.3	5.5	6.0	8.0	8.7	8.7	7.4
7. Transport, Storage and Communication	12.0	7.3	11.1	13.0	13.6	14.1	11.8
8. Financing Insurance and Real Estate	11.1	9.8	9.5	10.0	10.0	10.0	9.9
9. Community, Social and Personal Services	8.3	7.3	7.2	7.2	7.2	7.2	7.2
Total GDP	**8.0**	**5.8**	**7.3**	**8.5**	**9.0**	**9.2**	**8.0**
Industry (2–5)	7.2	4.0	6.6	8.4	9.4	9.8	7.6
Services (6–9)	9.7	7.6	8.3	9.4	9.7	9.9	9.0

Planning Commission recognised this fact only after several years of planned development in which benefits of economic growth did not trickle down to the poor and various disadvantaged groups of the society such as Scheduled Casts (SCs) scheduled Tribes (STs) and Other Backward Classes (OBCs). We can easily imagine a growth process which may not be sufficiently inclusive to ensure a spread of benefits to the mass of population.

Three Growth Scenarios

Perhaps recognising the uncertainty of achieving overall 8 per cent growth rate in the 12th Plan period, the Planning Commission in the 12th Plan document itself visualised three growth scenarios:

***Scenario 1*: Strong inclusive growth.** This was described as the future of India and was expected to ensure 8 per cent annual growth rate during the Twelfth Plan period along with the objective of 'inclusiveness' if we could implement a well-designed strategy addressing the key constraints holding back the economy. With appropriate steps taken to deal with **implementation and governance problems,** the wheels of government at all levels begin to move more smoothly. Local governance institutions and small enterprises were nurtured and had an opportunity to grow effectively, along with larger enterprises. Livelihood opportunities, along with community-based solutions and enterprises for addressing environmental issues, were seen to be sprouting. Many virtuous circles was expected to begin to operate in this scenario, raising confidence and trust.

***Scenario 2*: Insufficient Action.** This scenario reflected the outcome of insufficient policy action. While broad directions of policy may be endorsed at different levels, action might be incomplete or implementation might be poor, with the result that outcomes would be weaker than anticipated. Centralised government systems do not provide sufficient flexibility to cope with demands for decentralisation. Small enterprises and new entrepreneurs needed to be encouraged, but unless the business environment necessary for them to flourish was effectively transformed, the outcome would fall short of expectations. The policy conflict between subsidies and financial stability of the economy remained unresolved. In this scenario, growth of 8 per cent was not feasible. Growth could decline to between 6 per cent and 6.5 per cent, and inclusiveness would suffer.

***Scenario 3*. Policy Logjam.** This scenario reflected a situation where very little could be done for whatever the reason on many of the policy fronts identified in the Twelfth Plan. It was thought to be difficult to build growth momentum if critical supply constraints relating to energy and transport were not overcome. Investor confidence was likely to be severely eroded, and the lack of inclusiveness that results would lead to increased impatience and political logjam, putting the economy under severe stress. Vicious cycles would begin to operate and the growth rate could drift down to 5–5.5 per cent with serious loss on the inclusiveness front. In some ways, there was a danger of insufficient action scenario degenerating into a policy logjam scenario, if it persisted too long.

INVESTMENT IN THE TWELFTH PLAN

The ability to raise the rate of investment [ratio of gross fixed capital formation (GFCF) to GDP] is widely recognised as critical for the achievement of high economic growth rate. For annual output growth to average 8.0 per cent in the Twelfth Plan period, and to cross 9 per cent in the closing year, it is estimated that the fixed investment rate will have to increase by about 1.5 percentage points of GDP in 2016-17 over the level in 2011-12. The resulting trajectory of fixed investment over the Plan period is shown in Table 63.2. The fixed investment rate was targeted to increase to 35 per cent of GDP (at constant prices) by the end of the Twelfth Plan, yielding an average fixed investment rate of over 34.2 per cent of GDP for the Twelfth Plan period as a whole. These levels were marginally higher than what was achieved in the Eleventh Plan but they were broadly consistent with achieving an average real growth rate of around 8 per cent, allowing for acceleration in growth in the course of the Plan period. The gross domestic capital formation (*i.e.*, GDCF) or investment rate is planned to increase to 39.7% per cent of GDP in the *terminal year* (2016-17) of the Plan yielding average annual GDCF or investment rate of 38.8 per cent of GDP. This however implies a significant relaxation in the physical constraints that limit the economy in infrastructure and other key sectors.

Table 63.2. Investment as Ratio of GDP at Constant 2004-05 Prices

	11th Plan	Twelfth Plan Period					
	Average %	2012-13	2013-14	2014-15	2015-16	2016-17	Average
		Ratio to GDP per cent					
(*a*) Fixed Investment Rate	33.7	33.0	33.9	34.4	34.5	35.0	34.2
(*i*) Public	8.3	8.0	8.4	8.4	8.5	8.5	8.4
(*ii*) Private corporate	12.4	11.3	12.5	14.0	14.5	15.0	13.5
(*iii*) Household	13.0	13.5	13.0	12.0	11.5	11.5	12.3
(*b*) Stock	3.0	2.3	2.9	3.1	3.1	3.1	2.9
(*c*) Valuables	1.8	2.2	1.9	1.6	1.6	1.6	1.8
Gross Domestic Capital Formation (GDCF)	38.5	37.5	38.7	39.1	39.2	39.7	38.8
Errors and Omissions	–0.3						
Investment Rate	38.2	37.5	38.7	39.1	39.2	39.7	38.8

Furthermore, besides raising the rate of investment, the *Twelfth Plan emphasises that growth depends critically on productivity gains* as one of the key drivers of growth. Productivity gains flow from technological progress and makes additional contribution to growth after taking account of the effect of capital accumulation and growth in labour force. According to the Twelfth Plan, "The traditional sources of growth are not likely to be enough for India in the coming years and we must therefore focus much more on productivity improvements among all constituents: big businesses, MSMEs, farmers and even government."[5]

Composition of Investment: Public Sector Vs. Private Sector. The composition of fixed investment by source is also shown in Table 63.2. The public fixed investment rate (mostly investment by public enterprises) averaged 8.3 per cent in the Eleventh Plan, with a range of 7.8–8.8 per cent. It is projected to remain roughly in this range in the Twelfth Plan period averaging 8.4 per cent. Household fixed investment (which includes unincorporated business) averaged 13.0 per cent in the Eleventh Plan, with a range of 10.5–14.3 per cent. For the Twelfth Plan, household fixed investment was projected to average 12.3 per cent for the Plan period as a whole, it began higher at 13.5 per cent in the first two years, slowly reducing to 11.5 per cent in the final two years of the Plan as the corporate sector expanded its share.

It has been pointed out by the Planning Commission in the 12th Plan that **private corporate investment had now become the major driver of investment in recent years.** In 2003-04 private corporate fixed investment (at constant 1999–2000 prices) was only 6.2 per cent of GDP, while the overall fixed investment rate was 27.1 per cent. It rose to 9.1 per cent (at constant 2004–05 prices) in 2004-05 and to 11.9 per cent in 2005–06, when the overall fixed investment rate increased to 28.7 per cent in 2004-05 and to 30.5 per cent in 2005-06. Private corporate investment averaged 12.4 per cent in the Eleventh Plan but it was at a peak of 15.0 per cent in 2007-08, that is, the first year of the Eleventh Plan and declined in subsequent years to 11.6 per cent in 2011-12. If the overall fixed investment rate was to pick up in the Twelfth Plan, there had to be a recovery in private corporate fixed investment. Table 63.2 shows a gradual build-up in private corporate investment from 11.3 per cent in 2012-13 rising steadily to touch 15.0 per cent—the peak value achieved in 2007-08—in the last year of the Twelfth Plan. This would produce an average of 13.5 per cent for the Twelfth Plan as a whole; higher than the average of 12.4 per cent in the Eleventh Plan.

It is worth mentioning that *a large part of private corporate investment is now in the field of infrastructure—power generation, roads, ports, airports and telecommunications–and a lot of it is*

5 *The Twelfth Five Year Plan*, p. 4.

in the Public-Private Partnership (PPP) mode. The robust growth in private corporate investment is in part a reflection of the strategy of increasing the share of investment devoted to infrastructure and the recognition that private investment has to play a major part in this. Higher investment in infrastructure is critical for the revival of the investment climate as it would lead to enhanced investment in manufacturing.

MULTIDIMENSIONAL NATURE OF PLAN TARGETS

Traditionally, a Five Year Plan of India focuses on achieving a target of overall GDP growth rate and of its sub-sectors as growth of agriculture, industry and services. For the first time the Twelfth Five Year Plan fixes targets of several dimensions of growth process, namely, progress regarding reduction in poverty, increase in employment opportunities to reduce unemployment, the improvements in education of the primary, secondary and higher levels, improvement in nutrition and health of the people and progress in infrastructure including rural infrastructure. We explain below in brief the Plan targets in these aspects of growth process.

Reduction in Poverty

Next to GDP growth target, the target of reducing poverty occupies an important place in development strategy of a plan. The Twelfth Plan mentions that poverty as measured by Tendulkar Committee[6] declined from 37.2 per cent of population living below the poverty line in 2004-05 to 21.9 per cent in 2011-12, the end year of the Eleventh Five Year Plan, that is, 15.3 percentage points in just seven years. According to it, the poverty had declined at the rate of more than 2 percentage points every year during the period 2004-05 to 2011-12 whereas it had declined by 0.74 percentage point each year during 1993-94 to 2004-05. Though the poverty was declining, the absolute number of population living below the poverty line was still very large (270 million persons in 2011-12). In the Twelfth Plan, Planning, Commission has set a target of reducing head-count ratio of poverty by 10 percentage points by the end of Twelfth Plan over the level prevailing in 2011-12, that is, reducing it to just 11.9 per cent by 2016-17.

Employment Generation. In the Twelfth Plan, it is proposed to generate 50 million new jobs in the non-farm sector and to provide skill education to the equivalent number of persons.

Education. The Twelfth Plan has set a target of mean years of schooling to increase by seven years by the end of the Twelfth Plan. Besides, it plans to enhance access to higher education by creating two million new seats for each age group so as to fulfil the skill needs of the economy. Further, in regard to school enrolment, the gender and social gap currently existing between boys and girls and between Scheduled Castes (SCs), Scheduled Tribes (STs), Muslims and rest of the population will be removed by the end of Twelfth Five Year Plan.

Health and Nutrition. Promoting health is another critical dimension of building human capability. Expenditure on health by the government is only 1.2 per cent of GDP which is too low even compared to that of some of the developing countries. As a result, in 2011-12, less than 30 per cent of outpatient and less than half of inpatient healthcare capacity of the country was in the public sector and as a result the majority of the population relies on highly costly private healthcare facilities. Therefore, the Twelfth Five Year Plan proposes to expand public sector capacity in healthcare, especially in the rural areas. The following specific targets with regard to health have been set in the Twelfth Plan:

1. It is provided to bring about significant increase in life expectancy which was only 32 years at the time of independence and rose to 67 years in 2011-12 during the 11th Plan period.
2. Infant mortality rate (IMR) is another important dimension of human capability, which declined from 80 in 1991 to 66 in 2000 and at a faster rate to 47 in 2010 and is proposed to

6 According to Tendulkar Committee, poverty line corresponds to a family consumption of ₹ 3900 per month in the rural areas and ₹ 4,800 per month in the urban areas. A family consists of 5 members.

bring down further to 28 by the end of Twelfth Plan. Besides, maternal mortality rate (MMR) is proposed to be reduced it to 1 per 1000 by the end of the Twelfth Plan.

Further, it is provided to improve child-sex ratio (0 to 6 years), which has been a matter of serious concern as it implies that the society is denying life to female children. In this regard the target of child-sex ratio has been to raise it to 950 by the end of Twelfth Plan. Furthermore, to control the growth of population, *fertility rate* is to be reduced to 2.1 by the end of the Plan.

The poor learning abilities of children in our schools are partly due to high incidence of child malnutrition and undernutrition which is proposed to be reduced among children of 0-3 years half of what prevailed in 2005-07 according to the survey by National Family Health Survey–3 (NFHS-3).

Expansion in Infrastructure including Rural Infrastructure. One of the important reasons for slowdown in economic growth in the years 2011-12, 2012-13, and 2013-14 has been the lack of infrastructure facilities such as availability of power, transport, good highways, better ports and airports. The following targets have been set in the Twelfth Plan with regard to the expansion of infrastructure facilities:

1. Increase investment in infrastructure as a percentage of GDP to 9 per cent by the end of Twelfth Five Year Plan.
2. Increase the Gross Irrigated Area from 90 million hectares to 103 million hectares by the end of Twelfth Five Year Plan.
3. Provide electricity to all villages and reduce AT&C losses to 20 per cent by the end of Twelfth Five Year Plan.
4. Connect all villages with all-weather roads by the end of Twelfth Five Year plan.
5. Upgrade national and state highways to the minimum two-lane standard by the end of Twelfth Five Year Plan.
6. Complete Eastern and Western Dedicated Freight Corridors by the end of Twelfth Five Year Plan.
7. Increase rural teledensity to 70 per cent by the end of Twelfth Five Year Plan.
8. Ensure 50 per cent of rural population has accessed to 40 lpcd piped drinking water supply, and 50 per cent *gram panchayats to* achieve Nirmal Gram Status by the end of Twelfth Five Year Plan.

Environment Sustainability. As explained above, the Twelfth Five Year Plan emphasises that growth must not only be faster, but it should also be more inclusive and sustainable. With regard to environmental sustainability, the following two targets have been set.

1. It provides to increase green cover (as measured by satellite imagery) by one million hectare every year in the Twelfth Five Year Plan.
2. It is planned to increase 30,000 MW of renewable energy capacity in the Twelfth Plan period.

FINANCING THE TWELFTH PLAN

In Table 63.3 we give the financing pattern in the 12th Plan of financing public sector spending compared to the actual realisation in the Eleventh Plan. It will be seen from Table 63.3 that **balance from current revenue** (BCR) of the Centre as per cent of GDP is estimated to be 1.88 per cent of GDP for the 12th Plan. Note that balance from current revenue represents surplus of tax revenue and other non-tax revenue over the current expenditure of the Central Government. It is worth mentioning that for the Eleventh Plan while Planning Commission had projected BCR at 2.31 per cent but actually it turned out to be negative (–) 0.61 per cent. In the 12th Plan, the Planning Commission visualises unrealistically that with good tax buoyancy in tax revenue and a decline in non-plan expenditure, resources from balance from current revenue (BCR) will be 1.88 per cent of GDP in the 12th Plan.

The target of 3.0 per cent of fiscal deficit for 2016-17 implies the target of borrowing including net miscellaneous capital receipts (MCR) which will decline from 5.06 per cent in the Eleventh Plan to 3.35 per cent of GDP in the Twelfth Plan.

Table 63.3. Resources of the Centre in Eleventh and 12th Plans (as per cent of GDP)

Source of Funding	Eleventh Plan	12th Plan	% Change
1. Balance from current revenue (BCR)	– 0.61	1.88	2.49
2. Borrowing including net MCR	5.06	3.35	–1.71
3. Net Capital Flow from Abroad	0.24	0.00	–0.24
4. Gross Budgetary Support (GBS) to Plan (1 to 3)	4.69	5.23	0.54
5. Central Assistance to States and UTs' Plan	1.26	1.26	0.00
6. GBS for Central Plan (4 – 5)	3.43	3.97	0.54
7. Resources of BSEs	2.53	2.38	–0.15
8. Resources for Central Plan (6 + 7)	5.96	6.38	0.39

Source: Planning Commission.

Domestic Saving Rate. For the Twelfth Plan period the Planning Commission has set a saving target of 36.0 per cent of GDP in the last year of the plan. Their projection of **average level of domestic** saving rate for the entire 12th Plan period is 33.6 per cent of GDP, slightly higher than the 33.5 per cent recorded in the Eleventh Plan.

Current Account Deficit. On the basis of its projections of exports and imports of goods and also of invisibles, Planning Commission estimated the current account deficit of average **3.4 per cent of** GDP for the Twelfth Plan period as a whole. It was projected to be higher in the first two years and slightly moderate thereafter. The estimated current account deficit is higher than the normal comfort level of 2.5 per cent of GDP. To finance this higher than comfort level of current account deficit, namely, 3.4 per cent of GDP, the Planning Commission has emphasised that it required that capital account should be managed in a way that facilitates capital inflows.

Gross Budgetary Sources (GBS) of the Centre. The Finance Minister's announced that fiscal deficit of the Central Government would be reduced to 3 per cent in 2016-17. The 12th Plan therefore proposed to have higher collection of taxes including service tax (GST) so as to contain fiscal deficit to 3 per cent by 2016-17. Given the changed economic scenario, GBS is projected to grow from 5.13 per cent of GDP in 2012-13 to 5.2 per cent of GDP in 2016-17. The average gross budgetary sources for the Central Plan in Twelfth Plan stands at 5.23 per cent of GDP as against 4.69 per cent of GDP realised in the Eleventh Plan.

Gross Tax Revenue. The Gross Tax Revenue as a percentage of GDP was estimated to increase from 10.62 per cent in 2012-13 (BE) to at least the levels achieved in 2007-08. The tax revenue (net of States' share) increased from 7.60 per cent of GDP in 2012-13 to 8.79 per cent of GDP in 2016-17, averaging 8.27 per cent during the Twelfth Plan. Collection of direct tax remained higher than the indirect tax collection since 2008-09 and was projected to have similar trend during the Twelfth Plan. Corporate tax collection averaged 69.37 per cent of direct tax collection during the Twelfth Plan. It increased from 4.25 per cent of GDP in 2012-13 to 4.83 per cent of GDP in 2016-17 averaging 4.57 per cent of GDP, that is, 0.76 percentage points increase over the average Eleventh Plan realisation.

Subsidies. Subsidies in the first year of the Twelfth Plan had been taken as per 2012-13 (BE), which was somewhat higher when the final figures became available. With the reforms being undertaken, the total subsidies, as a proportion of GDP, have been projected to decline to 1.5 per cent by 2016-17. Inability to pass on increases in global oil prices to the consumers would have a substantial impact on resources for the Plan, if this situation was not rectified urgently.

Twelfth Plan: Resources of the Centre

The GBS (Gross Budgetary Support) available for the Plan is estimated at ₹35,68,626 crore at current prices. Central Assistance to the States, and UTs' Plan worked out to be ₹ 8,57,786 crore. IEBR of Central public sector enterprises (CPSEs) was estimated at ₹ 16,22,899 crore. *The total resources available for the Central Plan outlay have been, therefore, projected at ₹ 43,33,739 crore.* This is only an indicative outlay. The actual realisation would change depending on how resources position would be from year to year.

Borrowing and Fiscal Deficit. 12th Plan projects that borrowing by the government for funding Government budgetary resources for 12th Plan will be higher initially but is planned to decline gradually. The Centre's net borrowing which was 5.9 per cent of GDP in 2011-12 (RE) is estimated to decline to 5.1 per cent of GDP in 2012-13. The fiscal deficit as a percentage of GDP is further projected to decline to 4.5 per cent in 2013-14, 3.9 per cent in 2014-15 and 3.2 per cent in 2015-16 and 3.0 per cent of GDP in the last year of the Twelfth Plan.

A CRITICAL EVALUATION OF THE TWELFTH FIVE YEAR PLAN

Twelfth Five Year Plan suffers from several shortcomings. By presenting three alternative scenarios, namely, 'strong inclusive growth', 'insufficient action' and 'Policy logjam', shows that the Planning Commission itself was not certain about achieving its targets of its best scenario of 'Strong Inclusive Growth'. This makes its fixation of detailed targets of overall GDP growth rate, agricultural and industrial growth rates quite unrealistic. As a matter of fact, in the first two years, 2012-13 and 2013-14, lower growth rate of 5.1% and 6.9 per cent respectively, was achieved due to *policy paralysis* of UPA government which adversely affected the sentiments of the investors. For 8 per cent GDP growth to be achieved in the entire Twelfth Five Year Plan period, around 10 per cent growth is required to be achieved in the remaining three years which is not possible in view of the sluggish world demand for our exports and lack of adequate infrastructure facilities such as power. The agricultural and industrial growth rates will also fall short of the targets fixed for them. Therefore, to return to higher growth trajectory of achieving 9 per cent growth rate in the near future seems to be not possible.

That the 12th Plan lays stress on achieving more inclusive growth just represents pious wish as it points out that much of inclusive growth to be achieved depends on the private sector. The private sector, especially the corporate one, is driven by profit motive and generally hold a lot of market power to raise prices of goods to maximise their profits. Besides, the private corporate sector enterprises use capital-intensive technologies which generate little employment opportunities despite acceleration of investment and growth. Besides, there is firm evidence from the experience of developed countries that the working of the private sector has tended to concentrate income in the top 5 per cent of population. To hope that the private corporate sector will ensure generation of a lot of employment opportunities and help to reduce poverty, the two important aspects of inclusive growth, is just a wishful thinking without any valid reason. As regards private sector in medium and small enterprises, they do not have adequate funds on their own to make adequate investment. Further, landless labourers who suffer from acute poverty are often exploited by landlords.

As regards the target of generating new employment opportunities for 50 million persons in the non-farm sector in the Twelfth Plan period, it is just not feasible. The adviser to the Finance Ministry, Dr. Arvind Subramanian, has presented the evidence that employment elasticity of growth of output which was about 0.35 to 0.44 in the 1990s has dropped to close to 0.2 in the 2000s. Since labour force is increasing at a higher rate than employment growth, the generation of employment opportunities will be a challenge. The past Indian experience also shows that most of the employment opportunities in the non-farm sector are generated in the unorganised and informal sectors where productivity levels are very low and underemployment prevails on a large scale.

Similarly, the targets for expansion of infrastructure have been overstated. The targets of increasing the gross irrigated area from 90 million hectare to 103 million hectare, providing electricity to all villages, connecting all villages with all-weather roads, upgrading national and state highways to the minimum two-lane standard by the end of Twelfth Five Year Plan are too ambitions targets to be achieved.

Conclusion. In our view the Twelfth Plan is '*business as usual*' Ambitious targets have been set plan after plan but have not been realised and no lessons have been learnt from them. In view of the experience of the first three years of Twelfth Plan in which 6.4 per cent average annual GDP growth rate has been achieved, it does not appear feasible to achieve 8 per cent average annual GDP growth rate in the entire plan period. In view of this, various targets set for increase in education, health, infrastructure and environmental sustainability are unlikely to be realised.

THE INDIAN GROWTH MIRACLE

Though it seems surprising but it is a fact now that after Japanese Miracle, East Asian Miracle and Chinese Miracle there has been now *India's growth miracle*, as in the last 15 years (2000 to 2015) India achieved on an average annual growth rate of around 7.3 per cent while China's average annual growth rate during these fifteen years has been around 10 per cent. More surprisingly, in the four successive years (2004-2008). India achieved average annual growth rate of 9 per cent. Further, in the Eleventh Plan period (2007-12) there has been average annual GDP growth rate of 8 per cent which is the highest achieved in any Indian plan.

It is due to this high rate of GDP growth rate that, according to a World Bank's *International Comparison Program* (ICD) report, in 2011 India displaced Japan to become the world's *third biggest economy* in terms of GDP (based on purchasing power parity prices) ranked after the U.S. and China. India's miraculous growth in recent years can be seen from the fact that the previous International Comparison Program (ICP) survey report for the year 2005 had placed India in terms of GDP (at PPP prices) in the 10th place. So between 2005 and 2011 due to higher GDP growth rate India jumped from 10th place to the 3rd place in respect of GDP (at PPP prices). India's share in World GDP in terms of PPP was 6.4% in 2011 compared with China's 14.9 per cent and the U.S. 17.1 per cent, the latest ICP survey showed. The survey covered 199 countries. In 2011 ranking, India's economy was 37.1 per cent of the U.S. economy compared to 18.9 per cent in 2005. It may be noted that purchasing power parity (PPP) prices are used to compare economies and incomes of the people by adjusting for differences in prices in different countries to make a meaningful comparison. However, it is worthwhile to mention that due to large population, *in respect of per capita GDP, even in PPP terms*, India's rank in 2011 was placed at 127 in the 199 country ranking while China's rank was placed at 99 compared to 12th rank of the U.S.

INDIA'S GROWTH MIRACLE

Since 2003 Indian economy has emerged as one of the fastest growing economies of the world. In fact, next to China, India's growth rate from 2003-04 to 2014-15 has been highest in the world. This is often referred to as **India's growth miracle.** Before 1980s India's average growth rate stuck at around 3.6 per cent per annum which Late Prof. Raj Krishna called Hindu rate of growth. In the nineteen eighties India's average rate of economic growth rose to 5.6 per cent per annum and further in the 1990s and up till 2002-03 (*i.e.*, in 12 years period), India's average growth rate went up to 6.2% per annum under liberalisation and globalisation of the Indian economy. But from 2004-05 to 2007-08 India's average annual growth rate of GDP rose to over 9 per cent per annum. In 2008-09 while the advanced developed countries were experiencing recession *(i.e.*, negative growth), India succeeded in achieving 6.7 per cent growth rate which further rose to 8.6% in 2009-10 and 8.9% in 2010-11.

It will be seen from Table 64.1 (last row) that the GDP growth rate at factor cost (at 2004-05 prices) picked up from the year 2003-04. As compared to average GDP growth rate of around 6.2 per cent in 1991-2003, it was estimated at 8 per cent in 2003-04, 7.1 per cent in 2004-05, 9.5 per cent in 2005-06, 9.6 per cent in 2006-07, and 9.3 per cent in 2007-08. In the year of global financial crisis, it fell to 6.7 per cent in 2008-09. But even then it was well above other countries except China. The GDP growth rate again rose to 8.6 per cent in 2009-10 and to 8.9 per cent in 2010-11. In the next two years, 2011-12 and 2012-13 there was temporary slowdown in economic growth but as we shall explain later, in these two years due to adverse global factors, the growth rate declined in all countries including China. However, from 2013-14 onwards, India's growth rate has picked up while GDP growth rates in other countries of the world remain at lower levels. India's GDP growth rate has risen to 6.9 per cent in 2013-14 and to 7.3 per cent in 2014-15 and it is estimated to up to 7.6 to 7.8 per cent in 2015-16. With this India which has been the second fastest growing economy of the world since 2003 next only to China will overtake China in 2015-16 and is expected to become the fastest growing economy of the World. India's growth rate since 2004-05 is depicted in Fig. 64.1.

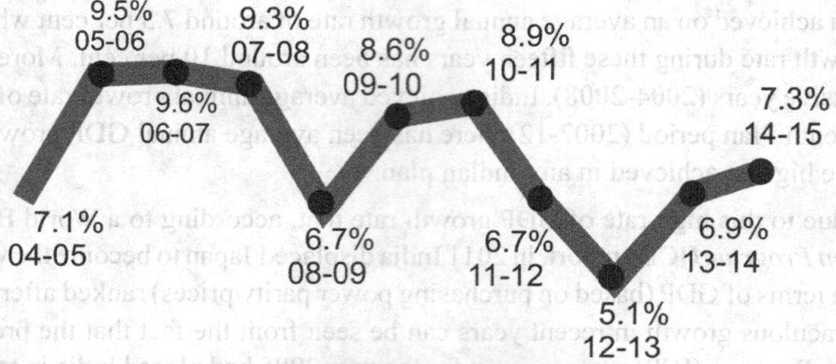

Fig. 64.1. *India's Growth of GDP in India in recent years*

Note. Up to the year 2011-12 growth rate is measured in terms *of GDP at factor cost* in old series, whereas in the last three years, growth is measured in *terms of increase in GDP at market prices* with 2011-12 as the base, in the new series.

Now, the question is how do we account for such a high growth rate in GDP from 2003-04 to 2014-15 in India. Growth depends mainly on rate of saving and investment (or, in other words, on rate of capital formation), and improvement in technology or capital-output ratio. In India, such as in other emerging economies, China, Singapore, Indonesia and South Korea, it was mainly increase in rate of saving and investment (*i.e.*, rate of capital formation) that brought about a sharp growth in GDP. Rates of gross domestic saving and capital formation and GDP growth since 2002-03 are given in Table 64.1. Prior to 2003-04 rate of gross domestic saving in India was around 24 to 26% of GDP. But, as will be seen from Table 64.1, from 2004-05 to 2007-08 (that is, prior to global financial crisis) domestic saving rate rose to 36.8 per cent of GDP in 2007-08 which pulled up the rate of investment or capital formation. As a result, average growth rate of GDP for the four years period (2004-08) rose to over 9 per cent. With this India became the second fastest growing economy of the world next only to China.

In keeping with the higher saving rate from 2003-04 onwards, **rate of fixed capital formation (GFCF)** rose from 24.1 per cent in 2003-04 to about 33 per cent of GDP in 2007-08 (see 5th row in Table 64.1). This higher growth rate of fixed capital formation caused 9 per cent plus average growth in GDP during 2004-05 to 2007-08. In 2008-09 global financial crisis (2007-09) and consequently global meltdown caused a fall in saving rate to 32.0% of GDP in 2008-09 but it rose again to 33.7% in both 2009-10 and 2010-11 before falling to 30.1% of GDP in 2011-12. The substantial increase in consumption

Table 64.1. Rate of Domestic Saving and Fixed Capital Formation, 2003–2012-13 (Old Series with 2004-05 Prices as the base)

	as % of GDP									
	2003-04	04-05	05-06	06-07	07-08	08-09	09-10	10-11	11-12	12-13
Gross Domestic Saving (GDS)	29.0	32.4	33.4	34.6	36.8	32.0	33.7	33.7	31.3	30.1
Household Saving	23.1	23.6	23.5	23.2	22.4	23.6	25.2	23.5	22.8	21.9
Private Corporate Sector Saving	4.6	6.6	7.5	7.9	9.4	7.4	8.4	7.9	7.3	7.1
Public Saving	1.3	2.3	2.4	3.6	5.0	1.0	0.2	2.6	1.2	1.2
Gross Fixed Capital Formation (GFCF)	24.5	28.7	30.3	31.3	32.9	32.3	31.7	31.7	30.6	30.4
Growth of GDP at factor cost	8.0	7.1	9.5	9.6	9.3	6.7	8.6	8.9	6.7	5.1

Source: CSO data after 2004-05 are based on new National Income Series with 2004-05 as the base. GDP growth rates for 2009-10, 2010-11, 2011-12 and 2012-13 are revised estimates.

expenditure under the fiscal stimulus measures to keep the growth momentum which caused drop in public saving rate to 1.0 per cent of GDP in 2008-09 as compared to 5.0 per cent in 2007-08. This financial crisis which caused negative growth of India's exports in 2008-09 slowed down the rate of economic growth in 2008-09 to 6.7 per cent. However, while advanced developed countries of the U.S., Japan and Europe experienced worst ever recession since the Great Depression of 1930s, India was successful in attaining the growth rate of 6.7 per cent in 2008-09. With the saving rate going up to 33.7 per cent and gross capital formation rate to 36.5 per cent of GDP in 2009-10 and revival of positive growth in exports in the second half of 2009-10, rate of growth of GDP rose to 8.6 % in 2009-10. In 2010-11 also with domestic saving rate equal to 33.7 per cent which along with capital inflows raised gross capital formation to around 36.5 per cent and, as a result, rate of GDP growth rose to 8.9 per cent in 2010-11 (RE). However, for the reasons explained below in 2011-12, growth rate of GDP fell further to 6.7 per cent, lowest in nine years. In 2012-13 growth rate in GDP fell further to 5.1 per cent but GDP growth rate picked up to 7.3 per cent in 2014-15.

The macroeconomic situation in India in 2013-14 and 2014-15 improved significantly. The release of the new series of national income accounts with 2011-12 as the base year revealed that the economy has been performing much better than what was thought earlier. In the face of sluggish global demand conditions, it is the increase in domestic demand that brought about the increase in GDP growth. In 2013-14 growth of GDP at constant (2011-12 market prices picked up to 6.9 per cent in 2013-14 and further to 7.3 per cent in 2014-15 (revised estimates). Most of the buoyancy in domestic demand can be traced to increase in consumption expenditure, especially by the Government. Whereas private final consumption expenditure at constant market prices increased by 6.2 per cent in 2013-14, 7.1 per cent in 2014-15, Government final consumption expenditure increased by 8.2 per cent in 2013-14 and 10.0 per cent in 2014-15.

Reasons for Substantial Rise in Saving Rate

Now, what has caused saving rate in India to rise substantially since 2004? Components of saving rate are : (1) household savings, (2) private corporate sector saving and (3) public saving. It will be seen from Table 64.1 that while household savings had stuck at around 23.5 per cent of GDP from 2002-03 to 2011-12 and therefore it cannot explain remarkable rise in overall saving rate in the Indian economy since 2004. It is the private corporate sector which registered a substantial rise in saving rate from 4.1 per cent of GDP in 2002-03 to 9.4 per cent of GDP in 2007-08, that is, the private corporate sector saving more than doubled in the five-year period. After dipping to 7.4 per cent of GDP in 2008-09, the year of global crisis, private sector saving again rose to 8.4 per cent of GDP in 2009-10 and around 8 per cent of GDP in 2010-11. It is this significant increase in corporate sector saving that resulted in higher rate of fixed capital formation which contributed to a big jump in annual growth rate to over 8 per cent in these years.

Besides, large increase in public saving since 2003 also contributed a lot to the increase in the overall saving rate and capital formation from 2003-04 to 2007-08. After 2007-08 due to fiscal stimulus, public saving and its contribution to capital formation or investment declined in the Indian economy. The public sector saving which was negative prior to 2003-04 turned positive and rose to 5 per cent of GDP in 2007-08. (See 4th row in Table 64.1). Thus private corporate sector and public savings together increased by around 10 per cent of GDP from 2003-04 to 2007-08, which brought about higher rate of overall saving and capital formation and ensured higher rate of economic growth. It will be seen from Table 64.1 that fixed capital formation which was 24.1% of GDP in 2002-03 rose to about 33% of GDP in 2007-08. No wonder that with such a high rise in fixed capital formation the average growth rate of GDP during the period 2004-08 rose to over 9%.

How do we explain the large increase in saving of the private corporate sector? It is primarily due to the increase in *profitability of private corporate sector* as measured by the **ratio of profit after tax (PAT) to sales,** which rose from 3.6% to 8% in the six years period, 2003-09.[1] Besides the rise in profitability of the private corporate sector, the companies also reduced dividend rate from half of profits to 1/4th of them. That is, the corporate companies retained (*i.e.*, saved) a greater amount of profits for their expansion or capital formation. Thus, the profits of the private corporate sector not only increased faster on account of higher economic growth but also the companies distributed less of them as dividends that resulted in substantial increase of corporate sector saving.

As regards the public savings, they rose from negative rate in 2003-04 to 5 per cent of GDP in 2007-08. It occurred due to *increase in tax revenue*, especially from the corporate sector. Thus, revenue from corporate tax rose from 1.9 per cent of GDP to 3.6 per cent during this period. Indeed, as a result of it since 2004 overall tax–GDP ratio rose from 8.9 per cent in 2003-04 to 11.9 per cent in 2007-08. This better tax performance along with Government control of its public expenditure under the Fiscal Responsibility Budget Management (FRBM) Act resulted in the fall in Central government's fiscal deficit to 2.5 per cent of GDP in 2007-08. Thus, the improved performance of both the private corporate sector and the public sector in the liberalisation era, especially during the period from 2003-04 to 2007-08, became the significant driver of faster economic growth of the Indian economy.

It may be further noted that rapid growth of some new sectors such as Telcom and IT which hardly existed before 2000 contributed a good deal to rapid economic growth since 2004. Besides, low interest rate policy of the Reserve Bank of India until 2008 made borrowing from the banks cheaper which created large demand for consumer durables such as cars, electronics and housing. This ensured relatively higher growth of consumer durables since 2003-04.

Temporary Slowdown in the Growth of the Indian Economy in 2011-12 and 2012-13

It may be noted that situation regarding saving in the two years (2011-12 and 2012-13) deteriorated, which adversely affected its potential growth rate. Saving as per cent of GDP fell to 31.3 in 2011-12 as against 36.8 per cent in the year 2007-08 (according to old series). This slowdown in saving rate prevented the Indian economy to grow at a faster pace. As explained above, high saving rate had allowed India to domestically finance a major part of its investment and slowdown in saving rate lowered the potential growth rate.

It may be noted that due to slowdown in savings in recent years has been seen in all three segments, household saving, private corporate saving and public saving (see Table 64.1). The fall in household savings has been due to high inflation. Because of high inflation the households had to spend more on consumer goods to maintain their usual standard of living which resulted in reduction of their savings. Besides, high inflation caused the *real* rate of interest earned on investment in bank deposits

1 Sumant Sinha, "Decoding the Saving Rate Miracle", *The Economic Times*, Oct. 22, 2010.

and other forms of financial savings that brought down the financial savings of the households who instead used their savings to buy gold, silver, real estate as hedge against inflation. This adversely affected productive investment.

It is worth mentioning that due to the poor recovery in the U.S. and European countries and uncertainty caused by Eurozone sovereign debt crisis, it was difficult to get sustained capital inflows to finance investment during the period, 2011-13. It was therefore necessary to increase domestic saving to finance increase in investment for attaining higher rate of economic growth.

Because in India at times of global recession in 2008-09 there was fiscal and monetary space, timely stimulus allowed the economy to recover fairly quickly to a growth of 8.6 per cent in 2009-10 and 8.9 per cent in 2010-11 (revised estimates). Since then a number of factors, both global and domestic, have led to a slowdown of the Indian economy. The slowdown in the Indian economy began in the second quarter of 2011-12 when the growth rate fell to 6.7 per cent from a level of 8.0 per cent in the first quarter and continued in the subsequent quarters. From the quarters 4 of 2011-12 and quarters 1 and 2 of 2012-13, growth had been in the range of 5.3 to 5.5 per cent. In the whole year 2011-12 the growth rate of GDP at factor cost was 6.7 per cent as against 8.6 per cent in 2009-10 and 8.9% in 2010-11 (revised estimates) but dropped to 5.1 per cent in 2012-13, the lowest in the ten years.

It may however be noted that slowdown in economic growth was not confined to India alone during this period. There had been a general slowdown in the global economy which was passing through a rather prolonged phase of uncertainty. The recovery from the global crisis of 2008-09 in the advanced economies had been slow and uneven, and a decisive resolution of sovereign debt problem of the Eurozone area had yet to be achieved. Having achieved a GDP growth of 5.1 per cent in 2010, the rate of growth in the global economy declined to 3.8 per cent in 2011 and further declined to 3.3 per cent in 2012, as per the World Economic Outlook released by the IMF in October 2012. The rate of growth of developed economies declined from 3.0 per cent in 2010 to 1.6 per cent in 2011 and was expected to decline further to 1.3 per cent in 2012. Even the emerging economies had slowed down during this period, partly as a result of the slowdown in their export markets. China's growth declined from 10.4 per cent in 2010 to 9.3 per cent in 2011 and was expected to be 7.8 per cent in 2012. Brazil's growth dipped from 7.5 per cent in 2010 to 2.8 per cent in 2011 and was expected to be 0.7 per cent in 2012 as shown in Fig. 64.2.

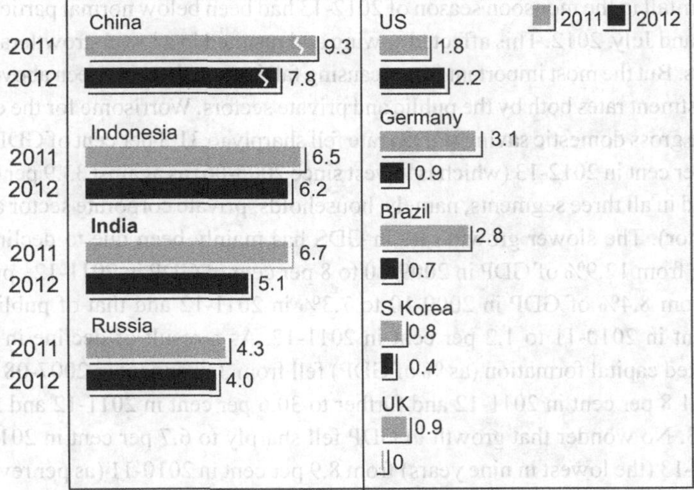

Source: IMF and World Bank Reports

Fig. 64.2. *Growth rates in major countries of the world in 2011 and 2012*

As stated above, slowdown in India's economic growth began in the second quarter of 2011-12 but the slowdown had been sharper in 2012-13. Whereas growth rate in the whole year 2011-12 fell to 6.7 per cent as against 8.6 per cent in 2009-10 and 8.9% in 2010-11, the growth rate in 2012-13 fell to 5.1 per cent. What accounts for this recent slowdown in India's economic growth rate?

The slowdown in growth rate in India in 2011-12 and 2012-13 can be explained in terms of both global factors and domestic factors. First, the slowdown in growth in developed economies and near recessionary conditions in Europe resulted not only in lower growth of international trade but also lower capital inflows. As a result, the growth rate of India's exports declined which contributed to the decline in overall growth rate and also caused problem of current account deficit (CAD). Besides, fall in capital inflows not only resulted in lower investment in the Indian economy but also made the problem of financing current account deficit (CAD) difficult.

Further, international price of crude oil remained high which led to the increase in fuel subsidy bill of the Indian government and drained away resources from public investment. This also adversely affected economic growth. Besides, high crude oil prices led to the widening of India's trade and current account deficits which caused sharp depreciation of rupee which adversely affected the sentiments of foreign investors.

Turning to the domestic factors, higher borrowing costs for the corporate sector due to RBI's high repro rate, the rate at which Reserve Bank lends to the commercial banks, discouraged investment by the corporate sector harming economic growth. The Reserve Bank of India continued to follow a relatively tight monetary policy to control inflation although there was some relaxation by it in lowering cash reserve ratio (CRR) and reducing repo rate by 0.50 per cent in April 2012 and 0.25 per cent in the end of January 2013. As a result of this tight monetary policy of RBI, the cost of borrowing remained at an elevated level and this had an impact on investment and growth in the Indian economy, particularly that of the industrial sector. The erratic power supply due to coal shortage caused delays in implementation of investment projects which made their financing more difficult and investors more cautious. Difficulties in getting clearances of various investment projects also resulted in lower investment. Further, various scams and corruption charges against several ministers and bureaucrats caused **policy paralysis** which made investors hesitant to make investment.

Besides, rainfall in the monsoon season of 2012-13 had been below normal particularly in the key months of June and July, 2012. This affected sowing and resulted in a lower growth rate of agriculture and allied sectors. But the most important factor causing fall in growth rate as seen above has been fall in saving and investment rates both by the public and private sectors. Worrisome for the economy's long-term growth rate gross domestic saving (GDS) rate fell sharply to 31.3 per cent of GDP in 2011-12 and further to 30.1 per cent in 2012-13 (which is lowest since 2005-06) as against 33.9 per cent in 2011-12. Savings declined in all three segments, namely, households, private corporate sector and government (*i.e.*, public sector). The slower growth rate in GDS has mainly been due to decline in household financial saving from 12.9% of GDP in 2009-10 to 8 per cent of GDP in 2011-12, private corporate saving sector from 8.4% of GDP in 2009-10 to 7.3% in 2011-12 and that of public sector saving from 2.6 per cent in 2010-11 to 1.2 per cent in 2011-12. As a result of decline in gross domestic saving, gross fixed capital formation (as % of GDP) fell from 33 per cent in 2007-08 to 31.7 per cent in 2010-11, to 31.8 per cent in 2011-12 and further to 30.6 per cent in 2011-12 and 30.4 per cent of GDP in 2012-13. No wonder that growth in GDP fell sharply to 6.7 per cent in 2011-12 and to 5.1 per cent in 2012-13 (the lowest in nine years) from 8.9 per cent in 2010-11 (as per revised estimates).

Table 64.2. Growth of GDP and its Components at Constant (2011-12) Market Prices (Per cent), 2012-13 to 2014-15 (New Series)

	2012-13	2013-14	2014-15
Total Final Consumption Expenditure	4.9	6.5	7.6
(1) Private final consumption expenditure	5.5	6.2	7.1
(2) Government final consumption expenditure	1.7	8.2	10.0
Gross Capital Formation*	2.6	–4.0	NA
(a) Gross fixed capital formation	–0.3	3.6	4.1
(b) Changes in stock	–6.2	–21.4	3.9
(c) Valuables	3.3	–48.7	28.2
Exports	6.7	7.3	0.9
Imports	6.0	–8.4	–0.5
Growth in GDP at constant market prices	5.1	6.9	7.3

Source: CSO and *Economic Survey*, 2014-15

*Gross Capital Formation adjusted for errors and emissions.

Revival of Growth. Growth in GDP at constant market prices and of its components for three years 2012-13, 2013-14 and 2014-15 according to new series (2011-12 as the base) is given in Table 64.2. It will be seen from this table that in 2013-14 and 2014-15 the growth of GDP has picked up; it is 6.9 per cent in 2013-14 and 7.3 per cent in 2014-15. In 2015-16, it is estimated that GDP growth will rise to around 7.8%. It will be further seen that there has been increasing trend in final consumption expenditure, with both private and government consumption expenditure growing in strength. Secondly, the fixed capital formation which is crucial for revival of economic growth has also picked up; it grew at 3.6 per cent in 2013-14 and 4.1 per cent in 2014-15 as against its negative growth in 2012-13. Thirdly, there is hardly any support to growth from exports in 2014-15. Exports grew only 0.9 per cent in 2014-15 as against 6.7 per cent in 2012-13 and 7.3 per cent in 2013-14. There has been deceleration in imports in 2013-14 and 2014-15 as well which is substantially due to sharp decline in international oil prices in 2014-15 that has reduced our oil import bill. Thus, it can be said that growth revival in 2013-14 and 2014-15 is mainly driven by domestic consumption and fixed capital formation.

India Emerging as the Fastest Growing Economy of the World

India's growth story is expected to dominate the headlines in the years to come as both the World Bank and the IMF predicting that from 1915-16 onward India will overtake China to become the fastest growing economy of the world. The World Bank in its report has estimated that India would achieve 7.5 per cent growth in 2015-16 while China's growth will be be around 6.8 per cent to 7 per cent. Further, according to World Bank forecasts, India's growth rate will accelerate to 7.9 per cent in 2016 and to 8 per cent in 2017. The Economic Survey 2014-15 estimates that India's GDP growth at market prices will be 8.1 to 8.5 per cent in 1915-16. The RBI's forecast for the year 2015-16 is 7.8 per cent. Economic indicators have shown signs of green shoots and policy makers expect that the momentum to sustained growth on the back of reforms that unfold in the years ahead. According to World Bank, acceleration in GDP growth will be driven by higher investment which is expected to grow at an average rate of 12% during 2015-2017. In our view with around 31.0% as the present (2014-15) saving rate and with capital inflow of around 2 per cent investment or capital formation will be around 33 per cent. With capital-output ratio estimated to be equal to 4, the growth rate of 8 per cent is quite feasible.

The achievement of 8 per cent growth rate is warranted by four factors. First, as mentioned above, higher rate of investment or capital formation made possible by increase in domestic saving and normal capital inflow of around 2% of GDP will help in achieving 8 per cent growth rate in the short run to medium term. Second, the Indian government has taken a number of economic reforms and is planning several more which has boosted investment sentiments of both the domestic and foreign investors. This is expected to have a positive impact on economic growth. Besides, investment proposals by investors are getting quick clearance by the government.

Third, an important factor that will boost growth will be provided by declining oil prices and increasing monetary easing by RBI made possible by fall in inflation rate. Decline in oil prices will reduce substantially the government expenditure on subsidies and thus releasing funds for investment. Stimulating the effects of tax cuts made in the budgets for 2014-15 and 2015-16, declining oil prices will add to spending power of households, thereby boosting consumption and growth. "Oil is also a significant input in production and its declining prices will shore up profit margins and hence balance sheets of the corporate sector."[2] Similarly, IMF says, "Growth in India will benefit from recent policy reforms, a consequent pick-up in investment and lower oil prices will raise real disposable incomes particularly among poor households." IMF report further says that inflationary pressures in the Indian economy are likely to ease gradually on account of lower credit prices and improved production capacity will prevent overheating in the medium term.

Table 64.3. Estimated GDP Growth Rate in Some Developed and Developing Countries

	2014	2015	2016	2017
High Income Countries				
US	2.4	2.7	2.8	2.4
Japan	0.0	1.1	1.7	1.8
UK	2.8	2.6	2.6	2.2
Russia	0.6	–2.7	0.7	2.5
Developing Countries				
China	**7.4**	**7.1**	**7.0**	**6.9**
Indonesia	5.0	4.7	5.5	5.5
Brazil	0.1	–1.3	1.1	2.0
Mexico	2.1	2.6	3.2	3.5
India	**7.3**	**7.5**	**7.9**	**8.0**
Pakistan	5.4	6.0	3.7	4.5
Bangladesh	5.6	6.3	6.7	6.7
South Africa	1.5	2.0	2.1	2.4
Iran	3.7	1.0	2.0	2.0
Nigeria	6.2	4.5	5.0	5.5

Source: World Bank, *Global Economic Report*, June 2015.

A few years ago no one had imagined that India would overtake countries like China, Japan, South Korea to become the fastest growing economy of the world. Till now China has been the fastest growing economy of the world. Now, both World Bank and IMF have estimated that beginning from the year 2015 (2015-16), India will overtake China and become the fastest growing economy of the World. In 2014 China's GDP grew at 7.4 per cent while India's GDP growth rate was 7.3 per cent. But China's growth rate is estimated to slip to 7.1 per cent in 1915, to 7.0 per cent in 2016 and further to 6.9 per cent in 2017.

On the other hand, India's growth rate will rise to 7.5 per cent in 2015, to 7.9 per cent in 2016 and further to 8.0 per cent in 2017 (see Table 64.3 that growth rate in High Income Countries such as US, UK, Japan, Soviet Russia is far behind that of India. The same is the case of growth rate in Indonesia, Brazil, Mexico, and South Africa which is much less than that of India.

India's Economic Survey 2014-15 has provided a graph given below comparing the growth rate of India and China. With the exception of few years, China's growth rate has been much higher since 1998 but from 2015 onwards India's growth will go above that of China.

Revised Growth Forecast by IMF

It may be noted that in its latest October 2015 report **"World Economic Outlook Update"** IMF has revised its growth forecast for the world and for both developed and developing countries. As shown in Table 64.4, according to these revised growth forecasts by IMF, India is likely to grow at

2 GOI, *Economic Survey,* Vol. I, 2014-15, p.70.

7.3 per cent in 2015, marginally lower than 7.5 per cent in its earlier estimates, and 7.5 per cent in 2016 as against its earlier estimate of 7.8 per cent in 2016.

However, despite the marginally lower growth forecast of India by IMF *India will remain the world's fastest growing economy* outpacing China's revised growth rate of 6.8 per cent in 2015, where recent shocks have sent ripples across the world. According to IMF, in India 'Growth will benefit from recent policy reforms, a consequent pick-up in investment and lower commodity prices. Besides, according to it, domestic demand in India is projected to remain strong. Furthermore, IMF report says "With China transitioning into an environment of lower growth, India could durably occupy the top growth spot among large emerging economies". However, it adds "in an environment of declining commodity prices, reduced capital flows to emerging markets and pressure on their currencies, and increasing financial market volatility, downside risks to the outlook have risen, particularly for emerging markets and developing economies."

Table 64.4. Revised Global Growth Rates by IMF (percent annual growth)

	2015	2016
World	3.1	3.6
United States	2.6	2.8
Euro Area	1.5	1.6
China	6.8	6.3
India	7.3	7.5

Source: IMF, '*World Economic Outlook: Adjusting to Lower Commodity Prices*, Oct. 2015.

It is evident from above that achievement of high GDP growth rates by India is quite extraordinary but more so because, unlike China, they have been achieved in a framework of parliamentary democracy with people enjoying fundamental rights to life, liberty and ownership of property. Laws regarding regulating the economy and government interventions in crucial fields have to be passed through Parliament where they are heatly debated. Therefore, to achieve 8 to 9 per cent GDP growth rate is no less than a miracle. If this growth momentum is maintained in future and advantage of demographic dividend is availed of by imparting appropriate skills to the growing labour force and providing them gainful employment, then India will catch up soon with the advanced developed countries.

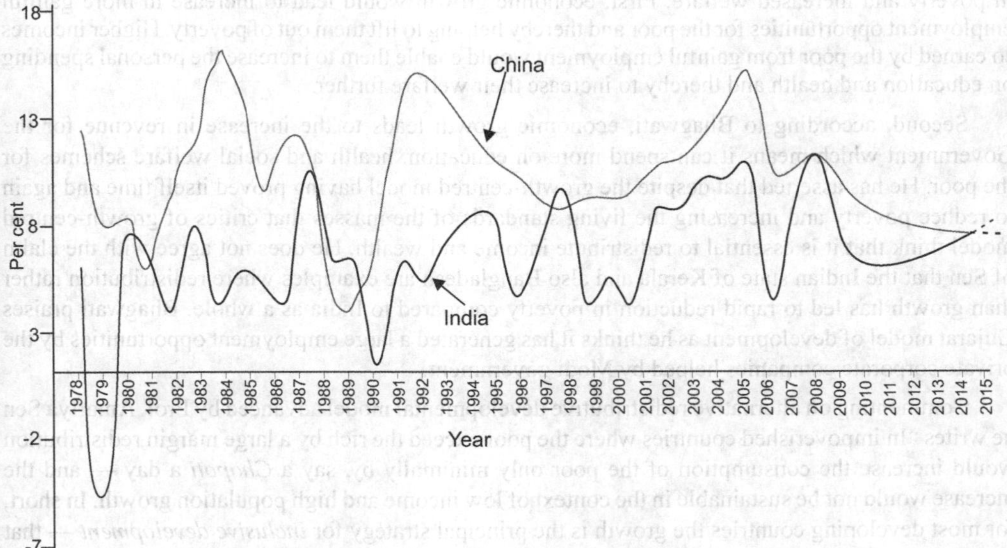

Fig. 64.3. *Real GDP growth: India and China*

IS GDP GROWTH ENOUGH FOR RAISING LIVING STANDARDS OF THE PEOPLE?

We have explained above that India's performance in terms of GDP growth has been quite good which has made possible for it to overtake China in this regard and has emerged as the fastest growing economy of the world from 2015-16 onwards. However, a pertinent question is whether GDP growth is enough for raising the standards of living of the people, especially bottom 40 per cent of population. It may be noted that in developing countries like India mere GDP growth in itself is not enough; it is meaningful if it uplifts the poor living below the poverty line and generate gainful employment opportunities for the unemployed. Besides GDP growth, it is required to fulfill the basic needs of the people, namely food security, good nutrition, healthcare and education which builds human capital and without which even growth cannot be sustained. It is for this reason that the Twelfth Five Year Plan pointed out that growth should not only be faster but also sustainable and inclusive. By inclusive growth we mean that benefits of growth must reach the poor and other marginalised sections of the society.

Bhagwati vs Sen on Growth, Distribution and Poverty

Regarding the importance of GDP growth in developing countries like India and approach towards it there has been intense debate between two prominent Indian economists, Prof Jagdish Bhagwati and Nobel Laureate Prof. Amartya Sen. We discuss below their views and approach towards growth, poverty and distribution of income.

Bhagwati's Approach. There is interesting ongoing debate between Sen and Bhagwati, two eminent India economists, about the issues of growth, distribution and poverty. Bhagwati focuses more on growth than distribution. He is one of the chief advocates of economic reforms involving liberalisation of economic controls (that is, removal of licensing and permits system and other restrictions on starting any industrial activity), the greater role of private sector in the growth process and globalisation, that is, liberalisation of foreign trade and foreign investment which he thinks will promote economic growth. However, *Bhagwati also regards emphasis on economic growth as an instrument of poverty reduction and social advancement of the masses*. He points out ways in which economic growth will cause reduction in poverty and increased welfare. First, economic growth would lead to increase in more gainful employment opportunities for the poor and thereby helping to lift them out of poverty. Higher incomes so earned by the poor from gainful employment would enable them to increase the personal spending on education and health and thereby to increase their welfare further.

Second, according to Bhagwati, economic growth leads to the increase in revenue for the Government which means it can spend more on education, health and social welfare schemes for the poor. He has asserted that despite the growth-centred model having proved itself time and again to reduce poverty and increasing the living standards of the masses that critics of growth-centred model think that it is essential to redistribute income and wealth. He does not agree with the claim of Sen that the Indian state of Kerala and also Bangladesh are examples where redistribution rather than growth has led to rapid reduction in poverty compared to India as a whole. Bhagwati praises Gujarat model of development as he thinks it has generated a large employment opportunities by the private corporate companies helped by Modi government.

Commenting on alternative redistributive developmental model advanced by Prof. Amartya Sen he writes "In impoverished countries where the poor exceed the rich by a large margin redistribution would increase the consumption of the poor only minimally by, say a *Chapati* a day — and the increase would not be sustainable in the context of low income and high population growth. In short, for most developing countries the growth is the principal strategy for *inclusive development* — that is, development that consciously includes marginalist and poorest members of the society."[3]

It is worth mentioning that Bhagwati advocates ***market-oriented strategy of growth*** in which the private sector plays a dominant role and further that Government should provide incentives and remove stifling controls over it. For achieving rapid economic growth he has therefore been a chief supporter of market-friendly economic reforms involving liberalisation, privatisation and globalisation, initiated in India by Dr. Manmohan Singh. These economic reforms, according to Bhagwati, would eliminate poverty and unemployment by bringing about rapid economic growth.

Evaluation of Bhagwati's Approach. Before explaining Sen's view about economic growth, poverty and redistribution some comments on Prof Bhagwati's market-oriented strategy of growth are in order. In our view as well as of Prof. Amartya Sen that though high rate of economic growth is necessary for tackling the problem of poverty and unemployment but not a sufficient condition for it. Whether a high rate of economic growth will help in reducing poverty depends on the composition of growth, the way growing output is produced as well as the distribution of benefits from it. Late Prof. Sukhamoy Chakraborty rightly writes, "*the rate of growth strategy is by itself an inadequate device to deal with the problem of generating employment opportunities. Much depends on the composition of the growth process and how growth is financed and how benefits from growth process are distributed.*"[4]

Empirical evidence also confirms that growth of the modern industrial sector does not generate adequate employment opportunities. In the post-economic reforms period in India during which Bhagwati's policies of liberalisation and globalisation have been implemented, employment growth in the modern organised sector (both in the public and private sectors) grew by 0.05 per cent per annum during 1994-2008 despite 7.2 per cent average annual growth achieved during this period as against 1.20 per cent per annum in the pre-reform period in the eighties. Due to dilution of the role of public sector in industrial growth in the economic reforms initiated in India since 1991 there has been negative growth in employment in it that has not been made up by adequate employment opportunities generated in the private sector which has been given more important and dominant role in the new industrial policy.

Besides, jobless nature of economic growth in India is also revealed by the recent 68th round of NSS conducted in 2011-12. According to this 68th round of NSS, overall employment rate in the Indian economy on the basis of usual states (both principal and subsidiary) has fallen to 38.6 per cent of population in 2011-12 from 39.2 per cent in 2009-10 and the absolute number of unemployed rose from 9.8 million persons in Jan 2010 to 10.8 million in January 2012, that is, one million increase in open unemployment in just two years.[5] This is despite the achievement of 8.9 per cent GDP growth rate in 2010-11 and 6.7 per cent in 2011-12 (revised estimates).

It is evident from above that it is not correct to say that rapid growth will necessarily generate employment opportunities and help in eradicating poverty. Much depends on what is being produced as to whether wage goods (especially food-grains and other essential goods, or luxury goods for those already well-off), and the techniques used for producing goods and services. If capital intensive techniques of production are employed for the production of industrial goods as has been the case in India, industrial growth will generate little employment opportunities and will therefore not lead to the reduction of poverty. As a matter of fact, in the first three decades of planning in India (1951-81) it was widely believed that benefits of growth would trickle down to the poor in the form of greater employment and higher wages. This is generally referred as **trickle-down theory**. After three decades of planning when it was realised that trickle-down effect did not work special employment and anti poverty schemes such as national rural employment scheme and Integrated Rural Development scheme were started.

3 Jagdish Bhagwati, 'Redistribution and Poverty', *Economic Times,* Oct. 31, 2011
4 Sukhamoy Chakravarty "Some Observation on Growth" *Seminar*, 1977
5 Jagdish Bhagwati, 'Redistribution and Poverty', *Economic Times,* Oct. 31, 2011

The second way in which Bhagwati thinks that higher growth will help in eliminating poverty and unemployment is that higher growth would yield more revenue to the Government which it can utilise it to spend more on schemes of promoting literacy, education, healthcare and other anti-poverty schemes such as MGNREGA (Mahatma Gandhi National Rural Employment Guarantee Act), Food Security Scheme). It is true that growth will yield more revenue through taxes but it does not follow that the extra revenue so obtained will be spent on social welfare and anti-poverty schemes and on building human resources through greater expenditure on education and health. For example, even after a substantial increase in revenue from direct taxes much of it is used to meet current revenue expenditure on non-productive activities and despite a large increase in tax revenue substantial amount of funds are borrowed from the market and thus incurring a *huge fiscal deficit*. And this huge fiscal deficit year after year has generated a persistent inflation which besides eroding the real incomes of the common man sends many people below the poverty line.

Further, the strategy of growth suggested by Bhagwati gives dominant role to the private sector without much regulation and control over it and, as the experience of post-reforms economic development reveals, this leads to glaring inequalities of income and wealth which are largely non-functional and *encourage conspicuous consumption* not conducive to promotion of economic growth. Strangely enough, Bhagwati advises the wealthy Indians to indulge less in conspicuous consumption; will the rich Indian entrepreneurs who have become billionaires and spend several crores on the wedding of their children and lead a highly luxurious life listen to Bhagwati's advice? To quote Bhagwati "The political sustainability of the growth first model requires both symbolic and material effects. While growth does benefit the poor: it often benefits the rich disproportionately. So, to keep the poor committed to the system as their economic aspirations are aroused, the wealthy would be well advised to indulge less in conspicuous consumption".[6]

It follows from above that single-minded focus on growth without regard to its composition, technology used for production and distribution of its fruits brought about by unfettered free private enterprise is not an adequate answer to the problem of poverty and unemployment in India. This is not to deny that growth is important but equally important is its composition, its employment-generating potential and distribution of its fruits. It is on these grounds that Amartya Sen has criticised Bhagwati's growth-first approach. We now turn to examine Sen's Approach to growth, distribution and poverty.

Prof. Amartya Sen on Growth, Poverty and Distribution

Prof. Amartya Sen has been an advocate of the approach that considers *building of capabilities of the people* through more education and healthcare of the poor. Besides, he advocates for enlargement of job opportunities for the poor and freedom of human choice as a means of eliminating poverty and promoting well-being of the people. Unlike Bhagwati, he does not consider growth first and then redistribute to solve the problems of poverty and unemployment. In his latest look '*An Uncertain Glory: India and its Contradictions*' coauthored with Jean Dreze he points out that rapid growth in India has coexisted with grossly inadequate social services (education and health) and physical services (safe water, electricity, drainage and sanitation).

Despite significant economic growth achieved in the last two decades (1991–2012) there still prevails widespread poverty in India. The poor and underprivileged people suffer from undernourishment, poor health, illiteracy, lack of education and skills to get gainful employment. Freedom from hunger and undernourishment, freedom from illness and freedom from illiteracy are essential requirements of economic growth. It is building of the capabilities of the poor and gain freedom from illness and illiteracy that Sen views as economic development. To quote him, "*economic growth cannot be sensibly treated as an end in itself. Development has to be more concerned with enhancing the lives we lead and freedom we enjoy*".[7]

6 Jagdish Bhagwati, 'Redistribution and Poverty', *The Economic Times,* Oct. 31, 2011

7 Amartya Sen, *Development as Freedom*, Oxford University Press, 2001, p. 43.

Thus, according to him, the challenge of development is to improve the quality of life, especially in a developing countries such as ours. A better quality of life generally calls for high standards of health and nutrition, less poverty, more equality of opportunity[8]. In his latest book, 'An *Uncertain Glory: India and its Contradictions*', he cites successful countries like Korea and China to argue that fast economic growth is not sustainable without strong development of human capital and essential infrastructure. India lags behind many countries at a similar level of development and even behind poor Bangladesh. In an interview with *Times of India* at the time of publication of its above mentioned book in July, 2013 he says, "despite great success in many ways over the last two decades the fact is that India is in a dreadful state in many ways. *Inequality is the primary aspect of it*. About economic growth I think there are two things about it. First, the way the Indian dialogue has developed there seems to be basic involvement about how growth happens. *No country in the world with such a fast sustained rate of economic growth has done so little towards having an educated and healthy labour force.* The way the debate has come it is now just '*we now have growth so we have to make it inclusive*'. *Now, these are not two distinct things*. If growth happens it depends on how it is happening. *If it happens because you have an educated and healthy labour force, then a lot of people are better placed to earn more income".*

It is evident from the above that, according to Sen, the State should begin with investment in education and healthcare of the people right away without waiting for first to become rich and then think of redistribution for achieving inclusive growth. He provides the example of Singapore, Taiwan, Korea, China which began with investment in education and healthcare of the people without waiting for first becoming rich. In their case, according to him, growth happened along with the poor benefitting from it by making earnings from the education and health acquired by them in the process of growth and in this way become a productive part of the society. He further thinks that growth will generate more resources and if they are ploughed back for further investment in building human capabilities, it will still generate rapid economic growth. He bemoans the fact that even after 60 years of development India has not achieved universal education. In response to Bhagwati's criticism he says that he is not against liberalisation and globalisation and did not support the license-permit system. But he emphasises that while economic reforms initiated by Dr. Manmohan Singh in 1991 *attempted to correct the overactivity of government in some fields* (*i.e.,* removing license-permit system by undertaking liberalisation and privatisation), *the need to correct government underactivity* in other areas has not really been addressed. As back as in 1998, he wrote, "the success of liberalisation and closer integration with the world economy may be severely impaired by India's backwardness in basic education, elementary healthcare, gender inequality and humilations".

It is because of absence of constructive activities of the State, namely, expansion in Government spending on healthcare and nutrition of the people that he has criticised 'Gujarat Model of Development'. Sen and his coauthor. Jean Dreze have supported the starting of **MGNREGA Scheme** because it helps the poor to obtain gainful employment giving them income which they can use to end their undernourishment and contribute to the improvement of their health. Similarly, they have supported the passage of *food security bill* which would ensure the poor people adequate food to remove their hunger and undernourishment which will enhance their capability to participate in the process of development.

Thus Sen believes that the State *must directly* deliver food, employment, education and healthcare rather than relying on trickle-down effect of economic growth achieved through the dominant role of private sector in a predominantly free-market economy. Besides, Sen is of the view that rapid economic growth achieved through liberalisation, privatisation and globalisation of the Indian economy has resulted in glaring income inequalities which besides being non-functional leads to conspicuous consumption of the few rich people. This has adversely affected resources available for growth and social spending by the Government on food security, education, employment and healthcare of the

8 *Ibid* p. 175.

poor people. According to him rapid growth would have been brought about by investing in India's most abundant resource, that is, investing in education and health of its people and thereby building up their capabilities for productive work, the present glaring income inequalities would not have been there and inclusive growth in real terms would have been achieved.

Evaluation of Sen's

Sen's view that a higher priority should be given to the investment in education and health and providing food and employment to the poor people in our growth strategy is a correct one and has been unjustly criticised by Bhagwati who believes in the efficiency of capitalism or free market economy to deliver rapid economic growth and enhanced welfare of the people.

However, Sen's present view of growth underplays the importance of investment in physical capital and physical infrastructure to promote growth. The expansion or accumulation of physical capital in both industry and agriculture is also of crucial importance for increase in productivity of labour force and growth of employment. In fact, in his earlier works (including 'Choice of Techniques') he had emphasized, accumulation of physical capital to accelerate economic growth. Besides, we need a growth strategy that ensures rapid growth of employment opportunities in the normal growth process. For this we require the *use of labour-intensive appropriate technologies* for use in small and medium enterprises rather than labour-displacing capital-intensive technologies generally used by our big corporate enterprises. Even if there is expansion of educated and healthy people, if adequate opportunities for their employment are not created, the education and skills acquired by them will be of no avail and their growth potential will remain unutilised. There is a lot of even educated unemployment in India. Further, the special employment schemes such as Mahatma Gandhi National Rural Employment Guarantee Scheme (MGNREGS) which Sen strongly recommends have generally found to be not resulting in the creation of productive assets. Further, these special anti-poverty employment schemes cannot ensure employment generation on a sustainable basis. *What is required is employment-oriented strategy of development so that employment opportunities increase through the regular growth process*.

It is worth mentioning that for bringing about rapid growth in GDP and employment the private sector on which Bhagwati relies for bringing about growth will not make adequate investment in infrastructure such as power, coal, roads, ports, irrigation projects which create external economies and hold back economic growth. Therefore, the State has to play a crucial role for adequate investment in infrastructure projects.

To conclude, what is required is a balanced growth involving investment in education, nutrition and health of the people as emphasised by Sen and adequate investment in expansion of physical capital goods and physical infrastructure. Besides, in India's growth strategy importance ought to be given to the growth of agriculture which produces *wage goods* and are essential for generation of employment opportunities and for ensuring price stability. Investment in agriculture has been neglected in India's growth strategy.

PART XII

Inequality, Poverty and Unemployment

- Income Inequality and Economic Growth
- Poverty and Economic Growth: International Perspective
- Problem of Poverty in India
- Disguised Unemployment and Capital Formation in Developing Countries
- Employment, Unemployment and Economic Growth

CHAPTER 65

INCOME INEQUALITY AND ECONOMIC GROWTH

Introduction

This chapter attempts to explain economic inequality, particularly income inequality, and how it changes as economic development proceeds in a developing economy. Its discussion is divided into three parts. In the first part we explain the meaning and concept of economic inequality and the methods of its measurement. In the second part we critically examine the rationale for social acceptance of some degree of income inequality. In this part we will critically examine how much inequality is justified on the basis of incentives to work more, to acquire skills and education and to promote more saving for increasing the rate of economic growth. In the third part we discuss Kuznets' famous *inverted U-hypothesis* about the impact of economic growth on the distribution of income. In the next part four we examine the relationship between economic growth and income inequality in the context of the Indian economy in the last six decades of planned economic development (1951-2011).

In the modern economics as we saw in Chapter 1, the distinction is now commonly made between the concepts of economic growth and economic development. Economic development means economic growth plus more desirable changes that must occur to raise the levels of living of the people at large. These other desirable things for economic development to occur are (1) reduction in economic inequalities, both of income and wealth, (2) reduction of absolute poverty which is the extreme form of inequality and (3) reduction in unemployment and underemployment.

The economic development requires a faster and more inclusive growth in GDP. The basic issue in economic development is not only how to achieve faster growth in GDP but also who benefits from growth.The principal objective of developing countries, especially of India, is to raise the levels of living of the people of a country. Therefore, economic growth will be of little value if it benefits only a few rich, keeping a good number of the population in the state of poverty and unemployment. This question of extreme inequality, that is, absolute poverty, and its relationship with economic growth will be examined in the next chapter.

It has now been found that many developing countries have experienced relatively higher rates of economic growth but much of the benefits of growth have not reached to the bottom of around 33 to 40 per cent of population and as a result they remained poor.

It may be noted that prime cause of inequality is not so much due to the differences in earnings from work *i.e.* labour services but because of the *highly skewed distribution of property or assets* and also of the *differential access of the people* to such facilities as education, health, housing and employment. Therefore, if the objective of economic equality is to be realised we have not only to improve the access of the people in general to the facilities of education, health, housing but also to redistribute assets (for example, land reforms). Besides, to ensure relative equality, adequate employment opportunities are to be generated to ensure earnings from work to labourers.

Inequality: Meaning and Measurement

Economists are primarily concerned with these inter-related types of inequalities, namely, inequality in *size distribution* of (a) income, (b) earnings from work (*i.e.* wages and salaries), and (c) wealth. Inequalities in earnings from work or labour services arise either from paid employment (*i.e.,* wages and salaries) or earnings of individuals from self employment in various types of economic activities.

Inequalities in incomes are described with reference to households or families and refers to the amounts received by all members of a household from all sources and shared by all its members, both earners and non-earners (including dependants and children). In the discussion of income inequalities what matters is how much a person or household receives regardless of whether income received is solely from work, from wage employment or from other sources such as rent from land, interest on financial capital, profits from business or dividends from shares of corporate companies or gifts or from inherited wealth. That is, in the concept of income inequalities we are not concerned with *functional distribution* but with the *size distribution of income*. Of course, functional distribution of income affects the size distribution of income. Incomes accrue to the households from the following three sources:

1. Income from work or earnings from labour services of the members of the family who are employed.
2. Income from wealth or assets possessed by a household or its individual members. The wealth consists of land and other non-renewable natural resources, tangible capital assets such as machines, equipment, buildings and financial assets belonging to households. Thus, rent from land, interest on financial capital and bank deposits and profits from enterprise and investment undertaken by the households or its members. Obviously, the distribution of income from wealth depends on distribution of wealth or assets among households in a society. The greater the inequality in the distribution of wealth or assets, the greater the inequality in income distribution.
3. The third source of income by households is the private or public transfer of income to the households as a result of unilateral income flows and cash transfers such as unemployment allowances, sickness benefits, old age pension, private transfers such as gifts, and remittances received from abroad by the households.

The income transfers from government also include free or subsidised supply of public services such as health and education to those who are incapable of funding them privately. It may be noted that transfer of income from government to individuals or households is essential in a welfare state and widely accepted as the function of the modern government in a democratic country.

MEASUREMENT OF INCOME INEQUALITY

To measure income inequalities economists arrange all individuals or households by ascending order of personal incomes. Then total population of individuals or households is divided into *quintiles* (*i.e.,* fifths) or *deciles* (*i.e.,* tenths) from the bottom to the top income groups, that is, in ascending order of income levels. It is then determined what percentage or proportion of total national income accrues to different quintiles or deciles of households. To give a concrete illustration we give in Table 65.1 the distribution of national income of India according to the ascending order of household disposable income of India for the years 1999-2000, 2005 and 2011.

It will be observed from Table 65.1 that in the year 1999-2000 the top of 20 per cent of households in India had 43.3 per cent share of consumption expenditure, whereas bottom 20 per cent of population had only 8.9 per cent share of consumption expenditure in India. This shows the gross inequalities in consumption expenditure and therefore income distribution in the year 1999-2000. In the year 2005, household survey of consumption expenditure revealed that the highest (*i.e.,* top) 20 per cent of the people had 45.3 per cent share of total consumption whereas the share of the lowest 20 per cent of population in consumption expenditure was only 8.1 per cent. This shows that between 1999-2000 and 2005 the inequality in consumption expenditure increased. This is also revealed by Gini Coefficient which was 36.8 in 2005 compared to 32.5 in 1999-2000.

Table 65.1. Distribution of Income/Consumption among Population in India: Percentage Share of Income/Consumption Expenditure

Percentage of Population	1999-2000	2005	2011
1. Lowest 10 %	3.9	3.6	3.7
2. Lowest 20%	8.9	8.1	8.5
3. Second 20%	12.3	11.3	12.1
4. Third 20%	16.0	14.9	15.7
5. Fourth 20%	21.2	20.4	20.8
6. Highest 20%	43.3	45.3	42.8
7. Highest 10%	28.5	31.3	28.8
Gini Coefficient	32.5	36.8	33.6

Source: World Bank, *World Development Indicators* for the years 2006 and 2015 and are based on '*Household Expenditure Survey*' data for the years.

Kuznets' Ratio

A popular method of measuring degree of income inequality is Kuznets' ratio after the name of Simon Kuznets who has been a pioneer in the study of income inequality. *Kuznets ratio is given by the income received by the top 20 per cent divided by the income of the bottom 40 per cent of the households or persons.* In India as is seen from Table 65.1 that 1999-2000 top 20 per cent of households had 43.3 per cent share of national consumption expenditure and the bottom 40 per cent households 21.2 per cent of national consumption expenditure. This gives us Kuznets' ratio to be equal to 43.3/21.2 = 2.04. Thus, the degree of consumption or income inequality in India in the year 1999-2000 as measured by Kuznets' ratio was 2.04 which is quite high. In 2005, Kuznets' ratio is 45.3/19.4 = 2.3 which is higher than in 1999-2000.

It is worth mentioning here that Kuznets' ratio measures the degree of income inequality between the two extremes of very poor and very rich in the country. How is income distributed within the remaining range of income distribution is not considered by Kuznets' ratio.

Kuznets' Curve

A very popular method of measuring income inequality is Kuznets' Curve which graphically measures inequality in income distribution. In order to draw Lorenz Curve we have first to find out *cumulative* percentage of households corresponding to cumulative percentage of income accruing to them. This is shown in Fig. 65.1 where cumulative percentage of households (*i.e.,* recipients of income)arranged from the poorest to the richest (in terms of size of income) are represented on the

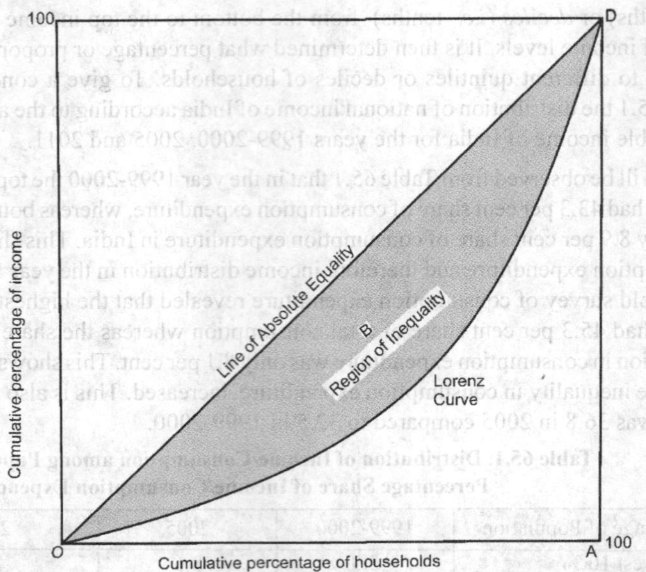

Fig. 65.1. *Lorenz curve showing income distribution*

horizontal axis and cumulative percentages of income of the households starting from the poorest to the richest are represented on the horizontal axis. Straight diagonal line *OD* shows equal distribution of income according to which every household receives the same income and therefore Lorenz Curve representing perfect or absolute equality of income will be a diagonal line. When the distrbution of income is less than perfect equality, Lorenz Curve will be below it, as shown by *OD* curve in Fig. 65.1. The line of perfect equality serves as a point of reference to which we compare actual or observed distribution of income in a society. The shaded area between the line of perfect equality and the actually obtained Lorenz Curve such as *OD* represents the observed distribution of income, that is, inequality in a society. This shaded area is therefore generally described as '*the region of inequality*'. The larger the deviation of Lorenz Curve depicting actual income distribution from the line of pefect equality the greater the inequality of actual distribution of income. Thus, in Fig. 65.2, the Lorenz Curve *H* (dotted)will indicate greater inequality of income distribution than the Lorenz Curve *L*. The maximum deviation of actual distribution from the line

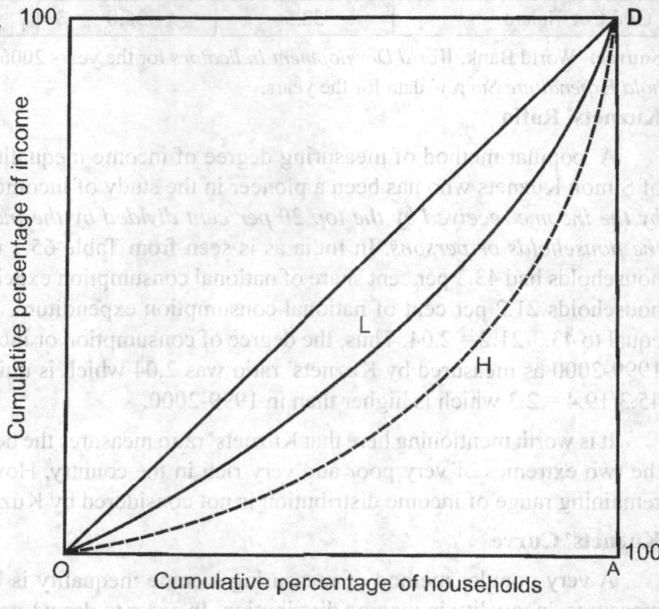

Fig. 65.2. *The Lorenz curves showing less and more inequality in income distribution*

of perfect equality will be represented by the area of a triangle *OAD* in Fig. 65.2. According Lorenz Curve criterion of income distribution, the farther the Lorenz curve to the line of absolute equality, the greater the inequality in the distribution of income. Thus in Fig. 65.2, the Lorenz curve *H* represents greater inequality in income distribution than Lorenz curve *L*.

Gini Coefficient as a Measure of Inequality

A conventional summary measure of inequality based on Lorenz curve is the Gini Coefficient named after the Italian economist who first suggested it in 1912. Gini Coefficient in Fig. 65.1 is given by the ratio of shaded area (*representing the actual deviation of observed income distribution from the line of perfect equality*) *to the area of triangle OAD*. Thus in 65.1, Gini Coefficient is given by the ratio of shaded area B to the total area of triangle OAD. Thus

$$\text{Gini Coefficient} = \frac{\text{The Shaded Area B}}{\text{The Total Area of Training } OAD}$$

It is worth mentioning the following four properties of Gini Coefficient:

1. First, the value of Gini Coefficient will be between zero (in case of perfect equality) and unity (in case of perfect inequality).
2. Second, since the Gini Coefficient is based on ratio of shares represented by a Lorenz curve, it is a relative measure of inequality in income distribution. This implies that the same Lorenz curve may refer to the distribution around different levels of income. This must be taken into account while comparing different income distributions.
3. In the third place, Gini Coefficient attempts to capture the extent of dispersion underlying the size distribution of income or consumption. Therefore, any statistical measure of distribution can be used to measure inequality in a given distribution of income.
4. Fourthly, the same Gini Coefficient may result from different Lorenz curves representing different income distribution patterns and therefore a *unique relationship* between the two does not exist. Let us illustrate this point with the help of Lorenz curve. Consider two Lorenz curves A and B with the same levels of mean income which cross each other as shown in Fig. 65.3. This situation of intersecting Lorenz curves represents conflict situation. In this case of income distribution share of income *accruing to certain sections* of the population is lower and others higher in one situation than in the other. In Fig. 65.3, according to Lorenz

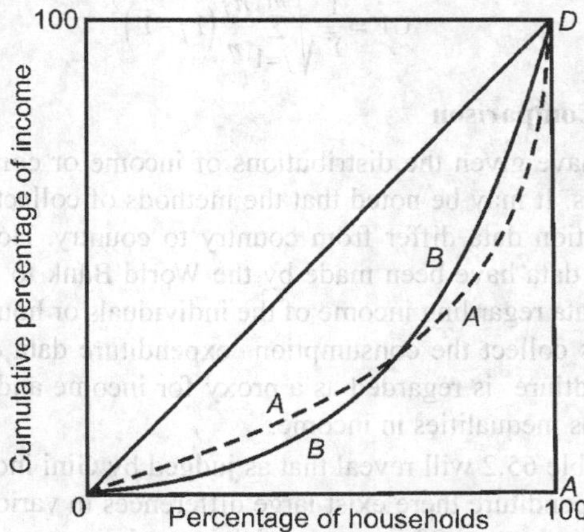

Fig. 65.3. *Two Lorenz curves representing conflict situation*

curve *A* in the households at the **bottom** of income distribution there is **more equality** and in households with higher income levels the income distribution is **more unequal**. The opposite is case *in Lorenz curve B in Fig. 65.3 where in the households at the bottom level there is more inequality*, while at the higher income level, income inequality is less. With the *level of mean income* being the same, the two Lorenz curves show different patterns of income distribution. The choice between such income distribution patterns represented by two Lorenz curves intersecting each other requires the *resolution of conflict situations* over which agreement regarding extent of inequality of income distribution may not be possible.

Coefficient of Variation (*CV*)

The coefficient of variation is a statistical measure of dispersion of income distribution. This measure gives more weight to larger deviation of households' income from mean and therefore represents better measure of income inequality than the '*mean absolute deviation*'. Coefficient of variation is the most common measure of dispersion of income that is generally used by statisticians and is based on standard deviation (σ) which squares all deviations from the mean. Since square of a number rises more than proportionately to the number itself, this implies greater weight being assigned to the larger deviations from mean. *The coefficient of variation is just the standard deviation divided by the mean* and, therefore, it reflects only relative incomes. Let there be *n* individuals and *m* is the number of distinct incomes and *j* denotes an income class and *nj* denotes the number of individuals earning income in each income class. The coefficient of variation of an income distribution is written as

$$CV = \frac{1}{\overline{Y}} \sqrt{\sum_{J=1}^{m} \frac{n_j}{n} \left(Y_j - \overline{Y}\right)^2}$$

In the above formula Y_j is income of an household, $\overline{Y}$ is the mean income, then $\left(Y_j - \overline{Y}\right)^2$ is the square of deviation of income of an household from the mean. With summing up of such squared deviations of incomes of all households and then taking a square root of it we get standard deviation. Thus standard deviation (σ) is given by

$$\sigma = \sqrt{\sum_{j=1}^{m} \frac{n_j}{n} \left(Y_j - = \overline{Y}\right)^2}$$

On dividing this standard deviation by the mean we have the following value of coefficient of variation:

$$CV = \frac{1}{\overline{Y}} \sqrt{\sum_{j=1}^{m} \frac{n_j}{n} \left(Y_j - \overline{Y}\right)^2}$$

Income Inequality: A Comparison

In Table 65.2, we have given the distributions of income or consumption of both developed and developing countries. It may be noted that the methods of collecting data, degree of coverage of income or consumption data differ from country to country. However, some adjustments in income or consumption data have been made by the World Bank to make them comparable. It is worth mentioning that data regarding income of the individuals or households is difficult to collect. Therefore, most surveys collect the consumption expenditure data of individuals or households and consumption expendtiure is regarded as a proxy for income and inequalities in consumption expenditure are treated as inequalities in income.

Now, a glance at Table 65.2 will reveal that as judged by Gini index, inequality in distribution income/consumption expenditure there exist large differences in various countries of the world. In India in the year 2011 the bottom 20 per cent of the population received 8.5 per cent of income/consumption whereas the top or highest 20 per cent had 42.8 per cent share of the national income or consumption. This shows that there exist quote a large inequalities of income/consumption despite the aim of the first Six Five Year Plans (1951 to 1990) to reduce inequalities of income. The degree of inequality in India is also revealed by Gini index of 33.6 (Note that Gini index is Gini Coefficient multiplied by 100).

Table 65.2. Distribution of Income of Consumption

Country	Year of Survey	Gini Index	Percentage Share of Income /Consumption of Subgroups						
			Lowest 10%	Lowest 20%	Second 20%	Third 20%	Fourth 20%	Highest 20%	Highest 10%
India	2011	33.6	3.7	8.5	12.1	15.7	21.8	42.8	28.8
Pakistan	2010	29.6	4.2	9.6	13.1	16.5	21.3	39.5	25.6
Bangladesh	2010	32.1	4.0	8.9	12.4	16.1	21.3	41.4	27.0
Sri Lanka	2009	36.4	3.4	7.7	11.4	15.3	21.0	44.6	30.0
China	2011	37.0	1.7	4.7	9.7	15.3	23.2	47.1	30.0
Brazil	2012	52.7	1.0	3.4	7.7	12.4	19.3	57.2	41.7
Kenya	2005	47.7	2.0	4.8	8.7	13.2	20.0	53.2	38.0
Indonesia	2011	38.1	3.4	7.6	11.3	15.6	21.8	43.7	28.2
Malaysia	2009	46.2	1.8	4.5	8.7	13.7	21.6	51.5	34.7
South Africa	2011	65.0	1.1	2.5	4.3	7.7	15.7	69.9	53.8
Thailand	2010	39.4	2.8	6.8	11.5	14.6	21.5	46.7	31.0
Philippines	2012	43.0	2.5	5.9	9.4	13.9	21.2	49.7	33.5
U.K.	2010	38.6	1.9	5.8	11.4	16.2	22.6	44.1	28.6
Canada	2010	33.7	2.7	7.1	12.4	16.8	22.7	41.0	25.7
U.S.	2010	41.0	1.4	4.7	10.4	15.8	23.1	46.0	29.6
Japan	2008	32.1	2.7	7.4	12.9	17.3	22.7	39.7	24.8
Sweden	2005	26.1	3.8	9.5	14.3	17.8	22.7	35.7	21.4
Norway	2000	25.8	3.9	9.6	14.0	17.2	22.0	37.2	23.4

Source: World Bank, *World Development Indicators,* 2015.

Now, the income distribution in China, which has been the fastest growing economy of the world in the last three decades, is noteworthy as since 1980s it has adopted the policy of privatisation and liberalisation with greater role to foreign investment to accelerate economic growth . It will be observed from Table 65.2 that in China in 2011, the top or the highest 20 per cent of population received 47.1 per cent of income/consumption while the bottom 20 per cent got only 4.7 per cent share of national income or consumption . It is the policy of privatisation and liberalisation of the economy that is responsible for the current large inequalities of income in China. Gini Coefficient in China in 2011 was 37.0 which is also quite high.

In Table 65.2, the worst developing country from the viewpoint of inequality is Brazil where Gini Coefficient in 2012 is 52.7 which is very high. Besides, in Brazil the top 20 per cent of population had 57.2 per cent share in national income/consumption, whereas the bottom 20 per cent received only 3.4 per cent share of it.

In the developed country of the US, inequalities in income distribution are quite large. In 2010, its Gini index was 41.0 which is quite high and in it while the top 20 per cent of population received 46 per cent of income, the bottom 20 per cent had only 4.7 per cent share in national income. In Japan, there exist less inequalities in income distribution where the highest 20 per cent of population had a share of 39.7 per cent in national income consumption, the bottom 20 per cent received 7.4 per cent of it.

Of special mention are the Scandinavian countries of Sweden and Norway which have developed and become rich while maintaining relative equality in income distribution. It will be seen from Table 65.2 that in Sweden and Norway Gini Index is 26.1 and 25.8 respectively which show lesser income inequalities in the distribution of income. In Sweden, the top 20 per cent of population had a share of 35.7 per cent in income/consumption whereas the lowest 20 per cent received 9.5 per cent of income. Gini index of income distribution of Sweden is equal to 26.1 which is quite small. The almost same situation regarding income distribution exists in Norway. The readers can themselves calculate Kuznets' ratio from income distribution data of various countries given in Table 65.2.

ECONOMIC GROWTH AND INEQUALITY: KUZNETS' INVERTED-U HYPOTHESIS

In his presidential address to the American Economic Association in 1955. Simon Kuznets put forward the hypothesis that relationship between per capita national income and the degree of inequality in income distribution may be of the form of inverted-U. Due to limitations of data he used an inequality measure of *"the ratio of income share of the richest 20 per cent of the population to the bottom 60 per cent of the population"*[1] known as Kuznets' ratio. According to the Kuznets' Inverted U-hypothesis, as per capita national income of a country increases, in the initial stages of growth, inequality in income distribition rises and after reaching the highest *degree in the intermediate* level the income inequality falls. This is shown in Fig. 65.4 where as a country develops and its per capita income rises, the degree of income inequality initially rises and after reaching the maximum level, it falls as GDP per capita increases further. As time series data of the transition of the poor underdeveloped countries from underdeveloped stage to the developed stage was not available, he used the data of cross section of countries including both developed and developing countries. In his 1955 study he calculated the Kuznets' ratios and found that *the developing countries tend to have a higher degree of inequality whereas the rich developed countries tend to have a lower degree of inequality.*

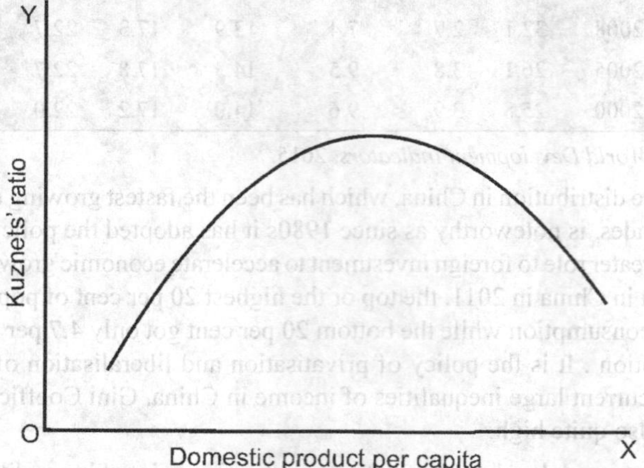

Fig. 65.4. *Kuznets' Inverted-U curve*

Later in his1963 study Kuznets provided further evidence of his inverted U-hypothesis regarding the relationship between inequality and economic growth. In this study he included eighteen countries, as in the earlier study, he included in this sample both the developed and developing countries. *From this later study he concluded that the share of upper income groups in the rich developed countries was signifcantly lower than their counterparts in the developing countries.*[2] This means income inequalities were higher in developing countries compared to those in the developed countries.

---

1 Simon Kuznets, "Economic Growth and Inequality" *American Economic Review,* 1955.

2 Simon Kuznets, "Quantitative Aspects of Economic Growth, Distribution of Income by Size", *Economic Development and Cultural Change*, Vol. 12, 1963.

Other economists have also carried out studies to test Kuznets' inverted U,-hypothesis. Due to the non-avilability of income distribution data of an individual country over time as it grows over time from an underdeveloped stage, like Kuznets, others have also generally used cross-section data of countries with a mixture of developed and developing countries to test Kuznets' inverted-U hypothesis regarding the relationship between changes in income inequality and economic growth. one such cross-section study with data of forty six countries classified into different income categories according to the per capita GDP in 1965 in US dollars was made by Paukert[3] using Gini Coefficient as a measure of inequality. Paukert's analysis of cross-section of countries also confirmed the inverted U-hypothesis of Kuznets and his findings are given in Table 65.3. As will be seen from Table 65.3 in less than $100 per capita GDP category countries, Gini Coefficient is 0.419 and as we go to the next category of countries with per capita GDP between $ 101 and $200, Gini Coefficient rises to 0.468 and in still higher categories of per capita GDP between $201 and 300 inequality as measured by

Table 65.3. Gini Coefficient in Cross-section of Countries

Income Category (1965 US $)	Average Gini Coefficient in Various Income Categories of Countries
Less than $100	0.419
$101 to $200	0.468
$201 to $300	0.499
$301 to $500	0.494
$501 to $1000	0.438
$1001 to $2000	0.401
$2001 and higher	0.365

Source: Paukert, F (1973), op. cit.

Gini Coefficient rises to 0.499. However, beyond this in still high income categories of countries, the value of Gini Coefficient goes on falling and in the highest income category of countries with per capital GDP $2001 and above, Gini Coefficient falls to 0.365. This is in accordance with Kuznets' inverted U-hypothesis regarding changes in income inequality as economic growth occurs.

Kuznets inverted U-hypothesis seems to hold well in later years, at least upto the year 1970. Montek Singh Ahluwalia used income distribution data of cross-section of countries and made estimates for the countries in near about the year 1970. Results of his study are given in Table 65.4.

Table 65.4. Inequalities of Income in GDP Per Capita

GNP Per Capita (in 1970 in $)	Number of Countries Included	Percentage of Income Recorded		Gini Coefficient	GNP Per Capita Mean ($)
		Lowest 40%	Highest 40%		
Under $ 150	10	15.6	51.3	0.402	101
$150 – $500	19	11.2	57.9	0.479	301
$ 500 – $1500	12	12.2	56.3	0.461	754
Developed Market Economics	13	16.1	43.5	0.358	2849
Socialist Countries	6	24.1	34.6	0.238	913

Source: Montek S. Ahluwalia, "Inequality, Poverty and Development", *Journal of Development Economics* 3, (1978). pp. 340-41.

3 Paukert F. (1973), "Income Distribution at Different Levels of Development: A Survey of Evidence," *International Labour Review*, 108, pp. 97-125.

From the above table inequality can be judged by any three measures, namely, share of bottom 40% of population in GNP, share of top 40% of population in **GNP** and Gini Coefficients in different income categories countries. It is worth mentioning that in 6th columnof Table 65.4 GNP per capita indicates the level of development of the economy. Using any of the three inequality measures it is found that the inequality first rises, then falls as per capita GNP increases as Kuznets' inverted -U hypothesis suggested. Changes in Gini ratio reveals that as average GNP per capita of countries increased from $101 to $301 Gini Coefficient increases from 0.402 to 0.479 and in countries with per capita GNP of $ 754 Gini Coefficient falls to 0.461 and then at mean GNP per capita of $ 2849, Gini Coefficient falls to 0.358.

Similarly, the share of **bottom 40%** of population in GNP indicates that it first falls and then rises again showing that inequality first rises and then falls. In accordance with this the share of highest 40 per cent in GNP first rises and then it falls.

An interesting fact is revealed by the last row of Table 65.4 which gives the data of 6 socialist countries around the year 1970. This reveals that degree of income inequality as per all the three inequality measures in them was much less compared to market capitalist countries. This is because in erstwhile socialist countries private ownership of tangible physical assets was generally abolished and therefore inequalities of income that arise mainly due to highly skewed distribution of assets and property did not exist in these socialist countries at that time. Even wage differentials in these countries were found to be less.

East Asian Countries and Kuznets' Inverted-U Hypothesis

It is woth mentioning that development experience in East Asian countries does not conform to the inverted-U hypothesis of Kuznets. In East Asian countries such as Japan, South Korea, Taiwan, Thailand, Indonesia and Malaysia, contrary to Kuznets' inverted -U hypothesis, in the initial stages growth was not associated with increase in inequality. Instead, the increase in national income was widely shared among its population and millions were lifted out of poverty. For example, in Malaysia and Thailand the incidence of poverty declined from about 50 per cent in 1960s to less than 20 per cent by the end of the 20th century[4]. Though the policies pursued by the various East Asian countries differed a lot, *but the common features of these countries were "high rates of investment in physical and human capital, rapid growth of agricultural productivity and declining fertility"*.[5] All these were conducive to economic growth with decline inequality in income distribution.

Explanation of Kuznets' Inverted-U Hypothesis

Leaving aside the case of East Asian countries where Kuznets' Inverted-U hypothesis regarding changes in inequality as a result of economic growth does not apply to a number of other countries, both the developed and developing countries, Kuznets' inverted U-hypothesis seems to apply well. What explanations have been offered for this inverted-U hypothesis. It is Arthur Lewis's famous model of '*Economic Development with Unlimited Supply of Labour*' that was put forward to explain the development process in a dual developing economy has also found to be highly useful to explain Kuznets' inverted-U hypothesis regarding the relation between economic growth and changes in income distribution over time. It may be noted that Lewis's development model like those of Ricardo and Marx was based on the assumption that the unlimited amount of labour was available for employment in modern industrial sector at a fixed real wage rate which was unlike the neoclassical economists who assumed that labour was a scarce factor of production to be bid away from alternative uses and therefore was not available in unlimited quantity for being employed for the growth of modern industrial sector.

---

4 See Joseph E. Stiglitz, *Fair Trade for All* (New York: Oxford University Press, 2005), pp. 14-15.

5 *Ibid.*

Lewis's labour-surplus model suggests that as economic growth takes place with withdrawal of surplus labour from low-productivity agriculture to the high-productivity modern industrial sector, income inequality will first increase and then after a point tends to decrease. This is therefore consistent with Kuznets' inverted U-hypotheses. In Lewis's labour-surplus model there are two reasons for increase in income inequality in the initial phase of economic development. First, the share of *profits or surplus of the capitalist's* (who in the Lewis's version of the model may be either private capitalists or government running State-owned enterprises) increases as the modern industrial sector expands. The second reason for increase in income inequality in the early stages of economic growth is that in the beginning of urban industrialisation, wages in the modern industrial sector, according to Lewis, are 30 per cent higher in real terms compared to the subsistence wage level in the traditional agricultural sector. This tends to increase the overall income inequality in the economy.

However, according to Lewis's model, *this tendency toward increasing inequalities is finally reversed as growth proceeds further and when all surplus labour has been fully withdrawn* from subsistence sector and absorbed in the modern sector. This is because when all surplus labour is productively absorbed in the modern sector, labour becomes scarce and as demand for labour by the modern sector further increases, the increment in wages are needed to bid away workers from the marginal uses. Thus, it is eventually rise in general wage level in Lewis's model that causes decline in income inequality and also leads to the elimination of poverty. Thus commenting on changes in income inequality as economic growth takes place in Lewis's model Debraj Ray writes, "*It should be quite clear that economic development viewed in this way cannot be evenly spread across the entire population at any one point in time. Initially only a few people get access to the progressive or modern sector. This view also suggests that the developed countries that have completed the transition from 'old' to the 'new' sectors should exhibit less inequality than the developing countries that are in the middle of transition process where individuals are in both sectors. The argument suggests that change is first uneven and then compensatory.*"[6]

The second factor that causes increase in income inequalities as a result of economic growth is that technological progress initially benefits relatively few industries that employ a relatively small number of workers. Thus technological progress in the developing countries initially can benefit only a fraction of the industrial economy benefiting only a small number of workers employed in the industrial sector. The modern capital-intensive farming is less applicable to the agriculture of the developing countries *that have a large number of workers in the rural sector* who are poor. The small and marginal farmers do not have access to bank credit to buy and use modern inputs such as fertilizers, high-yielding varieties (HYV) of seeds, pesticides, modern tools which are important inputs for adoption of green revolution technology. That is why, in the initial stages of the green revolution in India only rich farmers and landlords were mainly able to get benefits.

There is another way in which the technological progress can lead to the increase in inequality in developing countries. This is because *superior technology is biased against unskilled labour* and can be used only by the trained skilled manpower. However, in developing countries initially only unskilled labour is in surplus and needs to be productively employed and their larger supply tends to lower wage rate and this tends to increase inequality in income distribution in the initial stages of growth . To quote Debraj again, "The skill differentials are ultimately compensated by the growing educational status of the labour force but this is a slower process. When it does occur, inequality tends to decline"[7]

Lastly, without the bias of technological progress and without the dual economy structure industrialisation itself also leads to the large profits accruing to the capitalist class which owns financial resources and entrepreneurial ability seize the opportunities of making profits from industrial growth

6 Debraj Ray, *Development Economics* (New Delhi: Oxford University Press, 1998), pp. 210.

7 Debraj Ray, *op. cit.* p. 210.

that causes increase in income inequalities. However, it has been a general view among the economists that benefits of growth will *ultimately trickle down to the poor working class in the form of more employment and higher wages*, especially when the labour is organised into trade unions. But, as emphasized by Prof. Debraj Ray, in many developing countries labour is initially in surplus so that wages do not rise right away and laws that protect labour are either absent or difficult to implement. However, it has been a general belief among economists that with the passage of time, rise in wages will ultimately eat into profits and lower the share of profits. This will therefore eventually bring about greater equality in income distribution. It was therefore claimed that inequality in the present-day developed countries was less as compared to developing countries.

Conclusion

We have examined above Kuznets' inverted U hypothesis that suggests that in the growth process inequality first rises and then decline. The various factors and arguments have been advanced in favour of inverted-U hypotheses. However, as pointed out above, in case of East Asian countries such as Japan, South Korea, Taiwan, Thailand, Singapore where, contrary to Kuznets' inverted U-hypothesis, economic growth has resulted in the reduction in income inequality. This is *because the effect of economic growth on income distribution* has been influenced by economic policies pursued in these countries. For example, in countries of South Korea, Japan, Taiwan and other East Asian countries there had been redistribution of land and also other interventions by government in influencing economic activities that growth process worked to lower inequality in income distribution. *In our view, there is no single path of growth which first increases inequality and then decreases it and much depends on the character of growth and policies followed by the governments of countries in the growth process.* Many factors and policies influence growth and income distribution and *the view that each country* must travel through the inverted-U hypothesis is quite unwarranted.[8]

INCOME INEQUALITY, ECONOMIC EFFICIENCY AND ECONOMIC GROWTH

Inequality, Incentives and Efficiency

While movement towards reduction in economic inequality whether of income or wealth is generally regarded as socially desirable as it leads to increase in welfare of the society as a whole, but attempts have been made by some, especially those who are supporters of capitalism or a free market economy to defend income inequalities on grounds of adverse effect on economic efficiency and economic growth of reducing income inequalities. It is argued that a certain income distribution cannot be settled once and for all through redistribution because income distribution is a continuous process as production of goods and services goes on year after year and rewards for those who contribute to the production of goods and services are distributed every year. Therefore, the question arises if inequality in distribution of income or rewards for the services is reduced, *it may adversely affect the incentives to work hard and invest and as a result the production of goods and services may decline, that is, GDP or economic growth will be hurt*.

It is thus argued that attempts to bring about equality, that is, to reduce income inequalities may reduce the size of pie which is to be distributed. The lower size of pie will reduce the well-being of the people. On the other hand, the attempts to reduce income inequalities will lower the efficiency or productivity as the people with higher abilities or productivities will not utilize their abilities or capabilities fully or put in best of their efforts. As a result, productive efficiency of the economy will decline which will lower economic growth of the country, which it is argued is a necessary condition for improving the levels of living of the population. According to Late Prof. Suresh Tendulkar, "The work-incentive effect stands on a firmer ground. For one thing, interpersonal differences in the

8 For similar view, see Debraj Ray, *op.cit.*, p. 211 and Todaro and Smith *op.cit*, Tenth Edition, 2012, p. 233.

capacity to work and productivity of such work are established facts, although there is no agreement on the causes or measures of these differences. Again, while it may be possible to force a person to do a given job it is admitted that the efficiency with which he works will depend on the effort put in. This in turn is determined by the inherently individualised motivation factors which are influenced largely by the incentives provided in the shape of economic rewards."[9]

Related to the incentives required for full use of their capabilities is the question of incentives needed for the individuals to acquire education or higher skills or for the entrepreneurs to innovate. How can individuals or workers be induced to acquire higher skills and education to become more productive or entrepreneurs to innovate if they are to receive no more than the ordinary unskilled workers. It is thus argued that differential incomes or rewards are essential to achieve higher levels of productivity and growth.

The above incentive argument for inequalities of income has, however, a major loophole. Above argument would have been perfectly valid if perfect equality of income was intended to be established. As a matter of fact, nobody, not even the socialists, seeks to establish perfect or absolute equality of incomes. *What is wanted is that reasonable inequalities of incomes should be established. The reasonable inequalities of incomes are those that are just sufficient to furnish or maintain the incentives*. Inequalities of income beyond the point necessary to furnish incentives are not justified on grounds of higher productivity and growth. *Inequalities of income that prevail today are much more than what are required to furnish incentives to work hard and innovate or use their capabilities fully*. Prevailing inequalities of incomes are so glaring and non-functional that even a substantial reduction in them will not adversely affect the incentives and therefore the fear that the national production or growth will fall as a result of equalitarian policies is unfounded.

Besides, the present large income inequalities found in the free market economies are quite unrelated to the differential capabilities of the individuals and are mainly based on extraneous factors such as ownership of property or assets, the existence of certain economic and social institutions. Furthermore, the important question is how to find reasonable or functional income inequalities which should therefore be socially acceptable. This is a difficult question which cannot be answered unambiguously as this depends on value judgements of a society which can differ from one individual to another. Based on the value judgements of a society, preferably arrived at through democratic ways, we find *socially acceptable degree of inequality* which is of functional nature and sufficient to furnish incentives for individuals to put in their best efforts and use their capabilities fully and to acquire higher skills or education.

It is worth noting that there may be some trade-off between efficiency and equity, that is , some loss of efficiency may be sacrificed to have an equitable distribution of income, that is, a certain socially acceptable degree of income inequality.

It may be further noted that argument put forward for income inequality based on work-incentives does not apply to the people below the poverty line defined by minimum normative level of income just sufficient for subsistence. This is because *lower than minimum level of income and consumption prevent them to be effective participant in economic activity.* Due to their extremely low income they suffer from *undernourishment, have inadequate clothing, shelter* and healthcare. As a matter of fact, *the eradication of poverty is a precondition for building up their capabilities to work and improve their efficiency.*

Economists since Adam Smith have acknowledged the need for economic incentives for promoting economic growth and consequent inequality in economic rewards as the necessary price

9 Suresh D. Tendulkar, "Economic Inequality in the Indian Context" in Andre Beteille (ed.), *Equality and Inequality*, Oxford University Press, Delhi, 1983.

for furnishing economic incentives. An eminent economist, A.P. Lerner, drew distinction between *functional and dysfunctional* inequalities. The functional income inequalities are those that promote economic growth and dysfunctional are those that do not do so. Nevertheless, there is general abhorrence for growing income inequality and any reduction in it is universally taken as advancing equity. It is therefore, generally believed that government should intervene to bring about growth with equitable distribution of income especially in developing countries.

Therefore, in India, in the latest Five Year Plans (Eleventh and Twelfth Plans) the objective has been to achieve *inclusion growth*. It may be recalled that the concept of economic efficiency or what is called Pareto optimality takes the *distribution of income in a society as given* and explains how social optimum resource allocation is achieved. *It does not go into the question of optimum distribution of income in a society*. With a different income distribution, there will be different Pareto optimum. As a matter of fact, most government policies affect the distribution of income. This issue was even raised by classical economists Adam Smith and Ricardo who advocated free trade which benefits some and harms other members of the society. N. Kaldor and J.R. Hicks provided a welfare criterion according to which if as a result of government policy those who gain can compensate the loss and still remain better off, the new situation would represent an improvement over the existing one. However, the serious drawback of this criterion is that the *compensation visualised is potential and not real*. Therefore, for increase in actual welfare when any growth project is undertaken those who are displaced must adequately be compensated and also alternative gainful employment opportunities are provided to them.

Furthermore, the present inequalities of income reflect the *differences in opportunities* faced by various individuals. A man is the product of numerous forces acting upon him. Some forces work before his birth. The result of these forces is that an individual possesses certain inborn qualities. Other influences upon man come from environment in which he grows up. This environment consists of conditions of home, family, friends, teachers, and general surroundings. Both these hereditary and environmental forces come from outside man himself. An individual who is born with the silver spoon in his mouth and is therefore brought up in superior home influences and receives good education and training is not likely to acquire higher skills and education. He will be able to earn large income.

On the other hand, a person who is born in a poor family and is brought up in the environment of dust, disease and despair and who cannot obtain sufficient education and training because of the poverty of his parents is not likely to acquire higher skills and education. He will be able to earn only a meagre income. Under these circumstances, it cannot be said that the former individual *deserved success* and large income and the latter failure and meagre income. It is mere accident of birth and social conditions which have determined the success of the former individual and the failure of the latter. Each individual is the product of society. The wealth and richness of a man is mainly made possible by good heredity and favourable social environments. The poverty of the person who fails in life is due to bad heredity and unfavourable social environments. No one can claim with justification that his success and wealth are purely due to his personal efforts and that society has not contributed anything *towards it*.

Inequality, Saving and Capital Formation

From the viewpoint of economic growth, a forceful argument advanced to justify income inequalities is that inequality in the distribution of income promotes savings and capital formation. Because of their higher incomes rich people are in a position to make more savings, and invest them. As a result, capital formation takes place in the society. The greater the inequality in the distribution of income, the greater will be the rate of saving and investment. This increases the rate of capital formation. Capital formation is key to economic growth. A higher rate of capital formation brings about rapid economic growth and greatly increases the level of national production. It is argued that if the national income is equally distributed, that is, if income equality is brought about, average rate of saving will fall. With the fall in saving the rate of investment and capital formation will decline. As a result, level of national production and rate of GDP growth will go down making everybody poorer than before.

It is thus concluded that large incomes which accrue to the rich people are really beneficial since a good part of them is saved and invested. This promotes capital formation and economic growth which in turn raise the levels of living of the people. In this way, according to this view, *the rich are public benefactors*.

The relation between inequality and capital formation established above is doubtful and uncertain. It may be true that in a capitalist system large savings are made possible by the huge incomes accruing to the few rich people. But it is quite wrong to hold that the rate of savings and capital formation will necessarily decline in any other economic system having relative equality of incomes. Indeed it may be said that the large incomes accruing to the rich people are not adequately utilised for the purposes of capital formation. Quite a good amount of these high incomes is squandered away in *conspicuous consumption*. It is more conducive to capital formation if the surplus incomes of the rich come in the hands of the Government which can fully utilise them for investment in desired directions. Professor J.K. Galbraith, an eminent economist, apply remarks, "*To give individuals large incomes to encourage savings has elements of illogic. The rich man saves because he is able to satisfy all his wants and then have some left over. Such a saving, in other words, is residual after luxurious consumption. This obviously is not an especially efficient way to promote capital formation.*"[10]

Even empirical evidence does not support the view that large inequality in the distribution of income is helpful to capital formation or that the drastic reduction in inequality of incomes will discourage saving and capital formation. For instance, Norway, which had adopted effective policies to promote equality of incomes, has achieved since the Second World War one of the highest rates of capital formation and economic growth in the non-communist countries. In sharp contrast, Middle East countries, where inequality of income is perhaps the greatest, are among those with lowest rates of capital formation.

Further, large inequalities of income *may create economic instability* which may adversely affects investment and growth. Thus, Nobel Laureate Joseph E. Stiglitz in his recent book, "*The Price of Inequality*" points out that there is clear *association between inequality and economic instability*. According to him, in the US the people in top income-groups save a lot and relatively spend little, whereas the people in low and middle income groups save very little and spend all or most part of their incomes. This is the result of highly skewed income distribution and this reduces an aggregate consumption demand in a society which tends to reduce the level of GDP and thus causes economic instability.

However, in case of India when the *problem is more on supply side*, though large savings by the rich are good as they make large investment and growth possible but to rely on greater income inequalities to generate higher saving and investment is not the right approach. *Many East Asian countries such as Singapore, Malaysia, Taiwan, South Korea which achieved a higher rate of GDP growth from the mid-sixties to the mid-nineties did not experience the increase in income inequalities.* They were able to achieve high rates of economic growth with active participation of Government in their economies. Writing about growth miracle of East Asian countries, Joseph Sitglitz writes, "*Their economic model included a strong role for the public sector. They clearly did not blieve in free and unfettered markets but government played a critical role. Governments acted as catalyst which helped markets by providing the requisite physical and institutional infrastructure, by remedying market failures and by promoting saving and technology.*"[11]

---

10 Galbraith, J.K., *The Affluent Society*, p. 63.
11 Stiglitz, *op. cit.*

Further, Stiglitz writes, contrary to what has happened in India, "East Asian countries proved that the initial stages of development did not have to be associated with an increase in inequality. Instead the new prosperity was widely shared among the population and millions were lifted out of poverty. For example, in Malaysia and Thailand, the incidence of poverty declined from almost 50 per cent in the 1960s to less than 20 per cent by the end of the century."

Inequality is bad partly due to the fact that for any given average per capita income, the higher the inequality a larger number of people *lack the collateral to get loans from banks* or any other source because, they are not credit-worthy. With low incomes, the people cannot educate their children and cannot spend adequately on their healthcare. As a result, their children remain uneducated and undernourished. Besides, in case of India due to large income inequalities, as in other developing countries, the people in high income- brackets such as big capitalists, landlords, high salary persons spend lavishy on imported goods, luxury cars, palatial houses, gold and jewellery etc. which have *demonstration effect* on the middle-income group people and tend to lower overall saving rate of the society by increasing their propensity to consume. It is thus evident that income inequalities are bad for achieving higher rate of saving and economic growth.

High income inequalities also promote *rent seeking* by the rich people who through excessive lobbying, providing large donations to the political parties, bribing the ministers and bureaucrats succeed in getting licenses and permits as happened in India in case of allotment of 2G spectrum and coal blocks. When large financial resources are used for such rent seeking activities, they are diverted from their productive use which could have generated rapid growth.

We have seen earlier that, according to inverted-U hypothesis, as developing countries start growing in the initial stage inequalities of income will increase. On the basis of this hypothesis, the supporters of free market economy argued that increased inequality is a necessary condition for economic growth. However, relevant data collected by World Bank show that income inequality adversely affects economic growth.[12] Expressing the similar view Todaro and Smith write: "*A growth strategy based on sizable and gross income inequalities may in reality be nothing more than an opportunistic myth designed to perpetuate the vested interests and maintain status quo of the economic and political elites of developing nations, often at the expense of the great majority of general population.*"[13]

Society's Tolerance of Inequalities

Recently, a view has been expressed about the conditions or circumstances in which income inequalities can be socially tolerated. Late Prof. Suresh Tendulkar provided an economic rationale for rising income inequalities during periods of rapid economic growth because they cause upward *income mobility* for the people. Rapid economic growth throws up opportunities for the people to move from low income to higher income levels despite the fact that income inequalities as measured by Gini Coefficient remain quite large. Thus, rapid economic growth generates hope for the people to move to higher income level category and makes the existence of large income inequalities socially acceptable. However, according to Tendulkar, equity would be achieved in the *normal course of market functioning without* government intervention for reducing inequalities *if technological changes reduce the relative price of one or more necessities of life or by enhancing the supply and consumption of necessities like food.*[14] Two things must be noted about this view of Late Prof. Tendulkar. First, if a free market economy experiences rapid economic growth, it will promote equity without intervention by the government to reduce income inequalities. As it ensures upward income mobility, it will make

12 See Michael Bruno and Lyn Squire, "Why Worry about Inequality", *Economic Times*, Oct. 8, 1996

13 Todaro and Smith, *Economic Development*, 8th edition, 2003, p. 210.

14 Suresh Tendulkar, "Inequality and Equity during Rapid Growth Process" printed in *India's Economic Performance and Challenges*, Essays in Honour of Montek Singh Ahluwalia.

the existing income inequalities socially acceptable Second, Tendulkar considers that if food and other necessities of life become cheaper and become more available for consumption as a result of rapid economic growth, income inequalities will become socially acceptable. In other words, *if functioning of free market economy brings about rapid growth which causes absolute poverty to fall, the existing income inequalities will be socially acceptable*. In our view, this is an indirect argument for a free market economy established by the policy of liberalisation and privatisation adopted under the structural adjustment reforms.

Like Tendulkar, long ago Hirschman had also argued that in a rapidly growing economy the improvement in the well-being of others may signal a benign external environment and hope for the rest. This hope or 'expectations calculus' produces gratification that overcomes envy and raises society's tolerance for inequalities. A noted welfare economist Tibor Scitovsky was one of the earlier economists who suggested three criteria for social acceptability of inequalities. First, those inequalities that are based on merit or people's contribution to social product that can be considered as 'functional inequalities'. Second, those inequalities that arise even when there exist conditions of equality of opportunity which allow everyone to aspire to move up the income ladder. Third, those inequalities that prevail along with the improvement in the well-being of those at the bottom of the income ladder. This third criterion advanced by Scitovsky implies that if economic growth benefits the poor, the prevailing income inequalities will be socially tolerable.

CHAPTER 66

POVERTY AND ECONOMIC GROWTH: INTERNATIONAL PERSPECTIVE

POVERTY AND ECONOMIC GROWTH

Despite significant economic growth achieved during the last half a century, there still prevails widespread poverty in developing countries. The poor people suffer from undernourishment, poor health, illiteracy. Freedom from undernourishment, freedom from illness and freedom from illiteracy are the essential requirements of economic development. *It is the building up capabilities of the poor to gain freedoms in these respects which Amartya Sen calls development*.[1] Now, an important question is whether faster economic growth will necessarily solve the problems of poverty and development. In the fifties and sixties it was widely held that benefits of economic growth would trickle down to the poor. This is generally referred to as '*trickle down theory*'. It was then maintained that if you take care of economic growth, poverty will take care of itself.

But in the seventies there was a drastic change in the views of prominent development economists. They pointed that economic growth of GNP, though necessary, was not sufficient for eliminating poverty. This has been generally referred to as '*Dethronement of GNP*'. During the 1970s in India, it was realised that when the economy was growing at the rate of 4 to 5 per cent and with population growth of around 2 per cent annually at that time one could not rely on the 'trickle down' effect to reduce the problem of mass poverty. Therefore, to reduce poverty measures for making '*direct attack on poverty*' were suggested along with taking measures to accelerate economic growth. For this purpose development economists suggested special anti-poverty schemes such as starting of employment schemes, especially construction of rural public works, and strengthening of public distribution system for providing to the poor foodgrains and some other essential commodities at subsidised prices. However, in the late eighties and early nineties some world bank economists with the officials of US Government who met in Washington again reverted to the old view that economic growth benefits poor substantially even if no special pro-poor measures are adopted[2]. This provided a rationale for what is popularly called **Washington Consensus** which envisaged fiscal and structural adjustment reforms to accelerate economic growth in developing countries, first imposed on the Latin American countries and then on the developing countries of Malaysia, Indonesia and India.

In India there was an economic crisis in 1990-91 resulting from serious balance of payments problem and reduction of foreign exchange reserves to a very low level and flight of capital abroad. There was an urgent need for foreign aid from IMF and World Bank to tide over the crisis. But IMF and World Bank provided aid only if certain conditionalities were fulfilled. These conditionalities were nothing but implementation of fiscal and structural adjustment Programme (SAP) as contained in Washington Consensus. These economic reforms of fiscal consolidation and structural adjustment

1 See Amartya Sen, *Development as Freedom*, Alfred Knoph, New York 1999, p.43.

2 Author of the various provisions of Washington Consensus John Williamson writes, "The evidence says pretty clearly that growth benefits the poor, even if nothing is consciously done to make it pro-poor growth. *Benefits do trickle down*", in 'Washington Consensus and Beyond', *EPW*, April 12, 2003.

involved reduction in fiscal deficit and carrying out the policies of economic liberalisation, privatisation and globalisation. In 1991-93 most of these policies were implemented in India to accelerate economic growth and hoping that it will help to reduce poverty.

It may be further noted that the data collected by World Bank reveals that economic growth has led to the reduction in absolute poverty where it has been accompanied by *more equal distribution of assets*, especially land. Stressing this point Michael Bruno and Lyn Squire, two development economists of World Bank write."*Using the new data, we found that developing countries with a more equal distribution of assets—specifically land – grew more rapidly than countries with a less equal distribution of assets. Why is a more equal distribution of assets good for growth? One likely explanation involves credit. We know that investment is crucial for growth. The poor often cannot invest because they lack capital and they lack the collateral to borrow. In countries with a very unequal distribution of assets, many people find it difficult or impossible to invest, even in their own health and education.*"[3] They further write, "Economies in East Asia that had comparatively equal land distribution and aggressively pursued economic growth have achieved dramatic reductions in poverty. In Latin America, land distribution has generally been less equal, growth has been slower and less consistent, and poverty has remained stubbornly high".[4]

To reduce absolute poverty and to accelerate progress in human development, economic growth is of course necessary but not enough. World Development Report 2004 by World Bank rightly stressed that broad improvements in human welfare would not occur unless poor people receive wider access to affordable, better quality services in health, education, water, sanitation, and electricity. Without such improvements in services, freedom from illness and freedom from illiteracy — two of the most important ways poor people can escape poverty – will remain elusive to many.[5]

As we shall see in the next chapter, poverty in India has declined since 2004-05 but to attribute this decline in poverty to *economic growth alone* is not correct. In fact various special employment schemes, promotion of literacy, and strengthening of public distribution system to provide foodgrains at subsidised prices have also made important contribution to reduce poverty. Besides, as we shall see below to what extent poverty has declined is also a matter of great controversy because changes in methodology used for collecting household consumption expenditure data in NSS survey for 1999-2000, 2004-05 and 2009-10.

In our above analysis we have only given introduction to the issue of how economic growth affects poverty, we will discuss in detail in the next chapter the relation between economic growth and poverty.

In what follows we shall explain the concept of absolute and relative poverty and in the next chapter we will discuss the magnitude and trends of poverty in India. We shall also explain who are the poor and what are the causes of poverty in India. Besides, we will explain in the next chapter the different strategies adopted in different States of India to tackle the problem of poverty.

CONCEPTS OF POVERTY

It is not easy to measure poverty. Poverty is generally defined in absolute sense, though the concept of relative poverty is also important. We first explain the concept of absolute poverty. It may be noted that the concept of absolute poverty is measured with reference to income of the people which is required to meet the minimum basic needs. Through a survey method, consumption expenditure of the households is calculated to measure *income poverty*. Thus consumption expenditure is considered as a proxy for income. Both the concepts of poverty, namely *Head Count Ratio* (HCR) and *Poverty Gap* (PG) are measures of income poverty.

3 Michael Bruno and Lyn Squire, "Why Worry about Inequality?" *Economic Times*, Oct. 8, 1996.
4 *Ibid*.
5 World Bank, *World Development Report*, 2004.

Absolute Poverty

In this concept of poverty a person is poor if his income falls below a certain minimum level which is required to satisfy *minimum basic needs*. Now, the problem faced in measuring poverty is to specify the minimum basic needs or what is also called *minimum living standard* (MLS) that should be defined as *poverty line*. Then a person having an income or consumption expenditure below that poverty line will be described as poor in the absolute sense. Thus *norms* have to be fixed for minimum *calorie intake* of food, minimum clothing, minimum shelter, minimum healthcare which must be met for fulfilment of minimum basic needs or minimum standard of living. Then these norms have to be converted into *minimum consumption expenditure or income per capita* which will meet minimum basic needs or minimum living standard. Persons having income or consumption expenditure less than the minimum consumption expenditure defined as poverty line are called *poor in absolute sense*, that is, *living below the poverty line*. These poor will be living in condition of absolute human misery.

It is evident from above that to specify the poverty line in terms of consumption expenditure per capita, one needs the data about prices of goods that enter into basket of minimum basic needs. The two concepts of measuring absolute income poverty have been suggested: (1) *Head Count Ratio* (HCR) which is most widely used to estimate the incidence of poverty in countries. This refers to the number of people in a society living below the poverty line fixed on the basis of some minimum consumption level (2) The *Poverty Gap* which refers to the extent the income consumption of an individual falls short of the poverty line, that is, minimum income or consumption level. We explain below these two concepts in some detail.

Head Count Ratio. Thus, absolute poverty is measured by counting the number of persons or heads living below the specified poverty line in terms of minimum consumption expenditure or income per capita. Since this approach to measure absolute poverty is concerned with counting the number of persons or heads, this is generally referred to as *Head Count Ratio* approach to measure absolute poverty. If N stands for the number of population, H for the number of persons having consumption expenditure or income below that, then head count ratio of absolute poverty can be written as

$$\text{Head Count Ratio (HCR)} = \frac{H}{N}$$

It may be noted that to measure absolute poverty at the international level and to compare the incidence of extreme poverty in various countries, World Bank has specified \$ 1.25 a day in PPP (purchasing power parity) US dollar as poverty line norm. Recently \$2 a day in PPP is also being used by World Bank to estimate the incidence of poverty prevailing in various countries of the world. A shortcoming of head count ratio as a measure of poverty is that it *ignores the extent to which a poor person's income falls* below the poverty line. It is noteworthy that changes in the incidence of poverty over time in a country also poses a number of problems because it raises the question as to which price index number ought to be used to find the real income or consumption expenditure required to meet the minimum basic needs.

Poverty Gap. However the head count ratio as a measure of absolute poverty suffers from a major drawback. The head count ratio does not indicate the *severity or depth* of a poor person. For example, if poverty line for rural India is fixed at monthly per capita consumption expenditure at ₹ 150, then all those who have a per capita monthly income or consumption expenditure less than this would be counted as poor, no matter whether a person's monthly consumption expenditure is ₹ 75 or 125. Obviously, poverty is more severe in case of persons who have monthly consumption expenditure of ₹ 75 than of those who have monthly consumption expenditure or income of ₹ 125, To overcome this drawback absolute poverty is measured by poverty gap approach. Poverty gap concept seeks to measure severity or depth of poverty of a person. If Y_p stands for minimum income or consumption expenditure representing poverty line, Y_i stands for income or consumption expenditure of any individual, then $Y_p - Y_i$ will indicate the *severity or depth of this poverty*. In accordance with this, the total poverty gap (TPG) in an economy or a sector can be written as

$$TPG = \sum_{i=1}^{H} (Y_p - Y_i)$$

where H is the number of persons having per capita income or consumption expenditure less than the minimum living standard or consumption expenditure specified as poverty line.

Total poverty gap is considered as a better index of the extent of poverty in a country as it takes into account the severity or depth of the poverty of persons comprising a society.

Absolute poverty is bad because no civilised society can feel satisfied if its people exist in conditions of absolute human misery. Absolute poverty not only creates miserable living conditions for individuals, it also imperils social and political stability in a society. It is now a well recognised fact that the existence of absolute poverty raises the incidence of crime and creates law and order problems in a society. Therefore, all modern societies have started taking steps to alleviate absolute poverty.

Relative Poverty

As is well known, per capita income is only an average income per person and therefore does not represent a true index of social welfare. Social welfare in a society also depends on how the national income is distributed among the population. Poverty is in fact a relative concept. Relative poverty refers to *the people having income less than the average or mean per capita income of a country.* While the level of economic development of a country determines the mean per capita income of a country, inequalities in the distribution of income determines the number of poor people who have less than mean or average per capita income of a country.

Income of an individual in relation to the incomes of others in a country or region is an important determinant of welfare. Thus, greater the inequalities in income distribution, the lower the level of social welfare. It has been realised that greater income inequalities affect the capabilities of those who have relatively lower income through adversely affecting their access to credit from banks and other financial institutions and their capability to provide education to their children. Relative poverty reflects income inequalities in a country and like absolute poverty negatively affects social welfare. Income inequalities in a society is generally measured through estimating the value of *Gini coefficient*.

Social welfare function can be written as

$$W = (Y, I, P)$$

where

W = Social welfare

Y = Per capita income

I = Inequality index

P = Absolute poverty

Level of per capita income has a positive effect on welfare, whereas inequality (I) and absolute poverty (P) negatively affect welfare. That is, given the per capita income, the higher income inequality and absolute poverty the lower will be social welfare.

Why is Relative Poverty Bad? But what is so bad about relative poverty, that is, income inequality. Long ago Simon Kuznets using historical data from the first half of the 20th Century from three countries—England, Germany and the US pointed out that as a country industrialises and achieves economic growth, the gap between the rich and poor first widens (that is, income inequality increases) and then gradually narrows (that is, income inequality decreases). This is generally known as *Kuznets inverted U hypothesis*. To support their views, some advocates of free market economy argued that increased inequality was a necessary condition for accelerating economic growth. This view is not supported by the data collected by World Bank in case of countries.[6] In fact, it has now been found that income inequality adversely affects economic growth. This is due to the following factors.

6 See Michael Bruno and Lyn Squire, *op. cit.* and Todaro and Smith, *Economic Development*, 8th edition, 2003, pp. 209-210.

First, existence of income inequalities lowers the access to credit of those who are relatively poor. It is noteworthy that when low-income individuals cannot have adequate access to credit, they cannot provide good education to their children or start and expand business. Further, the recent findings indicate that with high inequality saving rate in the economy tends to be lower[7]. This is because empirical findings reveal that highest rate of marginal saving is found among the middle classes, whereas the rich spend a relatively larger fraction of their incomes on luxury goods, gold and jewellery, luxurious houses or seek safe havens abroad for depositing their savings in foreign banks and this causes capital flight. In short, the rich save and invest domestically a relatively smaller proportion of their income. Commenting on worldwide data Bruno and Squire write, "*Research shows that developing countries with a more equal distribution of assets grew more rapidly than countries with a less equal distribution of assets*"[8]

REGIONAL POVERTY ESTIMATES OF THE WORLD

World Bank has set a poverty line at $1.25 a day in terms of PPP 2005 US dollars. In Table 66.1, we have given the incidence of the poverty, given the poverty line at $1.25 a day PPP. It will be seen from this table that in the world as a whole (*i.e.*, total) 16.99 per cent of world population, which in absolute number amounts to over 1 billion people (1011.37 millions to be exact), lived below the poverty line in 2011. We will see later that both the percentage of world population and the number of world population living below this poverty line have been continuously declining.

Table 66.1. Regional Poverty Estimates of 2011

Region	Population below $1.25 a day PPP (Head Count Ratio)%	Poverty Gap at $ 1.25 a day PPP (%)	Number of Poor (Million)	Population (Million)
East Asia & Pacific	7.43	1.56	160.7	2027.27
Europe & Central Asia	0.49	0.14	2.35	479.13
Latin America & the Caribbean	4.63	2.17	27.63	596.77
Middle East and North Africa	1.69	0.35	5.64	333.78
South Asia	24.50	5.16	398.95	1628.35
Sub-Saharan Africa	46.85	19.20	415.7	883.43
Total World	16.99	5.05	1,011.37	5,952

Source: *World Development Indicators* 2015

From the regionwise data it will be seen from Table 66.1 that in the year 2011 Sub-Saharan Africa, poverty ratio was the highest at 46.85 per cent. This was followed by South Asia (which includes India) where the percentage of population living below the poverty line was estimated 24.50 per cent

7 See Joseph Zeira, Income Distribution and Macroeconomics, *Review of Economic Studies*, 60, (January 1993), and Gary Fields, *Distribution and Development: A New Look at the Developing World*, Cambridge, MIT Press, 2000, Ch. 10.

8 Bruno and Squire, "Why Worry about Inequality, *op.cit.*

in 2011. The number of people living below the poverty line ($1.25 a day PPP) was 415.7 million in Sub-Saharan Africa and 398.95 million in South Asia in 2011. These two regions together accounted for 80 per cent of the poor population of the world. In the East Asia and Pacific region 7.43% of the population living below the poverty line which in absolute number was 160 million. The developing countries of Lain America and the Caribbean, there prevails less poverty as head count ratio of poverty with international poverty line of $1.25 a day was estimated to be equal to 4.63 per cent.

Europe and Central Asia where mostly developed countries exist, the incidence of poverty at $ 1.25 a day is very low with only 0.49 per cent of population below the poverty line (head count ratio). The region of Middle East and North Africa covers oil rich countries and earn large income from export of oil. Therefore, the incidence of poverty is very low; only 1.69% of their population was below the poverty line of $ 1.25 a day.

As in case of Head Count Ratio (HCR), measure of poverty in terms of poverty gap at $ 1.25 a day varies in the different regions (See Column III in Table 66.1). Again the Sub-Saharan Africa and South Asia, poverty gap was larger with 19.20 and 5.0 per cent respectively.

The magnitude of poverty in various developing countries is quite uneven. In Table 66.2 we have given both head

Table 66.2. Percentage of Population below International Poverty Line

Country	Survey year	Population below $ 1.25 a day (%)	Poverty gap at $1.25 (%)	Population below $ 2 a day (%)	Poverty Gap at $ 2 a day (%)
Bangladesh	2010	43.3	11.2	76.5	30.4
Benin	2011	51.6	18.8	74.3	35.9
Bhutan	2012	2.4	0.5	15.2	3.3
Botswania	2009	13.4	4.0	27.8	10.2
Brazil	2012	3.8	2.1	6.8	3.3
Central African Republic	2008	62.8	31.3	80.1	41.2
China	**2010**	**6.3**	**1.3**	**18.6**	**5.5**
Guinea	2012	40.9	12.7	72.7	29.8
India	**2011**	**23.6**	**4.8**	**59.2**	**19.0**
Indonesia	2011	16.2	2.7	43.3	13.0
Jordan	2010	2.0	0.5	2.0	0.5
Kenya	2005	43.4	16.9	67.2	31.8
Malaysia	2009	2.0	0.5	2.3	0.5
Mexico	2012	2.82	0.5	4.1	1.0
Philippines	2012	19.0	4.0	41.7	14.1
Pakistan	2010	12.7	1.9	50.7	13.3
South Africa	2011	9.4	1.2	26.2	7.7
Sri Lanka	2009	4.1	9.7	23.9	5.4
Thailand	2010	2.0	0.5	3.5	0.6
Nigeria	2010	62.6	27.5	82.2	44.8
Nepal	2010	23.7	5.2	56.0	18.4
Zambia	2010	74.3	41.8	86.6	56.6

Source: *World Development Indicators*, 2015

count ratio of poverty and poverty gap at the international poverty line $ 1.25 a day and $ 2 a day. In this connection, the incidence of poverty in China and India are worth mentioning. China which achieved around 10 per cent GDP growth in the last over three decades has succeeded in substantial reduction in poverty. In 2010, percentage of population living below the International poverty line of $ 1.25 a day was only 6.3 per cent in China compared to 23.6 per cent in India. Similarly, poverty on the basis of poverty gap at $1.25 a day in China was quite low at 1.3 per cent compared to 4.8 per cent of India. It will also be seen that East Asian countries of Indonesia, Malaysia, Thailand which through their export-led growth strategy achieved quite a high GDP growth from the mid 1960s to 2000, poverty (both head count ratio and poverty gap) has substantially declined. In African countries, of Zambia, Guinea, Nigeria, Kenya, Central African republic the incidence of poverty is very high. On the other hand, in Latin American Countries of Mexico and Philippines the poverty both in respect of Head Count Ratio (HCR) and poverty gap at $1.25 a day is quite low.

Declining Poverty Rates at International Poverty Line

An important fact revealed by the poverty rates at international poverty line fixed at $1.25 a day of the world as a whole and in different regions is that they have been falling since 1980s (see Table 66.3). The percentage of population living below the international poverty line of $1.25 a day of the whole world fell from 51.9 per cent in 1981 to 41.7 per cent in 1990—a 10 percentage points fall in the decade. The percentage of total world population below the poverty line ($1.25 a day) further declined to 33.7 per cent in 1999, to 25.2 per cent in 2005 and to 16.99 per cent in 2011.

As will be seen from Table 66.3 the largest decline in poverty ratio with $1.25 a day as the poverty line took place in East Asia and Pacific where the poverty ratio declined from around 78 per cent in 1981 to 17 per cent in 2005 and the **number** of persons living below $1.25 a day fell more than 750 million in this region. It is worth mentioning that a largest part of decline in poverty ratio in this region was in China where incidence of poverty decreased from 84 per cent of population in 1981 to 16 per cent in 2005. It is in this period that China made a transition from socialist regime to privatisation and liberalisation of the economy with foreign investment playing an important role in its industrial development and succeeded in achieving around 10 per cent GDP growth rate.

Table 66.3. Falling Poverty Ratio (HCR) at International Poverty line of $1.25 a day (per cent)

Region	1981	1990	1999	2002	2005	2011
East Asia and Pacific	77.7	54.7	35.5	27.6	16.8	7.43
China	84.0	60.2	35.6	28.4	15.9	6.30
Europe and Central Asia	1.7	2.0	5.1	4.6	3.7	0.49
Latin America and Caribbean	12.9	11.3	10.9	10.7	8.2	4.63
Middle East & North Africa	7.9	4.3	4.2	3.6	3.6	1.69
South Asia	59.4	51.7	44.1	43.8	40.3	24.5
India	59.8	51.3	44.8	43.9	41.6	23.6
Sub-Saharan Africa	53.4	57.6	58.4	55.0	50.9	46.85
Total	51.9	41.7	33.7	30.5	25.2	16.99

Source: *World Development Indicators*, 2011 and 2015.

In the South Asia where India is situated the decline in poverty ratio was not so dramatic; poverty ratio in South Asia dropped from 59 per cent in 1981 be 40 per cent in 2005 and further to 24.5 per cent in 2011. It will be observed from Table 66.3 that in India percentage of population living below $ 1.25 a day fell from 59.8 in 1981 to 41.6 per cent in 2005 and further to 23.6 per cent in 2011. In sharp contrast to other regions, Sub-Saharan Africa the poverty ratio declined only slightly during this period, it fell from 57.6 per cent in 1990 to 50 per cent in 2005 (However, the decline in poverty ratio in Sub-Saharan Africa is not consistent as it rose in some years for example, it increased between 1981 and 1990) (See Table 66.3).

It may be noted that the target of Millennium Development Goal was to reduce the world poverty ratio to half by 2015 compared to what prevailed in 1990. As will be seen from Table 66.3 this target was achieved by 2011 as in 2011, world poverty ratio declined to 16.99 per cent compared to 41.7 per cent in 1990. It may be further noted that to reduce poverty ratio, the faster and sustained GDP growth rate is required. But it is now well recognised that GDP growth is necessary but not a sufficient condition for reduction in poverty. What is needed is that the character of GDP growth should be more inclusive with generation of adequate opportunities of gainful employment for the people.

Changes in Poverty Ratio with International Poverty Line of $ 2.0 a Day

Poverty line of $1.25 a day in terms of PPP is very low and the people living below this are *extremely poor* and are living at a bare subsistence level. The World Bank has now started estimating poverty in different countries with a higher poverty line of $ 2.0 a day in terms of purchasing power parity (at US dollar 2005). In Table 66.4 in case of some developing countries we have given the percentage of population living below $ 2 a day. Obviously, the poverty ratio with $ 2 a day as the international poverty line will be higher compared to that of $ 1.25 a day as the international poverty line. Thus, in case of India in 2011 while percentage of population living below the $ 1.25 a day was 23.6, whereas below $ 2.0 a day it was 59.2, that is, almost three times the former (See Table 66.2). Similarly, in China in the year 2010 the percentage of population living below $ 1.25 a day was 6.3 with $ 2.0 a day the poverty ratio shot up to 18.6, that is, three times greater than the former.

Further, even with $ 2.0 a day as the international poverty line, in the different regions of the world and the world as a whole, the poverty ratio has been declining since 1981. This is shown in Table 66.4 below where it will be seen that in the total world 69.4 per cent of population lived below $ 2.0 a day in 1981, the percentage fell to 63.4 in 1990–a fall of 6 percentage points in the decade and declined further to 57.1 in 1999 and further to 47.0 in 2005. In the region East Asia and Pacific, the percentage of population living below $ 2.0 a day which was 92.6 fell to 79.8 in 1990 and further to 61.8 in 1999 and to 38.7 in 2005. This large decline is due to the large fall in poverty ratio in China which is a part of this region. In case of South Asia which contains India the percentage of population living below on the higher international poverty line of $2 a day was 86.5 in 1981 which fell to 82.7 in 1990 and further to 77.2 in 1999 to 73.9 in 2005.

Table 66.4. Declining Poverty Ratio (HCR) at International Poverty line at $ 2.0 a day (Per cent)

Region	1981	1990	1999	2002	2005	2011
East Asia & Pacific	92.6	79.8	61.8	51.9	38.7	–
China	97.8	84.6	61.4	51.2	26.3	18.6
Europe and Central Asia	8.3	6.9	14.3	12.0	8.9	–
Latin America and Caribbean	24.6	21.9	21.8	21.6	17.1	–
Middle East and North Africa	26.7	19.7	19.0	17.6	16.9	–
South Asia	86.5	82.7	77.2	77.1	73.9	–
India	86.6	82.6	78.4	77.6	75.6	59.2
Sub-Saharan Africa	73.8	76.1	77.6	75.6	72.9	–
Total	69.4	63.4	57.1	53.3	47.0	–

Source: *World development Indicators 2011*

The New Index of Poverty: Multidimensional Poverty Index (MPI) by the United Nations

Human Development Report (HDR) 2010, measures poverty in terms of a new parameter namely "*Multidimensional Poverty Index* (MPI) which has replaced the *human poverty index* (HPI) since 1997. *The multidimensional poverty index* (MPI) *indicates the share of the population that is multidimensionally poor adjusted by the intensity of deprivation in terms of living standards, health and education.* According to this parameter, as will be seen from Table 66.5, India with a poverty index of 0.296 and poverty ratio of 41.6 per cent in terms purchasing power parity (PPP) of $ 1.25 a day and 28.6 per cent (as per national poverty line) is not favourably placed when compared with countries like China and Sri Lanka. In fact, the difference in population below the poverty line (BPL) as per multidimensional poverty index (MPI) and national poverty indicator widens substantially in case of India while for other countries there is less of difference and in some cases even a fall (see Table 66.5). This multidimensional poverty index has been prepared by the '*Oxford Poverty and Human Development Initiative*' for United Nations Development Programme (UNDP).

India's appalling record of inability to ensure basic levels of nutrition and other basic needs to its people is responsible for its huge poverty level as measured by the new international multidimensional Poverty Index (MPI). About 645 million people, that is, *55% of India's population is poor as measured by this composite index made up of 10 markers of health, education and standard of living achievement levels. This MPI attempts to capture more than just income poverty at the household level. It is composed of ten indicators: years of schooling and child enrolment (education),*

Table 66.5. Multidimensional Poverty Index

Country	Multidimensional Poverty Index*	Population below Income Poverty Line: PPP $ 1.25 a day 2000-2008**	Population below Income Poverty Line: National Poverty Line 2000-2008**
Poland	(41)	Less than 2	14.8
Malaysia	(57)	Less than 2	12.8
Russia	0.005 (65)	Less than 2	19.6
Brazil	0.039 (73)	5.2	21.5
Turkey	0.039 (83)	2.6	27
China	0.056 (89)	15.9	2.8
Sri Lanka	0.021 (91)	14	22.7
Thailand	0.006 (92)	Less than 2	–
Phillippines	0.067 (97)	22.6	–
Egypt	0.026 (101)	Less than 2	16.7
Indonesia	0.095 (108)	29.4	16.7
South Africa	0.014 (110)	26.2	22.0
Vietnam	0.075 (113)	21.5	28.9
India	0.296 (119)	41.6	28.6
Pakistan	0.275(125)	22.6	–
Kenya	0.302(128)	19.7	46.6
Bangladesh	0.291(129)	49.6	40.0

Source: HRD 2010.

Note: * Not all indicators were available for all countries; Caution should thus be used in making cross-country comparisons

** Data refer to the most recent year available during the period specified. Figures in parenthesis in column 2 *give ranking among 169 countries.*

child mortality and nutrition (health), electricity, flooring, drinking water, sanitation, cooking fuel and assets. Standard of living indicators of education and health has a 1/6 weight each living indicator has a 1/8 weight.

The data for the year 2008 also shows even in relatively rich Indian states such as Haryana, Gujarat and Karnataka more than 40 per cent of population is poor by the new multidimensional poverty index, while Kerala is the only state in which the poor are less than 20 per cent by this composite measure of poverty.

It is worth noting that **MPI measures both the incidence of poverty as well as its intensity.** In this multidimensional approach, a person is defined as poor if he or she is deprived of at least three of the ten indicators. By this definition 55% of India's poor is close to double of much criticised figure of official national poverty ratio of around 29 per cent Nutritional deprivation is overwhelming which is the largest factor responsible for overall poverty in India as half of all children in India are undernourished according to the National Family health Survey III (2005-06). Close to 40% of those who are defined as poor are also nutritionally deprived. In fact, the contribution of nutrition to the overall multidimensional poverty index (MPI) is greater in urban than in rural India.

Poverty by Caste Categories as per MPI. In Hindu population of India multidimensional poverty is highest among scheduled tribes with 81.4 per cent of them are poor followed by scheduled castes with 65.8 persons of poor, other backward classes (OBC) with 58.3% of them being poor and finally general Hindu population with 33 per cent counted as poor as per this composite measure. There is significant variation between the poverty incidence in various states as per the MPI and as per the Indian Planning Commission official figures based on head-count ratio. Bihar has by far the most poor of any State in the country with 81.4 per cent of its population defined as poor which is close to 12 per cent more than the next worst state of Uttar Pradesh. As per the Planning Commission figures 41.4 per cent of Bihar and 32.8 per cent of UP is poor. In a possible indication of inadequate access to health and education facilities which do not show up in income poverty, almost 60 per cent of North-East India and nearly 50 per cent of population of Jammu and Kashmir are poor as per the MPI while the Planning Commission figures of income poverty of these are around 16 per cent and 5 per cent respectively.

It is evident from above that India's method of poverty estimates by Planning Commission with focus primarily on subsistence expenditure or income are quite inadequate to capture the extent of poverty or deprivation in the country.

WORLD BANK'S NOTION OF SHARED PROSPERITY

Until recently World Bank has been concerned with reducing poverty in the developing countries and set a target of reducing poverty in 2015 half of what prevailed in 1990. Although poverty rates have fallen rapidly over the last three decades but as we have seen above more than 1 billion people of the world still live below the extreme poverty line of $ 1.25 a day. The existence of this extreme poverty is morally unacceptable given the world's resources and technology available. Now, the World Bank has set a target of reducing the extreme poverty of the people living below $ 1.25 a day to 3 per cent globally by 2030. This requires rapid and sustained growth in the developing countries and the measures to be taken by the government to ensure that benefits of growth reach the poor people.

Besides the goal of almost eliminating extreme poverty within a generation a special World Bank Group (WBG) has set a more ambitious goal of promoting what has been called *'Shared Prosperity'* By shared prosperity the World Bank Group means that a *sustainable growth in developing countries must ensure increase in the well-being of the less well-off sections of the society*. More specifically, under the goal of shared prosperity the World Bank will *strive to foster income growth of the bottom 40 per cent of the population in every country*. This goal of achieving shared prosperity is proposed to be well-aligned with the overall objectives of the Millennium Development Goals in the post

2015 Agenda. It has been pointed out by the World Bank Group that in the world there has been rising inequality in income distribution and social exclusion that has accompanied GDP growth in many countries poses a threat to social stability. While in the past the focus of the World Bank has been to achieve faster GDP growth and it was assumed that the benefits of economic growth would trickle down to the poor. Now, under the leadership of its new head Dr. Kaushik Basu, it has been recognised by the World Bank Group that the benefits of GDP growth will not automatically trickle down to the poor. Therefore, under the goal of share prosperity, according to it, *conscious efforts by the state have to be made so that the gains of economic growth must be adequately shared by the bottom 40 per cent of the population.* Thus, according to world Bank Group, "Our shared prosperity implies a *direct focus on the income of the less well-off* (that is bottom 40 per cent of population) as opposed to the common practice of focusing only on growth of GDP and implicitly relying on the "trickle down" impact of growth on the bottom of the distribution[9]". It may be noted that 'shared prosperity' notion of World Bank seems to be the same as the concept of *inclusive growth* laid down in the *Twelfth Five Year Plan* (2012–17) of India.

The three elements are considered to be central to the notion of shared prosperity are:

(1) Sustained economic growth.

(2) Reduction in income inequalities and achieving equity in income distribution.

(3) Differences in opportunities for various sections of the society.

We explain below the above three elements of shared prosperity.

Shared Prosperity and Economic Growth

Economic growth is thought to be necessary because it ensures an expansion in productive capacity of the economy which when utilised causes increase in the amount of goods and services required for increase in consumption of the people. Therefore, without economic growth, the living standards of the less well-off are unlikely to rise in the medium to the long run.

For example, growth of agriculture will increase the opportunities for a large part of the population (including small farmers and landless labourers). Economic growth is also important because it generates more employment for the people. Like agricultural growth, growth of small and medium enterprises will create higher incomes and larger employment opportunities for the poor people.

But for growth to be inclusive, the priority ought be given in the policy framework that ensures equitable distribution of growth in GDP or national income. The World Bank document on shared prosperity emphasises that for achievement of shared prosperity the growth in incomes should be accompanied by *decline in income inequality* as has been in the case of many Latin American countries during the past decade (2000-2010) and further that "sustained progress in shared prosperity is incompatible will a long-term increase in inequality.'[10]

It is evident from above that there is now distinct shift in the approach to development of the World Bank which along with IMF previously emphasised GDP growth alone in its structural adjustment reforms to be undertaken by the developing countries. Now, it refers to the two empirical research studies at the International Monetary Fund which find that the inequality of incomes is an obstacle to economic growth. Thus one such study finds that '*high inequality is associated with shorter growth episodes*'.[11] Similarly, another research study by W. Easterly suggests that '*structural inequality is a significant barrier to prosperity and growth in per capita income.*'[12]

---

9 World Bank, End Extreme Poverty and Promote Shared Prosperity, 2013, p. 20.

10 World Bank, *op.cit.*, p. 22.

11 A Berg, J. Osty and J. Zettelmeyer. 'What causes growth sustained' *Journal of Development Economics* 2012, 98 (2).

12 W. Easterly, 'Inequality does cause underdevelopment' *Journal of Development Economics*, 2007, 84 (2).

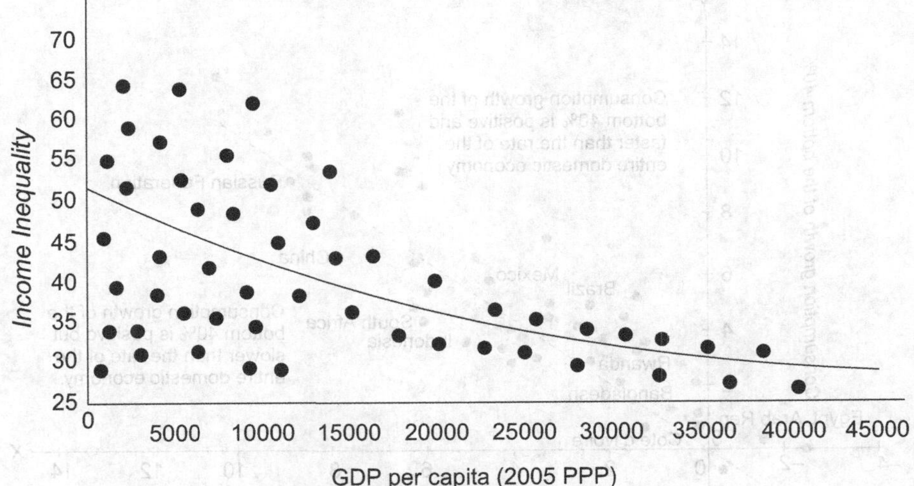

Fig. 66.1. *Inequality and GDP per capita low, middle and high income countries* (*circa* 2010)

More importantly, Ferreira and Ravallion[13] have found that sustained economic growth that raises the welfare of those at the bottom is not compatible with long run increase in income inequality. They point to the fact that in general *no country has grown beyond middle income level while maintaining a high level of inequality.* This is evident from Fig. 66.1 where data of income inequality and GDP per capita of various countries as shown by various dots representing them. A trend curve in the data is drawn which clearly shows that in countries with higher GDP per capita income inequality has declined. However, there is large variation in inequality among countries representing low and middle income countries. It further shows that where *income inequality is higher promoting shared prosperity will need that income of the bottom 40 per cent grow faster than average income of the population.*

It may be noted that for achievement of shared prosperity, income of the bottom 40 per cent of population must rise faster than the growth of the average income of the total population. *Thus though growth in GDP is necessary for higher performance in achievement of shared prosperity but it is not a sufficient condition for it*. This is because economic growth does not necessarily lead to the gains in incomes of the bottom 40 per cent of population. This is evident from the experience of the United States where per capita income of the bottom 40 per cent of population rose by just 7.5 per cent between 1975 and 2012 while mean income of the total households income increased by 40.5 per cent in the same period.[14]

The higher initial income inequality is a significant barrier to shared prosperity as well as GDP growth rate. It has been found that in 20 out of 55 developing countries in the decade of 2000-2010, real per capita consumption (or income) of the bottom 40 per cent of the population increased at the average rate of more than 5 per cent annually which is quite satisfactory. It is worth mentioning the empirical findings about the relationship between overall consumption (or income) growth and the consumption (or income) of the bottom 40 per cent of the population. As will be seen from Fig. 66.2

13 F. Ferreira and M. Ravallion (2009) Poverty and Inequality: The Global Context in W Salverda et al. *The Oxford Handbook of Economic Inequality,* Oxford University Press.

14 See *Shared Prosperity, Links to Growth, Inequality and Inequality of opportunity*. World Bank's Policy Research Working Paper 6649 by Ambar Narayan, Jaime Saavedra Chanduvi and Sailesh Tiwari, 2013, p.12.

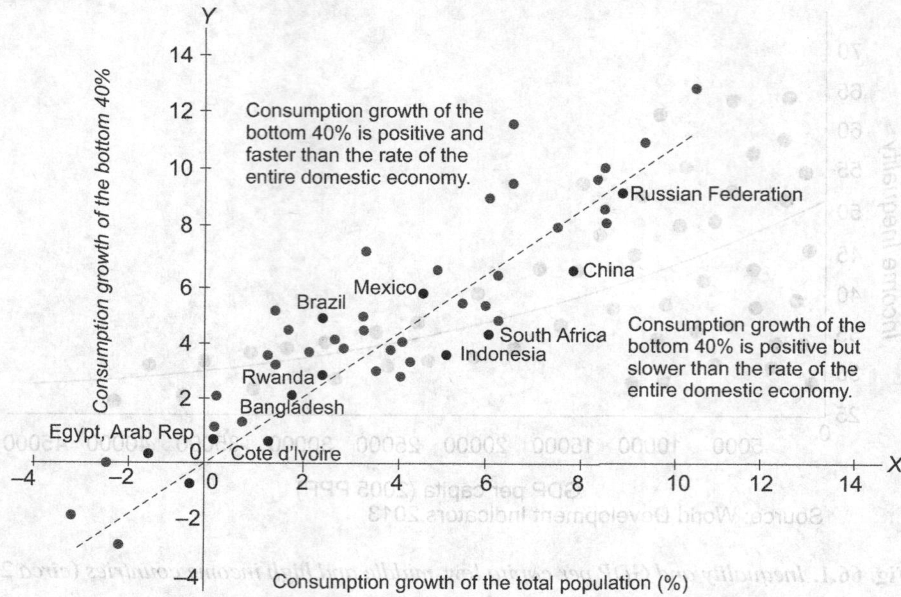

Fig. 66.2. *Shared prosperity indicator in selected countries (circa 2000-10)*

Source: World Bank database, based on household surveys from countries.

where data regarding percentage consumption growth of the total population (measured along the *X*-axis) and consumption growth of the bottom 40 per cent of population (measured along the *Y*-axis) of various countries are plotted; different dots in the figure represent different countries. A trend line has also been drawn which shows that there is a strong and positive relation between consumption of the bottom 40 per cent of population and consumption growth of the total population. This means *for achievement of shared prosperity growth in national income or consumption is necessary*.

The second important fact revealed by Fig. 66.2 is that in the decade, 2000-2010, 60 per cent of developing countries which include large Latin American Countries of Brazil and Mexico income (or consumption) of the bottom 40 per cent of population increased at a higher rate than the average growth of consumption (or income) of the total population.[15] This could *occur only if there was a decline* in income inequality. This clearly shows that *fall in inequality in income distribution is essential for promoting shared prosperity*. It will be seen from Fig. 66.2 that the countries which lies above the trend line such as Brazil, Mexico, though their percentage consumption growth of the total population is low, the percentage consumption growth of the bottom 40 per cent of population is relatively higher. Thus the *notion of shared prosperity that focusses on growth of bottom 40 per cent of population rather than average rate of GDP growth ensures improvement in living standards or welfare of the less well-off sections of population in a country*. It will also be observed from Fig. 66.2 that position of countries such as China, Indonesia, South Africa which lie below the trend line have relatively higher consumption growth of total population but greater income inequality, the consumption growth of bottom 40 per cent of population is lower.

Equality of Opportunity and Shared Prosperity

To foster shared prosperity requires ensuring equality of opportunity to all people, both children and male adults as well as women. It is only by providing equality of opportunity that production potential of every individual is maximised. Equality of opportunity in childhood and youth requires

15 World Bank, *End Extreme Poverty and Promote Shared Prosperity* 2013, p. 24.

adequate nutrition, healthcare and education so as to build human capital and raise productivity in the production process. During adulthood, ensuring equality of opportunity implies imparting appropriate skills and education, the taking care of their health and creation of employment opportunities and providing credit facilities to the young entrepreneurs so that they can set up their micro and small enterprises if not employed on wage basis in the organised sector. Thus, a World Bank research paper on shared prosperity[16] states that "Efforts to improve and equalise opportunities would lead to immediate rise in welfare along multiple (including non-monetary) dimensions particularly among the poor and the excluded. Over long term, it would also promote social mobility, reduce income inequality and enhance economic dynamism and prosperity for the economy as a whole". While the definitions of equality of opportunity by different economists and social thinkers vary significantly but the minimal view is that all children and adults must have access to basic goods and services such as safe water, adequate nutrition and healthcare, primary education so as to maximise human capability. In India, for example, there exists a gender gap in providing basic goods and services so that the girls and women are denied access to education, nutrition, healthcare and employment opportunities. To achieve shared prosperity women must be ensured equal opportunity with men.

Pathways to Shared Prosperity

There are many pathways for achievement of shared prosperity. Economic growth can insure improvement in living standards of bottom 40 per cent of population if it is broad based and generates a lot of opportunities for better quality jobs or gainful employment for all sections of the population. The state has to play a key role in promoting climate for investment in labour-intensive sectors. For generation of employment opportunities the government should link investment allowances to the magnitude of employment created by the industrial enterprises rather than to the amount of capital investment. Through fiscal incentives, the government should ensure that growth is diversified across multiple sectors. Besides, the Government should ensure "*ease of doing business*", improve competitiveness by preventing the emergence of monopolies and oligopolies in the production of goods and services. Besides, for the creation of adequate jobs, the government should encourage innovations or technological changes that are labour-absorptive rather than labour-displacing.

The second pathway to promote shared prosperity is to ensure that *growth is inclusive* through a specific structure of taxation, government expenditure and social programmes initiated by the government, especially those that make *investment in people* which build their capabilities and increase productivity and thereby promote economic growth with equity. For fostering shared prosperity, the tax structure should be such that gives incentives to the private sector but at the same time it should ensure equitable distribution of income in a society.

The third path to promote shared prosperity is to make investment by the government in social institutions so as to ensure equal *opportunities for all* including the marginalised sections of the society. For this purpose, the World Bank Group emphasizes that *rather than redistributing resources from one section of the society to another, the investment should be made for improving the capabilities of the people that increases their productivity and therefore promote growth and equity over time and across generations. With this the people will be able to better their lives on their own.*[17]

The evidence furnished by the World Bank Group gives many examples relating to developing countries where inequality of opportunity is still very high and despite growth made by them the circumstances at the time of birth of the individuals, the background and status of their parents, their gender and ethnicity still play a large part in determining his opportunity. To foster shared prosperity the World Bank document states, "The social contract for promoting equity and growth should aim to create an "opportunity society" where the human and productive potential of every individual regardless of gender, region, ethnicity or parental background is maximised. In childhood and youth,

16 See Ambar Narayan, Jaime Saavedra Chanduvi and Sailesh Tiwari, op. cit.

17 See World Bank, *"End Extreme Poverty and Promote Shared Prosperity"*, 2013, p. 28.

this would imply providing universal access to early childhood development, health, nutrition, education and basic infrastructure to build human capital and increase long-term productivity. This will enhance mobility on the economic and social ladder within and across generations."[18]

Further, a significant part of social contract aimed at creating conditions to promote shared prosperity is to ensure *gender equality.* Having equal opportunity with men and same access to facilities of educational healthcare, nutrition, sanitation would enable women to contribute to the best of their abilities in the development process. To quote the said World Bank Document, "Gender equality is not just a core development objective; it also enhances productivity, improves development outcomes for the next generation, and makes institutions more productive."[19]

LATEST ESTIMATES OF GLOBAL POVERTY BY WORLD BANK

On October 6, 2015 released its new estimates of global poverty in its report titled "*Ending Extreme Poverty and Sharing: Progress and Policies*". In this report World Bank has used a new updated international poverty line of $1.90 a day per person in 2011 PPP prices to measure extreme poverty in the world. *Thus in these latest estimates, the extreme poverty is defined as living at less than $ 1.90 a day*. It is important to note that this new poverty line has maintained the purchasing power of previous international poverty line of $ 1.25 (in 2005 PPP prices) living below which represented the extreme poverty earlier. Besides, the new extreme poverty line of $ 1.90 a day incorporates the new information on *differences in cost of living across countries* and the new PPP exchange rates. The estimates of global poverty based on the new international poverty line of $ 1.90 a day are given in Table 66.6.

Table 66.6. Estimates of Extreme Poverty based on the New International Poverty line ($ 1.90 a day in 2011 PPP prices)

Year	Number of poor (millions)	Poverty Ratio
1990	1,958	37.1
1999	1,747	29.0
2011	987	14.2
2012	902	12.8
2015*	702	9.6

* Projected

Source: World Bank Report "*Ending Extreme Poverty and sharing Prosperity: Progress and Policies*, 2015.

As will be seen from Table 66.6 the important fact revealed from the poverty estimates based on the new international poverty line of $ 1.90 a day is that the ratio of the poor people (*i.e.*, the people living below the new poverty line) to the total world population has declined from 37.1 per cent in 1990 to 29 per cent in 1999 and further to 12.8 per cent in 2012 and is projected to fall to the single digit of 9.6% in 2015. Similarly, in absolute number, the persons living below the new poverty line of $ 1.90 a day declined from 1,958 million in 1990 to 1,747 million in 1999 to 902 million in 2012 and is estimated to fall further to 702 million in 2015. This shows a significant achievement of the world community in reducing extreme poverty in the last 25 years, especially since 1999. About 1 billion people of the world have been lifted out of extreme poverty since 2000 (1747–702 = 1045 million). Most developing countries have experienced significant income growth of the bottom 40 per cent of their population in their income distribution. These poverty estimates based on new international poverty line and the new country level data on living standards shows that a quarter century long (1990-2015) reduction in extreme poverty in the developing countries (especially China and India) is moving the world closer to the historic goal of the UN of eradicating extreme poverty by the end of 1930 under its new sustainable development goals.

18 World Bank, *op. cit*, 28.

19 *Ibid.*

The new estimates of poverty are graphically shown in Fig. 66.3.

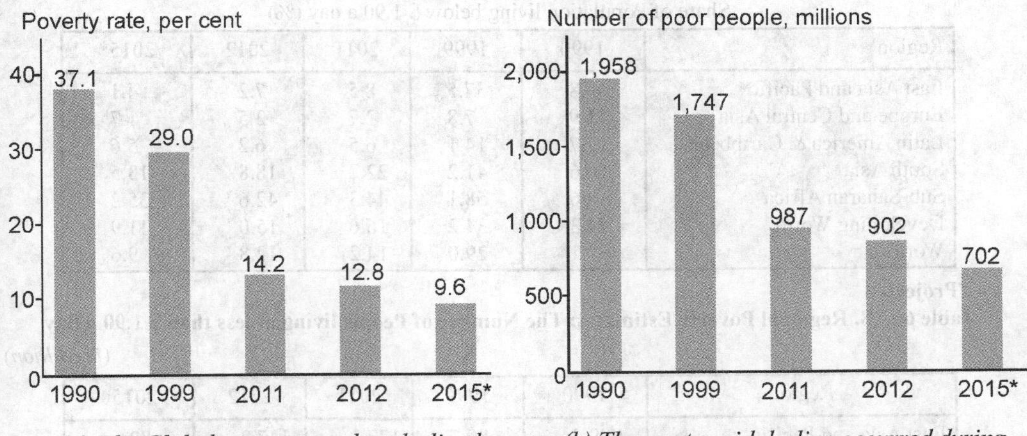

(a) *The Global poverty rate has declined significantly over the last 25 years*

(b) *The most rapid decline occurred during the 2000s*

Fig. 66.3. *Estimates of global poverty as per the new international poverty line of $ 1.90 a day*

The estimate of 1 billion people of the world being lifted out of poverty since 2000 and that in 2015, the global poverty would fall to single digit of 9.6 % are good news. Jim Yonk Kim, the president of World Bank group which prepared the report has said that, "This is the best story in the world today.........., these projections show us that we are in the first generation in human history that can end extreme poverty." He however has cautioned that with slowing global economic growth and many of the world's remaining poor people live in fragile and conflict affected states, the goal to end extreme poverty by 2030 is a highly ambitious target.

It may be further noted that the decline in poverty to 9.6 per cent of world population in 2015 is quite impressive but the number of people living in extreme poverty conditions, namely, 702 million persons in 2015, still remains unacceptably, high.

Regionwise New Poverty Estimates

We have seen above that global poverty has declined significantly over the last three decades. However, the progress in poverty reduction in different regions of the world has been quite uneven. As will be seen from Table 66.7A and B that extreme poverty is now more concentrated in Sub-Saharan Africa and South Asia. For the past several decades, the same three regions, namely, East Asia and Pacific (which includes China), South Asia (which includes India) and Sub-Saharan Africa account for 95 per cent of global poverty. The latest 2012 poverty estimates confirm this high degree of concentration (see Table 66.7A and 66.7B). Yet the composition of global poverty across these three regions has shifted overtime. There is large reduction in relative share of East Asia and Pacific in global poverty whereas the share of Sub-Saharan Africa in global poverty has risen to 43 per cent due to a slower pace of poverty reduction in this region along with rapid growth of population in it. However, the composition of global poverty across regions has shifted over the regions due to their uneven progress in reduction in poverty. Thus in East Asia and Pacific region, share of poor in total

Table 66.7A. Regional Poverty Estimates with updated International Poverty Line ($ 1.90 a day)

Share of Population living below $ 1.90 a day (%)

Region	1990	1999	2011	2012	2015*
East Asia and Pacific	60.8	37.5	8.5	7.2	4.1
Europe and Central Asia	1.9	7.8	2.7	2.5	1.7
Latin America & Caribbean	17.7	14.1	6.5	6.2	5.6
South Asia	50.6	41.2	22.2	18.8	13.5
Sub-Saharan Africa	56	58.1	44.3	42.6	35.2
Developing World	44.3	34.2	16.6	15.0	11.9
World	37.1	29.0	14.2	12.8	9.6

***Projected**

Table 66.7B. Regional Poverty Estimates: The Number of People living at less than $ 1.90 a day

(*in Million*)

Region	1990	1999	2011	2012	2015*
East Asia and Pacific	999.3	689.7	177.1	147.2	82.6
Europe and Central Asia	9.0	36.6	12.7	12.6	4.4
Latin America & Caribbean	78.0	77.2	37.2	37.1	29.7
South Asia	574.5	560.1	362.3	309.2	231.3
Sub-Saharan Africa	284.0	375.4	393.5	388.5	347.1
World	**1958.5**	**1746.6**	**987.4**	**902.0**	**702**

***Projected Source**: World Bank Report '*Ending Extreme Poverty and Sharing Prosperity*', progress and policies, Oct. 2015

population which was 60.8 per cent in 1990, fell to 37.5 per cent in 1999 and to 7.2 per cent in 2012 and is projected to fall further to 4.1 per cent in 2015. This has been due to rapid progress made in China in poverty reduction due to very high GDP growth rate. Similarly in South Asia, there has been good progress in poverty reduction due *mainly to substantial reduction in poverty in India the last over two decades*. Thus, in South Asia poverty ratio which was 50.6 per cent in 1990, fell to 41.2 per cent in 1999 and further to 18.8 per cent in 2012 and is projected to fall further to 13.5 per cent in 2015.

The share of Sub-Saharan Africa in global poverty has risen to 43 per cent due to a slower pace of poverty reduction in the region amidst rapid population growth. As will be seen from Table 66.7A, in Sub-Saharan Africa the poverty ratio fell from 56 to 42.6 per cent between 1990 and 2012. Though South Asia achieved more rapid poverty reduction over the past 30 years, yet, it is still home to about a third of the world's poor (see Table 66.7B). It will be seen from Table 66.7B that in 2012, as per new international poverty line of $ 1.90 a day in 2011 PPP prices, out of 902 million total world poor, 309 million people lived in South Asia and 388 million in Sub-Saharan Africa. Thus, *it is evident that extreme poverty is now concentrated in South Asia and Sub-Saharan Africa*. More focus is therefore needed to reduce extreme poverty in Sub-Saharan Africa and South Asia where most of the poor live.

In case of India, the World Bank Report 2015 says that, according to uniform Recall Period (URP) methodology, the per cent of population living below the poverty line (as per national estimates made by Tendulkar Committe) for 2011-12 is 21.2 per cent. According to it, though India has succeeded in significantly reducing poverty ratio but "*India was home to the largest number of poor in 2012* but its poverty rate is one of the lowest among those countries with the largest number of poor."

According to the report, strong economic growth and greater investment in physical and human capital in emerging economies, particularly in India and China, has led to the significant decline in poverty in the developing world.

CHAPTER 67

PROBLEM OF POVERTY IN INDIA

To eliminate poverty has been as important objective of planned economic development in India. Even before independence it was thought that without economic freedom and eradication of poverty, political freedom would be meaningless. In designing our strategy of development, the earlier Five Year Plans assumed that a fast rate of economic growth would by itself create adequate employment opportunities and achieve higher living standards for the poor. In addition, in the earlier plans, land reforms especially redistribution of land by imposing ceiling on land holdings, tenancy reforms aimed at protecting the tenants from eviction and charging high rents by landlords were expected to improve the living conditions of the rural poor.

But economic growth in the first two decades (1951–71) resulted in increase in national income at an average rate of 3.7 per cent per annum. Yet the achievement of this growth rate made little impact on the problem of poverty in India. Land reform legislations were not effectively implemented and remained on paper only. However, during the 1980s when average annual growth rate picked up to 5.6 per cent, poverty declined significantly. But from 1993–2004-05, the declined in poverty slowed down. But from 2004-05 to 2011-12, due to rapid economic growth and also starting on a large scale employment guarantee scheme poverty rate declined at a higher rate.

Dandekar-Rath Measure of Poverty

In the early seventies Dandekar and Rath[1] in their important study on poverty in India estimated that *per capita monthly consumption expenditure* of at least ₹ 14.2 at 1960-61 prices was required for a person to obtain a minimum subsistence diet of 2250 calories of food. On the basis of this norm of the poverty line, they estimated that, in 1960-61, 33 per cent of the Indian *rural population* lived below the poverty line, that is, they did not get even the above-mentioned minimum subsistence diet. For the *urban areas* they fixed ₹ 22.6 per person at the 1960-61 prices as the monthly minimum consumption expenditure required for minimum subsistence and estimated that in 1960-61 48.6 per cent of urban population did not obtain this subsistence, that is, they lived below the poverty line.

1 V.M. Dandekar and N. Rath Poverty in India, *Economic and Political Weekly*, Jan. 2 and Jan. 9, 1971.

Further, by making adjustments for changes in prices, they estimated that in the year 1968-69, 40 per cent of the rural population and 50 per cent of the urban population lived below the poverty line. Thus, according to the estimates of Dandekar and Rath, during 1961-69 the extent of rural poverty substantially increased, while urban poverty increased only marginally. Thus, contrary to popular perception, according to Dandekar and Rath study, the incidence of urban poverty was much greater than that of rural poverty. According to it, half of urban people lived below the poverty line.

Dandekar and Rath study on poverty prompted other scholars such as Dr. B.S. Minhas[2] and Pranab Bardhan[3] to make their own studies for estimating poverty in India, though there are some important difference in their estimates of poverty. A fact which was brought to light by these studies on poverty was that the first two decades of planned development did not make much impact on the problem of poverty. This gave rise to rethinking on the part of the Government and Planning Commission about revising strategy of development to solve the problem of poverty. Thus, in its Approach to Fifth Five Year Plan, (June 1972), Planning Commission states, "Economic development in the last two decades has resulted in an all round increase in per capita income and the proportion of the poor, defined as those living below a basic minimum standard of consumption has slightly come down. Yet the *absolute number of people below the poverty line today is just as large as it was two decades ago* and these people living in object poverty constitute between 40 and 50 per cent of all citizens".[4] Further it was realised in the approach paper that *to rely on economic growth alone* will involve too long a period for the solution of the problem of poverty. It was therefore suggested that *a direct attack* on the problem of poverty and unemployment be made if the objective of assuring minimum consumption levels were to be achieved within a foreseable future. Direct attack on poverty implies that *special employment schemes* be started so to assure more and fuller employment to the poor.

The study by Dandekar and Rath on poverty also gave rise to a severe controversy about the proper estimates of poverty and to what extent it had declined. This controversy still exists today with different scholars making different estimates of poverty. In what follows we shall study the various issues involved in estimating poverty and the extent to which it has declined during the last six decades of development (1951–2012). We shall also study the causes of prevailing poverty and the measures or strategy that should be adopted to tackle this problem.

Issues in Estimating Poverty

An important issue for estimating *poverty line* is to determine the *minimum nutritional requirement of a person in the rural and urban areas*. In this regard a widely accepted norm is the consumption of 2400 calories of food per day per person in the rural area and 2200 calories per day per person of food consumption in the urban areas. The next step is to convert the minimum consumption into money terms, that is, into minimum consumption expenditure. For this, appropriate prices separately for rural and urban areas have to be used. Besides, the expenditure on food that ensures the minimum calories intake, in recent years, minimum expenditure on healthcare, clothing, education and shelter is also included to determine the specified poverty line.

To estimate the variation in poverty over a period of time, poverty line has to be adjusted on the basis of change in prices over a period of time. For this appropriate price deflator has to be used and in regard to this several difficulties are faced. Thus, the following three elements affect the fixation of poverty line which determines the people below and above the poverty line.

1. Norm regarding minimum nutritional requirements of a person.
2. Minimum expenditure on healthcare, clothing, education and shelter is also included to fix the poverty line.

---

2 B.S. Minhas, *Planning and the Poor*, S. Chand and Co. 1973.

3 Pranav K. Bardhan, On the Incidence of Poverty in Rural India, *Economic and Political Weekly*, Annual Number Feb. 1973.

4 Planning Commission, *Approach to the Fifth Five Year Plan*, 1972, p. 3.

3. Use of what prices be made to convert the minimum nutritional requirement into money terms.
4. Choice of a price deflator to update the poverty line.
5. To adjust the number of households in different expenditure classes to determine the number of households below and above poverty line.

Various scholars have made different assumptions and different methods have been used to determine the above elements. This accounts for a wide difference in their estimates of the incidence of poverty. Such was the difference in various estimates of poverty that Planning Commission appointed an expert group headed by Late Prof. Lakdawala to suggest a proper methodology of estimating incidence of poverty in India. In 2010, again, an expert committee headed by Late Prof. Suresh Tendulkar was appointed and this committee's estimates of poverty in 2004-05 and 2011-12 came under heavy attack as it was alleged that the poverty line fixed by them was too low and therefore on this basis estimates of poverty was lower than expected. Therefore, another expert committee headed by Dr. Rangarajan was appointed in 2012 to go into the question of measuring the magnitude of poverty in India. Both Tendulkar committee and Rangarajan committee's estimates of poverty in India will be critically examined later in this chapter.

Now, for the last several years the Planning commission has been estimating the incidence of poverty in India at the national level and state level using the methodology of the expert group. Household's consumption expenditure data is taken from the large sample surveys made by NSSO at an interval of 5 years.

Trends in Poverty in India

These estimates of poverty made by the Planning Commission from 1973-74 to 2004-05 are given in Table 67.1 for the national level. It may however be noted the estimates of poverty for the year 1999-2000 are not quite comparable to those of the earlier years, as the *questionaire* used for the survey was changed. Therefore, the decline in poverty ratio in 1999-2000 is highly controversial. However, poverty estimates for 2004-05 are based on uniform recall period (URP) as the earlier ones and therefore they are comparable with 1993-94 estimates and of the previous years.

Three important changes occurred in regard to the extent of poverty since 1973-74. First, as is evident from Table 67.1 there has been a *continuous reduction in the incidence of poverty since 1973-74*. The percentage of households below the poverty line for All India (that is, rural and urban India combined) which was 54.9 per cent in 1973-74 declined to 51.3 per cent in 1977-78 and further to 44.5 per cent in 1983. For all India, poverty ratio further declined to around 38.9 per cent in 1987-88 and to 36 per cent in 1993-94. The poverty ratio for All India declined to 26 per cent in 1999-2000, which, was based on *mixed recall period* (MRP) and is not comparable with the 1993-94 poverty data which was based on *uniform recall period* (URP). According to uniform recall period (URP) basis poverty data of *National Sample Survey 2004-05,* poverty as ratio of population in case of all India declined to 27.8 per cent.

Table 67.1. Trends in Poverty in India

Years	Poverty Ratio (%)			Poor (million)		
	Rural	Urban	(All India Combined)	Rural	Urban	Total
1973–74	56.4	49.0	54.9	261	60	321
1977–78	53.1	45.2	51.3	264	65	329
1983	45.7	40.8	44.5	252	71	323
1987–88	39.1	38.2	38.9	232	75	307
1993–94	37.3	32.4	36.0	244	76	320
1999–2000 (MRP)	27.1	23.6	26.1	193	67	260
2004-2005 (URP)	28.3	25.7	27.8	221	80	301

Source: Planning Commission Estimates

A noteworthy fact is that rate of decline in poverty ratio during this period was much lower than the rate of economic growth. Thus while annual growth in GDP in real terms during 1993-94 to 2004-05 was 6.3%, the rate of reduction in poverty was much slower, 0.74 per cent per annum. Secondly, the rate of reduction in poverty ratio slowed down in the period 1993-94 to 2004-05, as compared to the pre-reforms period. Whereas decline in the poverty ratio was about 1.24 per cent per annum in the pre-reforms period, 1977-78 to 1987-88, it was only 0.74 per cent per annum during the post-reform period (1993-94 to 2004-05).

Second, the incidence of both rural poverty and urban poverty separately has also declined since 1973-74. As will be seen from Table 67.1, rural poverty ratio which was 56.4 per cent in 1973-74, fell to 45.7 per cent in 1983 and further to 37.3 per cent in 1993-94. In 2004-05, it was estimated to have fallen to 28.3 per cent (URP). Thus, there had been a marked decline in the *ratio of poor rural households* when comparing 2004-05 estimates with those of 1973-74. This is mainly due to agricultural growth but also due to increase in procurement prices during the period. Likewise, *poverty ratio in urban India* declined from 49 per cent in 1973-74 to 40.8 per cent in 1983 and to 32.4 per cent in 1993-94. In 2004-05, poverty ratio (URP) in urban India further fell to 25.7 per cent. ***An important fact revealed from these rural and urban poverty ratios is that the incidence of poverty in rural areas is greater than that in urban areas. This is contrary to estimates of rural and urban poverty in India.***

Third, the data regarding the incidence of poverty in various States of India during this period (1973-2004-05) reveal that the *secular decline in rural poverty ratio occurred in every individual state of the country,* although the extent of decline varied. However, it is important to note that in 2004-05 *rural poverty ratio* was still relatively high in Odisha, Bihar, Uttar Pradesh, Madhya Pradesh, Uttarakhand, Jharkhand and West Bengal as compared to 28.3 per cent at the All India level.

It may be noted that the NSS data about incidence of poverty reveal that there has been a *secular decline in urban poverty ratio* in every state of the country, although magnitude of this decline varies a good deal in different states. *It should be further noted that in 2004-05, in Odisha, Madhya Pradesh, Bihar and Uttar Pradesh, urban poverty ratio was relatively much higher than the poverty ratio at the urban national level of 25.7. It was 44.3% in Odisha, 34.6% in Bihar, 42% in Madhya Pradesh, 30.6% in Uttar Pradesh, and 32.6% in Karnataka.*

Latest Estimates of Poverty in India: 68th Round of NSS

In June 2013 the Planning Commission released the poverty estimates based on special 68th round of NSS based on poverty line fixed by an expert committee under the chairmanship of Prof. Suresh Tendulkar. These estimates gave rise to a lot of controversy about the true extent of poverty prevailing in India. Adjusted for price change, the *poverty line* based on Tendulkar Committee methodology was fixed at a daily expenditure of ₹ 27.20 per capita for rural areas and ₹ 33.3 per capita for urban areas for the year 2011-12. Based on this poverty line Tendulkar Committee calculated the poverty ratio and the absolute number of people living below the poverty line based on 68th National Sample Survey on consumption expenditure for the year 2011-12. It may be noted that for the sake of comparison, household expenditure data for the year 2004-05 had been used to make estimates of poverty for 2004-05. As will be seen from Table 67.2, during the period 2004-05 and 2011-12 there has been massive decline in poverty ratio. According to these estimates, poverty ratio for all India

Table 67.2. Estimates of Poverty in 2004-05 and 2011-12 Based on Tendulkar Committee Methodology

	Rural	Urban	Total
2004-05	41.8	25.7	37.2
2011-12	25.7	13.7	21.9

declined from 37.2 per cent in 2004-05 to 21.9 per cent in 2011-12, that is, 15.3 per cent fall in poverty in just seven years which amounts to 2.2 percentage points per year which is quite a large decline compared to 0.74 percentage points a year between 1993-94 and 2004-05. Further, it will be seen from Table 67.2 that there has been much larger decline in poverty ratio in rural areas, from 41.8 per cent in 2004-05 to 25.7 per cent in 2011-12, that is, 16.1 percentage points decline in seven years as compared to 12 percentage points in urban areas in these seven years. Based on this poverty line cut-off, there were 269 million poor people in India in 2011-12 against 407 million in 2004-05, that is, around *137 million persons were lifted out of poverty*. This means poverty declined at faster rate of 2.2 percentage points per year as against the reduction of 0.74 percentage point per year during the 1993-94 and 2004-05, that is, three times greater decline in poverty between 2004-05 and 2011-12 compared to the decline during the period 1993-94 and 2004-05.

It may be noted that the previous poverty estimates were based on National Sample Survey 2009-10. However, the Government did not consider the poverty number of 2009-10 as correct saying that it was a drought year and would not convey the true picture. For calculating the above poverty estimates the planning commission used Dr. Suresh Tendulkar Committee's methodology which factors in spending on education and health besides calorie intake to arrive at a poverty line in urban and rural areas. Accordingly, those whose daily consumption expenditure per capita on goods and services exceeds ₹ 33.33 in urban India and ₹ 27.20 per capita in rural India are not poor.

Now the greater decline in poverty between 2004-05 and 2011-12 has been explained by Planning Commission to faster GDP growth (average 8.2 per cent per annum) during this period. However, this is not fully correct. *Besides faster growth, starting of MGNREGS on a larger scale than before, sharp increase in procurement prices of farm products and in steady rise in rural wages during this period also contributed significantly to the fall in poverty during this period.* Furthermore, greater investment in infrastructure, greater access to education and healthcare which increased human capabilities also contributed to higher rate of growth during this period.

Better Performance in Poverty Reduction in Odisha and Bihar

An interesting feature of NSS data about poverty reveals that poverty in Odisha and Bihar have recorded the sharpest decline in poverty levels between 2004-05 and 2011-12, although the proportion of the poor in these states remains well above the national average. Latest data released by Planning Commission reveals that, according to poverty norm fixed by Tendulkar Committee in Odisha, the proportion of population below the poverty line (BPL) came down from 57.2% in 2004-05 to 32.6% in 2011-12, a decline of 24.6 percentage points.

In Bihar, which registered the fastest growth rate in the 11th Five-Year Plan (2007-12), the share of BPL in total population was estimated at 33.7% in 2011-12, compared to 54.4% in 2004-05, a reduction by 20.7 percentage points in seven years.

At the all-India level, BPL population was 21.9% – around 270 million. This means every fifth Indian lives below the poverty line. The Planning Commission as per recommendations of Tendulkar Committee has set the poverty line low, defining BPL as anyone earning ₹ 27.20 a day or less in villages and upto ₹33.30 in urban areas.

The poverty estimates however, vary from state to state. Although things seem to be looking up in the poor states, especially Bimaru States, which in absolute numbers amounts to still remain home to the maximum number of poor people in the country. While Uttar Pradesh has just under 30% of its population in the BPL group, the number adds up to almost 60 million. Bihar, despite the improvement, still has 33.7% which in absolute number amounts to 35.8 million poor, and ranks second, followed by Madhya Pradesh where 23.4 million or 31.6% of the population is below poverty line (BPL).

Table 67.3. BPL as % of Total Population

Sate	2004-05	2011-12	% change
WORST PERFORMERS			
Chhattisgarh	49.4	39.93	–9.75
Jharkhand	45.3	36.96	–8.36
Manipur	37.9	36.89	–1.01
Arunachal Pradesh	31.4	34.67	+ 3.27
Puducherry	14.2	9.69	–2.51
BEST PERFORMERS			
Odisha	57.2	32.6	–24.6
Bihar	54.4	33.74	–20.66
Goa	24.9	5.09	–19.81
Kerala	19.6	7.05	–12.58
Himachal Pradesh	22.9	8.06	–14.84
Punjab	20.9	8.26	–12.64

Among the Bimaru states, only Rajasthan has managed to do better than the national average (21.9%) with the share of BPL in total population has been estimated to fall to 14.7% in 2011-12, compared to 34.4% in 2004-05. In fact, Rajasthan now is a better performer than Gujarat, famous for its rapid growth and good infrastructure. Gujarat ruled by Narendra Modi had 16.6% people below the poverty line in 2011-12.

The other important trend coming from the latest poverty estimates, which have traditionally created controversy, is the fact *that rural India has seen faster improvement in poverty reduction than urban centres. The decline in poverty was steeper in rural areas as BPL population came down to 25.7% (2011-12)* from 42% (2004-05), around 17 percentage points as against around 12 percentage points decline in poverty ratio in urban areas.

On an all-India basis, there were 217 million poor in rural areas and 53 million poor in urban areas in 2011-12 as against 326 million and 81 million respectively, in 2004-05. That is, in absolute number, the poor people declined from 407 millions in 2004-05 to 270 million in 2011-12 that is, 137 million persons were lifted out of poverty and raised above the poverty line during these seven years.

Tendulkar committee poverty line was criticised as too low and therefore its poverty estimates based on it were challenged. The Government therefore appointed committee under C. Rangarajan to submit its report on a new methodology for fixing the poverty line. However, the Planning Commission in its press release pointed out that this *would only change the numbers, not the declining trend.* Planning Commission estimates were greatly critisised. It was pointed out that ₹ 27.7 of daily expenditure per capita in rural areas and ₹ 33.3 of daily per capita expenditure in urban area fixed as poverty line were too low and persons could hardly survive on such low expenditure. Many leaders said, it was a *joke on the poor.* In the year 2011, even Superme Court criticised these criteria of poor in the rural and urban India. This led to the Government to appoint a committee headed by Dr. C. Rangarajan to redifine the poverty line and prepare estimates of poverty ratio on that basis. Rangarajan Committee submitted its report in July 2014 which will be discussed in detail later in this chapter.

Amid a severe controversy regarding lower norms of poverty, Planning Commission Deputy Chairman Montek Singh Ahluwalia acknowledged that the poverty line based on the Tendulkar Committee methodology was a bit low and that it would be revised after Rangarajan panel submits its report. To quote him, "I am perfectly willing to agree that the poverty line fixed on the basis of

Tendulkar Committee is a bit low". He further says, "As the country becomes richer and the per capita income goes up, there is need to redefine the poverty line. *The latest numbers that planning commission have released, based on the Tendulkar Committee report, are absolutely rock-bottom numbers and gives us the number of poor who are actually the weakest group and therefore, should be the priority of the government*". Further, according to him, wherever the poverty line is drawn, poverty ratio has declined since 2004-05.

The poverty numbers for 2004-05 have been arrived at by the Planning Commission after taking into account per capita expenditure numbers from the 68th round of the National Sample Survery (NSS) as recommended by the Suresh Tendulkar expert committee on poverty estimation. *Prof. Tendulkar panel had suggested moving away from taking the calorie intake as the defining parameter for poverty line to a more comprehensive method of using per capita expenditure data on basic needs such as food, clothing, housing and services like health and education.*

The Planning Commission explained this sharp fall in poverty ratio, especially in the rural areas when India saw one of the worst droughts in 2009-10, with high growth of average 8.5 per cent achieved in India during 2004-05 to 2011-12 as will be seen from Table 67.4. It was asserted by

Table 67.4. Economic Growth in 2004-05 to 2011-12

Year	GDP Growth Rate %
2004-05	7.1
2005-06	9.5
2006-07	9.6
2007-08	9.3
2008-09	6.7
2009-10	8.6
2010-11	8.9
2011-12	5.1

the Planning Commission Deputy Chairman Dr. Montek Singh Ahluwalia that *benefits of high economic growth achieved during the period (2004-05 to 2011-12) trickled down to the poor and this resulted in the drastic fall in poverty.* It will be seen from Table 67.4 that a higher annual average of about 8.5 per cent growth in GDP was achieved during this period which, as claimed by the Planning Commission, brought down the poverty levels. This is despite the fact that India saw one of the worst droughts in 2009-10 and slowdown in economic growth in 2008-09 (due to global financial crisis) and in 2011-12.

However, as mentioned above, a significant factor that accounted for decline in poverty during this period was *larger spending by the government on social welfare programmes* such as Mahatma Gandhi Rural Employment Guarantee scheme (MGREGS) which was started in 2006. This scheme entitles 100 days of employment for one person per household at minimum of ₹ 100 per day to all rural households. This scheme not only provided employment to the poor households but also helped *pushing up wages in rural areas* and thereby further ensuring reduction in rural poverty. Since no such programme as MGREGS had been started in the urban areas there had been, as seen above, much lower decline in poverty ratio in urban India during this period.

Critique of Poverty Estimates

A severe controversy broke out when the Planning Commission released the estimates of poverty for 2011-12 based on the methodology recommended by an Expert Committee headed by Late Prof. Suresh Tendulkar. The adjusted for inflation figure of poverty line by Tendulkar committee was fixed at ₹ 33.3 in urban areas and ₹ 27.2 in rural areas at 2011-12 prices. The critics pointed out *whether anybody could survive* for a day on ₹ 33.3 in the urban areas and ₹ 27.2 in rural areas. Besides, it was reported by the Planning Commission that All India poverty ratio fell from 37.2 per cent in 2004-05 to 21.9 per cent in 2011-12, a sharp fall of 15.3 per cent in the poverty level in just 7 years, that is, at the rate of 2.2 percentage points per year as against 0.74 percentage point per annum in the period 1993-94 to 2004-05. This was quite unacceptable and critics asserted that planning commission indulged in statistical jugglery to show grand success of the UPA Government in reducing poverty significantly and achieving inclusive growth.

Besides while the earlier poverty estimates were based largely on food intake of 2400 calories per person per day in rural areas and 2100 calories per person per day in urban areas it was regarded as bare subsistence and the estimates of poor people below the poverty line (BPL) on this bench mark was in no way linked with the social benefits, especially the food and other items distributed through Public Distribution System. When the approach of BPL (Below Poverty Line) *targetting* was started under which social benefits provided by the Government was linked to the people below the poverty line (BPL), the use of poverty index for this purpose was quite unwarranted. Estimates of people below poverty line was a statistical exercise to measure the extent of poverty in India and to judge the performance of planned development with regard to the reduction of overall poverty in India. It was not good and fair to be used as benchmark for distribution of social benefits provided by the Government.

For distribution of social benefits we need to *identify actual persons* who are poor and need help by the Government. Prof Jean Dreze, an eminent Professor at the Delhi School of Economics, writes, "the whole idea of *'BPL targetting'* that is, of restricting various social benefits (in particular the public distribution system) to households below the poverty line', quickly transforms poverty line from a statistical benchmark into a real life social division. The division was all the more artificial as the identification of BPL households was highly unreliable. Indeed, the Planning Commission uses one method to count the poor and the ministry of rural development uses another method to identify them. This cannot work",[5] Criticising the methodology he writes that the Tendulkar committee "further complicated the matter by claiming for the first time that poverty line ensures *adequacy of actual private expenditure on food, education and health.* The ₹ 33 per person per day (the Tendulkar poverty line for the urban areas at today's prices) is wholly insufficient for the purpose is self evident from a common sense point of view. This is all the more glaring when one looks at the break down of ₹ 32 packet which includes, for instance just about *one daily rupee for health expenditure.* Yet the experts managed to rustle up technical arguments to substantiate their startling claims".[6]

Even as the critics accused the Government and the Planning Commission of tampering with poverty figures the Planning Commission, especially its Vice Chairman, stuck to its stand that poverty declined by 15.3 per cent between 2004-05 and 2011-12, a period when Congress and UPA were in power. However, due to strong criticisim of poverty estimates, changing its stand. Montek Singh Ahluwalia conceded that *poverty line was meant to reflect conditions of absolute poverty.* This poverty line is not the poverty line we think *a "person can comfortably survive* — the poverty line is a rock bottom bare subsistence kind of line."[7]

Further, due to severe criticism levelled against the government for a planning to link the social benefits of social welfare schemes to these poverty estimates, Planning Commission clarified that

5 Jean Dreze, The Poverty Trap, *The Hindustan Times*, July 2012.

6 ₹ 32 per person per day for the urban areas was calculated by the Planning Commission as per the poverty line drawn by Tendulkar committee prices and submitted to the Supreme Court in June 2011.

7 Statement Published in the *Times of India*, March 21, 2012.

food subsidies and other entitlements would not be linked to the new poverty line. Thus, it said that "entitlements for food subsidy benefits will not be linked to the number of persons estimated to be below the official poverty line". Further, *it clarified that poverty estimates will be used only to guage the performance* of the government in combating poverty.

In our view, the fall in all India poverty ratio by 15.3 percentage points in 2011-12 compared to 2004-05 as estimated by the Planning Commission appears to be too impressive. Besides, it cannot be claimed that poverty ratio declined due to the trickle-down effect of high economic growth rate achieved during 2004-05 and 2011-12. The fall in poverty, if any, is largely because of enhanced Government expenditure on social welfare schemes such as Mahatma Gandhi National Rural Employment Guarantee Scheme (MGNREGS) which has a lot of leakages and have *not created much durable productive assets* and therefore merely represents *cash transfers.* This way of poverty reduction is not a durable solution of the poverty problem. Besides, increase in wages in rural areas in general following the introduction of MGNREGS has also caused reduction in poverty in rural areas. However, it cannot be denied that higher economic growth would have some effect on poverty reduction as under the development programmes, a lot of construction activities has been involved in which *casual labour* has been employed on daily wages.

In our view *reduction in poverty as a result of economic growth depends on the character of economic growth.* Economic growth can lead to reduction in poverty if it generates adequate opportunities of productive employment at fair wages and if gross inequalities of income decline. On the contrary, Economic Survey 2012-13 of Government of India itself admits that economic growth in India has not generated much employment in the organised sector and further it has led to a large increase in income inequalities. Further, still in 2011 it was estimated that over 40 per cent of children in India was under-nourished and malnourished despite a 8% plus average GDP growth rate achieved. Under these circumstances, how can it be said that the poverty declined due to higher growth rate alone. This clearly shows that poverty estimates for 2011-12 released by the Planning Commission in June 2013 claimed to be based on Tendulkar Committee recommendations are not correct.

The criticism of these poverty estimates inside Parliament and outside was so severe that the Government appointed another committee headed by Dr. Rangarajan to propose new norms for poverty line and prepare new estimates of poverty level in India.

Rangarajan Committee Report on Poverty, July, 2014

As explained above, the estimates of poverty by the expert committee headed by Late Prof. Suresh Tendulkar was criticised on the ground that poverty line fixed at ₹ 27 for rural areas and ₹ 33 for urban areas was too low. According to the critics, no one can even subsist at these extremely low poverty norms of Tendulkar Committee. Besides, Tendulkar committee estimated that poverty ratio declined from 37.2 per cent of population in 2004-05 to 21.9 per cent in 2011-12. In absolute terms 269 million was estimated by the committee to be living below the poverty line in 2011-12. It was claimed by UPA Government that this showed that it was higher growth rate of over 8 per cent during the period of its rule that contributed to the significant decline in poverty ratio and the number of people living below the poverty line.

The Rangarajan Committee report on poverty estimates estimated India's poor to be much more than the previous estimates by Tendulkar Committee. The Rangarajan Committee estimated that for all India the poor accounted for 29.6 per cent of population instead of 21.9 per cent of Tendulkar Committee's estimate. In absolute numbers in 2011-12, according to Rangarajan Committee, 363 million Indians of the country's 1.2 billion people were poor, that is, lived below the poverty line as against 269 million poor estimated by Tendulkar Committee, that is, Rangarajan Committee estimated *94 million more poor people than Tendulkar Committee.*

It is worth mentioning that it was found that the poverty ratio steadily declined during 2004-05 and 2011-12, no matter which methodology is adopted. Dr. Rangarajan defended his estimates of poverty that 29.5 per cent or 363 million of India's population was poor saying that the poverty numbers provided by him were not conservative or lower estimates and in fact were at par with global estimates. According to him in preparing poverty estimates the World Bank also talks about purchasing power parity terms. In calculating poverty number, the World Bank now considers, their US $2 per day whereas, according to Rangarajan, their estimates of poverty are based on US$ 2.4 in terms of purchasing power parity. *Rangarajan emphasizes that their measure of poverty in no way can be considered as a criterion of entitlement to receive benefits from any Government programme meant to help the people*. According to him, these estimates of poverty are a mere measure of understanding how the economy is moving, that is, how economic growth affecting the poor of the economy.

According to the present general perception, it matters little to the standard of living of those who are counted and classified whether they are placed by one method, propounded by one eminent economist above the poverty line or below that as per another method propounded by another eminent economist. *The fact remains that, for most Indians their quality of life as measured by how much they consume has been improving steadily*. The task of the Government is to accelerate this process. However, this is not to belittle the importance of measuring poverty, however defined. The purpose of counting and identifying the poor is to *provide benefits* such as employment, food security, education by the Government to lift them out of poverty. Thus, according to Dr. Rangarajan, estimating and identifying the poor serves a useful purpose and not a mere academic exercise. In fact, Dr. Rangarajan's definition of poverty is based on "***basic standard***" of living' *including spending on food, education, transport and house rent*.

According to the Rangarajan panel, on state-wise poverty ratios Bihar witnessed the maximum dip in poverty ratios with the fall from 63.9% in 2009-10 to 41.3% in 2011-12 – a dip of about 22 percentage points. In absolute terms, it translates into 21 million people lesser poor people in the State. The fact resulted in Bihar losing the dubious tag of having the highest poverty ratio in India. Bihar has been replaced by BJP-ruled Chhattisgarh, where the panel has categorised 47.9% of the people as being poor. In 2009-10, 53.8% of Chhattisgarh's population was categorised as poor as per Rangarajan's definition of poverty based on "*basic standard of well being*" comprising spending on food, education, transport and house rent.

The panel's estimation shows that poverty is still a huge concern in Maoist effected States even though the UPA Government had spent over ₹ 4,600 crore in 83 districts over four years starting 2010-11 under its ambitious Integrated Action Plan (IAP) for bridging development deficiency in Left Wing Extremism hit areas. Apart from Maoist hit Chattisgarh, two other affected states Odisha and Jharkhand find themselves high on the poverty ratio scale.

According to Rangarajan Committee, around 45.9% of people in Odisha were poor in 2011-12 compared to 48.3% in 2009-10. In Jharkhand, 42.4% were poor in 2011-12 compared to 52.1% in 2009-10. A member of the panel, said, the estimation clearly showed that *effective implementation of poverty alleviation programmes can result in dip in numbers*. "Bihar is a case for study on how Government programmes can reduce poverty. But in contrast the same programmes have not helped in substantially reducing poverty in other Maoist affected States where impact of these programmes are not much", "he added. Eight districts of Bihar were also covered under IAP.

It is important to note that NDA Government did not accept Dr. Rangarajan Committee report. For assistance to states it still uses poverty estimates made by Tendulkar Committee.

India's Top 5 Poorest States as per Rangarajan Committee

■ Percentage of poor population

State	Percentage of poor population
Chattisgarh	47.9%
Odisha	45.9%
Madhya Pradesh	44.3%
Jharkhand	42.4%
Bihar	41.3%

Different Strategies for Poverty Reduction

It is worth noting that there is a *significant reductun in poverty* both in rural and urban areas from 1973-74 to 2011-12 in Punjab, Haryana, Kerala, Jammu & Kashmir, Goa, Delhi, Andhra Pradesh, Gujarat, Tamil Nadu, Karnataka and West Bengal. But in different states strategies of reducing poverty has been different. Thus, Punjab and Haryana have succeeded in reducing poverty through higher agricultural growth. Kerala has focussed on human resource development for reducing poverty. West Bengal has followed the path of vigorous implementation of land reform measures and empoverment of Panchayats. Andhra Pradesh has relied on direct public intervention in the form of Public Distribution System (PDS) of foodgrams to reduce poverty.

However, various special employment schemes such as Jawahar Rozgar Yojana, Integrated Rural Development Programme (IRDP) started after mid-seventies and sponsored by Central Governments have made significant contribution to the alleviation of poverty in the country. From 2006 UPA Government started National Rural Employment Gurantee Scheme (NREGS) on a large scale to ensure employment to members of poor households and thus to alleviate poverty.

Who are the Poor in India?

The knowledge about this is necessary for designing effective anti-poverty policies. Different sections of the poor face different structural and institutional obstacles which may require different strategies for reduction of poverty.

The distribution of total poor across different socio-economic groups reveals that around 45 per cent of poor rural households in 1993-94 belonged to landless *agriculture labour.* These agricultural labour are landless or own very small farming land. Next major group of poor is "*self employed in agriculture*" which consists of small and marginal farmers and accounted for around 28 per cent of total rural poor. These self-employed in agriculture are the families who suffer from acute under-employment. "*Self-employed in non-agriculture*" accounted for around 12 per cent of the rural poor. However, in various states the relative proportions of 'agricultural labour' and self-employed in agriculture in the total poor vary depending on the available employment opportunities on the one hand and land holding system on the other. It therefore follows that access to productive assets such as land is an important determinant of poverty in a country. Therefore, as a measure for alleviation of poverty in the earlier five year plans in India emphasis was laid on the implementation of land reforms which sought to ensure some land to the landless labourers and to ensure security of tenure to the tenants. However, in the last 45 years of planned development with the exception of W. Bengal no importance has been given by the States to the implementation of land reforms.

CAUSES OF POVERTY IN INDIA

As seen above, even under-estimates of poverty as made by Tendulkar Committee show that 269 million persons or 21.9 per cent of India's population live below the poverty line in 2011-12, that is, did not have sufficient consumption expenditure to meet minimum food intake in terms of calories and 70 per cent of the poor live in the rural areas. What are the causes of this mass poverty? We explain below some important causes of poverty in India.

1. Lack of Inclusive Economic Growth. The first important reason for mass poverty prevailing in India is lack of adequate economic growth in India. In the first three decades of planned development (1951–81) in India, annual average growth in national income had been 3.6 per cent. With 2.1 per cent per annum growth in population, per capita income grew by only 1.5 per cent per annum during this period. In addition, with the increase in saving rate from about 9 per cent in 1950-1951 to 20 per cent of GDP in 1979-80, increase in per capita consumption expenditure was too small to make any significant dent on the problem of poverty. Besides, because of prevailing income inequalities per capita consumption expenditure of the poor could have hardly risen.

In the next two decades of development (1981-2000) national income increased on an average by 5.5 per cent per annum. With about 2 per cent per annum growth in population, per capita income rose by 3.5 per cent which was quite high and, as seen above, did result in some decline in poverty ratio both in the rural and urban areas. But this could not sufficiently reduce poverty because land reforms could not be implemented in agriculture and industrial growth did not generate much employment opportunities. Besides strategy of growth benefited the rich more than it helped the poor. Capital intensive and labour-displacing technology was adopted in the growing industries. As a result, unemployment and underemployment increased. Besides, due to the increase in income inequalities during this period, rise in average per capita income could not bring about significant rise in per capita income of the weaker sections of the society. Further, trickle down effect of overall economic growth was operating only to a small extent. This is manifest from the fact that employment opportunities had been increasing at a very slow pace during this period. In fact, in NSS 2011-2012, usual status rate of unemployment increased. No wonder that even in 2011-12, 269 million persons or 21.9 per cent of population lived below the poverty line.

2. Sluggish Agricultural Performance and Poverty. Many economists have pointed out that in the year of good agricultural output, poverty ratio declines. Good performance in agriculture leads to more employment opportunities and fall in prices of food grains. More employment opportunities and lower food price cause poverty ratio to decline. The experience of Punjab and Haryana shows that with agricultural growth through use of new high yielding technology (popularly called green revolution), poverty ratio can be significantly reduced. However, in various states of the country such as Odisha, Bihar, Madhya Pradesh, Assam, East Uttar Pradesh, where poverty ratio is still very high new high-yielding technology has not been adopted on a significant scale and as a result agricultural performance has not been good. As a result, poverty prevails to a larger extent in them.

Further, Indian policy makers has neglected public sector investment in agriculture, *particularly irrigation* for quite a long period since 1980-81. As a result, irrigation facilities whose availability ensures adoption of new high-yielding technology and leads to higher productivity, income and employment, are available in not more than 40 per cent of cultivable land. As a result, many parts of the country remain semi-arid and rain-fed areas where agricultural productivity, income and employment cannot be sufficient to ensure significant reduction in poverty.

3. Non-implementation of Land Reforms. Equitable access to land is an important measure of poverty reduction. Access to adequate land, a productive asset, is necessary for fuller employment of members of an agricultural household. Most of the rural poor are agricultural labourers (who are generally landless) and self-employed small farmers owning less than 2 acres of land. They are unable to find employment throughout the year. As a result, they remain unemployed and underemployed for a large number of days in a year. No wonder that these landless agricultural labourers and self-employed small farmers remain poor. Land-reforms were intended to provide them equitable access to land.

An important type of land reforms was to redistribute land through implementation of ceilings on land holdings so that poor landless labourers and small farmers should have access to adequate land for having fuller employment and enough income to meet their basic needs. Another important land reforms measure related to tenancy reforms, which were intended to protect the poor tenants from eviction of land were cultivated by them and fixation of fair rents to be charged by the landlords. Further, ultimately ownership rights over land were to be conferred on the tenants cultivating the land. With security of tenure and fair rents they would have incentives to cultivate land and adopt the new green revolution technology. In this way with the implementation of land reforms, poor agricultural labourers, small farmers and tenants were expected to rise above the poverty line. But with the exception of West Bengal, and to some extent Kerala land reforms remain unimplemented with the result the rural poverty did not decline adequately. On the other hand, in West Bengal implementation of land reforms has led to a faster decline in rural poverty.

4. Rapid Population Growth. Rapid population growth since 1951 is another important factor responsible for persisting poverty in India. Population in India has increased from 36 crores in 1951 to 102.9 crores in 2001, that is, 66 crores people had been added to the Indian population in about 50 years since independence. Population of India further increased to 121 crore in 2011, that is, 18 crore people were further added to our population in these ten years (2001 to 2011). Rapid population growth causes excessive sub-division and fragmentation of holdings. As a result, per person available land has greatly declined so that households do not have access to sufficient land to produce enough output and income for them. Further, rapid growth of population increases the *dependency ratio*, that is, an earning member has more persons to support. This causes lower per capita consumption expenditure which is not enough even to meet the basic needs.

Rapid growth in population in India since 1951 has *caused lower growth in per capita income* causing lower living standards of the people. Besides, explosive growth in population has worked to reduce rates of saving and capital formation which are crucial factors for determining growth in income and employment. Though the rate of gross saving and investment rose from about 9 per cent of GNP to about 21 per cent in 1978-79. But, it fell to 18 to 19 per cent per annum in 1980. The rate of saving and real investment (*i.e.,* capital formation) remained almost stagnant at around 22 to 23 per cent per annum during the eighties and nineties. This has especially caused low rate of real investment in agriculture. This has adversely effected the growth in irrigation facilities which are important factor in determining income and employment in the rural economy.

We thus see that rapid population growth has adversely affected growth in per capita income, saving and capital formation which are so essential for reduction in poverty.

5. Unemployment and Underemployment. The existence of unemployment and under-employment in the Indian economy is another cause of poverty in India. Unemployment prevails more among casual labour whose proportion in labour force has been increasing and in their case unemployment and poverty go together. The unemployment has been caused by rapid growth of population and labour force on the one hand and relatively low rate of capital formation and economic growth on the other. Besides, the generation of employment opportunities by the organised sector has been quite insignificant. As a result, the demographic pressure on land has been increasing resulting in unemployment, and disguised unemployment in agriculture and the informal sector. Thus has caused low productivity, low incomes and poverty. According to the latest NSS survey, 2011-12, 5.7 per cent of labour force in rural areas and 5.5 per cent of labour force in urban areas were unemployed on the daily status basis. It is worth pointing out even daily status unemployment rate does not reflect accurately the extent of unemployment in India. In a country like India where social security system does not exist, poor cannot afford to remain unemployed for long. He takes up whatever work is available no matter how low the remuneration is. In fact, the poor work very hard and even for long hours and still are unable to earn enough income to meet their basic needs.

6. Slow Growth of Employment Opportunities in the Organised Sector. In the beginning of the planning era it was thought the organised sector over a period of 20 years will generate sufficient employment opportunities for the unemployed poor. The actual experience has belied these hopes. Take, for instance, the experience of the decade (1990–2000) of economic development. It is estimated that employment in the *total organised* sector (including both public sector and private sector) increased from about 26.4 million in 1990 to about 28 million in 2000, that is, in 10 years period, the organised sector which include industrial and services sectors as well as organised agriculture could generate employment for only 1.6 million people whereas labour force increased from about 340 million in 1990 to 406 million in 2001, that is, 66 million increase. The reason for this is the *use of capital-intensive techniques* in the production processes. These techniques are intended to save labour rather than employ it. Further, relative to the size of the total Indian economy, the organised sector is of very small size so that it is wishful thinking to expect that the growth of organised sector, that is, factory type industries and services using capital-intensive technologies, generally imported from the Western countries, would be able to generate enough employment opportunities.

7. Inflation and Food Prices. Rate of inflation and level of food prices is an important factor that cause poverty. Inflation, especially rise in food prices, raises the cost of minimum consumption expenditure required to neet the basic needs. Thus, inflation especially rise in food prices pushes down many households below the poverty line. That is why, Public Distribution System has been designed to provide foodgrains and other essential items such as Kerosene oil, standard cloth, pulses at subsidised prices, that is, prices which are lower than the free market prices. However, most of Public Distribution Ration Shops are located in the urban areas. Therefore, the rural poor which constitute around 70 per cent of the total poor cannot get much benefit from the food and poverty subsidies provided by the Government.

ECONOMIC GROWTH AND POVERTY

Whether economic growth necessarily reduces poverty has been a controversial issue. As pointed out above, it was first generally believed that benefits of economic growth would trickle down to the poor and thus alleviate poverty in the economy. This trickle-down effect of economic growth was thought to operate through an increase in employment opportunities and rise in real wages as a result of increase in productivity of workers. The favourable employment effect of economic growth depends on employment elasticity of output growth. The rise in real wages was thought to occur as a result of rise in wages of workers employed in agriculture and non-agricultural sector, both organised and informal.

The agricultural growth was visualised to cause reduction in food prices and greater availability of foodgrains along with employment growth in agriculture[8]. This would ensure reduction of poverty as it would enable the poor to meet their minimum consumption requirements. Besides, in this approach it was thought that the poor will also be benefitted by the multiplier effect of economic growth. According to this, benefits of growth are reaped first by the rich and subsequently by the poor when the rich spend their incomes leading to the rise in income and employment for the poor.[9] Further, as explained by T. N. Srinivasan[10] the multiplier effect also operates through economic growth raising the revenue of the government which if invested in *public goods and services* which are relatively consumed more by the poor would reduce non-income facets of poverty such as reduction in *infant mortality rate* and rise in *life expectancy* of the poor.

Further, some Indian economists, especially Prof, Jagdish Bhagwati and Arvind Panagariya of Columbia University (USA), who is now vice chairman of Neeti Aayog, have argued that economic growth leads to the increase in revenue of the Government which can be spent on special anti-poverty schemes. This will help in reducing poverty. This direct approach to poverty alleviation has in fact been adopted by the Indian Government by starting various special employment schemes such as National Rural Employment Gurantee Scheme (MGNREGS), Prime Minister's Sarak Yojana, mid-day meals in government schools and provision of food-subsidy through Public Distribution Scheme.

The reduction in poverty in the last 10 years (*i.e.,* since 2004-05) has been mainly due to the increase in Government expenditure on special anti-poverty schemes. However, it may be noted that increase in Government expenditure might be the result of higher fiscal deficit incurred rather than due to the large revenue generated through taxation as a result of higher rate of economic growth. As Paul Streeten has observed that *trickle down effect does not happen where assets and power are concentrated*. The Government did not act like Platonic guardian but reinforced the accrual of wealth

---

8 See Montek Singh Ahluwalia, Rural Poverty and Agricultural Performance in India, *Journal of Development Studies*, 1978, 14:13 pp. 298-323.

9 N. Kakwani and E.M. Pernia, What is Pro-Poor Growth *Asian Development Review*, (2000) Vol. 18, Number 1.

10 T.N. Srinivasan, Growth and Poverty Alleviation, Lessons from Development Experience, (2000), Paper presented at the Symposium, Asian Development Bank Institute, Tokyo.

to the rich and powerful. And it was not realised that investing in the developing countries' most abundant resource, its masses of poor people could be a paying proposition. This raises two issues. First, to what extent economic growth will cause reduction in poverty largely depends on the initial conditions of asset distribution. Since main asset in developing countries is land, if it is grossly unequally distributed, the benefits of agricultural growth will mainly go to the landlords with only small benefits to the landless labour, small and marginal farmers.

In India under the economic reforms initiated in 1991 involved liberalisation, privatisation and globalisation of the Indian economy have not paid any attention to the question of asset distribution (including the distribution of surplus land held by big landlords), and to the tenancy reforms. This explains why agricultural growth in India, though low it has been since 1991, has not led to any significant reduction in rural poverty, despite claims to the contrary by the Government and the Planning Commission.

It is due to the fact that strategy of economic growth pursued by the government failed to reduce poverty significantly that it has undertaken *special employment and anti-poverty schemes* to alleviate poverty in the country. Besides, benefits of growth have not reached the poor that Government has been providing subsidies on food, sugar, kerosene oil and distributing them through public distribution system to help them. The quotation from Paul Streeten[11] given above, indicates that ***"solution to the problem of poverty lies in developing countries undertaking greater investment in the masses of poor people.*** This can happen if Government spends a significant amount of its investment expenditure on human development, that is, on promotion of education and health of the poor. *Labour is essentially the only source of income for the poor people*. Therefore, increasing the productivity of labour through providing education and health care and technical skills to them provides a sustainable means of poverty reduction. Dreze and Amartya Sen have laid great stress on instrument role of education in enabling people to seize economic opportunities created by the growth process.[12]

The best example of this is Kerala where a very high rate of literacy of about 90 per cent, has provided most successful performance in rural poverty reduction. In contrast Bihar, the weakest of the large Indian States in terms of poverty reduction is *characterised by an abysmally low literacy rate*. In an important study Datt and Ravallion have also found that *initial levels of education affect the poverty-reducing effect of economic growth.*[13]

Moreover, the impact of economic growth on poverty reduction also depends on to what extent it is accompanied by inflation. Inflation determines the purchasing power of money wages and incomes earned by the poor people. A higher rate of inflation erodes to a large extent the purchasing power of wage earners as it affects the ability of the people to meet the specified level of consumption. Given the money wages, a higher rate of inflation will send more people below the poverty line. In the unorganised labour market wages of workers are not indexed to the cost of living, the rate of inflation accompanying economic growth has an adverse effect on poverty through its effect on real wages.

Further, for economic growth to have a significant impact on poverty depends not much on its trickle down effect but whether economic growth is pro-poor or what has been recently described as '*inclusive growth*'. However, our Planning Commission considers inclusive growth merely in terms of starting some special employment or anti-poverty schemes in which not only there are a lot of leakages but also do not result in the creation of durable productive assets. If economic growth has to be pro-poor or inclusive, the strategy of growth should be such that generates a lot of employment opportunities for the poor people in agricultural, industrial and services sectors at reasonable wages

11 Paul Streeten *'Thinking About Development'* Cambridge University Press, 1965.

12 See Dreze and Amartya Sen "*India's Development and Participation*" Oxford University Press, 2002.

13 See G. Datt and M. Ravallion, *"When is Growth Pro-Poor: Evidence from the Diverse Experiences of Indian States"* Policy Research paper, World Bank, Washington DC.

that enable them to meet their basic minimum needs. Such a pro-poor or inclusive growth strategy will, as mentioned above, involves adequate public expenditure on human resource development in the fields of education and health care which benefit the poor and enable them to participate in the activities that bring about expansion in output. Therefore, Kakwani and Pernia rightly defines pro-poor growth as "*growth that enables the poor to actively participate and significantly benefit from economic activity*".[14]

However, as pointed out by Gaurav Nayyar, "*Owing to the inherent advantages enjoyed by the rich in terms of material and human capital, the growth process generally tends to benefit the rich proportionately more than the poor*". Therefore, pro-poor and inclusive growth strategy requires building up human development which depends on increase in public expenditure on education and healthcare which depends on the poor people. Besides, pro-poor growth strategy also involves institutional reforms such as land reforms in agriculture aimed at distributing surplus land of big landlords among the landless agricultural workers and marginal and small farmers and also taking effective measures to protect the tenants and sharecroppers against exploitation by landlords.

Besides, inclusive growth strategy requires the adoption of labour-intensive technologies wherever feasible so as to generate adequate employment opportunities for the poor and unemployed. For this purpose reckless mechanisation of agriculture should be discouraged and appropriate fiscal measures be taken so that in the organised industries and service sector labour displacing technologies imported from abroad and unsuited to labour-surplus conditions of the Indian economy are not used in production of goods and services. Moreover, to provide gainful employment opportunities to the poor higher priority should be given to **investment in physical infrastructure**. It has been empirically found that *development of physical infrastructure* such as roads, irrigation facilities, and power (electricity) apart from creating direct employment has a large multiplier effect on both output and employment in agricultural and non-agricultural sectors.

Conclusion. To sum up, Government in India has relied on two approaches to alleviate poverty in India. The first approach is based on the thinking that benefit of economic growth will trickle down to the poor in the long run and if higher rate of economic growth is achieved, it will result in removal of poverty. Therefore, in this approach, emphasis was laid exclusively on attaining a higher economic growth to eradicate poverty. After 1980, it was realised that it would take a very long time for economic growth, even the higher rate, to cause reduction in poverty.

Therefore, according to the second approach, in the short run until economic growth alleviates poverty significantly special anti-poverty schemes such as Mahatma Gandhi National Rural Employment Scheme (MGNRES), providing food subsidies to the poor through public distribution system should be started. Evidence gathered so far indicates that both approaches have only limited success in reduction of poverty because of a lot of leakages in the money spent on the projects, a large chunk of benefits are bagged by the middle men. In 2011-12, according to 68 the round of NSS survey 21.9 per cent of population or in absolute number 269 million people were still living below the poverty line. Even this estimate was considered to be a gross underestimate of poverty in India. Therefore, as a result of severe criticism of these estimates by members of Parliament and many academicians and experts the Indian Government appointed another expert committee to go into the question again of proper methodology of estimating poverty in India and count the extent of poverty prevailing in India. Even the '*poverty line norm*' recommended by Suresh Tendulkar Committee had been challenged. The new expert committee headed by Dr. C. Rangarajan estimated that 29.6 per cent of India's population lived below the poverty line which in absolute number was equal to 363 million people which were greater by 94 million over Tendulkar Committee estimates. Rangarajan Committee's estimates were based on new poverty norm which included spending on food, clothing, education, transport and house rent.

14 Kakwani, N and E.M. Pernia, "What is Pro-Poor Growth", *Asian Development Review*, Vol. 18 Number 11 2000.

On the basis of 2011-2012 national sample, survey, the claim of the Planning Commission, that the higher rate of economic growth of average 8.5 per cent between 2004-05 to 2011-12 resulted in the decline in poverty at the rate of 2.2 per cent per annum during this period was not trustworthy as the growth strategy pursued during this period has been pro-rich rather than pro-poor. The policy of economic reforms of liberalisation, privatisation and globalisation has no doubt generated higher economic growth but its impact on the poverty has been very little as it has benefited the rich more. *Achievement of higher economic growth is not enough, much depends on the character of economic growth regarding whether growth strategy is pro-poor or pro-rich.* The higher rate of economic growth can help in reducing poverty significantly if it is employment oriented and involves human resource development of the poor, lowers inflation, especially food inflation, institutional changes to redistribute productive assets such as implementation of land reforms in agriculture, the greater priority to building up physical infrastructure which has a large multiplier affect. Such a pro-poor growth strategy has not been pursued in India.

MEASURES TO REDUCE POVERTY

We explain below various measures which should be taken to reduce poverty in India.

1. Changing Strategy of Economic Growth. In the fifties and sixties it was generally thought that poverty in India could be significantly reduced by accelerating economic growth. According to this view, benefits of economic growth will trickle down to the poor in the form of more employment opportunities, greater productivity and higher wages. With this it was expected that the poor will be raised above the poverty line.[15]

Various growth models put forward in the fifties and sixties such as Harrod-Domar growth model, Mahalanobis growth model, Lewis' model of economic development with unlimited supplies of labour suggested rapid growth of the modern industrial sector to tackle the problem of poverty in the long sun. For this purpose they suggested for increasing the rate of capital formation so as to generate more employment opportunities and increase productivity of labour. Though this is correct that higher rate of capital formation is necessary for accelerating economic growth and thereby for solving the problem of poverty, but this will not generate sufficient employment opportunities if labour-saving capital-intensive techniques of production are used in the process of growth. This was clearly brought out by the actual experience in India in the eighties and nineties whereas in the two decades of development, rate of growth in GDP achieved was in the range of 5.5 per cent to 6 per cent per annum there had been only little increase in employment opportunities, especially in the organised industrial sector. In the last ten years (since 2004-05) the rate of growth of employment has further declined despite the achievement of average 8 per cent GDP growth per annum. Therefore, while efforts should be made to accelerate economic growth but if it has to make a significant dent on the problem of poverty, the use of capital-intensive technologies imported from the Western countries should be avoided. In fact, we should pursue labour-intensive path of economic growth. Such monetary and fiscal policies should be adopted that provide incentives for using labour-intensive techniques.

2. Agricultural Growth and Poverty Alleviation. Agricultural growth has been recognised as an important factor that contributes to marked reduction in poverty. A study made by Montek Singh Ahluwalia, former member of Planning Commission, brought out clearly that agricultural growth and poverty are inversely related; the higher agricultural growth leads to lower poverty ratio. The experience of Punjab and Haryana in the late sixties and in the seventies confirmed this inverse relation between agriculture growth and poverty. The growth in agricultural output in these states propelled by the adoption of new-high yielding technology caused a marked reduction in poverty in these states. Rural poverty ratio in Punjab and Haryana declined to 6.4 and 8.3 per cent respectively in 1999-2000.

15 See Jean Dreze, the Poverty Trap, in *Hindustan Times*, July 2011.

Therefore, other States should follow the path of Punjab and Haryana for reduction of rural poverty. Thus, Late Prof. S. Chakravarty states, "*the solution to the problem of rural poverty requires that small farmers must also be given access to land-augmenting innovations*"[16]. By land augmenting innovations he means the new high-yielding technology represented by green revolution that occurred first in Punjab and Haryana.

However, *in the recent years relationship between agricultural growth and poverty reduction seems to have weakened*. For example, at all India level, employment elasticity of growth in agricultural output has been found to be zero during 1993-94–1999-2000 whereas it was 0.45 during 1977-78–1983.[17] It appears that at the all India level employment generated by new green revolution technology has been cancelled out by increasing mechanisation of agricultural operations in various parts of a country. Thus, even in the light of the finding of zero employment elasticity of agricultural output at the all India level, positive impact of agricultural growth on the incomes of small farmers and, more particularly on the wage income of agricultural labourors, cannot be denied.

To ensure marked decline in rural poverty through agricultural growth, rate of agricultural growth should be accelerated by increasing public investment in irrigation and other infrastructure. In recent years since 1980, rate of capital formation in agriculture has been declining. This trend has to be reversed by increasing public investment in agriculture, especially irrigation. Besides, higher agricultural growth can be achieved in semi-arid and rain-fed areas by increasing public investment in infrastructure and ensuring adequate access to credit to the small farmers.

3. Speedy Development of Infrastructure. An important measure to generate employment opportunities for the poor and to raise their productivity is the speedy development of infrastructure. Since private sector is not attracted to make adequate investment in infrastructure, public investment needs to be stepped up for its development. Infrastructure development consists of building of roads, highways, ports, telecommunication, power and irrigation. They involve mainly construction work which is highly labour intensive.

Besides, the availability of infrastructure such as power and irrigation greatly raise productivity of labour. C.H. Hanumantha Rao in his study of East and South East Asian Countries finds that reduction in rural poverty in them achieved through economic growth occurred due to the fact that physical infrastructure in them were already highly developed. To quote him, "*The experience of East and South East Asian Countries shows that the impact of development on rural poverty reduction has been greatest in situations where land reforms have been implemented effectively and a high priority has been accorded to infrastructure development, agriculture and human resource development within a liberalised economic policy framework*. These facts suggest, in the first place, that in a country like India where the physical and social infrastructure is inherited from the pre-liberalisation period is not strong and redistribution of land on a significant scale is not feasible, public investment needs to be stepped up for expending physical infrastructure in the less developed areas.[18]

4. Accelerating Human Resource Development. Besides physical infrastructure development, poverty can also be reduced through human resource development. Human resource development requires greater investment in educational facilities such as schools to promote literacy, technical training institutes and vocational colleges to import skills to the people. Further, human resource development requires healthcare by public investment in Primary Health Centres, dispensaries and hospitals.

16 Sukhamoy Chakravarty, *Development Planning, The Indian Experience* (1989) OUP, Delhi, p. 88.

17 Planning Commission (2001), *Report of the Task Force on Employment.*

18 C.H. Hanumantha Rao, *Economic Reforms, Agricultural Growth and Rural Poverty,* Sukhamoy Chakravarty Memorial Lecture delivered at the 17th Annual Conference of the Indian Economic Association, Chandigarh Dec. 28-30, 1995.

These human resource development not only directly generates a good deal of employment opportunities but also raises productivity and income of the poor. People equipped with skills, education and good health can easily get wage employment or self-employment with higher productivity. In this way human resource development helps in reducing poverty. The experience of East and South-East Asian Countries, referred to above, and Kerala in our country shows that poverty can be significantly reduced through investment in human resource development. However, private sector, guided as it is by profit motive, will not adequately invest in the human resource development.

5. Growth of Non-Farm Employment. For reduction of poverty growth of non-farm employment in the rural areas is of special importance. Non-farm employment is created in marketing (*i.e.,* petty trade), transportation, handicrafts, dairying, forestry, processing of food and other agricultural products, repair workshops. A study of poverty alleviation in Haryana[19] brings out that significant reduction in rural poverty in Haryana in spite of a reduction in employment opportunities in agriculture was due to the remarkable increase in non-farm employment. Similarly, a study of Andhra Pradesh[20] also shows that poverty declined more rapidly in the districts adjoining Hyderabad city due to large increase in non-farm employment.

6. Access to Assets. Rapid growth of population after independence has led to greater subdivision and fragmentation of agricultural holdings and lack of employment opportunities in industries and other non-farm sectors has worsened the conditions of agricultural labour and self-employed small farmers. With no land or little land they cannot engage themselves in self-employment activities for earning adequate income to meet their basic needs. Redistribution of land through effective redistribution, implementation of tenancy reforms so as to ensure security of tenure and fixation of fair rent would be important measures of reducing rural poverty. Except in case of West Bengal and Kerala land reforms have not been implemented to reduce rural poverty.

However, abolition of Zamindari system is the only land reform measure which had been faithfully implemented in several parts of the country. Other land reform measures, namely, ceilings on land holdings, protection of tenants against eviction, and regulation of fair rent by the Government have remained unimplimented except in case of West Bengal and Kerala. But without land reforms, a significant dent on the problem of rural poverty cannot be made. On small farms labour employment per hectare, output per hectare and double cropping are greater as compared to those of large farmers. Tenants who enjoy no security of tenure do not invest adequately in yield-increasing inputs to raise their productivity. The effective implementation of land reforms to ensure access to land and security of tenure are therefore essential for the reduction of poverty.

But, unfortunately, the present Planning Commission and the Government do not attach much importance to these much awaited land reforms. Citing the experience of East and South East Asia in which both rate of growth and poverty reduction has been remarkable Prof. C.H. Hanumantha Rao states, "their experience shows that the impact of development on rural poverty reduction has been greatest in situation where land reforms have been implemented effectively.[21]

7. Access to Credit. Availability of credit to the poor on easy terms can create the conditions for small farmers gaining access to productive resources such as HYV seeds fertilizers, construction of minor irrigation such as wells and tubewells. This will enable the small farmers to adopt high-yielding technology to raise their productivity. The new technology is size-neutral, that is, it can be adopted equally well by small farmers. But the adoption of new technology requires financial

19 Sheila Bhalla, Development, Poverty and Policy. The Haryana Experience, *Economic and Political Weekly*, Oct. 14-21, 1995.

20 G.Parthasarthy, Public Intervention and Rural Poverty, Case of Non-sustainable Reduction in Poverty in Andhra Pradesh, *Economic and Political Weekly*, Oct. 14-21, d 1995.

21 C. H. Hanumantha Rao, *op.cit.*

resources which are lacking with the small farmers. Besides, the non-farmer poor need credit for marketing, food processing, dairying, forestry, development of handicrafts which can provide them gainful employment. Important changes have been introduced in the credit delivery system in India. Expansion of network of rural branches of commercial banks after nationalisation and fixation of limits for compulsory lending to the priority sectors (which include agriculture, small-scale industries) and fixation of lower interest rates to be charged from the poor farmers and artisans some progress has been made in this regard.

However, banks and other financial institutions have not shown adequate response to provide adequate credit to them as they *consider the poor to be non-creditworthy.* Unless the banks and other financial institutions change their attitude toward supplying credit to the poor much success cannot be achieved to ensure adequate credit to the poor farmers and artisans. What they do need is short-term loan for working capital such as for purchasing raw materials, fertilizers, pesticides.

An important step in credit delivery system for the poor has been setting up of regional rural banks (RRB). Regional rural banks are primarily meant to meet the credit needs of the poor. The government should take effective steps to improve the functioning of these financial institutions so as to ensure availability of adequate credit to the poor.

8. Public Distribution System (PDS). Poor households spend nearly 80 per cent of their income on food. Therefore, an effective way of raising rural incomes and ensuring food security to the poor households is an assured supply of adequate quantity of foodgrains and other essential commodities at subsidised prices, that is, at prices which are lower than the market prices. A properly functioning public distribution system which is targeted to the poor households is an important element of the strategy for poverty reduction. The Central Government Organisation 'Food Corporation of India' procures the foodgrains from the farmers at the minimum support prices (MSP) and store them in their warehouses located throughout the country. The foodgrains so procured are allotted to the State Governments to be sold through the public distribution systems (*i.e.,* ration shops) at subsidised prices which are below market prices. The difference between the two prices is paid by the Central Government as subsidy. The expenditure on food subsidy has greatly increased in recent years. The ratio of release of foodgrains through PDS to total foodgrains production is around 10 to 13 per cent. Some economists have suggested lowering of subsidies. What is needed is to ensure subsidised foodgrains supply through PDS be made only to the targeted group of households living below the poverty line and not to all households. In this way the expenditure on food subsidy can be reduced significantly and only the poor will get the benefits of the subsidy. It is worth mentioning that Andhra Pradesh is a shinning example of using PDS to help the poor under ₹ 2 per kilogram of rice supplied through ration shops.

9. Direct Attack on Poverty: Special Employment Schemes for the Poor. It was realised in the early seventies that it would take a very long time for economic growth to generate enough employment opportunities to provide productive employment to all the unemployed and poor in the country. Therefore, a strategy of providing employment to the poor in the short run, special schemes of employing poor on rural public works was proposed by Dandekar and Rath in their now famous work "*Poverty in India*".

The special employment scheme of rural public works which was launched by the Government in 5th Five Year Plan constitutes a direct attack on poverty as it does not depend on the trickle-down effect of economic growth on the poor. There are mainly two types of such special anti-poverty schemes launched by the Government from time to time. First, there are several special schemes of providing *wage employment to the poor.* These include Mahatma Gandhi National Rural Employment Guarantee Scheme (MGNREGS) and Pradhan Mantri Sarak Yojna. It is centrally sponsored special employment scheme implemented by Gram Panchayats to generate wage employment for the rural poor. The approach of this scheme is to employ the poor on building *durable and productive community assets* such as roads, small irrigation facilities, school buildings, rural electrification. These durable productive assets after completion would create employment opportunities on sustained basis.

The second special employment scheme has been IRDP (*Integrated Rural Development Scheme*) under which self-employment of rural people is promoted by building their capacity in such activities as dairying, poultry, handicrafts, forestry. Financial assistance to them is arranged through banks for this purpose. Similarly, a third such special employment scheme is TRYSEM (*Training of Rural Youth for Self-Employment*) under which rural youth are given training and equipped with skills so that they can start some self-employment activity. Bank credit is arranged to financially support them.

With effect from April 1999, IRDP and TRYSEM schemes along with the schemes of *Development of Women and Children in Rural Areas* (*DWCRA*) and *Million Wells Scheme* (*MWS*) have been merged into a single scheme called *Swaran Jayanti Gram Swarozgar Yojana* (SGSY) which aim at promoting micro-enterprises by helping the poor to form *self-help groups* with the assistance from the Centre and States. If implemented in a right spirit, these schemes can make useful contribution to poverty reduction in the rural areas. However, the actual performance of these schemes has not been satisfactory. While a large amount of money is spent by the Government on payment of wages, durable productive assets to be used for future use are not generally created. Similarly, schemes for self-employment such as IRDP, TRYSEM are merely used to get loans from the banks and financial assistance from the States. They are not generally used for investment for viable schemes of productive self employment. This highlights the need for making reforms in these schemes so that they lead to the expansion of productive types of wage-employment and self-employment.

Chapter 68

Disguised Unemployment and Capital Formation in Developing Countries

The standard explanation for the existence of labour surplus or unemployment and underemployment in less developed countries like India is that as compared with the magnitude of population and labour force there is limited availability of capital which includes factories machines, tools and implements and also land–the means with which labour produces. Now, if the population grows faster than the stock of capital of a country, the entire addition to the labour force cannot be absorbed in productive employment, because not enough instruments of production will be there to employ them. Since in less developed countries, the stock of capital has not been growing fast enough to keep pace with the growth of population, the ability to offer productive employment is very limited. This has resulted in surplus labour, which as stated above, is manifested in the existence of huge magnitude of underemployment or disguised unemployment in agriculture and open unemployment in both the rural and urban areas. It is the low rate of saving and investment that has been responsible for the low rate of capital accumulation. In India before independence the rate of investment was around 5 per cent of national income.

The crux of the problem of economic development is to raise the rate of capital formation. In the preceding chapter we have discussed various measures to accelerate capital formation in developing economies. In the fifties an unorthodox method of financing capital formation was suggested by Ragnar Nurkse[1] of America and Professors Vakil and Brahmananda[2] of India. According to them, mass disguised unemployment existing in underdeveloped countries contains an important saving potential for capital formation. It can be mobilised and utilised to further economic development in the underdeveloped economies. Labour is said to be a great source of wealth and therefore the huge surplus labour represented by the disguised unemployed can be mobilised to create capital. In the present chapter we discuss the theory of saving potential of disguised unemployment with special reference to that of Nurkse. We shall describe at first what is precisely meant by disguised unemployment.

THE CONCEPT OF DISGUISED UNEMPLOYMENT

At the theoretical level, the existence of disguised unemployment in the case of overpopulated countries such as India has been hotly debated. However, Professor Ragnar Nurkse, Arthur Lewis, Gustav Ranis and John C.H. Fei, P.N. Rosenstein Rodan, Vakil-Brahmananda, Amartya Sen and many others are firmly of the view that in the densely populated countries such as India, Pakistan, Egypt

1 Ragnar Nurkse, *Problems of Capital Formation in Underdeveloped Countries*, Basil Blackwell, 1953.
2 C.N. Vakil and P.R. Brahmananda, *Planning in an Expanding Economy*, Vora & Co., Bombay 1956.

and Bangladesh, disguised unemployment in agriculture exists on a large scale. Some definitions of disguised unemployment are worth mentioning. Ragnar Nurkse defines the disguised unemployment in the following way: "These countries suffer from large-scale disguised unemployment in the sense that even *with the unchanged techniques* of agriculture, a large part of the population engaged in agriculture could be removed without reducing agricultural output. That is the definition of the concept of disguised unemployment as applied to *the situation with which we are concerned.* The same farm output could be obtained with a smaller labour force ... In technical terms, the marginal productivity of labour is zero."[3] Professor Rosenstein Rodan describing the disguised unemployment as the "basic concept which has a clear and unequivocal meaning" defines it as *"that amount of population in agriculture which can be removed from it without any change in the method of cultivation, without leading to any reduction in output"*.

From the above definitions of disguised unemployment, it is clear that its removal or withdrawal involves *ceteris paribus* condition. Thus, changes in the production techniques are especially ruled out. In estimating disguised unemployment, to quote Nurkse again, "We exclude technological advance, more equipment, mechanisation, better seeds, improvements in drainage, irrigation and other such conditions". It may, however, be noted that the concept of disguised unemployment does admit *changes in organisation of production and work* (as distinguished from *the changes in technology and the amount of capital equipment and other cooperating factors*) when some workers are withdrawn from agriculture. To quote Nurkse again, "One thing, " however, one needs not and probably cannot exclude and that is better organisation. If surplus labour is withdrawn from the land, the remaining people will not go on working in quite the same way. We may have to allow for changes in the manner and organisation of work including possibly a consolidation of scattered strips and plots of land.[4]

Another worth noting point about disguised unemployment is that *it is applicable to self-employed farmers of extended family system and does not apply to the wage employment which usually takes place on the large sized capitalist farms*. Thus, the U.N. group of experts writes "the significance of the term 'disguised' is that it is applied only to persons who are not normally engaged in wage employment, but are self-employed". They further write: "The term is not applied to wage labour; presumably employers will not employ a labourer for wages unless his labour increases the product."[5]

Prof. Amartya Sen's Analysis of Disguised Unemployment

Though the concept of disguised unemployment visualises production aspect of unemployment, it mainly manifests itself in idleness, that is, time not worked. In other words, disguised unemployment appears in the form of reduction in the hours worked in a day or a week and days in a week, or a month or year. As long as more work opportunities are available on the family farms, the additional labour is employed for that and as a result total output increases, though at a diminishing rate. When all the work opportunities on the farm are exhausted, no more addition to labour input will bring about increase in output. When the size of the families continues to increase due to the rapid growth of population and when alternative employment opportunities outside their families are not available, the additional members have to 'be absorbed on the family farms. Since on the family farms a point reaches beyond which no increase in labour input leads to the rise in total output, *additional workers are absorbed by sharing of the work among more workers rather than by increasing the quantum of labour input employed on the farms*. In other words, the same quantity of labour is now applied by more workers. As a result, the number of working hours performed by all labourers in a day, or week and days in a month or year are reduced.

Distinction between Marginal Productivity of Labourers and Marginal Productivity of Labour. In explaining the concept of disguised unemployment, Amartya Sen drawn the distinction between marginal product of *labourers* and marginal product of *labour*. He explain that it is the

3 R. Nurkse, *Problems of Capital Formation in Underdeveloped Countries*, p. 32.
4 *Op. cit.*, p. 33.
5 R. Nurkse, *op. cit.*

marginal productivity of labourers over a wide range which is zero and not the marginal productivity of Labour (*i.e.*, labour input) over a wide range of labour used. In fact, *marginal productivity of labour is just equal to zero at the margin.* Therefore, the distinction drawn between *Labour and Labourers* by Prof. Amartya Sen is significant since it helps in understanding the nature of disguised unemployment and the form in which it appears as well as in removing the apparent contradiction between the disguised unemployment and rational behaviour. Thus, Prof. Amartya Sen writes:

"This confusion arises because of not distinguishing between *Labour* and *Labourer*. *It is not that too much labour is being spent in the production process, but that too many labourers are spending it. Disguised unemployment thus normally takes the form of a smaller number of working hours per head per year*; for example, each of three brothers shepherding the sheep every third day. It is thus, the marginal productivity of the labourer, so to say, that is nil *over a wide range* and the productivity of labour may be just equal to zero at the margin. It may also take the *form of lower intensity of work with people 'taking it easy'*, *e.g.*, the peasant having time to watch the birds while working. If a number of labourers went away, the others would be able to produce about the same output working *longer and harder*. There is no contradiction between disguised unemployment and rational behaviour".[6] He further writes "In a family based peasant economy unemployment will naturally put on this disguise. A piece of land that can be cultivated fully by two, may actually be looked after by four, if a family of four working men having no other employment opportunity happens to own it."[7]

As is evident from Professor Sen's quotations given above, the disguised unemployment appears not only in the form of idle man hours (that is, all workers work for lesser hours of work than those considered standard or normal and remain idle for the rest) but also in the reduced intensity of work-hours performed. In other words, the disguised unemployment also creeps into work hours performed by labourers. This happens through what has been called *work-spreading* or *work-stretching devices*.

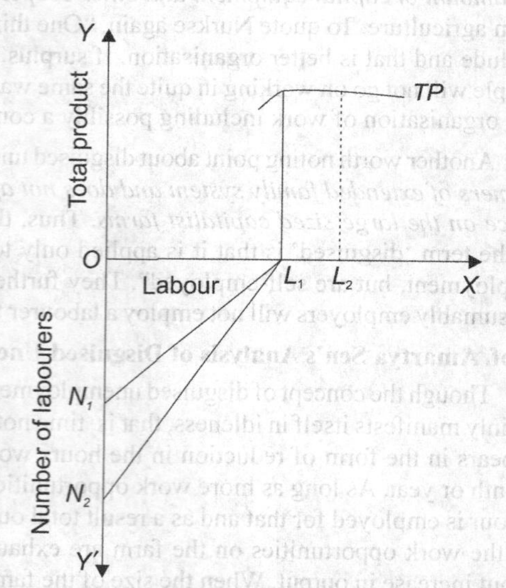

Fig. 68.1. *The emergence of disguised unemployment*

It is worth noting that not all sizes of farms suffer from disguised unemployment. As said above, large-sized farms generally use hired labour (or are cultivated through tenancy system) and granting that landlords of those farms operate on the principle of profit maximisation, no disguised unemployment will exist on those farms. As the size of the farms goes on declining, man-land ratio on them will be increasing. As the man-land ratio rises with the decrease in the size of farms, the average and marginal products of the labourers will diminish due to the operation of diminishing returns. Since a certain minimum ratio of land to labour is required even in the most labour-intensive agricultural processes, a point will reach when the further reduction in the size of the farm and consequently further increase in the man-land ratio will result in zero marginal product of labour.

Graphic Illustration of Sen's Concept of Disguised Unemployment. Let us graphically explain the concept of disguised unemployment as has been clarified by Prof. Amartya Sen. Consider Fig. 68.1 where along the *Y-axis* total output is measured and along the *X-axis*, labour (say labour hours) is

6 Amartya Sen, *Choice of Techniques*, Basil Blackwell, 1957.
7 2. *Ibid.*

measured. *TP* represents total product curve which in the beginning rises and after a point it becomes horizontal indicating thereby that total output remains constant after OL_1 amount of labour is used. Now, according to Amartya Sen, it will be irrational on the part of the family to put in more labour on the farm beyond OL_I since extra labour spent beyond OL_I does not add to total output. Thus, if the family goes beyond OL_1 and devotes OL_2 labour, then L_1L_2 labour input has been unnecessarily spent, for it has not brought any increment in output. Marginal product of labour is zero when OL_1 amount of labour is put in. Therefore, a rational family will put in OL_1 amount of labour.

But, according to Prof. Amartya Sen, the disguised unemployment occurs due to the fact that a given amount of labour is spent by too many labourers. Consider Fig. 68.1 again. Along the south, number of labourers are measured. Suppose in the beginning OL_1 amount of labour is being put in by ON_1 labourers who are working normal hours in a week. If now the size of the family expands and the *number of labourers* increases from ON_1 to ON_2 amount of land, other factors and technique of production remaining the same. As stated above, it will be futile and irrational to put in more labour beyond OL_1 even though the number of labourers in the family has increased. If the additional labourers do not get employment outside the family farm, the reaction of the family will be that the same amount of labour OL_1 be shared by ON_2 labourers. As a result, the number of work hours devoted by each labourer will be reduced. The total output; will not increase since the same amount of labour OL_1 is being put in. It follows therefore that the increase in the number of labourers from ON_1 to ON_2 has not resulted in any increment in total output; only the same amount of labour is being shared by ON_2 instead of ON_1. *Thus number of labourers N_1N_2 represents disguised unemployment since marginal productivity of a labourer over this range is zero*. Now if N_1N_2 labourers are withdrawn from the agricultural family, total output will not decline. With the withdrawal of N_1N_2 workers, the remaining workers will put in OL_1 labour so that each of them will work for normal hours.

The magnitude of disguised unemployment has been increasing in underdeveloped countries since the rate of capital accumulation has not, kept pace with the rapid growth of population. It has been estimated that 15 to 30 per cent of agricultural labour force is disguisedly unemployed in underdeveloped countries. This type of unemployment can be relieved by the development of non-agricultural sectors and by increasing the rate of capital formation that will open new avenues of employment. But the economies of such over-populated agricultural countries remained generally stagnant for a long time and economic development was too slow to absorb surplus farm labour. All this led to the emergence of the phenomenon of continuously mounting pressure of disguised unemployment. The increasing pressure of population has caused subdivision and fragmentation of holdings with all their attendant evils. The farm income has been going down in every generation. Low consumption of the unemployed presses has brought down the level of economic activity. Surplus available for investment is meagre. Thus mass disguised unemployment is a drag on economic progress. The problem can be solved only by stepping up the rate of investment above the rate of population growth. The central problem of economic growth in such countries is thus to create conditions under which rate of investment can be increased above that of growth of population.

DISGUISED UNEMPLOYMENT AND SAVING POTENTIAL FOR CAPITAL FORMATION

Nurkse regard disguised unemployment as saving potential. We have seen above that in the backward, overpopulated and predominantly agricultural countries there is mass unemployment; but it is disguised or hidden unemployment. The people live in joint families where a couple of earning members support a number of totally idle or partly employed members who are also ostensibly working. It is impossible to separate the employed from the unemployed and label the unemployed as such. That is why they are called *disguised unemployed.*

A little reflection will show that if unemployment is hidden, it is also a hidden source of potential saving which can be tapped for capital formation or investment purposes. What do we find in a state of disguised unemployment? Some productive workers support and feed some unproductive or idle workers. This they are able to do by consuming less themselves than they produce. They produce more than they consume and out of this surplus they continue feeding other members of the family, may be for years. Here are clearly a surplus funds which are available for capital formation if necessary steps in this direction are taken.

A new theory of relationship between consumption and investment emerges. The classical economists said it was necessary to consume less if capital was to be accumulated. Keynes said that both consumption and investment could increase at the same time. But the theory of saving potential in disguised unemployment says that capital formation is possible even if consumption is maintained at the present level: only the productive workers should not increase their consumption when the unproductive workers are taken off their lands. *"This is a compromise between classical notion of investment and consumption as inevitable alternatives and Keynesian idea of investment and consumption as possible complements"*.[8] This indicates a fundamental condition of capital formation in countries of mass disguised unemployment. The surplus or idle labour can be withdrawn without decreasing the total output. At present this idle labour is being fed in the family. When they are withdrawn and put to other jobs, clearly a consumable surplus will emerge which can be utilised for investment purposes. But it is very necessary that the productive workers should maintain their consumption at their original level and not swallow up the consumable surplus themselves.

The subsistence fund or consumable surplus made available by the productive workers can be utilised for financing other projects if the concealed saving potential is mobilised 100%, *i.e.*, if there are no leakages. Only in this way can capital formation through the use of surplus labour be self-financing. Now, what are the possible leakages? One leakage which we have already indicated is that as soon as the surplus labour is withdrawn the productive workers may raise their own consumption and the consumable surplus may disappear to that extent. The second possibility is that the formerly idle labour when put to productive jobs may increase their consumption so that the surplus food which they consumed before does not prove sufficient. These leakages must stop if the saving potential is to be successfully mobilised for purposes of capital formation or investment. It should be clearly understood that the food previously consumed by the disguised unemployed cannot be automatically released for feeding the productive workers engaged elsewhere. The farmers live very close to the subsistence level and they will not voluntarily save the surplus. Some coercive measures will have to be taken to prevent then from consuming the surplus. Taxing the things they buy, increase in rent, rationing and compulsory procurement are some such measures. The collective farms in Russia served an instrument of collection of the surplus.

It may be that with the best of intentions and effort it is not possible to plug all loopholes and stop leakages. In that case we shall have to look to some other supplementary or what is known as complementary saving. Saving may be done by other sector, say in urban areas, so that the idle workers when employed on capital projects like road building, draining, flood control, tool making, irrigation schemes, railways, houses and factories, may be fed partly by the savings of the rural people and partly by those of urban people. This is altogether a domestic source. But in case this is not sufficient food deficit can be met by imports from abroad. Some non-essential imports will have to be cut and or exports stepped up. Foreign grants or loans may be arranged. But external funds must not be used for increasing consumption; they must be used exclusively for productive purposes. The funds obtained from outside can exercise a multiplier or magnifying effect on the rate of capital formation because with their help it becomes possible to mobilise manifold saving potential associated with disguised unemployment.

Now let us understand in what pratical manner the saving potential in the disguised unemployment can be mobilised for capital formation. In other words, how can this surplus manpower be used for

8. R. Nurkse, *op. cit*

purposes of economic development and what problems will arise in this connection? There are two ways of utilising this surplus labour. One is to put this labour on some productive public projects in the locality in the rural areas such as construction of roads, irrigation tanks and canals, anti-flood works, anti-soil erosion works, etc. so that they continue to live in the family and be fed there as before. This is the simplest way and no problem arises. The hitherto unproductive workers now make a net addition to the nation's stock of capital. In the community development projects voluntary local labour is being utilised in this fashion. If these workers need some technical training, the process can start with a training course. Labour to be employed efficiently has to be supplied with some tools and machines. The projects first selected should be such as can be executed with the help of indigenous tools and equipment.

But difficulties arise when the surplus labour has to work away from homes in distant industrial centres. The productive members of the family cannot now be expected to feed the members who have been withdrawn. The surplus labour will now have to be paid a money wage and care will have to be taken to mobilise the consumable surplus. To sustain tempo of economic development wage rates may have to be kept low enforcing a sort of compulsory saving. Some system of deferred payments may have to be adopted. As we have already explained, measures will have to be taken on the other hand to see that the consumable surplus is not eaten up by increased consumption. Some element of compulsion will be required for achieving the objectives of economic development. In this respect socialist and totalitarian countries are better placed than free democratic societies.

Critical Evaluation of Disguised Unemployment as a Source of Capital Formation

The view put forward by Nurkse of the possibility of using disguised unemployment seems to be plausible and theoretically possible. But let us see how far it is practically feasible. As we have already said, the transfer of surplus labour can result in capital formation only if the level of consumption is prevented from rising and if the transfer does not cost much and transferred labour can be put on suitable jobs and are provided with suitable equipment without increasing much cost. This indeed is a very big 'IF'. Hence, the proposal to make use of surplus labour for capital formation suffers from serious limitations and there can be several leakages. That is why many economists do not subscribe to Nurkse's thesis. They admit that there is surplus labour in agriculture in the form of disguised unemployment. But owing to several difficulties they do not agree that its saving potential can be actually realised.

1. It is very likely that the consumption level of the labour left behind as well as of the labour transferred rises to nullify the saving potential. Since the consumption level is already very low, the agricultural output may fall when some labour is withdrawn unless consumption level is raised. Also, when surplus labour migrates from the rural to urban areas where the level of consumption is higher and the wages are higher too, the propensity to consume of the transferred labour is bound to go up. They will tend to consume more because they have now to put in more work. The workers who have been left behind in agriculture and whose dependents are now gone, will feel a little better off and will have more to eat. They will, therefore, be tempted to raise their level of consumption, when they have now more to eat. They must also consume more because they have now to work more to maintain the old level of output, since the number of workers has been reduced on account of transfer of some of their co-workers.

Thus, we see that when some labour is transferred from agriculture to other productive employment, the level of consumption of those who have been left behind and of those who are transferred, has a strong tendency to go up. The rise in consumption of the workers concerned will eat up the saving potential of disguised unemployment. In fact, the leakage in the savings potential will be substantial.

2. Another leakage will arise on account of the cost of transport. Costs will have to be incurred in transporting labour from villages to urban areas or to the sites of construction works started for

the purpose of absorbing surplus agricultural labour. There will be costs involved too in transporting food to feed the surplus labour that has been transferred to new areas. These costs of transport must be set off against the saving expected from the transfer of surplus labour from agriculture.

3. There are some other costs too which the scheme will involve. Obviously, labour cannot be dislodged from their native places and taken to other areas unless higher wages are offered. This will increase the cost of the investment works undertaken in this connection. Capital equipment will have to be supplied to the labour transferred to new projects. There will be additional administrative burden. Competent personnel will have to be engaged to supervise and organise the work. These costs may add up to a much higher figure than it is assumed and may substantially cut down the saving potential of disguised unemployment.

4. Besides, there is the difficulty of choosing suitable jobs for the transferred labour and to plant them in a convenient location. It may not be possible to start development projects in the vicinity of the village from which the workers are sought to be transferred. Further, these people have no training and can do only unskilled labour. They are tied to native place by a sentimental attachment. Unless the place of work is congenial and the working conditions are congenial, the transfer of labour may provoke adverse reaction. They may, in fact, return to their native place.

5. *Further, it is most likely that the type of people who are transferred from the villages are backward and poor. Hence, the amount of wage goods so released may not be very signification level. To extract surplus from poor families in which disguised unemployment prevails is not only difficult but unfair also. Consequently, the savings so made may not be substantial and worthwhile.*

6. Another difficulty relates to the procurement of foodgrains from the farming population left behind in agriculture and making it available to the transferred labour in their new places of work. Will the Government collect it by means of a tax or through procurement at fixed price or will it require the transferred labour to purchase it in the free market with the cash wages paid to them? It is very difficult to procure foodgrain and to arrange its distribution among the transferred labour. The Government will be powerless to collect such large quantities of foodgrains by means of a tax. If it is compulsorily procured at fixed prices, payment in cash will have to be made to the farmers and they will spend it on the purchase of the commodities. This means that the output of industrial consumer goods will have to be expanded.

In this way, consumption will increase which Nurkse's doctrine assumes to be kept at the previous level. If the distribution of foodgrains is left to the free market forces, the prices of foodgrains will be pushed up in the country and an inflationary situation will be created. The reason is that the consumption level of the transferred labour will go up and so also of the farmers left behind. On the one hand, the marketable surplus will be reduced and on the other the consumption of transferred labour will go up and the prices will rise. Thus, we see that the saving potential for capital formation in disguised unemployment is reduced and the possibility of price rise is increased which will impede economic growth in the country.

This doctrine may well work in communist countries like U.S.S.R. and China where the governments can compulsorily procure foodgrains from the farming population without paying any price and use it for feeding the transferred labour. The government there can also compel the people to keep their consumption at the old level. But such things are simply out of question in a democratic country like India. Hence, saving potential in disguised unemployment does not exist which be used for capital formation. It is true that people in India were persuaded to give their free labour for the community under the leadership of Acharya Vinoba Bhave but its impact was negligible. Also, under the community development programme in India people had been asked to give their free labour for the construction of roads, school buildings, construction of hospitals, minor irrigation works, etc. But this also made only a limited contribution to capital formation.

Thus, there are several difficulties in democratic countries like India in using saving potential of disguised unemployment for capital formation. Although it is admitted that there is a large-scale disguised unemployment in agriculture but its saving potential for capital formation is denied.

7. There is another formidable difficulty of identifying the disguised unemployed labour in agriculture. Who is going to pick and choose to transfer this labour elsewhere, the State or the farming families or such workers will themselves opt out? In actual practice, it will be found that the task is not only difficult but impossible. Agricultural operations provide work for all young and old and even children. Some persons are fully occupied some time and some others at other times. It is very difficult to lay finger on those workers whose marginal productivity is zero because calculation of marginal productivity itself is too difficult a task to be undertaken.

Conclusion

The difficulties mentioned above are quite real and the doctrine of surplus labour as a potential source for capital formation as propounded by Nurkse suffers from serious limitations. But the phenomenon of disguised unemployment in the labour surplus developing countries cannot be denied. It does not constitute a potential source of capital formation without putting undue strain on the economy. The developing countries, which suffer from capital deficiency but disguised unemployment does not contain saving potential for capital formation.

Solution of the Problem of Disguised Unemployment

In the underdeveloped countries, there is disguised unemployment not only in the agricultural sector, but there is also large-scale unemployment in the urban areas. In agriculture, unemployment is hidden and disguised but in the urban area it is open and visible. Now, the question is whether employment should be provided to those who are totally unemployed or to the partially employed or disguisedly unemployed people.

While there is not much scope of saving potential in disguised unemployment, the best thing would be to create employment opportunities for people who have no jobs. The wise course seems to be first to put the openly unemployed persons on the jobs and then solve the problem of disguised unemployment. Our view is that the best method of removing disguised unemployment is to increase employment opportunities and increase agricultural productivity through agricultural development. Employment and agricultural productivity can be raised by the use of modern agricultural inputs like high-yielding varieties of seeds, fertilizers in optimum, doses, pesticides and increase in irrigation facilities. With this new employment opportunities will be available in agriculture. For instance, more labour is required in a system of *multiple cropping*. If this system is extensively adopted, employment will certainly increase and disguised unemployment will decrease.

In this way, the problem of disguised unemployment or underemployment can be solved by raising agricultural productivity or by agricultural development. Since in disguised unemployment some workers do not get enough work to do and their removal will not reduce output, their marginal productivity is zero. But when there is a green revolution, as a result of which agricultural productivity goes up and more new employment opportunities become available, the problem of disguised unemployment will be automatically solved. Thus, we see that to remove disguised unemployment it is not necessary to withdraw those workers from agriculture whose marginal productivity is zero. But we should raise their marginal productivity in that very sector by improving agricultural productivity. This would solve their problem and there will be no difficulties that are faced in withdrawing the disguised unemployed labour and putting them to productive work elsewhere.

Chapter 69

Employment, Unemployment and Economic Growth

Unemployment in Developing Countries: Causes and Nature

Most of the unemployment in underdeveloped countries is of a different nature from that in advanced and developed countries. A major part of unemployment in developed countries is of cyclical nature which is due to *deficiency of aggregate effective demand.* But most of the unemployment in underdeveloped countries is not cyclical. Instead, it is a long-term problem. The major cause of unemployment and underemployment in developing countries like India is *the deficiency of the stock of capital* in relation to the needs of the growing labour force.

In the modern world, man by himself can hardly produce anything. Even the primitive man needed some elementary tools like bow and the arrow to engage in hunting for the earning of his livelihood. With the growth of technology and specialisation, he needs much more capital with which to engage him in the productive activity. If he is an agriculturist he needs not only a piece of land but also a plough, a pair of oxen, seeds and some foodgrains and other necessities of life to sustain himself during the period of sowing to the reaping of the harvest. In the industrial sector, he needs factories to work in and machines to work with. All these aids to production belong to the community's stock of capital. Now, if the working force grows faster than the stock of capital of a country, the entire addition of labour force cannot be absorbed in productive employment—because not enough instruments of production would be there to employ them. The resulting unemployment is known as the *long-term or chronic unemployment.*

A nation's stock of capital can be enlarged by increased investment which, in the absence of any unutilised resources, requires additional savings on the part of the community. The concern of the classical economists was to ensure that the rate of capital formation was kept sufficiently high so that employment opportunities were successively enlarged to absorb the additions to the working force of a country as a result of population growth. This is also the problem that developing countries like India are facing today. In recent years (between 1999-2000 and 2011-2012), the labour force in India has been growing at an annual rate of 2.2 per cent but our *rate of investment expressed as a percentage of our stock of capital* has not been growing fast enough rate to keep pace with the growth of population and therefore the country's ability to offer productive employment to the new entrants in the labour market has been severely limited. This manifests itself in two things—first, the prevalence of large-scale open unemployment in the urban areas as evidenced by the statistics of employment exchanges; second, it manifests itself in the form of open unemployment as well as disguised unemployment in agriculture.

It is a common knowledge that with minor changes in organisation and with the existing techniques, our agriculture can be looked after by a much smaller number of workers and they can be withdrawn from agriculture without reduction of agricultural output if alternative employment opportunities were available. Since employment opportunities in the formal non-agricultural sector have not been growing rapidly, the new entrants to the workforce are compelled to remain in agriculture on self-employment basis which perpetuates the phenomenon of *disguised unemployment* which means that people are engaged in occupations where their marginal productivity is very low (if not zero or negative) and that a shift to alternative occupations will increase their marginal productivity and add to national income of the country.

MEASUREMENT OF SURPLUS LABOUR OR UNEMPLOYMENT IN DEVELOPING COUNTRIES

The surplus labour in a developing economy such as ours manifests itself in (*a*) open unemployment, (*b*) underemployment and (*c*) disguised unemployment. Therefore, a realistic assessment of the magnitude of surplus labour that exists in the Indian economy should contain information about all these three forms of unemployment. However, the measurement of unemployment in an economy such as ours where self-employment is predominant and the bulk of productive activity is carried on within household enterprises is a difficult task. A slight difference in the definitions and criteria adopted to measure unemployment often makes enormous change in its magnitude. For example, late Professor Raj Krishna suggested the following four criteria to measure unemployment:

(*a*) *Time Criterion*: This refers to identifying those persons as unemployed who have no gainful work for less than some normal standard hours in a week or less than a certain normal standard days in a month or a year.

(*b*) *Willingness Criterion*: This calls a person unemployed when he is either seeking or is available for work at the prevailing wage rate.

(*c*) *Income Criterion*: This considers those persons unemployed or underemployed who have income (or expenditure) less than a certain '*poverty norm*' generally fixed on the basis of minimum calories required for subsistence.

(*d*) *Productivity Criterion*: This considers those persons as unemployed or underemployed who may be working but they have less than some normal standard of productivity.[1]

Thus, a change from time and willingness criteria to productivity criterion changes the estimate of rural unemployment for the year 1972-73 from 8.21 per cent of rural labour force (on daily status basis) to 33.7 per cent.[2]

Note that both willingness and time criteria have been used in India in the various rounds of National Sample Survey,[3] to measure unemployment in the economy. Productivity criterion has been used by Ashok Mathur, Shakuntala Mehra, Ashok Rudra and Amartya Sen to measure the extent of disguised unemployment in the Indian agriculture. Further, using household expenditure data from earlier rounds of NSS, Dandekar-Rath in their study of "*Poverty in India*" adopted income criterion to measure the magnitude of unemployment in the Indian economy.

Unemployment and Poverty Distinguished

However, it may be noted that the income criterion or poverty norm to measure unemployment suffers from several weaknesses. Poverty and unemployment are two different concepts. Many

1 Likewise, Prof. Amartya Sen has distinguished between *income aspect, production aspect* and *recognition aspect* of employment and defined unemployment accordingly. While his concept of unemployment based on 'production aspect' is the same as productivity criterion, his recognition concept of unemployment differs from "willingness criterion" only in that he calls all those persons as unemployed who are seeking work regardless of whether or not they already have some job. His income concept of unemployment, however, conceptually differs from the 'income criterion' in that it is "*concerned with that part of one's income which is received on condition that one works*" rather than earning of minimum income required for subsistence.

2 33.7 per cent of labour force is Sen's estimate of rural unemployment for the year 1972-73 on the basis of his productivity criterion.

3 See CSO, *National Sample Survey, 32nd round* (1977-78), Report No. 298, p. 20.

unemployed persons are poor, however, all poor persons are not unemployed. These poor persons who are not unemployed are engaged *in self-employment activities* with low earnings and low productivity. All poor persons are not unemployed and many employed persons are poor. Therefore, poverty should be distinguished from unemployment because of the following factors:

1. Unemployment and poverty are two different concepts and therefore it is not proper to consider the poor as unemployed or vice versa. Indeed, unemployment prevails even among members of the households with per capita expenditure well above the poverty line.
2. As has been pointed out by late Prof. Raj Krishna, poverty of the members of a household may not be due to unemployment or underemployment of its economically active persons but due to *higher dependency ratio*. A higher dependency ratio means on an earning member of a household there are too many members living on his earnings.
3. Poverty may be caused by low skills and low productivity of an employed person rather than unemployment. These are self-employed people who in order to survive make only meagre earnings. They include hawkers, persons repairing shoes, vegetable vendors, wood cutters. They are generally called *working poors*.

However, income criterion cannot be totally ignored for measuring unemployment in the Indian economy. The unemployment and underemployment are important causes of poverty, especially of landless agricultural labourers and urban casual workers, and that expansion in employment opportunities would greatly help alleviate the problem of poverty. Employment must be sufficiently *gainful* if the people are to meet their *basic needs and services*. However, unemployment does not always imply poverty, many youth who belong to relatively rich households remain unemployed as they do not find jobs according to their acquired skills, education and training nor does poverty imply unemployment. Hence the two concepts cannot be used interchangeably.

Measurement of Unemployment in India: Dantwala Committee Approach

Let us now first discuss the approaches to measure open unemployment and underemployment in India. On the basis of time and willingness criteria open unemployment and underemployment have been estimated using the following three approaches which were recommended by an expert committee headed by Prof. M.L. Dantwala.

(*i*) **Usual Status Approach.** This approach records only those persons as unemployed who had no gainful work for a *major time* during the 365 days preceding the date of survey and *are seeking or are available for work*. Thus, the estimates of unemployment obtained on the basis of usual status approach are expected to capture chronic open unemployment.

(*ii*) **Weekly Status Approach.** In this approach, current activity status relating to the week preceding the date of survey is recorded and those persons are classified as unemployed who did not *have gainful work even for an hour on any day in the preceding week and were seeking or were available for work*. The persons who may be employed on usual status approach may however become intermittently unemployed during some seasons or parts of the year. Thus, unlike the usual status approach, *weekly status approach would capture not only open chronic unemployment but also seasonal unemployment*. Besides, this approach provides weekly average rate of unemployment.

(*iii*) **Daily Status Approach.** As noted above, the weekly status approach records a person as employed *even if he works only for an hour on any day of the whole week*. It is thus clear that the weekly status approach would tend to underestimate unemployment in the economy because it does not appear to be proper to treat all those who have been unemployed for the whole week except an hour as employed. Indeed, the demand for labour in farming and non-farming households often fluctuates over a small period within a week. Hence the need for the use of daily status approach to measure the magnitude of unemployment and underemployment in India.

In the daily status approach current activity status of a person with regard to whether employed or unemployed or outside labour force is recorded *for each day in the reference week*. Further, for estimating employment and unemployment, *half-day has been adopted as a unit of measurement*. A person who works for 4 hours or more up to 8 hours on a day is recorded as employed for the full day and one who works for an hour or more but less than 4 hours on a day is recorded as employed for half-day. Accordingly, persons having *no* gainful work even for one hour on a day are described as unemployed for full day provided that they are either seeking or are available for work.

Thus, the *daily status approach would capture not only the unemployed days of those persons who are usually unemployed but also the unemployed days of those who are recorded as employed on weekly status basis*. Hence daily status concept of unemployment is more inclusive than those of usual status and weekly status approaches and would yield the number of unemployed person days in the year indicating the magnitude of both open unemployment and underemployment. They are therefore referred to as *person-days unemployed* in a year so as to distinguish them from *persons unemployed*. To measure rate of unemployment according to daily status approach, labour force in a year is also expressed in terms of person days. In fact, person days of unemployment measure unutilised time in terms of days in a year.

The estimates of unemployment on the basis of above three approaches are presented in Table 69.1. A comparison between different estimates of unemployment indicates that estimate of unemployment on the basis of current daily status (CDS) approach is the highest compared to the usual and principal status approaches in all the years shown in the table. As explained above, CDS approach captures intermittent unemployment (*i.e.,* underemployment), therefore it indicates a higher degree of unemployment. It may be observed from this table that according to NSS 2004-05 round, 2.3 per cent of labour force was unemployed on usual principal status basis and 8.2 per cent of labour force was unemployed on current daily status basis. Assuming the same unemployment rates, Planning Commission estimated current daily status unemployment to be of the order of 34.7 million persons in 2004-05 and 40 million persons in 2009-10.

Table 69.1. Magnitude of Unemployment in the Indian Economy (% of Labour Force)

Approach	1977-78	1983	1987-88	1993-94	1999-2000	2004-05	2009-10	2011-12
Usual Status	4.23	2.77	3.77	2.58	2.2	2.3	2.00	2.2
Current Weekly Status	4.48	4.51	4.80	3.6	4.4	4.4	3.6	NA
Current Daily Status	8.18	8.28	6.01	5.95	7.3	8.2	6.6	5.6

Source: Planning Commission, *Tenth Five Year Plan, and* GOI, *Economic Survey* 2014-15.

However, rates of unemployment on the basis of all three approaches were estimated to be lower in 2009-10 compared to 2004-05. Knowing that 2009-10 was one of a worst drought year, this fall in unemployment is doubtful. This is explained by the Planning Commission on the basis of starting of Mahatma Gandhi National Rural Employment Guarantee Scheme (MGNREGS) on a massive scale. In our view employment created under the employment guarantee scheme is neither genuine nor stable. Moreover, while the 11th Five Year Plan (2007-12) aimed at generation of 58 millions employment opportunities, 66th Round of NSS shows that increase in work opportunities increased to the tune of 18 millions under the current daily status (CDS) between 2004-05 and 2009-10. This shows that if labour force participation rate remained the same the rate of unemployment in 2009–10 must be higher than that in 2004-05.

It will be observed from Table 69.1 that as compared to 1993-94, *all rates of unemployment (usual status, weekly status and daily status)* increased in 2004-05 compared to the year 1999-2000. This clearly shows that economic reforms initiated since 1991 led to the worsening of unemployment situation in the Indian economy.

Thus, quite expectedly, the daily status approach which seeks to capture both open unemployment and underemployment reveals that quite a large magnitude of surplus labour exists in India. It will be seen from Table 69.1 that 8.2 per cent of labour force was found unemployed in 2004-05 on daily status basis. Assuming the same rate, Planning Commission estimated that the magnitude of daily status unemployment increased from 20 million persons in 1993-94 to 36.7 million persons in 2006-07. 66th round of NSS found that 6.6 of per cent of labour force was unemployed in 2009-10 on the bases of daily status approach, and 68th round of NSS found that daily status unemployment fell to 5.6% of labour force.

Critical Evaluation of Dantwala Committee's Measures of Unemployment

Note that, contrary to what could be expected, usual status unemployment is very low. This is for two reasons. First, a person to be identified as unemployed on usual status approach has to pass through a severe test, namely, he did not work for a *major time* during the 365 days preceding the date of survey. Now, in an economy where there is predominance of self-employed households engaged in family-based enterprises, it is quite easy for a person to have worked for some days even during the lean periods of the year and therefore get registered as employed rather than unemployed. Secondly, during the slack seasons of the year some persons, mainly women, withdraw themselves from the workforce. Therefore, instead of being counted as unemployed, they are treated as 'outside labour force', for they generally report as 'not available for work'. As a result, usual status unemployment estimates are relatively very low.

Further, it is noteworthy that both the usual and weekly status approaches reveal a rather small magnitude of surplus labour. This is because, as mentioned above, *both these approaches measure open unemployment in the country*. However, in India with predominance of selfemployed households and absence of social security system to support the people, they can hardly afford to remain absolutely unemployed. The new hands that are added to the labour force every year as a result of increasing population do not remain openly unemployed; they share employment and work with others so that there is more of underemployment and disguised unemployment rather than open unemployment.

However, even the daily status approach does not fully measure the magnitude of surplus labour in the Indian economy. Evidently, this also would have a tendency to underrecord unemployment as it considered a person working for only 4 hours (1/2 of the standard day) as fully employed and a person who worked for an hour (1/8th of the standard day) as employed for half-day. With this we are not able to measure disguised unemployment from daily status approach. In fact, as an alternative, hourly status approach measuring employment and unemployment in terms of man-hours would be more appropriate.

Further, the daily status approach-like the usual and weekly status approach, cannot fully capture disguised unemployment of those persons whose intensity of work and consequently productivity is very low even though they are employed for a long time. In India, as in other labour-surplus developing countries, people are generally found to be working longer hours and larger number of days than one is really required to do the given work by *stretching or spreading the work*. Therefore, *for the proper assessment of the magnitude of surplus labour that currently exists in the Indian economy, unemployment on the basis of daily/hourly status ought to be supplemented by a measure of disguised unemployment based on a norm of productivity or work-intensity*.

Despite the above limitations it is clear that daily status unemployment is a relatively better measure of the magnitude of surplus labour as it covers open unemployment as well as some amount of underemployment. It is evident from above that three measures of unemployment are based *mainly* on time criterion as stated by late Dr. Raj Krishna. The time criterion has been used in the above three measures of unemployment as they are based on the number of days in a year persons remain unemployed. Though the willingness criterion has been sought to be incorporated by asking the question from unemployed persons whether they are seeking to work or available for work. As far as seeking work is concerned it would have been relevant only if enough employment exchanges would have been there. In the rural India, employment exchanges do not exist. Even in urban areas, the unemployed people do not go to register their names for employment as it is a common knowledge that employment exchanges can arrange employment only for skilled and education and that too in a very small number of cases. Therefore, 'seeking for work', is not very relevant in labour surplus developing countries. Especially, women in rural India generally do not seek work outside their villages. The other question relating to 'willingness to work' is also sought to be obtained by asking question from unemployed whether they are "available for work". However, *without reference* to at what wages the work will be available is not very meaningful. Moreover, many female workers would neither be seeking nor available for work outside their village where they reside. Thus the three measures of unemployment suggested by Dantwala Committee which are being used by Planning Commission and Government are mainly based on time criterion regardless of earnings they make in their employment which can be described as gainful. They should be described as acutely underemployed or disguisedly unemployed if their employment in some work does not yield enough earnings to meet their basic needs.

Factors Determining Employment and Unemployment

Capital Accumulation and GDP Growth Rate. It is important to explain what factors determine growth of employment and therefore the emergence of unemployment. As explained above, unemployment in labour-surplus developing countries is due to shortage of cooperating factors such as capital stock (including land), relatively to labour force. In developing countries capital stock has not been increasing fast enough to keep pace with the growth of labour force. It is through rapid increase in investment or faster capital accumulation that the GDP growth can be accelerated.

According to ***Harrod-Domar model,*** the rate of growth of output depends upon the ratio of total investment to national income divided by the capital-output ratio, *i.e.*,

$$G = \frac{I}{v}$$

where

G = rate of growth of output,

I = rate of investment (as ratio of national income),

v = capital-output ratio.

As Harrod-Domar model assumes capital-output and capital-labour ratios to remain constant, increase in capital stock would imply increase in both output and employment. Therefore, Harrod, Domar model suggests that the rate of growth of both output and employment is determined by the growth of capital stock. Thus, according to this model, solution to the problem of unemployment lies in sufficient increase in the rate of investment or capital accumulation. Assuming a fixed capital-output ratio, Harrod-Domar Model lays stress on capital formation or investment to achieve a higher growth of output and employment. It is worth mentioning that this model does not distinguish between capital formation in industry and agriculture. Now, given the capital-output and capital labour ratio, faster growth of capital formation and GDP growth will lead to more employment being generated. Further, according to the model, investment or capital accumulation depends on rate of saving in the economy.

The basic solution to the problem of unemployment is therefore the faster rate of capital formation so as to enlarge employment opportunities. For this purpose, every possible encouragement should be given to the growth of domestic savings and their productive utilisation in increasing the rate of investment. In developing countries investment incentives for the private sector are very low and the State can assist in the process of capital formation directly as well as indirectly. Through a fiscal policy which encourages savings and investment and a sound monetary policy it can do much to encourage investors. The State itself can participate in the process of capital formation by undertaking such developmental activities as building infrastructure which do not attract the private investors.

Therefore, the State has got to assume a special role in speeding up the rate of economic development. The other line of attack has got to be on the rate of population growth. If population grows at a rapid rate, then to maintain the people even at their existing levels, large amounts of capital are needed which could otherwise have been used to raise the amount of capital available per man and hence to raise the living standards at a faster rate.

Employment Elasticity of Output

To what extent GDP growth will generate employment depends on *employment elasticity of output*. By employment elasticity of output we mean percentage growth in employment caused by one per cent growth in output. For the 1970s this author in his Ph.D dissertation[4] had calculated employment elasticity of industrial growth in India being equal to 0.5. Recent estimates show that, it has declined substantially. It was thought once that industrial growth would solve the unemployment problem in developing countries. Thus, India's first three Five Year Plans were based on sufficiently absorbing labour through industrial growth, so much that it would be able to withdraw surplus labour in the long term from agriculture and thus bring about structural change in the Indian economy. However, actual employment generation by industrial growth has been very disappointing. This is because of lower employment elasticity of growth of industrial output. As a result, employment growth has lagged behind. Let us explain employment growth with the following formula:

$$g(E_i) = e_{iY}.g(y_i)S_i$$

where $g(E_i)$ is employment growth in the *organised* industry as a percentage of total employment, e_{iY} = elasticity of employment with respect to growth of industrial output (*i.e.*, gross value added by the industry) and S_i is the *initial* share of industrial employment as a fraction of total employment. In India if initially the employment in the organised industrial sector as a fraction of labour force was 0.10, employment elasticity of growth of industrial output (*i.e.*, gross value added) as estimated by many being equal to 0.5 and if industrial growth rate of output $g(Y_i)$, was 6 per cent, then growth of industrial employment is given as under:

$$g(E_i) = 0.5 \times 6\% \times 0.10 = 0.3$$

Given the industrial growth equal to 6%, it means only 0.3 per cent of the labour force will get additional employment each year by the growth of the organised industrial sector while the labour force was growing at the rate of 2.2 per cent of labour force. This will actually be the case if *more capital-bias and labour-saving technologies* are not adopted by the industries. However, the trend in India has been to adopt highly capital-intensive or labour-saving technologies have been adopted by importing from the industrialised developed countries with the result that in the organised sector, employment growth has been very little.

Table 69.2. Employment Growth, GDP Growth and Employment Elasticity

	CENSUS		NSS		Labour Bureau
	1991 to 2001	2001 to 2011	1993-94 to 1999-2000	1999-2000 to 2011-12	2011-12 to 2013-14
Change in Employment (Millions)	88.4	79.2	25.5	73.4	9.15
Employment Growth (% per annum)	2.5	1.8	1.1	1.4	1.0
GDP Growth (% per annum)	5.7	7.7	6.8	7.3	4.6
Employment Elasticity	0.44	0.29	0.16	0.19	0.22

Source: *Economic Survey*, 2014-15 Vol. I, p. 11

4 *Development Strategy in a Labour Surplus Developing Economies Countries*, 1982, Unpublished Ph.D. Dissertation, Delhi School of Economics, Delhi University.

Important factor responsible for slow growth of employment in India is the decline in employment elasticity of growth of output. India's Economic Survey 2014-15 has clearly brought out by using employment growth in the economy as a whole and overall GDP growth of India. We give the data regarding measures of elasticity of employment from Census, NSS and Labour Bureau in Table 69.2. The measures of elasticity of employment of growth of output from Census figures for the period 1991 to 2001 was 0.44 which fell to 0.29 in the period 2001 to 2011. According to the Census 2011, the rate of growth of employment per annum during the period 2001-11 was 1.8 per cent per annum despite a high GDP growth of 7.7% per annum achieved during this period. Thus, even according to census estimates employment elasticity declined. Similarly, according to NSS data, during the period, 1993-94 to 1999-2000 employment elasticity of growth of output was still less at 0.16 and in the period 1999-2000 – 2011-12, it was found to be 0.19 even though GDP growth picked up to 7.3 per cent per annum. Labour Bureau, has estimated employment elasticity of growth of output equal to 0.22 between 2011-12 and 2013-14.

It is evident from above that employment elasticity of growth of output has declined since 2000. This reduction in employment elasticity has been mainly caused by the use of more capital-intensive technologies in production. Accordingly, the *relation between GDP growth and employment generation has greatly weakened.* It is worth quoting Economic Survey, 2014-15 which states that "Estimates of employment growth and its elasticity relative to economic growth vary widely. However tentatively one might say that employment growth and elasticity have decline in the 2000s compared to the 1990s. Since labour force is in excess of employment growth, labour absorption will be a challenge[5]

Factor Price Distortions

The other important cause of poor growth of employment opportunities and the existence of unemployment in labour-abundant developing countries is the prevailing factor price distortions. Ideally, the prices of capital and labour in an economy should reflect their *scarcity or shadow prices.* In labour abundant developing countries since capital is scarce, its price should be relatively higher and as labour is abundant, its price (*i.e.,* wages) should be lower. However, actually, in developing countries factor prices are distorted in the ways that capital is made artificially cheaper relative to labour, or to put in other words, price of labour (that is, wages) are made relatively higher and capital cheaper. As a result of these factor price distortions, the rational firms use capital-intensive methods to minimise their costs for a given level of output and thereby maximise profits. This makes employment of labour to grow slowly as industrial expansion takes place.

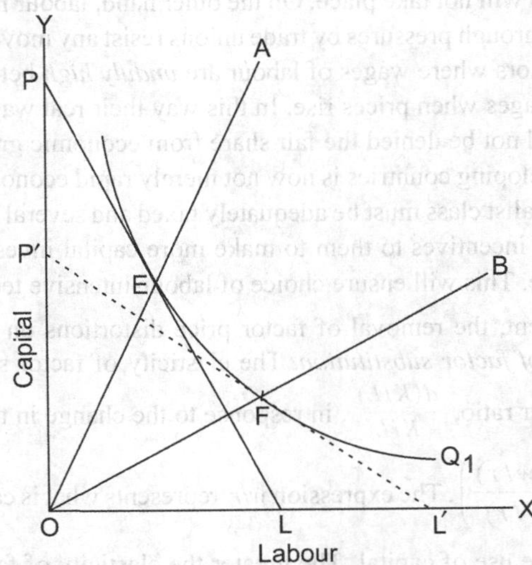

Fig. 69.1. *Factor price distortions and choice of a factor combination (i.e.Technique)*

5 GOI, *Economic Survey,* 2014-15, Vol., 1 p. 10.

Now the question arises why wages of labour are relatively higher. Under pressures of trade unions of labour and fixation of minimum wages by the Government make wages higher for those fortunate enough to get jobs in the modern sector. It is often pointed out that because of political pressures of trade unions that Government fixes wages at a relatively higher levels.

On the other hand, capital is artificially made cheaper by keeping interest rates lower which make capital equipment-cheaper to buy by borrowing from the banks or other financial institutions. Besides, there is often *overvaluation* of local currency in terms of foreign exchange which also makes the import of capital equipment cheaper. More important, in their fiscal policy Government provides liberal depreciation allowances, investment breaks, long tax holiday to induce capital investment. As a result of capital being made artificially cheaper and labour costlier, with steeper iso-cost line *PL*, the producer firms will choose a relatively capital-intensive method or technique of production as shown in Fig. 69.1 by point *E* on isoquant Q_1. In Figure 69.1 capital is measured along *Y*-axis and labour is measured along the *X*-axis. An isoquant Q_1 indicating a certain level of output has been drawn. When due to factor price distortions, capital is relatively cheaper and labour more expensive, we have iso-cost line *PL* which is tangent to isoquant Q_1 at point *E*. Thus, the producer will choose production technique (*i.e.*, factor combination) which is highly capital-intensive. Given these distorted factor prices, the producer firms will expand along the capital-intensive path shown by the line *OA* which will generate fewer employment opportunities.

Now, if the distortions in factor prices are removed and factor prices are made equal to their scarcity values, we will get the iso-cost line *P′L′* with which to produce output level Q_1 the producer will choose factor-combination *F* which is relatively more labour intensive. Given this labour-intensive technique, the firms will expand along the expansion path *OB* which indicate large increases in labour employment as output grows.

If the Government is serious about adequate increase in employment opportunities to solve the unemployment problem, it must correct the factor price distortions and *withdraw concessions given on the investment of capital* and try to fix wages at the *fair level* and not at unduly higher levels through labour reforms. However, the Governments are often reluctant to remove these factor price distortions as often there are political pressures especially by the capitalist class which through their lobbies insist that without adequate incentives in the form of liberal depreciation allowances, tax breaks on investment, longer tax holidays and other exemptions, investment will not increase and as a result rapid economic growth will not take place. On the other hand, labour in the organised industries and services sector which through pressures by trade unions resist any move to lower their money wages. In our view, in the sectors where wages of labour are *unduly high* better way to reduce them is not to raise their money wages when prices rise. In this way their real wages will fall. However, in our view, the labour should not be denied the fair share from economic growth in developing countries as the objective in developing countries is now not merely rapid economic growth but also inclusive growth. Profits of capitalist class must be adequately taxed and several exemptions in taxation which have been provided as incentives to them to make more capital investment must be withdrawn to make capital expensive. This will ensure choice of labour-intensive techniques.

Now, to what extent, the removal of factor price distortions on the use of labour will occur depends on *elasticity of factor substitution*. The elasticity of factor substitution is the percentage change in capital-labour ratio, $\frac{d(K/L)}{K/L}$, in response to the change in the ratio of price of labour to the price of capital $\left(\frac{d(w/r)}{(w/r)}\right)$. The expression *w/r* represents what is called *wage-rental ratio* where rental is the price of the use of capital. The greater the elasticity of factor substitution, the greater will be the effect of removal of factor-price distortions on the use of labour.

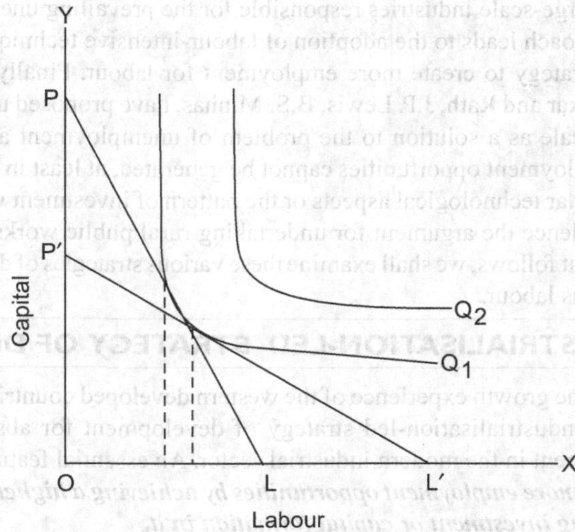

Fig. 69.2. *Relatively fixed factor proportion production function with low elasticity of factor substitution*

Some economists have pointed out that elasticity of substitution between factors is very low *as relatively fixed factor proportions* are actually found in the production processes in the real world as shown by the *isoqants* in Fig. 69.2. It will be seen from this figure that isoquants are almost right-angled and removal of factor price distortions, that is, raising the price of capital and lowering the wage rate will have a *very small effect* on the choice of technique or labour use. However, that is a very pessimistic view about the elasticity of factor substitution. Many empirical studies have found the elasticity of factor substitution ranges from 0.4 to 0.5. Even though in some industries the technology used is such that in the *core production process* factor proportions are relatively rigid, but in *subsidiary operations* such as material handling, packaging etc. there exist good scope for greater use of labour.

Various Development Strategies for Employment Generation in Developing Countries

In what follows we shall critically examine some well-known strategies of development, especially from the point of view of whether they provide an adequate answer to the problem of surplus labour in developing countries with special reference to India. Their critical evaluation will enable us to bring out the various policy measures which need to be adopted for designing an appropriate development strategy to ameliorate the problem of unemployment and underemployment in India. It is important to note that a development strategy for promoting the growth of employment is based on a particular diagnosis and explanation of the problem of surplus labour. As an explanation of unemployment and from the viewpoint of generation of new employment opportunities, the various employment strategies and aproaches have been proposed from time to time by different economists. The first important approach for generation of employment is what can be called **industrialisation-led strategy of development**. Some economists, prominent among whom are Nurkse, Lewis, Eckaus, Robinson, Mahalanobis, Hirschman, Fei-Ranis and Jorgenson, attribute unemployment in the developing countries to the lack of industrialisation and therefore suggest stepping up the rate of investment or capital formation for the expansion of modern industrial sector in which to absorb surplus labour.

On the other hand, Vakil and Brahmananda laid stress on wage-goods gap as a cause of unemployment and put forward a development strategy which assigned a high priority to wage-goods industries (especially agriculture) in the allocation of investment resources so as to increase the supply of wage goods which would enable us to generate more employment opportunities. Another group of economists led by Schumacher[6], Myrdal [7]and Singer hold the use of capital-intensive technology in the large-scale industries responsible for the prevailing unemployment in developing countries. This approach leads to the adoption of labour-intensive techniques as an essential part of the development strategy to create more employment for labour. Finally, some economists, more prominently Dandekar and Rath, J.P. Lewis, B.S. Minhas, have proposed undertaking of rural public works on a large scale as a solution to the problem of unemployment and poverty. According to them, adequate employment opportunities cannot be generated, at least in the short run, through any emphasis on particular technological aspects or the pattern of investment within the agricultural and industrial sectors. Hence the argument for undertaking rural public works to generate employment opportunities. In what follows, we shall examine these various strategies of development for productive absorption of surplus labour.

INDUSTRIALISATION-LED STRATEGY OF DEVELOPMENT

Influenced by the growth experience of the western developed countries, the several developing countries adopted industrialisation-led strategy of development for absorbing surplus labour in productive employment in the modern industrial sector. An essential feature of this approach is that ***it seeks to generate more employment opportunities by achieving a higher rate of industrial growth through accelerating investment or capital formation in it.***

Besides, this approach regards labour and capital as complementary inputs. In the developing countries the stock of capital and modern industries have not been growing at a rate fast enough to keep pace with the growth of population. As a result, the whole of growing labour force cannot be absorbed in productive employment because not enough capital is available to employ them. Thus this approach attributes the existence of unemployment and underemployment in developing countries to the lack of capital relative to the magnitude of labour force. A variety of growth models and development strategies come under this approach, all of these, though differing in some other aspects, lay stress on the importance of capital accumulation for generation of employment opportunities. We shall explain below some of the models of this industrial growth-led approach towards employment generation that fall in this category.

Industrialisation-Led Strategy of Development: Lewis Model

In their growth models for a dualistic economy with surplus labour, Lewis[8] and Fei-Ranis[9] regard capital as the crucial factor for the expansion of employment in the modern industrial sector. While their models suggest that rate of growth of employment depends upon the rate of capital accumulation and economic growth, it differs from Harrod-Domar model in the sense that they draw distinction between the two sectors of a less developed economy: (1) the subsistence agricultural sector which is characterised by surplus labour, low productivity and self-employment; and (2) the modern industrial sector which is characterised by wage employment and high productivity.

These growth models emphasise transfer of surplus labour from the subsistence agricultural sector to the modern industrial sector. And this *transfer of labour and expansion of employment opportunities in the modern industrial sector is determined by the rate of capital accumulation and industrial growth*. Therefore, the higher rate of capital accumulation and economic growth in the modern industrial sector over a number of years would enable us withdraw all the disguisedly unemployed labour from agriculture.

6 E.F. Schumacher, *Small is beautiful*, Board Briggs, London.
7 Gunnar Myrdal, *Asian Drama; An Enquiry into the Poverty of Nations*, Penguin Books, New York, 1968.
8 Arthur Lewis, Economic Development with Unlimited Supply of Labour, *Manchester School*, Vol. 22, 1954.
9 J.C.H. Fei, G. Ranis, *Development of the Labour Surplus Economy, Theory and Policy*, Irwin, Homesood, 1964.

It was assumed in this Lewis model of industrialisation that agriculture would adjust itself endogenously to the requirements of industrial growth. The assumption of unlimited supply of labour at *a given wage rate* implied that agriculture would adjust endogenously and release labour for industrial growth without lowering of agricultural production. Lewis realised that if on withdrawal of labour from agricultural productivity of labour falls, it would cause prices of agricultural output, especially food, to rise. The rise in food prices will lead to the rise in wage rates of labour in the industrial sector. The rise in wages would lower profits in the industrial sector and bring about stoppage of further industrial growth.

Heavy-Industry Strategy and Mahalanobis Growth Model

This growth model which formed the basis of development strategy adopted in India's Second and Third Plans also laid a great stress on the rate of capital accumulation for determining the rate of growth of employment. According to Mahalanobis, unemployment of labour is caused by the lack of capital stock. To employ a person in productive work, he needs to be equipped with adequate capital. Therefore, in order to generate more opportunities of productive employment more capital has to be accumulated. *Given a closed economy, the rate of capital formation, according to him, depends on the capacity of the economy to produce capital goods*. With this premise he showed that in order to achieve a high rate of economic growth and employment it *is necessary to accord a high priority to basic heavy industries producing capital goods* in the development strategy of a plan. It is worthwhile to mention that in Mahalanobis' opinion it is necessary to allocate relatively greater resources to basic heavy industries to achieve not only the objective of rapid economic growth but also of expanding opportunities for productive employment. With this, the stock of basic goods like steel, machinery, fertilizers, should be sufficiently increased to eliminate unemployment.[10]

It may be noted that Mahalanobis later realised that basic heavy industries, though important for determining the *long-term growth of employment*, will themselves not create adequate employment opportunities. In response to the need to create enough employment opportunities *in the short run*, he extended his two-sector model to four sectors wherein he kept the basic heavy industries sector intact but divided the consumption goods sector into three sub-sectors, namely: (1) factory enterprises sector, (2) household and small-scale sector, and (3) services sector.

It was the household and small-scale sector in his four-sector model which being labour-intensive was expected to create a good amount of employment opportunities. However, his four-sector model did not represent any essential change over his two-sector model in as much as it maintained the emphasis on basic heavy industries. Moreover, since adequate resources were not provided for the household and small-scale industries, nor was any effort made to improve their productivity so that they could successfully compete with the large-scale industries, they recorded a low growth rate in output and employment.

A Critical Appraisal of Industrialisation-led Strategy of Development and Employment

Industrialisation-led strategy of development rightly lays stress on the importance of capital goods for generating employment. Without some capital goods such as tools, implements, machinery and equipment, it is hard to generate productive employment in both the large-scale and small-scale industries. Likewise, capital inputs such as irrigation facilities, fertilizers, etc., play a crucial role for the productive absorption of labour in agriculture. Above all, shortage of infrastructure such as steel, power, cement and transport facilities serves as an important bottleneck for the expansion of output and employment in both industry and agriculture. Therefore, expansion in their supply would promote the growth of output and employment in the economy.

However, *industrialisation-led strategy of development did not sufficiently recognize the importance of wage-goods constraint for generation of employment opportunities*. Thus, at a time

10 P.C. Mahalanobis, "The Approach of Operational Research to Planning in India", Sankhya, Vol. 16, 1955.

when fixed capital goods alone were thought to be necessary, Vakil and Brahmananda[11] made a valuable contribution by highlighting the importance of wage goods for expansion of employment opportunities. But the assertion that the increase in the supply of wage goods alone is both a necessary and sufficient condition for creation of employment sounds quite unrealistic.[12] It is not a right approach to think of capital goods versus wage goods. Indeed, increase in the supply of both is needed to solve the problem of unemployment. The availability of wage goods serves as a constraint for generating wage-employment as without them the demand of the newly employed persons for wage goods would not be met. But if opportunities for productive employment are to be generated in the very first instance either in industry or in agriculture, labour needs to be provided with some capital goods.

It is worthwhile to note that growth of the modern industrial sector was expected to absorb not only the openly unemployed but also the disguised unemployed persons from agriculture. However, the actual experience belies the hopes of generating sufficient employment opportunities through industrial growth. For instance, an annual average rate of growth of around 6 per cent achieved by the industrial sector in India during the four decades (1956-96) and a very high increase in the rate of net capital formation (from 5.5 per cent in 1950-51 to 25 per cent of national income in 1995-96) had not been able to solve the problem of unemployment and underemployment in India. It is thus clear that not much employment opportunities can be generated *directly* through growth of modern industrial sector even with high rate of increase in its output.[13]

Industrialisation-led strategy based on Mahalanobis and Lewis models underplayed the importance of growth of agricultural output. Without the growth of marketable surplus of agricultural output, especially food, the sustained growth in the industrial sector could not be achieved. In the case of erstwhile Soviet Russia, the required food-surplus was procured *through forcible collection* from the farmers. In democratic countries like India forcible collection was ruled out. The neglect of agriculture in India in the Second Five Year Plan led to the food shortage in the early sixties. This caused not only inflation in the economy but we had to import foodgrains from the USA to feed our growing population.

A serious drawback of strategies of employment generation through industrial growth is that *they have ignored the possibilities of absorbing labour productively in agriculture*. These strategies regarded agriculture merely as the source of labour supply to the expanding industries. Even in growth models of Lewis and Fei-Ranis of a labour-surplus dual economy, and also of *Mahalanobis heavy-industry strategy of development* both surplus labour and dualism have been sought to be eliminated by way of shifting labour from agriculture to the modern industrial sector.[14] But there is ample scope for absorbing labour in the Indian agriculture provided proper agricultural policies

---

11 C.N. Vakil and P.R. Brahmananda, *Planning in an Expanding Economy*, Vohra & Co., Bombay, 1966.

12 It may be mentioned that Brahmananda later modified his wage woods strategy by incorporating in what he calls "*Integrated Wage-goods Complex*" which includes not only the wage-goods but also the capital goods required for the production of wage-goods. But the role of intermediate capital goods such as steel, cement, coal and power required for the production of wage-goods and also for investment sector had not been recognised by him even in his '*Extended Wage-goods Strategy*'.

13 Note that the growth of modern industrial sector generates few employment opportunities was also corroborated by the experience of Latin American countries such as Brazil, Argentina, Mexico, Columbia, Peru, Venezuela which have achieved annual rate of industrial growth ranging from 7.6 per cent to 10 per cent during the decades of nineteen fifties and sixties and still they faced the mounting problem of surplus labour.

14 It is important to note that Fei-Ranis have emphasised the importance of agricultural development in the growth process of a labour-surplus economy, but they have envisaged such a pattern of agricultural development which ensures more and more agricultural output for less and less use of labour input. Besides, the Second Five Year Plan based on Mahalanobis development strategy visualised reducing labour force in agriculture and employing a larger proportion of labour force in the modern industrial sector in the next 20 years.

are adopted. India employs much less labour per hectare than other countries like Japan.[15] A good amount of labour can be productively absorbed in the Indian agriculture through rapid growth of its output by increasing cropping intensity and irrigation facilities and through the adoption of new high yielding technology. Reckless mechanisation, that is, use of labour-displacing agricultural machines such as tractors, combine harvestors is to be avoided if more employment opportunities are to be created in agriculture.

Finally, most of the growth strategies which focussed on industrial growth for employment generation and *ignored the importance of institutional reforms, especially in agriculture, for promoting the expansion of employment opportunities*. Land reforms in agriculture such as redistribution of land and changes in the tenancy system can play an important role in increasing employment opportunities for landless labourers, small and marginal farmers and share-croppers. There exist large inequalities in land-ownership in India with the result that whereas a large number of rural households have either insufficient or no land to provide them adequate employment and income, a few families, on the other, own such a large amount of land that they cannot manage it efficiently. Consequently, there is underutilization of land and irrigation potential. Further, it has found from 'Farm Management Studies' in India that employment per hectare and cropping intensity are higher on small farms as compared to those on large farms. This may be taken to imply that redistribution of land through imposition and effective implementation of ceilings on land holdings will bring about increase in employment opportunities in agriculture.

To sum up, agriculture contains immense employment potential provided proper strategy for its development involving technological and institutional changes is adopted. This has, however, been ignored by the mainstream of the industrialisation-led strategies of development.

WAGE-GOODS STRATEGY OF DEVELOPMENT AND EMPLOYMENT IN THE DEVELOPING COUNTRIES

The industrialisation-led strategy of development explained above neglects the constraint of wage goods availability on employment generation.[16] In their criticism of the development strategy of Second and Third Five Year Plans, Vakil and Brahmananda advanced what is known as wage-goods strategy of development. According to them, unemployment and disguised unemployment in less developed countries are due to the deficiency of the supply of wage goods. They have argued that the magnitude of employment in less developed countries is determined by the available amount of wage goods. This is because whenever employment for new persons is created, say, in rural public works, it cannot be sustained unless adequate amount of wage goods, especially foodgrains, is available. Of course, when people are openly or disguisedly unemployed, they would be consuming some foodgrains. But in that situation their consumption would be very low because their budget would not allow them to consume more. Therefore, when they are given wage employment, their effective demand for wage goods will tend to increase. Hence, given the reasonable real wage rate (in terms of wage goods) we can calculate the total amount of wage goods required to obtain full employment. They call the difference between the required magnitude of wage goods and the actually

15 In the middle 1950s, labour input per hectare of net sown area was 530 working man days in Japan, as against only 137 in West Bengal in India.

16 Some of the models of capital formation do take into account the wage-goods constraint and provide for it. Thus, Nurkse thought that withdrawal of disguised unemployed will leave behind enough foodgrains to be mopped up for feeding the transferred people. Likewise, Lewis and Fei-Ranis also provide for the transfer of food from agriculture to feed the workers employed in expanding modern industrial sector. But the agricultural growth to make available sufficient quantities of foodgrains does not constitute the main thrust of the development designs of Nurkse, Lewis and Fei-Ranis, for the leading sector in their development models is the modern industrial sector.

available supply of wage goods as the '*wage goods gap*'.[17] Open and disguised unemployment in less developed countries like India, according to them, is due to the existence of this wage goods gap. The level of full employment can be attained only when this wage-goods gap is bridged by expanding the capacity to produce wage-goods.

We thus see that whereas in Mahalanobis' approach to growth and employment "the entire emphasis was on the role of fixed capital, Vakil and Brahmananda's entire emphasis was on the role of wage goods as capital."[18] It may be noted that in his later works Brahmananda modified his strategy in that he later assigned a high priority to what he calls '*Integrated Wage goods Complex*' which includes not only wage goods but also capital goods which are used for the production of wage goods. Since they consider the supply of wage-goods as the most important determinant of employment in less developed economies Vakil and Brahmananda proposed a development strategy which assigned the top priority to wage goods industries, especially agriculture, in the pattern of investment. That is why they severely criticized the development strategy adopted in India's Second and Third Plans which gave high priority to basic heavy industries producing fixed capital goods.

It may be noted that, like Nurkse, Vakil and Brahmananda believe that disguised unemployment in developing countries contains saving potential (in the form of wage goods) for capital accumulation. By withdrawing the disguised unemployed from agriculture, some amount of wage-goods would be released for providing wage employment in the investment sector. But, unlike Nurkse, they think that the surplus of wage goods so released will not be sufficient to provide employment to all the potentially available labour force. Therefore, they emphasised the expansion of the capacity to produce wage goods and for that purpose advanced a development strategy which envisaged greater allocation of investible resources to agriculture and other wage-goods industries.

A Critical Evaluation of Wage-Goods Strategy

The assertion by Vakil and Brahmananda that the growth in employment *solely and exclusively* depends upon the supply of wage goods and that the capital goods (that is, heavy-industry products) play no important role in the creation of employment opportunities is open to question. Under adequate organisation and entrepreneurial ability as well as optimum-institutional forms, two important bottlenecks, namely, capital goods bottleneck and wage goods bottleneck, are faced in creating opportunities for productive employment. For expansion in productive employment both these bottlenecks have to be overcome and to emphasise the breaking of one bottleneck, while making no attempt to tackle the other, is an unrealistic approach to the employment problem. Wage goods are required to meet the demands of the newly employed people, but if some people are to be employed in productive activities in the very first instance, they are required to be equipped with some capital goods. Further, for the production of wage goods themselves, capital goods are required. That is, labour is to be equipped with capital goods to produce wage goods. Professor Dantwala rightly points our that, *"it is a mistake to consider capital goods and wage goods as exclusive and unrelated categories. Anyone who studies the composition of inputs needed for transformation of traditional agriculture should be able to appreciate the inter-connection between the two."*

Thus, development strategy for rapid expansion of employment has to be such as will envisage the increase in production of both wage goods and capital goods. Thus, to talk of wage goods versus capital goods is a false issue and an unrealistic approach to the problem of employment since both are needed to generate employment; capital goods are required to make the employment productive

17 That the availability of wage goods is an important constraint on the growth of employment opportunities was first brought out by Ricardo (1815). In classical economics, wage-goods or wage fund have been treated as working capital as compared to fixed physical capital which consists of machines and equipment. Thus, importance given by Vakil and Brahmananda to wage goods for the generation of employment opportunities was merely a revival of the Ricardian thought.

18 Jagdish Bhagwati and S. Chakravarty, *Indian Economic Analysis*, (1971), p. 14.

and wage goods are needed to feed the workers provided with new employment, that is, to sustain their employment. To say this, however, does not imply that all capital goods industries should be necessarily developed at home and given higher priority in the allocation of resources. Which specific capital goods should be produced at home and which imported from abroad should be decided on the basis of resource endowments and comparative advantage conceived in the dynamic context.

DEVELOPMENT STRATEGY OF USING LABOUR-INTENSIVE TECHNOLOGY

An important school of thought led by Schumacher, Singer and Myrdal attributes the mounting problem of unemployment and underemployment in the developing countries to the use of capital-intensive technology. It has been observed that while industrial output in developing countries has increased at a reasonably good rate, growth of employment has lagged far behind. And this is said to be due to the use of capital-intensive technology. Thus, according to this school of thought, the creation of meagre amount of employment opportunities due to the use of capital-intensive technology on the one hand and the growth of population at an alarming rate on the other has resulted in the huge magnitude of surplus labour.

It is worthwhile to note here that the modern industries using capital-intensive technology not only create few new opportunities of employment but also destroy employment in the traditional household industries. This unfavourable impact of modern sector on the traditional employment is what Myrdal calls *backwash effect*. According to this school of thought, modern manufacturing enterprises using capital-intensive technology produce goods on a mass scale at lower cost per unit which drive out the products of traditional household industries from the market. As a result, a good number of people engaged in these household industries are displaced.[19] They add to either open or disguised unemployment in agriculture.

In this context, **labour migration model of Todaro** has often been invoked, especially by Singer, to explain the mounting problem of urban unemployment in developing countries. According to Todaro,[20] decision of rural workers to migrate to urban areas rests on the higher level of wage rate and the expectations of getting employment in the modern urban sector. A few employment opportunities at relatively higher wage levels created by capital-intensive technology in the modern urban sector attract many more rural workers than it is possible for it to absorb. This results in enormous increase in urban unemployment and underemployment.

Of course, Galenson-Leibenstein, M. Dobb, Amartya Sen have pointed out that *the use of capital-intensive techniques would generate more surplus resources which would be ploughed back into further investment and it would result in greater growth of employment than is possible through labour-intensive techniques*. But this has not been borne out by empirical evidence. For instance, estimates of saving and investment in India reveal that contributions of the public and the private corporate sectors to the domestic savings have not only been too small but have also recorded slow growth in the last six decades in spite of the fact that the capital-intensive technology has been used in them. On the contrary, it is the savings of the household sector (consisting of households and unicorporated enterprises) which often use labour-intensive technology that have greatly increased. This raises doubts about the argument that capital-intensive techniques necessarily generate more surplus and therefore greater growth of employment.

There is another important aspect of the use of capital-intensive technology which is worth mentioning. The *use of capital-intensive techniques creates high profit-wage ratio and thereby*

19 In his famous study of the industrial evolution in India, D.R. Gadgil, "*Industrial Evolution in Recent Times*", clearly brought out the decline of handicraft and displacement labour employed in them as a result of the growth of modern large-scale industries in India.

20. Michael, P. Todaro, "Income Expectations, Rural-Urban Migration and Employment in Africa", *International Labour Review*, Nov. 1971.

accentuates inequalities of income. These income inequalities create demand pattern oriented towards luxuries which are again produced by the use of capital-intensive techniques. This limits the size of market for labour-intensive goods consumed by the working classes. Thus, the use of capital-intensive techniques gives rise to a vicious circle which causes slow growth not only of direct employment but also of indirect employment through its effects on the pattern of demand.

Why in Developing Countries Capital-Intensive Technology is Used? Now, a pertinent question is why have the developing countries been using capital-intensive technology despite the fact that surplus labour prevails in them? There are two views about this. First, the alternative technology which though efficient but labour-intensive is generally not available. The available technology is the capital-intensive technology that was developed in the Western countries to suit their factor endowments. The Western technology is quite inappropriate for the developing countries which suffer from surplus of labour and shortage of capital. Now, given the technology imported from the Western countries, there is not much possibility of substitution of capital for labour. In view of this, Schumacher and Singer advocate for the development of what has been called *intermediate or appropriate technology*. Appropriate technology for the developing countries is that which though efficient should be labour-intensive so that it conforms to their factor endowments.

According to Schumacher, the development of appropriate technologies does not imply the discovery of altogether new principles of science and technology. What is required is the application of basic principles of modern science and technology to evolve the appropriate production techniques. These appropriate production techniques may be obtained by scaling down the advanced techniques by adapting them so as to make them more labour-intensive, or by scaling up handicrafts technique with the introduction of new tools and simple machines and thus improving economic efficiency of these techniques while maintaining their labour-intensity.

On the other hand, several other scholars such as Ranis, Blaug, Layard and Woodhall, Little, Scott and Scitovsky are of the view that the slow growth of employment opportunities in the industrial sector is not due so much to the lack of flexibility in the production function but to the **distortions in factor prices.**[21] Due to the various concessions and subsidies provided in taxation structure by the Government such as liberal investment or development rebate, policy of low interest rate and over-valued foreign exchange rate have caused the price of capital to be very low relative to its scarcity. On the other hand, the prevailing wage rates are too high for a labour-surplus economy due to the strong bargaining power of the trade unions in the organised sector. According to them, these distortions in factor prices induce the adoption of capital-intensive techniques in industries with the consequence that less labour is employed. In order to promote the use of more labour-intensive techniques, it is therefore imperative that all distortions in factor prices be corrected.

By emphasising the use of labour-intensive technology in developing countries, this strategy has brought into sharp focus the question of appropriate technological choices. In a labour-surplus economy the importance of the use of appropriate technology which is labour-absorptive and at the same time quite efficient can hardly be denied. However, appropriate technologies for various manufacturing industries just do not exist and a good deal of more research and development (R & D) would have to be undertaken before appropriate techniques are evolved for several industries. Of course, to encourage the development and use of appropriate techniques the various factor price distortions ought to be removed. Whereas, in view of the prevailing price situation, wage rates of industrial workers do not seem to be high, the effective price of capital is low. Therefore, the various concessions and rebates in taxes on various types of capital investment be drastically reduced and

21 Eckaus in his famous work '*Factor-Proportions Problem in Underdeveloped Countries*' showed that either factor-price disequilibrium or limited possibilities of substituting labour for capital can result in unemployment in less developed economies. Blaug, Layard and Woodhall in their study on educated unemployment have held high wage rates responsible for educated unemployment in India.

the lending rates of interest charged by banks and other financial institutions be raised so as to curb the tendency to substitute capital for labour.

As for technological choices in agriculture it may be noted that new high-yielding technology represented by a package of high-yielding varieties, fertilizers and pesticides is quite appropriate for a labour-surplus economy such as ours, for it not only raises yield per hectare substantially but is also labour-absorptive.

STRATEGY OF RURAL PUBLIC WORKS FOR EMPLOYMENT GENERATION

This approach seeks solution to the unemployment problem not through emphasising any particular pattern of resource allocation or technological choice but through special employment schemes, especially rural public works. This approach regards the regular development process as being incapable of alleviating the problem of unemployment and underemployment in the short run. The launching of rural works programme on a large scale had been especially advanced by Dandekar and Rath[22] to solve the problem of mass poverty which, they maintain, is mainly caused by unemployment and underemployment. Rural public works also constituted the main thrust of the recommendations of Bhagwati Committee on unemployment in India to tackle the problem of mass rural poverty and unemployment. Further, the scheme of rural public works as a major source of employment generation in rural areas has also been strongly recommended by J.P. Lewis,[23] K.N. Raj, M.L. Dantwala, and Raj Krishna. Besides, B.S. Minhas[24] also suggests massive rural works programme in his "*integrated programme of compulsory consolidation and land development*."[25]

Employment generation through Rural Public Works was undertaken in 1977-78 on a regular basis under the '*Food for Work Programme*' during the regime of Janata Government and was later adopted as a part of the Sixth Five Year Plan (1978-83). Under this scheme a major part of wages is paid in terms of foodgrains. The constraint of wage goods (*i.e.*, foodgrains) which stood in the way of implementation of earlier schemes of rural public works did not then exist. In the sixth and seventh plans rural public works programme continued under the scheme called **'National Rural Employment Programme' (NREP).** This programme intended to provide supplementary employment opportunities to the rural poor seeking work during the lean periods. Projects relating to soil and water conservation, irrigation, flood protection and drainage, field channels in irrigation command areas, construction and improvement of village tanks and ponds, school and dispensary buildings, improvements of village environment, hygiene and sanitation had been undertaken under this programme.

In the Eleventh Five Year Plan period new scheme called **Mahatma Gandhi National Rural Employment Guarantee Scheme** (MGNREGS) with focus on employment generation through rural public works was started under which one member of poor households has been guaranteed employment for hundred days in a year at specified wage rate. Though it has been reported that a large number of poor persons have been given employment under the scheme, the scheme suffers from various lacuna such as lack of awareness about rights and entitlements, lack of durable assets, faulty job cards and muster rolls. Therefore, there has been demand for recasting the scheme so as to create durable productive assets under the scheme and to stop the leakage of funds.

22 Dandekar, V.M. and Rath, N., *Poverty in India*, Indian School of Political Economy, Poona, 1971.

23 Lewis J.P., "The Public Works Approach to Low End Poverty Problem, *Journal of Development Planning*, Vol. 5.

24 Minhas, B.S., "Rural Poverty, Land Redistribution and Development Strategy", *Indian Economic Review*, Vol. 5, 1970.

25 In the strategy proposed by Minhas the scheme of rural public works is to be used for developing land and water resources after consolidation of land has been accomplished.

In recent years the scheme has come in for a lot of criticism. A major criticism is that MGNREGS funds are used for works of a non-permanent nature and therefore divert Government spending from the more productive sectors of the economy. To prevent wastes of scarce financial resources there is need to employ persons for making more durable and productive assets. Without the creation of permanent productive assets the money would evaporate. In view of the non-productive nature of assets created by employing poor persons merely to fulfil the targets by district administration, it has been asserted that *this employment guarantee scheme is just a cash transfer to the poor* rather than serving as a means of productive employment for the manpower.

Besides, in the scheme there has been a lot of leakages due to which the poor neither get full wages nor entire 100 days of employment are actually provided to a person of each poor rural household. This means a good deal of funds are siphoned off by the middlemen and do not reach the poor households. As no useful productive work is being done under the scheme, a former Rural Development Minister Jairam Ramesh had said that MGNREGA scheme had become a plan only for *'digging ditches.'* and the budget expenditure of ₹ 36,000 crore being annually spent on the scheme was just being wasted.

A MGNREGA survey conducted in Andhra Pradesh, Madhya Pradesh and Rajasthan and its report submitted recently to the Government has revealed that the average number of days worked per household in the projects under the scheme in 2010-11 was 45, 37, and 52 days for these States respectively as against 100 days per household guaranteed under the scheme. This shows hardly 50 per cent of the days that are being claimed by the poor, that is, the poor are not getting full employment opportunities guaranteed under the MGNREGS. It is therefore evident that MGNREGS suffers from implementation problems. In the years 2014-15, as will be seen from Table 69.2 that in recent years not only employment provided to the number of people has decreased but also *average days* of employment provided per household was 46 days in 2012-13 and 2013-14 but only 34 days in 2014-15 as against 100 days of employment per household in a year. Besides, as is evident from Table 69.2, another big problem being faced by the scheme is *large delay* in wage payments to the persons who worked under the scheme. Therefore, NDA government has decided to make *direct transfer of money* to the bank accounts of the households.

Table 69.3. Employment under MGNREGA

Items	2012-13	2013-14	2014-15*
Employment provided (persons)	4.99 crore	4.79 crore	3.60 crore
Average days of employment provided per household	46 days	46 days	34 days
Delay in wage payment	39 %	52 %	72 %

* Till Dec. 2014

Source: Compiled from Government Documents

One of the persistent complaints about the scheme is that *full wage* is not being received by the poor under the scheme due to various leakages from the funds allocated for the scheme. The findings of the survey conducted for AP, MP and Rajasthan mentioned above also reveal that average wage received per day by the workers employed under the scheme was ₹ 94, 98 and 79 in Andhra Pradesh; Madhya Pradesh and Rajasthan respectively which are far less than the wages fixed by the government. It is therefore evident that there is a lot of leakages in the scheme at the local level. That is, a good chunk of benefits under the scheme are grabbed by the middlemen who arrange employment work under the scheme. It has therefore often been found that district administration is hard put to spend sanctioned amounts and often resort to sanctioning unnecessary works and local functionaries hoarding job cards are able to grab a good deal of funds sanctioned for the works. This is a great lacuna in the scheme. Besides, due to lack of useful or productive projects in individual villages the poor are employed in unproductive and useless works. This prompted the former Union Minister for Rural Development to say that "how many ditches will you dig in a village, how much labour work you can do in building community assets such as schools, rural roads in a village or near by year after year, how many trees you can plant in a village or nearby year after year. There is a limit to such works or projects in individual villages".

In our view for the scheme to have utility in terms of creating productive assets *there is need for integrating the scheme with the rural development projects included in the five year plants.* This would require to employ people demanding work under the scheme far off from their villages. But this can be done by making available transport facilities to bring them to project places and back to their villages.

Further, the permissible works need to be expanded; especially *farm work* should be included in this guaranteed employment scheme. This will help in raising agricultural output apart from generating employment opportunities. This will also meet the complaint often made against the scheme that diversion of workers to the guaranteed employment scheme is affecting farm output. There is already demand that the MGNREGS be taken off during the peak season in agriculture when workers are badly needed for various agricultural operations. For engaging workers under the guaranteed scheme in farm work of private landlonds some funds can be collected from them to pay wages to the workers supplied to them.

Besides, the Government should include new types of rural works such as soil conservation measures, products of composts and bio-pesticides, other works related to sowing and harvesting activities such as threshing would help in raising farm output. Some of the funds can be collected from the landlords on whose land such farming related activities are undertaken under MGNREGA scheme. All these require to recast the employment guarantee scheme. However, for the success of such extended employment guarantee scheme there is need for **micro-level planning** which is not yet being done.

There can be hardly any two opinions that rural public works can be helpful in providing employment to the rural poor, especially the landless labourers and marginal farmers who remain without gainful work for a large number of days in a year. At the same time the programme can be used to build durable community assets which would promote rural development. Further, by providing alternative avenues of wage employment the rural works programme can ensure reasonable wages to the agricultural workers. But *the view that these rural public works should serve as a substitute for employment generation through a proper development strategy as was conceived by Dandekar and Rath and some others is open to question.* For, being construction activities, rural public works are, at best, an interim or short-run solution of the problem of unemployment and leave the question unanswered as to how the growing number of workforce will be productively employed in the long run. The lasting and long-term solution to the problem of unemployment and underemployment lies in framing a development strategy that involves not only acceleration of rate of capital formation but also technological and institutional changes which are appropriate for labour-surplus conditions of the Indian economy. However, the rural public works have an important role to play in an employment-oriented strategy. As stated above, with the scheme of rural public works we can build up durable assets or infrastructural facilities. Now, these assets or facilities will help in creating more employment opportunities in agriculture and rural industries in future. To fulfil this purpose, rural public works need to be integrated with the overall strategy of rural development rather than being formulated and implemented in isolation of it.